Majority and Minority

Majority and Minority

The Dynamics of Race and Ethnicity in American Life

Fifth Edition

Edited by

Norman R. Yetman
The University of Kansas

Allyn and Bacon
Boston London Toronto Sydney Tokyo Singapore

Managing Editor: *Susan Badger*
Series Editor: *Karen Hanson*
Series Editorial Assistant: *Laurie Frankenthaler*
Production Administrator: *Annette Joseph*
Production Coordinator: *Susan Freese*
Editorial-Production Service: *Spectrum Publisher Services, Inc.*
Manufacturing Buyer: *Megan Cochran*
Cover Administrator: *Linda K. Dickinson*
Cover Designer: *Suzanne Harbison*

Copyright © 1991, 1985, 1982 by Allyn and Bacon
A Division of Simon & Schuster, Inc.
160 Gould Street
Needham Heights, Massachusetts 02194

Previous editions of this book were published under the title *Majority and Minority:
The Dynamics of Racial and Ethnic Relations,* copyright © 1975, 1971 by Allyn and
Bacon.

 This textbook is printed on
recycled, acid-free paper.

Library of Congress Cataloging-in-Publication Data

Majority and minority : the dynamics of race and ethnicity in American
  life / edited by Norman R. Yetman. – 5th ed.
        p.   cm.
  Includes bibliographical references.
  ISBN 0–205–12950–1
  1. United States – Race relations.   2. United States – Ethnic
relations.   3. Minorities – United States.   I. Yetman, Norman R.
E184.A1M256   1991
305.8′00973 – dc20   90–23534
                                                              CIP

Printed in the United States of America

10 9 8 7 6 5   96 95 94 93

For Jill and Doug
with pride that they share the dream

Contents

Part 3   Patterns of Ethnic Integration in America   209

Part 4   Race and Ethnicity in 1980s America   379

Preface

Majority and Minority began in the late 1960s as a collaborative effort with C. Hoy Steele. The academic interests in race and ethnicity in American life that we shared were influenced by our personal commitments to the realization of a society free of social inequality and social injustice – the dream of which Martin Luther King, Jr., so eloquently spoke.

In the summer of 1970, during the final week of preparing the manuscript for the first edition of *Majority and Minority*, a local black youth was shot dead by a white policeman in Lawrence, Kansas. This event occurred amidst the greatest period of social unrest and conflict that this city had experienced since Quantrill's raid during the Civil War. Although this scenario occurred in cities throughout the nation during that period, the immediacy of the tragedy and its consequences in our own city and our own lives heightened the sense of urgency that has shaped the perspectives of the book throughout each subsequent edition. We sought to emphasize the *practical,* as well as the theoretical, need for a fundamental understanding of the dynamics of racial and ethnic relations. We were convinced of the irrelevance of analysis and understanding that are not complemented by action to alter existing systems of inequality.

This fifth edition appears twenty years after publication of the first edition. During these two decades many dramatic and far-reaching changes in American racial and ethnic relations have occurred. However, although racial tensions have not been so dramatically manifested as in the civil disorders that engulfed many American cities during the late 1960s, racial harassment and violence have persisted, and many of the racial inequalities that were the source of the protests of that period remain virtually unchanged. The persistence of racial conflict has, ironically, been most visible on the nation's college campuses, where more than 300 incidents of racial harassment or violence were reported between 1985 and 1990. Thus, rather than diminishing, racial and ethnic conflict has remained deeply engrained in American life, and the concerns that animated the first edition of *Majority and Minority* remain as urgent today as in 1970.

The basic assumption that has informed each edition of *Majority and Minority* has been that the study of racial and ethnic relations should focus primarily on patterns of differential power and intergroup conflict and should rely on sociological, rather than psychological, concepts. I have retained this orientation in this fifth edition. However, I have sought, above all, to respond to changing perspectives in the field. Foremost among the factors that have influenced my conceptualization, selection, and organization of materials has been the increased salience of and scholarly attention devoted to ethnicity throughout the world. These events demonstrate that ethnicity is not a superficial or fleeting factor in social life. Rather, it is critical to understanding the dynamics of modern societies in general and the United States in particular.

Given the enormous amount of literature on ethnic relations throughout the world, it would be impossible to provide the necessary breadth and depth of analysis to cover these phenomena worldwide. Consequently, I have restricted coverage to issues concerning race and ethnicity in American life. However, my focus on American society does not imply a lack of concern for comparative issues; nor should it reinforce the parochial perspective from which many American students view race and ethnicity. The major criterion for inclusion in this edition was that each article simultaneously explore both some aspect of race and ethnicity in the United States and a broader conceptual issue or model. Therefore, most articles address intergroup relations in general but use racial and ethnic relations from the United States as examples. I hope in this way to increase the volume's conceptual breadth and keep it attractive to students of race and ethnicity in American life.

One of the major objectives of this edition is to familiarize students with the *range* of conceptual perspectives or ways of interpreting American racial and ethnic relations. I have represented some of the most current issues scholars in the field have addressed. The primary audience for whom the book is intended is upper-division or graduate students; it is not intended as an introduction to the field. Nevertheless, to facilitate student interest and comprehension, I have edited several of the more difficult selections with an eye toward emphasizing their central conceptual issues. Moreover, I have expanded considerably the essays introducing each part to provide a context within which to consider each selection and to alert students to some of the salient issues that the selections raise.

I have retained the strong historical perspective of previous editions. I have tried to provide the historical depth necessary to understand the various ways in which different ethnic and racial groups have adapted to American society. Part 2 is explicitly devoted to historical perspectives, but the historical dimension is stressed throughout the entire book, making the placement of some articles arbitrary. Subsequent sections build on the historical base established in Part 2: patterns of ethnic integration in the American experience are examined in Part 3, and the present and future significance of ethnicity are addressed in Part 4. The most apparent changes from previous editions can be found in this section, which contains considerable material dealing with the most recent wave of immigration to the United States, and the implications of the changing patterns of immigration for the future of racial and ethnic relations in American life.

Acknowledgments

Special thanks go to those individuals who reviewed the manuscript at various stages for Allyn and Bacon: Gerry R. Cox, Fort Hays State University; Benjamin F. Hadis, Montclair State College; Gloria Nemerowicz, Monmouth College; Gary Sandefur, University of Wisconsin-Madison; David Sciulli, Texas A & M University; and Carol Stix, Pace University-Pleasantville.

I would like to express my thanks to all those who assisted me – in numerous ways – in preparing this fifth edition: Allyn and Bacon's Sociology Editor, Karen Hanson; Bob Antonio; Lori Houk-Stephens; Pat Johnston; Barbara Russiello; Anne Yetman; and Doug Yetman.

Introduction: Definitions and Perspectives

1

Among the most dramatic social phenomena of the 1980s was the resurgence of racial and ethnic rivalries, tensions, and hostilities throughout the world. Prejudice and discrimination and conflict and violence based on racial and ethnic distinctions are widely found throughout the world today – between black, white, colored, and Indian in South Africa; between English-speaking and French-speaking people in Canada; between Islamic Arabs and black Christians in the Sudan; between East Indians and blacks in Guyana; between Kurds and Iraqis in Iraq; between Tamils and Sinhalese in Sri Lanka; between Chinese and Malays in Malaysia; and between Krahn and Gio and Mano ethnic groups in Liberia. Indeed, in the last few decades more people have died in ethnic conflicts around the world than in the Korean and Vietnam wars combined.

Indeed, the political ferment that unleashed dramatic political changes throughout eastern Europe during the late 1980s was fed by a resurgence of historic ethnic and national rivalries and antagonisms. The Soviet Union was rent by interethnic conflicts, such as those between the Armenians and Azerbaijanis, as well as by demands from numerous other nationalities, such as Lithuanians, Latvians, Estonians, Georgians, ethnic Poles, and Ukrainians, for greater ethnic autonomy and even independence. Slavic nationalism in Yugoslavia, which earlier in the century had provided the spark that ignited World War I, has resurfaced, and conflicts among the country's several nationalities – Serbs, Croatians, Slovenes, Bosnians, Montenegrins, Macedonians, and Albanians – threaten the very existence of the nation. Prior to the fall of Rumanian strongman Nicolae Ceausescu in 1989, approximately two million Hungarians living in Rumania were subject to forced assimilation, the closing of Hungarian schools and social organizations, the suppression of the Hungarian language, and discrimination against those Hungarians who tried to retain their Hungarian ethnicity. Similar accusations of forced assimilation were raised by the Turkish minority in Bulgaria, where ethnic tensions led to the forced removal of thousands of Muslim Turks to Turkey.

Ethnic, Racial, and Caste Categories

Ethnicity

The word *ethnic* is derived from the Greek word *ethnos,* meaning "people." An *ethnic group* is socially defined on the basis of its cultural characteristics. *Ethnicity,* or the sense of belonging to a particular ethnic group, thus implies the existence of a distinct culture or subculture in which group members feel themselves bound together by a common origin, history, values, attitudes, and behaviors – in its broadest sense, a sense of peoplehood – and are so regarded by other members of the society.

This conception of ethnicity resembles what Robert N. Bellah and his colleagues have termed "communities of memory," in which people share an identity rooted in a collective history, tradition, and experience that can be both heroic and painful. However, a community of memory is not simply cultural, involving shared beliefs and ideas; it is sustained through social relations, by participation in the life of the community. Such participation, which Bellah has termed "practices of commitment," "define the patterns of loyalty and obligation that keep the community alive" (Bellah et al. 1985:152–155).

Ethnic groups differ in cultural characteristics as diverse as food habits, family patterns, sexual behaviors, modes of dress, standards of beauty, political orientations, economic activities, and recreational patterns. In American society, Chicanos, African-Americans, Jews, Poles, Filipinos, and white Anglo-Saxon Protestants can all be considered ethnic groups, however broad and diverse their internal compositions. Killian (1970) has argued that white Southerners also comprise an important ethnic group in American society. Ethnicity was an important factor in the 1976 presidential campaign of Jimmy Carter, whose candidacy evoked a sense of ethnic identity among many Southerners. It was explicitly articulated by Patrick Anderson, who served as Carter's aide:

> *Perhaps you have to be a Southerner to understand what [Jimmy Carter's candidacy] means to some of us. There is a great sense of personal pride and personal vindication involved, a sense that after losing for a long long time, our side is finally going to win one. I imagine that Jews and blacks will feel the same way when one of their own finally gets a shot at the White House.*
>
> *The emotions involved run deep, and are hard to communicate, but I think they must be considered by anyone who wants to understand why young Southerners . . . are driving themselves so relentlessly on Governor Carter's behalf. They are motivated, I think, not only by the personal ambition that afflicts us all, but by personal affection for the candidate, by political commitment to certain goals, and by a regional pride that has its roots many generations in the past. (Anderson 1976:21, emphasis added)*

Ethnic groups are inherently ethnocentric, regarding their own cultural traits as natural, correct, and superior to those of other ethnic groups, who are perceived as odd, amusing, inferior, or immoral. In Article 5, "A Theory of the Origin of Ethnic Stratification," Donald Noel (1968) suggests that ethnocentrism is a necessary, but not sufficient, condition for the emergence of ethnic stratification. According to Noel, a majority-minority relationship between two ethnocentric groups will not come about unless the groups are competing for the same scarce resources and, most important, one group possesses superior power to impose its will on the other.

Race

The terms *race* and *ethnicity* are often used interchangeably, but for analytic purposes they should be distinguished. Whereas an ethnic group is socially defined on the basis of its *cultural* characteristics, a race is socially defined on the basis of *physical* characteristics. A group is defined as a race when certain of its physical characteristics are selected for special emphasis by members of a society. Gerald Berreman (1972) contends in Article 1 that the definition of a group as a race is not a function of biological or genetic differences between groups, but of society's perceptions that such differences exist and that they are important—that they are related to other apparently innate mental, emotional, and moral differences, such as intelligence.

The term *race* has been an extremely loose concept; it has been used to refer to linguistic categories (Aryan, English-speaking), to religious categories (Hindu, Jewish), to national categories (French, Italian), and to mystical, quasiscientific categories (Teutonic). Because of this imprecision, several scholars have chosen to dispense with the term, preferring to subsume racially distinct groups under broadly defined ethnic groups. The wide range of social categories that have been considered races reinforces the notion that racial designations are artificial; they serve the function of separating certain social categories based on an arbitrary selection of physical or biologically transmitted characteristics.

The term *race* is meaningless in a biological sense, because there are no "pure" races. The crucial aspect of any ethnic or racial category is that the characteristics that distinguish it are *socially defined.* As Berreman notes, "systems of 'racial' stratification are social phenomena based on social rather than biological facts."

Many groups possess physically identifiable characteristics that do not become the basis for racial distinctions. The criteria selected to make racial distinctions in one society may be overlooked or considered insignificant or irrelevant by another. For instance, in much of Latin America skin color and the shape of the lips—important differentiating criteria in the United States—are much less important than are hair texture, eye color, and stature. A person defined as black in Georgia or Michigan might be considered white in Peru (Pitt-Rivers 1967).

The principle that racial differences are socially defined is vividly demonstrated by laws in the United States prohibiting interracial marriages. Until recently, many states stipulated that any person with one-fourth or more African ancestry (that is, with one black grandparent) was legally defined as "black" and therefore prohibited from marrying someone "white." However, some states enacted more restrictive definitions of race. A recent example occurred in Louisiana, when Susie Guillory Phipps, a light-skinned woman with Caucasian features and straight black hair, found that her birth certificate classified her as "colored." Phipps, who contended that she had been "brought up white and married white twice," challenged a 1970 Louisiana law declaring that anyone with at least one-thirty-second "Negro blood" was legally black. Under this law an individual who had one great-great-great-grandparent who was black (and thus had one-thirty-second "black" and thirty-one thirty-seconds "white" ancestry) was legally defined as black. Although the state's lawyer conceded that Phipps "looks like a white person," the state strenuously maintained that her racial classification was appropriate (Trillin 1986).

That racial classifications are social, not biological, categories is today nowhere more apparent than in South Africa, where all people are required to be classified in one of four legally defined racial categories—white, black, colored, and Indian. The lives of all South Africans, including the jobs they may hold, the schools they may attend, where they may live, and whom they may marry, are dramatically determined by the category in which they are placed. The arbitrary nature of such categories is revealed in circumstances in which an individual's legal racial classification—and the entire range of opportunities that flows from it—is changed. A South African newspaper recently reported:

> Nearly 800 South Africans became officially members of a different race group last year. . . . They included 518 coloreds who were officially reclassified as white, 14 whites who became colored, 7 Chinese [who are classified as "honorary whites"] who became white, 2 whites who became Chinese, 3 Malays [who are classified as colored] who became white, 1 white who became Indian, 50 Indians who became colored, 54 coloreds who became Indian, 17 Indians who became Malay, 4 coloreds who became Chinese, 1 Malay who became Chinese, 89 blacks who became colored, 5 coloreds who became black. (Usy 1988:27)

Racial distinctions are not restricted to skin pigmentation but can involve other physical characteristics as well. An excellent example is found in the small east African country of Burundi, which during the past twenty years has experienced waves of intergroup violence and conflict in which the principal distinction between antagonists has been stature.

Burundi is a landlocked country of central Africa, situated between the republics of Zaire and Tanzania. During its colonial period, which ended in 1962, Burundi was controlled by the Belgians. As in several other African countries, independence from European colonialism brought deep-rooted and long-repressed tribal rivalries to the surface. In 1972 a wave of violence swept the country. An estimated 100,000 people, or 3.5 percent of the population, were killed. A comparable annihilation in the American population would mean the deaths of about 8 million people.

The violence in Burundi reflects the rivalry of the country's two major racial groups: the Tutsi and the Hutu. The Tutsi, a tall and slender people among whom men average six feet in height, make up only about 15 percent of Burundi's population. For centuries before the arrival of European colonial powers, the Tutsi had held the Hutu, a people of smaller stature who stand slightly over four feet, in a form of serfdom. During the colonial period the Belgians supported the social divisions of a Tutsi aristocracy and a Hutu servant class. When independence was achieved in 1962, many Hutu were hopeful that, because they represented 85 percent of the population, the promise of majority rule would bring an end to Tutsi domination. However, Hutu frustration grew in the years following independence as the more politically astute Tutsi effectively blocked Hutu efforts to change the status quo.

In 1972 small bands of Hutu revolted against Tutsi rule. They killed and mutilated any Tutsi they could find, including women and children, as well as any Hutu who refused to join them. The Tutsi-dominated government of Burundi responded with a wave of counterviolence. In many villages all Hutu of any wealth, community influence, or educational level above grade school were systematically shot or beaten to death. The killing was selective, aimed at all influential Hutu. The objective of the annihilation of the Hutu elites was to crush any Hutu threat to Tutsi power. The Tutsi sought to eliminate "not only the rebellion but Hutu society as well, and in the process lay the foundation of an entirely new social order" (Lemarchand 1975:57).

This wave of genocide ensured Tutsi political and economic power in Burundi and led to the systematic exclusion of Hutu from the army, civil service, the university, and high schools. In 1988 the long-simmering tension between these two groups flared once again into violent conflict. At least 5,000 more people were killed in another Hutu uprising and the Tutsi reprisal that followed, and more than 50,000 Hutu fled to the neighboring country of Rwanda, where Hutu are the tribal majority (Brooke 1988; Perlez 1988). Because the principal criterion for distinguishing the majority Tutsi from the minority Hutu is a physical characteristic, stature, this violent conflict can be characterized as racial.

Caste

The concept of race has been closely related to that of *caste,* a system of social inequality characterized by rigidly separated social categories in which an individual's status is inherited and fixed. Indeed, Berreman contends that all systems of racial stratification and caste are qualitatively comparable. A caste system is a "hierarchy of endogamous divisions in which membership is hereditary and permanent" (Berreman 1969:226). A caste society can be conceptualized as occupying one end of a continuum, its polar opposite being a class society. The distinction is that in a caste system status is birth-ascribed; it is immutable, permanent, and fixed. In a class system, on the other hand, social mobility is possible because status is determined by achievement. However, pure caste and class systems do not exist. No stratification system is totally closed or totally open; virtually all societies display both ascription and achievement in some form (Tumin 1969).

Race might be a basis for status distinctions in a caste system; however, a caste system can also be organized without reference to hereditary physical characteristics so long as social categories are distinguished on the basis of traits believed to be birth-ascribed. The Japanese *Burakumin* – Japan's "invisible race" – represent an excellent example of a caste system without apparent racial distinctions. Physically indistinguishable from other Japanese, the *Burakumin* are acknowledged to be completely Japanese, but of such lowly social origins that they are constantly subjected to prejudice and discrimination (DeVos and Wagatsuma 1966).

The contemporary *Burakumin* are descendants of the untouchable *eta* caste. The degree to which the *eta* were despised by the rest of Japanese society is revealed in the name itself: *eta* means "filth abundant." Under the feudal system of Tokugawa, Japan, from the seventeenth to the nineteenth centuries, the *eta* occupied an outcaste status below the four superior castes (the ruling caste of warriors and administrators, the peasants, artisans, and merchants) that constituted Japanese society. The *eta* were discriminated against in every aspect of their lives, and a number of laws were enacted to reinforce their inferior status. For example, as outcastes they were restricted to the dirtiest, most defiling, and least desirable occupations (such as butchers, leatherworkers, grave tenders, and executioners). They were legally segregated from the rest of the Japanese people and forced to live in isolated ghettos. Moreover, they were required to walk barefoot and to wear special clothing that identified them as *eta*. Because they were considered innately inferior and "impure," their marriages were restricted to other *eta;* intermarriages with non-*eta* were virtually nonexistent.

The *eta* were legally "emancipated" during the mid-nineteenth century, and the laws that had formerly restricted their lives and discriminated against them were formally abolished. Although emancipation provided legal freedom, discrimination against the outcastes (subsequently known as *Burakumin,* or "village people") has persisted. Among the popular prejudices about the Burakumin that persisted well into the twentieth century were the following:

> *One rib is lacking; they have a dog's bone in them; they have distorted sexual organs; they have defective excretory systems; if they walk in the moonlight their necks will not cast shadows, and, they being animals, dirt does not stick to their feet when they walk barefoot. (Quoted in Neary 1986:558)*

Today there are an estimated one to three million *Burakumin* living in Japan, a nation of 123 million. During the twentieth century the *Burakumin* have organized social movements to protest the discrimination they continue to encounter in employment, education, and housing. Although the Japanese government has enacted legislation designed to end the cycle of poverty and discrimination and to improve their living conditions, *Burakumin* continue to be found in overcrowded slumlike ghettos, and their lives are characterized by low incomes, high unemployment, and high rates of dependence on welfare. They are often the "last hired and first fired." The *Burakumin* continue to be viewed by most Japanese as "mentally inferior, incapable of high moral behavior, aggressive, impulsive, and lacking any notion of sanitation or manners" (Wagatsuma 1976:245). The power of these stereotypes and the fear they elicit are reflected in the importance attached to family registration records, which certify "proper" social backgrounds. Such records are frequently required in connection with applications for jobs, loans, and admissions to schools. Above all, it is not unusual for families to undertake exhaustive investigations of the lineages of their children's prospective spouses to ensure that their families will not be "contaminated" by *eta* origins.

Thus the *Burakumin* occupy a pariah position in Japanese society, and their undesirable characteristics are perceived by upper-caste Japanese as attributable to biological inheritance; yet no physical differences can be detected between them. The similarity of the stereotypes of the *Burakumin* and of subordinate groups in other racial and caste systems is instructive. As Donald Horowitz points out in Article 2, "Whether or not there is an attempt to deny the common humanity of the subordinate group, the stereotype of such a group generally depicts it as irremediably slow, violent, lazy, unmannered, and dirty" (1985:27). Caste and racially stratified systems function in a similar manner. Thus, De Vos and Wagatsuma, on the basis of their analysis of the *Burakumin,* support Berreman's contention that racial and caste systems are analytically comparable: "From the viewpoint of comparative sociology or social anthropology, and from the viewpoint of human social psychology, racism and caste attitudes are one and the same phenomenon" (De Vos and Wagatsuma, 1966).

As the racial/ethnic conflict in Burundi and the caste status of the *Burakumin* in Japan demonstrate, in real life race, ethnicity, and caste are intimately related, and distinctions between them are difficult to make. Indeed, there has been considerable debate among social scientists concerning whether race relations are different in kind from ethnic relations or whether race relations can appropriately be subsumed under the broad rubric of ethnicity. Because in American society racial conflicts—those based on physical, rather than cultural, differences—have generally been more intense than ethnic conflicts, there has been a tendency to attribute a preeminence to the study of race relations. However, ethnic differences are capable of eliciting antagonisms and loyalties comparable in intensity and tenacity to those based on racial distinctions. For example, in his analysis of ethnically divided societies in Asia, Africa, and the Caribbean, Horowitz denies that race relations are somehow qualitatively different from intergroup relations based on language, religion, or putative common ancestry or origins. Such a notion, he contends, is based on two assumptions—that racial distinctions arouse "uniquely intense emotions and loyalties" and that such distinctions "serve as unusually reliable signs of individual identity. . . . Neither of these assumptions," he argues, "can be supported" (1985:42).

Therefore, it is appropriate to adopt an inclusive definition of ethnicity that emphasizes the different criteria—physical differences, language, religion, and putative common ancestry or origins—used to distinguish groups. Such an inclusive definition is consistent with Berreman's emphasis that the crucial feature of such phenomena is that group differences are attributed to ascriptive characteristics. Therefore, in subsequent discussion, this book treats "racial" relations as one dimension of ethnic relations and uses the terms "ethnic" and "ethnicity" in this broader and more inclusive sense.

Primordial and Situational Explanations

Why have people used racial and ethnic distinctions so frequently throughout history to rank a society's members? Why have racial and ethnic differences so often demarcated the lines of intergroup conflict? Two broad explanatory models have been advanced: the nonrational or primordialist perspective and the rational or situational perspective. The former position conceptualizes racial and ethnic identities as essentially biologically based, present at birth, instinctive, innate, and unchangeable, "attachments [that] seem to flow more from a sense of natural affinity than from social interaction" (Burgess 1978:266). The rational position, on the other hand, locates the sources of ethnicity in the structure and dynamics of human societies. From this perspective, race and ethnicity are functional, pragmatic, emergent, and constantly evolving and changing phenomena, "a rational group response to social pressures and a basis for group action, especially where no other exists. . . . Ethnicity [is] a strategy chosen to advance individual interest as the situation dictates" (Burgess 1978:267).

During the past three decades Pierre van den Berghe has been one of the most prominent, prolific, and penetrating scholars of race and ethnicity. In numerous publications (van den Berghe 1967, 1970, 1978, 1981), he has criticized American scholarship in the field of race and ethnicity for its narrow, myopic, and parochial focus on the United Sates, and he has urged sociologists to extend the range within which these phenomena are conceptualized to the wider context of evolutionary biology.

Van den Berghe argues for what has been broadly termed a primordialist perspective, one that sees racial and ethnic distinctions as deeply rooted in the basic nature of human sociality. He contends that kin selection and its corollary, nepotism, are the basic principles on which societies have been based for most of human existence; and that ethnic and racial distinctions are merely extensions of kinship principles. The pervasiveness of ethnic distinctions and ethnocentrism in human societies suggests that these phenomena are instrumental in establishing group boundaries. Most preliterate societies, for example, employ ethnic distinctions (such as language or body adornment), rather than racial ones, for the simple reason that they rarely encounter other peoples who are physically distinguishable from themselves. Racial distinctions, van den Berghe argues, are the consequence primarily of large-scale migrations, which have only occurred relatively recently in human history:

> Humans, like other animals, are selected to favor kin, and whatever does a quick, easy, and accurate job of differentiating kin and non-kin will be used. In most cases, and until recently, cultural criteria have been predominantly used. Physical criteria became salient only after large, strikingly different-looking populations found themselves in sudden and sustained contact. (van den Berghe 1978c:407–408)

Numerous authors have recently articulated the rational or situational approach to race and ethnicity, which emphasizes that definitions of ethnic and racial categories are *socially* defined phenomena. Edna Bonacich (1980a), for example, argues in Article 3 that an ethnic identity is not natural or inherent in the nature of the group itself; rather it is socially constructed, a reflection of the more deeply rooted dynamic of class. As a consequence, new ethnic or racial categories can emerge over time. Similarly, William Yancey and his colleagues (1976) contend that among groups of European immigrants to the United States a sense of ethnicity was produced, not by the cultural commonalities people shared, but by external factors. A sense of ethnicity was always "emergent" – that is, ethnic identity represented a response to the conditions in the cities in which they settled. Among these conditions were "common occupational positions, residential stability and concentration, and dependence on common institutions and services, [which were] in turn directly affected by the process of industrialization." Historians of American ethnic groups have pointed out that a sense of national identity was not brought by many immigrants from their homelands; it often crystallized in the United States. For example, Italians who immigrated to the United States did not think of themselves as Italians; rather, they defined themselves by their village or region. Consciousness of themselves as Italians emerged only as a consequence of their encounter with American society (Vecoli 1964).

Similarly, several of the racial categories discussed in Part 2 – American Indians, Asians, and Hispanics – are inclusive terms that ignore or obscure considerable internal diversity within each group. Edna Bonacich (1980a) notes that the Asian-American category is comprised of diverse and often antagonistic national elements, including Chinese, Japanese, Korean, Vietnamese, Thai, Khmer, and Asian Indian. Joane Nagel (1986) points out in Article 4 how the terms *American Indian* and *Native American* are consequences of their minority status in American society and obscure the substantial tribal (ethnic) differences among them. Simlarly, the terms *Hispanic* or *Latino,* which two decades ago were not even part of the common language, are increasingly employed to subsume into one category several extremely diverse ethnic categories. Although such distinctions are employed by social scientists, journalists, business people, and ultimately the people themselves, Cynthia Enloe (1981) has contended that the state has played a crucial role in defining these arbitrary social categories: "The state employs ethnic categories to suit its administrative-political needs. In so doing it requires individuals subject to certain laws to respond as 'Hispanics' or 'Indians' or 'Filipinos'."

Recently there has been a spate of newspaper and magazine accounts delineating the emergence of Asians or Hispanics as significant forces in American life. Indeed, in Part 2, reflecting this tendency to lump diverse groups together, I argue (as have numerous other social scientists and journalists) that at some point in the not-so-distant future Hispanics will exceed African-Americans as the nation's largest minority group. Likewise, in Article 23 (Part 4) Stanley Lieberson (1985) contends that there may be a new ethnic category emerging in American society: *unhyphenated whites,* whose European national origins are so obscure or so mixed that their only ethnic identity is in reference to American society. In each case, the ethnic categories – Italian, American Indian, Asian, Hispanic, and American – and the range of social, political, and economic opportunities available to members are socially and politically defined and created.

Ethnicity and Social Stratification

Because ethnicity has frequently been linked to relations of dominance and subordination and thus to a society's system of stratification, there has been a tendency to equate ethnic relations with majority-minority relations. However, the relationship between ethnicity and a system of social ranking is not invariable. Donald Horowitz agrees in Article 2 that, although it appropriate to consider many ethnic group relations in this way, "the relations of many other ethnic groups – on a global scale, most ethnic groups – are not accurately described as superior-subordinate relations." He distinguishes between *ranked* and *unranked* ethnic system, the latter characterized in cross-cultural and cross-national studies as "plural" societies.

However, because a ranking system involving relations of dominance and subordination has been so prominent a feature of ethnic relations, both today and in the past, in societies throughout the world, we will examine some of the key features of majority-minority relations.

The centrality of ethnicity to many of the recent upheavals in Eastern Europe serves as a reminder that the term *minority group* was originally derived from the European experience. Use of the term *minority* emerged in the context of the rise of nationalism and the nation-state in late eighteenth and early nineteenth-century Europe. In that context, it was used to characterize national or ethnic groups that had become subordinate to the peoples of another national or ethnic group through the imposition of, or shifts in, political boundaries. Although in the past two centuries many commentators have predicted that "minority" concerns and issues would wane as societies modernized, the extent to which long-simmering ethnic conflicts have resurfaced in the past decade reflects the tenacity of racial and ethnic identities and the significance of majority-minority relations in human societies.

Reflecting the usage developed from the experience of "nationality" (ethnic) groups in Europe, sociologists have continued to use the terms *majority* and *minority* to refer to social relations in which racial and ethnic criteria are employed in the society's system of stratification. The term *minority* has therefore been applied with greatest frequency to subordinate groups characterized by hereditary membership and endogamy – racial, caste, and ethnic groupings (Williams 1964:304; Wagley and Harris 1958:4–10).

A minority or *subordinate group* occupies an inferior position of prestige, wealth, and power in a society. Members of a minority group are typically excluded from full participation in a society; they are the object of discrimination by the majority group; and their life chances, when compared to those of the majority group, are circumscribed.

However, the distinctive feature of majority-minority relations – group differences in power – is not restricted to racial and ethnic relations alone, but can characterize other forms of social relations. Therefore, a more inclusive definition of minority, one not restricted to racial and ethnic relations, is appropriate. Joseph B. Gittler's comprehensive definition is consistent with this approach: "Minority groups are those whose members experience a wide range of discriminatory treatment and frequently are relegated to positions relatively low in the status structure of a society" (Gittler 1956:vii). This definition retains the crucial elements of the term's original meaning: the reference to a distinct group or social category occupying a subordinate position of prestige, privilege, and power.

The term *minority* does not refer to the numerical size of a group. Occasionally a so-called minority group will represent a numerical majority of the total population. For example, under the system of apartheid in South Africa today, blacks are a numerical majority (69 percent) of the total population; yet they are systematically excluded from full social, economic, and political participation. Similar situations have existed in some areas of the American South and in most colonial situations. For example, in 1910, although African-Americans represented more than 55 percent of the population of Mississippi and South Carolina, they were completely excluded from all political offices in these two states. Numerical superiority, therefore, does not necessarily ensure majority status. Many commentators have suggested that the terms *majority* and *minority* be replaced by *dominant* and *subordinate* to represent more accurately the differences in power. However, because *majority* and *minority* have been so widely used, I will continue to employ them here with the understanding that the crucial feature of the minority's status is its inferior social position, in which its interests are not effectively represented in the political, economic, and social institutions of the society. I will use the term *dominant* as a synonym for *majority* and *subordinate* as a synonym for *minority.*

Minorities and Conflict

Many different dimensions, such as race, ethnicity, and religion, have been used to distinguish a minority from the majority. However, as Donald L. Noel argues in "The Origin of Ethnic Stratification" (Article 5), ethnic, racial, or religious differences do not automatically generate conflict and social inequalities. Culturally, religiously, or racially distinct groups may coexist without a system of ethnic inequality developing. Majority-minority relations do not appear until one group is able to impose its will on another. By definition, minority groups are subordinate segments of the societies of which they are a part. Once people perceive ethnic differences and ethnic groups and then compete against each other, the crucial variable is power.

Power is the ability of one group to realize its goals and interests, even in the face of resistance. This power may be derived from the superior size, weapons, technology, property, education, or economic resources of the dominant group. Hence, minority groups are categories of people that possess imperfect access to positions of equal power, prestige, and privilege in a society. Superior power is crucial not only to the establishment of a system of ethnic stratification but, as Noel points out, also to its maintenance and perpetuation. Having obtained control of a society's institutions, a majority group generally strives to solidify and consolidate its position.

Although conflict is not always overt, continuous, or apparent in a social system based on structured inequality, the potential for conflict is continually present. The extent to which conflict or stability are manifested itself is related to social structure. Pierre van den Berghe (1967) has contrasted the patterns of race relations characteristic of two structurally different types of societies. Under the *paternalistic* type, characteristic of a traditional, preindustrial, predominantly agricultural society, race relations are highly stable and conflict is submerged–

a function of both the mechanisms of social control used by the dominant group and the symbiotic nature of relations between dominant and subordinate groups. On the other hand, race relations in a *competitive* setting – an urbanized and highly industrialized society characterized by a complex division of labor – are less likely to remain stable. Overt conflict, initiated by both the dominant and subordinate groups, frequently erupts.

However, even in the most stable situations, dominant groups view minority groups as potentially threatening to their position. This fact is nowhere more apparent than in the American slave system, which exemplifies van den Berghe's paternalistic type of race relations. Proponents of slavery – the so-called "peculiar institution" – frequently justified slaveholding on the grounds of the slave's docility, dependence, improvidence, and fear of freedom. Simultaneously, however, they saw slaves as "a troublesome presence" (Stampp 1956), they initiated elaborate mechanisms (such as patrols, passes, and legal prohibitions against literacy and the possession of weapons) to reduce resistance to the slave regime, and they employed brutal sanctions to discourage noncompliance with the prescribed subservient roles.

The social inequalities inherent in majority-minority relations are, as Berreman points out in Article 1, symbolically expressed in the institutionalized patterns of interpersonal relations between dominant and subordinate group members. Social interaction among majority and minority group members is never among status equals; it consistently involves what was known in the American context as "the etiquette of race relations," which involved restrictions on such activities as eating, touching, terms of address, marriage, sexual conduct, and social contact generally. Although the patterns of deference the slave system demanded persisted long after slavery was legally abolished, the American slave regime vividly exemplified this point. One primary objective of slave socialization was to implant in slaves a sense of personal inferiority. Slaves were taught to "know their place," to recognize the difference between the status of master and slave. Whites interpreted any impudence on the part of slaves as an effort to reject their subordinate role. Frederick Douglass, the great nineteenth-century African-American leader, recalled that slaves could be labeled disobedient and punished for a variety of actions, including "the tone of an answer; in answering at all; in not answering; in the expression of countenance; in the motion of the head; in the gait, manner and bearing of the slave" (Stampp 1956:145).

As events during the Black Protest Movement of the 1960s in the United States demonstrated, attempts by a subordinate group to alter traditional relationships between dominant and subordinate groups and to achieve autonomy and equality of status are strenuously resisted by the majority group. Allen D. Grimshaw has summarized the history of changes in black-white relations by pointing out that:

> The most savage oppression, whether expressed in rural lynching and pogroms or in urban race riots, has taken place when the Negro has refused to accept a subordinate status. The most intense conflict has resulted when the subordinate minority group has attempted to

disrupt the accommodative pattern or when the superordinate group has defined the situation as one in which such an attempt is being made. (Grimshaw, 1959:17)

Efforts to alter the relative power of the majority and the minority thus inevitably involve conflict between the two groups, the subordinate group attempting to decrease the inequalities in the system through a wide variety of means (including violence), the dominant group resorting to a multiplicity of techniques (also including violence – both legal and extralegal) to prevent such changes from occurring. Today, one of the settings in which these conflicts are most graphically and tragically apparent is South Africa, where whites have developed the repressive system of apartheid ("separate development"), and maintain it by one of the most repressive police states in the world. Despite minor recent concessions to blacks, the monopoly of power held by whites and their intransigent resistance to basic change offer little possibility that alteration of South Africa's power structure will be peaceful and nonviolent.

Majorities and Institutional Power

The discussion so far has suggested that the concept of minority group must always be considered in relation to a majority, or dominant, group. Although this conclusion may appear self-evident, until the 1970s only a meager amount of the voluminous research on racial and ethnic relations had been devoted to the characteristics and attributes of the majority group and the mechanisms by which the relationships between majority and minority are created, maintained, and altered. A notable exception was the work of Robert Bierstedt. In "The Sociology of Majorities," published more than four decades ago, Bierstedt wrote:

It is the majority . . . which sets the culture pattern and sustains it, which is in fact responsible for whatever pattern or configuration there is in a culture. It is the majority which confers upon folkways, mores, customs, and laws the status of norms and gives them coercive power. It is the majority which guarantees the stability of a society. It is the majority which requires conformity to custom and which penalizes deviation – except in ways in which the majority sanctions and approves. It is the majority which is the custodian of the mores and which defends them against innovation. And it is the inertia of majorities, finally, which retards the processes of social change. (Bierstedt 1948:709)

Bierstedt's statement, which places the primary emphasis in the analysis of majority-minority relations on the characteristics of the dominant group, not on those of the minority, reflects one of the major themes of this book. From this perspective, the principal focus of inquiry should be on the manner in which the dominant group controls the institutions of the society. As Preston Wilcox has argued, "Much of what has been written as sociology would suggest that . . . minorities suffer problems because of their unique characteristics rather than [because of] the systems which impinge upon them and the sanctioning of these systems by dominant groups" (Wilcox 1970:44).

Lack of recognition of the importance of societal patterns of institutional control has meant that frequently, as John Horton (1966) has pointed out, sociologists and laypeople alike frequently define social problems as a minority group's deviation from dominant societal norms and standards; seldom do they critically examine the society's institutions, values, and social processes themselves. The importance of an institutional approach to the analysis of mass protest and violence in America was forcefully articulated in 1969 by the Violence Commission, which was appointed by President Lyndon Johnson to examine and explain the mass protest that swept the country during the turbulent 1960s. Mass protest, the Commission contended,

> *must be analyzed in relation to crises in American institutions. . . . [It] is an outgrowth of social, economic, and political conditions. . . . Recommendations concerning the prevention of violence which do not address the issue of fundamental social, economic, and political change are fated to be largely irrelevant and frequently self-defeating. (Skolnick 1969:3)*

In other words, both the sources of, and the solutions to, problems of majority-minority conflict are institutional. Thus, the most realistic approach to their analysis must focus primarily on the majority group and the institutional structures of the society in question.

Examination of the ways majority group members typically approach intergroup conflict demonstrates the importance of an institutional perspective. As noted above, the majority determines whether a problem even exists—witness the classic statement advanced by proponents of the status quo in communities throughout America: "We have no problems here. Our _____ [insert appropriate minority group residing in the community] are happy." Whether or not one perceives social conditions as a problem depends on one's position within the social structure. As the Violence Commission noted, whether or not one classifies behavior as violent depends on whether one is challenging the existing institutional arrangements or seeking to uphold them (Skolnick 1969:3–4).

In an important article examining the functions of racial conflict, Joseph Himes (1966) has pointed out that conflict may have positive consequences: it can force the dominant group to be aware of, come to grips with, and respond to societal inequities. Himes argues that organized social conflict alters traditional power relations and the traditional etiquette of race relations. As the minority group develops the ability to mobilize power against the dominant group's interests, traditional race relations change to the point where minority grievances can be more realistically discussed and addressed. During the late 1950s and early 1960s, African-Americans, denied change through institutionalized political channels (voting, for example), used mass protest to mobilize power against the dominant group's entrenched interests. Nonviolent protest and conflict were integral strategies of power in the civil rights movement. Martin Luther King, Jr., one of history's most articulate advocates of the weapon of nonviolence, perceived that it represented a means of effecting a redistribution of power:

INTRODUCTION: DEFINITIONS AND PERSPECTIVES

Nonviolent direct action seeks to create such a crisis and foster such a tension that a community which has constantly refused to negotiate is forced to confront the issue. It seeks so to dramatize the issue that it can no longer be ignored. (King 1964:81)

If the dominant group acknowledges social problems at all, they invariably ascribe them to the characteristics of the subordinate group rather than to defects in the social system controlled by the majority group. For many years, discussion of black-white relations in America was described as the "Negro problem," a stance explicitly challenged by Gunnar Myrdal in his classic work, *An American Dilemma* (1944). Today, most white Americans deny that opportunities for black Americans are limited, and perceive that blacks themselves are primarily responsible for the conditions in which they find themselves (Schumann 1969; Kluegel and Smith 1982; Schuman, Steeh, and Bobo 1985).

This interpretation is also implicit in the idea of cultural deprivation (Baratz and Baratz 1970), or what Maxine Baca Zinn (1989) has termed the "cultural deficiency model" for explaining poverty and, especially, what has recently been termed the *underclass* – the most impoverished segment of American society. Found primarily in the nation's inner cities, the underclass is characterized by high unemployment, school dropouts, academic failures, out-of-wedlock births, female-headed families, welfare dependence, homelessness, and serious crime. According to the cultural deficiency model, these characteristics are attributable primarily to the internal deficiencies and instabilities of the minorities – primarily black and Hispanic – that make up the underclass. That is, cultural, family, and community and neighborhood factors, not the inadequate economic and educational opportunities, are the primary causes of the social dislocations experienced by the underclass. The cultural deficiency model focuses on the characteristics of minorities and deflects attention from the institutional factors that impinge upon them. In short, the emphasis in such a model is on the symptom rather than on the disease.

The resolution of intergroup conflict also reflects power differentials, for conflicts tend to be resolved within limits acceptable to the majority group. Efforts to alter the pattern of inequalities are therefore restricted to methods defined as legitimate or appropriate by the majority group, a requisite that seldom poses a threat to the continued functioning of the existing system. Nancy Oestreich Lurie's article, "The American Indian: Historical Background," (Part 2), which sketches the background of American Indian encounters with white Americans (Article 7), provides an excellent example of this pattern. Indian-white problems were always defined from the perspective of whites and generally involved the refusal of Native Americans to accede to white demands for cultural assimilation or for the cession of their lands. Native American values, needs, and desires were seldom, if ever, a consideration in the solution of such confrontations. According to the humanitarian Thomas Jefferson, if Indians did not conform to white cultural patterns, the only viable solution was their forcible removal.

The role of the majority group in delimiting the context within which solutions to problems of intergroup conflict can be reached is exemplified by the analysis and recommendations of the 1968 Kerner Commission report and the nation's reactions to it. Charged by President Lyndon Johnson with investigating the causes of the civil disorders that rent the nation for several years during the 1960s, the Commission concluded that the primary explanation was white racism. Moreover, it argued that, given the sustained and pervasive effects of racism, that "there can be no higher priority for national action and no higher claim on the nation's conscience" than the elimination of racism from American society (National Advisory Commission on Civil Disorders 1968:2). However, it warned that implementation of its recommendations would necessitate "unprecedented levels of funding and performance." Because implementation of these terms would be unpopular with the dominant group, the response to the Kerner report – both officially and unofficially – was to discredit or (perhaps more significant) to ignore its findings.

Because the conclusion that white racism was primarily responsible for the intense racial conflicts of the 1960s was unacceptable to most white Americans, the Commission's report demonstrated that majority solutions to social problems seldom entail basic alterations of the society's institutional patterns. On the one hand, the Kerner Commission indicted American institutions as the primary source of the racism that permeates the society. On the other hand, most of its recommendations involved changing blacks to conform to these institutions rather than substantially altering the institutions themselves. Such an approach, involving what Horton terms an *order model* of social problems, slights the basic institutional sources of racial inequality in American society, a subject that we will explore more fully in Parts 3 and 4.

Racism, Prejudice, and Discrimination

Prejudice and discrimination are important elements in all majority-minority relations. The term *prejudice* derives from two Latin words, *prae* "before" and *judicum* "a judgment." It denotes a judgment before all the facts are known. According to Gordon Allport, *prejudice* is "an avertive or hostile attitude toward a person who belongs to a group, simply because he [or she] belongs to that group, and is therefore presumed to have the objectionable qualities ascribed to the group" (Allport 1958:8). Prejudice thus refers to a set of rigidly held negative attitudes, beliefs, and feelings toward members of another group.

Prejudice often involves an intense emotional component. Thus, many white Americans consciously and rationally reject the myths of African-American inferiority but react emotionally with fear, hostility, or condescension in the presence of African-Americans. The forms of prejudice range from unconscious aversion to members of the out-group to a comprehensive, well-articulated, and coherent ideology, such as the ideology of racism.

Discrimination, on the other hand, involves unfavorable treatment of individuals because of their group membership. Prejudice and discrimination should not be equated. Prejudice involves attitudes and internal states, whereas discrimination involves overt action or behavior. Discrimination may be manifested in a multitude of ways: mild slights (such as Polish jokes); verbal threats, abuse, and epithets; intimidation and harassment (such as threatening phone calls); defacing property with ethnic slurs, graffiti, or symbols; unequal treatment (such as refusing to hire or promote qualified applicants); systematic oppression (such as slavery); or outright violence (vandalism, arson, terrorism, lynching, pogroms, massacres).

Because sociologists are primarily concerned with human behavior, the focus in this book is discrimination. Clearly, however, a close relationship frequently exists between prejudice and discrimination. Consequently, an extensive amount of research has been carried out concerning the nature and causes of prejudice. Attitude surveys conducted in the United States since the 1940s have shown a significant decline in antiblack prejudice; increasingly, white Americans have come to support broad principles of racial integration and equal treatment in public accommodations, employment, public transportation, schools, and housing. For example, in 1942, 32 percent agreed that whites and blacks should attend the same schools; by 1982 this figure was 90 percent. In 1944, 45 percent thought that blacks should have as good a chance as whites to get any kind of job; and by 1972, 97 percent agreed. The percentage approving integration in public transportation rose from 46 percent in 1942 to 88 percent in 1970. Moreover, whites have indicated increasing willingness to participate personally in desegregated settings (Schuman, Steeh, and Bobo 1985). These changes are a result of two factors. First, they reflect attitude changes among individuals over their lifetimes. Second, younger people generally exhibit less racial prejudice than their elders, and as younger, more tolerant, cohorts have replaced older, more prejudiced ones, overall racial prejudice has declined (Firebaugh and Davis 1988).

However, as Gerald Jaynes and Robin Williams (1989) point out in Article 26, the same striking agreement does not appear among Americans on how to combat discrimination or segregation. Although today white Americans endorse broad principles of nondiscrimination and desegregation in important areas of American life, they are much less likely to support policies for translating these principles into practice. For example, despite the strong support among white Americans for the principle of integrated education, the percentage of whites who felt that the federal government should ensure that black and white children attend the same schools declined between the 1960s and 1980s. Moreover, widespread white opposition was raised to busing as a means of desegregating schools (Schuman, Steeh, and Bobo 1985).

The substantial gap between people's support for broad principles of equality and their support for specific programs to implement these principles indicates the complexity of racial attitudes. The relationship between prejudicial attitudes and discriminatory behavior is equally complex. Prejudice does not always produce discrimination, although it has frequently been treated as the cause of discrimination. An individual, however, may be prejudiced without *acting* in a discriminatory manner. In recent years it has become less fashionable to express racial prejudice publicly. Overt forms of discrimination, such as exclusion from public accommodations, jobs, and colleges and universities—behaviors which in the past were tolerated by most whites—are now often prohibited by law and condemned by public opinion.

The distinction between prejudice and discrimination and the interrelationship between these two phenomena were first systematically developed by Robert Merton (1949) in his classic article, "Discrimination and the American Creed." "Prejudicial attitudes," Merton argued, "need not coincide with discriminatory behavior." Merton demonstrated the range of possible ways in which prejudice and discrimination interact by distinguishing among four types of individuals:

1. The unprejudiced nondiscriminator—the all-weather liberal
2. The unprejudiced discriminator—the fair-weather liberal
3. The prejudiced nondiscriminator—the fair-weather bigot
4. The prejudiced discriminator—the all-weather bigot

The unprejudiced nondiscriminator consistently adheres to the American creed of equality for all in both belief and practice. The unprejudiced discriminator, on the other hand, internalizes and may even articulate the ideals of the American creed but may acquiesce to group pressures to discriminate. Similarly, the prejudiced nondiscriminator conforms to social pressures not to discriminate despite harboring prejudices toward ethnic minorities. Finally, the prejudiced discriminator is, like the unprejudiced nondiscriminator, consistent in belief and practice, rejecting the American creed and engaging in personal discrimination.

Merton's discussion was critical to the recognition that whether prejudice becomes translated into discriminatory behavior depends on the social context. From this dynamic perspective it becomes impossible to understand the dynamics of majority-minority relations by examining prejudice alone; prejudice is most appropriately considered not as a causal factor but as a dependent variable. As Richard Schermerhorn has cogently suggested, prejudice "is a product of situations, historical situations, economic situations, political situations; it is not a little demon that emerges in people because they are depraved" (Schermerhorn 1970:6). To explain the dynamics of ethnic and racial relations fully, it is necessary to analyze the historical, cultural, and institutional conditions that have preceded and generated them.

During the past quarter century, the conceptualization of American race relations has undergone several significant changes. These changes have been profoundly influenced by the changing nature of race relations in the United States. Before the advent of the Black Protest Movement during the 1950s, social scientists focused their attention primarily on racial attitudes, because prejudice was thought to be the key to understanding racial and ethnic conflict. This perception of the essential dynamics of race relations is perhaps best illustrated in Myrdal's classic, *An American Dilemma,* in which he defined race prejudice as "the whole complex of valuations and beliefs which are behind discriminatory behavior on the part of the majority group . . . and which are contrary to the egalitarian ideals in the American Creed" (Myrdal 1944:52). Thus, as Paul

Metzger (1971) has pointed out, the liberal order model of race relations was predicated on the assumption that racial conflict in the United States was a problem of ignorance and morality that could best be solved by changing — through education and moral suasion — the majority's prejudicial attitudes toward racial minorities. "A great majority of white people in America," Myrdal wrote, "would be better prepared to give the Negro a substantially better deal if they knew the facts" (Myrdal 1944:48).

The black protest era of the 1950s and 1960s challenged the assumption that change in the patterns of racial inequality in American society could be brought about through a reduction in prejudicial attitudes alone. Sociologists and social activists focused increasingly on the dynamics of discrimination and sought means of eliminating discriminatory behavior. The numerous forms of direct protest, such as nonviolent sit-ins, boycotts, and voter registration drives, were tactics designed to alter patterns of discrimination. In keeping with this emphasis on discrimination were the legislative efforts undertaken to secure enactment of the Civil Rights Act of 1964, which outlawed discrimination in public accommodations and employment, and the 1965 Voting Rights Act, which provided federal support to ensure that African-Americans had the right to vote throughout the South.

However, the greatest racial unrest of the black protest era occurred after these legislative victories had been achieved. Whereas the earlier civil rights phase of the Black Protest Movement had been directed primarily against public discrimination and especially its manifestations in the South, the outbreak of urban riots in northern cities focused attention on the nature of racial inequalities affecting African-Americans throughout the entire nation. For several summers during the late 1960s, the nation was torn with racial strife. Parts of cities were burned, property damage ran into the millions of dollars, and the toll of dead — primarily, although not exclusively, blacks — numbered almost a hundred (National Advisory Commission on Civil Disorders 1968:116). In July, 1967, President Lyndon Johnson appointed a national commission (the Kerner Commission) to investigate the cause of these urban riots. In 1968 the commission issued its report, which concluded:

> *What white Americans have never fully understood — but what the Negro can never forget — is that white society is deeply implicated in the ghetto. White society condones it. . . . Race prejudice has shaped our history decisively in the past; it now threatens to do so again. White racism is essentially responsible for the explosive mixture which has been accumulating in our cities since the end of World War II. (National Advisory Commission on Civil Disorders 1968:203)*

Racism

Especially since the Kerner Commission concluded that the ultimate responsibility for the racial disorders of the 1960s should be attributed to "white racism," the term has been widely invoked to explain racial inequalities and conflict in American society. However, the term is extremely imprecise and ambiguous.

This imprecision enabled President Johnson, who had created the Commission, to ignore its findings and his successor, Richard Nixon, to condemn and deny them. Consequently, the term *racism* is in urgent need of clarification.

First, *racism* is a general term, subsuming several analytically distinct phenomena—prejudice and several forms of discrimination. Stokely Carmichael and Charles Hamilton distinguished between *individual* racism and *institutional* racism:

> *Racism is both overt and covert. It takes two closely related forms: individual whites acting against individual blacks and acts by the total white community against the black community. . . . The second type is less overt, far more subtle, less identifiable in terms of specific individuals committing the acts. But it is no less destructive of human life. . . . When white terrorists bomb a black church and kill five black children, that is an act of individual racism, widely deplored by most segments of the society. But when in that same city— Birmingham, Alabama—five hundred black babies die each year because of the lack of proper food, shelter, and medical facilities, and thousands more are destroyed and maimed physically, emotionally, and intellectually because of the conditions of poverty and discrimination in the black community, that is a function of institutional racism. (Carmichael and Hamilton 1967:4)*

However, as I will note more fully below, prejudicial attitudes are causal factors in Carmichael and Hamilton's conceptualization of institutional racism. Moreover, they do not distinguish between psychological and sociological factors in its operation.

Another problem in the use of the word *racism* is that although it lumps together all forms of racial oppression, it is not sufficiently inclusive. It does not encompass majority-minority situations based on criteria other than race—criteria such as religion, tribal identity, ethnicity, or gender. Therefore, in the following discussion, I have analytically distinguished the terms *racism, prejudice,* and *discrimination.*

The term *racism* has traditionally referred to an *ideology*—a set of ideas and beliefs—used to explain, rationalize, or justify a racially organized social order. There are two essential parts of racism: its content and its function. Racism is distinguished from ethnocentrism by insistence that differences among groups are biologically based. The in-group is believed to be innately superior to the out-group, and members of the out-group are defined as being "biogenetically incapable of ever achieving intellectual and moral equality with members of the in-group" (Noel 1972:157). Howard Schuman has offered a commonly accepted definition of racism:

> *The term* racism *is generally taken to refer to the belief that there are clearly distinguishable human races; that these races differ not only in superficial physical characteristics, but also innately in important psychological traits; and finally that the differences are such that one race (almost always one's own, naturally) can be said to be superior to another. (Schuman 1969:44)*

Racism's primary function has been to provide a rationale and ideological support – a moral justification – for maintaining a racially based social order. In other words, the assertion of the innate "natural" superiority or inferiority of different racial groups serves to justify domination and exploitation of one group by another. As Manning Nash has written, "no group of [people] is able systematically to subordinate or deprive another group of [people] without appeal to a body of values which makes the exploitation, the disprivilege, the expropriation, and the denigration of human beings a 'moral' act" (Nash 1962:288). In addition, an ideology of racism not only provides a moral justification for the dominant group of their positions of privilege and power; it also discourages minority groups from questioning their subordinate status and advancing claims for equal treatment.

Van den Berghe (1967:16–18) has suggested three major sources of Western racism. First, racism developed as a justification of capitalist forms of exploitation, particularly slavery in the New World. As Donald Noel has argued, "As slavery became ever more clearly the pivotal institution of Southern society, racism was continually strengthened and became an ever more dominant ideology" (Noel 1972:162).

Second, racism was congruent with Darwinian notions of stages of evolution and survival of the fittest, and with the idea of Anglo-Saxon superiority. According to these doctrines, those people in inferior social positions were destined to their station because they were least evolved or least fit in the struggle for existence. In 1870, Francis A. Walker, United States Commissioner of Immigration, characterized the most recent immigrants in the following manner:

> They are beaten men from beaten races; representing the worst failures in the struggle for existence. Centuries are against them, as centuries were on the side of those who formerly came to us. They have none of the ideas and aptitudes which fit men to take up readily and easily the problem of self-care and self-government. (Quoted in Saveth 1948:40)

The third explanation of racism, van den Berghe argues, is paradoxically related to the egalitarian ideas of the Enlightenment, which were expressed in the Declaration of Independence;

> Faced with the blatant contradiction between the treatment of slaves and colonial peoples and the official rhetoric of freedom and equality, Europeans and white North Americans began to dichotomize humanity between men and submen (or the "civilized" and the "savages"). The scope of applicability of the egalitarian ideals was restricted to "the people," that is, the whites, and there resulted . . . regimes such as those of the United States or South Africa that are democratic for the master race but tyrannical for the subordinate groups. The desire to preserve both the profitable forms of discrimination and exploitation and the democratic ideology made it necessary to deny humanity to the oppressed groups. (van den Berghe 1967:17–18)

As noted above, there has been a substantial decline in professions of racist attitudes among white Americans in the past half century; especially since 1970, white Americans have increased their approval of racial integration (Taylor, Sheatsley, and Greeley 1978; Schuman, Steeh, and Bobo 1985). In 1942, only 42 percent of a national sample of whites reported that they believed blacks to be equal to whites in innate intelligence; since the late 1950s, however, around 80 percent of white Americans have rejected the idea of inherent black inferiority. The Kerner Commission was therefore misleading in lumping all white antipathy toward blacks into the category of racism. Rather than believing blacks are genetically inferior, the dominant white ideology is one of free will: everyone can better their lot, if they are not too lazy to make the effort. This belief is not inherently racist, but a general judgment about human nature that can be applied to all sorts of human conditions or groupings. However, when applied to African-Americans, the belief system of free will is racist in that it refuses to recognize or acknowledge the existence of external impingements and disabilities (such as prejudice and discrimination) and instead imputes the primary responsibility for black disadvantages to blacks themselves. African-Americans, by this definition, are still considered inferior people; otherwise they would be as well off as whites.

If the term *racism* referred merely to the realm of beliefs and not to behavior or action, its relevance for the study of race relations would be limited. To restrict the meaning of racism to ideology would be to ignore the external constraints and societally imposed disabilities—rooted in the power of the majority group—confronting a racial minority. As Noel points out in Article 5, if one group does not possess the power to impose its belief system on another, ethnic stratification cannot occur. During the late 1960s and 1970s, when critics charged that the ideology of Black Power was "racism in reverse," African-American spokespersons responded that their critics failed to consider the components of differential power that enabled the ideology of white supremacy to result in white domination:

> There is no analogy—by any stretch of definition or imagination—between the advocates of Black Power and white racists. Racism is not merely exclusion on the basis of race but exclusion for the purpose of subjugating or maintaining subjugation. The goal of the racists is to keep black people on the bottom, arbitrarily and dictatorially, as they have done in this country for over three hundred years. (Carmichael and Hamilton 1967:47)

Therefore, the crucial component of a definition of racism is behavioral. Racism in its most inclusive sense refers to actions on the part of a racial majority that have discriminatory effects, preventing members of a minority group from securing access to prestige, power, and privilege. These actions may be intentional or unintentional. This broader conception of racism therefore entails discrimination as well as an ideology that proclaims the superiority of one racial grouping over another.

As noted above, *discrimination* refers to the differential treatment of members of a minority group. Discrimination in its several forms comprises the means by which the unequal status of the minority group and the power of the majority group are preserved. In the ensuing discussion, I distinguish between *attitudinal* discrimination, which refers to discriminatory practices attributable to or influenced by prejudice, and *institutional* discrimination, which cannot be attributed to prejudice, but instead is a consequence of society's normal functioning. Both of these types can be further elaborated according to the sources of the discriminatory behavior. In reality, these types are at times interrelated and reinforce each other. Seldom is discrimination against a minority group member derived from one source alone.

Attitudinal Discrimination

Attitudinal discrimination refers to discriminatory practices that stem from prejudicial attitudes. The discriminator either is prejudiced or acts in response to the prejudices of others. Attitudinal discrimination is usually direct, overt, visible, and dramatic. Despite increasing white acceptance of principles of non-discrimination and racial segregation, ethnic minorities, especially African-Americans, continue to be confronted with incidents of attitudinal discrimination. During the 1980s hundreds of incidents of intimidation, harassment, and vandalism occurred against racial minorities, including incidents on over 175 college campuses (Southern Poverty Law Center 1987; *Time* 1987; Magner 1989). The U.S. Justice Department reported 276 violent attacks by whites against blacks in 1986 alone. Between 1980 and 1988 the number of reported incidents of racial harassment and intimidation increased dramatically. In Kansas City, for example, the number of such incidents quadrupled between 1980 and 1988 (Penn 1989:B1).

In 1985 and 1986 alone, 45 cases were documented of arson and cross-burnings after minority families moved into predominantly white neighborhoods. Although such "move-in" violence was found throughout the entire nation, the majority of cases occurred in the North and Midwest. In Philadelphia an African-American couple were forced to move from their new home after they were threatened by a crowd of 400 whites, who jeered at them with taunts of "Beat it" and "We want them out" (*U.S. News and World Report* 1985:12). In Cleveland, a 66-year-old African-American woman was killed in her home when it was firebombed. In Chicago, a white neighbor of black victims of arson justified such violence to a reporter: "I don't think [arson] is right. But it's also not right for them to come into a neighborhood when it's all white" (Southern Poverty Law Center 1987:7).

Attitudinal discrimination does not always occur in so virulent or so direct a manner. It may be manifested less dramatically merely by the acceptance by members of the dominant group of social definitions of traditional subordinate group roles. Malcolm X, the charismatic black protest leader who was assassinated in 1965, recalled how his well-intentioned white high school English teacher, Mr. Ostrowski, was bound by cultural norms concerning the "proper" caste roles for blacks:

> *I know that he probably meant well in what he happened to advise me that day. I doubt that he meant any harm. . . . I was one of his top students, one of the school's top students—but all he could see for me was the kind of future "in your place" that almost all*

white people see for black people. . . . He told me, "Malcolm, you ought to be thinking about a career. Have you been giving it any thought? . . . The truth is, I hadn't. I have never figured out why I told him, "Well, yes, sir, I've been thinking I'd like to be a lawyer." Lansing certainly had no lawyers—or doctors either—in those days, to hold up an image I might have aspired to. All I really knew for certain was that a lawyer didn't wash dishes, as I was doing.

Mr. Ostrowski looked surprised, I remember, and leaned back in his chair and clasped his hands behind his head. He kind of half-smiled and said, "Malcolm, one of life's first needs is for us to be realistic. Don't misunderstand me, now. We all here like you, you know that. But you've got to be realistic about being a nigger. A lawyer—that's no realistic goal for a nigger. You need to think about something you can be. You're good with your hands—making things. Everybody admires your carpentry shop work. Why don't you plan on carpentry? People like you as a person—you'd get all kinds of work." (Malcolm X 1966:36)

Here we should recall Merton's distinction between the prejudiced discriminator and the unprejudiced discriminator. According to the definition advanced above, discrimination involves differential treatment of individuals because of their membership in a minority group. The term has traditionally referred to actions of people who arbitrarily deny equal treatment (for example, equal opportunity to obtain a job or to purchase a home) to minority group members because of the personal prejudices they harbor toward such groups. Such is the behavior of the prejudiced discriminator or all-weather bigot.

But discrimination can occur without the discriminator necessarily harboring prejudices. As Merton points out, an unprejudiced discriminator—the fair-weather liberal—can discriminate simply by conforming to existing cultural patterns or by acquiescing to the dictates of others who are prejudiced. Such discrimination can be attributed to the actor's conscious or unconscious perception of the negative effects that nondiscriminatory behavior will have. An employer or a realtor may genuinely disclaim any personal prejudice for having refused a minority group member a job or home. Perhaps they felt constrained by the negative sanctions of peers, or by the fear of alienating customers. In this case, the discriminatory actor's judgment would be based on the prejudicial attitudes of a powerful reference group. Although the heart and mind of the actors in our hypothetical situations may be devoid of any personal prejudice, nevertheless, the consequences—no job, no home—for the minority-group applicant are no different than if they were old-fashioned, dyed-in-the-wool bigots.

Attitudinal discrimination remains an important component of intergroup relations. One of the most prominent examples is the world of sports, which is perceived by most Americans to be devoid of racism. Although there have been substantial—even overwhelming—changes in the racial composition of sports teams during the past quarter of a century, the persistence of racial stacking (the placement of black and white players in certain positions, such as quarterback or wide receiver, in which they are stereotyped as best suited), the omission of African-Americans from leadership and outcome-control positions, and the relative dearth of African-Americans in second-team positions indicate discrimination is still a factor in player selection. The effects of attitudinal discrimination are even more pronounced at management levels: while African-Americans are overrepresented in player roles, there is a dearth of African-American executives, managers, coaches, scouts, and officials (Yetman and Eitzen 1982; Jaynes and Williams 1989:95–98).

Communication, including the mass media and everyday conversation, provides one of the most important means by which negative images and the powerlessness of minorities are (often unconsciously) perpetuated. Geneva Smitherman-Donaldson and Tevn van Dijk contend that the process of communication and discourse "essentially reproduces and helps produce the racist cognitions and actions of and among the white majority" (1988:18). They use the term *symbolic racism* to refer to communications that preserve or justify racist acts and policies.

> *Even more than physical racism (or sexism for that matter), symbolic racism allows for subtlety, indirectness, and implication. It may, paradoxically, be expressed by the unsaid, or be conveyed by apparent "tolerance" and egalitarian liberalism. Whereas the racial slur, the graffiti, or the old movie may be blatantly racist, many other present-day types of talk may communicate racism in a more veiled way.*
>
> *In everyday talk, underlying ethnic prejudices may indirectly appear in "innocent" stories about a black neighbor, or about a Turkish immigrant worker cleaning the office. Although such stories claim to tell the "facts," describe how "they" did it (wrong) again, or generally imply that "they" are stupid, lazy, welfare-cheats, criminal, or lack motivation to learn, the storyteller may, at the same time, emphasize that he has nothing against "them," and they are his "best friends." Yet the stories, spreading quickly in families, schools, or neighborhoods, and occasionally greatly magnified by media reproduction, contribute to the fundamental communication and reproduction of racism in society. (Smitherman-Donaldson and van Dijk 1988:18)*

Symbolic racism is manifested in a variety of communication contexts. Popular magazines and children's literature have been among the most conspicuous purveyors of racial stereotypes. Although social scientists have pointed out the racially biased nature of these publications for decades, a 1965 study found that of 5,206 children's trade books published from 1962 through 1964, only 349, or 6.7 percent, included one or more blacks (Larrick 1965:63–65; Berelson and Steiner 1946; Klineberg 1963; Teague 1968). Moreover, Tom Engelhardt (1971) has shown that the cultural stereotypes in American movies reinforce those found in other media forms. All positive, humanitarian virtues remain with whites: even if they represent the dregs of Western society, "any White is a step up from the rest of the world." Nonwhites, on the other hand, are depicted as alien intruders, helpless, dependent, or less than human. When they do assume center stage, they do so as villains—"the repository for evil." Finally, as Shirley Hune's analysis of Asian-American historical treatment demonstrates (Article 12), racial and ethnic stereotypes have been reinforced and legitimated by the omission, distortion, or misrepresentation of the role of racial and ethnic minorities in the nation's history books (see also Henry 1967 and Stampp et al. 1968). She shows how the assumptions of leading intellectuals—social scientists and historians in particular—have influenced policies and practices toward both

European and Asian immigrants. Therefore, whether undertaken consciously or unconsciously, intentionally or unintentionally, perpetuation of these symbolic biases serves to reflect and reinforce cultural beliefs in the racial inferiority of nonwhites.

Institutional Discrimination

Both forms of attitudinal discrimination defined above are ultimately reducible to psychological variables: the actor is prejudiced, defers to, or is influenced by the sanctions of a prejudiced reference group or the norms of a racially biased culture. Institutional discrimination, on the other hand, refers to organizational practices and societal trends that exclude minorities from equal opportunities for positions of power and prestige. This discrimination has been labeled "structural" by some scholars (*Research News,* 1987:9). Institutional or structural discrimination involves "policies or practices which appear to be neutral in their effect on minority individuals or groups, but which have the effect of disproportionately impacting on them in harmful or negative ways" (Task Force on the Administration of Military Justice in the Armed Forces 1972:19). The effects or consequences of institutional discrimination have little relation to racial or ethnic attitudes or to the majority group's racial or ethnic prejudices.

The existence of institutional inequalities that effectively exclude substantial portions of minority groups from participation in the dominant society has seldom been considered under the category of discrimination. According to J. Milton Yinger, discrimination is "the persistent application of criteria that are arbitrary, irrelevant, or unfair by *dominant standards,* with the result that some persons receive an undue advantage and others, *although equally qualified,* suffer an unjustified penalty" (Yinger 1968:449, italics added). The underlying assumption of this definition is that if all majority-group members would eliminate "arbitrary, irrelevant, and unfair criteria," discrimination would, by definition, cease to exist. However, if prejudice – and the attitudinal discrimination that emanates from it – were eliminated overnight, the inequalities rooted in the normal and impersonal operation of existing institutional structures would remain. Therefore, the crucial issue is not the equal treatment of those with equal qualifications, but access of minority-group members to the qualifications themselves.

Institutional discrimination is thus more subtle, covert, and complex, and less visible and blatant than attitudinal discrimination. Because it does not result from the motivations or intentions of specific individuals, but rather from policies that appear race-neutral, institutional discrimination is more impersonal than attitudinal discrimination and its effects are more easily denied or ignored. Nevertheless, it has the same discriminatory consequences for minority-group members. In examining institutional discrimination, therefore, it is more important to consider the *effect* of a particular policy or practice upon a minority group than it is to consider the *motivations* of the majority group.

Because it emphasizes the role of impersonal social forces, an institutional discrimination model focuses on the effects of broad structural factors in modern American society, especially in the economy. In their analysis of the under-class in Article 27, Loïc Wacquant and William Julius Wilson (1989) have identi-fied several broad economic factors that have recently contributed to the deterioration of social conditions in the black ghetto: the shift from goods-producing to service-producing industries, increasing labor market segmenta-tion, increased industrial technology, and the flight of industries from central cities.

This emphasis on the impact of broad structural changes raises the issue – a perennial concern among scholars in the field – of whether racial and ethnic relations are unique forms of structured social inequality or whether they are ultimately reducible to class factors. That the dynamics of race and ethnicity are influenced at a deeper level by class factors is Edna Bonacich's thesis in Article 3, "Class Approaches to Ethnicity and Race." Bonacich distinguishes between two broad types of social movements: *communalist,* which emphasize ethnic, racial, national, or tribal in-group solidarity and cut across class lines; and *class,* which emphasize common class interests and reject appeals to ethnic solidarity. From these two basic orientations she examines several class models (including the split labor market and middleman minority models that she has been instrumen-tal in developing) that have been advanced to explain the salience of ethnic and racial divisions in modern societies.

Having elaborated several variants of class-oriented models of racial and ethnic relations, Bonacich then seeks to develop an integrated class model. She suggests that the dynamics of race and ethnicity in the modern world in general, and in the contemporary United States in particular, must be conceptualized within the context of the world capitalist system. She contends that as the price of labor increases in developed nations, capital seeks alternative sources of labor. One consequence is the runaway shop, in which the labor is located in another country. The advantage of such an arrangement is that the capitalist is able to hire people who traditionally have worked for subsistence and, consequently, have low wage expectations. Moreover, such workers are unfamiliar with or disinclined to join trade unions, and their standards of living are lower than those of workers in developed countries. All these factors enable capitalists to hire workers at much lower wages than would be possible in the developed country.

An alternative to taking the employment opportunity abroad is to induce foreign workers to immigrate to the developed country, where, lacking many of the advantages available to indigenous labor, such as wages, medical and retire-ment benefits, workmen's compensation, and the like, they work under condi-tions that undermine the bargaining power of indigenous labor.

Bonacich demonstrates how communalist factors (race, ethnicity, or nation-ality) affect the multiplicity of possible relationships that can develop between capitalist and worker classes in the two different countries. Her analysis shows how closely linked are the issues of the expanding American underclass and, simultaneously, the recent upsurge in immigration, especially of illegal immi-grants, into the United States. On the one hand, the economic status of African-American workers, especially, has recently been severely affected by the flight of manufacturing jobs out of central cities in the industrial Northeast and Midwest to the suburbs, the Sunbelt, and overseas. On the other hand, illegal immigrants are encouraged to enter the United States, where they work under precarious economic and political conditions. "Immigrant labor, or the runaway shop to cheap countries or regions," writes Bonacich, "is used by capital in the form both of threat and reality to constrain its national working class." The nature and impact of these structural changes on the economy, and the increasing significance of contemporary immigration to these changes, will be discussed more fully in Part 4.

In her effort to develop an integrated model of race and ethnicity, Bonacich emphasizes the manner in which economic forces affect the dynamics of racial and ethnic relations and suggests that the state be considered as a "semi-autonomous" factor. However, numerous scholars (see especially Olzak and Nagel 1986) have recently drawn attention to the role of politics and the state in creating, heightening, and maintaining ethnic distinctions and divisions. From this perspective, the state is not merely a reflection of economic forces, but plays an independent role in the process of creating and maintaining ethnicity.

For example, Cynthia Enloe (1981) has shown how the civil bureaucracy, the judiciary, and the military each have contributed to the intensification of racial and ethnic divisions in American society. Similarly, in an analysis of public school desegregation within and between American cities and their suburbs, David James (1989) has shown that the state, by creating political boundaries that separate school districts and refusing to accept interdistrict desegregation, has been instrumental in creating school segregation and reinforcing patterns of social inequality. Suburban rings surrounding major American cities tend to have multiple school districts, and black suburbanites tend to be concentrated in areas close to the central cities. Therefore, because the Supreme Court has ruled that racial segregation *within* school districts is unconstitutional but that segregation *between* districts is not, whites can avoid living in school districts with large proportions of black students. Therefore, ethnicity cannot be adequately understood solely in reference to economic factors but must consider the actions of the state as well.

In "The Political Construction of Ethnicity" (Article 4), Joane Nagel emphasizes the situational, contextual nature of ethnicity – that it is a dynamic, ever-changing, and constantly emergent social construct that is continuously being created and recreated to be used in the competition for power and resources. She differs from Bonacich in her emphasis on the importance of the state and political factors in eliciting, heightening, and reinforcing ethnicity as an organizational resource around which competition for resources and power can be played out. Nagel contends that ethnicity may be *resurgent* (a revitalization of historic identities) or *emergent* (the creation of newly formed groups). (See, for example, Article 23, "A New Ethnic Group in The United States.") Her primary objective is to identify the conditions under which ethnic mobilization – "the process by which a group organizes along ethnic lines in pursuit of group ends" – occurs. Her analysis suggests that the state possesses a capacity – one frequently ignored by students of race and ethnicity – to shape ethnic relations and to generate ethnic awareness and identification, either intentionally or unintentionally. Her basic thesis is that because ethnicity in the modern world is a largely political phenomenon, because it arises out of the political structures and policies of the modern nation-state, it is unlikely that its significance will diminish in the near future. The implication is that, as the power of the American state continues to expand and penetrate all sectors of modern life, the salience of ethnicity is unlikely to decline. In all probability, ethnicity will continue to have an important influence, not because it reflects natural or primordial sentiments, but because the forces of the state elicit it. Nagel's argument, therefore, has special relevance to Part 4, in which we shall consider more fully the future of race and ethnicity in American life.

Race, Caste, and Other Invidious Distinctions in Social Stratification

Gerald D. Berreman

A society is socially stratified when its members are divided into categories which are differentially powerful, esteemed, and rewarded. Such systems of collective social ranking vary widely in the ideologies which support them, in the distinctiveness, number and size of the ranked categories, in the criteria by which inclusion in the categories is conferred and changed, in the symbols by which such inclusion is displayed and recognized, in the degree to which there is consensus upon or even awareness of the ranking system, its rationale, and the particular ranks assigned, in the rigidity of rank, in the disparity in rewards of rank, and in the mechanisms employed to maintain or change the system.

For purposes of study, such systems have been analysed variously depending upon the interests and motives of the analyst. One of the most frequently used bases for categorizing and comparing them has been whether people are accorded their statuses and privileges as a result of characteristics which are regarded as individually acquired, or as a result of characteristics which are regarded as innate and therefore shared by those of common birth. This dichotomy is often further simplified by application of the terms "achieved" versus "ascribed" status. Actually, what is meant is *non*-birth-ascribed status versus birth-ascribed status. The former is usually described as class stratification, referring to shared statuses identified by such features as income, education, and occupation, while the latter is frequently termed caste or racial stratification or, more recently, ethnic stratification, referring

to statuses defined by shared ancestry or attributes of birth.

Regardless of its characteristics in a particular society, stratification has been described as being based upon three primary dimensions: class, status, and power, which are expressed respectively as wealth, prestige, and the ability to control the lives of people (oneself and others).[1] These dimensions can be brought readily to mind by thinking of the relative advantages and disadvantages which accrue in Western class systems to persons who occupy such occupational statuses as judge, garbage man, stenographer, airline pilot, factory worker, priest, farmer, agricultural laborer, physician, nurse, big businessman, beggar, etc. The distinction between class and birth-ascribed stratification can be made clear if one imagines . . . two Americans, for example, in each of the above-mentioned occupations, one of whom is white and one of whom is black. This quite literally changes the complexion of the matter. A similar contrast could be drawn if, in India, one were Brahmin and one untouchable; if in Japan one were Burakumin and one were not; if in Europe one were Jew and one were Gentile; or if, in almost any society, one were a man and one a woman. Obviously something significant has been added to the picture of stratification in these examples which is entirely missing in the first instance – something over which the individual generally has no control, which is determined at birth, which cannot be changed, which is shared by all those of like birth, which is crucial to social identity, and which vitally affects one's oppor-

Reprinted from *Race* (Volume XIII, no. 4, April 1972) by permission of the author and The Institute of Race Relations, London.

tunities, rewards, and social roles. The new element is race (color), caste, ethnicity (religion, language, national origin), or sex. The differences in opportunities and behavior accorded people as a result of these criteria are described by such pejorative terms as racism, casteism, communalism (including especially ethnic and religious discrimination), and sexism. To be sure, the distinctions are manifest in class, status, and power, but they are of a different order than those considered in the first examples: they are distinctions independent of occupation, income, or other individually acquired characteristics. While the list includes a variety of criteria for birth-ascription and rank with somewhat different implications for those to whom they are applied, they share the crucial facts that: (1) the identity is regarded as being a consequence of birth or ancestry and hence immutable; (2) the identity confers upon its possessor a degree of societally defined and affirmed worth which is regarded as intrinsic to the individual; (3) this inherent worth is evaluated relative to that of all others in the society – those of different birth are inherently unequal and are accordingly adjudged superior or inferior, while those regarded as being of similar birth are innately equal. The crucial fact about birth-ascription for the individual and for society lies not so much in the source of status (birth), as in the fact that it cannot be repudiated, relinquished, or altered. Everyone is sentenced for life to a social cell shared by others of like birth, separated from and ranked relative to all other social cells. Despite cultural differences, therefore, birth-ascribed stratification has common characteristics of structure, function, and meaning, and has common consequences in the lives of those who experience it and in the social histories of the societies which harbor it.

The specific question motivating the present discussion is this: is social ranking by race absolutely distinctive, not significantly distinctive at all, or is race one criterion among others upon which significantly similar systems of social ranking may be based? While identifying the last of these as "correct" from my perspective, I shall insist that the answer depends entirely upon what one means by "race," and by "distinctive," and what one wishes to accomplish by the inquiry. No satisfactory answer can be expected

without comparative, cross-cultural analysis encompassing a number of systems of social differentiation, social separation, and social ranking, based on a variety of criteria, embedded in a variety of cultural *milieux,* analysed by reference to various models of social organization, and tested against accounts of actual social experience. The attempt to do this leads to a number of issues central and tangential to the study of stratification and race, some of which have been overlooked or given short shrift in the scholarly literature, while others are well discussed in particular disciplinary, regional, or historical specialties without necessarily being familiar to students of other academic domains to whose work and thought they are nevertheless relevant.

There is not space here to present ethnographic and historical documentation for particular instances of birth-ascribed stratification. I have done so briefly in another paper, citing five societies on which there is fortunately excellent published material vividly exemplifying the kinds of social system I refer to in this paper, and their implications for those who comprise them: Rwanda, India, Swat, Japan, and the United States. I recommend those accounts to the reader.[2]

MODELS FOR ANALYSIS

In the course of scholarly debate concerning the nature and comparability of systems of collective social ranking, a number of models and concepts have been suggested, implied, or utilized. A framework can be provided for the present discussion by identifying some of these and analysing whether and to what extent each is relevant and applicable to all or some systems of birth-ascribed social separation and inequality, with special attention to the five societies cited above.

Stratification

By definition, stratification is a common feature of systems of shared social inequality – of ranked social categories – whether birth-ascribed or not. Where membership in those categories is birth-ascribed, the ranking is based on traditional definitions of innate social equivalence and difference linked to a concept of differential intrinsic worth, rationalized by a myth of the origin, effect, and legitimacy of the system, perpetuated by differential power wielded by the high and the low, expressed in differential behaviors required and differential rewards accorded them, and experienced by them as differential access to goods, services, livelihood, respect, self-determination, peace of mind, pleasure, and other valued things including nourishment, shelter, health, independence, justice, security, and long life.

Louis Dumont, in *Homo Hierarchicus,* maintains that the entire sociological notion of stratification is misleading when applied to South Asia, for it is of European origin, alien and inapplicable to India. He holds that the term implies an equalitarian ideology wherein hierarchy is resented or denied, and that it therefore obscures the true nature of India's hierarchical society, based as it is on religious and ideological premises peculiar to Hinduism which justify it and result in its endorsement by all segments of Indian society. Stratification, he maintains, is thus a "sociocentric" concept which cannot cope with the unique phenomenon of Indian caste.[3] My response to this is twofold; first, the caste hierarchy based on the purity-pollution opposition, as Dumont insists, is well within any reasonable definition of stratification, for the latter refers to social structure and social relations rather than to their ideological bases; and second, Dumont's description of the functioning of, and ideological basis for, the caste hierarchy is idealized and similar to the one commonly purveyed by high caste beneficiaries of the system. Few low caste people would recognize it or endorse it. Yet their beliefs and understandings are as relevant as those of their social superiors to an understanding of the system. The low caste people with whom I have worked would find Dumont's characterization of "stratification" closer to their experience than his characterization of "hierarchy."[4]

Use of the stratification model focuses attention upon the ranking of two or more categories of people within a society, and upon the criteria and consequences of that ranking. Often, but not inevitably, those who use this concept place primary emphasis upon shared values and consensus, rather than power and conflict, as the bases for social ranking and its persistence. This emphasis is misleading, at best, when applied to

systems of birth-ascribed ranking, as I shall show. It is obvious, however, that while many systems of stratification are not birth-ascribed, all systems of social stratification, and any theory of social stratification must encompass them.

Ethnic Stratification
Probably the most recent, neutral, and nonspecific term for ascriptive ranking is "ethnic stratification." "An ethnic group consists of people who conceive of themselves as being alike by virtue of common ancestry, real or fictitious, and are so regarded by others,"[5] or it comprises "a distinct category of the population in a larger society whose culture is usually different from its own [and whose] members . . . are, or feel themselves, or are thought to be, bound together by common ties of race or nationality or culture."[6] Undoubtedly the systems under discussion fit these criteria. Use of the adjective "ethnic" to modify "stratification" places emphasis upon the mode of recruitment, encompassing a wide variety of bases for ascription, all of which are determined at birth and derive from putative common genetic makeup, common ancestry, or common early socialization and are therefore regarded as immutable. This commonality is held responsible for such characteristics as shared appearance, intelligence, personality, morality, capability, purity, honor, custom, speech, religion, and so forth. Usually it is held responsible for several of these. The ranked evaluation of these characteristics, together with the belief that they occur differentially from group to group and more or less uniformly within each group serves as the basis for ranking ethnic groups relative to one another.

Van den Berghe has held that "ethnic" should be distinguished from "race" or "caste" in that the former implies real, important, and often valued social and cultural differences (language, values, social organization), while the latter are artificial and invidious distinctions reflecting irrelevant (and sometimes non-existent) differences in physiognomy, or artificial differences in social role.[7] This is a useful point. In the recent sociological literature, however, "ethnic" has increasingly been used to refer to *all* social distinctions based on birth or ancestry, be they associated with race, language, or anything else. This is the usage adopted here. Moreover, as I shall elaborate in discussing pluralism below, race and caste entail the kinds of cultural distinctions cited by van den Berghe as diagnostic of ethnic diversity, for the social separation implied by those systems ensures social and cultural diversity. For example, van den Berghe's assertion that "nonwithstanding all the African mystique, Afro-Americans are in fact culturally Anglo-American,"[8] has been countered by ample evidence that the African origin, social separation, and collective oppression of blacks in America *has* resulted in an identifiable Afro-American culture.[9]

All systems of ethnic stratification are thus based on ancestry, approximating a theory of birth-ascription, and if the definitions set forth by advocates of this term are accepted, most systems of birth-ascribed stratification can properly be designated ethnic stratification. Perhaps the only recurrent exception is sexual stratification, wherein inherent, birth-ascribed, and biologically determined characteristics which are *independent* of ancestry are the basis for institutionalized inequality. This instance, exceptional in several respects, will be discussed separately below, and hence will not be alluded to repeatedly in intervening discussions although most of what is said applies to it also.

Caste

A widely applied and frequently contested model for systems of birth-ascribed rank is that of "caste," deriving from the example of Hindu India where the *jati* (almost literally, "common ancestry") is the type-case. *Jati* in India refers to interdependent, hierarchically ranked, birth-ascribed groups. The ranking is manifest in public esteem accorded the members of the various groups, in the rewards available to them, in the power they wield, and in the nature and mode of their interaction with others. *Jatis* are regionally specific and culturally distinct, each is usually associated with a traditional occupation and they are usually (but not always) endogamous. They are grouped into more inclusive, pan-Indian ranked categories called *varna* which are frequently confused with the constituent *jatis* by those using the term "caste." The rationale which justifies the system is both religious and philosophical, relying upon the idea of ritual purity and pollution to explain group rank, and upon the notions of right conduct *(dharma)*, just deserts *(karma)*, and rebirth to explain the individual's fate within the system. As an explanation of caste inequalities this rationale is advocated by those whom the system benefits, but is widely doubted, differently interpreted, or regarded as inappropriately applied by those whom the system oppresses.

Many students of stratification believe that the term "caste" conveys an impression of consensus and tranquility that does not obtain in systems of rigid social stratification outside of India. That notion, however, is no more applicable to, or derivable from Indian caste than any other instance of birth-ascribed stratification.[10]

If one concedes that caste can be defined cross-culturally (i.e., beyond Hindu India), then the systems under discussion here are describable as caste systems. That is, if one agrees that a caste system is one in which a society is made up of birth-ascribed groups which are hierarchically ordered, interdependent, and culturally distinct, and wherein the hierarchy entails differential evaluation, rewards, and association, then whether one uses the term "caste," or prefers "ethnic stratification," or some other term is simply a matter of lexical preference. If one requires of a caste system that it be based on consensus as to its rationale, its legitimacy, and the legitimacy of the relative rank of its constituent groups, then none of the examples mentioned here is a caste system. If one requires social tranquillity as a characteristic, then too, none of these is a caste system. If one allows that a caste system is held together by power and the ability of people within it to predict fairly accurately one another's behavior while disagreeing on almost anything or everything else, then all of these systems will qualify. If one requires a specifically Hindu rationale of purity and pollution and/or endogamy and/or strict and universal occupational specialization, then one restricts caste to India and to only certain regions and groups within India at that. If one requires for castes, as some do, a tightly organized corporate structure, then too one would exclude even in India some *jatis* and other groups commonly called "castes." (This, however, does seem to me to be the structural criterion which comes closest to differentiating Indian *jati* from other systems of birth-ascribed stratification, such as that of the United States. Corporateness evidently emerges as a response to oppression and as a mechanism for emancipation even where it has been previously minimal, e.g., in Japan, Rwanda, and the United States. Thus, the corporateness of Indian *jatis* may represent a late stage of development in caste systems rather than a fundamental difference in the Indian system.)

Jati in Hindu India and the equivalent but non-Hindu *quom* organization in Swat and Muslim India are each unique; yet both share the criteria by which I have defined caste, as do the tri-partite system of Rwanda and the essentially dual systems of Japan and the United States, and all share in addition (and in consequence, I believe) a wide variety of social and personal concomitants. Caste is a useful and widely used term because it is concise, well-known, and in fact (as contrasted to fantasy), the structural, functional, and existential analogy to Indian caste is valid for many other systems.

Race. Systems of "racial" stratification are those in which birth-ascribed status is associated with alleged physical differences among social categories, which are culturally defined as present and important. Often these differences are more imagined than real, sometimes they are entirely fictional and always a few physical traits are singled out for attention while most, including some which might differently divide the society if they were attended to, are ignored. Yet systems so described share the principle that ranking is based on putatively inborn, ancestrally derived, and significant physical characteristics.

Those who use this model for analysis generally base it upon the negative importance attached by Europeans to the darker skin color of those they have colonized, exterminated, or enslaved. A good many have argued that racially stratified societies are *sui generis;* that they are unique and hence not comparable to societies stratified on any other basis.[11] There is often a mystical quality to these arguments, as though race were an exalted, uniquely "real," valid, and important criterion for birth ascription, rendering it incomparable to other criteria. An element of inadvertent racism has in such instances infected the very study of race and stratification. In

fact, as is by now widely recognized, there is no society in the world which ranks people on the basis of biological race, i.e., on the basis of anything a competent geneticist would call "race," which means on the basis of distinctive shared genetic makeup derived from a common gene pool. "Race," as a basis for social rank is always a *socially* defined phenomenon which at most only very imperfectly corresponds to genetically transmitted traits and then, of course, only to phenotypes rather than genotypes. Racists regard and treat people as alike or different because of their group membership defined in terms of socially significant ancestry, not because of their genetic makeup. It could not be otherwise, for people are rarely geneticists, yet they are frequently racists.

To state this point would seem to be superfluous if it were not for the fact that it is continually ignored or contested by some influential scholars and politicians as well as the lay racists who abound in many societies. To cite but one well known recent example, Arthur Jensen, in his article on intelligence and scholastic achievement, maintains that there is a genetic difference in learning ability between blacks and whites in the United States.[12] Nowhere, however, does he offer evidence of how or to what extent his "Negro" and "White" populations are genetically distinct. All of those, and only those, defined in the conventional wisdom of American folk culture to be "Negro" are included by Jensen, regardless of their genetic makeup in the category whose members he claims are biologically handicapped in learning ability. Thus, large numbers of people are tabulated as "Negroes," a majority of whose ancestors were "white," and virtually all of Jensen's "Negroes" have significant but highly variable percentages of "white" ancestry. Although, also as a result of social definition, the "whites" do not have known "Negro" ancestry, the presumed genetic homogeneity of the "whites" is as undemonstrated and unexplored as that of the "Negroes." In short, there was no attempt to identify the genetic makeup or homogeneity of either group, the genetic distinctiveness of the two groups, or whether or how genetic makeup is associated with learning ability, or how learning ability is transmitted. This kind of reasoning is familiar and expectable in American racism, but not in a supposedly scientific treatise – a treatise whose author berates those who deplore his pseudo-science as themselves unscientific for failing to seriously consider his "evidence." The fallacy in Jensen's case is that he has selected for investigation two socially defined groupings in American society which are commonly regarded as innately different in social worth and which as a result are accorded widely and crucially divergent opportunities and life experiences. Upon finding that they perform differentially in the context of school and test performance, he attributes that fact to assumed but undemonstrated and uninvestigated biological differences. Thus, socially defined populations perform differently on socially defined tasks with socially acquired skills, and this is attributed by Jensen to biology. There are other defects in Jensen's research, but none more fundamental than this.[13] One is reminded of E.A. Ross's succinct assessment of over fifty years ago, that "race" is the cheap explanation tyros offer for any collective trait that they are too stupid or too lazy to trace to its origin in the physical environment, the social environment, or historical conditions."[14]

The point to be made here is that systems of "racial" stratification are social phenomena based on social rather than biological facts. To be sure, certain conspicuous characteristics which are genetically determined or influenced (skin color, hair form, facial conformation, stature, etc.) are widely used as convenient indicators by which ancestry and hence "racial" identity is recognized. This is the "color bar" which exists in many societies. But such indicators are never sufficient in themselves to indicate group membership and in some instances are wholly unreliable, for it is percentage rather than appearance or genetics which is the basis for these distinctions. One who does not display the overt characteristics of his "racial" group is still accorded its status if his relationship to the group is known or can be discovered. The specific rules for ascertaining racial identity differ from society to society. In America, if a person is known to have had a sociologically black ancestor, he is black regardless of how many of his ancestors were sociologically white (and even though he looks and acts white). In South Africa, most American blacks would be regarded as "colored" rather than

"black." Traditionally, in a mixed marriage, one is a Jew only if one's mother is a Jew. In contemporary India, an Anglo-Indian has a male European ancestor in the paternal line; female and maternal European ancestry are irrelevant. In racially stratified societies, phenotypical traits are thus never more than clues to a person's social identity.

As Shibutani and Kwan have noted, "a color line is something existing in the presuppositions of men."[15] ". . . What is decisive about 'race relations' is not that people are genetically different but that they approach one another with dissimilar perspectives."[16] Van den Berghe makes a similar point: "Race, of course, has no intrinsic significance, except to a racist. To a social scientist, race acquires meaning only through its social definition in a given society."[17]

This is illustrated by the title of DeVos and Wagatsuma's book, *Japan's Invisible Race*, dealing with the hereditarily stigmatized and oppressed Burakumin. The Japanese believe that these people are physically and morally distinct, and their segregation and oppression are explained on that basis when in fact they are not so at all. Instead they are recognizable only by family (ancestry), name, occupation, place of residence, life style, etc. The Burakumin thus comprise a "race" in the sociological sense of Western racism, but an "invisible" (i.e., not genetic or phenotypic) one. The authors subtitled the book, *Caste in Culture and Personality,* shifting the analogy from that of race (in the West) to that of caste (in India). The book could as well have been entitled: *Caste in Japan: Racial Stratification in Culture and Personality.*

The Japanese example brings up a point which needs to be made about the alleged uniqueness of "racial" stratification. *All* systems of birth-ascribed stratification seem to include a belief that the social distinctions are reflected in biological (i.e., "racial") differences. That is, caste and other ethnic differences are said to be revealed in physical makeup or appearance. Associated with these supposed natural and unalterable inherited physical characteristics are equally immutable traits of character, morality, intelligence, personality, and purity. This is the case in Japan, where no actual physical differences can be detected; it is true in India and Swat where physical stereotypes about castes abound but actual differences are minimal; it is true in Rwanda where the ranked groups are all black but are said to differ in stature and physiognomy as well as in culture; it is true in the United States where the physical differences are commonly and erroneously thought to be absolute. Cultural factors have to be relied upon in addition to whatever biological ones may be present, in order to make the important discriminations upon which ranked social interaction depends, and even then mistakes are frequently made. Throughout the world, people who look distinctive are likely to be regarded as socially different; people who are regarded as socially different are likely to be thought to look distinctive. They are also likely to be required to dress and act distinctively.

I suggest that, just as societies frequently dramatize the social differences among kin groups (e.g., sibs, clans, phratries) by giving to them totemic names and attributing to them characteristics of animals or plants, thereby identifying the social differences with biological species differences,[18] so also, societies with birth-ascribed status hierarchies dramatize and legitimize these crucial social differences by attributing to them innate biological, hence "racial," differences. As a result the concept of miscegenation arises, based on an ideology of innate difference contradicted by a persistent and recurrent perception of similarity by people of opposite sex across social boundaries.[19]

Thus, caste organization and ethnic stratification include racism; racial stratification is congruent with caste and ethnic stratification. Their ultimate coalescence is in the imputation of biological differences to explain and justify birth-ascribed social inequality. In this regard, sexual stratification can be seen to be a phenomenon of the same order.

This universality of racism in birth-ascribed stratification can be understood in the fact that physical traits not only dramatize social differentiation, but can also explain and justify it. The effect of such explanation is to make social inequality appear to be a natural necessity rather than a human choice and hence an artificial imposition. Social distinctions are man-made and learned; what man makes and learns he can unmake and unlearn. What God or biology has ordained is beyond man's control. The former may be defined as artificial, unjust, untenable, and

remediable; the latter as inevitable or divinely sanctioned. This is important because birth-ascribed stratification is widely or universally resented by those whom it oppresses (at least as it affects them), and advocated by those it rewards. Both categories share the human capability of empathy, and it inspires envy and resentment in the one and fear or guilt in the other. Racism— the self-righteous rationalization in terms of biology—is a desperate and perhaps ultimately futile attempt to counteract those subversive emotions.

In sum, "race," as commonly used by social scientists, emphasizes common physical characteristics (as does "sex"); "caste" emphasizes common rank, occupational specialization, endogamy, and corporate organization; "ethnic stratification" emphasizes cultural distinctiveness. These are real differences in meaning, but the degree of empirical overlap in systems so described, and the commonalities in the existential worlds of those who live within them are so great as to render the distinctions among them largely arbitrary, and irrelevant, for many purposes. Individual cases differ, but as types of social stratification, they are similar. With equal facility and comparable effect, they utilize as evidence of social identity anything which is passed on with the group: skin color, hair form, stature, physiognomy, language, dress, occupation, place of residence, genealogy, behavior patterns, religion. None is wholly reliable, all are difficult to dissimulate. In any case, strong sanctions can be brought to bear to minimize the temptation to "pass" among those who might be capable and tempted. As the case of India suggests and Japan confirms, social criteria can be as rigid as physical ones.

"Race" versus "Caste"

Considerable controversy has surrounded the terms "race" and "caste" when applied outside of the contexts in which they originated and to which they have been most widely applied: Western colonialism and Hindu India, respectively. This is understandable because there are important peculiarities in each of these situations, and to extend the terms beyond them requires that those peculiarities be subordinated to significant similarities. Systems of birth-ascribed inequality are sufficiently similar, however, to invite comparative study, and some general term is needed to refer to them. "Caste" has seemed to me more useful than "race," because it refers to social rather than allegedly biological distinctions, and it is the social distinctions which are universal in such systems. If it were a catchier term, "ethnic stratification" might replace both in the social scientific literature. Unfortunately it is not, so we must probably await a better term or tolerate continuing terminological dispute and confusion. In any case, it is the nature of birth-ascribed stratification—the ideas, behaviors, and experiences which comprise it, the effects it has on persons and societies and, quite frankly, the means by which it may be eliminated—in which I am interested. The words applied to it are of little importance. When I try to explain American race relations to Indians, I describe and analyze America as a caste stratified society, with attention to the similarities and differences in comparison with India. If I am trying to explain Indian caste stratification to Americans, I describe and analyse India as a racist society, with attention to the similarities and differences in comparison to the United States. I do this as a matter of translation from the social idiom of one society to the other. It is the most economic, vivid, and accurate way I know to convey these phenomena to people whose experience is limited to one system or the other. I do not think Indian caste *is* American race, or vice versa, but neither do I think that race stratification in America *is* race stratification in South Africa or that caste in India *is* caste in Swat, or that caste in the Punjab *is* caste in Kerala. Neither do I think racial stratification and racism are the same for blacks, Chicanos, and whites in America, or that caste stratification and casteism are the same for sweepers, blacksmiths, and Rajputs in Hindu India. There are features in all of these which are the same in important ways, and by focusing on these I think we can understand and explain and predict the experience of people in these diverse situations better than if we regard each of them as unique in every way.

Colonialism

The concept of colonialism has gained popularity in recent years for the analysis of racism and racial stratification in the West.[20] It therefore merits further discussion. This model focuses on the history of Western expansion and the exploi-tation of alien peoples, emphasizing notions of the superiority of the dominant, Western, white society whose members arrogated privilege to themselves through the exercise of power (usually technological, often military) to dominate, control, exploit, and oppress others. Racism has been an integral aspect of this process, for there usually have been differences in color between the colonizer and the colonized which were used to account for the alleged inferiority in ability, character, and mentality which in turn were used to justify colonial domination. Colonialism has been most often described as the result of overseas conquest, in which case the colonizing group has usually comprised a numerical minority. Less often colonialism has included conquest or expansion across national boundaries overland, but the results are the same, if the romance is less. These phenomena have recently come to be termed "external colonialism," in contrast to "internal colonialism," which refers to similar domination and exploitation, within a nation, of an indigenous, over-run, or imported minority. This distinction directs attention to the *locus* of colonial domination whereas the distinction between third-world and fourth-world colonies, cited above, directs attention to the *sources* of that domination.

While it has not been much easier to gain acceptance of the colonial model for analysis of American race relations than it has been to gain acceptance of the caste model, it is clear that here again, the problem is semantic rather than substantive. Some of those who argue persuasively the cross-cultural and multi-situational applicability of the colonial model deny such applicability for the caste model and in so doing use precisely the logic and data they deplore and regard as faulty when their intellectual adversaries deny applicability of "colonialism" outside of the classical overseas context.[21]

Colonialism, external and internal, is a process which has occurred repeatedly, in many contexts with many specific manifestations and many common results. It long antedates the recent period of European and American expansion. Caste stratification, racial stratification, ethnic stratification, and "pluralism" have been its recurrent products.[22] The point can be made with specific reference to caste in India. Rather than regarding colonialism as an antecedent condition which excludes traditional India from the category of racially or ethically stratified societies, it can well be used as a basis for assigning India historical priority among such societies, in the contemporary world. That is, traditional India may represent the most fully evolved and complex post-colonial society in the world. It is easy to obtain explanations of caste from informants or books in India which refer directly to the presumed early domination of primitive indigenes by advanced invaders. There is little doubt that the present caste system had its origins some 3,000 to 3,500 years ago in a socio-cultural confrontation that was essentially colonial. Low status was imposed on technologically disadvantaged indigenes by more sophisticated, militarily and administratively superior peoples who encroached or invaded from the north and west, arrogating to themselves high rank, privileges, and land. The large number of local and ethnically distinct groups on the subcontinent were fitted into a scheme of social hierarchy which was brought in or superimposed by the high status outsiders, culminating in the caste system we know today.[23] Social separation and social hierarchy based on ancestry became the essence of the system; colonial relations were its genesis. Even today, most tribal people—those who are geographically and economically marginal and culturally distinct—are incorporated into Hindu society, if at all, at the bottom of the hierarchy (except in those rare instances where they have maintained control over land or other important sources of income and power).

If one were to speculate on the course of evolution which ethnic stratification might take in the United States in the context of internal colonialism, of rigid separation, hierarchy, and discrimination which are part of it, and the demands for ethnic autonomy which arise in response to it, one possibility would be a caste system similar to, though less complex than that of India. The historical circumstances may be rather similar despite the separation of many hundreds of years, many thousands of miles and a chasm of cultural differences. Actually, development of the degree of social separation common in India seems at this point unlikely given the mass communications and mass education in the United States, its relative prosperity, and the rather widespread (but far from universal) commitment

to at least the trappings of social equality. But surely if anything is to be learned from history and from comparison, the case of the Indian subcontinent should be of major interest to students of American race and ethnic relations, social stratification, and internal colonialism.

In sum, colonialism is as inextricable from caste and race as caste and race are from one another. There may be instances of colonialism where birth-ascription is or becomes irrelevant, but every instance of caste, race, and ethnic stratification includes, and relies for its perpetuation upon, the kind of ethnic domination and exploitation that defines colonialism.

Class

Closely associated with each of the models discussed here is that of social class. Class is a matter of acquired status rather than of birth-ascription, and is in this respect distinct from race, caste, and ethnic stratification, with different social consequences. In a class system, one is ranked in accord with his behavior and attributes (income, occupation, education, life style, etc.). In a birth-ascribed system, by contrast, one behaves and exhibits attributes in accord with his rank. In a class system, individual mobility is legitimate, albeit often difficult, while in ascribed stratification it is explicitly forbidden. Systems of acquired rank—class systems—prescribe the means to social mobility; systems of ascribed rank proscribe them. As a consequence, a class system is a continuum; there are individuals who are intergrades, there are individuals in the process of movement, there are individuals who have experienced more than one rank. Miscegenation is not an issue because there are no ancestrally distinct groups to be inappropriately mixed. A birth-ascribed system is comprised of discrete ranks on the pattern of echelon organization, without legitimate mobility, without intergrades; the strata are named, publicly recognized, clearly bounded. Miscegenation is therefore a social issue. In a system of acquired ranks, the strata may be indistinct, imperfectly known, or even unknown to those within the system. In fact, there is considerable debate among students of stratification as to whether or not awareness of class is essential to a definition of class. Some hold that social classes are properly defined by social analysts who use such criteria as income to designate categories which may be entirely unrecognized by those in the society.

In a class system individuals regard themselves as potentially able to change status legitimately within the system through fortune, misfortune, or individual and family efforts. In a birth-ascribed system, individuals know that legitimate status change is impossible – that only dissimulation, revolution, or an improbable change in publicly accorded social identity can alter one's rank and hence life-chances.

Despite these differences, class is in no way incompatible with birth-ascribed systems. In fact, in so far as it is a term of categories of people ranked by income, occupation, education, and life style, it co-occurs with them. Low castes, despised races, ethnic minorities, and colonized people comprise economically and occupationally depressed, exploited classes who are politically and socially oppressed; high castes, exalted races, privileged ethnic groups, and colonizers comprise economically and occupationally privileged, power-wielding, elite classes who live off the labor of others. In this respect, class differences pervade and reinforce systems of birth-ascribed stratification. Furthermore, it is not unusual to find significant class differentials within a caste, racial, or ethnic group or within a colonized or colonial group.[24] That is, class, in the conventional sense, often occurs conspicuously within such groups, and may also bridge their boundaries without obscuring them. But it is not possible to analyze birth-ascribed stratification solely in terms of class, for no amount of class mobility will exempt a person from the crucial implications of his birth in such systems.

Those who have sought to identify the positions of European immigrants to America such as the Poles, Italians, and Irish, with the position of blacks, Native Americans, Chicanos, and Asians have failed to discern the essential fact that racism is the basis of American caste, and that it bestows upon those who experience it a unique social, political, and economic stigma which is not bestowed by class or national origin. Second generation white Europeans can meet all of the criteria for acceptance into the American white race-caste, for they are regarded as being only culturally different. A fifteenth generation American black, or a fifteen-hundredth generation American Indian cannot, for their differences are regarded as innate, immutable, and crucial. Equalitarianism has produced no "American dilemma" among racists, as Myrdal believed, simply because it is an equality for whites only, and its extension to other groups has moved slowly, painfully, and with vehement opposition, even where it has moved at all.

Systems of collective social rank, whether ascribed or acquired, are systems for retaining privilege among the powerful and power among the privileged, reserving and maintaining vulnerability, oppression, and want for those upon whom it can be imposed with minimal risk while retaining their services and their deference. In this way they are similar. In the principles of recruitment and organization by which that similarity is effected and in the individuals' prospects for mobility they differ, and those differences have important consequences for individual life experience and social processes in the societies which harbor them.

Pluralism

Pluralism is a model which has been applied to socially and culturally diverse societies since the writings of Furnivall on South-East Asia.[25] Cultural pluralism obtains when "two or more different cultural traditions characterize the population of a given society"; it is "a special form of differentiation based on institutional divergences."[26] Systems of birth-ascribed stratification are inevitably systems of social and cultural pluralism because they are accompanied by social separation. In a caste system, "Because intensive and status-equal interaction is limited to the caste, a common and distinctive caste culture is assured. This is a function of the quality and density of communication within the group, for culture is learned, shared and transmitted."[27] The same is true for any system of racial or ethnic stratification. M.G. Smith has noted, "It is perfectly clear that in any social system based on intense cleavages and discontinuity between differentiated segments the community of values or social relations between these sections will be correspondingly low. This is precisely the structural condition of the plural society."[28] And I have noted elsewhere that

> . . . castes are discrete social and cultural entities. . . . They are maintained by defining and maintaining boundaries between castes; they are threatened

when boundaries are compromised. Even when interaction between castes is maximal and cultural differences are minimal, the ideal of mutual isolation and distinctiveness is maintained and advertised among those who value the system. Similarly, even when mobility within, or subversion of the system is rampant, a myth of stability is stolidly maintained among those who benefit from the system.[29]

Mutual isolation of social groups inevitably leads to group-specific institutions (an important criterion for pluralism according to Furnivall), because members are excluded from participation in the institutions of other groups.

Caste, race, and ethnic stratification, like all plural systems, therefore, are systems of social separation and cultural heterogeneity, maintained by common or over-riding economic and political institutions rather than by agreement or consensus regarding the stratification system and its rationale.[30] This does not deny consensus, it only defines its nature:

In caste systems, as in all plural systems, highly differentiated groups get along together despite widely differing subjective definitions of the situation because they agree on the objective facts of what is happening and what is likely to happen—on who has the power, and how, under what circumstances, and for what purposes it is likely to be exercised. They cease to get along when this crucial agreement changes or is challenged.[31]

The constituent social elements of plural societies need not be birth-ascribed, and they need not be (and sometimes are not) ranked relative to one another, although by Furnivall's definition, one element must be dominant. In fact, unranked pluralism is the goal many ethnic minorities choose over either stratification or assimilation. But a system of birth-ascribed stratification is always culturally, socially, and hence institutionally heterogeneous, and thus pluralistic.

Hierarchy as Symbolic Interaction

I have elsewhere described the universality among social hierarchies of patterns of interaction which symbolize superiority and inferiority.[32] Social hierarchy, after all, exists only in the experiences, behaviors, and beliefs of those who comprise it. Interpersonal interaction becomes the vehicle for expression of hierarchy: for asserting, testing, validating or rejecting claims to

status. Almost every interaction between members of ranked groups expresses rank claimed, perceived, or accorded. When the hierarchy is birth-ascribed, the membership of its component groups is ideally stable, well-known, and easily recognizable. In such systems people are perceived by those outside of their groups almost wholly in terms of their group identity rather than as individuals. They are regarded as sharing the characteristics which are conventionally attributed to the group and they share the obligations, responsibilities, privileges, and disabilities of their group. In intergroup relations, therefore, one individual is substitutable for another in his group, for all are alike and interchangeable. This is the setting for prejudice, discrimination, bigotry, chauvinism, and is an ideal situation for scapegoating. These attitudes and their behavioral consequences are designated and deplored by such terms as racism, casteism, communalism (referring to ethnic chauvinism of various sorts), and recently, sexism. They are characterized by domination, deprivation, oppression, exploitation, and denigration directed downward; obedience, acquiescence, service, deference, and honor demanded from above. They result in envy, resentment, dissimulation, and resistance arising from below, balanced from above by fear, guilt, and that combination of arrogant self-righteousness and rationalization which is found in all such systems. Maya Angelou has aptly characterized the result in American race relations as "the humorless puzzle of inequality and hate"; "the question of worth and values, of aggressive inferiority and aggressive arrogance"[33] which confronts and exacts its toll not only from black Americans, but from the denizens of all those jungles of inherited inequality I call caste systems. It is this quality of interpersonal relations rather than any particular event or structural feature which struck me most vividly, forcefully, and surprisingly as similar in Alabama and India when I first experienced them for over a year each within a period of five years.[34] For me, this is the hallmark of oppressive, birth-ascribed stratification.

A specifically interactional definition of caste systems applies equally to all systems of birth-ascribed stratification: *"a system of birth-ascribed groups each of which comprises for its members the maximum limit of status-equal interaction, and between all of which interaction is consistently hierarchical.*"[35] The cultural symbols of hierarchical interaction vary; the presence and importance of such symbols is universal and essential to racism, casteism, and their homologs.

Hierarchy as Ideology

Dumont has emphasized the point that Indian caste is unique in that it is based on an ideology of hierarchy defined in terms of ritual purity and pollution.[36] He regards other systems of hierarchical social separation as non-comparable because of the inevitable differences in the ideologies supporting them. In the comparative framework which I advocate, I maintain simply that the Hindu rationale is one of several ideologies (cf. those of Islamic Swat, of the South Indian Lingayats to whom purity is irrelevant, of Rwanda, of Japan, and the United States) which can and do underlie and justify systems of birth-ascribed social hierarchy. Each is unique to the culture in which it occurs; each is associated with remarkably similar social structures, social processes, and individual experiences. I believe that anyone who has experienced daily life in rural India and the rural American South, for example, will confirm the fact that there is something remarkably similar in the systems of social relations and attitudes. I believe that anyone who has experienced daily life in an urban slum, a public market, or a factory in India and the Untied States would come to the same conclusion. That similarity is generated by birth-ascribed stratification and it is not concealed by differential ideologies.[37]

Contrary to another of Dumont's assumptions (shared with Cox), there is nothing incompatible between an ideology which underwrites a hierarchy of groups and a notion of equality within each group. This combination, in fact, is found not only in the United States where it accounts for the above-mentioned absence of a real "American dilemma" in race relations, but also in each of the other systems described here. Members of each ranked group are *inherently unequal* to those of each other group and are by birth *potentially equal* to those of their own group. More importantly, the existence of an ideology of hierarchy does not mean that this ideology is conceived and

interpreted identically by all within the system it is presumed to justify or even that it is shared by them. Acquiescence must not be mistaken for concurrence. Dumont's assumption to the contrary is the most glaring weakness in his analysis of Indian caste.[38]

Sexual Stratification

Finally, in my discussion of models for analysis, I turn to the controversial and sociologically puzzling matter of sex as a basis for social separation and inequality. The special problems which the sexual criterion poses for the student of stratification are both academic and substantive. The academic problems derive from the history of the study of stratification. Although the role of women in various non-Western societies has been discussed by anthropologists (including prominently Margaret Mead), and the position of women in European societies has been discussed by some social historians, the sexual dichotomy rarely appears in sociological works on stratification. That this criterion has been largely ignored or dismissed by stratification theorists is attributable to several factors, not the least of which is no doubt that members of the privileged sex have authored most of the work and to them such ranking has not been a problem and hence has not been apparent. Also, their culturally derived biases have been such that this kind of ranking was taken for granted as a manifestation of biological differences. "Many people who are very hip to the implications of the racial caste system . . . don't seem to be able to see the sexual caste system and if the question is raised they respond with: 'that's the way it's supposed to be. There are biological differences.' Or with other statements which recall a white segregationist confronted with integration."[39] The biological rationale – what Millett refers to as the "view of sex as a caste structure ratified by nature"[40] – recalls also the justification offered for all birth-ascribed dominance-exploitation relationships be they caste in India, Burakumin status in Japan, sexual roles, or any other. In each instance the plea is that these are uniquely real, significant, unavoidable, and natural differences, and therefore they must be acted upon. Thus, in an interview about their book, *The Imperial Animal,* which is said to claim that males have dominated human history because "the business of politics . . . is a business that requires skills and attitudes that are peculiarly male," anthropologists Robin Fox and Lionel Tiger were reported to have vehemently denied that their theory about the reasons for women's roles might be a sexist theory. " 'These are the facts, don't accuse us of making up the species,' Tiger said." And again, " 'Because this is a racist country, people relate sexism to racism.' But these two reactions are actually different because while there are no important biological differences between races, there are very important differences between the sexes."[41] Whether the differences are real or not (and who would deny that males and females differ in important ways?), the sociological and humanistic question is whether the differences require or justify differential opportunities, privileges, responsibilities, and rewards or, put negatively, domination and exploitation.

Birth-ascribed stratification, be it sexual, racial, or otherwise, is always accompanied by explanations, occasionally ingenious but usually mundane and often ludicrous, as to why putative natural differences *do* require and justify social differences. Those explanations are widely doubted by those whose domination they are supposed to explain, and this includes increasing numbers of women.

The substantive issues which becloud the topic of sexual stratification have to do with the mode of recruitment, the socialization, membership, and structural arrangements of sexually ranked categories. First, there is the fact that while sex is determined at birth, it is not contingent upon ancestry, endogamy, or any other arrangement of marriage or family, and is not predictable. It is the only recurrent basis for birth-ascribed stratification that can be defensibly attributed solely to undeniably physical characteristics. Even here there are individual or categorical exceptions made for transvestites, hermaphrodites, homosexuals, etc., in some societies as in the case of *hijaras* in India.[42] The significance (as contrasted to the fact) of the diagnostic physical traits – of sexual differences – is, however, largely socially defined, so that their cultural expressions vary widely over time and space. Second, as a concomitant to the mode of recruitment, males and females have no distinct ethnic or regional histories. It must not be overlooked, however, that they do have distinct social histories in every society. Third, the universal co-residence of males and females within the household precludes the existence of lifelong, separate male and female societies as such, and usually assures a degree of mutual early socialization. But note that it does not preclude distinct male and female social institutions, distinct patterns of social interaction within and between these categories, or distinguishable male and female subcultures (in fact the latter are universal) including, for example, distinct male and female dialects.

Partly as a consequence of these factors, the nature and quality of segregation of the sexes has not been defined by sociologists as comparable to that of the other ascriptive social categories discussed here. Nevertheless, most of the characteristics of birth-ascribed separation and stratification (racial, caste, ethnic, colonial, class, and pluralistic characteristics), and virtually all of the psychological and social consequences of inborn, lifelong superiority-inferiority relations are to be found in the relationship of males and females in most societies. These stem from similar factors in early socialization and from stereotypes and prejudices enacted and enforced in differential roles and opportunity structures, rationalized by ideologies of differential intrinsic capabilities and worth, sustained and defended through the combination of power and vested interest that is common to all birth-ascribed inequality. I have elsewhere contrasted some of the consequences of these assumptions and behaviors in the United States and India as reflected in the political participation of women in the two nations, although this is dwarfed by Millett's more recent work on male domination, its sources, and manifestations in the West.[43]

If we agree with van den Berghe that "race can be treated as a special case of invidious status differentiation or a special criterion of stratification,"[44] I think we are bound to agree that sex is another.

CONSEQUENCES OF INHERITED INEQUALITY

Assuming that there are significant structural and interactional similarities among systems of birth-ascribed stratification, the question can still be legitimately asked, "so what?" Is this merely a more or less interesting observation – even a truism – or does it have some theoretical or practical significance? My answer would be that it has both, for such systems have common and predictable consequences in the individual lives of those who live them and in the cumulative events which comprise the ongoing histories of the societies which harbor them.

> Caste systems are living environments to those who comprise them. Yet there is a tendency among those who study and analyze them to intellectualize caste, and in the process to squeeze the life out of it. Caste is people, and especially people interacting in characteristic ways. Thus, in addition to being a structure, a caste system is a set of human relationships and it is a state of mind.[45]

Their "human implications" are justification enough for studying and comparing systems of birth-ascribed stratification. There are neither the data nor the space to discuss these implications fully here, but I will suggest the nature of the evidence briefly, identifying psychological and social consequences. I am well aware that many features of such systems are found in all sharply stratified societies. Some are characteristic of all relationships of superordination and subordination, of poverty and affluence, of differential power. Others are found in all societies made up of distinct sub-groups whether stratified or not. It is the unique combination of characteristics in the context of the ideal of utter rigidity and unmitigable inequality which makes systems of stratification by race, caste, ethnicity, and sex distinctive in their impact on people, individually and collectively.

Psychological Consequences

Beliefs and attitudes associated with rigid stratification can be suggested by such terms as paternalism and dependence, *noblesse oblige,* arrogance, envy, resentment, hatred, prejudice, rationalization, emulation, self-doubt, and self-hatred. Those who are oppressed often respond to such stratification by attempting to escape either the circumstances or the consequences of the system. The realities of power and dependence make more usual an accommodation to oppression which, however, is likely to be less passive than is often supposed, and is likely to be unequivocally revealed when the slightest

change in the perceived distribution of power occurs. Those who are privileged in the system seek to sustain and justify it, devoting much of their physical effort to the former and much of their psychic and verbal effort to the latter. When these systems are birth-ascribed, all of these features are exacerbated.

Kardiner and Ovesey conclude their classic, and by now outdated, study of American Negro personality, *Mark of Oppression,* with the statement: "The psycho-social expressions of the Negro personality that we have described are the *integrated* end products of the process of oppression."[46] Although it is appropriate to question their characterization of that personality in the light of subsequent events and research, there is no doubt that such oppression has recurrent psychological consequences for both the oppressor and the oppressed, as Robert Coles has demonstrated in *Children of Crisis* and subsequent works.[47]

Oppression does not befall everyone in a system of birth-ascribed inequality. Most notably, it does not befall those with power. What does befall all is the imposition by birth of unalterable membership in ranked, socially isolated, but interacting groups with rigidly defined and conspicuously different experiences, opportunities, public esteem and, inevitably, self-esteem. The black in America and in South Africa, the Burakumin of Japan, the Harijan of India, the barber or washerman of Swat, the Hutu or Twa of Rwanda, have all faced similar conditions as individuals and they have responded to them in similar ways. The same can be said for the privileged and dominant groups in each of these societies, for while painful consequences of subordination are readily apparent, the consequences of superordination are equally real and important. Thus, ethnic stratification leaves its characteristic and indelible imprint on all who experience it.

The consequences of birth-ascribed stratification are self-fulfilling and self-perpetuating, for although low status groups do not adopt views of themselves or their statuses which are consistent with the views held by their superiors, they are continually acting them out and cannot avoid internalizing some of them and the self-doubts they engender, just as high status groups internalize their superiority and self-righteousness. The oppression of others by the latter serves to justify and bolster their superiority complex and to rationalize for them the deprivation and exploitation of those they denigrate. "Once you denigrate someone in that way," say Kardiner and Ovesey, "the sense of guilt makes it imperative to degrade the subject further to justify the whole procedure."[48] Gallagher notes that in the southern United States,

> By the attitudes of mingled fear, hostility, deprecation, discrimination, amused patronage, friendly domination, and rigid authoritarianism, the white caste generated opposite and complementary attitudes in the Negro caste. It is a touch of consummate irony that the dominant group should then argue that the characteristics which exhibit themselves in the submerged group are "natural" or "racial."[49]

The products of oppression are thus used to justify oppression.

Change and Emancipation

The self-reinforcing degradation described above combines with greed and fear of status-loss or revolt to comprise a dynamic of oppression which, in birth-ascribed stratification, probably accounts for the widespread occurrence of pariah status or untouchability. Elites characteristically justify oppression by compounding it; they enhance their own rewards by denying them ever more stringently to social inferiors, and they strive to protect themselves from challenges to status and privilege from below by rigidifying the status boundaries, reinforcing the sanctions which enforce them, and increasing the monopoly on power which makes the sanctions effective. This assures increasing social separation and hierarchical distance between groups until such time as it generates rebellion, reform, or disintegration.

The fact that social order prevails most of the time in any given instance of inherited inequality does not mean that all of those in the system accept it or their places within it willingly, nor does it mean that the system is either stable or static. It most often means that power is held and exercised effectively by those in superordinate statuses, for the time being. Such systems are based on conformity more than consensus, and are maintained by sanctions more than agreement. Nevertheless, change is inherent, resistance and mobility-striving are universal, and effective challenges to such systems are probably ultimately inevitable because the response they elicit from those they oppress is subversive. The possibility of acting out the subversion depends largely upon the balance of power among the stratified groups and the definitions of the situation their members hold. The processes of change and patterns of conflict which lead to them are major areas of commonality in such systems.[50]

The history of every caste system, of every racially stratified system, of every instance of birth-ascribed oppression is a history of striving, conflict, and occasional revolt. That this is not generally acknowledged is largely a result of the fact that most of these actions occur in the context of overwhelming power and uncompromising enforcement by the hereditary elites and are therefore expressed in the form of day-to-day resentment and resistance handled so subtly and occurring so routinely that it goes unremarked.[51] Even conspicuous manifestations are likely to be quickly and brutally put down, confined to a particular locality or group, and knowledge of their occurrence suppressed by those against whom they have been directed. These phenomena often can only be discovered by consulting and winning the confidence of members of oppressed groups, and this is rarely done.

Only the most spectacular instances of resistance, and the few successful ones are likely to be well-known. Immediately to mind come such martyrs to the cause of emancipation of oppressed peoples as the Thracian slave Spartacus, who led a rebellion against Rome; the American slave rebellion leaders Gabriel and Nat Turner, the white abolitionist John Brown, and the contemporary leaders of black emancipation in America, Martin Luther King, Medgar Evers, and others (too many of them martyred) among their fellow leaders and supporters, black and white. No doubt there are many more, most of them unknown and unsung, in the history of all groups whose members society condemns by birth to oppression. In the folk history of every such group, and in the memory of every member, are instances of courageous or foolhardy people who have challenged or outwitted their oppressors, often at the cost of their own foreseeable and inevitable destruction.

Better-known and better-documented than the individuals who led and sometimes died for them, are the emancipation movements which have occurred in most such societies – movements such as those for black power and black separatism in the United States, anti-casteism and anti-touchability in India, Hutu emancipation in Rwanda and Burundi, Burakumin emancipation in Japan, and anti-apartheid in South Africa. All have depended primarily upon concerted efforts to apply political, economic, or military power to achieve their ends. They have comprised direct challenges to the systems. Most have followed after the failure of attempts less militant, less likely to succeed, and hence less threatening to social elites – attempts towards assimilation or mobility within the systems such as those of status emulation.

Henry Adams characterized the slave society of Virginia in 1800 as "ill at ease."[52] This seems to be the chronic state of societies so organized – the privileged cannot relax their vigilance against the rebellious resentment of the deprived. That such rigid, oppressive systems do function and persist is a credit not to the consensus they engender any more than to the justice or rationality of the systems. Rather, it is a tribute to the effectiveness of the monopoly on power which the privileged are able to maintain. When in such systems deprived people get the vote, get jobs, get money, get legal redress, get guns, get powerful allies, get public support for their aspirations, they perceive a change in the power situation and an enhancement of the likelihood of successful change in their situation, and they are likely to attempt to break out of their oppressed status. These conditions do not generate the desire for change, for that is intrinsic; they merely make it seem worthwhile to attempt the change. Sometimes the triggering factor is not that the deprived believe conditions have changed so that success is more likely, but rather that conditions have led them to define the risk and consequences of failure (even its virtual certainty) as acceptable. Resultant changes are often drastic and traumatic of achievement, but they are sought by the oppressed and by enlightened people of all statuses precisely because of the heavy individual and societal costs of maintaining inherited inequality and because of its inherent inhumanity.

An important difference between the dynamics of inherited stratification and acquired stratification results from the fact that in the latter, power and privilege accompany achievable status, emulation is at least potentially effective, and mobility and assimilation are realistic goals. Therefore energies of status resentment may rationally be channelled toward mobility. Most immigrant groups in the United States, for example, have found this out as they have merged with the larger society after one or two generations of socialization. But in a system where inherited, unalterable group identity is the basis for rewards, emulation alone cannot achieve upward mobility, and assimilation is impossible so long as the system exists (in fact, prevention of assimilation is one of its main functions). Only efforts to destroy, alter, or circumvent the system make sense. In the United States, blacks, Chicanos, and Native Americans have found this out. Only in response to changes in the distribution of power is such inherited status likely to be re-evaluated and the distribution of rewards altered.

CONCLUSION

"Race" as the term is used in America, Europe, and South Africa, is not qualitatively different in its implications for human social life from caste, *varna*, or *jati* as applied in India, *quom* in Swat and Muslim India, the "invisible race" of Japan, the ethnic stratification of Rwanda and Burundi. Racism and casteism are indistinguishable in the annals of man's inhumanity to man, and sexism is closely allied to them as man's inhumanity to woman. All are invidious distinctions imposed unalterably at birth upon whole categories of people to justify the unequal social distribution of power, livelihood, security, privilege, esteem, freedom – in short, life chances. Where distinctions of this type are employed, they affect people and the events which people generate in surprisingly similar ways despite the different historical and cultural conditions in which they occur.

If I were asked, "What practical inference, if any, is to be drawn from the comparative study of inherited inequality – of ascriptive social ranking?" I would say it is this: There is no way to reform such institutions; the only solution is their dissolution. As Kardiner and Ovesey said long ago, *"there is only one way that the products of oppression can be dissolved, and that is to stop the oppression."*[53] To stop the oppression, one must eliminate the structure of inherited stratification upon which it rests. Generations of Burakumin, Hutu, blacks, untouchables, and their sympathizers have tried reform without notable success. Effective change has come only when the systems have been challenged directly.

The boiling discontent of birth-ascribed deprivation cannot be contained by pressing down the lid of oppression or by introducing token flexibility, or by preaching brotherly love. The only hope lies in restructuring society and redistributing its rewards so as to end the inequality. Such behavioral change must come first. From it may follow attitudinal changes as meaningful, status-equal interaction undermines racist, casteist, communalist, and sexist beliefs and attitudes, but oppressed people everywhere have made it clear that it is the end of oppression, not brotherly love, which they seek most urgently. To await the latter before achieving the former is futility; to achieve the former first does not guarantee achievement of the latter, but it increases the chances and makes life livable. In any case, the unranked pluralism which many minorities seek requires only equality, not love.

To those who fear this course on the grounds that it will be traumatic and dangerous, I would say that it is less so than the futile attempt to prevent change. Philip Mason spoke for all systems of inborn inequality when he called the Spartan oppression of the Helots in ancient Greece a trap from which there was no escape.

> *It was the Helots who released the Spartans from such ignoble occupations as trade and agriculture. . . . But it was the Helots who made it necessary to live in an armed camp, constantly on the alert against revolt. . . . They had a wolf by the ears; they dared not let go. . . . And it was of their own making; they had decided—at some stage and by what process one can only guess— that the Helots would remain separate and without rights forever.*[54]

That way, I believe, lies ultimate disaster for any society. A thread of hope lies in the possibility that people can learn from comparison of the realities of inherited inequality across space,

time, and culture, and can act to preclude the disaster that has befallen others by eliminating the system which guarantees it. It is a very thin thread.

ENDNOTES

1. Max Weber, *From Max Weber: Essays in Sociology,* H.H. Gerth and C.W. Mills, trans. and ed. (New York, Oxford University Press, 1946); W.G. Runciman, "Class, Status and Power?" in *Social Stratification,* J.A. Jackson, ed. (London, Cambridge University Press, 1968), pp. 25–61.

2. See for Rwanda: Jacques J. Maquet, *The Premise of Inequality in Ruanda* (London, Oxford University Press, 1961); for India: F.G. Bailey, "Closed Social Stratification in India," *European Journal of Sociology* (Vol. IV, 1963); Gerald D. Berreman, "Caste: The Concept," in *International Encyclopedia of the Social Sciences,* D. Sills, ed. (New York, Macmillan and The Free Press, 1968), Vol. II, pp. 333–9; André Béteille, *Castes Old and New* (Bombay, Asia Publishing House, 1969); Louis Dumont, *Homo Hierarchicus* (London, Weidenfeld and Nicolson, 1970); J.H. Hutton, *Caste in India, Its Nature, Functions and Origins* (London, Cambridge University Press, 1946); Adrian C. Mayer, "Caste: The Indian Caste System," in D. Sills, ed., op. cit., pp. 339–44; M.N. Srinivas, *Caste in Modern India and Other Essays* (Bombay, Asia Publishing House, 1962), and *Social Change in Modern India* (Berkeley, University of California Press, 1966); for Swat: Fredrik Barth, "The System of Social Stratification in Swat, North Pakistan," in *Aspects of Caste in South India, Ceylon and North-West Pakistan,* E. Leach, ed. (London, Cambridge University Press, 1960), pp. 113–48; for Japan: George DeVos and Hiroshi Wagatsuma, eds. *Japan's Invisible Race: Caste in Culture and Personality* (Berkeley, University of California Press, 1966); Shigeaki Ninomiya, "An Inquiry Concerning the Origin, Development and Present Situation of the *Eta* in Relation to the History of Social Classes in Japan," *The Transactions of the Asiatic Society of Japan* (Second series, Vol. 10, 1933); cf. Herbert Passin, "Untouchability in the Far East," *Monumenta Nipponica* (Vol. 2, No. 3, 1955); for the United States: Allison Davis, B. Gardner, and M.R. Gardner, *Deep South: A Social Anthropological Study of Caste and Class* (Chicago, The University of Chicago Press, 1941); John Dollard, *Caste and Class in a Southern Town* (Garden City, New York, Doubleday, 1957); Gunnar Myrdal, *An American Dilemma: The Negro Problem in Modern Democracy* (New York, Harper, 1944); Alphonso Pinkney, *Black Americans* (Englewood Cliffs, New Jersey, Prentice-Hall, 1969); Peter I Rose, ed., *Americans from Africa,* Vol. 1: *Slavery and its Aftermath* and Vol. II: *Old Memories, New Moods* (New York, Atherton Press, 1970). See also contrasts with South

Africa: Pierre van den Berghe, *South Africa, a Study in Conflict* (Berkeley, University of California Press, 1967); Latin America: Marvin Harris, *Patterns of Race in the Americas* (New York, Walker, 1964); Julian Pitt-Rivers, "Race, Color and Class in Central America and the Andes," *Daedalus* (Spring, 1967); the Caribbean: M.G. Smith, *The Plural Society in the British West Indies* (Berkeley, University of California Press, 1965); G.D. Berreman, *Caste and Other Inequities* (New Delhi, Meerut, 1979).

3. Dumont, op. cit.

4. Gerald D. Berreman, "A Brahmanical View of Caste: Louis Dumont's *Homo Hierarchicus*," *Contributions to Indian Sociology* (New Series, No. V, 1972).

5. Tamotsu Shibutani and Kian M. Kwan, *Ethnic Stratification: A Comparative Approach* (New York, Macmillan, 1965), p. 572.

6. H.S. Morris, "Ethnic Groups," in D. Sills, ed., op. cit., Vol. 5, p. 167.

7. Pierre van den Berghe, "The Benign Quota: Panacea or Pandora's Box," *The American Sociologist* (Vol. 6, Supplementary Issue, June 1971).

8. Ibid., p. 43.

9. Cf. Robert Blauner, "Black Culture: Myth or Reality?" in Rose, *Old Memories, New Moods*, pp. 417–43.

10. Gerald D. Berreman, "Caste in India and the United States," *The American Journal of Sociology* (Vol. LXVI, September, 1960); cf. Berreman, "A Brahmanical View of Caste . . . ," op. cit.

11. Oliver C. Cox, "Race and Caste: A Distinction," *The American Journal of Sociology* (Vol. L, March, 1945); cf. Oliver C. Cox, *Caste, Class and Race* (Garden City, New York, Doubleday, 1948).

12. Arthur R. Jensen, "How Much Can We Boost I.Q. and Scholastic Achievement?" *Harvard Educational Review* (Vol. 39, No. 1, Winter, 1969).

13. See the various articles comprising the "Discussion," of Jensen's article in *Harvard Educational Review* (Vol. 39, No. 2, Spring, 1969).

14. E.A. Ross, *Social Psychology* (New York, Macmillan, 1914), p. 3.

15. Shibutani and Kwan, op. cit., p. 37.

16. Ibid., p. 110.

17. Pierre van den Berghe, *Race and Racism* (New York, Wiley, 1967), p. 21.

18. Claude Lévi-Strauss, "The Bear and the Barber," *Journal of the Royal Anthropological Institute* (Vol. 93, Part 1, 1963).

19. Winthrop D. Jordan, *White over Black* (Baltimore, Penguin Books, 1969), pp. 137–8.

20. Robert Blauner, "International Colonialism and Ghetto Revolt," *Social Problems* (Vol. 16, No. 4, Spring 1969); Stokely Carmichael and Charles Hamilton, *Black Power* (New York, Random House, 1967); Frantz Fanon, *The Wretched of the Earth* (New York, Grove Press, 1966); O. Mannoni, *Prospero and Caliban: The Psychology of Colonization* (New York, Praeger, 1956); Albert Memmi, *The Colonizer and the Colonized* (Boston, Beacon Press, 1967).

21. Cf. Blauner, "Internal Colonialism . . . ," pp. 395–6.

22. Gerald D. Berreman, "Caste as Social Process," *Southwestern Journal of Anthropology* (Vol. 23, No. 4, Winter, 1967); Blauner, *Racial Oppression in America* (New York, Harper & Row, 1942); S.F. Nadel, "Caste and Government in Primitive Society," *Journal of the Anthropological Society of Bombay* (Vol. 8, 1954); J.S. Furnivall, *Colonial Policy and Practice: A Comparative Study of Burma and Netherlands India* (London, Cambridge University Press, 1948); M.G. Smith, *The Plural Society in the British West Indies* (Berkeley, University of California Press, 1965); James B. Watson, "Caste as a Form of Acculturation," *Southwestern Journal of Anthropology* (Vol. 19, No. 4, Winter 1963).

23. Cf. Irawati Karve, *Hindu Society: An Interpretation* (Poona, Deccan College Postgraduate and Research Institute, 1961).

24. Davis, Gardner, and Gardner, op. cit.; St. Clair Drake and Horace R. Cayton, *Black Metropolis* (New York, Harcourt, Brace, 1945); Dollard, op. cit.; Marina Wikramanayake, "Caste and Class among Free Afro-Americans in Ante-bellum South Carolina," paper delivered before the 70th Annual Meeting of the American Anthropological Association (New York, November 1971).

25. Furnivall, op. cit.; cf. Malcolm Cross, ed., *Special Issue on Race and Pluralism, Race* (Vol. XII, No. 4, April 1917).

26. M.G. Smith, op. cit., pp. 14, 83.

27. Gerald D. Berreman, "Stratification, Pluralism and Interaction: A Comparative Analysis of Caste," in *Caste and Race: Comparative Approaches*, A. deReuck and J. Knight, eds., p. 51.

28. M.G. Smith, op. cit., p. xi.

29. Berreman, "Stratification, Pluralism and Interaction . . . ," op. cit., p. 55.

30. Cf. Furnivall, op. cit.

31. Berreman, "Stratification, Pluralism and Interaction . . . ," op. cit., p. 55.

32. Ibid.; cf. McKim Marriott, "Interactional and Attributional Theories of Caste Ranking," *Man in India* (Vol. 39, 1959).

33. Maya Angelou, *I Know Why the Caged Bird Sings* (New York, Bantam Books, 1971), p. 168.

34. Cf. Berreman, "Caste in India and the United States," op. cit.

35. Berreman, "Stratification, Pluralism and Interaction . . . ," op. cit., p. 51.

36. Dumont, op. cit.

37. Cf. Berreman, "Caste in India and the United States," op. cit.; Berreman, "Caste in Cross-Cultural

Perspective . . . ," op. cit.; Berreman, "Social Categories and Social Interaction in Urban India," *American Anthropologist* (Vol. 74, No. 3).

38. Cf. Berreman, "A Brahmanical View of Caste . . . ," op. cit.

39. Kate Millett, *Sexual Politics* (New York, Avon Books, 1971), p. 19.

40. Casey Hayden and Mary King, "Sex and Caste," *Liberation* (April, 1966), p. 35; cf. Millett, op. cit.

41. Fran Hawthorne, "Female Roles Examined by Rutgers Professors," *Daily Californian* (Berkeley, 6 October, 1971), p. 5. See also Millett, op. cit., p. 57, for a summary of the common psychological traits and adaptational mechanisms attributed to blacks and women in American society as reported in three recent sociological accounts.

42. Cf. G. Morris Carstairs, *The Twice-Born* (Bloomington, Indiana University Press, 1958), pp. 59–62 et passim; Morris E. Opler, "The Hijarā (Hermaphrodites) of India and Indian National Character: A Rejoinder," *American Anthropologist* (Vol. 62, No. 3, June, 1960).

43. Gerald D. Berreman, "Women's Roles and Politics: India and the United States," in *Readings in General Sociology,* R.W. O'Brien, C.C. Schrag, and W.T. Martin, eds. (4th Edition, Boston, Houghton Mifflin Co., 1969). First published, 1966. Cf. Millett, op. cit.

44. van den Berghe, *Race and Racism,* op. cit., p. 22.

45. Berreman, "Stratification, Pluralism and Interaction . . . ," op. cit., p. 58.

46. Abram Kardiner and Lionel Ovesey, *Mark of Oppression* (Cleveland, The World Publishing Co., 1962), p. 387.

47. Robert Coles, *Children of Crisis* (Boston, Atlantic–Little, Brown, 1964); Robert Coles and Jon Erikson, *The Middle Americans* (Boston, Little, Brown, 1971).

48. Kardiner and Ovesey, op. cit., p. 379.

49. B.G. Gallagher, *American Caste and the Negro College* (New York, Columbia University Press, 1938), p. 109.

50. Berreman, "Caste as Social Process," op. cit.

51. Raymond Bauer and Alice Bauer, "Day to Day Resistance to Slavery," *Journal of Negro History* (Vol. 27, October 1942); Douglas Scott, "The Negro and the Enlisted Man: An Analogy," *Harpers* (October 1962), pp. 20–21; cf. Berreman, "Caste in India and the United States," op. cit.

52. Henry Adams, *The United States in 1800* (Ithaca, New York, Cornell University Press, 1961), p. 98.

53. Kardiner and Ovesey, op. cit., p. 387.

54. Philip Mason, *Patterns of Dominance* (London, Oxford University Press for the Institute of Race Relations, 1970), p. 75.

T W O

The Nature of Ethnic Affiliations

Donald L. Horowitz

THE STRUCTURE OF GROUP RELATIONS

The relationship between ethnicity and class has been subject to great confusion.[1] Much of the confusion can be dispelled by recognizing a simple distinction between ranked and unranked ethnic groups. The distinction rests upon the coincidence or noncoincidence of social class with ethnic origins. Where the two coincide, it is possible to speak of *ranked* ethnic groups; where groups are cross-class, it is possible to speak of *unranked* ethnic groups. This distinction is as fundamental as it is neglected. If ethnic groups are ordered in a hierarchy, with one superordinate and another subordinate, ethnic conflict moves in one direction, but if groups are parallel, neither subordinate to the other, conflict takes a different course.

Figure 1 depicts the two systems. The diagram, which is greatly simplified, obviously represents ideal types rather than actual systems. It also assumes, for the sake of clarity, that there are only two ethnic groups, A and B, though in most systems there are more than two.

As the figure shows, stratification in ranked systems is synonymous with ethnic membership. Mobility opportunities are restricted by group identity. In such systems, political, economic, and social status tend to be cumulative, so that members of Group B are simultaneously subordi-

nate in each of these ways to members of Group A.[2] Relations between the groups entail clearly understood conceptions of superordinate and subordinate status. Interactions partake of caste etiquette and are suffused with deference. The systems of race relations founded on African slavery in the Western Hemisphere were archetypical cases of ranked ethnic systems, but there are many others: relations between Hutu and Tutsi in Burundi, between Burakumin and other members of Japanese society, between Rodiya and other Sinhalese and Sri Lanka, between Osu and other Ibo in Nigeria, to name just a few.

In unranked systems, on the other hand, parallel ethnic groups coexist, each group internally stratified. Unlike ranked ethnic groups, which are ascriptively defined components of a single society, parallel groups are themselves incipient whole societies and indeed may formerly have constituted more or less autonomous whole societies.[3] Language suggests this: parallel groups in the Netherlands are aptly described as separate "pillars" (zuilen) and in Austria as "tribes" (from Stämme, meaning stems or tree trunks).[4] Although the question of group superiority is far from irrelevant in such a system, it is not settled. The groups are not definitively ranked in relation to each other, certainly not across the board. The term polydomainal has been applied to such a society.[5] The position of a group varies from one domain to another, none of them decisive in establishing superordination or subordination. Accordingly, transactions can occur across group lines without necessarily implying anything about a hierarchy of ethnic groups. In ranked systems, by contrast, roles are not merely consistent from one domain to another, but really comprise "a single role"; an actor "is never subordinate in one [domain] and superior in another."[6]

A similar distinction between ranked and unranked systems has been drawn by Max Weber. Weber uses "caste structure" to refer to hierarchically ordered groups and "ethnic coexistence" to denote parallel groups, and he notes some of the major differences:

> . . . the caste structure transforms the horizontal and unconnected coexistences of ethnically segregated groups into a vertical social system of super- and subordination. Correctly formulated: a comprehensive societalization integrates the ethnically divided commu-

Ranked Groups

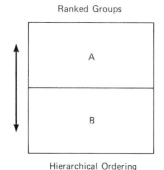

Hierarchical Ordering

Unranked Groups

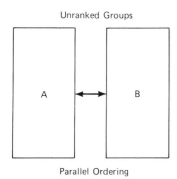

Parallel Ordering

FIGURE 1 *Ranked and Unranked Ethnic Systems*
Arrows indicate the direction of ethnic conflict.

nities into specific political and communal action. In their consequences they differ precisely in this way: ethnic coexistences condition a mutual repulsion and disdain but allow each ethnic community to consider its own honor as the highest one; the caste structure brings about a social subordination and an acknowledgement of "more honor" in favor of the privileged caste and status groups.[7]

As Weber suggests, the distribution of honor or prestige is a key difference.[8] In ranked systems, the unequal distribution of worth between superiors and subordinates is acknowledged and reinforced by an elaborate set of behavioral prescriptions and prohibitions. In unranked systems, relative group worth is always uncertain, always at issue.

RANKED AND UNRANKED SYSTEMS
IN PRACTICE

The distinction between these two types of systems is blurred in practice. Ranking is a pervasive aspect of social relations, which creeps into relations between individual members of unranked groups. A trader from unranked Group A may defer to an aristocrat from unranked Group B, while a servant from Group B may be subordinate to the same trader from Group A. What is more, ascriptive patterns of recruitment to these roles may develop. Merely because an unranked group has a full complement of statuses does not mean that its status pyramid has the same shape as that of other groups in the society or that every role is filled by a group member. Some unranked groups have larger elites than others; some have more intragroup social mobility; some leave particular functions to be performed by outsiders. Unranked systems assume elements of ranking, and, though for most purposes ethnic groups within them exist almost as autonomous societies, in some respects they are also interdependent parts of a common society.

Conversely, a subordinate ethnic group in a ranked system may produce an elite that defies the rules of ascriptive stratification. Clearly, the functional integration of ranked groups into a single society is far stronger than it is for unranked groups. Yet even here there are areas of ethnic autonomy. Neither type of system is pure,

and both are usually in a process of change, about which more shortly.

Despite the blurring, nearly all ethnic relationships can be identified as ranked or unranked. A key question is whether each group has a full complement of statuses or, to put the point differently, whether each of the groups in contact possesses a legitimately recognized elite. If so, the system is unranked.

Consider the case of Malaysia. There are high-status Malays who are members of the royalty or aristocracy and others who are members of the modern bureaucracy. There are high-status Chinese among the descendants of early traders and among the newer industrialists, professionals, and intellectuals. Although in the modern sectors there may be certain common criteria of stratification, there are also separate criteria for rank and prestige among the two groups. Each group has its own elite strata, so that the groups do not stand in a generalized hierarchical relation to each other. Each of these subsocieties can and does, as Weber suggested, consider its own "honor" to be the highest.

The clearest indicator of subordination, on the other hand, is the logical impossibility of an acknowledged upper class among the subordinate group.[9] That is not to say that all members of a superordinate group are of upper-class standing. This is most unlikely, and the line in Figure 1 that puts all members of Group A in a class above all of Group B is a distortion. In fact, any ideal-type conception that puts all members of a superordinate group in an economic class above all members of a subordinate group is something of a distortion. Within limits, a system of subordination can survive some dissonance between the economic status of the groups and that of its individual members, especially members of the superordinate group. For example, in Jamaica, traditionally stratified by color groups, the relatively few poor whites were viewed by their poor black neighbors as aberrations, rather than as glaring evidence of the quality of all.[10] Likewise, members of a subordinate group can and do acquire elite credentials acknowledged within their own community but not across ethnic lines. Carried far enough, however, either of these dissonant conditions can prove destabilizing to a ranked system: inferior members of a superordinate group threaten the myth of its superiority, and the growth of an elite among a subordinate group sooner or later creates aspirations for mobility and recognition incompatible with strictly ascriptive hierarchy.

Leadership selection constitutes another operational test of whether a ranked system exists. The leadership of a subordinate group must be acceptable to the superordinate group, which is usually in a position to reject unacceptable leaders. Influence or prestige within the subordinate group by itself is not enough. Lack of group autonomy in leadership selection is a sure sign of ethnic subordination.[11]

Unranked groups, on the other hand, select their leaders with relative autonomy, although the need to engage in bargaining across ethnic lines sometimes sets external limits on the selection. Because of this autonomy, unranked Groups A and B may throw up quite different types of leaders, in terms of social background, educational qualifications, personality, and relationship with their following. The relations of dissimilar ethnic elites can become a significant problem if they must interact on a regular basis.

The operating assumptions of the two types of systems, and the behavior appropriate to each, are vastly different. Ranked systems typically have ritualized modes of expressing the lower status or contamination of the subordinate groups. These may include restrictions on eating, dress, touching, sex, marriage, and social contact.[12] In Sri Lanka, the Rodiya are the closest thing the Sinhalese have to an outcaste group. Formerly, Rodiya women were required to go bare-breasted and, when this rule was abandoned, were forbidden to wear jackets.[13] Restrictions on education and occupation are also common. Stereotypes reflect the denial of prestige to subordinate groups, who are often depicted as a "contrast conception,"[14] the embodiment of all the vices disdained by the superordinate group. The Burakumin of Japan, whose earlier name, *Eta,* means "full of filth," are said to be "intellectually dull, disorderly, sexually loose, rude, violently aggressive and physically unclean."[15] The term *Rodiya* also means "filth," and the Rodiya, like other such groups in Asia, are said to have originated because of contact with "unclean activities," such as carrying corpses, slaughtering ani-

mals, or eating beef.[16] In Sulu, in the Southern Philippines, Tausug regard their subservient neighbors, the Samal Luwaan, as repulsive. The word *luwaan* means "that which was spat out," that is, rejected by God. There are myths that justify the low status of the Luwaan, including some stating that the Luwaan and the monkeys "come from the same race."[17] And, in Japan, Burakumin are sometimes referred to as *Yottsu,* meaning four and connoting four-legged beasts. Whether or not there is an attempt to deny the common humanity of the subordinate group, the stereotype of such a group generally depicts it as irremediably slow, violent, lazy, unmannered, and dirty. Indeed, such groups often do the dirty work.

Unranked groups obviously do not require methods of reinforcing and rationalizing ethnic subordination. Instead, a parallel group in contact and competition with others develops elaborate ways of reaffirming the superiority of its own culture, even while conceding limited spheres of cultural superiority to other groups. Malays, for example, admire the business skill of the Malaysian Chinese, but often regard Chinese behavior as crude and uncultured.[18] Creoles in Guyana and Trinidad readily grant the greater solidarity, thrift, and shrewdness of East Indians; yet Indians are referred to by the pejorative term *coolie* and are denied possession of certain traits that are highly valued in Creole society.[19] Indians, for their part, concede the physical strength of Creoles, but do not acknowledge the moral worth of presumed Creole behavioral patterns in general.[20] The Nigerian Kanuri likewise "are ambivalent about Ibo. In general, Ibo are disliked, mistrusted, and even despised. . . . Yet Kanuri grudgingly admire Ibo for their Western education, salaried jobs, and higher standards of living. . . ."[21] Stereotypes reflect these mixed evaluations. The Ceylon Tamils, for example, are seen by Sinhalese as poor and dirty, but also as thrifty and diligent.[22] Such mixed evaluations contrast vividly with the unmitigated denial of prestige and even of humanity that is reflected in stereotypes of subordinate groups in ranked systems.

Despite the common rigidity of ethnic stratification, relations between ethnic superiors and subordinates usually embody at least some elements of social cohesion and shared expectations, in addition to coercion and conflict. There may be a more or less explicit "premise of inequality,"[23] some degree of consensus on the aptitudes, rights, and obligations of the respective groups. In many settings, religion plays a role in legitimizing the ethnic hierarchy. Furthermore, there are elements of reciprocity and clientage that underpin the system. Typically, there is an exchange of protection of the subordinate for service rendered the superior. Benefits, such as increased personal security and even limited leeway for maneuver among competing superiors, usually accrue to those of subordinate status who accept the premise of inequality.[24] Adaptive behavior by the subordinate group to the requirements of its status is therefore common, and a substantial measure of predictability in relationships follows.

Relations among members of unranked ethnic groups are far less predictable. Characteristically, there is a lack of sufficient authority to establish a high level of reciprocity premised on inequality. Misunderstandings and misperceptions abound.[25] As there is less generalized domination, so there is also less generalized collaboration.

Ranked ethnic systems thus may possess more social cement than unranked at some stages of their development. This observation is consistent with experimental evidence that much potential aggression against superiors is inhibited, habits of deference as well as fear being what they are; more aggression against peers tends to be expressed.[26] But when the cement cracks in a ranked system, the edifice usually collapses: when ethnic hierarchies are undermined, they may undergo fundamental transformations.

The characteristics of ranked and unranked systems flow from their differing origins. In general, ranked systems are produced by conquest or capture. The ensuing domination lends itself to the establishment of upper and lower ranks, clientage relations, and an ideology of inferiority for the subordinate groups. The highly stratified ethnic system of Central Rwanda was the result of invasion and conquest, as were some equally stratified systems of Southern Africa and the Southern Philippines.[27] Slavery in North and South America was made possible by the equiva-

lent of conquest: the forced transportation of Africans to the New World. On the other hand, unranked systems are produced by invasion resulting in less than conquest, by more or less voluntary migration, or by encapsulation within a single territorial unit of groups that formerly had little to do with each other – or by some combination of these. Invasion short of conquest produced parallel groups in Nigeria and Sri Lanka, for neither Hausa-Fulani nor Ceylon Tamils were able to control the whole territory. Economically induced migration also created unranked systems in Malaysia, once Chinese and Indians arrived to mine tin and tap rubber, and in Guyana and Trinidad, where East Indians succeeded African labor on the sugar estates. And, in many cases, colonial rule brought together unranked groups that had had no previous contact, as well as those that had met on the battlefield or in the mines, shops, plantations, tea gardens, and other enterprises attracting ethnically differentiated work forces. Accordingly, their interactions were not those of clearly ranked superiors and subordinates but of unranked strangers.

Hierarchical groups are generally fairly well intermixed geographically. It seems evident that ranked subordination cannot long be sustained without a measure of spatial proximity to enforce it.[28] Parallel groups, however, may be either intermixed or regionally discrete. Typically, migration generates more geographic intermixture than does incomplete conquest.

Migration and incomplete conquest also give rise to different kinds of lingering historical grievances. A group whose conquest has been thwarted may nourish unfulfilled territorial ambitions, while a group whose land has been partly conquered may develop a domestic version of *revanche*.[29] An indigenous group that was colonized and forced to abide the entry of ethnic strangers for colonial economic purposes may later regard their presence as illegitimate *ab initio*.[30]

By now it should be clear that ranked and unranked systems are susceptible to different forms of ethnic conflict. Because the boundaries of ranked ethnic groups largely coincide with class lines, conflict in ranked systems has a class coloration. When warfare occurs, it takes the form of a social revolution.[31] The two post-independence changes of regime in Africa that can plausibly be called revolutionary – Rwanda in 1959 and Zanzibar in 1964 – were both the outgrowth of systems of ranked ethnic subordination.[32] (Ethiopia and Liberia are more debatable, but they, too, might fit the description.) The result was the overthrow of the former superordinates.

It is entirely different with unranked systems. They, too, are susceptible to serious conflict and violence, but with different goals. Unranked ethnic groups "act as if they were states in an international environment."[33] Interethnic elite relations partake of diplomacy. Ethnic leaders "form alliances that might remind the diplomatic historian of Renaissance Italy, and they deal with one another on the basis of sovereign equality."[34] They even make treaties: the Poona Pact and the Lucknow Pact in India, the Bandarinaike-Chelvanayakam Pact in Sri Lanka. The analogy to the international system is suggestive, not only with respect to alliance formation and negotiation across group lines, but also with respect to conflict and warfare. During the Sri Lanka riots of 1958, for example, the "refugee population, both Tamil and Sinhalese, was soon exchanged as hostages of war would be exchanged."[35] Unlike ranked groups, which form part of a single society, unranked groups constitute incipient whole societies.[36] It is not so much the politics of subordination that concerns them, though they are ever alert to threats of ethnic subordination, but rather the politics of inclusion and exclusion. These shadow societies often speak in the idiom of nations, referring, for example, to "the Dagomba nation" or to "Assamese nationalism." When ethnic violence occurs, unranked groups usually aim not at social transformation, but at something approaching sovereign autonomy, the exclusion of parallel ethnic groups from a share of power, and often reversion – by expulsion or extermination – to an idealized, ethnically homogeneous *status quo ante*.[37]

The confused relationship of class to ethnicity is now much clearer. On the one hand, it has often been stated that ethnic conflict is really class conflict. On the other, it has been said that ethnic conflict is an alternative or a barrier to class conflict. Both are true, but not in the broad way in which they have been asserted. Ethnic

and class conflict coincide when ethnicity and class coincide – in ranked systems. Class conflict, notes Ralf Dahrendorf, always entails "the arrangement of social roles endowed with expectations of domination or subjection,"[38] and this description applies equally to conflict between ranked ethnic groups. Ethnic conflict, however, impedes or obscures class conflict when ethnic groups are cross-class, as they are in unranked systems. There is, under those circumstances, a strong tendency to reject class conflict, for it would require either interethnic class-based alliances or intraethnic class antagonisms, either of which would detract from the ethnic solidarity that unranked ethnic conflict requires. Ethnic conflict in unranked systems usually goes hand in hand with conservative politics.[39]

THE INDICATORS OF ETHNIC IDENTITY

. . . I have not yet had a chance to explain what I mean by ethnicity. It may seem that we have gotten ahead of ourselves, but in fact the omission was intentional. The conception of ethnicity that I intend to put forward is rendered more understandable once the distinctions, especially between ranked and unranked systems, have been drawn.

Do we again wish to draw distinctions? Shall we separate "race" from "ethnicity," reserving race for differences of color?[40] Shall we sort out groups based on religion from those based on language or "nationality"? Although comparison is impeded by lumping together ranked and unranked cases or cases of conflict at the center with cases of conflict in dispersed pockets, comparison is facilitated by an inclusive conception of ethnicity that embraces differences identified by color, language, religion, or some other attribute of common origin.

The case for inclusiveness also rests on the contextual and in some ways accidental determination of attributes of difference. Group A speaks a language different from that of Group B, so language becomes the indicator of group identity in that relationship. But if, instead of Group B, the environment contained only Groups A and C, then religion or color or place of origin might differentiate the groups. In a typical multigroup environment, moreover, different attributes are invoked for differing group interactions. Indeed, it is apt to describe the attribute as belonging to the interaction as much as it belongs to the group. . . .

The suggestion that color-group relations necessarily differ in kind from other types of ethnic-group relations is generally based on one of two barely articulated assumptions: (1) that color differences are capable of arousing uniquely intense emotions and loyalties among the participants or (2) that color differences serve as unusually reliable signs of individual identity.[41] Neither of these assumptions can be supported, though the origin of each can readily be surmised.

The argument that color-group relations are especially conducive to hostility presumably derives from the aftermath of African slavery in the Western Hemisphere and perhaps also from the history of Western colonialism, which entailed subjugation of "non-white" by "white" peoples. To be sure, color preferences can be found in many parts of the world.[42] Quite often, color forms part of the imagery invoked in conflict relations. We have already seen this in the use of the work *khaek* for Malays in Southern Thailand, and there are comparable examples available for India, Sri Lanka, and Malaysia, all cases in which there is much color overlap among groups. But this is far from demonstrating the supposedly unique effects of color differences on group antipathy and cohesion.

What seems to have happened is that, because of the historical association of color differences with subordination and the conflict-laden efforts to overcome it, color differences are assumed to give rise to subordination and in general to severe conflict. In other words, the attempt is to explain the special harshness of a ranked system, such as slavery and Jim Crow, by the presence of somatic differences. Because it occurs in a context in which color has been linked with rigid stratification, the explanation mistakes the indicator for the substance of the relationship.

Elsewhere, as we have seen, hierarchical ethnic systems have been possible without color differences: between Tutsi and Hutu in Burundi (though there are other physical differences between those groups), between Tausug and Luwaan in the Philippines, between Burakumin and other Japanese in Japan, and between Osu

and other Ibo in Nigeria. By the same token, the peculiar passions supposedly aroused by color differences can also be generated without them. The Chinese penchant for the consumption of pork can be seized upon by the abstemious Malays as a sign of the uncleanliness and crudeness associated with the Chinese[43] in somewhat the same way as blackness became a symbol of pejorative traits associated with Africans in the New World. And, where there are alternative ways to divide groups up, color is not necessarily the preemptive differentiator. In Mauritania, for example, black Africans have attempted to forge political alliances with the so-called black Moors of Hartani, descendants of slaves who form a subordinate segment of the Moorish group. Not only have the appeals been unsuccessful, but in the ethnic riots of 1966 Hartani were in the vanguard of Moorish mobs that attacked black Africans.[44] Differentiators other than color were obviously more important.

The thesis that color-group relations are especially conducive to group cohesion and intergroup hostility is not merely insupportable in comparative terms; it is also historically inadequate. In the Western Hemisphere, slavery and its successor institutions did come to be identified with color. But color did not initially possess the stigma that it later did. In seventeenth-century North America, the English were originally called "Christians," while the African slaves were described as "heathens." The initial differentiation of groups relied heavily on religion. After about 1680, however, a new dichotomy of "whites" and "blacks" supplanted the former Christian and heathen categories, for some slaves had become Christians. If reliance had continued to be placed mainly on religion, baptism could have been employed to escape from bondage.[45] Color provided a "barrier" seemingly both "visible and permanent"[46] and therefore apt for maintaining a degrading and hereditary system of forced labor. To the extent that Christianity was a voluntary affiliation, the special place of color in American ethnic relations seems to have originated in the special desire of the slaveholders for a permanently servile group.[47] That purpose could be accomplished by redefining the indicia of ethnicity.

The distinction between color and other forms

of ethnic identification thus derives largely from the failure to distinguish between ranked and unranked systems of ethnic relations. The most significant way in which color differs from other varieties of ethnicity is its apparent immutability. But this characteristic is far more important in systems of ethnic stratification, where there is likely to be some attempt by members of the subordinate group to escape their identity, than it is in unranked systems.[48] Moreover, color had the comparative advantage in this respect only because the slaveholders regarded religion as mutable. Had they not held this view, had they refused to recognize the baptism of slaves, they would not have needed to resort to color. And, even then, the North American system of slavery, which placed such a premium on the visibility and permanence of the signs of identity, was obliged to resort to evidence of ancestry in the case of mulattoes who claimed to be descended of a free mother.[49] Even color can be changed in the course of generations.

This brings us to the second of the grounds on which color-group relations are asserted to be different from other types of ethnic relations: that color, because it is visible and permanent, is the most reliable indicator of identity. On this score, F.G. Bailey has argued that the visibility of color makes a hierarchical system based upon color differences easier to maintain over a large territory than is a hierarchical system based on nonvisible signs of difference.[50] Caste, according to Bailey, can only operate on a small scale, for, without a visible "rank sign," such as color, the caste origins of individual group members cannot be ascertained reliably for purposes of caste etiquette and avoidance.

This view seems plausible enough, but it can be shown to be inaccurate. What it reflects is the extent to which we think we depend on our eyes when in fact we depend as much or more on stimuli processed by the other senses. What we see is not always reliable, and what we hear and feel is not always less reliable than what we see. Moreover, even within the realm of what is visible, there is more than merely what is given at birth.

Bailey himself casts the first seeds of doubt, for he refers to the well-known phenomenon of collective caste mobility or even a shift for certain castes from ranked to unranked status. The impetus for this frequently occurred "when persons of humble caste achieved professional status as a lawyer or a Government servant," for they then "found themselves in difficulties with colleagues, most of whom belonged to higher castes."[51] Their response was to refuse to be subordinate and to claim a higher status for their caste. But then it is necessary to ask why persons of humble caste found themselves in such difficulty if indeed caste identification is impossible in a large-scale society. The answer seems plain: even in a government office or a bar association, far from village life, caste origins could easily be detected without a visible "rank sign."

This, in fact, is generally true. Where there are ambiguities of group membership, ways are found to make accurate identifications as fast as necessary. Color and phenotype are not the only visible cues, and in any case reliance need rarely be based on visible cues alone. In a North Indian village area, shopkeepers, using posture, bearing, gesticulation, clothing, and grammatical usage, in addition to physical features, were able, rapidly and rather reliably, to single out low-caste strangers for discriminatory service.[52] In the Nigerian riots of 1966, Northern mobs in search of Ibo sorted out Yoruba by their dress.[53] In Hindu-Muslim violence, circumcision is usually the definitive test of identity for male victims.[54] In the absence of so decisive a differentiator, Sinhalese mobs in the Sri Lanka riots of 1958 had to use a variety of indicators to identify Tamils. Methodically, they looked for men "who wore their shirts over their *vertis,* Tamil fashion," who had earring holes in their ears (a Tamil sign of "early parental affection"), or who could not on the spot "read and explain a piece from a Sinhalese newspaper."[55] Calling into operation as they did the wrath of the mob, these alternative tests of identity constitute a grim caution against acceptance of the figment of the pigment.

As the examples suggest, there is a continuum of cues, from visible to nonvisible. Among visible cues, there are, first of all, those that are birth-determined and bodily, such as color, physiognomy, hair color and texture, height, and physique. Then there are those that are not determined at birth but are also bodily: circumcision and earring holes, as we have seen, and also scarification, which indicates ethnic group and subgroup in parts of Africa, modification of earlobes in parts of Asia and Africa, the filing or removal of certain combinations of teeth among Masai, Luo, and Luhya in East Africa,[56] or the staining of teeth among Chagga in Tanzania from the brown water they drink. Still visible but behavioral rather than bodily, and certainly not determined by birth, are posture, bearing, gestures, dress, grooming, and display.[57] Perhaps in the same category are the short beards that identify Ahmadis in Pakistan, for, though bodily, they are not indelible, as holes, scars, and circumcision are. Finally, there are the nonvisible cues, many of which derive from language and culture: grammar, syntax, vocabulary, accent, and reading facility, to begin with, but also differences in names, as in Northern Ireland and the Punjab,[58] as well as food habits and mastery of the standard cultural repertoire, which may include such arcane items as the ability to recall Buddhist stanzas in their original Pali version, as commonly learned by Sinhalese children.[59]

On the average, perhaps, the more visible and the closer to birth, the more immutable and therefore reliable the cue. A name can be changed, a language learned, and clothing altered, but scars and height are more difficult to undo. Even here, the association is not perfect, for many of the birth-bodily cues are merely probabilistic, and cultural inventory items like speech patterns may be even more probative of identity. But this is a rather abstract way of putting the matter, for it is the combination of cues that constitutes the authoritative differentiator. Groups will use that mix of cues which they find most reliable. In Andhra Pradesh, Andhras often wear scarves around their necks, whereas Telanganas do not; Telangana speech has many Urdu words, Andhra speech fewer; Telangana food is more like Muslim food than the Andhra cuisine is; Telanganas prefer tea, Andhras coffee.[60] Of such small differences are identifications compounded, and the indicators of separate identity then also come to represent as symbols the traits said to be associated with the groups.[61]

No cue or combination of cues is wholly reliable. In one study, for example, physiognomy proved to be a reliable cue to Jewish identity on a more than random basis, but physiognomy,

speech, and gestures together were less reliable than physiognomy alone. When names were added to these cues, accuracy increased sharply.[62] There is some suggestion that the more salient the cleavage, or the more intense the conflict, the more accurate the identifications are likely to be.[63] Under acute conflict conditions, it will be more important to locate those cues that differentiate the largest number of members of the respective groups. But, even under the most severe conflict conditions, such as violent encounters in which rioters have the power to test ethnic identity systematically, mistakes are occasionally made.[64]

ENDNOTES

1. The distinctions elaborated in the following two sections were first presented in a much more cryptic form in Donald L. Horowitz, "Three Dimensions of Ethnic Politics," *World Politics* 23 (Jan. 1971): 232–44. Copyright © 1971 by Princeton University Press, to which I am indebted for permission to use this material.

2. F.G. Bailey, "Closed Social Stratification in India," *European Journal of Sociology* 4 (May 1963): 107–24, at 119.

3. Gerald D. Berreman draws a similar distinction: ". . . Castes are ranked components in a larger society comprised of analogous components. Tribes contrast to caste in that they are relatively independent and homogeneous systems of their own." "Structure and Function of Caste Systems," in George De Vos and Hiroshi Wagatsuma, eds., *Japan's Invisible Race* (Berkeley and Los Angeles: Univ. of California Press, 1966), 287. This is not the place to enter the debate over whether caste, in the precise usage of the term, is unique to India, for there is no doubt that ranked systems exist in many countries. Here and elsewhere in the text, wherever the word *caste* appears in a quotation, it is used in a sense equivalent to ranked ethnic groups. See ibid., 275. In India, of course, there are castes that have become essentially unranked groups, as Bailey, among others, has pointed out ("Closed Social Stratification," 119). This is one reason to adhere to the ranked-unranked terminology, rather than using a word like *caste*, which is now less precise.

4. Arend Lijphart, *The Politics of Accommodation: Pluralism and Democracy in the Netherlands* (Berkeley and Los Angeles: Univ. of California Press, 1968). William T. Bluhm, *Building an Austrian Nation* (New Haven: Yale University Press, 1973).

5. David H. Marlowe, "In the Mosaic: The Cognitive and Structural Aspects of Karen-Other Relationships," in Charles F. Keyes, ed., *Ethnic Adaptations and Identity:*

The Karen on the Thai Frontier with Burma (Philadelphia: Institute for the Study of Human Issues, 1979).

6. Bailey, "Closed Social Stratification in India," 119.

7. H.H. Gerth and C. Wright Mills, eds., *From Max Weber: Essays in Sociology* (New York: Free Press, 1958), 189.

8. Following Weber, Berreman ties caste to "criteria of intrinsic worth, honor, or purity," stating that "the fact that the paramount virtue is accorded differentially to birth-ascribed groups in a society is a common and distinctive characteristic of caste systems." "Structure and Function of Caste Systems," 281. Similarly, Bryce Ryan identifies caste with a system of ranks based on the hereditary distribution of "honor." *Caste in Modern Ceylon* (New Brunswick: Rutgers Univ. Press, 1953), 59.

9. See, e.g., John Dollard, *Caste and Class in a Southern Town,* 3d ed. (Garden City, N.Y.: Anchor Books, 1957), 65–67.

10. Fernando Henriques, *Family and Colour in Jamaica* (London: Eyre & Spottiswoode, 1953).

11. See Lewis C. Copeland, "The Negro as a Contrast Conception," in Edgar Thompson, ed., *Race Relations and the Race Problem* (Durham: Duke Univ. Press, 1939), 167.

12. Martin R. Doornbos, "Kumanyana and Rwenzururu: Two Responses to Ethnic Inequality," in Robert I. Rotberg and Ali A. Mazrui, eds., *Protest and Power in Black Africa* (New York: Oxford Univ. Press, 1970), 1090; Ryan, *Caste in Modern Ceylon,* 59, 74–75; George A. De Vos, *Japan's Outcasts: The Problem of the Burakumin* (London: Minority Rights Group, Report no. 3, 1971), 6.

13. Ryan, *Caste in Modern Ceylon,* 132–34.

14. Copeland, "The Negro as a Contrast Conception."

15. De Vos, *Japan's Outcastes,* 7; John Donoghue, "The Social Persistence of an Outcaste Group," in Melvin Tumin, ed., *Comparative Perspectives on Race Relations* (Boston: Little, Brown, 1969), 110–11.

16. Nandasena Ratnapala, *Sarvodaya and the Rodiyas* (Colombo, Sri Lanka: Sarvodaya Research, mimeo., 1979), 1–2.

17. Thomas M. Kiefer, *The Tausug: Violence and Law in a Philippine Moslem Society* (New York: Holt, Rinehart & Winston, 1972), 22–23.

18. Peter J. Wilson, *A Malay Village and Malaysia* (New Haven: HRAF Press, 1967), 25–29, 36.

19. Elliott P. Skinner, "Group Dynamics and Social Stratification in British Guiana," *Annals of the New York Academy of Sciences* 83 (Jan, 20, 1960): 904–12.

20. Morton Klass, *East Indians in Trinidad: A Study of Cultural Persistence* (New York: Columbia Univ. Press, 1961), 244.

21. Ronald Cohen, "Social Stratification in Bornu," in Arthur Tuden and Leonard Plotnicov, eds., *Social Stratification in Africa* (New York: Free Press, 1970), 243.

22. W. Howard Wriggins, *Ceylon: Dilemmas of a New Nation* (Princeton: Princeton Univ. Press, 1960), 232–33.

23. Jacques J. Maquet, *The Premise of Inequality in Ruanda* (London: Oxford Univ. Press, 1961). See Donoghue, "The Social Persistence of an Outcaste Group," 120–21.

24. For example, see C.C. Stewart, "Political Authority and Social Stratification in Mauritania," in Ernest Gellner and Charles Micaud, eds., *Arabs and Berbers: From Tribe to Nation in North Africa* (Lexington, Mass.: Lexington Books, 1972), 383; René Lemarchand, "Power and Stratification in Rwanda: A Reconsideration," *Cahiers d'Etudes africaines* 6 (Dec. 1966): 592–610, at 602–05; Dollard, *Caste and Class in a Southern Town,* 179, 212, 262, 282; Kenneth M. Stampp, *The Peculiar Institution: Slavery in the Ante-Bellum South* (New York: Random House, 1956); see also Michael Banton, *Race Relations* (New York: Basic Books, 1967), 87.

25. For an example, see Everett C. Hughes, *French Canada in Transition* (Chicago: Univ. of Chicago Press, 1943), 86.

26. Leonard Berkowitz, *Aggression: A Social-Psychological Analysis* (New York: McGraw-Hill, 1962), 76–78; Frances K. Graham, et al., "Aggression as a Function of the Attack and the Attacker," *Journal of Abnormal and Social Psychology* 46 (Oct. 1951): 512–20, at 516.

27. Lemarchand, "Power and Stratification in Rwanda"; I. Schapera, *Government and Politics in Tribal Societies* (New York: Schocken Books, 1967; originally published in 1956), 128; Kiefer, *The Tausug,* 22.

28. This is quite different from the position that, in the absence of a clear "rank sign," subordination is only possible on a localized basis. Compare Bailey, "Closed Social Stratification in India," 113, 120, discussed below. So long as geographic intermixture exists, large-scale systems can be ranked.

29. In Nigeria, the advent of British rule interrupted a Hausa-Fulani invasion southward, and after independence "many Southerners feared that the departure of the British had opened the way for its continuance"— a fear reinforced by occasional Hausa-Fulani utterances. Walter Schwartz, *Nigeria* (New York: Praeger, 1968), 76. See Richard L. Sklar, *Nigerian Political Parties* (Princeton: Princeton Univ. Press, 1963), 98 n.25. In Sri Lanka, Tamil invasions had resulted in a de facto partition of the island centuries before colonial rule. But the teaching of Sinhalese history kept the issue alive and gave it periodic political significance. In 1957, when the prime minister agreed to a decentralization that would have devolved considerable power on Tamil local authorities in the North and East, the opposition toured the country, displaying maps with a black footprint over the areas to be "ceded" to the Tamils. Robert N. Kearney, *Communalism and Language in the*

Politics of Ceylon (Durham: Duke Univ. Press, 1967), 117–18.

30. See, e.g., Elliott P. Skinner, "Strangers in West African Societies," *Africa* 33 (Oct. 1963): 307–20.

31. See Lemarchand, "Power and Stratification in Rwanda," 609–10.

32. See ibid.; René Lemarchand, "Revolutionary Phenomena in Stratified Societies: Rwanda and Zanzibar," *Civilisations* 18 (Mar. 1968): 16–49; Michael Lofchie, *Zanzibar: Background to Revolution* (Princeton: Princeton Univ. Press, 1965); John Okello, *Revolution in Zanzibar* (Nairobi: East African Publishing House, 1967); M. Catharine Newbury, "Colonialism, Ethnicity, and Rural Political Protest: Rwanda and Zanzibar in Comparative Perspective," *Comparative Politics* 15 (Apr. 1983): 253–80.

33. Michael C. Hudson, *The Precarious Republic: Political Modernization in Lebanon* (New York: Random House, 1968), 9.

34. Ibid., 135. James O'Connell refers to ethnic interaction as "international relations without safeguards." "Authority and Community in Nigeria," in Robert Melson and Howard Wolpe, eds., *Nigeria: Modernization and the Politics of Communalism* (East Lansing: Michigan State Univ. Press, 1971), 634–37.

35. Tarzie Vittachi, *Emergency '58: The Story of the Ceylon Race Riots* (London: André Deutsch, 1958), 91.

36. Cf. Clifford Geertz, "The Integrative Revolution: Primordial Sentiments and Civil Politics in the New States," in Geertz, ed., *Old Societies and New States* (New York: Free Press, 1963), 109–11.

37. For illustrations, see Lemarchand, "Power and Stratification in Rwanda," 609–10; Wilson, *A Malay Village and Malaysia,* 50.

38. *Class and Class Conflict in Industrial Society* (Stanford: Stanford Univ. Press, 1959), 165.

39. See, e.g., Myron Weiner, *Sons of the Soil: Migration and Ethnic Conflict in India* (Princeton: Princeton Univ. Press, 1978), 173; Samuel Decalo, *Coups and Army Rule in Africa* (New Haven: Yale Univ. Press, 1976), 177–78; Stein Rokkan, "Geography, Religion, and Social Class: Crosscutting Cleavages in Norwegian Politics," in Seymour M. Lipset and Stein Rokkan, eds., *Party Systems and Voter Alignments: Cross-National Perspectives* (New York: Free Press, 1967), 403, 423; Raymond E. Wolfinger, "The Development and Persistence of Ethnic Voting," in Lawrence H. Fuchs, ed., *American Ethnic Politics* (New York: Harper & Row, 1968), 180; Ed Cairns, "Intergroup Conflict in Northern Ireland," in Henri Tajfel, ed., *Social Identity and Intergroup Relations* (Cambridge: Cambridge Univ. Press, 1982), 281.

40. For the separate treatment of color differences, see Harold R. Isaacs, "Color in World Affairs," *Foreign Affairs* 47 (Jan. 1969): 235–50; Isaacs, "Group Identity and Political Change: The Role of Color and Physical Characteristics," *Daedalus* 96 (Spring 1967): 353–75.

41. For yet another distinction, see D. John Grove, "The Race vs. Ethnic Debate: A Cross-National Analysis of Two Theoretical Approaches," University of Denver Center on International Race Relations, *Studies in Race and Nations,* vol. 5, no. 4 (1973–74): 1–44, at 35.

42. See the contributions to the issue, "Color and Race," *Daedalus* 96 (Spring 1967).

43. Wilson, *A Malay Village and Malaysia,* 25.

44. For the background, see *Le Monde,* Feb. 19, 1966; Mokhtar Ould Daddah, "Rapport moral," presented at the Congrès ordinaire du Parti du Peuple, Aioun, Mauritania, June 24–26, 1966 (mimeo.), p. 9. I am also indebted to conversations with several Mauritanians. For a report on the status of the Hartani (sing. Haratin), see the *Washington Post,* May 31, 1981.

45. See Winthrop D. Jordan, *White over Black: American Attitudes Toward the Negro, 1550–1812* (Chapel Hill: Univ. of North Carolina Press, 1968), 91–98. See also Jeffrey R. Brackett, *The Negro in Maryland* (Baltimore: Johns Hopkins Univ. Press, 1889), 32, 38.

46. Jordan, *White over Black,* 96.

47. Cf. Dollard, *Caste and Class in a Southern Town,* 61, for the apocryphal story of a Negro found in a railroad car reserved for whites on a Southern train. Asked to move to the Jim Crow car, he announced he had "resigned" from the "colored race." Obviously, the reply sounds absurd in the Southern context only because color was an immutable indicator of subordinate identity. There is a double impossibility, physical and social: (1) color-group membership is fixed; (2) even if it were not, movement from one group to the other cannot be at the choice of a member of the subordinate group in a system of ethnic stratification.

48. The distinction made by Laponce between "minorities by force" and "minorities by will" is suggestive in this connection. J.A. Laponce, *The Protection of Minorities* (Berkeley and Los Angeles: Univ. of California Press, 1960), chap. 1. By the former, Laponce seems to refer mainly to subordinate groups in hierarchical systems; by the latter, to parallel groups excluded from political power.

49. Kenneth M. Stampp, *The Peculiar Institution,* 195–96.

50. "Closed Social Stratification in India," 113, 120. See also Bailey, *Politics and Social Change,* 126.

51. "Closed Social Stratification in India," 122.

52. James M. Sebring, "Caste Indicators and Caste Identification of Strangers," *Human Organization* 83 (Fall 1969): 199–207.

53. See the official Eastern version of the riots, *Nigerian Pogrom: The Organized Massacre of Eastern Nigerians* (Enugu: Eastern Regional Government, 1966), 15, 19.

54. See Manohar Malgonkar, *A Bend in the Ganges* (New Delhi: Orient Paperbacks, 1964), 367.

55. Vittachi, *Emergency '58,* 54.

56. R.D. Grillo, "Ethnic Identity on a Kampala Housing Estate," in Abner Cohen, ed., *Urban Ethnicity* (London: Tavistock Publications, 1974), 177.

57. Ibid.

58. Harold Jackson, *The Two Irelands—A Dual Study of Inter-Group Tensions* (London: Minority Rights Group, Report no. 2, 1971), 4; Khushwant Singh, *Train to Pakistan* (Bombay: IBH Pub. Co., 1970), 143. See also John Darby, "Group Interaction in Northern Ireland: The Literature" (unpublished manuscript, Colraine, Northern Ireland, 1982).

59. Vittachi, *Emergency '58,* 49.

60. Weiner, *Sons of the Soil,* 240.

61. Gordon W. Allport, *The Nature of Prejudice* (Garden City, N.Y.: Doubleday Anchor Books, 1958), 133–34.

62. Leonard D. Savitz and Richard F. Thomasson, "The Identifiability of Jews," *American Journal of Sociology* 64 (Mar. 1959): 468–75.

63. Cf. Launor F. Carter, "The Identification of 'Racial' Membership," *Journal of Abnormal and Social Psychology* 43 (July 1948): 279–86. Erving Goffman has emphasized the distinction between visible and nonvisible stigmata (often handicaps), arguing that persons with visible stigmata are "discredited," whereas persons with nonvisible ones are merely "discreditable" and can sometimes avoid being discredited by controlling information about themselves. *Stigma,* 48. If this distinction holds, it is only because most stigmata are probably not highly salient; if they were, the control of relevant information would be more difficult.

64. Vittachi, *Emergency '58,* 49; Aswini K. Ray and Subhash Chakravarti, *Meerut Riots: A Case Study* (New Delhi: Sampradyikta Virodhi Committee, n.d.), 11.

T H R E E

Class Approaches to Ethnicity and Race

Edna Bonacich

The field of ethnic and race relations has recently tended to be dominated by an assumption that race and ethnicity are "primordial" bases of affiliation, rooted in "human nature." This assumption is increasingly being challenged by authors who contend that, while race and ethnicity may appear to be primordial attachments, in fact they reflect a deeper reality, namely, class relations and dynamics. I believe that class approaches are the most fruitful way to study ethnicity and race. Not only are they more in accord with a "deeper"

level of reality that enables us to understand phenomena at the surface of society, but they also provide us with the tools for changing that reality. The purpose of this paper is to briefly review and criticize primordial assumptions about ethnicity and race, to present several class approaches to the subject in an effort to demonstrate the richness of available ideas, and finally, to attempt a tentative synthesis of some of these ideas.

Before we start, let us define our terms. Eth-

Reprinted from *Insurgent Sociologist* 10:2 (Fall, 1980) by permission.

nicity and race are "communalistic" forms of social affiliation, sharing an assumption of a special bond between people of like origins, and the obverse of a negative relation to, or rejection of, people of dissimilar origins. There are other bases of communalistic affiliation as well, notably, nationality and "tribe." For the sake of this discussion, I would like to treat all of these as a single phenomenon. Thus, ethnocentrism, racism, nationalism, and tribalism are similar kinds of sentiments, dividing people along lines of shared ancestry rather than other possible lines of affiliation and conflict, such as common economic or political interest.

Obviously there are other important bases of affiliation besides communalism. One important alternative form of solidarity is along class lines. Figure 1 presents schematically these two forms of affiliation and their interaction for capitalist societies. Needless to say, it is a very simplified sketch and could be elaborated along both dimensions, as well as by the addition of other dimensions. Still, the point to be made is that ethnic (or communalistic, or "vertical") forms of solidarity cross-cut class (or "horizontal") bases of affiliation. They represent competing principles, each calling on people to join together along one of two axes.

PRIMORDIALISM

The sociology of race and ethnic relations grew in reaction to a tradition that underplayed the importance of communalistic affiliations.[1] As many authors have pointed out, the early "classic" writers in sociology paid little heed to ethnicity.[2] They assumed that it would disappear with modernization and industrialization. Indeed, the early grand dichotomies, such as *gemeinschaft* and *gesellschaft,* assumed a movement from ethnic-type affiliations, based on irrational, kinlike bonds between people, to affiliation based on the rational principles of mutual interest and need. Organic solidarity would replace mechanical; horizontal bonds would destroy vertical ones. Ethnicity and race were "traditional" social forms. The exigencies of modern society would "liberate" people from these traditions.[3] It should be noted that this expectation was also held by early Marxists,

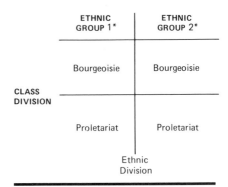

FIGURE 1 *Ethnicity and Class in the Capitalist Mode of Production*
Nationality, race, or tribe could be substituted for ethnicity.

who assumed that class solidarity would override national chauvinism (Nairn 1975; Blauner n.d.).

The obvious falseness of this premise, perhaps especially realized by American sociologists in the face of Nazi Germany, when one of the world's more "modern" societies proved capable of extreme racism, forced a reassessment. Similarly, the black uprising of the 1960s in the United States reawakened sociologists to the fact that the "race problem" was not simply disappearing. Clearly these "traditional" sources of solidarity were far more resistant to change than had been realized.

Several authors began to call for revisions in our thinking. Criticizing earlier writers, they demanded that race and ethnicity be given prominence as phenomena that could not be ignored. Some, for example, writers in the "plural society" school (Smith 1965; Kuper and Smith 1969) suggested that we place this phenomenon at center stage. As they correctly pointed out, almost every society in the world has some degree of ethnic and racial diversity, and for most it is apparently a pivotal point of division and conflict.

The polemic against the obvious inadequacies of the belief that ethnicity would disappear has led to another extreme position: the view that it is such a "natural" bond between people as to be immutable or "primordial." Geertz (1963:109) defines this concept as follows:

By a primordial attachment is meant one that stems from the "givens"—or, more precisely, as culture is inevitably involved in such matters, the assumed "givens"— of social existence: immediate contiguity and kin connection mainly, but beyond them the givenness that stems from being born into a particular religious community, speaking a particular language, or even a dialect of a language, and following particular social practices. These congruities of blood, speech, custom, and so on, are seen to have an ineffable, and at times overpowering, coerciveness in and of themselves. One is bound to one's kinsman, one's neighbor, one's fellow believer, ipso facto; as the result not merely of personal affection, practical necessity, common interest, or incurred moral obligation, but at least in great part by virtue of some unaccountable absolute import attributed to the very tie itself. The general strength of such primordial bonds, and the types of them that are important, differ from person to person, from society to society, and from time to time. But for virtually every person, in every society, at almost all times, such attachments seem to flow more from a sense of natural—some would say spiritual—affinity than from social interaction.

The primordial ethnic bond is assumed to have two faces. On the one hand, it leads to a special attachment to an "in-group" of similar people, on the other, to feelings of disdain or repulsion towards the "out-group" or people of dissimilar origins. "Ethnocentrism" is believed to be a "natural" human sentiment. For example, Gordon (1978:73) states:

The sense of ethnicity (in the larger definition of racial, religious, or national origins identification), because it cannot be shed by social mobility, as for instance social class background can, since society insists on its inalienable ascription from cradle to grave, becomes incorporated into the self. This process would appear to account for the widespread, perhaps ubiquitous presence of ethnocentrism, and perhaps even more crucially means that injury to the ethnic group is seen as injury to the self.

This idea derives from a biologically rooted conception of "human nature."[4]

Gordon may be more explicit than most in stating the assumption that ethnicity is rooted in human nature, but it is widespread (Williams, 1964:17–27) in the discipline. The naturalness of the ethnic bond is extended to "racial" categories, even as authors recognize that these have questionable validity. Thus such categories as "blacks"

and "whites" in the United States are treated as "groups." Whites naturally prefer the company of other whites, who are more similar to themselves, while disdaining the company of less similar blacks. The unquestioned assumption of the "group" nature of ethnic and racial "groups" extends even to authors who recognize that such groups may act as interest groups to attain political ends (Glazer and Moynihan 1975).

Accepting the primordialness of ethnicity leads to a certain logic of inquiry. Since ethnic and racial affiliation requires no explanation in itself, one concentrates on its consequences.[5] These may be negative, in the form of prejudice and discrimination against "out-groups."[6] Or they may be positive, providing people with a meaningful and rich group life.[7] In the process of concentrating on intra-"group" solidarity and inter-"group" hostility, little attention is paid to intra-ethnic conflict let alone cross-ethnic alliances.

There are at least three reasons for questioning the primordial nature of communalistic ties. First, there are boundary problems in defining ethnic and racial groups (cf. Barth 1969a; Patterson 1977). Because of the pervasive tendency for human beings to interbreed, a population of mixed ancestry is continually being generated. To consign these people to an ethnic identity requires a descent rule. There are a variety of such rules, including: tracing descent matrilineally (as found among the Jews), or by the presence of one particular ancestry (as in U.S. blacks), or by treating mixed ancestry as a separate ethnicity (as in the case of South African Coloureds), and so on. The variability in descent rules suggests their social rather than primordial nature. They reflect social "decisions," not natural, kin-like feeling.[8]

Apart from mixed ancestry problems, ethnic groups can redefine their boundaries in terms of whom they incorporate. As many authors (e.g. Yancey et al. 1976) have pointed out, several of the European immigrant groups to the United States, such as Italians, had no sense of common nationality until they came here. And the construction of "whites" out of the enmity between old and "new" European immigrants took decades to achieve. Similarly today a new ethnic group, Asian-Americans, is being constructed out of previously quite distinctive, and often hostile, national elements. That such a creation is social and political, rather than primordial, seems clear.

A second reason for questioning the primordial nature of ethnicity is that shared ancestry has not prevented intra-ethnic conflict, including class conflict. If one considers the history of societies which were relatively homogeneous ethnically, such as France or England, one finds not only intense class conflict, but even class warfare. Even in ethnically diverse societies such as the United States, within ethnic groups, class conflict is not unknown. White workers have struck against white-owned plants and been shot down by co-ethnics without concern for "common blood." Chinese and Jewish businessmen have exploited their ethnic "brothers and sisters" in sweatshops and have bitterly resisted the efforts of their workers to gain independence. The prevalence of intra-ethnic conflict should lead us to question the idea that ethnicity necessarily provides a bond between people, let alone a primordial one.

Third, conflicts based on ethnicity, race, and nationality, are quite variable. In some cases they are fierce; in others, despite the presence of groups with different ancestry, conflict is limited or non-existent. A full range of ethnic relations is found in the world, extending from complete assimilation of diverse ethnic elements (as in the case of various European nationalities which came to make up the "WASP" group in the United States), to the total extermination of one ethnic group by another (as in the genocide of the Tasmanians). This variability should, again, lead us to question the primordial nature of ethnicity, for if ethnicity were a natural and inevitable bond between people it should always be a prominent force in human affairs.

Of course, primordialists (e.g. Hoetink 1967) might reply that the level of conflict is based on the degree of difference between groups, in terms of color or culture. Thus variability in race and ethnic relations could be accounted for within a primordial framework. For instance, in the United States, degree of racial and ethnic difference would, on the surface, appear to account for patterns of assimilation or rejection (Warner and Srole 1945). Yet the U.S. pattern finds limited replications on a world scale. Some

of the worst ethnic-type conflicts have occurred among very similar groups, such as Protestants and Catholics in Northern Ireland, French and English-speaking Canadians, Ibos and other "tribes" in Nigeria, Chinese and native populations in Southeast Asia, and Jews and Germans in Nazi Germany, to name a few. The "degree of difference" seems quite inadequate to explain the emergence of conflict or its intensity.

For all these reasons, and there are probably others, we cannot simply accept communalistic groups as natural or primordial units. Ethnic, national, and racial solidarity and antagonism are all socially created phenomena. True, they are social phenomena which call upon primordial sentiments and bonds based upon common ancestry. But these sentiments and bonds are not just naturally there. They must be constructed and activated. It is thus incumbent upon us not to take ethnic phenomena for granted, but to try to explain them.

Recently a new school of thought has emerged. While not moving back to the earlier errors of the "founding fathers" in ignoring the importance of ethnicity, racism, and nationalism, it nevertheless holds that these phenomena cannot be taken for granted as natural; they need to be explained. Without ignoring communalistic affiliations we can ask: Under what conditions will ethnic or racial affiliation be invoked? Under what conditions will this lead to extreme conflict? And under what conditions will ethnicity or race subside as major axes of social organization and conflict? Class theories constitute one broad category of attempted explanation of the ethnic phenomenon. They share in common the notion that ethnic movements are not only essentially political rather than primordial, but that they have *material* roots in the system and relations of production.

CLASS THEORIES OF ETHNICITY

There is no single class approach to the question of ethnicity. Indeed, in recent years, considerable creative work has proceeded on several fronts, not all of which are in communication with one another. Different disciplines and subdisciplines, such as economic anthropology, urban sociology, and immigrant history, are all developing class approaches to ethnicity. Scholars interested in different areas of the world tend to communicate poorly with one another. Thus there are class theories of ethnicity in African or Latin American studies, about South Africa, the U.S.-Mexican border, about guest workers in Europe, and so one. In addition, an abundance of theoretical models is available, some of which operate at different levels, but all of which address ethnicity to some extent. These include: theories of labor migration and immigration, dependency theory, dual labor markets, split labor markets, internal colonialism, theories of middleman minorities, labor aristocracy theories, world systems theory, and more. Bringing all these literatures together is a huge task, well beyond the scope of this paper. My goal here is to present a few of the available ideas.

Before examining particular theories, let us briefly return to Figure 1 to define what is being talked about. Positive (integrative) movements along the vertical axis may be termed "nationalist" movements. These are efforts to mobilize people of different classes within the same ethnic group to join together. Negative (conflictual) movements along the horizontal axis represent within-class inter-ethnic antagonisms. These two types of movements constitute the two faces of ethnicity: in-group solidarity and out-group rejection. In contrast, negative movements along the vertical axis represent intra-ethnic class struggle, while positive movements along the horizontal axis reflect cross-ethnic class solidarity. Diagonal movements are ambiguous, having both class and ethnic content. For instance, a negative diagonal could represent national and colonial oppression or movements for liberation from such oppression. Our main concern here is with the explanation of ethnic-type movements, i.e., positive vertical and negative horizontal.

Note that the figure should apply to inter-ethnic relations regardless of the territorial location of these groups. They can each occupy a discrete geographical territory, or a segment of one nation may have conquered and settled among another,[9] or a segment of one nation may have moved or been brought in as laborers to the territory of another, and so on. While there are important differences between these situations (Lieberson 1961), they all juxtapose communalistic against class bases of affiliation.

Figure 2 presents very schematically several class approaches to the question of ethnic nationalism. They are intended not to represent a comprehensive coverage of all class theories of ethnicity but to illustrate the tremendous riches and diversity of ideas within a class orientation.

A. Nation-building

One of the simplest class theories of ethnicity or nationalism is that it is a movement reflecting an early stage of capitalistic development in which capitalists seek to integrate a "national" market. This movement achieved its peak in Europe in the late nineteenth century (Hobsbawm 1977). When capitalism became imperialistic, the national bourgeoisies of the various Western nations came into conflict with one another, leading ultimately to the two world wars (Lenin 1939). The participants in these wars espoused nationalist ideologies as a mechanism by which the capitalist class could mobilize workers to support their cause. Exponents of this view hold that workers are not nationalistic since they are all exploited. Rather, they are internationalist, sharing a common interest in the overthrow of capitalism which transcends national boundaries. Nationalism is thus a movement representing the interests of the bourgeoisie. (This is illustrated in Figure 2A by showing that antagonism between national bourgeoisies leads to efforts at national mobilization by the bourgeoisies. The workers are objects, not generators, of this effort.)

B. Super-Exploitation

The fact that workers of different nationalities have not easily joined with one another, and have apparently joined willingly with their "national bourgeoisie" in the oppression or exclusion of workers of other nationalities, revealed the limitation of this approach. Such cases as the U.S. South or South Africa, where white workers generally failed to join with blacks in a united working class movement, and instead identified with white capitalists and landowners, led to some rethinking on the issue. An adequate explanation of communalism must take into account worker interests in it too.

"Super-exploitation," a crude designation for several schools of thought, provided an answer. Probably the most common class approach to

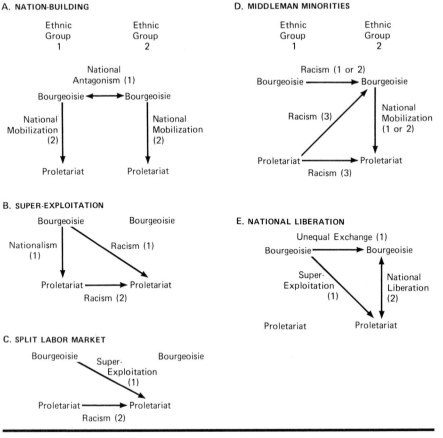

FIGURE 2 *Five Types of Class Theory of Ethnicity*

ethnicity, it sees ethnicity or race as markers used by employers to divide the working class. One segment of workers, typically dark-skinned, are more oppressed than another, the latter typically of the same ethnicity as the exploiters. This enables the dominant bourgeoisie to make huge profits from the former segment, enough to pay off the more privileged sector of the working class, who then help to stabilize the system by supporting it and acting as the policemen of the specially oppressed.[10]

For several authors in this tradition (e.g. Cox 1948), the super-exploitation of dark-skinned workers is rooted in the imperialistic expansion of Western European capitalism. Europe colonized the rest of the world in order to continue to accumulate capital more effectively. The ideol-

ogy of racism grew as a justification for the exploitation of colonized peoples: they were "naturally" inferior and needed Europeans to "help" them move into the modern world. Racist ideology developed not only in relation to people living in the distant colonies, but also toward people living in "internal colonies," (Allen 1970; Blauner 1972) where either white settlers had become established or colonized workers had been brought under some degree of coercion. Even when separated in politically differentiated territories, the working class of the imperialist power could be used to keep the colonized in line. Thus, with imperialism, the major axis of exploitation shifted from capitalist versus workers to oppressor "nations" and oppressed "nations."

Within a multi-ethnic society, having an especially exploited, ethnically delineated class serves several "functions" for the capitalist class: it can be used as a reserve army of labor, permitting flexibility in the system to deal with business cycles (Baran and Sweezy 1966); it allows employers to fill diverse labor needs, such as the "dual" requirements of a stable, skilled labor force in the monopoly and state sectors of the economy, and a flexible, unskilled, low wage labor force in the competitive sector (Gordon 1972; O'Connor 1973); it helps get done the "dirty work" that other workers are unwilling to do by creating a class that is desperate for work (Oppenheimer 1974); it helps in the accumulation of capital because wealth is extracted from the "under-developed" sector of ethnic group and passed on to the bourgeoisie of the dominant group (Blauner 1972; Frank 1967, 1969); and it helps to stabilize the system by keeping the working class fragmented and disorganized (Reich 1971; Szymanski 1976).

Within this broad perspective are found some major differences. One important issue of debate is whether white workers gain or lose from the racial oppression of minorities. The "internal colonialism" school supports the idea that white workers benefit, by being paid extra from the surplus taken from minorities, by being cushioned against unemployment, and by getting other psychological and political rewards. In other words, in this view, the racism of white workers is a "rational" response, rooted in their vested interest in imperialism.

In contrast, authors such as Reich and Szymanski contend that white workers lose from racism. Since workers of different ethnicity are pitted against one another, the working class movement is weakened, and all lose. Thus white worker racism is seen more as a product of manipulation by capital than a rational pursuit of self-interest by white labor.

Despite these differences, both schools of thought see ethnicity as created, or at least nurtured, by the bourgeoisie of the dominant ethnic group or nationality. It is used to mark off the super-exploited as inferior, through ideologies like racism. And it is used to bind the more advantaged workers to the ruling class through the ideology of ethnic solidarity, thereby masking conflicting class interests within that group.

White workers, for example, are taught that their whiteness makes them superior to other workers and gives them a common lot with their employers. A possibility is even held out to them that they too may become part of the ruling class because they are white. By the mobilization of ethnic solidarity, then, the capitalist class can induce these workers to support the system and align themselves against other workers. As Figure 2B suggests, the racism of dominant group workers is a secondary phenomenon, while that of the bourgeoisie is primary.

C. Split Labor Market

This approach places labor competition at the center of racist-nationalist movements, challenging the idea that they are the creation of the dominant bourgeoisie.[11] Uneven development of capitalism on a world scale, exacerbated by imperialist domination, generates "backwardness" or "under-development" for certain "nationalities." Workers of these nations, unable to defend themselves against exploitation of the severest kind, became "cheap labor" (arrow 1 in Figure 2C). The availability of cheap labor leads dominant workers to be displaced or threatened with displacement, since employers would prefer to hire cheaper labor. The threat of displacement may be accompanied by other changes in production, such as deskilling. Dominant group workers react to the threat of displacement by trying to prevent or limit capital's access to cheap labor, through efforts to exclude members of "cheap labor" groups from full participation in the labor market (arrow 2). That these exclusionary efforts have a "nationalist" or "racist" character is a product of historical accident which produced a correlation between ethnicity and the price of labor.

In contrast to the "super-exploitation" school of thought, split labor market theory argues that dominant group workers do not share a "national" interest with capital in the exploitation of colonized people, nor are they even fooled into believing they share such an interest. Rather, dominant group capital and labor are engaged in struggle over this issue. Capital wants to exploit ethnic minorities while labor wants to prevent them from doing so. However, in attempting to exclude ethnic groups from certain jobs, labor's reactions may be just as devastating to minority workers as direct exploitation by capital. Where the dominant working class is successful, minority workers are kept out of the most advanced sectors of the economy, suffer high unemployment rates, and so on. In sum, this approach suggests that there are two distinct types of racial-national oppression, one stemming from capital, and the other from labor.

Split labor market theory sees the question of whether white workers gain or lose from racism as a false, or at least oversimplified, issue. It suggests that white workers are hurt by the existence of cordoned-off cheap labor sectors that can be utilized by capital to undercut them. White labor's efforts to protect itself may prevent undercutting, in the short run; however, in the long run, it is argued, a marked discrepancy in the price of labor is harmful to all workers, permitting capital to pit one group against another.

D. Middleman Minorities

Middleman minority theories deal with a particular class of ethnic phenomena, namely groups which specialize in trade and concentrate in the petite bourgeoisie. Class explanations of this phenomenon vary. Some see these specialized minorities as creations of the dominant classes (not only bourgeoisies, since they arise in pre-capitalist societies as well) (Blalock 1967; Hamilton 1978; Rinder 1958). By marking a group off as ethnically distinct, it can be forced to occupy a distinctive class position that is of special use to the ruling class, namely, to act as a go-between to the society's subordinate classes, while bearing the brunt of hostility towards the elite. The racist reactions of subordinate classes against the middleman group can thus be seen as secondary or tertiary phenomena, manipulated by ruling classes to protect themselves. (There are parallels in this tripartite system to the construction of ethnic divisions within the working class. In both cases, the creation of two ethnically distinct subordinate classes which are pitted against one another helps to keep the elite in power.)

Another interpretation of middleman minorities is to see them as internally generated by the minorities themselves. Bonds of ethnic loyalty are used by the dominant class within the minority to mobilize the group economically. The use of ethnic sentiments enables the group's leaders to mobilize resources cheaply and effectively. One of the most important of these cheap resources is ethnic labor. By emphasizing ethnic bonds, the ethnic elite is able to minimize class division within the ethnic group, thereby keeping labor effectively controlled (Benedict 1968; Light 1972). In this interpretation, the racist reactions of dominant group members in part derive from fears of competition. The dominant business class, as well as the potential business class among subordinated segments of society, has access to a less pliable work force and fears being undercut. The dominant working class resents the competition of cheap-labor-based firms. Anti-middleman minority movements are seen (Bonacich 1973) to be rooted in these class antagonisms.

Several authors have pointed to a strong correlation between class position in the petty trader category, and ethnic solidarity. Not only does ethnic solidarity support trading, but the reverse holds true, namely, petty trading helps to hold the ethnic group together. Leon even coined the term "people-class" to express this coincidence. The argument follows that, when members of the ethnic group no longer occupy a unique class position, they will gradually lose their ties to the ethnic group and assimilate. Jews, according to Leon, who have ceased to be members of the petite bourgeoisie, have tended to disappear from the ranks of Judaism. If true, here is a clear example of the dominance of class over primordial roots of ethnic affiliation.

The people-class idea has also been used to describe groups that are not middleman minorities (or in the petite bourgeoisie). For instance, Leggett (1968) and Oppenheimer (1974) develop a similar conception of blacks in the United States. Blackness represents not merely a racial category, but a class category as well: sub-proletarian, marginal working class, etc.[12] As blacks become less exclusively identified with a particular class position, the salience of "race" as a category tends to decrease (Wilson 1978a). In other words, racial terminology and antagonism reflect, to some extent, the common and distinctive class position of blacks and reactions to that position. A similar approach is developed for U.S.

white ethnic groups by Hechter (1975) and Yancey et al. (1976), who see ethnic solidarity as linked to a concentration in particular occupations or subcategories of the working class.[13]

E. National Liberation

Partly growing out of the notion that some national groups are particularly oppressed or occupy a unique class position in world capitalism, is a concern for movements of national liberation. While these movements are clearly reactions to external domination and underdevelopment, considerable debate has ensued over the conditions under which "nationalist" reactions are appropriate. On the one hand is the principle of the right of "nations" to self-determination (Lenin 1968); on the other is the ambiguity of which groups actually constitute a viable nation and can therefore legitimately form separatist movements (Hobsbawm 1977). For instance, a major debate ensued over whether or not U.S. blacks constituted a "nation" in the South which could reasonably aspire to statehood. More recently, the "internal colonialism" model of the black experience again suggests the legitimacy of a "nationalist" solution, this time for northern, urban, ghetto-dwellers, a position that has been challenged by those who feel that class solidarity should take precedence.[14]

An important aspect of this issue is the question of whether it is necessary to go through a capitalist (or at least not fully socialist) phase in order to develop economically. Most Third World "peoples," particularly those in separate states, but also some minorities within states, still live and work under systems with feudal or pre-capitalist remnants, such as peasant agriculture, or migrate between pre-capitalist and capitalist sectors. It has been suggested that, under colonial conditions, a two-stage revolution is necessary: first, workers and peasants must join their incipient national bourgeoisie in overthrowing the foreign oppressor. Once the national bourgeoisie is sufficiently liberated to begin to develop the "nation" economically, and a true proletariat is formed, then intra-national class struggle and true socialist revolution become possible. Note that, in a way, we have come full circle, back to Type A, though under very different historical circumstances. Nationalism in the Third World can represent the interests of the bourgeoisie or petite bourgeoisie (Saul 1979) in establishing and consolidating modified forms of capitalism.

The necessity for a two-stage revolution has, of course, been challenged. On the one hand it is argued that the "national bourgeoisie" of oppressed nations is too linked to international capital to lead a liberation movement which will truly liberate. On the other, the ability of Third World peasants and other pre-capitalist classes as well as the incipient proletariat to engage in revolutionary movements has been proven. Indeed Third World peasant and proletarian movements have been far more successful on this score than the "developed" proletariat of Western Europe and the United States, though the degree to which these revolutions have produced truly socialist societies remains in question. Similarly, black workers in the United States, despite their sub-proletarian status (or perhaps more accurately, because of it) are undoubtedly more class conscious and ready for socialist revolution than the white working class (Leggett 1968, Geschwender 1978). Thus exclusively "nationalist" alliances are seen to be both undesirable and unnecessary, though colonized workers' movements against "white" capital still have a "national" component.

The debate is not so much concerned with explaining nationalist movements as prescribing when they are appropriate. However, implicit is an explanatory theme: movements for ethnic self-determination are likely to arise under conditions of colonial or neo-colonial rule; they represent a temporary class alliance between the colonized bourgeoisie (or incipient bourgeoisie) and workers-peasants, in response to colonial domination.[15]

As stated earlier, the five types of class theory are not intended to be definitive, but rather, illustrative of the multiplicity and complexity of ideas on this topic. Although I have presented them as if they were competing approaches, in fact they are not necessarily all incompatible. For instance, different kinds of communalistic movements may be appropriate to different stages of capitalist development. Thus the five approaches presented here may, to some extent, reflect sequential stages in the development of capitalism and imperialism. True, there are some genuine theoretical debates which need to be resolved one way or another, for example, whether or not most white workers have a vested interest in imperialist domination. I shall not, at this point, attempt to critically evaluate each of the various approaches since the criticism will be inherent in the synthesis attempted in the next section.

Before moving on to the synthesis, however, one lesson from this review needs to be stressed: "Nationalism" is not a unitary phenomenon. Not only must we distinguish between the nationalisms of the exploiters and the exploited (Mandel 1972), but also between nationalisms with different class roots, such as petit-bourgeois nationalism versus working-class nationalism. Indeed all four classes in our schema generate communalistic movement at times, and for quite different reasons. Some of the debates among class theorists may, in part, result from confusing different kinds of ethnic movements. To use the same example again, the debate over whether or not white workers have a vested interest in "racism" may confuse different kinds of racism: exploitation by the bourgeoisie versus exclusion by the working class. Any comprehensive class theory of ethnicity must take these differences into account.

TOWARDS AN INTEGRATED CLASS APPROACH

Since most of the important "ethnic relations" in the modern world have grown out of the rise of capitalism in Western Europe, and its resulting imperialist expansion, most of my analysis will concern this case. I assume that other capitalist imperialisms, notably that of Japan, produce a similar dynamic. Whether non-capitalist or state capitalist expansions, such as that of the Soviet Union, would fit the model, I do not know. The model will also not attempt to deal with pre-capitalist ethnic relations.

A promising new literature is developing which attempts to place ethnic phenomena within the context of the development of world capitalism.[16] The ideas which I am presenting here draw heavily upon their contributions.

A fully developed class analysis of ethnicity

needs to consider all of the possible class relations between "ethnic groups" that result from imperialism. These are schematically presented in Figure 3, and again we must note that the figure is simplified along both dimensions. One ought to consider not only other classes, but also, perhaps, a semi-autonomous role for the state. And "ethnic" relations between imperialist powers (as in Figure 2A), let alone between colonized peoples, have been omitted. A total analysis would include all of these. Still, even this very simplified version enables us to begin to chart the relationships and demonstrates some of the complexities of the problem.

Before we start to examine each of the relationships, it is important to point out that I am using the term "colonized" loosely here to refer to any form of external domination by a capitalist power. It may range from a minimum of unequal trade relations, through foreign investment, to total political domination.[17] In addition, the geographical position of both nationalities may vary: they may each remain primarily in their homelands, or members of the imperialist nation may move into the territory of the colonized nation, or members of the colonized nation may move to the territory of the imperialist power (as in labor immigration or importation). While geographic location obviously affects the nature of the rela-

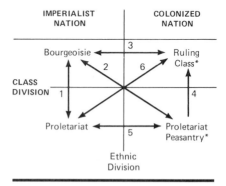

FIGURE 3 *Class and Ethnic Relations Resulting from Imperialism*

*The classes here are left somewhat ambiguous to indicate the possibility that full-blown capitalism has not yet emerged.

tions between national groups, there is, nevertheless, a fundamental similarity (or parallel) between these situations.

A final preliminary caution: the following attempt has numerous problems. For one thing, it is very general and abstract, glossing over differences in historical period let alone location. For another, it suffers from the ignorance, both theoretical and factual, of its author. My goal is mainly to *suggest* a way of tying these things together, and to stress that all the class relations generated by imperialism, in all its forms, need to be considered as a system if we are fully to understand the emergence of "nationalist" movements.

1. Class Relations within Imperialist Nations

Our analysis begins with class relations within imperialist nations. Needless to say, this encompasses the entire history of class struggle in the developed capitalist countries, a topic much too vast to cover here. I would like to examine one aspect of this topic, namely, the role of the "national" class struggle in the emergence of imperialism. While there is considerable debate over the roots of imperialism, it seems to me that one important push towards overseas expansion by capital comes from problems with its "national" working class. Put another way, as capitalism develops, the price of labor-power tends to rise, leading capital to seek cheaper labor-power (or commodities based upon cheaper labor-power) abroad.

The price of labor-power rises with the advance of capitalism for at least four reasons. First, increasing numbers of people are drawn from pre-capitalist modes of production into the proletariat until the potential national labor force is completely absorbed. We can see this process in the decline of independent farming and the rise of large cities, in the movement from self-employment to the predominance of wage and salary earners, and most recently, in the movement of women into the labor force. All of these shifts represent movements from pre-capitalist to capitalist relations of production. The complete absorption of the national labor force leads to a rise in the price of labor-power. Since the drive to accumulate capital continues unabated, the demand for labor exceeds supply, driving up the price.

Second, as workers become increasingly proletarianized, they are decreasingly able to provide any of the means of subsistence for themselves or their families. These need to be purchased from wages, which have to be increased in order to cover these new necessary expenses. In contrast, during transitional periods, when capitalism co-existed with pre-capitalist forms, part of the means of subsistence was provided by those forms. Women working in the home, processing food, making clothing, providing "free" child-care, and so on, meant that wages did not have to cover these items. But once the entire nation enters the proletariat, all goods and services become commodities, and they must be purchased with earnings.

A third factor in the rising cost of labor-power is that the social conditions of production become increasingly conducive to political organization among workers. In particular, large factories enable workers to compare their grievances and form organizations to protect their mutual interests. And their increasing divorce from their own means of subsistence, or any independent ownership of productive property, strengthens the motivation to organize. Thus, as capitalism advances, labor unionism develops and contributes to the rise in the price of labor-power.

Fourth, as capitalism develops, the rising demands of workers are likely to receive some state support. For example, under pressure from organized labor many advanced capitalist countries set minimum wages, regulate work conditions, provide old age pensions, and protect the rights of labor unions to provide independent representation for workers. In other words, the state helps to set national labor standards. In so doing, it provides a prop to the price of labor-power, helping both to maintain and raise it.

One important aspect of state intervention is protection against the use of the "army of the unemployed" to lower the price of labor-power in core industries. If left to their own devices, individual capitalists would respond to the rising cost of labor-power by introducing labor-saving machinery, throwing some people out of work, thereby putting competitive pressure on wages. Through "welfare" and unemployment insurance, the state cushions workers from the last aspect of this process, so that high levels of unemployment can, in fact, coexist with rising wages.

It is very important to recognize that a rise in the price of labor-power does not necessarily mean that workers are better off. The price goes up in part because the cost of living rises as people are increasingly dependent upon commodities. Many of these commodities are necessities (e.g., a car in Los Angeles), and in some cases their quality may be lower than when they were produced by unpaid family labor (e.g., homemade bread versus Wonder Bread). The rising price of labor-power may actually be associated with a decline in the quality of life.

Regardless of its impact on workers, the rising price of labor-power puts a squeeze on profits.[18] While there are various responses to this problem, including investment in labor-saving technology, one important response is to turn to new sources of labor-power. Having exhausted the national reserve army of the unemployed inaccessible because of welfare, capital looks overseas, especially to countries where capitalism is less fully developed, for "fresh troops." Essentially the process is one of continuing to absorb pre-capitalist modes of production and transforming their personnel into wage workers, except that now the process spills across national borders.

2. Relations between Imperialist Capital and Colonized Workers

Imperialist domination and exploitation of colonized workers is the fundamental root of "racism." Out of this exploitation grow efforts by imperialist capital to mobilize its "national" proletariat in support of colonial domination, utilizing racist, or nationalist, ideology. Also growing out of it are important divisions in the world's working class which lead to "nationalist" reactions on both sides.

As we have seen, capital tends to move overseas in search of cheaper labor-power. Labor is cheaper there for two reasons: first, the lower level of development decreases the price of labor-power; and second, imperialism itself distorts development, contributing to the perpetuation of a low price for labor-power beyond what might be expected under conditions of non-domination.

Let us deal briefly with each of these in turn.

Early stages of development are associated with the lower price of labor-power. Essentially the reason lies in the participation in pre-capitalist modes of production. In pre-capitalist modes, people mainly work for their own subsistence. When confronted with capitalist employers, they are likely, at first, to work for capital only on a supplementary basis. Most of their subsistence is provided by pre-capitalist forms. As a result, the capitalist employer need not pay the worker his or her complete subsistence, but only that part of it which is necessary to sustain the worker at that moment. In other words, the subsistence of his family, including health care, education, and housing, can be lifted out of the wage calculation. This enables employers in transitional economies to "earn" extraordinary rates of surplus value and at the same time to undersell competitors who use fully proletarianized work-forces.

Other features of attachment to pre-capitalist modes of production also contribute to "cheap labor." For one thing, "new" workers are unfamiliar with trade unions. For another, because they are less dependent on the wage-earning job, they have less incentive to form or join organizations to further their long-term collective interests as workers. Stable labor organizing goes hand-in-hand with permanent proletarianization. In general, the more completely dependent upon wage labor, the more developed will be the labor organizations of a group of workers.

Another factor which lowers the price of labor-power in less developed societies is a lower standard of living. Such items as housing, furniture, even diet, and certainly gadgetry of all kinds, vary from society to society, but tend to be more "substantial" in advanced capitalist societies. This may partly reflect real differences in necessities (e.g., an urban worker must have a means of transportation to get to work, must have a radio to find out certain kinds of information, must have a can-opener because much of his food comes in cans, etc.), but also seems to reflect different experiences and expectations, or what Marx terms an historical and moral element (Emmanuel 1972). Housing standards are a case in point. In one society, straw huts or shacks are perfectly acceptable. In another they are not even permitted.

Undoubtedly, these differences reflect the different levels of productivity of the two types of economy. Advanced capitalism spews forth an endless stream of commodities which come to be defined as necessities (in part through capitalist efforts). In poor, undeveloped societies, these necessities are luxuries which people have lived without for time immemorial. Imperialists can capitalize on these low expectations by lowering wages accordingly.

Imperialist capital introduces a special coercive element into the relations with colonized labor. Colonial and neo-colonial labor systems take on a variety of forms, e.g., the retention of peasant agriculture and crafts, but with increasing exaction of surplus from these workers; the retention of peasant agriculture associated with the migration of labor between the subsistence sector and capitalist enterprises; and the creation of plantation-type enterprises which employ semi- or fully-coerced labor full time. They all share however, a coercive element which cannot be imposed upon the working class of the advanced capitalist nation.[19]

Imperialist-type exploitation can also arise with immigrant workers. If the immigrants are still attached to pre-capitalist modes of production in the homeland, some of the factors which cheapen labor-power there apply to them as well. More importantly, just as imperialist capital can utilize special coercion in its relations with labor in the colonies, so can it towards immigrant workers. Special legal constraints, justified by "national" differences, can be set up for immigrants, such as the denial of citizenship rights. The legal disabilities of immigrants permit capital to act in an unrestrained manner towards this special class of workers. As Castells states: "The utility of immigrant labor to capital derives primarily from the fact that it can act towards it as though the labor movement did not exist, thereby moving the class struggle back several decades."[20] The same could be said for all types of colonized labor.

In sum, imperialist capital is willing and eager to make use of all potential sources of labor-power. Capitalism is a system that seeks to proletarianize the world. Pre-capitalist remnants in colonized territories, combined with the ability of imperialist capital to introduce coercive elements into labor relations, serve to retard the ability of colonized workers to fully participate in, or develop, a labor movement. Thus capital can "exploit" these workers (in the sense of extracting surplus from them, even if not always directly via the wage relationship) more thoroughly than it can exploit its own workers.

3. Relations between Imperialist Capital and Colonized Ruling Classes

Imperialism has important consequences not only for the workers in colonized societies, but also for their ruling classes, including the incipient bourgeoisie. The relationship between these two classes can take two major forms: on the one hand, imperialist capital can retard and undermine the development of a colonized ruling class. On the other hand, it can utilize this class to help them dominate colonized workers more effectively.

Imperialist undermining of colonial ruling classes can take many forms. Perhaps the simplest is the exaction of tribute, or simple stripping of some of the wealth from the invaded area. This may be achieved by taxation, for instance. At another level, the imperialist power can impose unequal treaties, forcing colonies or neo-colonies to accept trade from the more advanced economy, thereby having their crafts and infant industries undermined by cheap imports. At still a "higher" level, when foreign capital is invested in colonial societies, their ruling classes lose control over the direction of development. Profits and interest are drained out of the territory, while technologies are monopolized by foreign capital. Since power is unevenly distributed, benefit and wealth tend to accrue to the imperialist bourgeoisie, often at the expense of the colonized bourgeoisie. This unequal relationship may also arise with ethnic minorities within the imperialist nation so that their petite bourgeoisie is kept in a "dependent" position.

The other face of this relationship concerns the utilization of colonial leaders as "middlemen" to help imperialist capital penetrate the territory more effectively. Again, this occurs at many levels, from using the local rulers to collect taxes, to having them conduct the trade in imperialist commodities and in the goods produced by colonized workers. Perhaps the most important level is their role in helping to control colonized labor, the topic of our next section.

In sum, relationship 3 can be either competitive or cooperative. When the latter predominates, members of the colonial ruling class can become very wealthy, and develop a vested interest in the continuation of imperialism. Under such circumstances, there is little incentive to be "nationalist." When the relationship is competitive, however, nationalism is a likely response in the form of calling for the removal of "foreign domination." Both of these aspects may, of course, be present in the same territory, producing conflict within this class.

4. Relationship between Colonial Ruling Classes and Workers

The colonial ruling class can be used to make the "cheap labor" of colonial territories even cheaper, by the suppression and coercion of the workers. This suppression can take place at a variety of levels, from the individual entrepreneur or landholder, to the state, where oppressive "national" regimes can keep labor subdued for the benefit of foreign capital. The number of right-wing dictatorships propped up by foreign capital (aided by their states), which actively crush any movement that would improve the position of labor, need scarcely be mentioned. These intermediary classes often play a critical role in keeping the relations of production partially pre-capitalist.

"Nationalism" may be an important ideological tool in this effort. In particular, neo-colonial rulers may sometimes be able to persuade their workers to temper their demands, in the short run, in order to help the "nation" develop, and enable their exports to be competitive on the world market. While this effort may serve the interests of imperialist capital in its search for cheap labor, it also benefits colonial rulers and their bourgeoisies.

Ethnic minorities within capitalist societies may reveal both of these forms. The ethnic petite bourgeoisie can play a pivotal role in suppressing workers. Examples include labor contractors, padrones, and sweatshop owners. These people are able to take advantage of the vulnerable position of minority workers, while at the same time acting as intermediaries on behalf of big capital. They, too, can call upon "ethnic loyalty" as a technique of control. A garment sweatshop owner can appeal to his or her workers that it is in the "community interest" that the shop remain open, and provide jobs to community members. But this is conditional on their limiting their demands as workers, since the shop will only remain competitive if it can undersell others. Thus, ethnic solidarity can be used to retard the development of class consciousness as workers. Ultimately, this redounds to the benefit of big capital.

Since segments of the colonized ruling class are undermined by imperialist relations, another form of nationalism can emerge in this relationship, namely, an anti-imperialist alliance which calls for "national liberation." Although primordial symbolism may be invoked to bring the colonized ruling class together with workers and peasants, the coalition is still essentially the product of "class" forces: the exploitation of colonized labor, and the unequal competition between imperialist and colonial bourgeoisies.

In sum, two quite different nationalisms can emerge in this relationship. In one case, nationalism is used as a tool of exploitation; in the other, as a tool of liberation. The difference between these two may not always be easy to disentangle.

5. Relations within the Working Class

National divisions in the working class arise, in part, out of the material differences in the situations of different national segments. The working class of the imperialist nation has been able to organize and wrest some concessions from capital. Colonized labor (including migrant labor), in contrast, is under a double layer of oppression, both from the imperialist bourgeoisie and from middlemen. They are frequently still tied to pre-capitalist economic forms, limiting their ability to participate fully in a working-class movement. And they can be placed under special legal statuses (such as "illegal aliens") which are much more coercive than the situation with which the rest of the proletariat has to deal.

Since colonized workers are especially exploitable by capital, they pose a threat to the proletariat of the imperialist nation, who fear that their hard-won labor standards will be undermined. Immigrant labor, or the runaway shop to cheap-labor countries or regions, is used by capital in the form both of threat and reality to constrain its national working class. The local working class can respond to this threat either by trying to limit capital's access to cheap labor (protectionism), or by fighting to raise the labor standards of cheap labor (inclusionism). The first of these is a "nationalist" response, the second, "internationalist."

Both nationalist and internationalist responses are found among the workers of advanced capitalist countries. The issue is usually a point of struggle within the working-class movement. Factors that affect which choice is made include: the extent to which capital controls colonized labor (making it difficult to coordinate transnational efforts), the immediacy of the competitive threat, the completeness of proletarianization of workers in the imperialist nation (or the degree to which there are petit-bourgeois remnants),[21] and so on. Undoubtedly a very important factor is the ability of capital to manipulate "nationalist" sentiment by weeding out internationalist-oriented leaders from the working class movement.

Four quite different kinds of nationalism serve to divide the working class. First is imperialist capital's efforts to whip up nationalist sentiment among the workers to get them to support the oppression of the colonized. Second is the proletariat's own protectionist reactions (reinforced by segments of capital), which invoke nationalism (e.g., Buy American). Third is the nationalism generated by the colonial ruling class in an effort to keep colonized labor cheap for the benefit of international capital. And fourth is the nationalism promoted by colonized workers to overthrow the double and triple layers of oppression they face.

Neither set of workers has to respond in a nationalist manner, and segments of both frequently do not. But once nationalism is the dominant response, it tends to be mutually reinforcing such that each segment of the working class continues to distrust the other.

6. Relations between the Proletariat of Imperialist Nations and the Colonized Ruling Class

These two classes are often in a struggle for the affiliation of colonized workers; hence their relationship is typically conflictual. Colonized workers are either asked to join the working class

movement and become aware of their class antagonism with their ruling class (or middlemen), or they are asked to cooperate with the ruling class, which uses a nationalist pitch, to develop the "nation" (or ethnic community), and set aside class antagonisms.

To the extent that the colonized ruling class exercises control over "its" workers, they will be inaccessible to the proletariat of the advanced capitalist nation. Labor contractors, or sweatshop owners, for example, may be able to use a combination of coercion, paternalism, and desperation on the part of the workers, to keep them in the "nationalist" fold. If accomplished, another wedge is driven between the segments of the working class, and the dominant nation's proletariat continues to be threatened with displacement and undermining.

This kind of conflict can occur both within states and between them. For instance, at the international level, the existence of a right-wing, dictatorial, "nationalist" regime, which severely suppresses its workers, may preclude any efforts on the part of advanced capitalist workers to attempt to help raise labor standards in that country. The discrepancy in labor standards can be used by the ruling class to attract international capital, and as a basis for cheap exports. Within a single state, the leadership of a minority community may exercise a similar labor-control function, though on a much reduced scale, with the same effect of keeping labor standards low within the minority community, in part for the benefit of big capital.

Since both the ruling class and workers of colonized nations appear to conspire in maintaining the low level of labor standards, the advanced capitalist nation's proletariat is likely to have nationalist reactions. It sees all segments of the colonized nations as threatening its position, and may make crude generalizations about the nature of "those people." On the other side, protectionist reactions by labor in the imperialist nation may interfere with the plans of the colonized ruling class to penetrate international markets and may jeopardize the jobs of Third World workers in the affected industries.

In sum, there can be a major struggle between the workers of imperialist nations and colonial ruling classes over the affiliation of colonized workers to determine whether these workers will choose a nationalist or internationalist strategy emphasizing class or nationalist solidarity. Of course, such a struggle is only likely when the proletariat of the imperialist nation is not staunchly protectionist.

We have now briefly considered all six relationships represented in Figure 3. All interact with one another, creating "higher" levels of relationship. For example, if relationship 5, between the imperialistic proletariat and the colonized proletariat, becomes conflictual or nationalistic, imperialist capital can utilize the division to mute the class struggle of its national proletariat (relationship 1). This may lead workers in the imperialist nation to temper their demands and seek narrow concessions instead of revolutionary change. Thus nationalist division may be an important factor in the preservation of capitalism.[22] There are other such reverberations through the system: nationalism at one level tends to provoke counter-nationalism at other levels, while cross-national class alliances probably support one another.

Another point of elaboration, as suggested earlier, would be the addition of other classes and other ethnic groups. For instance, the imperialist nation's class structure includes important intermediary classes, such as managers and small business owners, which may foster nationalist reactions and make it more difficult for workers to support internationalist positions. Or, in the colonized nation, a special ethnic group may play the role of middleman, diluting the class struggle by turning it into an anti-ethnic (nationalist) movement against the middlemen.

In some cases, key classes may be absent, also with ramifications for nationalism. Thus, the fact that countries like Brazil and Mexico draw a less harsh "race line" than the United States and South Africa (both of which developed clear descent rules to protect the category "white") may in part be due to the absence of a large white working class in the former. There was, in other words, no sizable class to develop protectionist reactions against the absorption of colonized workers. Or the absence of a large middleman element among immigrant workers may make cross-ethnic worker alliances easier to establish, thus blurring the lines of national difference.

Needless to say, there are numerous issues this model has not addressed, such as the effects of technological change, labor productivity, geography, natural resources, and population density.[23] To understand the rise of nationalism, or its absence, in each particular case, such factors would have to be taken into consideration.

Despite its incompleteness, the model enables us to make four important points. First, nationalist movements are generated by each class, for different reasons, and with different content. Second, non-nationalist options are available to each class, and are often acted upon. The call upon "primordial attachments" frequently fails, indicating beyond doubt its lack of universality or inevitability. Third, the emergence of nationalist versus non-nationalist reactions depends upon the structure of the entire system of relationships. It is not simply an orientation that one group chooses to adopt in isolation. The emergence of nationalism is contingent upon where a group fits within the entire world capitalist system, and how others react to it. And fourth, despite the fact that nationalism calls upon "primordial" bonds of affiliation, it both grows out of the class relations generated by the development of capitalism and imperialism, and represents efforts to create alliances across class lines, or, alternatively, to prevent alliances from developing within major classes across national lines. In other words, nationalist movements are, at root, the product of class forces.

ENDNOTES

1. Perhaps this position was itself a reaction to the belief that race and ethnicity were "real" and marked off some nationalities from others as biologically superior or inferior.

2. Cf. Banton (1974); Glazer and Moynihan (1975); Rex (1970).

3. For a more complete exposition of this position, see Blumer (1965); pp. 220–253. For a criticism of this position see Wolpe (1970), pp. 151–179.

4. For a similar position see Isaacs (1975), pp. 29–52.

5. Perhaps I am overstating this case. Even authors who concentrate on the consequences of ethnic affiliations give some attention to origins. But these tend to be seen as rooted in the distant past, and firmly embedded in long-established cultural traditions, rather than requiring explanation in the present. Class theorists, in contrast, believe that ethnic affiliation must be created

or reproduced in the present for its persistence to be understood.

6. See for example, Simpson and Yinger (1972).

7. See for example, M. Gordon (1964). In addition, see authors interested in the rise of "white ethnicity," such as Greeley (1974); Novak (1971).

8. A good example of an effort to uncover the social or class meaning of descent rules is M. Harris (1964), in which he contrasts the United States' and Latin American descent rules for determining who is black.

9. This condition is itself quite variable depending on which classes move; i.e., a major distinction needs to be drawn between "white settler" colonies where members of the working class of the conquering nation settled in the colonized territory, and colonies where only foreign capitalists have been active. White settler colonies, such as the United States, Australia, and South Africa, have generally experienced much harsher ethnic problems, a fact that has raised considerable debate regarding competing explanations (Foner and Genovese 1969).

10. There is some debate over whether ethnically or racially oppressed workers are more exploited, in a technical sense, than dominant workers. The term "exploitation" refers to the amount of surplus value extracted from labor. Since ethnic minority workers are often employed in the most backward, unproductive sectors, the rate of surplus extracted from them may, in fact, be lower than for more privileged workers who work in the high-productivity, monopoly sector of the economy. Especially when minority workers suffer high rates of unemployment, it is difficult to see how surpluses are generated here (Willhelm 1971). Still, there are other mechanisms by which surplus is extracted from minority workers, such as "unequal exchange." It seems undeniable that some form of wealth moves from ethnically oppressed labor to the dominant bourgeoisie, even if not via direct employment as wage labor. In any case, this is a point of debate.

11. Bonacich (1972; 1975a; 1976; 1979). Some authors (Wilson 1978a) combine theories B and C, attributing them to different historical epochs.

12. Geschwender (1978) uses the concept "nation-class" more broadly to allow for class differentiation within oppressed ethnic groups. Thus blacks are differentiated by class, although disproportionately in the proletariat, but within each class they also experience "national oppression." Each case of coincidence between class and national categories is considered a "nation-class." Using a figure similar to Figure 1, Geschwender (1978, pp. 264–267), concludes that alliances and enmities can arise along both class and national axes.

13. The concept "people-class" needs to be distinguished from Gordon's (1964) concept of "eth-class." For Gordon, class means status group rather than relations to the means of production. Gordon's eth-classes are social groupings which feel comfortable together because of similarity in style of life. They are not political-economic interest groups. Gordon's is not a class theory of ethnicity; it accepts ethnicity as a primordial tie.

14. Harris (1972); Geschwender (1978), Chapters 4 and 5 review this debate.

15. Focus on the national liberation movements of the colonized tends to lead to a disregard of class dynamics within the dominating nationalities. As stated earlier, national oppression is seen to have taken the place of class oppression as the major axis of world capitalist exploitation. This viewpoint again puts ethnicity at center stage, though it recognizes that national domination and colonialism are rooted in capitalism rather than in the "national" tendencies of nations to despise one another. Still, by focusing on national oppression, writers in this school of thought tend to ignore the internal class dynamics of both national groups.

16. A sample of this literature includes Amin (1976); Bettelheim (1970); Burawoy (1976); Castells (1975); Geschwender (1978); Hechter (1975); Petras (1980); Portes (1978); and many others. For an effort to develop a theoretical statement integrating some of this literature, see Bonacich and Hirata (1979).

17. The use of the term "colonized" should not be taken as an endorsement of all the assumptions of the "internal colonialism" model.

18. An example of the "profit squeeze" argument is found in the work of Glyn and Sutcliffe (1971, 1972).

19. In some cases, the employees of foreign firms are among the most highly paid workers in a poor nation. They may be more fully proletarianized than other workers, and more likely to form unions. Foreign capital pays higher wages as a means of undercutting local manufacturers. Still, despite higher wages relative to other workers in the same country, they are paid considerably less than workers in the imperialist country.

20. Castells (1975), p. 52. Some of the differences in experience between Eastern European and non-European immigrants in the United States may be accounted for by this. Eastern Europe was less thoroughly dominated by the advanced capitalist societies of Western Europe. Thus the immigrants came under a less coerced status and were more readily able to joint the local labor movement.

21. This theme is developed, with respect to the United States, and its long tradition of an "independent household mode of production" associated with the availability of land and concomitant ability to withstand complete proletarianization, in Bonacich (1980). There I argue that this class, which oriented itself towards a pre-capitalist "golden age," contributed importantly to the generation of a powerful racist ideology. Since it often formed coalitions with the proletariat against the

"monopolists," the working-class movement sometimes developed a racist cast.

22. One may ask if nationalist movements are ever progressive. With important exceptions, I believe they are not. They always divide the working class movement. But sometimes they are necessary anyway, especially on the part of colonized workers who may have no other means to overthrow the double oppression

that can stem from imperialist capital's super-exploitation, combined with protectionist reactions by workers of the imperialist nation. Under such conditions, self-determination may be the only route to liberation. When this is the case, nationalism is progressive.

23. An attempt is made to deal with some of these issues in Bonacich and Hirata (1979) and Bonacich (1980b).

F O U R

The Political Construction of Ethnicity

Joane Nagel

I. THE RISE AND DECLINE OF ETHNICITY

The closing decades of the twentieth century find the world's real estate, and consequently its population, divided among a heretofore unprecedented number of sovereign states.[1] In light of their often arbitrary, sometimes capricious origins, the boundaries of this state system have remained surprisingly stable. Young (1976, p. 66) comments on the anomalously successful rupture of Pakistani territorial integrity that produced Bangladesh: "It is truly stupendous that this instance stands almost alone as the breakdown of an existing post-independence state in the three decades since World War II."

What is notable about Bangladesh is only its success, since the forces that amassed in pursuit of independence were, by 1971, abundantly familiar shapes on many national horizons—Biafra,

Katanga, Kurdistan, Eritrea, the Basque region, Québec, Northern Ireland, Southern Sudan, Azerbaijan, West Irian. These challenges to the postcolonial world map represented the extreme, separatist edge of a wave of subnational[2] mobilization sweeping across the world's states. The force and pervasiveness of subnationalism, not only in Asia and Africa, but in Scotland and Wales, Québec and Brittany, Flanders and Berne, found social scientists typically surprised. The presumed integrating effects of political and economic development (Deutsch 1966; Azkin 1964; Lipset and Rokkan 1967)—long under way in the West and accelerating during the postindependence mobilizations in the new states—had proved more centrifugal than conjunctive. Growing urban and industrial centers had become the

Reprinted with permission from Susan Olzak and Joane Nagel, eds., *Competitive Ethnic Relations.* Orlando, FL: Academic Press, 1986. Copyright © 1986 by Academic Press, Inc.

sites for cultural revivals, interethnic conflicts, and communal claims on resources and jurisdictions. Calls for devolution, autonomy, or independence had replaced the goals and rhetoric of the "integrative revolution" (Geertz 1963). The volume and timing of the subnational mobilizations provided a rare but clear disaffirmation of a body of social science theory. The processes of state- and nation-building had failed to manufacture national identities out of local linguistic, cultural, or religious affiliations. Indeed, just the opposite had occurred. Ethnic identity and organization clearly appeared to be strengthening in the face of economic and political development. This ethnic vitality was particularly disconcerting to social scientists because it contradicted what seemed clear evidence of integration.

In both new and old states, researchers had, for some time, reported the classic signs of assimilation: increases in native language loss and intermarriage and declines in traditional religious practices. Oddly, however, these trends did not appear to produce the expected result – i.e., the formation of national-level identities. Rather, observers noted a puzzling resurgence of ethnicity, which often involved shifting the level of ethnic identification from smaller boundaries to larger-level affiliations (Glazer and Moynihan 1963; Rudolph and Rudolph 1967; Horowitz 1971). For instance, the weakening of small-scale community-of-origin divisions in favor of larger linguistic identifications was reported among Italians in the United States (Child 1943; Firey 1974), Ibos in Nigeria (Horowitz 1977; van den Berghe 1971), Sindhi in Pakistan (Das Gupta 1975), Tamils in India (Young 1976), Malays in Malaysia (Smith 1970–1971), and Bagisu in Uganda (Kasfir 1979). Similarly, the amalgamation of linguistically, religiously, culturally, and geographically diverse groups into new larger-scale ethnic groupings was observed in the United States among "white ethnics" (Yancy et al. 1985), Native Americans (Enloe 1981; Jarvenpa 1985), and Hispanics and Latinos (Nelson and Tienda 1985; Padilla 1986). Cohen labeled such shifts in levels of identification, along with their apparent simultaneous weakening and strengthening of ethnic boundaries, "a sociological paradox" – that ethnic groups can appear to be "rapidly losing their cultural distinctiveness . . . [while] also emphasizing and exaggerating their cultural identity and exclusiveness" (1969, p. 1).

Hannan (1979) offers an interesting solution to this acculturation accentuation puzzle. Drawing on ecological theory, he argues that political and economic modernization are characterized by increases in organizational scale (particularly of economic and political units) and by increased "connectedness" (through economic and political interdependence) of various population segments. These increases in connectedness and scale of organization lead to a situation where larger and larger units interact, often competitively, with increasing frequency. In order for any contender in such a system to successfully confront (oppose, bargain with, extract resources from) these large-scale economic and political organizations, the contender (e.g., an ethnic group) should find it advantageous to organize "around larger scale cultural identities" (1979, p. 271). Thus, to the extent that ethnicity is a relevant and available basis for group organization, political and economic modernization should increase the likelihood that successful ethnic mobilization will occur along broader rather than narrower subnational identities. In a sort of social selection process, the boundaries around smaller affiliations dissolve in favor of larger affiliations, thereby accounting for the concurrent decline and growth in ethnicity, and so the puzzle is solved.

A. New Ethnicity

New ethnic mobilization can be *resurgent* (i.e., enacted by recently revitalized historical groupings) as among the Basques of Spain, the Bretons of France, the Welsh of Britain, the Quebecois of Canada, or *emergent* (Yancey, Eriksen, and Juliani 1976) (i.e., enacted by newly formed groups) as among the Ibo of Nigeria (Wolpe 1974), the Sikhs and Tamils of India (Horowitz 1975, p. 117; 1977, p. 12), the Native Indians of Canada (Robinson 1985), the Begisu of Uganda (Kasfir 1979, pp. 372–373), the North Tapanuli Batak of Indonesia (Liddle 1970, pp. 57–60).[3]

Both resurgent and emergent[4] ethnicity remind us that religious, linguistic, cultural, or somatic differences among a population are not reliable predictors of ethnic identification or group formation. Rather, the historical variations in ethnic mobilization observable in resurgent ethnicity, and the variations in organizational bases observable in emergent ethnicity, provide evidence of the mutability of ethnic boundaries that early researchers found so puzzling. Such fluidity is less disconcerting if we view ethnicity as partly ascribed and partly volitional, as situational, and as strategic. Rather than conceive of ethnic identification, conflict, or organization as the "natural" outgrowths of primordial divisions among a population (in, say, language, religion, or culture), the view of ethnicity as new stresses the nonfixed, fluid, and situational character of ethnic identification and points to the ascriptive and strategic nature of ethnic categories. This model of ethnic boundaries as emerging from social interaction follows from the theoretical work of Barth (1969a,b) and rests on empirical research conducted over the past two decades by a number of social scientists [among others Wallerstein (1960), Epstein (1967), Zolberg (1968), Melson and Wolpe (1971), Despres (1975), Schermerhorn (1970, 1978), Harris (1964), Young (1965, 1976), Enloe (1973) and van den Berghe (1971)]. The model has as its primary tenets (1) that ethnicity is largely an ascribed status that is situationally activated and (2) that ethnic boundaries are flexible, spatially and temporally fluid, and permeable – permitting the movement of personnel across them.

The view of ethnic identity as an ascribed or assigned status can be illustrated by the phenomenon of Sikhism "conversion" described by Garnett (Nayar 1966). In colonial India, the British preference for Sikh army recruits led to many quick conversions from Hinduism to Sikhism. Garnett reports that "it was almost a daily occurrence for – say – Ram Chand to enter our office and leave it as Ram Singh – Sikh recruit" (Nayar 1966, p. 65). Along similar lines, Haaland (1969) reports ethnic "switching" or the relabeling of individuals' ethnic affiliation as the result of changes in economic activity among Sudanese ethnic groups. That is, an individual's move from horticulture to herding was followed by a change in others' perception of his ethnicity. Both the Indian and Sudanese cases illustrate the role of external observers in determining salient ethnic identities. In fact, such outside designations can be so powerful as to supersede an individual's

beliefs about his "real" ethnic affiliation. For instance, ethnic distinctions that have meaning in certain situations (e.g., national origin distinctions among American "white ethnics" in urban political wards)[5] can become esoteric or meaningless in other settings (e.g., vis-à-vis blacks in Harlem or South Boston).

This situational character of ethnicity has led Horowitz to conclude that "ascriptive identity is heavily contextual" (1975, p. 118). A Native American is a Pine Ridge Sioux in Wounded Knee, South Dakota, but an Indian in Rapid City. Similarly, an Ibo is Onitsha or Owerri in the eastern states of Nigeria, but an Ibo or an Easterner in the North, and a Kurdish-speaking Iranian is a Barzani or Baradosti in the mountains, but a Kurd in Teheran. Thus an individual's ethnic affiliation at any point in time depends on the ethnic identities available to him or her in a particular situation. Sometimes there is a choice, and sometimes not.

While ethnic categories in a society are ascriptively delimited and the shifting of flexible ethnic boundaries may originate from forces outside the group in question (i.e., be ascriptive), shifts in ethnic boundaries may also originate from forces inside the group (i.e., be strategic). The coincidence of these two forces (ascriptive and strategic utility) is an especially powerful impetus to ethnic mobilization. When there exist social and political definitions that emphasize a particular boundary or affiliation (say, "Hispanic" in the United States) *and* when members of such an identified group perceive economic and/or political advantages to be derived from emphasizing that particular boundary (instead of, say, Puerto Rican, Cuban, or Chicano), then there exists a strong likelihood of mobilization on the basis of that designated identity. Since the most powerful ascriptive force in any state is the central government, there is a strong political character to much modern ethnic mobilization [Glazer and Moynihan (1975, p. 7) refer to ethnic groups as "interest groups"]. The next sections explore the political aspect of ethnic mobilization and argue for a view of ethnicity as politically constructed.

B. Ethnicity as a Strategic Mobilization

Tilly (1978, p. 69) defines mobilization as the process by which a group acquires resources and assures their delivery in pursuit of collective ends. Organization plays an essential role in the mobilization of any group. Both the ability to acquire and to deliver resources can be seen as a function of the degree of organization. Group organization, in turn, depends on commonality of interests as well as the extent of unifying structures within the group (Tilly 1978, p. 54). From this, ethnic mobilization can be defined as the process by which a group organizes along ethnic lines in pursuit of group ends. But when will ethnicity be selected as the basis of group organization?

The obvious answer, suggested already, is when such a choice provides social, economic, or political advantage. Stinchcombe (1975) argues that ethnic loyalty is a function of the degree to which one's ethnic affiliation provides one with necessary and important resources. But what is it about the modern world that has transformed ethnicity into a favored organizational strategy in competitive economic and political relations— into a perceived expedient and efficacious design for resource acquisition? The answer lies in the rise and expansion of national politics.

The political character of modern ethnicity has been noted by a large number of researchers, many of whom employ explicitly political indicators of ethnic mobilization [e.g., the proportion of the vote accruing to ethnically linked parties or candidates – see especially Hechter (1975), Olzak (1982), Ragin (1979)]. Despite this political approach to conceptualizing and measuring the dependent variable, the causal forces in these models are consistently economic, with such independent variables as sectoral labor distributions, economic differentiation, levels of industrial development, and standard of living indices [see especially Ragin (1979) and Neilsen (1980)]. Thus ethnic political mobilization is seen mainly as a response to the structure and operation of the economy, particularly to economic competition among mobilized ethnic contenders (Hannan 1979; Lauwagie 1979).

While economic organization and processes play an important role in ethnic identification, group formation, conflict, and collective action, the political orientation of much ethnic activism suggests a similarly important role played by *political* organization and processes. Further, while

the relationship between the economy and polity is a complex one, as Bell notes, "competition between plural groups takes place largely in the political arena" (1975, p. 161) due to the subordination of the economy to the polity. One reason for this subordination has been the trend, in both new and old states, toward an increased concentration of power in political centers (Parsons 1957; Tilly 1975b). The growth in political power through the political control of resources, the political regulation of social sectors, and the creation of political amenities prompted Geertz to describe the central government as "a valuable new prize over which to fight and a frightening new force with which to contend" (1963, p. 120). The power of this "new force" to determine the shape and extent of ethnic mobilization within a society is discussed next.

II. THE POLITICAL CONSTRUCTION OF ETHNICITY

This rise in ethnic mobilization around the world can be seen as a result of the nationalization and expansion of politics across states (Meyer, Boli-Bennett, and Chase-Dunn 1975; Tilly 1975b) and the increased willingness of governments to recognize ethnic groups as legitimate contenders (Glazer and Moynihan 1975). The nationalization and expansion of politics redirects increasing proportions of societal activity (ethnic and other) toward the political center. The recognition of ethnicity as a basis for political organization and claimsmaking legitimates ethnic mobilization. Thus we see a politicization and legitimation of ethnicity in modern states.

It is important here to clarify the role of ethnicity as both an *antecedent* as well as a *consequence* of particular political processes. It is an empirical fact that most countries contain ethnically diverse populations. It is not the assertion here that such diversity is solely or even primarily the result of political processes. However, the recognition and institutionalization of ethnicity in politics (1) *increases the level* of ethnic mobilization among all ethnic groups (e.g., among those previously mobilized as well as among those who mobilize for the first time in response to the politicization of ethnicity) and (2) *determines the boundaries* along which ethnic mobilization and/

or conflict will occur by setting down the rules for political participation and political access (e.g., should contenders organize on the basis of panethnic representation or on the basis of historical claims?).

Whether ethnicity is politically newly constructed or reconstructed, created or enhanced, formed or transformed, we can specify several mechanisms whereby ethnicity is politically constructed. They fall into two categories: the structure of political access and the content of political policies.

A. Political Access

PROPOSITION 1. *Within a state, ethnic mobilization is most likely when the structure of political access and participation is organized along ethnic lines.*

The structure of political access and the rules of participation can emphasize or minimize the salience of ethnicity in political contention. Both the regionalization and institutionalization of ethnic participation in the polity promote ethnic political mobilization.

1. Regionalization

HYPOTHESIS 1. *Ethnic mobilization will tend to occur along those ethnic boundaries that correspond to geographic political and administrative boundaries.*

There are two ways in which the organization of land and population within a state can promote subnational mobilization: first, by *reinforcing* existing ethnic differences, and second, by *creating* new ethnic groups.

a. *Reinforcement.*

When the boundaries of administrative or electoral units correspond to historical communal (cultural, religious, linguistic) divisions among a population, then those divisions tend to be politicized and reinforced. One reason for this is that political authorities' choice to use existing ethnoregional boundaries can be interpreted by all groups as recognition of those particular divisions of the population. In some cases the recognition can carry a positive message of uniqueness or special status, as the establishment of the Armenian Republic in the U.S.S.R. in 1922 or of the Jura canton in Switzerland in 1979. In other cases, the creation of regional units for particular

ethnic groups can be punitive and isolating, as the establishment of *Bantustans* "homelands" for black Africans in South Africa or of Indian reservations in the United States – both more like concentration camps than politically autonomous regions.

A second way ethnic mobilization can result from reinforcing existing ethnoregional boundaries by the superimposition of electoral or administrative regions is the tendency of political organizations and action to occur within bounded political units. Such regional mobilization can be on the part of the majority group in the unit or by minority groups who find themselves enclosed and are fearful of majority domination. The *Partei der Deutschsprachigen Belgien* (PDB) is an example of the latter. Constitutional plans for dividing Belgium into either French or Dutch language regions "precipitated the formation of a new language party [the PDB]" (Kane 1980, p. 138) when the German speakers' region was assigned to the French language category.

b. *Creation.*

The imposition of administrative or electoral boundaries around a segment of the population can go beyond reinforcing extant communal differences to actually create *new* ethnic identities. The Nigerian example is an apt one. The 1960 division of the Nigerian state into three regions that competed for access to and control of the central government resulted in the creation of three major regionally based, ethnically linked political parties (and many opposition parties in each region). The resulting ethnicization of politics led to the disintegration of the Nigerian political system and the secession of the Eastern Region (Biafra). The irony in this sequence of events is that the major ethnic groups in each of the three regions (the Ibos in the East, the Yoruba in the West, the Hausa in the North) were not historically united groups possessed of regional-level identities. Rather, these linguistic groups were historically organized into community-of-origin and kinship groups whose past internal relationships had been marked more by disinterest or contention than by unity (Sklar and Whitaker 1964, p. 621; Sklar 1963, p. 152; Coleman 1958, p. 343; Awolowo 1960; Paden 1973; Nafziger and Richter 1976, p. 93).

In a variety of countries the creation of administration units that serve as the bases for resource distribution has frequently led to mobilization among enclosed groups and to shifts in group identification from traditional boundaries to newly created administrative boundaries (Dresang 1974, p. 1606; van den Berghe 1971, p. 514; Young 1965, p. 245; Nafziger and Richter 1976, p. 93; Mazrui 1979, p. 260; Horowitz 1975, p. 133; Wallerstein 1960, p. 132). In the United States, not only does the federal Indian reservation system crosscut and ignore traditional tribal lands (U.S. Indian Claims Commission 1980), but reservation boundaries often fail to correspond to traditional tribal identity boundaries. The massive forced movement of the American Indian population onto reservation lands during the nineteenth century resulted in the fractionalization and/or the amalgamation of many traditional tribal organization and identity boundaries. The result is a different set of Indian tribes today than the set that existed a hundred years ago. An example of *fractionalization* is the Cherokee tribe whose members were relocated (via the "Trail of Tears") to Oklahoma; most stayed, but some returned to North Carolina. Today there are two Cherokee tribes, both officially recognized by the Bureau of Indian Affairs: the Cherokee Nation of Oklahoma and the Eastern Band of Cherokee Indians of North Carolina. These two tribes now not only are separated territorially, but have evolved separate political, economic, and social systems (Department of Commerce 1974; Bureau of Indian Affairs 1983). Examples of *amalgamation* can be found among many of the Pacific Northwest tribes, such as the Confederated Tribes of the Colville Reservation or the Tulalip Tribes of the Tulalip Reservation, both in Washington as well as elsewhere, as among the Confederated Tribes of the Flathead Reservation in Montana. All three communities are comprised of formerly autonomous groups that were socially, economically, politically, culturally, and linguistically diverse in varying degrees, but whose internal divisions have increasingly blurred over time to produce progressively homogeneous new tribes: the "Colville," "Tulalip," and "Flathead" tribes (Bureau of Indian Affairs 1983; U.S. Indian Claims Commission 1980). Horowitz (1975) provides further examples of

ethnic fractionalization and amalgamation in many countries, many often the result of the organization of political administration and access.

2. Participation.

HYPOTHESIS 2. *Ethnic mobilization will tend to occur along those ethnic boundaries that are officially recognized bases of participation.*

The official structuring of political participation along ethnic lines is an even more potent force in the construction of ethnicity than is regionalization. Whereas the administrative division of land and population along extant or potential communal boundaries provides a politically recognized, structurally facilitated basis for mobilization among both the enclosed groups as well as among other subpopulations, the organization of political participation along ethnic lines provides a rationale for, and indeed demands, the mobilization of political participation on the basis of ethnicity. The main reason for the rise in ethnic mobilization in states where political participation is structured ethnically is the tendency of such arrangements to transform ethnic groups into interest groups and to politicize ethnicity.

There are two main paths to ethnically structured political participation: (1) the constitutional (de jure) recognition of ethnicity as a basis for political representation [as in Belgium where electoral districts are designated as Dutch- or French-speaking (Heisler 1977; Kane 1980); in Fiji where an equal number of seats in the House of Representatives are assigned to Fijians and Indians (Norton 1977); or in India where Scheduled Caste (Untouchable) groups are guaranteed a specific proportion of seats in parliament and a designated quota of civil service posts (Dushkin 1972)]; or (2) the regionalization (de facto) of representation to adhere to ethnoregional boundaries [as in Switzerland where federal representation is officially by canton, but where cantons tend to be linguistically homogeneous (Connor 1977); in Malaysia where electoral districts are geographically determined, but where nine states are locally ruled by hereditary Malay rulers and where there exists a Malay advantage in the calculation of parliamentary and state constituencies (Means 1976; Musolf and Springer 1979, p. 34); or in Sri Lanka where the representation of minorities (e.g., Ceylon Tamils and Muslims) was adjusted upward by weighting minority-dominated regions and by appointing a small number of legislators (Wilson 1975)].

Whether explicit or de facto, recognition of religious, cultural, or linguistic affiliations as bases of political participation tends to promote ethnic group organization and to transform ethnic groups into political interest groups and thus tends to increase interethnic competition. The mobilization of the Scheduled Castes and subsequent intergroup hostility directed toward Untouchables in India illustrates this process. Untouchables represent the lowest sector of the traditional Indian (mainly Hindu) caste system. Although the group is comprised of linguistically and geographically diverse groups, special provisions for political participation and civil service representation resulted in the mobilization of these various groups into an increasingly self-aware subnational unit with a political party (the Republican Party) and a separatist fringe (Schermerhorn 1978; Dushkin 1972; Nayar 1966; Rudolph and Rudolph 1967).

The relationship between political recognition and ethnic mobilization is complex and probably more sequential than directional. The argument being made here is that of mobilization from above (Nettl 1967, p. 271). This is not to say that ethnic political organizations and political parties are mere creations of the writers of constitutions and do not reflect prior ethnic divisions among populations. It is to say, first, that the official recognition of ethnicity as a basis of political representation legitimizes, institutionalizes, and renders more permanent prior ethnically organized political participation—for example, the continued dominance of language parties in Belgian and Canadian politics even in the face of constitutional recognition and substantial concessions to various linguistic constituencies; and second, that the official recognition of ethnicity as a basis of political representation promotes new and parallel mobilization by formerly unorganized groups that face the prospect of exclusion from an ethnically defined political arena—for example, the rise of white ethnics in the United States, of German-speakers in Belgium, or of Italian and Portuguese nationality groups in Québec.

Both of the mechanisms for structuring political access along ethnic lines—regionalization and participation—often result in ironic, unintended consequences for the systems employing them (consequences that are repeated below in the various policy mechanisms). The irony in ethnic mobilization is best illustrated by the fact that such organizing principles are often conceived as a recipe for plural harmony (Lijphart 1977). While it is true that in some cases these organizational strategies are adopted to deal with historical communal hostilities, invariably they create a competitive atmosphere that encourages ethnic mobilization by both targeted groups (in order to gain access to the polity and all that such access provides), and by nontargeted groups as well (in order to avoid being excluded from the polity). Thus the invitation to mobilize extended to some groups (often with admirable intentions, as in the case of the Untouchables) ethnicizes the political process and expands the arena for ethnic competition.

B. Political Policies

PROPOSITION 2. *Within a state, ethnic mobilization is most likely when political policies are implemented that recognize and institutionalize ethnic differences.*

In addition to the ethnicization of political access through regionalization and ethnic participation provisions, there are four categories of political policy that are especially powerful in their implications for ethnic mobilization and in their ability to determine the boundaries along which such mobilization occurs: language policies, land policies, official designation policies, and resource distribution policies.

1. Language Policies.

HYPOTHESIS 3. *Ethnic mobilization will tend to occur along those ethnic boundaries that coincide with official language boundaries.*

Just as constitutionally guaranteed seats in parliament or positions in the civil service act to accentuate ethnic differences, language policies institutionalize ethnic diversity, politicizing linguistic divisions and rendering them permanent. Language policies range in their ability to institutionalize ethnicity according to their content. Most powerful is that of multiple official languages. While single official languages are difficult to select and implement and invariably provoke resistance, multiple official languages guarantee long-term or permanent linguistic division. Again, this is not to say that the adoption of several official languages *causes* all linguistic conflict in a state or that linguistic differences or hostilities are not present prior to the adoption. It is to say that such a policy institutionalizes and legitimates linguistic conflict and thus maintains and perpetuates it.

In order to fully understand the power of political policies to *create* linguistically based mobilization (rather than simply to respond to *prior* language group demands), we must suspend familiar notions of primordial ethnicity. The speaking of a common language, say Dutch or Scottish or Yoruba, does not automatically produce ethnic unity, group identification, an organizational substructure, or a shared culture. What it does produce is the ability to communicate within the group and the appearance of uniformity to outsiders. Mutual intelligibility, ascribed (presumed) community, and particular policies pursued by political authorities explain a good deal of linguistic mobilization in the modern world. Again, India provides a clear example of the political construction of linguistic mobilization.

The Indian constitution assigns 14 languages the status of "national languages" (Das Gupta 1970, p. 38).[6] The history of these designations began under British colonial rule with the formation of urban literary societies by educated speakers of various languages (Das Gupta 1970, pp. 69–97). The evolution from literary societies to linguistic social movements was the result of a two-stage process beginning with British colonial administrative practices and culminating in the competition associated with the establishment of an independent Indian state. Das Gupta (1975, p. 475) reports that "fashioning relatively larger language-based ethnic communities out of a mass of disparate segmental ethnicities . . . [was] facilitated by the system of the administrative division of India into provinces" by colonial authorities. This power of administrative boundaries to unify those enclosed has been discussed above. In In-

dia,[7] these administrative units became mobilized contenders for language and state status during the nationalist mobilization of the 1940s and 1950s. The creation of ethnic unity by British colonialists was not limited to the imposition of administrative boundaries. Civil service and military recruitment policies also encouraged the formation of ethnic unity and promoted subsequent mobilization. This was particularly true of the Sikhs, whose modern demands for autonomy are tied to British policies of separate treatment (Nayar 1966, pp. 55–74; Schermerhorn 1978, pp. 128–153).

In addition to the power of superimposed boundaries to promote group formation, the Indian example points out the more general relationship of state-building to subnationalism. That relationship is one of competition for political advantage. Such competition is organized ethnically where the rules of access or participation are articulated in ethnic terms. And one such articulation is in language policies. As Das Gupta neatly summarizes:

> Language demands, especially in developing nations, cannot be inferred from the nature of language groups. These groups tend to make demands only when social mobilization offers competitive opportunities and values. (1975, p. 487)

While preferred languages of administration, legislation, and education are generally those with official status, in some countries language policies governing education or administration are less sweeping and more situationally oriented. Bilingual education in the United States is one such case. While the United States has no official languages besides English (yet), the question of non-English language instruction has produced political mobilization among linguistic groups in favor of and opposed to bilingual education policies and has promoted parallel mobilization in school systems among language groups not initially included in bilingual programs. The debate surrounding bilingual education in the United States[8] has politicized linguistic differences among the American population and spawned a multitude of special interest organizations and official position statements from extant groups [see, for example, Novak (1978)].

2. Land Policies.

HYPOTHESIS 4. *Ethnic mobilization will tend to occur along those ethnic boundaries that coincide with officially allocated lands.*

In many states, communal groups are geographically concentrated. Besides the historic demographic forces (migration, geographic isolation, economic niche boundaries) that tend to separate groups and produce independent evolution, particular land policies can produce ethnogeographic concentration. These are of several sorts. One is the tendency of geographic administrative or electoral divisions to promote mobilization among enclosed groups as described above. Another is politically orchestrated or forced migration as in the case of the Shi'i Arab population in Iraq (Dann 1969) or the numerous refugee populations around the world (Portes and Stepick 1985). A third involves the allocation of land to particular ethnic groups as in the case of the Caribs of Dominica (Layng 1985), American Indian groups in Canada and the United States (Jorgensen 1978; Ponting and Gibbons 1980), or black Africans in South Africa (van den Berghe 1978a). A fourth includes political economic processes involving the siting and development of industries, as in the case of guestworkers in Western Europe (Mehrlaender 1980; Rist 1980) or urban enclaves of rural out-migrant ethnic groups in various African states (Cohen 1974).

An example of the capacity of land policies to shift ethnic boundaries as well as to promote ethnic mobilizations can be seen in the effect of U.S. Indian policy during the 1950s on pan-Indian ethnicity. Observers have noted that a good deal of American Indian political activity (protests, petitioning, lobbying) is organized along pan-Indian (e.g., Native American) rather than tribal (e.g., Jicarilla Apache, Rosebud Sioux, Tuscarora) boundaries. There is some evidence that this upward shift in political organization is paralleled by complementary upward shifts in identity and culture as well [see Stewart (1972) on the Native American Church, Hertzberg (1977), on pan-Indian organizations and movements, and Corrigan (1970) on pow-wows], producing what Thomas (1968, p. 84) has labeled "a new ethnic group, a new 'nationality' in America"–the Native American.

One explanation for this upward shift in ethnic boundaries can be found in U.S. Indian policy during the "termination" period (roughly 1946–1960). During this time an effort was being made to terminate, for once and for all, the unique trust relationship between Indian tribes and the U.S. government. Since the reservation system (a legacy of earlier federal Indian land policy) was central to the maintenance of the Indian-federal relationship, the desire to weaken reservation viability by population reduction led to a program of urban relocation of reservation Indians. Beginning with the Navajo-Hopi Rehabilitation Act of 1950, and continuing throughout the decade, through various "relocation" programs, the federal government engaged in an extended effort to move Indians from reservations to urban areas where they were to be assisted by government Indian centers in finding housing and employment (Jorgensen 1978). This population management program arising out of land policies was not incidental to the emergence of pan-Indian social and political organization among the tribally mixed populations residing in urban relocation areas. The fact that nearly half of the American Indian population is urban (U.S. Bureau of the Census, 1981) is largely the result of land policies that guaranteed impoverished reservations and provided incentives for urban migration (Nagel, Ward, and Knapp 1986).

3. Official Designations and Resource Distribution.

HYPOTHESIS 5. *Ethnic mobilization will tend to occur along those ethnic boundaries that are official ethnic designations for special treatment and/or political resource acquisition.*[9]

Policies of singling out particular ethnic groups for special treatment also tend to legitimate ethnic divisions and to emphasize certain boundaries over others. The power of official designations is obvious where negative policies such as genocide, internment, or deportation are concerned. However, neutral or positively intended official categories also operate to enhance ethnic mobilization. One fairly innocuous such designation is the census category. Horowitz (1975, p. 116) reports an emerging Yugoslav Muslim ethnic group whose legitimacy is partly based on census policy. Somewhat more powerful is the conception of "official" ethnic groups. In the

U.S.S.R. one chooses an official nationality at age 16 (Glazer and Moynihan 1975, p. 17); the choice has long-lasting economic and political implications (Allworth 1977). In the United States certain ethnic groups "count" for particular purposes (e.g., Affirmative Action), rendering them legitimate and encouraging organization and affiliation consistent with official boundaries rather than with more traditional or culturally relevant units (e.g., "Hispanic" as opposed to Mexican-American or Puerto Rican).

In terms of strategic organization for competitive advantage, the distribution of politically controlled resources according to ethnicity is an immensely powerful factor in ethnic mobilization. Part of Untouchable mobilization in India was attributable to the distribution of education scholarships, low-interest loans, and land on the basis of membership in Scheduled Castes (Nayar 1966, p. 319; Rudolph and Rudolph 1967, pp. 143–144). Dresang (1974) notes the mobilizing effects of the allocation of politically controlled jobs and resources in Zambia. And access to and control of central government resources has promoted ethnic mobilization among a variety of groups in Nigeria (Kirk-Greene 1971), among francophones in Canada (Smiley 1977, p. 190), and among blacks in the United States (Oberschall 1973, pp. 237–238).

Such "affirmative action" programs produce not only mobilization among designated groups, but can also lead to communal conflict in the form of "backlashes" *against* official groups; examples can be found in the same nations listed above: India, Nigeria, Canada, and the United States.

The role of officially designated political resource distribution in ethnic mobilization is not surprising, inasmuch as it parallels an argument arrived at by a somewhat different route in the social movements literature. A central tenet of the resource mobilization perspective is that successful mobilization depends on a combination of organization and resource acquisition (Jenkins and Perrow 1977; McCarthy and Zald 1973, 1977; Oberschall 1973; Tilly 1978; Walsh 1980). It follows that, *ceteris paribus,* those groups to whom political resources are available (set aside funds, special programs, low interest loans, etc.) are more likely to mobilize successfully than are nondesignated groups. Thus, the ethnic bound-

aries along which resources are distributed become the bases for mobilization.

While the power of the polity to define the "appropriate" bases for recognition and resource distribution increases the likelihood of mobilization among targeted groups, it must be remembered that to the extent that official designations are seen as advantageous, nondesignated groups will also seek recognition and expand the domain of ethnic politics. Thus recognizing and rewarding ethnicity for even one or a few groups in a state can promote parallel mobilization among nontargeted groups, and thus we see a general ethnicization of social, economic, and political life.

C. Ethnic Mobilization and the Nationalization of Politics

In addition to the role of political organization and policies in promoting ethnic mobilization, the trend in both old and new states toward national political structures encourages subnational mobilization. To the extent that ethnicity is politically constructed, the nationalization of politics should lead to increased nationally organized ethnic groups. A case in point is Guyana. In a preindependence election held in April 1953, a cross-section and majority of Guyana's subnationally mixed population [East Indians, 49%; Africans, 30%; Europeans, Amerindians, and others, 21% (Greene 1974, p. 2)] mobilized behind the People's Progressive Party (PPP) and its left-leaning leader Cheddi Jagan. In October 1953, fearing an alleged Communist takeover, British colonial authorities (at United States' urging) suspended the constitution and the PPP-dominated House of Assembly (Manley 1979, p. 6; Landis 1974, p. 256). The PPP continued to dominate subsequent elections in 1957 and 1961, although the ethnic consensus had begun to deteriorate, aided by British and American machinations and funding programs (Greene 1974) that strengthened the opposition party (the People's National Congress). The *coup de grace* was the introduction in the 1964 election of proportional representation, which changed the method of election to parliament from a locally focused, single-member constituency system to a nationally focused, proportional representation system. The shift to proportional representation had three results: (1) it nationalized political contention by moving campaigns out of local districts (where the party candidates stood off against one another, the winner going to parliament) to the national arena (where national proportion of the vote received by each party determined its number of representatives in parliament); (2) it centralized and nationalized political parties because campaigns became orchestrated at the national, not local, level; and (3) it ethnicized partisan politics because proportional representation refocused the voter from his or her district (and from which candidate would best represent local interests) to the national level where parties increasingly appealed to subnational loyalties as an easy and wider-issue basis for obtaining the vote. The logic of the vote shifted from the local candidate to the national party, and over time (between 1953 and 1964) a realignment of voters occurred, producing ethnic parties (Greene 1974) and a dramatic rise in communal conflict and hostility (Despres 1967; Landis 1974, p. 257).

III. CONCLUSION

It has been hypothesized and argued that the above political structural arrangements and policies promote ethnic mobilization. They provide the rationale for the selection of ethnicity as the basis for mobilization and designate the particular boundaries along which mobilization most likely occurs. Further, they provoke complementary mobilization among nondesignated groups. These structural arrangements and policies are often designed and implemented to avoid real or anticipated ethnic conflict. Whether or not they serve this end in the short term, in both the short and long term they act to spotlight diversity, to institutionalize ethnic differences, and to increase the level of ethnic mobilization and conflict.

As for the future, the political construction of ethnicity is probably no more potent a force than the political construction of nationalism. Both are situationally enhanced or diminished and rest on the same ideological bedrock of self-determination and representative government. The incentives for subnationalism appear at least as strong as those promoting nationalism at this juncture in world history, though the shifting ephemeral character of group organization must never be underestimated. The message is that ethnic nationalism is not the stuff of primordial, genetic, ancient differences, but is a child of the modern world with its multitude of fecund states and parturient political processes. The word for ethnicity is secular, not sacred.

ENDNOTES

1. From around 75 states at the beginning of World War II, to more than 150 at the present (Crawford 1979, p. 3).
2. Variously called "cultural pluralism" (Young 1976), "ethnonationalism" (Connor 1977), "communalism" (Melson and Wolpe 1971), "ethnicity" (Glazer and Moynihan 1975), "ethnopolitics" (Rothschild 1981).
3. Other groups described by social scientists as newly emergent are the Sinhalese of Sri Lanka (Horowitz 1977, p. 16), the Sindhi of Pakistan (Das Gupta 1975, p. 472), and the Naga of India (Schermerhorn 1978, p. 86).
4. Kilson refers to the phenomena of resurgent and emergent ethnicity as "neoethnicity . . . the revitalization of weak ethnic collectivities" (1975, p. 236); Singer (1962) and Despres (1975) label them "ethnogenesis"—the process whereby populations become (a) culturally differentiated and (b) corporately organized on the basis of that differentiation.
5. My thanks to Susan Olzak for this example.
6. They are Assamese, Bengali, English, Gujarte, Hindi, Kannada, Kashmiri, Malayalam, Marathi, Oriya, Punjabi, Tamil, Telugu, and Urdu (Das Gupta 1970, p. 46).
7. As in Nigeria (Melson and Wolpe 1971, p. 23), in Zaire (Young 1965, p. 245), in Malaysia (Horowitz 1975, p. 133), in Zambia (Dresang 1974 pp. 1605–1606), and in Iraq (Horowitz 1977, p. 11).
8. For instance, does bilingual education promote Spanish language retention or hinder economic advancement? The evidence is far from clear (Veltman 1981; Rodriguez 1981).
9. These hypotheses can be recast to predict relative rates of ethnic mobilization among states. By the argument presented here, the following also hold, all things being equal: (1) ethnic mobilization will tend to be greatest in those states where geographic, political, and administrative boundaries coincide with linguistic, cultural, or religious divisions among the population; (2) ethnic mobilization will tend to be greatest in those states where ethnicity is designated as a legitimate basis for political representation and/or participation; (3) ethnic mobilization will tend to be greatest in those states that recognize multiple official languages; (4) ethnic mobilization will tend to be greatest in those states with ethnic land policies; (5) ethnic mobilization will tend to be greatest in those states with official ethnic groups designated for special treatment and/or for the allocation of resources.

Historical Perspectives

2

The United States, which has been called a "nation of nations," is one of the most ethnically diverse societies in the modern world. Conflict for economic, social, and political preeminence among its numerous racial and ethnic groups has been one of the most salient features of the American experience. This section provides a brief overview of the history of American ethnic relations. Because they are so numerous, it would be impossible to examine the experience of all American ethnic groups in this brief section (for a comprehensive survey, see the superb essays in the *Harvard Encyclopedia of American Ethnic Groups*, edited by Stephen Thernstrom [1980]). The articles included here provide conceptual and substantive continuity to the volume as a whole. This survey of several of the major ethnic and racial categories that collectively comprise the American people is organized in roughly the chronological order of their migration to North America. We begin by sketching some key features of the experience of the earliest inhabitants – American Indians – and conclude with a discussion of some of the most recent immigrants to the United States.

American Indians

The first Americans migrated from Asia around 12,000 to 40,000 years ago, slowly dispersing throughout North, Central, and South America. Although the length of time that they inhabited the American continents is brief when compared to human societies elsewhere in the world, American Indian peoples developed a great diversity of cultures with widely different levels of technology, cultural complexity, and languages. The large and highly sophisticated Aztec, Inca, and Mayan civilizations contrast sharply with the simpler societies of the Yavapai, Onondaga, and Kansa. A good index of this diversity was the myriad number of languages found in the New World. Native American languages can be classed into about a dozen different stocks (each as distinct from the other as the Semitic from the Indo-European) and within each stock into languages as distinct as English from Russian. The Americas were linguistically as diverse as the Eurasian land mass (Ruhlen, 1987). Thus, as Cynthia Enloe has written, even "before the arrival of Europeans the American continent was already ethnically plural" (Enloe 1981:126). To the present day, substantial differences can be found among American Indians despite the popular perception among outsiders that they are a single distinct ethnic group.

The arrival of Europeans, however, significantly affected American Indian cultures. Examination of the effects of Indian-white contact shows the process by which a system of ethnic stratification develops. Ethnic stratification is a system of social ranking in which one ethnic group acquires greater power, privilege, and prestige than another (or others). An unequal relationship between two or more ethnic groups is not inevitable, however. In other words, some groups are not inherently dominant and others inherently subordinate. In Article 5, "A Theory of the Origins of Ethnic Stratification," Donald Noel suggests that three conditions are necessary for a system of ethnic stratification to be created: *ethnocentrism, competition, and differences in power.* Noel applied these conditions to the development of the caste system of black-white relations in the United States, but let us here examine how these variables influenced patterns of Indian-white relations.

Ethnocentrism is the idealization of the attributes of the group to which an individual belongs. People of all societies tend to think of themselves as the chosen people or, at the very least, as those at the center of humanity. People of any society tend to think their ways of doing things are correct, just, righteous, and virtuous – the way God intended. On the other hand, people tend to perceive the ways of other people as odd, incorrect, or immoral and to reject or ridicule groups from which they differ. Ethnocentrism seems to be an inevitable outgrowth of the socialization process, during which cultural values and standards of right and wrong, beauty and ugliness, and so forth are internalized.

European settlers regarded American Indians as heathen savages, possessing cultures vastly inferior to their own. Indeed, among many Puritans of New England, they were regarded as agents of Satan, to be exterminated by gunfire or disease. The European invaders considered agriculture a superior economic activity and an index of their own cultural superiority. Therefore they perceived the lands they entered to be "wilderness" – in their eyes, wild, unoccupied, and unused territory. Europeans also sought to Christianize the Indians and to eliminate their traditional religious practices. The ethnocentrism that underlay the missionary impulse is exemplified by the following speech by a Boston missionary to a group of Seneca Indians:

> *There is but one religion, and but one way to serve God, and if you do not embrace the right way, you cannot be happy hereafter. You have never worshipped the Great Spirit in a manner acceptable to him; but have all your lives been in great errors and darkness. To endeavor to remove these errors, and open your eyes, so that you might see clearly, is my business with you. (Washburn 1964:210)*

When two different ethnic groups come into initial contact, ethnocentrism is not restricted to one group. Rather, both sides respond with mutual ethnocentrism. Noel notes this reciprocal process when he cites the reply of representatives of the Six (Indian) Nations to an offer by the Virginia Commission in 1744 to educate Indian youth at the College of William and Mary:

Several of our young people were formerly brought up at Colleges of the Northern Provinces; they were instructed in all your sciences; but when they came back to us, they were bad runners, ignorant of every means of living in the woods, unable to bear either cold or hunger, knew neither how to build a cabin, take a deer, or kill an enemy, spoke our language imperfectly, were therefore neither fit for hunters, warriors, or counselors; they were totally good for nothing. We are, however, not the less obliged by your kind offer, though we decline accepting it; and to show our grateful Sense of it, if the Gentlemen of Virginia will send us a Dozen of their Sons we will take great care of their education, instruct them in all we know and make Men of them.

It is clear that the American Indian leaders felt their ways to be superior to those of the Virginians.

The second condition necessary for a system of ethnic stratification to develop is *competition*; that is, two or more individuals or groups must strive for a goal or objective that only one can achieve. From the beginning of Indian-European contacts, competition between the two groups centered around land. American Indian and white looked on land differently. The former emphasized the notion of *usufruct*, or user's rights. The land could be occupied, hunted, cultivated, and otherwise used as long as an individual wished. Once it was abandoned, it became available for the use of others. To Indian people, land therefore was not something that could be owned or bought or sold, as Europeans conceived of it. Many land transactions between Native Americans and Europeans were based on radically different conceptions of what rights were being conveyed.

A system of ethnic stratification ultimately rests on differences in power. Initial contacts between Indian and white usually took place in a context of equality and were not necessarily destructive of Indian cultures and societies. In fact, many items of white technology – especially guns, knives, cloth, fishhooks, pots, and other tools – were eagerly sought. For instance, it was only after the introduction of the horse by Europeans that the Plains Indian cultures flourished (Washburn 1964:66–70). The posture of equality is reflected by the white recognition of American Indian peoples as independent powers – nations (like the Cherokee Nation and the Navajo Nation) – and by numerous diplomatic treaties, gifts, and even politically arranged marriages. (The marriage of Pocahontas and John Rolfe, for example, was primarily a political match to ensure the survival of early Virginia colonists.)

Initially, the desire of Europeans for land they could cultivate did not strain Indian-white relationships; but as the number of Europeans increased throughout the seventeenth, eighteenth, and nineteenth centuries, their demand for land became the primary source of conflict with American Indians. Moreover, cultivation soon reduced the supply of game and forced an Indian retreat. The advance of European settlement eventually overwhelmed even the most resolute resistance. Armed with superior military technology and bolstered by increasing numbers, whites moved inexorably westward. As Europeans expanded westward, American Indian peoples were frequently expelled from their traditional settlements to lands beyond the immediate frontier. Removal was frequently legitimated by an underlying Anglo-Saxon ethnocentrism, exemplified by President Theodore Roosevelt's assertion that "this great continent could not have been kept as nothing but a game preserve for squalid savages" (quoted in Lurie 1968:66).

As control of lands they had formerly occupied increasingly passed to whites, the status of American Indians came increasingly to resemble what C. Matthew Snipp calls "captive nations" (Article 24). Their land base, which initially had been over two billion acres, dwindled to 155 million acres in 1871 and to 90 million acres in 1980 (Dorris 1981). Diseases carried by the Europeans, such as smallpox, scarlet fever, measles, and cholera, were fatal to large numbers of native peoples, who for centuries had been physically isolated from the Old World and had developed little or no resistance to these diseases. Epidemics ravaged American Indian peoples throughout American history, frequently killing more than half of a tribe. Washburn concludes that "unwittingly, disease was the white man's strongest ally in the New World" (1975:107). Moreover, substantial numbers of Indians died as a result of warfare with Europeans, policies of removal from ancestral lands, and deliberate extermination. The American Indian population, which had numbered between five and six million when Columbus reached the New World, dwindled to 237,000 by 1900 (Thornton 1987:32).

The reservation system that developed most fully during the nineteenth century symbolized both the end of the era of Indian-white equality and, as Snipp points out, political domination by whites. Most American Indians had to obtain passes to leave the reservation, were denied the vote, and were forcefully prohibited from engaging in native religious and ceremonial practices. Traditional patterns of authority were undermined because the administration and control of the reservation were placed in the hands of white agents. Reservation peoples lost control over their fate. As a consequence, they came to resemble a "captive nation" characterized by white political domination.

By the turn of the twentieth century, whites believed that American Indians were a vanishing race, and that the few remaining should be forced to assimilate–to give up their cultural heritages and to adopt the European values of rugged individualism, competition, and private enterprise. To ethnocentric whites, these values represented more "civilized" forms of behavior, in contrast to the "savage" practices of American Indians. Yet, despite efforts to extinguish them, traditional cultural values and practices persisted on the reservations, because they were usually isolated from the rest of society. In the last quarter of the nineteenth century, most white Americans agreed that forced assimilation–socialization to white culture–represented the most "humane" means of dealing with the dilemma of the American Indian's continued existence. Whites employed a strategy of destroying tribal governments, breaking up the reservations, and granting land to Indians on an individual basis. The federal government subsidized American Indian schools controlled by white religious groups. In many of these schools students were forcibly taken from their families, forced to adopt white styles of dress, and punished for speaking their own native languages (see Adams 1988).

In 1887, Carl Schurz, the German-born Secretary of the Interior justified these practices: "The enjoyment and pride of individual ownership of property is one of the most effective civilizing agencies" (U.S. Commission on Civil Rights 1961:122). Theodore Roosevelt, reflecting the late nineteenth-century Social Darwinist theory that emphasized the "survival of the fittest," agreed: "This will bring the whites and Indians into close contact, and while, of course, in the ensuing struggle and competition many of the Indians will go to the wall, the survivors will come out American citizens" (quoted in Washburn 1975:242).

The striking feature of American Indian life in the twentieth century has been its ability to endure. Despite pressures to force them to assimilate into the mainstream of American society, American Indians have tenaciously clung to their ancestral cultural values, standards, and beliefs. Although plagued by the nation's poorest health standards, the American Indian population increased by 1980 to nearly one and a half million, a five-fold increase since 1900. Moreover, the rise of ethnic consciousness and militancy during the 1960s and 1970s found expression among them, particularly among the younger and better educated.

As noted above, a substantial portion of American Indian lands were ceded to colonists and early settlers by treaties, first with the colonial British governments and later with the United States government. In signing these treaties, Indian peoples agreed to give up certain things (most frequently, land) in return for concessions and obligations by the government. Treaties therefore form the basis of the unique legal and political status of American Indians today. In contrast to other American racial and ethnic minorities, American Indian tribes "are due certain privileges, protections, and benefits of yielding some of their sovereignty to the United States" (Dorris 1981:54). Among these rights are the obligations of the federal government to protect their lands and to provide social, medical, and educational services.

After having forcibly removed many Indian peoples from their traditional settlements, the federal government frequently entered into treaties recognizing that Indians would retain sovereignty over their new lands in perpetuity – "as long as the grass shall grow and the rivers shall run." Despite persistent efforts to undermine the reservation system, these treaties did permit Indians to preserve some of their dwindling lands. Although the lands they hold today represent only a small portion of those guaranteed, they include vast and extremely valuable agricultural, water, timber, fishing, and energy resources. However, these resources are being developed and exploited primarily for external economic interests that are national and multinational. Snipp contends that the increasing attempts to develop and exploit American Indian resources for external economic interests reflect the shift from a captive nation status to internal colonialism. The former represented political domination but did not dramatically disrupt the economic lives of American Indian people. Internal colonialism, on the other hand, involves economic as well as political domination; as pressures for development of the scarce resources found on tribal lands continue, internal colonialism is likely to become more pronounced.

In response to their status as an internal colony, American Indians today are increasingly challenging their political and economic domination by outsiders, and are seeking to gain control over reservation resources. American Indian activists have mounted legal challenges to ensure that the federal government honors the terms of the solemn treaties it has made with Indian peoples. They have also developed organizations to advance Indian economic interests and resist external economic penetration and exploitation of their resources. One of the most prominent has been the Council of Energy Resource Tribes (CERT), which was formed in 1975 to increase American Indian control over the substantial coal, gas, oil, and uranium reserves that are found on Indian lands. As powerful economic and political pressures intensify over scarce and valuable Indian resources, such conflicts will increase (Erdrich and Dorris 1988).

European-Americans

The migratory movement of European peoples from the seventeenth through the twentieth centuries has been the greatest in human history. Since the beginning of the seventeenth century, more than seventy million people have emigrated from Europe; about three-fourths of this number came to the United States. For nearly two centuries—from the beginning of the seventeenth to the beginning of the nineteenth century—the European population of America was overwhelmingly Protestant and British.

The first European immigrants to settle permanently in what is now the United States were almost exclusively English. The first substantial English migration occurred between 1607 and 1660. The economic, legal, and political traditions that English settlers brought to America established the English character of American institutions, language, and culture. Ethnic groups who migrated later were forced to adapt to the cultural and social systems that the English had created.

Although the English comprised the greatest proportion of the total colonial population, the middle colonies (New York, New Jersey, Pennsylvania, Delaware) contained substantial settlements of Germans, Dutch, Scotch-Irish, Scots, Swedes, and French Huguenots. Because the middle colonies contained the greatest variety of European cultures, they provided a context within which interethnic relations among European peoples in American society can first be observed. Here the ideal of America as a *melting pot*, in which diverse cultures come together to form a new people, was first formulated. In 1782, a Frenchman, Hector St. John de Crevecoeur, wrote:

> *What then is the American, this new man? . . . Here [in America] individuals of all nations are melted into a new race of men, whose labours and posterity will one day cause great changes in the world. (Crevecoeur 1957:39)*

As we will consider more fully in Part 3, the idealistic notion of the melting pot has greatly influenced later conceptions of how the various cultures comprising the American people have adapted and interacted.

However, relations between ethnic groups in the middle colonies sometimes fell short of this ideal. Spurred by William Penn's promotional efforts during the late seventeenth and early eighteenth centuries, a substantial number of Germans settled in Pennsylvania, where they formed prosperous farming communities. Because the Germans insisted on maintaining their own language, churches, and culture, their presence generated some of the earliest recorded conflicts among European ethnic groups in America. In 1752, Benjamin Franklin openly expressed the widely held fears of the "Germanization" of Pennsylvania:

> *Why should the* Palatine Boors *[Germans] be suffered to swarm into our Settlements, and by herding together, establish their Language and Manners, to the Exclusion of ours? Why should* Pennsylvania, *founded by the* English, *become a Colony of* Aliens, *who will shortly be so numerous as to Germanize us instead of Anglifying them. . . ? [Cited in Dinnerstein and Reimers 1987:7]*

Thus, colonial attitudes toward immigrants were marked by considerable ambivalence. This same uncertainty still characterizes America's response to ethnic diversity. Throughout the American experience, immigrant groups have been regarded both positively and negatively. On the one hand, immigration has provided a steady source of labor necessary for the country's economic development and expansion. Until the twentieth century, inducements in the form of land, jobs, and exemption from taxation were offered to encourage settlement and thus to assist American economic development. Americans have also celebrated the idea of America as a haven for the oppressed, as in Emma Lazarus's classic poem, "Give me your tired, your poor/your huddled masses yearning to breathe free. . . ."

On the other hand, the concern expressed by Benjamin Franklin over the impact of ethnic diversity on the society's institutions has been a persistent one. Lazarus's poem, inscribed on the Statue of Liberty, further characterizes those "tired," "poor," "huddled masses" as "wretched refuse." Many immigrant groups have been perceived as wretched refuse. In practice, Americans have been less charitable than idealized accounts indicate. Americans have frequently rejected ethnic differences as alien and undesirable. Some ethnic groups in particular have been rejected or excluded as un-American and incapable of assimilating. Thus, while the labor of immigrants was accepted, their cultural traditions usually were not.

In 1790, when the first United States census was taken, the population of the new American nation was nearly four million. It was overwhelmingly British in composition, with the English comprising 60 to 80 percent of the population, and with other people from the British Isles (Scots, Welsh, and Scotch-Irish) contributing substantially. Between 1830 and 1930, the United States population experienced its greatest growth and change. During this period, the nation changed from a small group of tenuously related state governments to the most politically and economically powerful nation on earth. The frontier of unsettled land moved progressively westward and diminished at the same time that the country became the world's leading industrial nation.

Peoples of many lands contributed to this dramatic growth. Between 1830 and 1930, nearly thirty-five million immigrants entered the country, swelling its total population to more than 123 million. In contrast to the relative ethnic homogeneity of colonial immigration, the immigrants who arrived in the nineteenth and early twentieth centuries represented many different countries and peoples, including German, Russian, Mexican, British, Polish, Japanese, Scandinavian, Irish, Italian, Slavic, Greek, Chinese, and Portuguese. European immigration since 1790 has been divided into two broad categories: "old" immigrants from northern and western Europe and "new" immigrants from southern and eastern Europe (see Figures 2.1 and 2.2).

The "Old" Immigration

Immigration to the United States increased dramatically throughout the nineteenth century. In the peak year of the 1830s slightly more than 70,000 immigrants entered. By the 1850s this annual figure had increased to 400,000; by the 1880s to 650,000; and by the first decade of the twentieth century, there were several years in which more than one million immigrants were admitted.

Until the 1890s, immigration drew principally from countries of northern and western Europe: Germany, Ireland, Great Britain (England, Scotland, and Wales), and Scandinavia (Norway, Sweden, and Denmark). With the exception

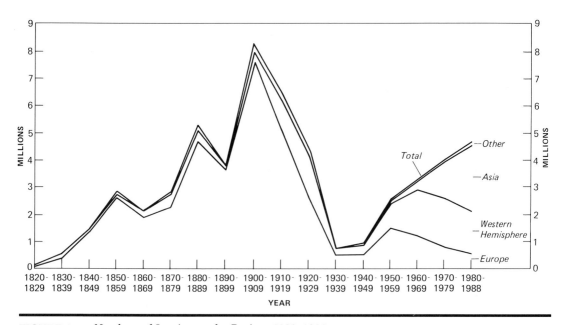

FIGURE 2.1 *Numbers of Immigrants by Region, 1820–1988*

Source: *1988 Statistical Yearbook of the Immigration and Naturalization Service*, pp. 11–12.

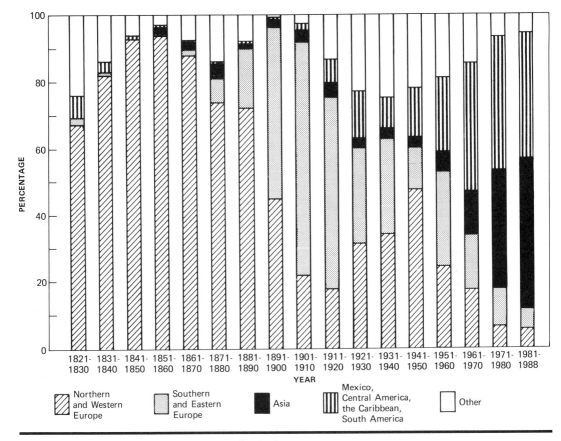

FIGURE 2.2 *Origins of U.S. Immigration by Region, 1821–1988*
Source: *1988 Statistical Yearbook of the Immigration and Naturalization Service,* pp. 11–12.

of the Roman Catholic Irish, the old immigration was substantially Protestant. These groups, again with the exception of the Irish, were attracted by the opportunities of free or relatively cheap land, and therefore often settled in the rural areas of the country. There were several common factors in their countries of origin that led people to emigrate: drastic population increases, displacement of traditional handicraft industries by the Industrial Revolution, an upheaval in agriculture that transformed traditional agrarian land patterns, and migration of substantial numbers of people from rural to urban areas. Above all, the promise of economic opportunity lured people to the United States.

The "New" Immigration

Immigration into the United States reached its peak between 1890 and the outbreak of World War I in 1914. During this period, the United States received more than fourteen million immigrants. As dramatic as the numerical increase during this period was the shift in the sources of immigration. Prior to the 1880s, immigrants had come almost exclusively from northern and western Europe. By the first decade of the twentieth century, however, more than 70 percent of all immigrants came from southern and eastern Europe. This shift brought large numbers of immigrants from a great variety of countries—Greeks, Croatians, Italians, Russians (primarily Jews), Poles, Hungarians, Czechs, and Lithuanians. These groups were culturally different from those who had previously migrated to this country. Unlike the old immigration, which was heavily Protestant and followed agricultural pursuits, the new immigrants were overwhelmingly Roman Catholic or Jewish and were drawn primarily to the economic opportunities in the nation's rapidly expanding cities. The changes in the ethnic composition of this immigration caused "native" whites to fear the impact of non-English cultures on American institutions.

The shift in immigration patterns coincided with the flowering of the ideology of "scientific" racism, which reached its height about the turn of the twentieth century. As noted in the introduction to Part 1, at this time scientific and lay opinion concurred in the idea of the inherent mental and moral inferiority of all those who were not of Anglo-Saxon or Teutonic ancestry. To already existing conceptions of black, American Indian, and Asian inferiority was added the notion of the racial inferiority and unassimilability of immigrant groups from southern and eastern Europe. Never before or since have racist ideologies been so pervasive and so intellectually respectable in the United States as they were at this time. Moreover, it is important to recognize that, as Shirley Hune points out in her critique of the assumptions of late nineteenth and early twentieth century historians and social scientists ("Pacific Migration to the United States," Article 12), these racist ideologies, which have had an enduring impact on policies and practices in American society throughout the twentieth century, were given intellectual legitimation by the nation's social elites—the "best and brightest."

These racist assumptions provided the foundations for American immigration policy from 1917 to 1965. The first general restrictive legislation, passed in 1917, was a literacy test, which was used precisely because it was believed that it would discriminate against "new" immigrants, limiting their numbers while still permitting substantial numbers of "old" immigrants to enter. In the ensuing decade, even more stringent restrictive measures were enacted, each one based on the assumption of the desirability of restricting immigration to those from the countries of the "old" immigration. In 1921 and 1924 further legislation designed to curtail new immigration was enacted. Finally, in 1929, the National Origins Quota Act, based (as was preceding legislation) on the rationale of ensuring the maintenance of Anglo-Saxon "racial" purity, became law. The law limited total immigration to 150,000 annually and established numerical quotas for each nation. Derived by a complicated calculation, each nation's quota was supposed to be "in proportion to its [the nation's] contribution to the American population." The measure assigned the highest quotas to those nations of northern and western Europe, whose "racial" stock was believed to coincide most closely with that of the original settlers of the country and who were therefore considered more assimilable and more desirable. More than four-fifths of the total quota was allocated to countries of the "old" immigration. For instance, Great Britain had an admission quota exceeding 65,000, but Italy was allocated fewer than 6,000, Hungary fewer than 1,000, and Greece a mere 310. Reflecting the racist assumptions on which it was based, the law excluded most Asians and Africans completely.

The uprooting that millions of immigrants experienced comprises one of the most dramatic sagas in American history. It has been widely described (Handlin 1951; Taylor 1971; Jones 1960, 1976; Seller 1977; Dinnerstein and Reimers 1987; Bodnar 1985; Archdeacon 1983). Moreover, the consequences of this massive migration — its effects on European immigrants and the manner in which they and their descendants adapted to American society — have been a source of considerable description, debate, and controversy among social historians and sociologists. In Part 3 we will examine in greater depth some of the competing explanations for differences in adaptation among ethnic groups in American society.

The blatantly racist immigration policies instituted in the 1920s were retained virtually intact until 1965, when the Immigration Act was enacted. Reflecting the egalitarian values of what Herbert Gans (1968) has termed the "equality revolution" of the 1960s, the Immigration Act of 1965 abolished the old national-origins quota system, increased the annual number of immigrants to 170,000, placed a limit of 20,000 for each country, and for the first time, established a limit (120,000) on immigration from the Western Hemisphere. It also established preferences for those who would be reunited with their families, for those with occupational skills needed in the United States, and for those emigrating for political reasons. Since 1968, when the provisions of the Immigration Act went into effect, traditional patterns of immigration to the United States have been transformed. No longer are most immigrants Europeans, let alone primarily from northern and western Europe. As we will note more fully in Part 4, today the predominant sources of immigration to the United States are Third World nations in Central and South America, the Caribbean, and Asia.

African-Americans

Racism, which provided a basis for restricting the immigration of southern and eastern European immigrants, has also been a pervasive characteristic of whites' interaction with blacks. From the earliest settlement to the present, the principal racial division in American society has been between white and black, between those of European ancestry and those whose ancestral origins can be traced to the African continent. From the arrival of the first African at Jamestown in 1619 to the present, the meaning attributed to the physical traits of black people has been more important than all other racial divisions in American society. African-Americans were enslaved for more than two centuries; and although more than a century has passed since slavery was legally abolished, the rationale for slavery that emphasized the racial and cultural differences between blacks and whites persists to this day. Today numbering more than thirty million — more than 12 percent of the total American population – African-Americans have been the largest racial minority in American society since the eighteenth century.

In Article 6, "The Declining Significance of Race," William Julius Wilson distinguishes among three major periods or stages of black-white relations in American history: preindustrial, industrial, and modern industrial. Let us review briefly here the African-American experience during the first two of these three periods. (We will examine the racial dynamics of the most recent period, the modern industrial stage, in Part 4).

During the preindustrial period, a plantation economy dominated and defined the lives of black people, the most important aspect of which was the institution of slavery. Slavery is a system of social relations in which some persons are involuntarily placed in perpetual servitude, are defined as property, and are denied rights generally given to other members of the society. Throughout human history, societies have limited the freedom and rights of particular classes of individuals. Other systems of servile status, such as serfdom, debt bondage, and indentureship, have involved some degree of unfreedom and rightlessness. What distinguishes these statuses from slavery is therefore not absolute. "Slaves are [simply] the most deprived and oppressed class of serviles" (Noel 1972:5). This definition of slavery is useful because it provides a standard against which social systems can be compared. In other words, if slavery is conceived as being located at the far end of a continuum ranging from absolute rightlessness, on the one hand, to absolute freedom on the other, one may examine each case of oppression in terms of its location between the extremes on this continuum.

Slavery was not an American invention. It existed in ancient civilizations, persisted throughout the Middle Ages and into modern times, was practiced legally until 1962 on the Arabian peninsula, and persists, unofficially, to this day. Although it has existed in many different societies throughout virtually the whole of human history, the introduction of national monarchies and the growing industrial and commercial revolutions in the sixteenth through the nineteenth centuries acted as catalysts for the development of Western slave systems, in which slave labor was an indispensable component of economic systems.

Even though there has been a surge of historical interest in the institution of American slavery (Elkins 1959; Davis 1966, 1975; Genovese 1974; Gutman 1976; Yetman 1970; Blassingame 1972; Rawick 1972; Fogel and Engerman 1974; Levine 1977), there has been a dearth of attention to the analysis of slavery as a social institution, and to the more general question of the nature and effects of institutional regimentation. The implications of an analysis of slavery in America could be used to examine the dynamics of other total institutions (Goffman 1961) and other dominant-subordinate relationships (serfdom, caste systems, racial or ethnic ghettos, and various aboriginal reservation systems) that have not yet been considered in these terms.

Article 5, "A Theory of the Origins of Ethnic Stratification," represents an effort to consider American slavery from a broader perspective. Donald Noel identifies three major conditions – ethnocentrism, competition, and differences in power – as necessary for the emergence of a system of ethnic stratification, and he uses American slavery as a case study with which to test the utility of his general propositions. However, if one closely considers Noel's arguments, it is problematic whether the important feature of black-white relations in the United States was slavery per se. Crucial to an understanding of the dynamics of black-white relations in the United States are the features that undergirded slavery, the so-called "peculiar institution": the conception of black inferiority and the capacity of the dominant group to restrict African-Americans to a permanent subordinate position.

Although slavery represented the most extreme form of institutionalized inequality between black and white in America, Leon Litwack (1961) has pointed out that during the slavery era the rights and privileges of free blacks also were severely circumscribed throughout the entire society. Oppression of African-Americans was by no means restricted to the South or to slaveholders; throughout the North, too, the freedom, rights, and privileges of free blacks were severely curtailed. At no time did the words *free person* or *freedom* mean the same thing to African-Americans as to whites. In many states, barriers to voting were initiated for blacks at the same time that restrictions for whites were being liberalized or eliminated. Court testimony and the formation of legal contracts and lawsuits by African-Americans were also forbidden in many states. Several states prohibited immigration; others required that blacks carry identification passes (as in modern South Africa). Excluded from public schools, African-Americans were generally denied the benefits of formal education. In addition to these officially imposed disabilities, blacks in most areas were subjected to ridicule, harassment, and occasional mob violence (Litwack 1961).

The most salient features of black-white relations in the United States, therefore, were that blacks, whether slave or free, occupied a lower caste status, and that severe sanctions were employed to restrict their freedoms. The American slave thus had to contend with the sanctions and effects of two inferior statuses—slave and lower caste—which were mutually reinforcing. Unlike many other slave societies, manumission was difficult, and people who had been freed could not anticipate assimilation into the society on an equal basis.

Immediately after the Civil War, a period of fluid race relations occurred. Bolstered by passage of the 13th Amendment, which abolished slavery; the 14th Amendment, which extended the equal protection of the law to African-Americans; and the 15th Amendment, which guaranteed the right to vote, African-Americans actively sought to realize the opportunities and responsibilities of their new status. Nevertheless, the reality of caste persisted. Patterns of black-white relations formed under slavery did not automatically change after emancipation: race relations continued to be based on a rigid caste system. The roles of African-Americans after their emancipation became well defined and tightly circumscribed. The new legal status conferred by emancipation and the Reconstruction Amendments did little to alter the patterns of social relations in the plantation South, or to promote the acquisition of new values, habits, and attitudes by either black or white. Former slaves were formally given liberty but not the means (that is, economic, political, educational, and social equality) to realize it. Blacks remained largely unskilled and illiterate, most of them living lives of enforced dependence on the still-dominant whites. The result was a black peasantry dominated by an agricultural system that ensured dependence on the land and isolation from the main currents of society.

Northern troops, which had occupied the South during the period of Reconstruction, were removed in 1877, and southern whites then resorted to a wide range of devices to ensure the maintenance of white dominance. Blacks, who during Reconstruction had voted and held public office, were systematically disenfranchised by a variety of mechanisms: white primary elections from which African-Americans were excluded; poll taxes; "grandfather clauses," which restricted voting to those (and their descendants) who had been eligible to vote before the Civil War; and literacy requirements, which, because they were selectively enforced, restricted even the most educated and literate African-Americans from exercising the constitutionally mandated right to vote.

Moreover, to ensure that white dominance would be perpetuated, the Jim Crow system of racial segregation was created. Historian C. Vann Woodward (1955) has described the extraordinary variety of state and municipal ordinances requiring racial separation that southern state legislatures enacted during the last decade of the nineteenth and first two decades of the twentieth centuries. The pervasiveness of the segregated system was signaled by a profusion of "Whites Only" and "Colored" signs that governed working conditions, public accommodations, state institutions, recreation, sports, cemeteries, and housing. In 1896, in the famous *Plessy v. Ferguson* decision, the United States Supreme Court provided judicial support for the doctrine of "separate but equal." Thereafter, virtually every aspect of contact between whites and blacks was legally regulated.

Finally, extralegal sanctions, including intimidation and violence in the form of lynching and terrorism, were employed to assure that the subservient status of African-Americans persisted long after slavery had been abolished. Writing in 1929, Charles S. Johnson, a pioneer African-American sociologist, noted the continuity between the slave plantation and rural Macon County, Alabama, during the 1920s:

> There have been retained, only slightly modified, most of the features of the plantation under the institution of slavery. . . . The Negro population of this section of Macon County has its own social heritage which, in a relatively complete isolation, has had little chance for modification from without or within. Patterns of life, social codes, as well as social attitudes, were set in the economy of slavery. The political and economic revolution through which they have passed has affected only slightly the social relationships of the community or the mores upon which these relations have been based. The strength and apparent permanence of this early cultural set have made it virtually impossible for new generations to escape the influence of the patterns of work and general social behavior transmitted by their elders. (Johnson 1934:16)

Similar reports noted the persistence of the slave plantation in many areas of the rural south well into the 1930s.

In response to these oppressive conditions, after the turn of the twentieth century African-Americans began to leave the South, a movement that has been called the Great Migration. Migrating primarily to Northern urban areas, African-Americans congregated in urban ghettos, geographically defined residential areas to which minority groups are restricted. Their transformation from an essentially rural to a predominantly urban people has been one of the most significant aspects in the African-American experience and one of the most important demographic changes in American history. In 1900, almost 90 percent of the black population lived in the South; in 1980, the percentage in the South had declined to only 53 percent. In 1900, blacks were primarily rural residents, with only 22.7 percent living in urban areas. By 1980, this percentage had increased to 81.3 percent, indicating that blacks have become a more urbanized population than whites. Although a substantial portion of the increase in the number of urbanized African-Americans was in the North, many were living in southern cities as well. Between 1900 and 1980, the percentage of the Southern black population residing in cities increased from 17.2 percent to 67.3 percent. Table 2.1 shows the percentage of the black population residing in major American cities for the years 1920, 1950, 1970, and 1980.

The massive movement of African-Americans out of the South changed race relations. Wilson has characterized this period as the *industrial* period of race relations. His description of the transition from preindustrial to industrial parallels van den Berghe's distinction between *paternalistic* race relations, which were characteristic of a plantation economy, and *competitive* race relations, which are found in an urban, industrial setting. In the industrial setting, competition for jobs generated considerable racial antagonism, tension, and conflict. (For a superb analysis of this conflict, see Tuttle 1972, especially Chapter 4).

TABLE 2.1 *African-American Population as Percent of the Total Population of the 12 Largest U.S. Cities,* * *1920, 1950, 1970, and 1980*

	1920†	1950†	1970	1980
New York	2.7	9.8	21.1	25.2
Los Angeles	2.7	10.7	17.9	17.0
Chicago	4.1	14.1	32.7	39.8
Philadelphia	7.4	18.3	33.6	37.8
Houston	24.6	21.1	25.7	27.6
Detroit	4.1	16.4	43.7	63.1
Dallas	15.1	13.2	24.9	29.4
San Diego	1.2	4.5	7.6	8.9
Phoenix	3.7	6.0	4.8	4.8
Baltimore	14.8	23.8	46.4	54.8
San Antonio	8.9	6.7	7.6	7.3
Indianapolis	11.0	15.0	18.0	21.8

Source: U.S. Census of 1920; U.S. Census of 1950; U.S. Bureau of the Census, *Negroes in the United States,* 1920–1932, Washington, D.C.: U.S. Government Printing Office, 1935; "Characteristics of the Population," *Statistical Abstract of the United States, 1972,* pp. 21–23; *Statistical Abstract of the United States, 1984,* pp. 28–30.

*These were the 12 largest cities in the United States in 1980.

†Figures pertain to "nonwhite" population, of which over 90 percent was black.

The Great Migration of African-Americans out of the South ultimately proved to be one of the most important factors underlying the Black Protest Movement that swept the nation during the late 1950s and 1960s. Although discrimination against African-Americans in education, employment, housing, and the administration of justice also prevailed in the North, a greater range of opportunities for blacks were available in northern urban areas than in the South. Especially after World War II, increasing numbers of African-Americans obtained college educations and found employment in skilled and white-collar occupations. These changes expanded the African-American middle class, which provided the primary source of leadership for the Black Protest Movement. The educated and articulate African-American middle class played an especially important role in providing legal challenges to the southern Jim Crow system, which culminated in the Supreme Court's 1954 *Brown v. Board of Education* decision that segregated schools were unconstitutional. The *Brown* decision, which overturned the 1896 separate-but-equal doctrine, symbolized the beginning of an era in which the legal basis for the caste system would crumble. In Part 4, we will examine the changing status of African-Americans during the past quarter century, the period that Wilson has identified as the *modern industrial* stage of American race relations.

Hispanic-Americans

Spanish-speaking Americans constitute one of the largest and most rapidly growing ethnic categories in contemporary American society. The *Hispanic* or *Latino* population totaled more than twenty million by 1989 – better than 8 percent of the U.S. population – and is growing five times as rapidly as the rest of the country. Demographers have estimated that, if Hispanic immigration (both legal and illegal) and fertility rates remain at their present levels, by the year 2020 Hispanics will number forty-six million and will exceed African-Americans as the country's largest ethnic minority category (Davis, Haub, and Willette 1983:39). This dramatic increase in the Hispanic population in the United States is the result of both higher Hispanic fertility rates and substantially increased rates of immigration from Latin America, especially from Mexico.

As we will see in Part 4, vast social inequalities, poverty, and political repression throughout the region all influence migration pressures in Latin America. A crucial dimension contributing to these problems is demographic: the recent rapid population growth in both Central and South America. During the 1950s, the total Latin American population was approximately the same as that of the United States – about 150 million. However, by 2025 it is expected to be 845 million, or about three times the estimate of the U.S. population at that time (Fallows 1983:45; Davis, Haub, and Willette 1983:39).

To refer to Spanish-speaking people as a single ethnic category is misleading. The terms *Hispanic* or *Latino*, which are of recent origin, obscure the great diversity of historical, cultural, and geographic backgrounds among them. The Hispanic category includes representatives from more than thirty Latin American nations, as well as from Spain and Portugal. More than three-fourths of them are of Mexican, Puerto Rican, or Cuban descent, but there are also substantial communities of people from Central and South America—for example, Dominicans, Colombians, Ecuadorians, Salvadoreans, Guatemalans, Nicaraguans, and several other Latin nationalities in the United States (see Levine 1987). These groups also differ in their socioeconomic status and in their regional distribution in the United States.

Mexican-Americans

Mexican-Americans, or Chicanos (from the Spanish *Mexicanos*), are the largest Hispanic group and (after African-Americans) the second largest ethnic minority group in American society. Today more than twelve and a half million Chicanos live in the United States, about 90 percent of them in the five southwestern states of Texas, New Mexico, Arizona, Colorado, and California.

Next to the North American Indians, with whom they share a common ancestry, they represent the oldest ethnic group in American society. The Chicano people are the biological and cultural descendants of the Spanish military and religious conquest of the native peoples of northern Central America. From the early 1600s to the mid-1800s, Spain, and, later, Mexico, colonized and exerted political, economic, and cultural dominance over the region. By the turn of the nineteenth century, Mexican culture, a mixture of Spanish and American Indian influences, was well established throughout what is today the southwestern United States.

The process of contact between Mexicans and the Anglo immigrants who settled in Texas in increasing numbers during the early nineteenth century provides another opportunity to test Noel's model of the emergence of ethnic stratification. Initially Anglo and Mexican peacefully coexisted, although each viewed the other with an antipathy and distrust that had grown out of two centuries of English and Spanish competition for world dominance. Mutual ethnocentrism between the two peoples occurred from the start, Anglos attributing "racial" inferiority to the darker-skinned Mexicans, and Mexicans seeing in the growing encroachment of the Americans confirmation of their stereotypes of Yankee aggressiveness and greed. Anglo and Mexican also differed in religion and class structure. To ensure their loyalty, the Mexican government required that Anglo colonists, most of whom were Protestants, become Roman Catholics as well as Mexican citizens. More offensive to the sensibilities of Anglo settlers, many of whom were from the South and were slaveholders, was the Mexican prohibition of slavery. Although slavery was illegal, Mexican society was highly stratified, with a small, wealthy upper class and a large class of the very poor. Anglo-Americans, literate and middle-class in outlook, developed a perception of the Mexican people as indolent and lazy (McLemore 1973).

Despite these differences, Anglo and Mexican Texans coexisted, cooperated, and together fought a common enemy, the Mexican central government controlled by Santa Ana. Both Anglos and Mexicans died fighting Santa Ana in the Alamo. After Santa Ana's defeat, however, competition for land became increasingly intense between Anglo and Mexican. The 1848 Treaty of Guadalupe-Hidalgo, in which Mexico ceded to the United States most of the land of the present-day Southwest, signaled the triumph of Anglo power. Despite the fact that the treaty guaranteed legal and property rights to Mexican citizens in the newly acquired territories, Mexican-Americans soon became the object of persistent discrimination. Anglos, especially in Texas, established a system of caste relations, which ensured Chicano political, social, and economic subservience. By the eve of the Civil War the American military conquest of Mexican lands in the Southwest had been completed. In the ensuing years those Mexicans who chose to remain in the annexed territories were largely dispossessed of both their land and the prominence they had occupied in Mexican society. By the turn of the twentieth century, Mexicans had been "relegated to a lower-class status, [in which] they were overwhelmingly dispossessed landless laborers, politically and economically impotent," which was justified by notions of racial inferiority (Estrada et al. 1981:109). For this reason, Alvarez (1973) has argued that the subjugation of this "creation generation" after the Mexican War was formative, in much the same sense that Bryce-Laporte (1969) has characterized slavery as "the contextual baseline of Black American experience."

Although a substantial proportion of the contemporary Chicano population is derived from the migrant generation that followed the surge of European immigration into the United States during the early twentieth century, the situation of Mexican immigrants differed substantially from that of European immigrant groups because Mexican immigrants entered a society that had already adopted a clearly defined lower-caste role for them, a result of the mid-nineteenth century conquest patterns of subordination.

Whereas the earliest Chicano population became an American minority through the annexation of Mexican lands by the United States, the primary source of the majority of the Chicano population in the United States has been immigration, both legal and illegal. This immigration, most of which has occurred during the twentieth century, has been instrumental in the economic development of the American southwest. As Leobardo Estrada and his colleagues indicate in Article 8, Mexican immigrants have provided a readily available and exploitable source of cheap labor, especially for the expansion of the railroad industry, mining, and above all, agriculture. Indeed, Mexican labor played an integral role in the dramatic expansion of agribusiness interests in the Southwest. During the first two decades of the twentieth century, many Mexicans fled to the United States from the upheavals of the Mexican Revolution. As European immigration to the United States was curtailed by the outbreak of World War I and the passage of the restrictive legislation of the 1920s, Mexican labor filled the growing demand for agricultural workers to replace those who had left for jobs in the nation's industrial sector. The defense employment boom generated by World War II produced a shift of the Chicano population away from rural areas and agricultural pursuits, while at the same time the *bracero* program, which ran from 1942 to 1965, ensured a continuing source of cheap agricultural labor from Mexico. As Douglas Massey ("The Social Organization of Mexican Migration to the United States," Article 25) points out, the general migration of Mexicans to work in the U.S. earlier in the twentieth century and the bracero program, in particular, played a major role in establishing the migration networks that sustain Mexican migration to the United States today.

Several indicators reveal that Mexican-Americans lag considerably behind the mainstream of American society in socioeconomic status. Despite some evidence of improvement among younger generations, Mexican-American educational attainment is less than that of both whites and African-Americans. They tend to be found in low-paying blue-collar and semiskilled occupations (although some evidence reveals that during the 1970s the proportion of Mexican-Americans in skilled, higher-paying occupations increased). As Table 2.2 indicates, in 1988 median family income of Mexican-Americans was only 64 percent of white median family income, having declined throughout most of the 1980s (U.S. Bureau of the Census 1990b).

Although Chicanos still comprise a substantial proportion of the nation's migratory farmworkers, today they are overwhelmingly—more than 80 percent—urban residents, especially in the major urban areas of the Southwest. Indeed, today more people of Mexican descent live in Los Angeles than any other city except Mexico City and Guadalajara. As their numbers and their concentration in urban areas has increased, Mexican-Americans, like other Hispanic groups, have also become an increasingly salient force in American politics, especially because of their substantial presence in the electorally significant states of Texas and California.

The other major groups of Spanish-speaking people are relatively recent immigrant groups who have settled primarily in urban areas on the East coast since the end of World War II. Although the number of immigrants from countries throughout the Caribbean and Central and South America has increased markedly during this period, the two Caribbean islands of Puerto Rico and Cuba have been the primary sources of this influx of Spanish-speaking peoples. These two groups provide an interesting contrast in backgrounds and adaptations to American society.

TABLE 2.2 *Median Family Income, 1988*

	Income	% of White Income
All races	$32,191	
White	33,915	
Black	19,329	56
Hispanic	21,769	64
Mexican	21,025	61
Puerto Rican	18,932	55
Cuban	26,858	79
Central & South America	24,322	71
Other Hispanic	23,666	69

Sources: U. S. Bureau of the Census, 1989b, 1990b.

Puerto Ricans

Among Hispanic groups, Puerto Ricans have a unique relationship with the United States. The island of Puerto Rico was ceded to the United States in 1898 after the defeat of Spain in the Spanish-American War. Despite changes in the twentieth century, the status of Puerto Rico has in many respects resembled a colonial dependency ever since. Although Puerto Ricans were granted American citizenship in 1917, they have retained their language and cultural traditions, different from the dominant language and culture of the United States. Puerto Ricans' determination to maintain their cultural distinctiveness has been an important element in the present debate over whether the island should become an independent nation, be the fifty-first American state, or retain its present commonwealth status.

Numbering 2.3 million people on the mainland, Puerto Ricans are today the largest Hispanic group outside the Southwest. Puerto Rican residents began migrating to the United States early in the twentieth century, but it was not until the advent of relatively cheap commercial air travel after World War II that they began to arrive in substantial numbers, settling primarily in New York City. Today about 40 percent of all Puerto Ricans live on the mainland, and because of the ease of travel to and from the island, it has been estimated that half of all island Puerto Ricans have at some time shared the mainland experience (Levine 1987:95). While Puerto Ricans continue to reside primarily on the East coast, especially in New York City, increasing numbers have recently begun to settle in midwestern and far western cities such as Chicago, Cleveland, and Los Angeles.

The Puerto Rican migration to the mainland must be seen in the context of the economic and political relationship between the United States and Puerto Rico, which Levine has characterized as "imperial development." The migration was prompted primarily by extremely high unemployment in Puerto Rico, and it has fluctuated in response to economic opportunities in the United States. Given the historic underdevelopment of the Puerto Rican economy, Puerto Rican immigrants to the United States have been overwhelmingly unskilled and have experienced difficulties in an increasingly technological society. Concentrated in blue-collar, semiskilled, and unskilled occupations and subjected to racial discrimination, Puerto Ricans are "the most socially and economically disadvantaged of Hispanic origin groups, with poverty, labor force participation and unemployment rates, and average earnings comparable to those of Native Americans and blacks" (Bean and Tienda 1987:286). In 1988, Puerto Rican median family income was 55 percent that of whites, the lowest figure of all American racial and ethnic minorities for which data were available (U.S. Bureau of the Census 1990b).

Cuban-Americans

Although Cuban immigrants to the United States have been recorded as early as the 1870s, the Cuban-American community today is comprised primarily of relatively recent political refugees. Approximately 750,000 Cubans have entered the United States since Castro's rise to power in 1959, and today they number more than one million. In contrast to most previous immigrations to the United States (with the notable exception of those fleeing from Nazi Germany during the 1930s), the initial Cuban emigrés tended to be drawn mainly from upper social and economic strata of Cuban society. Derived disproportionately from well-educated middle-class and upper-class professional and business backgrounds, they brought skills (educational, occupational, business, and managerial experience), entrepreneurial values, and substantial amounts of capital that enabled them to prosper and achieve rapid socioeconomic success. In less than thirty years since their initial migration, Cubans have become the most affluent of all Hispanics and a major economic force in a number of American cities, especially Miami, Florida, which they have transformed into a major international business and commercial center with important links throughout Latin America. (See Portes and Manning, "The Immigrant Enclave," Article 17.)

The most recent influx of Cubans – those who left Cuba during the so-called Freedom Flotilla or Mariel Boatlift of 1980 – numbered about 125,000. A substantial proportion of this recent migration was people of working-class and lower-class origins (Davis, Haub, and Willette 1983:23).

Asian-Americans

Asians are an extremely diverse category that includes Chinese, Japanese, Filipinos, Koreans, Asian Indians, Vietnamese, and several other national or ethnic groups. Compared to the many millions of Europeans who have migrated to the Untied States, Asian immigration has, until recently, been slight. At no time until the past two decades did the numbers of Asian immigrants ever approximate those from Europe. For example, Chinese immigration reached its peak during the decade from 1873 to 1882, when 161,000 Chinese entered the country. Peak Japanese immigration was reached during the decade between 1900 and 1909, when 139,000 entered. In contrast, between 1840 and 1920 there were thirty-one different years when the number of immigrants from a *single* European country alone exceeded 150,000. As Figures 1 and 2 reveal, the total number of immigrants from Asia, in general, and Japan and China, in particular, have been insignificant when considered in the context of American immigration as a whole. What is significant is the response that the presence of Asian immigrants generated, and the adaptation of Asians to the discrimination they encountered. By 1988 Asians numbered 6.5 million, or 2.6 percent of the American people.

However, as a result of changes in American immigration laws, which before 1965 had virtually excluded them, Asians are today proportionately the nation's fastest-growing minority. During the 1970s the Asian population increased by 141 percent, Hispanics by 39 percent, and African-Americans by 17 percent. Between 1980 and 1988 Asians constituted nearly half (48 percent) of all legal immigrants (Gardner, Robey, and Smith 1985; U.S. Immigration and Naturalization Service 1989). Historically, the Chinese and Japanese have been the most prominent Asian groups; Filipinos, Koreans, Asian Indians, and Vietnamese are relatively recent arrivals.

Early Immigrants: Chinese and Japanese

The earliest modern Asian immigrants were the Chinese, who migrated to North America beginning in the 1840s. During the next four decades more than 200,000 Chinese immigrants, primarily unskilled laborers, arrived. Filling a need for labor created by the economic development of the West in the mid-nineteenth century (especially in mining and in building the transcontinental railroad), the Chinese were initially welcomed. As their numbers increased, however, the Chinese became perceived as an economic threat to native labor, and racist opposition to them mounted. As a consequence, the Chinese were subjected to various forms of harassment, mob violence, and discriminatory legislation, including laws designed specifically to harass them. Finally, in response to anti-Chinese agitation in California, Congress passed the Chinese Exclusion Act of 1882, which was the first federal law to restrict immigration of a specific nationality to the United States. In contrast, more than thirty years were to pass before substantial restrictions were placed on European immigration (Hsu 1971; Lyman 1974; Nee and Nee 1974).

Anti-Asian sentiment, which pervaded the hysteria over Chinese immigration, was revived when the Japanese immigrated in the early twentieth century. Although the Japanese represented an extremely small proportion of the population of both California and the nation as a whole, their presence generated intense hostility. Like the Chinese before them, the Japanese were the object of legislation designed to harass and intimidate them. In 1906, the San Francisco Board of Education precipitated an international incident when it attempted to place all Japanese children, native and foreign-born, in a segregated Oriental school in Chinatown. Immediate protests from the Japanese ambassador ultimately led the school board to rescind its order; but the Board of Education's segregation efforts in reality were stymied only because President Theodore Roosevelt was able in 1907 to negotiate the so-called Gentleman's Agreement with Japan. Under this agreement, the American government agreed to end discrimination against Japanese living in the United States and Japan pledged to restrict visas of Japanese citizens to the United States to family members.

Even this accommodation failed to satisfy exclusionists, and in 1913 the California legislature enacted an alien land law barring the Japanese, who had become successful farmers, from owning agricultural land. As sentiment for the general restriction of immigration increased during the first three decades of the twentieth century, further limitations were placed on Asian immigration; in 1924 the Johnson-Reed Act prohibited completely all Asian immigration.

This anti-Asian agitation drew support from the same "scientific" sources that provided the intellectual respectability for racist thought described earlier (Matthews 1964). Ultimately, this fear of the "yellow peril" culminated in the forcible evacuation and relocation of more than 110,000 Japanese-Americans—more than half of them American citizens—by the federal government during World War II (Thomas and Nishimoto 1969; Grodzins 1966; Bosworth 1967; Kitano 1969; Daniels 1972). In Article 12, "Pacific Migration to the United States," Shirley Hune critically examines the ways in which Asian migration and adaptation to the United States has been conceptualized by historians and sociologists.

Despite early antipathy toward the Chinese and Japanese, and the particular hostility toward the Japanese during World War II, both groups have made substantial improvements in socioeconomic status. Both Chinese and Japanese today exceed all other racial groups, including whites, in educational attainments. By 1960, Japanese men and women had the highest median education of any racial group, and since then the educational achievements of Chinese- and Japanese-Americans have continued to increase. In Article 9 Charles Hirschman and Morrison Wong point out that by 1980 more than half of 20 to 21-year-old Asian-Americans were enrolled in school, compared with one-third of whites of the same age. So extraordinary have Asian educational attainments been that charges have been raised that many of the nation's most prestigious universities have placed limitations on the percentage of Asian students they would admit (Mathews 1987).

Similarly, a disproportionate percentage of Japanese and Chinese are found in professional occupational categories. Moreover, reflecting a decline in labor market discrimination against them, by the 1980s the income levels of American-born and immigrant Asians were not significantly different from those of whites who had comparable skills. However, there were differences in income levels among Asian groups: Japanese, Chinese, and Koreans earned more than whites; Filipinos, Asian Indians, and Vietnamese earned less. Moreover, poverty rates for native-born Chinese, Japanese, and Korean families were lower than for whites (U.S. Commission on Civil Rights 1988). Today the mean income of Japanese and Chinese men exceeds all other racial categories, including white males. Although they continue to encounter discrimination, the relative economic success of the Chinese and Japanese provides an interesting contrast to the status of other ethnic minorities in American society. Indeed, as we will consider more fully in Part 3, their socioeconomic success, in spite of the considerable discrimination against them, has led to the characterization of Asians as "model" minorities.

Later Immigrants: Filipinos, Koreans, Indochinese, and Indians

As the data in Figure 2.2 indicate, the numbers of several Asian groups — especially Chinese, Filipinos, Koreans, Indochinese, and Asian Indians — have recently increased dramatically. With the exception of the Chinese, whose presence in the United States was firmly established in the nineteenth century, these groups have emerged primarily since passage of the 1965 Immigration Reform Act.

Like Puerto Rico, the Philippine Islands were acquired by the United States from Spain in 1898 after the Spanish-American War, and the country has been economically dependent on the United States throughout the twentieth century, even after it gained its political independence in 1946. Because the Philippines was considered a territory of the United States, Filipinos were not initially subject to the immigration restrictions placed on other Asian groups. As residents of a U.S. possession, Filipinos were not included in the provisions of the 1924

Johnson-Reed Act that excluded immigration from elsewhere in Asia. Thus, when other Asian immigration was halted, Filipino laborers replaced the Chinese and Japanese as agricultural workers in California and Hawaii, and they also worked in the Alaskan salmon fisheries. However, in 1935, in the midst of the Great Depression, Filipino immigration was restricted as well. An annual quota of 50 Filipinos was established, and it was "liberalized" to 100 in 1946, when the Philippines was granted full political independence. Thus Filipino immigration between 1935 and 1965, when the Immigration Act eliminated national quotas, was negligible.

In 1960 Filipinos numbered only 176,000, a substantial portion of whom lived in Hawaii. The great preponderance of Filipino immigration to the United States, therefore, has come since 1965. The 1970 census recorded 343,000 Filipinos, and during the next decade their numbers more than doubled, to 782,000. Projections estimate that the Filipino population will have nearly doubled again by 1990, reaching a total of 1.4 million (Bouvier and Agresta 1987). However, because Filipinos, unlike other recent Asian immigrants, have not established identifiable ethnic communities, they have tended to be invisible, and their status as the largest Asian group in the United States today may therefore come as a surprise to many people. Similar to many other recent Asian immigrant groups, Filipino immigrants today have much higher educational levels than previous Filipino immigrants, and they have included high percentages of professional and technical workers, especially physicians and nurses. Despite these qualifications, Filipinos are much more likely than whites to work in occupations below their educational levels (Takaki 1989:434–436).

Koreans are also a relatively recent ethnic group in American society. Although a small number of Koreans, primarily agricultural laborers who migrated to Hawaii, were recorded in the census as early as 1910, as late as 1950 there were still fewer than 10,000 in the United States. A small portion of the increase since 1950 resulted from marriages of Koreans to members of the American armed forces stationed in Korea during and after the Korean War and from the adoption of Korean orphans.

However, most of the dramatic increase in Korean-Americans – to a projected 814,000 in 1990 – has occurred since the 1965 Immigration Act went into effect in 1968. Reflecting their relatively recent arrival, in 1980 nearly seven in ten Koreans (69.3 percent) had arrived in the previous decade (Xenos et al. 1987:256). Reflecting the post-Korean War modernization of South Korea, Koreans, like most other recent Asian immigrants, have had high educational attainments – for example, in 1980 more than 93 percent of Koreans had completed high school (Xenos 1987:270). Moreover, Koreans are more likely than the white population to be found in the two most prestigious and best paid occupational categories: executive, administrative, and managerial positions and the professions (Xenos et al. 1987). In contrast to the invisibility of the Filipinos, Korean communities have recently become very visible in several American cities, most notably New York City and Los Angeles. One of the most distinctive features of these communities has been the prominence of Korean small business enterprises, a phenomenon that is discussed in Part 3 (especially in Article 17, by Portes and Manning). Utilizing ethnic resources such as the *kae*, or rotating credit association, and capital accumulated in Korea, they have been especially prominent as proprietors of greengroceries, fish retail businesses, and dry cleaning establishments (Kim 1981; 1988; Light and Bonacich 1988; Takaki 1989:436–445).

The migration of Asian Indians to the United States began as early as the 1880s, when Hawaii's sugar planters recruited Indian workers to supply their labor needs. During the last decade of the nineteenth and the first two decades of the twentieth century small numbers of Indians – primarily male sojourners who worked in the railroad and lumber industries and in agriculture – immigrated to the U.S. mainland. Although these early immigrants were called "Hindus" by Americans, they included Muslims and Sikhs as well. Although Caucasian, they were included in the anti-Asian hysteria directed against the Chinese, Japanese, and Koreans and the subsequent legislation restricting Asian immigration. By the end of World War II, the Asian-Indian population numbered only 1,500 (Takaki 1989). Most Asian-Indians in the United States today, therefore, are products of the second wave of Indian migration begun after 1968. The 1980 census found 387,000 Indians, and this number is projected to increase to 684,000 by 1990 (Bouvier and Agresta 1987). Unlike earlier Indian immigrants, who were unskilled, this second wave has been overwhelmingly comprised of highly educated professionals. For example, 1980 census data revealed that nearly 90 percent of all Asian-Indian immigrants over the age of 25 had completed high school and two-thirds had completed college, in contrast to two-thirds of the total U.S. population who had completed high school and only one-sixth who had completed college (Bouvier and Gardner 1986:22).

Peoples from Indochina, the country's most recent arrivals, represent a diversity of ethnic groups from Vietnam, Laos, and Kampuchea (Cambodia). Most Indochinese have been refugees who have immigrated since the fall of Saigon in 1975. Projections place the total Indochinese population in 1990 at about 1.3 million, approximately two-thirds of whom are Vietnamese (Bouvier and Agresta 1987:292). It is anticipated that, because of the continuing social, political, and economic upheavals in southeast Asia, these numbers will continue to be reinforced in the near future. Many of the earliest Vietnamese immigrants were highly educated and possessed marketable technical skills. Later arrivals, including most Laotians and Kampucheans, have had fewer such resources and no established ethnic enclave to provide economic and social support. Consequently, their adjustment to American society has been much more difficult than that of many other recent Asian immigrants.

The recent increase of immigration from the Third World – especially from Latin American and Asia – has contributed substantially to some of the most dramatic changes in the ethnic composition of the United States in its history. Today nearly one-quarter of all Americans are of Native American, African, Hispanic, or Asian descent. By the year 2020 – approximately one generation – nearly one-third of the nation will be nonwhite (Quality Education for Minorities Project 1990:11). Any effort to comprehend both the short-term and long-term implications of these changes in the ethnic composition of American society must consider at least three basic factors: (1) recent changes in global political and economic structures; (2) structural changes in the American economy; and (3) the patterns of ethnic and racial relations that have previously been manifested in the American experience. In Parts 3 and 4 we will examine the nature of intergroup relations in, and ethnic adaptations to, American society. We will also speculate on how these recent trends may affect future patterns of race and ethnicity in the United States.

A Theory of the Origin of Ethnic Stratification

Donald L. Noel

While a great deal has been written about the nature and consequences of ethnic stratification, there have been few theoretical or empirical contributions regarding the causes of ethnic stratification.[1] It is the purpose of this paper to state a theory of the origin of ethnic stratification and then test it by applying the theory to an analysis of the origin of slavery in the United States. A number of recent contributions have clarified our knowledge of early Negro-white stratification[2] but there has been no attempt to analyze slavery's origin from the standpoint of a general theoretical framework. The present attempt focuses upon ethnocentrism, competition, and differential power as the key variables which together constitute the necessary and sufficient basis for the emergence and initial stabilization of ethnic stratification.

Ethnic stratification is, of course, only one type of stratification. Social stratification as a generic form of social organization is a structure of social inequality manifested via differences in prestige, power, and/or economic rewards. Ethnic stratification is a system of stratification wherein some relatively fixed group membership (e.g., race, religion, or nationality) is utilized as a major criterion for assigning social positions with their attendant differential rewards.

Prior to the emergence of ethnic stratification there must be a period of recurrent or continuous contact between the members of two or more distinct ethnic groups. This contact is an obvious requisite of ethnic stratification, but it is equally a requisite of equalitarian intergroup relations.

Hence, intergroup contact is assumed as given and not treated as a theoretical element because in itself it does not provide a basis for predicting whether ethnic relations will be equalitarian or inequalitarian (i.e., stratified). Distinct ethnic groups can interact without super-subordination.[3] Factors such as the nature of the groups prior to contact, the agents of contact, and the objectives of the contacting parties affect the likelihood of an equalitarian or inequalitarian outcome but only as they are expressed through the necessary and sufficient variables.[4]

THE THEORY AND ITS ELEMENTS

In contrast to intergroup contact per se, the presence of ethnocentrism, competition, and differential power provides a firm basis for predicting the emergence of ethnic stratification. Conversely, the absence of any one or more of these three elements means that ethnic stratification will not emerge. This is the essence of our theory. Each of the three elements is a variable but for present purposes they will be treated as attributes because our knowledge is not sufficiently precise to allow us to say what degrees of ethnocentrism, competition, and differential power are necessary to generate ethnic stratification. Recognition of the crucial importance of the three may stimulate greater efforts to precisely measure each of them. We shall examine each in turn.

Ethnocentrism is a universal characteristic of autonomous societies or ethnic groups. As introduced by Sumner, the concept refers to that

". . . view of things in which one's own group is the center of everything, and all others are scaled and rated with reference to it."[5] From this perspective the values of the in-group are equated with abstract, universal standards of morality and the practices of the in-group are exalted as better or more "natural" than those of any out-group. Such an orientation is essentially a matter of in-group glorification and not of hostility toward any specific out-group. Nevertheless, an inevitable consequence of ethnocentrism is the rejection or downgrading of all out-groups to a greater or lesser degree as a function of the extent to which they differ from the in-group. The greater the difference the lower will be the relative rank of any given out-group, but any difference at all is grounds for negative evaluation.[6] Hence, English and Canadian immigrants rank very high relative to other out-groups in American society, *but* they still rank below old American WASPs.[7]

Ethnocentrism is expressed in a variety of ways including mythology, condescension, and a double standard of morality in social relations. Becker has labeled this double standard a "dual ethic" in which in-group standards apply only to transactions with members of the in-group.[8] The outsider is viewed as fair game. Hence, intergroup economic relations are characterized by exploitation. Similarly, sexual relations between members of different groups are commonplace even when intermarriage is rare or prohibited entirely. The practice of endogamy is itself a manifestation of and, simultaneously, a means of reinforcing ethnocentrism. Endogamy is, indeed, an indication that ethnocentrism is present in sufficient degree for ethnic stratification to emerge.[9]

Insofar as district ethnic groups maintain their autonomy, mutual ethnocentrism will be preserved. Thus Indians in the Americas did not automatically surrender their ethnocentrism in the face of European technological and scientific superiority. Indeed, if the cultural strengths (including technology) of the out-group are not relevant to the values and goals of the in-group they will, by the very nature of ethnocentrism, be negatively defined. This is well illustrated in the reply (allegedly) addressed to the Virginia Commission in 1744 when it offered to educate six Indian youths at William and Mary:

Several of our young people were formerly brought up at Colleges of the Northern Provinces; they were instructed in all your sciences; but when they came back to us, they were bad runners, ignorant of every means of living in the woods, unable to bear either cold or hunger, knew neither how to build a cabin, take a deer or kill an enemy, spoke our language imperfectly, were therefore neither fit for hunters, warriors, or counsellors; they were totally good for nothing. We are, however, not the less obliged by your kind offer, though we decline accepting it; and to show our grateful Sense of it, if the Gentlemen of Virginia will send us a Dozen of their Sons we will take great care of their education, instruct them in all we know, and make Men of them.[10]

Ethnocentrism in itself need not lead to either interethnic conflict or ethnic stratification, however. The Tungus and Cossacks have lived in peace as politically independent but economically interdependent societies for several centuries. The groups remain racially and culturally dissimilar and each is characterized by a general ethnocentric preference for the in-group. This conflict potential is neutralized by mutual respect and admission by each that the other is superior in certain specific respects, by the existence of some shared values and interests, and by the absence of competition due to economic complementarity and low population density.[11]

The presence of competition, structured along ethnic lines, is an additional prerequisite for the emergence of ethnic stratification. Antonovsky has suggested that a discriminatory system of social relations requires both shared goals and scarcity of rewards,[12] and competition here refers to the interaction between two or more social units striving to achieve *the same scarce goal* (e.g., land or prestige). In the absence of shared goals members of the various ethnic groups involved in the contact situation would have, in the extreme case, mutually exclusive or nonoverlapping value hierarchies. If one group is not striving for a given goal, this reduces the likelihood of discrimination partly because members of the group are unlikely to be perceived as competitors for the goal. In addition, the indifference of one group toward the goal in effect reduces scarcity—i.e., fewer seekers enhance the probability of goal attainment by any one seeker. However, if the goal is still defined as scarce by members of one group they may seek to establish ethnic stratification in order to effectively exploit the labor of the indifferent group and thereby maximize goal attainment. In such a situation the labor (or other utility) of the indifferent group may be said to be the real object of competition. In any event the perceived scarcity of a socially valued goal is crucial and will stimulate the emergence of ethnic stratification unless each group perceives the other as: (1) disinterested in the relevant goal, *and* (2) nonutilitarian with respect to its own attainment of the goal.

In actuality the various goals of two groups involved in stable, complex interaction will invariably overlap to some degree and hence the likelihood of ethnic stratification is a function of the arena of competition. The arena includes the shared object(s) sought, the terms of the competition, and the relative adaptability of the groups involved.[13] Regarding the objects (or goals) of competition, the greater the number of objects subject to competition, the more intense the competition. Moreover, as Wagley and Harris observe, "It is important to know the objects of competition, for it would seem that the more vital or valuable the resource over which there is competition, the more intense is the conflict between the groups."[14] Barring total annihilation of one of the groups, these points can be extended to state that the more intense the competition or conflict the greater the likelihood – other things being equal – that it will culminate in a system of ethnic stratification. In other words, the number and significance of the scarce, common goals sought determine the degree of competition, which in turn significantly affects the probability that ethnic stratification will emerge.

The terms of the competition may greatly alter the probability of ethnic stratification, however, regardless of the intensity of the competition. The retention of a set of values or rules which effectively regulates – or moderates – ethnic interrelations is of particularly crucial significance. If a framework of regulative values fails to emerge, or breaks down, each group may seek to deny the other(s) the right to compete with the result that overt conflict emerges and culminates in annihilation, expulsion, or total subjugation of the less powerful group. If, in contrast, regulative values develop and are retained, competition even for vital goals need not result in ethnic stratification – or at least the span of stratification may be considerably constricted.[15]

Even where the groups involved are quite dissimilar culturally, the sharing of certain crucial values (e.g., religion or freedom, individualism, and equality) may be significant in preventing ethnic stratification. This appears to have been one factor in the enduring harmonious relations between the Cossacks and the Tungus. The influence of the regulative values upon the span of ethnic stratification is well illustrated by Tannenbaum's thesis regarding the differences between North American and Latin American slavery.[16] In the absence of a tradition of slavery the English had no established code prescribing the rights and duties of slaves and the racist ideology which evolved achieved its ultimate expression in the Dred Scott decision of 1857. This decision was highly consistent with the then widely held belief that the Negro "had no rights which the white man was bound to respect. . . ." By contrast the Iberian code accorded certain rights to the Latin American slave (including the right to own property and to purchase his freedom), which greatly restricted the extent of inequality between free man and slave.[17]

In addition to the regulative values, the structural opportunities for or barriers to upward mobility which are present in the society may affect the emergence and span of ethnic stratification. Social structural barriers such as a static, nonexpanding economy are a significant part of the terms of competition and they may be more decisive than the regulative values as regards the duration of the system. Finally, along with the goals and the terms of competition, the relative adaptive capacity of the groups involved is an aspect of competition which significantly affects the emergence of ethnic stratification.

Wagley and Harris assume that ethnic stratification is given and focus their analysis on the adaptive capacity of *the minority group* in terms of its effect upon the span and the duration of ethnic stratification. Thus they view adaptive capacity as:

> those elements of a minority's cultural heritage which provide it with a basis for competing more or less effectively with the dominant group, which afford protection against exploitation, which stimulate or retard its adaptation to the total social environment, and which facilitate or hinder its upward advance through the socioeconomic hierarchy.[18]

We shall apply the concept to an earlier point in the intergroup process—i.e., prior to the emergence of ethnic stratification—by broadening it to refer to those aspects of any ethnic group's sociocultural heritage which affect its adjustment to a given social and physical environment. The group with the greater adaptive capacity is apt to emerge as the dominant group[19] while the other groups are subordinated to a greater or lesser degree—i.e., the span of the stratification system will be great or slight—dependent upon the extent of their adaptive capacity relative to that of the emergent dominant group.

The duration, as well as the origin and span, of ethnic stratification will be markedly influenced by adaptive capacity. Once a people have become a minority, flexibility on their part is essential if they are to efficiently adjust and effectively compete within the established system of ethnic stratification and thereby facilitate achievement of equality. Sociocultural patterns are invariably altered by changing life conditions. However, groups vary in the alacrity with which they respond to changing conditions. A flexible minority group may facilitate the achievement of equality or even dominance by readily accepting modifications of their heritage which will promote efficient adaption to their subordination and to subsequent changes in life conditions.

Competition and ethnocentrism do not provide a sufficient explanation for the emergence of ethnic stratification. Highly ethnocentric groups involved in competition for vital objects will not generate ethnic stratification unless they are of such unequal power that one is able to impose its will upon the other.[20] Inequality of power is the defining characteristic of dominant and minority groups, and Lenski maintains that differential power is the foundation element in the genesis of any stratification system.[21] In any event differential power is absolutely essential to the emergence of ethnic stratification and the greater the differential the greater the span and durability of the system, other things being equal.

Technically, power is a component of adaptive capacity, as Wagley and Harris imply in their definition by referring to "protection against exploitation." Nevertheless, differential power exerts an effect independent of adaptive capacity in general and is of such crucial relevance for ethnic stratification as to warrant its being singled out as a third major causal variable. The necessity of treating it as a distinct variable is simply demonstrated by consideration of those historical cases where one group has the greater adaptive capacity in general but is subordinated because another group has greater (military) power. The Dravidians overrun by the Ayrans in ancient India and the Manchu conquest of China are illustrative cases.[22]

Unless the ethnic groups involved are unequal in power, intergroup relations will be characterized by conflict, symbiosis, or a pluralist equilibrium. Given intergroup competition, however, symbiosis is unlikely and conflict and pluralism are inevitably unstable. Any slight change in the existing balance of power may be sufficient to establish the temporary dominance of one group and this can be utilized to allow the emerging dominant group to perpetuate and enhance its position.[23]

Once dominance is established the group in power takes all necessary steps to restrict the now subordinated groups, thereby hampering their effectiveness as competitors,[24] and to institutionalize the emerging distribution of rewards and opportunities. Hence, since power tends to beget power, a slight initial alteration in the distribution of power can become the basis of a stable inequalitarian system.

We have now elaborated the central concepts and propositions of a theory of the emergence and initial stabilization of ethnic stratification. The theory can be summarized as follows. When distinct ethnic groups are brought into sustained contact (via migration, the emergence and expansion of the state, or internal differentiation of a previously homogeneous group), ethnic stratification will invariably follow if—and only if—the groups are characterized by a significant degree of ethnocentrism, competition, *and* differential power. Without ethnocentrism the groups would quickly merge and competition would not be structured along ethnic lines. Without competition there would be no motivation or rationale for instituting stratification along ethnic lines. Without differential power it would simply be impossible for one group to achieve dominance and impose subordination to its will and ideals upon the other(s).

The necessity of differential power is incontestable, but it could be argued that neither competition or ethnocentrism is dispensable. For example, perhaps extreme ethnocentrism independent of competition is sufficient motive for seeking to impose ethnic stratification. Certainly ethnocentrism could encourage efforts to promote continued sharp differentiation, but it would not by itself motivate stratification unless we assume the existence of a *need* for dominance or aggression. Conversely, given sociocultural differences, one group may be better prepared for and therefore able to more effectively exploit a given environment. Hence, this group would become economically dominant and might then perceive and pursue the advantages (especially economic) of ethnic stratification quite independent of ethnocentrism. On the other hand, while differential power and competition alone are clearly sufficient to generate stratification, a low degree of ethnocentrism could readily forestall *ethnic* stratification by permitting assimilation and thereby eliminating differential adaptive capacity. Ethnocentrism undeniably heightens awareness of ethnicity and thereby promotes the formation and retention of ethnic competition, but the crucial question is whether or not some specified degree of ethnocentrism is *essential* to the emergence of ethnic stratification. Since autonomous ethnic groups are invariably ethnocentric, the answer awaits more precise measures of ethnocentrism which will allow us to test hypotheses specifying the necessary degree of ethnocentrism.[25]

Given the present state of knowledge it seems advisable to retain both competition and ethnocentrism, as well as differential power, as integral elements of the theory. Our next objective, then, is to provide an initial test of the theory by applying it to an analysis of the genesis of slavery in the seventeenth century mainland North American colonies.

THE ORIGIN OF AMERICAN SLAVERY

There is a growing consensus among historians of slavery in the United States that Negroes were not initially slaves but that they were gradually reduced to a position of chattel slavery over several decades.[26] The historical record regarding their initial status is so vague and incomplete, however, that it is impossible to assert with finality that their status was initially no different from that of non-Negro indentured servants.[27] Moreover, while there is agreement that the statutory establishment of slavery was not widespread until the 1660s, there is disagreement regarding slavery's emergence in actual practice. The Handlins maintain that "The status of Negroes was that of servants; and so they were identified and treated down to the 1660s."[28] Degler and Jordan argue that this conclusion is not adequately documented and cite evidence indicating that some Negroes were slaves as early as 1640.[29]

Our central concern is to relate existing historical research to the theory elaborated above, *not* to attempt original historical research intended to resolve the controversy regarding the nature and extent of the initial status differences (if any) between white and Negro bondsmen. However, two findings emerging from the controversy are basic to our concern: (1) although the terms servant and slave were frequently used interchangeably, whites were never slaves in the sense of serving for life and conveying a like obligation to their offspring; and (2) many Negroes were not slaves in this sense at least as late as the 1660s. Concomitantly with the Negroes' descent to slavery, white servants gained increasingly liberal terms of indenture and, ultimately, freedom. The origin of slavery for the one group and the growth of freedom for the other are explicable in terms of our theory as a function of differences in ethnocentrism, the arena of competition, and power vis-à-vis the dominant group or class.[30]

Degler argues that the status of the Negro evolved in a framework of discrimination and therefore, "The important point is not the evolution of the legal status of the slave, but the fact that discriminatory legislation regarding the Negro long preceded any legal definition of slavery."[31] The first question then becomes one of explaining this differential treatment which foreshadowed the descent to slavery. A major element in the answer is implied by the Handlins' observation that "The rudeness of the Negroes' manners, the strangeness of their languages, the difficulty of communicating to them English notions of morality and proper behavior occasioned sporadic laws to regulate their conduct."[32] By itself this implies a contradiction of their basic thesis that Negro and white indentured servants were treated similarly prior to 1660. They maintain, however, that there was nothing unique nor decisive in this differential treatment of Negroes, for such was also accorded various Caucasian outgroups in this period.[33] While Jordan dismisses the Handlins' evidence as largely irrelevant to the point and Degler feels that it is insufficient, Degler acknowledges that "Even Irishmen, who were white, Christian, and European, were held to be literally 'beyond the Pale,' and some were even referred to as 'slaves'."[34] Nevertheless, Degler contends that the overall evidence justifies his conclusion that Negroes were generally accorded a lower position than any white, bound or free.

That the English made status distinctions between various out-groups is precisely what one would expect, however, given the nature of ethnocentrism. The degree of ethnocentric rejection is primarily a function of the degree of difference, and Negroes were markedly different from the dominant English in color, nationality, language, religion, and other aspects of culture.[35] The differential treatment of Negroes was by no means entirely due to a specifically anti-Negro *color* prejudice. Indeed, color was not initially the most important factor in determining the relative status of Negroes; rather, the fact that they were non-Christian was of major significance.[36] Although beginning to lose its preeminence, religion was still the central institution of society in the seventeenth century and religious prejudice toward non-Christians or heathens was widespread. The priority of religious over color prejudice is amply demonstrated by analysis of the early laws and court decisions pertaining to Negro-white sexual relations. These sources explicitly reveal greater concern with Christian-non-Christian than with white-Negro unions.[37] During and after the 1660s laws regulating racial intermarriage arose but for some time their emphasis was generally, if not invariably, upon religion, nationality, or some basis of differentiation other than race per se. For example, a Maryland law of 1681 described marriages of white women with Negroes as lascivious and "to the disgrace not only of the English but also [sic] of many *other Christian* Nations,"[38] Moreover, the laws against Negro-white marriage seem to have been rooted much more in economic considerations than they were in any concern for white racial purity.[39] In short, it was not a simple color prejudice but a marked degree of ethnocentrism, rooted in a multitude of salient differences, which combined with competition and differential power to reduce Negroes to the status of slaves.[40]

Degler has noted that Negroes initially lacked a status in North America and thus almost any kind of status could have been worked out.[41] Given a different competitive arena, a more favorable status blurring the sharp ethnic distinctions could have evolved. However, as the demand for labor in an expanding economy began to exceed the supply, interest in lengthening the term of indenture arose.[42] This narrow economic explanation of the origin of slavery has been challenged on the grounds that slavery appeared equally early in the northern colonies although there were too few Negroes there to be of economic significance.[43] This seemingly decisive point is largely mitigated by two considerations.

First, in the other colonies it was precisely *the few* who did own slaves who were not only motivated by vested interests but were also the men of means and local power most able to secure a firm legal basis for slavery.[44] The distribution of power and motivation was undoubtedly similar and led to the same consequences in New England. For the individual retainer of Negro servants the factual and legal redefinition of Negroes as chattel constitutes a vital economic interest whether or not the number of slaves is sufficient to vitally affect the economy of the colony. Our knowledge of the role of the elite in the establishment of community mores suggests that this constitutes at least a partial explanation of the northern laws.[45] In addition, the markedly smaller number of Negroes in the North might account for the fact that "although enactments in the northern colonies recognized the legality of lifetime servitude, no effort was made to require all Negroes to be placed in that condition."[46] We surmise that the laws were passed at the behest of a few powerful individuals who had relatively many Negro servants and were indifferent to the status of Negroes in general so long as their own vested interests were protected.

The explanation for the more all-encompassing laws of the southern colonies is rooted in the greater homogeneity of interests of the southern elite. In contrast to the northern situation, the men of power in the southern colonies were predominantly planters who were unified in their need for large numbers of slaves. The margin of profit in agricultural production for the commercial market was such that the small landholder could not compete and the costs of training and the limitations on control (by the planter) which were associated with indentured labor made profitable exploitation of such labor increasingly difficult.[47] Hence, it was not the need for labor per se which was critical for the establishment of the comprehensive southern slave system but rather the requirements of the emerging economic system for a particular kind of labor. In short, the southern power elite uniformly needed slave labor while only certain men of power shared this need in the North, and hence the latter advocated slave laws but lacked the power (or did not feel the need) to secure the all-encompassing laws characteristic of the southern colonies.

There is a second major consideration in explaining the existence of northern slavery. Men do not compete only for economic ends. They also compete for prestige and many lesser objects, and there is ample basis for suggesting that prestige competition was a significant factor in the institutionalization of slavery, North and South. Degler calls attention to the prestige motive when he discusses the efforts to establish a feudal aristocracy in seventeenth-century New York, Maryland, and the Carolinas. He concludes that these efforts failed because the manor was "dependent upon the scarcity of land."[48] The failure of feudal aristocracy in no way denies the fundamental human desire for success or prestige. Indeed, this failure opened the society. It emphasized success and mobility for "it meant that wealth, rather than family or tradition, would be the primary determinant of social stratification."[49] Although the stress was on economic success, there were other gains associated with slavery to console those who did not achieve wealth. The desire for social prestige derivable from "membership in a superior caste" undoubtedly provided motivation and support for slavery

among both northern and southern whites, slaveholders and nonslaveholders.[50]

The prestige advantage of slavery would have been partially undercut, especially for nonslaveholders, by enslavement of white bondsmen, but it is doubtful that this was a significant factor in their successfully eluding hereditary bondage. Rather the differential treatment of white and Negro bondsmen, ultimately indisputable and probably present from the very beginning, is largely attributable to differences in ethnocentrism and relative power. There was little or no ethnocentric rejection of the majority of white bondsmen during the seventeenth century because most of them were English.[51] Moreover, even the detested Irish and other non-English white servants were culturally and physically much more similar to the English planters than were the Africans. Hence, the planters clearly preferred white bondsmen until the advantages of slavery became increasingly apparent in the latter half of the seventeenth century.[52]

The increasing demand for labor after the mid-seventeenth century had divergent consequences for whites and blacks. The colonists became increasingly concerned to encourage immigration by counteracting "the widespread reports in England and Scotland that servants were harshly treated and bound in perpetual slavery" and by enacting "legislation designed to improve servants' conditions and to enlarge the prospect of a meaningful release, a release that was not the start of a new period of servitude, but of life as a free-man and landowner."[53] These improvements curtailed the exploitation of white servants without directly affecting the status of the Africans.

Farthest removed from the English, least desired, [the Negro] communicated with no friends who might be deterred from following. Since his coming was involuntary, nothing that happened to him would increase or decrease his numbers. *To raise the status of Europeans by shortening their terms would ultimately increase the available hands by inducing their compatriots to emigrate; to reduce the Negro's term would produce an immediate loss and no ultimate gain. By mid-century the servitude of Negroes seems generally lengthier than that of whites; and thereafter, the consciousness dawns that the blacks will toil for the whole of their lives. . . .*[54]

119

The planters and emerging agrarian capitalism were unconstrained in a planter-dominated society with no traditional institutions to exert limits. In this context even the common law tradition helped promote slavery.[55]

Ethnocentrism set the Negroes apart but their almost total lack of power and effective spokesmen, in contrast to white indentured servants, was decisive in their enslavement. Harris speaks directly to the issue and underscores the significance of (organized) power for the emergence of slavery:

The facts of life in the New World were such . . . that Negroes, being the most defenseless of all the immigrant groups, were discriminated against and exploited more than any others. . . . Judging from the very nasty treatment suffered by the white indentured servants, it was obviously not sentiment which prevented the Virginia planters from enslaving their fellow Englishmen. They undoubtedly would have done so had they been able to get away with it. but such a policy was out of the question as long as there was a King and a Parliament in England.[56]

The Negroes, in short, did not have any organized external government capable of influencing the situation in their favor.[57] Moreover, "there was no one in England or in the colonies to pressure for the curtailment of the Negro's servitude or to fight for his future."[58]

The Negroes' capacity to adapt to the situation and effectively protest in their own behalf was greatly hampered by their cultural diversity and lack of unification. They did not think of themselves as "a kind." They did not subjectively share a common identity and thus they lacked the group solidarity necessary to effectively "act as a unit in competition with other groups."[59] Consciousness of shared fate is essential to effective unified action but it generally develops only gradually as the members of a particular social category realize that they are being treated alike despite their differences. "People who find themselves set apart eventually come to recognize their common interests," but for those who share a subordinate position common identification usually emerges "only after repeated experiences of denial and humiliation."[60] The absence of a shared identification among seventeenth-century Negroes reflected the absence of a shared heritage from which to construct identity, draw

strength, and organize protest. Hence, Negroes were easily enslaved and reduced to the status of chattel. This point merits elaboration.

We have defined adaptive capacity in terms of a group's sociocultural heritage as it affects adjustment to the environment. Efficient adaptation may require the members of a group to modify or discard a great deal of their heritage. A number of factors, including ethnocentrism and the centrality of the values and social structures requiring modification, affect willingness to alter an established way of life.[61] Even given a high degree of willingness, however, many groups simply have not possessed the cultural complexity or social structural similarity to the dominant group necessary to efficient adaptation. Many Brazilian and United States Indian tribes, for example, simply have not had the knowledge (e.g., of writing, money, markets, etc.) or the structural similarity to their conquerors (e.g., as regards the division of labor) necessary to protect themselves from exploitation and to achieve a viable status in an emerging multiethnic society.[62]

By comparison with most New World Indians the sociocultural heritage of the Africans was remarkably favorable to efficient adaptation.[63] However, the discriminatory framework within which white-Negro relations developed in the seventeenth century ultimately far outweighed the cultural advantages of the Negroes vis-à-vis the Indians in the race for status.[64] The Negroes from any given culture were widely dispersed and their capacity to adapt *as a group* was thereby shattered. Like the Negroes, the Indians were diverse culturally but they retained their cultural heritage and social solidarity, and they were more likely to resist slavery because of the much greater probability of reunion with their people following escape. Hence, Negroes were preferred over Indians as slaves both because their cultural background had better prepared them for the slave's role in the plantation system (thus enhancing the profits of the planters) and because they lacked the continuing cultural and group support which enabled the Indians to effectively resist slavery.[65] By the time the Africans acquired the dominant English culture and social patterns *and* a sense of shared fate, their inability to work out a more favorable adaptation was assured by the now established distribution of power and by the socialization processes facilitating acceptance of the role of slave.[66]

CONCLUSION

We conclude that ethnocentrism, competition, and differential power provide a comprehensive explanation of the origin of slavery in the seventeenth-century English colonies. The Negroes were clearly more different from the English colonists than any other group (*except* the Indians) by almost any criterion, physical or cultural, that might be selected as a basis of social differentiation. Hence, the Negroes were the object of a relatively intense ethnocentric rejection from the beginning. The opportunity for great mobility characteristic of a frontier society created an arena of competition which dovetailed with this ethnocentrism. Labor, utilized to achieve wealth, and prestige were the primary objects of this competition. These goals were particularly manifest in the southern colonies, but our analysis provides a rationale for the operation of the same goals as sources of motivation to institutionalize slavery in the northern colonies also.

The terms of the competition for the Negro's labor are implicit in the evolving pattern of differential treatment of white and Negro bondsmen prior to slavery and in the precarious position of free Negroes. As slavery became institutionalized the moral, religious, and legal values of the society were increasingly integrated to form a highly consistent complex which acknowledged no evil in the "peculiar institution."[67] Simultaneously, Negroes were denied any opportunity to escape their position of lifetime, inheritable servitude. Only by the grace of a generous master, not by any act of his own, could a slave achieve freedom and, moreover, there were "various legal structures aimed at impeding or discouraging the process of private manumission."[68] The rigidity of the "peculiar institution" was fixed before the Negroes acquired sufficient common culture, sense of shared fate, and identity to be able to effectively challenge the system. This lack of unity was a major determinant of the Africans' poor adaptive capacity as a group. They lacked the social solidarity and common cultural resources essential to organized resistance and thus in the absence of intervention by a powerful ex-

ternal ally they were highly vulnerable to exploitation.

The operation of the three key factors is well summarized by Stampp:

> *Neither the provisions of their charters nor the policy of the English government limited the power of colonial legislatures to control Negro labor as they saw fit. . . . Their unprotected condition encouraged the trend toward special treatment, and their physical and cultural differences provided handy excuses to justify it. . . . [T]he landholders' growing appreciation of the advantages of slavery over the older forms of servitude gave a powerful impetus to the growth of the new labor system.*[69]

In short, the present theory stresses that *given* ethnocentrism, the Negroes' lack of power, and the dynamic arena of competition in which they were located, their ultimate enslavement was inevitable. The next task is to test the theory further, incorporating modifications as necessary, by analyzing subsequent accommodations in the pattern of race relations in the United States and by analyzing the emergence of various patterns of ethnic stratification in other places and eras.

ENDNOTES

1. The same observation regarding social stratification in general has recently been made by Gerhard Lenski, *Power and Privilege*, New York: McGraw-Hill, 1966, p. ix.

2. See Joseph Boskin, "Race Relations in Seventeenth Century America: The Problem of the Origins of Negro Slavery," *Sociology and Social Research*, 49 (July, 1965), pp. 446–455, including references cited therein; and David B. Davis, *The Problem of Slavery in Western Culture*, Ithaca: Cornell U., 1966.

3. A classic example is provided by Ethel John Lindgren, "An Example of Culture Contact Without Conflict: Reindeer Tungus and Cossacks of Northwest Manchuria," *American Anthropologist*, 40 (October-December, 1938), pp. 605–621.

4. The relevance of precontact and of the nature and objectives of the contacting agents for the course of intergroup relations has been discussed by various scholars, including Edward B. Reuter in his editor's "Introduction" to *Race and Culture Contacts*, New York: McGraw-Hill, 1934, pp. 1–18; and Clarence E. Glick, "Social Roles and Types in Race Relations" in Andrew W. Lind, editor, *Race Relations in World Perspective*, Honolulu: U. of Hawaii, 1955, pp. 239–262.

5. William G. Summer, *Folkways*, Boston: Ginn, 1940, p. 13. The essence of ethnocentrism is well conveyed by Catton's observation that "Ethnocentrism makes us see out-group behavior as deviation from in-group mores rather than as adherence to out-group mores." William R. Catton, Jr., "The Development of Sociological Thought" in Robert E.L. Faris, editor, *Handbook of Modern Sociology*, Chicago: Rand McNally, 1964, p. 930.

6. Williams observes that "in various *particular* ways an out-group may be seen as superior" insofar as its members excel in performance vis-à-vis certain norms that the two groups hold in common (e.g., sobriety or craftsmanship in the production of a particular commodity). Robin M. Williams, Jr., *Stranger Next Door*, Englewood Cliffs, N.J.: Prentice-Hall, 1964, p. 22 (emphasis added). A similar point is made by Marc J. Swartz, "Negative Ethnocentrism," *Journal of Conflict Resolution*, 5 (March, 1961), pp. 75–81. It is highly unlikely, however, that the out-group will be so consistently objectively superior in the realm of shared values as to be seen as generally superior to the in-group unless the in-group is subordinate to or highly dependent upon the out-group.

7. Emory S. Bogardus, *Social Distance*, Yellow Springs: Antioch, 1959.

8. Howard P. Becker, *Man in Reciprocity*, New York: Praeger, 1956, Ch. 15.

9. Endogamy is an overly stringent index of the degree of ethnocentrism essential to ethnic stratification and is not itself a prerequisite of the emergence of ethnic stratification. However, where endogamy does not precede ethnic stratification, it is a seemingly invariable consequence. Compare this position with that of Charles Wagley and Marvin Harris, who treat ethnocentrism and endogamy as independent structural requisites of intergroup hostility and conflict. See *Minorities in the New World*, New York: Columbia, 1958, pp. 256–263.

10. Quoted in T. Walker Wallbank and Alastair M. Taylor, *Civilization: Past and Present*, Chicago: Scott, Foresman, 1949, rev. ed., Vol. 1. pp. 559–560. The offer and counter-offer also provide an excellent illustration of mutual ethnocentrism.

11. Lindgren, *op. cit.*

12. Aaron Antonovsky, "The Social Meaning of Discrimination," *Phylon*, 21 (Spring, 1960), pp. 81–95.

13. This analysis of the arena of competition is a modification of the analysis by Wagley and Harris, *op. cit.*, esp. pp. 263–264. These authors limit the concept "arena" to the objects sought *and* the regulative values which determine opportunity to compete and then partly confound their components by including the regulative values, along with adaptive capacity and the instruments necessary to compete, as part of the "terms" of competition.

14. *Ibid.*, p. 263. They suggest that competition for scarce subsistence goals will produce more intense conflict than competition for prestige symbols or other culturally defined goals.

15. Discussing the ideological aspect of intergroup relations, Wagley and Harris note that equalitarian creeds have generally not been effective in preventing ethnic stratification. *Ibid.*, pp. 280ff. The operation of ethnocentrism makes it very easy for the boundaries of the in-group to become the boundaries of adherence to group values.

16. Frank Tannenbaum, *Slave and Citizen: The Negro in the Americas*, New York: Random House, 1963.

17. *Ibid.*, esp. pp. 49ff. Marvin Harris has criticized Tannenbaum's thesis, arguing that the rights prescribed by the Iberian code were largely illusory and that there is no certainty that *slaves* were treated better in Latin America. Harris in turn provides a functional (economic necessity) explanation for the historical difference in treatment of *free* Negroes in the two continents. See Marvin Harris, *Patterns of Race in the Americas*, New York: Walker, 1964, esp. Chs. 6 and 7.

18. Wagley and Harris, *op. cit.*, p. 264.

19. This point is explicitly made by Tamotsu Shibutani and Kian M. Kwan, Ethnic Stratification: A Comparative Approach, New York: Macmillan, 1965, p. 147; see also Ch. 9.

20. This point is made by Antonovsky, *op. cit.*, esp. p. 82, and implied by Wagley and Harris in their discussion of the role of the state in the formation of minority groups, *op. cit.*, esp. pp. 240–244. Stanley Lieberson's recent modification of Park's cycle theory of race relations also emphasizes the importance of differential power as a determinant of the outcome of intergroup contacts. See "A Societal Theory of Race and Ethnic Relations," *American Sociological Review*, 26 (December, 1961), pp. 902–910.

21. Lenski, *op. cit.*, esp. Ch. 3.

22. See Wallbank and Taylor, *op. cit.*, p. 95; and Shibutani and Kwan, *op. cit.*, pp. 129–130.

23. See *ibid.*, esp. Chs. 6, 9, and 12; and Richard A. Schermerhorn, *Society and Power*, New York: Random House, 1961, pp. 18–26.

24. Shibutani and Kwan observe that dominance rests upon victory in the competitive process and that competition between groups is eliminated or greatly reduced once a system of ethnic stratification is stabilized, *op. cit.*, pp. 146 and 235, and Ch. 12. The extent to which competition is actually stifled is highly variable, however, as Wagley and Harris note in their discussion of minority adaptive capacity and the terms of competition, *op. cit.*, pp. 263ff.

25. The issue is further complicated by the fact that the necessary degree of any one of the three elements may vary as a function of the other two.

26. The main relevant references in the recent litera-ture include Carl N. Degler, *Out of Our Past*, New York: Harper and Row, 1959 and "Slavery and the Genesis of American Race Prejudice," *Comparative Studies in Society and History*, 2 (October, 1959), pp. 49–66; Stanley M. Elkins, *Slavery: A Problem in American Institutional and Intellectual Life*, Chicago: U. of Chicago, 1959; Oscar and Mary F. Handlin, "Origins of the Southern Labor System," *William and Mary Quarterly*, 3rd Series, 7 (April, 1950), pp. 199–222; and Winthrop D. Jordan, "Modern Tensions and the Origins of American Slavery," *The Journal of Southern History*, 28 (February, 1962), pp. 18–30, and *White over Black*, Chapel-Hill: U. of North Carolina, 1968. See also Boskin, *op. cit.*, and "Comment" and "Reply" by the Handlins and Degler in the cited volume of *Comparative Studies* . . . , pp. 488–495.

27. Jordan, *The Journal* . . . , p. 22.

28. Handlin and Handlin, *op. cit.*, p. 203.

29. Degler, *Comparative Studies* . . . , pp. 52–56 and Jordan, *The Journal* . . . , pp. 23–27 and *White over Black*, pp. 73–74. Also see Elkins, *op. cit.*, pp. 38–42 (esp. fns. 16 and 19).

30. Our primary concern is with the emergence of Ne-gro slavery but the theory also explains how white bondsmen avoided slavery. Their position vis-à-vis the dominant English was characterized by a different "value" of at least two of the key variables.

31. Degler, *Out of Our Past*, p. 35. Bear in mind, how-ever, that slavery was not initially institutionalized in law or in the mores.

32. Handlin and Handlin, *op. cit.*, pp. 208–209.

33. *Ibid*. They note that "It is not necessary to resort to racist assumptions to account for such measures; . . . [for immigrants in a strange environment] longed . . . for the company of familiar men and singled out to be welcomed those who were most like themselves." See pp. 207–211 and 214.

34. Jordan, *The Journal* . . . , esp. pp. 27 (fn. 29) and 29 (fn. 34); and Degler, *Out of Our Past*, p. 30.

35. Only the aboriginal Indians were different from the English colonists to a comparable degree and they were likewise severely dealt with via a policy of exclusion and annihilation after attempts at enslavement failed. See Boskin, *op. cit.*, p. 453; and Jordan, *White over Black*, pp. 85–92.

36. The priority of religious over racial prejudice and discrimination in the early seventeenth century is noted in *ibid.*, pp. 97–98 and by Edgar J. McManus, *A History of Negro Slavery in New York*, Syracuse: Syracuse U., 1966, esp. pp. 11–12.

37. Jordan, *The Journal* . . . , p. 28 and *White over Black*, pp. 78–80.

38. Quoted in *ibid.*, pp. 79–80 (emphasis added). Also see pp. 93–97, however, where Jordan stresses the

necessity of carefully interpreting the label "Chris-tian."

39. See Handlin and Handlin, *op. cit.*, pp. 213–216; and W.D. Zabel, "Interracial Marriage and the Law," *The Atlantic* (October, 1965), pp. 75–79.

40. The distinction between ethnocentrism (the rejec-tion of out-groups *in general* as a function of in-group glorification) and prejudice (hostility toward the mem-bers of a *specific* group because they are members of that group) is crucial to the controversy regarding the direction of causality between discrimination, slavery, and prejudice. Undoubtedly these variables are mutu-ally causal to some extent but Harris, *op. cit.*, esp. pp. 67–70, presents evidence that prejudice is primarily a consequence and is of minor importance as a cause of slavery.

41. Degler, *Comparative Studies* . . . , p. 51. See also Boskin, *op. cit.*, pp. 449 and 454 (esp. fn. 14); Elkins, *op. cit.*, pp. 39–42 (esp. fn. 16); and Kenneth M. Stampp, *The Peculiar Institution*, New York: Knopf, 1956, p. 21. The original indeterminacy of the Negroes' status is reminiscent of Blumer's "sense of group position" theory of prejudice and, in light of Blumer's theory, is consis-tent with the belief that there was no widespread preju-dice toward Negroes prior to the institutionalization of slavery. See Herbert Blumer, "Race Prejudice as a Sense of Group Position," *Pacific Sociological Review*, 1 (Spring, 1958), pp. 3–7.

42. Handlin and Handlin, *op. cit.*, p. 210. Differential power made this tactic as suitable to the situation of Negro bondsmen as it was unsuitable in regard to white bondsmen.

43. Degler acknowledges that the importance of per-petuating a labor force indispensable to the economy later became a crucial support of slavery but he denies that the need for labor explains the origin of slavery. His explanation stresses prior discrimination which, in the terms of the present theory, was rooted in ethno-centrism and differential power. See *Comparative Studies* . . . , including the "Reply" to the Handlins, "Comment"; and *Out of Our Past*, pp. 35–38 and 162–168.

44. Elkins, *op. cit.*, pp. 45 (esp. fn. 26) and 48.

45. Historical precedent is provided by the finding that "The vagrancy laws emerged in order to provide the powerful landowners with a ready supply of cheap labor." See William J. Chambliss, "A Sociological Anal-ysis of the Law of Vagrancy," *Social Problems*, 12 (Sum-mer, 1964), pp. 67–77. Jordan, *White over Black*, pp. 67 and 69, provides evidence that the economic advan-tages of slavery were clearly perceived in the northern colonies.

46. Elkins, *op. cit.*, p. 41 (fn. 19).

47. By the 1680s "The point had clearly passed when white servants could realistically, on any long-term ap-

praisal, be considered preferable to Negro slaves." *Ibid.*, p. 48.

48. Degler, *Out of Our Past*, p. 3. Also see Hubert M. Blalock, Jr., *Toward a Theory of Minority Group Relations*, New York: Wiley, 1967, pp. 44–48.

49. Degler, *Out of Our Past*, p. 5; see also pp. 45–50. Elkins, *op. cit.*, esp. pp. 43–44, also notes the early emphasis on personal success and mobility.

50. Stampp, *op. cit.*, pp. 29–33, esp. 32–33. Also see J.D.B. DeBow, "The Interest in Slavery of the Southern Non-Slaveholder," reprinted in Eric L. McKitrick, editor, *Slavery Defended: The Views of the Old South*, Englewood Cliffs, N.J.: Prentice-Hall, 1963, pp. 169–177.

51. Stampp, *op. cit.*, p. 16; and Degler, *Out of Our Past*, pp. 50–51. Consistent with the nature of ethnocentrism, "The Irish and other aliens, less desirable, at first received longer terms. But the realization that such discrimination retarded 'the peopling of the country' led to an extension of the identical privilege to all Christians." Handlin and Handlin, *op. cit.*, pp. 210–211.

52. Elkins, *op. cit.*, pp. 40 and 48; and Handlin and Handlin, *op. cit.*, pp. 207–208.

53. *Ibid.*, p. 210.

54. *Ibid.*, p. 211 (emphasis added). That the need for labor led to improvements in the status of white servants seems very likely but Degler in *Comparative Studies . . .* effectively challenges some of the variety of evidence presented by the Handlins, *op. cit.*, pp. 210 and 213–214 and "Comment."

55. Elkins, *op. cit.*, pp. 38 (fn. 14), 42 (fn. 22), 43, and 49–52; and Jordan, *White over Black*, pp. 49–51.

56. Harris *op. cit.*, pp. 69–70.

57. The effectiveness of intervention by an external government is illustrated by the halting of Indian emigration to South Africa in the 1860s as a means of protesting "the indignities to which indentured 'coolies' were subjected in Natal, . . ." See Pierre L. van den Berghe, *South Africa, A Study in Conflict*, Middletown: Wesleyan U., 1965, p. 250.

58. Boskin, *op. cit.*, p. 448. Also see Stampp. *op. cit.*, p. 22; and Elkins, *op. cit.*, pp. 49–52.

59. Shibutani and Kwan, *op. cit.*, p. 42. See also William O. Brown, "Race Consciousness among South African Natives," *American Journal of Sociology*, 40 (March, 1935), pp. 569–581.

60. Shibutani and Kwan, *op. cit.*, Ch. 8, esp. pp. 202 and 212.

61. See the discussion in Brewton Berry, *Race and Ethnic Relations*, Boston: Houghton-Mifflin, 1965, 3rd ed. esp. pp. 147–149; Shibutani and Kwan, *op. cit.*, esp. pp. 217f.; and Wagley and Harris, *op. cit.*, pp. 40–44.

62. *Ibid.*, pp. 15–86 and 265–268.

63. *Ibid.*, p. 269; Harris, *op. cit.*, p. 14; and Stampp, *op. cit.*, pp. 13 and 23.

64. The Indians were also discriminated against but to a much lesser extent. The reasons for this differential are discussed by Jordan, *White over Black*, pp. 89–90; and Stampp, *op. cit.*, pp. 23–24.

65. Harris, *op. cit.*, pp. 14–16, an otherwise excellent summary of the factors favoring the enslavement of Negroes rather than Indians, overlooks the role of sociocultural support. The importance of this support is clearly illustrated by the South African policy of importing Asians in preference to the native Africans who strenuously resisted enslavement and forced labor. Shibutani and Kwan, *op. cit.*, p. 126. Sociocultural unity was also a significant factor in the greater threat of revolt posed by the Helots in Sparta as compared to the heterogeneous slaves in Athens. Alvin W. Gouldner, *Enter Plato*, New York: Basic Books, 1965, p. 32.

66. Shibutani and Kwan, *op. cit.*, esp. Chs. 10–12. Stampp observes that the plantation trained Negroes to be slaves, not free men, *op. cit.*, p. 12. Similarly, Wagley and Harris note that the Negroes were poorly prepared for survival in a free-market economic system even when they were emancipated, *op. cit.*, p. 269.

67. Davis asserts that while slavery has always been a source of tension, "in Western culture it was associated with certain religious and philosophical doctrines that gave it the highest sanction." *Op. cit.*, p. ix.

68. Wagley and Harris, *op. cit.*, p. 124.

69. Stampp, *op. cit.*, p. 22.

The Declining Significance of Race

William Julius Wilson

Race relations in the United States have undergone fundamental changes in recent years, so much so that now the life chances of individual blacks have more to do with their economic class position than with their day-to-day encounters with whites. In earlier years the systematic efforts of whites to suppress blacks were obvious to even the most insensitive observer. Blacks were denied access to valued and scarce resources through various ingenious schemes of racial exploitation, discrimination, and segregation, schemes that were reinforced by elaborate ideologies of racism.

But the situation has changed. However determinative such practices were in the previous efforts of the black population to achieve racial equality, and however significant they were in the creation of poverty-stricken ghettos and a vast underclass of black proletarians – that massive population at the very bottom of the social class ladder plagued by poor education and low-paying, unstable jobs – they do not provide a meaningful explanation of the life chances of black Americans today. The traditional patterns of interaction between blacks and whites, particularly in the labor market, have been fundamentally altered.

NEW AND TRADITIONAL BARRIERS

In the pre-Civil War period, and in the latter half of the nineteenth through the first half of the twentieth century, the continuous and explicit efforts of whites to construct racial barriers profoundly affected the lives of black Americans. Racial oppression was designed, overt, and easily documented. As the nation has entered the latter half of the twentieth century, however, many of the traditional barriers have crumbled under the weight of the political, social, and economic changes of the civil rights era. A new set of obstacles has emerged from basic structural shifts in the economy.

These obstacles are therefore impersonal, but may prove to be even more formidable for certain segments of the black population. Specifically, whereas the previous barriers were usually designed to control and restrict the entire black population, the new barriers create hardships essentially for the black underclass; whereas the old barriers were based explicitly on the racial motivations derived from intergroup contact, the new barriers have racial significance only in their consequences, not in their origins. In short, whereas the old barriers portrayed the pervasive features of racial oppression, the new barriers indicate an important and emerging form of class subordination.

It would be shortsighted to view the traditional forms of racial segregation and discrimination as having essentially disappeared in contemporary America; the presence of blacks is still firmly resisted in various institutions and social arrangements, for example, residential areas and private social clubs. However, in the economic sphere class has become more important than race in determining black access to privilege and power. It is clearly evident in this connection that many talented and educated blacks are now entering positions of prestige and influence at a rate comparable to or, in some situations, exceeding that of whites with equivalent qualifications. It is

Reprinted from *Society,* Jan./Feb. 1978 by permission of the author and The University of Chicago Press. © 1978 by The University of Chicago Press.

equally clear that the black underclass is in a hopeless state of economic stagnation, falling further and further behind the rest of society.

THREE STAGES
OF AMERICAN RACE RELATIONS

American society has experienced three major stages of black-white contact, and each stage embodies a different form of racial stratification structured by the particular arrangement of both the economy and the polity. Stage one coincides with antebellum slavery and the early postbellum era and may be designated the period of *plantation economy and racial-caste oppression.* Stage two begins in the last quarter of the nineteenth century and ends at roughly the New Deal era, and may be identified as the period of *industrial expansion, class conflict, and racial oppression.* Finally, stage three is associated with the modern, industrial, post-World War II era which really began to crystallize during the 1960s and 1970s, and may be characterized as the period of *progressive transition from race inequalities to class inequalities.* The different periods can be identified as the preindustrial, industrial, and modern industrial stages of American race relations, respectively.

Although this abbreviated designation of the periods of American race relations seems to relate racial change to fundamental economic changes rather directly, it bears repeating that the different stages of race relations are structured by the unique arrangements and interaction of the economy and polity. More specifically, although there was an economic basis of structured racial inequality in the preindustrial and industrial periods of race relations, the polity more or less interacted with the economy either to reinforce patterns of racial stratification or to mediate various forms of racial conflict. Moreover, in the modern industrial period race relations have been shaped as much by important economic changes as by important political changes. Indeed, it would not be possible to understand fully the subtle and manifest changes in race relations in the modern industrial period without recognizing the dual and often reciprocal influence of structural changes in the economy and political changes in the state. Thus different systems of production and/or different arrange-

ments of the polity have imposed different constraints on the way in which racial groups have interacted in the United States, constraints that have structured the relations between racial groups and that have produced dissimilar contexts not only for the manifestation of racial antagonisms, but also for racial group access to rewards and privileges.

In contrast to the modern industrial period in which fundamental economic and political changes have made the economic class position of blacks the determining factor in their prospects for occupational advancement, the preindustrial and industrial periods of black-white relations have one central feature in common: overt efforts of whites to solidify economic racial domination (ranging from the manipulation of black labor to the neutralization or elimination of black economic competition) through various forms of judicial, political, and social discrimination. Since racial problems during these two periods were principally related to group struggles over economic resources, they readily lend themselves to the economic class theories of racial antagonisms that associate racial antipathy with class conflict.

Although racial oppression, when viewed from the broad perspective of historical change in American society, was a salient and important feature during the preindustrial and industrial periods of race relations in the United States, the problems of subordination for certain segments of the black population and the experience of social advancement for others are more directly associated with economic class in the modern industrial period. Economic and political changes have gradually shaped a black class structure, making it increasingly difficult to speak of a single or uniform black experience. Although a small elite population of free, propertied blacks did in fact exist during the pre-Civil War period, the interaction between race and economic class only assumed real importance in the latter phases of the industrial period of race relations; and the significance of this relationship has grown as the nation has entered the modern industrial period.

Each of the major periods of American race relations has been shaped in different measure both by the systems of production and by the laws and policies of the state. However, the relationships between the economy and the state have varied in each period, and therefore the roles of both institutions in shaping race relations have differed over time.

ANTEBELLUM SOUTH

In the preindustrial period the slave-based plantation economy of the South allowed a relatively small, elite group of planters to develop enormous regional power. The hegemony of the southern ruling elite was based on a system of production that required little horizontal or vertical mobility and therefore could be managed very efficiently with a simple division of labor that virtually excluded free white labor. As long as free white workers where not central to the process of reproducing the labor supply in the southern plantation economy, slavery as a mode of production facilitated the slaveholder's concentration and consolidation of economic power. And the slaveholders successfully transferred their control of the economic system to the political and legal systems in order to protect their class interest in slavery. In effect, the polity in the South regulated and reinforced the system of racial caste oppression, depriving both blacks and nonslaveholding whites of any meaningful influence in the way that slavery was used in the economic life of the South.

In short, the economy provided the basis for the development of the system of slavery, and the polity reinforced and perpetuated that system. Furthermore, the economy enabled the slaveholders to develop a regional center of power, and the polity was used to legitimate that power. Since nonslaveholding whites were virtually powerless both economically and politically, they had very little effect on the developing patterns of race relations. The meaningful forms of black-white contact were between slaves and slaveholders, and southern race relations consequently assumed a paternalistic quality involving the elaboration and specification of duties, norms, rights, and obligations as they pertained to the use of slave labor and the system of indefinite servitude.

In short, the pattern of race relations in the antebellum South was shaped first and foremost by the system of production. The very nature of the social relations of production meant that the exclusive control of the planters would be derived from their position in the production process, which ultimately led to the creation of a juridicial system that reflected and protected their class interests, including their investment in slavery.

WORKERS' EMERGING POWER

However, in the nineteenth century antebellum North the form of racial oppression was anything but paternalistic. Here a more industrial system of production enabled white workers to become more organized and physically concentrated than their southern counterparts. Following the abolition of slavery in the North, they used their superior resources to generate legal and informal practices of segregation that effectively prevented blacks from becoming serious economic competitors.

As the South gradually moved from a plantation to an industrial economy in the last quarter of the nineteenth century, landless whites were finally able to effect changes in the racial stratification system. Their efforts to eliminate black competition helped to produce an elaborate system of Jim Crow segregation. Poor whites were aided not only by their numbers but also by the development of political resources which accompanied their greater involvement in the South's economy.

Once again, however, the system of production was the major basis for this change in race relations, and once again the political system was used to reinforce patterns of race emanating from structural shifts in the economy. If the racial laws in the antebellum South protected the class interests of the planters and reflected their overwhelming power, the Jim Crow segregation laws of the late nineteenth century reflected the rising power of white laborers; and if the political power of the planters was grounded in the system of producing in a plantation economy, the emerging political power of the workers grew out of the new division of labor that accompanied industrialization.

CLASS AND RACE RELATIONS

Except for the brief period of fluid race relations in the North between 1870 and 1890 and in the South during the Reconstruction era, racial oppression is the single best term to characterize the black experience prior to the twentieth century. In the antebellum South both slaves and free blacks occupied what could be best described as a caste position, in the sense that realistic chances for occupational mobility simply did not exist. In the antebellum North a few free blacks were able to acquire some property and improve their socioeconomic position, and a few were even able to make use of educational opportunities. However, the overwhelming majority of free northern Negroes were trapped in menial positions and were victimized by lower-class white antagonism, including the racial hostilities of European immigrant ethnics (who successfully curbed black economic competition). In the postbellum South the system of Jim Crow segregation wiped out the small gains blacks had achieved during Reconstruction, and blacks were rapidly pushed out of the more skilled jobs they had held since slavery. Accordingly, there was very little black occupational differentiation in the South at the turn of the century.

Just as the shift from a plantation economy to an industrializing economy transformed the class and race relations in the postbellum South, so too did industrialization in the North change the context for race-class interaction and confrontation there. On the one hand, the conflicts associated with the increased black-white contacts in the early twentieth century North resembled the forms of antagonism that soured the relations between the races in the postbellum South. Racial conflicts between blacks and whites in both situations were closely tied to class conflicts among whites. On the other hand, there were some fundamental differences. The collapse of the paternalistic bond between blacks and the southern business elite cleared the path for the almost total subjugation of blacks in the South and resulted in what amounted to a united white racial movement that solidified the system of Jim Crow segregation.

However, a united white movement against blacks never really developed in the North. In the first quarter of the twentieth century, management attempted to undercut white labor by using blacks as strikebreakers and, in some situations, as permanent replacements for white workers who periodically demanded higher wages and more fringe benefits. Indeed, the determina-

tion of industrialists to ignore racial norms of exclusion and to hire black workers was one of the main reasons why the industrywide unions reversed their racial policies and actively recruited black workers during the New Deal era. Prior to this period the overwhelming majority of unskilled and semiskilled blacks were nonunionized and were available as lower-paid labor or as strikebreakers. The more management used blacks to undercut white labor, the greater were the racial antagonisms between white and black labor.

Moreover, racial tension in the industrial sector often reinforced and sometimes produced racial tension in the social order. The growth of the black urban population created a housing shortage during the early twentieth century which frequently produced black "invasions" or ghetto "spillovers" into adjacent poor white neighborhoods. The racial tensions emanating from labor strife seemed to heighten the added pressures of racial competition for housing, neighborhoods, and recreational areas. Indeed, it was this combination of racial friction in both the economic sector and the social order that produced the bloody riots in East Saint Louis in 1917 and in Chicago and several other cities in 1919.

In addition to the fact that a united white movement against blacks never really developed in the North during the industrial period, it was also the case that the state's role in shaping race relations was much more autonomous, much less directly related to developments in the economic sector. Thus, in the brief period of fluid race relations in the North from 1870 to 1890, civil rights laws were passed barring discrimination in public places and in public institutions. This legislation did not have any real significance to the white masses at that time because, unlike in the pre-Civil War North and the post-Civil War South, white workers did not perceive blacks as major economic competitors. Blacks constituted only a small percentage of the total population in northern cities; they had not yet been used in any significant numbers as cheap labor in industry or as strikebreakers; and their earlier antebellum competitors in low-status jobs (the Irish and German immigrants) had improved their economic status in the trades and municipal employment.

POLITY AND RACIAL OPPRESSION

For all these reasons liberal whites and black professionals, urged on by the spirit of racial reform that had developed during the Civil War and Reconstruction, could pursue civil rights programs without firm resistance; for all these reasons racial developments on the political front were not directly related to the economic motivations and interests of workers and management. In the early twentieth century the independent effect of the political system was displayed in an entirely different way. The process of industrialization had significantly altered the pattern of racial interaction, giving rise to various manifestations of racial antagonism.

Although discrimination and lack of training prevented blacks from seeking higher-paying jobs, they did compete with lower-class whites for unskilled and semiskilled factory jobs, and they were used by management to undercut the white workers' union movement. Despite the growing importance of race in the dynamics of the labor market, the political system did not intervene either to mediate the racial conflicts or to reinforce the pattern of labor-market racial interaction generated by the system of production. This was the case despite the salience of a racial ideology system that justified and prescribed unequal treatment for Afro-Americans. (Industrialists will more likely challenge societal racial norms in situations where adherence to them results in economic losses.)

If nothing else, the absence of political influence on the labor market probably reflected the power struggles between management and workers. Thus legislation to protect the rights of black workers to compete openly for jobs would have conflicted with the interests of white workers, whereas legislation to deny black participation in any kind of industrial work would have conflicted with the interest of management. To repeat, unlike in the South, a united white movement resulting in the almost total segregation of the work force never really developed in the North.

But the state's lack of influence in the industrial sector of private industries did not mean that it had no significant impact on racial stratification in the early twentieth century North. The urban political machines, controlled in large measure by working-class ethnics who were often in direct competition with blacks in the private industrial sector, systematically gerrymandered black neighborhoods and excluded the urban black masses from meaningful political participation throughout the early twentieth century. Control by the white ethnics of the various urban political machines was so complete that blacks were never really in a position to compete for the more important municipal political rewards, such as patronage jobs or government contracts and services. Thus the lack of racial competition for municipal political rewards did not provide the basis for racial tension and conflict in the urban political system. This political racial oppression had no direct connection with or influence on race relations in the private industrial sector.

In sum, whether one focuses on the way race relations were structured by the system of production or the polity or both, racial oppression (ranging from the exploitation of black labor by the business class to the elimination of black competition for economic, social, and political resources by the white masses) was a characteristic and important phenomenon in both the preindustrial and industrial periods of American race relations. Nonetheless, and despite the prevalance of various forms of racial oppression, the change from a preindustrial to an industrial system of production did enable blacks to increase their political and economic resources. The proliferation of jobs created by industrial expansion helped generate and sustain the continuous mass migration of blacks from the rural South to the cities of the North and West. As the black urban population grew and became more segregated, institutions and organizations in the black community also developed, together with a business and professional class affiliated with these institutions. Still, it was not until after World War II (the modern industrial period) that the black class structure started to take on some of the characteristics of the white class structure.

CLASS AND BLACK LIFE CHANCES

Class has also become more important than race in determining black life chances in the modern industrial period. Moreover, the center of racial conflict has shifted from the industrial sector to the sociopolitical order. Although these changes can be related to the more fundamental changes in the system of production and in the laws and policies of the state, the relations between the economy and the polity in the modern industrial period have differed from those in previous periods. In the preindustrial and industrial periods the basis of structured racial inequality was primarily economic, and in most situations the state was merely an instrument to reinforce patterns of race relations that grew directly out of the social relations of production.

Except for the brief period of fluid race relations in the North from 1870 to 1890, the state was a major instrument of racial oppression. State intervention in the modern industrial period has been designed to promote racial equality, and the relationship between the polity and the economy has been much more reciprocal, so much so that it is difficult to determine which one has been more important in shaping race relations since World War II. It was the expansion of the economy that facilitated black movement from the rural areas to the industrial centers and that created job opportunities leading to greater occupational differentiation in the black community (in the sense that an increasing percentage of blacks moved into white-collar positions); and it was the intervention of the state (responding to the pressures of increased black political resources and to the racial protest movement) that removed many artificial discrimination barriers by municipal, state, and federal civil rights legislation, and that contributed to the more liberal racial policies of the nation's labor unions by protective union legislation. And these combined political and economic changes created a pattern of black occupational upgrading that resulted, for example, in a substantial drop in the percentage of black males in the low-paying service, unskilled laborer, and farm jobs.

However despite the greater occupational differentiation within the black community, there are now signs that the effect of some aspects of structural economic change has been the closer association between black occupational mobility and class affiliation. Access to the means of production is increasingly based on educational criteria (a situation which distinguishes the modern industrial from the earlier industrial system of production) and thus threatens to solidify the position of the black underclass. In other words, a consequence of the rapid growth of the corporate and government sectors has been the gradual creation of a segmented labor market that currently provides vastly different mobility opportunities for different segments of the black population.

On the one hand, poorly trained and educationally limited blacks of the inner city, including that growing number of black teenagers and young adults, see their job prospects increasingly restricted to the low-wage sector, their unemployment rates soaring to record levels (which remain high despite swings in the business cycle), their labor force participation rates declining, their movement out of poverty slowing, and their welfare roles increasing. On the other hand, talented and educated blacks are experiencing unprecedented job opportunities in the growing government and corporate sectors, opportunities that are at least comparable to those of whites with equivalent qualifications. The improved job situation for the more privileged blacks in the corporate and government sectors is related both to the expansion of salaried white-collar positions and to the pressures of state affirmative action programs.

In view of these developments, it would be difficult to argue that the plight of the black underclass is solely a consequence of racial oppression, that is, the explicit and overt efforts of whites to keep blacks subjugated, in the same way that it would be difficult to explain the rapid economic improvement of the more privileged blacks by arguing that the traditional forms of racial segregation and discrimination still characterize the labor market in American industries. The recent mobility patterns of blacks lend strong support to the view that economic class is clearly more important than race in predetermining job placement and occupational mobility. In the economic realm, then, the black experience has moved historically from economic racial oppression experienced by virtually all blacks to economic subordination for the black underclass. And as we begin the last quarter of the twentieth century, a deepening economic schism seems to be developing in the black community, with the black poor falling further and further behind middle- and upper-income blacks.

SHIFT OF RACIAL CONFLICT

If race is declining in significance in the economic sector, explanations of racial antagonism based on labor-market conflicts, such as those advanced by economic class theories of race, also have less significance in the period of modern industrial race relations. Neither the low-wage sector nor the corporate and government sectors provide the basis for the kind of interracial job competition and conflict that plagued the economic order in previous periods. With the absorption of blacks into industrywide labor unions, protective union legislation, and equal employment legislation, it is no longer feasible for management to undercut white labor by using black workers. The traditional racial struggles for power and privilege have shifted away from the economic sector and are now concentrated in the sociopolitical order. Although poor blacks and poor whites are still the main actors in the present manifestations of racial strife, the immediate source of the tension has more to do with racial competition for public schools, municipal political systems, and residential areas than with the competition for jobs.

To say that race is declining in significance, therefore, is not only to argue that the life chances of blacks have less to do with race than with economic class affiliation, but also to maintain that racial conflict and competition in the economic sector—the most important historical factors in the subjugation of blacks—have been substantially reduced. However, it would be argued that the firm white resistance to public school desegregation, residential integration, and black control of central cities all indicate the unyielding importance of race in the United States. The argument could even be entertained that the impressive occupational gains of the black middle class are only temporary, and that as soon as affirmative action pressures are relieved, or as soon as the economy experiences a prolonged recession, industries will return to their old racial practices.

Both of these arguments are compelling if not altogether persuasive. Taking the latter contention first, there is little available evidence to suggest that the economic gains of privileged blacks will be reversed. Despite the fact that the recession of the early 1970s decreased job prospects for all educated workers, the more educated blacks continued to experience a faster rate of job advancement than their white counterparts. And although it is always possible that an economic disaster could produce racial competition for higher-paying jobs and white efforts to exclude talented blacks, it is difficult to entertain this idea as a real possibility in the face of the powerful political and social movement against job discrimination. At this point there is every reason to believe that talented and educated blacks, like talented and educated whites, will continue to enjoy the advantages and privileges of their class status.

My response to the first argument is not to deny the current racial antagonism in the sociopolitical order, but to suggest that such antagonism has far less effect on individual or group access to those opportunities and resources that are centrally important for life survival than antagonism in the economic sector. The factors that most severely affected black life chances in previous years were the racial oppression and antagonism in the economic sector. As race declined in importance in the economic sector, the Negro class structure became more differentiated and black life chances became increasingly a consequence of class affiliation.

Furthermore, it is even difficult to identify the form of racial contact in the sociopolitical order as the source of the current manifestations of conflict between lower-income blacks and whites, because neither the degree of racial competition between the have-nots, nor their structural relations in urban communities, nor their patterns of interaction constitute the ultimate source of present racial antagonism. The ultimate basis for current racial tension is the deleterious effect of basic structural changes in the modern American economy on black and white lower-income groups, changes that include uneven economic growth, increasing technology and automation, industry relocation, and labor market segmentation.

FIGHTING CLASS SUBORDINATION

The situation of marginality and redundancy created by the modern industrial society deleteriously affects all the poor, regardless of race. Underclass whites, Hispano Americans, and Native

Americans all are victims, to a greater or lesser degree, of class subordination under advanced capitalism. It is true that blacks are disproportionately represented in the underclass population and that about one-third of the entire black population is in the underclass. But the significance of these facts has more to do with the historical consequences of racial oppression than with the current effects of race.

Although the percentage of blacks below the low-income level dropped steadily throughout the 1960s, one of the legacies of the racial oppression in previous years is the continued disproportionate black representation in the underclass. And since 1970 both poor whites and nonwhites have evidenced very little progress in their elevation from the ranks of the underclass. In the final analysis, therefore, the challenge of economic dislocation in modern industrial society calls for public policy programs to attack inequality on a broad class front, policy programs – in other words – that go beyond the limits of ethnic and racial discrimination by directly confronting the pervasive and destructive features of class subordination.

S E V E N

The American Indian
Historical Background

Nancy Oestreich Lurie

Thanks to work by generations of archeologists, ethnologists and historians, there is an enormous literature for intensive study of the prehistoric and historic cultures of the North American Indians and the effects of Euro-American influences on Indian Life.[1] This paper seeks only to provide a brief and general chronology of significant phases in the history of Indian-white contact as a background in understanding contemporary Indian life.

DISCOVERY AND EARLY CONTACT

It is commonly but incorrectly assumed that Indian societies, before Europeans arrived, were stable, and that they had existed in idyllic and unchanging simplicity since time immemorial, until Europeans made their first landfall and began disrupting and ultimately destroying native life. We now know, on the contrary, that their societies were developing and changing in important ways long before first contact. Archeological evidence reveals that prior to the discovery of America by Europeans, widespread trade routes stretched over the entire continent. Many of our important highways follow trails long familiar to the Indians. Furthermore, pottery, burial practices, grave goods, earthworks and other clues uncovered by the archeologist clearly show that new ideas arose in many different places and diffused to neighboring areas to be adapted to different natural environments, further elabo-

Reprinted from *The American Indian Today*, Stuart Levine and Nancy Oestreich Lurie, eds., by permission of the publisher, Everett Edwards, Inc., and the editors.

rated and passed on yet again. Religion, economic practices, and artistic and utilitarian productions were all subjected to the process. By the time of significant European contact along the east coast in the late sixteenth and early seventeenth centuries, a simple hunting and gathering economy was already giving way to a food production economy in the vast area south of the Great Lakes from the Mississippi River to the Atlantic Ocean. Domesticated corn, beans, squash and possibly other food plants as well as tobacco were in a process of northward spread from the lower Mississippi valley. They had undoubtedly been introduced from Mexican sources about one A.D., but by a process and routes not yet fully understood.

When Europeans first arrived, tribes in the northern Great Lakes region had only begun to experiment with gardening as a supplement to a diet based primarily on hunting and gathering, while tribes in the Southeast had already achieved populous, permanent settlements exhibiting marked social and material complexities as natural concomitants to the development of food production. The spread of cultural complexity was paced to some extent by the gradual selection of ever hardier varieties of what has been essentially a semi-tropical plant complex, but which now had to survive even shorter growing seasons. Warmer coastal regions permitted a somewhat faster diffusion of gardening than colder inland regions and in some cases peoples already accustomed to raising crops moved northward, displacing groups still largely dependent on hunting.

The establishment of permanent European settlements along the eastern seaboard and St. Lawrence River in the early seventeenth century required the assistance of Indians in providing food, information and skills to survive the first years in a new environment. As the fur trade took on importance, and with it competition among European nations for control of North America, the Indian tribes enjoyed a good deal of bargaining power and learned to use it astutely in their own interests in regard to both commercial and military activities. For many eastern tribes, it was the long period of the fur trade and not the aboriginal past which is recalled as a golden age.

Although the popular view is that a rapid demise was the fate of all Indians, generally it was the more fully agricultural and rigidly structured tribes which went under quickly and completely in the face of early European contact. Located close to the coasts to begin with and hemmed in by mountains or hostile tribes at their backs, these societies bore the first brunt of intense white competition for desirable land. Their more populous villages and accompanying social norms had developed prior to the advent of Europeans, which may have made for a certain inflexibility in adaptiveness. It should be borne in mind that in the seventeenth century, the difference in political and technological complexity between Indians and little groups of colonists was not so great as to suggest immediately to the tribes and powerful alliances of tribes that Europeans posed a serious threat to their future. Certainly, the relatively large and compact Indian villages with their gardens and stored surpluses of food were highly vulnerable both to new epidemic diseases and scorched earth campaigns in times of open hostilities when their continued presence in the region became a nuisance to the colonists. Thus, only remnants remain of once formidable alliances of tribes along the eastern seaboard, and many tribes noted as powerful and culturally sophisticated in the early British, French and Spanish chronicles have disappeared completely.

Further inland, the tribes were less fully committed to complexities attendant upon food production. They apparently benefitted from the greater flexibility and mobility of a hunting ethos as well as from the fact that Europeans were more interested in their country for furs than for colonization. Moreover, the nascent alliances and confederacies which had begun to develop inland were influenced and shaped in response to the Europeans who sought trade and friendship. These tribes accepted, made adaptations, and recognized as inevitable and even desirable that Europeans should be on the scene. When demand for their land eventually developed, as had happened so quickly on the coast, the inland Indians had established clear patterns for looking after their own interests as societies distinct from those of Europeans, despite their long association and extensive trade and more than occasional acceptance of white in-laws.

Beyond the St. Lawrence to the Arctic Circle,

there are still groups of people, Indian and Eskimo, who are essentially hunters. Even where ecological conditions might have eventually permitted aboriginal plant domestication, their contact with Europeans occurred before there was an intervening native food producing stage. In many instances, contact with outsiders has been so recent that the first encounters involved immediate introduction to features of highly industrialized society. Thus, there are Indian and Eskimo people who rode in airplanes before they even saw an automobile.[2] Some groups are still able to subsist largely off the land but have availed themselves rapidly and selectively of alien items to make the life of the hunter more efficient and comfortable: repeating rifles, gasoline "kickers" for canoes, even radios. Some are as fully committed to the fur trade as a way of life as the Indians of the eastern woodlands in the seventeenth and eighteenth centuries, while for others the fur trade is in its terminal stage, and they face painful adjustments experienced earlier by other groups living in a market economy.

Gardening also diffused into the Prairie and Plains region from Mississippian sources in aboriginal times, but was largely confined to river bottom lands where bone or stone implements could turn the loose soil. The people built substantial villages of timber-framed, mud-covered lodges and settled down to the elaboration of existence permitted by food production. The open plains, where coarse grass matted the earth, were exploited in brief, organized forays to take buffalo in quantity by such means as driving herds over cliffs. Having only dogs as beasts of burden, Indian people found the Plains dangerous, with uncertain and widely spaced sources of water. Only scattered bands of hunters wandered there on occasion.

Important contact with European people occurred only after the Plains had been made habitable for many tribes by the introduction of the horse. As herds of wild Spanish horses spread north, techniques of horsemanship diffused from Spaniard to Indian. Raiding for tamed animals from tribe to tribe became an important and exciting aspect of existence. The great herds of buffalo which a hunter approached on foot with trepidation could not be exploited efficiently

from horseback. The buffalo suddenly became an abundant and dependable food supply and source of housing, utensils and clothing as horses became available to more and more tribes. Some tribes were more or less pushed into the Plains as the pressure of white settlement forced one Indian group against another, but the Plains clearly attracted tribes to a new and exciting way of life as well. The gaudily befringed Indian in warbonnet astride his horse is the archetype of the American Indian all over the world, and we note with wonder the spectacular history of his distinctive way of life. It was made possible by native adaptations of an animal of European origin, achieved astonishing complexity to govern and give deep psychic and esthetic satisfaction to the life of large encampments, and collapsed with the disappearance of the buffalo in the short span of less than 200 years, roughly from 1700 to 1880. By then, the repeating rifle and commercial hunting, which hastened the demise of the buffalo, the windmill, barbed wire and the steel plow transformed the Plains into a rich grazing and grain area, no longer "The American Desert" of the early maps, fit only for Indians.

In the Southwest, agriculture had diffused directly from Mexico and stimulated elaborations of social life even earlier than in the Southeast, beginning perhaps about 1000 B.C. Changes in climate and invasions of hunter-raiders from the North saw shifts of settlements, abandonment of old villages and building of new ones before Europeans first visited the pueblos in 1539. Archeological studies show that the settled people of the Southwest, pueblos and other gardening villagers, had long exchanged items and ideas among themselves. Although actual relations with the Spaniards were frequently strained, they readily took over from the Spaniards a host of new objects, skills, plants, animals and ideas to make them peculiarly their own. Learning early the futility of overt aggression against the better armed Spaniards, the pueblo peoples particularly have developed passive resistance to a fine art in dealing with strangers in their midst—even holding hordes of modern tourists at arm's length with bland pleasantries while doing a brisk trade in hand crafts and fees for taking pictures.

The pueblos' once troublesome neighbors, the former raiders today designated as Navaho and

Apache, successfully incorporated elements of sedentary Indian cultures into their more mobile life in aboriginal times, and eventually they too made judicious selections from Euro-American culture, reworking and molding them to fit their own cultural predilections. The Southwestern Indians in general retain more obvious and visible symbols of their "Indianness" and for many white observers these are the only "real" Indians left. However, their modern material culture is far from aboriginal, distinctive though it may be. Like Indian groups throughout the country, the important criteria of identity rest in intangible attitudes, values, beliefs, patterns of interpersonal relations.

As in the East, native social and material elaboration in the West tended to thin out toward the North, limited by environmental factors. In the Great Basin, tiny bands of roving gatherers maintained a bare subsistence level of existence. Nevertheless, even some of the simple Basin societies were attracted by the horse-buffalo complex of the Plains and in an incredibly short time the Comanche, for example, had ventured out to become a Plains tribe *par excellence.*

North of the Basin, the relatively greater richness of the environment permitted the Plateau Indian to live much as the more favored northern hunters east of the Mississippi, even to enjoying a fur trade era, although of briefer duration. Gardening never reached this region in aboriginal times, but after contact the horse became important to many of the Plateau peoples.

In the West, there were several unusual situations where nature furnished dependable "crops" which man could harvest without first having sown. In central California, huge stands of oak accounted for regular supplies of acorns which the Indians converted into a nutritious flour by ingenious techniques of leaching out the bitter and somewhat toxic tannic acid. On the coast, enormous shell mounds are evidence of once large permanent settlements supported in large part by easily gathered mollusks. Many of the California Indians took quite readily to the ministrations of Spanish friars who began arriving in 1769, and set up mission compounds where they introduced the Indians to agricultural and other skills. Crowded together in the new villages, the Indians proved tragically susceptible to new dis-

eases. The eventual discovery of gold, the influx of lawless miners, and competition by the United States for control of California, in which Indian property and rights were often identified with Hispano-American interests, contributed to a rapid and widespread disorganization and decline among many of the California groups. The picture is, in fact, strikingly similar to the rapid depopulation and disruption of native life on the east coast.

Along the Northwest Coast from Oregon to Alaska, an abundance and variety of marine life and a northerly climate mitigated by the warm Japanese Current created ideal conditions for population growth and social elaboration which could be promoted in most places only through the development of food production. The peoples in this region had regularly traded, visited and fought among themselves when first European contacts were made by sailing ships out of Russia, England and the United States in the late eighteenth century. Trade soon flourished in which sea otter and other pelts were exchanged for both utilitarian and novelty items. The Northwest Coast peoples quickly earned a reputation for sharp bargaining and scant concern for the welfare of hapless seamen wrecked on their shores as they busily plundered ships' cargoes. An impressive way of native life became further enriched. Already skilled in working cedar with simple tools and clever methods of steaming, bending and sewing boards, the Indians soon appreciated that totem poles, storage boxes, house posts, masks and other objects could be enlarged and more ornately embellished with metal tools. However, indiscriminate slaughter of the peltry animals brought a rapid close to the coastal trade. Unlike the eastern tribes which foraged further and further west for fresh beaver areas, even to pushing out the resident tribes, the Northwest Coast people had no place else to go. The arrival of Lewis and Clark in 1806 heralded the opening of overland routes of settlement from the east and encroachment of farmers, miners and loggers. The later adaptations of the Coastal Indians have tended to center in fishing both for their own support and as commercial enterprise.

If we take a broad view of the entire continent from the end of the sixteenth century until well into the nineteenth century, we find that white contact stimulated new ideas, introduced new goods and even greatly accelerated the pace of cultural change in some cases. However, whites arrived on a scene where changes, experimentation, movements of people and diffusion of goods and ideas were already taking place. For the vast majority of tribes, there was time to develop attitudes and adaptations about the presence of whites which involved negotiation and selective borrowing of items rather than absorption into white culture and society. Exposure to similar opportunities to change, furthermore, did not lead to cultural homogeneity throughout the continent, since different Indian societies in different kinds of environments made different selections and adaptations in regard to white culture. The multiplicity of languages and local cultural identity persisted. When, from place to place, the nature of contact changed to one of intense competition for right to the land, the Indians were clearly at a disadvantage. However, even as their power to bargain waned, the various Indian groups continued to adapt to maintain their ethnic integrity. Because they made massive borrowings of European material items, which tended to be similar from place to place – guns, textiles, household utensils and tools – white people generally assumed they would soon gracefully phase out their social and cultural distinctiveness. However, we are still waiting for them to vanish.

TREATIES AND RESERVATIONS

When the United States and Canada finally emerged as the national entities controlling North America, increasingly determined to remain at peace with one another, Indian societies were obliged to deal exclusively with one or the other of these governments and were bereft of the opportunity to play the familiar game of favored nation in war and trade among competing powers – France, Spain, Britain and the young United States. Both Canada and the United States derive their Indian policies from guidelines which were already being laid down in the mid-seventeenth century in New England and Virginia. In the face of overwhelming defeat, the depleted and demoralized tribes in these areas were offered and accepted small parcels of land –

the first reservations – secured to them by treaties. These guaranteed homelands and other considerations, in the way of goods and religious and practical teachings, were to be compensation for the vast domains they relinquished. The Indians, in turn, pledged themselves to peace and alliance with the local colonies in case of war with hostile tribes or European enemies. In Virginia, in 1646, the regrouped remnants of the once powerful Powhatan Confederacy agreed in their treaty to pay a small annual tribute in furs to the colony, an interesting portent of things to come for their Indian neighbors to the West, as the fur trade was just beginning to loom importantly to the British.[3]

As the scattered and often competitive British colonies began to recognize their common interests in opposition to the French in the North and both Spain and France to the South, Indian policy became more firmly structured. By 1755, negotiations with Indians, particularly in regard to land, became the exclusive prerogative of the Crown acting through properly designated representatives. A northern and a southern superintendency were set up to regulate trade and undertake necessary diplomacy with the Indians. After the American Revolution, the southern superintendency ceased to exist as a British concern and the northern superintendency was moved from the area of New York State to Canada.

Canadian colonial governors handled Indian affairs locally until 1860 when responsibility in Ontario and Quebec was given directly to the Province of Canada. In 1867, the British North America Act placed Indian affairs under the jurisdiction of the Government of Canada. During the ensuing years, administrative headquarters were shifted between various offices and branches of the government, but policy itself tended to remain relatively consistent. Whenever possible, Canada dealt with tribes by treaty, including as many tribes under a common treaty as could be induced to sign in any particular region. Reserves were located in the tribes' homelands or in nearby, ecologically similar areas, the process being repeated from region to region as national interest in regard to allocation of land expanded west and north. Canada made its last treaty with some of the far northern Indians in 1923. A system to encourage understanding of modern principles of government provides for election of a chief and headmen in each "Band," the Canadian term for locally autonomous Indian groups. The number of headmen is determined by population size, with roughly one headman per 100 people. For some bands, such as the Iroquois groups along the southern border of Canada, this system is an uncomfortable imposition on their own patterns of semi-hereditary leadership, while for bands in the northern Territories, it has given a formal structure to an old system of leadership based on individual ability. The Canadian government has always cooperated with religious denominations in sharing responsibility for Indian affairs, especially in regard to education.

A few Canadian bands were by-passed in treaty negotiations and special provisions have been made for them to qualify for "Treaty Indian" benefits as well as conform to limitations placed on full citizenship by Treaty Indian status. A basic objective has been to encourage Indian people to declare themselves "nontreaty" as individuals and be accepted as full-fledged citizens. After 1950, most of the limitations on citizenship were lifted, even for Treaty Indians, in the hope of hastening the day when Indians would become assimilated. The Canadian government, however, has been generally more tolerant than the United States of ethnic distinctiveness and more agreeable to protecting Indian rights to their lands as defined by treaties.

Eskimo affairs, until 1966, were considered a separate concern, centering more in matters of trade and welfare than in questions of land. At present an effort is under way to consolidate and regularize Indian and Eskimo administration, stressing new experiments in economic development of native communities.

Perhaps the most distinctive feature of Canadian Indian history is the explicit recognition of old communities of stabilized Indian-white mixture, designated *Metis*. This is a sociological and not an official concept; the Metis are simply an ethnic group like Ukrainians or French Canadians, sharing none of the benefits of Indian status. They are considered different from Indians both by themselves and the Indian people who also represent some white admixture in the genealogies. In some cases, the actual kinship between certain Indian and Metis families is known

to both sides. Since Metis are generally found in the western Provinces and Territories, where there are large Indian populations, and suffer the same disabilities of isolation and inadequate education and perhaps even lower social status in the Canadian class system, there is an increasing tendency to group Metis and Indians in Canadian discussions of problems of poverty, employment, education and the like. The extent to which Metis and Indians themselves are interested in making common cause remains debatable.

The picture in the United States is much more complicated. In the first place there were and are more Indian people representing greater diversity of languages, cultures and ecological adaptations. Encroachment of whites on Indian land has always been a much more acute problem. After France ceased to be a consideration in the struggle for control of North America, many tribes allied themselves with the British against the Americans in the Revolution and War of 1812, or maintained a wary neutrality during these conflicts, waiting to see how they would turn out. Few tribes declared themselves clearly on the side of the Americans. Thus, from the start, American negotiations for land frequently followed recent hostile engagements with the tribes involved. The settlers' fears of disgruntled and warlike Indians, perhaps not yet entirely convinced they were defeated, gave added impetus to a policy designed to move Indian tribes far from the lands they ceded. In Canada, the relatively smaller populations of both Indians and whites as well as a history of friendlier relationships permitted comparatively easier negotiations for land and establishing reserves close to areas opening up for settlement.

Eventually, there was no place left to move Indians and the United States was also obliged to set up reservations in tribal homelands. Added to these many complications was the fact that in time American policy had to be adjusted to old Spanish arrangements in the Southwest where land grants established Indian title, a plan analogous but not identical to the British plan of treaties and reservations.

Following British precedent, the United States made Indian affairs a concern of the central government, but actual procedures were left vague. The Third Article of the Constitution merely empowered Congress to "regulate commerce with foreign nations, and among the several states, and with the Indian tribes." At first, administration was carried out through a system of government authorized trading posts, reminiscent of the British superintendencies. The army handled problems of hostile Indians. Peace negotiations and land sales, including arrangements for reservations, were carried out by special treaty commissions appointed as need demanded. The idea prevailed, as it had since colonial times, that changes in sovereignty over land did not abrogate the rights of possession of those who occupied the land, and that Indians should be recompensed for land which they relinquished. This concept was enunciated in the Northwest Ordinance confirmed in 1789 and extended to cover the tribes in the Louisiana Purchase in 1804. By the time the United States acquired Alaska, we had begun to equivocate on this philosophy, and questions of Indian and Eskimo land remain somewhat confused.[4]

The fact that the United States pledged itself to pay Indians for their lands at a time when there was virtually no national treasury has given comfort to those historians who would see the founding fathers imbued with the noblest of ideals. Cynics point out that it was cheaper and easier than trying to drive the Indians out by force. The price paid across the continent averaged well under ten cents an acre, and the government expected to recoup quickly by sale of land in large blocks to speculators at $1.25 an acre minimum. Moreover the debt on each treaty usually was paid under an annuity plan extending over thirty years. On the other hand, many of the tribes were not entirely naive and held out for payment in specie rather than the uncertain paper issues by banks in the early days of the republic.

Although successive efforts were made to establish a firm line between Indian and white holdings east of the Mississippi River, settlement continued to encroach on the Indian area, necessitating renegotiation of the boundary. By 1824, the demands of settlers, competition from illegal, private traders, and the diminishing returns of the fur trade led the government to abandon the trading business as basic to Indian affairs and concentrate on the land business. The Bureau of Indian Affairs was set up under the Department of War. When the Department of Interior was established in 1849 and Indian affairs were placed under its aegis, most of the eastern tribes had become located much as we find them today.

A few tribes on the seaboard occupy state reservations or are simply old Indian settlements, legacies of the colonial past which could be ignored. Along the Appalachians, particularly toward the southern end and elsewhere in the Southeast, there are isolated communities which identify themselves as Indian, such as the numerous Lumbee of North Carolina and adjoining states and the Houma of Louisiana. Their tribal affiliations are vague, because these people are the descendants of fugitive remnants of many tribes driven from the coasts, white renegades and, in some cases, runaway Negro slaves. These people are, in effect, Metis, but popular and official thinking in the United States has tended to more rigid classification than in Canada. Thus, rejected as white and reluctant to be considered Negro, the American Metis stress their identity as Indian. Those Indian societies which maintained a clear and unbroken tradition of tribal identity and stood in the path of settlement were exhorted, negotiated with and paid to move further west during the period of the 1820s and 1830s.

The United States entered into numerous treaties with these tribes and though it tried to deal with blocs of tribes as was done in Canada, this proved inexpedient. Both tribesmen and treaty commissioners tried to outmaneuver each other by devious diplomatic ploys. The Indians could play for delay in land sales by noting boundaries which had only Indian names and were unknown to the whites, so that final settlement would depend on formal surveys. The whites attempted to play one tribe off against another, and even one subband within a tribe against another, in the hope of leaving intransigent factions so isolated and unprotected that they would be forced to capitulate when their neighbors moved out. And then the factions would rally and claim the treaty had to include all parties with an interest to the land in question. Since treaties had to be ratified by Congress and the work of the commissioners was hampered by both budget allocations for their time and the desire to get back to Washington before Congress recessed, the Indians won compromises. The commissioners could afford to be philosophical as these loose ends could always be tied up in the next round of negotiations. There is little doubt that the Indian tribes hoped to make the best of what could only be a bad bargain, but to stick to that bargain once made, whereas the treaty makers from Washington took the treaties lightly, striving toward the final goal of general Indian removal to the less choice land west of the Mississippi acquired in the Louisiana Purchase.

Thus we find representatives of eastern tribes scattered from Nebraska to Oklahoma: Potawatomi, Winnebago, Miami, Shawnee, Kickapoo, Ottawa, Creek, Choctaw, Chickasaw, Cherokee, Seminole and others even including members of the League of the Iroquois such as Cayuga and Seneca. However, bands or small clusterings of families of many of these tribes managed to return to their homelands or held out against removal, arguing either the illegality of the treaty under which they were to move or misrepresentation by the government as to the quality of the new land or the terms whereby they and their possessions were to be transported. In some cases, this determination led to creation of reservations for them in their homelands, as in the cases of the Eastern Cherokee and Seminoles. Others, including some of the Potawatomi and Winnebago, were granted homesteads as individuals where it was hoped that they would become absorbed into the general rural white population. Popular indignation about the injustice shown one band of Potawatomi in Michigan led to the establishment of a small reservation for them under state jurisdiction. A group of Mesquakie (Fox) picked out and purchased their own land and applied for reservation status. Perhaps the most bizarre instance was the band of Kickapoo who just kept on going west and sought sanctuary in northern Mexico where they remain to this day, preserving many features of nineteenth century woodland Indian culture. In many cases, particularly in the Southeast, little groups simply managed to maintain themselves as Indian neighborhoods on property they were able to purchase, little noticed and bothering no one.

Several Iroquois tribes or portions of them who did not flee to Canada after the Revolution were granted their reservations in New York State by treaties signed during Washington's administration. Of these, the Oneida were induced to move to Wisconsin in the early 1830s along with the Stockbridge, a highly acculturated Algonkian group drawing its membership from remnants of coastal tribes, primarily the Mahicans. In Wisconsin, Michigan and Minnesota we find a number of tribes, Menomini, bands of Ojibwa and others who by various delaying tactics finally managed to get reservations in their homelands.[5]

There is no question that when it was a matter of the larger national interest, defined as the demands of settlers or speculators, the government made every effort to remove the Indians.[6] Humanitarians such as Jefferson expressed the hope that if Indian people conformed to the habits of rural whites they might remain in possession of what land they would need for this purpose, but if they would not change their ways, the only alternative was forceful persuasion and removal. The rationale for dispossession of the Indians has usually conformed to a logic summed up by Theodore Roosevelt in the late nineteenth century, "This great continent could not have been kept as nothing but a game preserve for squalid savages."[7] The myth of the hunter Indian, incapable or unwilling to rouse himself from the sloth of ancestral tradition in the face of new opportunities and the model afforded by civilized man, remains with us today. On close inspection, the problem seems to be less the Indian's inability to adapt than the unorthodoxy of his adaptations. Western cultures have a different history; our traditions evolved out of a stage of feudal peasantry which the Indians bypassed. So Indians react in unexpected but perfectly logical ways to our ideas and artifacts.

The essential problems which arise in the confrontation of different cultural systems, each changing and adapting its own way, are well illustrated in the fate of the Cherokee, who became literate as a result of exposure to the European idea of writing, but hit upon a syllabary rather than an alphabet to best convey the vagaries of their own tongue in written symbols. By the early nineteenth century, the Cherokee and other groups in the Southeast had built upon their growing aboriginal commitment to agriculture with new crops and implements brought by the Europeans. They were successfully self-sustaining from small farmsteads to large plantations, with many acres under cultivation and large herds of horses and cattle. But they wished to maintain themselves as distinct Indian societies, while acknowledging allegiance to the United States.

Decisions sympathetic to this outlook were expressed by the Chief Justice of the Supreme Court, John Marshall in 1831 (*The Cherokee Nation v. The State of Georgia*) and 1832 (*Samuel A. Worcester v. The State of Georgia*) but had little effect in protecting the Cherokee or any Indian tribes from private interests and states bent on their dispossession. Frontier statesmen, particularly during the administration of Andrew Jackson, could argue that Indians were different and therefore still clearly savage and a danger. Congress, as the body duly authorized to deal with Indian affairs, simply went around Marshall's decisions. It carried out the will of local states in regard to unwanted Indians, and provided for treaties and removals.

It must be noted that not all the proponents of the plan of Indian removal were motivated by selfish interests. There were missionaries and others who felt that removal of Indian tribes from the corrupting and demoralizing influences of frontier riff-raff would be in the Indians' best interest and allow them to establish a new and better life. However, even the kindest construction placed on this view must admit to its short-sightedness. Already resident on the land in the west were tribes whose interests were not consulted before newcomers were moved among them. They were often considerably less than hospitable. Furthermore, it was becoming obvious that the Plains area would not remain forever the habitation of buffalo hunters. By the time pioneers were spreading out into the Plains, instead of bypassing them on the way to the gold fields of fertile valleys of the west coast, there was really no place left to move Indians. There was also the danger that the plan of one, and later two, large Indian Territories in the West would allow tribes to see the advantages of alliance and make common cause against the white man. Therefore, most of the native tribes west of the Mississippi were placed in reservations which

are separated from one another yet in or near the original homelands. In contrast, large numbers of eastern Indians were clustered in Oklahoma.[8]

By 1849, when the Bureau of Indian Affairs was shifted from the Department of War to the newly created Department of the Interior, the eastern tribes had been "pacified," although troops were occasionally called in to round up returnees and get them back to their western reservations. The real problem, however, was the Plains Indians, who at this time were in the very midst of their great cultural florescence and were formidable and enthusiastic warriors. The efforts of Interior to get these tribes on reservations by negotiation, conciliation and persuasion were often confounded by the outlook of the War Department, which considered all Indians hostile, dangerous, and fair game. An unfortunate term, "ward," used by Marshall in his 1831 decision was revived. Marshall only intended a rough analogy in endeavoring to explain the responsibility of the federal government to protect Indian tribes against unauthorized usurpation of their lands: "Their relation to the United States resembles that of ward to his guardian." Because the Bureau "sometimes became the uneasy and unhappy buffer between Indians and the U.S. Army,"[9] it was decided in 1862 to designate the Indian tribes as "wards" of the Indian Bureau rather than let them be considered simply as "enemies" over whose fate the army would have jurisdiction to make decisions. Unfortunately, and without ever really having legal sanction, the term "ward" took on administrative connotations by which the Bureau exercised incredible control over the lives and property of individuals, much as a guardian would act for minor and even hopelessly retarded children.

THE END OF THE TREATY PERIOD

As noted, Canada took its Indian treaties more seriously from the start and has continued to respect them. In the United States, although important hostilities such as Little Big Horn and Wounded Knee were yet to come, it was apparent by 1871 that the process of "pacification" would continue at a rapid pace. The need to make treaties with so many different tribes and the embarrassment of making new treaties every time the demands of settlement required reduction of Indian acreage suggested to policy makers that Indian tribes were not really "nations" entitled to the respect and formality of treaties. Treaties required the unwieldy and expensive process of mutual agreement – albeit the United States held the greater power in dictating terms – and Senate ratification. Terms of existing treaties would be observed as long as the government found it practicable, but after 1871 no more treaties were made with Indian tribes. Instead, "agreements" were negotiated which were worded much like treaties and mistaken for treaties by many Indians, but which were administratively more expedient and not as binding in legalistic and even moral terms as far as the government was concerned. Champions of Indians' rights long endeavored to pique the conscience of the nation by pointing to our bad faith in entering into solemn treaties, "the highest law of the land," which we did not intend to keep.

It was the period from the 1870s to the 1920s during which the worst abuses occurred in regard to administration of Indian affairs. Most Indian people were denied the vote, had to obtain passes to leave the reservation and were prohibited from practicing their own religions, sometimes by force. Leadership and management of community affairs smacking of traditional forms and functions were either discouraged or ignored as proper representations of community interest. Children were dragooned off to boarding schools where they were severely punished if they were caught speaking their own languages. While these things all happened, shortage and rapid turnover of Bureau personnel, administrative apathy and occasional enlightenment at the local administrative level meant that the regulations were not always rigorously enforced. And the Indian societies themselves took a hand in playing off administrators, missionaries and other whites against each other to keep them busy while Indian people held the line in their determination to remain Indian. The ubiquity of factionalism in Indian societies which is so regularly deplored by those people, Indian and white, who are sincerely interested in helping Indian people make a better life, may actually have acted as an important mechanism of social and cultural survival for Indian groups. No outsider could gain

total dominance for his programs aimed in one way or another at reducing Indian distinctiveness. This suggestion, while admittedly speculative, seems worth bearing in mind when we turn to the contemporary scene where there seems to be a striving for common goals, in which factionalism for its own sake in avoiding undesirable goals may be giving way to what are really healthy differences of opinion based on habitual wariness in working toward positive objectives.

ATTEMPTS AT REFORM

Educated Indian people and their philanthropic white friends during the nineteenth century were generally as committed as the government to the view that the Indians' only hope was social and cultural assimilation into white society. The reservation system per se as well as the widespread peculation and dereliction in duty of reservation personnel were held responsible for impeding Indians in their course toward "civilization." This view tended to ignore the many non-reservation communities in the east which remained almost defiantly Indian, even where government experiments in granting stubborn "returnees" homesteads scattered among white neighbors did not automatically result in Indian assimilation or breakdown of a sense of community. If their conservatism in language, religion and other aspects of culture was noted at all, it was viewed optimistically as inevitably temporary. Ironically, one of the major measures of reform promoted by humanitarians turned out to exacerbate rather than alleviate Indians problems. This was the Indian Allotment Act of 1887. It was actually protested by some far-seeing people who recognized the opportunities it afforded for a tremendous Indian landgrab, but these voices were drowned out by those who considered themselves the Indians' true friends, righteously supported by those who stood to gain from the Allotment Act as predicted by the pessimists.[10]

The idea of allotment was that Indians could be assimilated into the white rural population in the space of a generation by granting them private property. Each individual was to receive his own acreage, usually coming to about 180 acres per family unit, and land left over after all allotments were made was to be thrown open to sale, the proceeds used to build houses and barns and to buy stock and equipment for the Indians to become farmers.

However, even by 1887, subsistence farming by individual families was giving way to large scale, single crop enterprises. Although allotments remained tax free for a period of twenty-five or thirty years, Indian people were not adequately informed nor technically prepared for managing farms. The result was that many of the allotments were lost through tax default or sold to pay debts which far-seeing whites had allowed Indians to run up against the day they would gain patents-in-fee to their land. Although the necessity for more protective provisions was soon recognized by the government, an unexpected complication rendered much of the land useless to its Indian owners. Some time between 1900 and 1910, a rapid decrease in Indian population leveled off and a steady rise set in. Original allotments were divided among increasing numbers of heirs. Given American laws of inheritance, there developed a common situation in which an individual might own forty or more acres, but as scattered fractions of land inherited from a number of ancestors who had received allotments. The easiest course was for the Indian Bureau simply to rent the land out in large parcels to white agriculturalists and stockmen and divide the proceeds among the many heirs. Some people could live on their rent money alone, often supporting less fortunate relatives as well. But, in most cases, rent money brought only a few dollars a year and a living was eked out by wage labor in planting and harvest seasons, forays to the cities to work in factories, and exploitation of the growing tourist industry in terms of sale of handcrafts and public dance performances.

As regulations on Indian movement off the reservations tended to relax, especially if people left to seek work, Indian people became increasingly better informed on the myriad opportunities to earn a living in industrial America besides the drudgery of farming. However, Indian communities persisted even where the allotment process had drastically reduced the land base. Indian people seemed to join circuses and wild west shows, seek out areas where relatively high wages were paid for crop work, or find their

way to industrial employment in the cities in a manner reminiscent of hunting, trading or war expeditions. They drifted back home periodically to seek help from relatives if they were broke or to share the spoils of the "hunt" with their kinsmen until it was necessary to forage again. They took to automobiles as enthusiastically as many had taken to ponies at an earlier time, becoming commuters to cities or other places where they could find work, returning daily or weekly or seasonally or by whatever schedule was practical. Some people spent most of their lifetimes in the city, but returned home to their tribesmen upon retirement. And these patterns persist today. Unlike the usual migrants, Indian people do not seem to perceive urban work as a break with the rural past, but merely as an extension of the peripheries of the territory which can be exploited economically. It is difficult to escape the conclusion that Indian people were "rurban" long before anyone coined the term or saw the industrial blending of city and country life as the direction in which the nation as a whole was to move.

Although Indian groups, with their characteristic close communal life, were persisting and increasing in size, the national outlook stressed rugged individualism and private enterprise. Both policy and administration of Indian affairs were oriented toward assimilating Indians as individuals into the general population. Tribal enterprises and industries were introduced only where the overwhelming argument of certain natural resources militated against allotment in severalty. Thus a few tribal forests and fishing groups provided regular employment and income on the reservation, but even in these cases Indian people were given little voice or purposeful training in management of tribal business. Beyond that, a number of areas escaped allotment either because the terrain made it impractical for subsistence farming or the problems created by allotment elsewhere had become apparent and the plan was simply shelved before more remote areas were included under it.

Other efforts to reform Indian administration gradually got around to matters of practical welfare. The Indian Bureau had always been a political pork barrel, appointments to various posts being handed out to party stalwarts. The pay was poor, but there were opportunities to shave budgets for personal gain. Allotment opened more opportunities to bribe officials to declare Indians "competent" to sell their land. The scandals of peculation, the complaints of sincere employees that the uncertainty of their jobs made it impossible to carry out decent programs, and the clear evidence of honest but unqualified and emotionally callous personnel all led to demands for improvement. Doctors and teaching staffs were put on civil service in 1892, and by 1902 all Bureau employees were on civil service except the Commissioner and Assistant Commissioner.

At the time of the First World War most of the Indian population was still without the vote and also not subject to conscription, but a surprising number of young men volunteered for the armed services and were recognized for remarkable heroism. This stirred the nation from complacency about Indian problems and in 1924 the franchise was extended to all Indians. Significantly, one Indian view, which found expression among tribes all over the country, considered the right to vote a pretty shabby reward and no more than further evidence of national disregard for Indian rights as established by treaties. The implication was that Indians volunteered in America's defense as loyal allies as pledged in treaties rather than as patriotic citizens.[11]

However, few white Americans were aware of this reaction to their magnanimous gesture, and concerned people continued efforts to understand why Indians had not yet been granted their proper place as assimilated Americans and to search for better means of accomplishing this end. The results of extensive investigation of Indian affairs by the Brookings Institution were published in 1928,[12] setting forth in concise and depressing detail just how bad things really were among Indian people under the federal jurisdiction, and suggesting means of improving the situation.

Although committed to the entrenched view that assimilation of Indians was both desirable and inevitable, the Brookings Report noted that this would take time and the settling of many just grievances harbored by the tribes before trust and cooperation could be expected of them. Throughout the Report we begin to see indications of a changing perspective on Indians' problems in the recommendations reached by objec-

tive investigators. For example, in speaking of administration as "leadership," the Report says:

> This phase "rights of the Indian" is often used solely to apply to his property rights. Here it is used in a much broader sense to cover his rights as a human being living in a free country. . . . The effort to substitute educational leadership for the more dictatorial methods now used in some places will necessitate more understanding of and sympathy for the Indian point of view. Leadership will recognize the good in the economic and social life of the Indians in their religion and ethics, and will seek to develop it and build on it rather than to crush out all that is Indian. The Indians have much to contribute to the dominant civilization, and the effort should be made to secure this contribution, in part because of the good it will do the Indians in stimulating a proper race pride and self-respect.[13]

Serious efforts to implement the Brookings recommendations were delayed as the nation entered the depression of the 1930s. With the election of Franklin D. Roosevelt and appointment of John Collier, Sr. as Indian Commissioner, a "New Deal" was also in store for Indian people. Collier's thinking went beyond the Brookings recommendations both in revising administrative procedures and in philosophy. He endeavored to set up mechanisms for self-government which would allow Indian communities to bargain as communities with the government and the larger society. He sought to teach them about a host of opportunities for community improvement and let them choose accordingly – revolving loan funds, tribal enterprises, resource development, land acquisition, tribal courts, educational programs. In many ways Collier's plan was inappropriate: too "Indian" for some tribes, not "Indian" enough for others, and characterized by unwarranted urgency and hard sell in some instances. For all that, Indian people recognized in large measure that Collier really understood what their grievances were about even if his methods were sometimes less than satisfactory or if Bureau personnel on the local level were often incapable of throwing off old habits of mind and behavior in carrying out the intent of the new administration. Where Collier and Indian people were in agreement was in the objective of restoring not the Indian culture of any past period but the kind of conditions and relationships which existed prior to the "ward" philosophy of Indian administration, a period when Indian people could still select and adapt innovations to find satisfactory patterns of their own for community life. Above all, Collier understood the need to secure an adequate land base for meaningful social experimentation and development.

Collier's administration and philosophy . . . were short-lived as views Congress would be willing to support. They were in effective operation for seven years at most. The Indian Reorganization Act was passed in 1934, time was required to inform Indian people and allow them to make decisions in regard to it, and by 1941 the nation was at war. Domestic programs, including those of the Indian Bureau, were naturally made secondary to the war effort. Wartime prosperity brought temporary alleviation of economic problems for many Indian communities. Collier remained in office until 1946, but it was becoming increasingly apparent that his administrative ideas were losing popularity with Congress.[14] After the war, when servicemen and factory workers returned home, Indian population, like that of the rest of the nation, had increased. Programs just started before the war had not been able to keep pace with the added pressures on the still limited sources of income of the reservations. Since the "Indian problem" suddenly loomed larger than ever, the easy explanation was Collier's revolutionary departure from the time-honored Indian policy of assimilation.

Because Indian people showed a marked aptitude for industrial work during the war, and it was obvious they would not succeed as farmers, the solution was simple. Relocate them in urban centers, preferably in each case as far from the home reservation as possible, and legislate the reservations out of existence so that Indian people could not run home when things got tough or share their good fortune periodically with kinsmen who lacked the gumption to get out on their own.

Like the grand scheme of 1887 to solve the Indians' problems by the simple expedient of allotment in severalty, the relocation-reservation termination plan of the 1950s was out of date for its time in terms of national, social and economic trends. If the ideal of the Allotment Act was to ensconce Indian people in a kind of average, small farm middle-class, which was actually disappearing, the ideal of the policy of the 1950s was primarily to get the government out of the Indian business and scant attention was paid to where Indian people might be able to fit in American life. Indian people opposed the policy of the 1950s, arguing for the alternative of community development through local industries and beefing up the long neglected educational programs. This, Indian people argued, would enable them to plan and manage intelligently in their own behalf community development and tribal enterprises. It would also make it possible for those individuals who wished to assimilate to enter the larger society at a decent economic and occupational level.

At the very time that suburbs were burgeoning, commuting was a way of life for much of the nation, and far-sighted people were anticipating greater segmentation of industrial operations and dispersing them to where the people live, Indian policy was based on models of concentrating population in large urban centers. Like the rural myth of the nineteenth century, mid-twentieth century policy promoted the myth of the "melting pot," whereby the ambitious immigrant worked his way out of the poor, ethnic neighborhood by frugality and hard work. Such thinking ignored a number of facts: (1) The agonies which such groups suffered during the period when they were exploited minorities living in urban slums. (2) The loss of a sense of community which such people suffered when, sometimes after repeated moves as a group to different urban neighborhoods, they finally "spun off" into the larger society. (3) The special reliance of Indian people on group identity, group membership and group decisions, which goes beyond anything comparable which the immigrant communities were able to establish. Immigrant communities usually were not communities when they came; their ethnic identities were, to a surprising extent, constructed in America. (4) The increasing difficulty of "making it" economically and socially in an economy which has much less use today for unskilled labor, and a society which sees color so strongly that many of its members still doubt that non-Caucasians are really capable of achieving middle-class standards.

The trends of social reform and legislation had taken increasing cognizance of the fact that the individual could no longer hope to go it alone, saving for the rainy days and providing for his old age. Studies of crime and mental health had begun to raise serious questions about the nature of modern, industrialized society in depriving the individual of a sense of community and meaningful engagement in life. But in the 1950s and to a great extent in the 1960s, it was considered unrealistic, impractical and perhaps even a little silly to suggest, as the Brookings Report did in 1928, that "The Indians have much to contribute to the dominant civilization, and the effort should be made to secure this contribution."[15]

Whether or not Indian people are potential models for satisfactory community life for the nation at large, one thing became clear during the 1950s. They were not happy with the solution to their problems of poverty offered by the government. Furthermore, it was soon obvious that the policy of the 1950s, like allotment in the 1880s, tended to create more new problems rather than solve old ones. By 1960, the presidential candidates of both parties recognized the need to reassess Indian affairs and find new directions for policy. At the same time, Indian people appeared to be more vocal and concerned with exercising a positive influence in regard to legislation affecting them. . . .

ENDNOTES

1. For more intensive study of the subject: William Brandon, *The American Heritage Book of Indians* (New York, 1961; paperback: Dell, 1964): more historical than ethnological. Harold Driver, *Indians of North America* (Chicago, 1961), a scholarly reference book with useful maps. Organized according to topics rather than culture areas. Wendell H. Oswalt, *This Land Was Theirs* (New York, 1966): good treatment of ten representative tribes across the country. Robert F. Spencer, Jesse D. Jennings, *et al.*, *The Native Americans* (New York, 1965): general introductory chapters followed by culture area descriptions and accounts of specific tribes within the areas, written for textbook use. Ruth Underhill, *Red Man's America* (Chicago, 1953), also a textbook, and in many ways still the best general introduction to the subject for the beginner. Wilcomb Washburn, ed., *The Indian and the White Man* (Garden City, N.Y., 1964), a fascinating compendium of documents from the period of early contact to the present day, including John Marshall's decisions of 1831 and 1832, and House Concurrent Resolution 108 – the termination bill referred to in this paper.

2. A small but revealing incident, illustrative of a kind of hunter's pragmatism, occurred in the Canadian Northwest Territories. When questioned about his first airplane ride, a Slave Indian was clearly enthusiastic but not awe-struck by modern technology – "Good! See moose sign. Come back, go find moose." Personal conversation, June Helm.

3. Nancy Oestreich Lurie, "Indian Cultural Adjustment to European Civilization," in James Morton Smith, ed., *Seventeenth Century America* (Chapel Hill, 1958), 33–60, discusses the Powhatan Confederacy and notes origins of the reservation system in North America.

4. Lurie, "The Indian Claims Commission Act," *the Annals of The American Academy of Political and Social Science* (May, 1957), 56–70, reviews the question of Indian land title, with special reference to an Alaskan case, 64–65.

5. The multitude of treaties in the United States and problems of boundaries are fully set forth in Charles J. Kappler, comp. and ed., *Indian Affairs, Laws and Treaties* (Washington, D.C., Vol. 2, *Treaties*, 1904); and Charles C. Royce and Cyrus Thomas, "Indian Land Cessions in the United States," *Annual Report* of the Bureau of American Ethnology, Smithsonian Institution, Vol. 18, Pt. 2 (Washington, D.C., 1896–97).

6. Cf. William T. Hagan, *American Indians* (Chicago, 1961), for a discussion of Indian rights vs. national interest.

7. Theodore Roosevelt, *The Winning of the West* (New York, 1889–1896), I, 90.

8. There are exceptions, however, as a few multi-tribe reservations were set up, particularly in the Northwest.

9. *Answers to Questions About American Indians,* Bureau of Indian Affairs (pamphlet), Washington, D.C., 1965, 7. The concept of ward, an equivocal term at best, is often confused with "trusteeship" which has legal meaning and refers to land, not people, in regard to the protective role of the federal government in regard to Indian affairs.

10. Before the general allotment act was passed in 1887, an earlier "pilot" allotment act was passed with specific reference to the Omaha Reservation in Nebraska in 1882. Cf. Lurie, "The Lady from Boston and the Omaha Indians," *The American West*, III, 4 (Fall, 1966), 31–33; 80–86.

11. This view of the vote is still found among some Indian people.

12. Lewis C. Merriam and associates, *The Problem of Indian Administration: Report on a Survey Made at the Request of the Honorable Hubert Work, Secretary of the Interior*, The Brookings Institution (Baltimore, 1928).

13. *Ibid.*

14. It is an open question whether the Indian Claims Commission Act, passed in 1946, represented the last of the Collier era or the beginning of the termination era.

The objective of the act is to provide restitution for Indian grievance, particularly in regard to non-payment or unconscionable consideration for land. However, as sentiment grew in favor of relocation and termination, one argument was that Indian communities would disperse once grievances were settled and only the hope of payment on old debts perpetuated Indian identity. Ide-

ally, claims payments would give Indian people the necessary stake to begin a new life as ordinary citizens far from the reservations. In actual fact, the amounts paid were relatively small on a per capita basis, and Indian communities persisted. Many tribes are still waiting for their claims to be settled.

15. Merriam, *The Problem,* 22–23.

E I G H T

Chicanos in the United States
A History of Exploitation and Resistance

Leobardo F. Estrada   *Reynaldo Flores Macías*
F. Chris García   *Lionel Maldonado*

This essay seeks to provide material that will contribute to an understanding of Chicanos[1] in the United States today. The task calls for a historical perspective on the Mexican people within the context of the U.S. political economy.

It is essential to examine first the early and continued influence of Mexicans in the development of what is today the southwestern United States. Unlike those who believe that social, political, and economic influences in the region were largely the result of Anglo penetration, we argue that practices and institutions indigenous to Mexicans were largely taken over by colonizing Anglos.[2] The military conquest of the Southwest by the United States was a watershed that brought about the large-scale dispossession of the real holdings of Mexicans and their displacement and relegation to the lower reaches of the class structure. Anglo control of social institutions and

of major economic sectors made possible the subsequent exploitation of Mexican labor to satisfy the needs of various developing economic interests.

Mexicans were not passive actors, simply accepting Anglo domination. Mexican resistance to exploitation has taken a great variety of forms since the conquest, contributing to the maintenance and perpetuation of cultural patterns among Mexicans living in the United States. These cultural patterns include: a national identity built around an "Indian" past; an Indianized Catholicism (*La Virgen de Guadalupe*); racial miscegenation (*mestizaje* – Indian and Spaniard – although almost as many Africans as Spaniards were brought to Middle America during the colonial period); and a regional, single language, Spanish. These patterns and practices, which distinguish the Mexican population from other

Reprinted by permission of *Daedalus,* Journal of the American Academy of Arts and Sciences, "American Indians, Blacks, Chicanos, and Puerto Ricans," 110:2 (Spring 1981), Cambridge, MA.

groups, have persisted even among those who left the Southwest for other regions of the United States.

THE MILITARY CONQUEST

Mexicans were incorporated into the United States largely through military conquest. The period that brought the northern reaches of Mexico under the U.S. flag begins approximately in 1836 with the Battle of San Jacinto, and ends in 1853 with the Gadsden Purchase. The military conquest was preceded by a period of Anglo immigration.

In 1810 Mexico began its struggle to gain independence from Spain, an objective finally achieved in 1821. Mexico, recognizing the advantage of increasing the size of the population loyal to its cause, granted permission to foreigners in 1819 to settle in its northern area, what is now Texas. Two years later Stephen Austin founded San Felipe de Austin: by 1830, one year after Mexico had abolished slavery, it is estimated that Texas had about twenty thousand Anglo settlers, primarily Southerners, with approximately two thousand "freed" slaves who had been forced to sign lifelong contracts with former owners.[3] This trickle of immigrants soon became an invading horde.

Immigrants into the territories of Mexico were required to meet certain conditions: pledge their allegiance to the Mexican government and adopt Catholicism. The settlers' initial acceptance of these conditions, however, soon turned to circumvention. The distance of the settlements from Mexico's capital city, together with the internal strife common in the period, made enforcement of these settlement agreements difficult, almost impossible. The foreigners' attitudes toward their hosts only aggravated the situation. Eugene C. Barker, a historian, wrote that by 1835 "the Texans saw themselves in danger of becoming the alien subjects of a people to whom they deliberately believed themselves morally, intellectually, and politically superior. Such racial feelings underlay Texan-American relations from the establishment of the very first Anglo-American colony in 1821."[4]

A constellation of factors—attitudes of racial superiority, anger over Mexico's abolition of slavery, defiance of initially agreed-upon conditions for settlement, and an increasing number of immigrants who pressed for independence from Mexico—strained an already difficult political situation. Direct and indirect diplomatic efforts at negotiation failed. The result was the Texas Revolt of 1835–36, which created for Anglo-Texans and dissident Mexicans the so-called independent Texas Republic, which was to exist until 1845. This republic, while never recognized by the Mexican government, provided the pretext for further U.S. territorial expansion and set the stage for the war between Mexico and the United States (1846–48).

Despite significant and conflicting regional interests in the war, imperialist interests allied with proponents for the expansion of slavery carried the day. When the United States granted statehood to Texas in 1845, almost a decade after recognizing it as a republic, war was inevitable; it was officially declared on May 13, 1846. It has been argued that U.S. politicians and business interests actively sought this war, believing Mexico to be weak, a nation torn by divisive internal disputes that had not been resolved since independence.[5]

When hostilities ended in 1848, Mexico lost over half its national territory. The United States, by adding over a million square miles, increased its territory by a third. Arizona, California, Colorado, New Mexico, Texas, Nevada, and Utah, as well as portions of Kansas, Oklahoma, and Wyoming, were carved out of the territory acquired.

The Treaty of Guadalupe Hidalgo, signed on February 2, 1848, officially concluded hostilities and settled the question of sovereignty over the territories ceded. A new border was established, and the status of Mexicans in the newly acquired U.S. territory was fixed. Mexicans were given one year to decide whether to relocate south of the new border, maintaining their Mexican citizenship, or remain on their native lands, accepting U.S. sovereignty. The treaty explicitly guaranteed that Mexicans who elected to stay in the United States would enjoy "all the rights of citizens of the [United States] according to the principles of the Constitution; and in the meantime shall be maintained and protected in the free enjoyment of their religion without restriction."

Mexican property rights were further defined

once the treaty had been approved by both governments. A Statement of Protocol, drafted by U.S. emissaries when the Mexican government reacted strongly to changes unilaterally made by the U.S. Senate, said:

> The American Government by suppressing the Xth article of the Treaty of Guadalupe Hidalgo did not in any way intend to annul grants of lands made by Mexico in the ceded territories. These grants preserve the legal value which they may possess, and the grantees may cause their legitimate [titles] to be acknowledged before the American tribunals.
>   Conformable to the law of the United States, legitimate titles to every description of property, personal and real, existing in the ceded territories, are those which were legitimate titles under the Mexican law of California and New Mexico up to the 13th of May, 1846, and in Texas up to the 2nd of March, 1836.

Subsequent events soon indicated that these "guarantees" were specious.

A final portion of Mexican land was acquired by the United States through purchase. James Gadsden was sent to Mexico City in 1853 to negotiate a territorial dispute arising from the use of faulty maps in assigning borders under the Treaty of Guadalupe Hidalgo. Mexico's dire need for funds to rebuild its war-ravaged economy influenced its agreement to sell more land. Gadsden purchased over 45,000 square miles in what is now Arizona and New Mexico, land the United States wanted for a rail line to California. The Gadsden Purchase territories were in time seen to contain some of the world's richest copper mines.

The importance for the United States of this imperialist war and the later Gadsden Purchase cannot be overstated. Vast tracts of land, rich in natural resources, together with their Mexican and Indian inhabitants, provided conditions very favorable to U.S. development and expansion. The United States had done very well in its "little war" with Mexico.

DISPOSSESSION AND DISPLACEMENT

The make matters worse, the social and economic displacement of Mexicans and their reduction to the status of a colonized group proceeded rapidly, in clear violation of the civil and property rights guaranteed both by treaty and proto-

col. In Texas, a wholesale transfer of land from Mexican to Anglo ownership took place. That process had started at the time of the Texas Revolt and gained momentum after the U.S.-Mexico War. Mexican landowners, often robbed by force, intimidation, or fraud, could defend their holdings through litigation, but this generally led to heavy indebtedness, with many forced to sell their holdings to meet necessary legal expenses. With depressing regularity, Anglos generally ended up with Mexican holdings, acquired at prices far below their real value.[6]

The military conquest, the presence of U.S. troops, racial violence, governmental and judicial chicanery – all served to establish Anglos in positions of power in economic structures originally developed by Mexicans. Anglos adopted wholesale techniques developed by Mexicans in mining, ranching, and agriculture.[7] Because this major transfer of economic power from Mexicans to Anglos varied by region, it is important to say something about each.

Texas, responding to a significant expansion in the earlier Mexican-based cattle and sheep industries, was quick to cater to increased world demands. Acreage given over to cotton also expanded, helped greatly by improvements in transport facilities. These industries helped create and develop the mercantile towns that soon became conspicuous features on the Texas landscape.[8] Mexicans, instead of reaping the economic rewards of ownership, found themselves only contributing their labor. Mexicans were increasingly relegated to the lower ranks of society. By the end of the century, ethnicity, merged with social class, made Mexicans a mobile, colonized labor force.

The social structure of *New Mexico* in the beginning was quite different from that of Texas. The state, sparsely populated, was more densely settled in the north, in and about Santa Fé, than in the south; communal villages with lands granted to each community were common in the north. Communal water and grazing rights were assigned by community councils; only homestead and farming land were privately owned. Southern New Mexico, by contrast, boasted *haciendas* that had been established by grantees. This system consisted of *patrónes,* with settlers recruited to perform the necessary chores. It was a social structure organized on a debt-peonage system.

Anglo penetration into New Mexico after the war was more limited and did not occur on a large scale until the mid-1870s. Indian and Mexican defense of the territory served to keep out many settlers. Only an established U.S. military presence in the area made it at all accessible to Anglo cattlemen and farmers. Encountering a diversified class structure among the resident Mexicans, the Anglos generally chose to associate with the U.S. armed forces, creating a quasi-military society in the process. By the early 1880s, however, the railroads had helped to stimulate a new economic expansion. There was a further swelling of the Anglo population, and as pressure for land increased, the process of Mexican dispossession also dramatically accelerated.

The dispossession process in New Mexico was achieved in part through taxation. The Spanish-Mexican traditional practice had been to tax the products of the land. Under the new Anglo regime, land itself was taxed. With agricultural income fluctuating greatly with climatic conditions, fixed land taxes placed severe burdens on both farmers and ranchers. Small-scale subsistence farmers were unprepared and generally unable to raise the capital to meet the newly imposed tax liabilities. The practice of transferring the title on land on which delinquent taxes were owed to the person making such payment caused many Mexicans to lose their land. Fraud, deceit, and manipulation were common. An associate justice of the Court of Private Land Claims wrote:

> *A number of grants have had their boundaries stretched and areas marvelously expanded. But this has been done mostly by Yankee and English purchasers and not by the original Mexican owners. Where boundaries were made by natural landmarks, such as a "white rock," and "red hill," or a "lone tree," another rock, hill or tree of like description could always be found a league or two farther off, and claimed to be the original landmark described in the grant documents.[9]*

Toward the end of the century, federal policies also operated to dispossess Mexicans of their land. The National Forest Service, for example, began taking over millions of acres from northern villages, which were rarely compensated for their losses. Inhabitants were now compelled to pay grazing fees on land that had originally belonged to the villages. The granting of large tracts of land to the railroads served further to confine Mexicans to increasingly smaller land bases.

The Court of Private Land Claims, established in 1891 to resolve conflicts over land claims in New Mexico, Colorado, and Arizona, existed for thirteen years; its Anglo judges had a very limited knowledge and understanding of Mexican and Spanish landowning laws, traditions, and customs. Their judgments, based on Anglo legal practices, greatly contributed to the dispossessions. In time, Anglos came to own four fifths of the New Mexican grant areas,[10] and this loss of land relegated the vast majority of Mexicans to a bleak economic and social existence.

Twenty or so prominent Mexican families in New Mexico joined with the Anglo interests in banking, ranching, and the railroads, expecting to maintain their own political, economic, and social advantages.[11] The alliance, however, was controlled by the Anglo faction, and was therefore always unequal.[12] In any case, efforts by this small proportion of the original Mexican families to hold on to their advantaged status had no positive effect for the vast majority of Mexicans. As in Texas, ethnicity and class merged, and Mexicans, dispossessed of their holdings, saw them taken by the Anglo elites that dominated the political and economic activities of the society.

Arizona offers the example of the development of a colonial labor force in yet another mode. Arizona, not a separate entity at the time of conquest, was originally part of New Mexico, administered from Santa Fé. The small Mexican population was concentrated in the south, largely in Tucson and Tubac. One of the reasons for the sparseness of the settlements was the failure of the Spanish missionaries to impose Christianity on the nomadic Indian inhabitants; another was the aridity of the soil, which made agricultural pursuits difficult. The presence of the U.S. Army in the 1880s began to have its effects on the region. The Army fought the Indians, allowing the mining of copper and silver to resume; it was soon to become a large-scale economic enterprise. As with other industries, Anglo ownership was the norm; Mexicans contributed their labor, employing the familiar techniques they had developed long before.[13] Railroads accelerated the migration of Anglos and the establishment of new towns. The growth of all these major industries called for a cheap wage labor pool. Mexicans who migrated north, mostly to work in these industries, discovered that the wages they received for tasks identical to their Anglo counterparts were considerably lower. Restricted to menial and dangerous work, and forced to live in segregated areas in the mining and railroad communities that had created their jobs, they felt the indignity of their situation.[14]

California differed from the other regions: New England clipper ships had established very early ties with California; Franciscans, founding missions in the area in the 1830s, forced Christianized Indians into agriculture and manufacturing, to work alongside mulatto and *mestizo* Mexicans. This labor force helped to make California—economically, politically, and socially distant—independent of Mexico City. Excellent climate and abundant natural resources contributed to make this the most prosperous province in Mexico. Strong ties bound the missions to the *ranchos*. Missions, given large parcels of land to carry out their Christianizing enterprise, were neighbors of private individuals who owned vast tracts of land. Eventually, however, the privately owned *ranchos* established their supremacy throughout the province.

Urban settlements also developed: Monterey was the center of northern California; *el Pueblo de Nuestra Señora, la Reina de los Angeles de Porciúncula,* the economic and social center of southern California. Other towns sprung up around the major forts and missions. The rigid feudal system of *patrón* and *peón,* typical of southern New Mexico, did not develop in California. The class system that emerged was three-tiered: wealthy landowners enjoyed political, economic, and social power, and constituted about 10 percent of the population; artisans, small-scale landowners, vaqueros, herders, and soldiers constituted the bulk of Californian society; Indians and lower class *mestizos* stood at the bottom of the class hierarchy.

A few Anglos had come to Alta California before the U.S.-Mexico War; some were recipients of land grants, and many of them apparently assimilated into Mexican society. After the Texas revolt, however, Anglo foreigners coming to California were more reluctant to mingle or assimilate, and openly showed their antagonism towards Mexicans. The U.S. government was at the same time stepping up its efforts to secure California. In 1842, in fact, the U.S. flag was prematurely raised in Monterey, when Commodore Thomas Jones imagined that the war with Mexico had already begun.

The transfer of land titles from Mexicans to Anglos in California differed significantly from the transfer of title in other areas conquered by the U.S. forces. To begin with, the vast majority of Mexicans did not own land in California. The original *Californios* began to lose title to their lands to better-financed Anglo newcomers very early; there was no possibility of competing with wealth established through banking, shipping, railroads, and other such enterprises. The holdings of these new elites ran into the hundreds of thousands of acres early in the nineteenth century.[15]

Congress established the Land Commission in 1851 to judge the validity of grant claims made by *Californios* whose titles came down through the Spanish and Mexican periods. The commission served mainly to hasten the process of dispossession. Litigation costs often involved a contingent lawyer's fee of one quarter of the land in question. Some Mexican landowners borrowed money at high interest rates to carry on their legal fights, and frequently found themselves in the end selling their lands to meet their debts. Anglo squatters only added to the burden; they formed associations to apply political pressure favorable to their own interests, and were generally successful in retaining land forcefully taken from Mexicans.[16] Violence and murder in California, as in other parts of the conquered territories, was the order of the day.

Gold discoveries in 1849 in northern California brought a massive influx of Anglo goldseekers. Although Mexicans had been working claims in the area for some time, those who now arrived entered as laborers. The Anglo-American foreigners, inexperienced and ignorant of mining techniques, depended on the Mexican/Spanish/Indian mining experience in Arizona, northern Mexico, and California for the technical knowledge required to develop mining in California. Large-scale borrowing of mining techniques, tools, and language, not to speak of geological knowledge, took place between 1840 and 1860. The highly prejudiced Anglo miners treated Mexican miners as they did Chinese laborers; illegal taxation, lynchings, robbings, beatings, and expulsion became daily occurrences. Gold-mining lasted only a short time. When it was over, Anglos in great numbers turned to agricultural pursuits. The Mexican and Chinese populations migrated to California's towns to become landless laborers.

Southern California showed a very different face. *Rancheros* managed to hold onto their land for at least a generation after the Gold Rush. But climate, in the end, defeated many of them. Floods, followed by severe droughts, undercut the economy of the region in the 1860s and again in the 1880s. These were not "good times" for California agriculture.

By the turn of the century, Mexicans had been largely dispossessed of their property. Relegated to a lower-class status, they were overwhelmingly dispossessed landless laborers, politically and economically impotent. Lynchings and murder of both Mexicans and Indians were so common that they often went unreported. Long-term residents of the region were reduced to being aliens in their native lands. The common theme that united all Mexicans was their conflict with Anglo society. The dominant society, profoundly racist, found it entirely reasonable to relegate Mexicans to a colonial status within the United States.

POLITICAL, MILITARY, AND CULTURAL RESISTANCE

Mexican resistance to Anglo hegemony took many forms. A great deal has been made of what individuals like Tiburcio Vásquez and Joaquín Murrieta were able to do; they, and others like them, became legendary for their resistance to Anglo domination. While many others resorted to the courts, a militarily conquered people, dispossessed and relegated to a subservient economic and political status largely justified by notions of racial inferiority, have seldom been successful in pressing their grievances to any equitable solution through a legal system controlled by the conquerors.

The political resistance that occurred varied from region to region, but almost always involved an accommodating elite who wanted to force the conqueror to stick to the "rules"—to abide by the Constitution, the Treaty of Guadalupe Hidalgo, and the like. In some areas, Mexicans went as delegates to constitutional conventions, winning at least some of the battles that the treaty negotiators had not been able to guarantee. In California, for example, it was significant that the franchise was not limited to white males. Legal recognition of the Spanish language was achieved for various periods in certain areas. Such political victories were won through struggle and resistance, yet they were rarely long-lived. Once there was Anglo control over a region—through military or police action, by economic advantage, or population size—there was no possibility of such "victories" being sustained.

The military resistance of Mexicans was never "official." Such actions were most often responses to individual or collective Anglo acts of violence against a Mexican, whether through lynching, rape, murder, or arson. The first person hanged in occupied California was a Mexican woman, three months pregnant, who had been raped by a drunken Anglo assailant. Her Mexican lover/husband who killed the Anglo was exiled; she was lynched.

The atrocities of the U.S.-Mexico war, especially along the Texas-Mexican border, continued; the Texas Rangers in time assumed the role once taken by the U.S. Army in Texas, Jacinto Treviño, Joaquín Murrieta, Chino Cortina, and Las Gorras Blancas are all examples of the "people's revolt" continuing well into the early twentieth century. Although Anglos called such men bandits, outlaws ("Mexican outlaws"), and desperados (from *desesperados*—those without hope, those who are desperate), Mexicans considered them heroes, often aiding and abetting their activities, if for no other reason than because they saw them as the only friendly force between themselves and the Anglo gun.

Many Anglos saw the Mexicans as a natural resource of the region that was to be domesticated and exploited. The Mexicans refused such a characterization; their resistance was a struggle to maintain their identity – control over their language, family, art, and religion – that involved them in a continuing relation with Mexico.

MEXICO AND ITS RELATIVE STANDING

Mexico, a nation with a long history of striving for social, political, and economic stability, seemed farther from its goal after its war with the United States than ever. The French invasion of Mexico in 1860 and the ensuing political instability only served to exacerbate many of Mexico's problems. When Porfirio Díaz became president of Mexico in 1876, he inaugurated policies that were intended to lead to rapid economic development. Federal government policies encouraged European and U.S. investments in railroads, mining, oil, and agriculture, especially cotton, sugar, coffee, and rubber. The attraction of foreign capital and investment was, however, too successful. By the time of the 1910 Revolution, foreigners owned three-quarters of Mexico's mines, more than half of its oil fields, and massive tracts of land. Huge cattle ranches, particularly in northern Mexico, were owned by foreigners. Five major rail lines in northern Mexico, built and owned by U.S. interests, were characteristic foreign investments. Foreigners, in sum, owned more capital in Mexico than its citizens.

It was one thing to be successful in attracting foreign capital; it was another to reap significant benefits from such a policy. The effects of large-scale foreign investment were neither anticipated nor always beneficial to Mexico. The five rail lines, for example, did little to integrate Mexico's national economy. All five ran unerringly north, connecting Mexico's markets and labor supply with ranching and commercial centers in the U.S. Southwest. Mexico's products made their way into the world market economy; they were not intended for internal markets and thus brought no great advantage to Mexicans, whose industrial economy remained massively underdeveloped.

Meanwhile, mechanization in agriculture displaced many Mexican workers; few could be absorbed into the modest industrial sector. Prices for food and related commodities doubled, and in some cases tripled, in the decades just before the 1910 Revolution. Real wages declined; inflation was consistently high. At the same time, Mexico's population was growing rapidly; it increased by 50 percent between 1875 and 1910. Not surprisingly, such pressures led to great discontent and ultimately to the Revolution of 1910. That even, in turn, created a large-scale movement of Mexicans unable to fit into the restricted Mexican economy. Galarza, in his moving autobiography, *Barrio Boy*,[17] tells how Mexicans in the interior were forced from the land, sought work wherever they might find it – generally on the railroads – and gradually made their way northward, along with products extracted from Mexico, with scant compensation.

THE U.S. SOUTHWEST AND BEYOND, 1900–1930

Foreign capital investments in Mexico retarded its economic independence. Far more was extracted than was left for internal development. The situation was made even more serious by events within the United States, particularly in the Southwest, where the local economy was developing and expanding. Initial U.S. demands for labor were large, particularly for agriculture, but also for sheep and cattle ranching. Between 1870 and 1900 the land given over to farming increased from 60,000 to nearly a million and a half acres.[18] Protective tariffs for agricultural products helped to expand the acreage under cultivation. The more powerful influence, however, was the effort by the federal government to bring water to arid regions. The Reclamation Act of 1902 significantly bolstered the struggling agricultural economy of the Southwest; the building of dams and reservoirs in the desert-like area created new prospects for a highly labor-intensive agricultural enterprise. Large areas in California, Texas, Arizona, and New Mexico were turned over to the cultivation of cotton, a commodity of increasing demand for the new industrial sectors of the world. When war came in 1914, Allied needs gave additional incentives for such agricultural expansion. Southwestern agriculture diversified; sugar-beet cultivation was another labor-intensive enterprise bolstered by a protective tariff and improved irrigation; California, Colorado, and Utah all profited. Fruits and vegetables – citrus, lettuce, spinach, beans, carrots, dates, cantaloupes, and nuts – became important commodities, particularly in California.

Agriculture played its own procreative role. It helped create industries for the processing, canning, packing, and crating of agricultural products. These tied in nicely with an expanding rail system that first linked east with west, and later, and more pragmatically, crisscrossed the Southwest to transport its products to new markets. Sheep and cattle ranching continued, creating yet new industries in meat processing and shipping.

Mining gained new momentum and new dimensions during this period. The manufacturing of machinery for ore extraction and processing became vitally important, first, with copper in Arizona and New Mexico, then, with quartz in Nevada, Colorado, and Arizona, and later, with petroleum in Texas and California. The petroleum industry had a multiplier effect; it rapidly became a major component in the nation's burgeoning chemical industry.

The lumber industry also grew. Texas, California, Arizona, and New Mexico identified timber-cutting very early as a profitable economic activity that called for new modes of processing and distribution. These in turn developed still other industries.

The common denominator for all this rapid growth in the Southwest was the availability of cheap labor. The majority of European immigrants flowing into the United States through New York were absorbed in the industrial economies of the Northeast and Midwest. The Southwest had its own source of readily available and exploitable labor in the colonized Mexicans who filled the lower ranks of the economic order. They were still developing communities throughout the Southwest and would in time become increasingly visible also in the Midwest.

The conditions that greeted new immigrants from Mexico were essentially like those Mexicans already in the United States knew only too well. There was powerful racial hostility; Mexicans were thought to be inferior beings and inherently unassimilable and foreign. Their economic niche was insecure; their work was often seasonal in nature. In agricultural and related pursuits they were forced into a dual-wage system where they received low wages, frequently below those received by Anglos for the same type and amount of work. Many found themselves barred from supervisory positions. The situation in mining and related industries was not much different.

The railroad companies offered only slightly better conditions. By 1908 the Southern Pacific and the Atchison, Topeka, and Santa Fe were each recruiting more than a thousand Mexicans every month. The vast majority worked as section crews, laying track and ensuring its maintenance. The major difference between this industry and others in which Mexicans found work was that it seemed somewhat more stable and less seasonal; wages, however, were uniformly low.[19]

The Southwest was growing; its urban centers – in most instances, expanded versions of earlier Mexican towns – were often inhabited by Mexicans overwhelmingly concentrated in the lower range of the urban occupational structure. The wage differentials common to the rural sector were not as obvious in the urban areas. Access to particular occupations and industries, however, was limited and channeled. There was no mobility out of the unskilled and semiskilled positions in which Mexicans found themselves. They formed a reserve labor pool that could be called up as the situation dictated. When the economy expanded and jobs were created, these might be filled by Mexicans in specific sectors. Contractions of the economy relegated Mexicans quickly to the ranks of the unemployed; it was then they were reminded that they could be technically subject to another "sovereign," Mexico.

Mexicans served the industrial economy in other ways, also. As a reserve labor pool, employers used them as a short of "strike insurance," much as female and child labor were used to undercut unionizing efforts in other parts of the country. Such policies tended to generate ethnic antagonism between working-class Mexicans and working-class Anglos. Trade union practices, which excluded Mexicans and contributed to their exploitation, also helped to maintain them as a reserve labor pool, forcing them in the end to organize their own unions and associations.

While the beginnings of a middle class among Mexicans is discernible at this time, it is important to emphasize that most of those who made up this incipient class were self-employed in small-scale service businesses (newspapers, retail stores, and the like) while a few were "professionals," mostly elementary and secondary school teachers (in segregated schools). This class was never absorbed into the general economy. Rather, these business ventures tended to be restricted overwhelmingly to the Mexican community. On a social level, members of this emerging middle class encountered substantial barriers to their acceptance in the larger society, further perpetuating the prevailing patterns of residential and social segregation.

The Mexican government regularly lodged formal complaints with the State Department, protesting the abusive treatment its citizens received from industrial, mining, and agricultural enterprises. Those protests went largely unheeded; the U.S. government generally chose not even to verify the assertions, let alone make efforts to correct abuses.

By the early 1920s Mexicans began to settle outside of the Southwest. Many were recruited by northern manufacturing interests; meat-packing plants and steel mills in the Chicago area; automobile assembly lines in Detroit, the steel industry in Ohio and Pennsylvania; and Kansas City's meat-packing plants. By 1930 about 15 percent of the nation's Mexicans were living outside the Southwest. In addition to the recruitment of Mexicans from northern Mexico and the American Southwest by the industrial sector, many others chose to settle out of the principal migrant agricultural stream. Regular routes had become established that connected South Texas with the Great Lakes and Plains states. Many Mexicans continued their odyssey, following the crops west through the northern tier of states, finally arriving in the Northwest, and then turning south again. Others journeyed from Texas to the South, then north along the Eastern seaboard. Still others went west for agricultural work. Mexicans in California worked the crops north through that state, into the Northwest, and then east through the Mountain states. Many settled out of the migrant stream in areas where they found work.[20]

MIGRATION 1900–1930

No precise figures are available on the number of Mexicans who migrated north (or south) across the paper-made border between Mexico and the United States before 1900. The fact is that the border was open to unrestricted immigration until the creation and organization of the Immigration and Naturalization Service (and the Border Patrol) in 1924. Even then, however, large parts of the 2,000-mile border were unguarded, making the accuracy of all immigration figures somewhat questionable. One estimate is that from 1901 to 1910 approximately 9,300 Mexicans, principally from central and eastern Mexico, came to the United States each year.[21] In the second decade of the century, Mexicans came principally from northeastern and west-central Mexico; it is thought that 1,900 or so came annually between 1911 and 1914. About 2,750 migrated annually from 1915 to 1919. Economic factors and the Revolution of 1910 spurred migration during this period. The third decade witnessed a very heavy Mexican migration to the United States. Between 1920 and 1924, more than 135,000 Mexicans (about 27,000 on an annual basis) left for the United States. Migration then tapered off to just under 109,000 between 1925 and 1930, about 18,000 per year. In all, about a quarter of a million Mexicans arrived in the United States during the first three decades of the twentieth century. No comparable figures are available on return migration.[22]

Included in the large wave of Mexican immigrants were a number of merchants, landowners, and intellectuals, many of whom had been displaced by the Revolution of 1910. Many settled in Texas; others established themselves in the Midwest, in cities like Kansas City; some went as far north as Milwaukee. Many, continuing with activities they had pursued in Mexico, became entrepreneurs in the United States. A greater number of Spanish-language newspapers, pamphlets, books, and articles appeared; analysis of the political effects of the Mexican Revolution became a staple item of such publications. Many Mexicans who crossed the border at this time, including this group of entrepreneurs, saw themselves as temporary expatriates who would one day return to Mexico when conditions there were more settled.

The population flow from Mexico during these decades represents one of the largest movements of people in the history of the world. The reasons are easily discoverable: there was an active labor recruitment by mining, railroad, and agricultural interests in the American Southwest, who justified the policies by arguing that Mexicans were uniquely suited for work that Anglo workers refused to do. The labor shortage resulting from U.S. involvement in World War I was another reason for the large upturn in demand. Mexico's Revolution of 1910 also induced many to leave. The net result, however, was that economic interests in the Southwest found an abundant source of cheap and exploitable labor.

The United States has been quite deliberate in permitting access to all immigrants except Asians. This policy of unrestricted immigration had significantly furthered national development. Immigrants took jobs in the industrial Northeast and Midwest that natives would not take, frequently at wages that tended to undermine unionizing activities. Immigrants served other purposes as well; for example, they traditionally constituted a disproportionate number of the enlisted men in the U.S. military forces.

Between 1917 and 1924, however, a combination of events caused the open-door policy to be changed, and free access to the United States was thereby ended. The sixty-year struggle of nativists and xenophobes to control the foreign population stimulated restrictionist legislation and promoted Americanization programs. The uneasy peace after World War I nurtured fear and distrust of all that was foreign, ranging from the League of Nations to immigrants. Old Yankee families in New England viewed with some misgivings the rising percentage of foreign-born around them. Organized skilled labor felt that its interests could be protected only by sharply curtailing cheap foreign labor. There were blocs of Southerners, Populists, and Progressives, each with its own reasons, wanting immigration to end.[23]

These groups were successful. Legislation passed in 1924 set national quotas on European immigrants to the United States. The year used as a base for calculating national quotas was 1890, a date chosen with care and deliberation, for in that year many more of the "older" immigrants from Northern and Western Europe had arrived in the United States. The law thus discriminated openly against the "new" immigrants from Eastern and Southern Europe. Justification for restrictive immigration was provided by the detailed study of the Immigration Commission. Appointed in 1907 by President Theodore Roosevelt, and chaired by Senator Dillingham, the commission issued its conclusions in 1911 in an impressive forty-two volume report, which was soon widely quoted. Its principal message was that the new immigration was essentially different from the old and that new immigrants were less capable of being Americanized. Oscar Handlin, critically reviewing the commission and its work, cites the overt bias of the commission's report, beginning with the acceptance of the very assumptions it was ostensibly charged with investigating:

> The old and the new immigration differ in many essentials. The former was . . . largely a movement of settlers . . . from the most progressive sections of Europe. . . . They entered practically every line of activity. . . . Many of them . . . became landowners. . . . They mingled freely with the native Americans and were quickly assimilated. On the other hand, the new immigration has been largely a movement of unskilled laboring men who have come from the less progressive countries of Europe. . . . They have . . . congregated together in sections apart from native Americans and the older immigrants to such an extent that assimilation has been slow.
>
> Consequently the Commission paid but little attention to the foreign-born element of the old immigrant class and directed its efforts almost entirely to . . . the newer immigrants.[24]

The commission's report reflected the racial bias and attitudes of the time. Handlin cites from *The Passing of the Great Race*, the immensely popular book by the distinguished anthropologist Madison Grant on these newer immigrants:

> The new immigration contained a large and increasing number of the weak, the broken, and the mentally crippled of all races drawn from the lowest stratum of the Mediterranean basin and the Balkans, together with hordes of the wretched, submerged populations of the Polish ghettoes. Our jails, insane asylums, and alms-

houses are filled with human flotsam and the whole tone of American life, social, moral, and political, has been lowered and vulgarized by them.[25]

These beliefs, although vigorously debated in scientific circles, were given validation by their wholesale incorporation in the Dillingham Commission's report. They gave intellectual support for restrictive immigration legislation.[26] If the Rogers Act, passed in 1924, was silent on the matter of Mexican immigrants who continued to arrive in great numbers, there was no comparable reticence by the Dillingham Commission, which had said of Mexicans:

Because of their strong attachment to their native land, low intelligence, illiteracy, migratory life, and the possibility of their residence here being discontinued, few become citizens of the United States. . . . In so far as Mexican laborers come into contact with native or with European immigrants they are looked upon as inferiors. . . . Thus, it is evident that in the case of the Mexican he is less desirable as a citizen than as a laborer.[27]

The Dillingham Commission, in common with later immigration legislation, officially sanctioned the social and economic niche of Mexicans: they were not good enough for citizenship but certainly acceptable as manual laborers. Why such "tolerance"? To begin with, there was a great social distance between the Mexican of the Southwest and the nativists of the Midwest and Northwest. Also, the continued expansion of the region's economy, particularly in railroads and agriculture, made the availability of a large labor force imperative. Social distance and the emerging economic needs of the Southwest resulted in a lax policy toward Mexican immigration when the country was otherwise obsessed by its restrictionist mood.[28]

The passage of the 1924 Immigration Act made Mexicans conspicuous by their continued free access to the United States. Debate on the issue continued to agitate Congress. A report prepared for the 1928 congressional hearings on Western Hemisphere immigration, which argued against Mexican immigration, suggests how some, at least, saw the Mexican:

Their minds run to nothing higher than animal functions—eat, sleep, and sexual debauchery. In every huddle of Mexican shacks one meets the same idleness, hordes of hungry dogs, and filthy children with faces plastered with flies, disease, lice, human filth, stench, promiscuous fornication, bastardy, lounging, apathetic peons and lazy squaws, beans and dried chili, liquor, general squalor, and envy and hatred of the gringo. These people sleep by day and prowl by night like coyotes, stealing anything they can get their hands on, no matter how useless to them it may be. Nothing left outside is safe unless padlocked or chained down. Yet there are Americans clamoring for more of these human swine to be brought over from Mexico.[29]

The Indian racial mixture was clearly a part of the cultural perception, little distinction being made between the two. The nativist drive for racial purity, emphasizing the superiority of the "white" race, denigrated the racial mixture characteristic of Latin America generally and of Indian nations like Mexico in particular. Yet no action was taken to curb the flow of Mexican immigrants. The powerful economic arguments for the continued importation of Mexican laborers had been articulated two years earlier before a congressional committee by John Nance Garner, who was to become Franklin Roosevelt's vice president: "In order to allow land owners now to make a profit of their farms, they want to get the cheapest labor they can find, and if they can get the Mexican labor it enables them to make a profit."[30]

At the same time, control of the "immigrant" population came to include measures that could be applied to the domestic Mexican population. The Americanization activities of the early twentieth century spread throughout the country and were used to bleach all vestiges in the national flock. These activities included intensive English instruction—with retribution for those who chose to speak other tongues—and success defined as a capacity to speak as did the English-speaking middle class; and intensive "civic" classes to socialist the "foreign" population. The norm for success became the Anglo middle class, and standardized IQ and achievement tests measured this success. The widespread institution of high schools that traced the population into occupational or college preparatory curricula, with immigrants and racial minorities tracked into the former—when they entered high schools at all—became common. English oral proficiency became a requirement for immigration, as did English literacy for voting. The latter was also aimed at blacks in the South, and spread throughout the United States as a mechanism of social control. Legislation mandating English instruction in the schools and English proficiency as a prerequisite to employment was targeted for various groups in different parts of the country. Segregated Mexican schools were maintained. In the early 1930s, through federal court litigation, segregation based on race was challenged, and segregation based on grouping for language instruction was initiated and legitimized.[31] Statehood for Arizona and New Mexico (which together had been one territory) was denied several times at the beginning of the century, in part because there were too many Mexicans in the territory. References were made to their "mongrel racial character," their inability to speak English, and therefore, presumably, their dubious allegiance to the United States. Despite racial conflict, physical abuse, cultural genocide, and economic exploitation, the Mexican population grew; however, where restrictionists had failed to limit Mexican immigration, the Great Depression succeeded.

THE GREAT DEPRESSION AND REPATRIATION

The decade of the Great Depression was another watershed for Mexicans. Social forces during this period significantly shaped the lives of Mexicans and are in many ways still responsible for their status half a century later. The decade began with a massive economic collapse that started late in the 1920s and continued until World War II. There was a major decline in economic activities, with wage rates in both industry and agriculture suffering, and rampant unemployment. With this came a major acceleration of government intervention in social welfare, with bureaucracies developing and expanding to meet the urgent needs of a dislocated populace. There was also a large-scale westward migration out of the Dust Bowl. In the Southwest, this was a time of accelerated rates of concentration into larger and larger units in both agriculture and mining, where increased mechanization led to a further displacement of labor. The industrial sector in the Southwest lagged behind the rest of the na-

tion and could contribute little to absorb either the locally displaced labor or the dust-bowl migrants. These major economic dislocations fell on Mexicans with even greater force than on other groups. Already relegated to a marginal status, Mexicans were particularly vulnerable. The situation worked to eliminate for all practical purposes further northward migration from Mexico.

The Great Depression had another sobering effect: it engendered a collective social atmosphere of insecurity and fear that set the tone in allocating blame for the major social and economic traumas. Mexicans were singled out as scapegoats and made to bear the guilt for some of the ills of the period. It was not long before great numbers of unemployed Mexicans, like other citizens in the country, found themselves on the rolls of the welfare agencies.

One response to the strain placed on limited economic resources throughout the country was the demand for large-scale repatriations. To reduce the public relief rolls and agitation to organize labor, the Mexican became both the scapegoat and the safety valve in the Southwest. It is estimated that in the early years of the Depression (1929–34) more than 400,000 Mexicans were forced to leave the country under "voluntary repatriation." Those who applied for relief were referred to "Mexican Bureaus," whose sole purpose was to reduce the welfare rolls by deporting the applicants.[32] Indigence, not citizenship, was the criterion used in identifying Mexicans for repatriation.

A 1933 eyewitness account of a Los Angeles repatriation scene suggests the mental frame of those responsible for the program:

It was discovered that, in wholesale lots, they could be shipped to Mexico City for $14.70 per capita. The sum represented less than the cost of a week's board and lodging. And so, about February 1931, the first trainload was dispatched, and shipments at the rate of about one a month have continued ever since. A shipment consisting of three special trains left Los Angeles on December 8. The loading commenced at about six o'clock in the morning and continued for hours. More than twenty-five such special trains had left the Southern Pacific Station before last April.

The repatriation programme is regarded locally as a piece of consummate statecraft. The average per family cost of executing it is $71.14, including food and trans-

portation. It cost one Los Angeles County $77,249.29 to repatriate one shipment of 6,024. It would have cost $424,933.70 to provide this number with such charitable assistance as they would have been entitled to had they remained—a savings of $347,468.40.[33]

Repatriations took place both in the Southwest and Midwest, where Mexicans, recruited to the area by employers with promises of work, had lived since the early twenties. Approximately half of the "returnees" actually were born in the United States.[34] Shipment to Mexico was a clear violation of both their civil and human rights. The Immigration and Naturalization Service, in concert with the Anglo press, identified the Mexican labor migrant as the source of (Anglo) citizen unemployment, for the increase of public welfare costs (and taxes), and as having entered the country "illegally" and in large numbers. The scapegoating tactics of an earlier nativist generation, with its xenophobic memories and myths, were used against the Mexicans. There was a good deal of sentiment also against Mexico's expropriation and nationalization of its oil industry, which U.S. oil companies had once controlled. Repatriation caused widespread dissolution of family and community, and contributed to an even more acute distrust among Mexicans of all government—local, state, or federal.

Some small efforts at organized resistance were made. Strikes and organizational campaigns were started in the agricultural and industrial sector. *La Unión de Trabajadores del Valle Imperial* and *La Confederación de Uniones Obreras Mexicanas* began late in the 1920s to try to ease the blow of the unfolding Depression through labor organizing and self-defense. There were similar, but less successful, efforts made in the mining industry. *La Confederación Regional Obrera Mexicana,* a Mexican industrial union affiliated with the American Federation of Labor, sought to encourage the formation of unions in California.

Mexican consuls, meanwhile, continued to lodge complaints with the federal government, protesting the treatment of Mexican citizens recruited to work in the United States. Official protests by Mexico generally were ignored, and the abuses went unchecked.

Despite all such efforts, the social and economic standing of Mexicans was seriously eroded by the Great Depression. Families were forcibly broken up by the repatriation efforts, as were

communities. The overall economic impact of trade union activities was limited, and failed to modify the underlying problem of relegating Mexicans to the lowest levels of the economic system.

WORLD WAR II TO 1960

World War II brought many changes. In the economic upturn that followed, there was a new demand for both industrial and agricultural labor. The movement to the cities accelerated. Regional economic needs and interests reasserted themselves; they were again instrumental in shaping national legislation in the agricultural arena. The bracero program, reestablished in 1942 and patterned after a similar program in effect from 1917 to 1920, was based on a bilateral agreement between Mexico and the United States, and was intended to supply labor for agriculture. The United States underwrote Mexicans' travel costs, insured a minimum wage, and guaranteed their just and equitable treatment. Agricultural interests were required to post a bond for every bracero and to abide by the agreements negotiated by the two governments. The program, in effect, was a federal subsidy of agriculture's labor needs.

Although intended only as a limited-term war measure to meet specific labor shortages in the agricultural sector, the advantages of the bracero program to both countries suggested its continuance. For Mexico, it was a temporary solution for high levels of unemployment, and made for a significant flow of capital to Mexico in wages earned and sent home. For U.S. agriculture, it gave promise of a steady supply of labor that was readily controlled and minimally paid, and for whom no long-term responsibilities were assumed.

The program, extended annually after the war, was formalized in 1951 as Public Law 78. The reasons given for the extension were labor shortages stemming from U.S. involvement in the Korean War; it is better understood as a continuation of the traditional U.S. manipulation and control of the flow of Mexican labor. The program was terminated in 1964, when annual immigration quotas of 120,000 were established for all the nations of the Western Hemisphere.

Large-scale abuses were common in the program.[35] Mexico protested these abuses, and each time the agreement was renegotiated, sought to protect its citizens from the inequitable wages and overt discrimination in working conditions, housing, and general treatment. The U.S. government relinquished the determination of wage rates to the agricultural employers, but continued to take responsibility for contracting and transporting Mexican laborers across the border. Nearly 5 million Mexicans came to the United States as a result of the program. The peak years were from 1954 to 1962, when 70 percent of all Mexicans involved in the program were working in the United States. We have no figures to tell us how many of these laborers returned to Mexico.

A steady flow of undocumented workers paralleled this importation of braceros. The undocumented proved to be a mixed blessing for agricultural interests. On the one hand, they were generally hired for wages substantially below the modest levels that agribusiness established for braceros, and bonds were not required to be posted for them. They were widely used as strikebreakers to thwart unionizing activities in agriculture. But there were obvious drawbacks. A labor pool made up of largely undocumented workers was very unstable. Since such workers were under no binding agreement to any employer, they were free to seek the highest wage, within the restrictions imposed by specific jobs and particular industries, and under the continuous threat that the employer would terminate the job by calling the Immigration and Naturalization Service just before he was to meet the payroll. To the extent that agribusiness failed to establish a uniform wage, there was a constant temptation for undocumented workers to move on in search of better employment. Moreover, since the undocumented worker was not covered by an agreement restricting him to agricultural tasks, he would always be attracted by industrial jobs in cities, where wages and working conditions were generally better. During World War II, the informal agreements between industry and agribusiness that prohibited the hiring of Mexican labor for factory work were in abeyance.

We understand today how an initial bilateral agreement between Mexico and the United States to supply braceros became in time a unilateral program dictated by U.S. agricultural interests, supported by the federal government.[36] Once agricultural employers took control of the bracero program, they sought to expand their control also over the undocumented worker. Agricultural entrepreneurs ended up by transporting undocumented workers to the border where they were immediately rehired as braceros, thereby transforming what was once an unregulated labor supply into a legal and semicontrolled work force bound to the agricultural sector.

After a regulated labor pool was firmly reestablished for agribusiness, in 1954 the Immigration and Naturalization Service vigorously launched "Operation Wetback." Undocumented workers, unstable and intractable as a labor source, were now to be removed. An astonishing 3.8 million Mexican aliens (and citizens) were apprehended and expelled in the next five years. Of the total number deported during that time, fewer than 2 percent left as a result of formal proceedings. The vast majority were removed simply by the *threat* of deportation. "Looking Mexican" was often sufficient reason for official scrutiny. The search focused initially on California and then Texas; it soon extended as far as Spokane, Chicago, St. Louis, and Kansas City.[37]

For urban Chicanos and Mexicans, World War II had effects similar to those for their rural cousins. On the positive side, war industries provided the semblance of occupational opportunity for many, though often in unskilled, semiskilled, and low-level service capacities. Still, the rigid tie between class and ethnicity seemed somewhat weakened.

World War II posed a major dilemma for the United States. In its official pronouncements and acts, the country strongly condemned the racism explicit in Nazism. Yet at the same time, the United States had a segregated military force. This was also a time when President Roosevelt issued Executive Order No. 9066, which authorized the internment of Japanese who were U.S. citizens and whose sole "crime" was living and working on the West Coast.

This contradiction also manifested itself in ugly confrontations between Mexicans and Anglos. The press, for its part, helped to raise feelings against Mexicans. The violent confrontations between servicemen and local police against Mexican residents began late in 1942 and continued until mid-1943. The overt racial bias of the press with regard to Mexicans has been thoroughly documented. It suggests the power of the press in shaping public opinion and in justifying major abuses by law enforcement and military personnel. The so-called zoot suit riots illustrate the power of the press in mobilizing prejudice:

> The zoot-suiters of Los Angeles . . . were predominantly Mexican youth with some Negro disciples, between the ages of sixteen and twenty. They wore absurdly long coats with padded shoulders, porkpie hats completed by a feather in the back, watch chains so long they almost touched the ground, and peg-top trousers tapering to narrow cuffs . . . at best, as one pundit observed, they were "not characterized primarily by intellect." They formed themselves into bands with flamboyant names: the "Mateo Bombers," "Main Street Zooters," "The Califa," "Sleepy Lagooners," "The Black Legion," and many more. Their targets for physical harm were members of the armed forces, with a special predilection for sailors. The latter fought back with devastating effect. The situation quickly deteriorated to the point that the Navy declared Los Angeles out of bounds. The city council outlawed wearing zoot suits for the duration and the city simmered down.[38]

Some investigators, more objective than the press, have reversed the roles, with the navy on the offensive and the Mexican young obliged to defend themselves. The firsthand accounts show that the police actually encouraged and supported the servicemen's aggression. And not only did the police refuse to halt the violence, they often contributed to it.[39]

Another celebrated incident was the so-called Sleepy Lagoon case in 1942. A Mexican youth was killed as the result of gang conflict. A sensationalist press soon gave the incident a wholly false character; it was thought to be the beginnings of an incipient crime wave led by insurgent Mexicans. Public pressure led the police to massive roundups. Twenty-four Mexican youths were arrested; seventeen were indicted and tried for murder. The defendants, beaten by the police and forced to appear in court in their unkempt and disheveled states, received scant sympathy. Despite the lack of tangible evidence, nine were convicted of murder, eight, of lesser crimes. These decisions, reversed two years later by the California District Court of Appeals as a direct result of efforts by outraged civil rights lawyers

and activists, tell much of the temper of the times. They also suggest why Chicanos and Mexicans are so suspicious of the U.S. law enforcement and legal systems. Mexicans believe that they consistently receive harsher sentences than Anglos for the same crime. They also believe that this explains their disproportionate representation in U.S. penal institutions.[40]

The Mexican community, in responding to the situation of World War II, acted as it had done in previous times of hostility and exploitation—with organizational efforts and litigation, and occasionally with armed resistance. Unity Leagues, created in the early 1940s, had as their principal purpose the election of Mexicans to city councils in Southern California communities; they also conducted voter registration drives, attempted fund-raising, and worked to get voters to the polls. The basic theme uniting these leagues was the fight against racial discrimination, particularly in the schools. The League of United Latin American Citizens (LULAC), founded in South Texas in 1928, expanded into a national organization in the post-World War II period, and was soon heavily involved in anti-discrimination activity, again particularly in the educational arena.

A landmark court decision in 1945 (*Méndez v. Westminster School District*) barred *de jure* segregation of Chicano students. A similar legal action in Texas in 1948 was also successfully pressed. The results of both court actions, as well as others during the 1950s, helped set the stage for the Supreme Court's *Brown v. Board of Education* decision in 1954, and clearly established the illegality of the deliberate segregation of Chicano and Mexican school children on the basis of race, and of bilingual education as a partial remedy for segregation. The success of these efforts served to encourage civil rights suits in other areas, notably against job discrimination in New Mexico.[41]

The refusal of local officials in Corpus Christi, Texas, in 1948, to allow the burial of a Chicano war hero in the local "for whites only" cemetery was the specific catalyst for the creation of the G.I. Forum. The Mexican community proudly emphasized two facts: Chicanos received the largest number of Congressional Medals of Honor during World War II, and despite forbidding interrogations by the North Koreans and

Chinese during the Korean War, no Chicano soldier ever "broke down." The collective memory of such Chicano military contributions fed the Mexican distaste of continued political gerrymandering, economic exploitation, physical abuse, and cultural repression at home.

The Mexican American Political Association, formed in 1959, had as its goal "the social, economic, cultural and civic betterment of Mexican Americans and all other Spanish-speaking Americans through political action." The association established chapters in voting districts with large concentrations of Mexican residents, and endorsed candidates for public office who could be counted on to work actively for social improvement.

Large numbers of Mexicans migrated to urban centers in the decades after World War II. There was a general optimism that life in the cities would be better than in the rural setting. The cities seemed to hold out the promise of better jobs, more adequate housing, and new educational possibilities. These early migrants to the cities came with visions of expanded opportunities, and believed that if they themselves did not achieve their aspirations, their children surely would. This optimism made tolerable the thwarted aspirations so many of these urban migrants soon came to feel. Since they outnumbered Mexicans already living in the cities, their optimism spread to the larger group.

Many of the postwar organizations were primarily self-protective, mutual-aid associations. They were formed principally to protect their numbers by offering services consistent with Mexican cultural traditions, in effect compensating for services withheld by the larger society. Organizations such as the G.I. Forum and LULAC entered the activist period of the 1950s and 1960s with an organizational base redirected toward activism. Their resources were considerable—a growing constituency, established legitimacy, and a solid leadership core. Their past history of noninvolvement in political affairs, their emphasis on assimilation, or working within the system, and their passive, nonactivist stance, drew criticism in the 1970s. Such groups, however, provided the foundation for attempts to improve the condition of the Mexican people.

THE CHICANO MOVEMENT 1965–1975

In the 1960s and early 1970s, activist, sometimes radical, organizations appeared. These organizations came to be known collectively as the Chicano movement. Often very critical of the basic assumptions of U.S. society, they sought fundamental transformations in the distribution of power in the United States. Many promoted radical alternatives, preferring socialism, for example, to the prevailing economic and political system. Others hoped to create various kinds of alternative or separatist institutions, with alternative schools, community control of law enforcement, health, educational, and political institutions, and the like. They were looking, in short, for a radical and equitable transformation of a racist society. Almost all such groups emphasized the distinctiveness of Mexican culture. They actively promoted Chicano cultural norms and values. Chicano culture represented the common ground that bound together all the members of the group. Political terms such as "Chicano" and *La Raza Nueva* were used to symbolize unity, and were intended to increase the cohesiveness of otherwise diverse elements.

Charismatic leaders appeared. Reies López Tijerina hoped to restore lost Spanish and Mexican land grants in New Mexico through the widely publicized and often dramatic activities of the *Alianza Federal de Pueblos Libres*. Rodolfo "Corky" Gonzáles, former prizefighter and disaffected Democratic party official, organized the Crusade for Justice and established several alternative community institutions in the Denver area. The miserable working conditions of Mexican agricultural laborers became the special concern of the United Farm Workers Organizing Committee, led by César Chávez.

Throughout the Southwest and Midwest, political and educational issues sparked new organizing activity. In Texas, José Angel Gutiérrez and others overthrew the minority Anglo-dominated governments of several South Texas cities and counties, primarily through a third party, *El Partido de La Raza Unida*. To secure educational change, students in secondary schools and colleges formed Chicano organizations to stage massive school walkouts. These organizations served as foci for various kinds of diffused activities;

they brought a variety of grievances under a single banner, and made a collective approach to these grievances possible.

Anglo decision-makers, reacting to the politics of direct action and confrontation, were sometimes repressive, sometimes progressive; many of the gains made could be attributed to the "threatening" activities of such militant organizations. The protest groups, however, were often short-lived. They called for a great expenditure of time and effort and involved considerable risk.

The student groups were ideologically very diverse: some were moderate-liberal; others were radical. The Mexican American Youth Organization, a precursor in Texas to the *Raza Unida* party, gave José Angel Gutiérrez, Mario Compeán, and others apprenticeship training in community-based and campus-based politics. *El Movimiento Estudiantíl Chicano de Aztlán,* a campus-based organization, was fairly radical and had many chapters throughout the Southwest; it was very active in support of the farm workers' movement and many other nonschool issues. The United Mexican American Students and the Chicano Youth Organization were other prominent student organizations during this period. Although such organizations often worked off-campus, they pushed also for increased recruitment of Chicano students and faculty, for opening new educational opportunities to Chicanos, and for curricula more relevant to Chicano concerns. Many of these demands were embodied in the new Chicano Studies programs developed in many colleges and universities.

The importance of these campus-based organizations cannot be overemphasized. They provided invaluable resources for both on-campus and off-campus activities. Many interacted with both staff and faculty. Student groups were effective agents of political mobilization; they had the idealism, ideological commitment, and the relatively supportive environment necessary for sustained organizational activities. Many of these campus organizations, however, were unable to contend with the rapid turnover of student populations, with increasing administrative intransigence, and internal division created by law enforcement *provocateurs* and ultraleftist organizations.

Prior to the 1970s there were few Chicano professional associations, which is not surprising, given the small number of Chicano professionals. As the system yielded to pressure, however, and greater numbers of Chicanos became teachers, lawyers, physicians, and business managers, organization became viable. Many started with less than a dozen members; in many of the academic disciplines, the formation of Chicano/Latino caucuses in major Anglo professional organizations was a necessary first step. Public and private foundations, responding to demands for increased numbers of Chicano professionals, provided support to foster organizational activity. Among these were the *Southwest Council de la Raza,* the Mexican American Legal Defense and Educational Fund (MALDEF), and the *National Task Force de la Raza.*

Until 1970, Mexicans were traditionally concentrated in the nonunion ranks of the U.S. economy. Starting in the early 1920s they attempted to form their own unions or to affiliate with unions in Mexico and the United States. The leadership of established industrial unions in this country was never Chicano, although some change is now taking place. Latino workers – Mexicans, Puerto Ricans, and others – are beginning to coalesce in organizations such as the Labor Council for Latin American Advancement.

With the establishment of "national" offices based in Washington, several Chicano organizations began to grow in the mid-1970s. Interorganizational cooperation between Chicanos and Latinos in general has become more common. There have been several attempts to weld "Hispanic" organizations together in some sort of federation, notably the newly created Forum of National Hispanic Organizations and the Hispanic Higher Education Coalition. In the late 1970s such Washington-based groups as the *National Council de la Raza,* MALDEF, and the Mexican American Women's National Association could coordinate to express the common concerns of Chicano organizations.

Chicanos have gravitated toward public employment, having found opportunities there, particularly in lower-status positions, somewhat more open than in the private sector. Organizations within the public sector, such as IMAGE, a nationwide group of employees that seeks to enhance the working conditions and positions of

Chicanos and other Latinos with the government, have emerged. Although there are few high-level government officials of Mexican origin, organizations of Latino officials have come into being. The National Association of Latino Elected and Appointed Officials tries to increase communication between Chicano and Latino decision-makers, particularly on the local level. The Congressional Hispanic Caucus, consisting of the six Latino members of Congress, is the group with the highest governmental status at the federal level.

Two broad coalitions of interests make up the major political parties in the United States, and in general, Chicanos have been exploited by both. Many of the successes of the Democratic party can be attributed to the 70 to 90 percent electoral support regularly given by Chicano voters. Minimal rewards, in the form of minor patronage and policy concessions, have been returned to the Chicano community by the Democratic party, which for the most part has taken the Chicano vote for granted. In very close elections, Democrats have made extravagant promises to Chicanos, but once the election is over, the Anglo Democratic leadership has generally failed to follow through. The Republican party has only limited appeal for Chicanos; Republican leaders have not made a very serious effort to broaden their base by attracting Chicano participation.

Minor parties, including socialist and Marxist-oriented parties, have not been very successful in recruiting Chicanos to their cause. The most successful third party movement for Chicanos, *El Partido de la Raza Unida* (LRUP), at the height of its influence in the early 1970s played a pivotal role in determining the outcome of several local elections, primarily in South Central Texas. In small localities with large Chicano populations, it succeeded in school, town, and county government elections, often stressing the unresponsiveness of the major parties, and arguing for cultural nationalism. The *Partido* provided an alternative that threatened the customary hegemonic position of the major parties. Both the Democratic and the Republican parties reacted by supporting minor institutional reform: they set up "Hispanic" offices within their party organizations, and the Democratic party went so far as to guarantee Chicano representation in its party structure.

Conflicts within its own ranks over strategic issues led *La Raza Unida* to fragment into smaller locally based units. Punitive measures sponsored by the State of Texas and specifically aimed at breaking up the *Partido* contributed to its decline. Modification in electoral laws proved problematic to third parties that attempted to place their candidates on the ballot. By raising the number of required petition-signers or voters received to qualify for inclusion on the ballot, third parties could be excluded.

By the late 1970s the organizational base of the Chicano community had been largely transformed. Many of the more radical and ideological organizations had either disappeared or were mere shadows of their former selves. Leaders who cut their political teeth in such organizations have become part of older, more broadly based organizations or have joined the new professional organizations that continue to advocate, with renewed spirit, specific political reforms. The organizational structure changes as collective and individual political sophistication continues to grow.

GROWTH AND NATIONAL VISIBILITY

The structural characteristics of the Chicano population suggest why Chicanos have gained national visibility. All demographic description starts by emphasizing the youthfulness of the Chicano population, the median age for Chicanos being seven years younger than the national population. A youthful population is one that will be active for a longer period, with the bulk of its members in an early phase of labor force participation, or only just beginning to prepare for that phase. A youthful population has its future before it; schooling, family formation, and child-rearing are crucial issues. And given their rapid numerical growth, Chicanos must play an increasingly important role in the United States in the next decades.

With journalistic phrases like "people on the move," "awakening giant," "emerging minority," and "sleeping giant," writers have drawn attention to the "sudden" visibility of Chicanos. Some are surprised by this visibility. Even the most casual traveler through the southwestern United States has observed the centuries-old Spanish and

Mexican influence on architecture, cuisine, language, art, music, and the very layout of towns and cities. Chicano presence in the Southwest has never been hidden. It is the sudden awareness that Chicanos also reside outside these traditional southwestern enclaves, and that Chicano issues are not simply regional in nature, that has drawn the continuing attention of the mass media. Indeed, the rapid *growth* and continuing *dispersion* of the Chicano population is producing the new national awareness.

The Chicano population has grown substantially over the last decade. Although this growth is attributed in part to improved methods of survey and enumeration by gathering agencies such as the Census Bureau, the greatest part of the increase comes from the real growth of the Chicano population. This growth rate has been conservatively estimated at 2.2 percent per year; a more liberal estimate is 3.5 percent per year. The first figure indicates a doubling of the Chicano population every twenty-five to twenty-seven years; the second, a doubling in less than twenty years.

This phenomenal rate of growth is in stark contrast with decreasing growth rates for the U.S. population as a whole. While U.S. birth rates are stabilizing at just above replacement level, the Chicano population is maintaining the highest rate of growth of all major racial and ethnic groups in the country. Early marriage and the emphasis placed on family accounts for these high fertility rates. Chicano families are generally about 24 percent larger than the average American family, and one in every five Chicano families consists of six or more persons.

There is, however, a trend toward lower birth rates. Younger Chicanas are having fewer children and spacing them out longer over the childbearing years. Still, even among younger and better-educated women, the emphasis on childbearing appears to remain strong; voluntary childlessness among married Chicanas, or those who were married, is virtually unknown.

The high fertility rates of Chicanos suggest major structural differences between them and the Anglo population. Although the Anglo birth rate has decreased owing to later marriages, birth spacing, and the use of contraceptives to synchronize childbearing with the demands of increased female employment, this has not always been the case. From the late 1930s to the early 1940s the United States had high rates of immigration and fertility; the two together produced a period of high population growth. The Chicano population explosion today is in many ways reminiscent of that earlier era, with high rates of immigration (both legal and undocumented) and birth rates. All signs point to a significant growth of the Chicano population in the 1980s.

There is now considerable discussion regarding total Hispanic population growth in the United States and whether this collective group will overtake blacks as the largest national minority group. Precise projections are impossible, since they depend on how long current high rates of growth in the Hispanic population are sustained. Still, it is now expected that the Hispanic population will become the largest minority in the United States in the foreseeable future. Further, since Chicanos make up the majority – 60 percent – of this population group, they will be among the more visible elements in what is increasingly referred to as the "Hispanization" of the United States.

If high birth rates are important, so also is immigration. The century-old relationship between the United States and Mexico continues to affect both nations. Immigrants, natural resources, and profits continue to flow north. Legal immigration from Mexico to the United States at present allows between forty and fifty thousand visas each year for permanent residence. Those looking for "commuter status," which allows them to work in the United States while living in Mexico, have to endure, barring political connections, a three-year waiting period.

Mexican workers caught in Mexico's economic sluggishness are aware that wages in the United States for identical work are sometimes seven times higher than at home, and many are thus led to risk illegal entry. Such illegal entry is only increased by the active recruitment by "coyotes," who transport Mexicans across the border for a fee. Undocumented workers are a significant part of the U.S. labor force, particularly for work that most American citizens regard as demeaning, low paying, dirty, and unstable. Undocumented workers have always come to the United States in circumstances of multiple jeopardy, as minorities unprotected from employer exploitation and abuse. Such conditions continue unabated today.

A majority of the undocumented workers in the United States come as sojourners in search of economic opportunity; few have any desire to remain here as permanent residents. Despite the widespread impression that Mexican undocumented workers come across the border in search of the promised land, *corridos,* or ballads, by and about them celebrate the less hostile, more familiar ambience they plan to return to.

The flow of immigration, both legal and undocumented, is extensive: more than a million persons annually are apprehended by the Border Patrol for seeking entry without inspection. Annual deportations, both voluntary and involuntary, continue to increase steadily. These statistics suggest improved enforcement capabilities; they also measure, however crudely, the growth in the number of Mexicans wanting to cross the permeable U.S.-Mexico border. That flow increases in part because of labor force needs. Jobs are available to Mexican migrants largely in the secondary labor market, where the lack of fringe benefits makes these low-paying, seasonal jobs unattractive to domestic workers. The Mexican worker historically has been desirable. Mexicans – particularly without legal rights and privileges – are especially desirable for agribusiness, marginal industries, seasonal work, or in businesses quickly affected by economic downturns.

Although only a small fraction of the undocumented workers come to the United States with any intention of staying, there is no reason to believe the Mexican immigration will cease, at least in the foreseeable future. The flow of nearly a century and a half, responding to the need for labor by U.S. employers, seems to argue against the possibility of immigration being terminated. The growth of the Chicano population, because of higher fertility and continued immigration, is increasingly visible. The continued dispersion of the Chicano population out of the Southwest into the industrial Midwest, particularly into cities like Chicago, Gary, Hammond, Kansas City, Detroit, Flint, and Saginaw, will go on. It is not difficult to understand the attraction of the Midwest: a Chicano worker with a high-school education will earn approximately $4,000 more per year there than his cousin can expect to earn in the Southwest.

Such differentials in income are significant. The Midwest, highly unionized and with a long-established industrial base, is very different from the Southwest, which is only now beginning to unionize, and where light manufacturing is still the rule. In the Southwest, also, labor-intensive industries in agriculture and mining are giving way to high-level service industries in aerospace, electronics, and petrochemicals that require a labor force that is technically trained. This new labor force tends to be made up largely of transplanted Easterners.

Chicanos in the Midwest, Pacific Northwest, Florida, and other parts of the United States need to be seen as a vanguard. Although farther removed from their origins, they still maintain and perpetuate their Mexican heritage. Their entry into an area is almost always followed by the rapid opening of small Chicano businesses that specifically cater to their needs. Spanish-language mass at the Catholic Church typically follows, along with Spanish-language radio programs and bilingual programs in the schools. The taking root of Chicano businesses, services, and traditions produces a Midwestern version of the Southwestern or Mexican environment. The ability of Chicanos to transfer their ethnic preferences from one location to another tells something of the strength and durability of their cultural ties.

Midwestern Chicanos, finding themselves among non-Chicano Latinos, necessarily interact, but not always easily or without hostility and suspicion. New patterns, however, are becoming evident as efforts at cooperative ventures are made. Chicanos in Milwaukee, Chicago, and Detroit, for example, discovering that they face problems very similar to those of other Latinos, seek to create coalitions that form the basis for a national Latino thrust. These contacts have understandably progressed further among Cuban, Puerto Rican, and Chicano leaders at the national level than at the local level, particularly as the strategy of nationally organized coalition-building has spread.

The dispersal of Chicanos has had positive and negative effects, making it obvious that Chicano issues cannot be dealt with simply as a regional (Southwestern) matter. Chicanos now reside in every state in the Union; the 1980s will undoubtedly see almost half the Chicano population residing outside the five southwestern states. Had the dispersal of Chicanos not occurred, most of the southwestern states would be overwhelmingly Chicano. Although the size of population does not automatically translate into political power, political negotiation and coalition-building would have taken very different forms if the Southwest had become a single and greater Chicano enclave.

CURRENT STATUS

Chicanos lag behind the rest of the U.S. population by every measure of socioeconomic well-being—level of education, occupational attainment, employment status, family income, and the like. Some say that Chicanos are no different from other immigrants who arrived in the United States impoverished, and who managed by hard work to gain advantages for their children, taking the first important step toward assimilation. The substantial achievements of the American-born first generation over that of the immigrant generation are thought to be conclusive. Such an optimistic view overlooks major changes in the society and the historical relationship of over a century and a half of racial discrimination and economic exploitation. Although economic expansion and dramatic social change characterized the postwar years, economic contraction and dislocation, possibly exaggerated by the new conservative retrenchment, are the hallmarks of more recent times. When the economy was productive and growing, Chicanos participated in that growth, at least through their labor. A close examination, however, suggests that the modest gains made in average income and occupational status during the 1950s and 1960s were lost in the 1970s. As one scholar explains:

When the 1975 occupational employment distributions for Anglos and Chicanos are compared to the Labor Department's revised estimates for 1985 employment opportunities, it is clear that the [1975] recession hurt the future income potential of Chicanos as well as their current incomes. In general, the recession has forced Chicanos into occupational groups for which future employment is expected to decline relative to the employ-

ment and in which relative wages can be expected to fall as well. Similarly, while Anglos were moving into those occupations that are expected to have the greatest future income potential, Chicanos were moving out, thus losing the ability to share in the expected relative wage increases that growth usually brings. By 1975, only 33 percent of Chicanos were located in expanding occupations. . . . The evidence supports the conclusion that our latest recession had a definite racial bias and that Mexican Americans received more than their share of economic hardship.[42]

Although second-generation and later Chicanos made large gains relative to those of the first generation, such gains did not allow for their thorough absorption into the economic and social structure of U.S. society. The data of the late 1970s suggest how different generations of Chicanos have fared.[43] The median education for second-generation Chicanos was 11.1 years, only two years more than for U.S.-born first-generation, but decidedly more than for the immigrant generation (5.8 years).

All generations of Chicano males are underrepresented in white-collar jobs; Mexican-born males are least likely to be found in such positions. Farm labor is the one area where there is a significant difference between the U.S.-born and immigrant Chicano populations.[44] Over 15 percent of Mexican-born men are employed as farm laborers, twice the number for sons of Mexican immigrants, five times the number of third-generation Chicanos. Labor force participation figures, however, also show that second-generation Chicanos had the highest unemployment rate, while the immigrant generation had the lowest. The data on incomes indicate first-generation Chicano families as having the highest median income, with the second-generation following, and the Mexican-born as having the lowest incomes. The range, however, was not great—about $1,500.

That Mexicans who have resided for the longest time in the United States—second generation—have the highest unemployment rates and only very modest representation in white-collar, professional, and managerial categories suggests the limited structure of opportunity for Chicanos. They are entering the industrial sector at a time when its socioeconomic structure is increasingly tertiary, demanding highly trained personnel in high-technology industries such as aerospace, communications, and the like. Although Chicanos may be making "progress" relative to their immigrant parents, they are actually falling farther behind when looked at in the context of the opportunity structure in an increasingly post-industrial social order and compared to the dominant population. Also, there is evidence that Chicano technical and occupational skills will increasingly limit them to the secondary labor market, with its unfavorable wage rates, limited fringe benefits, and general instability. These conditions to not promise either full equity or full participation for Chicanos in the decades immediately ahead. Still, that the Anglo population growth is at or near a steady state, with its income-generating population increasingly aging, suggests that the younger and expanding Chicano work force will be shouldering a growing and disproportionate burden in the future. Social Security, Medicare, Medicaid, and the myriad of other social programs funded from taxes on the work force will be more and more borne by youthful employed Chicanos.

Historically, Chicanos' economic rewards have been disproportionate to their contribution to U.S. industrial development. Now that the society is increasingly post-industrial, Chicanos find themselves still carrying the burden. The federal government, which played a prominent role throughout the history of Mexicans in the United States, has been repressive, supporting industries and employers, and generally frustrating Chicanos' efforts to advance. Many of the organizations developed by Chicanos were direct responses to these negative influences. The prediction seems to be unremitting governmental policies that will continue to deplete the resources of the Chicano community or leave it as disadvantaged as ever. But Mexico's new wealth, particularly its energy resources, may somewhat alter that prognosis, especially if Mexico retains control over those resources. A nation tends to treat descendants of foreign stock, even a militarily conquered population, with greater responsibility when it is obliged to negotiate with that foreign nation on an equal footing.

Still, the outlook for Chicanos is not very encouraging. Efforts by Chicano organizations to obtain justice and equality, and to share in society's bounties, have not been overwhelmingly successful. Whether these efforts stand a better chance of succeeding when external forces are more active in helping such efforts, only the future can tell.

ENDNOTES

This essay is a joint effort by the authors. The listing of names on the title page in no way indicates the extent of contribution. Rather, all four authors contributed equally.

1. The terms "Chicano" and "Mexican" are used interchangeably in this essay, because the U.S. Southwest and northern Mexico were initially a cultural and geographic unit, the border being only an invisible line between the two nations.

2. The term "Anglo" will be used to refer to U.S. residents of European origin. It is used, for convenience, as a generic term for all European immigrants to the United States.

3. Rodolfo Acuña, *Occupied America* (San Francisco: Canfield Press, 1972), p. 11.

4. Eugene C. Barker, *Mexico and Texas, 1821–1835* (New York: Russell and Russell, 1965), p. 52.

5. Acuña, *Occupied America.*

6. Ibid., p. 44ff; Mario Barrera, *Race and Class in the Southwest* (South Bend: University of Notre Dame Press, 1979), pp. 7–33; Matt S. Meier and Feliciano Rivera, *The Chicanos: A History of Mexican Americans* (New York: Hill and Wang, 1972), pp. 88–94.

7. Carey McWilliams, *North from Mexico* (Philadelphia: Lippincott, 1949).

8. Joan W. Moore, with Harry Pachon, *Mexican Americans,* 2d edition (Englewood Cliffs, N.J.: Prentice-Hall, 1976), pp. 13–14.

9. Barrera, *Race and Class in the Southwest,* p. 25.

10. Meier and Rivera, *The Chicanos,* p. 107.

11. Moore, with Pachon, *Mexican Americans,* p. 15.

12. Barrera, *Race and Class in the Southwest,* pp. 23–30.

13. McWilliams, *North from Mexico.*

14. Peter Baird, and Ed. McCoughan, *Beyond the Border: Mexico and the U.S. Today* (New York: North American Congress on Latin America, 1979); Barrera, *Race and Class in the Southwest;* Meier and Rivera, *The Chicanos.*

15. Ibid.

16. Barrera, *Race and Class in the Southwest,* p. 20.

17. Ernesto Galarza, *Barrio Boy* (South Bend, Ind.: University of Notre Dame Press, 1971).

18. Meier and Rivera, *The Chicanos,* p. 124.

19. Barrera, *Race and Class in the Southwest,* pp. 84–86.

20. Vernon M. Briggs, Jr., Walter Fogel, and Fred H. Schmidt, *The Chicano Worker* (Austin: University of Texas Press, 1977); Meier and Rivera, *The Chicanos.*

21. Manuel P. Servin, "The Pre-World War II Mexican-American: An Interpretation," *California Historical Society Quarterly,* 45 (1966): 325–38.

22. The migration figures at this time are characterized by imprecision. Leo Grebler, for example, in *The School Gap: Signs of Progress* (Advance Report 7, Mexican American Study Project [Los Angeles: University of California Press, 1967], has figures that are 20 percent higher than Servin's (Ibid.), and Barrera, in *Race and Class in the Southwest,* indicates that a comparison of Mexico's emigration statistics with U.S. immigration figures shows still higher numbers.

23. Oscar Handlin, *Race and Nationality in American Life* (New York: Anchor Books, 1957), pp. 93–94.

24. Ibid., pp. 101–2.

25. Ibid., p. 97.

26. Ibid., pp. 93–138.

27. William Paul Dillingham, *Report of the Immigration Commission,* vol. 1 (Washington, D.C.: Government Printing Office, 1911), pp. 690–91.

28. Acuña, *Occupied America,* pp. 123–50; Baird and McCoughan, *Beyond the Border,* pp. 21–35; Barrera, *Race and Class in the Southwest,* pp. 72–75.

29. "Mexican Immigration: A Report by Roy L. Garis for the Information of Congress," *Western Hemisphere Immigration,* Committee on Immigration and Naturalization, 71st Congress 2d session, 1930, p. 436.

30. Committee on Immigration and Naturalization, *Seasonal Agricultural Laborers from Mexico,* 69th Congress, 1st session, 1926, p. 24.

31. Moore, with Pachon, *Mexican Americans,* p. 40.

32. Meier and Rivera, *The Chicanos,* p. 163.

33. Moore, with Pachon, *Mexican Americans,* pp. 41–42.

34. Ernesto Galarza, *Merchants of Labor: The Mexican Bracero Story* (Santa Barbara, California: McNally-Loftin, 1964).

35. Ibid.

36. Ibid.

37. Ibid.

38. McWilliams, *North from Mexico,* pp. 227–58.

39. Roger Daniels and Harry H.L. Kitano, *American Racism: Explorations of the Nature of Prejudice* (Englewood Cliffs, N.J.: Prentice-Hall, 1970), p. 76.

40. Armando Morales, *Ando Sangrado: I Am Bleeding* (LaPuente, Calif.: Perspectiva Publications, 1972).

41. Meier and Rivera, *The Chicanos,* pp. 242–43.

42. Tim D. Kane, "Structural Change and Chicano Employment in the Southwest: Some Preliminary Changes," *Aztlan,* 45 (1973): 383–98.

43. Ibid., p. 29.

44. Philip Garcia and Lionel Maldonado, "America's Mexicans: A Plea for Specificity," (mimeo); Philip Garcia, "Nativity, Bilingualism and Occupational Attainment among Mexican American Men," (in press). The data summarized here are from a more detailed analysis of the 1970 Decennial Census and the March 1978 Current Population Survey. This section borrows from that more detailed analysis. Chicanos' attainments on selected racial characteristics are presented in terms of Mexican immigrants, first-generation and subsequent-generation Chicanos.

The Extraordinary Educational Attainment of Asian-Americans
A Search for Historical Evidence and Explanations

Charles Hirschman
Morrison G. Wong

Contrary to the popular image, Asian-Americans have not achieved equality in all spheres of American society. Their record of occupational and earnings attainment is positive relative to other minorities, but is still short of parity with the major population (Chiswick 1983a; Hirschman and Wong 1984; Jiobu 1976; Kitano and Sue 1973; Kuo 1981; Nee and Sanders 1985; Wong 1980b, 1982; Woodrum 1981). In the field of education, however, the record of Asian-Americans is one of consistent high achievement. In 1980, for the central college-going ages of 20 and 21, more than 50 percent of Asian-Americans were enrolled in school compared to about a third of whites at the same ages (U.S. Bureau of the Census 1984). For specific Asian populations, the percentages enrolled (at ages 20–21) were 62 percent for Japanese, 74 percent for Chinese, 38 percent for Filipinos, and 55 percent for Koreans (U.S. Bureau of the Census 1983a); data on years of completed schooling show comparable gaps between Asian-Americans and the majority population (see U.S. Bureau of the Census 1984). This extraordinary level of educational attainment among Asian-Americans is buttressed by a wide variety of other evidence including reports on classroom behavior, test scores, and an over-representation in institutions of higher education

(Bell 1985; Kitano 1976; Levine and Montero 1973; Lyman 1974; Montero and Tsukashima 1977; Petersen 1971; Schmid and Nobbe 1965; Schwartz 1970, 1971; U.S. Commission on Civil Rights 1978; Vernon 1982; Wong 1980b).

An important cause of Asian-American educational attainment has been selective immigration – a product of the reform 1965 Immigration Act (Wong and Hirschman 1983). More than half of Chinese- and Filipino-Americans are foreign-born, a category that includes a very high share of professional workers with university level education (Hirschman and Wong 1981). However, the educational attainments of native-born Asian-Americans, those fully exposed to the American educational environment, rival those of the foreign-born. To describe and explain the high educational attainments of native-born Asian-Americans are the objectives of our present inquiry.

If the educational achievements of Asian-Americans were of recent origin, then we could focus our inquiry on the last few decades, for which representative data are relatively abundant. However, it appears that Chinese and Japanese youth were making significant educational progress before World War II. An example of the historical depth of the Asian-American educational record is shown in Table 1. In 1910, the

Reprinted from *Social Forces* 65:1 (September 1986). "The Extraordinary Educational Attainment of Asian-Americans: A Search for Historical Evidence and Explanations," by Charles Hirschman and Morrison G. Wong. Copyright © the University of North Carolina Press.

percentages of Japanese and Chinese children attending school were significantly below (with the exception of 18–20-year-old Chinese youth) the comparable enrollment figures for white children. By 1920, the gap had been substantially narrowed for the younger age children and Asian-American enrollment rates for youth above age 16 exceeded white levels. By 1930, Asian-American children, at all ages, were more likely to be attending school than their white counterparts. Given the continued racism against Asians during this period, especially on the west coast (Daniels 1977; Nee and Nee 1972), these educational achievements are remarkable.

The coincidence of minority status and high educational attainment is not an unknown phenomenon. The most widely cited example is that of Jewish Americans, and the pattern may well be representative of other middleman minorities (Blalock 1967; Bonacich 1973; Chiswick 1983b; van den Berghe 1981). The reasons for this anomaly, however, are much in dispute (Ayal and Chiswick 1983; Brenner and Kiefer 1981). Are there additional resources available to some minority groups which allow for the mitigation of the effects of discrimination, or is there variation in opportunity structure for minority group achievement? Through an analysis of census data, we seek to document the trend in Asian-American educational attainment and to test several hypotheses that might explain it.

PRIOR RESEARCH

There is a considerable body of research on Asian-Americans and their position in American society (for general reviews, see Lyman 1974; Petersen 1971). The dominant explanation of the success of Asian-Americans is the cultural thesis. According to the cultural interpretation, successful minorities place a premium on ambition, persistence, and deferred gratification, and exhibit a strong desire for intergenerational social mobility (Glazer 1975; Rosen 1959).

Even among scholars who accept the cultural perspective, there is considerable disagreement on the source and content of the salient cultural values for Asian-Americans. According to one interpretation (Caudill 1952; Caudill and DeVos 1956), there is a significant overlap between the value systems of traditional Japanese society and the American middle class, both of which encourage education. However, Schwartz (1970, 1971) observes that many elements of traditional Japanese values, such as the emphasis on "collective" rather than "individual" action and respect for authority, are not those of middle-class whites. Similar claims about traditional Chinese culture – as exemplified by family unity, respect for elders and those in authority, industry, a high value on education, and personal discipline – have been proposed as the primary cause of the exceptionally high educational achievements of the Chinese in America (Hsu 1971; Sung 1967).

Another variant of the cultural perspective argues that rather than traditional Asian values, it is the acculturation of Asians to the American middle-class value system that accounts for their high level of achievement. Kitano (1976) says that one reason for the success of Japanese-Americans is their adoption of the values, skills, attitudes, goals, and expected behavior of the middle-class majority. Montero and Tsukashima (1977) found that Nisei (second-generation Japanese-Ameri-

TABLE 1   *Percent White, Chinese, and Japanese Youth Enrolled in School in the U.S. (Excluding Hawaii and Alaska): 1910, 1920, and 1930*

Age	White-NWNP*			Chinese			Japanese		
	1910	1920	1930	1910	1920	1930	1910	1920	1930
7–13	88.2	92.2	96.1	77.1	88.6	96.0	73.4	86.1	97.2
14–15	80.3	83.9	90.0	60.6	83.5	94.9	60.0	82.8	97.3
16–17	51.1	48.7	61.0	42.9	57.9	80.7	30.4	57.9	88.8
18–20	19.6	17.5	24.4	23.3	31.7	44.4	11.5	25.5	51.8

Source: U.S. Bureau of the Census (1922, Table 2; 1933a, Tables 8 and 11).

*Native white of native parentage.

cans) who were acculturated and identified themselves as Americans had higher educational attainment than the Nisei who remained within the traditional cultural world. Connor (1975), however, found a gradual decline in academic achievement of Japanese-Americans as they became more assimilated; longer residence in the United States led to more assimilation and less orientation toward achievement. Connor claims that the high academic achievement of Japanese-Americans was largely due to the denial of opportunities to participate in social and other extracurricular school activities in the pre-World War II period. In this setting, academic success was one of the few paths for achievement.

In spite of the contradictory claims made about the origins and impact of Asian-American cultural values on educational attainment, the general thesis is rarely challenged. A direct test of the hypothesis (or the several hypotheses) would require measurements of individual value orientations (preferably taken prior to the completion of schooling) along with other determinants of educational attainment (social class, family structure, environmental influences) which could then be evaluated in a multivariate analysis (e.g., Featherman 1971; Stryker 1984). To our knowledge, the necessary data for an analysis of the cultural hypothesis for Asian-American educational attainment do not exist.

There are, however, broader theoretical perspectives on the question of ethnic stratification in general, and Asian-American educational attainment in particular, that are more amenable to empirical investigation with extant data. Several forms of the cultural hypothesis, described above, suggest that ethnic values in interaction with the broader socioeconomic environment and opportunity structure influence Asian-American educational progress. An even bolder hypothesis is that ethnic organization and culture are, in large part, byproducts of the immigrant experience – the reception of the host community and the nature of available opportunities (Yancey, Ericksen, and Juliani 1976). The introduction of social structural determinants does not eliminate the role of cultural influences, but places them as intervening variables in the stratification process. Values can be interpreted as the mechanism by which social class, immigrant/nativity status, kinship organization, and oppor-

tunity structures influence educational and subsequent socioeconomic attainment. From this vantage point, it is possible to examine some of the potential influences on the trend in the educational attainment of native-born Asian-Americans. In this paper, we consider state of birth in the U.S. (a proxy for educational opportunities), the social class structure of the Asian-American population, and the occupational rate of return to education for Asian-Americans as potential explanations for their above average rate of educational progress in the early decades of the twentieth century.

ASIAN-AMERICANS: IMMIGRATION AND SETTLEMENT

Although the pace of Asian immigration to the United States has increased dramatically since the 1965 Immigration Act, the roots of Asian immigration extent back to the middle of the nineteenth century. As European immigrants began to arrive in increasingly large numbers on the east coast, a similar process was bringing Asians to the west coast and Hawaii. The reception experienced by Asian immigrants, however, was quite different. In addition to verbal and physical attacks, Asian immigrants faced official barriers enacted by state legislatures, Congress, and the courts – perhaps best symbolized by their legal status as "aliens ineligible for citizenship" (Bonacich 1984b, pp. 162–65).

The Chinese, the first Asian group to arrive in significant numbers, came during the 1850s to work in the gold mines in California and later on the railroads. Most of the Chinese immigrants were young men seeking new opportunities with hopes of eventually returning to China. Much of the white working class and small-scale independent craftsmen perceived Asians as "slave labor" for big business (Bonacich 1984b). Ethnic antagonism soon developed and violent attacks on the Chinese population were widespread (Nee and Nee 1972; Saxon 1971). Political pressures led to the Chinese Exclusion Act of 1882, which sharply curtailed working-class migration from China. This Act was renewed in 1892 and became a permanent feature of United States immigration policy in 1904. However, officials, merchants, teachers, students, travelers, and children of Chinese-American citizens were still allowed to enter, although they were subjected to considerable harassment (Lyman 1974; McKenzie 1928). The Chinese Exclusion Act was finally repealed in 1943 and Chinese immigration rose to modest levels in the late 1940s and the 1950s (Nee and Nee 1972). A new wave of Chinese immigration began in the 1960s with the Immigration Act of 1965, which struck down the racist national origin quotas of the 1924 legislation. The new law put a premium on family reunification and scarce occupational skills, with the result that many Chinese, especially those with high educational qualifications, were allowed to enter the United States.

The Japanese were the second Asian group to immigrate in large numbers to the United States. After the exclusion of the Chinese, Japanese immigrants became the new source of cheap labor on the west coast during the last years of the nineteenth century and the first decade of the twentieth century. Ethnic antagonism developed against the Japanese as it had against the Chinese before them (Daniels 1977). The decade of 1901–10 marked the peak of Japanese immigration. In the so-called "Gentlemen's Agreement" of 1908, Japan limited migration to the United States to nonlaborers. For the next fifteen years, Japanese immigration consisted mostly of "picture-brides" and the kin of Japanese already in the United States. The Immigration Act of 1924 barred further migration of Japanese to the United States. The Immigration and Nationality Act (McCarran-Walter) of 1952, by permitting immigration outside the quota system for immediate relatives of U.S. citizens and in other selected cases, allowed a moderate flow of Japanese to the United States in the mid-1950s. The Immigration Act of 1965 did not result in as large an increase in immigration from Japan as it did from other Asian countries.

The third major Asian stream to migrate to the United States, although much later, was from the Philippines. Filipinos initially began migrating to Hawaii to work on the sugar cane plantations (Sharma 1984). Migration of large numbers of Filipinos to the United States mainland did not begin until 1923, coming directly from the Philippines or indirectly through Hawaii (Burma 1951). Because Filipinos were considered nationals of the United States, they were not subject to the ban on Asian immigration. However, the Tydings-McDuffie Act of 1934 placed an "alien" status on Filipinos, thereby restricting Filipino immigration to fifty persons per year. The Immigration and Nationality Act of 1952, and especially the Immigration Act of 1965, led to the significant rise in the volume of Filipino immigration to the United States.

Based on decennial census data, Table 2 presents the historical record of Asian-American (Chinese, Filipino, Japanese) settlement in the United States, separately for Hawaii and the mainland, from the late 19th century to 1980. In addition to the number of Asian-Americans, the percent foreign-born is shown for each population. The last two columns of Table 2 shown the percentages of the total Asian-American population in Hawaii and on the mainland. A century ago, Chinese were the largest Asian population in the United States. From a peak in 1890, the number of Chinese-Americans declined (in absolute terms) until 1920. The very low proportion of Chinese women in the U.S. meant a much delayed development of a sizable second generation Chinese-American population, especially on the mainland. Nee and Wong (1985) argue that traditional Chinese ties to the homeland discouraged the emigration of Chinese women and the development of a settled Chinese family life in the United States. By 1910, there were more Japanese than Chinese in the U.S. (mainland plus Hawaii). Even with the phenomenal growth of the last two decades (1960–80), the total number of Japanese-, Chinese-, and Filipino-Americans was only 2.3 million in 1980 – about one percent of the total U.S. population (the total Asian and Pacific Islander population was 3.5 million in 1980; see U.S. Bureau of the Census 1981).

For the Japanese and Filipino populations, Table 2 shows the central role of Hawaii as the site of early immigration to the U.S. The movement of Chinese to the mainland began earlier and was always more substantial than their flow to Hawaii. During the first half of the twentieth century, only a quarter of all Chinese-Americans resided in Hawaii compared to half of Japanese- and Filipino-Americans. In recent decades, with renewed Asian immigration, the relative share of Asians on the mainland has increased even more. By 1980, two-thirds of Japanese-Americans, over

TABLE 2 *Census Counts* and Percent Foreign-Born of Japanese-, Chinese-, and Filipino-Americans in Hawaii and the U.S. Mainland, from the Late Nineteenth Century to 1980 (Population in Thousands)*

	Hawaii		Mainland U.S.		Total U.S.		% in	
	Pop.	%F.B.	Pop.	%F.B.	Pop.	%F.B.	Hawaii	Mainland
Japanese								
1980	240	9	476	37	716	28	34	66
1970	218	10	369	28	587	21	37	63
1960	203	12	270	29	473	21	43	57
1950	185	17	142	27	326	21	56	44
1940	158	24	127	37	285	30	55	45
1930	140	35	139	51	278	43	50	50
1920	109	56	111	73	220	64	50	50
1910	80	75	72	94	152	83	53	47
1900	61	92	24	99	85	94	72	28
(1896)	24	91	**	**	**	**	**	**
1890	12	**	2	**	14	**	86	14
Chinese								
1980	56	22	756	67	812	63	7	95
1970	52	11	381	52	433	47	12	88
1960	38	9	198	45	237	40	16	84
1950	32	11	118	47	150	39	21	79
1940	29	17	78	48	106	40	27	73
1930	27	28	75	59	102	50	26	74
1920	24	47	62	70	85	64	28	72
1910	22	67	72	79	93	75	24	77
1900	26	84	90	90	115	86	22	78
(1896)	22	90	**	**	**	**	**	**
1890	15	100	107	99	122	**	12	88
1880	**	**	105	99	**	**	**	**
1870	**	**	63	100	**	**	**	**
1860	**	**	35	**	**	**	**	**
Filipino								
1980	132	46	650	69	782	65	17	83
1970	95	35	241	60	336	53	28	72
1960	69	41	113	53	182	49	38	62
1950	61	55	62	64	123	60	50	50
1940	53	**	46	**	99	**	54	46
1930	63	**	45	**	108	**	58	42
1920	21	**	5	**	26	**	81	19
1910	2	**	**	**	2	**	**	**

Source: McKenzie (1928, p. 183); Schmitt (1968, Tables 17, 26, 27); U.S. Bureau of the Census (1943b, Table 4; 1953, Tables 28–30; 1963a, Table 44; 1963c, Table 8; 1973b, Tables 3, 18, 33; 1981, Table 1; 1983a, Table 161; 1983b, Table 94).

*Census counts for the same year vary depending on the base of complete count or sample data (see U.S. Bureau of the Census, 1963c, p. xi).

**Figures not available.

80 percent of Filipino-Americans, and 95 percent of Chinese-Americans lived on the mainland.

Because of the decline of immigration to Hawaii, the Asians in the islands, especially the Chinese and Japanese, are almost completely native-born. By 1980, about 90 percent of the Japanese, 80 of the Chinese, and one-half of the Filipinos in Hawaii were native-born. The transition to an American-born majority is also evident for the Japanese population on the mainland, where the proportion native-born has been over two-thirds for several decades. The early immigration of Japanese women allowed for the relatively rapid development of a second generation and even third generation Japanese-American population. The less balanced sex ratios of the Chinese and Filipino immigrant populations did not permit large second generation populations until recent decades. The sharp rise of Chinese and Filipino immigration that began in the late 1960s brought dramatic growth of these populations and reversed the increase in the proportion native-born.

IMMIGRATION AND THE DEVELOPMENT OF A "MIDDLEMAN MINORITY" COMMUNITY

The historical features of Asian immigration have had a marked imprint on subsequent patterns of stratification of the Asian-American population. Some of these features are common to all immigrant communities, but others are unique to Asian-Americans. An example of the former is the selectivity (on positive characteristics) of international migrants—a standard explanation for the relatively rapid socioeconomic gains of immigrants (Chiswick 1979; U.S. Department of Labor 1979). In addition, the often harsh experience of long-distance migration (and the breaking of past ties) seems to create an intense commitment to achievement in the new setting. This drive, coupled with the difficulties of finding employment (due to discrimination, language, and slow labor market adjustment), leads many immigrants into the small business or self-employed sector (Light 1984). But Asian-Americans, as the "middleman minority," have retained many of these features of an immigrant community.

In her classic "middleman minority" hypoth-

esis, Bonacich (1973) argues that the conditions of immigrant status (of being a sojourner community) can persist, even after generations of local residence, through the formation of an ethnic economy (also see Portes 1981; van den Berghe 1981). The ethnic economy counters the hostility of the host society by creating economic opportunities in family and other kin-based economic enterprises. Drawing on strong family ties and cultural traditions, such as "rotating credit associations" (Light 1972), middleman minorities reinforce ethnic solidarity and a sojourner outlook that inspires an intense commitment to work and economic accumulation.

How does the ethnic economy of middleman minorities lead to high educational aspirations for the children of immigrants? One feature of the ethnic economy is the sponsorship of opportunities for the next generation. This sponsorship helps to reinforce ethnic solidarity and to justify the sacrifice that is necessary to maintain low cost economic enterprises. A frequent element of sponsorship is likely to be investment in the education of children.

Another important feature of Asian immigration was the educational selectivity of different streams of immigrants. While the educational composition of recent Asian immigrants has been extraordinary (Chen 1977; North 1974; Pernia 1976), this was not always the case. Most of the early Asian immigrants to the United States, like their counterparts from Europe, arrived with only minimal educational qualifications. The important exception was early Japanese immigrants. Data from the 1960 Census show that Japanese immigrants, above age 65 in 1960, had a median eight years of schooling—comparable to the figure for the white population of the same age (U.S. Bureau of the Census 1963a, 1963c). This finding is corroborated by earlier studies which report a very selective pattern of Japanese immigration to the United States, particularly to the mainland (Ichihashi 1932; Kitano 1976; Petersen 1971; Strong [1934] 1970). This pattern parallels that of another successful minority group—Jewish immigrants in the late nineteenth and early twentieth centuries (Steinberg 1981). Immigrants with modest social class advantages (relative to other immigrants) may be better positioned to take advantage of available opportunities, including the sponsorship of schooling for their children.

Finally, the impact of restrictive immigration policies on Asian-American settlement and adaption needs to be considered. For Chinese, the open door policy ended early with the infamous Chinese Exclusion Act of 1882. After the immigration bar, Chinese immigration continued, but at much reduced levels. (Moreover, the exodus of return migrants meant that the absolute number of Chinese in the U.S. declined for several decades.) To get around the legal restrictions against Chinese immigration, a Chinese arrival had to fit rather narrow admission criteria or be a kin of a U.S. citizen. It seems reasonable to assume that these restrictions made the stream of immigration more selective. With the barrier to the immigration of Japanese laborers in the wake of the "Gentlemen's Agreement" there probably was a similar structural tendency for selectivity of Japanese migrants to the U.S.

Ironically, the racist character of U.S. immigration policy toward Asia, prior to 1965, may have strengthened the resources of the Asian communities in the U.S. for educational and economic advancement. The door, while not completely closed, limited the inflow of immigrants to a modest number of newcomers with above-average levels of education, often superior to that of the native white population in the United States. This certainly minimized pressures on the resident Asian communities to absorb and support a large number of new immigrants during the first half of the twentieth century. Moreover, the selective character of the immigrant stream strengthened the Asian-American community in a way that probably led to higher educational expectations for their children.

THE TREND IN ASIAN-AMERICAN EDUCATIONAL ATTAINMENT

Our first task is to chart the historical trend in educational attainment of native-born Asian-Americans relative to the majority population. Census data, our primary source, are limited in several respects. First, the standard census question on the number of school years completed

was not asked until the 1940 Census. Moreover, the tabulations for Asian-Americans in the published census reports were extremely limited until recent years.

However, it is possible to use fairly recent census data to study the historical trend in educational attainment. Because individuals rarely continue their formal schooling after reaching adulthood, it is possible to trace historical change across successive birth cohorts by examining the trend from the oldest to the youngest age group (of adults). Longitudinal inferences from cross-sectional data assume that the current population, arrayed by age, reflects the experiences of successive cohorts at earlier points in time. Differential mortality, as well as selective emigration, could reduce the representativeness of older age groups, although we think the impact is likely to be minor. With this caveat, we rely on 1960 and 1970 Census data.

To begin our inquiry, we examine the historical trend in educational attainment of Asian-Americans using 1960 published census reports. While based on only a 25 percent sample of the census population, these figures rest on a much firmer base than the estimates from the micro (public use sample) data. In particular, the estimates for the oldest age groups (which rest on quite small samples in the micro data) are not problematic with data from the published tables.

Table 3 shows the median years of completed schooling for whites and native-born Chinese, Filipinos, and Japanese by birth cohort and sex. An indicator of the inequality of two distributions, the Net Difference (ND) index, is shown in the last three columns of Table 3. For each age cohort, the distribution of whites by years of completed schooling is compared to the educational distribution for the Chinese, Filipino, and Japanese populations.

The ND index is based on each group's distribution in all locations along the educational continuum (Lieberson 1975). Assuming all possible pairings of individuals in the two populations, an index of .50 means that the educational attainment of whites will exceed the Asian level 50 percent more often than the educational attainment of the Asians will exceed the level of whites. If all white scores exceed all Asian scores,

TABLE 3 *Median Years of Completed Schooling and Net Difference Indexes of Whites and Native-Born Asian-Americans by Birth Cohort (Age in 1960) and Sex in the U.S.: 1960*

Birth Cohort	MEDIAN YEARS OF COMPLETED SCHOOLING				NET DIFFERENCE INDEX EDUCATIONAL INEQUALITY BETWEEN WHITES AND		
		Native-Born					
	White	Chinese	Filipino	Japanese	Chinese	Filipino	Japanese
Men							
1935–1939	12.4	13.4	12.3	12.9	−0.29	0.06	−0.28
1925–1934	12.3	13.3	12.1	12.7	−0.30	0.10	−0.23
1915–1924	12.4	12.5	10.2	12.4	−0.19	0.24	−0.14
1895–1914	9.3	9.0	7.2	10.9	0.08	0.39<	−0.06
Pre-1895	8.2	4.2	6.0	8.3	0.36	0.23	−0.01
Women							
1935–1939	12.4	12.9	12.4	12.9	−0.31	0.04	−0.34
1925–1934	12.3	12.7	12.1	12.5	−0.28	0.10	−0.24
1915–1924	12.2	12.4	9.2	12.3	−0.13	0.35<	−0.04
1895–1914	10.1	9.8	8.7	8.5	0.05	0.20	0.15
Pre-1895	8.5	3.8	7.7	6.1	0.45	0.14	0.32

Source: U.S. Bureau of the Census (1963a, Table 173; 1963c, Tables 21–23, 29–31).

the index is + 1.0. Conversely, if all Asian scores exceed all white scores, the ND is − 1.0. The value of zero means that the number of pairs in which whites exceed Asians is equal to the number of pairs in which Asians exceed whites.

In the oldest cohort (born before 1895), native-born Japanese men had educational levels comparable to those of white men – both groups had median values of a bit more than 8 years of schooling and the ND index is close to zero. Filipino and especially Chinese male educational levels were considerably below white levels for the oldest age group. In the next cohort (1895–1914), those who entered school in the first two decades of the century, Chinese and Japanese men made sharp advances, both absolutely and relative to whites. Japanese men pulled ahead with a median educational level 1.6 years above the comparable white figure. For this cohort, the median educational level for Chinese men more than doubled that of the oldest cohort, and they pulled almost equal with whites. While Filipino men registered absolute educational progress, the ND index shows they fell farther behind whites.

In later cohorts, Chinese and Japanese men

advanced beyond the educational levels of whites. This is much more evident in the ND index than in the comparison of median education attainment figures. The reason is that native-born Chinese and Japanese men with very low educational levels had virtually disappeared. The trend for Filipino men was somewhat different . After falling behind white gains in the 1895–1914 cohort, they began to narrow the gap in successive cohorts. They registered significant absolute and relative gains in the 1915–24 and 1925–34 cohorts. Filipino men were beginning to approach educational equality with white men in the cohorts that entered school in the 1940s.

The educational experience of native-born Asian-American women largely parallels that of men. Japanese women in the oldest cohort did not have quite the exceptional level of education that Japanese men had. In fact, it was Filipino women in the pre-1895 cohort whose educational attainments were closest to the white level (less than one year's difference). The next cohort (1895–1914) saw all Asian female groups make absolute educational gains, although Filipino women fell relatively behind. Japanese women closed the gap considerably, and Chinese women

THE EXTRAORDINARY EDUCATIONAL ATTAINMENT OF ASIAN-AMERICANS

made such remarkable progress that they approached educational equality with white women. Then, in later cohorts (as among males), Japanese and Chinese women were more educated than white women. For Filipino women, as for Filipino men, the educational advance was temporarily stalled, but with the 1925–34 cohort, Filipino women began to approach educational equality with white women.

The educational gains of native-born Asian-Americans early in the twentieth century might be explained by a variety of factors. The most obvious factor is that Asians were located in environments where educational opportunities were exceptionally favorable. The educational attainments of whites were a product of a national average of rural and urban places from all regions of the country. However, Asian-Americans were concentrated in California and Hawaii, where schools and educational opportunities may have been more accessible. To test this hypothesis, we turn to an analysis based on the micro data, which afford greater flexibility of analysis than do the published census tabulations.

STATE OF BIRTH
AND EDUCATIONAL ATTAINMENT

Based on public use sample data from the 1970 Census of Population, Table 4 presents mean years of schooling, subdivided into two components – graded schooling (0 to 12) and college (0 to 6) – for the native-born of the three major Asian populations and whites (excluding white Hispanics) by birth cohort and state of birth. In this table, we shift from *medians* to *means* as the measure of central tendency. Although educational means are more likely to be affected by outliers in the distributions, they are generally quite close to medians. Given that access to graded schooling (primary and secondary) and tertiary schooling (college and university) may differ, we examine both as elements of the educational stratification system. Another indicator of educational attainment, the percent attending college (those with 13 or more years of schooling) is also presented in Table 4. State of birth, assumed to represent the environment of subsequent schooling, is our proxy for the degree of educational opportunities. Asian-Americans are concentrated in Cali-

fornia and Hawaii, states where access to schooling may have been more favorable than in other regions of the United States. There are too few whites in Hawaii (in the public use sample) to provide reliable estimates for this analysis.

The trend in educational attainment of whites reflects the expansion of education in America during the twentieth century. The oldest cohort (born before 1905) received an average of between 9 and 10 years of schooling. Average education was slightly higher in California than elsewhere, although the level of college attendance was slightly lower in California. Average educational attainment increased steadily across successive cohorts, reaching above 13 years of schooling in California and only slightly less elsewhere for the youngest cohort (born in 1935–44 and whose schooling was centered in the 1950s). The components of educational growth were a trend towards almost universal completion of graded schooling and an increasing proportion attending college. Almost half of the youngest cohort of white men who were born in California attended college, but somewhat less than one-third of those from other states did.

The patterns of educational attainment for Japanese and Chinese do not fit the expectation for disadvantaged minorities. Native-born Japanese had comparable or higher educational attainments than whites for all the cohorts represented in this table. For the older cohorts, it seems that this Japanese parity with whites reflects roughly similar levels of graded and college schooling. Japanese from California did better than Japanese elsewhere (similarly to the differential for whites). It was the younger two Japanese cohorts, especially the youngest (born in 1935–44), whose educational attainments began to advance significantly above the white level. The slight Japanese edge in the 1925–34 cohort was due primarily to higher levels of secondary school completion. But the 1935–44 cohort of Japanese sharply increased their educational attainment through a dramatic jump in college attendance – e.g., 31 percentage points in California (from 44 to 75 percent). The increases in Hawaii and in other states were somewhat less, but still outstripped the educational gains of whites.

The educational achievements of native-born Chinese-Americans are no less impressive, but

TABLE 4 *Mean Years of Schooling (Graded and College)[a] and Percent Attending College of Whites and Native-Born Asian-Americans by Birth Cohort and State of Birth in the U.S.: 1970*

| | STATE OF BIRTH | | | | | | | | | PERCENT ATTENDING COLLEGE | | |
| | California | | | Hawaii | | | Elsewhere | | | California | Hawaii | Elsewhere |
	Total	Graded	College	Total	Graded	College	Total	Graded	College			
White[b]												
1935–44	13.3	11.8	1.5	**	**	**	12.2	11.3	1.0	51	**	32
1925–34	12.9	11.4	1.5	**	**	**	11.6	10.7	.9	47	**	26
1915–24	12.6	11.2	1.4	**	**	**	11.4	10.6	.8	35	**	23
1905–14	11.4	10.9	.5	**	**	**	10.4	9.8	.6	22	**	19
Before 1905	9.8*	9.6*	.2*	**	**	**	9.3	8.9	.5	10*	**	15
Japanese												
1935–44	14.3	11.9	2.4	13.7	11.9	1.8	13.0	11.4	1.7	75	52	48
1925–34	13.2	11.8	1.4	12.5	11.6	1.0	12.6	11.4	1.2	44	30	34
1915–24	12.6	11.6	1.0	10.8	10.3	.5	11.9	11.1	.7	33	15	23
1905–14	11.5	10.7	.8	9.2	8.7	.5	9.9	9.5	.3	25	12	13
Before 1905	10.3*	9.6*	.7*	6.8	6.8	0	9.6	9.1	.5	20	0	18
Chinese												
1935–44	14.3	12.0	2.3	13.9	11.8	2.0	12.9	11.1	1.8	69	54	47
1925–34	13.6	11.7	1.8	12.7	11.7	1.0	12.0	10.8	1.2	49	27	37
1915–24	13.6	11.6	2.0	12.1	10.9	1.2	10.8	10.2	1.2	52	30	16
1905–14	12.4*	10.8*	1.6*	10.7	10.1	.6	9.7	8.8	.9	35*	18	23
Before 1905	5.7*	5.3*	.4*	8.0	7.4	.6	8.0	7.7	.3	13*	12	8
Filipino												
1935–44	12.0	10.9	1.1	11.8	11.0	.8	11.0	10.4	.6	36	29	22
1925–34	12.4	11.4	.9	11.2	10.	.4	11.2	10.2	.9	43*	17	28
1915–24	**	**	**	**	**	**	9.8*	9.5*	.3*	**	**	20*
1905–14	**	**	**	**	**	**	8.6	8.3	.2	**	**	11
Before 1905	**	**	**	**	**	**	7.0	6.8	.2	**	**	9

Source: Public Use Sample of the 1970 Population Census.

*25 or less.

**Less than 10.

[a]Graded schooling ranges from 0 to 12 years, college from 1 to 6 years. All persons with 12 or more years of schooling are coded 12 for graded schooling; all with 12 or less years of schooling are coded 0 on the college variable.

[b]Whites of non-Hispanic origin.

the trajectory of historical change was somewhat different. For the oldest cohort of native-born Chinese, average educational levels were far below the white level, especially in California. In the next cohort (1905–14) whose schooling was centered in the 1920s, native-born Chinese registered sharp increases in their educational attainments (most strongly in California, but also in Hawaii and elsewhere) and reached parity with whites. An important component of the educational progress of native-born Chinese was above-average levels of college attendance (primarily in California). In successive cohorts, native-born Chinese maintained educational parity with whites; Chinese held a modest edge in California. Finally, in the youngest cohort, native-born Chinese jumped far ahead of their white counterparts – primarily through higher levels of college attendance (a pattern comparable to the shift in college attendance among native-born Japanese).

The analysis of the trend of educational attainment of native-born Filipinos rests on a much weaker empirical base. The number of cases in most cells is quite small and any interpretation of trends must be considered tentative. There has been a steady increase in native-born Filipino educational attainment with the most important shift occurring from the 1915–24 to 1925–34 birth cohort in Hawaii, where average education rose by almost two and a half years. Schooling continued to increase for the youngest cohort of native-born Filipinos in Hawaii, but there appears to have been a leveling off of educational gains (a small decline) for Filipinos in the rest of the U.S. Since this observation rests on a very small sample, further investigation is necessary to confirm this trend. Overall, there appears to have been a trend towards a narrowing of the white-Filipino educational gap, but parity had still not been achieved.

It appears that the societal discrimination of the first half of the twentieth century, although extensive, did not diminish the ability of Japanese- and Chinese-American families to support the education of their American-born children at levels comparable to or above that of the majority population. The cohort of American-born Chinese educated before World War I experienced an educational disadvantage, but this disap-

peared in the next cohort. Japanese and Chinese born in California did best of all, but those in other parts of the country also achieved educational levels equal to or above whites'. It appears that an explanation for Asian-American educational success cannot be specified in terms of favorable geographical settings alone.

CHANGES IN THE CLASS STRUCTURE OF ASIAN-AMERICANS

Changes in the social class composition of Asian-Americans might be another possible explanation for the rapid gains in Asian-American educational levels in the early decades of the twentieth century. The educational aspirations of children and their subsequent educational attainments are profoundly shaped by their socioeconomic origins, especially parental status (Duncan 1967; Hauser and Featherman 1976; Sewell and Hauser 1975). Families in the lower rungs of the social hierarchy are less able than middle-class families to provide the economic resources and social incentives to further the schooling of their children. To assess the changing socioeconomic structure of Asian-American families (the parents of the generation of native-born Asian-Americans schooled in the pre-World War II era), we chart the trend in the occupational structure of Chinese and Japanese men (relative to total employed men) from the population censuses of 1900, 1920, and 1930.

There are several conceptual and data limitations of our test of this hypothesis. Most basically, we cannot link data on family socioeconomic position and children's education, but can only see if there are parallel trends. Moreover, published data only allow for a look at the trend in occupational patterns of the adult population (by sex) as a whole, not separately for parents of school age children. We examine the occupations of men (realizing that this is only one dimension of family status) as a crude proxy of the social class structure of the Asian-American population. Changes in the occupational classification scheme for the 1940 Census caused us to limit our inquiry to the 1900, 1920, and 1930 censuses. (The published occupational tabulations of the 1910 Census combined the Chinese and Japanese populations.) Guided by earlier work on the matching of occupational categories from 1900 to 1930 (U.S. Census 1943b, Table 11), we have compiled the occupational distributions of Asian-Americans in comparable categories. Table 5 shows the occupational distributions of Chinese- and Japanese-Americans . . . and the ratio of the Asian to total workers (expressed as ratios of percentage distributions). . . .

In 1900, almost seven out of ten Chinese were in agriculture or in domestic and personal services. The stereotypical occupation of laundry workers employed a quarter of all Chinese men at the turn of the century. Chinese were underrepresented in almost all other occupations (see the ratios of less than 1 . . .), especially in higher status positions of public service, professional service, and clerical employment. Over the next three decades, the percentages of Chinese in agriculture (mostly farm laborers), mining, and manufacturing declined sharply, while there were corresponding increases in trade (from 10 to 17 percent) and especially in domestic and personal services (from 41 to 61 percent). Within this last category, the percentage of laundry workers remained at 25 percent, while the percentages of Chinese working as servants and waiters increased to 21 and 10 percent, respectively.

Although the Japanese began with a much higher proportion in agriculture (two-thirds worked in agriculture in 1900, mostly as farm laborers), there are some common trends in the Japanese and Chinese occupational structures: decline in agriculture and increases in trade and in domestic and personal services. Even though a third of Japanese men remained as farm laborers in 1930, this was only half the 1900 figure.

It is difficult to argue that these changes in the occupational distributions represent an upgrading in the social class structure of Asian-Americans. The proportions in higher status positions remained minimal and most Asians continued to work in low paid and low status occupations in 1930. Nonetheless, the changes in occupational structures might have created a more favorable environment for educational sponsorship of the next generation. Much of the growth of employment in trade, services, and even agriculture was tied to the entrepreneurial ethnic economy (Bonacich and Modell 1980; Light 1972). Within the small business sector,

education is likely to be seen as a means for success in a competitive environment. Unlike jobs in the manual sector or in traditional agriculture, family businesses often inspire high expectations for the future; these objectives may well be transmitted into high educational aspirations for the next generation.

OCCUPATIONAL RETURNS TO EDUCATION

Another possible explanation for the high levels of educational achievement among Asian-Americans might be the rate of economic returns to schooling. A common observation in the race relations literature is that the lower economic gains associated with minority education provided weaker incentives for continued schooling (Blau and Duncan 1967). This hypothesis suggests that the economic value of education influences the degree of support for schooling by the family and other social institutions. If education "matters," then parents and students will be motivated to invest in "human capital" as a channel for social mobility. Lieberson (1980, pp. 354–59) finds a more positive "feedback" of occupation on education for foreign-born whites than for blacks in 1940. He concludes that these patterns "affected educational incentives for the next generation of blacks in a radically different way than for the next generation of SCE (South, Central, and Eastern European) whites."

Table 6 presents a modest test of the "feedback" hypothesis, that is, that education offered some measure of occupational returns for the generations of Asian-Americans prior to World War II. From 1940 Census data, we compare the actual occupational distributions of native-born Chinese- and Japanese-Americans with their expected occupational distributions based on the assumption that education is translated into occupation in the same manner as for the total employed male population, and for the total nonwhite employed male population. The question is whether the Chinese and Japanese occupational "rate of return" to education is positive (similar to the expected distribution based on the nonwhite population). There are a host of methodological problems in these statistical "experiments" (the crudeness of the occupational categories, the differences in the age boundaries of the populations

TABLE 5 *Occupational Distribution of Male Chinese- and Japanese-American Gainful Workers in the U.S. (Excluding Hawaii and Alaska): 1900, 1920, and 1930*

Occupation[a]	PERCENTAGE DISTRIBUTION						RATIO TO TOTAL MALE WORKERS[b]					
	Chinese			Japanese			Chinese			Japanese		
	1900	1920	1930	1900	1920	1930	1900	1920	1930	1900	1920	1930
Agriculture, forestry, fishing	27	11	8	66	45	47	0.6	0.4	0.3	1.5	1.5	1.8
Farm laborers	21	8	6	62	26	31	1.1	0.7	0.6	3.3	2.2	3.1
Extraction of minerals	4	0	0	1	2	1	1.2	0.1	.0	0.3	0.7	0.6
Manufacturing and mechanical industries	13	9	7	8	12	7	0.5	0.3	0.2	0.3	0.4	0.2
Transportation and communication	3	2	2	13	8	5	0.4	0.2	0.2	1.6	1.0	0.5
Trade	10	16	17	4	9	14	0.9	1.5	1.3	0.3	0.8	1.1
Public service	1	0	0	1	0	0	0.5	0.2	0.1	0.7	0.1	0.1
Professional service	1	1	2	1	2	3	0.3	0.3	0.4	0.2	0.6	0.8
Domestic & personal service	41	58	61	8	20	20	11.2	16.5	13.2	2.1	5.6	4.2
Laundry	25	28	25	0	2	2	103.1	150.3	87.6	0.9	10.1	6.0
Servants	13	18	21	6	9	9	11.5	48.3	46.9	5.4	24.4	19.9
Waiters	1	6	10	1	1	1	18.6	22.7	0.1	3.7	2.3	
Clerical	1	2	2	0	2	2	0.3	0.3	0.4	0.1	0.3	0.3
Total gainful workers	100%	100%	100%	100%	100%	100%						

Source: U.S. Bureau of the Census (1904, Table 3; 1923, Table 5; 1933b, Tables 12, 13; 1943b, Tables 9, 11).

[a]The 1920 and 1930 occupational classifications are comparable at the major category level (except that communication occupations are not included with transportation in the 1920 classification). The 1900 classification, however, required considerable adjustment to estimate comparable 1900 occupational data. All adjustments are based on Alba Edwards' match of 1900 and 1930 Census occupational classifications (U.S. Bureau of the Census 1943b, Table 11). When it was necessary to split categories to fit the 1930 classification, proportional estimation, based on total male workers, as given by Edwards, was used.

[b]Ratio of the percentage distribution of Chinese- and Japanese-American workers to the percentage distributions of total male workers. A ratio greater than 1 represents an overrepresentation (proportional) of Chinese- and Japanese-American workers in that category.

TABLE 6 *Actual and Expected Occupational Distributions of Native-Born Chinese- and Japanese-American Men in the U.S. (Excluding Hawaii and Alaska): 1940*

| | CHINESE | | | JAPANESE | | |
| | | Expected[a] | | | Expected[a] | |
Occupation	Actual[b]	Total	Non-white	Actual[b]	Total	Non-white
Professional	4	3	4	3	9	10
Farmers	2	19	20	14	10	8
Managers, officials and proprietors	21	8	2	7	12	3
Clerical/sales	12	8	3	15	19	8
Craftsmen	2	13	5	2	14	6
Operatives	19	17	12	9	16	14
Domestic service	6	1	3	3	0	4
Other service	31	6	14	4	6	23
Farm laborers – wage	2	8	13	18	4	6
Farm laborers – unpaid	0	3	5	14	2	3
Nonfarm laborers	2	12	19	9	7	15
Not reported	1	1	1	1	1	1
Total[c]	100%	100%	100%	100%	100%	100%
Ns	11,039	12,915	12,915	15,241	7,460	7,460

Source: U.S. Bureau of the Census (1943c, Table 3; 1943d, Tables 6, 8).

[a]Expected occupational distributions of native-born Chinese and Japanese men; age 25 and above in 1940, based on their educational distributions and the outflow educational-occupational matrices of total employed men and total nonwhite employed men in 1940.

[b]Actual occupational distributions of native-born Chinese and Japanese men, age 14 and above in 1940.

[c]Columns do not always sum to totals because of rounding error.

by education and occupation, and the lack of controls for other influences) that caution against the interpretation of small differences.

The actual occupational distribution of native-born Chinese male workers in 1940 (note the major changes in occupational classification used in the 1940 Census from the classification of earlier censuses) was quite different from that expected for Chinese if the "rules of the game" (the education – occupational tradeoff system) for all men (total employed males) or nonwhite men (total nonwhite employed males) were applied. The Chinese were not able to turn their educational resources into some positive occupations (crafts) and were crowded into some unfavorable occupations (other service workers). On the other

hand, Chinese seem to have done relatively well in getting into the MOP (Managers, Officials, and Proprietors) and clerical/sales occupations and in avoiding the relatively unrewarding occupations of farmers, farm laborers, and nonfarm laborers. Comparison with the nonwhite population (about 90 percent black) shows that education was a more valuable resource for the occupational attainment of native-born Chinese.

Native-born Japanese men (who had a more favorable educational composition than did native-born Chinese men in 1940) do not appear to have done so well in translating their educational resources into occupations in 1940. If native-born Japanese men could have gotten the occupational rates of return of the total population, they (Japanese) would have had much higher representation in professional, MOP, and craft occupations. While native-born Japanese men did not get pushed to the lower ranks of blue-collar employment (operatives, nonfarm laborers) as did nonwhites as a whole, Japanese men did experience a serious problem in their overrepresentation as farm laborers (four times as high as for the total population with equivalent education).

In spite of this mixed picture, it seems that there was some positive feedback from occupation to education for Asian-Americans in 1940. This does not mean an absence of discrimination. The historical record is clear (Bonacich and Modell 1980; Cheng and Bonacich 1984; Daniels 1977; Ichihashi 1932) that both formal and informal barriers restricted the economic opportunities of Asian-Americans on the west coast for much of the first half of the twentieth century. But through various channels, perhaps the most important being the ethnic economy, Japanese and Chinese men appear to have been able to realize some economic returns to their education. Perhaps most importantly, they were able to avoid being thrust into the lower ranks of manual labor. These patterns may have provided critical reinforcement to the Asian-American cultural emphasis on education as a way to get ahead.

DISCUSSION AND CONCLUSIONS

The contemporary pattern of Asian-American education success has roots that extend back to the late nineteenth and early twentieth centuries. The historical record, however, is not simply a straightforward march from uneducated immigrants to a third or fourth generation with postgraduate degrees. Nor can an explanation that begins and ends with the high educational ambitions of Asian-Americans suffice as an interpretation. Both of these elements contain more than a grain of truth, but a closer examination of the evidence reveals a more complex picture.

For as far back as we can look with available census data, native-born Japanese-Americans have not been at an educational disadvantage (although enrollment data from 1910 for *all* Japanese children do proportionally show fewer attending school than among whites). In cohorts

born prior to World War I, native-born Japanese-Americans maintained educational parity with whites. Subsequent generations of Japanese-Americans have had educational attainments exceeding comparable white levels. For native-born Chinese-Americans, there was an educational disadvantage for the oldest cohort. But this seems to have disappeared for the cohorts born in the U.S. in the first two decades of the century. Then, as for Japanese-Americans, the educational levels of successive generations of Chinese-Americans rose sharply. The picture for native-born Filipino-Americans is more uneven. Starting off above Chinese-Americans, but below both whites and Japanese-Americans, native-born Filipinos lost ground educationally (in a relative sense), but have started to narrow the gap among younger generations. How can these trends be explained? The first element of our interpretation is the character of Asian immigration to the United States and the conditions of early settlement.

Several factors appear to have been common to Asian-American educational advancement, particularly for Japanese and Chinese. First, the closing of the door to further Asian immigration certainly lessened the pressures on the local ethnic community to absorb and support additional kinsmen. This may have allowed marginal resources to be invested in the education of children, rather than in supporting a growing ethnic enclave. In the middle decades of the twentieth century, the Japanese-American population grew very slowly and the Chinese-American population experienced an absolute decline in numbers for many years. Moreover, restrictive immigration policies meant that only highly selected Asians were allowed to enter the United States—immigrants who very often had educational qualifications superior to those of the native white population. One might expect parental education to serve as the minimal expectation for the next generation.

An important factor behind the educational progress of the second generation of Asian-Americans in the early decades of the century was the economic progress of their parents. Asian workers were unable to penetrate the higher echelons of the occupational ranks nor were they allowed to participate in the relatively well-paid skilled craft occupations of industrial work. Left to their own resources, Asians developed an ethnic economy that created an increasing number of jobs in trade and services. We suggest that this development was a major factor behind the educational gains of Asian-American children in the decades prior to World War II. Bonacich and Modell (1980, p. 152) suggest that educational ambition for second-generation Japanese-Americans grew out of the ethnic economy—that by providing their children with higher education, Japanese-American parents hoped to secure a means for their children to enter the ranks of the "independent professions, the pinnacle of the petit bourgeois world, or to take over the family business or farm and run it more efficiently." However, higher education of the Nisei had the unintentional consequence of being used as a stepping-stone to leave the ethnic economy. Instead of strengthening it, higher education often provided an avenue of escape.

Another factor is that Japanese and Chinese educational attainment seems to have "paid off" in occupational advancement even though Japanese and Chinese experienced considerable occupational discrimination. Education was a channel for the social mobility of Asians, partly because they were frozen out of some sectors of the econ-omy and were forced to create their own occupational niches in the ethnic economy.

As Asian-Americans have encountered a moderate amount of economic success in the postwar era, their educational attainments have shot up to record levels, with college graduation becoming the median level of attainment. While Asian-Americans born in California have been the most successful, the sharp rise in educational levels is evident in Hawaii and elsewhere. Since the ethnic economy and residential segregation appear to have lessened in recent years, it becomes more difficult to apply our earlier interpretation to the contemporary situation. One possible structural interpretation is that the high educational levels of the post-World War II generation of Asian-Americans are rooted in a subculture of professionalism as well as ethnicity. A disproportionate share of Asian-Americans are employed in professional and technical occupations (Hirschman and Wong 1981). Parents whose own careers are based on their educational credentials are likely to encourage and support the continued schooling of their children. Given this context, the very high levels of Asian-American education may well continue even though other aspects of Asian-American culture are losing their distinctiveness.

A Tale of Three Cities: Blacks, Immigrants, and Opportunity in Philadelphia
1850–1880, 1930, and 1970

Theodore Hershberg　　*Stephanie Greenberg*
Alan N. Burstein　　　*William L. Yancey*
Eugene P. Ericksen

Significant differences in socioeconomic conditions characterize the experience of black and white Americans. Why and how this happened, and what if anything should be done about it, are among the central questions of our time. Their answers have important implications for public policy. The crux of the matter can be put this way: were the burdens and disabilities faced by black Americans peculiar to their historical experience or were they simply obstacles which every immigrant group entering American society had to overcome?[1]

Over the years we have come to see how the study of the black experience requires a broader context than gross comparisons of whites with blacks. Recent research has finally recognized that white America consists of diverse groups and that the study of their distinct experiences requires a comparative ethnic perspective. While this constitutes a major advance, what remains conspicuously absent from the literature—especially from the history of blacks in cities—is an awareness that the study of the black experience necessitates an urban perspective as well.[2] Two

distinct environments embrace much of Afro-American history: plantation and ghetto.[3] Once the most rural of Americans, blacks are today the most urbanized. Unfortunately, the histories that have been written treat the city in passive terms, as a kind of incidental setting for the subject at hand; in order to learn how the "city" affected blacks it is necessary to construct a history which treats the city in dynamic terms. Such a history would conceive of "urban" as a "process" linking the experience of people to aspects of the particular environment in which they lived.[4] In this essay a comparative ethnic and an urban perspective are combined to further understanding of the black experience.

This essay will focus on Philadelphia's "opportunity structure." Such a term encompasses a wide variety of factors; although much more than the hierarchy of occupations defines an opportunity structure, the distribution of occupations is certainly central to the concept and may be considered its most important single attribute. For the sake of brevity, a vertical distribution of occupations will be used as a proxy measure for a

Reprinted from *A Tale of Three Cities: Blacks, Immigrants and Opportunity in Philadelphia: 1850–1880, 1930, and 1970* by Theodore Hershberg, Alan N. Burstein, Eugene P. Ericksen, Stephanie Greenberg, and William L. Yancey in volume no. 441 of THE ANNALS of the American Academy of Political and Social Science (January 1979). © 1979 by The American Academy of Political and Social Science. Reprinted by permission of the publisher and the authors.

group's place in the larger opportunity structure. The term "ecological structure," or the distribution in space of people, housing, jobs, transportation, and other urban elements, is understood as the material expression of the opportunity structure. A city's ecological structure can thus be considered as a major determinant of differential "access"—to jobs, housing, transportation, and services. Finally, the term "structural perspective" encompasses both the opportunity structure and its ecological form and is used here to characterize our overall conceptual approach.

The experience of black and white immigrant groups, then, must be understood within a changing urban environment, recognizing the effects that such environment had upon different groups of people at different points in Philadelphia's past. The ecological "rules" that explain important elements of the white immigrant experience do not explain, for most of Philadelphia's history, what happened to blacks. Where blacks were concerned the rules were inoperative, suspended as it were by the force of racism. Racism, particularly its manifestation in discriminatory hiring and housing practices, is the final dimension in the explanatory framework. The subsiding of the worst of racial discrimination in contemporary American life suggests that blacks will at last begin to be treated as other people. But the potential gains will not be realized because other offsetting changes have occurred simultaneously. Philadelphia's opportunity structure has altered radically for the worse, and the ecological manifestations of these changes leave blacks at a severe disadvantage: they find themselves in the wrong areas of the wrong city at the wrong time. Despite the lessening of racial discrimination, major changes in Philadelphia's opportunity and ecological structure prevent today's blacks from experiencing the successes enjoyed by the city's earlier immigrant groups.

UNIQUE ASPECTS
OF THE BLACK EXPERIENCE

Those who argue that the black experience was not unique fall into two categories. The first explanation of the socioeconomic differentials can be captured in single words—bootstraps—or opportunities. According to this point of view,

blacks, like all immigrant groups, had equal access to opportunities. If they took advantage of these opportunities—that is, if they pulled long enough and hard enough on their bootstraps—they made it. The bootstraps argument claims that everybody had it tough and that the problems faced by blacks were no tougher than those encountered by other immigrant groups entering American society. The message of this view for contemporary public policy is obvious: if blacks do not have a uniquely discriminatory past, they do not deserve to be the beneficiaries of compensatory legislation in the present.

The second explanation, known as the "Last of the Immigrants," rejects the bootstraps view of the past and concedes that blacks—in cities such as Philadelphia—were the victims of a peculiarly racist past. Such a concession, however, only documents how racist America was "back then," and suggests that time will be sufficient remedy. As late as 1910, the well-meaning holders of this viewpoint remind us, 90 percent of black Americans were rural and 80 percent were southern. Of all American blacks ever to live in cities, the vast majority settled in them after World War II: thus, in demographic terms, blacks can be considered as the last of the immigrants. Although this explanation differs from the notion of bootstraps in its view of the black past, its implications for public policy in the present are identical. We need not undertake any special legislation to ameliorate the condition of blacks today because the same process of assimilation through which European immigrants were integrated into the urban American mainstream will take care of black urban immigrants. Since the process of assimilation worked for other groups, it will work for blacks: all we need to do is stand by and give it time.[5]

THE ASSIMILATION PROCESS

Unfortunately, viewing blacks as the last of the immigrants is inaccurate and, in its false optimism, may ultimately prove to be as pernicious as the bootstraps explanation. Assimilation is not a mysterious process rooted in the individual, but is a combination of factors: opportunities available at a given time; housing stock; the nature and condition of the local, regional and national economy; the number of skilled and unskilled positions available in the labor force; the location of jobs; the transportation facilities; the fiscal circumstances of the local government; and the degree of discrimination encountered. Nor is there much validity in dealing with the assimilation process at the individual level; every immigrant group has its specially gifted members who "make it" despite the barriers erected by the host society. The concern here is with the experience of entire groups rather than the exceptionally talented few, and the focus is on the opportunity structure which affected all people and which regulated the degree of group progress.

The experience of blacks and immigrants will be compared at three points in Philadelphia's history. Although blacks were present in the city over the entire period, the reference to three cities reflects temporally distinct waves of immigrants to Philadelphia: the "Old" immigrants— Irish, Germans and British—who settled in the 1840s and 1850s; the "New" immigrants—Italians, Poles and Russian Jews—who arrived in the years between 1885 and 1914; and the "newest" immigrants—blacks—who came in their greatest numbers after 1945 (see Table 1).[6]

What happened to these groups depended not only upon what they brought with them from the Old World and the South—values, language, skills, urban and industrial experience—but what awaited them upon arrival in Philadelphia. It was not only that people with different backgrounds came to the city, but that the structure of opportunities that they found in Philadelphia was different as well; each time period represented a different stage in the city's urban-industrial development. And it was these differences that shaped a wide range of subsequent experience for each immigrant group. A full treatment of these differences would require discussion of a breadth of topics. This essay will focus on the changing opportunity structure and the residential experience of the black and white immigrants who lived in the designated three cities.

According to the accepted notion of the assimilation process, upon arrival in America immigrants settled in densely populated urban ghettos among friends and neighbors of the same ethnic background. A few, the most successful among them, were able to move out of the ghetto within

their own lifetime, but for most others, integration into the fabric of the larger society was the experience of their children and grandchildren. Several generations were required to complete the process. This point of view pervades our culture; we find it embedded in our literature, film and folklore. Its most recent and popular expression is found in Irving Howe's best-selling study, *World of Our Fathers*.[7]

Settlement in dense urban enclaves made sense. It was seen as the logical response of the newcomers to the hostility of the native population and to the strangeness of white Anglo Saxon Protestant culture at the societal core. It was rational as well—when understood as the natural tendency of the immigrants, faced with an unfamiliar new setting—to establish a secure and friendly place, to create a sense of the old Country in the new. A piece of Europe was transplanted in the streets of America.

The pervasiveness of this notion, however, did not rest solely on logic or cultural trappings. With the nation absorbing twenty million immigrants in thirty years at the turn of the last century, some scholars, particularly a group of sociologists at the University of Chicago, undertook major studies of the immigrant experience.[8] Their empirical observations corroborated those of the social reformers who were dealing with the problems of the immigrants, as well as those of the writers and artists who were capturing the immigrant saga in word and on canvas.

RESIDENTIAL SEGREGATION

Sociologists have maintained that the degree of residential segregation is an acceptable indicator of, or a proxy for, assimilation. An ethnically enclosed residential experience insulates a group from important mechanisms of assimilation, limits cross-cultural contacts that affect the socialization of the young, and has serious implications for subsequent experiences such as intermarriage, upward job mobility, and the formation of social ties. Thus, the lower the degree of segregation the greater the likelihood that a group is experiencing assimilation. The accepted notion of the assimilation process found what appeared to be scientific confirmation in the levels of segregation observed for northern

TABLE 1 *Ethnic Composition of Philadelphia: 1850–1970 (as Percent of Total Population)*

	1850	1880	1900	1930	1970
Blacks	4.8	3.6	4.8	11.3	33.6
Ireland*					
Born	17.6	11.9	7.6	2.7	0.4
Second		15.1	13.6	6.8	1.9
Stock		27.0	21.2	9.4	2.3
Germany					
Born	5.6	6.6	5.5	1.9	0.6
Second		9.6	9.6	4.8	1.4
Stock		16.2	15.1	6.7	1.9
Great Britain†					
Born		3.8	3.6	1.9	0.4
Second			4.8	3.2	1.1
Stock			8.4	5.1	1.5
Italy					
Born		0.2	1.4	3.5	1.3
Second			0.9	5.8	4.0
Stock			2.2	9.3	5.3
Poland					
Born		0.1	0.6	1.6	0.6
Second			0.3	5.8	1.8
Stock			0.9	7.4	2.4
USSR°					
Born		0.03	2.2	4.5	1.3
Second			1.3	5.3	3.2
Stock			3.6	9.9	4.5
Total Foreign					
Born	29.0	24.2	22.8	18.9	6.5
Second		30.4	32.1	31.7	16.6
Stock		54.6	54.9	50.6	23.1
Total Population	408,081	840,584	1,293,697	1,950,961	1,950,098

Sources: Figures for 1850 and 1880 are computed primarily from Philadelphia Social History Project compilations of the United States manuscript censuses of population. In 1880, figures for Italy, Poland, and USSR are taken from published United States Census totals. See Department of the Interior, Census Office, *Census of Population: 1880,* v. I., "Statistics of the Population of the United States at the Tenth Census," (Washington, D.C.: U.S. Government Printing Office, 1883), 540. Figures for 1900, 1930, and 1970 are computed from published United States Census totals. See Department of the Interior, United States Census Office, *Census of Population: 1900,* v. I, pt. 1, "Population," (Washington, D.C.: U.S. Census Office, 1901), 780, 866–905; U.S. Department of Commerce, Bureau of the Census, *Census of Population: 1930,* v. III, p. 2, "Population," (Washington, D.C.: U.S. Government Printing Office, 1932), 701–708; U.S. Bureau of the Census, *Census of Population: 1970,* v. I, "Characteristics of the Population," pt. 40, Pennsylvania – Section 1, (Washington, D.C.: U.S. Government Printing Office, 1973), 356.

*Includes Northern Ireland.

†Includes England, Scotland, Wales.

°Includes Russia, Lithuania, Estonia, Latvia.

Note: In 1880, "second generation" refers to native-born with *fathers* born in specified country. Native-born with native fathers and foreign-born mothers are classified as native. In 1900, 1930, and 1970, "second generation" refers to native-born with *fathers* born in specified country or, if father is native, with *mother* born in specified country. If parents are born in different foreign countries, birthplace of father determines parentage of native-born. "Stock" includes foreign-born plus second generation.

188

and midwestern cities in 1930. Expectations based on the accepted model were apparently confirmed by the data: old immigrants from Ireland, Germany and Britain, who had arrived in America in the 1840s and 1850s, were the least segregated residentially (20–30); while new immigrants from Italy, Poland and Russia, who came between 1885 and 1914, were considerably more segregated (50–60).[9] Here was proof – or so it seemed – that an assimilation process was operating in American cities; with the passage of time immigrants were being integrated into the mainstream. When the logic of this argument is applied to the high levels of segregation for urban blacks (70–80) observed in 1970, one is left with a comforting conclusion. With time, these latest newcomers will assimilate, as did earlier groups. The optimistic implications of this viewpoint for public policy are obvious: no legislation need be passed when a social process operates to generate the desired results.

Unfortunately, while the segregation scores are accurate, the interpretation is not. The data on white immigrant residential segregation are cross-sectional for 1930; when cross-sectional data are used to infer historical process they can distort history and lead to an erroneous conclusion. The low scores for the Irish and German immigrants – half the level observed for the Italians, Poles and Russian Jews – are not indicative of change over time from high to low segregation, and thus proof of an assimilation process; rather, they are the *retention* of segregation levels experienced by the Irish and German immigrants upon initial settlement (see Table 2).[10] In other words, the low segregation scores for the old immigrants, the higher scores for the new immigrants, and the highest scores for the blacks are not evidence for the existence of an assimilation process rooted in the individual and responsive to the passage of time, but are a reflection of changing structural conditions that awaited each wave of immigrants who settled in Philadelphia at three different points in time.[11]

THE NINETEENTH-CENTURY CITY: 1850–1880

Immigrant ghettos did not form in the nineteenth century manufacturing city. In simplest terms, no supply of cheap, concentrated housing existed to quarter the thousands of Irish and Germans who poured into the city seeking work in the 1840s and 1850s. As the manufacturing center of America and one of the largest in the Atlantic community, Philadelphia's job market was a magnet not only for immigrants, but for large numbers of native whites from the surrounding countryside.[12] The rapidly expanding population, which doubled between 1840 and 1860, reaching 565,000 by the latter year, far outstripped growth in the city's housing supply.

Thus newcomers found housing wherever they could. Since the large homes which faced each other on the main streets were expensive, most new settlement occurred in the smaller, cheaper houses and shanties that sprang up in sidestreets, lanes and back-alleys. Boarding with other families was quite common; one household in four took in lodgers. Population expansion in the pre-Civil War years led to sharply increased density, and growth in general was characterized by a "filling-in" process which ensured socioeconomic heterogeneity within a geographically compact city. The Irish and German immigrants, 18 and 6 percent of the 1850 population, respectively, were dispersed across the face of the city.

By 1880, when data are available to identify the American-born children of the immigrants, Irish stock were 30 percent and German stock 16 percent of the city's population. With these data, the residential patterns of the immigrants and their children can be reconstructed in detail. There were five identifiable clusters of Irish stock and one of German stock. However, only one person in five of Irish background and one person in eight of German background lived in such clusters. What is more, even in these areas which represented the heaviest concentrations of Irish and German stock in the city, each group composed only half of the population in their respective clusters.[13]

In 1850, the city's rudimentary transportation system – the horse-drawn omnibus lines which operated over mud and cobblestone streets – was irregular in service and prohibitively expensive for all but the wealthiest. Almost everyone lived within walking distance of their workplaces; indeed, for many at mid-century, home and work were not yet separated. Most blue-collar workers appear to have lived within a radius of half a mile of their jobs in 1850 with a median distance of two blocks.[14]

189

TABLE 2 *Indices of Dissimilarity from Native Whites: 1850, 1880, 1930–1970 (248 Tracts)*

	1850	1880	1930	1940	1950	1960	1970
Blacks	47	52	61	68	71	77	75
Puerto Ricans							
Stock						81	82
Ireland							
Born	30	32	28	32	29		
Second		31					
Stock		31	21			24	28
Germany							
Born	33	36	32	35	31		
Second		33					
Stock		34	27			25	26
Great Britain							
Born			24	23	22		
Stock			22			21	22
Italy							
Born			59	60	54		
Stock			58			47	48
Poland							
Born			54	55	46		
Stock			55			32	35
USSR							
Born			56	57	54		
Stock			53			50	52
Foreign							
Born	21	26					
Second		25					
Stock		25					
Other Foreign							
Born		27					
Second		21					
Stock		24					

Sources: Figures for 1850 and 1880 are computed from Philadelphia Social History Project compilations of the United States manuscript censuses of population. Figures for 1930–1970 are computed from tract-level data taken from the United States censuses.

Note: See Note for Table 1. "Stock" for 1960 includes foreign-born plus second generation which is defined as for 1900, 1930 and 1970. "Other Foreign-Born" refers to all immigrant groups except Irish and Germans.

Most jobs were concentrated within the city's historic core. Half of all manufacturing jobs, which accounted for one male worker in two, and an even greater proportion of nonmanufacturing jobs, were found within a few square blocks of Philadelphia's downtown. Industry— the location of manufacturing jobs—dominated the organization of the city's spatial arrangements. Workers' residential patterns reflected the spatial characteristics of their industries. For example, the residences of workers in concentrated, centralized industries were clustered in or adjacent to the city's core; those who labored in dispersed industries lived scattered across the city.[15]

Industry was more important than ethnicity in organizing the city's residential patterns. Workers of different ethnic groups employed in the same industry had residential characteristics – segregation, clustering, density and centrality – more in common with each other than with members of their own ethnic group. German leather workers, to choose a representative example of an ethnoindustrial type, were distributed over space more like Irish or native-white leather workers than like Germans in other industries. Under conditions of limited transportation and housing availability, workers had more in common residentially with coindustrial workers than with those of common cultural background.[16]

Another way of making this point is to examine the socioeconomic and demographic characteristics of the Irish population who lived in ethnic clusters. If ethnicity rather than industry were determining the organization of residence, the Irish in these areas should have resembled each other; the areas should have been similar pieces from a common cultural nucleus that was prevented from forming by the state of the housing market. Yet, when the areas are empirically examined, they turn out to be thoroughly distinct from each other. The characteristics of the Irish in each of the five clusters match the industrial opportunities available there; thus they differed markedly in occupational structure, unemployment rates, property holding, age and sex structure, household and family types.

The only major exception to the above generalizations were blacks. They were marginal to the rapidly industrializing urban economy of this period, and were considerably more segregated than white immigrants. They had few manufacturing jobs, even though they lived within easy access to more jobs of this type than any other ethnic group. Although the typical black worker lived within one mile of 23,000 manufacturing jobs – half again as many as were accessible to the typical Irish, German or native-white worker – he was refused employment (see Table 3).[17] Racism proved more powerful than the rules that normally governed spatially conditioned job access. In the few instances when blacks did obtain manufacturing jobs, they did not live close to their white coworkers. Rather they tended to live close to one another, regardless of industrial affiliation.[18]

It is fundamental to understand that, as the result of the new industrial order and the emergence of the factory system, all of this occurred within a context of widening occupational opportunity for whites. This is especially significant because the manufacturing sector has traditionally provided the first step up the occupational ladder to new arrivals to the city. Opportunities for upward mobility created by an expanding economy – which provided the bootstraps for the Irish and German immigrants – were so limited for blacks that they were virtually nonexistent. In 1847, for example, less than one-half of one percent of the adult black male work force could find jobs in the economy's dynamic new sectors such as iron and steel and machine tools. During the antebellum years, blacks were not only excluded from the new and well-paying positions, they were uprooted as well from many of their traditional unskilled

TABLE 3 *Distribution of Ethnic Groups by Accessibility to Manufacturing Jobs: 1880 (Males, 18+)*

	Blacks	Irish	Irish-Second	German	German-Second	Native-Whites	Total
Mean Jobs within 1 mile	23,289	15,179	14,985	18,894	17,863	15,313	16,074

Source: Figures are computed from Philadelphia Social History Project compilations of the United States manuscript census of manufactures.

Note: See Table 1.

jobs, denied apprenticeships for their sons, and prevented from practicing the skills they already possessed.[19] Little changed between 1850 and 1880; although the number and proportion of skilled positions increased significantly with the economy's expansion, which benefited the immigrants and especially their American born children, blacks experienced little or no progress (see Table 4). Thus, at least as far back as the mid-nineteenth century, the position of blacks in the city was unlike that of any other group.

Rapid growth in the years between 1850 and 1880 affected Philadelphia's ecological structure. The traditional view of immigrant residential settlement is firmly rooted in the original Park-Burgess notion of concentric zones, in which socio-economic status of the population increases with increasing distance from the center of the city.[20] It is this model which describes a city with a low status core and a high status periphery, and it is in the low status core that the immigrant ghettos are to be found. It is clear, however, that such a model did not fit the preindustrial city. In the preindustrial setting, transportation was poor and did not facilitate movement within the city. Since jobs and services were relatively centralized, the most desirable residences were those close to the center of the city. Thus the preindustrial model, postulated by Sjoberg, describes a city in which the most affluent live close to the center while the impoverished live on the periphery.[21]

In 1850, the residential pattern in Philadelphia could still be partially described by the preindustrial model. But in 1854, the City of Philadelphia merged with twenty-seven other political sub-divisions within Philadelphia County and the greatly enlarged city (it grew from 2 to 130 square miles) rapidly changed; consolidation led to the professionalization of the police and fire departments and the expansion of the public school system. But more importantly for what concerns us here, governmental rationalization facilitated the implementation of critical technological innovations in transportation and building construction. That, in turn, dramatically accelerated Philadelphia's transition to the modern form. Iron track was laid in the streets of the city in 1857; when the horse-drawn cars were hauled over the rail instead of street surfaces, the decline in fric-

tion made it possible to carry three to four times more passengers than had the omnibus. The effects of this transportation breakthrough were felt after the Civil War. The war brought boom times to certain sectors of the city's economy, but it retarded building construction as it accelerated capital accumulation. By the late 1860s the building industry, spurred by the new transportation technology, exploded in a surge of construction that continued into the twentieth century. The horse-car lines, which carried some 99 million passengers in 1880, led the way to residential and commercial deconcentration, while growth in the city's railroad network led to manufacturing decentralization; though the city's population more than doubled between 1850 and 1880, reaching 845,000 by the end of the period, the rate of building growth after 1870 far surpassed population growth.[22]

Population density declined; the average dwelling by 1880 (roughly 6 persons) contained almost one person less than it had in 1850. The modal housing type shifted from the free-standing or semi-detached three and four story dwelling to the two story row home. Moreover, houses that previously were erected by carpenters on demand were now built by large contractors anticipating the form of the modern tract development. Some 50,000 homes – one-third of the 1880 housing stock – were built in the preceding decade. The ratio of new population to new homes was 8 to 1 in the 1840s; by the 1870s, it had declined to 4 to 1.[23]

The dramatic growth during the latter period did not result in a duplication of the spatial patterns that characterized the 1850 city; the decade of the 1870s can be considered the beginning of modern urban form in Philadelphia. The shuffling of the occupational universe brought about by the process of industrialization – the creation of jobs with new skills and the dilution of others, the emergence of bureaucracy and a managerial class – coincided with the city's ability to accommodate wholly new changes in land use specialization. Not only did industry and commerce accelerate their carving up of urban space, but social differentiation and spatial differentiation proceeded in tandem. Social differences in work – wages, status and work environments – now began to be mirrored in increasingly homogeneous

TABLE 4 *Occupational Distribution of Males, 18+, by Ethnicity: 1850, 1880 (as Percent of Ethnic Group)*

1850	Blacks	Irish	German	Foreign-Born°	Native-Whites*
High White Collar and Professional	1.1	1.4	2.6	1.8	8.9
Low White Collar and Proprietary	4.2	11.2	13.6	12.0	23.2
Artisan	17.1	42.1	67.3	49.6	57.0
Specified Unskilled	44.0	11.2	3.9	9.1	6.3
Unspecified Unskilled	33.3	33.9	12.3	27.6	4.3
Totals	4,245	25,389	10,633	36,022	51,930
(Row %s)	(4.5)	(27.5)	(11.5)	(39.1)	(56.3)
Dissimilarity from all Native-Whites*	67	34	18	26	—

1880	Blacks	Irish	Irish-Second	German	German-Second	Foreign-Born°	Native-Whites†	Native-Whites*
High White Collar and Professional	1.0	1.2	1.7	1.9	1.8	1.5	5.5	4.6
Low White Collar and Proprietary	6.6	18.3	22.4	23.6	26.0	20.5	33.7	31.2
Artisan	14.0	31.8	43.5	57.9	54.0	42.6	42.7	43.8
Specified Unskilled	52.2	19.5	18.4	10.5	13.0	15.8	12.8	13.7
Unspecified Unskilled	26.2	29.2	14.0	6.1	5.2	19.7	5.3	6.7
Totals	9,043	38,035	21,780	26,780	12,690	64,743	105,165	139,635
(Row %s)	(4.2)	(17.8)	(10.2)	(12.5)	(5.0)	(30.3)	(49.3)	(65.4)
Dissimilarity from Native-Whites of Native-White Parents†	60	31	15	16	12	17	—	—
Dissimilarity from all Native-Whites*	58	28	12	14	10	15	—	—

Sources: Figures are computed from Philadelphia Social History Project compilations of the United States manuscript censuses of population.

*Includes second generation Irish and Germans.

†Excludes second generation Irish and Germans.

°Includes Irish and Germans only.

Note: See Note for Table 1.

residential settings. The supervisors and clerks who left the shop floor for wood-paneled offices now sought to leave their older heterogeneous neighborhoods for new residential areas where they could live with people more like themselves. The differentiation of residential areas along class, racial-ethnic and life-cycle lines accelerated. The more affluent Irish and German immigrants and their children started to join native-whites in an exodus from the city's center to new modern neighborhoods developing at its peripheries. Over the ensuing thirty years, large residential areas of cheap concentrated housing in the old city center were vacated, making room for the next wave of immigrants and ensuring that the residential patterns of the new immigrants would be far more segregated than those experienced by the old immigrants.

THE EARLY TWENTIETH-CENTURY CITY: 1900–1930

The availability of cheap, old housing concentrated in close proximity to plentiful manufacturing jobs contributed to the considerably higher levels of residential segregation of the Italians, Poles, and Russian Jews who settled in the industrial city of the early twentieth century.[24] The forces set in motion in the 1870s proceeded apace, led by the tract development of the row house, and major changes in transportation technology. The trolleys were electrified in the 1890s, the elevated train and subway were introduced in the early decades of the next century, and the automobile made its appearance shortly thereafter.

The new means of transportation made it possible to open large outlying areas of the city for residential settlement.[25] Unlike building practices in other major cities, Philadelphia's landlords erected few tenements at this time. The row house remained the modal-housing type; in 1915 roughly nine houses in ten were of this architectural form.[26] The emergence of the street-car suburbs and the row house ensured the continued decline in residential density. Despite an increase in the city's population to almost two million by 1930, the average density per dwelling fell to 4.2 persons. Philadelphia richly deserved its nickname as "The City of Homes."

The city's economy did not change dramati-

cally over the half century between 1880 and 1930.[27] Its most salient feature remained its diversification. Despite the entrance of some new industries, most notably in the electronics field, Philadelphia's economy was characterized by the same range of activities found in the nineteenth century: textiles, apparel, printing, publishing, foundry, and machines. Two important changes were noticeable in 1930. First, although the number of manufacturing jobs increased 60 percent over the period, it fell as a proportion of all jobs (from 48 to 31 percent) and increased far less rapidly than did the population as a whole; second, changes in transportation and production technologies began to accelerate the shift of manufacturing activity from the city's center to outlying areas. The full impact of these changes, however, would not be felt until the 1960s and 1970s.

The new occupational opportunities that emerged tended to be located in the economy's white-collar sector (see Table 5). By and large, expanding jobs were found in the professional, white collar or service categories; faced with discrimination, language difficulties and limited educational backgrounds, few blacks and immigrants worked in these desirable positions. As a result, "New" immigrants found their occupational opportunities more limited in this period than the "Old" immigrants had encountered in the nineteenth century; improvements in the overall occupational distribution of black workers during these years were at best marginal.

The socioeconomic differentiation of the city's space that resulted from transportation innovation, the decentralization of manufacturing and greater housing availability produced an urban form well described by the Chicago School model of concentric zones. At furthest remove from the center, in the street-car suburbs, lived white-collar and highly skilled "aristocrats of labor"; largely, these groups were composed of native-whites and the successful descendants of Irish, German and British immigrants. Although the automobile suburbs would not emerge until after World War II, roughly one person in seven in Philadelphia was sufficiently well-off to commute regularly to work by auto in 1934 (this is almost the same proportion of the work force that could afford regular use of the horse-drawn street cars in their "journey-to-work" in 1880).[28]

In the zones surrounding the manufacturing

and retailing core lived the bulk of the working classes, largely "new" immigrants and blacks, roughly one-third of whom walked to work. In general, ethnic concentrations were located near concentrations of industrial employment.[29] This is particularly true of the Italian and Polish areas. Workers living in these neighborhoods were overrepresented in industrial occupations. Once again, the relationships between the occupational distribution of immigrant groups and the location of their jobs and residences can be seen.[30] The principal exception were Russian Jews who, after initial settlement in South Philadelphia, established neighborhoods in the nonindustrial streetcar suburbs in the west and northwestern areas of the city. Workers here were disproportionately found in wholesale and retail rather than industrial jobs.

By 1930 native whites and old immigrants had moved into better jobs and were able to use their greater income to ensure more housing choice; they lived in many different areas of the city characterized by greater housing value and distance from the center. As a result, they were less segregated. The relationship between occupational segregation and residential segregation was a close one. The data suggest that the segregation of newer immigrants was not complete because their occupational segregation was not complete; and, as in the nineteenth century, work location took precedence over the desire to live in an ethnic neighborhood in the residential location decision.

Blacks again stand in sharp contrast. Although they continued to live in and near areas characterized by high industrial concentrations, blacks were excluded from industrial work. Although 80 percent of the blacks in the city lived within one mile of 5,000 industrial jobs, less than 13 percent of the black work force found gainful employment in manufacturing. Blacks earned their livelihood as best they could, concentrating as they had in the last century, in menial, domestic and largely unskilled low-paying occupations (see Tables 5 and 6).

THE MODERN CITY: 1970

Modern Philadelphia bears little resemblance to earlier periods. Technological change has continued to alter urban form and the means of crossing its increasingly inhabited spaces. Automobile suburbs have emerged in all directions and a wide-range of choice characterizes the housing market. Philadelphia's population peaked in 1950 at 2.1 million and was, in 1970, exactly as it had been in 1930: 1.95 million. Population density, however, continued to decline, reaching three persons per dwelling in 1970 – almost exactly half of what it had been in 1850.

Significant changes affected the city's economy. Some 75,000 manufacturing jobs were lost between 1930 and 1970, and the appearance of new jobs in the service sectors have not made up the loss. In this regard, Philadelphia's experience resembles that of many older industrial cities in the Northeast. Large manufacturing employers have abandoned the city for regions with lower taxes, and a work force of nonunionized labor. The location of the remaining manufacturing activity has changed significantly. The earlier shift in production technology, from coal and steam to electricity, combined with important changes in transportation technology in the post-World War II years, produced a marked decentralization of manufacturing jobs. The advent of the interstate highway system, connecting with urban expressways – and the emergence of the trucking industry – has led to the suburbanization of manufacturing activity in industrial parks in the surrounding SMSA. Of every ten manufacturing jobs in the city, the three-mile ring from the city's center held nine jobs in 1880, six in 1930 and four in 1970 (see Table 7).

These changes have had important consequences for Philadelphia's blacks – the city's most recent immigrants. Their numbers increased from 221,000 in 1930 to 645,000 in 1970, and their proportion of the city's population increased from one-tenth to one-third. Today's blacks inherit the oldest stock of deteriorated housing once inhabited by two earlier waves of immigrants, but the jobs which once were located nearby and provided previous newcomers with avenues for upward mobility are gone. Precisely at the moment in time when the worst of the racist hiring practices in industry appear to have abated, the most recent black immigrants find themselves at considerable remove from the industrial jobs that remain and thus are unable to repeat the essential experience of earlier white immigrants. When understood in light of changes

195

TABLE 5 *Occupational Distribution of Males and Females, 10+, by Ethnicity: 1900, 1930 (as Percent of Ethnic Group)*

1900	Blacks	Ireland	Germany	Great Britain	Italy	Poland	Russia	White Foreign-Born	Second Generation Foreign-Born	Native-White of Native Parents
Professional	1.6	2.8	3.7	5.2	3.5	0.6	2.0	2.5	4.5	7.5
Owners and Executives	1.5	5.6	8.6	8.3	7.0	3.7	12.6	8.0	7.1	9.6
Clerks and Sales	1.0	8.9	8.6	10.4	1.6	2.3	6.9	4.2	13.6	17.4
Trade and Transportation	10.8	11.5	7.0	7.0	6.4	4.4	7.5	6.9	9.9	10.3
Manufacturing	8.2	40.2	54.3	56.2	32.6	55.5	62.8	47.3	49.2	40.4
Domestic and Personal										
Service	54.1	18.0	11.1	8.2	12.4	4.8	4.5	17.4	8.9	8.8
Laborers	21.6	10.7	4.0	3.2	34.8	25.9	3.0	11.0	4.6	3.4
Agriculture	0.6	1.0	1.0	0.9	1.4	1.4	0.4	1.2	0.7	1.1
Other	0.6	1.3	1.5	0.6	0.3	1.4	0.3	1.5	1.5	1.5
Dissimilarity from Native-Whites of Native-White Parents†	64	18	17	16	35	38	25	23	10	—

1930	Blacks	White Foreign-Born	Total Native-White
Professional	2.4	3.9	8.5
Owners and Executives	1.5	13.6	8.6
Clerks and Sales	2.6	9.3	27.8
Trade and Transportation	17.1	7.9	9.3
Manufacturing	12.6	42.8	33.7
Domestic and Personal Service	43.4	12.4	6.0
Laborers	17.6	7.3	2.5
Agriculture	0.6	0.9	0.4
Other	2.1	2.0	3.2
Totals	118,890	203,692	565,481
(Row %)	(13.4)	(22.9)	(63.7)
Dissimilarity from all Native-Whites*	61	26	—

Sources: Figures are computed from published United States Census totals. See Department of the Interior, United States Census Office, *Census of Population: 1900*, v. II, pt. II, "Population," (Washington, D.C.: U.S. Census Office, 1902), 583, 585; U.S. Department of Commerce, Bureau of the Census, *Census of Population: 1930*, v. IV, "Population," (Washington, D.C.: U.S. Government Printing Office, 1933), 1412–1415.

*Includes second generation Irish and Germans.

†Excludes second generation Irish and Germans.

Note: See Note for Table 1.

TABLE 6 *Location of Ethnic Populations by Distance from City Center and Access to Industrial Jobs: 1930 (Percent of Foreign Stock Living in Census Tract with the Following Characteristics)*

	Within 3 Miles of City Center	Within 1 Mile of 5,000 or More Industrial Jobs	Of Those Who Are within 3 Miles of City Hall, Percent with Access to 5,000 or More Industrial Jobs	Of Those Who Are beyond 3 Miles of City Hall, Percent with Access to 5,000 or More Industrial Jobs
British	.305	.614	.816	.520
Irish	.411	.610	.791	.483
German	.336	.633	.838	.529
Polish	.404	.815	.943	.724
Russian	.565	.537	.778	.223
Italian	.794	.714	.801	.627
Blacks	.786	.799	.882	.489
Native Whites	.393	.593	.803	.472
Total	.469	.643	.829	.473

Sources: Figures are computed from tract-level data taken from the United States Census.

Note: See Note for Table 1.

in the city's economy as a whole, especially the decline of manufacturing activity and the demand for unskilled labor, it is plain to see that blacks in 1970 Philadelphia are faced with a very different set of circumstances from those which existed in the nineteenth and early twentieth centuries.

The uniqueness of the black experience can be understood in yet another way. Blacks have always been the most segregated group in Philadelphia; this was true in the years 1850–1880, when blacks constituted but 4 percent of the city's population; in the years 1900–1930, when they were roughly 8 to 12 percent; and in 1970, when 33 percent of the city was black. Thus population size alone cannot explain their consistently higher levels of segregation; indeed, despite the fact that smaller groups requiring less housing are often the most segregated, as the size and proportion of the black population increased over time, so did their segregation from native whites: 47 (1850), 52 (1880), 61 (1930), 75 (1970) (see Table 2). This development is tied to the rapid growth of new suburban housing after World War II; whites settled in these automobile

suburbs, and in classic "trickle down" manner, blacks inhabited the older housing vacated by whites.[31]

What sets the contemporary black experience off from that of earlier white immigrants (and earlier black Philadelphians), however, is not simply the consistently higher level of segregation. A new measure of residential experience has been developed that asks what proportion of a typical person's census tract consisted of the same group; for example, what percentage of the population in the typical black person's census tract was black? In this measure of "dominance," the composition of the areal unit is sought. On the other hand, the Index of Segregation asks what percentage of a group would have to move to another location in the city to achieve a distribution throughout each areal unit in the city equal to their proportion of the city's total population.

Using the dominance measure, the striking differences that distinguish blacks from white immigrants can be seen.[32] The typical Irish immigrant in 1880 and the typical Italian immigrant in 1920, for example, shared a similar aspect of

TABLE 7 *Percent Manufacturing Jobs at Given Distances (in Miles) from Center of Philadelphia: 1850–1970*

Distance	1850*			1880†			1930°			1970°		
	#	%	Cum %	#	%	Cum %	#	%	Cum %	#	%	Cum %
0–0.99	30,366	60.9	60.9	78,111	47.2	47.2	52,794	18.8	18.8	32,380	15.7	15.7
1.00–1.99	15,576	31.3	92.2	44,848	27.1	74.3	62,062	22.1	40.9	26,812	13.0	28.7
2.00–2.99	1,353	2.7	94.9	20,521	12.4	86.7	48,582	17.3	58.2	23,305	11.3	40.0
3.00–3.99	192	0.4	95.3	4,634	2.8	89.5	39,596	14.1	72.3	31,143	15.1	55.1
4.00–4.99	387	0.8	96.1	3,806	2.3	91.8	42,404	15.1	87.4	37,536	18.2	73.3
5.00+	1,959	3.9	100.0	13,570	8.2	100.0	35,384	12.6	100.0	55,067	26.7	100.0
Total Jobs:	49,833			165,489			280,823			206,243		

Source: Figures for 1850 and 1880 are computed from Philadelphia Social History Project compilations of the United States manuscript censuses of manufactures. Figures for 1930 and 1970 are computed from tract-level data taken from the Pennsylvania Industrial Directory.

*Center is 3rd and Market.

†Center is 7th and Market.

°Center is 14th and Market.

their residential experience. When the hypothetical immigrant in each era walked through his neighborhood, what kind of people might he have met? The Irishman in 1880 lived with 15 percent other Irish immigrants, 34 percent Irish stock, 26 percent all foreign born persons and 58 percent all foreign stock. The typical Italian immigrant in 1930 had an almost identical experience. He lived with 14 percent other Italian immigrants, 38 percent Italian stock, 23 percent all foreign born persons and 57 percent all foreign stock.[33] In striking contrast, the typical black in

1970 lived in a census tract in which 74 percent of the population was black (see Table 8). What is more, the "dominance" of blacks has risen steadily since 1850 when it was 11 percent; it was not until 1950, however, that the typical black lived in a census tract with a black majority. Ghettos are the product of the post-World War II city.

The black residential experience differs from that of white immigrants in yet another important regard. As ethnic occupational segregation decreased over time – that is, as white immigrant groups gained access to a broader range of occu-

TABLE 8 *Indices of Dominance: 1850, 1880, 1930–1970 (248 Tracts)*

	1850	1880	1930	1940	1950	1960	1970
Blacks	11	12	35	45	56	72	74
Ireland							
Born	24	15	3	2	2		
Second		19					
Stock		34	8			5	3
Germany							
Born	9	11	4	3	2		
Second		14					
Stock		25	11			5	3
Great Britain							
Born			4	3	2		
Stock			12			5	3
Italy							
Born			14	13	9		
Stock			38			23	21
Poland							
Born			7	6	4		
Stock			20			9	8
USSR							
Born			14	12	9		
Stock			28			17	14
Foreign							
Born	32	26	23				
Second		32	34				
Stock		58	57				
Native-White	68	44					
Other Foreign							
Born	7	8					
Second		7					
Stock		14					

Source: See Sources for Table 2.

Note: See Notes for Tables 1 and 2.

pations – their residential segregation decreased. Quite the opposite was true for blacks: despite the occupational desegregation produced in recent decades by the opening of new job opportunities for blacks, their residential segregation has increased over time.

As measured by the Index of Dissimilarity, the differences between the occupational distributions of blacks and native-whites did not fall below 60 percent until 1940 when it reached 52 percent. After 1930, comparisons can be made only with all whites (native and foreign-born combined); it fell to 42 percent in 1950, 29 percent in 1960 and 25 percent in 1970. The significance of the relatively sharp decline in occupational dissimilarity between blacks and whites after World War II, especially in the decade of the 1950s, however, should not be exaggerated (see Table 9). In a 1975 survey of adult males in the Philadelphia Urbanized Area, blacks reported a mean income of $3,000 below whites even after

the effects of age, education and occupation were controlled.[34]

SUMMARY AND CONCLUSIONS

Systematic data on levels of segregation, as measured by the index of dissimilarity and our measure of ethnic dominance, make clear that a "Tale of Three Cities" is the story of three distinct waves of immigrants, three distinct opportunity structures and ecological forms, and three distinct settlement patterns. In each of the three cities, immigrants interacted with the urban structure they encountered and produced markedly different residential patterns.

The first city – the industrializing city of the mid-nineteenth century – was settled by large numbers of Irish, Germans and British of the "Old" immigration. They established integrated residential patterns which have persisted throughout the twentieth century.

TABLE 9 *Occupational Distribution of Males and Females, 16+, by Ethnicity: 1970 (as Percent of Ethnic Group)*

	Blacks		Puerto Ricans		Whites*	
	City	SMSA	City	SMSA	City	SMSA
Professional	7.7	8.1	4.4	5.3	15.1	17.2
Owners and Executives	2.5	2.5	1.4	1.9	7.0	8.8
Clerks and Sales	21.6	20.4	14.7	13.2	32.7	29.9
Trade and Transportation	5.2	5.3	4.3	3.4	3.8	3.4
Manufacturing	30.1	30.1	52.8	49.3	27.6	27.6
Domestic and Personal Service	22.7	23.1	13.8	14.2	8.0	7.8
Laborers	8.0	8.0	6.8	8.4	3.1	3.0
Agriculture	0.6	0.8	0.8	3.9	0.1	0.6
Other	1.7	1.6	0.8	0.5	2.5	1.5
Totals	232,192	279,703	6,270	10,749	525,058	1,570,045
(Row %)	(30.4)	(15.8)	(0.8)	(0.6)	(68.8)	(83.6)
Dissimilarity from *All* whites	24	25	36	37	–	–

Source: Figures are computed from published United States Census totals. See U.S. Bureau of the Census, *Census of Population: 1970* v. I, "Characteristics of the Population," pt. 40, Pennsylvania-Section 1, (Washington, D.C.: U.S. Government Printing Office, 1973), 395, 400, 451, 456, 499, 504.

*Includes a small number of non-black non-whites, i.e., Chinese, etc.

The second city – the industrial city of the early twentieth century – was home for even greater numbers of Italians, Poles, and Russian Jews of the "New" immigration. The residential patterns they formed were much more segregated than those of their predecessors. Yet even here the stereotypic notions of settlement and adjustment to conditions in the New World require some qualification. The experience of initial segregation in working and lower class ghettos and subsequent occupational and residential mobility, as Sam Warner and Colin Burke pointed out, is a limited case in American history: limited to the "New" immigrants in the largest cities at the turn of the last century.[35] And, as the dominance data make clear, most immigrants never lived in ghettos if they are understood as places inhabited, only or largely, by a single ethnic group.

The third city – "post-industrial" modern Philadelphia – was the destination for thousands of black migrants largely from the Southeast. Their segregation and dominance scores have increased steadily from 1850. Unlike earlier groups, today's blacks live in isolated ghettos.[36]

Changes in the patterns of ethnic settlement, can only be fully understood within the context of an ecological explanation that focuses upon changes in the housing market, industrial base, transportation, production, and communication technologies. The ecological perspective makes it possible to explain the changing measures of segregation and dominance, important aspects of the ethnic experience, and the uniqueness of the black experience.

The many significant changes in the relationship between work and residence that characterized Philadelphia's growth over the last century had direct implications for the location, character and stability of ethnic communities. Under constraints of expensive transportation and limited housing, industrial affiliation had a greater impact on the residential choice of immigrants than did their ethnicity.

To the degree that specific ethnic neighborhoods were based on their concentration in nearby industrial employment, the stability of these neighborhoods has depended upon the stability of jobs. When contemporary observers seek explanations for stable neighborhoods, for example, they find strong ethnic ties; yet their analyses all too often confuse causes with effects. The strong ethnic ties are themselves the product of stable neighborhoods; the stability of the neighborhood results from the continuing presence of industrial employment opportunities. The black slums in 1970, for example, were located primarily in areas that had no manufacturing jobs in 1930.[37]

This structural view then suggests that the presence of nearby industrial employment reinforces the stability of white ethnic communities, and it is the industrial concentrations of white ethnics rather than ethnic culture or historical accident that underlies resistance to black invasion. Previous research by Burgess and Duncan and Lieberson has suggested that historical accidents or differences in ethnic tolerance for blacks accounts for their differential resistance to black settlement.[38] The results presented here indicate that the frequently expressed stereotypes of resistant Poles, Italians, and fleeing Russian Jews are applicable only when one does not consider the impact of the ecological structure of the city, the position of these groups in the occupational structure, and their location and access to industrial employment. The reason that white ethnics on Chicago's South Side were able for so many years to prevent black residential penetration has more to do with the continued presence of their job opportunities in the nearby stock yards and steel mills than with cultural factors. The lack of adjacent industrial turf explains the rapid racial turnover that characterized Harlem's transition from an upper middle-class suburb to a lower-class slum in the early decades of the twentieth century.[39] These same factors emerge from an examination of the ghettos of blacks and Puerto Ricans in contemporary Philadelphia; unlike the earlier white ethnic villages, these racial ghettos have not formed around abundant employment opportunities; they emerged instead in economically depressed residential areas which were abandoned by affluent whites who moved to more distant suburbs seeking greater socioeconomic homogeneity, better schools, and more spacious housing.

A decade ago the *Report of the National Advisory Commission on Civil Disorders* asked why "the Negro has been unable to escape from poverty and the ghetto like the European immigrants?" Their answer stressed historical factors.[40] They pointed to the changing nature of the American economy, to slavery and its legacy of racial discrimination, and to the decline of patronage and services when urban black voters win political power.

To the arguments of the Kerner Commission, three further points can be added. First, it is clear that the changing opportunity structure and the different ecological arrangements of the city provide the basic parameters within which the experience of white ethnics and blacks must be understood. To assume a constant opportunity structure and an unchanging ecological form is to seek explanations for differences in ethnic settlement and adjustment in the cultural origins of ethnic groups and thus to misdirect inquiry from the obvious. Cultural factors come into play only within the larger structure of the urban environment.[41] Second, the impact of housing and industrial location – the constraints that work and residence imposed on earlier immigrants – are significant. Western European immigrants came at the most propitious time; both the highly skilled Germans and British, and the relatively unskilled Irish, found ample opportunities. Even though the industrial base of the city began to decline at the turn of this century, it is clear that Eastern European immigrants, when compared with post-World War II blacks, settled in what must be considered the "ghettos of opportunity." Finally, the experience of blacks stands in sharp contrast to that of white ethnics. Not only has their segregation increased over the last century – contrary to the standing theory of assimilation – but it is also clear that blacks have been forced to settle in the oldest industrial and residential areas of the city – areas which have been left behind by the processes of modern urban-industrial development.

There is little to be gained by continuing a debate among advocates of structural and cultural points of view where one is posed to the exclusion of the other. Both play critical explanatory roles. Structural considerations explain well the occupational and residential experience of white immigrants who settled in mid-nineteenth and early twentieth-century Philadelphia; they do not explain the black experience. Here the explanation must be racism. If it is understood as a cultural factor, then culture explains why blacks who lived in Philadelphia at the same time fared so badly despite the twin structural advantages of abundant industrial opportunities and residential location where these opportunities were particularly plentiful. If racial discrimination had been absent in earlier Philadelphia, blacks should have done at least as well if not better than their white immigrant contemporaries.

In modern Philadelphia racism has somewhat abated, but the twin structural advantages of the past have disappeared. Thus structural constraints loom large today; though different from the racial barriers that prevented advancement in the past, they function just as effectively. They retard the economic progress of all groups – blacks and whites alike – who still inhabit the depressed areas of a city with a declining opportunity structure.

Although the Bootstraps and the Last of the Immigrants explanations for the socioeconomic differential that characterize blacks and whites today are of markedly different types, they have the same implications for public policy: do nothing. Both explanations are false and based on a mistaken understanding of our history. Why these points of view persist is important to comprehend. They are accepted in large part because they justify things as they are now. And in legitimating the status quo, these two views demonstrate how what is believed about the past affects the present – not in abstract scholarly logic, but in the material daily life of real people, not only in Philadelphia, but across the nation. Since our sense of history – conscious or not – exercises a real power in the present, it should sensitize us to the dangers of a historical social science.[42] This essay provides an empirically grounded and interdisciplinary historical perspective so often absent in discussions of contemporary social problems and their solutions.

The Bootstraps explanation looks to the past, but however heroic the sound which comes from praising the courage and stamina of earlier white immigrants, it rings totally untrue when applied to the historical experience of blacks. The Last of the Immigrants explanation looks to the future, but the conditions that blacks face in modern

Philadelphia are so different from those which earlier groups found that the analogy is thoroughly inappropriate. Unless major structural changes and perhaps some form of preferential treatment are undertaken at all levels of public and urban policy, it is doubtful that assimilation and economic progress for blacks will be possible. The approaches which blacks utilize to enter the American mainstream will certainly not be the same as those used by white immigrants; of necessity, they may have to be devised in ways yet unanticipated. As a national policy is formulated to revitalize our cities, it must be remembered that racial discrimination, though less pervasive, persists. The challenge is to recognize how our cities have changed and to use this understanding to provide real bootstraps for blacks so that they may indeed become the last of the immigrants.

ENDNOTES

1. This essay is based on the research of five authors, all Research Associates of the Philadelphia Social History Project which collected and made machine-readable the data for the nineteenth century. For further information about the PSHP and its interdisciplinary approach to research see Theodore Hershberg, "The Philadelphia Social History Project: A Methodological History" (Ph.D. diss., Stanford University, 1973), and "The Philadelphia Social History Project: A Special Issue," *Historical Methods* 9 (1976): 2–3. The twentieth-century data were collected by William Yancey and Eugene Ericksen. PSHP data form the basis for Alan N. Burnstein, "Residential Distribution and Mobility of Irish and German Immigrants in Philadelphia, 1850–1880" (Ph.D. diss., University of Pennsylvania, 1975); the nineteenth and twentieth century data were used in Stephanie Greenberg, "Industrialization in Philadelphia: The Relationship between Industrial Location and Residential Patterns, 1880–1930" (Ph.D. diss., Temple University, 1977).

"A Tale of Three Cities" attempts to synthesize the findings reported in these dissertations and in a number of separate journal articles and unpublished papers. Many of these papers appear in *Toward an Interdisciplinary History of the City: Work, Space, Family and Group Experience in Nineteenth Century Philadelphia*, ed. Theodore Hershberg (New York: Oxford University Press, 1979); hereafter cited as *Interdisciplinary History of the City*.

2. Recent monographs on urban black communities provide an ethnic and racial perspective on the black experience but fail to adequately treat its urban context.

See Gilbert Osofsky, *Harlem: The Making of a Ghetto: Negro New York, 1890–1920* (New York: Harper and Row, 1963); Allan H. Spear, *Black Chicago: The Making of a Negro Ghetto, 1890–1920* (Chicago: University of Chicago Press, 1967); Seth M. Scheiner, *Negro Mecca: A History of the Negro in New York City, 1865–1920* (New York University Press, 1965); David M. Katzman, *Before the Ghetto: Black Detroit in the Nineteenth Century* (Urbana: University of Illinois Press, 1973); John W. Blassingame, *Black New Orleans, 1860–1880* (Chicago: University of Chicago Press, 1973).

An exception is Kenneth L. Kusmer, *A Ghetto Takes Shape: Black Cleveland 1870–1930* (Urbana: University of Illinois Press, 1976). Following in the tradition of W.E.B. DuBois, *The Philadelphia Negro: A Social Study* (Philadelphia, 1899; New York: Schocken Press, 1965) and St. Clair Drake and Horace R. Cayton, *Black Metropolis: A Study of Negro Life in a Northern City* (New York: Harper and Row, 1945), Kusmer discusses how the urban environment affected the collective experiences of blacks in late nineteenth and early twentieth century Cleveland.

3. For an interpretative overview of Afro-American history that develops this theme see August Meier and Elliot Rudwick, *From Plantation to Ghetto*, 3d. ed. rev. (New York: Hill and Wang, 1976).

4. The concept "urban as process" is elaborated in Theodore Hershberg, "The New Urban History," *Journal of Urban History* 5 (November 1978).

5. This point of view is held by many in positions of considerable influence in our society. In discussing the impact of the Bakke case with a black clerk in a Washington, D.C., bookstore, no less than Chief Justice Warren E. Burger was quoted as saying that ". . . his grandparents had come from Europe and were illiterate and it had taken 150 years for his people to improve themselves." Miss Audrey Hair, the bookstore clerk, said: "I asked him if he didn't think 300 years was enough time for my people?" New York *Times*, 5 November 1978, p. 6. The "Last of the Immigrants" explanation is cogently presented by Nathan Glazer, "Blacks and Ethnic Groups: The Difference, and the Political Difference It Makes," in *Key Issues in the Afro-American Experience*, ed. Nathan I. Huggins, Martin Kilson, and Daniel M. Fox (New York: Harcourt Brace Jovanovich, 1971), pp. 193–211. A more popular expression can be found in Irving Kristol, "The Negro Today Is Like the Immigrant of Yesterday," New York *Times* Magazine, 11 September 1966.

No particular author is identified with the Bootstraps explanation; rather it is considered endemic in American culture and is associated with a racist interpretation of the black experience; that is, blacks failed because they are racially inferior.

6. Sam Bass Warner has also described "three" Phila-

delphias: "The Eighteenth-Century Town" of 1770–1780; "The Big City" of 1830–1860; and "The Industrial Metropolis" of 1920–1930; *The Private City: Philadelphia in Three Periods of Its Growth* (Philadelphia: University of Pennsylvania Press, 1968); see also Warner, "If All the World Were Philadelphia: A Scaffolding for Urban History, 1774–1930," *American Historical Review* 74 (October 1968).

A more recent study also identified "three cities": the "commercial" city of the eighteenth and early nineteenth centuries, the "industrial" city of the late nineteenth and early twentieth centuries, and the "corporate" city of the post World War II period; see David Gordon, "Capitalist Development and the History of American Cities," in *Marxism and the Metropolis: Perspectives in Urban Political Economy,* ed. Larry Sawers and William K. Tabb (New York: Oxford University Press, 1978).

The differences here reflect purpose. Warner initially wanted to demonstrate to historians that systematic data were available with which to document the major changes that occurred in the urban environment over the last two centuries. His major purpose in *The Private City,* however, had far less to do with changes in the city's opportunity and ecological structure than with the failures of urban life in a capitalist economy; he attributes urban problems to the pursuit of private profit at the expense of the public good. Where these once coincided in the colonial city, they diverged permanently with the emergence of the urban industrial order in the nineteenth century. Gordon's purpose was to classify cities according to stages in their historical economic development, arguing that urban form and the requirements of capitalism are inextricably linked to each other. Our purpose differs; we wished to characterize the particular kind of economy and environment that awaited the settlement of three temporally distinct waves of immigrants. Thus we have designated our three cities as "The Industrializing City," "The Industrial City," and "The Post-Industrial City."

7. (New York: Harcourt Brace and Jovanovich, 1976).

8. See for example Robert E. Park, "The Urban Community as a Spatial Pattern and a Moral Order," in *The Urban Community,* ed. Ernest W. Burgess (Chicago: University of Chicago Press, 1926); Louis Wirth, *The Ghetto* (Chicago: University of Chicago Press, 1928); Ernest W. Burgess, "Residential Segregation in American Cities," *Annals of the American Academy of Political and Social Science* 140 (1928): 105–115; Robert E. Park, *Human Communities* (Glencoe, IL: Free Press, 1952).

9. Stanley Lieberson, *Ethnic Patterns in American Cities* (Glencoe, IL: Free Press, 1963). The Index of Segregation expresses the percentage of a group that would have to move to another location in the city to achieve a distribution throughout each areal unit equal to their proportion of the city's total population; the Index measure is often expressed as a whole number ranging from 0 (no segregation) to 100 (complete segregation). For a detailed explanation of the Index of Segregation, see also Otis Dudley Duncan and Beverly Duncan, "Residential Distribution and Occupational Stratification," *American Journal of Sociology* 60 (1955): 493–503; Otis Dudley Duncan and Beverly Duncan, "A Methodological Analysis of Segregation Indexes," *American Sociological Review* 20 (April 1955); Karl E. Taeuber and Alma F. Taeuber, *Negroes in Cities: Residential Segregation and Neighborhood Change* (Chicago: Atheneum, 1965), pp. 195–245.

10. The dissimilarity scores reported in Table 2 are calculated in the same manner as the Index of Segregation but describe the degree of difference from native whites as opposed to the remainder of the city's population. The scores reported in Tables 2 and 8, moreover, *are based on identical areal units.*

Tract level data were not collected by the nineteenth-century U.S. Census Bureau. For the 1930 and 1970 censuses, Philadelphia was divided into 404 and 365 tracts respectively. To achieve compatible boundaries, it was necessary to collapse these into 248 tracts. The much smaller PSHP areal units for the nineteenth century – 7,100 rectangular grids one and one-quarter blocks square – were aggregated up to the level of the 248 census tracts. Areal compatibility was thus achieved across the entire 120 year period. For information on the construction of the PSHP grid areal unit, see Hershberg, "The PSHP: A Methodological History," pp. 150–87; and "The PSHP: A Special Issue," pp. 99–105.

11. Given the standing notion of the assimilation process, moreover, the decline in residential segregation over the period 1930–1970 is less than might be expected: the greatest decline was found among Polish stock (55% in 1930 to 35% in 1970), but Italian stock fell only slightly (58% to 48%), and Jewish stock did not change (53% to 52%). See Table 2.

12. Bruce Laurie and Mark Schmitz, "Manufacture and Productivity: The Making of an Industrial Base in Nineteenth-Century Philadelphia," in Hershberg, *Interdisciplinary History of the City.*

13. Hershberg, "The PSHP: A Methodological History," pp. 285–323; see especially Tables 21 and 23; A. Burstein, "Patterns of Segregation and the Residential Experience" in Hershberg, "The PSHP: A Special Issue," pp. 105–113.

14. Hershberg, Harold Cox, Richard Greenfield and Dale Light Jr., "The Journey-to-Work: An Empirical Investigation of Work, Residence, and Transportation in Philadelphia, 1850 and 1880," in Hershberg, *Interdisciplinary History of the City.* Although the estimated journey to work doubled between 1850 and 1880, reaching a radius of one mile and a median of one-half

mile, the absolute distances involved remained quite short.

15. Greenfield, Hershberg, and William Whitney, "The Dynamics and Determinants of Manufacturing Location: A Perspective on Nineteenth-Century Philadelphia"; Greenberg, "Industrial Location and Ethnic Residential Patterns"; both in Hershberg, *Interdisciplinary History of the City.*

16. Greenberg, "Industrialization in Philadelphia."

17. Greenberg, "Industrial Location and Ethnic Residential Patterns," in Hershberg, *Interdisciplinary History of the City;* and Greenberg, "Industrialization in Philadelphia."

18. On the other hand, given black overrepresentation in such service occupations as waiter and porter, their residential pattern was functional: the single large black residential concentration was located adjacent to the city's largest concentration of hotels, restaurants and inns in the downtown area.

19. Hershberg, "Free Blacks in Antebellum Philadelphia: A Study of Ex-slaves, Freeborn and Socioeconomic Decline," *Journal of Social History* 5 (December 1971); and "Free-born and Slaveborn Blacks in Antebellum Philadelphia," in *Slavery and Race in the Western Hemisphere* ed. Eugene Genovese and Stanley Engerman (Princeton: Princeton University Press, 1975).

The characteristic difficulties that blacks faced in finding employment were described by Joshua Bailey, member of the Board of Managers of the Philadelphia Society for the Employment and Instruction of the Poor. Bailey wrote in his diary that "Employers express themselves willing to receive such an one (a young 'colored' man) into their shops, but they cannot dare to do it knowing the opposition such an act would meet from their workmen who will not consent to work with colored persons" (10 January 1853).

The process of adjustment to conditions in the New World was a difficult one for all newcomers—black and white immigrants alike. Yet the historical record makes clear that much about the black experience was different—sometimes in degree, other times in kind. Blacks were victims of frequent race riots and saw their homes, schools and churches burned again and again. Though legally a free people and citizens, only members of the black race were denied the right to vote in the State of Pennsylvania after 1838. They occupied the worst housing in the Moyamensing slum and suffered from the greatest degree of impoverishment. Their mortality rate was roughly twice that of whites, and the death of black men early in their adult lives was the major reason that blacks were forced, far more often than whites, to raise their children in fatherless families; see F.F. Furstenberg, Jr., Hershberg and J. Modell, "The Origins of the Female-Headed Black Family: The

Impact of the Urban Experience," *Journal of Interdisciplinary History* 6 (September 1975).

For the occupational experience of the white immigrant work force, see B. Laurie, Hershberg and G. Alter, "Immigrants and Industry," *Journal of Social History* 9 (December 1975) and B. Laurie and M. Schmitz, "Manufacture and Productivity."

20. Robert Park, Ernest W. Burgess, and Roderick D. McKenzie, eds., *The City* (Chicago: University of Chicago Press, 1928).

21. Gideon Sjoberg, "The Preindustrial City," *American Journal of Sociology* 60 (1955): 438–45; Gideon Sjoberg, *The Preindustrial City: Past and Present* (Glencoe, IL: Free Press, 1960).

22. Hershberg, et al., "The Journey-to-Work."

23. Ibid. We do not wish to leave the impression that the decline in population densities over the period was due solely to the increased availability of housing. Declining population densities were also tied to declining fertility, a process experienced over at least the last century in Western Europe and North America.

When the city is divided into concentric rings of roughly one mile, the inner two rings lost population consistently over the period. The first ring fell from 206,000 persons in 1880 to 67,000 in 1970; and in the second ring population fell from 241,000 in 1880 to 135,000 in 1970. Although contemporary population density gradients from the center outward are not level, their smoothing over time is one of the striking changes in urban population structure.

24. For an excellent discussion of the Polish experience in Philadelphia in the first two decades of the twentieth century, and less detailed but useful information on other immigrant groups in the city at the same time, see Carol Golab, *Immigrant Destinations* (Philadelphia: Temple University Press, 1978).

25. Sam Bass Warner, Jr., has described this process for late nineteenth-century Boston, *Street Car Suburbs: The Process of Growth in Boston, 1870–1900* (Cambridge, MA: Harvard University Press, 1962).

26. Golab, *Immigrant Destinations*, p. 153.

27. Greenberg, "Industrialization in Philadelphia," see Chap 6, "Changes in the Location of Jobs Between 1880 and 1930 and the Composition and Stability of Urban Areas in 1930," pp. 139–182.

28. Greenberg, "Industrialization in Philadelphia," Chap 6; Hershberg, *et al.*, "The Journey-to-Work."

29. Ericksen and Yancey, "Work and Residence in an Industrial City," *Journal of Urban History* (1979).

30. The relationship between work and residence was for Polish immigrants in 1915 what it had been for the Irish and German immigrants in the nineteenth century. Golab summarizes their experience in these words: "Each Polish settlement (and there were nine such areas) directly reflected the industrial structure of

the neighborhood in which it was located. It was the availability of work that determined the location of the Polish colony, for the Poles were invariably employed in the neighborhoods where they resided." *Immigrant Destinations*, p. 113.

A similar conclusion was reached by E.E. Pratt in his study of immigrant worker neighborhoods: *Industrial Causes of Congestion of Population in New York City* (New York: Columbia University Press, 1911).

31. William Alonso, "The Historic and the Structural Theories of Urban Form: Their Implications for Urban Renewal," in Charles Tilly, ed., *An Urban World* (Boston: Little, Brown, 1974), 442–446.

32. The "dominance" measure not only operates to homogenize the experience of the two earlier waves of white immigrants, it also calls into question too great a reliance on the Index of Segregation as a useful tool to infer social experience. To the extent that cross-cultural contacts are central to our thinking about the socialization of the young and subsequent mobility and assimilation experience, the dominance measure, in getting more directly at who lives near whom, may be a better measure than the Index of Segregation; indeed we have seen that although some groups can be twice as segregated as others – as the new immigrants were compared to the old – they can display identical levels of dominance. Although the thrust of this essay is not methodological, we think in time that the uses of the Index of Segregation, particularly the assumptions that underlie its correlation with a wide range of social behaviors, be carefully reconsidered. We are not claiming that the Index of Segregation is without value, but rather that in many instances it may be (and has been) inappropriately applied. The socioeconomic correlates of the Index of Segregation and our new measure of dominance remain a topic for empirical investigation.

Although when compared to the black experience the differences between the old and new immigrants appear small indeed, there were differences nonetheless. While the dominance measures for the white immigrant groups were approximately equal, this does not mean that they had the same residential *pattern*. In order for the new immigrants, proportionally smaller than the old immigrants, to achieve so much higher measure of segregation than, and measures of dominance equal to the old immigrants, they would have had to be considerably more clustered. Thus, relative to the entire settled area of the city, the residential pattern of the new immigrants must have been much more compact than that of the old. Accordingly, an examination of the dimensions of segregation reveals that while the very localized experiences of the old and new immigrants may have been the same, the old immigrants had access to more diverse areas of the city. See Burstein, "Patterns of Segregation."

33. Golab's description of 1915 immigrant residential patterns corroborates the argument presented here: "No immigrant group in the city ever totally monopolized a particular neighborhood to the extent that it achieved isolation from members of other groups." Golab, *Immigrant Destinations*, p. 112.

34. Ericksen and Yancey, "Organizational Factors and Income Attainment: Networks, Businesses, Unions," unpublished paper (Temple University, 1978). This result is consistent with those reported in many national studies.

The occupational dissimilarity scores are reported at the bottom of each occupational table. The scores can be interpreted in the same manner as the segregation scores: the percent of blacks who would have to shift to another occupational strata in order to approximate the same distribution as whites.

35. Sam Bass Warner and Colin Burke, "Cultural Change and the Ghetto," *Journal of Contemporary History* 4 (1969): 173–187.

36. Puerto Ricans, a much smaller group than blacks, are in fact the most recent immigrants to the city and are also slightly more segregated than blacks; see Table 2.

37. Gladys Palmer, *Recent Trends in Employment and Unemployment in Philadelphia* (Philadelphia: Works Project Administration, Philadelphia Labor Market Studies, 1937).

38. Burgess, "Residential Segregation"; Otis Dudley Duncan and Stanley Lieberson, "Ethnic Segregation and Assimilation," *American Journal of Sociology* 64 (January 1959): 364–74.

39. Gilbert Osofsky, *Harlem: The Making of a Ghetto*. While carefully documenting the real estate boom and bust that followed the construction of the elevated lines which connected Harlem with lower Manhattan, Osofsky overlooked entirely the significance of the work-residence relationship in his explanation of the dramatic changes in Harlem's racial demography.

40. (New York: Bantam Books, 1968); see chapter 9, "Comparing the Immigrant and Black Experience," pp. 278–282. For a convincing critique of the "Last of the Immigrants" theory that focuses on patterns of intra- and inter-generational occupational mobility and supports our argument nicely, see Stephan Thernstrom, *The Other Bostonians: Poverty and Progress in the American Metropolis* (Cambridge, Mass.: Harvard University Press, 1973), chapter 10, "Blacks and Whites," pp. 176–219. "By now . . . ," Thernstrom concluded, somewhat too optimistically in our opinion, "American Negroes may face opportunities and constraints that are fairly analogous to those experienced by the millions of European migrants who struggled to survive in the American city of the late nineteenth and early twentieth centuries. But until very recently, the problems of black men in a white society were different in kind

from those of earlier newcomers. . . . The main factor that will impede black socioeconomic progress in the future will be the forces of inertia that have been called passive or structural discrimination" (pp. 218–219).

41. Yancey, Ericksen and Richard N. Juliana, "Emergent Ethnicity: A Review and Reformulation," *American Sociological Review* 41 (June, 1976): 3.

42. See Stephan Thernstrom, "Further Reflections on the Yankee City Series: The Pitfalls of a Historical Social Science," *Poverty and Progress: Social Mobility in a Nineteenth-Century City* (Cambridge, Mass.: Harvard University Press, 1964), pp. 225–239; and Michael B. Katz, "Introduction," *The People of Hamilton, Canada West: Family and Class in a Mid-Nineteenth Century City* (Cambridge, Mass.: Harvard University Press, 1975), p. 1.

Patterns of Ethnic Integration in America

3

The dominant conceptual framework in the analysis of American ethnic and racial relations has been an assimilation model. One of the earliest and most influential statements of the assimilation model was embodied in the classic "race relations cycle" advanced by sociologist Robert E. Park in 1926:

> In the relations of races there is a cycle of events which tends everywhere to repeat itself. . . . The race relations cycle, which takes the form . . . of contacts, competition, accommodation, and eventual assimilation, is apparently progressive and irreversible. Customs regulations, immigration restrictions, and racial barriers may slacken the tempo of the movement; may perhaps halt it altogether for a time, but cannot change its direction; cannot, at any rate, reverse it. (Park 1950:150)

According to the assimilation model of intergroup contact, interethnic relations inevitably go through successive stages of competition, conflict, accommodation, and assimilation. In Article 12 Shirley Hune documents the widespread and enduring impact of Park's assimilation model and his notions of immigrant social psychology.

In Part 2 Noel ("The Origins of Ethnic Stratification") focused on the first phase of Park's race relations cycle: the *origins* of ethnic stratification. However, the succeeding stages in Park's cycle are more problematic. For example, Lieberson (1961) contends that the Park race relations cycle is inadequate because it fails to recognize that differences in power relations in the original contact situations produce different stratification outcomes. Lieberson distinguishes between two different situations of ethnic stratification: one in which the migrating group is the dominant ethnic group (migrant superordination) and one in which the group residing in the region at the time of contact is dominant (indigenous superordination). In migrant superordination, the economic, political, and cultural institutions of the subjugated indigenous population are undermined. However, because the subordinate indigenous group seeks to maintain its traditional institutions, conflict with the dominant group can persist over long periods of time. This situation, exemplified by Indian-white relations in the United States, is classic colonialism, in which the subordinate group strenuously resists assimilation. When the migrating group is subordinate, on the other hand, its decision to enter another society is more likely to be voluntary, and it is much more likely to accept assimilation into the dominant society, as exemplified by the experience of most European immigrants to America.

Most discussions of assimilation in the United States have focused on the adaptation of immigrant groups that have voluntarily entered American society. The experience of African-Americans, whose ancestors were involuntarily imported from Africa, does not fall into either contact situation – migrant or indigenous subordination. Wilson (1973) maintains that slave transfers constitute a third major contact situation, the one in which the power and coercion of the dominant group is greatest. In contrast to colonization, in which the indigenous group, although subordinate, is able to maintain elements of its own cultures, slave transfers involve the forcible and involuntary uprooting of people from families and traditional cultures, which places them in a much greater dependent relationship with the dominant group (Wilson 1973:19–20). The extent to which differences between migrant superordination, indigenous superordination, and slave transfers have affected the nature of intergroup relations has been the subject of considerable controversy among social scientists, especially as they have sought to compare the patterns of integration among different ethnic groups and to develop explanations for the differences that exist.

An important assumption of the assimilation model has been that, as American society became more modernized, ethnic and racial distinctions would become insignificant or eventually disappear. According to this conception, the forces of modernity – democratic and egalitarian political norms and institutions, industrialization, urbanization, and bureaucratization – place increasing emphasis on rationality, impersonality, status by achievement, physical and social mobility, and equal opportunity. Traditional social systems, in which social position is based on racial and ethnic origins rather than on individual merit, become increasingly burdensome (and even expensive) to maintain. Thus, the Southern caste system, in which selection was based on the irrational ascriptive criterion of race, was perceived by advocates of an assimilation model as a vestige of a premodern, agrarian society that ultimately and inevitably would be undermined as the modernization process transformed the society by emphasizing a selection process based on merit, credentials, and skills.

This position was nowhere more clearly articulated than in Gunnar Myrdal's *An American Dilemma,* probably the most important book ever written on the subject of American race relations. Published in 1944, *An American Dilemma* became an instant classic and exerted a profound influence on white America by drawing attention to the dynamics of race in American society in a way that had not been accomplished since the elimination of slavery. Myrdal's title reflected his basic thesis: the American creed of "liberty, equality, justice, and fair opportunity" was violated by the subservient status to which African-Americans had been relegated. Myrdal felt that the contradiction between white America's deeply felt professions of equality and brotherhood, on the one hand, and its treatment of African-American people, on the other, presented an "embarrassing" dilemma that made for "moral uneasiness" in the hearts and minds of white Americans. He also optimistically thought that the primary thrust of American institutions was in a direction that would ultimately undermine the last vestiges of the racial caste system.

The assumption that the forces of modernization will progressively weaken the ties of race and ethnicity has been questioned, however (see, for example, Bonacich's discussion in Article 3). In his classic essay, "Industrialization and Race Relations," Herbert Blumer (1965) noted that the projected effects of industrialization are not, in reality, inevitable. An emphasis on rationality may not make job opportunities available to the best qualified individuals irrespective of race; rather, the goal of efficiency and social harmony may impel managers *rationally* to discriminate because to hire minority applicants might disrupt the efficient and harmonious functioning of the enterprise. "*Rational* operation of industrial enterprises which are introduced into a racially ordered society may call for a deferential respect for the canons and sensitivities of that racial order" (Blumer 1965:233). In other words, modernization and industrialization do not necessarily change the order of majority-minority relations; rather, these processes adapt and conform to existing systems of racial etiquette, as the debate over economic sanctions against the South African system of apartheid demonstrates. Blumer contended that changes in race relations in the workplace are brought about not by an inherent dynamic of the modernization process but by forces outside the world of work.

Assimilation as Ideology

Assimilation involves efforts to integrate or incorporate a group into the mainstream of a society. The objective of assimilation is a homogeneous society. In general, the assimilation model of racial and ethnic contact assumes that the unique and distinctive characteristics of a minority will be erased and the minority's culture, social institutions, and identity will be replaced by those of the dominant group.

Critics of the assimilation model have charged that it reflects a "liberal" view of the manner in which racial and ethnic diversity should be resolved. That is, an assimilationist perspective has frequently served an ideological function of specifying how racial and ethnic groups *should* relate to each other, instead of assessing the process whereby they *do* interact. In many circumstances, assimilationist analyses have served to legitimize the basic ideology of American society as a land of opportunity. Metzger (1971) has argued that, in general, the assimilationist perspective assumes that

> *The incorporation of America's ethnic and racial groups into the mainstream culture is virtually inevitable. . . . Successful assimilation, moreover, has been viewed as*

synonymous with equality of opportunity and upward mobility for the members of minority groups; "opportunity," in this system, is the opportunity to discard one's ethnicity and to partake fully in the "American Way of Life." In this sense, assimilation is viewed as the embodiment of the democratic ethos. (Metzger 1971:628–629)

Myrdal's monumental *An American Dilemma* reflected this general liberal notion of how racial and ethnic groups should come together in American society. The basic framework within which Myrdal conceptualized American race relations is perhaps most clearly reflected in his examination of the nature of African-American culture and community life. To the extent to which African-American culture diverged from dominant white culture patterns Myrdal considered it a "distorted development, or a pathological condition, of the general American culture." Therefore, the primary thrust of black efforts toward institutional change in American society should be toward acquiring the characteristics of the dominant group. "It is to the advantage of American Negroes as individuals and as a group," wrote Myrdal, "to become assimilated into American culture, to acquire the traits held in esteem by the dominant white Americans."

One of the implications of such a model is that frequently the sources of ethnic conflict are perceived to reside not within the structure of society but within the "pathological" or "maladjusted" behavior of the minority group. In such circumstances resolution of ethnic conflict involves a minority group adapting to the standards of the majority. As we will note more fully in the introduction to Part 4, the Black Protest Movement of the late 1960s and early 1970s was in many respects a reaction against such an assimilationist stance.

Majority Policies toward Racial and Ethnic Minorities

The nature of the assimilation process and the extent to which various racial and ethnic groups should be permitted or permit themselves to be integrated, incorporated, or absorbed into American society has been the source of considerable controversy. In his now classic analysis, *Assimilation in American Life* (1964), Milton Gordon (Article 11) distinguished among three ideologies – Anglo-conformity, the melting pot, and cultural pluralism – that have been used to explain the dynamics of intergroup relations in American life.

Anglo-Conformity/Transmuting Pot

The principal assimilationist model in the American experience has emphasized conformity by minority groups to dominant group standards – the desirability and necessity of maintaining English social institutions, language, and cultural patterns. Termed Anglo-conformity, this model assumes that an ethnic minority should give up its distinctive cultural characteristics and adopt those of the dominant group. It can be expressed by the formula A + B + C = A, in which A is the dominant group and B and C represent ethnic minority groups that must

conform to the values and life styles of the dominant group; they must "disappear" if they wish to achieve positions of power and prestige in the society
(Newman 1973:53).

A policy of Anglo-conformity not only seeks a homogeneous society organized around the idealized cultural standards, social institutions, and language of
the dominant group; it also assumes the inferiority of the cultures of other ethnic
groups. Many first- and second-generation Americans retain vivid and painful
recollections of the ridicule of their cultural ways and the pressures for them to
become "Americanized." Many tried to rid themselves of their traditional beliefs
and practices. A daughter of Slovenian immigrant parents recalled her childhood:

> In the 9th grade, a boy said to me, "You talk funny." I wondered what he meant. I listened
> to my friends, and I did not think they "talked funny." Then, that great American
> experiment, the public high school, opened my ears. I heard the English language spoken as
> I had never heard it spoken. . . . I began to hear that I did indeed pronounce my words
> differently, and so did my friends. I practiced [English] in secret, in the bathroom, of course,
> until I could pronounce properly the difficult "th" sound, which seemed the most distinctive
> and, therefore, the most necessary to conquer. How superior I felt when I had mastered this
> sound. . . ! Alas, however, I refused to speak Slovenian. (Prosen 1976:2–3)

Such a conception of how a minority group should relate to the majority is
not unique to the United States. Consider, for example, the statement of an
Australian Minister for Immigration concerning the objective of his country's
immigration policy:

> It is cardinal with us that Australia, though attracting many different people, should
> remain a substantially homogeneous society, that there is no place in it for enclaves or
> minorities, that all whom we admit to reside permanently should be equal here and capable
> themselves of becoming substantially Australians after a few years of residence, with their
> children in the next generation wholly so. (Opperman 1966)

For this model to be applicable to majority-minority relations in societies other
than the United States the culture-specific term *Anglo-conformity* must be replaced by the more general term *transmuting pot* (Cole and Cole 1954).

The Melting Pot

Like Anglo-conformity, the objective of a *melting pot* policy is a society without
ethnic differences. More tolerant than a policy of Anglo-conformity, the melting
pot ideal sees ethnic differences as being lost in the creation of a new society and
a new people—a synthesis unique and distinct from any of the different groups
that formed it. Unlike Anglo-conformity, none of the contributing groups is
considered to be superior; each is considered to have contributed the best of its
cultural heritage to the creation of something new. The melting pot ideal can be
expressed by the formula $A + B + C = D$, in which A, B, and C represent the
different contributing groups and D is the product of their synthesis (Newman
1973:63). As Ralph Waldo Emerson expressed it in the mid-nineteenth century:

As in the old burning of the Temple at Corinth, by the melting and intermixture of silver and gold and other metals a new compound more precious than any, called Corinthian brass, was formed; so in this continent—asylum of all nations—the energy of Irish, Germans, Swedes, Poles, and Cossacks and all the European tribes—of the Africans and of the Polynesians—will construct a new race, a new religion, a new state, a new literature. (Quoted in Gordon 1964:117)

The melting pot conception has been perhaps the most widely idealized popular conception of how ethnic groups have been integrated into American society. As both Gordon and Hune point out, the melting pot notion has pervaded American intellectual life and popular culture. It was a prominent feature of Frederick Jackson Turner's 1893 frontier thesis, which for generations provided the most definitive and compelling interpretation of what was most distinctive about American society. According to Turner, "in the crucible of the frontier the immigrants were Americanized, liberated, and fused into a mixed race." (Turner 1894/1966:12)

Pluralism

Pluralism, on the other hand, rejects the inevitability of cultural assimilation. As the term has been applied to American society, pluralism is a system in which groups with different cultural practices can coexist and be preserved but simultaneously embrace common values and beliefs and participate in common economic, political, and social institutions. According to this notion, the strength and vitality of American society is derived from the many different ethnic groups that have made it a "nation of nations." Each group should be permitted to retain its unique qualities while affirming its allegiance to the larger society. It can be expressed by the equation $A + B + C = A + B + C$, in which A, B, and C are each ethnic groups that maintain their distinctiveness over time (Newman 1973).

This is a much narrower conception of ethnic coexistence than is implied in the use of the term in many other societies. In the American conception of pluralism, diverse ethnic groups maintain some elements of cultural distinctiveness but accept core elements of the dominant culture and seek participation in the mainstream economic and political institutions. However, in addition to possessing cultural heterogeneity, most genuinely "plural" societies are characterized by "mutually incompatible institutional systems—social structures, value and belief systems, and systems of action" (Horowitz 1985:136).

The three types that Gordon delineated can be placed on a continuum ranging from lesser to greater minority-group integrity and autonomy. Each type merges imperceptibly with the adjacent type. For example, Anglo-conformity is much closer to the melting pot than it is to pluralism. Moreover, the range of possible alternatives can be logically extended. Examination of the history of racial and ethnic contact in the United States and throughout the world makes it apparent that Anglo-conformity (the transmuting pot), the melting pot, and pluralism do not exhaust the theoretical possibilities or the historical examples of the consequences of intergroup contact. A policy of genocide, at one extreme, permits less minority autonomy, obviously, than does a policy based on the transmuting pot model. At the other extreme, *separatism,* or complete autonomy for the minority group, comprises a more expansive ideology than pluralism. When all of these ideologies are placed on a continuum, the result looks like Figure 3.1 below. Let us review the alternative possible dominant policies toward racial and ethnic minorities suggested by this continuum.

Genocide/Extermination

The most repressive and destructive dominant-group policy toward a minority group is *extermination* or *genocide,* which denies the minority's very right to live. The objective of a policy of extermination is to eliminate or substantially reduce the minority group. The post-World War II International Genocide Convention, which was convened in response to the atrocities committed by the Nazi regime between 1933 and 1945, developed the following definition of genocide:

> . . . any of the following acts committed with intent to destroy, in whole or in part, a national, ethnic, racial, or religious group as such: (a) killing members of the group; (b) causing serious bodily or mental harm to members of the group; (c) deliberately inflicting on the group conditions of life calculated to bring about its physical destruction in whole or in part; (d) imposing measures intended to prevent births within the group; (e) forcibly transferring children of the group to another group. (O'Brien 1968:516)

Although efforts to exterminate minorities are not confined to the modern era, some of the most notorious instances of genocide have occurred in the twentieth century. In 1915 1.5 million Armenians were massacred by the Turks. As noted in Part 1, in the small African country of Burundi more than 100,000 minority Hutu (about 3.5 percent of the population) were murdered by the dominant Tutsi people in 1972, and in 1988 another 20,000 were killed. During the 1970s approximately one million Cambodians – 30 percent of the population – were killed or died from hunger, disease, and overwork as a result of conditions created by the American bombing that devastated the country and by atrocities committed by the Khmer Rouge. The country's ethnic and religious minorities, especially the Muslim Chams, were special targets for extermination by the Pol Pot regime (Kiljunen 1985; Kiernan 1988). During their 1975 invasion of East Timor, Indonesians indiscriminately wiped out entire villages, killing over 100,000 in a population of less than one million. Moreover, the Indonesian destruction of East Timorese farms and villages led to famine, starvation, and disease, as a consequence of which "half a generation of Timorese children has been rendered mentally retarded" (Sidell 1981:50).

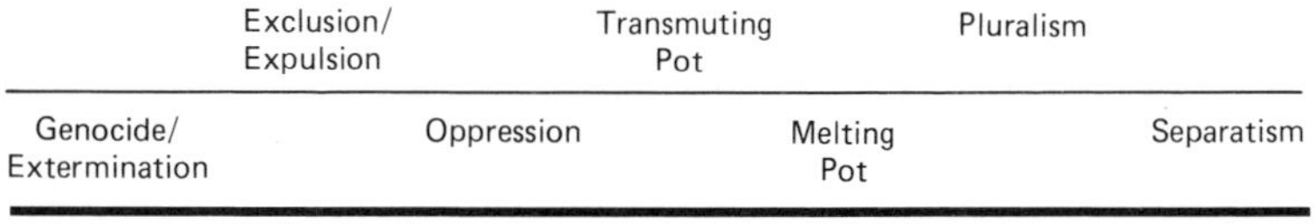

Exclusion/Expulsion		Transmuting Pot		Pluralism	
Genocide/Extermination	Oppression		Melting Pot		Separatism

FIGURE 3.1 *Types of Dominant Group Policies Toward Racial and Ethnic Minorities*

A clearly articulated policy of genocide was most systematically implemented under the Nazi extermination program, in which Hitler's objective was
the extinction of several million Jews and other "non-Aryan" groups (such as
Gypsies). Between 1935 and 1945 more than six million people perished as a
consequence of this policy.

In American society, a policy of genocide was one of the several pursued by
dominant whites in their effort to wrest control of the country's vast lands from
the American Indians. The slogan "the only good Indian is a dead Indian" was
common among frontier whites, who consistently encountered Indian resistance
to their continued encroachment on Indian lands. As noted in Part 2, by the turn
of the twentieth century, the American Indian population of the United States
had been brought to the point of virtual extinction by a combination of European
diseases, disintegration of tribal cultures, and an aggressive military policy by the
federal government.

Because genocide violates the sanctity of human life, an ideology of racism is
often developed to justify it. Racism involves a belief in the inherent superiority
of one racial group and the inherent inferiority of others. Its primary function is
to provide a set of ideas and beliefs that can be used to explain, rationalize, and
justify a system of racial domination. By denying that a racial minority has
human qualities or by depicting it as subhuman or destructive of human values
and life, the minority's extermination is made morally justifiable and acceptable.
For example, in 1876 an Australian writer defended efforts to annihilate the
native people of New Zealand (Maoris), Australia, and Tasmania: "When exter-
minating the inferior Australian and Maori races . . . the world is better for
it. . . . [By] protecting the propagation of the imprudent, the diseased, the defec-
tive, the criminal . . . we tend to destroy the human race" (quoted in Hartwig
1972:16).

Expulsion and Exclusion

Extermination clearly represents the most extreme dominant-group method for
dealing with the existence of minorities and the potential for interethnic conflict
in a multicultural society. The objective of extermination is to reduce or eliminate contact between majority and minority and to create an ethnically (or
racially) homogeneous society. A similar rationale underlies *expulsion,* the ejec-
tion of a minority group from areas controlled by the dominant group. Minorities
are told, in essence, "Because you differ from us so greatly, you have no right to
live among us."

Expulsion can be of two types: *direct* and *indirect* (Simpson and Yinger
1985:19–20), which are often interrelated. Direct expulsion occurs when minorities are forcibly ejected by the dominant group, often through military or other
governmental force. A policy of direct expulsion was at no time more pronounced in American history than during the nineteenth century, when thousands of American Indians were removed from the East to areas beyond the
Mississippi River. During World War II, 110,000 Japanese-Americans, most of

them United States citizens, were forcibly removed from their homes and placed in detention camps in remote areas of the country.

Several noted instances of expulsion have occurred throughout the world in the past decade. In 1989 more than 310,000 Bulgarians of Turkish descent (of a Bulgarian Turkish community estimated at between 900,000 and 1.5 million), whose ancestors had lived in Bulgaria for generations, fled to Turkey, forming one of Europe's largest refugee populations since World War II. Some Turks were forcibly expelled by Bulgarian authorities, while others were subjected to forced assimilation and repression of their Muslim faith, were forced to take Slavic names, and were beaten and abused for speaking Turkish in public (Haberman 1989:1). On two separate occasions—in 1983 and 1985—the government of Nigeria resorted to mass expulsion. In 1983 Nigeria expelled about 2 million immigrants from the neighboring countries of Ghana, Cameroon, Benin, Chad, and Niger. In 1985 another 700,000 people were forced to leave (*The Economist* 1985). In Israel, Meir Kahane, an American-born rabbi, has gained considerable political support for his proposal to resolve the problem of Arab-Jewish tensions in that country by forcibly removing all Arabs from Israel and its occupied territories and making Israel into an exclusively Jewish state (Friedman 1985:1).

Indirect expulsion occurs when harassment, discrimination, and persecution of a minority become so intense that members "voluntarily" choose to emigrate. Harassment and persecution of minorities, particularly religious minorities, has led many groups to seek refuge in the United States. Persecuted Protestant sects were among the earliest European immigrants to the American colonies, and the tradition of America as an asylum for the oppressed has continued to be a prominent feature of American ideals. The exodus of millions of Jews from eastern Europe during the late nineteenth and early twentieth century is another example of this process.

Underlying an expulsionist policy is the desire to achieve or retain ethnic or racial homogeneity. This end may occur not only when an ethnic group is expelled from the society, but also when a host society refuses to admit another group because that group is perceived as a threat to the society's basic institutions. Refusal to admit groups because of cultural or racial characteristics can be termed *exclusion*. As noted in Part 2, between 1917 and 1965 American immigration policy was based on the assumption that immigrants from southern and eastern Europe and Asia represented a threat to the biological, social, and political fabric of American society and therefore should be excluded, or their entrance substantially restricted.

Oppression

Oppression is exploitation of a minority group by excluding it from equal participation in a society (Turner, Singleton, and Musick 1984:1–2). Oppression "depends on exclusiveness rather than exclusion" (Bonacich 1972:555). Positions of higher prestige, power, and income are reserved exclusively for dominant group members. Unlike extermination, expulsion, or exclusion, a system of oppression accepts the existence of minorities but subjugates them and confines them to inferior social positions. The majority group uses its power to maintain its access to scarce and valued resources in a system of social inequality.

Slavery, in which the slave's labor was a valuable resource exploited by the slaveowner, was an example of oppression in American society. As we noted in the introduction to Part 2, even after slavery was legally abolished, the Jim Crow system of racial segregation that ensued was organized to exploit blacks for the benefit of the dominant whites. After taking a tour of the South at the turn of the twentieth century, a prominent journalist remarked on the exploitative nature of black-white relations:

> One of the most significant things I saw in the South—and I saw it everywhere—was the way in which the white people were torn between their feelings of race prejudice and their downright economic needs. Hating and fearing the Negro as a race (though often loving individual Negroes), they yet want him to work for them; they can't get along without him. In one impulse a community will rise to mob Negroes or to drive them out of the country because of Negro crime or Negro vagrancy, or because the Negro is becoming educated, acquiring property and "getting out of his place"; and in the next impulse laws are passed or other remarkable measures taken to keep him at work—because the South can't get along without him. (Baker 1964:81)

A classic contemporary example of oppression is the South African system of *apartheid*, or "separate development," which functions to maintain the privileged position of whites, who enjoy one of the highest standards of living in the world but who represent only 15 percent of the country's population. On the other hand, South African blacks, who comprise more than two-thirds (69 percent) of the population, are excluded from genuine participation in the nation's political system and are legally confined to rural reserves, or "homelands," that represent only 13 percent of the land. However, black labor provides a cheap labor supply for South African mines, farms, manufacturing, and domestic help that is essential to the South African economy and the system of white privilege. Therefore, the entire system of state controls restricting black political power, residence, and education is designed to perpetuate the system of white privilege (Cohen 1986).

Separatism

At the other end of the continuum from genocide is *separatism*, which is the most tolerant and expansive of the several majority group policies or practices that we have considered. Like pluralism, *separatism* implies social and cultural equality among ethnic groups, not the superiority of one. Both pluralism and separatism accept and encourage—even celebrate—cultural diversity. Separatism differs from pluralism in that the former includes some form of geographic and social separation.

In the American experience pluralism and separatism have seldom been advocated by the majority; the primary advocates of each stance have been minority spokespersons. The basic difference between policies of pluralism or separatism and exclusion is that under the former the minority chooses to place itself apart, whereas under the latter the separation is dictated by the majority group. Under separatism the majority does not require separation of ethnic and racial groups; it simply permits it.

Throughout the American experience many ethnic groups have tried to avoid pressures of forced assimilation with the dominant society by embracing a form of ethnic pluralism as the most appropriate means of adjusting to American society. The adjustment of the immigrant Irish typifies a pluralist response that is characteristic of many other ethnic groups. Although the objects of discrimination by Protestant Americans, the Irish avoided much of the hostility directed toward them by creating a society within a society, a separate institutional system centered around the Roman Catholic church. The institutional system that developed around the church – its schools, hospitals, orphanages, asylums, homes for the aged, charitable and athletic organizations, and informal groups – integrated the Irish community and served to maintain Irish-American solidarity and identity (Yetman 1975).

Separatism, on the other hand, involves minimal interaction by a minority group with the majority. The impulse for separatism frequently has been created by considerable conflict with the majority group and a desire to avoid a recurrence of discrimination or subjugation. For example, this impulse was an important factor contributing to the creation of the state of Israel. A separate nation was also the objective of the pre-Civil War colonization movement that aimed to return American slaves to Africa and of the African-American Back-to-Africa campaign of Marcus Garvey during the 1920s.

The idea of separate ethnic areas or states has been advocated by spokespersons of a number of different ethnic groups in the United States – by African-Americans, Indians, and Germans, among others. Religious groups such as the Amish, the Hutterites, and the Doukhobors that seek to protect their unique identity from the influences of the larger society have been among the foremost advocates of separatism. Having endured great persecution for their beliefs during the mid-nineteenth century, members of the Church of Jesus Christ of Latter Day Saints (the Mormons) sought to isolate themselves from the corrupting influences of the larger society by establishing, in the words of a Mormon hymn,

> . . . a place which God for us prepared
> Far away in the West
> Where none shall come to hurt or make afraid
> There the Saints will be blessed.

The transmuting pot, melting pot, and pluralism are all assimilation ideologies that imply the integration of majority and minority groups in some manner, whereas expulsion, exclusion, oppression, and separatism imply some form of minority group separation. The crucial distinction between separation ideologies is whether the separation of the minority group is achieved voluntarily or involuntarily, and whether the minority is relatively autonomous or relatively powerless. Thus, *exclusion* refers to separation by the decision of the majority group, whereas *separatism* means that the minority group has decided to place itself apart and is not prevented from doing so by the dominant group.

The case of American Indians demonstrates that these policies are not mutually exclusive; one or more of them may be embraced simultaneously or in different historical periods. In the early years of the republic, United States policy moved from genocide to expulsion and exclusion (the reservation system). Since the late-nineteenth century, the ideology of Anglo-conformity has been predominant, with exclusion an acceptable alternative. For example, as Lurie observed in Part 2, the purpose of governmental actions such as the Indian Allotment Act of 1887 was to force Indians to assimilate culturally. Even though many Indians would have welcomed separatism, their confinement to reservations has more closely resembled exclusion, because the reservations have been substantially controlled by the federal government and other extensions of white society (for example, missionaries and traders).

Neither Anglo-conformity nor exclusion permits American Indians to exercise free choice. To assimilate or adopt the European-derived norms, values, and cultural standards of the larger American society means to cease being an American Indian culturally. On the other hand, to be restricted to the reservation is to have life choices and chances severely circumscribed by powerful external forces. In spite of these exigencies, there seems little likelihood that the stubbornly purposeful maintenance of Indian traditions, values, and aloofness from the rest of the society will be surrendered. Even in urban areas, where increasing numbers have migrated since World War II, American Indians are resisting assimilation and forming their own ongoing communities.

Dimensions of Assimilation

In "Assimilation in America" (Article 11), Milton M. Gordon recognizes that each of the three theories – Anglo-conformity, melting pot, and cultural pluralism – on which his analysis focuses are primarily ideologies; that is, prescriptive models of how the process of intergroup relations in American society *should* proceed. He contends, therefore, that such idealized conceptions are of limited utility in analyzing precisely how diverse ethnic groups in American society have interacted.

Gordon argues that in order to assess accurately how extensively different ethnic groups have intermingled, it is essential to recognize that assimilation is not a single phenomenon but involves several related but analytically distinct processes. The three most important of these processes are cultural assimilation, structural assimilation, and marital assimilation, each of which may take place in varying degrees (Gordon 1964:71).

Popular discussions of assimilation usually are concerned with *cultural assimilation,* or what Gordon terms *behavioral assimilation* or *acculturation* – that is, the acquisition of the *cultural* characteristics of the dominant group, including its values, beliefs, language, and behaviors. However, many ethnic groups have become fully acculturated to the dominant American cultures – they have lost most traces of their ancestral cultures – but still have not been able to achieve full *social* participation in the society. Sharing the same language, norms, and cultural characteristics does not ensure access to informal social organizations, clubs, cliques, and friendship groups. Even sharing membership in secondary groups such as schools, jobs, and community and political organizations does not necessarily provide access to primary-group associations for those who have been culturally assimilated.

Because it is possible for a group to become culturally assimilated but to remain socially excluded, isolated, or segregated, it is important to distinguish cultural assimilation from *structural assimilation,* which involves social interaction among individuals of different ethnic and racial backgrounds. Two types of structural assimilation can be distinguished: secondary and primary. *Secondary structural assimilation* is the ethnic or racial integration of settings characterized by impersonal secondary relationships: jobs, schools, political organizations, neighborhoods, and public recreation. However, even sharing participation in such secondary groups does not necessarily involve primary-group associations – relationships that are warm, intimate, and personal. *Primary structural assimilation* is the ethnic integration of primary relationships, such as those found in religious communities, social clubs, informal social organizations, close friendships, and family relationships. Finally, the third subprocess, which is closely related to and, Gordon maintains, follows from primary structural assimilation, is *marital assimilation,* amalgamation or intermarriage among different ethnic or racial groups.

These distinctions enable us to compare and contrast the relative degree of integration or separation of different ethnic groups in American society in a relatively systematic fashion. Considerable research has been directed to developing empirical indicators with which to measure assimilation; among the indicators are years of schooling, income levels, occupational characteristics, segregation indices, and rates of intermarriage. (See Hirschman 1983, for an excellent review of these efforts.)

One of the important issues in assessing Park's original model of the assimilation process, however, is whether rates of assimilation are changing over time. In other words, are there differences between the first generation (the immigrants themselves), the second generation (the American-born offspring of immigrants), the third generation (the grandchildren of immigrants), and subsequent generations?

There have been two basic interpretations of the effect of generational differences on ethnicity. *Straight-line theory,* most closely identified with Herbert Gans (see Article 22, "Symbolic Ethnicity," in Part 4), predicts increasing assimilation with each succeeding generation. According to this model, English would be more likely to be spoken in the home, occupational characteristics would be higher, and there would be higher rates of intermarriage among the second generation than among the first, and, moreover, these trends toward assimilation would increase with each succeeding generation.

A contrasting model of the assimilation process was proposed by the historian Marcus Lee Hansen. Hansen contended that whereas children of immigrants seek to shed evidence of their foreignness as fully as possible and to "become American," the immigrants' grandchildren – the third generation – seek to rediscover their roots and retain their ethnic distinctiveness. He formulated the notion of the *third generation return:* "What the son wishes to forget, the grandson wishes to remember" (Hansen 1938:9). This model, which has become known as *Hansen's Law,* suggests that increasing assimilation with each succeeding generation is not inevitable. Instead, there can be variations among generations in rates of assimilation; the third generation, in particular, may identify more closely with their grandparents' ethnic backgrounds than did their parents, producing a cultural or ethnic revival.

In one of the most celebrated interpretations of American religious life, Will Herberg (1955) employed a variant of Hansen's Law to account for changing patterns of religiosity in America. Herberg argued that because American religious communities have been so strongly linked to ethnicity, Hansen's model could be extended to explain patterns of religious practice among American ethnic groups. According to Herberg, religiosity was high among the first generation, but because it was perceived as something "foreign" and thus something to escape, it declined among the second generation. For the third generation, however, affiliation with and participation in one of the three broad American religious traditions – Protestantism, Catholicism, and Judaism – provided a socially acceptable way in which to maintain ethnic identity in modern society. Therefore, Herberg argued, members of the third generation would tend to have higher rates of religious participation than their second-generation parents.

Herberg's bold and imaginative interpretation stimulated considerable controversy. In one important study, Abramson (1975) showed that empirical data do not support the three-generations hypothesis as a general interpretation of the process of immigrant adjustment. Analyzing data on the religious beliefs and behavior of ten religioethnic groups, Abramson found great variation in generational patterns of religiosity. In general there was little support for the hypothesized decline-and-rise pattern; only one of the ten religioethnic groups in his study (Eastern European Catholics) conformed to the pattern. Although more groups manifested a consistent decline in religiosity over three generations, there were a sufficient number of alternative patterns (for example, an increase in religiosity in the second generation) to preclude unequivocal support for a straight-line interpretation. Abramson's study reveals that although ethnicity is still a salient factor affecting religious behavior, the diversity of experiences among American ethnic groups (such as the differences among Irish, Polish, and Italian Catholics) has been so great as to challenge the appropriateness of any general models of immigrant adjustment.

Scholars have challenged the assimilation model on a variety of grounds, especially Park's view that assimilation is a linear process leading ultimately from cultural to marital assimilation and the disappearance of ethnic identity. However, as Nagel argued in "The Political Construction of Ethnicity" (Article 4), ethnicity remains a viable and vital force in modern societies precisely because it is functional and provides a source of emotional support and social solidarity in an increasingly fragmented and anonymous society. Thus Portes and Bach (1985), in their study comparing the adaptations of Cuban and Mexican immigrants to the United States, conclude that these immigrants' cultural and socioeconomic adaptation to American society, rather than being impeded, is facilitated by the maintenance of ethnic identity and close ethnic ties.

> Those immigrants more able to relate effectively to various aspects of life in America are often those who most strongly adhere to personal relationships within their own communities. Awareness of barriers and, at times, outright hostility confronting them in the outside has its counterpart in the reaffirmation of primary relations within protected ethnic circles. . . . Rather than abandoning personal relationships within their own groups, immigrants who have moved farthest into the outside world seem to rely more heavily on such bonds. Ethnic resilience, not assimilation, is the theoretical perspective more congruent with this interpretation. This resilience is not, however, a force leading to collective withdrawal, but rather a moral resource, an integral part of the process of establishing and defining a place in a new society. (Portes and Bach 1985:333)

In other words, maintaining ethnic primary group supports may actually enhance cultural and secondary structural assimilation.

Assimilation, therefore, is not a unidimensional or unilinear phenomenon, leading ultimately to an ethnically homogeneous society. Recognizing the multidimensional nature of assimilation, Gordon deplored the tendency to use the term in an inclusive way, and he argued it was essential to identify its several forms. For example, he argued that, although extensive cultural assimilation had taken place in American life through the 1950s, there was only limited evidence of structural assimilation. For Gordon, a more accurate description of the realities of ethnic relations in American life at that time was *structural pluralism*, in which racial, ethnic, and, in particular, religious categories "retained their separate sociological structures."

To what extent has assimilation proceeded nearly thirty years after Gordon published his classic essay? It is impossible to review all of the voluminous research on the several dimensions of assimilation here, but we will examine several salient issues suggested by this literature. We will focus especially on the three key areas of socioeconomic status—income levels, occupational status, and educational attainment—as well as spatial assimilation and patterns of intermarriage.

Socioeconomic Assimilation

By almost any measure, descendants of southern and eastern European immigrants (Italians, Jews, Poles, Greeks, Hungarians) have become structurally assimilated into American life to a degree that few would have predicted at the end of World War II. During the 1950s one of the most striking findings in the social science literature dealing with assimilation was the rapid socioeconomic mobility of Jews, who, like most other "new" immigrant groups entering the United States between 1890 and 1915, had arrived virtually penniless

(Strodtbeck 1958). By the 1960s, despite the relatively brief time in which they had resided in the United States, Jews had come to exceed all other ethnic groups (including the once-dominant white Anglo-Saxon Protestants) on the most common measures of socioeconomic status: median family income, educational attainment, and occupational prestige. The extremely rapid rise in the socioeconomic status of Jews historically contrasted sharply with other "new" immigrant groups (primarily southern and eastern European Catholics) who, with Jews, had entered American society in the massive wave of immigration near the turn of the twentieth century. In Article 15, "Education and Ethnic Mobility," Stephen Steinberg discusses some of the explanations for these differential rates of mobility.

By the early 1970s, however, Andrew Greeley (Article 13), the prolific sociologist and novelist, was able to celebrate what he characterized as the "ethnic miracle." Using extensive national social-survey data compiled between 1945 and 1970, Greeley contended that despite their lowly socioeconomic status three generations ago, "the ethnics have made it." By 1970 the income levels of Irish, German, Italian, and Polish Catholics were exceeded only by Jews, not by white Anglo-Saxon Protestants, who in many accounts were still defined as the "establishment," or the "core" group to which all other ethnic groups compared themselves. In overall educational achievement, Polish, Italian, and Slavic Catholics still lagged somewhat behind the national white average, but when parental educational levels were held constant, Catholic ethnics showed higher educational levels than any other ethnic group except Jews. Indeed, Irish Catholics, once among the most despised and unfavorably stereotyped of all European ethnic groups, had by 1970 become "the richest, best educated, and most prestigious occupationally of any gentile religioethnic group." Thus, Greeley concluded, "In a very short space of time, the length of one generation, more or less, the American dream has come true" for European Catholic ethnic groups.

Neidert and Farley (1985) report similar, although not identical, findings in their analysis of differences in socioeconomic status in a 1979 national survey of American ethnic groups. Their data show that occupational returns for educational attainment tend generally to increase with each succeeding generation, thus providing strong support for a straight-line theory of assimilation. They also found that, although ethnic differences exist in educational attainment, occupational prestige, and per capita income among non-English European ethnic groups, they were not at a disadvantage compared to those of English ancestry. Indeed, those of Russian (primarily Jews), Eastern European, and Asian ancestries were especially successful, whereas those most disadvantaged were of Mexican, African-American, and American Indian origins.

In Article 14, "The Economic Progress of European and East Asian Americans," Suzanne Model provides an excellent review of the literature on ethnic group differences in economic attainment in the United States. She notes that numerous researchers have reported striking patterns of social mobility among Asians. During the past two decades, especially, there has been a notable change in the perception of Asians in American society. As we noted in Part 2, Asians, primarily Chinese and Japanese, have been the object of considerable discrimination throughout their history in America. Indeed, so unfavorable were the perceptions of Asians by whites that they were, unlike any European ethnic groups, virtually excluded from immigrating to the United States for more than half a century. Moreover, in one of the most notorious instances of racism in American history, American citizens of Japanese descent were subjected to the humiliation of incarceration in detention camps during World War II.

Today, however, the unfavorable stereotypes that were widely embraced by white Americans before, during, and immediately after World War II have been supplanted by perceptions of Asians as "model minorities," who, despite discrimination, have demonstrated remarkable patterns of educational, occupational, and financial success (Hurh and Kim 1989). As Hirschman and Wong pointed out in Article 9, the educational levels of Japanese, Chinese, and Filipinos – immigrant as well as native-born – today equal or exceed those of whites. These high levels of educational attainment are particularly pronounced among the younger segments of the population. Moreover, Asians are overrepresented in higher-status occupations, especially the professions. Although income levels among those of comparable occupational backgrounds tend to be lower than whites, overall income levels for native-born Japanese, Chinese, and Filipino males are about the same as for white males. Nevertheless, Hirschman and Wong caution against generalizing from these selected indices of secondary structural assimilation to other dimensions of assimilation. They conclude that Asian-Americans tend to remain greatly underrepresented in many sectors of the dominant economy, society, and polity. Moreover, Hurh and Kim (1989) have shown that Asians with comparable educational attainments, occupational prestige, and hours worked per week earn less than their white counterparts. Thus images of Asian-American "success" obscure both the relatively heavier investments required for Asians to achieve such income levels and the discrimination to which they are still subject. It is because of images of Asian success that they encounter discrimination as a consequence of their minority status; Asians tend to be excluded from governmental programs designed to address such discrimination.

Hurh and Kim suggest that the widespread perception of the success image of Asian-Americans has an additional consequence. If the situation of Asian-Americans appears favorable, it is only in reference to the greater disadvantages of other minorities – African-Americans, Hispanics, and American Indians. Indeed, the "model minority" stereotype of Asians serves to reinforce negative stereotypes of these other minorities and to blame them for the social, economic, and political conditions under which they find themselves.

However, the patterns of educational, occupational, and financial achievement found among European and Asian ethnic groups are not duplicated among Hispanics and African-Americans. Bean and Tienda (1987) and Davis, Haub, and Willette (1983) have demonstrated that substantial gaps separate Hispanics from the Anglo population on these dimensions. Davis, Haub, and Willette anticipate that because there is evidence of increasing Hispanic educational attainments with each succeeding generation, the gap between Hispanics and Anglos in levels of educational achievement should narrow in the future. On the other hand, the historic concentration of Hispanics in lower-paid, less-skilled occupations has persisted, and since 1972 the ratio of Hispanic to white income declined from 71 percent in 1972 to 64 percent in 1989. Moreover, during the same period of time the Hispanic poverty rate rose from 22 percent in 1972 to 26 percent in 1989 (U.S. Bureau of the Census 1990d). However, among Hispanic groups there are obvious disparities, most prominently those between Cubans, whose early migration, especially, was comprised substantially of middle-class and professional people (see Portes and Manning, Article 17), and Puerto Ricans, who were much more likely to have had lower levels of educational attainment and fewer occupational skills than Cubans.

As we will note more fully in Part 4, similar patterns have characterized African-American socioeconomic status. During the 1970s, the African-American community in general experienced gains in educational attainment and political participation. Paralleling the decline in income among Hispanics, though, the overall financial condition of black families deteriorated. However, as Wacquant and Wilson note in Article 27, "The Cost of Racial and Class Exclusion in the Inner City" (Part 4), such generalizations obscure the increasing economic divergence within the African-American community. Wilson contends that in the past two decades blacks have had occupational opportunities unprecedented in the African-American experience in America. On the other hand, the economic distress of the African-American underclass, in particular, of female-headed families, has grown increasingly acute.

Spatial Assimilation

Each of the dimensions mentioned above – years of schooling, occupational distribution, and income levels – in itself reveals little about the extent of social assimilation, integration, or incorporation of different ethnic groups in a society. In a genuinely plural society with unranked parallel social structures, for example, it is hypothetically possible for two or more ethnic groups to manifest high educational attainment, occupational status, and income levels without substantial physical interaction.

Patterns of residential integration have been one of the most frequently examined indices of assimilation. Massey and Mullan (1984) have referred to it as *spatial assimilation* and defined it as "the process whereby a group attains residential propinquity with members of a host society." Numerous scholars (such as Hershberg et al. 1979; Lieberson 1963, 1980: Marson and Van Valey 1979; Pettigrew 1979; Roof 1979; and Taeuber 1990) have shown that there is a close interrelationship between housing and jobs, educational opportunities, and income. Therefore, an ethnic group's spatial location is a crucial variable affecting its overall socioeconomic position. Residential location affects life chances in a wide variety of ways, including "cost and quality of housing, health and sanitary conditions, exposure to crime and violence, quality of services (the most important of which is education), and access to economic opportunity, as well as a host of less tangible factors ranging from the character of one's children's playmates to the kinds of role models they emulate" (Massey and Mullan 1984:838).

In *A Piece of the Pie: Black and White Immigrants since 1880* (1980), Stanley Lieberson undertook an exhaustive comparative analysis of the experiences of African-Americans and "new" European immigrants in twentieth-century America. His examination of the patterns of residential segregation of African-Americans and various "new" immigrant groups revealed several important features. First, at the beginning of the period of massive immigration from southern and eastern Europe (the last decade of the nineteenth century), blacks living in northern cities were less spatially segregated than the new European groups that were beginning to arrive. Second, the residential segregation of African-Americans increased during the twentieth century, a process that correspondingly cut them off from participation in most of the activities of the larger community. The position of blacks in northern cities deteriorated from the turn of the twentieth century onward. Moreover, the patterns of residential segregation of African-Americans and southern European immigrant groups moved in opposite directions: at the same time that the rates of spatial assimilation for African-Americans were declining, rates were increasing for southern and eastern European immigrants. Thus the deterioration of African-Americans' position in northern urban areas occurred at precisely the time that the position of immigrant whites was beginning to improve.

As we noted in Part 2, the massive migration of African-Americans out of the South to the North and from rural areas to the nation's cities has been one of the most important demographic shifts in American history. Today, African-Americans are much more likely to live in metropolitan areas than are whites. Moreover, the percentage of metropolitan blacks who reside in central cities is more than double that of whites, creating the urban racial polarization that is one of the basic racial demographic facts of American life today (Pettigrew 1979:122; see Taeuber 1990 for an excellent review of historical trends in racial residential patterns).

These patterns of residential segregation are not comparable to the immigrant neighborhoods or enclaves in which "new" immigrant groups congregated around the turn of the century. First, although they were spatially isolated, at no time were immigrant neighborhoods as homogeneous or their spatial isolation as pronounced as in black neighborhoods today. In other words, the spatial isolation of white ethnics was never so extreme as that of African-Americans during the last half-century. From their examination of the experience of African-Americans and ethnic groups in Philadelphia, Hershberg and his colleagues (Article 10, "A Tale of Three Cities") report:

> The typical Irish immigrant in 1880 and the typical Italian immigrant in 1930 . . . shared a similar aspect of their residential experience. When the hypothetical immigrant in each era walked through his neighborhood, what kind of people might he have met? The Irishman in 1880 lived with 15 percent other Irish immigrants, 34 percent Irish stock, 26 percent all foreign-born persons and 58 percent all foreign stock. The typical Italian

immigrant in 1930 had an almost identical experience. He lived with 14 percent other Italian immigrants, 38 percent Italian stock, 23 percent all foreign born persons and 57 percent all foreign stock. In striking contrast, the typical black in 1970 lived in a census tract in which 73 percent of the population was black.

Second, as noted above, patterns of ethnic segregation were not enduring but began to break down relatively quickly, whereas the characteristic feature of racial residential segregation since 1940 has been its persistence (Sorensen, Taeuber, and Hollingsworth 1975; Taeuber 1983, 1990).

One prominent measure that sociologists have developed to determine the extent of residential segregation or spatial isolation is the segregation index, or *index of dissimilarity.* With this measure a score of 100 represents complete racial segregation, in which every city block is 100 percent black and 0 percent white or vice versa; conversely, a score of zero represents a housing pattern in which members of different racial and ethnic groups are distributed in a completely random fashion and each city block has the same percentage of blacks and whites as the city's overall population.

Taeuber (1990) analyzed trends in the index of dissimilarity between whites and nonwhites from 1940 to 1988 for 109 large cities. The average segregation index was 85 in 1940, 87 in 1950, 86 in 1960, 75 in 1980, and 76 in 1988 (Taeuber 1990:144–145). However, the segregation index was even higher for the 28 cities that had an African-American population of more than 100,000 in 1980. Already highly segregated by 1940, the patterns of racial residential isolation remained relatively stationary during the 1950s and 1960s. By 1970 the average segregation index for the twenty-eight American cities with African-American populations of more than 100,000 was 87; by 1980 the index for these cities had declined to 81, although in some (such as Chicago and Cleveland) the index remained above 90 (Taeuber 1983). Although the overall spatial assimilation increased during the 1970s more rapidly than in the preceding three decades, this trend did not continue through the 1980s.

These data document the highly segregated residential patterns that have characterized American cities during the modern industrial period. Despite declines in the previous two decades, by 1980 the general pattern of spatial isolation for African-Americans was still more pronounced than for any other racial or ethnic group in American history. Moreover, the declines in residential segregation that did occur were so modest as to make problematic whether substantial increases in spatial assimilation for African-Americans are likely in the near future. These conclusions are reinforced by Massey and Denton's study of residential segregation trends during the 1970s (Article 19).

One source of this racial polarization has been the increasing suburbanization of American society, especially of the white population, including the white ethnic groups that formerly resided in central cities. The process of suburbanization has involved not only residences, but also schools, churches, synagogues, commercial enterprises, and industry. The suburban movement of business and industry, which has further isolated inner-city residents from job opportunities, has been especially important in this regard. During the 1970s, for example, Chicago lost more than 200,000 manufacturing jobs; New York lost 600,000 (Wilson 1981a:39).

Many different discriminatory mechanisms have contributed to this pattern of residential segregation. Among them have been restrictive covenants, neighborhood protection associations, and block-busting practices that serve to exclude racial minorities. Another crucial aspect of housing discrimination is home loans. A study that analyzed over 10 million applications for home loans from every savings and loan association in the country between 1983 and 1988 showed that black applicants were rejected more than twice as often as white applicants. Moreover, the applications of high-income blacks were rejected more often than those of low-income whites (Dedman 1989).

Even if these practices had not been employed, federal government policies would have ensured that the suburban population would be overwhelmingly white and that African-Americans would be relegated primarily to the inner cities. Most important was the decision by the federal government to permit private enterprise to meet the great demand for housing that had developed during the Depression and World War II. As a result, suburban housing was built almost exclusively for those who could afford to pay, while people unable to meet financing requirements were forced to accept housing vacated by those moving to the suburbs. On the other hand, low-cost, government-subsidized housing, which attracted a primarily black clientele, was constructed mostly in center cities rather than in the suburbs (Grier and Grier 1965). Therefore, organized neighborhood resistance to proposals for low-income and moderate-income housing is often a veiled form of attitudinal discrimination that serves to reinforce the patterns of residential segregation.

In "A Tale of Three Cities" (Article 10), Hershberg and his associates note the crucial importance of residential proximity to jobs in American history. For many whites, occupational opportunities have been the primary factor in determining where to live. Blacks, on the other hand, have been circumscribed by racial exclusion. In the nineteenth century, when they resided in close proximity to occupational opportunities, African-Americans were arbitrarily excluded from jobs. Today, when employment discrimination has declined, they are excluded by physical distance. Pettigrew assesses the implications of the continuing spatial isolation of African-Americans:

> This massive metropolitan pattern of housing segregation has now become the principal barrier to progress in other realms. Indeed, the residential segregation of blacks and whites has emerged as a functional equivalent for the explicit state segregation laws of the past in that it effectively acts to limit the life chances and choices of black people generally. (Pettigrew 1979:124)

Today, despite federal fair-housing legislation, a Supreme Court decision that declared housing discrimination illegal, generally more favorable racial attitudes by whites toward African-Americans, and a substantial growth of the black middle class, residential segregation still persists on a massive scale in the United States.

Is the residential segregation of African-Americans a result of racial discrimination, or is it a reflection of the generally lower overall class position of blacks? Taeuber and Taeuber (1965) have shown that the residential segregation of African-Americans is not primarily a result of black income levels, which, they maintain, can account for only a small portion of residential segregation. High-income whites and blacks do not live in the same neighborhoods, nor do low-income whites and blacks. Nevertheless, if, as Wilson argues, class factors have increasingly come to affect the life chances of American racial and ethnic minorities—not merely African-Americans, but Hispanics and American Indians, as well—then these other minorities should experience comparable forms of residential segregation.

However, critics dispute the arguments that the effects of structural economic changes are equally devastating to other contemporary racial and ethnic minorities such as Hispanics and American Indians. Rather, they argue, because race remains an important determinant of opportunity in American life, other minorities, even those from comparable class locations, have been and will be able to experience spatial assimilation more easily than African-Americans.

Massey and Mullan (1984) found substantial differences in the changes that occurred during the 1960s in the residential patterns of Hispanics and African-Americans: "A barrio-centered residential pattern simply does not typify the experience of Hispanics in the same way that a ghetto-centered pattern typifies that of blacks" (Massey and Mullan 1984:870). African-Americans who moved into previously white neighborhoods found that their presence led to white flight, but Hispanics did not:

> *Residential succession [an exodus of current residents] is likely to follow the entry of Hispanics into an Anglo area when the incoming Hispanics are poorly educated and foreign, with low occupational statuses and incomes, and when the tract is near an established black or Hispanic area. In contrast, residential succession follows black entry into an Anglo area no matter what the objective social characteristics of the incoming blacks. . . . Because the Anglo response to Hispanic invasion is not universally one of avoidance and flight, Hispanics are much better able than blacks to translate social into residential mobility. . . .*
>
> *[Moreover,] the social status required of blacks before they are not threatening to Anglos appears to be significantly higher than that required of Hispanics. In other words, a black lawyer or doctor may be able to move into a mixed neighborhood with other professionals, but a black plumber or bricklayer cannot buy into a working-class Anglo neighborhood. What is required for black spatial assimilation is a quantum leap in social status. (Massey and Mullan 1984:851–852, 854, 856)*

Massey and Mullan conclude that "Anglos avoid blacks on the basis of race, not class," whereas the converse was more likely to be true for Hispanics.

In "Trends in the Residential Segregation of Blacks, Hispanics, and Asians" (Article 19), Massey and Denton extended the analysis of racial segregation through the 1970s. They note that during that decade minority populations increased at a much more rapid rate than whites in most metropolitan areas (SMSAs). Although African-Americans experienced slight declines in spatial isolation in 1980 when compared with 1970, they remained by far the most isolated of the three minority groups. Black segregation from whites declined in some smaller cities in the south and west, but it remained virtually unchanged in the large cities of the northeast, where a substantial majority of urban blacks live. Hispanic segregation from Anglos was substantially less than black segregation, but it increased slightly in areas of heavy Hispanic immigration and population growth. Asians had high levels of spatial assimilation and low social isolation.

Massey and Denton argue that suburbanization is a key factor affecting the processes of residential segregation. As minorities experience socioeconomic mobility, they try to move to better neighborhoods, which, in post-World War II America, has generally meant the suburbs. In moving to the suburbs, the opportunities of African-Americans are much more limited than those of either Hispanics or Asians. Although affluent Hispanics and Asians are able to translate improved socioeconomic status into spatial assimilation in the suburbs, black suburban movement is largely restricted to predominantly black suburbs immediately adjacent to central cities. Therefore, blacks who are able to move from deteriorating central city neighborhoods are likely to move to equally segregated suburbs. Massey and Denton's conclusions concerning trends during the 1970s reinforce Massey and Mullan's findings for the 1960s: Asians and Hispanics (except for Puerto Ricans, who are more likely than other Hispanics to be identified as black) do not experience residential isolation and barriers nearly so restrictive as those encountered by blacks. In regard to residential segregation in American life, "it is not race that matters, but black race."

Unlike Wilson, who contends that economic class factors will in the future effect similar life chances for African-Americans and Hispanics, Massey and Mullan contend that because blacks are unable to translate economic mobility into spatial assimilation in the same manner as Hispanics, "the discrepant patterns of black and Hispanic spatial assimilation portend very different futures for these groups." Because residential integration has strong effects on other patterns of social interaction, such as friendships, marriage, and schooling, African-Americans are likely to remain socially and spatially isolated in the United States. They therefore dispute the notion that Hispanics can be seen as an underclass in the same way as blacks: "Unlike blacks, [Hispanics] are able to translate social mobility into residential mobility. Hispanics are simply not trapped in the barrio in the same way that blacks are trapped in the ghetto" (Massey and Mullan 1984:870).

Marital Assimilation

Gordon maintains that once structural assimilation has occurred, other dimensions of assimilation—most importantly, intermarriage, or what he terms *marital assimilation* or *amalgamation*—will follow. Marital assimilation, he claims, represents the final outcome of the assimilation process, in which "the minority group (ultimately) loses its ethnic identity in the larger host or core society" (Gordon 1964:80).

The extent to which marital assimilation has occurred among different ethnic groups has been the subject of considerable research. One of the most celebrated interpretations of intermarriage patterns among white Americans was the "triple melting pot" thesis, which saw intermarriage increasing across ethnic lines but keeping within the three religious communities of Protestants, Catholics, and Jews (Kennedy 1944, 1952). Although this interpretation was integral to Herberg's discussion (1955) of general patterns of ethnic identity, discussed above, subsequent analyses have raised a considerable number of questions concerning its validity (Peach 1981; Hirschman 1983). Richard Alba's analysis of ethnic marriage patterns among American Catholics (Article 21, Part 4) reveals increasing rates of religious intermarriage, which in turn "point to a decline in the salience of religious boundaries for a good part of the Catholic group." This general inference concerning the waning significance of religious boundaries could be extended to Protestants, with whom Catholics most frequently intermarry, as well. In other words, religious affiliation is declining in salience as a factor influencing mate selection.

Recent analyses suggest that white ethnic groups generally have demonstrated substantial marital assimilation, especially among third and fourth generations and those from higher occupational categories. In national studies of assimilation among American Catholics, Alba (1976, 1981) and Alba and Kessler (1979) found that as early as 1963 marriage outside ethnic groups was extensive. Rates of intermarriage were most pronounced among the third generation and among the youngest adult members of each ethnic group. Similarly, in a study of ethnic consciousness in Providence, Rhode Island, Goering found that among the Irish and Italians only 15 percent of the first generation had married outside their own ethnic group, whereas 63 percent of the third generation had done so (Goering 1971:382n). Finally, utilizing the 1979 population survey on ancestry, Alba and Golden (1986) found high rates of intermarriage among Europeans but, except for Native Americans, relatively low rates between Europeans and non-Europeans, especially blacks. Intermarriage rates were higher for "old" immigrant European ancestry groups (British, Irish, German, and Scandinavian) than for "new" immigrant ancestry groups (Italian, Polish, Russian, and Slavic). They conclude that today "ethnicity carries much less weight than in the past for the choice of a spouse" (Alba and Golden 1986:219).

Further evidence of the trend toward greater social and marital assimilation is shown in the rates of intermarriage for American Jews. Jewish rates of intermarriage vary by city. For example, in New York City less than one-sixth (14 percent of men and 12 percent of women) of Jews marrying had non-Jewish spouses, whereas in Denver more than half of married spouses were born as gentiles (Cohen 1988:27). The national rate of Jewish intermarriage with non-Jews increased from approximately 3 percent between 1900 and 1940 to nearly one-third (32 percent) between 1966 and 1972 (Massarick n.d.:10). Since 1976 these rates of Jewish intermarriage have continued to rise (Mayer 1983:viii). This trend has raised concerns among many Jews that the future of the American Jewish community may be threatened (Glazer 1987; Cohen 1988).

Even more dramatic is the increasing rate of marital assimilation among Asians. Tinker (1973) found that more than half of the marriages of Japanese were to non-Japanese. Montero (1981), basing his analysis on 1970 census data, found that, except for American Indians, the rates of intermarriage among Asians were higher than among any other racial category. Levine (1989) has reported that 60 percent of the Sansei (third generation Japanese-Americans) have Caucasian spouses. Similarly, Wong (1989) documented a major increase in intermarriage among Chinese-Americans during the past half century. Whereas Chinese-American marriages were basically endogamous up to the 1930s, by 1980 over 30 percent of Chinese marriages were to non-Chinese, primarily whites.

However, the patterns of extensive intermarriage for European ethnic groups, Chinese, Japanese, and American Indians are not duplicated among Hispanics and, especially, African-Americans. Black-white marriages are especially infrequent—in 1980 only 2.7 percent of black men were married to white partners, while less than one percent (0.8%) of black women were married to white men (U.S. Bureau of the Census 1985:175). While the number of black-white marriages more than tripled between 1970 and 1988, such unions still represented only 0.41 percent of all marriages in the United States. In general, intermarriage rates among different racial and ethnic categories are influenced by such factors as cultural similarities, generational status, residential dispersion, and socioeconomic status. For example, there are considerable regional variations in intermarriage rates, ranging from a low intermarriage rate of 1.6 percent for black males in the South to a high of 12.3 percent in the West (Tucker and Mitchell-Kernan 1990).

Why Assimilation Rates Vary

Analyses of race and ethnicity in American life have frequently reflected social and political controversies within the broader society. As we noted in Part 1, the research agenda in the field of racial and ethnic relations—issues considered and questions posed—frequently has been drawn from social policy concerns, not from sociological theory alone.

One of the most striking changes in the research agenda in the field of racial and ethnic relations over the past decade has been a shift to a broadly comparative perspective. Some scholars have taken a cross-cultural perspective, examining the dynamics of race and ethnicity throughout the world (for example, Burgess 1978; Francis 1976; Glazer and Moynihan 1975; Gordon 1978; Hechter 1975; Henry 1976; Horowitz 1985; Olzak and Nagel 1986, Rose 1976).

However, the black protest activity of the 1950s and 1960s, which sought to eliminate the chasm historically separating African-Americans from the American mainstream, contributed substantially to a resurgence of interest in ethnicity that focused on other ethnic groups in American society as well. Since the late 1970s research dealing with ethnicity in American society has proliferated (for example, Dinnerstein and Reimers 1983, 1987; Greeley 1976; Kinton 1977; Lieberson 1980; Mindel and Habenstein 1976; Patterson 1977; Seller 1977; Sowell 1978, 1980, 1981; Steinberg 1981). This shift from a focus almost exclusively on black-white relations to an examination of the role of ethnicity in American life was stimulated in part by the conflicts that emerged from African-Americans' claims for equal participation and opportunity. As Steinberg has pointed out, "That the ethnic resurgence involved more than nostalgia became clear as racial minorities and white ethnics became polarized on a series of issues relating to schools, housing, local government and control over federal programs" (Steinberg 1981:50).

The resentment fueled by these conflicts with African-Americans were reflected in the question frequently posed by white ethnics: "If we made it, why can't they?" If Greeley's characterization of the "ethnic miracle" is correct, if Jews, Poles, Italians, and the Irish today have "made it," how have they been able to do so while other groups have not? How do we account for the "extraordinary success story" of Catholics and Jews, who had to overcome poverty, discrimination, illiteracy, and chronic overcrowding in America's urban ghettos?

Explanations for differences in socioeconomic status – levels of income, educational attainment, and occupational prestige – among American ethnic groups that formerly were debated informally and privately in bull sessions, dinner parties, and cocktail parties have increasingly become the focus of formal inquiry by social scientists, whose interpretations have become part of the public discourse. During the past decade, especially, there have been numerous comparative studies of American ethnic groups: advancing explanations for the differences in achievement levels among American ethnic groups has become a major preoccupation of specialists in the field.

Several explanations for the differences among American ethnic groups have been advanced. Although there are considerable differences among them, they can be divided into two broad categories: those that emphasize qualities and characteristics internal to an ethnic group, and those that emphasize the influence of factors external to an ethnic group, forces over which members of the group have no control.

Internal Explanations

An internal model conceives an ethnic group's adaptation, adjustment, achievement, or assimilation to be the result primarily of the traits, qualities, or characteristics that the group brings with it – the group's own "personality," if you will. The emphasis in this argument is on the inheritance of behavioral traits and characteristics and on continuity of these traits across generations. In other words, proponents believe that groups possess certain identifiable characteristics that are transmitted and perpetuated from generation to generation.

Biology

The most simplistic of the internal explanations is a biological or genetic argument: American ethnic groups have different *biological* endowments, innately different mental, emotional, and moral characteristics that are biologically transmitted from generation to generation.

For instance, during the last decade of the nineteenth century and the first two decades of the twentieth, differences between the political, social, and economic institutions of Anglo-Saxon and non-Anglo-Saxon peoples were "scientifically" attributed to biologically transmitted and relatively immutable "racial" traits. Thus Senator Henry Cabot Lodge, in an 1896 Senate speech condemning continued unrestricted immigration by peoples from southern and eastern Europe, argued that the Anglo-Saxon capacity for democracy was instinctual:

> The men of each race possess an indestructible stock of ideas, traditions, sentiments, modes of thought, an unconscious inheritance from their ancestors, upon which argument has no effect. What makes a race are their mental and, above all, their moral characteristics, the slow growth and accumulation of centuries of toil and conflict. These are the qualities which determine the social efficiency as a people, which make one race rise and another fall. (Lodge 1896:2819)

Lodge, and most other intellectuals of the day, believed that the "old" immigrants from northern and western Europe (the British, Germans, and Scandinavians) were descended from common ancestors who were "historically free, energetic, and progressive," whereas Slavic, Latin, and Asiatic races were "historically downtrodden, atavistic, and stagnant" (Solomon 1956:111).

Given these assumptions, which were supposed to be scientifically valid, unrestricted immigration meant the introduction of millions of unassimilable people who lacked the "superior" instincts of northern and western Europeans. The absence of these instincts, Lodge believed, would ultimately bring about the "decline of human civilization." Much of the "scientific" research concerning racial inequality in the last half of the nineteenth and first half of the twentieth centuries involved examination of physical differences and differences in intelligence test performances among American racial and ethnic groups. Frequently, inferences from such studies were cited as "evidence" of the biological inferiority of non-Anglo-Saxon groups and then used to justify their subordinate status.

As we pointed out in Part 1, the conceptions of "race" entertained by Lodge, which were, in one form or another, shared by virtually all American social scientists at the turn of the twentieth century, are radically different from prevailing scientific notions today. Biological arguments enjoy little legitimacy among contemporary social scientists (for a critique of the use of such arguments in conjunction with intelligence testing, see Weinberg 1983). The important difference resides in the understanding of the *process* by which behavioral traits and characteristics are transmitted. Traits that once were considered to be "instinctual," innate, and biologically inherited are today conceived to be learned—a product not of the genes but of socialization. Culture, rather than biology, is considered the primary determinant of the traits and characteristics of ethnic groups.

Culture

The most prominent contemporary internal explanation attributes an ethnic group's position in a society's stratification system to its *cultural* characteristics: the values, attitudes, beliefs, store of knowledge, customs, and habits learned in the family and the community. Some groups are believed to possess cultural traits that make for success in American society – such as high achievement motivation, industriousness, perseverance, future orientation, ability to postpone immediate gratification for later rewards, and so forth. Groups that have internalized such values succeed, whereas those lacking them are doomed to failure. Those who have succeeded have done so because of the traits that their cultural tradition bequeathed them. A group's low socioeconomic status can be attributed to the fact that its cultural inventory did not include the requisite values, attitudes, and personal qualities. An underlying assumption of a cultural interpretation, therefore, is that "American society provides ample opportunity for class mobility and it is [the minority's] cultural institutions – 'home and family and community' – that are problematic" (Steinberg 1981:119). Whether an ethnic group succeeds or fails, it is perceived as being responsible for its own fate – what William Ryan (1971) has called a "blaming the victim" ideology. By implication, those who have been less successful than others can ensure their entrance into the mainstream of American society by becoming more fully culturally assimilated, by adopting the cultural values of the dominant group.

Hershberg and his associates have identified two variants of the cultural argument: the "bootstraps" and "last of the immigrants" explanations. The *bootstraps* explanation for the socioeconomic success of white ethnics and Asians is that they were able to overcome the disabilities with which they were confronted because through hard work, industry, perseverance, self-reliance, and thrift, they exploited as fully as possible the economic opportunity that America afforded. They pulled themselves up by their own bootstraps, without governmental assistance. Thus Greeley (see Article 13, "The Ethnic Miracle") contends that when "new" immigrants began their struggle for upward mobility in the first two decades of the twentieth century,

> There were no quotas, no affirmative action, no elaborate system of social services, and heaven knows, no ethnic militancy. There was no talk of reparations, no sense of guilt, no feeling of compassion for these immigrants. . . . Hard work, saving, sacrifice – such is a tentative explanation of the "ethnic miracle."

The other, sometimes complementary, explanation is the *last-of-the-immigrants* argument. According to this argument, ethnic socioeconomic success is only a matter of time, and those ethnic groups who have most recently migrated to the nation's cities (Chicanos, Puerto Ricans, American Indians, and in particular, African-Americans) must not be impatient with their present position at the bottom of the economic ladder. In several generations they will inevitably repeat the experience of European ethnic groups and climb into the American economic, educational, and political mainstream. Thomas Sowell, for example, contends that today's patterns of white flight from the central cities to the haven of suburbia are merely repeating the process of ethnic succession that has long been a characteristic feature of America's ethnically diverse cities; ethnic groups who arrive first move when their territory is invaded by a new and "inferior" ethnic group (Sowell 1981:277–278).

As noted above, Andrew Greeley subscribed to a cultural explanation in his analysis of the post-World War II socioeconomic achievements of Catholic and Jewish Americans. He contends that these achievements were the consequence of "something in the culture of the immigrants themselves." However, the cultural argument has been nowhere more clearly and effectively articulated than by Thomas Sowell, an economist who has written widely concerning American ethnic groups (Sowell 1978, 1980, 1981). Sowell contends that the variations in rates of socioeconomic status and achievement among American ethnic groups can best be explained by examining a group's cultural inheritance. "Whether in an ethnic context or among peoples and nations in general, much depends on the whole constellation of values, attitudes, skills, and contacts that many call a culture and that economists call 'human capital.' " That is, different rates of achievement among American ethnic groups are a result of differences in the cultural inventories that have been transmitted to them. The different values, attitudes, and moral disciplines that comprise each group's cultural inheritance, which "can be more important than biological inheritance," therefore provide the crucial ingredients that account for success or failure in American society. On the one hand, ethnic groups "that arrived in America financially destitute have rapidly risen to affluence, when their cultures stressed the values and behavior required in an industrial and commercial economy." On the other hand, "groups today plagued by absenteeism, tardiness, and a need for constant supervision at work or in school are typically descendants of people with the same habits a century or more ago" (Sowell 1981:282, 284).

For example, an emphasis on education has often been cited as an explanation for the extremely high levels of achievement among Jews. In a widely noted cultural explanation of differences in ethnic group achievement levels, Fred Strodtbeck (1958) argued that Jewish goals, values, and cultural norms were more compatible with the dominant values of American society than were those of other ethnic groups. In particular, the value of education, learning, and scholarly inquiry was long expressed in the intellectual tradition of orthodox Jewish culture. Jewish immigrants placed high prestige on education and educational attainments: the scholar was venerated and accorded respect. As Abraham Cahan wrote in his classic novel of Jewish immigrant life, *The Rise of David Levinsky,* "The ghetto rang with a clamor for knowledge. . . . To save up some money and prepare for college seemed to be the most natural thing to do" (Cahan 1966:156). By contrast, most Catholic "new" immigrants came from peasant backgrounds where formal education and learning were alien and remote. Southern Italian immigrants, who in many respects were typical of Catholic "new" immigrants, came from a society in which formal education clashed with traditional values. For them, education and learning were regarded as a threat to the integrity and strength of the family. Unlike Jews, Italian parents saw little value in education and did not encourage their children toward educational attainments (Strodtbeck 1958; Vecoli 1964).

Social Class

The traditional cultural explanation for the rapid mobility of Jewish immigrants (as contrasted to Catholic "new" immigrants) stressed the high value placed on education, learning, and scholarly achievement among immigrant Jews. However, Steinberg rejects the interpretation that Jewish *values* are the explanation for their success. Instead, he focuses on the impact of the different social-class backgrounds of entering immigrants. In "Education and Ethnic Mobility" (Article 15) he points out that although Jewish and Catholic "new" immigrants entered the United States with about the same meager amounts of money, their occupational backgrounds were not identical. Immigrant Jews came overwhelmingly from towns and cities of eastern Europe, where they had had extensive experience with manufacturing and commerce. More than two-thirds of Jewish immigrants were skilled workers, professionals, or merchants, as opposed to only one-sixth of southern Italians and one-sixteenth of Polish immigrants. More than two-thirds of Italian and three-fourths of Polish immigrants were unskilled laborers or farmers, in contrast to about one-seventh of entering Jews. The skills the Jews brought with them to the United States were needed by an expanding American economy and enabled them to enter at a higher status level than most unskilled immigrants. These occupational backgrounds and experiences of immigrant Jews enabled their children—the second generation—to acquire relatively easily the middle-class skills that were a prerequisite for entrance into the professions, in particular academic pursuits.

Jewish and Catholic "new" immigrants differed on another important characteristic: literacy. About one-fourth of all Jews entering the United States between 1899 and 1910 were unable to read and write, whereas more than half (54 percent) of southern Italians and one-third (35 percent) of Poles were illiterate. Similarly, because many Italians and Poles immigrated to the United States as temporary workers and did not intend to settle permanently in this country, they were much less likely to learn to speak English than were Jews, most of whom were fleeing religious persecution in eastern Europe and did not intend to return there. This stronger commitment to settlement in the United States increased the process of cultural assimilation for Jews. Italians and Poles, whose frames of reference remained in the old country, were much more likely to resist assimilation to American culture, a factor that greatly limited the occupational mobility of the second generation.

Steinberg shows how these background factors affected the occupational mobility of Jews and Catholics within the academic profession. Because professionals, especially academics, tend to be drawn from professional, managerial, and small-business backgrounds, individuals whose parents had such characteristics were favored in their access to such pursuits. Hence, the social class characteristics of Jewish and Catholic "new" immigrants were important influences on their patterns of occupational mobility. It was not simply that Jews embraced cultural values that extolled education and revered learning. It was rather "that cultural factors have little independent effect on educational outcomes, but are influential only as they interact with class factors. Thus, to whatever extent a reverence for learning was part of the religious and cultural heritage of Asians and Jews, it was activated and given existential significance by their social class circumstances" (Steinberg 1981:132).

The implication of Steinberg's analysis is that the social class characteristics of different American ethnic groups have played a crucial role in influencing the socioeconomic status of their descendants. As Portes and Bach have recently argued in their comparison of Mexican and Cuban immigrants to the United States, "the class composition of the different immigrant flows . . . played a decisive role in determining their modes of incorporation and subsequent economic destiny in the United States" (Portes and Bach 1985:48).

Culture and Social Class: A Synthesis

The prominence of small business enterprises among immigrants is one of the most widely documented and debated phenomena in recent ethnic group literature (Cheng and Bonacich 1984; Bonacich and Light 1988; Kim 1981; Waldinger 1987). In Article 16, "Immigrants and Ethnic Enterprise in North America," Ivan Light notes that since 1880 the foreign-born have been overrepresented in American small businesses, and he asks why immigrants should have higher rates of self-employment than native-born minorities. Light has sought to develop a synthesis of the role of cultural and class factors that more adequately explains this disproportion and, by implication, variations in ethnic socioeconomic status as well.

Light argues that immigrants may utilize either *ethnic resources* or *class resources* in developing business enterprises. The traditional "ethnic only," or what Light terms the "orthodox" cultural, argument of Greeley and Sowell is that a "tradition of enterprise" is part of the cultural inventory that certain immigrant groups (such as Jews or Japanese) bring with them. In this "orthodox" cultural explanation of entrepreneurship, a version of Weber's Protestant Ethic, immigrant cultural endowments are transferred relatively intact and unmodified from the old country to the new. On the other hand, a "class only" argument, represented here by Steinberg, explains immigrant socioeconomic success as a function of immigrants' class position—most importantly, the human capital or educational and technical skills that immigrants bring with them as a result of their class position.

Light argues for a much more complex and dynamic model. He contends that it is not merely the cultural baggage or endowments that is crucial in determining the mode of economic incorporation into a new society; instead, cultural attributes are but *one* aspect of ethnic resources which can be drawn upon to promote entrepreneurship. The experience or process of migration and alien status themselves elicit certain distinctive responses from immigrants that contribute to the establishment of entrepreneurship; alien status releases "latent facilitators" that provide entrepreneurial resources independent of immigrants' cultural endowments. Among these factors are relative satisfaction—that many immigrants from low wage countries are frequently willing to accept economic conditions that Americans are not; reactive solidarity—that ethnic minority status promotes ethnic solidarity, networks, and mutual aid organizations (such as rotating credit associations); and that many immigrants come as sojourners, who, wishing to amass money as quickly as possible, consume little and save much. Through each of these mechanisms the resources with which to establish small businesses are created.

Class resources, on the other hand, may be either cultural or material. The former include bourgeois values and attitudes that are, as Steinberg stressed, a function of class position, not of an entire culture. Material resources include property and money to invest. Light contends that, whereas ethnic resources were most important in establishing immigrant entrepreneurship in the past, as the class backgrounds of contemporary immigrants (Koreans, Hongkongese, Cubans, Iranians) have shifted, class resources in the form of money, human capital, and bourgeois cultural values have increasingly played a prominent role. Therefore, Light argues that traditional cultural and class explanations are inadequate; entrepreneurial activity will be most pronounced when class resources are combined with ethnic resources; comprehending the dynamics of immigrant entrepreneurship today must take account of both factors.

The Enclave Economy Model

The emphasis on ethnic solidarity that is a crucial dimension of Light's ethnic enterprise model is also central to the immigrant enclave model, which emphasizes the social mobility opportunities that work in an immigrant enclave affords. As previously mentioned, in a dual or segmented labor market model, minorities and women are likely to be relegated to low-wage, dead-end jobs in the "peripheral" or "secondary" labor market, which provides few opportunities for promotion. Because immigrant workers are likely to be incorporated into the secondary sector of the economy, their prospects for mobility and, hence, assimilation into the receiving society are likely to be limited. Given the preference for skills in recent American immigration policy, a substantial portion of immigrants to the United States in the past two decades has been highly skilled and educated professionals and managers. For example, the 1980 Census revealed that nearly half (45.6 percent) of all African immigrants and more than two-thirds (69.9 percent) of all Asian Indian immigrants had completed college (Bouvier and Gardner 1986:22). These highly skilled workers are much more likely to be incorporated into the "core" or "primary" sector of the economy than those who are less skilled. Therefore, social diversity of recent immigrants and the changing nature of the American economy have undermined the validity of a traditional model of assimilation in which immigrant groups enter the bottom rungs of the socioeconomic hierarchy and over a period of time gradually experience social mobility.

On the other hand, Alejandro Portes and his associates (Wilson and Portes 1980; Portes and Bach 1980, 1985; Portes and Rambaut 1990; Portes and Stepick 1985; Portes and Jensen 1989) contend that the incorporation of immigrants into the economy is not simply a function of the immigrants' skill levels or whether they enter the primary or secondary sector of the economy. Rather, they emphasize that the immigrant community is itself a major factor influencing the range of opportunities available to individual immigrants and, as a consequence, their adaptation to a new society. They have developed the concept of an enclave economy, which focuses on the manner in which several immigrant groups have been incorporated into the American economy. A critical element of the enclave model is the presence of coethnics with sufficient capital to provide employment opportunities for newly arrived immigrants. In an enclave economy, immigrant workers are not trapped in the secondary sector of a segmented labor market. Although immigrants are forced to work hard for low wages, their opportunities for upward mobility are not blocked, as is the case for most workers in the secondary labor market. Workers in an immigrant enclave "can be empirically distinguished from workers in both the primary and secondary labor market. Enclave workers will share with those in the primary sector a significant economic return to past human capital investments. Such a return will be absent among those in the 'open' secondary labor market" (Wilson and Portes 1980:302). In other words, the human capital resources (education and skills) brought from the home country will result in greater economic returns for individuals located in an ethnic enclave economy than those in the outside labor market; an individual entering an enclave economy will ultimately fare better economically than someone with exactly the same level of skills who does not have the advantages of incorporation into an enclave.

In Article 17, "The Immigrant Enclave," Portes and Robert D. Manning use the enclave model to explain the incorporation of four ethnic groups—the Jews, Japanese, Koreans, and Cubans. As we saw earlier, the relative economic successes of each of these groups has been variously attributed to a cultural explanation, on the one hand, and a social class explanation on the other. Portes and Manning emphasize the crucial role of ethnic communal factors and social solidarity in facilitating the adjustment not only of immigrant Jews and Japanese around the turn of the twentieth century, but also of the Koreans and Cubans, the vast majority of whom are relatively recent immigrants, to the United States. Each of these groups, they contend, has demonstrated a similar tendency to activate resources through what Light has termed "reactive solidarity" and ultimately to accumulate sufficient capital to establish an enclave economy that facilitates economic mobility for their compatriots. Unlike comparable low-wage work in the secondary labor market, employment in an enclave enterprise therefore provides the potential for advancement.

The enclave model has been subjected to considerable criticism. For example, Sanders and Nee (1987) found that an enclave economy did not provide overall economic benefits to its participants. Immigrants living outside the enclave had higher socioeconomic status than those living in it. Moreover, they found that immigrant workers in the enclave economy received lower wages than workers in the outside economy. They questioned how truly effective employment in an enclave economy is in facilitating a worker's movement into self-employment.

Responding to recent criticisms of the enclave model, Portes and Leif Jensen (1989) refined the notion to refer to a situation in which individuals both live in a community comprised predominantly of coethnics and work in enterprises owned by coethnics. In an analysis of the Cuban enclave economy in Miami, they found that self-employed entrepreneurs earned significantly higher incomes if they were located within the enclave. In other words, Cuban entrepreneurship had a positive effect on earnings when it occurred within the enclave economy. Self-employment produced significantly higher increases in earnings among Cubans employed in the enclave when compared with those employed outside the enclave. Moreover, employment in Cuban firms did not reduce the earnings of fellow Cubans. Indeed, for women it actually increased them. Thus Portes and Jensen reject the thesis that small ethnic businesses are economically successful because they exploit their coethnics – the pattern in which entrepreneurship is economically advantageous for employers but at the expense of their coethnic employees. They found "no indication of a pattern of overall disadvantage or lower human capital returns among employees in enclave firms" (Portes and Jensen 1989:943).

External Explanations

In contrast to a cultural explanation of ethnic group achievement and assimilation, an *external* or *structural* explanation emphasizes the external constraints, disabilities, limitations, and barriers to which a group is subjected and which serve as obstacles to achievement. Some groups (for example, African-Americans) have been confronted with substantial barriers that have circumscribed the resources available to them and precluded their full and equal participation in society. As noted in Part 2, there is a range of possible dominant-group policies that, to a greater or lesser degree, limit the options available to a minority group. These range from extermination to discrimination in many different forms.

A cultural explanation tends to minimize or dismiss the role of external factors, especially in contemporary American society. Sowell, for example, contends that the intergroup animosities and discrimination that existed in American society in the past have lessened in intensity and "in some respects disappeared" (Sowell 1981:7). Such a perspective presupposes that social structure is blind to group differences and does not play a significant role in affecting patterns of ethnic group achievement. Put another way, it assumes that the social structure is neutral when it comes to racial and ethnic factors, and that individuals from all ethnic backgrounds have relatively equal opportunities to succeed.

Moreover, a cultural interpretation assumes that external barriers are insignificant in affecting group outcomes because the opportunities of all American ethnic groups have at one time or another been circumscribed in some way. All American ethnic groups, Sowell writes, "have been discriminated against to one degree or another. Yet some of the most successful – such as the Orientals – have experienced worse discrimination than most, and the extraordinary success of Jews has been achieved in the face of centuries of anti-Semitism" (Sowell 1981:6).

Finally, a cultural model assumes that the distinctive traits and capacities that characterize a group will manifest themselves in spite of harsh and restrictive treatment by other groups. Thus, Sowell argues that the characteristics of "working harder and more relentlessly" will overcome even the most pronounced adversity (Sowell 1981:283).

Each of these assumptions has been vigorously challenged by critics who contend that the structural barriers confronting Chicanos, Puerto Ricans, American Indians, and, in particular, African-Americans have been more severe and repressive than those encountered by "new" immigrants or even by Asians.

The most apparent external barrier distinguishing the experience of African-Americans has been the disability of race, which has subjected blacks, in both the South and the North, to discrimination far more severe than experienced by any European ethnic groups. For example, Lieberson's analysis (1980) demonstrates that prejudice and discrimination against African-Americans in Northern cities intensified rather than diminished during the first few decades of the twentieth century. At the same time that spatial isolation declined for "new" immigrants it increased markedly for African-Americans. Moreover, the discrimination that African-Americans encountered in education and employment was never so consistently a feature of the experience of "new" immigrant groups. These findings are reinforced by Hershberg's analysis of Philadelphia, which shows that historically the occupational opportunity structure for African-Americans has never been as open as that for white immigrants and that, because of increased residential segregation, blacks have been excluded from recent occupational opportunities.

The experience of Asians, in particular the Japanese and the Chinese, frequently is cited to support the claim that being nonwhite is not an insurmountable barrier to achievement in American society. In other words, Asian success casts considerable doubt on the notion that nonwhite racial status is inherently a liability to achievement. Indeed, Asians are frequently cited as "model minorities" because they have been able to succeed despite extremely virulent forms of discrimination. They have been able to do so, Sowell writes, because of their cultural traits of "effort, thrift, dependability and foresight, [which] built businesses out of 'menial tasks' and turned sweat into capital" (Sowell 1981:7).

However, Asians were not forced to endure the historical experience of slavery and the discriminatory barriers that persisted on a pervasive scale after its legal elimination. Moreover, unlike African-Americans, the number of Asians in the United States was never so large as to represent a real threat to the existing white population. Even in California, the state in which Asians have been most highly concentrated, the highest-ever proportion of Japanese in the state's population was 2.1 percent, and the Chinese proportion was even smaller (Peterson 1971:30). When these extremely small numbers of Asians appeared to increase even slightly, the perceived threat they represented was reduced by changes in American immigration laws that effectively limited Asian population to a tiny proportion of the total (Lieberson 1980:368). Moreover, Nee and Wong (1985:20) suggest that the number of African-Americans who migrated to the West during and after World War II exceeded the small Asian population. Their increased presence, and the greater prejudice toward them on the part of white Americans, lessened the impact of anti-Asian discrimination and thus facilitated Asian-American socioeconomic mobility.

Emphasizing the caste dimensions of the experiences of African-Americans, Chicanos, Puerto Ricans, and Native Americans, John Ogbu (1978) contends that there have been qualitative differences between the experiences of the Chinese and Japanese in the United States and the experiences of what he characterizes as *caste minorities:* African-Americans, Chicanos, Puerto Ricans, and American Indians. Because Asians have not been subjected to the systematic economic subordination of caste minorities, their academic performance has not been comparably impaired (Ogbu 1978:21–25). Ogbu rejects a cultural interpretation of the minority status of African-Americans and other American minorities. Most cultural explanations, he argues, explicitly or implicitly assume that the socioeconomic inequality between blacks and whites is caused, at least in part, by differences in the school performance and educational attainment of the two races [and] that this inequality would largely disappear if only blacks would perform like whites in school (Ogbu 1978:43–44).

From Ogbu's perspective, however, black inequality has not been caused so much by poor academic performance as poor academic performance is the product of African-American perceptions that academic achievement will not be rewarded, because of the discriminatory job ceiling that African-Americans historically have encountered. In other words, Ogbu argues that the absence of high educational aspirations, high achievement motivation, and a future orientation on the part of some minority-group members is a response to external circumstances, to their realistic perception that their opportunities in the work world are extremely restricted. Lower school performance is merely a symptom of the broader and more central societal problem of caste. Minority educational achievement will be improved only when there is a dramatic societal commitment to ending discrimination in jobs and housing, and to including American minorities in the decision-making process in institutions throughout the whole of American society. "The only lasting solution to the problem of academic retardation," he writes, "is the elimination of caste barriers" (Ogbu 1978:357).

From a structural perspective, therefore, it is the opportunity structure, not minority values, that accounts for the different socioeconomic positions occupied by different ethnic groups. It is the opportunity structure, not minority values, that must first be changed in order to reduce the inequalities in American society.

The structure of opportunity may be limited by what we have termed attitudinal discrimination, which is motivated by prejudices against racial or ethnic minorities. For example, as noted above, although there is evidence of a decline in attitudinal discrimination in employment from two decades ago, it still remains a potent force perpetuating patterns of residential segregation in America. However, a structural model also focuses on the objective economic circumstances that confront the so-called caste minorities today, and compares them with those that ethnic groups, in particular "new" immigrants, encountered in the past.

William Julius Wilson has been among the foremost critics of a cultural perspective. As noted in Part 2, in *The Declining Significance of Race* (1978), Wilson divided the history of American race relations into three periods or stages—the preindustrial, industrial, and modern industrial, each reflecting changes in the nation's economic structure. Wilson acknowledged that in contemporary American society—the modern industrial period—attitudinal discrimination is still pervasive in many areas, such as housing, education, and municipal politics, and serves as a barrier to black participation in society's mainstream. However, he contended that in the economic sphere, institutional, not attitudinal, discrimination has become the primary source of continuing black inequalities. In the economic life of African-Americans, "class has become more important than race in determining black access to privilege and power." (See Article 6, "The Declining Significance of Race," in Part 2.)

Wilson's thesis is based on the contention that during the modern industrial era African-American economic status has been influenced by substantial structural economic changes "such as the shift from goods-producing to service-producing industries, the increasing segmentation of the labor market, the growing use of industrial technology, and the relocation of industries out of the central city" that, in themselves, have little to do with race (Wilson 1981a:38).

As a result of these changes in the economic structure, the structure of the African-American community has been altered. On the one hand, "educated blacks are experiencing unprecedented job opportunities in the growing government and corporate sectors, opportunities that are at least comparable to those of whites with equivalent qualifications." This advance has come about as a result of the expansion of salaried, white-collar positions and of changes in the role of government. Before the modern industrial era, the state merely reinforced patterns of race relations established in the economic sector. Recently, in response to the civil rights movement, the government has stood in formal opposition to discriminatory barriers. Indeed, with the enactment of affirmative action programs in the 1960s, government undertook the initiative in combatting discrimination.

On the other hand, the social conditions of the African-American underclass have deteriorated in the last quarter of a century. In his most recent book, *The Truly Disadvantaged* (1987), Wilson focuses on the crisis of the underclass in the inner city, where the broad economic changes mentioned above have caused extremely high levels of unemployment. Earlier in the twentieth century, relatively uneducated and unskilled native and immigrant workers were able to find stable employment and income in manufacturing. Today, however, the process of deindustrialization has created an economic "mismatch" between the kinds of jobs available and the qualifications of inner city residents lacking highly sophisticated educational and technical skills. On the one hand, manufacturing jobs, which do not require advanced skills, have moved from inner cities to the suburbs, to the Sun Belt, or overseas. On the other hand, the jobs created in the cities demand highly technical credentials for which most inner city residents are unqualified. Thus many inner city residents find themselves without prospects for work. Moreover, as many stable working-class and middle-class residents with job qualifications have moved from the inner cities into better residential neighborhoods, the stability of neighborhood social institutions (such as churches, schools, newspapers, and recreational facilities) has been undermined and the social fabric of community life has deteriorated. The underclass has become increasingly isolated, socially and economically. "Today's ghetto residents face a closed opportunity structure." In Article 27, "The Cost of Racial and

Class Exclusion in the Inner City," Loïc Wacquant and Wilson describe the impact of institutional and structural changes in triggering a process of "hyper-ghettoization" or concentration of the very poor.

Wilson's argument has been subjected to considerable criticism. One of the most frequent criticisms is that, in stressing the nonracial structural sources of the underclass, he ignores or underestimates the role of race. For example, Massey and Denton (Article 19) contend that "race continues to be a fundamental cleavage in American society." In an elaboration of this position, Massey (1990) has argued that, while industrial restructuring contributed significantly to the increasing concentration of urban poverty during the 1970s, racial segregation was *the* critical factor. Because African-Americans are more highly residentially segregated, regardless of their socioeconomic characteristics, than any other American racial or ethnic group, they were more vulnerable to the cumulative impact of the economic dislocations that occurred throughout the seventies.

Other critics have argued that Wilson's analysis tends to obscure continuing attitudinal discrimination in the economic sphere; not only is the contemporary underclass a consequence of historical patterns of racial discrimination, but such discrimination continues today to affect black economic opportunities and life chances. For example, Steinberg has challenged Wilson's use of the "mismatch" explanation for black exclusion from the expanding service sector of the economy. The "mismatch" hypothesis, he contends, "seriously underestimates the color line in the world of work" (Steinberg 1989:289). It overlooks the large number of jobs that do not require extensive education, training, and skills and it ignores the virtual exclusion of African-Americans from certain segments of the labor market.

Moreover, the "mismatch" hypothesis ignores the extent to which many relatively unskilled service sector jobs have been taken by recent immigrants. As the articles by Light, Portes, Manning, and Waldinger point out, recent immigrant groups are increasingly settling in America's urban centers. The presence of immigrants has raised the issue of whether immigrants take jobs away from native-born workers, especially native-born minorities. Most studies have concluded that immigrants do not displace native workers. However, Elizabeth Bogen has argued that native workers experience considerable discrimination from the proprietors of the ethnic businesses that have recently proliferated in the nation's center cities. "Ethnic hiring networks and the proliferation of immigrant-owned small businesses in [New York City] have cut off open-market competition for jobs; there are tens of thousands of jobs in New York for which the native-born are not candidates" (Bogen 1987:91). Vernon Briggs has further argued that a major factor contributing to the migration during the 1980s of blacks from the North to the south was the dramatic increase in immigrant settlers in major urban areas in the North. Because blacks outside the South are concentrated overwhelmingly in urban areas, especially in the inner cities, "the urban black population has borne the brunt of the competition with immigrants for jobs, training opportunities, community services, and housing" (Briggs, 1990:A14).

In Article 18, Roger Waldinger ("Changing Ladders and Musical Chairs") argues that the shift to a postindustrial global economy has transformed the ethnic division of labor in America's major urban centers. His analysis focuses on the economic and social changes that have accompanied the decline of manufacturing and the rise of a service-oriented economy in New York City, the nation's largest and historically most ethnically diverse city. Waldinger disputes the "mismatch" hypothesis and the thesis that ethnic minorities are essential to maintain low cost services for the city's affluent residents. Instead, he argues that the substantial decline since 1950 in jobs previously held by whites provided opportunities for ethnic occupational realignment – for nonwhites to replace whites in the city's labor force. However, what was distinctive about the manner in which nonwhites succeeded whites was the salience of distinct economic niches in which different ethnic groups were concentrated. For example, blacks tended to concentrate in public sector jobs, whereas immigrants were more likely to be found in a wide range of small, ethnically distinct businesses. Waldinger argues that ethnic-network recruiting tends to exclude nonethnics and thus to reinforce the ethnic identification of specific occupations. The tendency for ethnic enterprises to hire coethnics has an especially significant impact on native-born blacks, who as a consequence are excluded from occupational opportunities controlled by immigrants as well as those dominated by native-born whites. He concludes that "native blacks are the big losers in the new ethnic division of labor."

Assimilation in America
Theory and Reality

Milton M. Gordon

Three ideologies or conceptual models have competed for attention on the American scene as explanations of the way in which a nation, in the beginning largely white, Anglo-Saxon, and Protestant, has absorbed over 41 million immigrants and their descendants from variegated sources and welded them into the contemporary American people. These ideologies are Anglo-conformity, the melting pot, and cultural pluralism. They have served at various times, and often simultaneously, as explanations of what has happened – descriptive models – and of what should happen – goal models. Not infrequently they have been used in such a fashion that it is difficult to tell which of these two usages the writer has had in mind. In fact, one of the more remarkable omissions in the history of American intellectual thought is the relative lack of close analytical attention given to the theory of immigrant adjustment in the United States by its social scientists.

The result has been that this field of discussion – an overridingly important one since it has significant implications for the more familiar problems of prejudice, discrimination, and majority-minority group relations generally – has been largely preempted by laymen, representatives of belles lettres, philosophers, and apologists of various persuasions. Even from these sources the amount of attention devoted to ideologies of assimilation is hardly extensive. Consequently, the work of improving intergroup relations in America is carried out by dedicated professional agencies and individuals who deal as

best they can with day-to-day problems of discriminatory behavior, but who for the most part are unable to relate their efforts to an adequate conceptual apparatus. Such an apparatus would, at one and the same time, accurately describe the present structure of American society with respect to its ethnic groups (I shall use the term "ethnic group" to refer to any racial, religious, or national-origins collectivity), and allow for a considered formulation of its assimilation or integration goals for the foreseeable future. One is reminded of Alice's distraught question in her travels in Wonderland. "Would you tell me, please, which way I ought to go from here?" "That depends a good deal," replied the Cat with irrefutable logic, "on where you want to get to."

The story of America's immigration can be quickly told for our present purposes. The white American population at the time of the Revolution was largely English and Protestant in origin, but had already absorbed substantial groups of Germans and Scotch-Irish and smaller contingents of Frenchmen, Dutchmen, Swedes, Swiss, South Irish, Poles, and a handful of migrants from other European nations. Catholics were represented in modest numbers, particularly in the middle colonies, and a small number of Jews were residents of the incipient nation. With the exception of the Quakers and a few missionaries, the colonists had generally treated the Indians and their cultures with contempt and hostility, driving them from the coastal plains and making the western frontier a bloody battleground where eternal vigilance was the price of survival.

Reprinted by permission from *Daedalus,* Journal of the American Academy of Arts and Sciences, Boston, Massachusetts, Volume 90, Number 2 (Spring 1961), pp. 263–285.

Although the Negro at that time made up nearly one-fifth of the total population, his predominantly slave status, together with racial and cultural prejudice, barred him from serious consideration as an assimilable element of the society. And while many groups of European origin started out as determined ethnic enclaves, eventually, most historians believe, considerable ethnic intermixture within the white population took place. "People of different blood" [sic] – write two American historians about the colonial period, "English, Irish, German, Huguenot, Dutch, Swedish – mingled and intermarried with little thought of any difference."[1] In such a society, its people predominantly English, its white immigrants of other ethnic origins either English-speaking or derived largely from countries of northern and western Europe whose cultural divergences from the English were not great, and its dominant white population excluding by fiat the claims and considerations of welfare of the non-Caucasian minorities, the problem of assimilation understandably did not loom unduly large or complex.

The unfolding events of the next century and a half with increasing momentum dispelled the complacency which rested upon the relative simplicity of colonial and immediate post-Revolutionary conditions. The large-scale immigration to America of the famine-fleeing Irish, the Germans, and later the Scandinavians (along with additional Englishmen and other peoples of northern and western Europe) in the middle of the nineteenth century (the so-called "old immigration"), the emancipation of the Negro slaves and the problems created by post-Civil War reconstruction, the placing of the conquered Indian with his broken culture on government reservations, the arrival of the Oriental, first attracted by the discovery of gold and other opportunities in the West, and finally, beginning in the last quarter of the nineteenth century and continuing to the early 1920s, the swelling to proportions hitherto unimagined of the tide of immigration from the peasantries and "pales" of southern and eastern Europe – the Italians, Jews, and Slavs of the so-called "new immigration," fleeing the persecutions and industrial dislocations of the day – all these events constitute the background against which we may consider the rise of the theories of assimilation mentioned above. After a necessarily foreshortened description of each of these theories and their historical emergence, we shall suggest analytical distinctions designed to aid in clarifying the nature of the assimilation process, and then conclude by focusing on the American scene.

ANGLO-CONFORMITY

"Anglo-conformity"[2] is a broad term used to cover a variety of viewpoints about assimilation and immigration; they all assume the desirability of maintaining English institutions (as modified by the American Revolution), the English language, and English-oriented cultural patterns as dominant and standard in American life. However, bound up with this assumption are related attitudes. These may range from discredited notions about race and "Nordic" and "Aryan" racial superiority, together with the nativist political programs and exclusionist immigration policies which such notions entail, through an intermediate position of favoring immigration from northern and western Europe on amorphous, unreflective grounds ("They are more like us"), to a lack of opposition to any source of immigration, as long as these immigrants and their descendants duly adopt the standard Anglo-Saxon cultural patterns. There is by no means any necessary equation between Anglo-conformity and racist attitudes.

It is quite likely that "Anglo-conformity" in its more moderate aspects, however explicit its formulation, has been the most prevalent ideology of assimilation goals in America throughout the nation's history. As far back as colonial times, Benjamin Franklin recorded concern about the clannishness of the Germans in Pennsylvania, their slowness in learning English, and the establishment of their own native-language press.[3] Others of the founding fathers had similar reservations about large-scale immigration from Europe. In the context of their times they were unable to foresee the role such immigration was to play in creating the later greatness of the nation. They were not all men of unthinking prejudices. The disestablishment of religion and the separation of church and state (so that no religious group – whether New England Congregationalists, Virginian Anglicans, or even all Protestants combined—could call upon the federal government for special favors or support, and so that man's religious conscience should be free) were cardinal points of the new national policy they fostered. "The Government of the United States," George Washington had written to the Jewish congregation of Newport during his first term as president, "gives to bigotry no sanction, to persecution no assistance."

Political differences with ancestral England had just been written in blood; but there is no reason to suppose that these men looked upon their fledgling country as an impartial melting pot for the merging of the various cultures of Europe, or as a new "nation of nations," or as anything but a society in which, with important political modifications, Anglo-Saxon speech and institutional forms would be standard. Indeed, their newly won victory for democracy and republicanism made them especially anxious that these still precarious fruits of revolution should not be threatened by a large influx of European peoples whose life experiences had accustomed them to the bonds of despotic monarchy. Thus, although they explicitly conceived of the new United States of America as a haven for those unfortunates of Europe who were persecuted and oppressed, they had characteristic reservations about the effects of too free a policy. "My opinion, with respect to immigration," Washington wrote to John Adams in 1794, "is that except of useful mechanics and some particular descriptions of men or professions, there is no need of encouragement, while the policy or advantage of its taking place in a body (I mean the settling of them in a body) may be much questioned; for, by so doing, they retain the language, habits and principles (good or bad) which they bring with them."[4] Thomas Jefferson, whose views on race and attitudes towards slavery were notably liberal and advanced for his time, had similar doubts concerning the effects of mass immigration on American institutions, while conceding that immigrants, "if they come of themselves . . . are entitled to all the rights of citizenship."[5]

The attitudes of Americans toward foreign immigration in the first three-quarters of the nineteenth century may correctly be described as ambiguous. On the one hand, immigrants were much desired, so as to swell the population and importance of states and territories, to man the farms of expanding prairie settlement, to work the mines, build the railroads and canals, and take their place in expanding industry. This was a period in which no federal legislation of any consequence prevented the entry of aliens, and such state legislation as existed attempted to bar on an individual basis only those who were likely to become a burden on the community, such as convicts and paupers. On the other hand, the arrival in an overwhelmingly Protestant society of large numbers of poverty-stricken Irish Catholics, who settled in groups in the slums of Eastern cities, roused dormant fears of "Popery" and Rome. Another source of anxiety was the substantial influx of Germans, who made their way to the cities and farms of the mid-West and whose different language, separate communal life, and freer ideas on temperance and sabbath observance brought them into conflict with the Anglo-Saxon bearers of the Puritan and Evangelical traditions. Fear of foreign "radicals" and suspicion of the economic demands of the occasionally aroused workingmen added fuel to the nativist fires. In their extreme form these fears resulted in the Native-American movement of the 1830s and 1840s and the "American" or "Know-Nothing" party of the 1850s, with their anti-Catholic campaigns and their demands for restrictive laws on naturalization procedures and for keeping the foreign-born out of political office. While these movements scored local political successes and their turbulences so rent the national social fabric that the patches are not yet entirely invisible, they failed to influence national legislative policy on immigration and immigrants; and their fulminations inevitably provoked the expected reactions from thoughtful observers.

The flood of newcomers to the westward expanding nation grew larger, reaching over one and two-thirds million between 1841 and 1850 and over two and one-half million in the decade before the Civil War. Throughout the entire period, quite apart from the excesses of the Know-Nothings, the predominant (though not exclusive) conception of what the ideal immigrant adjustment should be was probably summed up in a letter written in 1818 by John Quincy Adams, then Secretary of State, in answer to the inquiries of the Baron von Fürstenwaerther. If not the earliest, it is certainly the most elegant version of the sentiment, "If they don't like it here, they can go back where they came from." Adams declared:[6]

They [immigrants to America] come to life of independence, but to a life of labor—and, if they cannot accommodate themselves to the character, moral, political and physical, of this country with all its compensating balances of good and evil, the Atlantic is always open to them to return to the land of their nativity and their fathers. To one thing they must make up their minds, or they will be disappointed in every expectation of happiness as Americans. They must cast off the European skin, never to resume it. They must look forward to their posterity rather than backward to their ancestors; they must be sure that whatever their own feelings may be, those of their children will cling to the prejudices of this country.

The events that followed the Civil War created their own ambiguities in attitude toward the immigrant. A nation undergoing wholesale industrial expansion and not yet finished with the march of westward settlement could make good use of the never faltering waves of newcomers. But sporadic bursts of labor unrest, attributed to foreign radicals, the growth of Catholic institutions and the rise of Catholics to municipal political power, and the continuing association of immigrant settlement with urban slums revived familiar fears. The first federal selective law restricting immigration was passed in 1882, and Chinese immigration was cut off in the same year. The most significant development of all, barely recognized at first, was the change in the source of European migrants. Beginning in the 1880s, the countries of southern and eastern Europe began to be represented in substantial numbers for the first time, and in the next decade immigrants from these sources became numerically dominant. Now the notes of a new, or at least hitherto unemphasized, chord from the nativist lyre began to sound—the ugly chord, or discord, of racism. Previously vague and romantic notions of Anglo-Saxon peoplehood, combined with general ethnocentrism, rudimentary wisps of genetics, selected tidbits of evolutionary theory, and naive assumptions from an early and crude imported anthropology produced the doctrine that the English, Germans, and others of the

"old immigration" constituted a superior race of tall, blonde, blue-eyed "Nordics" or "Aryans," whereas the peoples of eastern and southern Europe made up the darker Alpines or Mediterraneans—both "inferior" breeds whose presence in America threatened, either by intermixture or supplementation, the traditional American stock and culture. The obvious corollary to this doctrine was to exclude the allegedly inferior breeds; but if the new type of immigrant could not be excluded, then everything must be done to instill Anglo-Saxon virtues in these benighted creatures. Thus, one educator writing in 1909 could state:[7]

These southern and eastern Europeans are of a very different type from the north Europeans who preceeded them. Illiterate, docile, lacking in self-reliance and initiative, and not possessing the Anglo-Teutonic conceptions of law, order, and government, their coming has served to dilute tremendously our national stock, and to corrupt our civic life. . . . Everywhere these people tend to settle in groups or settlements, and to set up here their national manners, customs, and observances. Our task is to break up these groups or settlements, to assimilate and amalgamate these people as a part of our American race, and to implant in their children, so far as can be done, the Anglo-Saxon conception of righteousness, law and order, and popular government, and to awaken in them a reverence for our democratic institutions and for those things in our national life which we as a people hold to be of abiding worth.

Anglo-conformity received its fullest expression in the so-called Americanization which gripped the nation during World War I. While "Americanization" in its various stages had more than one emphasis, it was essentially a consciously articulated movement to strip the immigrant of his native culture and attachments and make him over into an American along Anglo-Saxon lines—all this to be accomplished with great rapidity. To use an image of a later day, it was an attempt at "pressure-cooking assimilation." It had prewar antecedents, but it was during the height of the world conflict that federal agencies, state governments, municipalities, and a host of private organizations joined in the effort to persuade the immigrant to learn English, take out naturalization papers, buy war bonds, forget his former origins and culture, and give himself over to patriotic hysteria.

After the war and the "Red scare" which followed, the excesses of the Americanization movement subsided. In its place, however, came the restriction of immigration through federal law. Foiled at first by presidential vetoes, and later by the failure of the 1917 literacy test to halt the immigrant tide, the proponents of restriction finally put through in the early 1920s a series of acts culminating in the well-known national-origins formula for immigrant quotas which went into effect in 1929. Whatever the merits of a quantitative limit on the number of immigrants to be admitted to the United States, the provisions of the formula, which discriminated sharply against the countries of southern and eastern Europe, in effect institutionalized the assumptions of the rightful dominance of Anglo-Saxon patterns in the land. Reaffirmed with only slight modifications in the McCarran-Walter Act of 1952, these laws, then, stand as a legal monument to the creed of Anglo-conformity and a telling reminder that this ideological system still has numerous and powerful adherents on the American scene.

THE MELTING POT

While Anglo-conformity in various guises has probably been the most prevalent ideology of assimilation in the American historical experience, a competing viewpoint with more generous and idealistic overtones has had its adherents and exponents from the eighteenth century onward. Conditions in the virgin continent, it was clear, were modifying the institutions which the English colonists brought with them from the mother country. Arrivals from non-English homelands such as Germany, Sweden, and France were similarly exposed to this fresh environment. Was it not possible, then, to think of the evolving American society not as a slightly modified England but rather as a totally new blend, culturally and biologically, in which the stocks and folkways of Europe, figuratively speaking, were indiscriminately mixed in the political pot of the emerging nation and fused by the fires of American influence and interaction into a distinctly new type?

Such, at any rate, was the conception of the new society which motivated that eighteenth-century French-born writer and agriculturalist,

J. Hector St. John de Crèvecoeur, who, after many years of American residence, published his reflections and observations in *Letters from an American Farmer*.[8] Who, he asks, is the American?

> He is either an European, or the descendant of an European, hence that strange mixture of blood, which you will find in no other country. I could point out to you a family whose grandfather was an Englishman, whose wife was Dutch, whose son married a French woman, and whose present four sons have now four wives of different nations. He *is* an American, who leaving behind him all his ancient prejudices and manners, receives new ones from the new mode of life he has embraced, the new government he obeys, and the new rank he holds. He becomes an American by being received in the broad lap of our great Alma Mater. Here individuals of all nations are melted into a new race of men, whose labours and posterity will one day cause great changes in the world.

Some observers have interpreted the open-door policy on immigration of the first three-quarters of the nineteenth century as reflecting an underlying faith in the effectiveness of the American melting pot, in the belief "that all could be absorbed and that all could contribute to an emerging national character."[9] No doubt many who observed with dismay the nativist agitation of the times felt as did Ralph Waldo Emerson that such conformity-demanding and immigrant-hating forces represented a perversion of the best American ideals. In 1845, Emerson wrote in his Journal:[10]

> I hate the narrowness of the Native American Party. It is the dog in the manger. It is precisely opposite to all the dictates of love and magnanimity; and therefore, of course, opposite to true wisdom. . . . Man is the most composite of all creatures. . . . Well, as in the old burning of the Temple at Corinth, by the melting and intermixture of silver and gold and other metals a new compound more precious than any, called Corinthian brass, was formed: so in this continent, — asylum of all nations, — the energy of Irish, Germans, Swedes, Poles, and Cossacks, and all the European tribes, — of the Africans, and the Polynesians, — will construct a new race, a new religion, a new state, a new literature, which will be as vigorous as the new Europe which came out of the smelting-pot of the Dark Ages, or that which earlier emerged from the Pelasgic and Etruscan barbarism. La Nature aime les croisements.

Eventually, the melting-pot hypothesis found its way into historical scholarship and interpretation. While many American historians of the late nineteenth century, some fresh from graduate study at German universities, tended to adopt the view that American institutions derived in essence from Anglo-Saxon (and ultimately Teutonic) sources, others were not so sure.[11] One of these was Frederick Jackson Turner, a young historian from Wisconsin, not long emerged from his graduate training at Johns Hopkins. Turner presented a paper to the American Historical Association meeting in Chicago in 1893. Called "The Significance of the Frontier in American History," this paper proved to be one of the most influential essays in the history of American scholarship, and its point of view, supported by Turner's subsequent writings and his teaching, pervaded the field of American historical interpretation for at least a generation. Turner's thesis was that the dominant influence in the shaping of American institutions and American democracy was not this nation's European heritage in any of its forms, nor the forces emanating from the eastern seaboard cities, but rather the experiences created by a moving and variegated western frontier. Among the many effects attributed to the frontier environment and the challenges it presented was that it acted as a solvent for the national heritages and the separatist tendencies of the many nationality groups which had joined the trek westward, including the Germans and Scotch-Irish of the eighteenth century and the Scandinavians and Germans of the nineteenth. "The frontier," asserted Turner, "promoted the formation of a composite nationality for the American people. . . . In the crucible of the frontier the immigrants were Americanized, liberated, and fused into a mixed race, English in neither nationality nor characteristics. The process has gone on from the early days to our own." And later, in an essay on the role of the Mississippi Valley, he refers to "the tide of foreign immigration which has risen so steadily that it has made a composite American people whose amalgamation is destined to produce a new national stock."[12]

Thus far, the proponents of the melting pot idea had dealt largely with the diversity pro-

duced by the sizeable immigration from the countries of northern and western Europe alone—the "old immigration," consisting of peoples with cultures and physical appearance not greatly different from those of the Anglo-Saxon stock. Emerson, it is true, had impartially included Africans, Polynesians, and Cossacks in his conception of the mixture; but it is was only in the last two decades of the nineteenth century that a large-scale influx of peoples from the countries of southern and eastern Europe imperatively posed the question of whether these uprooted newcomers who were crowding into the large cities of the nation and industrial sector of the economy could also be successfully "melted." Would the "urban melting pot" work as well as the "frontier melting pot" of an essentially rural society was alleged to have done?

It remained for an English-Jewish writer with strong social convictions, moved by his observation of the role of the United States as a haven for the poor and oppressed of Europe, to give utterance to the broader view of the American melting pot in a way which attracted public attention. In 1908, Israel Zangwill's drama, *The Melting Pot,* was produced in this country and became a popular success. It is a play dominated by the dream of its protagonist, a young Russian-Jewish immigrant to America, a composer, whose goal is the completion of a vast "American" symphony which will express his deeply felt conception of his adopted country as a divinely appointed crucible in which all the ethnic division of mankind will divest themselves of their ancient animosities and differences and become fused into one group, signifying the brotherhood of man. In the process he falls in love with a beautiful and cultured Gentile girl. The play ends with the performance of the symphony and, after numerous vicissitudes and traditional family opposition from both sides, with the approaching marriage of David Quixano and his beloved. During the course of these developments, David, in the rhetoric of the time, delivers himself of such sentiments as these:[13]

America is God's crucible, the great Melting Pot where all the races of Europe are melting and reforming! Here you stand, good folk, think I, when I see them at Ellis

Island, here you stand in your fifty groups, with your fifty languages and histories, and your fifty blood hatreds and rivalries. But you won't be long like that, brother, for these are the fires of God you've come to—these are the fires of God. A fig for your feuds and vendettas! Germans and Frenchman, Irishmen and Englishmen, Jews and Russians—into the Crucible with you all! God is making the American.

Here we have a conception of a melting pot which admits of no exceptions or qualifications with regard to the ethnic stocks which will fuse in the great crucible. Englishmen, Germans, Frenchmen, Slavs, Greeks, Syrians, Jews, Gentiles, even the black and yellow races, were specifically mentioned in Zangwill's rhapsodic enumeration. And this pot patently was to boil in the great cities of America.

Thus around the turn of the century the melting-pot idea became embedded in the ideals of the age as one response to the immigrant receiving experience of the nation. Soon to be challenged by a new philosophy of group adjustment (to be discussed below) and always competing with the more pervasive adherence to Anglo-conformity, the melting-pot image, however, continued to draw a portion of the attention consciously directed toward this aspect of the American scene in the first half of the twentieth century. In the mid-1940s a sociologist who had carried out an investigation of intermarriage trends in New Haven, Connecticut, described a revised conception of the melting process in that city and suggested a basic modification of the theory of that process. In New Haven, Ruby Jo Reeves Kennedy[14] reported from a study of intermarriages from 1870 to 1940 that there was a distinct tendency for the British-Americans, Germans, and Scandinavians to marry among themselves—that is, within a Protestant "pool"; for the Irish, Italians, and Poles to marry among themselves—a Catholic "pool"; and for the Jews to marry other Jews. In other words, intermarriage was taking place across lines of nationality background, but there was a strong tendency for it to stay confined within one or the other of the three major religious groups, Protestants, Catholics, and Jews. Thus, declared Mrs. Kennedy, the picture in New Haven resembled a "triple melting pot" based on religious division, rather than a "single melting pot." Her study indicated, she stated, that

"while strict endogamy is loosening, religious endogamy is persisting and the future cleavages will be along religious lines rather than along nationality lines as in the past. If this is the case, then the traditional 'single-melting-pot' idea must be abandoned, and a new conception, which we term the 'triple-melting-pot' theory of American assimilation, will take its place as the true expression of what is happening to the various nationality groups in the United States."[15] The triple melting-pot thesis was later taken up by the theologian Will Herberg, and formed an important sociological frame of reference for his analysis of religious trends in American society, *Protestant-Catholic-Jew.*[16] But the triple melting-pot hypothesis patently takes us into the realm of a society pluralistically conceived. We turn now to the rise of an ideology which attempts to justify such a conception.

CULTURAL PLURALISM

Probably all the non-English immigrants who came to American shores in any significant numbers from colonial times onward—settling either in the forbidding wilderness, the lonely prairie, or in some accessible urban slum—created ethnic enclaves and looked forward to the preservation of at least some of their native cultural patterns. Such a development, natural as breathing, was supported by the later accretion of friends, relatives, and countrymen seeking out oases of familiarity in a strange land, by the desire of the settlers to rebuild (necessarily in miniature) a society in which they could communicate in the familiar tongue and maintain familiar institutions, and, finally, by the necessity to band together for mutual aid and mutual protection against the uncertainties of a strange and frequently hostile environment. This was as true of the "old" immigrants as of the "new." In fact, some of the liberal intellectuals who fled to America from an inhospitable political climate in Germany in the 1830s, 1840s, and 1850s looked forward to the creation of an all-German state within the union, or, even more hopefully, to the eventual formation of a separate German nation, as soon as the expected dissolution of the union under the impact of the slavery controversy should have taken place.[17] Oscar Handlin, writing of the sons of Erin in mid-nineteenth-century Boston, recent refugees from famine and economic degradation in their homeland, points out: "Unable to participate in the normal associational affairs of the community, the Irish felt obliged to erect a society within a society, to act together in their own way. In every contact therefore the group, acting apart from other sections of the community, became intensely aware of its peculiar and exclusive identity."[18] Thus cultural pluralism was a fact in American society before it became a theory—a theory with explicit relevance for the nation as a whole, and articulated and discussed in the English-speaking circles of American intellectual life.

Eventually, the cultural enclaves of the Germans (and the later arriving Scandinavians) were to decline in scope and significance as succeeding generations of their native-born attended public schools, left the farms and villages to strike out as individuals for the Americanizing city, and generally became subject to the influences of a standardizing industrial civilization. The German-American community, too, was struck a powerful blow by the accumulated passions generated by World War I—a blow from which it never fully recovered. The Irish were to be the dominant and pervasive element in the gradual emergence of a pan-Catholic group in America, but these developments would reveal themselves only in the twentieth century. In the meantime, in the last two decades of the nineteenth, the influx of immigrants from southern and eastern Europe had begun. These groups were all the more sociologically visible because the closing of the frontier, the occupational demands of an expanding industrial economy, and their own poverty made it inevitable that they would remain in the urban areas of the nation. In the swirling fires of controversy and the steadier flame of experience created by these new events, the ideology of cultural pluralism as a philosophy for the nation was forged.

The first manifestations of an ideological counterattack against draconic Americanization came not from the beleaguered newcomers (who were, after all, more concerned with survival than with theories of adjustment), but from those idealistic members of the middle class who, in the decade or so before the turn of the century,

had followed the example of their English predecessors and "settled" in the slums to "learn to sup sorrow with the poor."[19] Immediately, these workers in the "settlement houses" were forced to come to grips with the realities of immigrant life and adjustment. Not all reacted in the same way, but on the whole the settlements developed an approach to the immigrant which was sympathetic to his native cultural heritage and to his newly created ethnic institutions.[20] For one thing, their workers, necessarily in intimate contact with the lives of these often pathetic and bewildered newcomers and their daily problems, could see how unfortunate were the effects of those forces which impelled rapid Americanization in their impact on the immigrants' children, who not infrequently became alienated from their parents and the restraining influence of family authority. Were not their parents ignorant and uneducated "Hunkies," "Sheenies," or "Dagoes," as that limited portion of the American environment in which they moved defined the matter? Ethnic "self-hatred" with its debilitating psychological consequences, family disorganization, and juvenile delinquency, were not unusual results of this state of affairs. Furthermore, the immigrants themselves were adversely affected by the incessant attacks on their cultures, their language, their institutions, their very conception of themselves. How were they to maintain their self-respect when all that they knew, felt, and dreamed, beyond their sheer capacity for manual labor—in other words, all that they *were*—was despised or scoffed at in America? And—unkindest cut of all—their own children had begun to adopt the contemptuous attitude of the "Americans." Jane Addams relates in a moving chapter of her *Twenty Years at Hull House* how, after coming to have some conception of the extent and depth of these problems, she created at the settlement a "Labor Museum," in which the immigrant women of the various nationalities crowded together in the slums of Chicago could illustrate their native methods of spinning and weaving, and in which the relation of these earlier techniques to contemporary factory methods could be graphically shown. For the first time these peasant women were made to feel by some part of their American environment that they possessed valuable and interesting skills—that they too had something to offer – and for the first time, the daughters of these women who, after a long day's work at their dank "needletrade" sweatshops, came to Hull House to observe, began to appreciate the fact that their mothers, too, had a "culture," that this culture possessed its own merit, and that it was related to their own contemporary lives. How aptly Jane Addams concludes her chapter with the hope that "our American citizenship might be built without disturbing these foundations which were laid of old time."[21]

This appreciative view of the immigrant's cultural heritage and of its distinctive usefulness both to himself and his adopted country received additional sustenance from another source: those intellectual currents of the day which, however overborne by their currently more powerful opposites, emphasized liberalism, internationalism, and tolerance. From time to time an occasional educator or publicist protested the demands of the "Americanizers," arguing that the immigrant, too, had an ancient and honorable culture, and that this culture had much to offer an America whose character and destiny were still in the process of formation, an America which must serve as an example of the harmonious cooperation of various heritages to a world inflamed by nationalism and war. In 1916 John Dewey, Norman Hapgood, and the young literary critic Randolph Bourne published articles or addresses elaborating various aspects of this theme.

The classic statement of the cultural pluralist position, however, had been made over a year before. Early in 1915 there appeared in the pages of *The Nation* two articles under the title "Democracy *versus* the Melting-Pot." Their author was Horace Kallen, a Harvard-educated philosopher with a concern for the application of philosophy to societal affairs, and, as an American Jew, himself derivative of an ethnic background which was subject to the contemporary pressures for dissolution implicit in the "Americanization," or Anglo-conformity, and the melting-pot theories. In these articles Kallen vigorously rejected the usefulness of these theories as models of what was actually transpiring in American life or as ideals for the future. Rather he was impressed by the way in which the various ethnic groups in America were coincident with particular areas and regions, and with the tendency for each

group to preserve its own language, religion, communal institutions, and ancestral culture. All the while, he pointed out, the immigrant has been learning to speak English as the language of general communication, and has participated in the over-all economic and political life of the nation. These developments in which "the United States are in the process of becoming a federal state not merely as a union of geographical and administrative unities, but also as a cooperation of cultural diversities, as a federation or commonwealth of national cultures,"[22] the author argued, far from constituting a violation of historic American political principles, as the "Americanizers" claimed, actually represented the inevitable consequences of democratic ideals, since individuals are implicated in groups, and since democracy for the individual must by extension also mean democracy for his group.

The processes just described, however, as Kallen develops his argument, are far from having been thoroughly realized. They are menaced by "Americanization" programs, assumptions of Anglo-Saxon superiority, and misguided attempts to promote "racial" amalgamation. Thus America stands at a kind of cultural crossroads. It can attempt to impose by force an artificial, Anglo-Saxon oriented uniformity on its peoples, or it can consciously allow and encourage its ethnic groups to develop democratically, each emphasizing its particular cultural heritage. If the latter course is followed, as Kallen puts it at the close of his essay, then,[23]

The outlines of a possible great and truly democratic commonwealth become discernible. Its form would be that of the federal republic: its substance a democracy of nationalities, cooperating voluntarily and autonomously through common institutions in the enterprise of self-realization through the perfection of men according to their kind. The common language of the commonwealth, the language of its great tradition, would be English, but each nationality would have for its emotional and involuntary life its own peculiar dialect or speech, its own individual and inevitable esthetic and intellectual forms. The political and economic life of the commonwealth is a single unit and serves as the foundation and background for the realization of the distinctive individuality of each nation that composes it and of the pooling of these in a harmony above them all. Thus "American civilization" may come to mean the perfection of the cooperative harmonies of "European civiliza-

tion"—the waste, the squalor and the distress of Europe being eliminated—a multiplicity in a unity, an orchestration of mankind.

Within the next decade Kallen published more essays dealing with the theme of American multiple-group life, later collected in a volume.[24] In the introductory note to this book he used for the first time the term "cultural pluralism" to refer to his position. These essays reflect both his increasingly sharp rejection of the onslaughts on the immigrant and his culture which the coming of World War I and its attendant fears, the "Red scare," the projection of themes of racial superiority, the continued exploitation of the newcomers, and the rise of the Ku Klux Klan all served to increase in intensity, and also his emphasis on cultural pluralism as the democratic antidote to these ills. He has since published other essays elaborating or annotating the theme of cultural pluralism. Thus, for at least forty-five years, most of them spent teaching at the New School for Social Research, Kallen has been acknowledged as the originator and leading philosophical exponent of the idea of cultural pluralism.

In the late 1930s and early 1940s the late Louis Adamic, the Yugoslav immigrant who had become an American writer, took up the theme of America's multicultural heritage and the role of these groups in forging the country's national character. Borrowing Walt Whitman's phrase, he described America as "a nation of nations," and while his ultimate goal was closer to the melting-pot idea than to cultural pluralism, he saw the immediate task as that of making America conscious of what it owed to all its ethnic groups, not just to the Anglo-Saxons. The children and grandchildren of immigrants of non-English origins, he was convinced, must be taught to be proud of the cultural heritage of their ancestral ethnic group and of its role in building the American nation; otherwise, they would not lose their sense of ethnic inferiority and the feeling of rootlessness he claimed to find in them.

Thus in the twentieth century, particularly since World War II, "cultural pluralism" has become a concept which has worked its way into the vocabulary and imagery of specialists in intergroup relations and leaders of ethnic communal groups. In view of this new pluralistic emphasis, some writers now prefer to speak of the "integration" of immigrants rather than of their "assimilation."[25] However, with a few exceptions,[26] no close analytical attention has been given either by social scientists or practitioners of intergroup relations to the meaning of cultural pluralism, its nature and relevance for a modern industrialized society, and its implications for problems of prejudice and discrimination—a point to which we referred at the outset of this discussion.

CONCLUSIONS

In the remaining pages I can make only a few analytical comments which I shall apply in context to the American scene, historical and current. My view of the American situation will not be documented here, but may be considered as a series of hypotheses in which I shall attempt to outline the American assimilation process.

First of all, it must be realized that "assimilation" is a blanket term which in reality covers a multitude of subprocesses. The most crucial distinction is one often ignored—the distinction between what I have elsewhere called "behavioral assimilation" and "structural assimilation."[27] The first refers to the absorption of the cultural behavior patterns of the "host" society. (At the same time, there is frequently some modification of the cultural patterns of the immigrant-receiving country, as well.) There is a special term for this process of cultural modification or "behavioral assimilation"—namely, "acculturation." "Structural assimilation," on the other hand, refers to the entrance of the immigrants and their descendants into the social cliques, organizations, institutional activities, and general civic life of the receiving society. If this process takes place on a large enough scale, then a high frequency of intermarriage must result. A further distinction must be made between, on the one hand, those activities of the general civic life which involve earning a living, carrying out political responsibilities, and engaging in the instrumental affairs of the larger community, and, on the other hand, activities which create personal friendship patterns, frequent home intervisiting, communal worship, and communal recreation. The first type usually develops so-called "secondary relationships," which tend to be relatively impersonal and segmental; the latter type leads to "primary relationships," which are warm, intimate, and personal.

With these various distinctions in mind, we may then proceed.

Built on the base of the original immigrant "colony" but frequently extending into the life of successive generations, the characteristic ethnic group experience is this: within the ethnic group there develops a network of organizations and informal social relationships which permits and encourages the members of the ethnic group to remain within the confines of the group for all of their primary relationships and some of their secondary relationships throughout all the stages of the life cycle. From the cradle in the sectarian hospital to the child's play group, the social clique in high school, the fraternity and religious center in college, the dating group within which he searches for a spouse, the marriage partner, the neighborhood of his residence, the church affiliation and the church clubs, the men's and the women's social and service organizations, the adult clique of "marrieds," the vacation resort, and then, as the age cycle nears completion, the rest home for the elderly and, finally, the sectarian cemetery – in all these activities and relationships which are close to the core of personality and selfhood – the member of the ethnic group may if he wishes follow a path which never takes him across the boundaries of his ethnic structural network.

The picture is made more complex by the existence of social class divisions which cut across ethnic group lines just as they do those of the white Protestant population in America. As each ethnic group which has been here for the requisite time has developed second, third, or in some cases, succeeding generations, it has produced a college-educated group which composes an upper middle class (and sometimes upper class, as well) segment of the larger groups. Such class divisions tend to restrict primary group relations even further, for although the ethnic-group member feels a general sense of identification with all the bearers of his ethnic heritage, he feels comfortable in intimate social relations only with those who also share his own class background or attainment.

In short, my point is that, while *behavioral assimilation* or acculturation has taken place in America to a considerable degree, *structural assimilation,* with some important exceptions has not been extensive.[28] The exceptions are of two types. The first brings us back to the "triple-melting-pot" thesis of Ruby Jo Reeves Kennedy and Will Herberg. The "nationality" ethnic groups have tended to merge within each of the three major religious groups. This has been particularly true of the Protestant and Jewish communities. Those descendants of the "old" immigration of the nineteenth century, who were Protestant (many of the Germans and all the Scandinavians), have in considerable part gradually merged into the white Protestant "subsociety." Jews of Sephardic, German, and Eastern-European origins have similarly tended to come together in their communal life. The process of absorbing the various Catholic nationalities, such as the Italians, Poles and French Canadians, into an American Catholic community hitherto dominated by the Irish has begun, although I do not believe that it is by any means close to completion. Racial and quasi-racial groups such as the Negroes, Indians, Mexican-Americans, and Puerto Ricans still retain their separate sociological structures. The outcome of all this in contemporary American life is thus pluralism – but it is more than "triple" and it is more accurately described as *structural pluralism* than as cultural pluralism, although some of the latter also remains.

My second exception refers to the social structures which implicate intellectuals. There is no space to develop the issue here, but I would argue that there is a social world or subsociety of the intellectuals in America in which true structural intermixture among persons of various ethnic backgrounds, including the religious, has markedly taken place.

My final point deals with the reasons for these developments. If structural assimilation has been retarded in America by religious and racial lines, we must ask why. The answer lies in the attitudes of both the majority and the minority groups and in the way these attitudes have interacted. A saying of the current day is, "It takes two to tango." To apply the analogy, there is no good reason to believe that white Protestant America has ever extended a firm and cordial invitation to its minorities to dance. Furthermore, the attitudes of the minority-group members themselves on the matter have been divided and ambiguous. Particularly for the minority religious groups, there is a certain logic in ethnic communality, since there is a commitment to the perpetuation of the religious ideology and since structural intermixture leads to intermarriage and the possible loss to the group of the intermarried family. Let us, then, examine the situation serially for various types of minorities.

With regard to the immigrant, in his characteristic numbers and socio-economic background, structural assimilation was out of the question. He did not want it, and he had a positive need for the comfort of his own communal institutions. The native American, moreover, whatever the implications of his public pronouncements, had no intention of opening up his primary group life to entrance by these hordes of alien newcomers. The situation was a functionally complementary standoff.

The second generation found a much more complex situation. Many believed they heard the siren call of welcome to the social cliques, clubs, and institutions of white Protestant America. After all, it was simply a matter of learning American ways, was it not? Had they not grown up as Americans, and were they not culturally different from their parents, the "greenhorns"? Or perhaps an especially eager one reasoned (like the Jewish protagonist of Myron Kaufmann's novel, *Remember Me to God,* aspiring to membership in the prestigious club system of Harvard undergraduate social life) "If only I can go the last few steps in Ivy League manners and behavior, they will surely recognize that I am one of them and take me in." But, alas, Brooks Brothers suit notwithstanding, the doors of the fraternity house, the city men's club, and the country club were slammed in the face of the immigrant's offspring. That invitation was not really there in the first place; or, to the extent it was, in Joshua Fishman's phrase, it was a " 'look me over but don't touch me' invitation to the American minority group child."[29] And so the rebuffed one returned to the homelier but dependable comfort of the communal institutions of his ancestral group. There he found his fellows of the same genera-

tion who had never stirred from the home fires. Some of these had been too timid to stray; others were ethnic ideologists committed to the group's survival; still others had never really believed in the authenticity of the siren call or were simply too passive to do more than go along the familiar way. All could not join in the task that was well within the realm of the sociologically possible – the build-up of social institutions and organizations within the ethnic enclave, manned increasingly by members of the second generation and suitably separated by social class.

Those who had for a time ventured out gingerly or confidently, as the case might be, had been lured by the vision of an "American" social structure that was somehow larger than all subgroups and was ethnically neutral. Were they, too, not Americans? But they found to their dismay that at the primary group level a neutral American social structure was a mirage. What at a distance seemed to be a quasi-public edifice flying only the all-inclusive flag of American nationality turned out on closer inspection to be the clubhouse of a particular ethnic group – the white Anglo-Saxon Protestants, its operation shot through with the premises and expectations of its parental ethnicity. In these terms, the desirability of whatever invitation was grudgingly extended to those of other ethnic backgrounds could only become a considerably attenuated one.

With the racial minorities, there was not even the pretense of an invitation. Negroes, to take the most salient example, have for the most part been determinedly barred from the cliques, social clubs, and churches of white America. Consequently, with due allowance for internal class differences, they have constructed their own network of organizations and institutions, their own "social world." There are now many vested interests served by the preservation of this separate communal life, and doubtless many Negroes are psychologically comfortable in it, even though at the same time they keenly desire that discrimination in such areas as employment, education, housing, and public accommodations be eliminated. However, the ideological attachment of Negroes to their communal separation is not conspicuous. Their sense of identification with ancestral African national cultures is virtually nonexistent, although Pan-Africanism engages the interest of some intellectuals and although "black nationalist" and "black racist" fringe groups have recently made an appearance at the other end of the communal spectrum. As for their religion, they are either Protestant or Catholic (overwhelmingly the former). Thus, there are no "logical" ideological reasons for their separate communality; dual social structures are created solely by the dynamics of prejudice and discrimination, rather than being reinforced by the ideological commitments of the minority itself.

Structural assimilation, then, has turned out to be the rock on which the ships of Anglo-conformity and the melting pot have foundered. To understand that behavioral assimilation (or acculturation) without massive structural intermingling in primary relationships has been the dominant motif in the American experience of creating and developing a nation out of diverse peoples is to comprehend the most essential sociological fact of that experience. It is against the background of "structural pluralism" that strategies of strengthening intergroup harmony, reducing ethnic discrimination and prejudice, and maintaining the rights of both those who stay within and those who venture beyond their ethnic boundaries must be thoughtfully devised.

ENDNOTES

1. Allen Nevins and Henry Steele Commager, *America: The Story of a Free People* (Boston, Little, Brown, 1942), p. 58.
2. The phrase is the Coles'. See Stewart G. Cole and Mildred Wiese Cole, *Minorities and the American Promise* (New York, Harper & Brothers, 1954), ch. 6.
3. Maurice R. Davie, *World Immigration* (New York, Macmillan, 1936), p. 36, and (cited therein) "Letter of Benjamin Franklin to Peter Collinson, 9th May, 1753, on the condition and character of the Germans in Pennsylvania," in *The World of Benjamin Franklin, with Notes and Life of the Author,* by Jared Sparks (Boston, 1828), vol. 7, pp. 71–73.
4. *The Writings of George Washington,* collected by W.C. Ford (New York, G.P. Putnam's Sons, 1889), vol. 12, p. 489.
5. Thomas Jefferson, "Notes on Virginia, Query 8"; in *The Writings of Thomas Jefferson,* ed. A.E. Bergh (Washington, The Thomas Jefferson Memorial Association, 1907), vol. 2, p. 121.
6. *Niles Weekly Register,* vol. 18, 29 April 1820, pp. 157–158; see also Marcus L. Hansen, *The Atlantic Migration, 1607–1860,* pp. 96–97.
7. Ellwood P. Cubberly, *Changing Conceptions of Education* (Boston, Houghton Mifflin, 1909), pp. 15–16.
8. J. Hector St. John de Crèvecoeur, *Letters from an American Farmer* (New York, Albert and Charles Boni, 1925; reprinted from the 1st edn., London, 1782), pp. 54–55.
9. Oscar Handlin, ed., *Immigration as a Factor in American History* (Englewood, Prentice-Hall, 1959), p. 146.
10. Quoted by Stuart P. Sherman in his Introduction to *Essays and Poems of Emerson* (New York, Harcourt Brace, 1921), p. xxxiv.
11. See Edward N. Saveth, *American Historians and European Immigrants, 1875–1925* (New York, Columbia University Press, 1948).
12. Frederick Jackson Turner, *The Frontier in American History* (New York, Henry Holt, 1920), pp. 22–23, 190.
13. Israel Zangwill, *The Melting Pot* (New York, Macmillan, 1909), p. 37.
14. Ruby Jo Reeves Kennedy, "Single or Triple Melting-Pot? Intermarriage Trends in New Haven, 1870–1940," *American Journal of Sociology,* 1944, 49:331–339. See also her "Single or Triple Melting-Pot? Intermarriage in New Haven, 1870–1950," *ibid.,* 1952, 58:56–59.
15. Kennedy, "Single or Triple Melting-Pot? . . . 1870–1940," p. 332 (author's italics omitted).
16. Will Herberg, *Protestant-Catholic-Jew* (Garden City, Doubleday, 1955).
17. Nathan Glazer, "Ethnic Groups in America: From National Culture to Ideology," in Morroe Berger, Theodore Abel, and Charles H. Page, eds., *Freedom and Control in Modern Society* (New York, D. Van Nostrand, 1954), p. 161; Marcus Lee Hansen, *The Immigrant in American History* (Cambridge, Harvard University Press, 1940), pp. 129–140; John A. Hawgood, *The Tragedy of German-America* (New York, Putnam's, 1940), *passim.*
18. Oscar Handlin, *Boston's Immigrants* (Cambridge, Harvard University Press, 1959, rev. edn.), p. 176.
19. From a letter (1883) by Sanuel A. Barnett; quoted in Arthur C. Holden, *The Settlement Idea* (New York, Macmillan, 1922), p. 12.
20. Jane Addams, *Twenty Years at Hull House* (New York, Macmillan, 1914), pp. 231–258; Arthur C. Holden, *op. cit.,* pp. 109–131, 182–189; John Higham, *Strangers in the Land* (New Brunswick, Rutgers University Press, 1955), p. 236.
21. Jane Addams, *op. cit.,* p. 258.
22. Horace M. Kallen, "Democracy *versus* the Melting-Pot," *The Nation,* 18 and 25 February 1915; reprinted in his *Culture and Democracy in the United States,* New York, Boni and Liveright, 1924; the quotation is on p. 116.
23. Kallen, *Culture and Democracy . . . ,* p. 124.
24. *Op. cit.*
25. See W.D. Borrie *et al., The Cultural Integration of Immigrants* (a survey based on the papers and proceed-

ings of the UNESCO Conference in Havana, April 1956), Paris, UNESCO, 1959; and William S. Bernard, "The Integration of Immigrants in the United States" (mimeographed), one of the papers for this conference.
26. See particularly Milton M. Gordon, "Social Structure and Goals in Group Relations"; and Nathan Glazer, "Ethnic Groups in America: From National Culture to Ideology," both articles in Berger, Abel, and Page, *op. cit.*; S.N. Eisenstadt, *The Absorption of Immigrants* (London, Routledge and Kegan Paul, 1954) and W.D. Borrie *et al., op. cit.*

27. Milton M. Gordon, "Social Structure and Goals in Groups Relations," p. 151.
28. See Erich Rosenthal, "Acculturation without Assimilation?" *American Journal of Sociology,* 1960, 66:275–288.
29. Joshua A. Fishman, "Childhood Indoctrination for Minority-Group Membership and the Quest for Minority-Group Biculturism in America," in Oscar Handlin, ed., *Group Life in America* (Cambridge, Harvard University Press, forthcoming).

T W E L V E

Pacific Migration to the United States
Trends and Themes in Historical and Sociological Literature

Shirley Hune

HISTORICAL PERSPECTIVES AND THEIR IMPACT ON PACIFIC MIGRATION LITERATURE

The Asian Immigrant as "Invisible" or "Exceptional"

The migration of peoples from the countries and islands of Asia and the Pacific rim is but one phase of the movement of the world's population to the United States. Until the development of the field of Asian American Studies[1] over the past two decades, the major trend in U.S. immigration history has been to omit this phase, to treat it peripherally, or at best, to view the migrations from Europe and Asia as separate phenomena and not as integral parts of American civilization. A cursory glance over the general literature on immigration might lead one to conclude that either the Pacific migration never happened, that it was unimportant, or that it was too unique to be

Reprinted by permission of the author. This essay is a revised and excerpted version of a larger study, *Pacific Migration to the United States: Trends and Themes in Historical and Sociological Literature* (Washington, D.C.: Smithsonian Institution, 1977). For a critique of contemporary Asian American works through the 1970s, consult the original publication. Excerpts of the contemporary perspectives also appear in Hyung-chan Kim (ed.), *Asian American Studies: An Annotated Bibliography and Research Guide* (Greenwood Press, 1989): 237–249.

considered as part of the general history of the United States. An explanation for this major trend in immigration historiography can be found in the social backgrounds, training, and ideological perspectives of American historians. John King Fairbank, in his presidential address to the American Historical Association in December 1968, noted critically that American historians have not only been parochial and "myopic" but *ahistorical.* They have viewed America primarily in its relationship with Europe, ignoring its long interaction with East Asia and the impact of U.S.-East Asian relations on the internal development of the United States since the early 19th century (Fairbank, 1969). Elsewhere, Fairbank has suggested that the tendency to view East Asia, particularly China, as "unique" has not only limited the perspective of American historians but also led them to view U.S.-East Asian relations as "special" and different (Fairbank, 1972). Although Fairbank is concerned here with East Asia and U.S.-East Asia relations, his comment on the "myopia" of American historians sheds some light on why immigrants from East Asia have been omitted, neglected, or treated as an exceptional case in American immigration history.

This trend began as early as the late nineteenth century with the first generation of professional historians at a time when Asian immigrants had been present in the United States for forty years. The idea of the United States as a "nation of nations" is so much a part of our everyday language that it may be surprising to realize that immigration has not always been a field of study in American history. Edward Saveth in *American Historians and European Immigrants, 1875–1925* found that the first generation of academic historians paid little attention to the role immigrants played in the development of the nation. Their interests centered around politics and the uniqueness of the American nation with the subject of European immigrants as a side issue. If European immigrants were an aside, Asians were nowhere to be seen (Saveth, 1948).

By the last two decades of the nineteenth century, history had become an academic profession in the United States. The university began to train and employ historians and historians were increasingly applying the "scientific method" to the study of history (Higham, 1973). However

professional these historians believed themselves to be, their assumptions blinded them from acknowledging the place and role of immigrants in the development of the United States. These historians were generally male, Protestant, and from the middle and upper classes. They were descendants of early Anglo-Saxon stock and proud of their English heritage. Their intellectual training was intertwined with current European thought. They came to maturity in the age of Social Darwinism when racist ideology thrived on the doctrine of natural selection which justified excluding Blacks and other "inferior" races from determining their own destiny. During this same period, America received large numbers of immigrants from Southern and Eastern Europe and only a small number from Asia. Historians of that time were confident of the superiority of their origins and yet fearful of African Americans and "new" immigrants. They viewed American civilization largely as a part of Europe, albeit an exceptional extension of Western civilization.[2] As members of the ruling elite, these historians saw themselves as the guardians of that culture and civilization and hoped that the newcomers would adapt themselves to Anglo-Saxon institutions.

Although these scholars professed to be "scientific," their ideas were formulated in an age in which racist assumptions were virtually unquestioned. Also in an age of nationalism and imperialism, the United States acquired an empire in the Caribbean and Asia at this time. Historians (and political scientists) asserted that the genius of the nation could be found in the "Teutonic" origins or "germ theory" of its political institutions, practices and ideas. Anglo-Saxon peoples of the world, it was argued, were especially destined to rule. The impact on historical writing was to focus attention primarily on institutions and their "Teutonic" origins, with limited attention to the role of people in the nation's development. Immigrants, especially non-Western European peoples, were peripheral to their concerns (Saveth, 1948).

Racism and Assimilation

It was left largely to journalists and missionaries in the late nineteenth century to contribute materials on Asians.[3] An exception to this general tendency on the part of historians to ignore the presence of Asian immigrants was Hubert Howe Bancroft, who wrote several volumes on the Pacific regions.[4] His writings were, however, generally racist, reflecting the current ideology of the day. Descended from California's first families, he was a state "booster." For Bancroft, California was to be the height of Western civilization from which "the seed of Anglo-Saxon culture" would be scattered "among the retrograde nations of the south and orient."

Like others of his time, Bancroft viewed immigrants in narrow terms. While acknowledging that immigrants and Africans had contributed to America through their labor and skill, he questioned the social cost to society and saw their presence as a potential problem. He opposed assimilation of non-Anglo-Saxons, maintaining that would only debase American civilization.

Bancroft never intended for Asians to become citizens or to participate in government. He regarded Asian immigrants as aliens and thought even less of Asian women. His statement, "We want the Asiatic for our low-grade work, and when it is finished we want him to go home and stay there until we want him again," typified what the average American thought about Asians: they were available for exploitation and then discarded (Bancroft, 1912:357).[5] Bancroft's assertions were similar to those used by restrictionists in their efforts to exclude Asian immigrants during this period. Thus, while Bancroft included the Pacific migration in his history of the Far West, his biased descriptions contributed more to the support of anti-Asian movements than to scholarly work.

A second factor contributing to the "invisibility" of the Pacific migration has been the historian's belief in assimilation. By the turn of the twentieth century, the prevailing ideology held by American historians had shifted away from the theory of "Teutonic" origins to an assimilationist ideology. This belief system has had an impact on the study of immigration to this day. In a self-criticism of the profession, Rudolph Vecoli has pointed out that serious research on immigration and ethnicity had been neglected because of the overwhelming belief that each immigrant would be transformed by the environment and republican institutions into a "new" person—an American (Vecoli, 1970). From the days of J. Hec-

tor St. John de Crèvecoeur, the notion of assimilation, the process of Americanization, or the idea of the U.S. as a "melting pot" has been part of the American Creed. This was generally believed to be not only desirable but also natural and inevitable. However, it was not until the end of the nineteenth century that some "scientific" basis was found for this commonly held belief.

In 1893 Frederick Jackson Turner presented his famous paper on "The Significance of the Frontier in American History," an interpretation of American civilization that shaped the perspective of the next generation of historians and revolutionized American historiography by turning its focus inward and away from Europe. America's uniqueness grew out of the westward migration of its peoples across the expanding American frontier. The impact of settlement on the people gave them a common experience, and thus, a common identity. On the frontier peoples of different origins were molded into one. The frontier hypothesis thus lent scholarly credibility to the ideology of America as a melting pot and to the expectation that differences among Americans would soon disappear. Therefore, immigrants were not a subject worthy of serious study (Vecoli, 1970).

Turner's impact on immigration history only reinforced the trend to omit, neglect, or treat the Asian immigrant in a separate or exceptional manner. The racist ideology of the "Teutonic" origins theory had left little room for Asians to be seen in any context other than as temporary sources of labor. The frontier thesis, on the other hand, split the migration process of Europeans and Asians into two separate and distinct experiences. As American historians described it, the history of the nation followed the migration of peoples, ideas and institutions from across the Atlantic and then across the frontier. The United States, therefore, is interconnected with Europe, and its unique character is the product of the interaction of its people with their American environment. American historians ignored or overlooked the fact that peoples, ideas and institutions could come from across the Pacific; that East Asia was intimately interrelated with the history of the United States; and that the western U.S. was undergoing agricultural and industrial development that would have an impact on the entire country. As long as their eyes remained fixed on the Atlantic and the frontier, they could not explain the significance of the Asian presence in America. In this circumscribed view of the world, the Pacific migration could only be understood as atypical. For example, in the preface to her classic reference work on immigrants, Edith Abbott (1924) concluded that "the study of European immigration should not be complicated for the student by confusing it with the very different problems of Chinese and Japanese immigration" (Abbott, 1924:9).

The assimilationist and European biases in the frontier thesis further reinforced the belief in the superiority of Anglo-Saxon peoples. It appeared that the frontier experience could transform only Atlantic immigrants into Americans. There was, then, a clear distinction made between immigrants who were not only culturally, but racially, different. In a period in which the ideology of biological racism prevailed alongside that of assimilation, Asians were viewed as inferior and unassimilable. Not even the frontier or republican institutions could transform Asians into Americans.

The Twentieth Century: "Scientific" Immigration Studies

Modern immigration studies are said to have begun in 1921 with Arthur M. Schlesinger's article, "The Significance of Immigration in American History," published in the *American Journal of Sociology* (Schlesinger, 1921). Written at the end of the restrictionist movement, the article is a reappraisal of American viewpoints on immigration and immigrants. Restrictionists had stressed the contributions of Anglo-Saxons to American life and institutions. With the passage of national origins quotas in the 1920s, most Americans could assume that the immigration "problem" was over. Schlesinger's article sought to change American perspectives based on his belief that immigration should not be viewed as a "social problem" but as a "dynamic factor in America's development." He also represented a generation of American historians interested in a "new history" which was to broaden the discipline and encompass some aspects of the social sciences.

These pioneers in immigration studies, Schlesinger, George Stephenson, Thomas Blegan, Carl

Wittke and, later, Marcus Lee Hansen, were all midwesterners intimately involved in the immigrant experience as sons of Scandinavian and German immigrants (Commager, 1962:3–7). They reacted against the thinking of the first generation of professional historians of Anglo-Saxon heritage who had seen little value in the study of immigration and had generally hoped that immigrants would quickly become Americanized (i.e., conform to the Anglo-Saxon norm).

In spite of this new emphasis on "scientific" studies of immigration, American perspectives on Asians in the United States had not changed fundamentally. While the immigrant experience was now an acknowledged part of American history and civilization, it was still narrowly regarded as an experience for Europeans only. Even Schlesinger's new viewpoint ignored the existence of non-Europeans. For him, America's "national purpose" was "to create a democracy of diverse cultures" which would include the heritages of people from "every *European* background" (Schlesinger, 1921:85).

Asians were relegated to an aside in major surveys of U.S. immigration of this period. In a first attempt at a synthesis of American immigration, George Stephenson left his discussion of Asians to a separate section entitled "The Oriental Immigration." In excluding Asians from the main body of his work, Stephenson separated them from his description of the political aspects of American immigration history (Stephenson, 1926). Furthermore, Carl Wittke, who expanded Schlesinger's theme into a full length book, characterized Oriental immigration as a brief and strange interlude in the general account of the great migration to America (Wittke, 1940).

These pioneers of "scientific" immigration studies were Turnerians at heart. Although the emphasis on racial stock as a basis for determining history began to be discredited by the 1920s, the perspective of American historians remained fixed upon the Atlantic and the frontier. As a consequence of this myopia, the persistence of racism, the cultural chauvinism of immigration historians, and the concept of the frontier as a melting pot, the Pacific migration continued to be treated extraneously to the general immigrant experience, and thereby as a nonintegral part of American civilization. Perhaps Asians would just go away as Hubert Howe Bancroft hoped; but Asians remained and historical studies began to appear. Notable works in the early period are Mary Coolidge's *Chinese Immigration* (1909), Bruno Lasker's *Philipino Immigration to the Continental United States and Hawaii* (1931), and Yamato Ichihashi's *Japanese in the United States* (1932). Despite some serious shortcomings, they remain standard reference tools.

Marcus Lee Hansen, writing in the 1940s, is considered the first serious student of American immigration. Although his work altered American perspectives on immigration, Hansen reinforced certain assumptions held by earlier Euro-biased historians. Deeply influenced by Frederick Jackson Turner, he applied Turner's concept of the frontier and its influence on the development of America to that of Europe. For Hansen, the immigrant experience was not confined to the frontier, but was part of a larger phenomenon which included a European experience. He envisaged immigration not as a "problem" but as a "process" encompassing both emigration and settlement (Hansen, 1940a; 1940b). In addressing himself to the conditions and forces in Europe which contributed to the emigration of Europeans, Hansen gave the immigrant experience a broader historical perspective by relating it to events outside the United States (Spear, 1961).

While Hansen moved away from the racist assumption that there was a fundamental difference between "old" and "new" immigrants, he reinforced the belief in the exclusiveness of the experience of Atlantic immigrants. Hansen was unable to break from a Eurocentric or Eurobiased view of American history, or the Turnerian notion of American civilization in which the nation is developed in an east to west progression as people interact with the frontier. He also believed in the inevitability of assimilation. Clearly, if the immigration process was to be explained within the limitations set by Turner, then there would be no place for Asians in the development and formation of American civilization.

Despite this serious drawback, immigration historiography owes a debt to Hansen because of his stress on the "emigration" aspect of the American experience. Literature on the Asian American experience reflects this change in immigration thought. For example, Barth (1964), Hoso-

kawa (1969), Kim (1971), Conroy and Miyakawa (1972), Lyman (1974), and many others all examine the society from which Asians came and the circumstances leading to their emigration to the United States. Students of immigration thereafter asked not only who came but from where and why.

Oscar Handlin took up where Turner and Hansen left off. He followed immigrants from Europe to America and traced their settlement and adjustment patterns in urban areas (for example, see Handlin, 1951). Another product of the "new history," many of his ideas were influenced by the social science thinking of the time. Although Handlin, like Hansen, did not contribute directly to studies on Pacific migration, his work altered American perspectives on immigration which, in turn, has affected writing and research on Asians.

By the middle of this century, the idea of America as a culturally pluralistic society began to attract popular attention. Yet, the main concern of academics studying immigration remains centered around the assimilation of culturally diverse groups into the American mainstream. Handlin's work reinforced assimilationist ideology, although he views it in somewhat more complex terms. For Handlin, the immigrant group's settlement often resulted in a period of heightened group consciousness, but the process of acculturation, conflict and assimilation was inevitable. Handlin's process of immigrant adjustment incorporated the work of sociologist Robert E. Park, whose work will be discussed later in this essay. While Park suggested that immigrants as individuals pass through a cycle of rejection and accommodation before acceptance, Handlin applied this cycle of adjustment to the immigrant group and adapted Park's cycle to the study of socio-economic mobility. Handlin maintained that an immigrant group would become assimilated once it had achieved a certain stage of socio-economic mobility. With time, hard work, and the "tolerance" of their neighbors, an immigrant group could overcome even racism to achieve the American Dream (Greer, 1974, especially Part 1). He does not distinguish between racial and ethnic groups, but regards the experience of colonists, immigrants, and former slaves as essentially the same. In *The Newcomers*, he considered

Blacks from the American South and Puerto Ricans as merely the latest arrivals to share in the American experience. Responding to the need for cheap labor in the cosmopolitan cities of America, they have come to play out roles first assumed by European immigrants (Handlin, 1959). The city thus becomes Handlin's crucible for the process of assimilation.

Handlin's concept of the American immigrant experience has had enormous impact. His views of acculturation, conflict, and group mobility are a part of the contemporary perspective on immigrants found in recent studies of the Asian American experience. R.H. Lee (1960), Sung (1967), and Hsu (1971) represent examples of Handlin's influence on the process of Chinese American adaptation. Petersen (1966), and the many essays in Conroy and Miyakawa (1972), examine various aspects of Japanese American assimilation and acculturation, while Navarro (1974) discusses how newly arrived Filipinos become acculturated in America.

Handlin added a new dimension to American immigration studies. He did not confine his studies to the Atlantic migration and he also acknowledged the role that racial prejudice has played in American life (Handlin, 1957). However, Handlin's concepts rested on certain false assumptions, including the notion that racism was a temporary phenomenon of individual miseducation and misunderstanding which would soon be overcome. He assumed that Americans had an unlimited capacity for economic growth and would always find room for newcomers. This perspective of the immigrant group experience also rested on the belief that "newcomers" and other racial and ethnic groups would be accepted by earlier immigrants and allowed to share in the economic abundance of America. Thus, Handlin held out great promise for racial minorities to fully participate in the American Dream.

Far from being the "invisible" immigrants, Asians, and particularly Japanese Americans, were regarded as "exceptional" because they were a "model" minority group. In spite of the discrimination they had endured, it was argued that Asians had managed, largely through hard work and traditional culture, to overcome even racism

and attain a certain amount of socio-economic success. Under the influence of Handlin's assimilation perspective, scholarly work on Pacific migration has been concerned with what is seen as the rapid socio-economic mobility of Chinese and Japanese Americans as compared with other minority groups. Petersen has described this "anomaly" of the Japanese American experience throughout his works (1966 and 1971). R.H. Lee (1960), Sung (1967), and Hsu (1971) suggest that Chinese Americans' participation in the American Dream is within grasp if only they reach out for it. Other scholars sought to explain this unique group achievement through specific studies of Japanese and Chinese personality and culture. Thus the Pacific migration, formerly an "invisible" and unassimilable group, is now recognized for its exceptionalism. The Handlin model of group mobility, achievement and ultimate assimilation has helped support the popularly held belief of Asian exceptionalism. This exceptional "success" story (positive though it may be) has been challenged by Asian American scholars and proved lacking in evidence. (For example, Chun, 1980; Hurh and Kim, 1983; and Suzuki, 1977.)

Finally, in 1960, with Maldwyn Jones' *American Immigration,* there is a change in the interpretation of Pacific migration and all other non-European migrations (Jones, 1960). His study was the first survey to incorporate the Pacific migration into the general context of American immigration without treating it as separate or different. (It is interesting to note that Jones is a British scholar of American civilization and not a native-born American.)

In summary, the predominant trend in historical literature is the *neglect* of the Pacific migration phase of American immigration. At best, American historians have considered this phase too unusual to be considered part of the general American experience. For the most part, this perspective of Pacific migration supported by historians was influenced by their Eurocentric or Eurobiased view of the world, their racism and cultural chauvinism, and the ideology of assimilation. An important consequence of this trend in American immigration historiography has been the limited research and study of the Asian American experience. As a self-fulfilling prophecy, the absence of materials on Pacific migration contributes to the belief of its insignificance to an understanding of American civilization.

Some historians did contribute to the field of Pacific migration studies. In the next sections, I will examine two other trends in the literature — the Asian immigrant as "contribution" and the Asian immigrant as "object."

The Asian Immigrant "Great" Man or Woman as "Contribution"

A further review of the historical literature on Asians in America suggests that they have been studied in terms of what "contributions" they have made to the United States. This narrow perspective is not restricted to Pacific immigrants alone but applied to all immigrants. Although it originated at the turn of the century, this interpretation of the immigrant experience still influences the contemporary literature.

Immigration as an aspect of U.S. history was not seriously considered until the first two decades of the twentieth century. Immigrants or the children of immigrants were the first recorders of immigration history. In turning (as each generation has) to re-examine past history immigrants reinterpreted their historical role in a new but also limited perspective. Where immigrant groups had previously been either omitted from U.S. history or treated peripherally, they now become accounted for in terms of their "contribution" to the society.

During this period, a number of general portraits of predominantly European immigrant groups appeared. Each portrait emphasized the special character of its ethnic or racial stock, its cultural and intellectual "gifts" to America, and the compatibility of the group's heritage with such traditional American characteristics as love of liberty and democracy (for example, Faust, 1909; Burgess, 1913; Capek, 1920. The subtitles of these books reflect the fervor with which they wrote about their national groups). These studies generally praised the exceptional immigrant and listed the great men and women of science and the arts who had made major "contributions" to their newly adopted country.

The next generation of immigration historians considered these first works by the immigrants themselves to be amateurish. However, these immigration studies must be considered in conjunction with the period in which they appeared.

The beginning of this century was marked by a long and bitter public debate over the restriction of southern and eastern European immigrants. (Asian groups had already been substantially restricted from entry.) Many Americans, mostly of Anglo-Saxon ancestry, suspected "new" immigrants of being potential social threats to the stability of U.S. civilization because of their different cultural heritages and their low social class status. Sensitive to these generalized attacks and to continued references to them as a "problem" in American society, immigrant groups made an effort to stress their *positive* aspects as against the negative ones attributed to them by supporters of the restrictionist movement. Therefore, these first immigrant group histories were written largely by immigrants in defense of their existence in the United States. That many still relied upon the value and contribution of their racial "stock" to justify their presence suggests that racist interpretations of the development of America were still influential. Other immigrant groups which could not defend their value along racial lines because of their distinct difference from the Anglo-Saxon norms were often left with little recourse but to seek the sympathy of the American people and attempt to dispel myths and stereotypes. Under these circumstances one of the first surveys of the Asian American experience appeared. In *The Real Chinese in America* (1923), J.S. Tow (then Secretary of the Chinese Consulate General at New York) defended the presence of the Pacific migration. The purpose of the book, he stated, was "to give the general American public a fuller knowledge and a better understanding of the Chinese people in the United States."

In the decades that followed, immigration historians directed greater attention to historical methodology, but their perspective on American immigration did not change greatly. This emphasis on "contributions" is neither confined to any historical period nor is it limited to "insiders" writing the history of their own immigrant group. Contemporary materials reveal that Pacific migration literature has not escaped this trend. For example, in S.W. King's *Chinese in American Life*

(1962), Betty Lee Sung's *Mountain of Gold* (1967), Bill Hosokawa's *Nisei: The Quiet Americans* (1969) and H. Brett Melendy's *The Oriental Americans* (1972), one finds general accounts of Chinese or Japanese immigration with special references to their "contributions" to the United States. It is through such accounts that one learns of Asian American Nobel Prize winners, scientists, war heroes, academicians, artists, and other notables.

Notwithstanding the positive objectives and attributes of this distinct trend in immigration historiography, the emphasis on immigrant "contributions" has resulted in an incomplete and one-sided portrait of U.S. immigration. When the study of immigration becomes focused on a few "great" individuals and their "contributions," one learns very little about the group as a whole or the other members of the immigrant community. Similarly, when U.S. immigrants are studied with regard to what they can do for the United States vis-à-vis cultural and social accomplishments, we suffer from a dearth of information about their economic and political influence upon U.S. society. Not only were studies of the everyday existence of immigrants and their communities neglected, but we learn even less about changes in mainstream U.S. society which resulted from the presence of different immigrant groups. Therefore, while it is important to recognize the accomplishments of outstanding Asian Americans and to acknowledge the significance of Asian cuisines, art and architecture, much of the history of Asian peoples in the United States still remains to be written.

The Asian Immigrant as "Object"

A third major trend has been the tendency of historians to study what happened to Asians rather than to record what they did. This is not to suggest that all work in this area be dismissed. In fact, much of the work is outstanding. But, it is important to point out that this perspective once again has distorted Asian American history. Here Asians are portrayed primarily as passive victims rather than participating members in U.S. society. The reader can only assume after a review of the literature that Asian Americans are objects rather than the subjects of historical events. Furthermore, Asians become part of United States history only insofar as something terrible is being

done to them, and are historically ignored during all other periods.

For example, the major focus of historical research on Asians has been the various movements organized in opposition to the Pacific migration. These studies have generally fallen into two categories, the first of which relates to movements to restrict Asian immigration. Such works as Coolidge (1909), Bailey (1934), Cross (1935), Sandmeyer (1939), Daniels (1962), Saniel, ed. (1967), Hess (1974), and Saxton (1971) are among the many attempts to explain the origins of different movements to restrict Chinese, Japanese, Filipino and Indian ("Hindu") immigration to the Untied States. A second field of research has centered around the Japanese American concentration camps during World War II. McWilliams (1944), Grodzins (1956, 1966), tenBroek et al. (1954), Bosworth (1967), Girdner and Loftis (1969), and Daniels (1971 and 1975) are but a few of the numerous monographs and articles explaining the events leading up to the decision to relocate Japanese American citizens. While these works and others like them tell us much about the circumstances and the persons who opposed Asians, this approach to Asian American history ignores the Asians themselves in these most important circumstances of their lives.

SOCIOLOGICAL PERSPECTIVES AND THEIR IMPACT ON PACIFIC MIGRATION LITERATURE

Integration

After the 1920s, much of the study of American immigration was taken up by social scientists, especially sociologists. When they turned their attention to the migration phenomenon, social scientists generally focused on one particular facet—the immigrant in American society. Out of this concern grew the interest and research into the field now commonly referred to as "majority-minority" or "race and ethnic relations."

During the early part of the twentieth century, the social sciences gained new credibility with the challenges they posed to racial theories of social development. In spite of this, social scientists were constrained by their own perspectives in a manner similar to historians. First, as members of the "old" immigration, the Anglo-American world was their point of reference as well. There was a tendency, then, to view the "new" immigrant as an *outsider* – a type of stranger. Secondly, American social science thought was heavily influenced by an order-consensus or structural-functionalist ("system paradigm") approach to society. This view of society has generally been supported by those favoring the maintenance of the status quo and has often been identified with the established professionals in the social sciences (Horton, 1966).

Briefly, in this approach society is viewed as a dynamic system of many integrative parts held together in delicate balance. Changes in any of the parts may lead to a dysfunction or imbalance in the system. It is expected, though, that a new consensus would help reintegrate the parts and re-establish the equilibrium. The emphasis in this concept of society is on social stability and harmony (Armstrong, 1975; Horton, 1966).

The assumption of a "system paradigm" of American society led many social scientists to consider that the major issue of the twentieth century was the presence of so many "outsiders." How could a single nation be formed out of such a racially, ethnically and culturally varied population with a minimum of disruption and disorder? This consideration followed from the prevailing belief that only through a homogeneous society and a consensus of values could American society avoid conflict and exist in harmony. Diversity symbolized disunity and this, in turn, would weaken the viability of the American society. The solution to this potential problem appeared to be the integration of these different groups into the dominant society. Sociologists, therefore, became interested in studying not the immigrants, *per se,* but the *integration process* of the immigrant stranger into American majority society. Because social scientists defined American society largely in cultural terms, they were concerned primarily with the cultural integration or acculturation of racial and ethnic groups. Pacific migration literature has also reflected this bias. In the following section, I will examine the major social theories of integration and discuss their impact on the study and research of Asian Americans.

The Assimilationist Model and Asian Americans

The most persistent model of American integration has been that of assimilation. The idea of the United States as a melting pot had been popularly conceived and expressed long before the appearance of sociologist Robert E. Park. Historians had often relied upon the "frontier" to complete the transformation of the immigrant into an American. However, it was not until Park outlined his race-relations cycle that social scientists had a model that would explain how the melting pot would be achieved in structural terms.

According to Park, the integration of diverse peoples into the American mainstream consisted primarily of the *adjustment* of its newcomers to the dominant society. He developed a theory of intergroup relations known as the race-relations cycle to explain this process of adjustment. Park categorized stages through which races would pass: contact, conflict, accommodation, and assimilation. This process was considered to be generally applicable to all situations of intergroup relations and historical development. The cycle was evolutionary, progressive, irreversible, and inevitable. Ultimately, not only would there be an homogeneous American society but also an homogeneous world society. This concept lent scientific credibility and authority to the popularly held belief in America as a melting pot.

Park's theory reflected the influence of American anthropologists who were the first social scientists to systematically challenge the notion of racial determinism. By perceiving differences between peoples as primarily cultural rather than racial, the problem of integration became a cultural one. Therefore, the assimilation process could be seen as a course of acculturation. But, what of the situation of racially defined groups such as Asians or Blacks? How would they be integrated into the mainstream society which had historically excluded them? Racism, as viewed by Park and others in this period, was defined as prejudice and regarded primarily as a problem of attitude. It was believed that attitudes could be changed through continued intergroup contact and new information. It would follow, then, that since the race-relations cycle was inevitable and progressive, racial prejudice would be overcome in a matter of time (Park, 1950). Although Park's theory could not be proven empirically (and was occasionally contradicted by the findings of his own research team on the Pacific Coast), this concept was generally accepted by both laypeople and professionals. It has left an indelible mark on American thought with respect to immigrant and/or minority groups and their relationship with majority society (Lyman, 1973).

Park's race-relations cycle only exemplified the assimilationist bias and "system paradigm" perspective of American social scientists. His model was well received, in part, because it represented what so many people wanted. Americans were generally relieved that the diverse members of its society could be integrated with a minimum of disruption. Similarly, minority group members eager to accept the American Dream were anxious to believe that in due time racial prejudice and xenophobia would be overcome. For the time being, they overlooked some of the underlying assumptions in Park's model. In advocating integration, American social scientists assumed that the homogeneous culture and society would be basically Anglo-Saxon. They also assumed that the "outsiders" shared these values and ideals, and that they concurred with this view of U.S. society. The assimilation process was not to be a two-way process as some immigrants had hoped, for immigrant cultures were still considered inferior. Another fundamental assumption was the belief that consensus was good for America and diversity, because of its potential for conflict, was bad.

Consequently, numerous studies of the adjustment of Asian Americans as they progress towards the inevitable and idealized goal of assimilation have appeared. Gonzalo (1929) was concerned with the various stages of social adjustment for the Filipinos. Bogardus (1930) outlined a seven stage race-relations cycle and concluded that Chinese and Japanese immigrants were already well on their way to assimilation, though not without some difficulties. Filipinos (and Mexicans) he noted, were in the middle of the cycle. Ichihashi (1932) described the gradual but favorable assimilation progress of Japanese Americans while Smith (1925 and 1936) examined some of the difficulties, especially among second generation "Orientals." A study made by Fisk University in 1946, using personal interviews and life histories, illustrated some of the experiences Chinese and Japanese immigrants encountered in "adjusting" in America. R. Lee (1952) observed how Chinese Americans were rapidly adopting the cultural patterns of the dominant society, and Cheng (1953) analyzed Asian assimilation in Hawaii. These same concerns are echoed in the contemporary literature of R.H. Lee (1960) and Sung (1967), who anxiously await a more complete integration of Chinese Americans into the mainstream, while Fong (1965) focused on different aspects relating to the assimilation of Chinese college students, and a number of articles in Conroy and Miyakawa (1972) have extended the work begun by Ichihashi on Japanese American assimilation.

With the path to the new utopia in sight, social scientists were left merely to attempt to describe its coming. Thus the immigrant and/or minority group experience was examined for its stage in the race-relations cycle and the rapidity with which adjustment (i.e., assimilation) took place. Ichihashi (1932) was optimistic about the rate and state of Japanese American assimilation. R.H. Lee (1960) could not understand why Chinese Americans did not assimilate faster since she saw conditions as very favorable. Kitano (1969) found that, by and large, Japanese American adaptation followed Park's cycle to a high degree since prejudice and discrimination had been overcome to a greater extent than previously imaginable. Other social scientists directed their attention to empirical studies in an attempt to measure the changes taking place. Accordingly, Glick (1938) studied Chinese immigrants in Hawaii and noted their shifting group loyalties and increased identification with the local community as an indication of their progressive assimilation into their newly adopted society; Briggs (1954) observed Japanese American youth and concluded that, because of their close association with Caucasians, they were already well adjusted into American society; and DeFleur and Cho (1957) conducted a sample survey of urban first generation Japanese American women in an effort to measure their degree of assimilation.

Having concluded the inevitability of the assimilation process, some social scientists turned to the study of the impact of adjustment upon the immigrant's personality.

The Social Psychology of the Immigrant: The "Marginal" Asian American

Robert E. Park significantly influenced social theory relating to immigrants in a second area by suggesting that the migration process should be studied for its impact upon the personality. This opened up yet another area of research – the social psychology of immigrants. Park maintained that the acculturation process involved a psychological adjustment which took place in the *mind* of the immigrant. It was in the mind where one could best observe the "changes and fusions of cultures" and "best study . . . the processes of civilization and culture" (Park, 1928).

Park introduced the concept of the "marginal man" – a new personality type (Park, 1928:881–893). Some anthropologists had suggested that different cultures produced different personality types. Park attempted to explain the personality in terms of the social consequences which result when an individual's original culture conflicts with a new culture. The meeting of cultures through the process of migration represented an advance in the development of civilization, for new ideas and institutions were often created. However, it could also be a dislocating experience for the individual. In such a situation, whether or not an individual is a cultural or racial hybrid (product of intermarriage), he or she becomes a new personality type. This individual, as Park described it, lives and shares "intimately in the cultural life and traditions of two distinct peoples." However, one is never able to break from the past, nor is one fully accepted by the new society because of "racial prejudice." One is "on the margin of two cultures and two societies," which are "never completely interpenetrated and fused" (Park, 1928:892). Because of this internal conflict in the immigrant's mind, it was believed that the "marginal man" was apt to be an unstable character.

During the 1950s Everett Stonequist further developed the "marginal man" concept, conceptualizing it as part of a life cycle in which the individual becomes aware of one's dualism and experiences a "crisis." This crisis is a personal one which often does not take place within the first generation of immigrants. However, the second generation – the children of immigrants – are most likely to experience the personal crises of cultural conflicts. However, Stonequist was more optimistic than Park about the future of the "marginal man." Whereas Park felt that marginality might be a permanent condition, Stonequist saw some long-range positive aspects. He identified the "marginal man" among the first persons in an ethnic community to adjust to the new society and move towards complete assimilation (Stonequist, 1935, 1937).

The "marginal man" concept drew scholarly attention towards a social psychological interpretation of the immigrant/minority group experience. Assimilation (immigration adjustment) was regarded as a cultural process to be understood in social psychological terms. The Pacific migration literature reflects that emphasis on cultural conflict and personality adjustment or maladjustment. The study of the adaptation of Pacific immigrants was particularly susceptible to this interpretation of their experience in the United States, especially by Asian Americans themselves, because of the widely-held presumption that their cultural background was so different from European Americans that adjustment would be extremely difficult, though not impossible.

A survey of the literature reveals, for example, that Smith (in 1928) was concerned about the changing personality traits among second generation Asians and (by 1934) with the important role of the marginal man in Hawaii. Louis (1932) and Chang (1934) both offered programs to assist second generation Chinese Americans in their assimilation process. Rojo (1937) described how he had observed the Filipino personality changing as a result of the American experience. Many studies were made of the social psychological adjustment of Japanese Americans during the World War II camp experience. Bogardus (1943), in particular, pointed out cultural conflicts between first and second generation Japanese in the camps; and DeVos (1955) attempted to assess some general problems of maladjustments in acculturating Japanese Americans.

This interest in personality adjustment has continued to influence even contemporary literature in which cultural conflict is increasingly being studied as a major contributor to the problem of self-identification. In this regard, some of the studies have been authored by social scientists who are themselves second, third, or fourth generation Asian Americans: Sommers (1960), Fong (1965), Callao (1973), and Cordova (1973) have examined various aspects of cultural conflict, adjustment and identity crises in Asian Americans, especially among its youth, while S. Sue and D.W. Sue (1971), Maruyama (1973), and D.W. Sue (1973) have explored the concept of a distinct Asian American personality structure that is neither traditionally Asian nor American. Thus, adjustment and personality remain leading concerns in the literature, especially among Asian American social scientists.

Although Park's two concepts (the race-relations cycle and the "marginal man") have been criticized for their theoretical weaknesses and lack of empirical evidence, they nevertheless garnered wide acceptance.[6] Consequently, much of Pacific migration literature pertains to assimilation. For at least four decades, social scientists have been primarily concerned with the social integration of racial and ethnic groups into the majority society, disregarding attendant political and economic aspects. Furthermore, the emphasis upon the social psychological phase of the Asian American experience, to the neglect of all other sides of their life in the United States, continues to confuse the total picture of the Pacific migration phenomenon.

Why did the ideas of Park and others leave such a profound mark on immigration literature? These concepts were influential and deemed credible partly because they rested upon certain assumptions which American social scientists held in common. Racist ideas still persisted although they were now cloaked in cultural terms.

The exchange of a racial definition of integration for a cultural one neither lowered the structural barriers to the mainstream, nor changed racist attitudes. American social scientists assumed that there was a definable American culture, that it was constant and that it was superior to any that newcomers might bring with them. Thus, it was expected that "outsiders," being of inferior background, would adjust (assimilate) to the dominant culture. There was little or no suggestion that the majority society would have to adapt in any way. Those who did not conform (i.e., acculturate) were viewed as deviants and considered not only maladjusted but a potential threat to the social order. On the other hand, social scientists, many of whom were representative of progressive thinking, also assumed that "outsiders" would eventually be accepted by the dominant group. Underlying these assumptions was an idealized conception of American society as a culturally homogeneous population adhering to common values, which would, in turn, help ensure a stable and orderly nation.

Moreover, the emphasis on social psychological aspects of the adjustment process placed the burden of adaptation upon the individual and removed the majority society and its institutions from any responsibility for facilitating integration. Rather than fault the social structure when assimilation failed to take place, the immigrant was blamed. One suffered from cultural conflict or a dual personality. In other words, the immigrant, not society, was maladjusted. The foundation was thus laid for what William Ryan has called "blaming the victim" when assimilation was not achieved.[7] Conflict, which U.S. social scientists feared most, was confined (according to Park's and Stonequist's analyses) within the individual. All conflict was personal and occurred in the minds and souls of those individuals attempting to reap the rewards promised by the American Dream. Once conflict was *internalized,* there was little danger to the social order, or so the social scientists assumed.

One of the unfortunate consequences of this ideology was the popular acceptance of these sociological formulations, especially by racial and ethnic groups themselves. They came to blame themselves for their failure to become accepted, and felt guilty when they tried to preserve their own culture. Therefore, cultural conflict and identity crises of the psychological variety are, in part, a creation of social scientists.

Cultural Pluralism as a Model of Integration

It was not until the beginning of the 1960s that social scientists searched for an increased "understanding of the meaning and processes of 'integration' " (*Daedalus,* 1961) beyond Park's race-relations cycle. Social scientists were discovering what many Americans already knew, but some were afraid to talk about: the melting pot did not exist. Milton Gordon, for example, asserted that assimilation was a more complex process than Park could have envisioned and that it involved many sub-processes. He called for a distinction between assimilation which was "behavioral" and assimilation which was "structural." He also argued that assimilation, as many ethnic groups had come to understand it, was in reality a demand for Anglo-conformity (Gordon, 1964). At the same time, Glazer and Moynihan revealed that ethnic group identification in New York City had been maintained well into the third and fourth generations (Glazer and Moynihan, 1963). As an alternative to the assimilationist model of integration, many social scientists sought to explain this persistence of ethnicity through the concept of cultural pluralism.

As Gordon has noted, cultural pluralism was a fact in American society long before it became a theory (Gordon, 1961). The concept was first introduced by Horace Kallen in an article in the *Nation* in 1915. Writing in a period of anti-foreign hysteria and intense debate on the impact of immigrants, Kallen defended the idea of a culturally pluralistic society. He stated that America was composed of a "mosaic of peoples" with different backgrounds and heritages. This cultural variation, developed through "continuous free and fruitful cross-fertilization of its many cultures," made the U.S. great. This diversity, however, did not mean disharmony. According to Kallen, America's unity was protected by its democratic institutions, which permitted the best opportunity for people to develop and perfect themselves. Rather than eliminate differences, democracy would perfect and conserve them. Thus, a culturally pluralistic society represented a more ideal goal for America than the melting pot (Kallen, 1915).

Nevertheless, assimilationist ideology continued to dominate; not until after World War II was the notion of cultural pluralism popularly accepted and then primarily by ethnic group leaders who wanted to preserve their cultural traditions and who chafed under the pressures of Anglo-conformity. Proponents of cultural pluralism expressed the right for peoples to maintain a separate cultural identity within the confines of a common civilization. Even before it attracted the attention of social scientists, the notion of a culturally pluralistic society had influenced the writings of American immigration historians, such as Carl Wittke and Louis Adamic (for a review of the concept of ethnic pluralism in American thought, see Higham, 1975:196–230).

Social scientists embraced the concept of cultural pluralism in an attempt to re-define American society realistically rather than in its preconceived ideal. Despite these efforts the concept of cultural pluralism has not been developed much beyond Kallen's formulation (Gordon, 1961:90).

Nonetheless, many social scientists and historians have adopted cultural pluralism as an alternative conceptual model of American society. The immigrant experience is being reinterpreted in accordance with a culturally pluralistic view of America. Although assimilation remains an important theme in the literature relating to Pacific migration, this perspective has been applied to the Asian American experience as well.

For example, Melendy (1972) devoted his concluding chapters to a description of the Chinese and Japanese "joining the pluralistic society." New imagery has replaced the overworked phrases of "joining the mainstream" and the "melting pot," which were associated with the assimilationist model. Hosokawa (1969:497) likened the change in the nation from an all-American melting pot to an "all-American stew in which each of the ingredients remains identifiable." Similarly, Kitano (1969:145) believed that "the distinctive contribution of Oriental, of Mexican, of African, and many other cultures, could greatly improve the flavor of the bland American brew." He envisioned different cultural groups living side by side in harmony. Although he was later to modify his interpretation, Kitano was hopeful that the Japanese American experience had foreshadowed a new future in race relations where racial prejudice and discrimination were archaic issues.

Cultural pluralism was acceptable as an alternative model of integration because it seemed to work and was agreeable to so many people. Many white Americans suspected that assimilation, taken to its logical extent, might lead to racial amalgamation. Cultural pluralism was a preferable form of integration for members of the dominant group reluctant to accept "outsiders" because it could be interpreted as voluntary separation. Others, especially minority group members, were pleased that one could be an ethnic and still be considered an American.

Despite this shift from assimilation to cultural pluralism, social scientists had not fundamentally altered their perspective of an ideal American society. The study of immigrant and minority group integration remained a major trend in sociological thought. Well into the 1960s many social scientists still held an order-consensus approach to the study of society and continued to focus on the same problem of how to form a unified society out of a diverse (and socially unequal) population with the least amount of disturbance to the status quo. The social integration of immigrant and/or minority groups was still seen as a means of securing a stable and unified society, but social scientists were less concerned with achieving this goal through a culturally homogeneous population. They believed that adjustment could take place without Anglo-conformity. Consensus was still desired, but it was to be achieved on a new basis. Far from being viewed as a weakness in America, cultural diversity was now recognized as a strength. Not only was American civilization enriched, but the concept of cultural pluralism implied a means of reducing conflict between the dominant mainstream culture and America's many substreams, thus helping to preserve the status quo. Unity and harmony were to be achieved by a common allegiance to values other than cultural forms, namely, the American economic system and the American way of life.

In summary, sociological thought on the immigrant in America since the 1920s has been heavily influenced by a "system paradigm" perspective of American society. Social science research in the fields of immigration and majority-minority relations has been constrained by this view. The predominant trend in sociological literature has centered upon the integration of minority groups into the majority society and the social psychological adjustment of the "outsider." This one-sided interpretation of the immigrant/minority group experience in the United States is reflected in the literature on the Asian American experience.

During the past two decades the emergence of ethnic studies on American campuses has provided the scholarly opportunity to correct many of the omissions, distortions, and biases in the historical and sociological literature relating to the minority group experience. Space does not permit me to do justice here to the impact of the establishment of Asian American studies on research and scholarship. The following is merely suggestive. Historians have taken a bottoms-up (non "great man or woman") perspective and begun to retrieve a buried past using neglected archival sources. The new interpretation finds Asian Americans to be creative and dynamic participants in American history. For example, there are major studies on the significant role of Asian Americans in California's agricultural history (Chan, 1986; and Lukes and Okihiro, 1985). Daniels (1988), Ichioka (1988), and Jensen (1988) provide the fullest and most balanced studies to date of Chinese and Japanese immigrants since 1850, the Issei generation, and Asian Indian immigrants respectively. Ronald Takaki (1989), using the voices of Asian Americans through their personal testimonies, has synthesized the histories of all the Asian American groupings into a single integrative narrative. Recent studies on Asian American women (Asian Women United of California, 1989) and Vietnamese Americans (Freeman, 1989) also give voice to individual and collective experiences.

Asian American social scientists, like their historian counterparts, have also turned their attention to the political and economic dimensions of the Asian American experience. One notable study is L. Cheng and E. Bonacich's *Labor Immigration under Capitalism* (1984) which develops a theory of labor migration within a global framework. Research has expanded into all facets of Asian American life – past and present – such as education, economic enterprises, women and work, marriage and family, political participation, and much more. Scholars are exploring the extent to which ethnic identities and organizations are maintained. At the same time new social formations have been created which are distinctly Asian American. In the field of "majority-minority relations," Asian communities in the U.S. have yet to be assimilated structurally. What remains to be explored in detail are the ways in which the majority structure has been transformed not only economically, but politically and culturally by the presence of Asians and others.

For current developments in Asian American

studies, consult *Amerasia Journal* and the anthologies of the Association for Asian American Studies entitled *Reflections on Shattered Windows,* edited by Gary Y. Okihiro et al. (1988); *Frontiers of Asian American Studies,* edited by Gail M. Nomura et al. (1989); and *Asian Americans: Comparative and Global Perspectives,* edited by Shirley Hune et al. (1990).

ENDNOTES

1. For an assessment of the current place of Asian American Studies in higher education, see Shirley Hune, "Opening the American Mind and Body: The Role of Asian American Studies," *Change* (Nov./Dec. 1989):56–63.

2. Interestingly, Joseph S. Roucek (1969) has argued that American historians have also been biased against Central and Eastern Europe. These areas have never been considered part of Western civilization. This opposition has been reflected not only in the historical and social science literature, but in U.S. immigration policy as well.

3. For example, see Charles Morley's translation of Henryk Sienkiewicz's report, "The Chinese in California" (Morley, 1955). Mark Twain also made some acute observations in Clemens, 1972, especially pp. 350–355. Issues of *The Overland Monthly* contain many articles by missionaries and clergymen about Chinese living in the United States.

4. For additional details on Bancroft's writings on Asians, see Bancroft, 1888; 1890; 1912.

5. More recently, this concept has become institutionalized into U.S. and Western European immigration policy. One might look at the U.S. bracero program with Mexico, the temporary workers programs, or, in Western Europe, the present day Guest Worker contract system.

6. For an excellent critique of Park's race-relations cycle and its impact on race relations theory in the context of Black America, see Lyman, 1973. Park's "marginal man" concept has been re-evaluated by Goldberg, 1941; Green, 1947; and Golovensky, 1952.

7. William Ryan has argued with this tendency on the part of social scientists to find fault with the "victim" rather than the social structure developed, though unintentionally, to rationalize maintenance of the status quo. By this, they distort social reality and oppose fundamental social change (Ryan, 1971).

T H I R T E E N

The Ethnic Miracle

Andrew M. Greeley

The neighborhood is a 10-square-block area with almost 14,000 people, an average of 39.8 inhabitants per acre—three times that of the most crowded portions of Tokyo, Calcutta, and many other Asian cities. One block contains 1,349 children. A third of the neighborhood's 771 buildings are built on "back lots" behind existing structures; the buildings are divided into 2,796 apartments, with a ratio of 3.7 rooms per apartment. More than three quarters of the apartments have less than 400 square feet. Tenants of the 556 basement apartments stand knee-deep in human ex-

Reprinted with permission of the author from *The Public Interest* 45 (Fall 1976), pp. 20–36.

crement when even moderate rainstorms cause plumbing breakdowns. Garbage disposal is a chronic problem—usually, trash is simply dumped in the narrow passageways between buildings. Nine thousand of the neighborhood's inhabitants use outdoor plumbing. The death rate is 37.2 per thousand per year.

These are the poorest of the poor people, making less than three quarters of the income of nonminority-group members in the same jobs. The rates of desertion, juvenile delinquency, mental disorder, and prostitution are the highest in the city here. Social disorganization in this neighborhood, according to all outside observers—even the sympathetic ones—is practically total and irredeemable.

Blacks? Latinos? Inhabitants of some Third World city? No—Poles in Chicago in 1920.

The neighborhood is still there. You drive in from O'Hare airport and see the towering spires of St. Mary of the Angels, St. Stanislaus Kostka, and Holy Trinity. If you turn off at Division Street you will see the manure boxes are gone, and so are the backyard buildings, the outdoor plumbing, the sweatshops over the barns, the tuberculosis, the family disorganization, the violence, and the excessive death rates.

For the most part, the Poles are gone too. Some of them remain, sharing a much more pleasant (and brightly painted) neighborhood with Puerto Ricans. Where have the Poles gone? Farther northwest along Milwaukee Avenue, even out into the suburbs—they are now a prosperous middle class. How have they managed to make it, this most despised of all the white immigrant groups? It is no exaggeration to say that no one really knows, and that the success of the southern and eastern European immigrant groups who frantically crowded into the Untied States before the First World War is as unexplained as it is astonishing. Indeed, rather than to attempt an explanation, many Americans—including some from those very same ethnic groups—prefer to deny the phenomenon of ethnic success.

Yet the "ethnic miracle" is one of the most fascinating stories in the history of the United States, an American success story, an accomplishment of the "system" in spite of itself; and while the "ethnic miracle" does not necessarily provide a model for later groups (in fact, it almost

certainly does not), it does offer insights into how American society works that social-policy-makers can ill afford to ignore.

"SOCIAL DISORGANIZATION"?

The neighborhood I described is called the "Stanislowowo" after St. Stanislaus Kostka, its parish church. At one time, it was the largest Catholic parish in the world (40,000 members) in the second largest Polish city in the world. Nobody in the United States between 1900 and 1920 did its parishioners any favors. In five of the years before the First World War, more than one million foreign immigrants poured into the country. They were ignorant, illiterate, and dirty; they spoke little English if any at all; their families, the sociologists of the time assured us, were chronically "disorganized." They had no tradition of freedom and responsibility; they lacked political maturity. They were a bad bet to assimilate into American society.

Was there poverty and suffering in the Stanislowowo and neighborhoods like it? That was largely the fault of the immigrants themselves, Americans were told by their elites. The Dillingham Commission on immigration assured the rest of the country that the Italians were inherently disposed to criminal behavior and that the Polish family lacked stability—both groups were racially inferior. The walls of restrictive immigration legislation were quickly erected after the war to end immigration. Large-scale "Americanization" campaigns were begun to try to teach these illiterate peasants the virtues of good Americans, and there was great hope that the public high schools would mold the children of the immigrants (the parents were beyond hope) into good, loyal, dutiful citizens.

There were no quotas, no affirmative action, no elaborate system of social services, and, heaven knows, no ethnic militancy (although it need not follow that there should not be these things for the more recent immigrants to the big cities of the United States). There was no talk of reparation, no sense of guilt, no feelings of compassion for these immigrants. The stupid, brutal, but pathetic heroes of Nelson Algren's novels were about as much as most Americans recognized; "Scarface" and "Little Caesar" of the motion pictures were taken to be typical of the Italians who got beyond street cleaning, ditch digging, garbage collection, and waiting on tables. It is safe to say that in the 20th century, no urban immigrants have been so systematically hated and despised by the nation's cultural and intellectual elites. The stereotypes may be more sophisticated now, but they still portray the ethnics as hateful and despicable. Stanley Kowalski has been replaced by Don Corleone, but both still represent the white ethnic as a bluecollar, racist, hard-hat, chauvinistic "hawk"—even though available statistical evidence does not support the myth of the Godfather or the bigot, and lends no credence to the ethnic joke.

Closely related to the thesis of the racial inferiority of the eastern and southern European immigrants was the theory of their cultural inferiority. "Social disorganization" was the explanation of the plight of the Stanislowowians offered by the "Chicago school" of sociology. The cultural values of the immigrants were not able to absorb the shock of the immigration experience and the resultant confrontation with the more "modern" values of the host society. Crime, generational conflict, family disorganization, prostitution, and juvenile delinquency were the effects of this unequal meeting of a peasant and a modern culture. Several generations of scholars, administrators, and social workers were raised on such scholarly books as *The Gang, The Gold Coast and the Slum,* and *The Polish Peasant in Europe and America*—which were in whole or in part about the Stanislowowo; much of the reform legislation of the 1930s was designed from that perspective. The problem with the poor was not their poverty but their "social disorganization" and "alienation." Fortunately for the ethnics, they stopped being poor before the reformers could set up high-rise public housing and dependency-producing welfare legislation to "undisorganize" them.

Across the Chicago River from "St. Stan's" is the infamous Cabrini-Green high-rise public housing project, one of the most evil things that good intentions have every produced—a monstrosity that causes the very "social disorganization" it was designed to eliminate. It is a slum far worse than the author of *The Gold Coast and the Slum* could have imagined, and while the death rate may not be as high as it was in the Stan-

islowowo in 1901, the human demoralization in Cabrini-Green is far worse. (*Cooley High* of movie fame was once the parochial high school for St. Stan's.) If contemporary welfare, urban renewal, and public housing legislation had existed a half century ago, the Poles might still be poor, and sociologists might still be writing books about how the Polish family structure—one of the strongest in America—is "disorganized."

One need not conclude that there ought to be no government intervention to help and protect the poor. On the contrary, the "ethnic miracle" might have happened more quickly if the government had intervened to prevent discrimination and to facilitate the rise out of poverty. But the "ethnic miracle" at least raises questions as to whether social legislation would be more effective if it were to respect the culture and family life of the poor and fight poverty directly, rather than with most useless attempts to correct "alienation" and "social disorganization." There obviously are individuals and families so badly traumatized by either poverty or misguided efforts to "unalienate" them (or combinations of both) that they cannot cope with problems or urban living without help from society. But the "ethnic miracle" suggests that such help should be aimed at making them think and act not like psychiatrically oriented social workers but rather like the more successful members of their own cultural community.

A half century ago, the "disorganization" models of the "Chicago school" of sociology looked like a big change from the biological racism of the Immigration Commission. In retrospect, and in light of the "ethnic miracle," one is permitted to wonder if in fact the theory of "social disorganization" was not a more subtle but equally pernicious form of "cultural racism"—and one not absent by any means from the reform legislation of the 1960s.

EXPLANATION FOR SUCCESS

The 1920s and 1930s were bad times for the immigrants and their children. The fierce nativism of the 1920s and the grim and frustrating Great Depression of the 1930s kept them pretty much in the poverty of the immigrant neighborhoods. Only a few managed to claw their way out into middle-class respectability. But in the three decades since the end of the Second World War, an extraordinary economic and social phenomenon has occurred: The ethnics have made it. The Italians are now the third richest religio-ethnic group in American society—second only to Jews and Irish Catholics—and the Poles earn almost $1,000 a year more than the average white American in metropolitan areas of the North. In the middle 1940s, the curve of college attendance for young people for both Italians and Poles began to swing upward, so that by the 1960s, Poles and Italians of college age were *more* likely to attend college than the national average for white Americans.

Without anyone's noticing it, those who were doomed to be failures by their race, religion, language, and family backgrounds have now succeeded. Few of them are wealthy, some are still poor; but on the average their incomes are substantially higher than those of other white Americans living in the same cities and regions of the United States. Many Americans reject in principle the possibility of such a miracle; some of the ethnic leaders themselves (in a perhaps unintentional ethnic joke) vigorously deny the success of their own people; yet the data are beyond any reasonable doubt. In a very short space of time, the length of one generation, more or less, the American dream has come true; and some of the people who were children in the Stanislowowo in 1920 have lived to see and to enjoy the achievement of their dream. Even the Stanislowowo has changed for those who remain. The well fed, neatly dressed, scrupulously clean children who troop out of St. Stanislaus Kostka on a spring afternoon—grandchildren, perhaps, of the women who worked 60 hours a week in sweatshops filled with the stench of manure—are clearly the offspring of an affluent society.

There is doubtless much wrong with the United States of America, and we will doubtless hear all about it in the course of the 200th anniversary of the republic; but sometimes things have gone well—despite almost conscious efforts to make them go badly. The success of the eastern and southern European immigrant groups at the turn of the century is one of America's success stories. The achievements of the Jews have been well known for some time; only recently

have we discovered that the Italians and the Poles have also done remarkably well. We do not like to admit it. Very few agencies or scholars, whose responsibility it is to study and understand American society, show any interest at all in the extraordinary success story of those against whom the immigration acts of 1920 were directed. It seems that we couldn't care less about finding an explanation.

Perhaps it was the public school—maybe good, solid American education undid the work of a thousand years of oppression and misery. The evidence, however, suggests the opposite. The success of the Polish and the Italians seems to have come *first* in income, then in education, and finally in occupation (and, as we shall see later, they are still impeded somewhat in occupational achievement).[1]

The few scholars who pay any attention to immigration have begun to wonder whether the conventionally understood progression from education through occupation toward economic success is all that helpful a model. Among the Asian immigrants to the United States, and among the Sephardic Jews in Israel, income parity seems to come before educational and occupational parity. In the Sephardic families, for example, with everyone working—husband, wife, and children—equality of family income with the Ashkenazics has already been achieved, although educational and occupational parity lag behind. It would seem very likely that most immigrant groups must first achieve some kind of basic financial success, and only then can they exploit the advantages of educational and occupational mobility and concomitant opportunities for even more dramatic income achievement.

However patriarchal the family structures may have been, the women of the ethnic immigrants went to work from the beginning—long before it became an upper-middle-class fashion. The income of many wage earners in a family no doubt provided an economic base for the ethnics to make their initial breakthrough—which occurred, perhaps, sometime in the early 1950s. (Data on neighborhood concentration of various ethnic communities indicate that the Poles finally began to move out from the center of the city at that time.) But by 1970, the women in Polish and Italian families were no more likely to have jobs than their nonethnic counterparts in the large cities of the North. So the income achievement of the southern and eastern European Catholics cannot be explained by multiple wage earners in the family – though there is a possibility that many of the men and some of the women may also have second and third jobs.[2]

EDUCATION AND INCOME MOBILITY

The mean education of Polish, Italian, and Slavic Catholics ("Slavic" means non-Polish eastern Europeans) is substantially below the national white average of 11.56 years. The Poles and the Italians have little more than 11 years of education, the Slavs fall under 11 years (Table 1). However, when one looks at educational achievement *given parental educational level,* the Catholic ethnics have higher academic achievement than do British Americans; indeed it is higher than anyone else in the country save for the Jews – and the Italians have an even higher achievement than Jews.

Furthermore, if one considers college attendance by the various age cohorts (an indication of educational decisions made by an ethnic collectivity at a time when a given cohort was of college age), one can see that the slope of college attendance for the three southern and eastern

European ethnic groups turned sharply upward in the 1940s; by the 1960s, it had crossed the national average.[3]

While Irish Catholics are not significantly different from British Protestants in occupational achievement, the three more recent Catholic ethnic groups were substantially beneath the national average in occupation and did not make up the difference even when parental education and their own education was taken into account. In order words, the Polish, Slavic, and Italian Catholics were not getting the occupational prestige to which their education seemed to entitle them in comparison with British Protestants.

However, despite their lower occupational achievement, the Catholic ethnic groups (save for the Slavs) earn more money than their British counterparts, and when the pertinent background variables are taken into account these differences become statistically significant. Indeed, the net advantage of Italians over British Protestants in income is higher even than that of the Jews. In other words, while they may not get the kind of jobs their education entitles them to, the Catholic ethnics seem to make more money than their occupational level entitles them to. On the face of it, it would appear that, like Avis, they try harder (Table 2).[4]

In sum, eastern and southern European Cath-

TABLE 1 *Education and Religio-Ethnicity*

Religio-Ethnic Group	Years of Education
Jewish	13.9
Irish Catholic	12.8
British Protestant	12.41
German Catholic	11.59
National white average	11.56
German Protestant	11.34
Scandinavian Protestant	11.32
Polish Catholic	11.11
Italian Catholic	11.07
Irish Protestant	10.95
"American" Protestant	10.93
Slavic Catholic	10.84

Source: National Opinion Research Center. (Used by permission.)

TABLE 2 *Real Family Income and Religio-Ethnicity*

Religio-Ethnic Group	1974 Income
Jewish	$14,577
Irish Catholic	13,451
German Catholic	12,543
Italian Catholic	12,473
Polish Catholic	12,257
British Protestant	12,208
National average for whites	11,892
German Protestant	11,500
Slavic Catholic	11,499
Scandinavian Protestant	11,284
Irish Protestant	10,714
"American" Protestant	10,572

Source: National Opinion Research Center. (Used by permission.)

olics do more with their parents' education in terms of their own education than do other Americans, and they also do more with their occupation in terms of income earned than do other Americans. However, they apparently still are not able to convert education into the same level of occupational prestige as that of Jews and British Protestants.

A word should be said in passing about a slightly earlier "ethnic miracle," that of the Irish Catholics, who are the richest, best educated, and most prestigious occupationally of any gentile religio-ethnic group—the comparison again being made with their appropriate counterparts, those living in metropolitan regions in the North. Irish-Catholic college attendance for those of college age surpassed the national average as long ago as 1910, and has remained substantially above the average ever since, passing even the Episcopalians in the 1960s. The Irish Catholic income advantage over British Protestants is $1,243 a year (trailing behind the $2,369-a-year advantage of Jews). Many of those who are willing to admit that the Poles and Italians may have achieved rough parity with the rest of the country find the spectacular success of Irish Catholics almost impossible to swallow.

There may be an important social policy hint in the apparent primacy of income in the "assimilation" of the early 20th-century immigrants. Subject to much more careful investigation, *one might take it as a tentative hypothesis that the school is a rather poor institution for facilitating the upward mobility of minority groups—until they first acquire some kind of rough income parity.* The naive American faith that equality of education produces equality of income seems to have been stood on its head in the case of the ethnics. For them, better income meant more effective education.[5]

Nor did the public schools play the critical "Americanization" role that such educators as Dr. James B. Conant expected them to play in the 1940s and 1950s. Even taking into account parents' education and income, the most successful of the ethnics—educationally, occupationally, and economically—went to parochial schools, and they did so at a time when the schools were even more overcrowded than they are today, staffed by even less adequately trained teachers, and administered by an even smaller educational bureaucracy than the very small one that somehow manages to keep the parochial schools going today. Again, a social policy hint: Maybe what matters about schools for a minority group is, as my colleague Professor William McCready has remarked, that "they are *our* schools" (whoever "we" may be).

THE LEGACY OF THE IMMIGRANTS

So one must still face the puzzle: Despite the virtually unanimous opinion of educated Americans a half century ago, the children and the grandchildren of eastern and southern European immigrants have achieved not only economic equality but economic superiority, on the average, in the United States. They were not supposed to be able to do it; to many people it is incredible that they have done it; and to almost everyone the explanation of their success is obscure. Now we see that the ethnics in the quarter century between the end of the Second World War and the end of the Vietnamese War did exactly what the Jews had done in the previous quarter century—and with apparent ease.

How did they manage it? The immigrants themselves were ambitious. Perhaps they were the enterprising and courageous young people in their own societies—and young they were. When we see movies like *Hester Street,* many of us are astonished to discover that the immigrants from eastern and southern Europe were disproportionately young, and either unmarried or just recently married. We all have a recollection of an old grandparent whom we knew during childhood, and without giving the matter much thought, we tend to imagine the immigrants themselves as old—forgetting that the old *babushka* or *mamacita* was once as young as we were.

The immigrants came from a Europe which, as one American historian has remarked, "invited desertion." The population expansion of the middle 19th century had created a land-hungry peasant class for whom there was no room either on the farms or in the cities. They came to the United States seeking the "good life," the kind of life that owning land made possible. They were fully prepared to work hard; indeed, a life of anything but hard work was beyond their comprehension. They would work hard to make money. "All the Italians want is money," remarked an observer around 1910, and like devout practitioners of the Protestant ethic, they would sacrifice to save as much money as they could. In 1905, when Poles were still pouring into the city of Chicago, 15 per cent of the money in Chicago savings-and-loan institutions was already in Polish-owned associations, a remarkable achievement for people who were scarcely off the boat. Credit buying was taboo; "cash money" paid for everything. Desperately poor people themselves, with scores of generations of poverty behind them, the immigrants could imagine no other way to live besides scrimping, sacrificing, saving. America did them no favors, gave them no special treatment, in fact discriminated against them, forced them into the most menial occupations and the most miserable housing, and exploited them through the most corrupt political structures in the country. Americans hated them, despised them, condemned them, and eventually tried to bar their relatives from joining them; they joked about them, stereotyped them, and tried to change them into "good Americans" by making them ashamed of their own heritages.

The Poles and the Italians, like the Irish and the Jews before them, bitterly resented such treatment, but they did not grow angry at the United States, for even though it did them no favors, it still provided them with two things they would never have had in the old country: personal freedom and the opportunity to convert the hard work they took for granted into economic progress. In the old country, hard work got you nothing; in the United States it got you, or at least your children or their children, a chance.

Hard work, saving, sacrifice – such is a tentative explanation of the "ethnic miracle." Ironically, the Catholic ethnics turned out to be very good at these "Protestant" and "American" traits that the Dillingham Commission thought they could never learn. To work hard, to save, to be ambitious for oneself and one's children – the immigrants needed no "Americanization" to learn that way of life. They came here with a dream; it was not that they expected something for nothing, but rather that their hard work would earn them something. For some of them, for many of their children, and for most of their grandchildren the dream came true.

Is that how it happened? It would seem so, though until much more careful study of the history of immigrant families is done, we will not know for sure. And it should be done in the relatively near future, while some of the immigrants and their oldest children are still alive to be interviewed. But curiously enough, many Americans, including ethnics like Michael Novak, are much more eager to believe that the American dream has not come true for the ethnics. If it hasn't, then there is nothing to explain.

In the process of economic achievement, have the ethnics "assimilated"? Have they absorbed the values and beliefs and behavior patterns of the host culture? To begin with, they came with many values in common. They were, after all, products of the same white-European, Judaeo-Christian heritage. They learned to speak English quickly, they wore the same clothes, listened to the same radio and television programs, read the same newspapers; and yet a remarkable diversity of values, attitudes, styles, opinions, and behavior has persisted. Affection and authority, for example, are recognizably different in Jewish, Italian, Polish, and Irish families, as are the styles with which they approach politics, the ways in which they consume alcohol, and the ultimate views they hold about human nature and the nature of the universe.

ETHNICITY AND AMERICAN CULTURE

Furthermore, these differences do not seem to diminish with the number of generations ethnics have been in the United States or with the amount of education they have had. In a loose, pluralistic society like the United States, economic success and rather harmonious adjustment to other groups can be achieved while still maintaining a partially distinctive culture. Indeed, such a distinctive culture can be maintained without having to be self-conscious about it. The Irish propensity for politics and alcohol, for example, and the Polish propensity to vote (Poles have the highest voting rates of any American religio-ethnic group) are not affected by ethnic self-consciousness or militancy. The anxiety of the Dillingham Commission and its nativist successors about whether diversity threatened America's "common culture" missed the whole point: In America the common culture validates diversity in theory, if not in practice. You can be anything you want – religiously, culturally, stylistically – so long as you are committed to the fundamental political principles of the republic.

Ethnicity is not a way of looking back to the old world. Most of the immigrants were only too happy to get the hell out of it. Ethnicity is rather a way of being American, a way of defining yourself into the pluralistic culture which existed before you arrived. The last thing in the world the new ethnic upper-middle class wants is to define themselves out of the common American culture. Why should they? America may have done them no favors, but it still has been better to them than any society their families ever knew.

So the militant ethnic somewhere out there in "middle America" – hard hat on his head and gun in his hand, ready to tear society apart by resisting the advances of the nonwhite immigrants – is almost entirely a fiction of the imagination of liberals and leftists in the media and the academy. The ethnic may not always like some of the things he sees and hears on television, but his standard of living has doubled at least in the last quarter century, so he is not angry at the "American way"; he is not about to do anything to endanger his still precarious respectability and affluence. He may rejoice that the black activism of the 1960s has legitimated his somewhat more explicit and conscious pride in heritage, but the "ethnic revival" or the "new ethnic militancy" is largely another fiction of the liberal imagination.

Nor has the ethnic turned to the right. He is neither a "rugged individualist" nor a political reactionary, as many left-liberal commentators would so dearly like to believe. On social legislation, the Italian, Polish, and for that matter, Irish Catholics are still left of center, still members of the New Deal coalition. They did not disproportionately defect from the Democratic party to vote against George McGovern, nor were they strong supporters of George Wallace in the 1968 Presidential election. The myth of the massive Polish vote for Wallace is so powerful that it is practically impossible to debunk; yet the Poles were the most likely of all gentile groups to vote for Hubert Humphrey, and substantially less than the six percent non-Southern vote for Wal-

lace was recorded among Polish Catholics. It would surely be inaccurate to think of the children, grandchildren, and great grandchildren of the ethnics as left-wing liberals or militant integrationists (most militants seem to live in the suburbs), but on virtually every political and social issue facing the country today, the ethnics are either at the center or to the left of it. Their Irish coreligionists are either close to or just behind the Jews on most measures of liberalism. I do not expect such data to be believed, because too many people have too much emotional energy invested in the opposite opinion. The data, nevertheless, are impossible to ignore.

So the "ethnic miracle" was accomplished without the complete loss of values or family structures – and without a right-wing backlash either. Indeed it was accomplished without any notable desertion from the Democratic party. The Stanislowowians and their children and grandchildren apparently made it despite their Polish values and family structure.

But is the word "despite" appropriate? Might there be a possibility that there was something in the culture of the immigrant that actually facilitated the "ethnic miracle"? Preliminary but sophisticated research conducted both at the Department of Labor and the National Bureau of Economic Research (NBER) suggests that Catholics and Jews are more successful in American society than Protestants because of some special factor at work in their early childhood – perhaps a closer and more intense attention from parents. As Thomas Juster of the NBER observes, "Economists and other social scientists have recently begun to pay close attention to the possible role of preschool investments in children by parents as it affects subsequent educational attainment . . . [and to the] possible influence on earnings of different amounts of parental time spent with preschool or school-age children. . . . Taking account of family background factors like father's and mother's education and occupation, variables for both Jewish and Catholic religious preference have a significant (positive) impact on reported earnings relative to respondents' reporting of Protestant preference. . . . Plausible hypotheses are that they reflect differences in the cultural background to which the respondents were exposed during formative years or differences in the quality or quantity of parental time inputs. . . ."

Not only the Dillingham Commission but even the Protestant ethic has been stood on its head; the familial culture of the ethnics, their stubborn differences in family values, may well have turned out to be an economic asset. In the absence of further research, such a possibility will remain an intriguing speculation.[6]

STATUS VERSUS INCOME

Is all well then for the ethnics? Not quite. Their educational mobility is the highest in America, and their income achievement goes beyond what one would expect, given their education and occupation. However, they do not achieve the occupational status appropriate for their education.

Interestingly enough, this discrepancy occurs at the upper end of the educational and prestige hierarchies. Poles and Italians do as well in occupational prestige as anyone else if they do not go to college. However, among those who have attended college, Poles and Italians have notably lower occupational-prestige scores. For those who attended college, the "cost" of being Polish or Italian is about one-third as high as the cost of being black, and more than half that of being Spanish-speaking.

How can one explain this underrepresentation of the college-educated ethnics in the occupational-prestige levels to which their education should entitle them? In the past, many social scientists would have attributed the difference to a lack of energy, or ambition, or "need achievement" among the ethnics. However, the considerable economic achievement of the ethnics makes this explanation implausible. Others would suggest that the ethnics are more likely to devote psychic energy to income than to prestigious occupations – to become insurance brokers, for example, instead of college professors.

James Coleman and his colleagues asked the same question in their study of how blacks and whites maximize their resources in obtaining jobs. Using a technique called "canonical correlations," they concluded that there is a tendency for blacks to seek income in jobs, and whites to seek

status. It would appear that British Protestants, Irish Catholics, and Polish Catholics follow exactly the same pattern of "investing" their education into status and income as do Coleman's whites (indeed, to almost the same numerical weights). To paraphrase Coleman, the status attributes of jobs attract British, Irish, and Polish ethnics; the income attributes of jobs attract Italians and Jews. The occupational disadvantage of the Italians relative to their education may be a result of an "overinvestment" in income achievement, which parallels that of the Jews. (The Jews have higher occupational status than their education "entitles" them to, but they achieve even higher income than their occupation "entitles" them to.) However, no such strategy exists for the Poles and the Irish, and the substantial underrepresentation of college-educated Poles and the moderate underrepresentation of college-educated Irish Catholics in higher prestige positions cannot be explained by a differential strategy. Thus the question of discrimination must necessarily remain open, at least for these groups.

Whatever the explanation – and much more careful research than is likely to be done would be required for certainty – it is a matter of everyday observation that Italian, Polish, and even Irish Catholics are largely absent from the world of the elite private universities, the large foundations, the national mass media, the big financial institutions (as opposed to manufacturing corporations), and certain of the intellectually oriented government agencies. At a national meeting concerned with the lack of women and nonwhite scholars this was attributed to the "intellectual inferiority produced by Catholic religious belief." Women and blacks, I was told, are absent because of discrimination, Catholic ethnics because their religion interferes with intellectual achievement. This explanation was offered with a straight face and obvious sincerity.

In fact, since 1960 Catholics have not been underrepresented in those groups pursuing academic careers, finishing dissertations, publishing articles, or even obtaining tenured appointments at the major state universities. The myth of Catholic intellectual inferiority simply will not stand up to examination in the light of valid empirical evidence – at least not for Catholics who are under 35, presumably the grandchildren of the immigrants. (Given where the eastern and southern European immigrants began, what is surprising is not that their children did not become scholars in proportionate numbers but that their grandchildren did.) If a religio-ethnic group is intellectually good enough to get its young people on the faculties of Michigan, Wisconsin, and California but not quite good enough to make it at Columbia, Yale, Harvard, or Chicago, one begins to wonder what subtle criteria for intellectual excellence are being used at the elite private schools.

There would be very few who would question that the lower occupational scores of the blacks who attended college are the result of discrimination. Unless one can come up with solid evidence for another explanation, intellectual honesty should compel one to take very seriously the possibility that the same explanation should be applied to the lower scores of Polish, Irish, and Italian Catholics.

RECOVERING THE PAST

If there is any ethnic militancy at all, it is to be found not in the vast middle and lower reaches of income and occupational prestige but rather among the elite, those college-educated and graduate-school-educated ethnics who bump up against the residual nativism still present in the upper strata of American society. It is not the Slovakian steelworkers but the Michael Novaks who are the most likely to be angry—and with good reason. Or, as far as that goes, it is not the Irish cop or the Irish politician or the Irish attorney who grows angry at elite nativism, for they either do not encounter it or it does not affect them. (The reader may judge for himself whether the author of this article is an angry militant.)

Those of us who stand on the shoulders of the immigrants are ill at ease with our predecessors. Their raw acquisitiveness embarrasses us, and their sacrifices and sufferings cause us pain. It is hard to admit that we owe a great deal to those who came before us. We repress memories of places like the Stanislowowo in the same way we repress memories of such disasters as the Spanish Influenza or the Great Depression; they are too terrible and too close for us to think about very much. It took a long, long time before a movie

like *Hester Street* could be made, and it may be another generation or two before the descendants of those brave, strong, ambitious young people who swarmed into this country between 1890 and 1914 will be able to relax sufficiently to place those urban pioneers alongside the other brave people who came over the Appalachian mountains a century earlier to pioneer an unexplored continent. The miracle of the frontier is now a standard part of American mythology. Perhaps by the tricentennial the ethnic miracle will have become one of the respected marvels of the American story.

ENDNOTES

1. The empirical evidence on which this article is based comes from an analysis of a composite file assembled from 12 National Opinion Research Center (NORC) national sample surveys. (For a complete report see *Ethnicity, Denomination, and Inequality,* Sage Publications, Beverly Hills, California, 1976.) The composite sample numbers some 18,000 respondents and, despite serious limitations, still represents the best collection of data currently available on American religio-ethnic groups. The United States Census cannot ask a religious question, and only recently has the Census monthly "Current Population Survey" (CPS) begun to ask an ethnic question intermittently. However, since Polish Jews and Polish Catholics are combined under the rubric "Pole," and Irish Protestants (disproportionately rural southerners and more numerous than Catholics) are combined with Irish Catholics, the CPS data are useful only with respect to Italians. The NORC composite statistics, however, have been compared with the results of the CPS (50,000 respondents). There are only slight variations between the two; in the case of the Italians, a group for which the NORC data and CPS data are roughly comparable, there is virtually no difference in the statistics on education, occupation, and income. Unfortunately, until funding agencies are willing to support better data collection, composite survey data will provide the only available evidence for scholarly investigation.

2. Nor do the 25 years of prosperity between 1945 and 1970 explain the "ethnic miracle," though they obviously created an environment in which such a miracle could occur. For not only did the ethnics improve their income during that quarter century, as did virtually everyone else, but they improved it *disproportionately.* At the end of the quarter century, not only were they better off than in 1945, they had improved their relative position in comparison with the rest of the population. Prosperity, in other words, provided the opportunity

for the "ethnic miracle," but the miracle itself was a response to the opportunity.

3. The analytic technique used is a form of dummy-variable multiple-regression analysis in which each ethnic group becomes a dummy variable and is compared with the British Protestant group. The "net differences" among groups are arrived at by adding to the regression equation the dummy variables for region and for metropolitan residence, as well as for the number of years of the mothers' and fathers' education. Subsequent net differences are arrived at by adding individual educational achievement and occupational prestige to the regression equation. This method is somewhat different from that used in *Ethnicity, Denomination, and Inequality* and is more "conservative" statistically, permitting estimates of the statistical significance of observed differences. I am grateful to Christopher Jencks for suggesting the technique to me. College attendance was measured according to the log of the "odds ratio" of attendance to non-attendance for each age cohort. Tests of statistical significance were used to determine that the slope of the three ethnic groups was different from the national slope.

4. Since the analytic technique used in this article is somewhat different from that used in *Ethnicity, Denomination, and Inequality*, there are minor differences in the tables between this article and the longer report. In addition, a different technique was used to take into account cost-of-living changes to bring income from surveys taken in the 1960s into line with income reported in surveys taken in the 1970s. Hence, income figures here are slightly higher than those in the longer report.

5. It should be noted that I do not intend to suggest a comparison between the white immigrants of the turn of the century and the more recent nonwhite immigrants to the city. The path of upward mobility which worked for one group at one time does not necessarily work for another group at another time. Comparisons may be interesting and suggestive, but they should not be pushed too far. The Polish immigrants were indeed abject and miserable, unwanted and humiliated – but they were still white. On the other hand, the apparent historical phenomenon of income preceding rather than following education for the ethnics does seem to add weight to the argument of those who presently wonder whether too much has been expected of education as a corrective of social pathology in the last two decades. The experience of the ethnics is interesting in itself; whatever hints for current social policy may be obtained from their study should be considered no more than that – certainly not as blueprints for imitation. Occasionally one hears an ethnic complain "Why can't 'they' work hard like we did?" but the evidence shows that most ethnics are well aware that nonwhites have to put up with greater obstacles. The irony of their comment is aimed not so much at the more recent immigrants but rather at those of the intellectual and cultural elite who despised the ethnics when they were poor, and have contempt for them now that they are middle-class. As the Irishman said, "Where were you when we needed help?"

6. Let it be noted again that while ambition, hard work, and strong family support for achievement may have been the path to upward mobility for the white ethnics, it does not follow that the same path can or must be followed by more recent immigrants. The ethnic miracle is worth studying in itself even if it has no pertinence to more recent social problems or provides only useful insights for considering those problems.

The Economic Progress of European and East Asian Americans

Suzanne Model

INTRODUCTION

The economic success of the descendants of immigrants from Europe and East Asia stands in marked contrast to the earnings disadvantages suffered by blacks, some Hispanic minorities, and American Indians. The resumption of mass immigration to the U.S. in 1965 provides yet other sets of peoples against whom the achievements of European and East Asian Americans can be measured. These disparities prompt scholars and policy makers to inquire: What factors proved decisive in bringing at least some American ethnics into the economic mainstream? Did these conditions require that some groups advance at the expense of others? What information is still needed to determine whether past success stories can be expected to repeat themselves?

This essay seeks some answers to these questions through an interdisciplinary review of scholarship devoted to the economic achievements of those European and East Asian immigrants who arrived before the 1924 Johnson-Reed Act, and to their progeny. The review focuses primarily on the larger, non-Anglo-Saxon ethnic groups whose economic performance is well documented. While the contextual nature of ethnic stratification requires some attention to other contending groups, this review is restricted to instances of intergroup relations relevant to the economic outcomes of Europeans and East Asians.

To help the reader grasp the concreteness of ethnic stratification, research on the relative position, past and present, of the groups in question is summarized, and the sorts of measurement problems that plague any effort to generalize about the economic position of American ethnic groups are discussed. Following some documentation of ethnic rankings, a critical summary of historically based explanations for the observed ethnic outcomes is offered. The organization of this summary reflects the variety of factors that scholars have associated with ethnic economic achievement. Beginning at the individual level of analysis and moving toward the social structural, the survey examines culture, resources, demographic factors, and labor market conditions. The rationale governing this order of presentation is primarily pedagogical, as all factors are assumed to interact with one another. The essay concludes with a brief summary of major research trends and some recommendations on topics in need of further clarification.

Problems in Measurement

The term "inequality" demands referents: Who is unequal to whom and in what respects? A variety of racial, national, linguistic, religious, and cultural markers may delineate ethnic groups. But even the scholar who is analytically clear on the choice of a group may find that empirical sources fail to distinguish the group of interest. Similarly problematic is the isolation of an appropriate category for baseline comparisons. Should the selected group be compared to a national average (Greeley 1976a)? To white natives of native parentage (Lieberson 1980)? (This choice places all

Reproduced, with permission, from the *Annual Review of Sociology*, Volume 14, © 1988 by Annual Reviews Inc.

third generation Americans in the reference category.) To those of British descent (Neidert & Farley 1985, Alba 1988)? Scholars concerned with religious distinctions may also require a benchmark group that is sensitive to denominational affiliation (Roof 1979b).

Historians of stratification face significant problems in choosing outcome variables. Since the U.S. Census did not ask any questions on income until 1940, much of the research on earlier economic differentiation has relied on occupational status measures. Although some sociologists have argued that occupational status has been relatively stable throughout the period of interest (Treiman 1977, Hauser 1982), historians are less convinced, and many have created their own occupational scales (Thernstrom 1973, Hershberg & Dockhorn 1976, Decker 1978). In other instances, researchers have shown great ingenuity in accessing records of wealth and property (Griffen & Griffen 1978, Gabaccia 1984, Morawska 1985).

For any given outcome variable, investigators usually elect to focus on either gross or net differences (Roof 1981). In general, the introduction of control factors reduces the advantage of the more successful. But a group's distribution on a control variable is often both a result and a cause of ethnic position; hence it is worthy of study in its own right.

The choice of a unit of analysis for the dependent variable introduces a final difficulty. Studies at the individual level tell investigators a good deal about the intersection of ability and opportunity but overlook the variety of family-based strategies that enhance economic well-being. Should the income of the entire family or only that of the primary breadwinner be used to gauge ethnic achievement? Group differences in the number of earners and in family structure could influence ethnic rankings.

The Relative Success of American Ethnic Groups

Given the sets of caveats just outlined, any attempt to generalize about ethnic stratification would seem very dangerous. Indeed, distinguishing some groups well enough to offer historically grounded conclusions about their economic trajectories remains a challenge. Nevertheless, several groups have been sufficiently isolated to decipher general trends. When gross outcomes are considered, neither the choice of benchmark groups nor the selection of a dependent variable radically alters the general ranking of groups. The introduction of control variables has a leveling effect, but since such variables also remove some of the explanation for group differences, control variables are a topic more appropriate for later portions of this review.

Even a cursory investigation of ethnic stratification reveals that the myth that all immigrants entered the American economy at the bottom does not square with the facts (Steinberg 1981). Despite the unavailability of reliable income data until the mid-twentieth century, the occupational distributions published by the U.S. Census provide an impression of general group rankings. Perhaps the simplest way to measure ethnic economic position is to compare the proportion of unspecified laborers across backgrounds. The earliest collected data combine the sexes and cover the small number of groups well established by 1870. Among non-Anglo-Saxons, these figures show German immigrants least overrepresented proportionately in the unspecified laborer category, Scandinavians next, while the Irish are most overrepresented (Hutchinson 1956). A much larger selection of groups was tabulated in 1900, by which time large numbers of South and East Europeans were joining their Northern European neighbors in choosing American shores. These figures, disaggregated by sex, show that among male immigrants, Russians—who were primarily Jews (Rosenthal 1975)—were least overrepresented as unspecified laborers; they were followed by Scandinavians, Central Europeans, Irish, Eastern Europeans, and Italians in that order (Hutchinson 1956). Moreover, the differences among the nationalities were often quite large.

The earliest complete data on income appear in the 1950 PUMS files. Hirschman & Kraly (1986a) have distinguished the earnings of the males therein by national background. Their figures reveal that the incomes of first and second generation Russians and Romanians (both assumed to be predominantly Jewish) were highest. The first and second generations of most Northern European groups fell between the Jews and native whites of native parents, the reference group in their analysis. The Irish, however, surpassed native whites of native parents only in the second generation, a trajectory paralleled by most Eastern European Gentiles. Southern European Gentiles and an undifferentiated Middle East/Asia group also exhibited intergenerational improvement, though only sufficient to match the earnings level of the reference group.

Data on the native born compiled by Chiswick (1986a) from the 1970 census indicate that Jewish, Chinese, and Japanese males all outearned native whites of native parentage. Finally, Greeley's (1976a) creation of a composite NORC sample for the years 1963–1974 provides data on family income by ethnoreligious self-identification. Here Jewish families rank highest, followed by Irish, Italian, German, and Polish Catholics in that order. Households that identified themselves as British or American Protestant earned *less* than any of those above.

Since none of these studies includes significance tests for group differences, the wisest conclusion is that members of most pre-1924 immigrant backgrounds now fare at least as well as do other white Americans (Jencks 1983). The several explanations for these results occupy the remainder of this review.

EXPLANATIONS FOR ETHNIC ACHIEVEMENT

Culture

Culture has long been considered a vehicle for transmitting attitudes, beliefs, and values, which, in turn, influence economic decisions. Variations in cultural legacy, therefore, could translate into significantly different economic behaviors. There is some disagreement, however, about which cultural systems are most compatible with industrial capitalism as well as about the dynamics of cultural change (Tilly 1974, Schooler 1976, Henrietta 1977, Sowell 1981).

The writings of Max Weber set the agenda for much of the culturalist debate. Weber (1958) argued that Protestant theology, particularly the secular asceticism of Puritanism and Calvinism, provided a major impetus for the birth of capitalism. Over Weber's objections, Sombart (1971) maintained that Judaism reinforced many of the

same traits. Later, Bellah (1957) argued that persons in certain segments of Japanese society idealized diligence and frugality during the Tokugawa period.

If these formulations help to explain the economic outcomes of immigrants and their descendants, researchers must show that similar religious outlooks have persisted in America in ways that cause economic differences. Lenski's (1961) survey of Detroit residents detected a link between the low economic position of Catholics and their weak commitment to values claimed for Weber's Protestant ethic. A recent study of similar questions by Woodrum (1985) finds that religious practices had a small but significant association with income and self-employment among Japanese immigrants. Yet, neither of these efforts establishes causal direction or rules out competing hypotheses. Woodrum's (1985) work, for example, neglects to incorporate an important strand of research on the relevance of culture to Asian success, namely Light's (1972) observation that the Chinese and Japanese brought with them the institution of rotating credit associations, an institution that proved vital in financing their small businesses. Jewish immigrants, also well known for their entrepreneurial endeavors, transplanted a related organization, the free loan society, from Europe to America (Tenenbaum 1986).

An additional cultural phenomenon associated with the success of entrepreneurial groups is their exceptionally strong ascriptive ties, within both family and group. These bonds facilitate the accumulation of resources and the exploitation of labor in a manner that renders ethnic enterprise extremely competitive, even in a rational, capitalist society (Ianni 1972, Light 1972, Bonacich 1973, Bonacich & Modell 1980).

This judgment, that precapitalist kinship ties profited immigrant businessmen, illustrates the kinds of criticism recently mounted against the view that the authoritarian, paternalistic world of traditional communities provided inadequate preparation for survival in modern, capitalist societies (Greeley 1982). Studies now indicate that the industrial-preindustrial dichotomy has been overdrawn and that a variety of strategies were functional in both environments. To cite another example, communal associations served as useful, though different, cultural legacies for proletarian *and* entrepreneurial groups (Cummings 1980). From a narrow economic standpoint, the most valuable services that proletarian ethnic associations offered were insurance protection and home mortgages (Barton 1975, Briggs 1978, Bodnar et al. 1982). A somewhat broader perspective, though, suggests that the formal and informal opportunities these organizations provided to obtain job information, to mediate disputes, and to enforce social control brought indirect but no less valuable material benefits (Parot 1981, Cinel 1982, Oestreicher 1983, Stolarik 1985).

In sum, current research indicates that all immigrant groups selected from their cultural traditions some mechanisms that remained economically utilitarian in their new homes. The persistence of these legacies is testimony to the complexity of modern society, not to the obstinacy of the ethnics. Scholars continue to debate the contribution of culture because of the theoretical and empirical difficulties associated with isolating purely cultural variables. Later sections of this review evaluate some efforts in this direction.

Resources

Scholars have devoted considerable energy to examining relationships between economic outcomes and a wide range of immigrant characteristics, including the socioeconomic status of workers' parents and worker's own expectations, education, English proficiency, job skills, and experience. So far, nearly all of this work has been limited to males. (For an exception, see Roos & Hennessy 1987.)

With respect to family background, few European immigrants hailed from the most poverty-stricken classes within their homelands (Barton 1975, Cinel 1982, Doyle 1983). Moreover, it is generally believed that migration is a selective process that attracts the more motivated and talented within a population (Blau & Duncan 1967, Chiswick 1979). Despite this favorable self-selection of individuals within the place of origin, there are several reasons for expecting differences between groups to emerge at destination.

Lieberson (1980), for instance, proposes that to induce the migration of the economically motivated, wages at destination will be somewhat higher than wages at origin. He argues that this relationship will reproduce the gap among workers from different sending regions once they enter the migratory setting. Another factor that affects wages is the permanency of the relocation. Persons who intend only a transient stay are usually willing to accept poorer pay and working conditions than those who view their move as permanent (Rosenblum 1973, Piore 1979).

Research has confirmed some of these expectations. For instance, an ecological relationship exists between human capital levels and degrees of industrialization in a way that implies the reproduction of wage differentials across countries. Those immigrants who reported more education – natives of Northern Europe and, to a lesser but not insignificant extent, the Jews and the Japanese – set out from more economically developed environments (Kitano 1969, Steinberg 1981, Bodnar 1985, Hirschman & Kraly 1986b, Hirschman & Wong 1986). Similarly, skill levels ran highest among German and Jewish immigrants, (Kessner 1977, Kessler-Harris & Yans-McLaughlin 1978), although the abilities of other immigrant groups have probably been underestimated because many nationalities had some experience as migratory laborers in nonagricultural pursuits (Briggs 1978, Morawska 1988a). Unfortunately, data on the individual transfer of job skills from the old world to the new are inadequate.

The resources just described influenced group earnings, but outcomes also were affected by the varying ability of groups to convert their resources into economic rewards. Recent reanalyses of data assembled by the U.S. Immigration Commission indicate that, among equally "resourceful" immigrants, those from Britain and Western Europe reaped higher monetary rewards than those from Ireland, and Eastern or Southern Europe (McGouldrick & Tannen 1977, Blau 1980). Among the latter groups, other data sources reveal that intragenerational advancement was likewise rather limited, though with considerable regional and temporal variation (Thernstrom 1973, Barton 1975, Bodnar et al. 1982, Hareven 1982, Zunz 1982).

Studies devoted to the trajectories of later generations of ethnics record that both resource gaps and achievement shortfalls diminished. Several investigations concur in concluding that the children of Jews and East Asians reached educational parity with other Americans early in this century and later surpassed the schooling levels of most benchmark groups (Lieberson 1980, Gorelick 1981, Dinnerstein 1982, Hirschman & Wong 1986). Cohort analysis shows that Irish Catholics have registered respectable educational levels since World War I, while Catholics from Southern and Eastern Europe dramatically improved their educational profiles after World War II (Lieberson 1980, Greeley 1976, Alba 1988).

Efforts to explain the educational achievements of later generation ethnics have stimulated vigorous debates over the preeminence of culture versus structure. The most common cultural interpretation of East Asian and Jewish educational achievement credits ancient traditions that revered scholarship and learning (Kitano 1969, Dinnerstein 1982, Brumberg 1986). The cultural basis for Catholic educational achievement is less obvious, though in the case of the Irish, the early prominence of Irish-dominated Catholic colleges may have been valuable. On the other hand, structuralists have associated a modicum of parental economic security with the extended schooling of the next generation (Lieberson 1980, Hirschman & Falcon 1985). In the case of the Jews, several investigations lend support to the notion that they did not act on their educational ambitions until extended schooling was financially both feasible and rewarding (Berrol 1976, Steinberg 1981, Morawska 1988b).

Many studies have explored the ability of later generation ethnics to translate their resources into economic outcomes. Historical work on intergenerational occupational mobility reveals that, when paternal occupational status is controlled, the sons of Irish, Italian, and Polish immigrants had a harder time accessing the better occupations than did the sons of Germans and Jews (Thernstrom 1973, Kessner 1977, Griffen & Griffen 1978, Harzig 1983, Smith 1985, Model 1988a). Multivariate analyses of more recent data, however, indicate that European ethnics differ little from other whites in the translation of educational achievement into occupation and income (Duncan & Duncan 1968, Duncan et al. 1972, Neidert & Farley 1985). A much documented exception arises in the case of Jews, who have experienced significantly higher translations of education into both job status and earn-

ings, perhaps since the turn of the century (Kessner 1977, Duncan et al. 1972, Chiswick 1985). Conclusions about the Chinese and Japanese are less consistent, with some researchers uncovering evidence of inadequate returns and others not (Chiswick 1983b, Hirschman & Wong 1984, Nee & Sanders 1985, Roos & Hennessy 1987).

To summarize, research on immigrant resource levels indicates substantial group differences in the distribution of human capital and human capital returns; these differences have diminished but not totally disappeared with the passage of generations. Not all these differences are disadvantageous. Indeed, according to Chiswick (1979), sons of economically motivated immigrants generally earn more than sons of the native born, when human resources and demographic characteristics are equal. The next section reviews the impact of these demographic characteristics.

Demographic Factors

Under this rubric, the major variables considered are sex ratios, fertility, geographic locations, and the ethnic-racial composition of local labor markets. The effects of the first two and of the last two are strongly intertwined.

Among groups whose members frequently planned to repatriate – Southern and Eastern Europeans and East Asians – sex ratios initially favored males because women's role was to remain behind, tending the family holdings until the men returned (Lyman 1974, Yans-McLaughlin 1977). Those groups departing with the more permanent intentions, the Irish, Scandinavians, Germans, and Jews, migrated as families or individuals and had more balanced sex ratios as a result (Kessler-Harris & Yans-McLaughlin 1978, Bade 1985, Bodnar 1985). Within these broad categories, however, cultural and structural factors promoted considerable intergroup variation (Hutchinson 1956).

The presence of relatively normal sex ratios heightened financial needs because larger proportions of immigrants were married. Family life required abandoning the marginal living quarters and extreme self-denial characteristic of sojourners, who remitted most of their earnings to their loved ones abroad, where a small sum went a good deal further than in America. Many observers believe that the delayed family formation of Southern and Eastern Europeans, and especially of the Chinese, retarded their economic progress (Lyman 1974, Kessler-Harris & Yans-McLaughlin 1978, Nee & Wong 1985).

The fertility rate of immigrant women usually ran higher than that of native women, though there were differences associated with both ethnicity and time of migration (U.S. Immigration Commission 1911). Until well into the twentieth century, urban poverty motivated higher fertility because large families meant more offspring who could ultimately contribute to family coffers (Goldin 1981, Sharpless & Rury 1980, Ewen 1985, M. Cohen 1988). Because immigrants were frequently poorer than natives, their higher fertility was partly a reflection of their economic distress.

As the twentieth century progressed and child labor became less necessary or desirable, later generation ethnics began to limit family size. Researchers continue to debate the degree to which economic factors explain the remaining group differentials (Bean & Marcum 1978). In general, Catholics exhibited relatively high fertility compared to the entrepreneurial minorities (Lenski 1961, Chiswick 1986a, Goldscheider 1986). These trends contradict the view that ethnic enterprise profited from a pool of unpaid family laborers, reinforcing instead a picture of entrepreneurs eager and able to educate their small families. Chiswick (1983b, 1985, 1986a,b) offers a relevant hypothesis on this point. He argues that groups for whom children are more expensive will have smaller families and higher quality children than those for whom children are less costly. Among the factors Chiswick associates with greater child costs are favorable attitudes toward contraception, urban residence, and higher maternal educations. Interestingly, most of the groups he cites as illustrative of the small family strategy have been heavily entrepreneurial.

Still, most of the groups considered here ultimately secured respectable educational investments, a fact that may also reflect their residential concentration in Northern cities, where better educational opportunities first surfaced (Lieberson 1980). In other ways, however, researchers note that northern cities had drawbacks. From at least the late nineteenth until the early twentieth century, European immigrants of identical nationality groups fared better in the smaller, commercial cities of the "urban frontier" than in established northern communities (Conzen 1976, Vinyard 1976, Burchell 1980, Cinel 1982, DiLeonardo 1984).

Investigators disagree about the reasons for this pattern. Some argue that more talented immigrants were disproportionately likely to initiate internal migration (McCaffrey 1985); others claim the converse (Thernstrom 1973). Geographic differences in job opportunities certainly played a part (Blauner 1972, Golab 1977), but the allocation of immigrants within these opportunities was also a function of the ethnic-racial mix in local labor markets. Debate clouds conclusions about the economic effects of variation in the proportion of co-ethnics (Kirk & Kirk 1978, Conk 1981, Faires 1983, Harzig 1983, Suhrbur 1983), but scholars concur that Europeans especially prospered in cities containing high proportions of more stigmatized, non-European minorities (Hopkins 1968, Barr 1970, Bonacich 1973, Burchell 1980, Cinel 1982).

In Northern labor markets, not all European groups could escape the stint at the bottom of the labor queue that they successfully avoided elsewhere (Golab 1977, Cizmic 1983, Orsi 1985, Stolarik 1985). This situation did not change until the hiatus and eventual termination of overseas immigration and the arrival in the North of large numbers of less skilled and less demanding blacks (Lieberson 1980, Zunz 1982). These blacks offered the white laboring classes of the North the same exemptions from undesirable employment that their counterparts in the South and West had enjoyed earlier. In this sense, it may be said that the upgrading of some groups has depended upon the oppression of others.

A full appreciation of the impact of location, however, requires accounting for the economic opportunity structure that immigrants and their children encountered, as well as the distributive mechanisms operating to link these workers to their jobs. These issues comprise the final substantive portion of this essay.

Labor Market Variables

The Structure of Opportunity. Immigrants entering American labor markets found their opportunities very much a function of time and place. Those Northern Europeans who arrived before the close of the frontier and before the rise of mass production could still put land to the plow or indulge in entrepreneurial craftsmanship. The Irish avoided the countryside, however, and accepted unskilled urban laboring jobs instead (Kessler-Harris & Yans-McLaughlin 1978, Bodnar 1985). As manufacturing quickened, most urban immigrants and their children joined the Irish in becoming increasingly proletarianized (Zunz 1982, Levine 1986). The urban Germans, for instance, many of whom were artisans, discovered that the markets for their skills declined (Griffen & Griffen 1978, Keil 1983). Nineteenth century economic fluctuations meant that those groups whose mass migration began earlier were more dispersed among jobs and less likely to display intergenerational persistence in those jobs than did the groups who began to arrive after industrial take-off (Hutchinson 1956).

By the turn of the century, a few industries had risen to dominance in some of the larger inland cities (Bodnar et al. 1982, Zunz 1982, Keil & Jentz 1983), while in many smaller centers single companies reigned supreme (Hareven 1982, Morawska 1985). Within the confines of place, skill purportedly remained a crucial determinant of wages, though some writers maintain that skill itself is socially constructed (Granovetter & Tilly 1988). Struggles among workers, between workers and gatekeepers, and within the political sphere all influenced decisions about which jobs were labeled skilled and which not (Conk 1978, Keil 1983). The greater resources and organizational capacities of so-called skilled workers brought them meaningful unionization (Dawson 1983, Suhrbur 1983, Jackson 1984). Among ethnic Americans, the prime beneficiaries of these efforts were the earlier arriving Northern Europeans.

Indeed, it was the relative docility of Southern and Eastern Europeans that attracted industrial employers to these nationals in the first place (Erickson 1957). But it did not take long for the less skilled immigrants to articulate their discontent over low pay and atrocious working conditions. Employers responded by dividing workers along racial and ethnic lines, crushing collective action by force, and placating disaffection by means of company unions (Green 1980, Gordon et al. 1982, Bukowczyk 1984). As labor historians

have ably demonstrated, immigrant workers occasionally overcame these obstacles (Nelli 1985, Barrett 1986, Hoerder 1986, Gordon et al. 1982). But in most industries, the enormous political and economic clout of capital assured the triumph of ownership until the thirties (Montgomery 1986).

During the Depression, a combination of worker agitation, government action, and employer receptivity secured the legitimation of new, industrially based unions (Brody 1971, Rosenblum 1973, Piore 1979). Scholars remain divided about the motives for the heightened contentiousness of immigrants and their children (Piore 1979, Bodnar 1985, Morawska 1985) but not about the results. Internal labor markets, seniority rules, and fringe benefits brought financial security to many working class ethnics, while the more recently arrived blacks absorbed the vagaries of the business cycle (Bonacich 1972, 1976; Lieberson 1980; Gordon et al. 1982).

Considerable research effort has been directed at identifying which employment opportunities most benefited from these changes. Writers sympathetic to a labor market segmentation perspective have distinguished desirable jobs from undesirable on the basis of a dichotomy that separates a core (large, monopolistic, capital intensive firms) from a periphery (small, competitive, labor intensive firms) (Gordon et al. 1982). This distinction, however, has been severely criticized on theoretical and empirical grounds (Hodson & Kaufman 1982). More germane to the present discussion is the lack of research directed at matching ethnic distributions and manufacturing locations. Which groups benefited most from industrial unions is a question deserving further scrutiny.

One of the few well-documented instances of immigrant concentration has been the small business of Jews and East Asians. Some writers have suggested that this specialization represents a third option, the ethnic enclave, which is theoretically distinct from the core of periphery sectors (Portes & Bach 1985). The major framework for understanding these groups, however, has been middleman minority theory (Bonacich 1973, 1979; Bonacich & Modell 1980; van den Berghe 1981: Ch 7). A surprisingly wide range of economic activities – agriculture, light manufacture, trade, and personal services – have responded to the entrepreneurial tactics of immigrants.

Information about the kinds of endeavors that absorbed first and second generation immigrant women has been easier to assemble because female job opportunities were so restricted. Nineteenth and twentieth century ethnic women earners, most of them young and unmarried, worked primarily in light industry – especially clothing, textiles, and tobacco – as well as in various types of domestic service (Tentler 1979, Bose 1984, Glenn 1984). Some of the garment trades offered unionized protection, but such advantages were the exception rather than the rule. Teaching enjoyed popularity among the more educated, first the Irish and later the Jews (Gorelick 1981, Moore 1981, Bose 1984). Married women usually contributed to family finances in ways compatible with household responsibilities, such as by engaging in home manufacture, serving as unpaid assistants in a family business, or caring for boarders (DiLeonardo 1984, Ewen 1985). Unfortunately, the documentation of married women's economic contribution is scanty and uneven.

Social scientists have devoted more attention to the occupational status of ethnic males than to any other attribute. Investigations of occupational data are useful in showing the movement from manual to nonmanual jobs, but they obscure the process behind this result. These studies reveal considerable shifts out of blue collar jobs, for Jews in the twenties and thirties and among most other ethnics in the years following World War II (Blau & Duncan 1967, Greeley 1976, Dinnerstein 1982, Lieberson 1980). Yet, even at the occupational level, more could be done to describe the distributions of the groups considered here. That the Jews, Japanese, and Chinese have disproportionately flocked to certain professions is well known (Bonacich & Modell 1980, Goldscheider 1986). But scholars have ignored the more recent, detailed occupational distributions of most European groups, perhaps under the assumption that such an analysis would prove uninformative.

The Allocation of Opportunity. Given the current lack of sophistication about where ethnics have worked in recent decades, it is not surprising that more is known about how immigrants and jobs were matched in the nineteenth and early twentieth centuries than thereafter. Two themes dominate this literature: how discrimination affected opportunity and how interpersonal sponsorship brought applicants jobs.

While few immigrant groups emerged unscathed from the attacks of American nativism (Higham 1963), its virulence varied both across time and across groups. Some investigators stress the significance of physical and cultural differences in stimulating discrimination (Gordon 1964, Sowell 1981), but marxian analysis faults the capitalist pursuit of profits and the differential cost of labor (Bonacich 1972, 1973, 1976, 1984a,b; Reich 1981). Groups prized by employers for their low wage demands – the Chinese or Italians, for example – suffered more intensely than groups engaged in activities peripheral to capitalist expansion – for example, the Germans and Scandinavians. Disagreement continues regarding the relative responsibilities of capitalists and higher priced labor in fomenting discriminatory incidents, but the significance of economic competition is not in doubt (Olzak 1987).

Immigrants were randomly distributed neither by industry nor occupation. Ethnic stereotypes among employers and gatekeepers, as well as a group's premigration skills and wage demands, combined to channel certain groups into particular industries: the Irish and later the Italians into construction, the Bohemians into cigarmaking, the Poles into steel (Korman 1967, Lopreato 1970, Golab 1977). Most of the initial labor distribution was handled by urban labor agencies (Erickson 1957). Over time, however, employers discovered that their present workers performed admirably as recruiting agents. Each worker was potentially in touch with large numbers of kin and fellow villagers both in this country and overseas (Erickson 1957, Bodnar et al. 1982, Hareven 1982, Morawska 1985, 1988a). Employers' satisfaction with this form of recruiting perpetuated the association between industry and ethnicity, sometimes into the second and later generations (Granovetter & Tilly 1988, Model 1988b).

Blatant discrimination was more overt at the

level of the occupation than the industry. For example, through the first quarter of the twentieth century, Central and Eastern Europeans in the steel industry found that gatekeepers consistently allocated the more arduous and dangerous jobs to "Hunkies" (Morawska 1985). Hareven (1982) reports greater tolerance within the textile industry, where ethnic barriers rose only at the level of overseer.

The main route to escaping such restrictions was to work for oneself or one's co-ethnics. All immigrants were disproportionately represented as traders and dealers—a fact that is probably related to the limitations they experienced in the broader labor market (Conk 1981). However, for entrepreneurial groups, self-employment and working for the self-employed became the primary adaptation, partly because of the vehement opposition that members of these groups encountered in the majority economy. Among Jews, entrepreneurship was already typical in Europe and was transplanted to America, first by German Jews, and later, with their help, by Jews from other nations (Rischin 1962, Decker 1978, Toll 1982). In the case of East Asians, opposition in this country was so strong that steps were taken to exclude Asians as immigrants, citizens, and landowners (Petersen 1978, Bonacich 1984a,b). The retreat into ethnic enterprise did not assure immunity from attack, but it did reduce vulnerability.

Asians and Jews entered coethnically owned enterprises in much the same way that other workers found jobs—through personal sponsorship. The main difference was that employers might recruit workers themselves. Shared ethnicity implied a variety of social contacts between owners and workers which the latter could exploit to obtain labor. Frequently the bond of a common hometown formed the bridge between the prospect and the intermediary, who might be a future boss or simply a future co-worker (Light 1972, Zenner 1980,—see Waldinger 1986 for a contemporary account).

As mentioned above, both middleman minorities and proletarian ethnics have increased their representation in mainstream, white collar careers. But how some immigrant children and grandchildren moved out of their early spheres and secured these new jobs is not clear. Research

into the procurement of white collar positions suggests that interpersonal sponsorship remains significant, though shared ethnicity is perhaps less characteristic of the participants (Granovetter 1974). The hypothesis that ethnically heterogeneous social bonds guided the job search of later generation ethnics parallels the hypothesis that they entered ethnically heterogeneous occupational and industrial environments. These hypotheses require testing.

CONCLUSION

The evidence reviewed here documents how immigrants with differing values, abilities, and goals secured a variety of economic opportunities, some unattractive, others less so. The analysis suggests that the improvements recorded by these groups are the outcome of specific historical forces rather than the simple passage of generations. The cessation of overseas immigration, the exodus of blacks from the South, the triumph of industrial unionism, and the upgrading of the American occupational structure comprise the most frequently cited explanations (Blau & Duncan 1967, Piore 1979, Lieberson 1980). Some groups, especially the middleman minorities, were positioned to take advantage of these changes more rapidly and more effectively than others, but none remained impervious to these events. Whether ethnics now enjoy proportionate representation in all spheres of wealth, power, and influence in this country remains debated (Roof 1981, Alba & Moore 1982, Slavin & Pradt 1982), but their broad progress is not in question.

This review has emphasized that the greatest gaps in scholarly knowledge about ethnic mobility surround the mechanisms through which the above mentioned structural shifts affected economic trajectories. How have European and East Asian groups been distributed across occupational, industrial, and authority structures as the twentieth century progressed? What circumstances impelled different groups to extend their education? What tactics linked educated ethnic applicants to their new white collar jobs? And to what extent have investigators overlooked intra-ethnic variations in socioeconomic mobility?

Better answers to these questions would assist

scholars in approaching one of the most serious dilemmas the nation now faces, the plight of currently disadvantaged groups. Existing scholarship indicates that many of the changes that upgraded the less privileged early immigrant groups depended on economic growth and demographic shifts not likely to be repeated. Nevertheless, more refined analyses are needed before social scientists should accept this disturbing conclusion.

F I F T E E N

Education and Ethnic Mobility
The Myth of Jewish Intellectualism and Catholic Anti-Intellectualism

Stephen Steinberg

"If our children don't go to school, no harm results. But if the sheep don't eat, they will die. The school can wait but not our sheep." An Italian peasant, quoted in Leonard Covello, *The Social Background of the Italo-American School Child,* 1967.

Horace Mann, the architect of the common school, once described education as "the great equalizer." Implicitly Mann recognized that the schools would function within the context of class inequality, providing the less privileged members of society with opportunities for social and economic advancement. In *Democracy and Education* John Dewey also wrote that "it is the office of the school environment . . . to see to it that each individual gets an opportunity to escape from the limitations of the social group in which he was born, and to come into living contact with the broader environment."[1] To this day, it is an article of faith in American society that education

is the key to material success, and the key to eliminating social inequalities as well.

Consistent with this liberal faith in education, two general assumptions run through the social science literature on education and ethnic mobility. The first is that those ethnic groups that have taken advantage of educational opportunities have, for that reason, enjoyed comparative mobility and success. The second assumption is that the values of some groups have been conducive to intellectual achievement, whereas other groups have been saddled with anti-intellectual values or other cultural traits that discouraged their children from pursuing educational opportunities. This "theory" is thus a variant of the more general theory of ethnic success discussed earlier.

As before, issue arises not with the fact that ethnic groups vary in educational attainment, but with the assumption that this reflects the operation of cultural factors, such as the degree to which education is valued. How do we know that some ethnic groups value education more highly? Because they have a superior record of educational attainment. Obviously, it is incorrect to infer values from the outcome, and then to posit these values as causal factors. To prove the cultural thesis, it is necessary to furnish independent evidence that some groups placed special value on education, and that this factor operated in its own right as a determinant of educational achievement.

Yet a number of writers have claimed such evidence by pointing to the cultural systems of certain ethnic groups that are thought to be compatible or incompatible with the requirements of modern education. This argument is commonly made with respect to Asians and Jews, both of whom have in fact achieved higher levels of education than most other groups in American society.

For example, in his book on Japanese-Americans William Petersen begins with the factual observation that "since 1940, the Japanese have had more schooling than any other race in the American population, including whites."[2] He then proceeds to explain the high educational levels of Japanese-Americans as an outgrowth of a particular set of cultural values. On the basis of his examination of the records of Japanese students at Berkeley during the late 1950s and early 1960s, Petersen writes: "Their education had been conducted like a military campaign against a hostile world, with intelligent planning and tenacity. . . . In a word, these young men and women were squares."[3] Irrespective of Petersen's questionable metaphor (would enterprising Jewish or Italian students be described as waging a military campaign, or is this imagery reserved for the Japanese?), his characterization of such students as "squares" is most revealing. According to Petersen, the "cultural traditions" of Japanese produced diligent, persevering, and industrious students who eschewed the pleasures of the moment in their dogged pursuit of long-range goals. Like the "old-fashioned boys" in Horatio Alger's novels, it is the squares who ultimately triumph.

In her praise of Chinese educational achievement, Betty Sung is even more explicit in tracing this to a specific "cultural heritage." According to Sung:

> Chinese respect for learning and for the scholar is a cultural heritage. Even when a college degree led to no more than a waiter's job, the Chinese continued to pursue the best education they could get, so that when opportunities developed, the Chinese were qualified and capable of handling their jobs. Other minorities have not had the benefit of this reverence for learning.[4]

For Sung, the Chinese reverence for learning is not merely characteristic of Chinese-Americans, but is a product of cultural heritage rooted in centuries of history.

Of course, it is the Jews who are most often acclaimed, in folklore and social science alike, as a "people of the book." The implication here is that Jews owe their intellectual prominence to a reverence for learning that is rooted in their religious culture and that has been passed down through the ages. There is hardly a study of Jews in America that does not cite a "Jewish passion for education" as a major factor, if not *the* major factor, in explaining Jewish mobility. A typical exposition of this idea is found in Marshall Sklare's 1971 book on *America's Jews:*

> Jewish culture embraced a different attitude toward learning from that which characterized the dominant societies of eastern Europe. This Jewish attitude was part of the value-system of the immigrants. It pertains to learning in general, though in the traditional framework it is most apparent with respect to the study of religious subjects.[5]

According to Sklare and numerous others, the high valuation that Jews traditionally placed on religious learning was, in the New World, transferred to secular learning, and with this cultural head start, the children of Jewish immigrants were quick to climb the educational ladder.

A large number of empirical studies have documented Jewish intellectual achievements. It is known that, compared with most other groups, Jews are more likely to go to college, especially highly competitive colleges, to excel once they are there, and to go on to graduate and professional schools. Studies have also shown that Jews are disproportionately represented among the teaching faculties of the nation's colleges and universities and this is especially so in the leading research institutions.[6] Still other studies have shown that Jews have produced more than their share of eminent scholars and scientists, and of course there has been much preoccupation with the fact that Marx, Freud, and Einstein, three of the towering figures of modern history, have been Jewish.[7] As in the case of Jewish economic success, the fact of Jewish intellectual prominence can hardly be disputed. Rather it is the interpretation of this fact – specifically, the notion that Jewish educational achievements result from a reverence for learning embedded in Jewish history and culture – that is problematic.

An alternative to this cultural theory is a social class theory that does not deny the operation of cultural factors, but sees them as conditional on preexisting class factors. Whereas the cultural theory holds that certain groups placed unusually high value on education, which resulted in greater mobility, the class theory turns this proposition around, and holds that economic mobility occurred first, and this opened up channels of educational opportunity and engendered a corresponding set of values and aspirations favorable to education. Obviously, education allowed these groups to consolidate and extend their economic gains, but these were gains that initially occurred in the occupational marketplace without the benefit of extensive education.

This is not to deny the well-documented fact that Japanese, Chinese, and Jews all placed high value on education; nor does the class theory deny that reverence for education may be rooted in the traditional belief systems of these groups. Where the class theory differs from the cultural theory is in its emphasis on the *primacy* of class factors. That is to say, it is held that cultural factors have little independent effect on educational outcomes, but are influential only as they interact with class factors. Thus, to whatever extent a reverence for learning was part of the religious and cultural heritage of Asians and Jews, it was activated and given existential significance by their social class circumstances. Without this congruence between culture and circumstance, it is hardly conceivable that these groups could have sustained their traditional value on education, or that it would have actually resulted in higher levels of educational achievement.

THE MYTH OF JEWISH INTELLECTUALISM

Can Jewish intellectual traditions, rooted in premodern and prescientific systems of thought, explain the academic achievements of Jews in twentieth-century America? This is the question raised by anthropologist Miriam Slater, who did a "content analysis" of Jewish scholarly traditions. Slater shows that the style and content of traditional Jewish scholarship were fundamentally at odds with the requirements of modern secular education, and if anything would have operated as a deterrent to educational achievement in America. For example, whereas shtetl learning involved a ritualistic preoccupation with Talmudic legalisms, Western education is highly pragmatic, innovative, and oriented toward lucrative employment in the marketplace. In Slater's view it was a striving for material success, and not a passion for learning, that spurred Jews up the educational ladder.[8]

Slater is not the first to suggest that the specific content of traditional Jewish education was incompatible with modern secular education. For example, in his study on the historical evolution of science, Lewis Feuer writes of Talmudic scholarship that "this sterile type of 'learning' and disputation was an obstacle to the development of science among Jews, a hurdle they had to surmount."[9] In *World of Our Fathers* Irving Howe also comments that "scholarship often degenerated into abysmal scholasticism. Intellect could be reduced to a barren exercise in distinctions that had long ago lost their reality."[10] A less dispassionate view of traditional Jewish pedagogy is found in Michael Gold's autobiographical novel *Jews Without Money:*

> Reb Moisha was my teacher. . . . What could such as he teach any one? He was ignorant as a rat. He was a foul smelling, emaciated beggar who had never read anything, or seen anything, who knew absolutely nothing but this sterile memory course in dead Hebrew which he whipped into the heads and backsides of little boys.[11]

In his own fashion, Gold concurs with Slater's view that Jewish scholarship was "discontinuous" with secular education in America.

Yet the issue that Slater raises is a spurious one. What sociologists have argued is not that

Jewish intellectual traditions were important in and of themselves, but rather that they fostered a positive orientation toward learning that was easily adapted to secular education. In his novel *The Rise of David Levinsky,* Abraham Cahan explores how Old World values were recast in the New World. Formerly a Talmudic scholar in Russia, David Levinsky yearns to go to City College. Gazing at the "humble spires" of a City College building, he thinks to himself: "My old religion had gradually fallen to pieces, and if its place was taken by something else . . . that something was the red, church-like structure on the southeast corner of Lexington Avenue and Twenty-third Street. *It was the synagogue of my new life."*[12] This last phrase epitomizes the transfer of a traditional value on learning from religious to secular education which, according to the conventional wisdom, accounts for the rapid economic mobility that Jews experienced in America.

Yet in Cahan's novel, Levinsky never fulfills his ambition to go to City College; instead he makes a fortune as an entrepreneur in the garment industry. Is this mere fiction or does Cahan's character typify the pattern of Jewish mobility? In other words, was it generally the case that Jews achieved economic mobility *before* their children climbed the educational ladder? Indeed, this is the conclusion of a recent study by Selma Berrol on "Education and Economic Mobility: The Jewish Experience in New York City, 1880–1920."[13]

Berrol's inventory of educational facilities in New York City at the turn of the century shows that the schools could not possibly have functioned as a significant channel of mobility. Still in an early stage of development, the public school system was unable to cope with the enormous influx of foreigners, most of whom were in their childbearing ages. Primary grade schools were so overcrowded that tens of thousands of students were turned away, and as late as 1914 there were only five high schools in Manhattan and the Bronx. If only for this reason, few children of Jewish immigrants received more than a rudimentary education.

Berrol furnishes other data showing that large numbers of Jewish students ended their schooling by the eighth grade. For example, in New York City in 1908 there were 25,534 Jewish students in the first grade, 11,527 in the seventh, 2,549 in their first year of high school, and only 488 in their last year.[14] Evidently, most immigrant Jewish children of this period dropped out of school to enter the job market.

Nor could City College have been a major channel of Jewish mobility during the early decades of the twentieth century. Until the expansion of City College in the 1930s and 1940s, enrollments were not large enough to have a significant impact on Jewish mobility. Furthermore, Jewish representation at the college was predominantly German; Berrol estimates that in 1923 only 11 percent of CCNY students had Russian or Polish names.

In short, prior to the 1930s and 1940s, the public schools, and City College in particular, were not a channel of mobility for more than a privileged few. It was not until the expansion of higher education following the Second World War that City College provided educational opportunities for significant numbers of Jewish youth. However, by this time New York's Jewish population had already emerged from the deep poverty of the immigrant generation, and had experienced extensive economic mobility.

It was the children of these upwardly mobile Jews who enrolled in City College during the 1930s and 1940s. For them, education was clearly a channel of mobility, but it accelerated a process of intergenerational mobility that was already in motion, since their parents typically had incomes, and often occupations as well, that were a notch or two above those of the working class in general. As Berrol concluded:

> . . . *most New York City Jews did not make the leap from poverty into the middle class by going to college. Rather, widespread utilization of secondary and higher education* followed *improvements in economic status and was as much a result as a cause of upward mobility.*[15]

The conclusion that economic mobility preceded the Jewish thrust in education is also suggested by Herbert Gutman's analysis of 1905 census data.[16] Gutman did a comparison of two immigrant Jewish neighborhoods on New York's East Side: Cherry Street, one of the section's poorest neighborhoods, made up largely of rank-and-file workers; and East Broadway, a somewhat more prosperous neighborhood largely inhabited by businessmen and professionals. The contrast between the two neighborhoods in terms of the mobility patterns of the next generation is striking. On Cherry Street almost all of the children in their late teens had left school and gone to work, generally at low-status, blue-collar jobs that barely raised them above the level of their parents. However, the children of the more affluent families on East Broadway were making a breakthrough into higher-status white-collar occupations and the professions.

Though Gutman's data are far from conclusive, they are consistent with other historical data suggesting that economic success was a precondition, rather than a consequence, of extensive schooling. There is no evidence to indicate that the children of Jewish rank-and-file workers received more education than other immigrant children of the same social class. If this assumption is correct, then the greater overall success that Jews experienced stems from the fact that Jews had an occupational head start compared to other immigrants, that this resulted in an early economic ascent, which in turn allowed more of their children to remain in school and avail themselves of educational opportunities.

Precisely at the time that Jews were overcoming the poverty of the immigrant generation, there was a vast increase in educational opportunity, another fortuitous wedding of historical circumstance that facilitated Jewish mobility. As the economy matured, the demand increased for a more educated labor force. This set in motion a long series of educational reforms leading to an expansion and overhaul of the nation's educational institutions. Especially in the northern industrial states where Jews were concentrated, there was a trend toward much heavier public investment in schools and colleges. The curricula were also changing away from their classical traditions toward science, vocational training, and professional education, and thus were more compatible with the talents and aspirations of children born outside the upper class.

One ramification of the educational expansion of the period was that teaching itself emerged as a significant profession. Between 1898 and 1920, the number of teachers in the New York City schools increased from 10,008 to 24,235, the largest numerical increase in any profession.[17] And among Russian Jews who graduated from City College between 1895 and 1935, more entered teaching than either medicine or law.[18] But it was not until a second major expansion of higher education after the Second World War that Jews began to show up in large numbers on the faculties of American colleges and universities.[19] Not surprisingly, they tended to enter new and expanding fields in the social and natural sciences. In all these ways, the stages of economic and educational development within the Jewish population coincided with stages of growth and change in American educational institutions.

What conclusion, then, can be drawn concerning the relationship between Jewish cultural values and Jewish educational achievements? It goes without saying that the educational levels that Jews finally attained would not have been possible without a corresponding set of supportive values that encouraged education, defined college as a suitable channel for social and economic mobility, and idealized intellectual achievement. But were these values distinctively part of a religious and cultural heritage, or were they merely cultural responses of a group that had acquired the economic prerequisites for educational mobility at a time when educational opportunities abounded?

There is a sense in which both these questions can be answered affirmatively. Even if Jews placed no special value on education, their social class position undoubtedly would have led them to pursue educational opportunities anyway. But Jews *did* place a special value on education, and this helped to impart the pursuit of educational opportunities with deeper cultural significance. Given the role of study in Jewish religion, the transfer of these values to secular learning tended to legitimate and sanctify a worldly desire for social and economic improvement. But these values only assumed operational significance in their interaction with a wider set of structural factors, especially the advantageous position of economically mobile Jews and the favorable structure of educational opportunity that they encountered. It was because education carried with it such compelling social and economic rewards that the traditional value on education was activated, redefined, and given new direction.

Had immigrant Jews remained trapped in poverty and deprived of educational opportunities, it is unlikely that Jewish intellectual life would have advanced beyond the archaic scholasticism that immigrant Jews carried over with them from Europe. Conversely, other immigrant groups that started out with less favorable cultural dispositions with respect to education rapidly developed an appetite for education once they achieved a position in the class system comparable to that of Jews a generation earlier.

THE MYTH OF CATHOLIC ANTI-INTELLECTUALISM

In matters of education, Catholics stand in historical counterpoint to Jews, lagging behind in areas where Jews have excelled. This has sometimes led to invidious comparisons between the two groups. For example, Thomas O'Dea, a leading Catholic scholar, wrote in 1958:

> It is doubtful that even the Irish immigrants, perhaps the poorest of the nineteenth-century arrivals to these shores, were much poorer than the eastern European and Russian Jews who came after 1890, except possibly in the worst years of the Irish potato failure in the 1840s. Yet these eastern Jews . . . have contributed a larger proportion of their children and grandchildren to academic and scholarly life than have Catholic immigrants as a whole.[20]

Having assumed that Catholics and Jews started out in the same place in the class system, O'Dea implicitly dismisses class factors as irrelevant to the question of why Jews have produced a greater number of scholars. As already shown, however, although Jewish immigrants were poor, they had social class advantages in the form of literacy and occupational skills, that resulted in more rapid economic mobility. Thus, O'Dea's unfavorable comparison between Catholics and Jews is based on a false assumption.

Yet O'Dea's failure to consider class factors has been characteristic of nearly half a century of social research, and has resulted in a castigation of Catholicism itself for the underrepresentation of Catholics among the nation's scientists and scholars. For example, in 1931 Scientific Monthly published an article on "Scientific Eminence and Church Membership," in which the authors reported that Unitarians were 1,695 times more likely than Catholics to be listed among the nation's eminent scientists. The data seemed to give credence to the popular stereotype of the Catholic Church as a dogmatic and authoritarian institution that restricts free thought and scientific inquiry. The authors thus concluded that "the conspicuous dearth of scientists among Catholics suggests that the tenets of the church are not consonant with scientific endeavor."[21]

Several decades later, in his book on Anti-Intellectualism in American Life, Richard Hofstadter also scored Catholics for having "failed to develop an intellectual tradition in America or to produce its own class of intellectuals. . . ."[22] Like earlier writers, Hofstadter automatically assumed that the low level of Catholic representation among scholars is symptomatic of an anti-intellectualism rooted in Catholic religion and culture.

The same inference is made in Kenneth Hardy's 1974 study of the "Social Origins of American Scientists and Scholars," published in Science magazine.[23] Hardy ranked American undergraduate colleges in terms of their "scholarly productivity," as measured by the relative number of their graduates who went on to receive Ph.D.s Like women's colleges and southern colleges, Catholic colleges turn out to be low in scholarly productivity. Hardy's interpretation of these findings is altogether circular. He assumes ipso facto that those institutions low in productivity are marked by anti-intellectual, anti-democratic, and antihumanitarian values that are antithetical to scholarship. But the only evidence he has that institutions have such retrograde values is that they are low in productivity. On this flimsy basis, he portrays Catholic colleges, as well as women's colleges and southern colleges, as culturally to blame for the fact that relatively few of their students go on to earn Ph.D.s.

A more plausible explanation, however, is that such colleges tend to attract students from less privileged backgrounds who have lower academic qualifications from the start, and who are less likely to aspire to careers that entail graduate education. Indeed, Alexander Astin has shown that it is not the attributes of colleges that determine their productivity of future Ph.D.s, but rather the attributes of the students they recruit.[24] In fact, those Catholic colleges that maintain high entrance standards—for example, Georgetown University, Boston College, Loyola University, and the Catholic University of America—all have above-average records for producing future Ph.D.s. Thus, there is no basis for attributing the generally lower rates of scholarly productivity of Catholic colleges to the intellectual quality of these institutions, much less to a specific set of anti-intellectual values rooted in the Catholic religion.

Why, then, have Catholics produced fewer scholars and scientists than other groups? What was the meshing of culture and circumstance that obstructed educational progress for Catholics? As a first step in addressing this issue, it is necessary to consider the varied ethnic composition of the Catholic population. It makes little sense to treat Catholics as a monolith, especially given the fact that the ethnic groups that make up the nation's Catholic population occupy such different positions in the class system. As Andrew Greeley has shown, Irish and German Catholics rank well above the national average on measures of income, occupation, and education, while Poles, Italians, Slavs, and French are closer to average.[25] These differences themselves suggest that religion may be less important as a factor in explaining social class outcomes than factors associated with the nationality of particular groups. In order to explore this further, it will be useful to focus on Italians, since they constitute the largest Catholic group in the last great wave of immigration, and because Italians have often been singled out as a group whose values are said to be inimical to education.

Most Italian immigrants came from the underdeveloped provinces of Southern Italy, where they worked as landless peasants. This helps to explain not only why Italians were less mobile than other groups, but also why they would have exhibited different attitudes toward education. Obviously, immigrants from peasant backgrounds were not likely to have the same outlook upon education as other immigrants, including Northern Italians, who came from more industrially advanced sectors of their countries of origin. In his book *The Social Background of the Italo-American School Child,* Leonard Covello had this to say about the sources of the Southern Italian's low valuation of formal education:

> As a peasant, unable to perceive things in abstracto, and as a man of the soil, he perceived education in association with material benefits. He saw the need to educate his children only insofar as the school provided means for bettering one's economic condition, or for breaking through the caste system. But since few precedents existed where a peasant's son became anything but a peasant, the contadino almost never entertained the possibility of his son's becoming a doctor, a lawyer, or embarking on some other professional career.[26]

Given the fact that Italian peasants were tied to the soil, formal education had little value for individual or collective survival.

A more basic reason for the high rate of illiteracy that prevailed among Italian immigrants was that schools were poor or nonexistent. As John Briggs has shown in a recent study, in areas where education was available, illiteracy was far less prevalent. On the basis of a painstaking analysis of educational statistics in the early 1900s, Briggs reached the following conclusion:

> Literacy, then, was closely associated with the quality and quantity of schooling available in southern Italy. The lower social classes had little control over the provision of public schooling. They took advantage of it where it existed. Illiteracy resulted where it was lacking or was offered only under extremely inconvenient circumstances. Clearly, the prevalence of illiteracy among emigrants is not a good criterion of their attitudes toward education, nor is it an indication of the inappropriateness of their traditional culture for their futures as urbanites. Such evidence is better viewed as a measure of past opportunity than as a prediction of future response to schooling.[27]

To whatever extent Southern Italians exhibited negative attitudes toward education, in the final analysis these attitudes only reflected economic and social realities, including a dearth of educational opportunities.

A number of ethnographic studies of Italians in the United States have also found evidence of unfavorable attitudes toward education, and have implicitly chastised Italians for not being more zealous in pursuit of educational opportunities. But, once again, it is necessary to ask whether Italian attitudes toward education were simply a carryover from Europe, as is commonly assumed, or whether they were responses to conditions of Italian life in this country as well.

This issue arises, for example, in interpreting

the results of a 1958 study by Richard Otis Ulin on "The Italo-American Student in the American Public School," which was based on a comparison of students from Italian and Yankee backgrounds in Winchester, Massachusetts. Ulin found that the Italian students generally had poorer academic records, and he ascribed this to cultural orientations inherited from Southern Italy. The most important cultural flaw, according to Ulin, is a tendency toward fatalism and an inability to plan for the future. As Ulin writes:

> One can see much of the same Wheel of Fortune attitude that left the South Italian peasant praying for rain but neglecting to dig an irrigation ditch, hoping for a remittance from America or for a windfall in the national lottery. These are sentiments which are echoed today in the currently popular tune, which interestingly enough, has Italian lyrics, "Che Sera, Sera" ("What Will Be, Will Be").[28]

Aside from Ulin's stereotypical view of the Italian peasant, what evidence is there that his Italian subjects in Winchester exhibit a "wheel of fortune attitude" toward life?

Ulin bases his conclusion on comments by Italian students such as the following: "I know other guys who worked their _____ off in school and they got good grades and now they got lousy jobs. It's just the way the ball bounces." But Ulin offers no evidence to support his claim that such attitudes are rooted in Southern Italian culture. On the contrary, it could be argued that his Italian subjects are expressing attitudes that are typical of the working class and in all likelihood accurately reflect the world as it actually exists for these working-class students in Winchester, Massachusetts. At least this is what is implied by another student, whom Ulin also construes as expressing a fatalistic attitude:

> Listen, they [the teachers] can talk all they want about how everybody in Winchester has an equal chance. Do they think us kids from the Plains have an equal chance? In the pig's eye! The West Side kids get all the breaks. They don't have to work after school. The teachers go out of their way to help them. And if they want to go to college, their old man will give 'em the dough.[29]

What these students appear to be expressing is not a cultural disregard for education, but a recognition of the fact that, unlike their more afflu-

ent Yankee peers, their chances of reaching college are slim, and consequently their futures are not likely to depend upon their school performance. Like the men on *Tally's Corner*, they have adjusted their aspirations and their strategies to what they can realistically hope to achieve.

The view that cultural factors explain the low academic achievement of Italians has also been advanced in a study by Fred Strodtbeck that compared Italian and Jewish students on a number of value measures that predict educational performance. The largest differential was on the item: "Planning only makes a person unhappy because your plans hardly ever work out anyway." Only 10 percent of Jewish students in his sample, but 38 percent of Italians, answered in the affirmative. Strodtbeck interprets such responses as an indication of the extent to which individuals have developed a sense of self-mastery, which he speculates is more often found in Jewish families because they are more democratic, and for this reason produce more motivated, secure, and achieving children. Not only does this interpretation involve a perilous leap from rather scant data, but there is evidence in Strodtbeck's data that what he measured were not ethnic differences, but class differences. When Strodtbeck compared Italian and Jewish students of the same social class background, there was no longer any difference between them.[30] In other words, the reason that the Jews in his original comparison were more likely to exhibit such traits as a future-time orientation, self-mastery, and democratic family relationships was that these qualities are generally characteristic of the middle class, regardless of the ethnic character of the groups involved.

In short, if Italians and other Catholics have not excelled academically, this cannot be blamed on a value system that discouraged education, since these values themselves only reflect the operation of social class factors and the unfavorable structure of educational opportunity that confronts the lower classes generally. As in the case of Jews, Catholics had to secure an economic foothold before their children could make significant advances up the economic ladder. But given the relative disadvantages associated with the peasant origins of most Catholic immigrants, more time was required to establish this foothold. Since the Second World War, however, Catholics have substantially improved their collective position in the class system. On the basis of national surveys extending from 1943 to 1965, one study concluded that:

> At the end of World War II, Protestants in the United States ranked well above Catholics in income, occupation, and education; since then Catholics have gained dramatically and have surpassed Protestants in most aspects of status.[31]

If the above historical interpretation is correct, then the fact that Catholics are achieving economic parity with the rest of the population should bring an end to patterns of Catholic underrepresentation among the nation's scholars and scientists.

THE CHANGING RELIGIOUS COMPOSITION OF AMERICAN HIGHER EDUCATION

About a decade ago the Carnegie Commission on Higher Education conducted a massive survey of approximately 60,000 faculty in 303 institutions of higher learning across the nation.[32] From this landmark study it is possible to chart historical trends in the religious background of American scholars and scientists and, indirectly, to test the proposition that Catholicism is inherently anathema to intellectual achievement.

Table 1 reports the religious background of faculty in four different age groups, and of graduate students planning a career in college teaching.

In evaluating these figures it should be kept in mind that Catholics make up roughly 26 percent of the national population, Protestants 66 percent, and Jews 3 percent.

The data in Table 1 show unmistakably that there has been a gradual uptrend in Catholic representation over the past several decades. Among the oldest cohort of faculty, Catholics are only 15 percent, but this figure increases among younger age groups to 17, 19, and 20 percent. Among graduate students who plan a career in college teaching, the figure again rises to 22 percent. Since Catholics make up 26 percent of the national population, it is clear that they are rapidly approaching the point of being represented among faculty in the same proportion as in the nation as a whole.

In the case of Jews, the data indicate a pattern of overrepresentation. Though only 3 percent of the national population, Jews were already 5 percent of the oldest cohort of faculty, and this proportion gradually rose to 10 percent, where it has leveled off. The largest increase in Jewish representation occurred with the 45–54 age group, which indicates that Jews made their major breakthrough in college teaching during the expansion of higher education after World War II.

The increasing representation of Catholics and Jews among college faculty has resulted in a proportionate decrease of Protestants. Between the oldest cohort and the youngest, Protestants have gone from being overrepresented to being underrepresented relative to their proportion of the

TABLE 1 *The Religious Background of College Faculty of Different Ages (All Institutions)*

| Religious Background | Age of Faculty | | | | Graduate Students Planning a Career in College Teaching |
	55 or More	45–54	35–44	34 or Less	
Protestant	76%	69%	63%	63%	58%
Catholic	15	17	19	20	22
Jewish	5	8	10	10	10
Other	2	3	4	4	4
None	2	3	4	3	6
Total	100%	100%	100%	100%	100%

Source: Stephen Steinberg, *The Academic Melting Pot* (New York: McGraw-Hill, 1974), p. 104. Reprinted by permission of the Carnegie Foundation for the Advancement of Teaching.

national population. Given the Protestant decrease and the Catholic increase, it can now be said that Catholics and Protestants have achieved parity with each other.

The same trends emerge even more clearly when the ranking universities are examined (this includes seventeen "top" institutions such as Columbia, Harvard, Johns Hopkins, Northwestern, etc.). Jewish representation in these institutions is considerably higher than among colleges and universities generally, and Protestant and Catholic representation is somewhat lower. But the *trend* is even more pronounced than before (see Table 2). That is, Catholic representation in these ranking institutions has steadily increased; there has been a corresponding decrease of Protestants; and the Jewish proportion reached a peak with the expansion of higher education after the Second World War and then leveled off. As far as Catholics are concerned, all the evidence leads to the conclusion that they are belatedly taking their place in American higher education.[33]

Further insight into the different mobility patterns of Protestant, Catholic, and Jewish scholars can be gleaned from data on the class origins of faculty in the Carnegie survey. Respondents were asked about the occupation of their fathers; the category labeled "working class" includes both blue-collar workers and those in low-level white-collar occupations such as clerical and sales workers. The data, reported in Table 3, are consistent with the historical data analyzed above.

In the first place, relatively few Jewish scholars, and many more Catholics, have their origin in the working class. The figure for Jews is 25 percent; for Protestants, 32 percent; for Catholics, 45 percent. What is especially notable is that even among older age cohorts, relatively few Jewish faculty come from working-class backgrounds.

An unusually large number of Jewish faculty had fathers who owned small businesses. Indeed, this is the case of slightly over half the Jews in the oldest age category, and a third of those in the youngest age category. As observed earlier, many Jewish immigrants were able to use their prior experience in commerce as an avenue of economic mobility. The data now indicate that it is the children of these businessmen who went on to become scholars and scientists in disproportionate numbers. On the other hand, the Jewish working class has never been a major source of Jewish scholars.

The pattern is quite the opposite for Catholics. In every age cohort four out of every ten Catholic scholars come from working-class backgrounds, and on the basis of what is known about the occupational concentrations of Catholics in the society at large, it is safe to assume that Catholic scholars are typically coming not from the bottommost strata, but rather from stable working-

TABLE 2   *The Religious Background of College Faculty of Different Ages (The Top-Ranking Universities Only)*

| Religious Background | Age of Faculty | | | | Graduate Students Planning a Career in College Teaching |
	55 or More	45–54	35–44	34 or Less	
Protestant	72%	64%	57%	55%	52%
Catholic	10	11	13	16	20
Jewish	12	16	19	18	16
Other	2	3	5	4	5
None	4	6	6	7	7
Total	100%	100%	100%	100%	100%

Source: Stephen Steinberg, *The Academic Melting Pot,* op. cit., p. 107. Reprinted by permission of the Carnegie Foundation for the Advancement of Teaching.

TABLE 3 *Social Class Origins of College Faculty by Religion and Age*

Religious Background Father's Occupation	Age				
	55 and More	45–54	35–44	34 or Less	Total
Protestant					
Professional	26%	22%	22%	25%	23%
Managerial*	13	16	17	20	17
Owner, small business	17	16	15	13	15
Farm	19	14	12	9	13
Working class**	25	32	34	33	32
Total	100%	100%	100%	100%	100%
Catholics					
Professional	10%	14%	13%	16%	14%
Managerial*	19	18	19	22	20
Owner, small business	22	16	17	13	16
Farm	9	6	5	4	5
Working class**	40	46	46	45	45
Total	100%	100%	100%	100%	100%
Jews					
Professional	13%	14%	17%	26%	19%
Managerial*	14	11	13	17	14
Owner, small business	52	45	44	33	41
Farm	2	1	0	1	1
Working class**	19	29	26	23	25
Total	100%	100%	100%	100%	100%

Source: Stephen Steinberg, *The Academic Melting Pot,* op. cit., p. 92. Reprinted by permission of the Carnegie Foundation for the Advancement of Teaching.

*Includes corporate officials and owners of large businesses.

**Includes skilled and unskilled workers and low-level white-collar workers such as clerical and sales workers. Armed Forces personnel are also included, though they constitute a negligible 1 percent of the sample.

class occupations that offer an adequate, if marginal, livelihood. This is a more precarious economic base than existed for Jews, which helps to explain the lower representation of Catholics in the academic profession.

CONCLUSION

Given the disadvantages with which Catholic immigrants started life in America, it is not surprising that they required another generation or two to produce their numerical share of scholars and scientists. Thomas O'Dea is too quick to dismiss immigration and problems of assimilation as factors bearing on "the absence of intellectual life" among Catholics.[34] The fact that the great majority of Catholic immigrants came from peasant backgrounds was of enormous consequence. Not only did high levels of illiteracy slow the pace of cultural adjustment, but Catholic immigrants also lacked the kinds of occupational skills that facilitated economic mobility for other groups. These conditions also presented formidable obstacles to intellectual achievement, especially in light of the class character of American higher education, and the many factors producing a far lower rate of college attendance among lower-class children. However, as Catholics have gradually improved their position in the class system, their children are going to college with greater frequency, and as in every group, a certain number of them pursue academic careers and become scholars of distinction. The scenario is no different for Catholics than for other groups. It has only taken longer to play itself out.

ENDNOTES

1. Quoted in Samuel Bowles and Herbert Gintis, *Schooling in Capitalist America* (New York: Basic Books, 1976), p. 21.

2. William Petersen, *Japanese Americans* (New York: Random House, 1971), p. 113.

3. Ibid., pp. 115–16.

4. Betty Lee Sung, *The Story of the Chinese in America* (New York: Macmillan, 1967), pp. 124–25.

5. Marshall Sklare, *America's Jews* (New York: Random House, 1971), p. 58.

6. Stephen Steinberg, *The Academic Melting Pot* (New York: McGraw-Hill, 1974), chap. 5.

7. Tina Levitan, *The Laureates: Jewish Winners of the Nobel Prize* (New York: Twayne Publishers, Inc., 1960); Nathaniel Weyl and Stefan Possony, *The Geography of Intellect* (Chicago: Henry Regnery, 1913), pp. 123–28.

8. Miriam Slater, "My Son the Doctor: Aspects of Mobility Among American Jews," *American Sociological Review* 34 (June 1969): 359–73.

9. Lewis S. Feuer, *The Scientific Intellectual* (New York: Basic Books, 1963), p. 303.

10. Irving Howe, *World of Our Fathers* (New York: Harcourt Brace Jovanovich, 1976), pp. 8–9.

11. Michael Gold, *Jews Without Money* (New York: Avon Books, 1961; orig. edition 1930), p. 43.

12. Abraham Cahan, *The Rise of David Levinsky* (Colophon Books: New York, 1960), p. 169 (italics added).

13. Selma C. Berrol, "Education and Economic Mobility: The Jewish Experience in New York City, 1880–1920," *American Jewish Historical Quarterly*, March 1976, pp. 257–71.

14. Ibid., p. 261.

15. Ibid., p. 271.

16. Gutman's unpublished data are summarized by Irving Howe in *World of Our Fathers*, op. cit., pp. 141–44.

17. Sherry Gorelick, *City College and the Jewish Poor.* (New Brunswick, NJ: Rutgers University Press), p. 167. *The World Almanac, 1923* (New York: The Press Publication Co., 1923), p. 549.

18. Gorelick, ibid., p. 165.

19. Steinberg, op. cit., p. 106.

20. Thomas O'Dea, *American Catholic Dilemma* (New York: Sheed & Ward, 1959), p. 87.

21. Harvey D. Lehman and Paul A. Witty, "Scientific Eminence and Church Membership," *Scientific Monthly* 33 (December 1931), pp. 548–49.

22. Richard Hofstadter, *Anti-Intellectualism in American Life* (New York: Random House, 1963), p. 136.

23. Kenneth Hardy, "Social Origins of American Scientists and Scholars," *Science*, vol. 185, August 9, 1974, pp. 497–506. Also, my critique in *Change* magazine, June 1976, pp. 50–51, 64.

24. Alexander Astin, " 'Productivity' of Undergraduate Institutions," *Science* 136 (April 1962); *Predicting Academic Performance in College* (New York: Free Press, 1971), pp. 129–35.

25. Andrew Greeley, *Why Can't They Be Like Us?* (New York: Dutton, 1971), pp. 67–68; "The Ethnic Miracle," *Public Interest*, Fall 1976, pp. 20–36.

26. Leonard Covello, *The Social Background of the Italo-American School Child*, edited with an introduction by Francesco Cordasco (Totowa, N.J.: Rowman and Littlefield, 1972), p. 256.

27. John W. Briggs, *An Italian Passage* (New Haven: Yale University Press, 1978), p. 64.

28. Richard Otis Ulin, "The Italo-American Student in the American Public School," unpublished Ph.D. dissertation, Harvard University, 1958, p. 157.

29. Ibid., p. 156.

30. Fred L. Strodtbeck, "Family Interaction, Values, and Achievement," in Marshall Sklare, *The Jews* (New York: Free Press, 1958), pp. 161–62.

31. Norval D. Glenn and Ruth Hyland, "Religious Prejudice and Worldly Success," *American Sociological Review* 32 (February 1967), pp. 84–85.

32. For methodological details regarding these surveys, see Martin Trow and Oliver Fulton, *Teachers and Students* (New York: McGraw-Hill, 1975), pp. 297–371.

33. Though the Carnegie surveys did not query respondents about their ethnic background, it is safe to assume that the Irish have contributed disproportionately to the Catholic increase, since they have higher levels of income and education in the population at large. See Andrew Greeley, "The Ethnic Miracle," op. cit.

34. O'Dea, op. cit., p. 93.

Immigrant and Ethnic Enterprise in North America

Ivan Light

In the decade 1820–30, 80 percent of free white Americans owned their own means of livelihood (Corey, 1966:113). This decade was the highwater mark of self-employment in America, and subsequent trends have shown an almost uninterrupted decline. Generations of sociologists have declared that business self-employment in the modern United States has become an economic anachronism which is in the process of disappearance (Light, 1979:31). Following Marx on this point, they have observed that the progressive concentration of capital reduced the once numerous class of free entrepreneurs that existed in the last century. Indeed, three decades ago C.W. Mills (1951) already showed the steady decline of agricultural and non-agricultural self-employment in the United States between 1870 and 1950:

> A larger number of small businesses are competing for a smaller share of the market. The stratum of urban entrepreneurs has been narrowing, and within it concentration has been going on. Small business becomes smaller, big business becomes bigger (Mills 1951:24).

After Mills wrote this evaluation the decline of self-employment in the American labor force unambiguously continued until 1973. In that year a slim majority of American farmers continued to be self-employed, but less than 7 percent of nonfarm workers were self-employed (Ray, 1975). Given these trends, government and business analysts agreed that the probability of self-employment had become poorer than in the past and its

rewards correspondingly more meager (Cingolani, 1973:8–10; Special Task Force, 1973:21). In this economic context, social scientists generally concluded that small business self-employment was incompatible with capitalist economic concentration and could be expected to slide into oblivion for this reason (Bottomore, 1966:50; O'Connor, 1973:29–30; Horvat, 1982:11–15; Auster and Aldrich, 1984).

However, on the cultural side, sociologists had to explain the atavistic persistence of entrepreneurial values and ambitions in the American labor force (Chinoy, 1952; Walker and Guest, 1952) as well as the extent of self-employment among the wage-earning population (Lipset and Bendix, 1959:102–3, 177–81). Given the USA's *laissez-faire* traditions (Meyer, 1953) it was easy to understand entrepreneurial ambitions and frustrated aspirations as cultural residuals of an economically bygone era (Vidich and Bensman, 1960:305–6). Thus Riesman (1950) juxtaposed the "inner-directed" old-fashioned individualism of yesteryear's entrepreneurs with the glad-handed "other-direction" of corporate executives, finding in this contrast a shift in the modal personality from the former to the latter. In a similar exercise, Miller and Swanson (1958:123) found that achievement imagery in the American middle class had shifted away from self-employment toward bureaucratic careers in corporate hierarchies. Bell's (1976:84) analysis of the "cultural contradictions of capitalism" identified the Puritan tradition as a self-destructive rationality

Reprinted from *Ethnic and Racial Studies* 7:2 (April 1984) by permission of Routledge & Kegan Paul PLC.

whose adolescent heirs had discarded the disciplines of planning and work in favor of "voluptuary hedonism."

Entrepreneurship's protracted decline provided a neat illustration of cultural lag, the belated adjustment of superstructure to changes in production relations (Aronowitz, 1973:257). A small business economy needed entrepreneurial motivations in its labor force. When the economic basis of small business deteriorated, socialization lagged behind, continuing to produce entrepreneurial ambitions and values in lifelong wage workers (Lynd and Lynd, 1937:70). The temporary result was a glut of disappointed aspirants for small business self-employment, a situation of imbalance between supply and demand (O'Connor, 1973:29–30). Ultimately, the market's surplus of aspiring entrepreneurs reached back into the socialization system, causing reallocation of motivational resources away from this overpopulated occupation in diminishing demand. As salaried workers corrected their aspirations for realistic prospects, the social origins of American small business owners declined (Newcomer, 1961:490; Meyer, 1947:347; Mills, 1966). By 1952 the "creed of the individual enterpriser" had become "a working class preoccupation" (Lipset and Bendix, 1966:462).

ETHNIC AND IMMIGRANT ENTERPRISE IN AMERICA

Taken very generally, cultural lag still offers a satisfactory explanation of what happened to entrepreneurial individualism in twentieth-century America. However, the cultural lag orthodoxy encounters two serious objections, one empirical, the other conceptual. First, as Giddens (1973: 177–8) has observed, the *rate* of decline in self-employment was never so rapid as Marxists had expected even though the direction of change was mostly negative. Moreover, in the specific period 1972–9, "the number of self-employed Americans rose by more than 1.1 million, reversing decades of steady decreases" (Fain, 1980:3). This stabilization suggests that a plateau in self-employed population firmly supports an ideology of entrepreneurship among a minority (see Table 1). This conclusion is particularly appealing since Boissevain (1984) has reported that in 1978 "Common Market countries registered a net increase in the number of entrepreneurs and family workers" thus reversing their postwar trend of decline.

Second, cultural lag orthodoxy depends upon a simplifying, inaccurate assumption of homogeneity in economy and labor force. A homogeneous economy means uniformity in industrial

TABLE 1   *Self-Employed and Unpaid Family Workers in the United States, 1948–79 (Number in Thousands)*

1948	1948	1958	1968	1972	1979
Non-agricultural industries					
Total employed	51,975	56,863	72,900	78,929	94,605
Self-employed	6,109	6,102	5,102	5,332	6,652
Percent of total	11.8	10.7	7.0	6.8	7.0
Unpaid family workers	385	588	485	517	455
Percent of total	0.7	1.0	0.7	0.7	0.5
Agriculture					
Total employed	6,309	4,645	3,266	3,005	2,993
Self-employed	4,664	3,081	1,985	1,789	1,580
Percent of total	73.9	66.3	60.8	59.5	52.8
Unpaid family workers	1,318	941	550	467	304
Percent of total	20.9	20.3	16.8	15.5	10.1

Source: T. Scott Fain, "Self-Employed Americans: Their Number Has Increased," *Monthly Labor Review* 103 (1980): Table 1, p. 4.

conditions among the various sectors as well as a uniform rate of capitalist concentration in each. Labor force homogeneity means all workers are identical in values, attitudes, skills, employment access, and return on human capital. Both assumptions are unrealistic. The USA economy actually consists of a plurality of sectors which differ in respect to industrial conditions, capitalist concentration, and rates of change. O'Connor's (1973) distinctions between competitive, monopoly and state sectors need attention, and this tripartite division could easily be augmented in the interest of exactitude (reviewed in Kallenberg and Sorenson, 1979). Additionally, the USA labor force consists of unequally situated groups which differ in cultural heritages. At the very least, one must distinguish the immigrant, the nonwhite, and the native white labor force sectors. Workers in these sectors experience differential returns on human capital, rates of under- and unemployment, welfare and legislative support, and career opportunities.

Given variation in the economy and labor force, uneven resolution of cultural lag follows. On the one hand, some business sectors retain contrary-to-trend compatibility with entrepreneurial activities. On the other, some working populations retain atavistic aspirations for business self-employment. In point of fact, immigrant and nonwhite workers cluster heavily in the economy's competitive sector within which, by definition, a small business milieu persists (Waldinger, 1982:1–2; Zenner, 1982:474; Auster and Aldrich, 1984). Thus, on structural grounds alone, there is reason to predict that old-fashioned entrepreneurial ideology should remain among immigrant and minority sector workers long after native white workers have resigned themselves to salaried and wage employment in the monopoly and state sectors.

This situation is not really novel. In actual fact, the foreign-born have been overrepresented in American small business since 1880 and probably earlier (Light, 1980:33; Higgs, 1977:92). Two explanations seem plausible. The first is disadvantage in the labor market. Such disadvantage causes foreigners to concentrate in small business because they suffer under- and unemployment as a result of poor English, unvalidated educational credentials, discrimination, and so

forth (Reitz, 1980:191). Anyone who is disadvantaged in the labor force derives from this unfortunate situation a special incentive to consider self-employment, and the greater his disadvantage, the greater his incentive. The unemployed apple vendors of the Great Depression epitomize the resourcefulness of workers who, unable to find wage-earning jobs, turn to any and every pitiful self-employment from economic desperation.

However, labor markets' disadvantage cannot be the whole explanation of this phenomenon, because some immigrant and ethnic minority groups have higher rates of urban self-employment ("entrepreneurship") than do others (Goldscheider and Kobrin, 1980:262–75; Boissevain, 1984; Jenkins, 1984). Given equal disadvantage why do some foreign groups have higher rates than others, and why should the foreign-born in general have higher rates of business self-employment than disadvantaged native minorities, especially blacks (Handlin, 1959:74)? Native blacks are more disadvantaged than native whites, yet the blacks' rates of business self-employment have been and remain lower than the native whites' rates and much lower than the foreign-born rates despite presumptively higher disadvantage of the blacks (Light, 1972, 1979; Wright et al., 1982:724).

ORTHODOX AND REACTIVE CULTURAL CONTEXTS

The orthodox answer to this issue has fastened upon transplanted cultural endowments of various ethnic minority groups. Derived from Max Weber, this model of entrepreneurship has claimed that individuals introject cultural values in the course of primary socialization. When a group's values and motivations encourage business enterprise, cultural minorities produce socialized adults who prosper in business. The prototype is Weber's (1958a) Protestant sectarians who espoused the values of diligence in a calling, thrift, profit, and individualism. These values and attendant motivations caused adult sectarians to prosper in business. With appropriate adjustments, this model might account for the anomalous and persistent overrepresentation of selected cultural minorities in self-employment. American examples include Jews, Chinese, Japanese, Greeks, Macedonians, West Indians, Dominicans, Gypsies, Iraqi Christians, Lebanese, Koreans, and Arabs.[1] In all such cases, cultural theory has explained business overrepresentation and/or success in terms of intact, unmodified cultural heritages. A fine example is the migration of Gypsy fortunetellers. Before debarkation in New York City, the Gypsies already knew how to tell fortunes, and their cultural baggage included ready-to-use skills (crystal balls, tarot cards, palmistry) other groups simply lacked. Gypsy practice of these skills in the Untied States only involved the utilization of a cultural tradition for the specific purpose of self-employment (Sway, 1983).

This view has merit, but research in ethnic enterprise has disclosed its inadequacy. In reality, immigration and alien status release latent facilitators which promote entrepreneurship independently of cultural endowments (Turner and Bonacich, 1980:145, 148). Three facilitators are especially important. The first is psychological satisfaction arising from immigration to a high-wage country from a low-wage country. Immigrants in the United States have recurrently proven willing to accept low money returns, long hours of labor, job-related danger, and domestic penury in order to maintain business self-employment. Relative to their countries of origin, even adverse conditions look good to immigrants and, until fully adapted to the American standard of living, immigrants obtain satisfaction from squalid proprietorships that would not attract native-white wage earners. This is *relative satisfaction*.

A second, much-documented reaction is enhanced social solidarity attendant upon cultural minority status. Chain migrations create immigrant communities with extraordinarily well-developed social networks. Numerous studies have shown that these social networks create resources upon which immigrant co-ethnics can draw for business purposes (Light, 1972; Bonacich, 1973, 1975b; Bonacich and Modell, 1980; Wilson and Portes, 1980). "The cornerstone of an ethnic subeconomy is the communal solidarity of a minority group" (Hraba, 1979:374). Insofar as reactive solidarity encourages immigrant entrepreneurship, a situation has brought out a collective response which is not cultural in the ortho-

dox sense (Young, 1971). A concrete example is the influence of immigrant *Landsmannschaften* upon business enterprise. Immigrant *Landsmänner* belong to a primary group which did not exist as such in their country of origin. Thus, among Japanese of Los Angeles *Hiroshimakenjin* formed a solidaristic subgroup within the metropolitan population—all the brothers hailed from Hiroshima. On the other hand, contemporaneous residents of Hiroshima did not share the sense of local solidarity so the immigrants had obviously created a solidarity abroad that did not exist in Hiroshima, their city of origin (Modell, 1977:99–117). This is a *reactive* solidarity which required alien status to liberate, and as such is quite different from the practice of fortunetelling by immigrant Gypsies.

The third endowment is sojourning (Siu, 1952). Sojourning arises when immigrants intend to repatriate, and derive from this intention a desire to amass as much money as possible as quickly as possible. As Bonacich (1973) has shown, sojourning implies a battery of entrepreneurial motivations which give middlemen minorities an advantage in business competition over nonsojourners. Admittedly, the cultural status of sojourning is uncertain, and the phenomenon arguably arises liturgically as well as situationally (Light, 1979:33–4). Nonetheless, sojourning is a frequent (but not invariant) accompaniment to international immigration, and its presence provides an economic edge to the foreign born in small business enterprise (Zenner, 1982:458; Portes, Clark and Lopez, 1981–2:18).

Light's (1980:34–6) distinction between reactive and orthodox cultural contexts of entrepreneurship is a new one necessitated by the rapidly growing literature on this topic, but anticipated by earlier writers (Young, 1971). Orthodox and reactive contexts in Light's rubric correspond closely to what Turner and Bonacich (1980:145, 148) elsewhere identified as cultural and situational variables. In both cases, authors responded to the tendency of ethnic business researchers to "talk past" real issues on the one hand or, on the other, to engage in "unnecessary and wasteful polemics" about pseudo-issues (Turner and Bonacich, 1980:145, 147). Authorities agree that, however named, the conceptual distinctions identified do not necessitate an empirical repugnance because different variables can contribute to the entrepreneurship of the same ethnic groups. Old-fashioned cultural analysis (Belshaw, 1955) stressed only orthodox etiologies, thus creating the erroneous implication that only culturally intact transmission affected entrepreneurship (Freedman, 1959). Conversely, Bonacich's (1973) model of "middleman minorities" ignored orthodox contributions, focusing only upon reactivities. In Light's (1972) treatment of prewar blacks and Asians in the USA the overrepresentation of Asians in business proprietorships is credited to reactions arising from relative satisfaction and immigrant solidarity *as well as* to rotating credit associations, culturally transmitted institutions fitting the orthodox model (see also Woodrum, Rhodes and Feagin, 1980:1245).

Orthodox, reactive, or mixed entrepreneurship arises when only-orthodox, only-reactive or mixed orthodox and reactive components of entrepreneurship figure in an empirical analysis. On the face of the available evidence, some groups belong in one, other groups in another category. The crucial evidence arises from two comparisons. On the one hand, the foreign-born in general have been overrepresented in American small business since at least 1880 and are still overrepresented. On the other hand some foreign-born groups have higher rates of business self-employment than do others. For example, Jews have been and remain extraordinarily entrepreneurial whereas Irish have been lower than the foreign-born average (Goldscheider and Kobrin, 1980). The general overrepresentation of the foreign-born betokens a situationally-induced responsiveness to self-employment. This responsiveness is *prima facie* evidence for a reactive model. On the other hand, the higher than average rates of selected foreign-born groups suggest unique cultural endowments. Unique endowments imply cultural heritages transmitted intact, the orthodox cultural model. The best fit of theory and evidence occurs when theory acknowledges the additive possibilities of orthodox and reactive components. On this view, the foreign-born in general experience the reactive entrepreneurship arising from their alien situation, but middleman minorities (Jews, Chinese, Greeks, etc.) add to this reaction their culturally intact heritages of sojourning entrepreneurship

(Bonacich and Modell, 1980:Ch. 2). As a result, rates of entrepreneurship are higher among middleman minorities than among the foreign-born in general, and higher among the foreign-born than among the native-born whites.

ETHNIC AND CLASS RESOURCES

Efforts to explain ethnic and immigrant entrepreneurship invariably turn up batteries of special causes. That is, the immigrants developed higher than average rates of entrepreneurship because they drew upon special resources which native groups lacked. In Barth's (1962) terminology these facilities constitute entrepreneurial "assets" but the term resources is more general and does not lend itself to confusion with financial assets (Light, 1980:35). *Ethnic resources* are any and all features of the whole group which coethnic business owners can utilize in business or from which their business benefits (Reitz, 1982; Wallman, 1979a:ix; 1979b:10). Thus, ethnic resources include orthodox cultural endowments, relative satisfaction, reactive solidarities, sojourning orientation, and these four encompass all types of ethnic resources empirically described in the existing literature (cf. Turner and Bonacich, 1980: 152). As such, ethnic resources should be distinguished from class resources. *Class resources* are cultural and material. On the material side, class resources are private property in the means of production and distribution, human capital, and money to invest. On the cultural side, class resources are bourgeois values, attitudes, knowledge and skills transmitted intergenerationally in the course of primary socialization (DiMaggio, 1982:190–1). An established bourgeoisie equips its youth with appropriate class resources, and, having them, the youth are well endowed to prosper in a market economy. Class resources exist, and sociological theory has amply and basically acknowledged their importance. An analytical dispute has arisen, however, when studies of ethnic entrepreneurship have sought to distinguish ethnic resources from class resources. The mainstream view ignored ethnic resources, assuming that only class resources do or even can exist. On this view, an ethnic bourgeoisie is just a bourgeoisie rather than a bourgeoisie which has unique access to ethnic resources.

In principle, class and ethnic resources might occur singly or in combination. This compatibility yields four basic etiologies: class-only, ethnic-only, class-ethnic mixed, and no resources. A class-only etiology explains ethnic minority or immigrant entrepreneurship strictly on the basis of class origins, property, money, and human capital. Class-only explanation is Type 1 in Table 2. Ethnic-only analysis omits the above, focusing explanation wholly upon ethnic resources such as cultural heritages, reactive solidarities, sojourning, and relative satisfaction. Ethnic-only explanation is Type 2 in Table 2. Mixed analysis combines elements of ethnic and class analysis to suit empirical cases of entrepreneurship. Mixed explanation is Type 3 in Table 2. Since class-only analysis is most compatible with a macro-theory of the economy, the mixed and ethnic-only analytic possibilities signal a newly discovered frontier of theoretical controversy. If the latter types exist, class macro-theory needs adjustment to take into account complexities currently ignored.

The North American literature contains no examples of class-only or ethnic-only resource-mobilizing entrepreneurial subgroups. All the empirical cases are mixed. The evidence thus reduces the theoretical polarities to ideal types. Admittedly some cases of ethnic minority or immigrant entrepreneurship weigh more heavily on one side or the other of this class/ethnic balance. Especially in the past, immigrant entrepreneurship seems to have depended more heavily upon ethnic resources than it currently does. Turn-of-the-century Chinese and Japanese immigrants in California are the best-documented illustrations. Disadvantaged in the general labor market, they turned in extraordinary proportion to self-employment, apparently mobilizing ethnic resources very effectively to this end (Light, 1972; Modell, 1977; Bonacich and Modell, 1980). Post-1970 Asian immigrants in North America continue to mobilize ethnic resources to support business ownership, but the balance has shifted toward money, human capital, and bourgeois culture. Thus, all cases of Asian entrepreneurship have been mixed, but in the last half-century the balance has appreciably swung from ethnic toward class resources (Thompson, 1979).

In contemporary American and Canadian society, immigrant entrepreneurship still combines ethnic and class resources, thus creating an empirical problem of sorting out each contributor and assessing its contribution. Thorny as is this measurement problem the empirical dualism is clear especially in the important cases of political refugees from the Third World. To a substantial extent, Korean, Vietnamese, Taiwanese, Hong Kong, Cuban, and Iranian immigrants now in the United States derived from property-owning upper classes in their countries of origin.[2] Fearing or experiencing sociopolitical turmoil in their homelands, these refugees entered the United States with only capital, money to invest, and bourgeois cultural values. Accordingly, it is no

TABLE 2 *Ethnic and Class Resources of Entrepreneurship*

| | RESOURCE BASIS | | | |
| | Ethnic | | Class | |
	Orthodox	Reactive	Material	Cultural
1. Class-only	O	O	X	X
2. Ethnic-only	X	X	O	O
3. Mixed	X	X	X	X
4. Mixed: class predominant	x	x	X	X
5. Mixed: ethnic predominant	X	X	x	x
6. No resources	O	O	O	O

O = none

x = some

X = much

surprise that their involvement in small business has been extensive, their success in it remarkable, and their achievement much celebrated in popular media (Ramirez, 1980). On a class-only model the small business success of these refugees reflects only the class resources they brought with them, and any group of wealthy refugees would have created as many small businesses. Ethnicity conferred nothing: this is the null hypothesis.

Class resources indisputably help, but empirical research suggests that a class-only explanation is inadequate. An immigrant bourgeoisie utilizes ethnic resources in supplementation of class resources. The two best-studied examples are Cubans in Miami, and Koreans in Los Angeles.[3] Wilson and Portes (1980; Portes, 1981; Wilson and Martin, 1982) found that about one-third of Cubans in Miami were employed in Cuban-owned business and another fragment were self-employed. For the Cubans returns on human capital were more favorable among the self-employed than among those employed for wages in the competitive sector. Indeed, returns on human capital were equivalent to those in the primary sector. Explaining this success, Wilson and Portes (1980:315) conclude:

> Immigrant entrepreneurs make use of language and cultural barriers and of ethnic affinities to gain privileged access to markets and sources of labor. . . . The necessary counterpart to these ethnic ties of solidarity is the principle of ethnic preference in hiring and of support of other immigrants in their economic ventures.

Since these resources would be unavailable in Cuba, the Cuban immigrant bourgeoisie acquires access to ethnic resources in Miami where they are members of a cultural minority. To a substantial extent, these reactive resources permit the Cubans to thrive in small business and even to outperform the native whites in this sphere despite the material advantages of the latter.

Bonacich, Light and Wong (1977; see also Light, 1980; Bonacich and Jung, 1982) have looked into the entrepreneurial success of 60,000 Koreans in Los Angeles. In 1980, approximately 40 percent of employed Korean men headed small firms (Yu, 1982:54).[4] An additional 40 percent of Koreans worked in these firms so only about 20 percent of the Korean immigrants found

employment in non-Korean-owned firms or government agencies. Admittedly, the Korean immigrants were highly educated: on one account nearly 70 percent of men had college degrees compared with only 15 percent of Los Angeles County residents in general. Additionally, the Koreans brought with them sums of capital rarely less than $25,000 and sometimes millions. On the other hand, these class resources supplemented ethnic resources; they did not exclude them. As among the Cubans in Miami, Koreans in Los Angeles made effective business use of language and cultural barriers distinguishing coethnics from the general population, reactive social solidarity, nepotistic hiring, and formal and informal mutual support networks. Additionally, Koreans made some use of rotating credit associations,[5] nationalistic appeals for labor peace, vertical and horizontal integration of firms, informal and formal restraints of trade,[6] and political connections with City Hall developed by leading Korean business organizations. In all these respects, Korean entrepreneurship drew upon ethnic resources, not merely upon class resources.

COLLECTIVIST AND INDIVIDUALIST STYLES OF ENTREPRENEURSHIP

Textbook treatments of entrepreneurship have long begun with the economistic assumption that small business owners are individualists. Indeed, the term "entrepreneurial individualism" remains in general currency as a reflection of this persisting assumption. Underlying the microeconomic theory of the firm are the class resources of the bourgeoisie which provide facilities for individual business owners. In Schumpeter's famous image, these entrepreneurs behave like spectators in a crowded stadium during a rainstorm. Feeling rain, each spectator independently decides to raise his umbrella, and decides to put it away when the sun once again comes out. In this analogy, the material resource is the umbrella, and the cultural resource is the trained wisdom to utilize it properly. But each entrepreneur thinks and acts independently albeit in utilization of class-linked resources.

Accepting Schumpeter's (1934:81, n.1, 2) class-only model of entrepreneurship,[7] sociology has, however, parted company with neoclassical economics on the issue of consciousness. Insofar as a resource-transmitting bourgeoisie develops self-consciousness, this consciousness becomes a class resource capable of affecting the economic success of members. Thus, elitist studies of the American upper class have long claimed that debutante cotillions, preparatory schools, swank vacation resorts, exclusive suburbs, and stuffy downtown clubs reflect and forge upper-class consciousness (Useem, 1980:53–8). Group consciousness enhances the chances of individual bourgeois to monopolize access to material and status rewards. For instance, clubs provide a private place to concoct business and political deals or to arrange marriages. Admittedly the importance of bourgeois group consciousness has not been so systematically examined in its economic as in its political ramifications. However, class-only theories of the bourgeoisie have acknowledged the development of an entrepreneurial collectivism which enhances the competitive chances of the individual members of the bourgeoisie. Evaluating two generations of social research on the American business elite, Useem (1980:58) finds "internal cohesion" strikingly in evidence. "Unity is far more extensively developed at the top than anywhere else in the class structure."

A similar evolution has characterized sociological studies of ethnic business (Jenkins, 1984). Classical sociologists called attention to cultural endowments which governed the style of business ownership, and explained in historical context the transition from merchant to bourgeois. The prototype was, of course, Weber's (1958a) Protestant sectarians whose economic style reflected religio-cultural values. Their disciplined lifestyle caused them to prosper in business, but they were expected to do so as noncooperating individuals standing or falling on individual merits. Of course, there is no denying that under some cultural or situational conditions, small business owners can be individualistic nor that introjected values of hard work, thrift, and economic rationality encourage business survival and success.[8] Bechofer et al.'s (1974) study of Scottish business owners in Edinburgh depicts individualistic business conduct. Jarvenpa and Zenner (1979) reported the same individualism among Scots in the Canadian fur trade. On the other hand, even Weber overstated the extent of individualism among Protestant sectarians and, aware of this error, was more careful (1958b) in some writings. Historical research among Puritan business owners in seventeenth-century New England has not disclosed the expected individualism. On the contrary, Bailyn (1955), Hall (1977), and Griffen and Griffen (1977:150) concluded that observantly Calvinist business owners in New England were active participants in commercial networks knit together on the basis of extended kinship and friendship, these networks actually linking ports of origin in the British Isles and New England cities.

In the same sense, cultural treatments of middlemen minorities in North America began with the assumption that cultural subgroups acted out their values in enterprising individualism based upon hard work, thrift, rationality, and self-denial (Auster and Aldrich, 1984). In this model, immigrant entrepreneurs drew upon a cultural tradition, then fanned out into the economy in individualistic search for profitable opportunities. Equipped with cultural resources, co-ethnics knew how to make the most out of such business opportunities as they encountered – but each did so as an isolated individual.

There is, of course, no question that ethnic values and motivations do affect individual behavior. However, ethnic research has shown there exists a largely ignored dimension of collective action which goes beyond individualistic value or motivational effects, important as those are (Leff, 1979). This is the dimension of entrepreneurial collectivism in the ethnic minority (Young, 1971:140–1; Cummings, 1980b). Collective styles of entrepreneurship depend upon group resources in which business owners only participate insofar as they maintain active, adult participation in community life (Herman, 1979:84). For example, a rotating credit association requires cooperators to establish a reputation for trustworthiness in the ethnic community, and this reputation depends in turn upon active involvement (Light, 1972:Ch. 2). Similarly, an immigrant or ethnic informational network confers benefits upon business owners, but to obtain these benefits an owner needs to belong to the network. Isolates cannot share network information so this ethnic resource only benefits participants in ethnic community networks. Finally, trade guilds may regulate and control internal competition, but the benefits of collusion in restraint of trade accrue to members. Isolates suffer the consequences of collusion by others.

In principle, class and ethnic resources both confer potentialities for individualist or collectivistic styles of business management. As before, however, all empirical cases in the literature have been mixed. For instance, Koreans in Los Angeles have utilized both class and ethnic resources, and these resources have here supported individualistic and there collectivistic entrepreneurship. Taken together, Korean entrepreneurship in Los Angeles is a pastiche of ethnic and class resources and individualist and collectivist styles. On the other hand, the balance of individualism and collectivism in immigrant entrepreneurship appears to have shifted in three generations. Chinese and Japanese immigrants in California at the turn of the century utilized entrepreneurial strategies which were more collectivistic than those currently utilized by Chinese immigrants in Toronto (Chan and Cheung, 1982). In the same manner, Polish, Finnish, Irish, Mormon, and Jewish entrepreneurship appears to have undergone a shift in this century away from an immigrant-generation dependence upon collective resources toward a native-born generation dependence upon individual resources.[9]

Two related changes explain this shifting balance. On the one hand, the competitive sector has become smaller in size and the price of admission higher in response to capitalist concentration. Ethnic collectivism may be less adequate than in the past. On the other hand, upward social mobility has conferred class resources upon native-born ethnics whose progenitors did not have them. Specifically, native-born descendants of immigrant business owners enter the business sector with money, education, and skills their forebears lacked. Possessing class resources, immigrant and ethnic minority entrepreneurs become more individualistic in style. Thus, impoverished immigrants needed to combine their small amounts of capital in rotating credit associations in order to assemble a sum large enough to finance small business. Dependent upon kinsmen and landsmen for initial capital, immigrant business owners could not thereafter

operate their businesses as if they were isolated individualists. With personal money to invest, the descendants of these immigrants and contemporary "new" immigrants no longer need to borrow from kin and friends (Kim, 1977). Therefore, they establish their business enterprises without rotating credit associations, and operate them in a more individualistic manner.[10] Similarly, poor immigrants did not understand inventories or balance sheets so they turned to kin and friends for advice in business management. Equipped with MBAs, their descendants and North America's new immigrants possess the business skills they need as class resources. Therefore, they do not need to turn for management advice to informal, ethnically linked agencies, and they are free to operate their business enterprises as if they were isolated individuals. In this manner, access to class resources may obviate collectivism in ethnic enterprise – but not exclude it altogether. In Toronto, Thompson (1979) reports, a bipolar business class has actually emerged as a result of these processes. On the one side are the old-fashioned, ethnic-dependent Mom and Pop store owners; on the other, Hong Kong millionaires operating investment corporations. "The new stratum of entrepreneurial elites differs in both origin and lifestyle from the traditional merchant elites who for years controlled the [Chinese] ethnic community" (Thompson, 1979:311).

In principle, ethnic and immigrant small business ought to run out of solidarity to exploit because cultural assimilation and higher education undercut the ascriptive solidarities from which immigrant-generation business owners derived the resources to power their business network (Turner and Bonacich, 1980:157). Much evidence suggests that over generations ethnic resources do decay for this reason (Bonacich and Modell, 1980:Chs. 6, 9; Borhek, 1970; Goldscheider and Kobrin, 1980; Montero, 1981). "Over the long run," Reitz (1980:231) observes, "there is a progressive trend toward abandonment of ethnic group ties for all groups in which long-term experience can be measured." However, the rate of deterioration has been much slower than sociologists once expected (Wilensky and Lawrence, 1979). The indisputable profitability of ethnic capitalism is an apparent cause of this retardation. Especially relative to equally qualified members of the same ethnic group in the general labor market, owners of ethnic sector business enterprises earn high incomes in business. Big profits make ethnic business attractive (Wilson and Portes, 1980:314; Sway, 1983; Reitz, 1982; Bonacich and Modell, 1981:257). Ethnic business owners identify with their ethnic community and participate actively in it. They provide the leadership for ethnic institutions. Ethnic attachments also persist more strongly among wage workers whose workplace is a co-ethnic firm whose language is that of the homeland, not English (Bonacich and Modell, 1980; Reitz, 1980; Woodrum, Rhodes and Feagin, 1980:1240–52). These two classes often account for between 40 and 80 percent of the total ethnic population. Ethnic-owned businesses "help prop up other institutions which recruit and maintain ethnic membership" (Reitz, 1980:223). Ethnicity supports the ethnic economy, and the ethnic economy supports ethnic perpetuation (Bonacich and Modell, 1981:257).

NO RESOURCES ENTREPRENEURSHIP

The preceding analysis offers a satisfactory account of why equally disadvantaged ethnic and immigrant minorities display unequal rates of entrepreneurship: survival and success depend upon group resources. Groups with more resources outperform groups with less; and groups with class resources are individualistic whereas groups with ethnic resources are collectivistic. On this view, entrepreneurship is highest when disadvantaged immigrant minorities are well endowed with class and ethnic resources; endowment with one or the other is intermediate; and negligible endowment in both class and ethnic resources implies correspondingly low rates of entrepreneurship.

Behind this conclusion lies the assumption that immigrant minorities' rate of business ownership is a fair measure of their entrepreneurship. The rate of business ownership has been operationally defined as self-employed per 1000 in the urban labor force.[11] A major objection to this definition, it is increasingly clear, arises from the inadequacy of published statistics (Karsh, 1977; Light, 1979:39–40; US Small Business, 1980). "The Census has a completely nonsociological way of defining 'self employment' " (Wright

et al., 1982:712n). US statistics routinely exclude petty traders without fixed business premises, no-employee firms, illegally operated firms in legitimate industries, and firms producing unlawful goods or services. Since minorities and immigrants bulk very large in such firms, their exclusion from official tabulations results in undercounts of minority-owned business enterprise as well as theoretical misperception of the whole phenomenon of ethnic entrepreneurship. No one knows how many untabulated firms exist nor what is their distribution among various sectors of the labor force.

The case of native-born Americans is instructive because blacks are disadvantaged but native-born. All statistical and ethnographic sources have uniformly reported that rates of business self-employment among urban blacks have been and remain lower than among even native-white, let alone the foreign-born (Light, 1972, 1979, 1980). At the same time, ethnographic sources have stressed the importance of "hustling" as an economic activity among underclass urban blacks (Valentine, 1978; Glasgow, 1980:9, 90; Light, 1977b). Hustling involves piecing together a livelihood by operating a variety of legal, semi-legal, and sometimes illegal business activities. Legal enterprises of urban blacks include street corner and door-to-door peddling of trinkets, objets d'art, junk, salvage, and fire-damaged merchandise. Unlawfully conducted legal enterprises include unlicensed taxicabs, unlicensed pharmacies, unlicensed medical services, welfare cheating, tax-evading labor services and so forth. Illegal enterprise includes gambling administration, pimping, prostitution, narcotics vending, and other victimless crimes (Light 1977a, 1977b). Predatory crimes include armed robbery, burglary, shop-lifting, and all similar activities. All these self-employed activities are entrepreneurial in that they involve risk and uncertain return (Harbison, 1956:365). Although comprehensive statistics are lacking, there seems little doubt that urban blacks are as overrepresented in marginal legal and unlawfully operated self-employment as crime statistics indicate they are in illegal enterprise and predatory crime. Taken together, this package suggests much higher than average self-employment among economically marginal blacks in unmeasured business at the same time that official statistics reveal much lower than av-erage self-employment in measured business.

Given the presumptively high rates of black self-employment in these undocumented indus-tries, it is improper to conclude that native blacks are less entrepreneurial than other economically disadvantaged immigrants and ethnic minorities. It rather appears that native-born blacks have elaborated an alternative, heavily illegal, highly individualistic style of coping with protracted economic marginality. Compared to the foreign-born in general, and middleman minorities in particular, native-born blacks are low in ethnic resources of entrepreneurship, but share eco-nomic disadvantage (Wong, 1977; Light, 1972:Chs. 2, 6–8; Venable, 1972:30). Compared to native whites, native blacks are high in eco-nomic disadvantage, low in class resources of entrepreneurship, but similar in respect to ethnic resources of entrepreneurship. Table 3 docu-ments these contrasts. Low on ethnic resources of entrepreneurship but high in economic disad-vantage, native-born blacks were compelled to depend upon class resources in which they have been underendowed for centuries. As an overall result, marginal black enterprises have not bro-ken into the circle of legal, officially enumerated small business enterprises. Their problem has been nonpromotion of their very large class of petty but invisible enterprises such that a visible

minority enjoy upward social mobility within the legitimate, competitive sector (Glasgow, 1980: 189). It is in the assistance of upward mobility that ethnic and class resources make themselves appreciably manifest (Gelfand, 1981:185, 190). Given labor force disadvantage, chronic unem-ployment or both, any ethnic or immigrant mi-nority resorts to self-employment, but only re-sources make possible the promotion of marginal enterprises into small businesses whose long-term profitability brings along the social mobility of proprietors, their kin, and their heirs (Wilson and Martin, 1982:155–7).

SUMMARY AND CONCLUSION

Uneven development has created economic en-claves within which small business can still be profitable. Success in small business requires, however, a combination of class and ethnic re-sources with some evidence indicating the for-mer have increased their importance in the last generation. Nonetheless, ethnic resources pers-ist, and immigrant and ethnic minority groups are overrepresented in small business in large part because their access to ethnic resources per-mits them to outcompete native workers. In this comparative respect native whites and blacks are similar but the native blacks lack class resources and additionally suffer labor market disadvan-

TABLE 3   *Profiles of Entrepreneurship*

	Comparison Groups			
	Middleman Minorities	Foreign-Born	Native Blacks	Native Whites
Rotating credit associations	+			
Precapitalist commercial background	+			
Landsmannschaften	+	+		
Extended kinship	+	+		
Relative satisfaction	+	+		
Sojourning	+			
Unpaid family labor	+	+		
Labor force disadvantage	+	+	+	
Ineligible for public welfare	+	+		
Language barrier	+	+		
Special consumer demands	+	+		

tage which gives them a motive to seek self-employment income. Underclass blacks do find this income in the form of hustling, but hustling has by and large failed to create firms that are large and legal enough to achieve visibility in government statistics.

Ethnic resources of entrepreneurship often depend upon premodern values and solidarities. So long as these survive in the ethnic community, co-ethnic business owners are able to utilize them in business, achieving advantage over fully proletarianized, native-born workers among whom blacks are conspicuous. In theory, ethnic capitalism and cultural assimilation should first undercut and then demolish precapitalist solidarities, thus eliminating an ethnic group's competitive edge in small business. In the perspective of history, this self-destruction probably occurs. However, its rate should not be exaggerated. Ethnic enterprises still earn handsome financial returns, and these substantial rewards prop up the ethnicity upon which owners depend for resources. Profitability brakes the rates of deterioration of ethnic solidarity, supports the persistence of ethnic-owned firms in the competitive sector, and perpetuates the whole competitive sector.

ENDNOTES

An earlier version of this paper was presented at the 10th World Congress of the International Sociological Association, Mexico City, August 19, 1982.

1. See Gelfand, 1981; Chs. 4, 5; Goldscheider and Kobrin, 1980; Light, 1972:Ch. 5; Light and Wong, 1975; Wong, 1977; Sassen-Koob, 1981:30–1; Modell, 1977; Bonacich and Modell, 1981; Lovell-Troy, 1980, 1981; Chock, 1981; Sway, 1983; Sengstock, 1967; Bonacich, Light and Wong, 1977; Blackstone, 1981; Herman, 1979:90; Zenner, 1982; Waldinger, 1982; Yu, 1982; Bonacich and Jung, 1982.

2. "Most of the refugees are ethnic Chinese, most of whom were shopkeepers or businessmen who had little future under a communist system." "Bleak Outlook for Vietnam refugees," *East/West* (San Francisco), June 20, 1979:1. See also: McMillan, 1982; Rogg, 1971:480; Chan and Cheung, 1982; Thompson, 1979; Wilson and Portes, 1980.

3. But two recent studies have produced important new documentation. In New York City's garment industry, Waldinger (1982) reported extensive and critically important utilization of ethnic networks among Dominican entrepreneurs. In Los Angeles's taxi industry, Russell (1982) documented the mutual assistance common among Soviet Jews seeking to break into the occupation.

4. A similar situation apparently exists in New York City, site of the second largest Korean settlement in the United States. See Illsoo Kim, 1981:110; see also "Faced with prejudice and language difficulties, New York Koreans turn to private business," *Koreatown* (Los Angeles), December 14, 1981:8–9.

5. "$400,000 *kye* broke," *Joong-ang Daily News* (Los Angeles: in Korean), February 20, 1979; Kim, 1981:210–11.

6. "Markets agree to cut down on competition," *Korea Times English Section* (Los Angeles), November 23, 1981:1. "KCCI asks bizmen for more cooperation," *Korea Times English Section*, February 6, 1980; "Fifteen Korean chambers unite," *Koreatown*, November 17, 1980; "Prosperity of shops leads community development." *Korea Times English Section*, November 22, 1976.

7. Schumpeter's (1934) views are endorsed in Beveridge and Oberschall, 1979:207, 225, 229; criticized in Jones and Sakong, 1980:211; reviewed in Hagen, 1968:221–7.

8. "When individuals go into business they must be prepared to lower standards of living and make personal sacrifices until their firms begin to prosper," Cingolani, 1973.

9. See Chap. 4–10 in Cummings (ed.), 1980.

10. In the wake of extremely high interest rates, white Californians began to utilize the *Pandero*, a Brazilian rotating credit association, for purposes of home purchase. In this situation, a class-based, individualistic style reverted to old-fashioned collectivism as class resources became inadequate because of high interest rates. See DeWolfe, 1982.

11. Gerry and Birkbeck (1981) and Portes (1981) argue that marginal self-employed of the Third World are "thinly disguised wage workers" because of their indirect economic dependencies upon big firms. However, Aldrich and Weiss (1981) have shown that a linear relationship exists between employment size and business owners' incomes, and linearity persists in the USA when non-employer firms are introduced. "Owners without employees are simply the 'poorest of the poor' among small capitalists. This group . . . should be assigned to the owner class in future research."

SEVENTEEN

The Immigrant Enclave
Theory and Empirical Examples

Alejandro Portes
Robert D. Manning

I. INTRODUCTION

The purpose of this chapter is to review existing theories about the process of immigrant adaptation to a new society and to recapitulate the empirical findings that have led to an emerging perspective on the topic. This emerging view revolves around the concepts of different modes of structural incorporation and of the immigrant enclave as one of them. These concepts are set in explicit opposition to two previous viewpoints on the adaptation process, generally identified as assimilation theory and the segmented labor markets approach.

The study of immigrant groups in the United States has produced a copious historical and sociological literature, written mostly from the assimilation perspective. Although the experiences of particular groups varied, the common theme of these writings is the unrelenting efforts of immigrant minorities to surmount obstacles impeding their entry into the "mainstream" of American society (Handlin, 1941, 1951; Wittke, 1952; Child, 1943; Vecoli, 1977). From this perspective, the adaptation process of particular immigrant groups followed a sequential path from initial economic hardship and discrimination to eventual socioeconomic mobility arising from increasing knowledge of American culture and acceptance by the host society (Warner and Srole, 1945; Gordon, 1964; Sowell, 1981). The focus on a "core" culture, the emphasis on consensus-

building, and the assumption of a basic patterned sequence of adaptation represent central elements of assimilation theory.

From this perspective, the failure of individual immigrants or entire ethnic groups to move up through the social hierarchies is linked either to their reluctance to shed traditional values or to the resistance of the native majority to accept them because of racial, religious, or other shortcomings. Hence, successful adaptation depends, first of all, on the willingness of immigrants to relinquish a "backward" way of life and, second, on their acquisition of characteristics making them acceptable to the host society (Eisenstadt, 1970). Throughout, the emphasis is placed on the social psychological processes of motivation, learning, and interaction and on the cultural values and perceptions of the immigrants themselves and those who surround them.

The second general perspective takes issue with this psychosocial and culturalist orientation as well as with the assumption of a single basic assimilation path. This alternative view begins by noting that immigrants and their descendants do not necessarily "melt" into the mainstream and that many groups seem not to want to do so, preferring instead to preserve their distinct ethnic identities (Greeley, 1971; Glazer and Moynihan, 1970). A number of writers have focused on the resilience of these communities and described their functions as sources of mutual support and collective political power (Suttles,

Reprinted with permission from Susan Olzak and Joane Nagel, eds. *Competitive Ethnic Relations.* Orlando, FL: Academic Press, 1986. Copyright © 1986 by Academic Press, Inc.

1968; Alba and Chamlin, 1983; Parenti, 1967). Others have gone beyond descriptive accounts and attempted to establish the causes of the persistence of ethnicity. Without exception, these writers have identified the roots of the phenomenon in the economic sphere and, more specifically, in the labor-market roles that immigrants have been called on to play.

Within this general perspective, several specific theoretical approaches exist. The first focuses on the situation of the so-called unmeltable ethnics – blacks, Chicanos, and American Indians – and finds the source of their plight in a history of internal colonialism during which these groups have been confined to specific areas and made to work under uniquely unfavorable conditions. In a sense, the role of colonized minorities has been to bypass the free labor market, yielding in the process distinct benefits both to direct employers of their labor and, indirectly, to other members of the dominant racial group (Blauner, 1972; Geschwender, 1978). This continuation of colonialist practices to our day explains, according to this view, the spatial isolation and occupational disadvantages of these minorities (Barrera, 1980).

A second approach attempts to explain the persistence of ethnic politics and ethnic mobilization on the basis of the organization of subordinate groups to combat a "cultural division of labor." The latter confined members of specific minorities to a quasi-permanent situation exploitation and social inferiority. Unlike the first view, the second approach does not envision the persistence of ethnicity as a consequence of continuing exploitation, but rather as a "reactive formation" on the part of the minority to reaffirm its identity and its interests (Hechter, 1975; Despres, 1975). For this reason, ethnic mobilizations are often most common among groups who have already abandoned the bottom of the social ladder and started to compete for positions of advantage with members of the majority (Nagel and Olzak, 1982).

A final variant focuses on the situation of contemporary immigrants to the United States. Drawing on the dual labor market literature, this approach views recent immigrants as the latest entrants into the lower tier of a segmented labor market where women and other minorities already predominate. Relative to the latter, immigrants possess the advantages of their lack of experience in the new country, their legal vulnerability, and their greater initial motivation. All of these traits translate into higher productivity and lower labor costs for the firms that employ them (Sassen-Koob, 1980). Jobs in the secondary labor market are poorly paid, require few skills, and offer limited mobility opportunities. Hence, confinement of immigrants to this sector insures that those who do not return home are relegated to a quasi-permanent status as disadvantaged and discriminated minorities (Piore, 1975, 1979).

What these various structural theories have in common is the view of resilient ethnic communities formed as a result of a consistently disadvantageous economic position and the consequent absence of a smooth path of assimilation. These situations, ranging from slave labor to permanent confinement to the secondary labor market, are not altered easily. They have given rise, in time, either to hopeless communities of "unmeltable" ethnics or to militant minorities, conscious of a common identity and willing to support a collective strategy of self-defense rather than rely on individual assimilation.

These structural theories have provided an effective critique of the excessively benign image of the adaptation process presented by earlier writings. However, while undermining the former, the new structural perspective may have erred in the opposite direction. The basic hypothesis advanced in this chapter is that several identifiable modes of labor-market incorporation exist and that not all of them relegate newcomers to a permanent situation of exploitation and inferiority. Thus, while agreeing with the basic thrust of structural theories, we propose several modifications that are necessary for an adequate understanding of the different types of immigrant flows and their distinct processes of adaptation.

II. MODES OF INCORPORATION

In the four decades since the end of World War II, immigration to the United States has experienced a vigorous surge reaching levels comparable only to those at the beginning of the century

(National Research Council, 1985, chapter 2). Even if one restricts attention to this movement, disregarding multiple other migrations elsewhere in the world, it is not the case that the inflow has been of a homogeneous character. Low-wage labor immigration itself has taken different forms, including temporary contract flows, undocumented entries, and legal immigration. More importantly, it is not the case that all immigrants have been directed to the secondary labor market. For example, since the promulgation of the Immigration Act of 1965, thousands of professionals, technicians, and craftsmen have come to the United States, availing themselves of the occupational preference categories of the law. This type of inflow, dubbed "brain drain" in the sending nations, encompasses today sizable contingents of immigrants from such countries as India, South Korea, the Philippines, and Taiwan, each an important contributor to U.S. annual immigration.

The characteristics of this type of migration have been described in detail elsewhere (Portes, 1976, 1981). Two such traits deserve mention, however. First, occupationally skilled immigrants – including doctors, nurses, engineers, technicians, and craftsmen – generally enter the "primary" labor market; they contribute to alleviate domestic shortages in specific occupations and gain access, after a period of time, to the mobility ladders available to native workers. Second, immigration of this type does not generally give rise to spatially concentrated communities; instead, immigrants are dispersed throughout many cities and regions, following different career paths.

Another sizable contingent of entrants whose occupational future is not easily characterized *a priori* are political refugees. Large groups of refugees, primarily from Communist-controlled countries, have come to the United States, first after the occupation of Eastern Europe by the Soviet Army, then after the advent of Fidel Castro to power in Cuba, and finally in the aftermath of the Vietnam War. Unlike purely "economic" immigrants, refugees have often received resettlement assistance from various governmental agencies (Zolberg, 1983; Keely, 1981). The economic adaptation process of one of these groups, the Cubans, will be discussed in detail in this chapter. For the moment, it suffices to note that all the available evidence runs contrary to the notion of a uniform entry of political refugees into low-wage secondary occupations; on the contrary, there are indications of their employment in many different lines of work.

A third mode of incorporation has gained the attention of a number of scholars in recent years. It consists of small groups of immigrants who are inserted or insert themselves as commercial intermediaries in a particular country or region. These "middleman minorities" are distinct in nationality, culture, and sometimes race from both the superordinate and subordinate groups to which they relate (Bonacich, 1973; Light, 1972). They can be used by dominant elites as a buffer to deflect mass frustration and also as an instrument to conduct commercial activities in impoverished areas. Middlemen accept these risks in exchange for the opportunity to share in the commercial and financial benefits gained through such instruments as taxation, higher retail prices, and usury. Jews in feudal and early modern Europe represent the classic instance of a middleman minority. Other examples include Indian merchants in East Africa, and Chinese entrepreneurs in Southeast Asia and throughout the Pacific Basin (Bonacich and Modell, 1980, chapter 1). Contemporary examples in the United States include Jewish, Korean, and other Oriental merchants in inner-city ghetto areas and Cubans in Puerto Rico (Kim, 1981; Cobas, 1984).

Primary labor immigration and middleman entrepreneurship represent two modes of incorporation that differ from the image of an homogeneous flow into low-wage employment. Political refugees, in turn, have followed a variety of paths, including both of the above as well as insertion into an ethnic enclave economy. The latter represents a fourth distinct mode. Although frequently confused with middleman minorities, the emergence and structure of an immigrant enclave possess distinct characteristics. The latter have significant theoretical and practical implications, for they set apart groups adopting this entry mode from those following alternative paths. We turn now to several historical and contemporary examples of immigrant enclaves to clarify their internal dynamics and causes of their emergence.

III. IMMIGRANT ENCLAVES

Immigration to the United States before World War I was, overwhelmingly, an unskilled labor movement. Impoverished peasants from southern Italy, Poland, and the eastern reaches of the Austro-Hungarian Empire settled in dilapidated and crowded areas, often immediately adjacent to their points of debarkation, and took any menial jobs available. From these harsh beginnings, immigrants commenced a slow and often painful process of acculturation and economic mobility. Theirs was the saga captured by innumerable subsequent volumes written from both the assimilation and the structural perspectives.

Two sizable immigrant groups did not follow this pattern, however. Their most apparent characteristic was the economic success of the first generation, even in the absence of extensive acculturation. On the contrary, both groups struggled fiercely to preserve their cultural identity and internal solidarity. Their approach to adaptation thus directly contradicted subsequent assimilation predictions concerning the causal priority of acculturation to economic mobility. Economic success and "clannishness" also earned for each minority the hostility of the surrounding population. These two immigrant groups did not have a language, religion, or even race in common and they never overlapped in significant numbers in any part of the United States. Yet, arriving at opposite ends of the continent, Jews and Japanese pursued patterns of economic adaptation that were quite similar both in content and in their eventual consequences.

A. Jews in Manhattan

The first major wave of Jewish immigration to the United States consisted of approximately 50,000 newcomers of German origin, arriving between 1840 and 1870. These immigrants went primarily into commerce and achieved, in the course of a few decades, remarkable success. By 1900, the average income of German-Jewish immigrants surpassed that of the American population (Rischin, 1962). Many individuals who started as street peddlers and small merchants had become, by that time, heads of major industrial, retail, and financial enterprises.

The second wave of Jewish immigration exhibited quite different characteristics. Between 1870 and 1914, over two million Jews left the Pale of Settlement and other Russian-dominated regions, escaping Czarist persecution. Major pogroms occurred before and during this exodus (Dinnerstein, 1977). Thus, unlike most immigrants of the period, the migration of Russian and Eastern Europe Jews was politically motivated and their move was much more permanent. In contrast to German Jews, who were relatively well educated, the Yiddish-speaking newcomers came, for the most part, from modest origins and had only a rudimentary education. Although they viewed the new Russian wave with great apprehension, German Jews promptly realized that their future as an ethnic minority depended on the successful integration of the newcomers (Rischin, 1962). Charitable societies were established to provide food, shelter, and other necessities, and private schools were set up to teach immigrants English, civics, and the customs of the new country (Howe and Libo, 1979).

Aside from its size and rapidity of arrival, turn-of-the-century Jewish immigration had two other distinct characteristics. First was its strong propensity toward commerce and self-employment in general in preference to wage labor; as German Jews before them, many Russian immigrants moved directly into street peddling and other commercial activities of the most modest sort. Second was its concentration into a single, densely populated urban area – the lower East Side of Manhattan. Within this area, those who did not become storekeepers and peddlers from the start found employment in factories owned by German Jews, learning the necessary rudiments for future self-employment (Sowell, 1981, chapter 4).

The economic activities of this population created, in the course of two decades, a dense network of industrial, commercial, and financial enterprises. Close physical proximity facilitated exchanges of information and access to credit and raw materials. Characteristic of this emerging Jewish enclave is that production and marketing of goods was not restricted to the ethnic community, but went well beyond it into the general economy. Jews entered the printing, metal, and building trades; they became increasingly prominent in jewelry and cigar-making; above all, the garment industry became the primary domain of

Jewish entrepreneurship, with hundreds of firms of all sizes engaged in the trade (Rischin, 1962; Howe and Libo, 1979).

The economic success of many of these ventures did not require and did not entail rapid acculturation. Immigrants learned English and those instrumental aspects of the new culture required for economic advancement. For the rest, they preferred to remain with their own and maintained, for the most part, close adherence to their original religion, language, and values (Wirth, 1928, 1956; Howe, 1976). Jewish enclave capitalism depended, for its emergence and advancement, precisely on those resources made available by a solidaristic ethnic community: protected access to labor and markets, informal sources of credit, and business information. It was through these resources that upstart immigrant enterprises could survive and eventually compete effectively with better-established firms in the general economy.

The emergence of a Jewish enclave in East Manhattan helped this group bypass the conventional assimilation path and achieve significant economic mobility in the course of the first generation, well ahead of complete acculturation. Subsequent generations also pursued this path, but the resources accumulated through early immigrant entrepreneurship were dedicated primarily to furthering the education of children and their entry into the professions. It was at this point that outside hostility became most patent, as one university after another established quotas to prevent the onrush of Jewish students. The last of these quotas did not come to an end until after World War II (Dinnerstein, 1977).

Despite these and other obstacles, the movement of Jews into higher education continued. Building on the economic success of the first generation, subsequent ones achieved levels of education, occupation, and income that significantly exceeded the national average (Featherman, 1971; Sowell, 1981, chapter 4). The original enclave is now only a memory, but it provided in its time the necessary platform for furthering the rapid social and economic mobility of the minority. Jews did enter the mainstream of American society, but they did not do so starting uniformly at the bottom, as most immigrant groups had done; instead, they translated resources made available by early ethnic entrepreneurship into rapid access to positions of social prestige and economic advantage.

B. Japanese on the West Coast

The specific features of Japanese immigration differ significantly from the movement of European Jews, but their subsequent adaptation and mobility patterns are similar. Beginning in 1890 and ending with the enactment of the Gentlemen's Agreement of 1908, approximately 150,000 Japanese men immigrated to the West Coast. They were followed primarily by their spouses until the Immigration Act of 1924 banned any further Asiatic immigration. Although nearly 300,000 Japanese immigrants are documented in this period (Daniels, 1977), less than half of this total remained in the United States (Petersen, 1971). This is due, in contrast to the case of the Jews, to the sojourner character of Japanese immigrants: the intention of many was to accumulate sufficient capital for purchasing farm land or settling debts in Japan. Hence this population movement included commercial and other members of the Japanese middle class who, not incidentally, were explicitly sponsored by their national government.

The residential patterns of Japanese immigrants were not as concentrated as those of Jews in Manhattan, but they were geographically clustered. Almost two-thirds of the 111,010 Japanese reported in the U.S. Census of 1920 lived in California. Further, one-third of California's Japanese residents lived in Los Angeles County in 1940, while another one-third lived in six nearby counties (Daniels, 1977). However, it was not the residential segregation of Japanese immigrants but rather their occupational patterns that eventually mobilized the hostility of the local population.

Japanese immigrants were initially welcomed and recruited as a form of cheap agricultural labor. Their reputation as thrifty and diligent workers made them preferable to other labor sources. Nativist hostilities crystallized, however, when Japanese immigrants shifted from wage labor to independent ownership and small-scale farming. This action not only reduced the supply of laborers but it also increased competition for domestic growers in the fresh-produce market. In 1900, only about 40 Japanese farmers in the entire United States leased or owned a total of 5000 acres of farmland. By 1909, the number of Japanese farmers had risen to 6000 and their collective holdings exceeded 210,000 acres (Petersen, 1971). Faced with such "unfair" competition, California growers turned to the political means at their disposal. In 1913, the state legislature passed the first Alien Land Law, which restricted land ownership by foreigners. This legislation did not prove sufficient, however, and, in subsequent years, the ever-accommodating legislature passed a series of acts closing other legal loopholes to Japanese farming (Petersen, 1971).

These proscriptions, which barred most of the Japanese from the lands, accelerated their entry into urban enterprise. In 1909, Japanese entrepreneurs owned almost 3000 small shops in several Western cities. Forty percent of Japanese men in Los Angeles were self-employed. They operated businesses such as dry-cleaning establishments, fisheries, lunch counters, and produce stands that marketed the production of Japanese farms (Light, 1972).

The ability of the first-generation *Issei* to escape the status of stoop labor in agriculture was based on the social cohesion of their community. Rotating credit associations offered scarce venture capital, while mutual-aid organizations provided assistance in operating farms and urban businesses. Light (1972) reports that capitalizations as high as $100,000 were financed through ethnic credit networks. Economic success was again accompanied by limited instrumental acculturation and by careful preservation of national identity and values. It was the availability of investment capital, cooperative business associations, and marketing practices (forward and backward economic linkages) within the ethnic enclave that enabled Japanese entrepreneurs to expand beyond its boundaries and compete effectively in the general economy. This is illustrated by the production and marketing of fresh produce. In 1920, the value of Japanese crops was about 10% of the total for California, when the Japanese comprised less than 1% of the state's population; many retail outlets traded exclusively with a non-Japanese clientele (Light, 1972; Petersen, 1971).

During the early 1940s, the Japanese ethnic economy was serious disrupted but not elimi-

nated by the property confiscations and camp internments accompanying World War II. After the war, economic prosperity and other factors combined to reduce local hostility toward the Japanese. Older *Issei* and many of their children returned to small business, while other second-generation *Nisei*, like their Jewish predecessors, pursued higher education and entered the white-collar occupations *en masse*. This mobility path was completed by the third or *Sansei* generation, with 88% of their members attending college. Other third-generation Japanese have continued, however, the entrepreneurial tradition of their parents (Bonacich and Modell, 1980). Like Jews before them, Japanese-Americans have made use of the resources made available by early immigrant entrepreneurship to enter the mainstream of society in positions of relative advantage. The mean educational and occupational attainment of the group's 600,000 members surpasses at present all other ethnic and native groups, while its average family income is exceeded among American ethnic groups only by the Jews (Sowell, 1981).

IV. CONTEMPORARY EXAMPLES

As a mode of incorporation, the immigrant enclave is not only of historical interest since there are also several contemporary examples. Enclaves continue to be, however, the exception in the post-World War II period, standing in sharp contrast to the more typical pattern of secondary labor immigration. Furthermore, there is no guarantee that the emergence and development of contemporary ethnic enclaves will have the same consequences for their members that they had among turn-of-the-century immigrants.

A. Koreans in Los Angeles

The Korean community of Los Angeles is a recent product of liberalized U.S. immigration laws and strengthened political and economic ties between the two nations. Since 1965–1968, South Korean immigration to the United States has increased sixfold, swelling the Korean population of Los Angeles from less than 9000 in 1970 to over 65,000 in 1975. Approximately 60% of Korean immigrants settle in Los Angeles. In addition to increasing the size of this population flow, U.S.

immigration law has altered its class composition. Korean immigrants come predominantly from the highly educated, Westernized, Christian strata of urban Korea. Their median educational attainment of 16 years is equivalent to an undergraduate education in the United States (Kim 1981; Portes and Mozo, 1985).

Light (1979, 1980) attributes the business impulse of Korean immigrants to their "disadvantage" in the general U.S. labor market. It derives, he argues, from their inability to speak English rather than from discrimination by American employers. Bonacich (1978b; Bonacich, Light, and Wong, 1977), in comparison, describes Korean entrepreneurship as a situational response to the growing commercial vacuum arising from the consolidation of monopoly capitalism and the subsequent decline of small business. In this view, ethnic enterprise constitutes a disguised form of cheap labor that provides inexpensive goods and services for the center economy.

The origins of Korean enterprise may be uncertain but its existence is indisputable. Bonacich estimates that 4000 or one-fourth of all Korean families in Los Angeles County owned their businesses in 1976. The propensity for self-employment among this minority is three times greater than among the total urban labor force of Los Angeles (Bonacich, 1978b). Light consulted published Korean business directories, which are biased against firms with nonethnic clients, and arrived at a conservative estimate of 1142 Korean businesses with the Los Angeles Metropolitan Area.

Korean entrepreneurs, like Jewish and Japanese immigrants before them, are highly dependent on the social and economic resources of their ethnic community. Some immigrants managed to smuggle capital out of Korea, but most rely on individual thrift and ethnic credit systems. For instance, a Korean husband and wife may save their wages from several service and factory jobs until enough capital is accumulated to purchase a small business. This process usually takes 2 or 3 years. Rotating credit systems (gae), which are based on mutual trust and honor, offer another common source of venture capital. This economic institution could not exist without a high degree of social solidarity within the ethnic community. There are more than 500 community social and business associations in Los Angeles, and nearly every Korean is an active member of one or more of them. In addition, Korean businessmen have utilized public resources from the U.S. Small Business Administration as well as loans and training programs sponsored by the South Korean government (Light, 1980; Bonacich et al., 1977).

The ability of the Korean community to generate a self-sustaining entrepreneurial class has had a profound impact on intraethnic labor relations and patterns of ethnic property transfers. For example, labor relations are enmeshed in extended kinship and friendship networks. In this context of "labor paternalism," working in the ethnic economy frequently entails the obligation of accepting low pay and long hours in exchange for on-the-job training and possible future assistance in establishing a small business. Hence, employment in the ethnic economy possesses a potential for advancement entirely absent from comparable low-wage labor in the secondary labor market.

Along the same lines, business practices are fundamentally influenced by cultural patterns. Koreans patronize coethnic businesses and frequently rely on referrals from members of their social networks. Korean-owned businesses, moreover, tend to remain in the community through intraethnic transactions. This is because economic mobility typically proceeds through the rapid turnover of immigrant-owned enterprises. A common pattern of succession, for instance, may begin with a business requiring a relatively small investment, such as a wig shop, and continue with the acquisition of enterprises requiring progressively larger capitalizations: grocery stores, restaurants, gas stations, liquor stores, and finally real estate. This circulation of businesses within the ethnic economy provides a continuous source of economic mobility for aspiring immigrant entrepreneurs. Table 1 presents data illustrating both the significant presence of Koreans in the liquor business in the Los Angeles area and the pattern of intraethnic business transfers among Koreans and other Oriental minorities.

The Korean economy is clearly thriving in Los Angeles. Its emerging entrepreneurial class and accumulating assets have created new employ-

TABLE 1 *Liquor License Transfers in Hollywood, California, 1975*

| | Sellers | | | Buyers as |
Buyers	Korean (%)	Chinese (%)	Japanese (%)	Percent of All Buyers
Korean	79.0	18.5	16.7	15.0
Chinese	9.0	70.4	0.0	6.7
Japanese	4.0	0.0	50.0	3.9
All other	7.5	11.1	33.3	74.4
Total (%)	100.1	100.0	100.0	100.0
Number	67	27	18	641

From Light (1980, pp. 33–57).

ment opportunities for an expanding immigrant community. As in the previous historical examples, the principal characteristic of this structure is a dense network of diversified enterprises that provide goods and services both for the ethnic community and for the general market. It is this characteristic that most clearly differentiates an immigrant enclave from the assortment of restaurants and small shops commonly established by other immigrant minorities to cater to their particular cultural needs.

In 1975, Korean enterprises were overrepresented in retail trade and to a minor extent in wholesale trade (Light, 1980). This sectoral concentration no doubt reflects the recent arrival of most immigrant entrepreneurs and thus the fact that many of them are still in an early phase of business succession. Over time, however, successful Korean enterprises should be able to penetrate more highly capitalized sectors of industry and commerce. The initiation of this trend is already apparent in the presence of immigrant-owned firms in intermediate industries such as construction, manufacturing, and transportation and public utilities. Although underrepresented in these sectors due to large capital requirements and stiff outside competition, the emergence of these firms points to the growing diversity of the ethnic economy. With continuing capital accumulation and continuing immigration from Korea, it is unlikely that this process will lose momentum in the near future.

B. Cubans in Miami

Over the past 20 years, nearly 900,000 Cubans or about 10% of the island's population have emi-

grated, mostly to the United States. The overwhelming proportion of the Cuban population in America, estimated at roughly 800,000, resides in the metropolitan areas of south Florida and New York (Diaz-Briquets and Perez, 1981). This movement of Cuban emigrés has not been a continuous or socially homogeneous flow. Instead, it is more accurately described as a series of "waves," marked by abrupt shifts and sudden discontinuities. This pattern has supported the emergence of an enclave economy through such features as spatial concentration, the initial arrival of a moneyed, entrepreneurial class, and subsequent replenishments of the labor pool with refugees coming from more modest class origins.

In 1959, when Fidel Castro overthrew the regime of Fulgencio Batista, the Cuban community in the United States numbered probably less than 30,000 (Jorge and Moncarz, 1982). The political upheavals of the Revolution, however, precipitated a massive emigration from the island. Not surprisingly, the Cuban propertied class, including landowners, industrialists, and former Cuban managers of U.S.-owned corporations, were the first to leave, following close on the heels of leaders of the deposed regime. In the first year of the exodus, approximately 37,000 emigrés settled in the United States; most were well-to-do and brought considerable assets with them (Thomas and Huyck, 1967). After the defeat of the exile force in the Bay of Pigs, in April 1961, Cuban emigration accelerated and its social base expanded to include the middle and urban working classes (Clark, 1977). By the end of 1962, the first phase of Cuban emigration had concluded and over 215,000 refugees had been admitted to the

United States. The emerging Cuban community in south Florida, unlike earlier Japanese and contemporary Korean settlements, was thus fundamentally conditioned by political forces (Portes and Bach, 1985; Pedraza-Bailey, 1981).

Political factors continued to shape the ups and downs of Cuban emigration as well as its reception by American society over the next two decades. In this period, three additional phases can be distinguished: November 1962 to November 1965, December 1965 to April 1973, and May 1973 to November 1980, including 74,000 in the second phase, 340,000 in the third, and 124,769 in the last (Portes and Bach, 1985, chapter 3). This massive influx of refugees to south Florida generated local complaints about the social and economic strains placed in the area. Accordingly, the policy of the Cuban Refugee Program, originally established by the Kennedy Administration, was oriented from the start to resettle Cubans away from Miami. Assistance to the refugees was often made contingent on their willingness to relocate. Although over 469,000 Cubans elected to move by 1978, many subsequently returned to metropolitan Miami (Clark, 1977; Boswell, 1984). There is evidence that many of these "returnees" made use of their employment in relatively high-wage Northern areas to accumulate savings with which to start new business ventures in Miami. By 1980, the Cuban-born population of the city, composed to a large extent of returnees from the North, was six times greater than the second largest Cuban concentration in New Jersey (Boswell, 1984).

Although a number of Cuban businesses appeared in Miami in the 1960s, they were mostly restaurants and ethnic shops catering to a small exile clientele. An enclave economy only emerged in the 1970s as a result of a combination of factors, including capital availability, access to low-wage labor provided by new refugee cohorts, and the increasingly tenuous hope of returning to Cuba. Cuban-owned firms in Dade County increased from 919 in 1967 to about 8000 in 1976 and approximately 12,000 in 1982. Most of these firms are small, averaging 8.1 workers (Diaz-Briquets, 1985; Portes and Bach, 1985, chapter 6). Cuban firms in such sectors as light manufacturing, including apparel, footwear, beverages, cigars, and furniture, construction, agriculture (sugar), and finance and insurance have ceased supplying an exclusively ethnic clientele to become integrated into the broader local economy. Although the Cuban market in south Florida has also grown in size, the key for success among the larger immigrant-owned firms has been to make use of community resources – labor, credit, and information – to compete with better established outside enterprises (Wilson and Martin, 1982).

This strategy seems to have paid off: between 1969 and 1977, the number of Cuban-owned manufacturing firms almost doubled and construction enterprises virtually tripled. In terms of average gross annual receipts, Cuban manufacturing firms went from a very modest $59,633 in 1969 to $639,817 in 1977, a 1067% increase. By 1972, average gross receipts of Cuban-owned enterprises in Miami exceeded that of Hispanic businesses in other cities, including Los Angeles, which has the largest concentration of such firms (Boswell, 1984; Jorge and Moncarz, 1982). With the exception of banks and other large companies, Cuban service firms continue to depend on an ethnic clientele. The latter, however, has expanded with the growth of both Cuban and other Hispanic populations in the city; service firms have become accordingly larger and more diversified, including restaurants, supermarkets, private clinics, realty offices, legal firms, funeral parlors, and private schools.

The Cuban enclave has been the subject of intense study in recent years. Jorge and Moncarz (1981, 1982) and Diaz-Briquets (1985) have reported on the size and composition of refugee-owned firms in Miami and compared them both with others in the same metropolitan area and with Hispanic enterprises elsewhere. Table 2 presents data drawn from one of these studies on the number of Cuban-owned firms and their relative size in comparison with those owned by other Hispanic groups and black Americans. Although Cuban enterprises are not the most numerous in absolute terms, they are larger on the average and more numerous relative to respective population. Keeping in mind that sizable Cuban exile immigration started only in 1959 and that the first signs of a Cuban business community did not appear until the late 1960s, the data provide a vivid illustration of the dynamism of the process.

Along similar lines, Wilson and Martin (1982) conducted a sophisticated input-output analysis

TABLE 2 *Firm Ownership Among Cubans, Other Hispanics, and Blacks*

	All Firms			Firms with Paid Employees		
Ownership	Number of Firms	Firms per 100,000 Population	Gross Receipts per Firm ($1000)	Number of Firms	Firms per 100,000 Population	Employees per Firm
Cuban	30,336	3650.5	61.6	5888	672.4	6.6
Mexican	116,419	1467.7	44.4	22,718	286.4	4.9
Puerto Rican	13,491	740.0	43.9	1767	96.9	3.9
South Central or South American	26,301	2573.5	38.1	4900	479.4	3.0
All Spanish origin (except other Spanish)	219,355	1889.7	47.5	41,298	355.8	5.0
Black	231,203	872.9	37.4	39,968	150.9	4.1

From Diaz-Briquets (1985).

of business relationships among refugee-owned firms in south Florida and compared them with the predominant pattern among black-owned enterprises in the area. In relation to the latter, Cuban firms were shown to have a high degree of interdependence, with substantial internal "sourcing" among manufacturing and construction firms as well as heavy use of commercial and financial services. This analysis provided the first solid quantitative evidence of a dense network of enterprises at the core of the enclave economy.

These and other studies of immigrant businesses in Miami have been conducted on the basis of secondary data. Paralleling them, other research sought to examine the consequences of these activities for individual mobility through primary data collection. A longitudinal study, initiated in 1973, provided data for an extensive series of statistical analyses on the topic. By 1973 most of the Cuban upper and middle classes had left the country; thus, the 590 adult males interviewed originally in this study came overwhelmingly from lower occupational strata, mostly petty services and industrial blue collar work (Portes, Clark, and Bach, 1977). Despite these modest origins, a sizable number of sample members managed to move out of wage work and into self-employment after only a few years in the country. Between 1973 and 1976, 8% ac-

quired their own businesses, and by 1979, 21.2% had done so. Adding the self-employed to those working in other Cuban-owned firms, almost half of the sample was found to participate in the enclave labor market in 1979 (Portes and Bach, 1985).

A discriminant analysis conducted on the basis of the 1976 follow-up survey clearly differentiated between refugees employed in enclave firms and those working in either segment of the general labor market. In addition, the analysis found a distinct and significant payoff for human capital brought from Cuba among refugees in the enclave economy (Wilson and Portes, 1980). This analysis was replicated with data from a second follow-up, conducted in 1979, yielding essentially identical results (Portes and Bach, 1985). The positive consequences of the enclave mode of incorporation for individual mobility are also reflected in other findings from the same study, three of which may be cited for illustration:

1. Years of education in Cuba, which have little or no payoff for occupational attainment in either the primary or the secondary labor markets, have the strongest positive effect in the enclave. The same pattern holds true for the effect of occupational aspirations.

2. Refugees employed in the enclave are not at a disadvantage with respect to those in the primary labor market either in terms of average income or rewards for human capital. The situation of both groups is far more advantageous than that of refugees employed in the secondary sector.

3. Self-employment in the enclave is the most remunerative occupation on the average. In 1979, the median monthly earnings of employees in this sample was $974, in comparison with $1194 for the self-employed without workers, and $1924 for the self-employed with at least one salaried worker. Although the number of the latter is small, there is every indication that it is likely to increase in the future.

V. CONCLUSION: A TYPOLOGY OF THE PROCESS OF INCORPORATION

Having reviewed several historical and contemporary examples, we can now attempt a summary description of the characteristics of immigrant enclaves and how they differ from other paths. The emergence of an ethnic enclave economy has three prerequisites: first, the presence of a substantial number of immigrants with business experience acquired in the sending country; second, the availability of sources of capital; and third, the availability of sources of labor. The latter two conditions are not too difficult to meet. The requisite labor can usually be drawn from family members and, more commonly, from recent arrivals. Surprisingly perhaps, capital is not a major impediment either since the sums initially required are usually small. When immigrants did not bring them from abroad, they could be accumulated through individual savings or pooled resources in the community. It is the first condition that appears critical. The presence of a number of immigrants skilled in what Franklin Frazier (1949) called the art of "buying and selling" is common to all four cases reviewed above. Such an entrepreneurial-commercial class among early immigrant cohorts can usually overcome other obstacles; conversely, its absence within an immigrant community will confine the community to wage employment even if sufficient resources of capital and labor are available.

Enclave businesses typically start small and cater exclusively to an ethnic clientele. Their expansion and entry into the broader market requires, as seen above, an effective mobilization of community resources. The social mechanism at work here seems to be a strong sense of reciprocity supported by collective solidarity that transcends the purely contractual character of business transactions. For example, receipt of a loan from a rotating credit association entails the duty of continuing to make contributions so that others can have access to the same source of capital. Although, in principle, it would make sense for the individual to withdraw once his loan is received, such action would cut him off from the very sources of community support on which his future business success depends (Light, 1972).

Similarly, relations between enclave employers and employees generally transcend a contractual wage bond. It is understood by both parties that the wage paid is inferior to the value of labor contributed. This is willingly accepted by many immigrant workers because the wage is only *one* form of compensation. Use of their labor represents often the key advantage making poorly capitalized enclave firms competitive. In reciprocity, employers are expected to respond to emergency needs of their workers and to promote their advancement through such means as on-the-job training, advancement to supervisory positions, and aid when they move into self-employment. These opportunities represent the other part of the "wage" received by enclave workers. The informal mobility ladders thus created are, of course, absent in the secondary labor market where there is no primary bond between owners and workers or no common ethnic community to enforce the norm of reciprocity.

Paternalistic labor relations and strong community solidarity are also characteristic of middleman minorities. Although both modes of incorporation are similar and are thus frequently confused, there are three major structural differences between them. First, immigrant enclaves are not exclusively commercial. Unlike middleman minorities, whose economic role is to mediate commercial and financial transactions between elites and masses, enclave firms include in addition a sizable productive sector. The latter may comprise agriculture, light manufacturing, and construction enterprises; their production, marketed often by coethnic intermediaries, is directed toward the general economy and not exclusively to the immigrant community.

Second, relationships between enclave businesses and established native ones are problematic. Middleman groups tend to occupy positions complementary and subordinate to the local owning class; they fill economic niches either disdained or feared by the latter. Unlike them, enclave enterprises often enter in direct competition with existing domestic firms. There is no evidence, for example, that domestic elites deliberately established or supported the emergence of the Jewish, Japanese, Korean, or Cuban business communities as means to further their own economic interests. There is every indication, on the other hand, that this mode of incorporation was largely self-created by the immigrants, often in opposition to powerful domestic interests. Although it is true that enclave entrepreneurs have been frequently employed as subcontractors by outside firms in such activities as garment-making and construction (Bonacich, 1978b), it is incorrect to characterize this role as the exclusive or dominant one among these enterprises.

Third, the enclave is concentrated and spatially identifiable. By the very nature of their activities, middleman minorities must often be dispersed among the mass of the population. Although the immigrants may live in certain limited areas, their businesses require proximity to their mass clientele and a measure of physical dispersion within it. It is true that middleman activities such as moneylending have been associated in several historical instances with certain streets and neighborhoods, but this is not a necessary or typical pattern. Street peddling and other forms of petty commerce require merchants to go into the areas where demand exists and avoid excessive concentration of the goods and services they offer. This is the typical pattern found today among middleman minorities in American cities (Cobas, 1984; Kim, 1981).

Enclave businesses, on the other hand, are spatially concentrated, especially in their early stages. This is so for three reasons: first, the need for proximity to the ethnic market which they initially serve; second, proximity to each other,

which facilitates exchange of information, access to credit, and other supportive activities; third, proximity to ethnic labor supplies on which they crucially depend. Of the four immigrant groups discussed above, only the Japanese partially depart from the pattern of high physical concentration. This can be attributed to the political persecution to which this group was subjected. Originally, Japanese concentration was a rural phenomenon based on small farms linked together by informal bonds and cooperative associations. Forced removal of this minority from the land compelled their entry into urban businesses and their partial dispersal into multiple activities.

Physical concentration of enclaves underlies their final characteristic. Once an enclave economy has fully developed, it is possible for a newcomer to live his life entirely within the confines of the community. Work, education, and access to health care, recreation, and a variety of other services can be found without leaving the bounds of the ethnic economy. This institutional completeness is what enables new immigrants to move ahead economically, despite very limited knowledge of the host culture and language. Supporting empirical evidence comes from studies showing low levels of English knowledge among enclave minorities and the absence of a net effect of knowledge of English on their average income levels (Light, 1980; Portes and Bach, 1985).

Table 3 summarizes this discussion by presenting the different modes of incorporation and their principal characteristics. Two caveats are necessary. First, this typology is not exhaustive, since other forms of adaptation have existed and will undoubtedly emerge in the future. Second, political refugees are not included, since this entry label does not necessarily entail a unique adaptation path. Instead, refugees can select or be channeled in many different directions, including self-employment, access to primary labor markets, or confinement to secondary sector occupations.

Having discussed the characteristics of enclaves and middleman minorities, a final word must be said about the third alternative to employment in the lower tier of a dual labor market. As a mode of incorporation, primary sector immigration also has distinct advantages, although

TABLE 3 *Typology of Modes of Incorporation*

Variable	Primary Sector Immigration	Secondary Sector Immigration	Immigrant Enclaves	Middleman Minorities
Size of immigrant population	Small	Large	Large	Small
Spatial concentration, national	Dispersed	Dispersed	Concentrated	Concentrated
Spatial concentration, local	Dispersed	Concentrated	Concentrated	Dispersed
Original class composition	Homogeneous: skilled workers and professionals	Homogeneous: manual laborers	Heterogeneous: entrepreneurs, professionals, and workers	Homogeneous: merchants and some professionals
Percent occupational status distribution	High mean status/low variance	Low mean status/low variance	Mean status/high variance	Mean status/low variance
Mobility opportunities	High: formal promotion ladders	Low	High: informal ethnic ladders	Average: informal ethnic ladders
Institutional diversification of ethnic community	None	Low: weak social institutions	High: institutional completeness	Medium: strong social and economic institutions
Participation in ethnic organizations	Little or none	Low	High	High
Resilience of ethnic culture	Low	Average	High	High
Knowledge of host country language	High	Low	Low	High
Knowledge of host country institutions	High	Low	Average	High
Modal reaction of host community	Acceptance	Discrimination	Hostility	Mixed: elite acceptance/mass hostility

they are of a different order from those pursued by "entrepreneurial" minorities. Dispersal throughout the receiving country and career mobility based on standard promotion criteria makes it imperative for immigrants in this mode to become fluent in the new language and culture (Stevens, Goodman, and Mick, 1978). Without a supporting ethnic community, the second generation also becomes thoroughly steeped in the ways of the host society. Primary sector immigration thus tends to lead to very rapid social and cultural integration. It represents the path that approximates most closely the predictions of assimilation theory with regard to (1) the necessity of acculturation for social and economic progress and (2) the subsequent rewards received by immigrants and their descendants for shedding their ethnic identities.

Clearly, however, this mode of incorporation is open only to a minority of immigrant groups. In addition, acculturation of professionals and other primary sector immigrants is qualitatively different from that undergone by others. Regardless of their differences, immigrants in other modes tend to learn the new language and culture with a heavy "local" content. Although acculturation may be slow, especially in the case of enclave groups, it carries with it elements unique to the surrounding community – its language in-

flections, particular traditions, and loyalties (Greeley, 1971; Suttles, 1968). On the contrary, acculturation of primary sector immigrants is of a more cosmopolitan sort. Because career requirements often entail physical mobility, the new language and culture are learned more rapidly and more generally, without strong attachments to a particular community. Thus, while minorities entering menial labor, enclave, or middleman enterprise in the United States have eventually become identified with a certain city or region, the same is not true for immigrant professionals, who tend to "disappear," in a cultural sense, soon after their arrival (Stevens et al., 1978; Cardona and Cruz, 1980).

Awareness of patterned differences among immigrant groups in their forms of entry and labor market incorporation represents a significant advance, in our view, from earlier undifferentiated descriptions of the adaptation process. This typology is, however, a provisional effort. Just as detailed research on the condition of particular minorities modified or replaced earlier broad generalizations, the propositions advanced here will require revision. New groups arriving in the United States at present and a revived interest in immigration should provide the required incentive for empirical studies and theoretical advances in the future.

EIGHTEEN

Changing Ladders and Musical Chairs
Ethnicity and Opportunity in Post-Industrial New York

Roger Waldinger

If New York City's brush with fiscal insolvency in the mid-1970s signaled the end for the United States' urban-industrial economies, its revival in the 1980s heralds the emergence of the nation's largest cities as world service centers. For the smokestack cities of the industrial heartland, with their specialized concentrations of industrial capital and labor, there is seemingly no replacement for the run-of-the-mill production activities that are steadily eroding under the twin impact of technological change and international competition. But in the largest urban agglomerations—Chicago, Los Angeles, and most important, New York—the advent of a post-industrial economy, centered around information processing, the coordination of large organizations, and the management of volatile financial markets, has triggered a new phase of growth.

In the course of this transition from goods to services, the demographic base of the United States' largest urban places has been transformed. The era of the post-industrial transformation brought the city two distinctive, largely nonwhite inflows: a movement of displaced blacks from the technological backwaters of the agrarian South; and more recently, a wave of newcomers from the labor-surplus areas of the developing world, in numbers that rival the great immigrations at the turn of the twentieth century.

Thus the city of services is also an increasingly nonwhite city; the central question in urban research is consequently the relationship of the city's new population base to its present economic functions. How do the new, minority population groups fit into the new urban economy? One story holds essentially that they don't. This is the tale of "two cities," of the "new urban reality" of elites and of largely minority poor, in which the city's advanced service base has rendered useless those low-skill residents who earlier had been recruited for those inner-city manufacturing jobs now irrevocably gone.[1] Another story holds that, far from being useless, the minority population are the new drawers of water and hewers of wood. The large urban economy, as this story has it, has not only been transformed, it has been polarized. In this version, the rich need the poor to provide low-cost services, to maintain the city's underbelly, and to prop up what remains of the depressed manufacturing sector.[2]

This paper offers an alternative view. The prism is that of New York City, where the economic sea change is most in evidence and the era of a "majority-minority" city, split almost evenly between whites and native and foreign nonwhites, seems close at hand.[3] The main argument is inspired by a point developed by Stanley Lieberson in his book, *A Piece of the Pie;* namely, if nonwhites are low in the hiring queue, their access to good jobs is greater where the size of the preferred, white group is smaller. Reformulated to account for change over time, this proposition

Reprinted from *Politics and Society,* 15:4 (1986–87) by permission of the author and publisher.

suggests that compositional changes in which the proportion of whites declines set in motion a vacancy chain, allowing nonwhites to move up the job hierarchy as replacements for whites.[4] What I will show is that in New York the massive succession of new populations – occurring simultaneously with the structural transformations noted above – mediated the impact of the shift from goods to services in precisely this way. The driving force for change was a decline in the size of the white population and an upward shift in the social structure of those whites who remained. In the course of occupational change, however, a pattern more complex than a simple one-for-one replacement transpired; after reviewing empirical data from the 1970 and 1980 Censuses of Population, I will develop an explanation for the new ethnic division of labor that emerged from this process.

ECONOMIC AND DEMOGRAPHIC TRANSFORMATIONS

New York shifted from goods to services earlier than did the rest of the United States. In 1950, proportionally fewer New Yorkers worked in manufacturing than was true for the nation as a whole, and thereafter goods-production employment swiftly declined. Although the 1950s and 1960s were boom times for the local economy, these two decades saw a steady decline of New York's manufacturing sector; this erosion slowed only in the late 1960s, when the nation's super-heated economic environment kept New York's old and obsolescent plant in demand. However, the falloff in goods production was more than compensated by two other developments. The more important one was the continued buildup of New York's white-collar, corporate complex. Changes in technology brought new jobs in communications (television) and transport (air); a robust economy led to growth in advertising; the merger mania of the 1960s and the expansion of government regulation meant additional work for New York's corporate offices; and the burst of economic growth in the 1960s spurred a buildup of jobs on Wall Street. While expansion of the private white-collar sector thus took up part of the slack created by the decline of manufacturing, public employment burgeoned in the 1960s,

thus further offsetting any losses in the manufacturing sector.

The apogee of New York's growth was reached in 1969; thereafter the decline was brutal and swift. Nixon's attempt to curb inflation sparked off a minor recession in 1969; for New York City, however, the downswing produced major job losses. Although the rest of the nation soon pulled out of the doldrums, jobs continued to seep out of New York. The root problems were twofold. The 1970s marked the passage to a new stage of intensified interregional and international competition in which capital became increasingly footloose and a revolution in communications and transportation technology accelerated the relocation of jobs from high- to lower-cost areas. Under the impact of this change, New York's manufacturing complex – with its antiquated and inefficient infrastructure, outdated plant, and high-cost labor – could no longer compete. Moreover, the 1970s were also bad times for the once-vibrant white-collar sector. Wall Street went from bull market to bear market as falling stock market prices reflected the weakening U.S. economy and the squeeze on large corporate profits. To cut costs, securities firms sought to reduce their back-office operations, filled mainly with low-level clerical functionaries; this marked the first phase of office automation, and it hastened the winnowing-out process. Further job losses occurred as large corporations moved their headquarters to the suburbs – an increasingly frequent event in the 1970s. The weakening of export sectors brought inevitable decline to local-economy industries: the city's very large wholesaling/retailing complex was particularly hard hit.[5]

Then, in 1977, the erosion stopped; since that time, the city's economy has marched steadily forward. The precise causes of the turnaround are still a matter of debate, but what appears to have happened is that New York's role as a purveyor of advanced services generated a new set of agglomeration economies that first halted and then reversed the city's economic decline. New York is now principally host to activities centered on the processing of information and the transaction of high-level business deals, all of which are increasingly international in scope. The city's pull on these activities is in part due to its size, which both permits extensive specialization in legal, financial, consulting, and other services and attracts the massive corps of highly trained talent on which an international post-industrial business depends. For a variety of reasons—the volatility of financial markets, the importance of discretion, the absence of routinization—many of these factors rely on face-to-face communication and hence are bound together. Gradually, the strength of the export-oriented advanced services has spilled over into the local-economy industries, which now show renewed vigor. Manufacturing remains the weak reed, however, although even in this sector the pace of decline has slowed a bit.[6]

Table 1 traces the changes in the city's economy for the 1970–1980 period. By stopping in 1980, which I do in order to obtain the detailed data on ethnic characteristics available only from the decennial censuses, I capture little of New York's post-1977 growth. Yet the table does highlight most of the trends discussed above, including the disastrous plunge in manufacturing and retailing (the historical loci of low-level jobs), the sizable upswing in private-sector professional and business services, and the slight increase in financial jobs (later to become a torrent), all of

which now constitute the heart of the city's advanced sector.

Thus, New York City's economy has gone from boom to bust to better times. It would be churlish to quarrel with the city's recent success in generating new jobs. Yet the worry is that the demographic changes in New York over the past three decades have been equally as transforming as the economic shifts, and it is not at all clear how the city's new population groups fit into this new economic base.

The demographic transformation of New York can be divided into two phases. Phase 1, which began with the end of World War II and lasted to the end of the 1960s, involved the exodus of the city's white population and the massive in-migration of displaced black sharecroppers from the South and of Puerto Ricans uprooted by that island's modernization. In Phase 2, the white exodus continued, but the black and Puerto Rican inflows halted, to be replaced by a vast influx of newcomers from abroad. The starting point for this change was the liberalization of U.S. immigration laws in 1965; as Table 2 shows, New York has since been a mecca for immigrants, much as it had been in the early twentieth century. Between 1966 and 1979, the city absorbed

TABLE 1   *New York City Employment, 1970–1980 (in thousands)*

Sector	1970	1980	Change	Percentage Change
Construction	105,500	74,080	−31,420	−29.8
Manufacturing	608,500	490,760	−117,740	−19.3
TCU	264,100	197,360	−66,740	−25.3
Wholesale	158,400	136,800	−21,600	−13.6
Retail	444,400	376,580	−67,820	−15.3
FIRE	320,000	321,520	1,520	0.4
Business services	171,400	185,000	13,600	7.9
Personal services	140,800	98,300	−42,500	−30.2
Professional services	370,800	434,820	64,020	17.3
Miscellaneous	48,300	52,080	3,780	7.8
Public sector	518,300	508,000	−10,300	−2.0
Total	3,150,500	2,875,300	−275,200	−8.7%

Sources: 1970, 1980 *Census of Population,* Public Use Microdata Sample.

Note: TCU, transportation, communications, and utilities; FIRE, finance, insurance, and real estate.

TABLE 2 *Immigration, United States and New York City, 1966–1979 (in thousands)*

Years	United States	New York City	NYC as Percentage of U.S.
1966	323.0	61.2	18.9
1967	362.0	66.0	18.2
1968	454.4	75.4	16.6
1969	358.6	67.9	18.9
1970	373.3	74.6	20.0
1971	370.5	71.4	19.3
1972	384.7	76.0	19.8
1973	400.1	76.6	19.1
1974	394.9	73.2	18.5
1975	386.2	73.6	19.1
1976	500.5	90.7	18.1
1977	462.3	76.6	16.6
1978	601.4	88.0	14.6
1979	460.3	82.4	17.9
1966–79	5,834.0	1,053.6	18.1%

Sources: U.S. Department of Justice, Immigration and Naturalization Service, *Statistical Yearbook of the Immigration and Naturalization Service,* annual editions.

over one million legal immigrants; the 1980 census recorded 1,670,000 foreign-born New Yorkers, of whom 928,000 had come to New York City after 1965. The new immigration, as can be seen from the data presented in Table 3, has mainly brought the Third World to the First World. Despite the city's large population of European immigrants, Latin Americans, Caribbeans, and Asians have accounted for the lion's share of the new arrivals.[7]

How well suited are these New Yorkers to the city's evolving economy? The postwar migrants arrived with low levels of schooling, and the Puerto Ricans among them were further handicapped by a lack of English-language facility. Yet because they arrived at an opportune time, they found a place in New York's then-thriving economy. But many of those initial entry-level jobs have since been lost. Although the skill and education levels of black and Puerto Rican New Yorkers have been upgraded in the interim, it is not clear that these levels have risen as quickly as job requirements. The same questions apply

to the immigrants. Although some component of the new immigration consists of a "brain drain," the majority of newcomers arrive with low- or mid-level skills. The proportion of all immigrants reporting prior professional or related experience has fallen steadily since 1971; the available data indicate that the share of professionals among the newcomers to New York City is lower still.

Thus, the characteristics of New York's new demographic base seem compatible with either of the two stories of the urban post-industrial transformation mentioned in the introduction. On the one hand, the low skill and educational levels of the minority populations should make them poorly matched with the rising job requirements of post-industrial employers. On the other hand, the substantial and constant flow of recent immigrants suggests that the problem is not so much a paucity of entry-level jobs as an absence of opportunities to move from bottom to top.

TABLE 3 *Immigrants Arrived in United States, 1965–1980, and Living in New York City, 1980*

Country of Origin	Number in NYC
Dominican Republic	98,410
Jamaica	76,280
China	62,420
Haiti	43,780
Italy	42,000
Trinidad/Tobago	34,300
Colombia	33,200
Ecuador	32,960
USSR	32,640
Guyana	29,420
Greece	26,000
Cuba	23,520
India	20,680
Philippines	18,920
Korea	17,620
Barbados	14,520
Yugoslavia	14,260
Panama	12,120
Poland	10,760
England	10,520
Israel	10,260

Source: 1980 *Census of Population,* Public Use Microdata Sample.

ETHNIC SUCCESSION AND EMPLOYMENT CHANGE: ANOTHER VIEW

There is, however, another possible interpretation of the fit between New York's economic functions and its demographic base. Table 4 presents data from the Public Use Microdata Samples of the 1970 and 1980 Censuses of Population (the first was a 1 percent sample; the second a 5 percent sample). Although the decennial censuses are somewhat dated for my purposes, they are unique, and hence indispensable, for the detailed data on ethnic and occupational characteristics that they provide.

Table 4 organizes the population according to eight synthetic ethnic groups, classified by ethnicity (white, black, Hispanic, Asian) and nativity (native- or foreign-born), and shows the number of jobs held by each group in New York City in 1970 and 1980. The fourth column in the table shows the number of jobs each group would have lost had its losses been proportional to the decline suffered by the overall economy during this period, when employment fell by 8.56 percent, from 3,191,370 jobs in 1970 to 2,918,183 in 1980. The table then indicates how many jobs the group actually lost and the difference between expected and actual employment losses.

Here is where we begin to glimpse a different set of dynamics affecting the process of job change in post-industrial New York. The reason

is that the biggest job losers over the course of the 1970s, both quantitatively and proportionally, were whites! In fact, native and foreign-born whites together lost almost twice as many jobs as the total job loss for all New Yorkers.[8]

Why so many whites lost jobs during this period is difficult to say – some undoubtedly began to work in the suburbs after moving there (and we know that there was substantial white out-migration to the suburbs during this time); some joined the vast tide of migrants headed to the Sunbelt; some simply left the labor force (it is worth remembering that the large cohort of European immigrants who arrived between 1900 and 1915 reached retirement age during this period). But the reasons for white job loss are not nearly as interesting as its possible effects: my basic hypothesis, as noted in the introduction, is that the position of nonwhites depends on the proportion of the preferred group – whites – in the labor force. Where the white proportion declines as radically as it did in New York, we can expect ethnic realignment as opportunities open up for nonwhites to take over better jobs.[9]

To what extent did compositional changes produce such effects? I attempt to answer this question by focusing on four ethnic groups: native whites, native blacks, foreign Hispanics, and foreign Asians. The choice of the four was made partially for reasons of expediency; that is, to avoid a blizzard of tables and numbers. More

TABLE 4 *Changes in Employment for Ethnic Groups, New York City, 1970–1980*

	EMPLOYMENT		JOB CHANGE			
Group	*1970*	*1980*	*Expected*	*Actual*	*Actual − expected*	*A − E/ 1970 Empt*
WhNb	1,785,200	1,382,980	− 155,939	− 402,220	− 246,281	− 13.8%
WhFb	417,400	315,520	− 36,460	− 101,880	− 65,420	− 15.7
BlNb	462,700	440,180	− 40,417	− 22,520	+ 17,897	+ 3.9
BlFb	55,500	170,320	− 4,848	+ 114,820	+ 119,668	+215.6
AsNb	8,000	10,460	− 699	+ 2,460	+ 3,159	+ 39.5
AsFb	31,200	108,740	− 2,725	+ 77,540	+ 80,265	+257.3
HisNb	242,000	232,640	− 21,139	− 9,360	+ 11,779	+ 4.9
HisFb	132,700	205,520	− 11,591	+ 72,820	+ 84,411	+ 63.6

Sources: See Table 1.

Note: Wh, white; Bl, black; His, Hispanic; As, Asian; Nb, native-born; Fb, foreign-born. Data in this and all following tables for employed New York City residents, age 16 and over.

important, each group's fate is important in and of itself. In both 1970 and 1980, native whites were the dominant and most numerous group in the labor market; hence any change, not only in their number but in their position, would be of consequence to all others. The progress of native blacks is a question of obvious concern; it is this group, above all, that has been the main focus of affirmative action and equal opportunity programs over the past two decades. Foreign-born Hispanics are of interest because they have apparently moved into the lower rungs of the city's economy and exemplify, if any group does, the situation of newcomers confined to the bottom stratum of the labor force. Finally, Asians have played a distinctive and more specialized economic role than the other groups and seem akin to the earlier European immigrants in their predilection for small business and entrepreneurship.

To assess the impact of compositional change, I have used a technique known as "shift-share" analysis. The virtue of the procedure is that it decomposes the effects attributable to the factors of particular interest here: composition (or "group size" in Tables 5–8), industry change, and "share," a residual term that reflects the shifts in the ethnic division of labor. Each of the following tables shows an ethnic group's employment in 1970 and 1980 in columns 1 and 2 and the group's employment change over the course of the decade in column 3. The next four columns detail the components of job change.

Column 4 shows "group size," the possibility that change in an industry is due to changes in a group's relative size (after adjustments have been made for the impact of the local economy's decline). In calculating this effect, I assume that job change in each industry is proportional to the change in relative size for the group (as shown in the last column of Table 4).

Column 5 indicates "industry change," the possibility that groups gained or lost jobs because the industries on which they had been dependent in 1970 waxed or waned over the course of the decade. In calculating this effect, I assume that a group's gain or loss in an industry is proportional to total employment change in the industry (given in Table 1, column 4).

Column 6 reveals the interactive effect of "industry change" and "group size," which shows

whether the two factors worked in opposing or reinforcing directions. This effect is calculated by adding group size effects (col. 4) and industry effects (col. 5).

Column 7 indicates "share," the possibility that a group's employment in an industry increased or declined, net of "group size" and "industry change." This component is calculated by subtracting the "interactive effect" (col. 6) for an industry from the net change in that industry (col. 3).

Finally I sum the industry calculations in each component to produce a total figure for the group.

Table 5 presents data on job change for native whites. Total employment among this group declined by almost one-fourth (col. 3), and whites lost employment in every sector with the exception of professional services and miscellaneous (the latter consists mainly of entertainment), and they sustained sizable losses in the financial (FIRE) and business service sectors. The main sources of these losses (col. 4) was the decline in the size of the native white labor force. Whites also lost substantial numbers of jobs due to industry change (col. 5), but fewer than would have been expected had white job loss been proportionate to the decline in the total economy. Additional jobs were lost because native whites suffered a net loss in their share of particular industries; not only did white shares fall in declining industries like manufacturing and the public sector, but they also slipped in the expanding business service and FIRE components of the advanced service sector. As indicated by the 1970/1980 index of dissimilarity–which measures the net 1970–1980 change in native whites' distribution among the various industries–this group's position at the end of the decade differed considerably from its position at the beginning.

Table 6 presents the data on job change for native blacks. Overall, native black employment declined over the decade; the sharpest falloffs were registered in personal services; retailing; transportation, communications, and utilities; repair services; and manufacturing; however, employment increased in the public sector and in the three advanced service sectors–professional services, FIRE, and business services. Because blacks had started the period in industries that were to decline severely as a result of the city's

TABLE 5   *Components of Job Change: Native Whites, 1970–1980*

	EMPLOYMENT			CHANGE DUE TO			
	(1)	(2)	(3)	(4)	(5)	(6)	(7)
				Group	Industry	Interactive	
Sector	1970	1980	Change	Size	Change	Effect	Share
Const	57,400	34,620	−22,780	−7,918	−17,095	−25,014	2,233
Mfg	304,800	189,620	−115,180	−42,049	−58,976	−101,026	−14,154
Trans	156,400	104,800	−51,600	−21,576	−39,523	−61,100	9,499
Whole	99,100	74,200	−24,900	−13,672	−13,514	−27,185	2,285
Retail	245,900	173,480	−72,420	−33,924	−37,527	−71,450	−969
FIRE	209,900	181,200	−28,700	−28,957	997	−27,960	−739
Busserv	108,200	98,660	−9,540	−14,927	8,585	−6,345	−3,198
Persserv	43,400	24,440	−18,960	−5,987	−13,100	−19,087	127
Profserv	222,700	236,680	13,980	−30,723	38,450	7,727	6,253
Misc	33,300	36,120	2,820	−4,594	2,606	−1,987	4,808
PubSec	304,100	229,160	−74,940	−41,953	−6,043	−47,996	−26,944
Total	1,785,200	1,382,980	−402,220	−246,281	−135,140	−381,421	−20,799

Sources: See Table 1.

Note: 1970/1980 index of dissimilarity: 7.8. Const, construction; Mfg, manufacturing; Trans, transportation, communications, utilities; Whole, wholesale; FIRE, finance, insurance, and real estate; Busserv, business services; Persserv, personal services; Profserv, professional services; Misc, miscellaneous (agriculture, mining, entertainment); PubSec, public sector.

economic crisis, the main source of native black job loss was industry change. Blacks experienced a net loss in share, mainly due to erosion in older, blue-collar sectors like manufacturing, transport, retailing, and personal services. By contrast, the shift to services was not inimical to blacks' access to employment: the black share increased in both business services and FIRE and declined only marginally in professional services (a sector in which blacks did register a net increase in jobs). More important than services was the public sector, where a very sizable increase in share almost offset the losses suffered in other sectors. Overall, considerable reshuffling in black employment among industries transpired, as indicated by the 1970/1980 index of dissimilarity of 10.9.

Table 7 shows the data for the Hispanic foreign-born. This group experienced increases in every industry, including advanced services. In contrast to blacks, the foreign-born Hispanics' greatest gains came in two sectors where native black employment suffered considerable erosion over the same period: manufacturing and retailing. Like native blacks, foreign Hispanics began

this period in industries that were to perform poorly over the next ten years: hence, the net job losses attributable to industry change, but, in contrast to blacks, Hispanics replaced whites in the industries from which the latter withdrew. Virtually all of the gain in foreign Hispanic employment was due to a change in the group's size. Column 7 is once again a source of considerable interest. Foreign Hispanics gained in their net share of individual industries only to a very limited extent. Only in manufacturing, a sector in which they were already concentrated, did foreign Hispanics make a sizable increase in share. The end result was that foreign Hispanics ended the decade in much the same industries as they began, as the very low 1970/1980 index of dissimilarity shows.

Table 8, which contains the data for the Asian foreign-born, presents still another picture. As with the Hispanics, Asians gained jobs in every industry; similarly, change in group size was the engine of their increase in employment. Foreign Asians' net change increased over the period, but only slightly. Column 7 points to significant shifts

TABLE 6   *Components of Job Change: Native Blacks, 1970–1980*

	EMPLOYMENT			CHANGE DUE TO			
	(1)	*(2)*	*(3)*	*(4)* Group Size	*(5)* Industry Change	*(6)* Interactive Effect	*(7)* Share
Sector	1970	1980	Change				
Const	12,900	8,100	−4,800	499	−3,842	−3,343	−1,457
Mfg	59,900	51,920	−7,980	2,316	−11,590	−9,273	1,293
Trans	45,800	32,580	−13,220	1,772	−11,574	−9,802	−3,417
Whole	13,500	13,120	−380	522	−1,840	−1,319	939
Retail	51,600	41,660	−9,940	1,996	−7,874	−5,879	−4,061
FIRE	34,100	36,580	2,480	1,319	162	1,480	999
Busserv	22,900	25,840	2,940	886	1,817	2,703	237
Persserv	41,100	20,560	−20,540	1,590	−12,406	−10,816	−9,724
Profserv	46,700	56,440	9,740	1,806	8,063	9,869	−129
Misc	6,400	4,300	−2,100	248	501	748	−2,848
PubSec	127,800	149,080	21,280	4,943	−2,540	2,403	18,876
Total	462,700	440,180	−22,520	17,897	−37,443	−19,545	−2,975

Sources: See Table 1.

Note: 1970/1980 index of dissimilarity: 10.9. Const, construction; Mfg, manufacturing; Trans, transportation, communications, utilities; Whole, wholesale; FIRE, finance, insurance, and real estate; Busserv, business services; Persserv, personal services; Profserv, professional services; Misc, miscellaneous (agriculture, mining, entertainment); PubSec, public sector.

in Asians' share of individual industries. On the one hand, those sectors that contain a preponderance of low-level jobs and that have historically been an important source of Asian employment—personal service, manufacturing, and retailing—show either a loss in share (retailing and personal services) or a slight gain (manufacturing). On the other hand, sizable gains in share were made in two of three advanced service sectors—FIRE and professional services. Thus, although change in group size accounted for the bulk of net job change, Asians also repositioned themselves significantly—as indicated by the high 1970/1980 index of dissimilarity.

OCCUPATIONAL REPOSITIONING

Of course, it is one thing to gain access to the growth sectors of the economy; quite another, to get employed in those same industries in higher-level jobs. The shift in economic function from goods to services altered the occupational profile of New York's economy, further swelling the white-collar component. The net white-collar gain, from 59 percent employed in white-collar jobs in 1970 to 62.5 percent in 1980, was relatively slight because quite sizable gains in professional and managerial employment were offset by still heavier losses in clerical and sales jobs. Still, the overall increase in white-collar jobs means that some minority and immigrant gain in white-collar employment could be expected simply on the basis of their shift into service industries. Yet the sectoral shifts analyzed above might also be compatible with the "hewer of wood" story; namely, that the gains registered by native blacks, foreign Hispanics, and foreign Asians in the advanced service sectors reflected nothing more than their hiring as cleaners, janitors, and so on.

Table 9 shows the changes in white-collar employment for the total labor force and for the four ethnic groups at issue in this paper. As the third column shows, the total number of white-dollar jobs declined by almost 68,000, but far steeper declines were experienced by native whites. The white-collar job loss for this group was three times the decline for the total economy; it lost

TABLE 7 *Components of Job Change: Foreign-Born Hispanics, 1970–1980*

	EMPLOYMENT			CHANGE DUE TO			
	(1)	*(2)*	*(3)*	*(4)* Group Size	*(5)* Industry Change	*(6)* Interactive Effect	*(7)*
Sector	1970	1980	Change				Share
Const	3,900	4,040	140	2,481	−341	2,140	−2,000
Mfg	44,200	70,720	26,520	28,116	−13,164	14,952	11,568
Trans	7,200	10,860	3,660	4,580	−1,393	3,187	473
Whole	5,700	8,480	2,780	3,626	−777	2,849	−69
Retail	19,500	29,880	10,380	12,404	−2,976	9,428	952
FIRE	12,300	18,680	6,380	7,824	58	7,883	−1,502
Busserv	7,200	13,000	5,800	4,580	5,718	5,151	649
Persserv	8,500	13,340	4,840	5,407	−2,566	2,841	1,999
Profserv	16,000	17,860	1,860	10,178	2,763	12,940	−11,080
Misc	800	2,560	1,760	509	63	571	1,189
PubSec	7,400	16,100	8,700	4,707	−147	4,560	4,140
Total	132,700	205,520	72,820	84,412	−17,909	66,503	6,317

Sources: See Table 1.

Note: 1970/1980 index of dissimilarity: 5.0. Const, construction; Mfg, manufacturing; Trans, transportation, communications, utilities; Whole, wholesale; FIRE, finance, insurance, and real estate; Busserv, business services; Persserv, personal services; Profserv, professional services; Misc, miscellaneous (agriculture, mining, entertainment); PubSec, public sector.

TABLE 8 *Components of Job Change: Foreign-Born Asians, 1970–1980*

	EMPLOYMENT			CHANGE DUE TO			
	(1)	*(2)*	*(3)*	*(4)* Group Size	*(5)* Industry Change	*(6)* Interactive Effect	*(7)*
Sector	1970	1980	Change				Share
Const	100	1,160	1,060	257	−30	227	833
Mfg	7,200	25,920	18,720	18,522	−1,393	17,130	1,590
Trans	800	4,520	3,720	2,058	−202	1,856	1,864
Whole	1,400	6,160	4,760	3,602	−191	3,411	1,349
Retail	10,100	27,060	16,960	25,983	−1,541	24,442	−7,482
FIRE	1,200	9,000	7,800	3,087	6	3,093	4,707
Busserv	1,400	3,920	2,520	3,602	111	3,713	−1,193
Persserv	2,100	4,340	2,240	5,402	−634	4,769	−2,529
Profserv	3,700	16,680	12,980	9,519	639	10,158	2,823
Misc	400	580	180	1,029	31	1,060	−880
PubSec	2,800	9,300	6,500	7,203	−56	7,148	−648
Total	31,200	108,740	77,540	80,265	−3,260	77,005	435

Sources: See Table 1.

Note: 1970/1980 index of dissimilarity: 12.2. Const, construction; Mfg, manufacturing; Trans, transportation, communications, utilities; Whole, wholesale; FIRE, finance, insurance, and real estate; Busserv, business services; Persserv, personal services; Profserv, professional services; Misc, miscellaneous (agriculture, mining, entertainment); PubSec, public sector.

jobs in three of the four white-collar categories; only in the managerial category was there a net white gain, and in this instance, native whites obtained just over a third of the new managerial jobs created over the course of the decade. By contrast, native blacks, foreign Asians, and foreign Hispanics made very substantial gains in every white-collar category, with the exception of sales jobs for native blacks.

To what extent changes in occupational position can be linked to shifts in group size can be grasped by examining the last three columns of Table 9. The fourth column tells us how many jobs a group would have lost or gained had its employment in an occupation changed in proportion to its total employment; the fifth column shows the difference between actual and expected employment; and the sixth shows this dif-

TABLE 9   *White-Collar Occupational Shifts, 1970–1980*

| | EMPLOYMENT | | | *Expected* | *Actual − A − E/1970* | |
	1970	*1980*	*Change*	*Change*	*Expected*	*Employment*
	Employment, All Demographic Groups					
White-collar	1,860,300	1,792,340	−67,960	−162,499	94,539	5.1%
PTK	500,600	533,560	32,960	−43,728	76,688	15.3
Managerial	250,100	314,960	64,860	−21,846	86,706	34.6
Sales	226,200	177,920	−48,280	−19,759	−28,521	12.6
Clerical	883,400	765,900	−117,500	−77,166	−40,334	−4.6
	White, Native-Born					
White-collar	1,248,800	1,044,020	−204,780	−281,364	76,585	6.1
PTK	355,000	335,380	−19,620	−79,984	60,364	17.0
Managerial	172,100	196,740	24,640	−38,776	63,416	36.8
Sales	159,400	112,880	−46,520	−35,914	−10,606	−6.7
Clerical	562,300	399,020	−163,280	−126,691	−36,589	−6.5
	Black, Native-Born					
White-collar	206,400	242,320	35,920	−10,046	45,966	22.3
PTK	43,100	56,460	13,360	−2,098	15,458	35.9
Managerial	14,100	25,960	11,860	−686	12,546	89.0
Sales	14,900	13,840	−1,060	−725	−335	−2.2
Clerical	134,300	146,060	11,760	−6,537	18,297	13.6
	Hispanic, Foreign-Born					
White-collar	52,700	72,520	19,820	28,919	−9,099	−1.7
PTK	11,900	15,700	3,800	6,530	−2,730	−22.9
Managerial	5,900	13,980	8,080	3,238	4,842	82.1
Sales	5,100	7,680	2,580	2,799	−219	−4.3
Clerical	29,800	36,160	6.360	16,353	−9,993	−33.5
	Asian, Foreign-Born					
White-collar	15,300	61,320	4,602	38,024	7,996	52.3
PTK	7,600	25,400	17,800	18,888	−1,088	−14.3
Managerial	3,000	12,400	9,400	7,456	1,944	64.8
Sales	400	5,180	4,780	994	3,786	946.4
Clerical	4,300	18,340	14,040	10,687	3,353	77.9

Source: See Table 1.

Note: PTK, professional, technical, and kindred.

ference as a percentage of 1970 employment. One conclusion is that in addition to the replacement demand arising from the disproportionate white decline, native whites created further vacancies by repositioning themselves within the white-collar hierarchy. A second conclusion, however, is that the nonwhite population became further differentiated in the process of moving into the white-collar jobs left vacant by whites. Foreign Asians were the greatest beneficiaries of succession, both in numbers and in proportion. Although gains in professional employment were less than expected on the basis of total employment growth, the disproportionately large gains in managerial and, especially, sales employment suggest that job growth for Asians was linked to the strength of the Asian American subeconomy. Although black gains were not as great as those of Asians, blacks' increase in white-collar jobs was still substantially greater than expected, with the result that by 1980 more than half of all native blacks were employed in white-collar jobs. As noted above, only in sales was there any black loss in employment, suggesting that employers continue to assume aversion by white to face-to-face contact with blacks in selling jobs and/or competition with immigrants, whose gains in retailing have already been observed. Although native blacks and foreign Hispanics further penetrated the white-collar sector, foreign Hispanics lost ground. Net white-collar job gains for this group were slight; because total foreign Hispanic employment increased substantially during this period (see Table 4), the proportion of this group working in white-collar jobs actually declined between 1970 and 1980.

EXPLAINING OCCUPATIONAL CHANGE

How is one to understand the pattern of job change that emerged over the course of the 1970s? To answer this question, the accounting scheme used thus far will not suffice since what it tells us—to what extent job change was proportional or not to some other quantity (for example, the change in a group's size or in an industry's size)—is precisely what needs to be explained. The puzzle is why, for example, foreign Hispanics gained more jobs than expected in a declining sector like manufacturing, even when an adjustment is made for the increase in group size,

or why gains for native blacks in the public sector similarly outweighed the shift attributable to their relative increase in group size.

To develop such an explanation, we need some model of job change. The simplest model assumes that groups are ranked in a more or less stable order in which whites are at the top, and the other nonwhite groups follow, with their positions determined in part by skill, in part by employers' preferences. Under these conditions, job growth at the top of the hierarchy would benefit whites, whose march up the totem pole would in turn open up positions for everyone else. Conversely, should the overall economy, or even particular sectors, turn down, whites' average position might be depressed, but they would still hold on to their jobs on the first-in, last-out principle; nonwhites would be pushed further down or possibly off the queue. What we've seen so far, of course, shows that both the cyclical and structural changes of the 1970s produced little such effect. With the exception of blacks, industry change proved not to be the most important contributor to job gain or loss; and at a more disaggregated level, whites lost jobs in growing industries (FIRE, business services), whereas nonwhites gained jobs in declining industries (manufacturing and retailing for Asians and Hispanics, the public sector for all three nonwhite groups).[10]

This model falls short in assuming that population composition remains constant. But in this case, compositional change was far-reaching, with the preferred group (whites) shrinking in size; what the queue model would then suggest is that the average position of whites improves (as competition among whites for more favorable positions lessens) and that nonwhites in turn move up the pecking order as replacement for whites who have either moved up or moved out. When compositional change is far-reaching—as in this case—it also alters gatekeeping mechanisms. Keeping blacks or other minorities out of jobs is one thing when there are plenty of whites among whom to choose, but the costs of discrimination rise when there are fewer whites competing for the available jobs. Similarly, there is a high level of arbitrariness in entry-level requirements. It is well documented that the majority of blue-collar employers do most of their skill training on the job floor and that their hiring criteria are designed mainly to screen out "bad prospects" not unskilled workers. By contrast, office employers often prefer that "pink-collar" workers obtain their clerical skills before employment. But there is ample evidence of considerable variation among otherwise similar office employers with respect to skill requirements and provision of on-the-job training; this suggests that hiring procedures can be altered if changes on the supply side require that new labor force groups be recruited.[11]

Just how the process of replacement worked itself out in New York—and its implications for nonwhite employment—is illustrated by the cases of the two sectors in which white losses in total employment and in share were most severe: the public sector and manufacturing.

Total employment in the public sector declined after 1974 under the impact of New York City's fiscal crisis; the number of workers on local government payrolls did not begin to rise until 1981; and as of late 1985, the size of the local-government sector was 91 percent of its 1974 peak. However, jobs were shed mainly through attrition, not layoffs, which meant that the bulk of withdrawals from the public sector were made by civil servants high in seniority, who also happened to be overwhelmingly white. Thus, although municipal employment fell from 285,856 in 1975 to 236,596 in 1979, the nonwhite share of employment in this sector actually climbed from 32.5 percent to 36.8 percent. A further consequence of the fiscal crisis was that the real earnings of municipal employees plummeted, reducing the available supply of white labor, who had access to better-paying jobs. Once hiring resumed and municipal payrolls began to swell, the bulk of the jobs went to nonwhites; by 1985, 42 percent of New York City's employees were nonwhite, as were 52 percent of the workers hired that year. These jobs were mainly allocated to blacks. In 1985, blacks made up four-fifths of the city's nonwhite employees; although up-to-date data on the nativity of city workers is not available, the 1980 pattern, in which 85 percent of black public employees were native-born, is unlikely to have changed.[12]

Similar conditions apply in the case of manufacturing, for which the best illustration is probably the garment industry, the most important component of New York's industrial base. A shortage of labor has been a recurring problem for this industry since World War II, and it has cycled through a series of different migrant and immigrant groups in its search for an appropriate labor supply. Several factors—declining relative hourly wages; seasonal swings in employment, which added a large gap in fulltime, full-year earning power to the differential in hourly wages; and the industry's low prestige, itself a product of its image as an immigrant enclave—led the industry to recruit first blacks and then Puerto Ricans to replace whites, who either left for other employment or no longer sought work in the industry. Nonetheless, as late as 1970, 59 percent of the city's blue-collar garment workers were white. In the following decade, the bottom of the market fell out; those firms that hung on did so at the price of workers' wages—which fell relative to wages in the rest of New York's already depressed manufacturing sector—and deteriorating working conditions. Seasonality became even more pronounced, producing diminishing weekly wages. Consequently, whites dropped out of the industry's effective labor supply: by 1980, less than 35 percent of the industry's blue-collar workers were white, and the high median age of those who remained suggested that few replacements were forthcoming. Similar deterrents affected native black and native Hispanics, for whom the opening of opportunities in offices and services provided preferable alternatives. Hence, compositional changes led to recruitment of new, mainly Asian and Hispanic immigrants. As of the early 1980s, the consensus among garment employers was that "if there were no immigrants, the needle trades would be out of New York."[13]

But if these cases illustrate the ways in which replacement demand arose, they also suggest that the queue model of occupational change remains simplistic in terms of its understanding of the process of nonwhite for white succession. Instead of moving up the ladder in an orderly and steady way, the different groups appear to have concentrated in distinctive economic niches. Thus, the public sector, a declining industry, became a stronghold of blacks, but an employer of little importance for either foreign Asians or Hispanics. By contrast, these two groups piled up in retailing and manufacturing, industries in which blacks lost out severely.

What impedes orderly succession up the queue is the tendency of groups to branch off into particular fields and then to monopolize particular jobs through a process of occupational closure. A variety of actors determines the branching pattern. Groups may enter the labor market with skills that influence their initial placement: Greeks from the province of Kastoria, where a traditional apprenticeship in furmaking is common, tend to enter the fur industry; Israelis move into diamonds, a traditional Jewish business centered in New York, Tel Aviv, and Antwerp; Indians from Gujarat, previously traders, become small storeowners. Language facility may similarly be a barrier to, or a facilitator of, specialization. English-language ability has steered West Indians into a heavy concentration in health care, where the importance of interpersonal communication has been an impediment to immigrants that are not native speakers. By contrast, Koreans arrive with professional degrees, but because they are poor English speakers—according to the 1980 census, 40 percent of adult Koreans in New York said that they spoke English poorly or not at all—and lack the appropriate licenses, they turn to retailing. Alternatively, specializations may arise in those fields where exclusionary barriers are weakest. Thus, the continuing attraction of public-sector jobs to native blacks is a reflection of past and present discrimination: opportunities for black upward mobility in large, private organizations have consistently lagged behind the public sector, which has proved more susceptible to pressure for affirmative action. A final influence stems from differences in predisposition: an important consideration here, congruent with the garment industry case reviewed above, is that immigrants tend to be more favorably disposed toward low-level, low-status jobs than natives, in part because they come as temporary migrants, in part because they continue to evaluate jobs, even after settlement, in terms of still lower-quality employment back home.[14]

Once these patterns are established, however, the tendency toward occupational closure is strong because networks of information and support are often ethnically bounded. Thus, newcomers move and settle down under the auspices of co-ethnics; due to a preference for familiarity, the efficiency of personal contacts, and social distance from the host society's institutions of assistance, they then pile up in fields where settlers have made an early beachhead. Thus, in the garment industry, for example, Dominicans became pleaters, Chinese from Hong Kong went into sewing and stitching, and immigrants from Taiwan concentrated in knitting. Ties between immigrants and co-ethnic employers are an important part of this process: many ethnic firms serve as way stations for newly arrived immigrants looking for jobs or recruit workers primarily among immigrants from a common hometown.[15] Alternatively, institutional processes of job placement may be organized around ethnic lines. Thus, in New York, the black quest for political equality has not produced much power, but it has at least yielded training programs, community agencies, and "captive" departments of city and, to a lesser extent, state government where the bulk of personnel, from agency chief to file clerk, is black.

Such positional advantages often cumulate over time, leading the circle to close. Different industries hold out different pathways for getting ahead: in a small-business industry, like retailing or construction, the key is to start out on one's own; in an industry where large organizations predominate, like hospitals, mobility takes place through the acquisition of credentials, seniority, or a combination of the two. Consequently, initial placement is a crucial condition of subsequent movement: the immigrant garment cutter, the salesman, or the waiter is more likely to have the necessary ingredients of business success—contacts, information, knowhow—than is the hospital worker or government employee, who by contrast knows more about how to move up in the organizational hierarchy than how a small firm might be run. A further factor is that ethnic-network recruiting has a strong exclusionary bias: if you're not a member of the club, you may not be welcomed. In some instances, this is because ethnic group membership is the source of job-relevant knowledge, such as in the case of the ethnic restaurant. More commonly, group membership is valued because it is a source of trust and a promise of "good behavior": for this reason, Korean greengrocers serving minority neighborhoods hire other Koreans rather than black youths.[16] Finally, ethnic boundaries are closed in order to maintain valued resources, the pattern one observes in the construction industry, where persistently high levels of white employment are maintained because fathers recruit and train sons.[17] Similarly, the Hispanic charge that blacks have gained public-sector jobs at their expense suggests that similar processes may be at work in this case.[18]

PATTERNS OF DISPLACEMENT

The emergence of a new ethnic division of labor suggests the possibility of displacement, and hence a dynamic that may not simply complicate but blunt the impact of compositional change. The first hint of displacement is visible in Table 4: although native blacks lost fewer jobs than was to be expected on the basis of the decline of New York's economy alone, the absolute numbers of employed blacks nonetheless declined. Further evidence of competition appears in Tables 5–8. Whereas immigrants gained jobs in every industry and did particularly well in declining sectors like manufacturing and retailing, blacks lost jobs in every instance, with the exception of the public sector and the three branches of the advanced service sector – FIRE, business services, and professional services. Furthermore, blacks suffered a net loss in share, making their most substantial gain in the public sector – an industry of diminishing attractiveness for whites.

More compelling still is that immigrants retained strong job attachments, despite the decline of New York's economy, but native black and native Hispanic ties to the labor market weakened. The basic pattern, as shown in Table 10, which disaggregates employment-population, labor force participation, and unemployment rates by sex for 25–65 year olds, finds immigrants doing better than native minorities on all three indicators. Evidence of displacement is strongest for men: witness especially the sharp falloff in native black and Hispanic employment-to-population rates and the growing foreign black/native black and foreign Hispanic/native Hispanic disparities on all the indicators. Because the shift from goods to services brought greater job opportunities for females, all women gained in employment and in

access to the labor force, regardless of nativity and ethnicity. Still, immigrant women appeared to enjoy significant competitive advantages over their native counterparts since the native-foreign gap in employment and labor force participation was actually greater among black and Hispanic women than among males.

Native blacks are thus the big losers in the new ethnic division of labor; their vulnerability is rooted in their reliance on public-sector employment on the one hand and the persistence of low self-employment rates, on the other hand. Blacks have concentrated in government because they have found public jobs more accessible than private employment and more likely to offer far better opportunities for internal promotion. Not only are native blacks overrepresented in government, but they are also overrepresented in public-sector managerial and professional ranks. In 1980, when native blacks made up just under 10 percent of all professionals and managers in the private and public sectors, they comprised 21 percent of government employees in these same two occupations.[19] Moreover, opportunities for public-sector employment extend to the highest levels. Data for 1986 show that 16 percent of the top managers in New York City government were black.[20]

These positions are also effective vehicles for movement into higher social class: Peter Eisinger's recent study of high-level black civil servants in New York's Human Resources Administration showed that "high-level black civil servants are far more likely to have grown up in working- and lower-class families than in solidly middle-class families" and were also more likely to be of lower-class origin than were their white counterparts.[21] Regardless of position in civil service ranks, public employment offers a key component of middle-class status: stability. As noted earlier, the falloff in public-sector employment resulting from New York's fiscal crisis took place through accelerated retirements, rather than layoffs of recently hired staff. Indeed, throughout the 1975–83 period, when New York City's budget remained under tight constraints, 100 percent of the changes in New York City labor costs came from compensation, rather than employment.[22]

Although the public sector is not an unrewarding niche, the evidence of declining black job

TABLE 10 *Labor Force Activity Rates, 25–65-year-old Adults, 1970–1980*

	WhFb	WhNb	BlFb	BlNb	AsFb	AsNb	HisFb	HisNb
Employment to Population Rates (Percent Population Employed)								
Males, 1970	86.7%	88.0%	89.6%	80.9%	84.3%	69.1%	89.6%	80.0%
Males, 1980	83.0	82.6	81.0	66.9	86.9	88.1	82.0	71.3
Females, 1970	47.8	51.0	68.4	50.2	56.6	67.6	57.6	29.6
Females, 1980	52.8	58.9	76.5	58.2	67.9	71.6	57.3	37.9
Labor Force Participation Rates (Percent Population in Labor Force)								
Males, 1970	89.8%	90.4%	92.0%	84.0%	85.2%	73.8%	91.9%	83.2%
Males, 1980	87.4	86.4	88.1	74.5	90.5	92.2	88.2	78.1
Females, 1970	44.8	49.2	67.0	48.3	55.0	61.8	53.4	28.0
Females, 1980	48.9	58.1	71.0	54.0	65.6	67.5	51.5	34.0
Unemployment Rates (Percent Labor Force Unemployed)								
Males, 1970	3.5%	2.7%	2.6%	3.6%	1.1%	6.4%	2.5%	3.8%
Males, 1980	5.0	4.4	8.1	10.2	4.0	4.5	7.0	8.7
Females, 1970	6.3	3.7	2.0	3.9	2.9	8.7	7.3	5.4
Females, 1980	7.4	4.8	7.2	7.3	3.4	5.7	10.1	10.2

Sources: See Table 1.

Note: Wh, white; Bl, black; As, Asian; His, Hispanic; Fb, foreign-born; Nb, native-born.

attachment suggests the difficulties in extending those advantages to the private sector. Blacks' underrepresentation among the ranks of entrepreneurs, both petty and large, has left blacks vulnerable to the exclusionary mechanisms that characterize the small-business sector and have led to substantial displacement of blacks, especially from lower-level positions. Moreover, government efforts and instruments designed to achieve equal opportunity have been ineffective in altering those exclusionary mechanisms, especially in sectors where more desirable positions are to be found.

In contrast to blacks, immigrants are prevalent among the ranks of New York's petty entrepreneurs: in 1980, the self-employment rate for foreign-born males was 12.7 percent, compared with 3.3 percent for native black males. Going into business appears to be an important component of the immigrant settlement process: only the most recent newcomers are self-employed at a rate below that of the native-born; after ten years in the United States, self-employment rates exceed those for the native-born and continue to climb with length of stay. The reasons for immigrants' drift into self-employment are various: in part, the buildup of immigration populations creates demand for special products and services that other immigrants are best suited to provide; in part, immigrants have benefited from opportunities for succession in small-business industries like retailing, garment manufacturing, or taxis, which no longer recruit entrepreneurs from the traditional ethnic sources of supply; in part, there is a predisposition toward starting out on one's own precisely because exclusion from jobs on the grounds of language problems, skill inadequacies, or discrimination leaves self-employment the best source of reward in light of the restricted opportunities at hand.[23]

Whatever the precise sources of immigrants' thrust into business, the emergence of immigrant economic enclaves closes off sectors that had previously been open to blacks. One case in point is that of food retailing, where supermarkets, employing large numbers of blacks in both fulltime, high-paying, and parttime, minimum-wage jobs, compete with small, immigrant-owned firms. For the immigrant firms, the importance of maintaining control over the labor force and the preference for employing trusted insiders serve to strengthen the tie to family or ethnic labor and deter them from employing Americans, as the following quote from the president of the Korean Produce Retailers Association suggests: "We should be especially cautious in employing Americans because union officials may encourage them to become union members. Once they belong to the union, extra expenses such as overtime payments, the hourly minimum wage, and social security taxes follow. . . . Small Korean fruit and vegetable stores cannot afford to pay all these extra costs."[24] This pattern of competition may well explain why the black losses in the retailing sector overall exceeded the shift attributable to either population change or industry decline.[25]

There is also a line between immigrant business success and the growth of opportunities for the broader ethnic community that is dynamic in a way that has no parallel in the relationship between blacks and the public sector; this linkage is actually a further source of black displacement. The failure rate among small businesses is appallingly high, and immigrant businesses go under even more frequently than do white-owned businesses. The crucial difference, however, is that immigrants are far more likely than whites to start up new businesses in low-status, high-risk lines like garments or retailing. And because it is immigrants, not native blacks, who provide the replacements to existing white entrepreneurs, it is immigrant labor that is used to staff the new businesses – not the native blacks who might have been employed in the earlier white-owned concern.[26] In addition, the ties between immigrant consumers and merchants ensure that resources remain encapsulated within the ethnic economy, thus producing multiplier effects. The multiplier effects are greatest when resources are generated by the "export activities" of ethnic businesses – that is, the revenues produced through transactions with nonimmigrant customers; but the likelihood that immigrants, whatever their source of income, make substantial purchases of services or products supplied by co-ethnics means an increase in expenditures for local ethnic suppliers and services. By contrast, the potential multiplier effects generated by public-sector employment among native blacks are largely lost. Due to the low self-employment

rates among blacks, resources are siphoned out of the community and captured by immigrants, who are overrepresented as "middleman" entrepreneurs in black communities.[27]

The low self-employment rate among blacks has negative consequences in and of itself since it means that there is no private-sector industry to which blacks have privileged access. As a result, traditional exclusionary mechanisms that have barred black entry into preferred jobs continue to operate. The best example is construction, where whites actually *increased* their share of jobs between 1970 and 1980 and blacks suffered a decline both in employment and in share. The same trends extend into the present, a period of vigorous activity in the industry. The 40 percent increase in construction employment registered since 1980 has led the construction unions to double enrollment in their apprenticeship programs (some of which had folded during the mid-1970s); however, black enrollment has remained virtually stagnant and has actually declined in the more desirable, so-called mechanical trades (carpentering, plumbing, electrical work).[28]

The obstacles to minority gains in construction lie in the marriage between the family and union systems of training and in the weakness of those government instruments designed to uncouple these systems. Although the construction unions play crucial roles in mobilizing and training the skilled labor force through apprenticeship programs and hiring halls, these activities are congruent with the workings of informal social networks. Thus, most training is done on-the-job through informal instruction by journeymen; the most crucial components of the learning process take place on small jobs where the apprentice works on a one-to-one basis with a journeyman; contractors often rely on the hiring hall only to supplement the pool of workers with whom they have established attachments; and close personal ties to contractors are important in breaking into the various construction trades and staying employed. For these reasons, outsiders have experienced severe difficulties in gaining entry.

Government efforts have enlarged access to apprentice programs, but black apprentices appear to receive inferior training, suffer higher dropout rates than do whites, and receive fewer regular job placements once journeyman status is obtained. Indeed, the entire formal component of the training system can be bypassed if need be, as illustrated by the following quote from a court-appointed administrator for one New York construction local that had failed for several years to comply with an earlier consent degree:

Contractors would delegate the hiring of many workers to a maintenance foreman who was a member of the same union. So they just bypassed the hiring hall. While the union business agent was sitting there in the hall saying "I don't understand why nobody calls me anymore," workers who were part of the buddy system were being hired directly by the contractor. We found that 80 percent of the hires were made outside of the hiring hall.[29]

Union resistance to attempts at integration has led the government to establish alternative training programs, in which contractors doing government work must hire a certain proportion of "trainees." Since the "trainees" lack apprenticeship status, they have no guarantee of continued activity in the trade once a government project is over, and thus the proportion of trainees graduating into journeyman status is low. Similar requirements oblige contractors to hire minority journeymen on public projects. These stipulations are equally ineffective in upping the proportion of minorities doing private-sector work because contractors respond by "checkerboarding," circulating minority craftworkers among their public projects while keeping a high ratio of whites employed on private work.[30]

CONCLUSION

What place is there for minorities in the post-industrial economies of U.S. cities? As this paper suggests, the conventional answers to the question do not provide a reliable guide to the trends in the premier post-industrial urban center – New York. The most widespread interpretation – that the shift from goods to services has engendered a skills mismatch in which minorities have lost economic function – receives no backing at all. Despite major structural changes, nonwhite employment increased substantially; the local economy absorbed large numbers of newcomers characterized by precisely those attributes presumably

not in demand and concentrated in those sectors most sharply affected by industrial decline. Nor is there much support for the thesis of polarization. Rather than being confined to the depressed sectors of the economy, all nonwhite groups gained jobs in the growth industries of the advanced service sectors; all groups gained in white-collar employment in every category (with the exception of native blacks in sales jobs); among blacks and Asians, the increase in white-collar employment considerably exceeded the gain predicted on the basis of population change alone; even Hispanics, whose situation most closely approximates the predictions of the polarization thesis, showed only the slightest slippage in their share of white-collar jobs.

Rather, the data in this paper confirmed the basic argument delineated in the introduction and adumbrated in latter sections: that composition is a crucial factor in the occupational position of nonwhites and that changes in the size of the white population set the stage for an upward realignment of nonwhite workers. In New York, the shift from goods to services went hand-in-glove with a decline in the availability of white workers, creating a replacement demand for nonwhite workers. Overall, the falloff in white employment greatly exceeded the shrinkage in the local economy: the simple outflow of whites from the New York economy left vacancies into which nonwhite workers could step. Although the size of the white labor force diminished, it also repositioned itself over the course of the 1970s: shifts in the distribution of whites, out of clerical and sales jobs and out of public-sector jobs in particular, created further opportunities for nonwhite succession.

Replacement is only part of the story. As nonwhites succeeded whites, they came to specialize in distinct economic niches – a pattern arising from diverse sources, but self-reinforcing over time as a result of occupational closure. Consequently, the impact of compositional change was blunted by a trend toward ethnic competition, reflected in a declining employment total and share for native blacks.

In conclusion, these findings suggest that research on the post-industrial transformation of U.S. cities and its impact should be redirected. Rather than another paper emphasizing the mismatch between urban employers and the urban, nonwhite population, what is needed is a closer look at the interaction between population dynamics and labor demand and more attention to the complex process by which groups are sorted among jobs and labor markets.

ENDNOTES

1. George Sternlieb and James Hughes, "The Uncertain Future of the Central City," *Urban Affairs Quarterly,* 18, no. 4 (1983): 455–72; John Kasarda, "Entry-Level Jobs, Mobility, and Urban Minority Employment," *Urban Affairs Quarterly* 19, no. 1 (1983): 21–40; idem, "Urban Change and Minority Opportunities," in *The New Urban Reality,* ed. Paul Peterson (Washington, D.C.: Brookings Institution, 1984), 33–67.

2. Bennett Harrison, "Rationalization, Restructuring and Industrial Reorganization in Older Regions: The Economic Transformation of New England since World War II," Working Paper no. 72, Joint Center for Urban Studies of MIT and Harvard University (Cambridge, Mass., 1982); Saskia Sassen-Koob, "The New Labor Demand in Global Cities," in *Cities in Transformation,* ed. Michael Smith (Beverly Hills, Calif.: Sage Publications, 1984).

3. Calculations based on Bureau of Labor Statistic data show that New York ranks first among major U.S. cities in its share of private-sector employment in services and next-to-last, after government-dominated Washington, D.C., in share provided by goods production (Bureau of Labor Statistics, *Geographic Profile of Employment and Unemployment, 1983,* Bulletin 2216 [Washington, D.C.: GPO, 1984], table 27). The 1980 Census of Population found that 48 percent of New Yorkers were nonwhite.

4. In *A Piece of the Pie* (Berkeley: University of California Press, 1980), Lieberson argues that "the occupational composition of a given ethnic or racial group will vary between communities in accordance with the group's proportion of the population and in accordance with the racial-ethnic composition of the city" (p. 297).

5. For further discussion of New York City's economy, with reference to the problems of the industrial regions of the Northeast, see the essays in *Post-industrial America: Metropolitan Decline and Inter-regional Job Shifts,* ed. George Sternlieb and James Hughes (New Brunswick, N.J.: Center for Urban Policy Research, 1976).

6. Important accounts of New York's economic revival, within the context of the changing economic functions of U.S. cities, are Robert Cohen, "The New International Division of Labor, Multinational Corporations, and Urban Hierarchy," in *Urbanization and Urban Planning in Capitalist Societies,* ed. Michael Dear and Al-

len Scott (New York: Methuen, 1981), 287–315; and Thierry Noyelle and Thomas Stanback, *The Transformation of American Cities* (Totowa, N.J.: Rowan & Allenheld, 1984).

7. Details on these demographic changes can be found in Emanuel Tobier, "Population," in *Setting Municipal Priorities: American Cities and the New York Experience,* ed. Charles Brecher and Raymond Horton (New York: New York University Press, 1984), 19–42; and "Foreign Immigration," in *Setting Municipal Priorities, 1983,"* ed. Brecher and Horton (New York: New York University Press, 1982), 154–201.

8. Data from the censuses report employment for New York City residents only; this raises the possibility that the disproportionate decline in white employment represents a shift in residence from city to suburb and not a drop in white share. Commuting is not especially prevalent in the New York City area, especially in comparison with other major U.S. cities, and the proportion of New York City residents who commute out to the suburbs is very low. However, commuters gained almost 50,000 jobs between 1970 and 1980, with the result that the commuter share of employment rose from 18 to 21 percent. Since the bulk of this increase was due to the rise in the number of nonwhite commuters, the job patterns of New York City residents should resemble the job patterns of all workers with jobs located in New York City (calculated from Bureau of the Census, *Census of Population, 1970,* Subject Reports PC [2]-CD, Journey to Work, table 2; Bureau of the Census, *Census of Population, 1980,* Subject Reports, PC80-2-6D, Journey to Work, table 2). Another source of possible distortion would be undercounting of New York's illegal immigrant population. However, due to special efforts to improve coverage of immigrants and other groups, the Census Bureau appears to have significantly improved its coverage. The bureau's own estimates are that less than 1 percent of the total residential population was missed in its enumeration. Indeed, the census was quite successful in counting illegal immigrants: it is estimated that slightly over 2 million of the 7.5 million foreign-born persons counted in the 1980 census were illegal. Moreover, even if the undercount of immigrants were equal to the undercount of the most difficult to count groups – 35–45 year-old black men – this would increase the immigrant population by only 6 percent. For further discussion, see R. Warren and J. Passell, "A Count of the Uncountable: Estimates of Undocumented Aliens Counted in the 1980 Census" (Unpublished paper, Bureau of the Census, 1983).

9. Strictly speaking, several factors account for the decline of New York's white population between 1970 and 1980. Since whites had an older age structure than nonwhite groups, the death rate was higher for whites;

similarly, the white birthrate was lower and actually slowed between 1970 and 1980; finally, there was substantial out-migration of whites during this period. Of the three factors, out-migration provided the most substantial contribution to population loss. Where whites migrated to – whether to the suburbs or to other regions of the United States – is difficult to determine. However, the decline in the population of the entire New York Metropolitan Region by over one million during this same period suggests that there was substantial movement to other regions. For further details, see Tobier, "Population."

10. For fuller elaboration of the queuing model, see Lieberson, *A Piece of the Pie*, 296–99; and Lester Thurow, *Generating Inequality* (New York: Basic Books, 1975), chap. 4.

11. Peter Doeringer and Michael Piore, *Internal Labor Markets and Manpower Analysis* (Lexington, Mass.: Lexington Books, 1971); Paul Osterman, "The Mismatch Hypothesis and Internal Labor Markets," *Proceedings of the 36th Annual Meeting of the Industrial Relations Research Association, 1982* (Madison, Wisc.: Industrial Relations Research Association, 1983.

12. Data on public employment from Mary McCormick, "Labor Relations," in *Setting Municipal Priorities: American Cities and the New York Experience,* ed. Charles Brecher and Raymond Horton (New York: New York University Press, 1984), 301–2; Raymond Horton, "Human Resources," in Charles Brecher and Raymond Horton, *Setting Municipal Priorities, 1986* (New York: New York University Press, 1985), 170–203; Press Release, Office of the Mayor, Jan. 2, 1986.

13. A fuller discussion is presented in chap. 3 of my book, *Through the Eye of the Needle: Immigrants and Enterprise in New York's Garment Trades* (New York: New York University Press, 1986).

14. This draws on material discussed in ibid., chap. 2; for more material on Israelis, see Josef Korazim and Marcia Freedman, "Self-employment and the Decision to Emigrate: Israelis in New York City," *Contemporary Jewry* (forthcoming); labor force patterns in the fur industry are discussed in a study I prepared, with Thomas Bailey, for the New York Office of Economic Development, "Displacement Pressures on Manhattan Manufacturing Industries and Job Retention Strategies" (1983); the observation about Gujarati merchants is based on a study I am presently conducting on white, Indian, Korean, and Hispanic business owners.

15. Several studies, in addition to my own, underline the importance of network recruiting among a number of different groups in a variety of industries; see, e.g., Thomas Bailey, *Immigrant and Native Workers: Contrasts and Competition* (Boulder, Colo.: Westview, 1987), chaps. 2–3; Bernard Wong, *A Chinese-American Commu-*

nity (Singapore: Chopmen, 1980); and Harry Herman, "Dishwashers and Proprietors: Macedonians in Toronto's Restaurant Trade," in *Ethnicity at Work,* ed. Sandra Wallman (London: Macmillan, 1979).

16. See Illsoo Kim, *The New Urban Immigrants: The Korean Community in New York* (Princeton: Princeton University Press, 1981), 112.

17. Thus, Bailey points out that in construction, "the union structure based on informal ties . . . perpetuates the barriers to outsiders that are inherent in the industry's informal structure. For example, membership in the operating engineers locals – the possession of a union book – has traditionally passed from father to son. Training for this trade was mostly informal. In fact, until a recent court order required that the two operating engineers locals in New York establish a training program, there was no formal training for this trade in the city." A fuller discussion is reported in chap. 6 of his *Immigrant and Native Workers.*

18. Thus, Angelo Falcon points out in "Black and Latino Politics in New York City: Race and Ethnicity in a Changing Urban Context" (*New Community,* forthcoming) that "many Latinos complain that blacks use the term 'minority' to increase their political leverage, while excluding Latinos from the benefits that ensue from this strategy." He goes on to show that Latinos are far less well represented than blacks in New York City and New York State employment at all levels of work.

19. Data calculated from Public Use Microdata Sample, 1980 Census of Population.

20. See Lydia Chavez, "Koch and Hispanic-Issue Panel Differ," *New York Times,* Aug. 3, 1986, 28.

21. Peter Eisinger, "Local Civil Service Employment and Black Socio-economic Mobility," *Social Science Quarterly,* 67, no. 2 (1986): 171.

22. Raymond Horton, "Fiscal Stress and Labor Power," *Proceedings of the 38th Annual Meeting of the Industrial Relations Research Association* (1985), 304–15.

23. For a fuller explanation of the development of ethnic business, see chap. 2 in Waldinger, *Through the Eye of the Needle.*

24. Quoted in Kim, *The New Urban Immigrants,* 115.

25. This discussion of blacks and immigrants in food retailing is based on a study of youth employment that I conducted with Thomas Bailey for the New York City Office of Economic Development, "Marginal and Out of Work: The Youth Employment Problem in New York City" (1984); the findings from the retail food case study appear in chap. 5 of Bailey's *Immigrant and Native Workers;* other conclusions have been reported in Waldinger and Bailey, "The Youth Employment Problem in the World City," *Social Policy,* 16, no. 1 (1986), 55–59.

26. For further elaboration, see Waldinger, *Through the Eye of the Needle,* chap. 5.

27. For a discussion of the role of Koreans as middle-men merchants in black communities and the conflicts that this has precipitated, see Kim, *The New Urban Immigrants*, 257–59; and Jin H. Yu, *The Korean Merchants in the Black Community* (Philadelphia: Philip Jaison Memorial Foundation, 1980).

28. Thomas Bailey and Roger Waldinger, "Labor Force Adjustments in a Growing Construction Industry" (Report prepared for the Port Authority of New York and New Jersey, Feb. 1987). The following paragraphs draw on this report (and the fieldwork done for it) as well as the material found in Bailey, *Immigrant and Native*

Workers; and Marc Silver's *Under Construction: Work and Alienation in the Building Trades* (Albany: SUNY Press, 1986), esp. chap. 3.

29. Quoted in Bailey, *Immigrant and Native Workers,* chap. 6.

30. For further discussion of the continuing disparities in the on-the-job experience of apprentices and "trainees" employed on government projects, as well as the legal history of this issue, see *Problems of Discrimination and Extortion in the Building Trades* (Report prepared by the Mayor's Office of Construction Industry Relations, City of New York, 1982).

N I N E T E E N

Trends in the Residential Segregation of Blacks, Hispanics, and Asians 1970–1980

Douglas S. Massey
Nancy A. Denton

INTRODUCTION

The 1970s were a period of tumultuous change in American cities, as conditions likely to affect the spatial distribution of racial and ethnic groups shifted radically over the decade. Levels and patterns of black, Hispanic, and Asian residential segregation were particularly affected by changes in five areas of national life: federal law, public attitudes, social class, immigration, and the economy.

The year 1968 saw the culmination of a de-

cades-long struggle for black civil rights that progressively dismantled the legal supports for segregation (Farley 1984, pp. 2–5). In the famous *Brown v. Topeka* decision of 1954, the U.S. Supreme Court overturned earlier decisions supporting racial discrimination in public schools. In 1964, the Civil Rights Act banned discrimination in public accommodations, supported the integration of schools, outlawed discrimination involving federal funds, and forbade discrimination in employment. The Voting Rights Act of 1965 attacked the systematic political disen-

Reprinted from *American Sociological Review* 52, 1987, pp. 802–825, by permission of the authors and the American Sociological Association.

franchisement of black voters and brought them into the electoral process. Finally, and most important for present purposes, the Civil Rights Act of 1968 banned racial discrimination in the sale or rental of housing. Although the 1970 census revealed little change since 1960 in the very high levels of black segregation (Sorensen et al. 1975; Van Valey et al. 1977), observers at the time noted that fair housing laws had had little time to operate, and looked forward to 1980, when they hoped racial segregation would be reduced.

Over the course of the 1960s and 1970s, there was a sharp improvement in racial attitudes among whites. The percentage of whites opposed to residential integration steadily fell (Greeley and Sheatsley 1974; Taylor et al. 1978), until by 1972 85 percent agreed that it would make no difference to them "if a Negro with just as much income and education" moved onto their block (Pettigrew 1973; 1979). By the mid-1960s, opposition to integration in public and informal settings had almost disappeared (Sheatsley 1966; Greeley and Sheatsley 1974), and over the course of the 1970s, blacks and whites mixed increasingly on the job, in the media, in sports, and in public life generally.

As a result of more tolerant racial attitudes and anti-discrimination legislation, economic opportunities for blacks also increased during the 1970s, leading to the development of a large and increasingly affluent black middle class (Freeman 1976; Wilson 1978a; Farley 1984). By 1980 more blacks than ever had access to the levels of income and economic resources that have permitted other groups to achieve spatial assimilation in American society. Some observers suggest that the black middle class largely abandoned poor areas to move into middle-class neighborhoods, exacerbating the spatial isolation of low-income minority members (Auletta 1982; Wilson 1987).

Immigration to the United States from Latin America and Asia increased over the past decade. Sweeping changes in U.S. immigration law took effect in 1968 and eliminated the discriminatory national origins quotas (Keely, 1979), and undocumented migration rose markedly. During the 1970s, some 4.5 million legal immigrants and at least 2 million illegal immigrants entered the country (Massey 1981a; Passel and Woodrow 1984; Passel 1986), mostly from Asia and Latin America. They settled primarily in large urban areas such as Los Angeles, New York, Chicago, and Miami, rapidly augmenting Hispanic and Asian populations.

The rapid growth of ethnic and racial minorities through immigration is relevant to residential segregation in two ways. First, it stimulates negative attitudes of natives towards immigrant groups such as Hispanics and Asians (Harwood 1986). The reaction is particularly strong towards undocumented migrants and especially pronounced among native blacks (Harwood 1986; Muller and Espenshade 1985). Second, migration chains tend to concentrate immigrant groups in specific neighborhoods (Massey 1986b). New arrivals enter areas where they have friends or relatives. After becoming established, they find permanent homes in the same area, leading to consolidation and further ethnic-enclave growth.

Finally, the 1970s were a decade of urban economic and demographic upheaval. The postwar movement of people and jobs out of central cities into suburban areas continued, although at a slower pace, and the rural-urban shift of population slowed and then reversed itself (Fuguitt 1985). Job creation and population growth during the 1970s were more rapid in nonmetropolitan areas than in the largest urban areas. Some observers argue that these forces increased the spatial isolation of minorities, segregating them within depressed inner-city neighborhoods (Kain 1968, 1974; Kain and Quigley 1975; Straszheim 1980).

It is difficult to say, a priori, how these five sets of changes affected racial and ethnic segregation patterns in American cities. Lessening prejudice against blacks and other minorities, the ongoing impact of civil rights legislation, and the rise of the black middle class no doubt acted to reduce segregation. But rapid immigration and metropolitan decentralization probably increased it. In this paper, we measure recent trends in racial and ethnic segregation using 1970 and 1980 census data on blacks, Hispanics, and Asians in 60 large U.S. metropolitan areas, and then analyze interurban variation in the degree of segregation to explain the patterns we observe.

PATTERNS OF SEGREGATION CIRCA 1970

Studies of blacks in 1970 generally found a high degree of spatial segregation between the races, with indices ranging from about .600 to .900 (using the index of dissimilarity). Segregation was particularly strong in large metropolitan areas with high black concentrations. The average level of black-white segregation in 237 SMSAs in 1970 was .695 (Van Valey et al. 1977), but in the 29 largest urbanized areas it averaged .831 (Massey 1979a). Black segregation did not decline with rising socioeconomic status (Farley 1977b; Simkus 1978; Massey 1979b), and average black socioeconomic status was not highly related to interurban variation in black segregation (Massey 1979a, 1981b). However, segregation was related to black-white occupational differentiation in southern cities (Roof et al. 1976). Lieberson and Carter (1982a) estimate that 85 percent of black segregation in 1970 was attributable to involuntary causes.

The pace of black suburbanization increased during the late 1960s and early 1970s (Farley 1970; H. Rose 1976; Guest 1978; Logan and Schneider 1984), with relatively young and well-educated blacks moving out of central cities into white suburban neighborhoods (Clay 1979; Lake 1981; Spain and Long 1981). But the relative number of suburban blacks in 1970 was quite small, and blacks in suburbs were still quite segregated (Massey 1979a; Logan and Stearns 1981; Schneider and Logan 1982; Logan and Schneider 1984). Nonetheless, several researchers have argued that black suburbanization will eventually lower levels of black residential segregation (Frey 1985; Clark 1986).

Levels and patterns of Hispanic segregation in 1970 differed markedly from those of blacks. Hispanic-Anglo segregation was quite modest in 1970, with segregation scores ranging from .307 to .646 in the 29 urbanized areas studied by Massey (1979a), yielding an average of .444 (again using the index of dissimilarity). In a sample of 35 southwestern central cities, Lopez (1981) found an average score of .545. Segregation declined sharply with rising socioeconomic status and generations spent in the United States (Massey 1979b, 1981c), and was markedly lower in suburbs than in central cities (Massey 1979a). Only

the Puerto Rican population of New York contradicted these findings; their segregation was quite high and did not decline with rising socioeconomic status or suburbanization (Massey 1979a, 1979b, 1981b; Jackson 1981). Massey and Bitterman (1985) attributed this pattern to the relatively large number of Puerto Ricans with black ancestry.

Several studies also examined the segregation of blacks and Hispanics using indices of spatial isolation and interaction, which measure the probability of residential contact within and between groups. . . . In urban areas where they are substantial minorities, the two groups display quite different patterns of spatial interaction. Blacks typically experience a low probability of contact with whites and a relatively high degree of spatial isolation, while Hispanics display relatively high probabilities of contact with Anglos and modest spatial isolation (Lieberson and Carter 1982b; Massey and Blakeslee 1983; Massey and Mullan 1984), again with the exception of Puerto Ricans in New York (Massey and Bitterman 1985).

There was no systematic study of Asian segregation done for 1970, but preliminary work from the 1980 census suggests that patterns of Asian segregation closely parallel those of Hispanics, with low-to-moderate levels of segregation from whites that decline with rising socioeconomic status and increasing acculturation (Langberg and Farley 1986; Langberg 1986). These early studies covered only 35 metropolitan areas, however, and were limited in the amount of socioeconomic background information they could consider. To date, no study has systematically compared patterns of black, Hispanic, and Asian segregation across a large sample of urban areas.

SOURCES OF DATA

The data used in this study were taken from the 1970 Fourth Count Summary Tapes and the 1980 Summary Tape File 4 (STF4) from the U.S. Bureau of the Census (1970b, 1980). They provide counts of whites, blacks, Hispanics, and Asians in census tracts of Standard Metropolitan Statistical Areas (SMSAs). We selected tracts in the 50 largest SMSAs, plus tracts in 10 other metropolitan areas (mainly in the southwest) that contained relatively large numbers of Hispanics. . . . The term "Hispanic" refers to Spanish Americans in 1970 and persons of Spanish origin in 1980. Although comparability is not perfect, it produces reasonable results and is preferable to using the Spanish origin definition in both census years. . . .

A final problem emerges because Hispanics are an ethnic group, while whites, blacks, and Asians are racial groups, and Hispanics can be white, black, or Asian. Fortunately, Hispanics were cross-classified by race in 1970 as well as 1980. White Hispanics, black Hispanics, and Asian Hispanics were therefore subtracted from the respective white, black, and Asian populations; throughout this article the term "Anglo" refers to non-Hispanic whites and the terms "black" and "Asian" indicate non-Hispanic blacks and Asians. We use the term "Asian" to refer to a group that includes Asians, Pacific Islanders, and a very small number of persons of other race.

Obviously, the terms "Hispanic" and "Asian" mask considerable underlying diversity in national origins and characteristics (Massey 1985; Wong 1986; Bean and Tienda 1987). Hispanics encompass relatively well educated, high-income Cubans as well as poorly educated, low-income Puerto Ricans, and Asians run the gamut from Chinese electrical engineers to poor Vietnamese refugees. Both populations display considerable generational diversity. It is clear that "Hispanics" and "Asians" do not really exist as coherent minority groups except in a weak sense; the census categories are convenient labels that have been externally imposed.

These groups are, nonetheless, those for which the Census Bureau supplies the richest and most detailed information at the census-tract level. Patterns of segregation for individual Asian and Hispanic groups will be studied in future reports. Our strategy here is to use data on Hispanics and Asians to study patterns of ethnic and racial segregation, recognizing the inherent limitations in doing so and trying to adjust interpretations accordingly. In the case of Hispanics, our task is aided somewhat by the fact that the constituent groups have different regional concentrations – Mexicans in the southwest, Puerto Ricans in the northeast, and Cubans in Florida –

so that in studying Los Angeles, New York, and Miami we are in some sense isolating Mexicans, Puerto Ricans, and Cubans. . . .

MEASURES OF SEGREGATION

There is a voluminous and controversial literature on the measurement of residential segregation (for recent reviews see James and Taeuber 1985; Stearns and Logan 1986; and White 1986). In preparing this study, we undertook a systematic empirical evaluation of all indices of segregation identified from an exhaustive survey of the methodological literature, some 19 in all (Massey and Denton unpublished). Each measure was computed to assess the degree of segregation between blacks, Hispanics, Asians, and Anglos in 1980, and the results were intercorrelated and factor analyzed. Each index was found to load very strongly on one of five underlying factors: evenness, exposure, centralization, concentration, or clustering. This article focuses on the first two of these dimensions. . . .

Evenness is the differential distribution of minority and majority members across census tracts within an urban area. A minority group is said to be segregated if it is unevenly distributed over tracts. Evenness is maximized and segregation minimized when all tracts have the same relative number of minority members as the whole urban area. . . .

The second dimension is exposure, which refers to the degree of potential contact between minority and majority members within census tracts of urban areas. Exposure indices measure the extent to which minority and majority members must physically confront one another by virtue of sharing a common tract of residence. The degree of minority exposure may be conceptualized as the likelihood that minority and majority members share a common neighborhood. . . .

TRENDS IN INTERGROUP EXPOSURE

One cannot interpret trends in intergroup exposure without considering changes in population size and ethnic composition in the 60 SMSAs under study. Unfortunately, limitations of space prevent us from tabulating this information here, so we refer to an unpublished table giving the number and proportion of minority and majority members in each metropolitan area (available on request). These data reveal a widespread decline in Anglo population relative to blacks, Hispanics, and Asians. In the 60 SMSAs, Anglos increased by 233,000 persons, compared to respective increases for blacks, Hispanics, and Asians of 2.5 million, 3.0 million and 1.8 million. As a result, Anglos' share of the metropolitan population fell by an average of 5 percentage points, while the other groups' share increased from 1.5 to 2.4 points. The percentage of Anglos fell in 56 of the 60 SMSAs, and Anglos sustained absolute losses in 24 cases. By way of contrast, the percentage of blacks fell in only 8 cases, and the percentage of Hispanics in 10, and no SMSA reported absolute declines for these groups. All SMSAs showed an increase in the percentage Asian, but most began the decade with very small Asian populations.

Over the decade of the 1970s, minorities became increasingly preponderant in most SMSAs. By 1980 blacks exceeded 20 percent of the metropolitan population in 12 of the areas under study, including Chicago and New York. They comprised 40 percent of metropolitan Memphis and 32 percent of metropolitan New Orleans. Hispanics similarly exceeded 20 percent of the population in 10 SMSAs, including Los Angeles and Miami, which experienced particularly strong shifts in composition. In both areas the percentage the Anglos fell by 15 percentage points, while the percentage of Hispanics grew by 9 and 12 points, respectively. Hispanics were majorities or near majorities in Corpus Christi, El Paso, and San Antonio. Asians represented a much smaller share of the population in all cities. They constituted the largest proportion in San Francisco, where they were 11 percent of the population, followed by 9 percent in San Jose. Asians exceeded 5 percent of the metropolitan population in seven cases, all on the west coast, and, with the exception of Seattle, all in California.

Table 1 presents 1970 and 1980 indicators of residential exposure for minority and majority groups in the 60 SMSAs. To conserve space, 1970–1980 changes are not shown. Since the information in this table is substantial, we focus primarily on the averages at the bottom of the table, and on five "key metropolitan areas" that

contain significant numbers of all three minority groups: Chicago, Los Angeles, Miami, New York, and San Francisco. Discussion of other metropolitan areas will be general, except when a particular pattern of segregation draws our attention.

Of the many residential contact probabilities shown in Table 1, two are especially revealing: the isolation index, . . . which measures the average probability of group X members sharing a tract with themselves (i.e., blacks with blacks, Hispanics with Hispanics, or Asians with Asians); and the interaction index, . . . which measures the probability that group X members have of sharing a tract with Y members, in this case Anglos (i.e., blacks with Anglos, Hispanics with Anglos, or Asians with Anglos). The increasing prevalence of minorities in nearly all of the SMSAs suggests a decrease in Anglo-interaction probabilities and an increase in isolation indices, other things being equal.

Black trends run opposite this prediction, however, suggesting there has been some improvement in their spatial position over the past decade. The probability of contact with other blacks declined by an average of .062 over the decade, from .553 in 1970 to .491 in 1980, while the average probability of interaction with Anglos increased from .333 to .376. Black isolation decreased in 50 of the 60 SMSAs and the likelihood of Anglo contact increased in 47 cases. Given that the effect of compositional change was in the opposite direction, one might be led to conclude that civil rights legislation and more tolerant white attitudes finally had an effect in decreasing levels of black segregation in U.S. cities.

This initial optimism is dispelled somewhat by a closer look at the data. In spite of declines over the past decade, blacks remain by far the most spatially isolated of the three minority groups. Average black isolation (.491) is 2.5 times that of Hispanics (.201) and 10 times that of Asians (.047). In some SMSAs, such as Chicago, the level of black isolation (.828) is extremely high and has changed little over the past decade (it was .855 in 1970). The probability of residential contact with Anglos was only .125, which is actually *lower* than the proportion of blacks in Chicago (.199), indicating that a very rigid pattern of racial seg-

TABLE 1 *Probabilities of Residential Contact Between Blacks, Hispanics, Asians, and Anglos in 60 Metropolitan Areas, 1970–1980*

| | GROUP'S PROBABILITY OF CONTACT WITH: | | | | | | | |
| | Anglos | | Blacks | | Hispanics | | Asians | |
Metropolitan Area and Group	1970	1980	1970	1980	1970	1980	1970	1980
KEY METROPOLITAN AREAS								
Chicago								
Anglo	.926	.881	.027	.036	.040	.059	.008	.026
Black	.118	.125	.855	.828	.023	.038	.005	.009
Hispanic	.649	.499	.085	.093	.251	.380	.021	.031
Asian	.721	.736	.099	.075	.109	.105	.076	.087
Los Angeles-Long Beach								
Anglo	.812	.720	.023	.038	.141	.180	.027	.065
Black	.153	.165	.703	.604	.110	.188	.037	.046
Hispanic	.523	.347	.063	.084	.378	.501	.046	.074
Asian	.534	.489	.112	.080	.242	.286	.123	.152
Miami								
Anglo	.766	.649	.042	.074	.189	.263	.004	.014
Black	.174	.206	.752	.642	.073	.143	.002	.011
Hispanic	.487	.341	.045	.067	.465	.583	.005	.011
Asian	.618	.526	.088	.146	.289	.311	.008	.018
New York								
Anglo	.862	.820	.051	.056	.076	.092	.012	.033
Black	.210	.164	.588	.627	.193	.189	.013	.021
Hispanic	.389	.330	.236	.232	.361	.400	.022	.040
Asian	.558	.556	.136	.119	.197	.184	.116	.143
San Francisco-Oakland								
Anglo	.805	.763	.041	.053	.109	.095	.052	.095
Black	.292	.299	.560	.511	.098	.104	.059	.092
Hispanic	.671	.582	.085	.113	.192	.193	.066	.120
Asian	.587	.564	.095	.097	.121	.116	.210	.232
OTHER METROPOLITAN AREAS								
Albany-Schenectady-Troy								
Anglo	.966	.955	.023	.028	.007	.008	.004	.009
Black	.704	.690	.283	.279	.008	.015	.005	.016
Hispanic	.948	.909	.036	.066	.012	.014	.004	.011
Asian	.944	.908	.041	.066	.008	.010	.007	.017
Albuquerque								
Anglo	.679	.662	.012	.017	.297	.292	.015	.032
Black	.436	.516	.097	.051	.454	.388	.015	.050
Hispanic	.425	.448	.019	.019	.544	.506	.016	.030
Asian	.543	.578	.016	.029	.420	.348	.026	.048
Anaheim-Santa Ana-Garden Grove								
Anglo	.881	.821	.004	.010	.101	.115	.017	.056
Black	.509	.651	.174	.038	.305	.241	.026	.074
Hispanic	.773	.610	.017	.020	.194	.310	.021	.064
Asian	.839	.750	.009	.015	.131	.161	.026	.077

(continued)

TABLE 1   continued

Metropolitan Area and Group	Anglos 1970	Anglos 1980	Blacks 1970	Blacks 1980	Hispanics 1970	Hispanics 1980	Asians 1970	Asians 1980
				GROUP'S PROBABILITY OF CONTACT WITH:				

Metropolitan Area and Group	Anglos		Blacks		Hispanics		Asians	
	1970	1980	1970	1980	1970	1980	1970	1980
OTHER METROPOLITAN AREAS								
Atlanta								
Anglo	.925	.886	.062	.091	.011	.013	.002	.011
Black	.213	.237	.780	.748	.005	.010	.002	.005
Hispanic	.860	.736	.115	.228	.022	.022	.003	.014
Asian	.819	.821	.161	.144	.013	.018	.007	.018
Austin								
Anglo	.853	.797	.039	.059	.104	.128	.004	.018
Black	.269	.397	.524	.368	.206	.226	.002	.011
Hispanic	.514	.524	.148	.137	.336	.326	.002	.019
Asian	.827	.724	.062	.069	.101	.186	.011	.023
Bakersfield								
Anglo	.847	.790	.017	.026	.124	.151	.014	.036
Black	.248	.365	.488	.346	.250	.262	.021	.032
Hispanic	.557	.481	.077	.059	.349	.421	.031	.046
Asian	.597	.646	.065	.040	.303	.257	.062	.066
Baltimore								
Anglo	.919	.887	.067	.090	.009	.009	.005	.015
Black	.216	.259	.772	.723	.008	.009	.004	.009
Hispanic	.753	.705	.224	.263	.017	.015	.006	.017
Asian	.789	.785	.186	.178	.011	.011	.015	.026
Birmingham								
Anglo	.768	.787	.227	.201	.004	.007	.001	.005
Black	.544	.486	.451	.502	.004	.007	.001	.004
Hispanic	.669	.691	.319	.295	.009	.009	.003	.004
Asian	.674	.728	.309	.257	.007	.007	.007	.007
Boston								
Anglo	.966	.946	.017	.022	.011	.018	.007	.015
Black	.376	.345	.567	.551	.045	.080	.013	.025
Hispanic	.787	.653	.145	.185	.052	.129	.017	.033
Asian	.822	.768	.071	.080	.028	.047	.080	.105
Buffalo								
Anglo	.961	.946	.024	.035	.010	.011	.005	.009
Black	.267	.335	.712	.635	.016	.022	.006	.009
Hispanic	.820	.751	.118	.157	.050	.077	.012	.016
Asian	.875	.867	.082	.087	.025	.022	.019	.024
Cincinnati								
Anglo	.943	.926	.049	.062	.005	.005	.003	.007
Black	.401	.441	.591	.543	.004	.009	.004	.007
Hispanic	.890	.799	.096	.183	.010	.010	.004	.008
Asian	.823	.854	.162	.127	.006	.007	.008	.013
Cleveland								
Anglo	.952	.936	.033	.041	.010	.013	.005	.010
Black	.170	.180	.819	.804	.007	.010	.004	.006

TRENDS IN THE RESIDENTIAL SEGREGATION OF BLACKS, HISPANICS, AND ASIANS

TABLE 1 continued

	GROUP'S PROBABILITY OF CONTACT WITH:							
	Anglos		Blacks		Hispanics		Asians	
Metropolitan Area and Group	1970	1980	1970	1980	1970	1980	1970	1980
OTHER METROPOLITAN AREAS								
Cleveland								
Hispanic	.815	.771	.114	.133	.065	.082	.008	.015
Asian	.837	.836	.131	.122	.018	.022	.015	.021
Columbus								
Anglo	.944	.917	.046	.065	.006	.008	.004	.011
Black	.355	.407	.635	.575	.007	.009	.003	.010
Hispanic	.850	.822	.131	.152	.014	.013	.005	.014
Asian	.891	.832	.090	.130	.008	.010	.011	.029
Corpus Christi								
Anglo	.704	.643	.009	.015	.286	.333	.003	.010
Black	.116	.186	.363	.267	.517	.544	.009	.005
Hispanic	.321	.317	.043	.042	.635	.636	.002	.006
Asian	.545	.591	.109	.021	.344	.377	.009	.015
Dallas-Fort Worth								
Anglo	.908	.866	.033	.050	.055	.068	.006	.016
Black	.189	.272	.760	.646	.049	.074	.003	.009
Hispanic	.700	.619	.107	.124	.186	.240	.009	.018
Asian	.818	.796	.069	.078	.098	.101	.017	.026
Dayton								
Anglo	.960	.937	.031	.049	.005	.006	.003	.008
Black	.258	.339	.733	.650	.005	.007	.004	.005
Hispanic	.878	.837	.106	.145	.012	.010	.005	.008
Asian	.867	.904	.118	.077	.007	.007	.008	.012
Denver-Boulder								
Anglo	.890	.867	.011	.026	.090	.086	.011	.022
Black	.235	.455	.596	.411	.153	.110	.020	.026
Hispanic	.661	.649	.052	.048	.274	.275	.018	.031
Asian	.753	.773	.063	.054	.166	.143	.022	.033
Detroit								
Anglo	.936	.919	.047	.054	.013	.015	.004	.013
Black	.222	.204	.759	.773	.014	.015	.006	.009
Hispanic	.775	.736	.173	.186	.046	.065	.007	.015
Asian	.753	.806	.217	.153	.020	.019	.011	.023
El Paso								
Anglo	.550	.480	.015	.033	.427	.470	.009	.020
Black	.337	.405	.053	.050	.604	.525	.007	.022
Hispanic	.266	.229	.017	.021	.715	.741	.006	.011
Asian	.488	.435	.016	.040	.485	.506	.016	.023
Fort Lauderdale								
Anglo	.954	.919	.016	.034	.026	.040	.004	.008
Black	.113	.262	.873	.702	.013	.031	.002	.005
Hispanic	.893	.852	.064	.087	.039	.053	.004	.009
Asian	.886	.866	.072	.075	.030	.047	.011	.013

(continued)

TABLE 1 continued

Metropolitan Area and Group	GROUP'S PROBABILITY OF CONTACT WITH:							
	Anglos		Blacks		Hispanics		Asians	
	1970	1980	1970	1980	1970	1980	1970	1980
OTHER METROPOLITAN AREAS								
Fresno								
Anglo	.754	.713	.014	.025	.206	.221	.029	.045
Black	.210	.313	.522	.377	.248	.278	.026	.039
Hispanic	.551	.469	.046	.046	.376	.446	.033	.045
Asian	.640	.618	.040	.042	.273	.292	.057	.053
Gary-Hammond-E. Chicago								
Anglo	.927	.901	.028	.038	.042	.054	.003	.007
Black	.121	.142	.804	.773	.073	.081	.002	.004
Hispanic	.552	.538	.223	.220	.223	.237	.005	.006
Asian	.804	.815	.111	.107	.079	.065	.006	.013
Greensboro-Winston-Salem								
Anglo	.896	.867	.097	.121	.004	.006	.003	.007
Black	.432	.487	.561	.501	.003	.007	.004	.006
Hispanic	.835	.765	.151	.217	.010	.011	.004	.007
Asian	.772	.810	.207	.171	.005	.007	.016	.013
Houston								
Anglo	.836	.783	.070	.078	.089	.116	.006	.025
Black	.254	.283	.664	.593	.078	.109	.005	.016
Hispanic	.585	.517	.141	.134	.269	.328	.011	.022
Asian	.659	.699	.149	.120	.184	.137	.015	.045
Indianapolis								
Anglo	.941	.929	.049	.057	.007	.007	.003	.007
Black	.346	.361	.645	.623	.007	.009	.003	.007
Hispanic	.874	.824	.109	.156	.014	.012	.003	.008
Asian	.861	.852	.125	.127	.008	.009	.005	.013
Jersey City								
Anglo	.826	.717	.051	.052	.118	.201	.007	.031
Black	.394	.260	.528	.604	.073	.111	.008	.027
Hispanic	.602	.456	.048	.050	.345	.465	.010	.032
Asian	.696	.566	.098	.100	.190	.260	.021	.078
Kansas City								
Anglo	.945	.921	.033	.044	.019	.023	.004	.013
Black	.236	.282	.742	.690	.017	.020	.004	.009
Hispanic	.798	.773	.103	.106	.092	.104	.007	.019
Asian	.823	.840	.113	.094	.035	.037	.009	.030
Louisville								
Anglo	.950	.929	.043	.058	.005	.006	.002	.007
Black	.308	.357	.687	.633	.003	.005	.002	.005
Hispanic	.912	.851	.076	.132	.009	.009	.003	.009
Asian	.896	.871	.092	.106	.006	.008	.007	.015
Memphis								
Anglo	.858	.815	.132	.169	.006	.008	.003	.009
Black	.214	.228	.780	.759	.004	.009	.002	.004

TABLE 1   continued

| | GROUP'S PROBABILITY OF CONTACT WITH: | | | | | | | |
| | Anglos | | Blacks | | Hispanics | | Asians | |
Metropolitan Area and Group	1970	1980	1970	1980	1970	1980	1970	1980
OTHER METROPOLITAN AREAS								
Memphis								
Hispanic	.705	.524	.281	.456	.011	.013	.003	.007
Asian	.695	.728	.294	.248	.005	.010	.006	.015
Milwaukee								
Anglo	.961	.934	.020	.034	.014	.021	.005	.012
Black	.239	.269	.739	.695	.016	.026	.007	.011
Hispanic	.817	.706	.076	.112	.098	.162	.010	.022
Asian	.863	.838	.091	.094	.028	.045	.018	.025
Minneapolis-St. Paul								
Anglo	.973	.953	.009	.017	.009	.011	.009	.020
Black	.552	.622	.399	.307	.022	.021	.028	.051
Hispanic	.898	.870	.039	.047	.049	.048	.014	.039
Asian	.908	.861	.048	.059	.014	.020	.030	.062
Nashville-Davidson								
Anglo	.927	.901	.064	.086	.006	.006	.003	.007
Black	.296	.375	.697	.611	.004	.008	.002	.006
Hispanic	.869	.751	.114	.229	.013	.012	.004	.009
Asian	.818	.814	.161	.159	.010	.008	.012	.019
Nassau-Suffolk								
Anglo	.941	.924	.026	.030	.029	.035	.004	.012
Black	.538	.445	.412	.469	.045	.073	.006	.014
Hispanic	.871	.781	.066	.111	.060	.096	.005	.013
Asian	.895	.867	.062	.069	.034	.043	.010	.022
New Orleans								
Anglo	.829	.797	.120	.141	.047	.047	.003	.015
Black	.257	.274	.713	.688	.028	.027	.002	.012
Hispanic	.720	.708	.203	.212	.074	.063	.003	.017
Asian	.723	.613	.220	.251	.049	.046	.008	.093
Newark								
Anglo	.906	.872	.056	.065	.033	.046	.005	.018
Black	.261	.218	.670	.692	.064	.078	.007	.012
Hispanic	.581	.481	.245	.241	.167	.263	.010	.016
Asian	.686	.757	.217	.149	.085	.066	.015	.029
Norfolk-Virginia Beach-Portsmouth								
Anglo	.879	.809	.102	.155	.011	.015	.009	.024
Black	.254	.351	.735	.628	.007	.010	.004	.012
Hispanic	.782	.736	.182	.217	.022	.020	.016	.030
Asian	.775	.767	.137	.173	.021	.019	.069	.047
Oklahoma City								
Anglo	.941	.893	.019	.044	.017	.023	.024	.041
Black	.203	.386	.772	.569	.014	.021	.010	.026
Hispanic	.867	.810	.069	.087	.038	.056	.027	.049
Asian	.901	.854	.038	.062	.020	.029	.042	.057

(continued)

TABLE 1   continued

| | GROUP'S PROBABILITY OF CONTACT WITH: | | | | | | | |
| | Anglos | | Blacks | | Hispanics | | Asians | |
Metropolitan Area and Group	1970	1980	1970	1980	1970	1980	1970	1980
OTHER METROPOLITAN AREAS								
Paterson-Clifton-Passaic								
Anglo	.899	.874	.049	.043	.048	.071	.004	.012
Black	.377	.240	.485	.489	.135	.260	.006	.011
Hispanic	.579	.368	.209	.241	.207	.375	.010	.016
Asian	.706	.690	.140	.110	.147	.170	.013	.031
Philadelphia								
Anglo	.921	.912	.062	.061	.013	.016	.004	.012
Black	.287	.257	.682	.696	.025	.035	.006	.013
Hispanic	.634	.500	.254	.267	.106	.216	.009	.017
Asian	.720	.743	.225	.185	.032	.033	.024	.040
Phoenix								
Anglo	.868	.866	.012	.018	.108	.096	.014	.021
Black	.311	.484	.385	.225	.291	.265	.020	.030
Hispanic	.602	.591	.064	.062	.321	.321	.026	.033
Asian	.703	.738	.039	.039	.237	.186	.043	.048
Pittsburgh								
Anglo	.958	.952	.034	.037	.005	.005	.003	.006
Black	.454	.446	.535	.541	.006	.008	.004	.005
Hispanic	.888	.861	.095	.119	.013	.013	.004	.007
Asian	.890	.908	.094	.070	.006	.007	.011	.016
Portland								
Anglo	.960	.934	.012	.017	.013	.019	.014	.030
Black	.538	.606	.426	.316	.019	.026	.017	.054
Hispanic	.931	.904	.030	.036	.023	.028	.016	.033
Asian	.931	.889	.027	.045	.016	.020	.027	.047
Providence-Warwick-Pawtucket								
Anglo	.973	.956	.016	.017	.006	.016	.004	.012
Black	.717	.601	.254	.253	.012	.086	.017	.063
Hispanic	.932	.769	.041	.110	.019	.085	.008	.039
Asian	.895	.781	.075	.118	.011	.057	.020	.047
Riverside-San Bernardino-Ontario								
Anglo	.829	.782	.026	.037	.135	.152	.013	.031
Black	.515	.586	.254	.160	.222	.226	.016	.032
Hispanic	.636	.601	.052	.057	.302	.316	.017	.031
Asian	.739	.733	.045	.048	.200	.182	.025	.041
Rochester								
Anglo	.952	.929	.032	.047	.011	.014	.005	.010
Black	.460	.487	.495	.442	.040	.061	.005	.010
Hispanic	.725	.614	.188	.254	.082	.120	.006	.013
Asian	.905	.875	.061	.081	.015	.025	.017	.019
Sacramento								
Anglo	.848	.817	.030	.043	.091	.088	.035	.055
Black	.557	.577	.260	.209	.136	.138	.055	.083

TABLE 1   continued

Metropolitan Area and Group	GROUP'S PROBABILITY OF CONTACT WITH:							
	Anglos		Blacks		Hispanics		Asians	
	1970	1980	1970	1980	1970	1980	1970	1980
OTHER METROPOLITAN AREAS								
Sacramento								
Hispanic	.736	.691	.059	.080	.163	.165	.048	.069
Asian	.707	.699	.060	.078	.122	.111	.118	.116
St. Louis								
Anglo	.944	.927	.043	.055	.010	.009	.004	.009
Black	.227	.257	.765	.729	.006	.009	.003	.005
Hispanic	.877	.804	.098	.168	.022	.019	.004	.010
Asian	.848	.865	.132	.109	.011	.011	.009	.016
Salt Lake City-Ogden								
Anglo	.937	.924	.005	.007	.046	.046	.014	.024
Black	.707	.815	.111	.041	.152	.108	.033	.037
Hispanic	.868	.861	.019	.018	.096	.089	.019	.034
Asian	.899	.884	.014	.012	.065	.066	.024	.040
San Antonio								
Anglo	.698	.660	.021	.043	.276	.283	.007	.015
Black	.159	.297	.511	.360	.328	.334	.005	.010
Hispanic	.279	.276	.044	.046	.675	.670	.007	.009
Asian	.470	.573	.042	.055	.482	.354	.012	.020
San Diego								
Anglo	.851	.808	.016	.029	.115	.117	.024	.052
Black	.323	.421	.419	.263	.221	.233	.061	.094
Hispanic	.708	.582	.069	.079	.198	.269	.040	.080
Asian	.689	.631	.088	.076	.187	.194	.059	.111
San Jose								
Anglo	.811	.763	.012	.026	.146	.135	.036	.082
Black	.597	.565	.059	.066	.308	.260	.046	.120
Hispanic	.645	.547	.027	.048	.296	.317	.040	.099
Asian	.746	.655	.019	.043	.189	.194	.053	.116
Seattle-Everett								
Anglo	.946	.914	.013	.021	.016	.019	.025	.048
Black	.446	.544	.427	.294	.020	.030	.108	.138
Hispanic	.894	.854	.033	.052	.031	.026	.043	.072
Asian	.762	.768	.099	.087	.025	.026	.117	.124
Tampa-St. Petersburg								
Anglo	.907	.895	.046	.051	.044	.046	.003	.008
Black	.361	.422	.580	.515	.058	.056	.002	.007
Hispanic	.642	.706	.106	.104	.250	.182	.003	.009
Asian	.871	.840	.067	.089	.056	.058	.005	.013
Tucson								
Anglo	.821	.812	.017	.021	.154	.147	.012	.023
Black	.481	.611	.194	.088	.313	.276	.023	.033
Hispanic	.485	.509	.035	.033	.467	.431	.032	.039
Asian	.520	.628	.034	.031	.420	.305	.067	.050

(continued)

TABLE 1 continued

Metropolitan Area and Group	GROUP'S PROBABILITY OF CONTACT WITH:							
	Anglos		Blacks		Hispanics		Asians	
	1970	1980	1970	1980	1970	1980	1970	1980
OTHER METROPOLITAN AREAS								
Washington, D.C.								
Anglo	.892	.812	.070	.118	.027	.033	.011	.039
Black	.208	.280	.772	.680	.014	.022	.007	.020
Hispanic	.803	.705	.142	.196	.043	.054	.013	.047
Asian	.777	.741	.169	.162	.033	.042	.022	.057
Average								
Anglo	.883	.849	.040	.053	.068	.077	.010	.023
Black	.333	.376	.553	.491	.103	.110	.014	.026
Hispanic	.709	.642	.106	.131	.173	.201	.014	.028
Asian	.760	.749	.104	.099	.108	.107	.032	.047

regation must have been imposed. Even in El Paso, where Hispanics make up roughly 66 percent of the SMSA, the likelihood of Anglo contact was .299.

The high degree of black spatial isolation is put into better perspective when average contact probabilities are tabulated by basic SMSA characteristics. The first three columns of Table 2 show black-Anglo interaction probabilities classified by region, SMSA size, minority population size, total population growth, and rate of minority immigration, where the latter variable is defined as the intercensal rate of growth in the foreign-born population. . . .

This table reveals that increases in the probability of black-Anglo interaction were by no means general across U.S. metropolitan areas. They occurred primarily outside the largest size category in rapidly growing SMSAs of the south and west that contained relatively few blacks. The greatest increases were in places like Anaheim, Austin, Bakersfield, Denver, Ft. Lauderdale, Fresno, Oklahoma City, and Portland. The large, slowly growing metropolitan areas of the northeast and north central states, where the vast majority of urban blacks live, did not show marked changes. Places like Baltimore, Chicago, Cleveland, and St. Louis had very low Anglo contact probabilities ranging from .125 to .257, with little change over the decade. In Detroit, Newark,

New York, and Philadelphia, the likelihood of contact with Anglos actually *decreased*. The only real exception to this pattern was Washington, DC, where "gentrification" apparently was responsible for a decrease in black spatial isolation (Lee et al. 1985), although it is arguable whether this type of integration represents a stable outcome. In short, there is little evidence that large black ghettos in the north became less isolated spatially from the mainstream of American society during the 1970s. Integration occurred primarily in small and mid-sized cities that contained relatively few blacks.

At first glance, recent trends in Hispanic exposure probabilities also provide cause for pessimism. Increasing spatial isolation and declining contact with Anglos was the most common pattern for Hispanics during the 1970s, holding in about half of the SMSAs listed in Table 1. The average level of Hispanic isolation rose from .173 to .201, and the probability of Anglo interaction fell from .709 to .642. There was considerable variation around this pattern, however, and as Table 2 shows, large declines in the probability of Anglo interaction were by no means general. They were concentrated particularly in the northeast, in large metropolitan areas with relatively low rates of total population growth, in large Hispanic populations, or in areas with high rates of Hispanic immigration.

TABLE 2 *Average Minority-Anglo Interaction Probabilities in 60 SMSAs Classified by Selected Metropolitan Characteristics, 1970–1980*

Metropolitan Characteristic	MINORITY GROUP								
	Blacks			Hispanics			Asians		
	1970	1980	Change	1970	1980	Change	1970	1980	Change
Region									
Northeast	.421	.374	−.047	.730	.623	−.107	.799	.774	−.025
North Central	.270	.302	.032	.806	.748	−.058	.833	.837	.003
South	.256	.322	.066	.673	.618	−.055	.741	.729	−.012
West	.410	.498	.088	.667	.608	−.059	.699	.690	−.009
SMSA Population									
Largest	.267	.268	.001	.699	.608	−.091	.737	.739	.002
Bigger	.352	.424	.072	.742	.676	−.066	.786	.764	−.022
Smaller	.387	.429	.042	.786	.731	−.055	.812	.797	−.014
Smallest	.325	.382	.056	.610	.554	−.056	.705	.696	−.009
Minority Population									
Largest	.219	.231	.013	.572	.488	−.084	.707	.689	−.018
Bigger	.336	.355	.018	.619	.564	−.055	.796	.777	−.019
Smaller	.328	.395	.067	.812	.748	−.064	.757	.756	−.001
Smallest	.449	.522	.073	.834	.770	−.064	.779	.774	−.005
Rate of Population Growth									
Fastest	.372	.472	.100	.619	.580	−.038	.716	.700	−.016
Faster	.314	.383	.069	.699	.644	−.054	.733	.730	−.003
Slower	.345	.356	.012	.781	.696	−.084	.796	.776	−.020
Slowest	.301	.290	−.010	.739	.648	−.091	.795	.790	−.005
Rate of Minority Immigration									
Highest	.285	.362	.078	.747	.656	−.092	.781	.770	−.011
Higher	.395	.434	.039	.780	.715	−.065	.768	.757	−.011
Slower	.329	.368	.038	.740	.678	−.062	.784	.786	.002
Slowest	.321	.338	.017	.570	.522	−.048	.706	.684	−.022
Average	.333	.376	.043	.709	.642	−.067	.760	.749	−.011

Note: Number of SMSAs in different regions are as follows: Northeast (14), North Central (11), South (19), West (16). The remaining variables are classified into equal quartiles of 15 SMSAs each.

In other words, declining Hispanic contact with Anglos appears to have been a consequence of shifting population composition. Hispanic spatial isolation rose markedly when a large and rapidly growing Hispanic population combined with a declining Anglo population to cause a rapid increase in the proportion Hispanic. Chicago, Los Angeles, Anaheim, Miami, Paterson, Newark, and Jersey City all experienced sizeable absolute and relative increases in their Hispanic populations (data not shown). Not surprisingly,

each area also recorded a decline in the likelihood of contact with Anglos and an increase in the degree of Hispanic isolation.

Even after these pronounced increases, moreover, Hispanic isolation indices remain considerably below those of blacks. Whereas Hispanic isolation in Chicago increased from .251 to .380, the 1980 figure for blacks was .828. In Los Angeles the Hispanic isolation index of .501 still compares favorably to the black index of .604, even though Hispanics are a much larger share of the population than blacks (28 percent compared to 12 percent, so that, other things equal, they should be *more* isolated than blacks). Similar contrasts stand out in Miami, Jersey City, Newark, Paterson, and other urban areas with large and growing Hispanic populations.

With respect to exposure probabilities, Asians stand directly apart from blacks and Hispanics because they represent a much smaller share of the population in most SMSAs. Even in San Francisco, Asians are only 11 percent of the metropolitan population, and their average over all SMSAs is just under 3 percent. Naturally, with such small relative numbers in all metropolitan areas, Asians experience very low levels of spatial isolation and very high likelihoods of Anglo contact. The average isolation index in 1980 was only .047, and the average probability of Asian interaction with Anglos was .749. The maximum isolation index occurred, of course, in San Francisco, where it stood at .232 in 1980, up from .210 a decade before. The probability of interaction with Anglos was .564. Similarly, in Los Angeles and New York, isolation indices were around .150, and Anglo interaction probabilities were in the range of .500 to .550.

In the largest Asian concentrations in the United States, therefore, the probability of sharing a census tract with another Asian was always less than .250, while the likelihood of sharing a tract with an Anglo was always .500 or greater. Obviously, Asian enclaves exist in some SMSAs, but it seems clear that most Asians do not live in them. Rather, they display a remarkably high level of spatial assimilation and little isolation. Given these facts, and the relative paucity of Asians in most SMSAs, it is nor surprising that the classifications of Table 2 reveal few meaningful patterns. The pattern everywhere seems to be one of small increases from a very low level of spatial isolation in 1970, accompanied by modest decreases in the probability of Asian-Anglo interaction.

TRENDS IN RESIDENTIAL DISSIMILARITY

Unlike the exposure indices reported above, the index of dissimilarity has no *mathematical* relationship to the minority composition of the population (Duncan and Duncan 1955), but it may be a *behavioral* relationship (Lieberson 1980; Lieberson and Carter 1982a). If one assumes that Anglos desire to minimize contact with minorities, then the relative number of minority members has profound implications for spatial behavior. Suppose that all Anglos are willing to tolerate no more than a .10 probability of residential contact with blacks. If blacks are 10 percent of the urban population, then this desire can be satisfied without imposing residential dissimilarity. With each tract 10 percent black, all Anglos are satisfied and the index of dissimilarity is 0. If blacks are 40 percent of the population, however, spatial unevenness has to be imposed on blacks. If no tract containing whites is to exceed 10 percent black, then some tracts will have to be all black, leading to high indices of residential dissimilarity.

Other things equal, therefore, a rising minority percentage within an urban area leads to rising levels of dissimilarity if Anglos seek to limit residential contact with minorities. But other things are rarely equal, and a rising minority percentage may also be associated with lower indices of dissimilarity if the shift in composition stems from rapid minority immigration. When existing minority enclaves cannot accommodate new migrants, they must settle in predominantly majority areas. Even if minority entry leads ultimately to Anglo population loss and eventual succession, in the short run a decline in segregation may ensue, as happened for blacks in many northern cities between 1950 and 1960 (Taeuber and Taeuber 1965).

During the 1970s, black migration to northern cities virtually ceased (Wilson 1981a), so the decline in black-Anglo dissimilarity shown in Table 3 is especially noteworthy. Most metropolitan areas experienced a clear lowering of black segregation over the decade (in 54 of 60 cases), and on average black segregation fell by almost .100, from .792 to .694, suggesting substantial progress in the desegregation of U.S. metropolitan areas. Again, however, a closer look at the data dampens optimism about the extent of recent racial integration.

Table 4 shows average dissimilarities classified by selected metropolitan characteristics. Although black segregation declined in all metropolitan categories, the decline was strongest in the south and the west, especially the latter. As

TRENDS IN THE RESIDENTIAL SEGREGATION OF BLACKS, HISPANICS, AND ASIANS

TABLE 3 *Residential Dissimilarity of Blacks, Hispanics, and Asians from Anglos in 60 U.S. Metropolitan Areas, 1970–1980*

| | DISSIMILARITY BETWEEN ANGLOS AND: | | | | | | | | |
| | Blacks | | | Hispanics | | | Asians | | |
Metropolitan Area	1970	1980	Change	1970	1980	Change	1970	1980	Change
Key SMSAs									
Chicago	.919	.878	−.041	.584	.635	.051	.558	.439	−.120
Los Angeles	.910	.811	−.099	.468	.570	.102	.531	.431	−.100
Miami	.851	.778	−.073	.504	.519	.015	.392	.298	−.094
New York	.810	.820	.010	.649	.656	.007	.561	.481	−.080
San Francisco	.801	.717	−.084	.347	.402	.055	.486	.444	−.042
Other SMSAs									
Albany-Schenectady	.677	.617	−.060	.348	.324	−.024	.383	.354	−.030
Albuquerque	.575	.398	−.177	.457	.425	−.032	.340	.305	−.034
Anaheim-Santa Ana	.839	.458	−.381	.320	.416	.096	.274	.249	−.026
Atlanta	.821	.785	−.036	.359	.329	−.031	.458	.291	−.167
Austin	.772	.620	−.152	.507	.441	−.067	.451	.216	−.235
Bakersfield	.834	.644	−.190	.508	.545	.037	.460	.287	−.172
Baltimore	.819	.747	−.072	.442	.381	−.061	.473	.389	−.084
Birmingham	.378	.408	.031	.285	.221	−.065	.379	.261	−.118
Boston	.812	.776	−.036	.486	.579	.093	.499	.474	−.025
Buffalo	.870	.794	−.076	.484	.491	.007	.484	.437	−.047
Cincinnati	.768	.723	−.045	.378	.303	−.075	.433	.330	−.103
Cleveland	.908	.875	−.033	.523	.554	.031	.450	.358	−.093
Columbus	.818	.714	−.105	.441	.330	−.111	.446	.370	−.076
Corpus Christi	.835	.717	−.118	.559	.516	−.042	.525	.297	−.228
Dallas-Ft. Worth	.869	.771	−.098	.425	.478	.052	.439	.291	−.149
Dayton	.869	.780	−.089	.434	.328	−.106	.417	.306	−.111
Denver-Boulder	.876	.684	−.192	.474	.474	.000	.363	.266	−.097
Detroit	.884	.867	−.017	.479	.451	−.029	.461	.375	−.086
El Paso	.528	.347	−.181	.496	.512	.016	.363	.237	−.126
Ft. Lauderdale	.956	.816	−.140	.276	.255	−.022	.449	.318	−.131
Fresno	.784	.624	−.161	.408	.454	.047	.351	.229	−.122
Gary-Hammond	.914	.906	−.008	.591	.562	−.028	.420	.350	−.070
Greensboro-Winston-Salem	.654	.560	−.094	.482	.322	−.159	.482	.350	−.131
Houston	.781	.695	−.087	.453	.464	.011	.427	.346	−.081
Indianapolis	.817	.762	−.055	.383	.332	−.051	.402	.360	−.042
Jersey City	.753	.765	.013	.548	.488	−.060	.465	.450	−.015
Kansas City	.874	.789	−.085	.437	.421	−.017	.412	.308	−.105
Louisville	.810	.717	−.092	.389	.271	−.118	.458	.341	−.117
Memphis	.759	.716	−.044	.390	.406	.016	.408	.301	−.107
Milwaukee	.905	.839	−.066	.537	.562	.025	.494	.386	−.108

(continued)

TABLE 3   continued

| | DISSIMILARITY BETWEEN ANGLOS AND: | | | | | | | | |
| | Blacks | | | Hispanics | | | Asians | | |
Metropolitan Area	1970	1980	Change	1970	1980	Change	1970	1980	Change
Other SMSAs									
Minneap.-St. Paul	.856	.683	−.172	.491	.409	−.082	.452	.369	−.083
Nashville-Davidson	.777	.699	−.077	.418	.366	−.052	.521	.388	−.133
Nassau-Suffolk	.744	.755	.011	.291	.362	.070	.422	.345	−.077
New Orleans	.731	.683	−.048	.318	.251	−.068	.459	.427	−.031
Newark	.814	.816	.002	.604	.656	.052	.502	.344	−.158
Norfolk-Va. Beach	.757	.631	−.126	.363	.284	−.079	.519	.347	−.172
Oklahoma City	.911	.709	−.202	.346	.312	−.034	.320	.231	−.089
Paterson-Clifton	.779	.815	.037	.610	.722	.112	.466	.404	−.061
Philadelphia	.795	.788	−.007	.540	.629	.089	.491	.437	−.053
Phoenix	.819	.594	−.225	.484	.494	.009	.441	.328	−.113
Pittsburgh	.750	.727	−.023	.508	.419	−.089	.535	.456	−.079
Portland	.835	.685	−.150	.319	.250	−.069	.330	.271	−.059
Providence-Warwick	.756	.731	−.025	.502	.567	.065	.523	.495	−.028
Riverside-San Ber.	.686	.488	−.197	.373	.364	−.009	.319	215	−.104
Rochester	.745	.674	−.071	.559	.588	.029	.454	.341	−.113
Sacramento	.688	.559	−.129	.347	.364	.018	.476	.355	−.121
St. Louis	.847	.813	−.034	.354	.339	−.014	.428	.329	−.099
Salt Lake-Ogden	.774	.532	−.242	.362	.307	−.056	.293	.260	−.032
San Antonio	.834	.636	−.199	.591	.572	−.019	.442	.266	−.176
San Diego	.834	.643	−.191	.331	.421	.090	.413	.405	−.009
San Jose	.607	.487	−.120	.402	.445	.043	.254	.295	.041
Seattle-Everett	.819	.682	−.137	.303	.213	−.090	.466	.333	−.133
Tampa-St. Peters	.799	.726	−.073	.560	.484	−.076	.380	.299	−.081
Tucson	.708	.466	−.242	.526	.519	−.007	.526	.365	−.162
Washington, D.C.	.811	.701	−.110	.318	.305	−.013	.365	.268	−.097
Average	.792	.694	−.098	.444	.434	−.010	.437	.342	−.095

with the exposure indices, the largest declines were registered in rapidly growing urban areas with small black populations, places such as Albuquerque, Anaheim, and Austin, rather than in large black concentrations such as Chicago, Detroit, or Cleveland. Large, declining metropolitan areas in the northeast and north central regions, which house the majority of urban blacks, remained very segregated and displayed relatively little change over the decade, especially in the northeast. The 30 largest black SMSAs averaged a decline of only −.050, compared to an average change of −.116 in the next smallest quartile and −.173 in the smallest. In Cleveland, Los Angeles, New York, Detroit, Newark, and St. Louis, the index of dissimilarity remained well above .800 with changes in the range of −.010 to −.040. In New York, Newark, Jersey City, Paterson, and Philadelphia, the level of dissimilarity increased or stayed the same. Chicago again displayed the highest level of black segregation, with a dissimilarity index of .878. As before, there is little evidence that blacks in large, northern ghettos are achieving residential integration.

Since Hispanic population growth varied considerably across urban areas (data not shown) the pattern of change in residential dissimilarity was highly variable: 33 SMSAs experienced a decline in Hispanic dissimilarity from Anglos, and 27 showed an increase (see Table 3). On average, the increases balanced the declines, so the average level of dissimilarity changed very little over the decade, falling slightly from .444 to .434, and remaining well below the average level of black-Anglo dissimilarity.

As with the exposure probabilities, a closer look at Tables 3 and 4 indicates that trends in Hispanic-Anglo dissimilarity largely reflect patterns of Hispanic immigration over the past decade. The largest Hispanic communities also

TABLE 4 *Average Residential Dissimilarity of Three Minority Groups from Anglos in 60 SMSAs Classified by Selected Metropolitan Characteristics, 1970–1980*

Metropolitan Characteristic	Blacks			Hispanics			Asians		
	1970	1980	Change	1970	1980	Change	1970	1980	Change
Region									
Northeast	.775	.756	−.019	.511	.540	.029	.482	.418	−.064
North Central	.865	.802	−.063	.469	.436	−.034	.448	.357	−.091
South	.773	.673	−.100	.424	.384	−.040	.435	.308	−.127
West	.774	.592	−.182	.402	.417	.015	.395	.315	−.080
SMSA Population									
Largest	.824	.779	−.045	.699	.608	−.091	.479	.390	−.089
Bigger	.817	.682	−.135	.742	.676	−.066	.400	.315	−.085
Smaller	.776	.680	−.095	.786	.732	−.054	.428	.341	−.087
Smallest	.750	.635	−.116	.610	.554	−.056	.439	.321	−.119
Minority Population									
Largest	.835	.784	−.050	.460	.495	.035	.496	.370	−.069
Bigger	.773	.721	−.053	.476	.481	.005	.408	.316	−.092
Smaller	.814	.698	−.116	.428	.408	−.020	.461	.359	−.102
Smallest	.747	.574	−.173	.414	.353	−.060	.439	.322	−.117
Rate of Population Growth									
Fastest	.766	.587	−.179	.431	.431	.000	.393	.297	−.096
Faster	.763	.648	−.115	.406	.371	−.035	.427	.304	−.123
Slower	.816	.750	−.066	.427	.421	−.006	.448	.370	−.078
Slowest	.823	.791	−.032	.514	.516	.002	.478	.395	−.083
Rate of Minority Immigration									
Highest	.782	.678	−.104	.490	.521	.031	.429	.315	−.114
Higher	.767	.652	−.115	.438	.376	−.062	.438	.345	−.093
Slower	.823	.722	−.101	.419	.404	−.015	.445	.345	−.100
Slowest	.795	.724	−.071	.431	.436	.005	.434	.362	−.072
Average	.792	.694	−.098	.444	.434	−.010	.437	.342	−.095

Note: Number of SMSAs in different regions are as follows: Northeast (14), North Central (11), South (19), West (16). The remaining variables are classified into equal quartiles of 15 SMSAs each.

tended to experience the greatest immigration and the fastest growth over the decade (tabulation not shown). They also recorded the most dramatic increases in spatial dissimilarity. Smaller, slowly growing Hispanic communities experienced little immigration and showed declines in spatial dissimilarity. The former were located primarily in the northeastern and western regions, while the latter were concentrated in the north central and southern regions. Hispanic dissimilarity therefore increased in Los Angeles, Anaheim, and Paterson, and declined in Greensboro, Dayton, and Columbus. Significantly, large Hispanic communities that did not experience rapid growth, such as those in New York, Denver, El Paso, Phoenix, Tucson, and San Antonio, showed little or no change in dissimilarity over the decade. Hispanic immigration and population growth thus appear to be the driving forces behind trends in Hispanic-Anglo dissimilarity during the 1970s.

Asians also experienced substantial immigration and rapid population growth over the past decade. In the vast majority of SMSAs, the Asian population at least doubled, and in some cases it tripled or quadrupled (data not shown). But with a few exceptions, such as San Francisco, New York, and Los Angeles, there was no recognizable Asian enclave upon which to build. Entering the urban environment, Asians probably sought residences near one another, but there were few Asian neighborhoods in existence, so Asian growth typically entailed entry into Anglo neighborhoods. It is not surprising, therefore, that the trend in Asian residential dissimilarity from 1970 to 1980 was one of universal decline. As Table 3 shows, Asian dissimilarity fell in 59 of 60 cases. In areas where there were very few Asians in 1970, the declines were spectacular: −.235 in Austin and −.228 in Corpus Christi, each of which had only about 1,000 Asians in 1970. Where well-known Asian neighborhoods existed, as in San Francisco, declines were still registered, but they were more modest (−.042).

In 1980, the level of Asian residential dissimilarity varied in a narrow range from .216 to .456. The average value was .342, a remarkably low level of spatial segregation, roughly equivalent to the 1970 levels for the "old" European ethnic groups (British, German, Irish, Scandina-

vian) (Massey 1985). If Asian migration continues, however, this level will most likely increase as Asian enclaves emerge and become poles of attraction for new immigrants. The fact that over the 1970s Asian spatial isolation increased (Table 1) while dissimilarity fell (Table 3) suggests that many areas of recent Asian settlement contain the seeds of new enclaves. But at this time, the level of Asian segregation remains very low. Even in San Francisco, Asian-Anglo dissimilarity was only .444, half the level of the highest black-Anglo dissimilarity index (in Chicago) and two-thirds the highest Hispanic-Anglo index (in New York).

EXPLAINING THE PATTERNS

The foregoing section has shown that, despite recent declines in some metropolitan areas, the level of black segregation remains quite high, especially in cities where the majority of urban blacks live. Hispanic segregation is relatively moderate, although it has increased substantially in areas of rapid immigration. Asian segregation is very low, even in cities with large Asian populations. Behind these generalizations, however, lies considerable variability, particularly among Hispanics and blacks. Dissimilarity indices for blacks ranged from .408 to .878 in 1980, while those for Hispanics varied from .213 to .656. Similarly, black-Anglo interaction probabilities ranged from .125 to .815, while Hispanic-Anglo probabilities varied from .229 to .910.

In this section we attempt to account for interurban variation in segregation by estimating statistical models derived from a theoretical perspective developed in earlier research (Massey and Mullan 1984; Massey and Denton 1985; Massey 1985). The perspective argues that spatial assimilation is driven by social mobility and, among immigrant groups, by acculturation, and that these variables affect spatial integration through the intervening step of suburbanization. Because these processes are strongly conditioned by the structural context provided by specific urban environments, metropolitan-level characteristics must be explicitly controlled.

As a minority group's socioeconomic status increases, its members seek to improve their spatial position in urban society, which typically involves moving into neighborhoods with greater prestige, more amenities, safer streets, better schools, and higher-value homes (Massey et al. forthcoming). Accomplishing these goals usually brings a minority group into greater spatial contact with majority members and promotes residential integration. Among immigrant-origin populations such as Hispanics and Asians, moreover, acculturation increases the desire of minority members to live in neighborhoods where majority members predominate (acculturation is not relevant to the case of American blacks, of course). Both socioeconomic mobility and acculturation reduce the social distance between minority members and native whites, so the former's entry into a neighborhood does not spark hostility, resistance, and systematic out-migration by the latter. Over time, therefore, social mobility and acculturation bring about the spatial assimilation of minority groups in urban society.

Although changes in socioeconomic status and acculturation may lead directly to spatial assimilation, in the United States an important intervening process is suburbanization. In post-war America, the process of racial and ethnic integration has been inextricably bound up with movement to the suburbs, where levels of segregation are generally lower and Anglos predominate (Golant and Jacobsen 1978). To the extent that suburban residence may be precluded for some minority groups because of discriminatory housing practices, an important avenue of residential integration may be closed off.

Processes of social mobility and acculturation are strongly affected by the larger structural context of urban society (Massey 1985). An important structural element is the housing market. During periods of rapid home construction and residential expansion, such as occurred between 1945 and 1970, residential mobility is accelerated and the process of spatial assimilation encouraged. A second factor is the state of the urban economy, which acts as a structural constraint on social mobility and, hence, spatial assimilation. During periods of economic growth, widespread social mobility generates demand for improved housing in more desirable, typically suburban, neighborhoods and leads to considerable residential mobility, which in turn facilitates integration. A third contextual element is the history of immi-

gration into the urban area. During periods of rapid immigration, social networks channel minority members into existing areas of minority settlement, raising the overall level of segregation if the ethnic enclave can accommodate the newcomers, and lowering it when growth spills over into surrounding Anglo neighborhoods (Taeuber and Taeuber 1965). The arrival of new immigrants also lowers the average level of acculturation within the ethnic group, dampening motivations for mobility and integration. Finally, any analysis of segregation must control for the physical stock of the city. Cities built up before the Second World War have ecological structures that are more conducive to segregation (Hershberg et al. 1979), with densely settled cores and tightly packed working-class neighborhoods clustered around old factories.

Our analytic strategy is to operationalize this simple model, using information available from the census, and to estimate OLS regression models in an effort to account for interurban variation in black, Hispanic, and Asian segregation in 1980. Three dependent variables are considered: the proportion of group members living in the suburbs, the probability of contact with Anglos (from Table 1), and residential dissimilarity from Anglos (from Table 3). Because all three variables have a limited range, we transform them into logits before conducting the regression analyses. Indicators of overall acculturation and socioeconomic status are computed for each of the three minority groups and regressed, across metropolitan areas, on their respective segregation measures, controlling for metropolitan structure. Minority populations with high average levels of acculturation and socioeconomic status are hypothesized to have higher probabilities of Anglo contact, lower levels of dissimilarity from Anglos, and higher proportions living in the suburbs.

Acculturation is operationalized by computing the proportion of minority members who report speaking English well, and the proportion of minority members who are native born. Since 98 percent of blacks are born in the United States and are native English speakers, acculturation is not relevant for them and these variables are not employed in the black models. Socioeconomic status is measured in both absolute and relative terms. Absolute status is measured by median family income and relative status by the degree of occupational dissimilarity between minority members and Anglos. Income provides economic resources that make residential mobility possible, and rising occupational status decreases the minority group's social distance from Anglos, thereby reducing their potential threat and making entry into Anglo neighborhoods less problematic. We therefore expect the probability of Anglo contact to be a positive function of income and a negative function of occupational dissimilarity; we also expect residential dissimilarity to be negatively related to income and positively related to occupational dissimilarity. Educational variables were not included in the equations because they were found to be highly collinear with the other two indicators.

Structural context is measured by five indices computed at the metropolitan level. The state of the housing market is indicated by the average rate of growth in the median value of housing between 1970 and 1980, with a high rate of inflation indicating a tight market and a relative shortage of housing. The state of the economy is indicated by the annual rate of growth in metropolitan employment between 1970 and 1980. The relative age of a metropolitan area is measured by the median age of growth in metropolitan employment between 1970 and 1980. The relative age of a metropolitan area is measured by the median age of the housing in it. Recent trends in immigration are measured by the average annual growth rate of the foreign-born population within each minority group, and relative population growth is measured by computing the minority-Anglo growth differential (minority rate minus Anglo rate). Positive values of the latter variable indicate a predominance of minority over Anglo growth, and negative values indicate the opposite. "Minority" refers to the group in question (blacks, Hispanics, or Asians), rather than the three groups added together.

Three other factors are taken into account in the statistical models. First, we control for the relative proportion of minority members in the metropolitan area. Population composition is mathematically related to the likelihood of contact with Anglos, and the relative number of minority members has strong implications for spatial behavior generally. Second, we control for the effect of ethnic/racial composition *within* the minority groups themselves, measuring the proportion of Hispanics who are Mexican, Cuban, or Puerto Rican, and the proportion of Asians who are Japanese, Chinese, Korean, Vietnamese, or Indian. We also control for the proportion of Hispanics who are black, since prior work has shown this to be an important variable affecting Hispanic segregation (Massey and Bitterman 1985). . . . The analysis proceeds in three phases. First we analyze the process of minority suburbanization, then consider the impact of socioeconomic, cultural, and structural variables on Anglo-interaction probabilities, and, finally, measure the effect of these variables on spatial dissimilarity from Anglos. The last two steps control for the level of suburbanization as a predetermined variable.

Table 5 begins the analysis by examining the determinants of minority suburbanization for blacks, Hispanics, and Asians in 59 metropolitan areas (Nassau-Suffolk has no central city and therefore no suburbs). Because the vast majority of blacks are native born, measures of acculturation were not included for this group. None of the socioeconomic or metropolitan structural variables has a significant effect on the level of black suburbanization, and no variance is explained by the model. The intercept corresponds to a very low level of suburbanization, about .150, and, in fact, the average in the 59 SMSAs was only .282 (compared to .482 for Hispanics and .530 for Asians). Neither socioeconomic status nor metropolitan context influences the level of black suburbanization, which remains quite limited.

In contrast, interurban variation in Hispanic and Asian suburbanization is highly related to socioeconomic status. Consistent with expectations, lower Hispanic-Anglo occupational dissimilarities and higher Hispanic incomes are associated with greater suburbanization. Asian suburbanization is likewise positively related to income and the relative number of native born: as income and the proportion of natives rise, so does the relative number of Asians living in suburbs. Table 5 contains one coefficient that is opposite the expected direction. English language

TABLE 5 *Logistic Regression of Selected Variables on the Proportion of Blacks, Hispanics, and Asians Living in Suburban Areas of 59 Metropolitan Areas*

Independent Variables	MINORITY GROUP					
	Blacks		Hispanics		Asians	
	B	SE	B	SE	B	SE
Level of Acculturation						
% Native Born	–	–	2.008	2.504	7.029*	4.274
% Speaking English well	–	–	−8.144*	4.443	5.995	4.642
Socioeconomic Status						
Median family income	−0.069	0.104	0.100*	0.606	0.101*	0.606
Occup. dis. from Anglos	3.814	4.797	−7.912**	3.847	−0.635	3.370
Hispanic Composition						
% Black Hispanics	–	–	1.398	1.971	–	–
% Mexican	–	–	−1.207	0.976	–	–
% Cuban	–	–	−0.500	2.037	–	–
% Puerto Rican	–	–	−1.306	1.625	–	–
Asian Composition						
% Japanese	–	–	–	–	−3.721	4.948
% Chinese	–	–	–	–	1.118	2.242
% Korean	–	–	–	–	0.396	4.076
% Vietnamese	–	–	–	–	−2.323	5.371
% Indian	–	–	–	–	1.277	3.874
Metropolitan Context						
Housing inflation rate	9.650	6.534	12.418**	5.177	7.697	9.337
Employment growth rate	−4.368	13.298	−9.512	12.750	−23.184*	14.101
Growth rate of for. born	−0.211	3.017	−4.269*	2.595	2.823	2.931
Anglo growth differential	9.719	10.963	4.730	9.094	6.641	6.532
Median age of housing	−0.028	0.031	−0.001	0.034	−0.038	0.028
Group's % of population	−0.041	2.534	−3.360**	1.547	−15.318	15.001
Selectivity Correction						
P-1	−0.380	0.763	−1.648**	0.625	0.693	0.800
Intercept	−1.697	2.249	6.235	4.373	−8.605**	3.911
Adjusted R^2	0.000		0.301**		0.162**	
N	59		59		59	

Note: The Nassau-Suffolk SMSA has no central city.

*$p < .10$.

**$p < .05$.

ability among Hispanics is *negatively* related to suburbanization, a finding that is difficult to interpret.

Suburbanization of Hispanics and Asians is apparently not affected by the ethnic composition of these groups, but is influenced by elements of metropolitan context. Hispanic suburbanization is greater in areas with a relative scarcity of housing (see the coefficient for housing inflation), while Asian suburbanization is lower in areas that experienced rapid economic growth (see the coefficient for labor force growth). Both of these findings are somewhat anomalous, since tighter housing markets normally restrict residential mobility and suburbanization, while economic growth usually promotes integration by fostering group mobility. Consistent with earlier reasoning, however, the level of Hispanic suburbanization is lower in areas that experienced higher immigration over the prior decade, and in areas with a high proportion of Hispanics.

In spite of a few anomalous coefficients in the Hispanic and Asian models, results consistently show that blacks are highly disadvantaged in the suburbanization process. Not only are levels of black suburbanization quite low, but they are unrelated to any of the explanatory variables we examined. Hispanic and Asian suburbanization, in contrast, are explained largely by objective indicators of socioeconomic status and acculturation, and they are also related to structural trends within metropolitan areas. With rising socioeconomic status, progressive suburbanization of these two groups should occur; their levels of suburbanization are already considerably above that of blacks.

Table 6 carries the analysis of spatial assimilation a step further by considering the effect of acculturation and socioeconomic status on Anglo interaction probabilities, controlling for the level of suburbanization, which is predetermined. The proportion of variance explained by the black model is roughly half that explained by the Hispanic model, but about the same as the Asian model. The probability of black contact with Anglos is determined principally by relative occupational dissimilarity from Anglos and by the proportion of blacks in the metropolitan area. In other words, there is some evidence of a process of spatial assimilation among blacks: as social distance from Anglos decreases, the likelihood of residential contact with them increases. But black suburbanization is unrelated to the probability of Anglo contact. To the extent that spatial assimilation occurs, therefore, it happens independently of suburbanization, primarily through occupational mobility rather than spatial mobility to the suburbs.

Hispanic-Anglo contact, in contrast, is highly related to suburbanization as well as acculturation and socioeconomic status. Hispanic spatial assimilation is promoted strongly by English language ability, as one would expect, but is inversely related to income and the proportion native born, contrary to predictions. The latter anomalous relationships are difficult to explain, but perhaps reflect the fact that suburbanization has been controlled. If movement to the suburbs is the primary channel of spatial assimilation, then SES or acculturation might be unrelated or even negatively related to Anglo contact after its effect is removed.

Contextual variables also affect the likelihood of Hispanic contact with Anglos, being greater in areas where Hispanic growth dominates over that of Anglos. Rapidly growing Hispanic populations cannot always be accommodated within existing Hispanic enclaves, and spillover into adjacent Anglo areas increases residential contact between the two groups. The probability of Anglo interaction is also strongly affected by the racial composition of Hispanics, being markedly lower in SMSAs where a large share of Hispanics are black, underscoring the salience of race in American society.

The Asian model presents a somewhat different vision of spatial assimilation. Asian-Anglo contact is not related to indicators of SES or acculturation, but is affected by several contextual variables, and by the relative number of Chinese. In contrast to the case of Hispanics, high rates of Asian population growth and immigration reduce the likelihood of contact with Anglos. Since Asians are not likely to have saturated enclaves in most SMSAs, spillover into Anglo areas does not occur. Rapid growth through immigration in this case promotes the formation of new enclaves through chain migration, thereby reducing contact with Anglos. The Chinese, being the largest and oldest Asian group, tend to have more established enclaves ("Chinatowns"), so the proportion of Chinese is negatively associated with Anglo contact.

In both the Asian and Hispanic models, suburbanization is very strongly related to the probability of Anglo contact. It is an endogenous variable predetermined by SES and acculturation. Thus, although the *direct* effects of acculturation and SES on Anglo contact may be weak and inconsistent, these variables have important *indirect* effects through their impact on the likelihood

TABLE 6 *Logistic Regression of Selected Variables on the Probability of Hispanic, Black, and Asian Contact with Anglos in 60 SMSAs*

| | MINORITY GROUP | | | | | |
| | Blacks | | Hispanics | | Asians | |
Independent Variables	B	SE	B	SE	B	SE
Level of Acculturation						
% Native Born	−	−	−2.338**	0.927	−1.107	2.354
% Speaking English well	−	−	8.458**	1.695	−3.968	2.519
Socioeconomic Status						
Median family income	−0.043	0.055	−0.045**	0.023	−0.007	0.033
Occup. dis. from Anglos	−5.093**	2.567	0.423	1.493	2.792	1.795
Level of Suburbanization						
% of group in suburbs	0.077	0.430	0.699**	0.264	0.792**	0.399
Hispanic Composition						
% Black Hispanics	−	−	−5.124**	0.732	−	−
% Mexicans	−	−	0.168	0.362	−	−
% Cubans	−	−	0.277	0.751	−	−
% Puerto Ricans	−	−	−0.088	0.603	−	−
Asian Composition						
% Japanese	−	−	−	−	0.617	2.651
% Chinese	−	−	−	−	−2.206*	1.197
% Korean	−	−	−	−	−0.572	2.172
% Vietnamese	−	−	−	−	4.215	2.870
% Indian	−	−	−	−	1.752	2.066
Metropolitan Context						
Housing inflation rate	−1.836	3.512	−1.870	2.014	−2.695	5.029
Employment growth rate	2.029	7.018	1.334	4.719	−8.039	7.741
Growth rate of for. born	0.510	1.587	0.924	0.986	−2.833*	1.581
Anglo growth differential	4.265	5.825	7.554**	3.354	−8.123**	3.518
Median age of housing	−0.023	0.016	0.010	0.013	−0.021	0.015
Group's % of population	−2.390*	1.333	−3.166**	0.590	−0.780	8.114
Selectivity Correction						
P-1	−0.549	0.402	−0.245	0.244	−0.020	0.431
Intercept	1.672	1.182	−4.509**	1.685	5.998**	2.148
Adjusted R^2	0.357**		0.876**		0.360**	
N	60		60		60	

*$p < .10$

**$p < .05$

of suburban residence. For Asians and Hispanics, suburbanization is a key step in the larger process of spatial assimilation, one that is largely closed to blacks.

The importance of suburbanization in the process of desegregation is reaffirmed by the results of Table 7, which considers the determinants of residential dissimilarity. Indicators of accultura-

tion and SES are again weakly (in the case of Asians) or inconsistently (in the case of Hispanics) related to segregation, but suburbanization is strongly related to dissimilarity for both groups. As before, suburbanization has no impact on the level of black-white segregation.

The black model explains significantly less variance than the Hispanic or Asian models, with

TABLE 7 *Logistic Regression of Selected Variables on the Dissimilarity of Blacks, Hispanics, and Asians from Anglos in 60 SMSAs*

| | MINORITY GROUP | | | | | |
| Independent Variables | Blacks | | Hispanics | | Asians | |
	B	SE	B	SE	B	SE
Level of Acculturation						
% Native Born	−	−	−2.139**	0.758	0.742	0.947
% Speaking English well	−	−	−4.923**	1.386	−0.003	1.013
Socioeconomic Status						
Median family income	0.076*	0.044	0.010	0.018	0.004	0.013
Occup. dis. from Anglos	2.844	2.049	1.693	1.220	−0.847	0.723
Level of Suburbanization						
% of group in suburbs	−0.258	0.343	−0.577**	0.216	−0.416**	0.161
Hispanic Composition						
% Black Hispanics	−	−	0.617	0.598	−	−
% Mexicans	−	−	−0.047	0.296	−	−
% Cubans	−	−	0.509	0.614	−	−
% Puerto Ricans	−	−	−0.219	0.493	−	−
Asian Composition						
% Japanese	−	−	−	−	−2.245**	1.066
% Chinese	−	−	−	−	0.316	0.481
% Korean	−	−	−	−	0.132	0.873
% Vietnamese	−	−	−	−	−0.711	1.154
% Indian	−	−	−	−	0.769	0.831
Metropolitan Context						
Housing inflation rate	−1.230	2.803	−0.356	1.646	4.985**	2.022
Employment growth rate	−9.443*	5.601	−4.876	3.857	−3.088	3.113
Growth rate of for. born	0.252	1.267	0.332	0.806	0.928	0.636
Anglo growth differential	−8.326*	4.650	−5.427**	2.742	−2.164	1.415
Median age of housing	0.020	0.013	0.004	0.010	0.022**	0.006
Group's % of population	−0.183	1.063	−0.120	0.482	−3.984	3.263
Selectivity Correction						
P-1	0.804**	0.321	0.231	0.199	0.366**	0.173
Intercept	−0.194	0.944	2.226	1.377	−1.162	0.864
Adjusted R^2	0.445		0.786		0.593	
N	60		60		60	

*$p < .10$

**$p < .05$

only three substantive variables being marginally significant. The rate of employment growth and the rate of black population increase are both negatively associated with dissimilarity from Anglos. In other words, metropolitan areas with slow economic growth and growing black populations (older industrial cities with large black ghettos) are associated with a high degree of resi-

dential segregation. Contrary to expectations, rising black income produced a significant increase, rather than a decrease, in segregation.

As before, results for Hispanics present an inconsistent picture of spatial assimilation, once suburbanization is controlled. Hispanic segregation falls with rising English language ability, as expected, but rises with an increasing prevalence of the native born, contrary to theoretical predictions. Rapid Hispanic population growth promotes lower levels of segregation, probably through the spillover effect noted earlier. Among Asians, neither acculturation nor SES affects residential dissimilarity once suburbanization is controlled. Anglo-Asian dissimilarity is affected primarily by contextual and compositional factors, with segregation being greater in tighter housing markets and older SMSAs, and being markedly lower among Asian populations with a relatively large number of Japanese.

Taken together, the last three tables suggest that the spatial assimilation of Hispanics and Asians occurs primarily through movement to the suburbs. Indicators of acculturation and assimilation are strongly related to suburbanization for both groups, but once suburbanization is controlled, they are weakly and inconsistently related to indicators of segregation. For blacks, this avenue to residential desegregation appears to be closed. None of the variables we considered are related to black suburbanization, and the level of black suburbanization is, in turn, unrelated to either measure of residential segregation.

Suburbanization is, therefore, a key factor in the spatial assimilation of all three groups. For Hispanics and Asians, ongoing processes of suburbanization have generated low-to-moderate levels of residential segregation that reflect underlying socioeconomic differences and structural shifts. For blacks, significant barriers to suburban settlement perpetuate high levels of residential segregation that are resistant to socioeconomic or structural effects.

DISCUSSION

Our results indicate that blacks, Hispanics, and Asians occupy very different positions in urban society. The contrast in the spatial situations of the groups is well-illustrated by a quick look at San Francisco, where each group represents about 11 percent of the population. In 1980, the probability of black contact with Anglos was .299, compared to .582 for Hispanics and .564 for Asians; and black-Anglo dissimilarity stood at .717, with respective figures of .444 and .402 for Asians and Hispanics. In other words, given the same relative numbers, blacks are nearly twice as segregated as Hispanics or Asians.

Our analyses suggest several conclusions about race and residence in U.S. cities. First, there has been remarkably little change in the status quo since 1970. Articles that contrasted patterns of Hispanic and black segregation using 1970 census data arrived at nearly the same conclusions as we did. In both 1970 and 1980 there is little evidence of a significant process of spatial integration among blacks in large metropolitan areas. The level of black segregation is not strongly related to indicators of socioeconomic status, SES is unrelated to black suburbanization, and the level of black suburbanization has no influence on segregation. In short, a key step in the process of spatial assimilation for other groups, suburbanization, plays no role in black integration. Some blacks may be moving to suburban areas, but this movement does not seem to be related to their socioeconomic characteristics, and it has had no measurable impact on the overall level of black segregation. Either blacks are moving to suburbs in numbers too small to make a difference, or suburbs and central cities are equally segregated.

A second conclusion is that the forces of racial change that transformed American society during the 1970s have had a marginal impact on the spatial behavior of blacks and whites in American cities. Despite the advent of fair housing legislation, more tolerant white racial attitudes, and a growing black middle class with income sufficient to promote residential mobility, the segregation of blacks in large cities hardly changed. If the black middle class has abandoned the black poor, it has not been by moving to Anglo neighborhoods, at least on a significant scale. Most blacks continue to reside in predominantly black neighborhoods, even in cities with relatively large and affluent black middle classes, such as New York, Chicago, and Philadelphia.

The patterns of segregation we have described also speak to the meaning of race in American society. The high degree of black residential segregation, and its relative imperviousness to socioeconomic influences, suggest that race continues to be a fundamental cleavage in American society. Yet it is not race per se. Asians are also members of nonwhite racial groups, easily identifiable as such by Anglo whites, but there is little evidence that Anglos harbor significant prejudice against them when it comes to sharing urban residential space. Asians are characterized by very low levels of residential segregation, even in urban areas where they particularly concentrate. It is not race that matters, but black race.

This fact is underscored by the case of black Hispanics. We found that a relatively large number of black Hispanics was significant in reducing the likelihood of contact with Anglos. Other research has shown that black Hispanics are highly segregated from other groups, including white Hispanics (Goldstein and White 1985; Massey and Mullan 1985; Massey and Bitterman 1985). Blacks are apparently viewed by white Americans as qualitatively different and, by implication, less desirable as neighbors, than members of other racial or ethnic groups.

For blacks seeking integration into the mainstream of American society, the issue of race is still very much alive. Blacks may have won political freedom, and may have made substantial progress in attaining their economic goals, but they have yet not achieved the freedom to live wherever they want. If black residential integration has occurred at all, it has not been through residential mobility within metropolitan areas where the vast majority of blacks live, but through movement to small and mid-sized cities that presently contain few black residents. Perhaps the growth of black populations in these smaller metropolitan areas will be the means by which residential integration will finally occur in the United States.

Race and Ethnicity in 1980s America

4

As we indicated in Part 1, by 1988 members of the largest racial and ethnic categories (African-Americans, Hispanics, Asians, and American Indians) comprised nearly one-quarter (24.4 percent) of the population of the United States (U.S. Bureau of the Census 1990). This figure represented the highest proportion of non-Europeans in the United States population since it became an independent nation in the late 18th century.

Therefore, rather than diminish in intensity, it is probable that issues of race and ethnicity will assume even greater significance in American society during the 21st century. By the year 2000 – in less than a decade – one-third of all school-age children will be either African-American, Hispanic, Asian, or American Indian (American Council on Education 1988). Furthermore, in some states (such as California) the majority of working age adults in 2000 will be members of these minorities (California Assembly Office of Research 1986). If current birth and immigration rates continue, by the last quarter of the 21st century these minorities will comprise a numerical majority of the population. (Quality Education for Minorities 1990). Therefore, in the near future "minority" peoples will affect the nation's prosperity more substantially than ever before in American history. All Americans, especially those who will be economically dependent on the productivity of the working age population, will be directly affected by the manner in which racial and ethnic inequalities in American life are addressed.

This section will focus on several recent trends in American majority-minority relations: the impact of recent demographic changes, including the changing nature of immigration to the United States; the recent surge of interest in ethnicity and ethnic pluralism among European-Americans; and the changing status of African-Americans.

Demographic Changes in the 1970s and 1980s

In order to comprehend the dynamics of ethnic relations during the past two decades (and to anticipate the future), it is useful to examine briefly some of the demographic changes that occurred during that time. Table 4.1 below provides the basic data for several broad racial and ethnic categories.

African-Americans, the nation's largest racial minority, today total more than 30 million, or more than the entire population of Canada or of Sweden, Denmark, Norway, Finland, and Iceland combined. As in 1970, African-Americans continue to live overwhelmingly in urban areas, especially in the nation's largest cities. Today New York City has a black population of more than one and three-quarters million, more than any other city in the world and more than any state (besides New York state) in the country. Chicago has more African-Americans than Mississippi or South Carolina; and Philadelphia more than Arkansas and Kentucky combined. During the 1980s blacks continued to be more likely than whites to live in urban areas, especially in central cities. However, during this period, for the first time in this century, the proportion of blacks living in the

TABLE 4.1 *Racial and Hispanic Population in the United States, 1970–1989*

	Number (in thousands)			Percent Distribution		
	1970	1980	1989	1970	1980	1989
Total	203,212	226,546	248,762	100.0	100.0	100.0
White	177,749	188,341	209,326	87.5	83.2	84.1
Black	22,580	26,488	30,788	11.1	11.7	12.4
American Indian, Eskimo, and Aleut	827	1,418	1,737	0.4	0.6	0.7
Asian and Pacific Islander	1,539	3,501	6,881	0.8	1.5	3.5
Chinese	435	806	1,079†	0.2	0.4	–
Filipino	343	775	1,051†	0.2	0.3	–
Japanese	591	701	776†	0.3	0.3	–
Asian Indian	NA	362	526†	–	0.2	–
Korean	69	355	542†	0.0	0.2	–
Vietnamese	NA	262	634†	–	0.1	–
Hispanics*	9,073	14,609	20,528	4.5	6.4	8.3
Mexican-American	4,532	8,740	12,565	2.2	3.9	5.1
Puerto Rican	1,429	2,014	2,330	0.7	0.9	0.9
Cuban	544	803	1,069	0.3	0.4	0.4
Other	2,566	3,051	4,111	1.2	1.3	1.6

Sources: U.S. Bureau of the Census 1973a, 1973b, 1984, 1990b, 1990c. Gardner, Robey, Smith, 1985.

NA – Not available.

*Hispanics also included in white, black, and "other" categories.

†Data for specific Asian categories are for 1985.

South increased, growing from 52 percent in 1980 to 56 percent in 1988 (U.S. Bureau of the Census 1989b:2).

During the 1970s and 1980s the number of Hispanics more than doubled, increasing from 9 million in 1970 to more than 20 million in 1988. During the 1980s the Hispanic population grew by 34 percent, an increase greater both proportionately and numerically than that of the African-American population, which grew by 13 percent. California had the greatest number of Hispanics: more than six and one-half million, or about 34 percent of the nation's total. Texas and New York together accounted for a nearly comparable number, thus bringing the Hispanic populations in these three states alone to nearly two-thirds (65 percent) of the Hispanics in the country overall (U.S. Bureau of the Census 1990b). Reflecting its historical role as the nation's—indeed the world's—most ethnically diverse city, New York City was the American city with the largest Hispanic population. In 1980 African-Americans and Hispanics together comprised more than 42 percent of New York's population.

Among the most striking demographic changes of the 1970s and 1980s was the growth of the Asian population, which quadrupled between 1970 and 1988. During the 1980s, the overall Asian population increased by 70 percent, with the most dramatic increases occurring among Koreans, Filipinos, Chinese, and In-dochinese. By 1980 Chinese and Filipinos had both surpassed in number the Japanese, who until 1980 had been the largest Asian national group. Regionally, Asians were concentrated in the West, especially in California, which had more Chinese, Japanese, Filipinos, Koreans, and Vietnamese than any other state.

The growth in the Hispanic and Asian populations in the 1970s and 1980s were both affected by dramatic increases in immigration, which was a result of three factors. First was the passage of the Immigration Act of 1965, which dramatically changed America's immigration policy. As noted in Part 2, the 1965 law eliminated racial or ethnic discrimination from immigration policy. It also placed a priority on family reunification and facilitated the admission of political refugees. Finally, about 20 percent of the visas were allocated to immigrants on the basis of their skills.

Since the late 1960s, the number of immigrants has increased substantially. During the 1980s, the number averaged over 625,000 annually, compared to 282,000 in the decade prior to 1965. In 1989, more than 1.1 million immigrants were admitted, a number greater than in any year since 1914. Moreover, experts estimate that there is a net annual increase of 100,000 to 200,000 illegal immigrants (Bouvier and Gardner 1986). (Net legal immigration is calculated by subtracting the number of people leaving the country from the number entering the country.) Given the declining birth rate of the native-born American population, immigrants now comprise a greater percentage of the nation's total population growth than they have since the first two decades of the twentieth century—approximately 25 percent of the population increase, in contrast to 6 percent in 1940.

Even more dramatic than the increase in numbers, however, were the changes in the immigrants' countries of origin. Until enactment of the 1965 law, immigrants into the United States had been overwhelmingly from European countries, ranging from a high of 96 percent of all immigrants during the 1890s to

59 percent during the 1950s. Today only a small percentage (10 percent in 1988) of immigrants come from Europe; the predominant sources are Third World nations in Asia, Central and South America, and the Caribbean. While European immigration was declining, Asian immigration increased from 6 percent in the 1950s to 42 percent in 1988, and immigrants from the Western Hemisphere (not including Canada) rose from 23 percent to 41 percent. In 1988 *none* of the ten leading countries from which the United States received immigrants – Mexico, the Philippines, Haiti, Korea, the People's Republic of China, Dominican Republic, India, Vietnam, Jamaica, and Cuba – was a traditional European source.

Moreover, the settlement patterns of this "new immigrant wave" differ from previous flows into the United States. Whereas previous immigrants settled primarily in the industrial states of the Northeast and Midwest (New York, Illinois, New Jersey, Ohio, Pennsylvania), immigrants today are much more dispersed geographically. States with the largest foreign-born populations in the 1980s were California, New York, Florida, Illinois, and Texas (U.S. Bureau of the Census 1982c:14–19).

The changes in America's immigration laws have affected the occupational composition of the present immigrant population as well as the country of origin. Today the range of immigrants' occupations closely resembles that of the native population. Whereas immigrants during the first two decades of the twentieth century were overwhelmingly unskilled blue-collar workers, preferences today for those with skills needed by the United States has meant that immigrants entering now are much more highly educated than in the past. (Hirschman and Wong confirmed this trend among Asian immigrants in Article 9.) Physicians, nurses, scientists, architects, artists, entertainers, engineers, and others with highly technical skills have contributed to a "brain drain," first from Europe and later from Third World nations that can least afford to lose such skills. Today the overall educational level of immigrants is nearly comparable to that of the United States' population as a whole. For example, 16.2 percent of American adults aged 25 and over have completed college, whereas 15.8 percent of immigrants have done so. Immigrants from Asia and Africa are especially well educated; almost half of African (46 percent) and Asian (44 percent) immigrants in 1980 had completed college (Bouvier and Gardner 1986:24). About half of all Asian immigrants between 1966 and 1975 were professionals; for Asian Indians the figure was 90 percent (U.S. Commission on Civil Rights, 1988:5).

On the other hand, the preference for skills has meant that, unlike the peak years of American immigration between 1840 and 1920, it has become almost impossible for unskilled laborers to enter the United States unless they can claim a close family relationship or political refugee status. Therefore, increasingly, the less highly skilled have resorted to illegal means of entering the country. Today the largest category of immigrants consists of those who enter the country illegally (although as we noted earlier, the estimated annual net increase from illegal immigrants is lower than from legal immigrants). In 1986 1.8 million illegal immigrants from 93 countries were apprehended, with the vast majority from Latin America (Bouvier and Gardner 1986:36–38). However, *apprehensions* of illegal immigrants are a misleading index of the number living in the United States at any one time, since the same person may be apprehended several times during a year, or even a week or a day. Moreover, a substantial proportion of these undocumented aliens, especially those from Mexico, reside in the United States only for short periods of time and then return to their countries of origin. The most recent estimates of the total number of illegal aliens living in the United States range from 1.5 to 3.5 million (Simon 1989:283–284).

Almost from its enactment, the 1965 immigration legislation proved inadequate to reduce the flow of cheap labor to the United States. During the late 1960s and 1970s the number of illegal immigrants apprehended increased dramatically, from 110,000 in 1965 to 1,251,000 in 1983 (Zolberg 1989b). As the number of apprehensions of undocumented aliens increased, so also did political pressures for the United States "to take control of its borders." Responding to these pressures, in 1986 Congress enacted the Immigration Reform and Control Act (IRCA), which represented a compromise among a disparate group of political interests. On the one hand, the law established sanctions for those employers who hired illegal aliens. On the other hand, it provided an "amnesty"–a grant of permanent residence–for illegal aliens who could prove that they had lived continuously in the United States since 1982. IRCA thus addressed primarily illegal immigration but left legal immigration intact.

Finally, in the 1990 Congress enacted a comprehensive overhaul of American immigration policy, which increased from 500,000 to 700,000 the numbers of immigrants admitted annually. It also eliminated most of the social and political restrictions (against Communists and homosexuals, for example) adopted during the McCarthy era of the 1950s. Finally, while it retained the priority on the reunification of immediate family members, it substantially increased opportunities for highly skilled workers–scientists, artists, athletes, inventors, and professionals–and entrepreneurs willing to invest in businesses in the United States.

Refugees represent the second major factor contributing to the swell of immigrants entering the United States. Determining who can enter the country as a refugee is essentially a political judgment, made by the federal government. Given that there are an estimated 18.5 million political and economic refugees in the world today under the government's definition, the moral and political pressures to admit refugees are considerable. Although refugees from more than 100 different nations have been admitted, official government policy has given special treatment to those fleeing Communism, and the vast majority to enter the United States in the past two decades have been from Cuba and Vietnam. By 1988, nearly one million Cubans and more than 500,000 Vietnamese had been admitted–both groups coming from nations where American-supported governments had been supplanted by Communist regimes. However, the refugee quotas established under the 1965 law and its subsequent revisions proved inadequate to respond either to the global refugee pressures or to the specific pressures represented by groups such as the Cubans and the Vietnamese. In some instances, as in the case of the Vietnamese, special laws were passed to enable the president to respond to emergency situations. In others, such as the case of the Cuban "Freedom Flotilla" in 1980, the political power of the Cuban-American community and the propaganda value of thousands fleeing Fidel Castro's regime permitted a *de facto* circumvention of the law.

However, as indicated by the cases of the Haitians and the Salvadorans, whose plight has been less widely publicized, the admission of refugees for political reasons does not apply to non-Communist regimes, even those that are equally oppressive. Thus in 1984 the Reagan administration planned to offer legal status and citizenship opportunities to more than 100,000 Cubans who entered the United States during the Freedom Flotilla but failed to extend the same privileges to 7,200 Haitian refugees who had fled their nation in small boats at approximately the same time (Pear 1984:1). There has been no groundswell of support for those fleeing government-sponsored terror in El Salvador, nor for the Haitians seeking to escape the nation's poverty and its political repression.

Massey (1981a:58) and Portes (1979) suggest that a third factor contributing to the recent increase in immigrants has been the emergence of an international pattern of migration between low and high income countries starting in the 1960s (see also Piore 1979). This pattern has contributed to the rise in legal immigration to the United States, but it has had a particular impact on illegal immigration, especially from Mexico and the Caribbean.

Traditionally, historians and social scientists have used a dualistic, "push-pull" model to explain immigration to the United States (Archdeacon 1983; Bodnar 1985; Handlin 1951; Jones 1960; Taylor 1971; Seller 1977; Dinnerstein and Reimers 1987). They have identified numerous "push" factors, such as population increases, economic deprivation, and religious and political repression, that impel people to leave their homelands. They have also identified "pull" factors, such as economic opportunity and abundance, and freedom of religious and political expression, that have lured immigrants to the United States.

A widespread assumption concerning the newest immigrant wave is that, as in the past, migration pressures – the push factors – are internal to those countries. In the past, the United States has been perceived to influence these migration pressures only to the extent that it offers a beacon of hope for emigrants to escape lives of economic impoverishment or political repression. Thus, the push factors that have impelled people to emigrate have been the consequence of policies, practices, and social arrangements that the United States has been relatively powerless to control or influence.

This traditional push-pull model is inadequate to explain forces stimulating immigration today. Pull factors, though greatly influenced by the pervasiveness of the mass media in even the remotest corners of the world, remain *qualitatively* the same as ever: the United States remains the epitome of economic abundance, affluence, and opportunity in the minds of people around the world. However, starting after World War II, the push factors producing immigration no longer lay largely outside U.S. influence. In the past four decades, the United States has emerged as the world's dominant economic, political, and military power. This transformation has reshaped international relations as well as expanded U.S. influence on the internal affairs of many of the world's states. The major difference between immigration today and in the past, then, is the economic and political impact of the United States in those countries that have been among the major sources of immigration. In other words, the increased numbers of immigrants entering the United States are an indirect – and sometimes direct – consequence of American policies and practices. Furthermore, American ideas and actions – economic, social, and political – have created or contributed to the conditions that have led to the uprooting of people in many societies, a number of whom have immigrated to the United States as a result.

Douglas Massey's analysis (Article 25) emphasizes the formative role of official American policies in creating the networks that today sustain the migration of undocumented Mexican workers to the United States. The contention that American policies and practices have been instrumental in stimulating the increasing exodus of Mexican workers from the United States is reinforced by the research of Alejandro Portes (1979), who has argued that, paradoxically, it is Third World economic *development,* not underdevelopment, that has contributed significantly to the growing pressures for emigration. The American model of economic development, with its emphasis on consumerism and consumption, and American economic forces have transformed the social structures of many developing societies. Simultaneously unemployment, underemployment, and income inequalities preclude access by the majority of the population of developing countries to these consumer goods. "In the eyes of the Mexican worker," Portes writes, "the United States stands as the place where the benefits of an advanced economy, promised but not delivered by the present national development strategy, can be turned into reality." Thus, ironically, the very forces generated by the American economic system and exported extensively to the economic life of Third World societies, have been instrumental in attracting the massive influx of immigrants to the United States.

Two implications can be drawn from this interpretation. First, given the thrust of the modernization process and the impact of American political and economic power throughout the world, the United States will continue to attract immigrants – legal and illegal – from Third World sources. This continuation of immigration for the foreseeable future will likely reinforce and recreate the ethnic diversity that, almost from its founding, has characterized American society. Second, although migration pressures are manifested in different ways in different countries, they frequently derive their impetus from American economic and political power abroad. Thus comprehension of the dynamics of American immigration today cannot begin at America's borders. Rather, it must encompass the examination of the migration pressures in countries of origin as well. As Aristide R. Zolberg points out in Article 29, "The New Waves," contemporary international migration in general and immigration to the United States in particular must be conceptualized more broadly as an integral component and consequence of a modern global economy characterized by dramatic inequalities between societies. Given the interdependent nature of the global economy and the continued inequalities between rich and poor countries, Zolberg contends that the continued exploitation of foreign labor by wealthy nations, the lessening of exit prohibitions from Communist countries, and the growing refugee crisis in the developing world ensure that immigration pressures on the United States and other Western nations will continue to remain an important factor affecting public policies throughout the last decade of the twentieth century.

The Ethnic Revival

The "new immigrant wave" became a significant phenomenon just when ethnicity and the celebration of America's ethnic diversity became more fashionable than ever before. The main theme of the ethnic revival of the 1970s was the rediscovery and reassertion of the importance and value of cultural pluralism and a simultaneous rejection of Anglo-conformity and the melting pot, which envision an ideal society as culturally homogeneous rather than culturally diverse. African-Americans, Blacks, Chicanos, Puerto Ricans, American Indians, and Asians each asserted their cultural distinctiveness and rejected what they perceived as efforts to impose on them the culture of the white middle class.

Each of these assertions of cultural identity and distinctiveness can be seen as an effort at ethnic mobilization – "the process by which a group organizes along ethnic lines in pursuit of collective political ends" (Nagel and Olzak 1982:127). In Article 4, "The Political Construction of Ethnicity," Joane Nagel provides an explanation for the emergence of recent tribal, pan-tribal, and pan-Indian movements. She sees such movements as responses to external stimuli; in particular, to policies of the American federal government that control resources available to Indians.

However, the primary impetus for the ethnic revival of the 1970s came from the so-called "white ethnics." Spokespersons for the ethnic revival maintained that the movement represented a spontaneous and broadly based reassertion of ethnic pride, not only of intellectuals but of the frequently ignored, unarticulated, and pervasive sentiments of working-class ethnics as well. Michael Novak, the grandson of Slovakian immigrants and author of *The Rise of the Unmeltable Ethnics* (1971), was one of the foremost proponents of the new ethnicity. He identified two basic elements in the movement: a sensitivity to and appreciation of the importance of ethnic pluralism; and a self-conscious examination of one's own cultural heritage (Novak 1971:17). Another prominent spokesman, Andrew Greeley, the Irish-American sociologist, priest, and novelist, noted several ways in which this ethnic "consciousness raising" was expressed: increased interest in the literacy, intellectual, and artistic culture of one's ethnic background; visits to one's ancestral homeland; and increased use of one's ancestral language (Greeley 1975:149–151).

The case for a broadly based ethnic revival was supported by considerable impressionistic evidence. In 1969, for the first time, the Census Bureau asked Americans about their ethnic backgrounds. Those interviewed were given seven choices from which to select: German, English, Irish, Spanish, Polish, Italian, and Russian (and "mixed" or "other"). Thirty-eight percent of the respondents (equivalent to 75 million Americans) placed themselves in one of the seven categories. Three years later, when the Census Bureau conducted a similar survey, Americans appeared much more conscious of, or willing to indicate, their affiliation with an ethnic group. This time nearly 50 percent (equivalent to 102 million) identified with a specific national group. Moreover, during the late 1960s and early 1970s numerous ethnic groups developed organizations, such as the Italian-American Civil Rights League, that were designed to combat negative

perceptions of their group. Such self-consciously ethnic organizations also mobilized to obtain financial resources from the federal government and private
foundations in order to fund activities to rekindle or awaken ethnic consciousness. In 1972 the Ethnic Heritage Studies Act gave federal government sanction
to the ethnic revival by providing financial assistance to promote ethnic studies.
The Act gave, in the words of one of its sponsors, "official recognition to ethnicity
as a positive constructive force in our society today" (quoted in Polenberg
1980:246).

The notion of an ethnic revival was also reflected in increased academic
attention to ethnicity. History, literature, and sociology courses that had focused
almost exclusively on African-Americans during the 1960s broadened their scope
to include other ethnic groups in the 1970s. Indeed, student enrollments declined
in black studies courses and there were instances in which ethnic courses
supplanted race courses completely. The increasing salience of ethnicity was also
symbolized by the founding of several journals devoted to its analysis: *Ethnicity*
(1974), *Journal of Ethnic Studies* (1974), *Ethnic and Racial Studies* (1978), *MELUS
(Multiethnic Literature in the United States)* (1975), and the *Journal of American
Ethnic History* (1981). Finally, one of the most salient indices of the rediscovery of
ethnicity was the publication in 1980 of the *Harvard Encyclopedia of American
Ethnic Groups,* the most comprehensive resource available on the subject today
(Thernstrom 1980). Publication of the *Encyclopedia* under the aegis of the nation's
most prestigious university press reflects the primacy that ethnicity has been
accorded over the last two decades.

What are the reasons for this resurgence of ethnicity? Foremost was the
impact that the Black Protest Movement had on the self-definition of other ethnic
groups, in particular white ethnics. On the one hand, the emphasis on black
pride and on understanding African-American culture, stimulated by the civil
rights movement of the late 1950s and 1960s, led many white ethnics to consider
their own heritages more closely. Moreover, the "roots phenomenon" emerged
among white ethnics that both reflected and was stimulated by the celebrated
television saga, "Roots," which was based on Alex Haley's attempt to trace and
construct his ancestral origins on the African continent.

On the other hand, spokespersons for white ethnics criticized what they
perceived as the myopia of the white, liberal, basically Protestant Establishment.
They contended that liberal academics and journalists, especially, were oblivious
to the discrimination to which white ethnics historically had been subjected, and
tended to portray white ethnics as the primary source of racism towards blacks.
For many white ethnics, who felt that they had been the object of derision by
liberals, such charges reinforced their perception that the conditions of their lives
had not been given the same sympathetic treatment as was given to African-
Americans, Chicanos, Puerto Ricans, and American Indians. Novak contends
that from the white liberal perspective, the latter were "legitimate" minorities but
that the idea of white ethnics as minorities was unacceptable. The white ethnic's
perspective, Novak wrote, was that "he is being asked to pay the entire price of
the injustices done to blacks – he who is living on the margin himself – while
those who are enriched pay nothing" (Novak 1975:112). Thus the ethnic revival

was in some respects a defensive response to external pressures, particularly in its opposition to an increasingly strident Black Protest Movement, rather than a positive, liberating affirmation of identity.

In another sense, however, the movement had less to do with factors external to the white ethnic groups than with the nature of these groups' adaptation to American society. Richard Alba (Article 21 and 1988) has shown how the experience of ethnicity among southern and eastern Europeans is affected by age and cohort. Older cohorts were far more likely to have been raised in homes in which a language other than English was spoken, to have had both parents from the same ethnic background, and not to have attended college. Members of younger cohorts, on the other hand, were much more likely to have grown up in homes in which only English was spoken, to have had ethnically mixed ancestry, and to have attended college. Moreover, members of younger cohorts were much more likely to have married spouses from different ethnic and religious backgrounds and to have switched religious affiliations than were members of the older cohorts. By the 1970s the fourth generation of the southern and eastern European immigrants was entering adulthood. As the distance from their ancestral roots increased, their identification with them weakened. The decline of the ancestral language, the dispersion of ethnic neighborhoods, decreasing participation in and identification with the traditional religious community (primarily among Catholics, especially those under thirty years of age), and increased rates of ethnic intermarriage contributed to the dwindling of a meaningful ethnic identity.

Another major factor was what Greeley termed the "ethnic miracle," which we discussed in Part 3. The increased economic, educational, and occupational mobility Greeley documented indicated that white ethnics have moved into the mainstream of American society, where their identification with their ethnic origins has become increasingly remote.

Moreover, there is considerable evidence that ethnicity as a source of social cohesion is decreasing, especially among the third and fourth generations. In Article 22, "Symbolic Ethnicity," Herbert Gans disputes the notion of an enduring ethnic revival, arguing that cultural and social assimilation continue to take place in American society. Ethnicity is no longer rooted in group membership or cultural patterns but instead has become symbolic, a matter of choice, an ethnicity of "last resort." In his study of an Italian-American community in Boston in the 1960s, Gans did not find a sense of ethnic identity to be increasing. Instead, he found a straight-line decline in ethnicity over three generations. That is, ethnicity was less significant in each succeeding generation (Gans 1962). Similarly, a study by Sandberg showed a constant decline in ethnic consciousness, identification, and cohesion among Polish-Americans in Los Angeles; by the fourth generation, ethnicity had ceased to play an important role in their lives (Sandberg 1974). Finally, these findings are reinforced by increased rates of ethnic intermarriage, which were discussed in Part 3.

Thus, paradoxically, at precisely the moment that white ethnics have become the most fully assimilated into American society, culturally and socially, their interest in and identification with their ethnic roots has also become the most pronounced. In *The Ethnic Myth* Stephen Steinberg argued that ". . . the impulse to recapture the ethnic past is a belated realization that ethnicity is rapidly diminishing as a significant factor in American life" (Steinberg 1981:73).

Although neither is especially sympathetic to the notion of an ethnic revival, both Irving Howe (1977) and Herbert Gans ("Symbolic Ethnicity") suggest another source of the surge of interest in things ethnic. In an interpretation reminiscent of Herberg's (1955) explanation of the surge of religiosity a generation earlier, they find that ethnicity provides a fashionable, socially acceptable source of personal identity in an increasingly homogenized America. In Howe's words,

> We are all aware that our ties with the European past grow increasingly feeble. Yet we feel uneasy before the prospect of becoming "just Americans." We feel uneasy before the prospect of becoming as indistinguishable from one another as our motel rooms are, or as flavorless and mass-produced as the bread many of us eat. (Howe 1977:18)

Thus, although there appears to be widespread interest today among many European-Americans in retrieving or maintaining a sense of ethnic identity (what Gans called *symbolic ethnicity*), precisely how deep and enduring the ethnic revival will remain is problematic (for a similar interpretation, see Hirschman 1983).

Finally, Stanley Lieberson suggests in Article 23, "A New Ethnic Group in the United States," that a substantial number of Americans have no sense of ethnic group identity other than a general notion that they are American. The European origins of these "unhyphenated whites," as Lieberson dubs them, are either so remote or so mixed that they are able to define themselves, in true melting pot or transmuting pot fashion, only as American. Lieberson's article raises the intriguing question of whether his findings herald the continual decline of ethnicity among people of European extraction. Or, if ethnicity is situational and emergent, is it more likely that unhyphenated whites will coalesce into novel ethnic groupings fully derived from the American experience in the future?

The Status of African-Americans

Near the end of World War II, Gunnar Myrdal, a Swedish economist and later a Nobel Prize winner, published *An American Dilemma* (1944), a massive two-volume study of American race relations that he had conducted with the financial support of the Carnegie Corporation. The book examined in greater depth than any previous study the subordinate political, economic, and social status of African-Americans and the prospects for change of that status. The book's title reflected Myrdal's basic premise that American race relations were essentially a moral problem in the hearts and minds of Americans—that the caste status that constrained African-Americans in virtually every aspect of their lives represented a violation of what he called the "American creed" of equality and brotherhood. The book became an immediate classic, influencing an entire generation of academics, students, clergy, and social workers, and providing the intellectual backdrop for the attack upon segregation during the 1950s and 1960s. The book's influence extended to the Supreme Court, which cited it in the historic 1954 *Brown v. Board of Education of Topeka* decision.

The pace of change in American race relations in the years following publication of *An American Dilemma* was more rapid than even Myrdal had anticipated. During the next two decades resolution of the glaring contradiction between American ideals and African-Americans' second-class citizenship became the nation's most prominent domestic political issue. Reflecting this focus, in 1965, in an introduction written for a series of essays entitled "The Negro American" in the scholarly journal *Daedalus,* President Lyndon Johnson wrote: "Nothing is of greater significance to the welfare and vitality of this nation than the movement to secure equal rights for Negro Americans" (*Daedalus* 1965:743). Johnson's crucial role in achieving passage of the landmark 1964 Civil Rights Act and the 1965 Voting Rights Act and his War on Poverty program are ample evidence that his support was not merely rhetorical.

Johnson wrote these words at the zenith of personal and national attention to the status of African-Americans. However, reflecting the unrest created by their continued exclusion from the mainstream of American life, a wave of urban uprisings by blacks swept American cities during the mid-1960s. These uprisings claimed a toll of over 100 lives and millions of dollars in property damage. President Johnson responded by appointing a blue-ribbon commission to investigate the causes of the civil disorders and to recommend ways in which the conditions that triggered them might be addressed. In 1968 the National Commission on Civil Disorders (popularly known as the Kerner Commission, after its chair, Illinois Governor Otto Kerner) attributed the primary responsibility for the outbreaks to "white racism" and warned that American society was moving toward "two societies, one black, one white – separate and unequal." It concluded that "there can be no higher claim on the Nation's conscience" than to eliminate "deepening racial division" by a "compassionate, massive, and sustained" commitment of resources and energy (National Advisory Commission on Civil Disorders 1968).

Johnson, by that time preoccupied with the escalation of the war in Vietnam, ignored the commission's recommendations, just as his successor, Richard Nixon, disputed its basic conclusions. Subsequently, despite several significant private and governmental efforts to implement programs to achieve racial equality, the status of African-Americans no longer occupied the prominence in the American consciousness that it did in 1965. By 1981, the editors of an issue of *Daedalus* devoted to American racial minorities would write, "It is a measure of the distance we have traveled in sixteen years that is almost unthinkable to image any white politician today making such a statement as Johnson's in 1965, giving such primacy to the issue of racial equality" (*Daedalus* 1981:vi).

Nevertheless, as the decade of the 1980s came to a close, several assessments appeared that sounded alarm at the glacial pace of progress for minorities in general and African-Americans in particular (American Council on Education 1988; Quality Education for Minorities Project 1990). Most detailed of these reports was *A Common Destiny: Blacks and American Society,* a comprehensive analysis of black social, political, and economic trends since World War II. The study, conducted by a national commission of distinguished scholars, concluded that despite many significant gains by African-Americans, "there are striking resemblances between the description of 1968 [in the Kerner Report] and the position of black Americans reflected in our findings. To the extent that such continuity of black status persists, it derives from persisting basic conditions not yet removed by either private initiative or the national actions that have been taken, much less by those repeatedly proposed but never fully taken" (Jaynes and Williams 1989:xi).

The basic conclusions of this study are found in Article 26. As its authors point out, the status of African-Americans since World War II has been affected by four major societal developments: the urbanization and northward migration of blacks, the Civil Rights Movement of the 1950s and 1960s, post-World War II economic expansion, and the curtailment of economic growth since the early 1970s. We will examine some aspects of the continuities and changes in the status of African-Americans.

There can be little doubt that the rise of black militancy was one of the most momentous developments of the turbulent 1960s. Each year during the decade, the scale of racial conflict and violence escalated. In retrospect, the beginnings appear relatively subdued. In 1960, the most dramatic events involved drugstore sit-ins in Greensboro, North Carolina, a tactic that quickly spread throughout the South. In the following years, the pace and intensity of protest increased dramatically. Civil disorders engulfed cities throughout the country, with great loss of property and lives. In the heated climate of those years, four of the most important figures in the movement for African-American equality were the victims of assassins' bullets. Two of them, Malcolm X and Martin Luther King, Jr., were black; two, John Kennedy and Robert Kennedy, were white.

Between 1960 and 1970, the goals and means of the Black Protest Movement underwent substantial changes. As is characteristic of much social change, yesterday's radicalism became today's moderation. Many ideologies and tactics that came to be defined as moderate would have appeared unthinkably radical to concerned individuals – black and white – a decade earlier. Joseph C. Hough, Jr., has characterized this change as the "stretching of the extremism spectrum":

> About 1953 I had my first conversation with [a friend in the South] about race relations, and he and I agreed that while the Negro deserved a better chance in America, we must be careful to oppose two kinds of extremists – the NAACP and the Ku Klux Klan. In 1955, we had another conversation, and again we agreed that Negroes ought to be able to attend desegregated public schools, but that we should oppose two kinds of extremes – White Citizens Councils and Martin Luther King. In 1966, this same friend said to me, "If we could get the good whites and the good Negroes to support Martin Luther King, perhaps we could put the brakes on these SNCC and CORE people and also put a stop to this ridiculous revival of the Ku Klux Klan. (Hough 1968:224–225)

By the late 1960s, the forms and direction of African-American protest had shifted from the moderate civil rights movement to a more militant black power movement. The civil rights movement of the 1950s and early 1960s had been based essentially on an order model of society; the primary goal had been integration into the mainstream of the dominant society, and the primary means were nonviolent. As Skolnick (1969) pointed out, the civil rights movement "operated for the most part on the implicit premise that racism was a localized malignancy within a relatively healthy political and social order; it was a move to force American morality and American institutions to root out the last vestiges of the 'disease' " (Skolnick 1969:31).

The fundamental ideological thrust of the black power movement, on the other hand, derived from a conflict model of societal functioning. In response to the intransigence and unresponsiveness of white America, articulate African-American spokespersons increasingly questioned the capacity of traditional goals and means to ensure the dignity and autonomy of black people in a white society. After the Kerner Commission's report was published in 1968, militancy among African-Americans, particularly among the young, increased even further. Perhaps the most important shift in attitudes among African-Americans was the growing recognition that the racial problems were national and could not be confined to the South; that nonviolence was merely a *tactic* in a power struggle and in many instances was useless to obtain black equality and autonomy; and that racism was rooted in the society's institutions. Consequently, the primary efforts of the black power movement were to obtain a more equitable distribution of power in the many institutional spheres of American life and to search for new ideological forms, or cultural alternatives to those of white America.

For African-Americans, however, the 1960s were a decade of progress: during this period blacks experienced their greatest gains since their emancipation in 1865. These gains were brought about by the unprecedented efforts of federal, state, and local governments and private organizations to remove inequalities and redress injustices that had for years relegated African-Americans to second-class citizenship.

Most visible and dramatic were the legal changes made by the federal government. For the first time in American history the three branches of the federal government acted in concert on behalf of African-Americans. The Supreme Court, whose *Brown v. The Board of Education* decision had outlawed segregated schools in 1954, substantially extended the implications of the *Brown* decision, and symbolized the beginning of a new era for blacks. It outlawed state laws prohibiting racial intermarriage and racial discrimination in the rental and sale of private and public property. Moreover, it decisively rejected efforts by local school districts to evade its desegregation rulings, and unanimously supported school busing as one means of achieving that goal. President Lyndon Johnson, a Southerner, provided the most unequivocal moral and political support of African-American aspirations of any president in American history. Through his leadership, the Congress enacted legislation that outlawed discrimination in public accommodations, employment, housing, voting, and education. In addition, his Great Society economic programs provided federal funds to enhance occupational and educational opportunities for blacks.

By the end of the 1960s African-Americans, particularly the better educated and more highly skilled, had made substantial gains, both economically and educationally. One of the best indices of these changes was black median family income, which in 1959 was only half of white median family income. By 1964 it had risen to 54 percent of white income and by 1969, reflecting the economic expansion and prosperity that characterized the decade, as well as national efforts to reduce black inequalities, it had risen to 61 percent. Thus, although problems remained acute for poorly educated and unskilled African-Americans, the efforts of the 1960s had clearly produced some impressive advances.

However, the civil rights movement, which during the 1960s had generally displayed consensus concerning both goals and tactics despite internal differences, was now in disarray. Part of the reason was the movement's very success in achieving impressive legislative and judicial victories in the 1960s. The disarray also reflected the fact that for many African-Americans the optimism of the early 1960s had been shattered by the failure of these legislative changes to institute meaningful changes in their lives. It became increasingly apparent that the abolition of legal barriers to public accommodations and suburban housing, for example, did not address the essential problems of a substantial portion of the African-American population. The erosion of the fragile consensus among African-Americans was symbolized by the outbreaks of the civil disorders of the late 1960s, which did little to allay conscious and unconscious white anxieties concerning African-American demands for substantial changes in the status quo. As many whites grew weary of what they perceived as government support for lawlessness, and tired of the constant media attention to blacks, the conservative mood of the country increased, contributing to the 1968 election of Richard Nixon to the presidency.

By the early 1970s, the impetus and fervor of the black power movement was spent. The frequency of mass social unrest dramatically declined during the decade. American involvement in Indochina formally ended and the civil disorders that rent many American cities during the 1960s did not recur on an equally massive scale. The sense of concern for social justice affecting many white Americans was replaced by an indifference, even an aversion, to the problems of racial minority groups in the country. Indeed, the activism of the so-called concerned generation of the 1960s was replaced by a stance of "benign neglect." Compared to the progress achieved during the 1960s, the 1970s and 1980s were, at best, a period during which the rate of African-American advance slowed appreciably; at worst it was a time of retrogression and retrenchment.

The most dramatic advances for African-Americans since the 1960s were in the political arena. The tactics of public confrontations, boycotts, and demonstrations, which in the late 1950s and early 1960s had been successful in effecting social change, were supplanted in the 1970s by more traditional political activity. "Politics is the civil-rights movement of the 1970s," said Maynard Jackson, the black mayor of Atlanta (Sitkoff 1981:229). Such a stance was possible because of the increase in African-American political strength brought about by the Voting Rights Act of 1965, which provided federal protection for black efforts to register and vote in states throughout the South. The percentage of Southern blacks registered to vote increased from 35 percent in 1964 to 65 percent in 1969. In Alabama the increase was from 19 to 61 percent, in Mississippi from 7 to 67 percent; and in Georgia from 27 to 60 percent (Polenberg 1980:192).

The increases in African-American voters throughout the South substantially increased their political representation. In 1964 there were only 103 blacks holding elected offices (ranging from local school board member to president) among the early half-million elected officials in the entire country. By 1970 this number had increased to 1,400 and by 1989 to 7,200, two-thirds of them in the South, including the nation's first black governor – Douglas Wilder of Virginia. Moreover, the number of African-American mayors had increased from none in 1965 to nearly 300 in 1989, including four of the nation's six largest cities – New York, Los Angeles, Philadelphia, and Detroit. Finally, by 1991 the Congressional Black Caucus, comprised of African-American members of the House of Representatives, claimed a membership of 26 out of the 435 seats in that body.

Because of their strategic location in the major metropolitan areas of key industrial states, the combined voting strength of African-Americans could swing close elections. This power was demonstrated first in 1960, when John Kennedy's narrow victory over Richard Nixon was due to the substantial margin he obtained from black voters in the industrial Northeast and Midwest. It was even more noteworthy in the 1976 election, when over 90 percent of more than six and one-half million black voters voted for Jimmy Carter. Carter owed his victory margin in most of the Southern as well as several Northern states – and thus his election as a whole – directly to the overwhelming support of African-American voters. Although his legislative record did not match his campaign promises to African-Americans, Carter appointed more black officials to the judiciary and to prominent positions in the executive branch of the federal government than all previous presidents combined. Finally, the increasing significance of African-American political power was made abundantly clear during the 1980s, when Jesse Jackson's presidential candidacy not only electrified the black community (and was instrumental in registering thousands of new black voters), but gained the support of a substantial number of white voters as well.

Despite these highly visible changes, by 1989 African-Americans remained only about 1.5 percent of all elected officials in the country, a percentage not even closely approximating their nearly 12 percent of the total population. In the South, where blacks comprise more than 20 percent of the population, only 3 percent of the elected officials were black. Moreover, in many instances the political power that black elected officials do have today is limited by the fact that they are politically isolated. Moreover, given the exodus of white middle-class residents and businesses to the suburbs, African-Americans often find they have gained political power without the financial resources with which to provide the jobs and services (educational, medical, police and fire protection) that their constituents most urgently need.

Since the civil rights movement of the 1950s and 1960s, African-Americans have also experienced substantial gains in education. In 1957 the proportion of whites aged 25–29 who had completed high school (63.3 percent) was almost double the proportion of blacks (31.6 percent). By 1987 the proportions of each racial group who were high school graduates were nearly equal – 86.3 percent for whites and 83.3 percent for blacks. Moreover, between 1957 and 1987 the ratio of white to black college graduates declined. In 1957 11 percent of whites but only 4 percent of blacks aged 25–29 had completed four or more years of college, but by 1987 comparable figures were 23 percent for whites and 11.4 percent for blacks (U.S. Bureau of the Census 1988a:75–76). In the early 1970s a steadily increasing percent of blacks began attending college, so that by 1977 the percentage enrolled was virtually equal to that of whites, a dramatic change when compared to the college attendance rates of blacks as late as the mid-1960s (Jones 1981). However, during the 1980s the gains of the 1960s and early 1970s eroded, threatening to reverse the movement toward educational equality. Since 1976 black college attendance and completion rates have declined, as has the proportion of black students enrolled at four-year colleges and in graduate and professional schools (American Council on Education 1988:8). The percentage of black high school graduates entering college fell from 48 percent in 1977 to 36.5 percent in 1986 (Jaynes and Williams 1989:338–339). In 1976 African-Americans earned 6.4 percent of all bachelor's degrees awarded but only 5.7 percent in 1987 (*New York Times* 1990:11). Moreover, these figures on college attendance and graduation rates obscure the fact that, although black students are today found in a much wider range of educational institutions than ever before (including the nation's most selective and prestigious colleges and universities), a disproportionately large percentage attend two-year junior and community colleges, and about one-third attend historically black colleges.

These statistics also obscure substantial qualitative differences in African-American educational achievement. As the 1990s began, black students remained as racially isolated as they were in 1972. Ironically, black students in the South today are far more likely to attend racially integrated elementary and secondary schools than are black students in other regions of the country, although the desegregation achieved during the 1960s and early 1970s in the South was beginning to erode by the late 1980s. Because of the patterns of residential segregation in most American cities, 70 percent of black children outside the South attend schools that are comprised predominantly of minority children. The situation is most acute in the nation's twenty-five largest central city school districts, which enroll more than one-fourth (27.5 percent) of all African-American children. These districts have experienced substantial declines in white enrollment; by 1986 only 3 percent of the nation's white students were enrolled in them. (Orfield and Monfort 1988; Orfield, Monfort, and Aaron 1989). In the late 1960s and early 1970s this pattern of marked racial isolation led to the increasing use of busing to achieve racially balanced schools. However, even in circumstances in which there was overwhelming evidence of state responsibility for the creation and support of the residential segregation that created racial imbalance in public schools, whites responded with intense opposition to using busing as a remedy for the ensuing racial segregation. The importance of this resistance was reflected in the spate of congressional proposals to restrict the courts' use of busing as a remedy for metropolitan segregation. Thus, although there have been significant educational advances for

African-Americans during the past two decades, whether these gains are endur-ing and whether they can be translated into higher economic status remains problematic.

Thus the trends in both the political and educational areas indicate qualified improvements for African-Americans. However, no such progress has taken place in the economic sphere, perhaps the most important institutional category. The economic gains of the 1960s were eroded by inflation, two recessions, and substantial reductions in federal, state, and local governmental commitments to racial progress. The economic recovery championed by the Reagan and Bush administrations during the 1980s did little to enhance the economic status of African-Americans, which has shown little improvement since the mid-1960s. Although many blacks have experienced socioeconomic mobility during the past decade, African-Americans remain underrepresented in high-status professional, technical, and managerial positions, and overrepresented in service occupations, traditionally recognized as low-status jobs in American society (Farley and Allen 1987). Since 1970 the income gap separating black and white has widened substantially. Black median family income, which rose from 50 percent of white median family income in 1959 to 61 percent in 1969, declined to 56 percent in 1989. The gap in terms of absolute dollars more than quadrupled, from a difference of $3,800 in 1969 to more than $15,766 in 1989 (U.S. Bureau of the Census 1990d). One of the factors contributing to this decline was a substantial increase in poor black families, who were likely to be unemployed or under-employed. However, even among full-time wage and salary workers, the ratio of black to white income declined during the 1980s (Swinton 1990:50).

However, measures of income inequality alone do not adequately measure the disparities between black and white in economic status. To obtain a more accurate picture of the racial distribution of economic resources, it is necessary to examine wealth, which includes savings, investments, homes, and property. Wealth represents accumulated or "stored-up" purchasing power.

Most studies of the distribution of wealth in American society have relied on measures of *net worth,* the difference between a household's assets and liabilities. In 1984 the Census Bureau conducted the most comprehensive study yet under-taken of the net worth (which includes assets such as homes, bank accounts, stocks and bonds, and liabilities such as mortgages and loans) of American households. The study found that nearly one-fifth of American families had zero or negative net worth—that is, their financial liabilities exceeded their assets. It also found that the net worth of a typical white household was 12 times that of a black household and eight times that of an Hispanic household. The median net worth for white households was $39,135; for black households, $3,397; and for Hispanic households, $4,913 (U.S. Bureau of the Census 1986:19).

However, the net worth of many Americans who have accumulated some wealth is held almost exclusively in the equity that they have in their homes and automobiles. Oliver and Shapiro (1989a, 1989b) have therefore argued that the most accurate measures of the concentration of wealth in the United States should exclude equity in homes and vehicles, because these assets can seldom be converted to other purposes (such as financing a college education, establishing or expanding a business, or paying for emergency medical expenses). They suggest that a more appropriate measure of wealth is *net financial assets,* household wealth after the equity in homes and vehicles has been deducted. If this measure (rather than net worth) is used, figures on the overall wealth of American households and inequalities in the distribution of wealth in American society change dramatically; net financial assets tend to be much more heavily concentrated among the very wealthy. "Whereas the top 20 percent of American households earn over 43 percent of all income, the same 20 percent holds 67 percent of net worth and nearly 90 percent of net financial assets" (Oliver and Shapiro 1989a).

The disparities between black and white in net financial assets are even more pronounced than those for net worth. White households had a median net worth of $39,000, but median net financial assets of about only $5,000. Black households, on the other hand, had a median net worth of $3,400, but median net financial assets of zero. Among blacks wealth was even more heavily concentrated than among whites—two-thirds of all black households have zero or negative net financial assets. On the other hand, 99 percent of all net financial assets among blacks are owned by the wealthiest one-fifth of the black community. Oliver and Shapiro conclude that blacks are therefore much more disadvantaged than whites when measures of wealth, especially net financial assets, rather than income, are used.

With the exception of three years during the 1970s, the annual black unemployment rate has been at least double that for whites since 1954, and during the 1980s the gap between white and black unemployment rates actually increased. In 1988 black unemployment stood at nearly 12 percent (11.7 percent) of the black labor force, having risen to 2½ times the rate for whites (U.S. Bureau of the Census 1990a:9). Unemployment was most acute for black teenagers. Despite declines in unemployment among all categories of workers since 1983, nearly one-third (32.4 percent) of black teenagers were unemployed in 1988, a figure also 2½ times higher than that for white teenagers (13.1 percent). Moreover, the National Urban League, whose research division annually surveys African-American households, contends that the official unemployment rate substantially underrepresents real unemployment because it does not include discouraged workers who have dropped out of the labor force entirely. They also note that the unemployment data cited above are national averages and obscure the variations among different cities, in some of which, the Urban League estimates, the jobless rate for black teenagers during the 1980s may have risen to as high as 80 percent. Thus the overall economic status of African-Americans appears to have deteriorated during the 1970s and 1980s.

However, as William Julius Wilson (1978a, 1987) has pointed out, this deterioration in economic status was not felt uniformly throughout the black community. During the 1970s, middle-class blacks made impressive economic advances. The number of blacks in professional and managerial positions increased to 2½ times what it had been in 1965. Indeed, between 1975 and 1980 the largest gains in black employment were in higher-status occupations. During this period the number of African-Americans employed increased by 1.3 million, over half of them in managerial, professional, and craft jobs (Hill 1981:22). Moreover, Wilson notes that prior to 1960 the ratio of black income to white income actually decreased as educational attainment increased, but that this pattern has now been reversed: the higher the black educational level, the more closely incomes approximate those of whites.

However, Wilson argues that because of macrostructural changes in the American economy, a growing division has emerged among African-Americans between the middle class and a steadily increasing underclass – the nation's most impoverished social category, many of whom live in persistent poverty. Found predominantly in the nation's inner cities, the underclass is characterized by high rates of unemployment, out-of-wedlock births, female-headed families, welfare dependence, homelessness, and serious crime. Although those included in the underclass include some whites and, increasingly, Hispanics, its existence is most pronounced and most visible in the black ghettos of northern cities in the United States.

The nature and causes of the growing underclass have been the subject of considerable controversy. In Article 28, "Family, Race, and Poverty in the Eighties," Maxine Baca Zinn distinguishes between two broad ideologies or models – the cultural deficiency and the macrostructural – that have been used both by social scientists and laypeople to explain the underclass phenomenon. These two models roughly correspond to the "internal" and "external" explanations of ethnic group achievement developed in the Introduction to Part 3. The cultural deficiency model emphasizes shortcomings either in the minority's culture or family system or in a welfare system believed to encourage personal traits that prevent people from pulling themselves out of poverty. The cultural deficiency model locates the explanation for the underclass in the cultural or psychological characteristics of its members.

A macrostructural explanation of the underclass, on the other hand, focuses on the decline of opportunity structures. As noted in Part 3, William Julius Wilson has been one of the most prominent and articulate spokespersons for this perspective. In *The Truly Disadvantaged* Wilson has argued that the growth of the urban underclass has resulted from major structural changes in the American economy that have caused extremely high levels of inner city unemployment. Earlier in the twentieth century, relatively uneducated and unskilled native and immigrant workers were able to find stable employment and income in the manufacturing sector of the economy. However, most of the nation's major manufacturing centers in the industrial states of the North and Midwest have experienced dramatic declines in manufacturing, as such jobs have moved from the inner cities to the suburbs, the Sun Belt, or overseas. The service jobs that have been created in the inner cities demand credentials for which most relatively unskilled inner city residents are unqualified, and they lack access (both physical and social) to suburban employment. Thus unskilled inner city residents find themselves without prospects for work.

Moreover, as those stable working-class and middle-class residents with job qualifications have moved from the inner cities to better residential neighborhoods, the stability of neighborhood social institutions (such as churches, schools, newspapers, recreational facilities, and small businesses) has been undermined, and the social fabric of community life has deteriorated. Those remaining in such neighborhoods, increasingly the "most marginal and oppressed of the black community," have become increasingly socially isolated. Loïc Wacquant and Wilson (Article 27) refer to this loss of community social institutions and increasing concentration of the extreme poor as *hyperghettoization*.

Whereas Wilson's analyses have focused primarily on the black underclass, Maxine Baca Zinn points out in Article 28 that similar macrostructural conditions have affected Hispanics, especially Puerto Ricans and Mexicans. Increases in Hispanic poverty have been most pronounced in those regions (such as the Northeast and Midwest) in which broad structural changes in the economy have occurred. "The association between national economic shifts and high rates of social dislocation among Hispanics provides further evidence for the structural argument that economic conditions rather than culture create distinctive forms of racial poverty" (Zinn 1989).

Therefore, the major thrust of both Wilson's and Zinn's arguments is that, although the African-American and Hispanic underclass both reflect a legacy of racial discrimination, class factors have become critical in sustaining the underclass today. Lacking the necessary training and job skills for positions in the modern economy, members of the underclass are instead the victims of broad economic and technological changes in American society. Even if all racial prejudice and discrimination were eliminated, African-American and Hispanic members of the underclass would still lack the necessary qualifications with which to participate in the mainstream of the economy and would continue to be found primarily in the low-paying, unskilled sector where unemployment is extremely high. In the economic sphere institutional, not attitudinal, discrimination has become critical to sustaining African-American and Hispanic inequalities.

Thus the economic problems confronting African-Americans are those of structural discrimination. The thrust of Wilson's thesis is that major attention must be directed not only to the removal of racial barriers (which he acknowledges still confront African-Americans in education, politics, and especially in housing) but to the very structure of the American economy and its inability to provide opportunity for the substantial segment of its population. The challenge for American society in the next decade, therefore, is not only to ensure that the barriers of racial discrimination continue to recede, but that class barriers now precluding minority access to economic opportunities are also eliminated.

However, Zinn questions the utility of a structural model for explaining the role of gender in poverty. She contends that both the cultural deficiency and macrostructural models have similar underlying conceptions about gender and gender roles. Both models "assume that the traditional family is a key solution for eliminating racial poverty. . . . Both models rest on normative definitions of women's and men's roles . . . and traditional concepts of the family and women's and men's roles within it." Both, therefore, tend to ignore the role of gender in explaining poverty.

Although her article focuses primarily on explanations of African-American and Hispanic poverty, Zinn's analysis raises important questions concerning the ways in which racial and ethnic phenomena are affected by gender. Until recently, there has been a tendency in the literature of racial and ethnic relations in the United States to generalize about these phenomena without considering gender. However, scholars have increasingly focused on the manner in which gender intersects with race and ethnicity.

For example, Geschwender and Carroll-Seguin (1990) have recently pointed out that failure to recognize that the historical experiences of African-Americans created patterns of female labor force participation different from those of European-Americans has contributed to the myth of African-American progress toward achieving economic equality. Historically African-American women have been much more likely to work outside the home than European-American women, and consequently the "labor and earnings of African-American women have made a much greater relative contribution to the economic survival of the African-American family" (1990:289). However, indices of family income tend to ignore the relative contribution of wives to two-parent family incomes, thus giving a misleading impression of overall economic improvement among blacks. Geschwender and Carroll-Seguin point out that black and white women have had generally divergent patterns of labor force participation. Rates for European-American women are highest among working class families and decline as the husband's income increases. However, because the incomes of African-American men are lower than those of European-American men, more than one income is necessary to achieve comparable family income levels. Therefore, the rate of labor force participation for African-American women *increases* as their husbands' income increases. Geschwender and Carroll-Seguin conclude that whatever improvements two-parent African-American families have made in the past two decades are because African-American wives "have been far more likely to work, and to work full-time. . . . Thus, the earnings of African-American wives constituted a much greater percentage of total family income than was the case among European-Americans" (1990:298).

Comprehending the significance of racial differences in gender economic roles therefore is critical to comprehending fully the dynamics of race relations during the 1990s.

The Future of Race and Ethnicity in American Life

At the 1963 March on Washington, Martin Luther King, Jr., delivered one of the most memorable speeches ever uttered by an American. In this address he spoke of his dream for the future:

> *I have a dream . . . [of] that day when all God's children, black men and white men, Jews and Gentiles, Protestants and Catholics, will be able to join hands and sing in the words of that old Negro spiritual, "Free at last! Free at last! Thank God almighty, we are free at last." (quoted in Oates 1982:255)*

400

Within two years of his historic address two of the most far-reaching pieces of federal legislation to help African-Americans realize this dream – the 1964 Civil Rights Act and the 1965 Voting Rights Act – were enacted. Moreover, as noted above, the predominant thrust of public policy during the late 1960s was to undermine and deny the legitimacy of the forces of ethnic and racial particularism – to eliminate the formal barriers that had previously relegated certain racial and ethnic groups to second-class citizenship. These efforts were suffused with an optimism that racial and ethnic criteria would cease to be salient issues in American life, that the dream of racial and ethnic equality of which King had so eloquently spoken would be realized.

Today, nearly thirty years after King's historic address, despite the repudiation of racist ideologies and substantial changes in many facets of society, race and ethnicity remain prominent features of American life. Civil rights legislation and well-intentioned commitments on the part of many whites have not eliminated controversies over racial and ethnic matters. For example, social programs such as affirmative action, busing, and bilingual education, all of which were implemented in order to remedy the effects of past discrimination and to achieve greater equity among racial and ethnic groups, have been denounced by scholars and politicians who contend they contravene the very goals of equality for which they were enacted. Indeed, far from withering away, debates concerning what constitutes a racially and ethnically just society, and what are the appropriate mechanisms with which to achieve it, show little sign of diminishing in intensity.

Most important, however, is that these debates creatively and dramatically be translated into public policies that imaginatively address the racial and ethnic inequalities in American life documented throughout this book. The urgency with which this goal should be considered is reflected in the 1988 report *One-Third of a Nation.* Prepared by a commission co-chaired by former presidents Jimmy Carter and Gerald Ford, the report warned that the future prosperity of the United States was jeopardized by the nation's failures to address the problems confronted by its racial and ethnic minorities.

> *America is moving backward – not forward – in its efforts to achieve the full participation of minority citizens in the life and prosperity of the nation. . . . In education, employment, income, health, longevity, and other basic measures of individual and social well-being, gaps persist – and in some cases are widening – between members of minority groups and the majority population. . . . If we allow these disparities to continue, the United States inevitably will suffer a compromised quality of life and a lower standard of living. . . . In brief, we will find ourselves unable to fulfill the promise of the American dream. (American Council on Education 1988:1)*

The ability of the United States to respond to the challenges posed by its continuing ethnic inequalities will, in large measure, determine the nation's stature in the estimation of the world during the twenty-first century.

Making Sense of Diversity
Recent Research on Hispanic Minorities in the United States

Alejandro Portes
Cynthia G. Truelove

INTRODUCTION

Hispanics are those individuals whose declared ancestors or who themselves were born in Spain or in the Latin American countries. Until recently, this rubric did not exist as a self-designation for most of the groups so labeled; it was essentially a term of convenience for administrative agencies and scholarly researchers. Thus, the first thing to be said about this population is that it is not a consolidated minority, but rather a group-in-formation whose boundaries and self-definitions are still in a state of flux. The emergence of a Hispanic "minority" has so far depended more on actions of government and the collective perceptions of Anglo-American society than on the initiative of the individuals so designated.

The principal reason for the increasing attention gained by this category of people is its rapid growth during the last two decades which is, in turn, a consequence of high fertility rates among some national groups and, more importantly, of accelerated immigration. In addition, the heavy concentration of this population in certain regions of the country has added to its visibility. Over 75% of the 14.5 million people identified by the 1980 Census as Hispanics are concentrated in just four states – California, New York, Texas, and Florida; California alone has absorbed almost one third (U.S. Bureau of the Census 1983a).

The absence of a firm collective self-identity among this population is an outcome of its great diversity, despite the apparent "commonness" of language and culture which figures so prominently in official writings. Under the same label, we find individuals whose ancestors lived in the country at least since the time of independence and others who arrived last year; we find substantial numbers of professionals and entrepreneurs, along with humble farm laborers and unskilled factory workers; there are whites, blacks, mulattoes, and mestizos; there are full-fledged citizens and unauthorized aliens; and finally, among the immigrants, there are those who came in search of employment and a better economic future and those who arrived escaping death squads and political persecution at home.

Aside from divisions between the foreign and the native-born, there is no difference of greater significance among the Spanish-origin population than that of national origin. Nationality does not simply stand for different geographic places of birth; rather it serves as a code word for the very distinct history of each major immigrant flow, a history which molded, in turn, its patterns of entry and adaptation to American society. It is for this reason that the literature produced by "Hispanic" scholars until recently has tended to focus on the origins and evolution of their own national groups rather than to encompass the diverse histories of all those falling under the official rubric.

The bulk of the Spanish-origin population – at least 60% – is of Mexican origin, divided into sizable contingents of native-born Americans and immigrants. Another 14% come from Puerto Rico and are U.S. citizens by birth, regardless of whether they were born in the island or the mainland. The third group in size is made up of Cubans who represent about 5% and who are, overwhelmingly, recent immigrants coming after the consolidation of a communist regime in their country. These are the major groups, but there are, in addition, sizable contingents of Dominicans, Colombians, Salvadoreans, Guatemalans, and other Central and South Americans, each with its own distinct history, characteristics, and patterns of adaptation (Nelson & Tienda 1985, U.S. Bureau of the Census 1983, U.S. Immigration and Naturalization Service 1984).

The complexity of Hispanic ethnicity is a consequence, first of all, of these diverse national origins which lead more often to differences than similarities among the various groups. Lumping them together is not too dissimilar from attempting to combine turn-of-the-century Northern Italian, Hungarian, Serbian, and Bohemian immigrants into a unit based on their "common" origin in various patches of the Austro-Hungarian empire. A second difficulty is that most Spanish-origin groups are not yet "settled," but continue expanding and changing in response to uninterrupted immigration and to close contact with events in the home countries. This dense traffic of people, news, and events between U.S.-based immigrant communities and their not-too-remote place of origin offers a far more challenging landscape than, for example, the condition of European ethnic groups whose boundaries are generally well defined and whose bonds with the original countries are increasingly remote (Glazer 1981, Alba 1985).

THE PRINCIPAL STRANDS
OF THE SOCIOLOGICAL LITERATURE
ON THE HISPANIC POPULATION

This diversity of phenomena under a common label is reflected in the research literature and makes it, in turn, complex and difficult to summarize. To attempt this task with some hope of success, it is necessary to set limits to the discussion that are perforce narrower than those of the topic as a whole. In this essay, we limit ourselves to reviewing the sociological literature, with only passing reference to that coming from other disciplines, and we do so by deliberately focusing greater attention on some specific areas than on others. Since this choice is necessarily arbitrary, it is only fair to present at the start a brief overview of what the sociological literature on Hispanics encompasses at present.

A first general topic fits within the realm of historical sociology, namely the origins and evolution in time of each national group. As mentioned above, we do not have so far a history of Hispanics as such, but rather histories of individual national groups written, more often than not, by scholars of the same minority. Mexicans are the oldest and largest Spanish-speaking minority, and thus it is not surprising that most of this literature deals with the nineteenth and early-twentieth century origins of this group and its subsequent patterns of adaptation. Julian Samora's *Los Mojados: The Wetback Story* (1971), a text which combines historical material with results of contemporary field research, is perhaps the best and best-known in this tradition, but others come close behind, including the early 1970s review volume *The Mexican-American People* by Grebler et al. (1970), the many books on migrant laborers by Ernesto Galarza (1964, 1970, 1977), Mario Barrera's carefully researched *Labor and Class in the Southwest* (1980), and Alfredo Mirandé's recent *The Chicano Experience* (1985). With few exceptions, historical accounts of the Mexican-American population are written from a critical perspective, using as a theoretical framework ideas drawn from dependency, internal colonialism, class conflict, and related approaches.

A similar theoretical bent is apparent in the less abundant literature on Puerto Ricans which features as one of its earliest distinguished contributions C. Wright Mills' *Puerto Rican Journey* (Mills et al. 1950). Puerto Rican scholars in the island have tended to focus on the condition and the peculiar political status of their nation, and thus the literature on the mainland minority has been, by and large, the product of U.S. based scholars. Worthy of mention in this regard are Joseph Fitzpatrick's *Puerto Rican Americans* (1971), Elena Padilla, *Up from Puerto Rico* (1958),

Virginia Sánchez-Korrol, *From Colonia to Community* (1983), recent works by Bonilla & Campos (1981, 1982), and the Center of Puerto Rican Studies' *Labor Migration under Capitalism* (1979). In a more anthropological vein, this migrant community was also the subject of Oscar Lewis' famous *La Vida, a Puerto Rican Family in the Culture of Poverty* (1966).

Historical accounts of the Cuban community are still less common, due no doubt to its recent emergence. The gap is being rapidly filled by such works as Boswell & Curtis' *The Cuban-American Experience* (1984), Jose Llanes' celebratory *Cuban-Americans: Masters of Survival* (1982), and Silvia Pedraza-Bailey's (1985a) historical essay on the post-1959 exodus. Contrary to the critical orientation of most histories of Spanish-origin groups, those relating to Cubans tend to be of the struggle-and-success type, reflecting the distinct origin and present condition of this minority. Other groups are mostly too small or too recent to have acquired their own biographers. Among exceptions worth mentioning are Glen Hendricks' *The Dominican Diaspora* (1974), focused on the history of migration and current situation of this group in the New York area, and Ramiro Cardona & Isabel Cruz's (1980) Spanish-language study of Colombian migration to the United States and return patterns.

A second related strand is the more recent inquiry into determinants of contemporary out-migration. Unlike the historical literature based, for the most part, on secondary sources, the distinguishing trait of this second line of research is original field work in Mexico, Cuba, Puerto Rico, the Dominican Republic, and other sending countries. The principal example is the study initiated by Reichert & Massey (1979, 1980) and completed recently by Massey (1986a, 1987) on determinants of out-migration and return migration from four Mexican communities. A similarly ambitious study on Dominican out-migration by Pessar (1982) and Grasmuck (1984) featured in-depth field research in remote rural areas combined with a large survey of popular neighborhoods in Santiago, the Dominican Republic's second largest city. A somewhat different example is Robert Bach's (1985) insightful analysis of the domestic conditions giving rise to the Mariel exodus of 1980, which is based on personal observation and informant interviews with government officials in Cuba.

These and other studies have done much to dispel prior myths about the origins of migration in economic destitution or individual psychological distress. They have instead consistently supported three themes: first, that the very poor seldom emigrate because they lack the means or the knowledge to undertake such long-distance journeys; second, that the principal causes of migration are rooted in structural contradictions in sending countries reflected, at the individual level, in such situations as underemployment, landlessness, and a growing gap between normative consumption patterns and income; third, that once a migration flow begins, it tends to become self-sustaining through the emergence of strong social networks linking places of origin and destination. (See also Cornelius 1977, Reichert 1981, and Portes & Bach 1985).

A third significant strand of the literature is the study of the demography of the Spanish-origin population, both native and foreign-born, including such aspects as regional distribution, residential segregation, fertility, and rates of intermarriage. Unlike historical studies, demographic research has tended to accept the characterization of this population under a single ethnic label, in part because much of the census data on which it depends is organized in this manner. However, after a number of studies, it has also become clear that differences in population characteristics among groups included under a common term frequently exceed their similarities. Thus, although all Hispanics share a high and increasing urban concentration (U.S. Bureau of the Census 1983c), individual nationalities differ significantly in fertility (Bean et al. 1985), intermarriage rates (Fitzpatrick & Gurak 1979), and residential patterns and segregation (Massey 1981b), Díaz-Briquets & Pérez 1981). The explanation for these differences must be sought in variables other than those generally available in the census public-use tapes. A recent summary study by Bean & Tienda (1987) reviews the existing literature on the demography of Hispanic-Americans within a broad sociological framework that avoids the facile generalization of the past.

The remaining three principal areas of study

are those to which the rest of the chapter are dedicated. They pertain, respectively, to the economic and labor market situation of the different national groups, their language use, and their patterns of political organization and citizenship. These are the areas where recent sociological research has tended to concentrate and are also those where the distinct characteristics and heterogeneity of the Spanish-origin population emerge most clearly.

LABOR MARKET CHARACTERISTICS AND ATTAINMENT

A good part of the literature on this population focuses on comparisons of its labor market performance and general socioeconomic condition with those of other ethnic groups and the U.S. population at large. The sociological literature on these issues has sought to answer three questions: First, are there significant differences in the condition of Hispanic groups both in comparison with the U.S. population and among themselves? Second, are there significant differences in the *process* by which education, occupation, and income are achieved? And this, if there are differences in this process, what are their principal causes?

Table 1 presents a summary of descriptive statistics, drawn from the 1980 census. Aside from age and nativity, included as background information, the rest of the figures indicate that the socioeconomic performance of Hispanics is generally inferior to that of the U.S. population as a whole and, by extension, that of the white non-Hispanic majority. This is true of education, occupation, income, and entrepreneurship (measures by rates of self-employment), although less so of labor force participation especially among females.

The same figures also indicate major disparities among Spanish-origin groups. In general, mainland Puerto Ricans are in the worst socioeconomic situation, a fact manifested by high levels of unemployment, female-headed families, and poverty, and correspondingly low levels of education, occupation, and income. Mexicans occupy an intermediate position, although one consistently below the U.S. population. To be noted is that the size of this group, which represents the

majority of all Hispanics, has a disproportionate weight in aggregate figures that purport to describe the Spanish-origin population as a whole.

A more favorable situation is that of Cubans – whose occupation, family income, and self-employment rates come close to U.S. averages – and of the "Other Spanish" group, which behaves in a similar manner. This last category is a sum of immigrant groups too small to be counted individually, plus those who declared their ancestry as Spanish-origin without further specification. Because of this heterogeneity, it is difficult to provide a meaningful interpretation either of the absolute condition of this category or of the processes that have led to it.

This basic picture of the situation and heterogeneity of the Spanish-origin population is familiar to sociologists working in this field (Nelson & Tienda 1985, Pérez 1986, Pedraza-Bailey 1985b). More interesting is the question of the causal factors that produce the above differences. Here the basic question is whether the condition of a specific minority is explainable entirely on the basis of its background characteristics or whether it is due to other factors. If members of a given group are found to attain socioeconomic positions comparable to native-born Americans with similar human capital endowments, then the observed differences can be imputed to the group's current average levels of education, work experience, and other significant causal variables. If, on the other hand, differences persist after equalizing statistically the minority's background, then other factors must come into play. If the gap is one of disadvantage, discrimination is generally assumed to play a role; if the gap is advantageous to the minority, then collective characteristics of the group are explored in search of a possible explanation.

Several analyses, especially those of educational attainment, tend to support the "no difference, no discrimination" hypothesis. This is the conclusion reached, for example, by Hirschman & Falcón (1985) after a broad-gauged study of educational levels among religio-ethnic groups in the United States. However, these authors also report that, after controlling for all possible relevant predictors, the Mexican educational attainment still falls 1.4 years below the norm.

Similarly, in a study of occupational attain-

TABLE 1   *Selected Characteristics of Spanish-Origin Groups, 1980*

Variable	Mexicans	Puerto Ricans	Cubans	Other Spanish	Total
Number – millions	8.7	2.0	0.8	3.1	226.5
Median age	21.9	22.3	37.7	25.5	30.0
Percent native born	74.0	96.9	22.1	60.5	93.8
Percent female headed families	16.4	35.3	14.9	20.5	14.3
Median years of school completed[a]	9.6	10.5	12.2	12.3	12.5
Percent high school graduates[a]	37.6	40.1	55.3	57.4	66.5
Percent with 4 + years of college[a]	4.9	5.6	16.2	12.4	16.2
Percent in labor force[b]	64.6	54.9	66.0	64.6	62.0
Percent females in labor force[b]	49.0	40.1	55.4	53.4	49.9
Percent married women in labor force[c]	42.5	38.9	50.5	45.7	43.9
Percent self-employed[d]	3.5	2.2	5.8	4.5	6.8
Percent unemployed	9.1	11.7	6.0	8.0	6.5
Percent professional specialty, executive, and managerial occupations – males	11.4	14.1	22.0	19.0	25.8
females[d]	12.6	15.5	17.9	17.2	24.7
Percent operators and laborers – males	30.4	30.9	23.1	23.8	18.3
females[d]	22.0	25.5	24.2	19.9	11.7
Median family income	14,765	10,734	18,245	16,230	19,917
Median income of married couples with own children	14,855	13,428	20,334	16,708	19,630
Percent of families with incomes of $50,000 +	1.8	1.0	5.2	3.6	5.6
Percent of all families below poverty level	20.6	34.9	11.7	16.7	9.6

Source: U.S. Bureau of the Census 1983a: Tables 39, 48, 70; 1983b: Tables 141, 166–171.

[a]Persons 25 years of age or older.

[b]Persons 16 years of age or older.

[c]Women 16 years of age or older; husband present and own children under 6 years of age.

[d]Employed persons 16 years of age or older.

ment based on the 1976 Survey of Income and Education (SIE), Stolzenberg (1982) concludes that the causal process is essentially the same among all Spanish-origin groups and that, after standardizing individual background characteristics, no evidence of Spanish-origin ethnic group net effects remains. However, Stolzenberg includes in the analysis a series of state dummy variables in order to control for the possible confounding of geographic location and ethnicity. What he does, of course, is to insure a priori that ethnic differences would be insignificant because of the high concentration of particular groups in certain states. Including "Florida" as a causal predictor, for example, pretty much eliminates the distinct effect of Cuban ethnicity since this group has chosen to concentrate in that state; the same is true for New York and the Puerto Ricans.

Even with state dummies included, significant ethnic effects on occupational attainment remain in Stolzenberg's analysis of the Mexican and Cuban groups. The Mexican coefficient is negative, indicating lower occupational levels than those expected on the basis of the group's average characteristics; the Cuban effect is, however, positive, indicating above-average attainment, and this becomes much stronger when state controls are deleted. A subsequent and more carefully specified analysis of SEI wage data by Reimers (1985) yields similar conclusions. After controlling for selection bias and human capital predictors, Reimers finds that male Puerto Rican wage levels fall 18% below the average for white non-Hispanic men; those of Mexicans and other Hispanics are 6% and 12% below, respectively. These sizable differences are interpreted as evidence of labor market discrimination. Cuban men, however, receive wages 6% *above* white non-Hispanics of similar human capital endowment. These differences lead the author to conclude: "The major Hispanic-American groups differ so much among themselves . . . that it makes little sense to lump them under a single "Hispanic" or "minority" rubric for either analysis or policy treatment" (Reimers 1985:55).

This basic conclusion is supported by studies based on different and more recent data sets which also tend to replicate the finding of significant disadvantages in occupational and earnings attainment for Mexicans and, in particular, Puerto Ricans and a small but consistent advantage for Cubans, relative to their human capital levels (Nelson & Tienda 1985, Pérez 1986, Jasso & Rosenzweig 1985: Table 4).

These differences lead naturally to the more sociologically intriguing question of their possible cause. The argument that there is discrimination in the labor market will not do because such explanation does not clarify why discrimination operates differentially among presumably similar groups and not at all in certain cases. Thus, there is no alternative but to dig into the particular characteristics and history of each group in search of suitable answers. To do this, we must abandon not only the general label "Hispanic," but also leave behind the residual category "Other Spanish." This is necessary not because of lack of substantive importance of the groups that form it, but because the category is itself too heterogeneous to permit a valid summary explanation. Left are the three major Spanish-origin groups – Mexicans, Puerto Ricans, and Cubans.

When comparing the socioeconomic performance of these groups, two major riddles emerge: First, why is it that Mexicans and Puerto Ricans differ so significantly in such characteristics as labor force participation, family structure, and poverty as well as in levels of wage discrimination. Second, why is it that Cubans register above-average occupations and family incomes relative to their levels of human capital. The below-average socioeconomic condition of the first two groups is *not* itself a riddle since the historical literature above has fully clarified the roots of exploitation and labor market discrimination in both cases. What historical accounts do not explain is why the present condition of these groups should be so markedly different. Similarly, the absolute advantage of Cubans relative to other Spanish-origin groups is not mysterious since it is well known that this minority was formed, to a large extent, by the arrival of upper and middle-class persons who left Cuba after the advent of the Castro Revolution. The riddle in this case is why the collective attainment of Cubans should exceed, at times, what can be expected on the basis of their average human capital endowment.

A fairly common explanation of the latter result is that Cubans were welcomed in the United States as refugees from a communist regime and thus received significant government aid denied to other groups. This explanation is mentioned in passing by Jasso & Rosenzweig (1985:18), among other authors, and is vigorously defended by Pedraza-Bailey (1985b) in her comparative study of Cuban and Mexican immigrants. However, this interpretation runs immediately against evidence from other refugee groups who have received equal or more generous federal benefits than Cubans, but whose socioeconomic condition is more precarious. Southeast Asian refugees, for example, benefited from the extensive aid provisions mandated by the 1980 Refugee Act, more comprehensive and generous than those made available to Cubans during the sixties; however, levels of unemployment, poverty, and welfare dependence among most Southeast Asian groups continue to exceed those of almost every other ethnic minority (Tienda & Jensen 1985, Bach et al. 1984).

The favorable governmental reception of Cubans in the United States is certainly a factor contributing to their adaptation, but it must be seen as part of a complex which may be labelled the distinct *mode of incorporation* of each immigrant minority. This alternative interpretation says that the condition of each group is a function both of average individual characteristics and of the social and economic context in which its successive cohorts are received. A sociological explanation to the above riddles is found in the distinct models of incorporation of the three major Spanish-origin groups.

Mexican immigrants and new Mexican-American entrants into the labor force tend to come from modest socioeconomic origins and have low average levels of education. In addition, however, they enter labor markets in the Southwest and Midwest where Mexican laborers have traditionally supplied the bulk of unskilled labor. Social networks within the ethnic community tend to direct new workers toward jobs similar to their co-ethnics, a pattern reinforced by the orientation of employers. Lacking a coherent entrepreneurial community of their own or effective political representation, Mexican wage workers are thus thrown back onto their own individual resources, "discounted" by past history and present discrimination against their group (Barrera 1980, Nelson & Tienda 1985). Because many Mexican workers are immigrants and a substantial proportion are undocumented (Passel 1985; Bean et al. 1983, 1986; Browning & Rodríguez 1985), they continue to be seen by many employers as a valuable source of low-wage pliable labor. This employer "preference," which may account for the relatively low average rates of Mexican unemployment, creates simultaneous barriers for those with upward mobility aspirations.

Puerto Rican immigrants fulfilled a similar function for industry and agriculture in the Northeast during an earlier period, but with two significant differences. First, they entered labor markets which, unlike those of the Southwest, were highly unionized. Second, they were U.S. citizens by birth and thus entitled to legal protection and not subject to ready deportation as were many Mexicans. These two factors combined over time to make Puerto Rican workers a less pliable, more costly, and better organized source of labor. Employer preferences in the Northeast thus shifted gradually toward other immigrant groups—West Indian contract workers in agricul-

ture (DeWind et al. 1977; Wood 1984) and Dominican, Colombian, and other mostly undocumented immigrants in urban industry and services (Sassen-Koob 1979, 1980; Glaessel-Brown 1985; Waldinger 1985). Lacking an entrepreneurial community to generate their own jobs and shunted aside by new pools of "preferred" immigrant labor in the open market, Puerto Ricans in the mainland confronted a difficult economic situation. Record numbers have migrated back to the Island during the last two decades, while those remaining in the Northeast continue to experience levels of unemployment and poverty comparable only to those of the black population (Bean & Tienda 1987: Ch. 1, Centro de Estudios Puertorriqueños 1979).

The Cuban pattern of adaptation is different because the first immigrant cohorts created an economically favorable context of reception for subsequent arrivals. This was due to the fact that the bulk of early Cuban migration was composed of displaced numbers of the native bourgeoisie rather than laborers (Pérez 1986). These refugees brought the capital and entrepreneurial skills with which to start new businesses after an early period of adaptation. Ensuing middle-class waves followed a similar course, leading eventually to the consolidation of an enclave economy in South Florida. The characteristics of the Cuban enclave have been described at length in the sociological literature (Wilson & Portes 1980, Portes & Manning 1986, Wilson & Martin 1982). The strong entrepreneurial orientation of the earlier Cuban cohorts is illustrated by census figures on minority-business ownership, presented in Table 2.

In 1977, when these data were collected, black- and Mexican-owned businesses were the most numerous in absolute terms, reflecting the size of the respective populations. In per capita terms, however, Cuban-owned firms were by far the most numerous and the largest both in terms of receipts and number of employees. Figures in the bottom rows of Table 2 suggest that the relative weight of Miami Cuban firms among Hispanic-owned businesses has continued to grow since 1977. By 1984, five of the ten largest Hispanic-owned firms in the country and four of the ten largest banks were part of the Cuban enclave, at a time when this group represented barely 5% of the Spanish-origin population.

TABLE 2 *Spanish-Origin and Black-Owned Firms in the United States.*

Variable	Mexicans	Puerto Ricans	Cubans	All Spanish	Black
Number of firms, 1977	116,419	13,491	30,336	219,355	231,203
Firms per 100,000 population	1,468	740	3,651	1,890	873
Average gross receipts per firm ($1000)	44.4	43.9	61.6	47.5	37.4
Firms with paid employees, 1977	22,718	1,767	5,588	41,298	39,968
Firms with employees per 100,000 population	286	97	672	356	151
Average employees per firm	4.9	3.9	6.6	5.0	4.1
Average gross receipts per firm with employees ($1000)	150.4	191.9	254.9	172.9	160.1
Ten largest Hispanic industrial firms, 1984:					
Percent located in area of group's concentration[a]	40	10	50	100	NA
Estimated sales ($1,000,000)	402	273	821	2,317	NA
Number of employees	5,800	1,100	3,175	10,075	NA
Ten largest Hispanic-owned banks and savings banks, 1984:					
Percent in area of group's concentration[a]	40	20	40	100	NA
Total assets ($1,000,000)	1,204	489	934	2,627	NA
Total deposits ($1,000,000)	1,102	434	844	2,380	NA

Sources: Bureau of the Census (1980); *Hispanic Review of Business* (1985).

[a]Southwest locations for Mexicans; New York and vicinity for Puerto Ricans; Miami metropolitan area for Cubans.

For our purposes, the significance of an enclave mode of incorporation is that it helps to explain how successive cohorts of Cuban immigrants have been able to make use of past human capital endowment and to exceed at times their expected level of attainment. Employment in enclave firms has two principal advantages for new arrivals: First, it allows many to put to use their occupational skills and experience without having to wait for a long period of cultural adaptation. Second, it creates opportunities for upward mobility either within existing firms or through self-employment. The bond between co-ethnic employers and employees helps fledgling immigrant enterprises survive by taking advantage of the cheap and generally disciplined labor of the new arrivals. The latter benefit over the long term, however, by availing themselves within the enclave of mobility chances that are generally absent in outside employment.

A longitudinal study of Cuban and Mexican immigrants conducted during the 1970s provides an illustration of different patterns of adaptation, conditioned by the presence or absence of an enclave mode of incorporation. By the early 1970s, the middle-class emigration from Cuba had ceased, and new arrivals came from more modest socioeconomic origins, comparable to those of Mexican legal immigrants. The study interviewed samples of Cuban refugees and Mexican legal immigrants at the time of their arrival during 1973–1974. The study followed both samples for six years, interviewing respondents twice during that interval. Results of the study have been reported at length elsewhere (Portes & Bach 1985). Table 3 presents data from the last follow-

TABLE 3 *The Socioeconomic Position of Cuban and Mexican Immigrants after Six Years in the United States*

Variable	Mexicans (N = 455)	Cubans (N = 413)
Percent in city of principal concentration	23.7	97.2
Percent who speak English well	27.4	23.7
Percent home owners	40.2	40.0
Percent self-employed	5.4	21.2
Percent employed by other Mexicans/Cubans	14.6	36.3
Average monthly income[a]	$ 912	$1057
Average monthly income of employees in large Anglo-owned firms[a]	$1003	$1016
Average monthly income in small nonenclave firms[a]	$ 880	$ 952
Average monthly income in enclave firms[a]	NA	$1111
Average monthly income of the self-employed, Cubans[a]	NA	$1495

Source: Portes & Bach 1985: Chs. 6–7.

[a] 1979 dollars

up survey, which took place in 1979–1980. The first finding of note is the degree of concentration of Cuban respondents, 97% of whom remained in the Miami metropolitan area. By comparison, the Mexican sample dispersed throughout the Southwest and Midwest, with the largest concentration – 24% – settling in the border city of El Paso.

Otherwise, samples were similar in their knowledge of English – low for both groups after six years – and their rates of home ownership. They differed sharply, however, in variables relating to their labor market position. More than a third of 1973 Cuban arrivals were employed by co-ethnic firms in 1979, and one fifth had become self-employed by that time; these figures double and quadruple the respective percentages in the Mexican sample. Despite their concentration in a low-wage region of the United States, the Cuban average monthly income after six years was significantly greater than that among Mexicans.

However, a closer look at the data shows that there were no major differences in income among those employed in large Anglo-owned firms, commonly identified as part of the "primary" labor market. Nor were there significant income differences among those employed in the smaller firms identified with the "secondary" sector; in both samples, these incomes were much

lower than among primary sector employees. The significant difference between Cuban and Mexican immigrants in the study lies with the large proportion of the former employed in enclave firms where their average income was actually the highest of those in both samples. In addition, Cuban immigrants who had become self-employed exceeded the combined monthly income of both samples by approximately $500 or one half of the total average.

No comparable empirical evidence at present supports the mode-of-incorporation hypothesis as an explanation of the observed occupational and income differences among Mexicans and Puerto Ricans. This is due to the scarcity of comparative studies between Puerto Rican patterns of attainment and those of other minorities. (For a recent exception, see Tienda & Lee 1986.) The available information points, however, to the gradual displacement of Puerto Ricans by newer immigrant groups as sources of low-wage labor for agricultural and urban employers in the Northeast (DeWind et al. 1977, Glaessel-Brown 1985). This evidence is congruent with the interpretation of the current situation of one group – Mexicans – as an outcome of its continued incorporation as a preferred source of low-wage labor in the Southwest and Midwest and with that of the other – Puerto Ricans – as a consequence of its increasing redundancy for the same labor market in its principal area of concentration.

KNOWLEDGE OF ENGLISH

In this section, we consider some evidence concerning language use among different Spanish-origin groups. According to the 1980 Census, roughly half of the population of the United States who spoke a language other than English spoke Spanish. The absolute number, 11.5 million, would make the United States one of the largest Spanish-speaking countries in the world although, as with the Spanish-origin population itself, use of the language tends to be highly concentrated in a few states – California, Texas, New York, and Florida. The highest state concentration, however, is in New Mexico where close to one-third of the population retains use of the language (Moore & Pachón 1985:119–122).

The data in Table 4 indicate that the major gap in English proficiency is between the native and the foreign-born. Over 90% of native-born Hispanics reported speaking English well, the figure being essentially invariant across major national groups. The proportion among the foreign-born varies however, between one-half and two-thirds of the respective populations. Note that, because the overwhelming majority of Cubans are foreign-born, the total proportion of this group who reported speaking English well is actually much lower than among the other minorities.

Despite an apparently rapid language assimilation after the first or immigrant generation, there is evidence that self-reports of English proficiency are often exaggerated relative to actual knowledge and that language difficulties are not limited to the foreign-born. According to Moore & Pachón (1985:119), four out of five Hispanics reporting difficulties with English were U.S. citizens. This result is, in part, a consequence of the predominance of the native-born in this population, but this suggests that the process of language acquisition is less than straightforward.

These conclusions are supported by results displayed in the middle rows of Table 4, drawn from the longitudinal study of Cuban and Mexican immigrants described above. The data show that levels of English knowledge, as measured by an objective index, changed remarkably little over the six years of the study and were almost as low in 1979 as at the time of arrival in 1973.[1] In addition, self-reports of English competence were much higher than actual performance, a result which casts some doubt on the validity of Census reports, based on subjective evaluations. Similar results, reported in the following rows of the table, were obtained in a survey of 1980 Cuban (Mariel) refugees after three years of U.S. residence.

Although it is almost certain that linguistic assimilation will occur over the long run, the resilience of Spanish over time and the apparent difficulty for many immigrants in learning English even after a substantial period of residence in the country is noteworthy. Three factors seem to play a central role in producing these results. First, the generally low levels of education among most Spanish-origin immigrants tend to make acquisition of new language more difficult. Second, continuing immigration and the ebb-and-flow pattern occurs between countries of origin and U.S. communities of destination (Moore & Pachón 1985:121, Browning & Rodríguez 1985, Massey 1987). Third, the tendency of Spanish-origin groups to concentrate in certain geographic areas and of new immigrants to move into them also lessens the need to learn English for everyday living. The particular characteristics of the Cuban enclave in Miami make it possible for new arrivals to live and work within the confines of the ethnic community, a pattern which significantly contributes to the low levels of English acquisition reported above. Other groups, however, also tend to concentrate in their own neighborhoods; this eases the process of adaptation of newcomers but slows their language learning.[2]

Adaptation studies of immigrants and second-generation natives generally report high levels of satisfaction with life in the United States and commitment to remain in the country. Spanish-origin groups are no exception (Rogg & Cooney 1980, Cardona & Cruz 1980, Browning & Rodríguez 1985). Among immigrants, there is a consistent correlation between length of time in the United States and plans to stay permanently – recent immigrants are more likely to voice return plans, but the proportion of would-be returnees drops rapidly with time (Massey 1986b, Gras-

TABLE 4 *Self-Reports and Objective Measures of English Knowledge*

Variable	Cubans		Mexicans		Puerto Ricans	
	Native	Foreign-Born	Native	Foreign-Born	Born in Mainland	Born in Puerto Rico
Percent who report speaking English well, 1980[a]	94.3 (3,503)[b]	58.0 (29,888)	92.6 (177,149)	45.4 (93,422)	96.1 (19,078)	69.5 (43,677)
Percent who report speaking English well—immigrants, 1979[c]		38.3 (413)		46.2 (452)		
Percent scoring high in knowledge of English Index, 1979[c]		16.0		17.3		
1973		12.3 (590)		14.5 (822)		
Percent who report speaking English well—Mariel entrants, 1983[d]		33.7 (558)				
Percent scoring high in knowledge of English Index, 1983[d]		22.6				

	Cuban Immigrants[c]		Mexican Immigrants[c]	
	1976	1979	1976	1979
Percent satisfied with their present lives	(427)	(413)	(439)	(454)
	81.3	93.7	79.1	78.8
Percent planning to stay permanently in the U.S.	88.5	95.9	85.2	88.3
Major adaption difficulties experienced in the United States, percent:[e]				
Lack of English	42.3	49.1	43.9	28.7
Unemployment, low wages, etc.	29.4	20.1	30.6	39.6
Customs, cultural adaption	10.2	6.2	11.0	9.6
Family problems	3.0	3.3	4.2	4.7
Health problems	10.5	17.0	6.1	8.2
Other	4.6	4.3	4.2	9.2

Sources: Nelson & Tienda 1985: Table 1; Portes & Stepick 1985: Table 4; authors' tablulations.

[a]Data from 5 percent Public Use Sample, 1980 Census.

[b]Sample sizes in parentheses.

[c]1973–1979 longitudinal study of Cuban and Mexican Immigrants.

[d]Survey of 1980 (Mariel) Cuban Refugees settled in the Miami Metropolitan area.

[e]Respondents indicating at least one major problem.

muck 1984, Portes & Bach 1985:273). The bottom rows of Table 4 provide illustrative evidence of these trends. Note, however, that next to the predictable economic difficulties, the principal problem reported by Cuban and Mexican immigrants is lack of knowledge of English. Language problems were the adaptation difficulty mentioned most frequently by both groups after three years in the United States, and this continued to be the modal response among Cuban refugees after six years. Hence, despite the protection and comfort offered by the ethnic community, recent immigrants are subjectively aware of the impairment created in their lives by lack of fluency in the language of the surrounding society.

POLITICAL BEHAVIOR AND CITIZENSHIP

Differences between Spanish-origin groups are again highlighted by their political concerns, organization, and effectiveness. Regardless of national origin, a major gap separates the native-born—whose interests are always tied to their situation in the United States—and immigrants—whose political allegiance and organized actions often relate to events in the country of origin. The political sociology of Hispanic-Americans can thus be conveniently summarized under two main topical categories: first, the goals and actions of established groups, including the native-born and naturalized citizens; and second, the political orientations and, in particular, the problematic shift of nationality among immigrants.

Ethnic Politics

Moore & Pachón (1985: Ch. 10) provide a lucid summary of the politics of major Spanish-origin groups. Their overview can be supplemented by studies of Mexican-Americans by Camarillo (1979), Barrera (1980), Murguía (1975), and de la Garza & Flores (1986); of Puerto Ricans by Falcón (1983), Bonilla & Campos (1981), and Glazer & Moynihan (1963); and of Cubans by Boswell & Curtis (1984), Llanes (1982), and Fagen et al. (1968).

The political history of Mexican-Americans bears considerable resemblance to that of American blacks, both in their earlier subordination and disenfranchisement and in subsequent attempts to dilute their electoral power through such devices as literacy tests, gerrymandering, and co-optation of ethnic leaders. The two groups are also similar in their contemporary reactions to past discrimination. Mexican-Americans differ from black Americans, however, in one crucial respect, namely their proximity to and strong identification with the country of origin. Attachment to Mexico and Mexican culture is strongly correlated with a sense of "foreignness," even among the native-born and, hence, with lower rates of political participation (García 1981). This reluctance to shift national allegiances appears to have represented one of the main obstacles in the path of effective organizing by Mexican-American leaders.

Despite these obstacles, a number of organizations did emerge which articulated the interests of one or another segment of the minority. These ranged from the earlier *mutualistas* and the *Orden de Hijos de América* to the subsequent League of United Latin American Citizens (LULAC) and the GI Forum, created to defend the interests of Mexican-American World War II veterans (Moore & Pachón 1985:176–86). The 1960s marked a turning point in Mexican-American politics. Inspired in large part by the black example, a number of militant organizations emerged that attempted to redress past grievances by means other than participation in the established parties. A number of radical student and youth organizations were created and a third party, La Raza Unida, won a series of significant electoral victories in Texas.

Although the more militant demands of these organizations were never met and most of them have ceased to exist, the organizations succeeded where more conventional tactics had failed in the past: in mobilizing the Mexican-American population and creating a cadre of politicians who could forcefully defend its interests before national leaders and institutions. Today, the still-existing LULAC and MALDEF (the Mexican-American Legal Defense Fund) are among the most powerful and active Hispanic organizations. By 1984, 10 out of 11 members of the Hispanic Caucus in Congress represented districts with a heavy Mexican-American population (Roybal 1984).

Unlike Mexicans, Puerto Ricans are U.S. citizens by birth and thus do not face the obstacle to political participation posed by naturalization proceedings. In addition, the Puerto Rican migrant population is concentrated in New York, a city and state with a long tradition of ethnic politics. A number of factors have conspired, however, to reduce the political weight of this population over the years. These include lack of knowledge of English, generally low levels of education and occupation among the migrants, and the resistance of established political "clubs" – in the hands of Jews, Italians, and other older immigrants – to admitting Puerto Ricans. In addition, the strong sojourner orientation of many migrants has reduced their interest in and attention to local politics. For many years, Puerto Rican activism on the mainland was targeted on demands for improvements in the economic and political status of the Island rather than of the New York community (Falcón 1983, Jennings 1977).

Although concern for the welfare of Puerto Rico has not been abandoned, events and needs of the mainland communities gradually gained priority during the post-World War II period. Puerto Rican politics paralleled the course followed by Mexicans and blacks during the 1960s. Militant youth organizations like the Young Lords and the Puerto Rican Revolutionary Workers' Organization made their appearance. Significant advances in mainstream politics occurred when a number of Puerto Ricans won local and state offices. Like Mexicans, Puerto Ricans vote overwhelmingly Democratic. By 1982, there were six Puerto Rican state legislators in New York, and a joint Black and Puerto Rican Caucus had been established. During the 1970s, Puerto Ricans also elected their first state senator and first congressman. At present, Congressman Robert García, elected by the Bronx (18th) District, is the eleventh member of the Hispanic Caucus in the U.S. House and still the sole Puerto Rican representative.

Two other congressional districts in New York City and two in the New Jersey suburbs have concentrations of Hispanic population that would make the election of additional Puerto Rican legislators viable (Moore & Pachón 1985:186–90). This will depend, however, on increasing the levels of registration and voting among Puerto Ricans and on securing the support of naturalized immigrants from other Latin American countries who – like Colombians and Dominicans – compose an increasing proportion of the area's population.

Like Mexicans, first-generation Cuban immigrants face the riddle of naturalization and, like Puerto Ricans, they tend to remain preoccupied with events in their country. Like both groups, Cubans generally speak little English on arrival, and this also conspires against effective participation. Despite these obstacles, Cuban-Americans have become a potent political force in South Florida. The mayors of the largest cities in the area – Miami and Hialeah – are Cuban, as are those of several smaller municipalities, and so are numerous city and county commissioners. Cuban-Americans are influential in the local Republican party and have elected a substantial delegation to the state legislature. Observers agree that it is only a matter of time before this community sends its first representative to Congress from Florida's 17th and 18th districts. Meanwhile, a political action group funded by exiled businessmen – the Cuban-American National Foundation – has lobbied effectively in Washington for such causes as the creation of Radio Marti and the appointment of Cubans to federal offices (Botifoll 1984, Boswell & Curtis 1984: Ch. 10, Petersen & Maidique 1986).

Until the mid-1960s, the attention of Cuban refugees was riveted on the Island and the hope of return after the overthrow of the Castro regime. Two major events reduced these hopes: first, the defeat of the Bay of Pigs invasion in 1961, and second, the U.S.-U.S.S.R. agreement of 1962 which removed Soviet missiles from Cuba in exchange for an American pledge to prevent the refugees from launching new military attacks. Both events took place under the Kennedy Administration, and Cubans have blamed the Democrats for them ever since. As hopes for return became dimmer and the refugee community turned its attention inwards, Cubans naturalized in record numbers and lined solidly behind the Republican Party. With their support, Republicans – a minor force in Florida politics before that time – have become an increasingly serious power contender (Nazario 1983).

There are recent indications, however, that the monolithic conservatism of the Cuban vote may be more apparent than real. It is true that

Cubans overwhelmingly supported President Reagan and other Republican candidates for national office in 1980 and 1984; it is also true that they continue to oppose, almost to a man, any foreign policy initiative perceived as "soft" on Communism. However, the vote in local elections has become more progressive and more likely to be guided by local concerns and issues. For example, during the last mayoral election in Miami, the Republican candidate finished a distant last. The final race was between two Cuban-Americans—a conservative banker supported by the Latin and Anglo business communities and a more progressive Harvard-trained lawyer. The latter won handily, primarily because of the support of the Cuban grassroots vote. Similarly, there are indications that Cuban representatives in the state legislature tend to be more concerned with populist issues, especially those involving ethnic minorities, than are fellow Republicans.[3]

An important topic for future research is the apparent trend toward convergence of the political organizations representing major Spanish-origin groups. As seen above, there is little similarity in historical origins or present socio-economic situation among these groups. There is, however, the realization among certain political leaders of a basic communality of interests (in such issues as the defense of bilingualism and a common cultural image) and of the significance of strength in numbers. Thus, if the term "Hispanic" means anything of substance at present, it is at the political level. An indication of this trend is the emergence of the National Association of Latin Elected Officials (NALEO), a strong organization which groups Mexican, Puerto Rican, and Cuban congressmen, state legislators, and mayors (Moore & Pachón 1985:194–98).

Citizenship

The first step for effective political participation by any immigrant group is acquisition of citizenship. Table 5 presents data showing how different the rates of naturalization have been among the foreign-born in recent years. During the 1970s, naturalized Mexican immigrants represented only 6% of the total, despite the sizable potential pool of eligible individuals—the largest among all nationalities, representing close to 20% of all legal admissions during the preceding de-

cade. By contrast, Cuban immigrants—a much smaller group—contributed 12% of all naturalizations, exceeding the figure for Canada despite the much larger number of eligible Canadian immigrants. The rest of Latin America contributed only 3%, but this is due to the relative small size of the cohorts of legal immigrants from the region before the 1970s.

The remaining columns of the table present data for the 1970 immigrant cohort that are representative of trends during recent years. Highest rates of naturalization correspond to Asian immigrants—mostly Chinese, Indians, South Koreans, and Filipinos—and to Cubans. Citizenship acquisition among these groups represented close to half of the legal admissions from the respective source countries in 1970. Intermediate rates—close to a fifth of the immigrant cohort at the beginning of the period—are found among West Europeans and Central and South Americans. The lowest rates, less than 7%, correspond to immigrants from the two contiguous countries: Mexico and Canada. Mexican immigrants are also the slowest to naturalize, as indicated by their peak year of naturalizations during the decade—the ninth—or two full years behind the norm for all countries (Warren 1979, Portes & Mozo 1985).

The analytical literature on determinants of these differences comprises two separate strands: First, there are studies that attempt to explain variation among nationalities, and second, there are those that focus on proximate causes within a particular group. A pioneer contributor to the first or comparative literature was Bernard (1936), who identified literacy, education, and occupational prestige as major causes of differences in rates of naturalization between "old" and "new" European immigrants, as defined at that time. Subsequent studies have generally supported Bernard's hypothesis.[4]

In addition, more recent quantitative studies have identified other variables, such as the political origin of migration and the geographical proximity of the country of origin as causally significant. Refugees from communist-controlled countries naturalize in greater numbers, other things being equal, than do regular immigrants. Those from nearby countries, especially those nations that share land borders with the United

TABLE 5 *U.S. Citizenship Acquisition for Selected Countries and Regions, 1970–1980*

	Naturalized 1971–1980	Percent of Total	Cohort of 1970[b]	Naturalized during Next Decade	Percent of Cohort	Peak Year during Decade[c]
Cuba	178,374	12	16,334	7,621	47	8th (2444)
Mexico	68,152	5	44,469	1,475	3	9th (404)
Central and South America	40,843	3	31,316	6,161	20	9th (1480)
Canada	130,380	9	13,804	856	6	8th (182)
West Europe	371,683	25	92,433	17,965	19	7th (5103)
Asia	473,754	32	92,816	44,554	48	7th (15129)
Totals[a]	1,464,772		373,326	94,532	25	7th (27681)

Source: U.S. Immigration and Naturalization Service, *Annual Reports*, various years.

[a]All countries. Column figures do not add up to row total because of exclusion of other world regions – Africa, Eastern Europe, and Oceania.

[b]Number of immigrants admitted for legal permanent residence.

[c]Year of most numerous naturalizations during the decade after legal entry. Actual number naturalized in parentheses.

417

States, tend to resist citizenship change more than others. Both results seem to reflect the operation of a more general factor, which may be labelled the potential "reversibility" of migration: Immigrants for whom it is more difficult to return because of political conditions at home or the high cost and difficulty of the journey tend to naturalize at higher rates than those for whom return is but a simple bus ride away (Jasso & Rosenzweig 1985, Portes & Mozo 1985).

Studies of proximate determinants of citizenship have generally focused on those specific minorities with the lowest propensities to naturalize. Mexican immigrants are notorious in this respect; their collective behavior has given rise to a huge gap between the pool of potentially eligible citizens (and voters) and its actual size. Accordingly, several recent studies have sought to identify the principal determinants within the Mexican immigrant population of both predispositions and behaviors with respect to adopting U.S. citizenship. This research comprises both quantitative analyses (García 1981, Grebler 1966) and ethnographic observations (Alvarez 1985, Fernández 1984, North 1985, Cornelius 1981). Several studies have noted a correlation between social psychological variables, such as self-identity as a Mexican, attitudes toward U.S. society, and hopes of returning to Mexico with plans for naturalization. With few exceptions, however, these results are based on cross-sectional data, and hence, it is not possible to determine whether these subjective orientations play a causal role in individual decisionmaking or whether they are simply post-factum rationalizations.

Studies that focus on more objective variables have identified such characteristics as length of U.S. residence, level of education, knowledge of English, age, marital status, citizenship of the spouse, and place of residence as potentially significant. In general, propensity to naturalize emerges from these studies as an outcome of a complex of determinants that include: (a) individual needs and motivations, (b) knowledge and ability, and (c) facilitational factors. Those Mexican immigrants whose stake in America is limited to a low wage job intended to support a family or future investments in Mexico have little motivation to obtain U.S. citizenship. Those, on the other hand, who have acquired property, whose spouses or children are U.S. citizens, and who begin to feel barriers to upward mobility because of their legal status have much greater incentive to initiate the process (Alvarez 1985, Portes & Curtis 1986).

Motivation is not enough, however, because citizenship acquisition is not an easy task. For most immigrants, it requires knowledge of English and some knowledge of U.S. civics in order to pass the naturalization test. Thus, better educated immigrants, those who have lived in the country longer and are more informed about it, tend to face fewer obstacles than do the others. Finally, there is the question of external facilitation. Two factors play the most significant roles in this respect: social networks and the conduct of official agencies in charge of the process. Networks limited to Mexican kin and friends tend to be unsupportive of the naturalization process (García 1981, Fernández 1984), while those that include U.S.-born or U.S.-naturalized relatives and friends may facilitate it.

The key governmental agency involved in this process is the U.S. Immigration and Naturalization Service (INS), and its behavior toward applicants has been found decidedly mixed. Ethnographic research has identified "fear of the INS" as a significant deterrent of naturalization among Mexican immigrants (Alvarez 1985). In *The Long Gray Welcome,* an in-depth study of the agency's naturalization procedures, North (1985) outlines the numerous obstacles—from heavy backlogs to arbitrary examiners—often thrown in the way of poor and little-educated immigrants. Confronted with such barriers, the appropriate question may not be why so few Mexicans naturalize, but why so many decide to and succeed in doing so.

CONCLUSION

Unlike research on European ethnic minorities, where the topic of interest is increasingly historical in orientation, the study of Spanish-origin groups involves very contemporary issues which are likely to persist and gain relevance in the future. An important question is whether the label "Hispanic" itself will endure. As seen above, political leaders from various groups have started to cooperate, at least in a limited manner, in the pursuit of common interests. In addition, governmental, journalistic, and academic use of the term will reinforce its currency. On the other hand, the economic and social conditions of the groups so labelled appear to be evolving in increasingly separate and distinct ways. In addition to differentiation among the major groups discussed above, others – such as Dominicans, Colombians, and Salvadoreans – are growing rapidly and will surely add to the overall complexity of the picture. Whatever the fate of the general term of reference, research on Spanish-origin minorities is likely to become more nuanced and sophisticated as scholars learn to appreciate the distinct identity and economic situation of each and as new groups are targeted for study.

This review of the sociological literature has been neither exhaustive nor representative of all substantive concerns. Readers interested in a more extensive discussion may consult a number of recent book-length summaries including Moore & Pachón's *Hispanics in the United States* (1985) and the demographically oriented but highly readable study, *The Hispanic Population of the United States* by Bean & Tienda (1987). Nevertheless, themes touched in the limited space of this chapter – modes of labor market incorporation and their consequences; language acquisition; naturalization and political participation – are likely to remain central ones for these ethnic minorities and for the roles which, individually and collectively, they will play in American society.

ENDNOTES

1. This measure – the knowledge of English Index (KEI) – consists of translations to nine words and phrases at elementary and junior high school levels of comprehension. Factor analysis performed on each sample at each point of time indicated consistently unidimensional structure. Internal consistency reliability, as measured by Cronbach's alpha, exceeded .90 in every survey.

2. Of Mexican immigrants interviewed in 1979 for the longitudinal study described above, 70% concentrated in central-city areas and almost the same proportion – 66% – reported that their neighborhood was predominantly Mexican or Mexican-American. Thus, the ethnic *barrio* was the place of residence for a majority of this immigrant sample, not only at arrival but after six years of U.S. residence.

3. Unpublished material from authors' interviews with community leaders in Miami during 1985. See also Portes (1984).

4. The single exception – a study by Barkan & Khoklov (1980) which specifically addresses Bernard's model – is based on a questionable operationalization of variables and a faulty use of the factor analytic method.

The Twilight of Ethnicity among American Catholics of European Ancestry

Richard D. Alba

The vitality of ethnicity in advanced industrial societies like that of the United States recently has become accepted generally as a fact, although there has been little consensus about the reasons for it. With some oversimplification, two basic explanations can be discerned. According to one, ethnicity is rooted in primordial sentiments that throb beneath the veneer of an industrial order. That is, ethnic communities and cultures serve vital human needs because they provide enduring personal identities amid the social flux of a rapidly changing society and also provide communities of solidarity that are larger than face-to-face groups and are smaller than the whole society. According to the other explanation, ethnicity flourishes along the lines of fracture in the stratification order, revitalized if not recreated by the struggle over access to privilege. Ethnicity is reinforced by common socioeconomic position that may be imposed from outside a group by majority groups seeking to solidify their privileges; or it may emerge from a group's natural history, as the peculiarities of the opportunities open to it and the disabilities inherent in its culture lead to a rough congruence between group membership and social class position.

The Catholic ethnic groups of European origins, the focus of this article, hold a position of strategic importance for evaluating these recent understandings of ethnicity in the United States.

This is not to deny the variations among them in culture, American experience, and socioeconomic success, but some common features stand out in most treatments of them.[1] They are generally believed to persist in strong ethnic affiliations, a persistence which has been seen from the vantage points of both explanations. In the main, the Catholic groups came from underdeveloped rural areas of Europe and were often recruited from the poorest strata of these societies. With some notable exceptions, they tended to settle in the major urban areas of the Northeast and the Midwest, where they clustered together in intensely ethnic communities that retain an ethnic character even today. This concentration gave rise to a view of Catholic ethnics as having merely transplanted their peasant solidarities from rural Europe to urban America – a view that seemed to explain their apparent lack of mobility. This lack is ascribed to cultural values finely attuned to the needs of survival in rural Europe, but incapacitating in urban, industrial America. Indeed, groups like the Poles and Italians have come to occupy a peculiar place in the iconography of inequality in America, often used by the mass media in symbolic evocations of working-class life. Were these and other Catholic groups to be assimilating, that fact would indicate a clear need for a reevaluation of our current assumption about ethnicity's vitality.

Reprinted from "The Twilight of Ethnicity among American Catholics of European Ancestry" by Richard D. Alba in volume no. 454 of THE ANNALS of the American Academy of Political and Social Science. © 1981 by the American Academy of Political and Social Science.

The Catholic groups are comparatively recent settlers in the United States. There were few Catholics in the former colonies at the end of the eighteenth century.[2] The Catholic population grew rapidly through immigration during the nineteenth century and the first few decades of the twentieth. The Irish were the first large Catholic group to arrive, their immigration swelling to a flood during the famine years in the 1840s and 1850s. There were also many Catholics among the immigrants from Germany, and they too began coming in large numbers around the middle of the nineteenth century. Later in the nineteenth century, immigration from southern and eastern Europe began in earnest, bringing many Polish and other eastern European Catholics and those from Italy. This so-called new immigration reached a crescendo during the early years of the twentieth century, before being stifled by the restrictive immigration laws of the 1920s. There has not been a mass immigration of European Catholics since then.[3]

CHARACTERISTICS OF CATHOLIC ETHNIC GROUPS TODAY

To arrive at an assessment of the current situation of the Catholic groups, it is necessary to use national survey data, since the Census does not ask about religion. For this article, I have used the National Opinion Research Center's (NORC) annual General Social Survey, combining the surveys for the years 1973–78 to make certain that statistics are based on ample numbers of individuals.[4] Some important characteristics of the Catholic groups are shown in Table 1, which also shows the same characteristics of all white Protestants and of Protestants of British ancestry for purposes of comparison. Religion in Table 1, it should be noted, is the religion in which an individual was raised.

In terms of numbers, individuals who were raised as Catholics make up slightly more than a quarter of the adult American population. The vast majority of this group is composed of persons who trace their ancestry to European nations, and among them is a sizable minority who do not identify themselves in terms of a single nationality. The NORC survey asks the respondent to name the "countries or part of the world"

from which his or her ancestors came. In the event that more than one country is named, the respondent is asked to indicate the country to which he or she feels "closer." Still, many respondents cannot make such a choice or cannot name any country in response to the first question, and for these the survey yields no information about national background. This is true for over 11 percent of white Catholics, most of whom name more than one country—there are few who do not name any. Since this lack of an ethnic identification is likely to be associated with many generations of family residence in the United States, the bulk of this minority is probably descended from northern and western European ancestors.

Of those who are ethnically identified, either because their ancestry is from a single country or because they feel closer to one country, four Catholic groups are especially prominent in size. The largest of these is composed of Italian-Americans, who make up over 4 percent of the American population and nearly 17 percent of white Catholics. The second and third largest are composed, respectively, of those from German-speaking countries and of those from Ireland. Each of these groups accounts for nearly 4 percent of the American population and about 14 percent of white Catholics. Polish-Americans constitute the last of the four major groups; they are slightly more than 2 percent of the American population and 8 percent of the Catholic population.[5]

Several simple indices roughly delineate the current situations of these major Catholic groups. One is generational distance from the point of immigration, with each new generation likely to represent another step in processes of assimilation. The first generation is the immigrant one itself; the second generation is born in America of immigrant parents; the third and four generations have immigrant grandparents and great-grandparents, respectively. The generational distribution of the major Catholic groups conforms to their order of arrival, but indicates that most adult members of these groups are within living memory of the immigrant experience. Although large proportions of Irish and German Catholics, as well as of British Protestants, belong to the third and later generations, the modal generation of the two Catholic groups is the third, while nearly three quarters of British Protestants be-

TABLE 1 *Selected Characteristics of Major Catholic Ethnic Groups of European Ancestry*

	Percentage of Population	Percentage Not Identified Ethnically	Percentage Third Generation or Later[†]	Percentage in Urban North[‡]	Percentage Who Attended College	Percentage with Multiple Ancestry
*All White Catholics**	25.9	11	62	38	31	30[§]
Italian	4.3	–	34	53	29	20
German (including Austrian)	3.8	–	79	33	26	31
Irish	3.6	–	85	42	42	41
Polish	2.1	–	52	52	25	20
*All White Protestants**	56.7	25	88	13	31	36[§]
British (English, Welsh, Scotch)	13.4	–	88	16	46	39

Source: National Opinion Research Center's General Social Surveys, 1973–78.

Note: Combined N = 8984.

*Religion is religion raised.

[†]Generation is available only for the 1977 and 1978 surveys.

[‡]The urban North is defined as the large urban areas and their suburbs in the Northeast and the Midwest.

[§]For each religious group, the percentage base includes only those who are ethnically identified to aid comparability to percentages among nationality categories.

long to the fourth or a later generation. A smaller proportion of Polish Catholics belongs to these later generations, and the smallest proportion of all, one third, is found among Italian Catholics. Even in the 1970s, more than half of adult Italian-Americans are the children of immigrants.

In contrast with Protestant Americans, the major Catholic groups of European origins are concentrated in the large cities of the Northeast and the Midwest and in their suburbs. The concentration is greatest for the two most recently arrived groups, Polish and Italian Catholics, and is least for German Catholics, who are unusual among the Catholic groups because they settled in rural America in large numbers. But even they are more concentrated in the urban North than are American Protestants or those of British ancestry. This urban concentration is important because for the better part of this century, these places experienced tremendous economic growth, with profound consequences for the Catholic groups that we shall soon see.

Two last indices bear directly on assimilation. Although assimilation can be thought of as having several dimensions, two stand out: acculturation and structural – or social – assimilation. Acculturation may involve only the taking on of some of the cultural traits of the host society – perhaps only those that are minimally necessary for participation in the economic and political institutions of the host society. It need not imply the dissolution of ethnic communities or the waning of ethnic identities. Structural assimilation, on the other hand, the entry into socially intimate relations like friendship and marriage with individuals from outside the ethnic groups, has profound consequences for ethnic group life. At the extreme, large-scale structural assimilation usually signifies the disappearance of ethnic boundaries that constrain social relations and the imminent full assimilation of an ethnic group.[6]

I have used educational attainment – more specifically, the percentage of a group's members who attend college – as an index of acculturation. It serves as an index in two senses, since educational institutions promote the acculturation of those who pass through them and also tend to select for the best educational credentials those individuals who already are acculturated.[7] Obviously, educational attainment holds another significance: it is closely related to subsequent occupation and income. Within the range of educational attainment, college attendance represents a crucial threshold.

In the aggregate, the educational differences among ethnic groups seems to indicate serious disadvantages for most of the major Catholic groups. To be sure, there is not a statistically significant difference in the college attendance rates of British Protestants and Irish Catholics, the most successful of all the Catholic groups in this, as in other ways.[8] But the other major Catholic groups are distinctly less likely than these two groups to have been to college. The relative lack of success of Italian and Polish Catholics reflects the comparative recency of their arrival in America and, according to a familiar argument, the education-hobbling values they brought with them from rural Europe. The educational attainment of German Catholics is probably hindered by their lower concentration in the urban areas of the North.

Of the various forms that structural assimilation can take, interethnic marriage looms large. Not only does it involve an enduring relationship across ethnic boundaries between two individuals, but it generally leads to some degree of social intimacy between their families and means that their children will be raised in an ethnically heterogeneous milieu. A direct measure of interethnic marriage is not available in the NORC data, but an indirect one, resulting from intermarriages in preceding generations, is, namely, the percentage of a group's members who report multiple national ancestry. This too is reported in Table 1.

Clearly indicated in the pattern of multiple ancestry is the relative salience of ethnic boundaries among the more recently arrived Catholic groups. Only one fifth of those who identify themselves as Polish and Italian Catholics trace their ancestry to more than one country, while two fifths of Irish Catholics and British Protestants do; German Catholics fall in between these two poles. In the case of British Protestants – as is true to a lesser extent of Irish and German Catholics – the extent of multiple ancestry is underestimated greatly in Table 1 because many others who could trace a part of their ancestry to this group undoubtedly are included among the individuals who are unable to give a single ethnic identification.

THE TRAJECTORY OF ASSIMILATION

So far, this portrait of the Catholic groups seems familiar, but it is too static. For the two indices of assimilation, the aggregate group differences in Table 1 are misleading and fail to reveal the powerful dynamics affecting the Catholic groups and bringing about a convergence between them and others in America. Those dynamics are traceable in two ways: by generations and by age. The significance of generations has been noted already, but time measured in generations is not the only kind of time that correlates with assimilation processes. Changes in the nature of the opportunities available to the members of a group – that result, for example, from a waning of prejudice toward its members – generally are visible in differences among age categories. That is, as these historical shifts occur, the opportunities available to an individual who matures, say, 20 years later than another are different from what they were for the earlier person, even when both belong to the same generation.

The changes occurring among the Catholic groups are illustrated in Table 2. This table gives a crude sense of the magnitude of change through a comparison of two birth cohorts in each group, those born before World War I and those born after World War II. The changes associated with generations are not represented directly. They are represented indirectly, however, since the younger members of each group, those born after World War II, are more likely to belong to the third or fourth generations than are its older members.

The trends in Table 2 are sharply etched. In terms of educational attainment, few among the German, Italian, and Polish Catholics born before World War I had attended college – only about 1 out of 10 in each group. This proportion compares with over a quarter of the older Irish Catholics and nearly two fifths of British Protestants. But nearly everything has changed among those born after World War II. About half the Irish, Italian, and Polish Catholics have attended college, the same proportions as found among British Protestants. Only Germans, the Catholic

group least concentrated in urban areas, deviate from this rate – about one third of them have attended college. The younger members of the urban Catholic groups, in other words, have caught up.[9]

Convergence is visible also in multiple ancestry. In the older group, there are virtually no Italian Catholics and very few Polish ones with ethnically mixed ancestry. More substantial proportions of the older German and Irish Catholics – about one fifth and one quarter, respectively – have mixed ancestry, and the largest proportion is found unsurprisingly among British Protestants, over one third of whom have mixed ancestry. But profound changes are visible in the younger group. Two fifths of Italian and Polish Catholics born after World War II report mixed ancestry, a proportion which is repeated among German Catholics and British Protestants. Fully half of those identified as Irish Catholics have ancestry other than Irish as well.

It should be remembered at this juncture that multiple ancestry lags by a generation after intermarriage, and thus the rates of multiple ancestry in Table 2 are likely to be considerably lower than the rates of intermarriage for the same groups. And by the evidence of a survey of American Catholics collected in 1963, they are. Generally speaking, large majorities of the third- and fourth-generation members of the major Catholic groups and of their youngest members also had married across ethnic boundaries. Among those who were 30 years old or younger in 1963, for example, 82, 74, 65, and 69 percent of Irish, German, Polish, and Italian Catholics, respectively, had intermarried.[10]

THE SIGNIFICANCE OF THE TRENDS IN COLLEGE ATTENDANCE AND INTERMARRIAGE

What are we to conclude about the positions of the major Catholic groups in American society? The enormous differences between the older and younger cohorts in Table 2 demonstrate beyond the shadow of a doubt a growing ethnic convergence, but it would be wrong to infer from that fact the disappearance of ethnic differentiation in the near future. In the case of educational attainment, the current equality in rates of college at-

TABLE 2 *Change by Birth Cohort of Selected Characteristics of Major Catholic Ethnic Groups*

	Birth Cohort	Percentage Not Identified Ethnically	Percentage Who Attended College	Percentage with Multiple Ancestry	Percentage Who Married Interreligiously*
All White Catholics	Before WWI	8	15	17	30
	After WWII	12	42	41	44
Italian	Before WWI	—	6	2	21
	After WWII	—	49	40	40
German	Before WWI	—	12	21	41
	After WWII	—	32	38	51
Irish	Before WWI	—	26	27	18
	After WWII	—	59	52	40
Polish	Before WWI	—	11	7	20
	After WWII	—	51	41	35
All White Protestants	Before WWI	25	21	25	11
	After WWII	25	39	42	24
British	Before WWI	—	38	35	9
	After WWII	—	52	43	24

Source: National Opinion Research Center's General Social Surveys, 1973–78.

Note: Combined N = 8984.

*Based on the religions in which respondents and their spouses were raised.

tendance need not imply the complete disappearance of educational and other socioeconomic differences. It may well be that the groups that have only recently entered higher education in large numbers, such as the Italians and Poles, are more concentrated than others in two-year colleges and in less prestigious public colleges and universities.

Some hesitation is also necessary in drawing conclusions about acculturation. A widely held position is that the acculturation of the Catholic groups, as indeed of many other American ethnic groups, has occurred in terms of a public American culture – and note that we speak here of secular, not religious, culture – but that behind an Americanized facade, ethnic subcultures quietly live on, receiving their chief expression in terms of the values concerned with home, family and community. The extensive research of Andrew Greeley demonstrates that some cultural differences among aggregate ethnic categories are visible in current survey data,[11] although this demonstration is not as conclusive as it seems at first sight because aggregate categories contain considerable numbers of less acculturated older persons and those from the first and second generations. Still, some ethnic cultural variation is compatible with growing educational equality.

Yet this growing equality should not be left without some recognition that it does clearly imply profound cultural change. The Italians, the most intensively studied of the Catholic groups, provide a compelling illustration. They frequently have been portrayed as bearers of cultural values that inhibit educational achievement. Indeed, the starkest of these portraits, drawn from the life of the group in America and in the Mezzogiorno and containing some spillover from descriptions of Italian-American organized crime, have resonated with echoes of the "culture of poverty." Amoral familism, fatalism, and a constricting loyalty to the family above all else – these and other overlapping concepts suggest a group that is tied to the lower rungs of the social ladder by its cultural chains.[12] Projected against this background, the increase in the rate of college attendance among Italian Catholics looks stunning. One cannot escape concluding that a decline in adherence to the core values of

the ethnic subculture has happened, since it is at the very center of this core, in the emphasis on certain family values, that a key impediment is located.

In addition, a profound weakening of ethnic boundaries seems indicated by the rising rates of intermarriage that are visible behind the patterns of multiple ancestry in Table 2, although it must be acknowledged that we ought to know more about the consequences of intermarriage than we do. The most often studied type of intermarriage is interreligious marriage, but its consequences are likely to be different from those of marriage across nationality boundaries, since American culture firmly supports membership in some religious denomination, and family pressures tend to bring about the conversion of one spouse to the religion of the other.

Even though interreligious marriage serves as an indicator of weakening religious boundaries, detachment from religious group membership is not its usual consequence. The limited evidence about marriage across nationality lines suggests that it entails quite a different outcome. For one thing, this kind of intermarriage appears to go hand in hand with the attenuation of ethnic subcultures, since ethnicity has a weaker relation to specific attitudes and behaviors among the intermarried and those with multiple ancestry than it does among those who marry within their own ethnic group. Also, interethnic marriage is linked to a broader relaxation of ethnic boundaries, since the personal networks of intermarried individuals, and also of individuals with multiple national ancestries, include friends and relatives drawn from a wider ethnic spectrum than found in the more ethnically homogeneous networks of the in-married.[13]

The final piece of evidence about the meaning of interethnic marriage lies in the pattern of intermarriage itself, in the matrix of who marries whom. The expectations that flow from the familiar notion of "social distance" would lead one to suspect that when individuals marry across ethnic boundaries, they usually choose partners from one of the few groups that are culturally and socially close to their own. But in fact this happens only to a minor degree, at least among marriages between partners from the Catholic groups of European origins.[14] In the main, then, intermarriage between members of these Catholic groups functions like a "melting pot."

The emergence of separate melting pots within religious boundaries was the thesis of the most prominent essay on ethnicity of the 1950s – Will Herberg's *Protestant-Catholic-Jew.* In Herberg's view, ethnicity was an enduring feature of American life, but it was destined to transmute itself before reaching a stable form. Rising rates of intermarriage across nationality lines but within religious boundaries would weaken ethnicity based on national ancestry while strengthening ethnicity based on religious group membership. In the case of Catholics, intermarriage would bring about a Pan-Catholic group by submerging national cultural differences and giving rise to a uniform American Catholicism.

Speaking against the emergence of a Pan-Catholicism, however, are the increasing rates of interreligious marriage depicted in Table 2. Over 40 percent of Catholics born after World War II have married individuals not raised as Catholics, with the vast majority of these marriages to persons raised as Protestants. Increases in interreligious marriage have occurred among all four major Catholic ethnic groups, although in every case recent rates are still a considerable distance from those obtainable if religious boundaries lost their meaning altogether. Since Catholics are only a quarter of the population, three quarters of them would marry non-Catholics if this happened.

Nevertheless, the increasing rate and substantial magnitude of interreligious marriage on the part of Catholics point to a decline in the salience of religious boundaries for a good part of the Catholic group. These facts suggest that the most significant aspect of rising rates of marriage across nationality lines is that they signal a general decline in the importance of ethnic and religious boundaries for Catholics of European descent.

Does this decline mean the complete submergence of ethnic identity? It would appear not, on the basis of the evidence in Table 2. Despite the extent of intermarriage, the proportion of Catholics who lack an ethnic identification has risen only modestly between the older and younger cohorts and remains at a low level even among those born after World War II, only 12 percent of whom do not identify with some nationality group. But just because the vast majority of Catholics retain some ethnic identification does not mean that we should conclude that little has changed. Ethnic identities are likely to be far more circumscribed in scope and practice for individuals in ethnically heterogeneous milieus, such as the intermarried, than they are for individuals in ethnically homogeneous ones.

The great extent of intermarriage among young Catholics in juxtaposition with their retention of some ethnic identification seems in accord with Herbert Gans's notion of "symbolic ethnicity." Briefly, Gans suggests that ethnicity has become increasingly peripheral to the lives of many upwardly mobile members of ethnic groups. But they do not relinquish ethnic identity entirely; rather, they adapt it to their current circumstances, selecting from an ethnic heritage a few symbolic elements that do not interfere with the need to intermix socially with persons from a variety of ethnic backgrounds. This symbolic identification with the ethnic group allows individuals to construct personal identities that contain some ethnic "spice," but it reflects an ethnicity in disarray. One key to the character of symbolic ethnicity is its voluntaristic nature, so that the symbolic elements differ from one individual to another, removing the basis for group cohesion.[15]

CONCLUSION

Ethnicity, then, appears to be subsiding among the Catholic ethnic groups, although not disappearing entirely. At this juncture, one may wonder where this leaves the widely accepted belief in an "ethnic resurgence" among Catholic, as among other, ethnic groups. My own suspicion is that this ethnic resurgence was more in the eyes of beholders than it was in events among the Catholic ethnics and, moreover, that the increased visibility of ethnicity was paradoxically a product of the same forces sapping ethnicity's vitality. During the 1970s, ethnicity could be celebrated precisely because assimilation had proceeded far enough that ethnicity no longer seemed so threatening and divisive. Ethnicity was made more visible by the penetration of

Catholic ethnics into positions of prominence in American life.[16]

To understand the reasons for the increasing assimilation of the Catholic ethnic groups, it is important to recognize the significance of the fact that the Catholic groups entered American society as voluntary immigrants; they were not incorporated forcibly through conquest and enslavement, as were Blacks and some other minority Americans. Their mode of entry was so fateful because, simply put, immigrant groups have had greater freedom than others to determine where they settle and what occupations they pursue.[17]

The greater latitude afforded immigrant groups combined in the case of some of the major Catholic groups with peculiarities of time, place, and circumstance to promote their social mobility and eventually their assimilation. Three of the major Catholic groups, the Irish, Italians, and Poles, and a number of smaller ones settled in the major cities of the Northeast and the Midwest; their mobility was spurred by the economic dynamism of these places over a good part of the nineteenth and twentieth centuries. Economic dynamism is a key because the chances in the occupational structure that accompany advancing industrialization generate a large-scale mobility that does not have a zero-sum character. Expansion of the middle and upper levels of the occupational hierarchy allows the children of those at lower levels to rise without having to displace the children of those at higher ones. Many children and grandchildren of immigrants were beneficiaries of this sort of structural mobility; as they moved upward, the equal-status contact between them and others that resulted made ethnic boundaries seem less and less meaningful.

There were, of course, many other contingencies that affected the assimilation of the Catholic groups. Without any pretense of exhaustiveness, a few must be mentioned,

The assimilation of the Catholic groups was made easier by the great distance of American shores from their European homelands, preventing a back-and-forth movement that would have periodically renewed ethnic sentiments and loyalties. For similar reasons, assimilation was made easier by the restrictive immigration laws of the 1920s, which eliminated mass immigration as a continuing source of revitalization for ethnic communities.

The order in which groups came was also consequential. That later Catholic groups were preceded by the Irish, who were able to garner a strong measure of political power by virtue of their command of the English language and their familiarity with political institutions derived from English models, probably created channels of mobility for the later groups that would have been harder to open otherwise.

And lastly, there were many idiosyncrasies in group cultures or in the opportunities in a specific place at a specific time that helped to shape ethnic mobility. One need not subscribe to all the mythology surrounding the Mafia, for example, to acknowledge that organized crime has provided a ladder of mobility for some Italians and members of some other groups.

Ethnicity appears to be nearing twilight among the Catholic ethnic groups whose forebears immigrated to the United States in the nineteenth and early twentieth centuries. The approach of this twilight is deceptive, for a fading glow from the intense ethnicity of the earlier part of the century remains. And it is a twilight which may never turn into night. For the foreseeable future, some individuals will retain strong affiliations with the Catholic groups, and immigrants will replace a few of those whose affiliations have lapsed. But the Catholic ethnic groups, so prominent a feature of the American social landscape for the better part of this century, seem destined as groups to recede into the background, at the same time that many Americans descended from these groups, still tinged by the ethnicity of their ancestors, move into the social heartland of America.

ENDNOTES

1. Two introductions to ethnicity among American Catholics are as follows: Harold Abramson, *Ethnic Diversity in Catholic America* (New York: John Wiley & Sons, 1973); and Andrew Greeley, *The American Catholic: A Social Portrait* (New York: Basic Books, 1977) (hereafter cited as *The American Catholic*). Also important, even though limited to New York City, is Nathan Glazer and Daniel Patrick Moynihan, *Beyond the Melting Pot* (Cambridge: The M.I.T. Press, 1970).

2. Greeley, *The American Catholic*, p. 35.

3. Sources for immigration statistics are as follow: *His-*

torical Statistics of the United States, Colonial Times to 1970, part I (Washington: U.S. Department of Commerce, 1975), pp. 105–6; and *Statistical Abstract of the United States, 1979* (Washington: U.S. Department of Commerce, 1979), pp. 89–90.

4. The combined surveys yield a total of 8984 cases with racial, religious, and nationality information. It should be noted that the sampling universe for these surveys is limited to the English-speaking population, and consequently, Spanish-speaking Americans are underrepresented. This is not a matter of concern for this article, which focuses on Catholics of European ancestry.

5. With the exception of Italian-Americans, the literature devoted to these groups is sparse. Two studies of Irish Catholics are as follows: Andrew Greeley, *That Most Distressful Nation* (Chicago: Quadrangle, 1972); and Marjorie Fallows, *Irish Americans* (Englewood Cliffs, NJ: Prentice-Hall, 1979). On Polish Catholics, there are as follows: Helena Znaniecki Lopata, *Polish Americans* (Englewood Cliffs, NJ: Prentice-Hall, 1976); and Neil Sandberg, *Ethnic Identity and Assimilation: The Polish American Community* (New York: Praeger, 1974). To my knowledge, there is no contemporary sociological study of German-Americans. The literature on Italian-Americans is too large to be cited fully here. Two classics are as follows: William F. Whyte, *Street Corner Society* (Chicago: University of Chicago Press, 1943); and Herbert Gans, *The Urban Villagers* (New York: The Free Press, 1962). Another useful essay is by Joseph Lopreato, *Italian Americans* (New York: Random House, 1970).

6. These are, simplified for my purposes, the familiar concepts from Milton Gordon's *Assimilation in American Life* (New York: Oxford University Press, 1964), ch. 3.

7. This is as true of the Catholic educational system as it is of others. See Andrew Greeley and Peter Rossi, *The Education of Catholic Americans* (Chicago: Aldine, 1966).

8. See Greeley, *The American Catholic*, ch. 3.

9. That the Catholic ethnics are now very mobile is argued persuasively by Greeley in *The American Catholic*, ch. 3.

10. Richard Alba, "Social Assimilation Among American Catholic National-Origin Groups," *Am. Soc. Review*, 41: 1030–46 (Dec. 1976) (hereafter cited as "Social Assimilation").

11. For example, see Greeley, *The American Catholic*.

12. Edward Banfield, *The Moral Basis of a Backward Society* (New York: The Free Press, 1958); Richard Gambino, *Blood of My Blood* (New York: Doubleday, 1974), ch. 8; and Carmi Schooler, "Serfdom's Legacy: An Ethnic Continuum," *Am. J. Soc.*, 81: 1265–86 (May 1976).

13. Richard Alba, "Ethnic Networks and Tolerant Attitudes," *Public Opinion Quarterly*, 42: 1–16 (spring 1978); and Alba, "Social Assimilation."

14. Richard Alba and Ronald Kessler, "Patterns of Interethnic Marriage Among American Catholics," *Social Forces*, 57: 1124–40 (June 1979).

15. Herbert Gans, "Symbolic Ethnicity: The Future of Ethnic Groups and Cultures in America," *Ethnic and Racial Studies*, 2: 1–20 (Jan. 1979).

16. For data on the growing representation of Catholics in the academic world, see Stephen Steinberg, *The Academic Melting Pot* (New York: McGraw-Hill, 1974).

17. Robert Blauner, *Racial Oppression in America* (New York: Harper & Row, 1972), ch. 2.

Symbolic Ethnicity
The Future of Ethnic Groups and Cultures in America

Herbert J. Gans

INTRODUCTION

One of the more notable recent changes in America has been the renewed interest in ethnicity, which some observers of the American scene have described as ethnic revival. This paper argues that there has been no revival, and that acculturation and assimilation continue to take place. Among third and fourth generation "ethnics" (the grand and great-grandchildren of Europeans who came to America during the "new immigration"), a new kind of ethnic involvement may be occurring, which emphasizes concern with identity, with the feeling of being Jewish or Italian, etc. Since ethnic identity needs are neither intense nor frequent in this generation, however, ethnics do not need either ethnic cultures or organizations; instead, they resort to the use of ethnic symbols. As a result, ethnicity may be turning into symbolic ethnicity, an ethnicity of last resort, which could, nevertheless, persist for generations.

Identity cannot exist apart from a group, and symbols are themselves a part of culture, but ethnic identity and symbolic ethnicity require very different ethnic cultures and organizations than existed among earlier generations. Moreover, the symbols third generation ethnics use to express their identity are more visible than the ethnic cultures and organizations of the first and second generation ethnics. What appears to be an ethnic revival may therefore only be a more visi-

ble form of long-standing phenomena, or of a new stage of acculturation and assimilation. Symbolic ethnicity may also have wider ramifications, however, for David Riesman has suggested that "being American has some of the same episodic qualities as being ethnic."[1]

ACCULTURATION AND ASSIMILATION[2]

The dominant sociological approach to ethnicity has long taken the form of what Neil Sandberg aptly calls straight-line theory, in which acculturation and assimilation are viewed as secular trends that culminate in the eventual absorption of the ethnic group into the larger culture and general population.[3] Straight-line theory in turn is based on melting pot theory, for it implies the disappearance of the ethnic groups into a single host society. Even so, it does not accept the values of the melting pot theorists, since its conceptualizers could have, but did not, use terms like cultural and social liberation from immigrant ways of life.

In recent years, straight-line theory has been questioned on many grounds. For one thing, many observers have properly noted that even if America might have been a melting pot early in the 20th century, the massive immigration from Europe and elsewhere has since then influenced the dominant groups, summarily labelled White Anglo-Saxon Protestant (WASP), and has also decimated their cultural, if not their political and

Reprinted from *Ethnic and Racial Studies* 2:1 (January 1979) by permission of Routledge & Kegan Paul Ltd., publishers.

financial power, so that today America is a mosaic, as Andrew Greeley has put it, of subgroups and subcultures.[4] Still, this criticism does not necessarily deny the validity of straight-line theory, since ethnics can also be absorbed into a pluralistic set of subcultures and subgroups, differentiated by age, income, education, occupation, religion, region, and the like.

A second criticism of straight-line theory has centered on its treatment of all ethnic groups as essentially similar, and its failure, specifically, to distinguish between religious groups like the Jews and nationality groups like the Italians, Poles, etc. Jews, for example, are a "peoplehood" with a religious and cultural tradition of thousands of years, but without an "old country" to which they owe allegiance or nostalgia, while Italians, Poles and other participants in the "new immigration" came from parts of Europe which in some cases did not even become nations until after the immigrants had arrived in America.

That there are differences between the Jews and the other "new" immigrants cannot be questioned, but at the same time, the empirical evidence also suggests that acculturation and assimilation affected them quite similarly. (Indeed, one major difference may have been that Jews were already urbanized and thus entered the American social structure at a somewhat higher level than the other new immigrants, who were mostly landless laborers and poor peasants.) Nonetheless, straight-line theory can be faulted for virtually ignoring that immigrants arrived here with two kinds of ethnic cultures, sacred and secular; that they were Jews from Eastern – and Western – Europe, and Catholics from Italy, Poland and elsewhere. (Sacred cultures are, however, themselves affected by national and regional considerations; for example, Italian Catholicism differed in some respects from German or Polish, as did Eastern European Judaism from Western.)

While acculturation and assimilation have affected both sacred and secular cultures, they have affected the latter more than the former, for acculturation has particularly eroded the secular cultures which Jews and Catholics brought from Europe. Their religions have also changed in America, and religious observance has decreased, more so among Jews than among Catholics, although Catholic observance has begun to

fall off greatly in recent years. Consequently, the similar American experience of Catholic and Jewish ethnics suggests that the comparative analysis of straight-line theory is justified, as long as the analysis compares both sacred and secular cultures.

Two further critiques virtually reject straight-line theory altogether. In an insightful recent paper, William Yancey and his colleagues have argued that contemporary ethnicity bears little relation to the ancestral European heritage, but exists because it is functional for meeting present "exigencies of survival and the structure of opportunity," particularly for working class Americans.[5] Their argument does not invalidate straight-line theory but corrects it by suggesting that acculturation and assimilation, current ethnic organizations and cultures, as well as new forms of ethnicity, must be understood as responses to current needs rather than only as departures from past traditions.

The other critique takes the reverse position; it points to the persistence of the European heritage, argues that the extent of acculturation and assimilation has been overestimated, and questions the rapid decline and eventual extinction of ethnicity posited by some straight-line theorists. These critics call attention to studies which indicate that ethnic cultures and organizations are still functioning, that exogamous marriage remains a practice of numerical minorities, that ethnic differences in various behavior patterns and attitudes can be identified, that ethnic groups continue to act as political interest groups, and that ethnic pride remains strong.[6]

The social phenomena which these observers identify obviously exist; the question is only how they are to be interpreted. Straight-line theory postulates a process, and cross-sectional studies do not preempt the possibility of a continuing trend. Also, like Yancey, et al., some of the critics are looking primarily at poorer ethnics, who have been less touched by acculturation and assimilation than middle class ethnics, and who have in some cases used ethnicity and ethnic organization as a psychological and political defense against the injustices which they suffer in an unequal society.[7] In fact, much of the contemporary behaviour described as ethnic strikes me as working class behaviour, which differs only slightly among various ethnic groups, and then largely because of variations in the structure of opportunities open to people in America, and in the peasant traditions their ancestors brought over from the old country, which were themselves responses to European opportunity structures. In other words, ethnicity is largely a working-class style.[8]

Much the same observations apply to ethnic political activity. Urban political life, particularly among working class people, has always been structured by and through ethnicity, and while ethnic political activity may have increased in the last decade, it has taken place around working class issues rather than ethnic ones. During the 1960s, urban working class Catholic ethnics began to politicize themselves in response to black militancy, the expansion of black ghettoes, and governmental integration policies which they perceived as publicly legitimated black invasions of ethnic neighborhoods, but which threatened them more as working class homeowners who could not afford to move to the suburbs. Similarly, working and lower-middle class Catholic ethnics banded together in the suburbs to fight against higher public school taxes, since they could not afford to pay them while they were also having to pay for parochial schools. Even so, these political activities have been *pan-ethnic*, rather than ethnic, since they often involved coalitions of ethnic groups which once considered each other enemies but were now united by common economic and other interests. The extent to which these pan-ethnic coalitions reflect class rather than ethnic interests is illustrated by the 1968 election campaign of New York City's Mario Proccaccino against John Lindsay. Although an Italian, he ran as a "candidate of the little people" against what he called the "limousine liberals."

The fact that pan-ethnic coalitions have developed most readily in conflicts over racial issues also suggests that in politics, ethnicity can sometimes serve as a convenient euphemism for anti-black endeavors, or for political activities that have negative consequences for blacks. While attitude polls indicate that ethnics are often more tolerant racially than other Americans, working class urban ethnics are also more likely to be threatened, as home-owners and job holders, by black demands, and may favor specific anti-black

policies not because they are "racists," but because their own class interests force them to oppose black demands.

In addition, part of what appears as an increase in ethnic political activity is actually an increase in the visibility of ethnic politics. When the pan-ethnic coalitions began to copy the political methods of the civil rights and anti-war movements, their protests became newsworthy and were disseminated all over the country by the mass media. At about the same time, the economic and geographic mobility of Catholic ethnic groups enabled non-Irish Catholic politicians to win important state and national electoral posts for the first time, and their victories were defined as ethnic triumphs, even though they did not rely on ethnic constituents alone, and were not elected on the basis of ethnic issues.

The final, equally direct, criticism of straight-line theory has questioned the continued relevance of the theory, either because of the phenomenon of third-generation return, or because of the emergence of ethnic revivals, Thus, Marcus Hansen argued that acculturation and assimilation were temporary processes, because the third generation could afford to remember an ancestral culture which the traumatic Americanization forced the immigrant and second generations to forget.[9] Hansen's hypothesis can be questioned on several grounds, however. His data, the founding of Swedish and other historical associations in the Midwest, provided slender evidence of a widespread third generation return, particularly among non-academic ethnics. In addition, his theory is static, for Hansen never indicated what would happen in the fourth generation, or what processes were involved in the return that would enable it to survive into the future.[10]

The notion of an ethnic revival has so far been propounded mostly by journalists and essayists, who have supplied impressionistic accounts or case studies of the emergence of new ethnic organizations and the revitalization of old ones.[11] Since third and fourth generation ethnics who are presumably participating in the revival are scattered all over suburbia, there has so far been little systematic research among this population, so that the validity of the revival notion has not yet been properly tested.

The evidence I have seen does not convince me that a revival is taking place. Instead, recent changes can be explained in two ways, neither of which conflicts with straight-line theory: (1) Today's ethnics have become more visible as a result of upward mobility; and (2) they are adopting the new form of ethnic behavior and affiliation I call symbolic ethnicity.

THE VISIBILITY OF ETHNICITY

The recent upward social, and centrifugal geographic mobility of ethnics, particularly Catholics, has finally enabled them to enter the middle and upper middle classes, where they have been noticed by the national mass media, which monitor primarily these strata. In the process they have also become more noticeable to other Americans. The newly visible may not participate more in ethnic groups and cultures than before, but their new visibility makes it appear as if ethnicity had been revived.

I noted earlier the arrival of non-Irish Catholic politicians on the national scene. An equally visible phenomenon has been the entry of Catholic ethnic intellectuals into the academy, and its flourishing print culture. To be sure, the scholars are publishing more energetically than their predecessors, who had to rely on small and poverty-stricken ethnic publishing houses, but they are essentially doing what ethnic scholars have always done, only more visibly. Perhaps their energy has also been spurred in part by the need, as academics, to publish so that they do not perish, as well as by their desire to counteract the anti-ethnic prejudices and the entrenched vestiges of the melting pot ideal which still prevail in the more prestigious universities. In some cases, they are also fighting a political battle, because their writings often defend conservative political positions against what they perceive — I think wrongly — as the powerful liberal or radical academic majority. Paradoxically, a good deal of their writing has been nostalgic, celebrating the immigrant culture and its Gemeinschaft at the same time that young Catholic ethnics are going to college partly in order to escape the restrictive pressures of that Gemeinschaft. (Incidentally, an interesting study could be made of the extent to which writers from different ethnic groups, both of fiction and non-fiction, are pursuing nostalgic, contemporary or future-oriented approaches to ethnicity, comparing different ethnic groups, by time of arrival and position in the society today, on this basis.)

What has happened in the academy has also happened in literature and show business. For example, although popular comedy has long been a predominantly Eastern European Jewish occupation, the first generation of Jewish comic stars had to suppress their ethnicity and even had to change their names, much as did the first generation of academic stars in the prestigious universities. Unlike Jack Benny, Eddie Cantor, George Burns, George Jesel and others, the comics of today do not need to hide their origins, and beginning perhaps with Lenny Bruce and Sam Levinson, comics like Buddy Hackett, Robert Klein, Don Rickles and Joan Rivers have used explicitly Jewish material in entertaining the predominantly non-Jewish mass media audience.

Undoubtedly, some of the academics, writers and entertainers have undergone a kind of third generation return in this process. Some have re-embraced their ethnicity solely to spur their careers, but others have experienced a personal conversion. Even so, an empirical study would probably show that in most cases, their ethnic attitudes have not changed; either they have acted more publicly and thus visibly than they did in the past, or in responding to a hospitable cultural climate, they have openly followed ethnic impulses which they had previously suppressed.

ETHNICITY IN THE THIRD GENERATION

The second explanation for the changes that have been taking place among third generation ethnics will take up most of the rest of this paper; it deals with what is happening among the less visible population, the large mass of predominantly middle class third and fourth generation ethnics, who have not been studied enough either by journalists or social scientists.[12]

In the absence of systematic research, it is even difficult to discern what has actually been happening, but several observers have described the same ethnic behavior in different words. Michael Novak has coined the phrase "voluntary ethnicity"; Samuel Eisenstadt has talked about

"Jewish diversity"; Allan Silver about "individualism as a valid mode of Jewishness," and Geoffrey Bock about "public Jewishness."[13] What these observers agree on is that today's young ethnics are finding new ways of being ethnics, which I shall later label symbolic ethnicity.

For the third generation, the secular ethnic cultures which the immigrants brought with them are now only an ancestral memory, or an exotic tradition to be savored once in a while in a museum or at an ethnic festival. The same is true of the "Americanization cultures," the immigrant experience and adjustment in America, which William Kornblum suggests may have been more important in the lives of the first two generations than the ethnic cultures themselves. The old ethnic cultures serve no useful function for third generation ethnics who lack direct and indirect ties to the old country, and neither need nor have much knowledge about it. Similarly, the Americanization cultures have little meaning for people who grew up without the familial conflict over European and American ways that beset their fathers and mothers: the second generation which fought with and was often ashamed of immigrant parents. Assimilation is still continuing, for it has always progressed more slowly than acculturation. If one distinguishes between primary and secondary assimilation, that is, out of ethnic primary and secondary groups, the third generation is now beginning to move into non-ethnic primary groups.[14] Although researchers are still debating just how much intermarriage is taking place, it is rising in the third generation for both Catholic ethnic groups and Jews, and friendship choices appear to follow the same pattern.[15]

The departure out of secondary groups has already proceeded much further. Most third generation ethnics have little reason, or occasion, to depend on, or even interact with, other ethnics in important secondary group activities. Ethnic occupational specialization, segregation, and self-segregation are fast disappearing, with some notable exceptions in the large cities. Since the third generation probably works, like other Americans, largely for corporate employers, past occupational ties between ethnics are no longer relevant. Insofar as they live largely in the suburbs, third generation ethnics get together with their fellow homeowners for political and civic activities, and are not likely to encounter ethnic political organizations, balanced tickets, or even politicians who pursue ethnic constituencies.

Except in suburbs where old discrimination and segregation patterns still survive, social life takes place without ethnic clustering, and Catholics are not likely to find ethnic subgroups in the Church. Third generation Jews, on the other hand, particularly those who live in older upper-middle class suburbs where segregation continues, if politely, still probably continue to restrict much of their social life to other Jews, although they have long ago forgotten the secular divisions between German (and other Western) and Eastern European Jews, and among the latter, the division between "Litwaks" and "Galizianer." The religious distinction between German Reform Judaism, and Eastern European Conservatism has also virtually disappeared, for the second generation that moved to the suburbs after World War II already chose its denomination on status grounds rather than national origin.[16] In fact, the Kennedy-Herberg prediction that eventually American religious life would take the form of a triple melting-pot has not come to pass, if only because people, especially in the suburbs, use denominations within the major religions for status differentiation.

Nevertheless, while ethnic ties continue to wane for the third generation, people of this generation continue to *perceive* themselves as ethnics, whether they define ethnicity in sacred or secular terms. Jews continue to remain Jews because the sacred and secular elements of their culture are strongly intertwined, but the Catholic ethnics also retain the secular or national identity, even though it is separate from their religion.[17]

My hypothesis is that in this generation, people are less and less interested in their ethnic cultures and organizations – both sacred and secular – and are instead more concerned with maintaining their ethnic identity, with the feeling of being Jewish, or Italian, or Polish, and with finding ways of feeling and expressing that identity in suitable ways. By identity, I mean here simply the socio-psychological elements that accompany role behavior, and the ethnic role is today less of an ascriptive than a voluntary role that people assume alongside other roles. To be sure, ethnics are still identified as such by others, particularly on the basis of name, but the behavioral expectations that once went with identification by others have declined sharply, so that ethnics have some choice about when and how to play ethnic roles. Moreover, as ethnic cultures and organizations decline further, fewer ethnic roles are prescribed, thus increasing the degree to which people have freedom of role definition.

Ethnic identity can be expressed either in action or feeling, or combinations of these, and the kinds of situations in which it is expressed are nearly limitless. Third generation ethnics can join an ethnic organization, or take part in formal or informal organizations composed largely of fellow-ethnics; but they can also find their identity by "affiliating" with an abstract collectivity which does not exist as an interacting group. That collectivity, moreover, can be mythic or real, contemporary or historical. On the one hand, Jews can express their identity as synagogue members, or as participants in a consciousness-raising group consisting mostly of Jewish women. On the other hand, they can also identify with the Jewish people as a long-suffering collectivity which has been credited with inventing monotheism. If they are non-religious, they can identify with Jewish liberal or socialist political cultures, or with a population which has produced many prominent intellectuals and artists in the last 100 years. Similar choices are open to Catholic ethnics. In the third generation, Italians can identify through membership in Italian groups, or by strong feelings for various themes in Italian, or Neapolitan or Sicilian culture, and much the same possibilities exist for Catholics whose ancestors came over from other countries.

Needless to say, ethnic identity is not a new, or third generation phenomenon, for ethnics have always had an ethnic identity, but in the past it was largely taken for granted, since it was anchored to groups and roles, and was rarely a matter of choice. When people lived in an ethnic neighborhood, worked with fellow ethnics, and voted for ethnic politicians, there was little need to be concerned with identity except during con-

flict with other ethnic groups. Also, the everyday roles people played were often defined for them by others as ethnic. Being a drygoods merchant was often a Jewish role; restaurant owners were assumed to be Greek; and bartenders, Irish.

The third generation has grown up without assigned roles or groups that anchor ethnicity, so that identity can no longer be taken for granted. People can of course give up their identity, but if they continue to feel it, they must make it more explicit than it was in the past, and must even look for ways of expressing it. This has two important consequences for ethnic behavior. First, given the degree to which the third generation has acculturated and assimilated, most people look for easy and intermittent ways of expressing their identity, for ways that do not conflict with other ways of life. As a result, they refrain from ethnic behavior that requires an arduous or time-consuming commitment, either to a culture that must be practiced constantly, or to organizations that demand active membership. Second, because people's concern is with identity, rather than with cultural practices or group relationships, they are free to look for ways of expressing that identity which suit them best, thus opening up the possibility of voluntary, diverse or individualistic ethnicity. Any mode of expressing ethnic identity is valid as long as it enhances the feeling of being ethnic, and any cultural pattern or organization which nourishes that feeling is therefore relevant, providing only that enough people make the same choice when identity expression is a group enterprise.

In other words, as the functions of ethnic cultures and groups diminish and identity becomes the primary way of being ethnic, ethnicity takes on an expressive rather than instrumental function in people's lives, becoming more of a leisure-time activity and losing its relevance, say, to earning a living or regulating family life. Expressive behavior can take many forms, but it often involves the use of symbols – and symbols as signs rather than as myths.[18] Ethnic symbols are frequently individual cultural practices which are taken from the older ethnic culture; they are "abstracted" from that culture and pulled out of its original moorings, so to speak, to become stand-ins for it. And if a label is useful to describe the third generation's pursuit of identity, I would propose the term symbolic ethnicity.

SYMBOLIC ETHNICITY

Symbolic ethnicity can be expressed in a myriad of ways, but above all, I suspect, it is characterized by a nostalgic allegiance to the culture of the immigrant generation, or that of the old country; a love for and a pride in a tradition that can be felt without having to be incorporated in everyday behavior. The feelings can be directed at a generalized tradition, or at specific ones: a desire for the cohesive extended immigrant family, or for the obedience of children to parental authority, or the unambiguous orthodoxy of immigrant religion, or the old-fashioned despotic benevolence of the machine politician. People may even sincerely desire to "return" to these imagined pasts, which are conveniently cleansed of the complexities that accompanied them in the real past, but while they may soon realize that they cannot go back, they may not surrender the wish. Or else they displace that wish on churches, schools, and the mass media, asking them to recreate a tradition, or rather, to create a symbolic tradition, even while their familial, occupational, religious and political lives are pragmatic responses to the imperatives of their roles and positions in local and national hierarchical social structures.

All of the cultural patterns which are transformed into symbols are themselves guided by a common pragmatic imperative: they must be visible and clear in meaning to large numbers of third generation ethnics, and they must be easily expressed and felt, without requiring undue interference in other aspects of life. For example, Jews have abstracted rites de passage and individual holidays out of the traditional religion and given them greater importance, such as the bar mitzvah and bas mitzvah (the parallel ceremony for 13 year old girls that was actually invented in America). Similarly, Chanukah, a minor holiday in the religious calendar, has become a major one in popular practice, partly since it lends itself to impressing Jewish identity on the children. Rites de passage and holidays are ceremonial; and thus symbolic to begin with; equally important, they do not take much time, do not upset the everyday

routine, and also become an occasion for family reunions to reassemble family members who are rarely seen on a regular basis. Catholic ethnics pay special attention to saints' days celebrating saints affiliated with their ethnic group, or attend ethnic festivals which take place in the area of first settlement, or in ethnic churches.

Consumer goods, notably food, are another ready source for ethnic symbols, and in the last decades, the food industry has developed a large variety of easily cooked ethnic foods, as well as other edibles which need no cooking, for example, chocolate matzohs which are sold as gifts at Passover. The response to symbolic ethnicity may even be spreading into the mass media, for films and television programs with ethnic characters are on the increase. The characters are not very ethnic in their behavior, and may only have ethnic names—for example, Lt. Colombo, Fonzi, or Rhoda Goldstein—but in that respect, they are not very different from the ethnic audiences who watch them.

Symbolic ethnicity also takes political forms, through identification or involvement with national politicians and international issues which are sufficiently remote to become symbols. As politicians from non-Irish ethnic backgrounds achieve high state or national office, they become identity symbols for members of their group, supplying feelings of pride over their success. That such politicians do not represent ethnic constituencies, and thus do not become involved in ethnic political disputes only enhances their symbolic function; unlike local ethnic politicians, who are still elected for instrumental bread-and-butter reasons, and thus become embroiled in conflicts that detract from their being symbols of ethnic pride.

Symbolic ethnicity can be practiced as well through politically and geographically even more distant phenomena, such as nationalist movements in the old country. Jews are not interested in their old countries, except to struggle against the maltreatment of Jews in Eastern Europe, but they have sent large amounts of money to Israel, and political pressure to Washington, since the establishment of the State. While their major concern has undoubtedly been to stave off Israel's destruction, they might also have felt that their own identity would be affected by such a disaster. Even if the survival of Israel is guaranteed in the future, however, it is possible that as allegiances toward organized local Jewish communities in America weaken, Israel becomes a substitute community to satisfy identity needs. Similar mechanisms may be at work among other ethnic groups who have recently taken an interest in their ancestral countries, for example the Welsh and Armenians, and among those groups whose old countries are involved in internal conflict, for example the Irish, and Greeks and Turks during the Cyprus war of 1973.

Old countries are particularly useful as identity symbols because they are far away and cannot make arduous demands on American ethnics; even sending large amounts of money is ultimately an easy way to help unless the donors are making major economic sacrifices. Moreover, American ethnics can identify with their perception of the old country or homeland, transforming it into a symbol which leaves out its domestic or foreign problems that could become sources of conflict for Americans. For example, most American Jews who support Israel pay little attention to its purely domestic policies; they are concerned with its preservation as a state and a Jewish homeland, and see the country mainly as a Zionist symbol.

The symbolic functions of old countries are facilitated further when interest in them is historical; when ethnics develop an interest in their old countries as they were during or before the time of the ancestral departure. Marcus Hansen's notion of third-generation return was actually based on the emergence of interest in Swedish history, which suggests that the third generation return may itself only be another variety of symbolic ethnicity. Third generations can obviously attend to the past with less emotional risk than first and second generation people who are still trying to escape it, but even so, an interest in ethnic history is a return only chronologically.

Conversely, a new symbol may be appearing among Jews: the Holocaust, which has become a historic example of ethnic group destruction that can now serve as a warning sign for possible future threats. The interest of American Jews in the Holocaust has increased considerably since the end of World War II; when I studied the Jews of Park Forest in 1949–50, it was almost never

mentioned, and its memory played no part whatsoever in the creation of a Jewish community there. The lack of attention to the Holocaust at that time may, as Nathan Glazer suggests, reflect the fact that American Jews were busy with creating new Jewish communities in the suburbs.[19] It is also possible that people ignored the Holocaust then because the literature detailing its horrors had not yet been written, although since many second generation American Jews had relatives who died in the Nazi camps, it seems more likely that people repressed thinking about it until it had become a more historical and therefore a less immediately traumatic event. As a result, the Holocaust may now be serving as a new symbol for the threat of group destruction, which is required, on the one hand, by the fact that rising intermarriage rates and the continued decline of interest and participation in Jewish religion are producing real fears about the disappearance of American Jewry altogether; and on the other hand, by the concurrent fact that American antisemitism is no longer the serious threat to group destruction that it was for first and second generation Jews. Somewhat the same process appears to be taking place among some young Armenians who are now reviving the history of the Turkish massacre of Armenians some sixty years later, at a time when acculturation and assimilation are beginning to make inroads into the Armenian community in America.

I suggested previously that ethnicity per se had become more visible, but many of the symbols used by the third generation are also visible to the rest of America, not only because the middle class people who use them are more visible than their poorer ancestors, but because the national media are more adept at communicating symbols than the ethnic cultures and organizations or earlier generations. The visibility of symbolic ethnicity provides further support for the existence of an ethnic revival, but what appears to be a revival is probably the emergence of a new form of acculturation and assimilation that is taking place under the gaze of the rest of society.

Incidentally, even though the mass media play a major role in enhancing the visibility of ethnicity, and in communicating ethnic symbols, they do not play this role because they are themselves ethnic institutions. True, the mass media, like other entertainment industries, continue to be dominated by Jews (although less so than in the past), but for reasons connected with anti-semitism, or the fear of it, they have generally leaned over backwards to keep Jewish characters and Jewish fare out of their offerings, at least until recently. Even now, a quantitative analysis of major ethnic characters in comedy, drama and other entertainment genres would surely show that Catholic ethnics outnumber Jewish ones. Perhaps the Jews who write or produce so much of the media fare are especially sensitive to eth-nic themes and symbols; my own hypothesis, however, is that they are, in this case as in others, simply responding to new cultural tendencies, if only because they must continually innovate. In fact, the arrival of ethnic characters followed the emergence and heightened visibility of ethnic politics in the late 1960s, and the men and wom-en who write the entertainment fare probably took inspiration from news stories they saw on television or read in the papers.

I noted earlier that identity cannot exist apart from a group and that symbols are themselves part of a culture, and in that sense, symbolic ethnicity can be viewed as an indicator of the persistence of ethnic groups and cultures. Sym-bolic ethnicity, however, does not require func-tioning groups or networks; feelings of identity can be developed by allegiances to symbolic groups that never meet, or to collectivities that meet only occasionally, and exist as groups only for the handful of officers that keep them going. By the same token, symbolic ethnicity does not need a practiced culture, even if the symbols are borrowed from it. To be sure, symbolic culture is as much culture as practiced culture, but the latter persists only to supply symbols to the for-mer. Indeed, practiced culture may need to per-sist, for some, because people do not borrow their symbols from extinct cultures that survive only in museums. And insofar as the borrowed materials come from the practiced culture of the immigrant generation, they make it appear as if an ethnic revival were taking place.

Then, too, it should be noted that even sym-bolic ethnicity may be relevant for only some of the descendants of the immigrants. As intermar-riage continues, the number of people with par-ents from the same secular ethnic group will continue to decline, and by the time the fourth generation of the old immigration reaches adult-hood, such people may be a minority. Most Cath-olic ethnics will be hybrid, and will have diffi-culty developing an ethnic identity. For example, how would the son of an Italian mother and Irish father who has married a woman of Polish-Ger-man ancestry determine his ethnicity, and what would he and his wife tell their children? Even if they were willing, would they be able to do so; and in that case to decide their children's eth-nicity, how would they rank or synthesize their diverse backgrounds? These questions are empir-ical, and urgently need to be studied, but I would suggest that there are only three possibilities. Either the parents choose the single ethnic iden-tity they find most satisfying, or they become what I earlier called pan-ethnics, or they cope with diversity by ignoring it, and raise their chil-dren as non-ethnic.

THE EMERGENCE OF SYMBOLIC ETHNICITY

The preceding observations have suggested that symbolic ethnicity is a new phenomenon that comes into being in the third generation, but it is probably of earlier vintage and may have already begun to emerge among the immigrants them-selves. After all, many of the participants in the new immigration were oppressed economically, politically and culturally in their old countries, and could not have had much affection even for the village and regions they were leaving. Conse-quently, it is entirely possible that they began to jettison the old culture and to stay away from ethnic organizations other than churches and unions the moment they came to America, saving only their primary groups, their ties to relatives still left in Europe, and their identity. In small town America, where immigrants were a numer-ically unimportant minority, the pressure for im-mediate acculturation and assimilation was much greater than in the cities, but even in the latter, the seeds for symbolic ethnicity may have been sown earlier than previously thought.

Conversely, despite all the pressures toward Americanization and the prejudice and discrimination experienced by the immigrants, they were never faced with conditions that required or encouraged them to give up their ethnicity entirely. Of course, some of the earliest Jewish arrivals to America had become Quakers and Episcopalians before the end of the nineteenth century, but the economic conditions that persuaded the Jamaican Chinese in Kingston to become Creole, and the social isolation that forced Italians in Sydney, Australia, to abolish the traditional familial male-female role segregation shortly after arriving, have never been part of the American experience.[20]

Some conditions for the emergence of symbolic ethnicity were present from the beginning, for American ethnics have always been characterized by freedom of ethnic expression, which stimulated both ethnic diversity, and the right to find one's own way of being ethnic that are crucial to symbolic ethnicity. Although sacred and secular ethnic organizations which insisted that only one mode of being ethnic was legitimate have always existed in America, they have not been able to enforce their norms, in part because they have always had to compete with other ethnic organizations. Even in ethnic neighborhoods where conformity was expected and social control was pervasive, people had some freedom of choice about ethnic cultural practices. For example, the second generation Boston Italians I studied had to conform to many family and peer group norms, but they were free to ignore ethnic secondary groups, and to drop or alter Italian cultural practices according to their own preference.

Ethnic diversity within the group was probably encouraged by the absence of a state religion, and national and local heads of ethnic communities. For example, American Jewry never had a chief rabbi, or even chief Orthodox, Conservative and Reform rabbis, and the European practice of local Jewish communities electing or appointing local laymen as presidents was not carried across the ocean.[21] Catholic ethnics had to obey the cardinal or bishop heading their diocese, of course, but in those communities where the diocese insisted on an Irish church, the other ethnic groups, notably the Italians, kept their distance from the church, and only in parochial

schools was there any attempt to root out secular ethnic patterns. The absence of strong unifying institutions thus created the opportunity for diversity and freedom from the beginning, and undoubtedly facilitated the departure from ethnic cultures and organizations.

Among the Jews, symbolic ethnicity may have been fostered early by self-selection among Jewish emigrants. As Liebman points out, the massive Eastern European immigration to America did not include the rabbis and scholars who practiced what he called an elite religion in the old countries; as a result, the immigrants established what he calls a folk religion in America instead, with indigenous rabbis who were elected or appointed by individual congregations, and were more permissive in allowing, or too weak to prevent, deviations from religious orthodoxy, even of the milder folk variety.[22] Indeed, the development of a folk religion may have encouraged religious and secular diversity among Jews from the very beginning.

Still, perhaps the most important factor in the development of symbolic ethnicity was probably the awareness, which I think many second generation people had already reached, that neither the practice of ethnic culture nor participation in ethnic organizations were essential to being and feeling ethnic. For Jews, living in a Jewish neighborhood or working with Jews every day was enough to maintain Jewish identity. When younger second generation Jews moved to suburbia in large numbers after World War II, many wound up in communities in which they were a small numerical minority, but they quickly established an informal Jewish community of neighborly relations, and then built synagogues and community centers to formalize and supplement the informal community. At the time, many observers interpreted the feverish building as a religious revival, but for most Jews, the synagogue was a symbol that could serve as a means of expressing identity without requiring more than occasional participation in its activities.[23] Thus, my observations among the second generation Jews of Park Forest and other suburbs led me to think as far back as the mid 1950s that among Jews, at least, the shift to symbolic ethnicity was already under way.[24]

THE FUTURE OF ETHNICITY

The emergence of symbolic ethnicity naturally raises the question of its persistence into the fifth and sixth generations. Although the Catholic and Jewish religions are certain to endure, it appears that as religion becomes less important to people, they, too will be eroded by acculturation and assimilation. Even now, synagogues see most of their worshipers no more than once or twice a year, and presumably, the same trend will appear, perhaps more slowly, among Catholics and Protestants as well.

Whether the secular aspects of ethnicity can survive beyond the fourth generation is somewhat less certain. One possibility is that symbolic ethnicity will itself decline as acculturation and assimilation continue, and then disappear as erstwhile ethnics forget their secular ethnic identity to blend into one or another subcultural melting pot. The other possibility is that symbolic ethnicity is a steady-state phenomenon that can persist into the fifth and sixth generations.

Obviously, this question can only be guessed at, but my hypothesis is that symbolic ethnicity may persist. The continued existence of Germans, Scandinavians, and Irish after five or more generations in America suggests that in the larger cities and suburbs, at least, they have remained ethnic because they have long practiced symbolic ethnicity.[25] Consequently, there is good reason to believe that the same process will also take place among ethnics of the new immigration.

Ethnic behavior, attitudes, and even identity are, however, determined not only by what goes on among the ethnics, but also by developments in the larger society, and especially by how that society will treat ethnics in the future; what costs it will levy and what benefits it will award to them as ethnics. At present, the costs of being and feeling ethnic are slight. The changes which the immigrants and their descendants wrought in America now make it unnecessary for ethnics to surrender their ethnicity to gain upward mobility, and today ethnics are admitted virtually everywhere, provided they meet economic and status requirements, except at the very highest levels of the economic, political, and cultural hierarchies. Moreover, since World War II, the eth-

nics have been able to shoulder blacks and other racial minorities with the deviant and scapegoat functions they performed in an earlier America, so that ethnic prejudice and "institutional ethnism" are no longer significant, except again at the very top of the societal hierarchies.

To be sure, some ethnic scapegoating persists at other levels of these hierarchies; American Catholics are still blamed for the policies of the Vatican, Italo-Americans are criticized for the Mafia, and urban ethnics generally have been portrayed as racists by a sometime coalition of white and black Protestant, Jewish, and other upper-middle class cosmopolitans. But none of these phenomena, however repugnant, strike me as serious enough to persuade many to hide their ethnicity. More important but less often noticed, white working class men, and perhaps others, still use ethnic stereotypes to trade insults, but this practice serves functions other than the maintenance of prejudice or inequality.

At the same time, the larger society also seems to offer some benefits for being ethnic. Americans increasingly perceive themselves as undergoing cultural homogenization, and whether or not this perception is justified, they are constantly looking for new ways to establish their differences from each other. Meanwhile, the social, cultural and political turbulence of the last decade, and the concurrent delegitimation of many American institutions have also cast doubt on some of the other ways by which people identify themselves and differentiate themselves from each other. Ethnicity, now that it is respectable and no longer a major cause of conflict, seems therefore to be ideally suited to serve as a distinguishing characteristic. Moreover, in a mobile society, people who move around and therefore find themselves living in communities of strangers, tend to look for commonalities that make strangers into neighbors, and shared ethnicity may provide mobile people with at least an initial excuse to get together. Finally, as long as the European immigration into America continues, people will still be perceived, classified, and ranked at least in part by ethnic origin. Consequently, external forces exist to complement internal identity needs, and unless there is a drastic change in the allocation of costs and benefits with respect to ethnicity, it seems likely that the larger society will also encourage the persistence of symbolic ethnicity.

Needless to say, it is always possible that future economic and political conditions in American society will create a demand for new scapegoats, and if ethnics are forced into this role, so that ethnicity once more levies social costs, present tendencies will be interrupted. Under such conditions, some ethnics will try to assimilate faster and pass out of all ethnic roles, while others will revitalize the ethnic group socially and culturally if only for self-protection. Still, the chance that Catholic ethnics will be scapegoated more than today seems very slight. A serious economic crisis could, however, result in a resurgence of anti-semitism, in part because of the affluence of many American Jews, in part because of their visibly influential role in some occupations, notably mass communications.

If present societal trends continue, however, symbolic ethnicity should become the dominant way of being ethnic by the time the fourth generation of the new immigration matures into adulthood, and this in turn will have consequences for the structure of American ethnic groups. For one thing, as secondary and primary assimilation continue, and ethnic networks weaken and unravel, it may be more accurate to speak of ethnic aggregates rather than groups. More important, since symbolic ethnicity does not depend on ethnic cultures and organizations, their future decline and disappearance must be expected, particularly those cultural patterns which interfere with other aspects of life, and those organizations which require active membership.

Few such patterns and organizations are left in any case, and leaders of the remaining organizations have long been complaining bitterly over what they perceive as the cultural and organizational apathy of ethnics. They also criticize the resort to symbolic ethnicity, identifying it as an effortless way of being ethnic which further threatens their own persistence. Even so, attacking people as apathetic or lazy, or calling on them to revive the practices and loyalties of the past have never been effective for engendering support, and reflect instead the desperation of organizations which cannot offer new incentives that would enable them to recruit members.

Some cultural patterns and organizations will survive. Patterns which lend themselves to transformation into symbols and easy practice, such as annual holidays, should persist. So will organizations which create and distribute symbols, or "ethnic goods" such as foodstuffs or written materials, but need few or no members and can function with small staffs and low overheads. In all likelihood, most ethnic organizations will eventually realize that in order to survive, they must deal mainly in symbols, using them to generate enough support to fund other activities as well.

The demand for current ethnic symbols may require the maintenance of at least some old cultural practices, possibly in museums, and through the work of ethnic scholars who keep old practices alive by studying them. It is even possible that the organizations which attempt to maintain the old cultures will support themselves in part by supplying ethnic nostalgia, and some ethnics may aid such organizations if only to assuage their guilt at having given up ancestral practices.

Still, the history of religion and nationalism, as well as events of recent years, should remind us that the social process sometimes moves in dialectical ways, and that acculturative and assimilative actions by a majority occasionally generate revivalistic reactions by a minority. As a result, even ethnic aggregates in which the vast majority maintains its identity in symbolic ways will probably always bring forth small pockets of neotraditionalism—of rebel converts to sacred and secular ways of the past. They may not influence the behavior of the majority, but they are almost always highly visible, and will thus continue to play a role in the ethnicity of the future.

SYMBOLIC ETHNICITY AND STRAIGHT-LINE THEORY

The third and fourth generation's concern with ethnic identity and its expression through symbols seem to me to fit straight-line theory, for symbolic ethnicity cannot be considered as evidence either of a third generation return or a revival. Instead, it constitutes only another point in the secular trend that is drawn, implicitly, in straight-line theory, although it could also be a point at which the declining secular trend begins to level off and perhaps straightens out.

In reality, of course, the straight-line has never been quite straight, for even if it accurately graphs the dominant ethnic experience, it ignores the ethnic groups who still continue to make tiny small bumps and waves in the line. Among these are various urban and rural ethnic enclaves, notably among the poor; the new European immigrants who help to keep these enclaves from disappearing; the groups which successfully insulate themselves from the rest of American society in deliberately-enclosed enclaves; and the rebel converts to sacred and secular ways of the past who will presumably continue to appear.

Finally, even if I am right to predict that symbolic ethnicity can persist into the fifth and sixth generations, I would be foolish to suggest that it is a permanent phenomenon. Although all Americans, save the Indians, came here as immigrants and are thus in one sense ethnics, people who arrived in the seventeenth and eighteenth centuries, and before the mid-nineteenth century "old" immigration, are, except in some rural enclaves, no longer ethnics even if they know where their emigrant ancestors came from.

The history of groups whose ancestors arrived here seven or more generations ago suggests that eventually, the ethnics of the new immigration will be like them; they may retain American forms of the religions which their ancestors brought to America, but their secular cultures will be only a dim memory, and their identity will bear only the minutest trace, if that, of their national origin. Ultimately, then, the secular trend of straight-line theory will hit very close to zero, and the basic postulates of the theory will turn out to have been accurate—unless of course by then America, and the ways it makes Americans, has altered drastically in some now unpredictable manner.

ENDNOTES

1. Personal communication. Incidentally, David Riesman is now credited with having invented the term ethnicity as it is currently used. (Hereafter, I shall omit personal communication footnotes, but most of the individuals named in the text supplied ideas or data through personal communication.)

2. For reasons of brevity, I employ these terms rather than Gordon's more detailed concepts. Milton Gordon, *Assimilation in American Life,* New York, Oxford University Press, 1964, Chapter 3.

3. Neil C. Sandberg, *Ethnic Identity and Assimilation: The Polish-American Community,* New York, Praeger, 1974. The primary empirical application of straight-line theory is probably still W. Lloyd Warner and Leo Srole, *The Social Systems of American Ethnic Groups,* New Haven, Yale University Press, 1945.

4. See e.g., Andrew Greeley, *Ethnicity in the United States,* New York, Wiley, 1974, Chapter 1.

5. W. Yancey, E. Ericksen and R. Juliani, "Emergent Ethnicity: A Review and Reformulation," *American Sociological Review,* Vol. 41, June 1976, pp. 391–403, quote at p. 400.

6. The major works include Greeley, op. cit.; Harold J. Abramson, *Ethnic Diversity in Catholic America,* New York, Wiley, 1973; and Nathan Glazer and Daniel P. Moynihan, *Beyond the Melting Pot,* Cambridge, MIT Press, 2nd ed., 1970.

7. Class differences in the degree of acculturation and assimilation were first noted by Warner and Srole, op. cit.; for some recent data among Poles, see Sandberg, op. cit.

8. Herbert J. Gans, *The Urban Villagers,* New York, Free Press, 1962, chap. 11. See also Dennis Wrong, "How Important is Social Class," in Irving Howe, ed., *The World of the Blue Collar Worker,* New York, Quadrangle, 1972, pp. 297–309; William Kornblum, *Blue Collar Community,* Chicago, University of Chicago Press, 1974; and Stephen Steinberg, *The Academic Melting Pot,* New Brunswick, Transaction Books, 1977.

9. Marcus L. Hansen, *The Problems of the Third Generation Immigrant,* Rock Island, Ill., Augustana Historical Society, 1938; and "The Third Generation in America," *Commentary,* Vol. 14, November 1952, pp. 492–500.

10. See also Harold J. Abramson, "The Religioethnic Factor and the American Experience: Another Look at the Three-Generations Hypothesis," *Ethnicity,* Vol. 2, June 1975, pp. 163–177.

11. One of the most influential works has been Michael Novak, *The Rise of the Unmeltable Ethnics,* New York, Macmillan, 1971.

12. Perhaps the first, and now not sufficiently remembered, study of third-generation Jews was Judith Kramer and Seymour Leventman, *The Children of the Gilded Ghetto,* New Haven, Yale University Press, 1961.

13. Geoffrey Bock, "The Jewish Schooling of American Jews," unpublished Ph.D. Dissertation, Graduate School of Education, Harvard University, 1976.

14. The notion of primary assimilation extends Gordon's concept of marital assimilation to include movement out of the extended family, friendship circles and

other peer groups. In describing marital assimilation, Gordon did, however, mention the primary group as well. Gordon, op. cit., p. 80.

15. The major debate at present is between Abramson and Alba, the former viewing the amount of intermarriage among Catholic ethnics as low, and the latter as high. See Abramson, "Ethnic Diversity in Catholic America," op. cit.; and Richard Alba, "Social Assimilation of American Catholic National-Origin Groups," *American Sociological Review*, Vol. 41, December 1976, pp. 1030–1046.

16. See e.g., Marshall Sklare and Joseph Greenblum, *Jewish Identity on the Suburban Frontier*, New York, Basic Books, 1967; Herbert J. Gans, "The Origin and Growth of a Jewish Community in the Suburbs: A Study of the Jews of Park Forest," in Marshall Sklare, ed., *The Jews: Social Pattern of an American Group*, New York, Free Press, 1958, pp. 205–248, and Herbert J. Gans, *The Levittowners*, New York, Pantheon, 1967, pp. 73–80. These findings may not apply to communities with significant numbers of German Jews with Reform leanings. There are few Orthodox Jews in the suburbs, except in those surrounding New York.

17. Sandberg, op. cit. and James Crispino, *The Assimilation of Ethnic Groups: The Italian Case*, New York, Center for Migration Studies, 1979.

18. My use of the word symbol here follows Lloyd Warner's concept of symbolic behavior. See W. Lloyd Warner, *American Life: Dream and Reality*, Chicago, University of Chicago Press, 1953, Chapter 1.

19. See Nathan Glazer, *American Judaism*, Chicago, University of Chicago Press, 2nd ed. 1972, pp. 114–115.

20. On the Jamaica Chinese, see Orlando Patterson, *Ethnic Chauvinism*, New York, Stein and Day, 1977, Chapter 5; on the Sydney Italians, see Rina Huber, *From Pasta to Pavlova*, St. Lucia, University of Queensland Press, 1977, Part 3.

21. For a study of one unsuccessful attempt to establish a community presidency, see Arthur A. Goren, *New York Jews and the Quest for Community*, New York, Columbia University Press, 1970.

22. Charles S. Liebman, *The Ambivalent American Jew*, Philadelphia, Jewish Publication Society of America, 1973, Chapter 3. Liebman notes that the few elite rabbis who did come to America quickly sensed they were in alien territory and returned to Eastern Europe. The survivors of the Holocaust who came to America after World War II were too few and too late to do more than influence the remaining Jewish orthodox organizations.

23. Gans, "The Origin of a Jewish Community in the Suburbs," op. cit.

24. See Herbert J. Gans, "American Jewry: Present and Future," *Commentary*, Vol. 21, May 1956, pp. 422–430, which includes a discussion of "symbolic Judaism."

25. Unfortunately, too little attention has been devoted by sociologists to ethnicity among descendants of the old immigration.

A New Ethnic Group in the United States

Stanley Lieberson

It is the thesis of this paper that there is a major and extraordinarily important ethnic shift underway in the United States: the growth and expansion of a new white ethnic group. This new white group is characterized by several features.

There is a recognition of being white, but lack of any clearcut identification with, and/or knowledge of, a specific European origin. Such people recognize that they are not the same as some of the existing ethnic groups in the country such as Greeks, Jews, Italians, Poles, Irish, and so forth. The vast bulk of persons meeting these conditions are of older Northwestern European origins, but there are also some persons from newer European sources of immigration shifting into this group. Indeed, for reasons to be given below, I would expect more to do so in the years ahead.

There is some difficulty in finding an appropriate name for this group. The term WASP is inappropriate for two reasons: first, it is often used in a pejorative sense; second, it is not clear that this new group is restricted to persons of Anglo-Saxon origin or to Protestants. For lack of an appropriate alternative, I will refer to this group as *unhyphenated whites*—as distinguished from all whites. Note that my thesis is not that the term *unhyphenated whites* means the elimination of some other specific ethnic groups such as, say, Germans. It is perfectly appropriate to recognize that there are some persons of German ancestry who would declare themselves to be German-American or some such variant, and that

there would be others of German ancestry who would fit into the unhyphenated white category.

This conclusion about a new white ethnic group stems from several factors that are not as widely appreciated as they might be. First, there is a tendency to see ethnic and racial categories as static, unchanging entities—a perception that is probably correct in the short term, but radically in error when viewed from the long-range, historical perspective. To be sure, it is widely recognized that the degree of identification with an ethnic group may fluctuate over time as a function of various social conditions. But less clearly understood is the fact that the group categories themselves may shift over time and, moreover, short-term vacillations in identification may well be hiding strong long-term shifts. Second, the understanding of the mechanisms that permit shifts in ethnic classification and identification is inadequate. Third, there are fundamental causes of changes that have not been recognized. Finally, there are data that are at least consistent with this thesis about a newly forming ethnic group, but they have not been interpreted in this way.

ETHNIC AND RACIAL GROUPS IN FLUX

Racial and ethnic groups are not merely static entities, but also products of labelling and identification *processes* that change and evolve over time. Differentials in fertility, mortality, and mi-

A revised and abridged version of a paper given in April, 1984 at the SUNY-Albany Conference on Ethnicity and Race in the Last Quarter of the 20th Century. A special debt is owed to Guy E. Swanson, who suggested the term *unhyphenated whites*.

gration are not the only forces responsible for the expansion or decline in their numbers. Beyond this, gradual shifts occur in the sets and subsets of groups found in a society such as to lead to both new combinations and new divisions. This continuous process of combining and recombining means that the very existence of a given group is not to be taken for granted; groups appear and disappear. Ethnic groups such as Mexicans or Puerto Ricans are essentially very recent in nature, resulting from interethnic contacts only since the expansion of Europe into the New World. In similar fashion, the Coloured population in South Africa is a recent group. But it would be the case for many older ethnic groups as well; the English ethnic population in the United Kingdom, for example, is obviously a hybridized population descending from contact and expansion involving a number of groups.

These processes can be so gradual that they may run for hundreds of years before anything close to a complete shift occurs (an estimate that is probably conservative). Ethnic origin, from this point of view, is both a status and a process. At any given time, we are most likely to see the state of affairs reported by the population – it is less easy to see the process of ethnic change that is also going on. Indeed, some of the difficulties that researchers and census takers experience in using data on racial and ethnic groups reflect the processes of ethnic and racial change themselves. Part of the difficulty in asking people about their ethnic or racial origins is actually due to a social fact that is telling us something about the flux in the concepts and identifications themselves.

In short, when examining the racial and ethnic groups found in a given society, there is a tendency to take for granted their existence. In fact, a given racial or ethnic group does not go back to the origins of the human species. Rather, each ethnic group was created out of dynamic processes that took place over periods far longer than a given individual's lifespan. Just as various species in the plant and animal worlds are continuously changing – even though it is normally possible to point to this species or that – so, too, ethnic groups are under continuous flux in terms of their birth, maintenance, and decline. If people are asked for their ethnic ancestry at a given time, they are apt to give answers that largely fit

into the rubrics established and conventional at the time. Responses that do not fit these rubrics tend to be viewed as errors, or as failures of the enumeration instrument, or of the enumerator, or what have you. And that is often the case. But in addition, there is a continuous flux in the categories themselves and in who defines himself or herself (or is defined by others) as belonging in these categories. In this manner, there are shifts in racial and ethnic populations. Because we are dealing with populations, it is perfectly possible, particularly at some intermediate stage of change, for some persons of X ancestry to identify themselves as belonging to ethnic group X while an increasing proportion with X ancestry are now reporting themselves as Y.

MECHANISMS OF SHIFT

How might the ethnic/racial origins reported in a country shift without being the result of differentials in birth, death, and international migration? No matter what causal force underlies the change (and we shall see that there are many), ultimately it must operate through a limited number of mechanisms. There are really four main ways of thinking about a respondent's ancestry. One deals with the true ancestral origins for a given respondent, i.e., what we would learn about the respondent if roots could be traced back to some specific temporal point. We can call this the *true ancestral origin* or AO_t. The second are the origins that the respondent *believes* to be his or her ancestral origins at a given specified point in time. In most cases, then, AO_b is the only indicator available of AO_t. It is an imperfect indicator, but nevertheless one would hope that there is some reasonably strong association between reported and actual ancestral origins. The third and fourth measures refer to *identification*. This is either self-identification *(SI)*, or what a person declares as the group(s) he/she identifies with; *or* the ethnic label imposed on the person by others *(OI)*.

These four variables are actually oversimplified in the sense that there are subsets of each that could be considered in greater detail than is possible here. Even AO_t, the true ancestral origins, is more complicated than it might seem at first glance. If it were possible to trace somebody's ancestry backwards in time, there would be no "natural" stopping point at which one would say, "At last, here is this person's ancestry." One could always go further back and find earlier combinations of characteristics that led to the ones just recognized. The only natural stopping points are really societal ones. In a study of the ancestral origins of the United States population, chances are the investigator is interested in the defined ancestral roots at the time of arrival in the New World. However, for ancestors who were here prior to the expansion of Europe in the sixteenth century, we would simply want to know what the ancestors were at that time rather than earlier, e.g., Indian tribes rather than origins at the time these peoples crossed into the New World much earlier. Therefore, conclusions about ancestral origins—if we were to imagine the capability of actually determining each person's true roots as far back in time as we wanted—would depend on where one decided to stop. In similar fashion, then, beliefs about ancestral origins would also have certain complications that depended on the "generational span" covered by ancestors in the information passed on to offspring. One source of distortion, then, is the societal process of intergenerational transmission. Under any circumstance, if it were possible for an investigator to correctly trace the actual ancestral history of each respondent as far back as relevant, there is no doubt that the information obtained in such a manner would differ in many cases from what was reported as the respondent's ancestral origins. Presumably there is some sort of correlation between reported and true origins, but who can say how close it is?

Because the self-identification reported to others can be affected by both the audience and the social context, there are several subtypes of *SI*. Indeed, private self-identification can even be totally different from any public declaration of ethnic identification. As a matter of fact, ethnic or racial cases of "passing" are exactly that—situations where someone's publicly declared identification is intentionally different from the person's private self-identification. At the very least, we can say that the social context may affect both an individual's self-identification *and* the identification reported to someone else.

As for the identification imposed by others, *OI*, it is almost certain that parents will be a

powerful force since in most cases it is from them that one obtains at least the initial sense of self-identification. However, this is not a simple, cut-and-dried matter. More than one single message may be conveyed to the offspring even from within the family, particularly if parents have different identifications. Beyond this, outsiders can have certain notions of who one is that are at variance with the identification learned at home. In turn, individuals can be swept into social movements and other events during their lifetime that end up redefining their self-identification. The power of outside identifications can range enormously. The Pass Laws of South Africa and the policies of Nazi Germany represent extreme versions of this, where in effect the state will not allow certain options at all. Thus persons of partial Jewish ancestry were suddenly identified as Jews by the State in a way that could not be avoided. The current use of a self-enumeration procedure in the United States Census gives respondents considerable freedom to report their own identification. However, this complete freedom does not mean that reported origins or identification is a free-floating matter, since self-identification is still affected by the identification placed on the individual by others and this in turn affects the voluntary response in a census or any other context.

Societal forces are more than simply *imposed*, pure and simple, on the population. And, of course, it is these forces that are especially important to consider in studying self-identification and response in a country such as the United States. (Incidentally, until very recently, there was not complete freedom for respondents in the United States to declare whatever ancestry they wanted. Instructions to enumerators indicated very specific rules about accepting certain responses from persons of mixed, non-white origins. Likewise, there used to be various state laws that defined blacks in very specific descent terms.) In other words, self-identification is a complicated variable, affected by a variety of societal forces. Pass Laws and completely laissez-faire policies may represent the extremes of political forces, but the actual responses in laissez-faire situations are not without their strong informal pressures. For example, the response a person of mixed-white origins receives, based on his or her distinctive surname, may well lead to the less visible and unidentified origin fading.

In summary, one can visualize obtaining four items of information for each respondent: self-identification (vaguely defined, since there would be contextual effects on the SI that is reported); AOb, which refers to what the respondent believes is his or her ancestral origin; AOt, the historically *true* origins at the time the various ancestors arrived in the New World or, if Native Americans, at the outset of the sixteenth century; and OI, the identification imposed by others. One can also visualize measuring the association between various pairings of these attributes. There is, for example, the linkage between true ancestral origins and what one believes them to be; the association between self-identification and believed origins; and the linkage between self-identification and true origins. Presumably there are positive associations between each of these pairs, but it is an open question – and one not readily answered – as to how strong they would be. In the case of self-identification and believed origins, for example, I think we can expect a fairly strong linkage, if only because modifications in one of these will tend to modify the other; if not within one's lifespan, then at least in the course of a few generations. If SI and AOb are highly linked, such that shifts in one lead to shifts in the other, it would mean that changes in self-identification will cause the association between *believed* and *true* ancestry to drift apart and become progressively weaker. Thus the linkage between self-identification and true ancestral origins, as well as the linkage between true and believed origins, should get progressively weaker over time.

Given these distinctions, it is clear that many studies of race and ethnic relations are truncated or warped to some unknown degree. If one examines the assimilation of, say, persons of Italian ancestry, then those that either do not identify or are not aware of their Italian ancestry are fully lost. Such a subset of the population with Italian ancestry is almost certain to differ from the entire set of persons who could have accurately reported themselves of that origin. The loss or truncation is certainly affected by the research instrument. The 1980 U.S. census and 1979 Current Population Survey conducted by the census both allowed for multiple responses, but the National Opinion Research Center studies of ethnic origin in the General Social Survey and earlier census surveys did not.

TWO FORMS OF CHANGE

Changes in ethnic grouping can occur either within the life span of a respondent or inter-generationally. It is easy to visualize a variety of ways through which changes of the latter type can take place. If there is intermarriage and inter-breeding, then the lineage of the descendants becomes more complicated with each passing generation. The potential of dropping off and simplifying ethnic matters becomes great. Even endogamous mating does not necessarily avoid simplification when there are Old World geographic complications and subtleties that can be lost in each succeeding generation. For example, the descendants of Swiss-Germans do not always know that their ancestors drew a sharp distinction between Swiss-German (as opposed to being German-German) nor do they always know that being Swiss does not convey any ethnic ancestry at all. Boundary changes, incorrect and/or over-simplified knowledge of various settings, confusion, and the like all affect intergenerational continuity even in relatively simple settings.

Schools and religious institutions may or may not serve to reinforce and maintain ethnic identification. Much of this depends on governmental policies. In some countries, for example, linguistic differences between the ethnic groups lead to separate schools and these, in turn, mean setting off an ethnic marker for each child at a very early age. (Obviously de jure ethnic/racial school segregation can and does occur for other reasons as well.) In the United States, the existence of public schools and the mixture of ethnic groups found within some of the denominations offering private schooling (e.g., Roman Catholics and Lutherans) probably does less to maintain specific ethnic identity among white groups than occurs in some other nations.

It is by no means inevitable that a full and correct transmission of ethnic ancestry will occur through the family. First, there are distortions through the increasingly common circumstances in which many children spend part or all of their life in a household with at least one of the parents absent through divorce, desertion, or death. Intergenerational knowledge can easily be affected in situations where one or both parents die before their offspring reach adulthood; children are abandoned; or children are raised by relatives on one side of the family. Beyond this, there are also circumstances where promiscuity may literally lead to ignorance of one parent's origins. Finally, there is the possibility of intentional discontinuities between parents and children, in which parents attempt to hide certain ethnic origins or in some other way de-emphasize certain knowledge.

In addition, there are children with only a modest interest in their ancestral origins, children who do not focus on the topic. Others become interested too late to obtain accurate information from parents who, by then, are deceased. To be sure, such a situation presupposes a special type of society, one where a significant number of children are not that interested in the answer *and* one where it is not automatically learned regardless of a child's initial interest. In similar fashion, there may be parents who have little or no interest in discussing ancestral histories with their offspring. In all of this, of course, we can visualize an intergenerational shift in largely one direction: from knowledge to ignorance, from detail to blur. Thus, unless exceptional effort is made, it is unlikely for knowledge about ancestral origins to be reclaimed in later generations. Such events mean that some members of later generations will be unable to provide any ethnic identification at all, but it also means badly warped responses that are either totally or largely inaccurate on the part of others. Questions on ancestry, for *some* respondents, begin to approximate a sociological form of the ink blot test.

Ethnic identification may also change *within* someone's lifespan through a variety of ways. One force is analogous to the intergenerational simplifying process, except here within someone's own lifespan a complicated ancestral history slowly changes and is simplified by forgetting or unlearning some parts of it. Even some details of a relatively simple ancestral history can be distorted and changed during a person's lifetime. In either case, we would find a deterioration in the detail with which ancestral history is reported. Certainly, too, there is the question of self-identification, particularly after people reach an age where they are removed from parental pressures and control. At such a point, certain changes in self-identification are freer to come out.

The identification imposed by others on a given respondent will also influence intragenerational changes. It is my impression that regions of the country vary considerably in the degree to which residents can "spot" or identify members of different groups. If this impression is correct (or if for other reasons someone experiences variation in the degree to which others are attuned to ethnic ancestry), then the identification imposed by others affects the propensity for someone to identify himself or herself in a certain manner.

CAUSES

What social forces cause shifts in identification, ancestral knowledge, and in the categories themselves? By contrast, what keeps such shifts from occurring in other contexts? As a general rule, one should recognize that social organization and ethnic delineations tend to be linked. Changes in the identification of groups, by either others or themselves, in the long run affect the organizational structure of racial and ethnic populations. On the other hand, changes in the organizational structure of racial and ethnic populations generate new identifications (again by themselves or imposed by others) that reflect their structural positions within the society. A series of forces can thus be visualized as operating to affect identification, the known ancestral origins, and the ethnic categories found in a population. Needless to say, they are not always mutually exclusive in any given context.

1. It is important to recognize that social pressures towards shift are sometimes of an idiosyncratic nature. Ryder (1955) has demonstrated this rather nicely for Canada with respect to residents of German ethnic origin during World War II. The sharp, downward decline in the numbers reporting themselves as German suggested a definite misreporting and reflected the unpopularity of being German. In this case (and in other below), we can see how such changes might be

especially likely for persons of mixed ethnic origins; it would simply be a matter of emphasizing one origin at the expense of another. If a historically idiosyncratic or unique feature were to operate for a relatively long time, there is a strong chance that the consequence would be a shift in self-identification and knowledge of ancestral origin, which would then persist even if the cause was later to disappear. This is because of the natural drift mechanism described below.

2. An ethnic ranking system means that members of some groups enjoy prestige and various advantages, whereas others face handicaps or even punishments. This suggests that, other things being equal, there will be a net change toward the direction that generates positive rewards and prestige, and away from those categorizations and classifications that generate disadvantages and lower status. Insofar as groups differ in their prestige and in the real advantages and disadvantages that perceived membership offers, one might expect subtle and less-than-subtle shifts towards more desirable, or less disadvantaged, origins at the price of others. This could occur for those without any claims to such ancestries, and certainly for those of mixed ancestry. Thus under some circumstances, ethnic origins will be lost, identifications changed, and perhaps new nomenclature used as a device for avoiding social disadvantages. A nice example of the latter, by the way, is the use of *Czech* as an ethnic identifyer in the United States instead of *Bohemian*, the latter having certain unfavorable connotations in an earlier period.

To be sure, this is not the only response possible to such a ranking and reward system. Responses of a far different nature involve combatting disadvantages through legislation, protests, group organization, and the like. Acquiescence is another response, not unknown at least for the short-term. It is only possible to speculate, at this point, whether ancestral loss is less likely during periods of intense, organized effort by a group to alter its disadvantaged situation. During such periods ethnic awareness is likely to be intensified and reinforced by organized efforts; slight or partial shifts away from the group identification are also likely to be branded as betrayals or traitorous acts. (Under such circumstances, by the way, a different form of distortion can occur: the de-emphasis of other ancestries among the mixed members of groups aroused to protest and combat their disadvantaged situation.) But overall, where there is ethnic shift, it is in the direction towards groups that provide more advantageous positions in the ethnic hierarchy.

3. The very opposite factor to that discussed above is a natural drift mechanism; namely, indifference to one's ethnic origin, which leads to the loss of detailed or even partially accurate information on ancestry. Once this occurs, it is unlikely for details to be recovered in later generations, although there is the possibility via grandparents or other relatives such as aunts and uncles. Hence, for the most part, any de-emphasis or loss of interest in ethnic origins leads to permanent losses of information and, as a consequence, possibly newer and vaguer and simpler identification schemes. In that sense, change can occur only in the direction towards distortion or new delineations.

One feature of this drift is that it is more likely to occur in some directions than in others. As a general rule, voluntary drifts in identification are never towards greater disadvantages, but either maintain or improve one's position within the system. The drift is limited to shifts toward memberships and identifications that are beneficial, or at least not harmful. Hence it is unlikely for people to give up distinctions that are beneficial by merging or joining them with categories that are beneath them in prestige and/or other rewards. A broader and vaguer ethnic delineation may then develop, if it is not disadvantageous when compared with the more precise ancestral delineations that previous generations would have given. As we shall see below, this is what I believe is going on with respect to the development of a new unhyphenated-white ethnic group.

4. Government and other major institutions vary over time, and between societies, in how much formal attention they pay to ethnic/racial categories. But it is unlikely that the subject will be totally ignored in any multiethnic situation. As a consequence, at least some formal bureaucratic rules and definitions are always used and that such rules will be too simple to take into account the entire range of ethnic/racial complexities and the existing array of self-identifications is virtually guaranteed. Furthermore, the rules almost

certainly deviate from the reality in the direction of meeting the needs of the dominant population and/or the organizations themselves (Petersen, 1969). This means that government and other organizational forms of control affect the ethnic delineation process. Because various organizational processes formally identify ethnic lineage, they can leave less room for distortion than there could be otherwise (except when the distortions are in the governmental delineations themselves, such as when one-sixteenth black and fifteen-sixteenths white is defined as "black"). But organizational forms of control are relevant because they offer advantages to some identifications and disadvantages to others. For example, being on Indian tribal rolls can provide certain rewards in the United States at this time, so there is an incentive to remain on such rolls and to be sure that one's offspring (in the case of persons of mixed origins) are aware of their Indian heritage.

Governmental and other institutional delineations of racial and ethnic categories (and the criteria for inclusion) are almost certain to differ from all the subtle permutations and combinations of identification and ancestry held by the populations themselves. The net effect is a massive set of distortions due to these influences, combined with efforts by members of different groups to adjust to these delineations (in order to take advantage of the rewards from some categories and to escape the handicaps of others).

5. Also affecting the shifts, and their direction, is the nature of the identification system. This can be visualized as ranging from a totally coercive system, where identification is imposed on the individual by the government or some other institution, to the other extreme, where identification is voluntary and completely a matter of self-declaration. As noted earlier, South Africa, with its Pass Laws, and Germany during the Nazi era, represent one such extreme on the *coercive-voluntary continuum.* The laissez-faire disposition toward race in Brazil represents the other extreme. The United States is somewhere between an imposed coercive system and a purely voluntaristic one. In addition, there have been fluctuations over time, as in the cases of blacks and American Indians. For most white groups in the United States, however, ethnic/ancestral affiliations are in principle voluntary,

i.e., there is no governmental or other *formal* institutional constraint on the affiliation claimed. Likewise, the civil rights legislation at present encourages some persons to maintain particular identifications, at least in certain contexts, in order to enjoy special programs and considerations.

6. Intergroup conflicts have consequences for labelling and identification. Certainly the dominant group's interaction with subordinate groups has a direct impact on the organization of the subordinates. The terms *Native American* or *American Indian* are examples of this, involving a new classification scheme (new in the sense of post-European conquest) that incorporates within it ethnic groups (tribes) whose sense of oneness is a function only of the presence of the white groups and the fact that they share a common condition. In that sense, the ethnic lines and boundaries are to be viewed as floating—as a function of the interactions with other groups and, particularly, the behavior of the dominant groups toward them. In similar fashion, any sense of a common bond among the various black ethnic groups of South Africa must be a function of the behavior directed toward them by the dominant white population and, as a consequence, the common situation that they find themselves in. Another example in the United States is the newly developing Latino identification for various groups descending from Spanish-speaking ancestors.

An important reason for the shift of ethnic identification is also possible simply because the scale and nature of the contact is different. This is particularly striking for migrant peoples who originally saw themselves in their homelands as members of a given town or, at best, province or region. In the context of the United States, however, they find themselves in contact with others from the same national homeland who, although different, still have far more in common with them than do the vast bulk of persons with whom they now co-exist. Moreover, these persons are all given a common label by the larger society, for whom these distinctions are of no interest. This was an important force among many immigrant groups to the United States who had identified with a much narrower unit prior to emigration.

In this case, the ecological-demographic context is significant: numerically smaller groups are less likely to be singled out as distinctive by the dominant group. But of course this hinges in part on the distinctiveness of the group (cultural, physical, spatial isolation, religious, and the like), the number of other groups present, and the importance to the dominant group of making specific distinctions. But the dominant group also has a propensity to simplify the situation and description of subordinate groups. The errors and distortions made by the dominant group, insofar as they are of consequence for the life chances of the groups subjected to these actions, do in the long run affect the identifications of the groups themselves and tend to draw them into new bonds.

7. Internal group pressures, although a necessary product of some of these other forces, themselves merit at least brief separate mention. In the course of interethnic/racial conflicts, groups often generate elaborate rituals and pressures to maintain members' identification. Self-identification becomes a central part of the socialization process and becomes defined in the context of respect for parents, extended family, and friends. These thrusts toward group identification are really no different from those exerted by the larger society or nation to maintain allegiance to itself or, on the other hand, the loyalties that other groups in conflict attempt to promote (e.g., labor unions, teams, etc.). Aside from the powerful pull of primary-group ties, there is also a glorification of the group through such mechanisms as learning of a noble history, belief in its special and unique qualities, tales of heroes who sacrificed much for it, and the like. Such developments, at least for the short run, can well reduce inter- and intragenerational shifts.

EMPIRICAL CONSEQUENCES

The above analysis suggests that censuses and other survey data on racial and ethnic groups are characterized by all sorts of volatile and erratic qualities. These and other inconsistencies need not be interpreted as *errors* in either enumeration procedures or in respondent behavior, although such errors cannot be ruled out. Rather, such difficulties may well reflect the flux outlined above in the nature of race and ethnic relations in the society. It is not easy to deal with this topic as

an empirical problem. The birth of new ethnic groups, and the shifts among others, do not necessarily occur overnight in a cataclysmic fashion. Although the rates of change are probably not linear, they are probably more gradual than sudden. For example, it is rather unlikely that a vast segment of the population of England awoke one day to discover they were neither Saxons nor Normans nor Angles nor Jutes, but were rather English. Likewise there is now evidence supporting the contention that a new white ethnic group is evolving in the United States.

Two important statistical developments are noteworthy. The U.S. government asked a straight ethnic-origins question in the 1980 decennial census as well as in important sample surveys taken in recent years. The population was asked, "What is this person's ancestry?" Multiple entries were accepted and recorded. In addition, the census asked separate questions on Spanish/Hispanic origin or descent and one that seemed to elaborate on the old color or race question. Second, the General Social Survey (GSS), conducted by the National Opinion Research Center, has been asking a question on ethnic origin since 1972. Its question construction and treatment of multiple entries are of interest to us because they are different from that found in the census, and hence can provide additional clues as to what is going on. The NORC surveys asked, "From what countries or part of the world did your ancestors come?" If more than one country was named, the respondent was asked to indicate the one they felt closest to. If they couldn't decide, then tney were recorded separately without any group entered.

Both the 1980 census and the 1979 current population survey accepted *American* as an ethnic ancestry response, but it was discouraged and collected only as a response of last resort. First of all, the use of *American* as a suffix, as in Mexican-American, Italian-American, and so forth was rejected by the census in their coding procedures. A Mexican-American response was counted as Mexican, likewise Italian-American was shortened to Italian, and so on. Even more significantly, the 1979 CPS, which was based on interviews (in contrast to the mail-back procedure in 1980) explicitly instructed its interviewers as follows:

Some persons may not identify with the foreign birth-place of their ancestors or with their nationality group and may report the category "American." If you have explained that we are referring to the nationality group of the person or his or her ancestors before their arrival in the United States, and the person still says that he or she is "American," then print "American." [Emphasis added.]

American was also discouraged in the 1980 census with the instructions specifying that "Ancestry (or origin or descent) may be viewed as the nationality group, the lineage, or the country in which the person or the person's parents or ancestors were born before their arrival in the United States."

Nevertheless, out of a total United States population of 226.5 million in 1980, there were an estimated 13.3 million who gave "American" or "United States" as their ancestry. Just under 6 percent of the population could not name any specific ancestries—or chose not to; in the 1979 survey, the percentage was slightly higher, 6.3 (U.S. Bureau of the Census, 1983a, Table E: 4). To appreciate the importance of this number, consider three additional facts. First, "American" is a major ethnic response, ranking fifth in the nation. To be sure, it trails by a massive amount the 50 million reporting English, the 59 million indicating German, the 40 million with Irish ancestry, and the 21 million who indicated black (the actual number indicating black on the census *race* question is nearly 8 million greater than the number obtained on this ethnic item. But "American" narrowly edges out such groups as French and Italian, and, by much greater margins, exceeds other leading ancestry responses such as Scottish, Polish, Mexican, American Indian, and Dutch (see U.S. Bureau of the Census 1983a: 2).

Second, there is a strong bias against the "American" response. The decision to exclude American as an acceptable multiple response is understandable, even though other multiethnic responses were accepted and recorded by the Census Bureau in both 1979 and 1980. One assumes that many persons used the word "American" along with another ancestry response only as a way of indicating that they were true-blue citizens of the United States, being neither sojourners nor of questionable loyalty. But certainly, there may have been respondents who indicated themselves as, say, Irish-Americans or

some such, not for this reason but in order to convey the complexity of their mixed ancestry and/or the limits of their identification with the group specified. in this regard, the figures for various specific groups combine persons who made such a response exclusively with those who picked the specified group in addition to one or in some cases, two other groups. In 1980, for example, there were 40 million persons recorded as having Irish ancestry; only 25.7 percent of these reported Irish ancestry exclusively (10.3 million) whereas nearly 30 million of these included at least one other ethnic group. Now obviously many of the mixed Irish respondents would pick Irish if they were forced to select only one group, but it is clear that there are more members of the Irish than the American ethnic group in the United States. Nevertheless, it is also clear that these census procedures work toward an undercount of the population who call themselves unhyphenated white or the equivalent.

Finally, a large number of respondents do not report any ancestry, about 23 million respondents in both 1979 and 1980; in effect, about one-tenth of the entire population. It is reasonable to assume that at least some of these would be classified as part of this new group of white Americans who are unable to specify any ethnic ancestry.

The General Social Survey (GSS) conducted by the National Opinion Research Center is relevant to these results. From 1972 through the census year of 1980, there were 1,288 respondents who could not name *any* country at all when asked, "From what countries or part of the world did your ancestors come?" This amounts to 10.7 percent of those responding to the question. In addition, there were 339 who selected "America" in response to the ancestral geography question used in the GSS. Thus about 13.5 percent of the American population could name no country or simply took the America response. The percentage unable to name any country is larger than all but the respondents indicating German, England and Wales, black, and those unable to choose a preference between countries. Both the census and the NORC approaches indicate substantial segments of the population who are unable to specify a conventional ethnic response.

Whites are only about 45 percent of the respondents indicating "American" on the GSS, and they are about 74 percent of the much larger number who cannot name *any* ancestral country. Between these two categories, it means that 9.2 percent of the entire population are whites who are either unable to report an ancestral nation or indicate simply that they are American. Confining ourselves to NORC survey data only for whites, one finds that the unhyphenated-white component amounts to 10 percent of all whites in the period between 1972 and 1980. Thus the number of whites responding as either Americans or unable to name any ancestry is an important component of the entire white population of the United States.

At this point, there are three issues to address. First, is there further evidence that a significant part of the white population is in what might be thought of as an ethnic flux leading toward a new American ethnic group? Second, who are these people who report themselves as American in the census or are unable to indicate any country in the GSS survey? Finally, what are the trends with respect to the unhyphenated white group in the future?

EVIDENCE OF FLUX

There are two separate indications of enormous flux in the ethnic responses among many whites. These come from comparisons of ethnic responses obtained for the same individuals a year apart and the generational makeup of "Americans" and other new residual responses.

Inconsistency

A rare test of consistency and shift was provided by the Current Population Surveys conducted by the Bureau of the Census in 1971, 1972, and 1973. Not only was there a certain degree of overlap in the respondents interviewed in each year with those interviewed in the preceding, but in each case respondents were asked to report their ethnic origin. The same question was asked in March of each year: "What is . . .'s origin or descent?" Of special interest here is the fact that the same people were matched in adjacent years. Hence we have a rare opportunity to "match" the ethnic origin reported for the same person a year later.

There is remarkably low consistency in the ethnic origins reported for persons one year later:

in only 65 percent of the cases was the same ethnic response obtained for the respondent one year later. In other words, in fully one-third of the match-ups, a different response was obtained one year later. These inconsistencies in part reflect procedural difficulties related to the manner in which the data were collected, but intergroup differences in the level of inconsistency suggest that something else is going on – something that might be a true flux or vacillation in the ethnic responses that some people are giving. The degree of fluidity varied greatly between groups in a manner that is quite consistent with the theoretical perspective discussed above. Consistency ranged from nearly 80 to more than 95 percent for Poles, Cubans, Italians, Mexicans, blacks, and Puerto Ricans. On the other hand, the consistency was much lower for white groups from Northwestern Europe, the so-called old European stocks who have many ancestors going back a large number of generations in the United States. Little more than half of the respondents giving English, Scottish, or Welsh in 1971 reported a similar response a year later. Thus inconsistency varies in a systematic way: the older-stock white populations from Northwestern Europe, containing substantial components with many generations of residence in the United States, have much lower levels of consistency than either blacks or whites from relatively more recent sources of immigration such as Italy and Poland.

Such a pattern of inconsistency is exactly what one might expect if flux within the white population increases by generations of residence in the United States. This would be compatible with the simple hypothesis that there is a decline in the ties and knowledge of ancestral homelands such that knowledge of – and identification with – such origins declines sharply, if all factors are held constant.

Generational Comparisons

It is one matter to hypothesize that an increase in the confusion and uncertainty about ancestral origins (as well as perhaps indifference) is a pathway to the development of a new ethnic conception; it is another matter to provide evidence of such a claim. However, the evidence is fairly convincing on this matter.

The NORC survey permits a distinction in terms of four generations, applying the procedure described by Alba and Chamlin (1983). Some 57 percent of the entire U.S. population is at least fourth generation, i.e., the United States is the country of birth for themselves, both of their parents, and all four of their grandparents. Among unhyphenated whites (those unable to name any ancestral country or those choosing "American"), 97 percent were at least fourth generation. Thus unhyphenated whites make up fully 16 percent of all Americans with at least four generations' residence in the country, and therefore about 20 percent of the non-black population with at least four generations' residence in the United States. By contrast, new unhyphenated whites are one percent or less of the third, second and first generations. This sharp difference by generation – with such small percentages for earlier generations – suggests that the data are quite meaningful. One would be suspicious if many of the immigrants or their offspring were unable to state the countries or part of the world from which their ancestors came, and/or if the American response was given after only such a short generational stay in the United States.

An added hypothesis about ethnic origins is suggested by the distinctive regional distribution of these unhyphenated whites. Compared with all whites, unhyphenated whites are especially likely to be found in the South, particularly in the South Atlantic states. Thirty-eight percent of all unhyphenated whites are found in the South Atlantic states, and 67 percent are in the entire South. By contrast, only about 30 percent of the entire white population surveyed by NORC lives in the South. The distribution of unhyphenated whites, in varying degrees throughout the rest of the nation, is less than other whites. This difference from the rest of the country could reflect several different forces:

1. The historically large black population of the South could lead to a relative deemphasis of ethnic distinctions.
2. The white ethnic composition of the South is of proportionately greater numbers of various Northwestern European origins. Perhaps they are especially likely to shift, after taking into account their number of generations in the country.
3. The relative absence of significant new Eu-

ropean immigration has meant that there is less renewal of ethnic ties for older groups and less regeneration of ethnic issues for them in the sense of reminding the older groups of white subdivisions.

4. On the other hand, regional differences could simply reflect the fact that proportionately more of the whites found in a particular region are of 4 or more generations' residence. It is certainly true that there has been only moderate migration to the South for quite some time. So it might well be that the average length of generations within the 4-plus category is greater among those in the South.

The available data are not really adequate to evaluate most of these interpretations. But one can at least compare the distribution of all 4-plus generation whites in the United States with that for unhyphenated whites. Among all whites in the United States, about 53 percent have at least four generations of residence in the country. By contrast, 80 percent of whites in the South have 4-plus generations of residence in the country. This reflects the fact that various white immigrant groups have not, for the most part, found the South an attractive destination. A much larger segment of the Southern white population can trace its ancestry back for a longer span. The concentration of unhyphenated whites in the 4-plus generation category, coupled with the fact that 4-plus generation whites are more likely to be found in the South, would lead one to expect that there would be proportionately more unhyphenated whites in the South. But the concentration is even greater: two-thirds of unhyphenated whites are found in the South, whereas half of all 4-plus generation whites are located in this part of the country (67 versus 46 percent).

CHARACTERISTICS

Neither the census nor the GSS data allow for determination of the true ancestral origins (AO_t) of those reporting themselves as unhyphenated white. Indeed, as the surveys are now constructed, all one can obtain is either some belief about such origins (AO_b), some declaration of self-identification, or a mixture of the two. This means that one of the more interesting questions cannot be answered at this time, to wit, the ancestral origins of those who became unhyphenated whites.

Nevertheless, the census and GSS do permit examination of some of the social characteristics of this population, which in turn, can be compared with the entire white population. The data below are drawn from various GSS data sets obtained between 1972 and 1980.

Not only is the new white ethnic population disproportionately located in the South, but it is especially concentrated in rural areas. In the United States as a whole, 33 percent of all unhyphenated whites are located in what NORC refers to as *Open Country*. By contrast, 17 percent of all whites are located in the open country. This is more than a reflection of regional differences and the former's concentration in the South. Some 27 percent of all whites living in the South are found in open country; by comparison 42 percent of unhyphenated whites living in the South are in these rural areas. It is not easy to determine whether these are areas with relatively little ethnic heterogeneity and where shift is thereby encouraged. All of this is speculative at this point.

The vast majority of unhyphenated whites were raised as Protestant (87 percent) when compared with all whites in the country (64 percent). Although Roman Catholics are clearly less likely to report themselves in this category (8 percent compared with 29 percent of the total white population), it is significant that the category is not exclusively Protestant. If the theoretical exposition presented earlier is valid, one may speculate that the Roman Catholic component will increase in the years ahead, particularly with generational changes. Among those giving either of the unhyphenated white responses, less than 0.5 percent reported themselves as having been raised as Jews.

As a general rule, the unhyphenated white population tends to be of lower socioeconomic status (SES) than the entire white population in the United States. Unhyphenated whites also have considerably lower levels of educational attainment. For example, 15 percent of all whites had four or more years of college, compared with 4 percent of unhyphenated whites. By contrast,

19 percent of the latter had no more than seven years of schooling, compared with 7 percent of all whites. Also noteworthy are some important occupational differences, with the proportion of unhyphenated whites in professional-technical occupations amounting to less than half that found for all whites. There is a massive difference in the opposite direction with respect to concentration in the relatively unskilled operatives-transport category.

The overall occupational prestige score for all whites is 40.7 and 38.9, respectively, for men and women. For purposes of calibration, it is about 31 for black men and women. The score for unhyphenated white men, 36.0, falls just about midway between all white men and black men; the mean prestige score for unhyphenated women is 33.6, considerably close to the level for black women than all white women. In the ten-word vocabulary test used by NORC, the average number of correct responses for all whites is 6.17, compared with 4.54 for unhyphenated whites. This is the lowest score obtained for any of the larger populations, specified as part of a general study of the topic, being very slightly lower than the level obtained for blacks. The general cross-tabulation between educational attainment and vocabulary for the entire population was used to determine the expected number for unhyphenated whites that takes into account their lower educational levels and the obvious influence of education on vocabulary. Using this variant of standardization, one would have expected 5.22 correct words for unhyphenated whites; thus their actual level is even lower than would be expected after taking their levels of education into account.

In regard to conventional political labels, there are only modest differences between whites as a whole and this new ethnic group. About the same percentages are Democrats (subclassified as "strong" or "not very strong"), independents of one sort or another, or Republicans (likewise subdivided). At most, the differences between all whites and unhyphenated whites in any of these categories is no more than 3 percentage points. In similar fashion, there are only modest differences between them in their self-conception along liberal-conservative lines. The biggest gap is rather modest, with 40 percent of all whites and 44 percent of unhyphenated whites describing themselves as "moderate." There are some bigger differences with respect to specific political issues, but for the most part the new unhyphenated white group is not distinctive in conventional political terms.

On the normative issues that were considered, somewhat larger gaps turned up, but for the most part they are hardly of the magnitude to suggest a strikingly unique subset of whites. There are some differences with respect to values for children. Given a list of characteristics, subjects were asked to select the most desired characteristic for a child to have. The three most common ones picked by all whites in the country were honesty (39 percent of those able to choose one characteristic), sound judgment (17 percent), and obeys parents (13 percent). By contrast, these characteristics were picked by 41, 12, and 21 percent of unhyphenated whites as the most desirable. Admittedly, the new ethnic population tends to favor obedience more than do whites generally (a difference of 8 percentage points) and are less concerned about sound judgment, but the gaps are not terribly great. In fact, about 40 percent of both groups pick honesty as the most important characteristic. Of course this type of measure is not necessarily a good substitute for observing actual behavior. More of a gap turns up on some specific political issues, suggesting that unhyphenated whites are more conservative than the total white population. The former are more likely to think that too much is being spent to improve conditions of blacks (41 versus 29 percent for all whites) and are less likely to object to the level of military spending (19 versus 28 percent thinking too much is spent). There is a particularly large difference with respect to the civil liberties question; that is, whether a communist should be allowed to make a speech. Two-thirds of unhyphenated whites thought a communist should *not* be able to, whereas close to 60 percent of all whites thought just the opposite. (Persons who did not respond or indicated "don't know" and the like are excluded from the computations.) On the other hand, the gap is very small (4 percentage points) between unhyphenated whites and all whites with respect to favoring the death penalty. In short, the results are mixed with regard to the

attitudinal-normative qualities of the new white group. On some dimensions they are very close to all whites and on others there are moderate to fairly large differences.

A FINAL NOTE

In recent years, considerable attention has been given to two related theses about white ethnic groups in the United States:

1. The rediscovery and re-emphasis of ethnic identification among white groups in recent years. Presumably the assertions of black pride and black awareness served as a catalyst for this new emphasis among white ethnic groups.
2. The presumed failure of the ethnic melting pot to work as advertised and believed for many years.

It may well be that the melting pot is beginning to work in a different way than has been discussed in the literature. Instead of different groups acting increasingly alike, perhaps a *new* population is in process of forming. Whether this is the case requires much more evidence than is possible to present here. The strongest evidence will come from the 1990 census, when it will be possible to make longitudinal comparisons; specifically, whether there is an increase in the unhyphenated white response for each age- and generational-specific cohort as it ages. At the present time, the proportions giving such responses seem to be concentrated in the older age groups, but with data for one period it is impossible to separate the age, cohort, and period effects.

A second issue pertains to meaning of the responses. Given the relatively low SES positions held by the unhyphenated white population (as measured with NORC data) there is always the possibility that people giving these responses are selective on various characteristics and are not truly representative of a new ethnic thrust. In this regard, the two subsets of the population defined as unhyphenated white with NORC data—those reporting themselves as American as opposed to those unable to name a group—do differ on some dimensions. For example, the specifically American subset appear to be *relatively* higher in SES, less likely to reside in the South, and more Catholic compared to the other subset. But they are still different from all whites. Obviously, this deserves more examination. Under any circumstance, it would be helpful to understand why the population giving these responses are relatively concentrated in lower SES positions. Further clues may well develop when the

census data on American whites are examined. The concentration in the South, in my estimation, is less of a puzzle since it is more a matter of choosing and evaluating several plausible explanations for the fact. However, an evaluation of these different causal forces may well help provide important clues about what factors are generating this new ethnic group in America.

T W E N T Y - F O U R

American Indians and Natural Resource Development
Indigenous People's Land, Now Sought After, Has Produced New Indian-White Problems

C. Matthew Snipp

I. INTRODUCTION

Stemming from agreements made in the 19th century, American Indians occupy a unique niche in the political and economic structures of the United States. These agreements removed American Indians to isolated areas where they now have access to potentially vast resources in the form of water, timber, fisheries, and energy minerals. The growing demand for these resources is in several important ways reshaping

the relationship between Indians and the rest of American society. A dramatic example is that, since the mid-1970s, holdings in energy resources such as gas, coal, oil, and petroleum have given a small number of tribes the power to control raw materials considered vital for the well-being of the national economy.

In an earlier article,[1] I briefly reviewed the literature pertinent to resource development on tribal lands and outlined a simply typology for describing the changing political and economic

Reprinted from the *American Journal of Economics and Sociology*, 45:4 (October 1986) by permission of the author and publisher.

status of American Indians in the wake of natural resource development. This typology remedies several shortcomings in the development literature by taking into account the special legal and historical status of North American Indians. By highlighting the changing status of American Indians before and after development, this typology is primarily intended as a heuristic device for characterizing, in simple terms, an otherwise highly complex process spanning a long period of U.S. history.

The transformation of the political and economic status of American Indians before and after development can be described in terms of two distinctive phases of development: "captive nations" and "internal colonies." Captive nationhood describes the status of American Indian tribes following their subordination to the United States, and before natural resource development. An especially important point is that the captive nation status is mainly a political condition established and maintained through the legal doctrine of tribal sovereignty. During the 19th century, military and bureaucratic measures were used to restrict the powers of tribal leaders, rendering Indians as "sovereign wards of the State." Captive nationhood expresses the limited powers of self-government retained by tribal leaders after their conquest by the United States. Although the status of captive nation insures a measure of political autonomy, it also has made American Indians heavily dependent on federal authorities for diverse types of assistance.

Surrendering their autonomy to become captive nations had little effect on the economic life of most Indian tribes. If anything, it further impoverished Indian people by denying them access to traditional pursuits such as hunting, fishing, and trapping. In relation to the development of natural resources, the dependence and economic vulnerability cultivated among Indian tribes in their tenure as captive nations paved the way for their emergence as internal colonies. Resource development on Indian lands is hastening the process of internal colonialism and this process is revolutionizing the status of American Indian tribes on a scale equal to the restriction of their political powers in the 19th century. As internal colonies, Indian lands are being developed primarily for the benefit of the outside, non-

Indian economy. The tribes have been relatively unsuccessful in capturing the material benefits of development to be used as tribal public revenue, and some observers claim that Indians are now exposed to subtle new forms of economic exploitation, in addition to the political dominance they have experienced as captive nations.

The captive nation–internal colony distinction implies a gradual process by which political domination is translated into economic exploitation. Internal colonialism is a type of economic relationship that has developed out of the political dominance established with the creation of captive nations. Resource development on Indian lands is the mechanism by which tribes are transformed from captive nations into internal colonies. Documenting the changing political and economic position of American Indians requires a survey of historical events as evidence. Other types of data are inadequate for capturing the richness and complexity of this process. This paper has two objectives. The first is to review the historical circumstances by which formerly autonomous Indian tribes were transformed into captive nations. The second objective is to establish how the practices of internal colonialism are manifest in resource development on Indian lands. Collectively, this information should build support for the captive nation–internal colony typology as a way of conceiving the changing status of American Indians.

II. CAPTIVE NATIONS: THE DEVELOPMENT OF UNDERDEVELOPMENT

Showing how American Indian tribes were gradually moved into their status as captive nations illustrates a process that at once led to their political subjugation and facilitated their survival as inhabitants of isolated social enclaves. This process is characterized by alternating trends in social policy that swing between measures aimed at annihilating Indians and Indian culture, and vigorous efforts intended to preserve the remnants of tribal life. The status of American Indian tribes as captive nations did not result from sudden tribal capitulation or from scattered social policies. Captive nationhood is the product of slowly evolving social policies toward Indians beginning with the British administration of colonial America.[2]

Prior to American independence, American Indian tribes enjoyed the political status of fully independent sovereigns and were treated accordingly by the British crown. In recognition of military realities, British authorities enacted policies designed to curry good will with the east coast tribes. Edmund Atkin, one of the British officials responsible for Indian policy wrote:

> The importance of Indians is now generally known and understood. A doubt remains not, that the prosperity of our colonies on the continent will stand or fall with our interest and favor among them. While they are our friends, they are the cheapest and strongest barrier for the protection of our settlements; when enemies, they are capable of ravaging in their method of war, in spite of all we can do, to render these possessions almost useless.[3]

For the British, safeguarding their colonial interests meant developing a set of policies which would provide for equitable relations with the tribes. With this purpose in mind, colonial agents adopted a three-pronged strategy for managing diplomatic relations. Essentially, the British attempted to (1) centralize authority in the conduct of negotiations, (2) upgrade the standards for business ethics among traders dealing with Indian groups and, (3) formalize the procedures for negotiating land cessions from the tribes.

These goals were fully embraced by the Royal Proclamation of 1763 which would later influence U.S. Indian policies. Consistent with British goals, the Royal Proclamation contained four major provisions. It recognized the territorial rights of tribes to lands which they had not formally relinquished by sale or by cession. A second proviso prescribed a boundary line beyond which White settlement would be forbidden. Third, it provided for the removal of White settlers living on Indian lands and, last, it set forth a principle for peacefully acquiring future territory.[4]

The British policies, and especially the 1763 Proclamation, are important because they set the tone for the handling of Indian affairs after the American revolution. In 1783, the Indian Committee of Congress recommended that the U.S. government should enter negotiations with the tribes. In these discussions, the U.S. should try "neither to yield or to require too much."[5] Peaceful negotiations were preferable over what many influential policy makers regarded as the unac-ceptably high cost of military action. This opinion gained further influence with the support of George Washington. Several years later, these sentiments were re-expressed in two major pieces of legislation. One act, Ordinance for the Regulation of Indian Affairs (1786), established an Indian Department and strict rules for the governance of trade. A second act, Ordinance for the Government of the Northwest Territory, contained the framework for Northwestern territorial governance and declared that:

> The utmost good faith shall always be observed towards the Indians, their lands and property shall never be taken from them without their consent; and in their property rights and liberty, they shall never be invaded or disturbed, unless in just and lawful wars authorized by Congress; but laws founded in justice and humanity shall from time to time be made, for preventing wrongs being done to them, and for preserving peace and friendship with them.[6]

In the years shortly after U.S. independence, American Indians still exercised sovereign authority over their lands and people.

This authority was relatively short-lived as it was curtailed by the convergence of several events. Continuing immigration from Europe was a leading cause of expansionary pressures to the south and west of the original thirteen colonies. Between 1790 and 1830, the American population more than tripled from 4 to 13 million.[7] This period is significant because the pressures to expand U.S. territory were decisive in the election of Andrew Jackson in 1828. Prior to his election, Jackson commanded the U.S. troops against the Creek tribe. The Creek Wars of 1813 represented a major defeat for the Creek tribe and signified the growing strength of the U.S. military. The Creek defeat also compromised the image of Indian tribes as major military threats. After his election, Jackson added to his military success by effectively lobbying for the wholesale removal of all Indians east of the Appalachians.[8] In 1830, the Indian Removal Act provided for the relocation of eastern tribes such as Cherokee, Choctaw, Seminole, Creek, and Chickasaw to territory in eastern Oklahoma. Implementing this act established the U.S. government's absolute dominance over these tribes.

While Jackson and his supporters moved to strip all vestiges of tribal authority, Chief Justice

John Marshall of the Supreme Court affirmed the principle of tribal sovereignty in a series of landmark decisions. These decisions offered a limited vision of tribal authority and continue to serve as the foundation of modern legal doctrines favoring sovereignty. In two decisions, Marshall expressed the view that American Indian tribes are "domestic, dependent nations" subject to the authority of the Federal government. In *Cherokee Nation v. Georgia*,[9] Marshall ruled that Indian tribes did not have the same status as a foreign power because:

> It may well be doubted, whether those tribes which reside within the acknowledged boundaries of the United States can, with strict accuracy, be denominated foreign nations. They may, more correctly, perhaps, be denominated domestic dependent nations. . . . They are in a state of pupilage; their relations to the United States resembles that of a ward to his guardian.

Marshall elaborated this theme in *Worcester v. Georgia*[10] by declaring that "Indian nations had always been considered as distinct, independent, political communities, retaining their original natural rights. . . . A weaker power does not surrender its independence – its right to self-government – by associating with a stronger nation, and taking its protection." These passages illustrate the manner in which the subordinate political status of American Indians became ensconced in American legal doctrine. It also illustrates the meaning of the term "captive nation." Events surrounding the Jacksonian attacks and the Marshall defense redefined the political status of American Indians from autonomous sovereigns to captive nations with limited rights of self-government.

Events after 1830 were presaged by Jackson's reaction to Marshall's opinions: "John Marshall has made his decision; let him enforce it."[11] The westward expansion and ensuing Indian Wars were smoothed by the signing of 70 treaties by 1870. Many of these treaties were never ratified by Congress and nearly all were summarily disregarded. By 1871, the domination of American Indians was virtually assured, and Congress confidently approved the legislation which forbade further treaty negotiations. At the close of the decade, 1880, military hostilities were concluded at the expense of $500 million,[12] and the most hostile tribes were quarantined on reservations under military surveillance.

The apparent contradictions of the captive nationhood and the concept of sovereign wardship annoyed the authorities responsible for developing Indian policy in the late 19th century. Indian Affairs Commissioner Edward P. Smith complained in 1873 that, "This double condition of sovereignty and wardship involves increasing difficulties and absurdities. . . . So far, and as rapidly as possible, all recognition of Indians in any other relation than strictly as subjects of the United States should cease."[13]

Jacksonian Indian policy reached its peak in the late 1880s. As a means for severing the federal responsibility implied by wardship, Congress enacted a series of bills between 1878 and 1887 which culminated in the passage of the General Allotment Act (also known as the Dawes Severalty Act). The Allotment Act broke up tribal lands into small tracts that were haphazardly dispensed among tribal members. The rationale for this policy was to encourage Indians to become small farmers by giving them small plots of land. Owning and cultivating allotted land was supposed to hasten their incorporation into American society. Many American Indian tribes possessed little interest or knowledge of farming and much of the allotted land was eventually acquired by non-Indians. Allotment was seen as a failure mostly because it did not speed Indian acculturation.[14]

Counterbalancing the Jacksonian influence, the Indian Reorganization Act of 1934 was a legislative breakthrough and a centerpiece of the New Deal for Indians. This act formally encouraged tribes to take a more active role in their self-governance. It stopped short of re-instituting traditional tribal authority structures because they were perceived as undemocratic. Instead, it called for the formation of tribal councils modeled after western ideals of democratic organization. This act specified that federally recognized tribal councils must be democratically elected and formally organized with constitutions and bylaws. The actions of these councils are subject to scrutiny by the Bureau of Indian Affairs (BIA) and must not violate principles established in federal law. To this day, federal authorities do not recognize the authority granted by tribal traditions that are not in accordance with the basic principles of the Indian Reorganization Act.[15]

After World War II, Jacksonian sentiments re-emerged in policies designed to eliminate federal obligations by promoting Indian assimilation. The BIA established "relocation" programs which encouraged reservation Indians to move to designated urban centers such as Chicago, Minneapolis, and Los Angeles.[16] This policy tilt was formally recognized in 1953 by House Concurrent Resolution 108 (H.C.R. 108). It placed Congress on record as favoring the termination of federal involvement in Indian affairs. The initiatives following H.C.R. 108 made available to non-Indians 1.4 million acres of land and severed relations with tribes in four states.[17] The adverse effects of termination were felt immediately in the loss of basic services such as health and education.

In 1954, the Menominee tribe of Wisconsin was the first to be denied recognition following H.C.R. 108. Symbolizing the failure of these measures and their eventual reversal, legislation was enacted in 1973 which restored the Menominee as a federally recognized tribe.[18] In the same year, the Congress also passed the Indian Self-Determination Act which calls for greater tribal authority in the administration of reservation affairs without diminishing government obligations. The importance of this act is comparable to the legislation authorizing the reorganization of tribal governments. These bills are representative of another swing in public policy toward strengthening tribal powers. The most recent expression of this position appears in the final report of the American Indian Policy Review Commission to the U.S. Senate. This document strongly affirms the legitimacy of tribal sovereignty and emphasizes a more forthright recognition of federal responsibilities.[19]

Involved in the continuing debate over the status of American Indians, the intellectual descendants of John Marshall advocate recognition of limited tribal authority and rights of self-governance. The Jacksonian position argues for policies that deny the legitimacy of tribal organization and would disperse Indians as a distinct segment of American society. As different as these ideological extremes in Indian policy may seem, they are jointly responsible for moving American Indians into increasingly marginal economic situations, and for creating the conditions that make underdevelopment possible. Measures intended to promote the assimilation and acculturation of Indians, such as the Allotment Acts, discounted the legitimacy of tribal authority and were a corrosive influence on tribal organization. Lapses in tribal authority were closely followed by actions that dispersed collectively-held tribal lands and resources. Once these lands and resources were lost, competing policies aimed at the preservation of tribal rights returned a depleted and dwindling resource base to Indian control. Gravitating between the positions of Marshall and Jackson, American Indians have been alternately isolated from society, stripped of their resources, then re-isolated as captive nations. The repetition of this cycle has pushed Indian tribes to the outer fringes of the U.S. economy.

To illustrate this process, around 1881 hostilities had ceased and most tribes had been removed to reservations. Congress had started enacting allotment legislation but it was yet to be fully implemented. In this year, Indians resided on about 156 million acres of reservation land.[20] In the twenty years following allotment, reservation lands fell to 85 million acres in 1900. And in 1928, they reached an all time low of 30 million acres. In less than 50 years, 126 million acres of Indian land were removed from tribal possession. Considering that much of this land was acquired by non-Indians, this loss was made more critical by population growth which enlarged the number of Indians in 1880 from 244,000 to 332,000 in 1930.[21] As a result, the per capita land base changed from 516 acres per person in 1880 to 90 acres per person in 1930, an 83 percent reduction. Even allowing for measurement error, this represents a cataclysmic change in the land available to sustain a population, especially considering that most Indian land is located in agriculturally unproductive areas. At the same time that Indian land was dwindling, a series of land management acts[22] were reassigning former Indian land to homesteaders and encouraging settlers to consolidate land holdings.[23] As their only remaining resource diminished, the restoration of tribal government in 1934 brought back Indian leadership to preside over a constituency impoverished by earlier policies.

III. INTERNAL COLONIES: PERPETUATING UNDERDEVELOPMENT

During the formative years of American capitalism, Indians were viewed as impediments to expansion and exempt from economic interests. Underdevelopment among American Indians resulted from the events related to their political subjugation, and except for the outright expropriation of their land, this preceded the economic relations associated with internal colonialism. The defining mark of internal colonization, economic penetration by outside interests, occurred after the marginal economic position of Indian tribes had been established by earlier legal and military action. From this perspective, internal colonialism is an extension of practices that add economic dominance to the already subordinate political status of the tribes. It should be no surprise that the instruments of internal colonization are not unlike the ones which established political dominance.

Acting on Congressional and Presidential authority, the U.S. military was primarily responsible for curtailing tribal autonomy, stopping short of Jacksonian inspired annihilation. Along with military force, treaties are the legal documents most closely identified with this era of Federal-Indian relations. Treaty agreements and the subsequent removal of Indian tribes sealed their fate as captive nations. Treaty negotiations have been outlawed and the military is no longer responsible for Indian affairs. Lease agreements and the Bureau of Indian Affairs have replaced these institutions in the conduct of contemporary Indian affairs.[24] As the catalysts of internal colonialism, leases facilitate economic penetration by granting access to Indian resources, and with Congressional and executive authority, the BIA administers virtually all leasing agreements.

Resembling minority workers in split labor markets,[25] Indians are exploiting whatever resources are available because their poverty and economic dependency leaves them with few alternatives. The subsequent intrusion of large scale capital investments for the benefit of non-Indian interests, along with poverty and dependency, complete the classic image of internal colonialism. As exporting colonies, Indians are mainly suppliers of agricultural and forest commodities, and mineral resources. The resources most often subject to lease agreements include agricultural land, lumber, water, and energy resources. Because of the scale and potential worth, energy resources are often perceived as the most significant but this has not always been the case. The process of economic penetration began much earlier than the discovery of coal and gas in the west.

Agriculture

The leases of tribal agricultural lands represent the earliest traces of colonial relations. This began in the late 19th century, stimulated by the allotment acts.[26] Allotted lands which are leased under the supervision of the BIA have been especially vulnerable. In 1960, more than 1.5 million acres of the 6 million administered for Indian heirs by the BIA were leased by non-Indians,[27] further shrinking the land base available for the Indian population. Two other factors promote the leasing of agriculturally productive lands to non-Indians. For some tribes, cash crop farming is an alien concept and consequently, they have little interest or expertise in agriculture as a livelihood. For many others, the capital requirements of farming are major impediments which have been repeatedly documented.[28] Financially pressed Indian land owners have few alternatives to leasing their property. Over the past 50 years, ranches and farms have consolidated and become larger, and farm land has become scarcer and more valuable. This has accelerated the leasing of Indian land and created pressures on the Federal Government to make more land available for longer periods of time. In the early 1960s, the lease terms on Indian lands were further liberalized by Congress,[29] providing for agreements up to 99 years.

Common types of agriculture practiced on Indian lands include livestock grazing, dry land farming, and irrigated crops. Traditionally, Indian farmers are most concentrated in grazing which is the least profitable of the three types of farming. Non-Indian lessees are more likely to be engaged in profitable dry land and irrigation farming.[30] Of the productive acreage belonging to American Indians, non-Indians lease 60 percent of irrigated lands, 75 percent of dry farm land, and only 20 percent of the less productive grazing land.[31] Besides having smaller proportions of the most productive lands, American Indians generally have smaller and less productive farms than non-Indians. For example, in the 1950s, most cattle herds on Indian ranches usually consisted of 100 or less animals.[32] Despite the small farm size and low productivity, livestock grazing is a major source of income for many Indians. In 1972, prior to major price increases for energy, livestock grazing provided $78 million in gross revenues compared to $49 million from mineral leases and royalties, and $38 million for timber leases.[33]

The productiveness of Indian lands could be increased by putting additional acreage under irrigation. The BIA estimated in 1974 that at least 400,000 acres could be brought into production with irrigation technology. Most of these lands are in the arid southwest and plains states where water is a scarce and valuable resource.[34] In these regions, the tribes are confronted by a serious dilemma. They may use their water for agricultural production which will be exported from the reservation, or they may export their water directly to rapidly expanding metropolitan areas such as Tucson, Arizona.

Water

In 1908, the Supreme Court case of *Winters v. United States*[35] established the principle that Indian tribes retain the rights to the water on their reservations, except for water relinquished in treaties and other types of agreements. Since the *Winters* decision, the rights of Indian tribes to claim this resource have been defined in a massive and complex body of case law. These decisions alternately deny and reaffirm tribal claims and the case is still in the midst of unfolding. In 1983, pending litigation over water rights involved over 60 water basins and 100 Indian communities.[36]

Much of this litigation results when non-Indians expropriate water without the benefit of lease agreements. Litigation over water rights is costly and protracted but it is the only recourse for most tribes wishing to preserve their resources. For example, in 1913, the Paiute Tribe first pressed their claims on the Truckee River in California. This claim was not settled until 1983 – the Paiutes lost their rights to all but a small portion of the river.[37] The importance of water as a resource is vividly illustrated by the experiences of the Papago and the Ak Chin reservations. Earlier in this century, the Ak Chin reservation cultivated nearly 11,000 acres of farmland but the demand for water created by the rapid growth of Phoenix, Arizona depleted local aquifers until less than 4,000 acres were cultivated in 1980.[38] The Papago, near Tucson, cultivate less than 1 percent of 25,000 acres of tillable soil because water is unavailable.

Despite the scarcity of water and the extended legal struggles over its ownership, water leases and royalties are trivial revenue sources for southwest reservations. These reservations have provided water for urban development throughout this region and received almost nothing in return. The Navajo are the largest tribe in this region and are probably the largest losers to date. To participate in a large irrigation project planned by the Bureau of Reclamation, the Navajo ceded their rights to the San Juan River. Congressional approval was given to this project in 1962 and construction began shortly after Congress acted. The Navajo portion of this irrigation system is yet to be built after 21 years. In another instance, they ceded their rights to 50,000 acre-feet of the Colorado River in exchange for special consideration in hiring at the Central Arizona Project, a large power generating station. Except for a few unskilled jobs, the promised positions have not materialized and the Navajo are alleging widespread discrimination in hiring and promotion.[39] Related to energy development, the Navajo also sold the Peabody Coal Company 3,000 acre-feet of unreplenishable aquifer water for a coal slurry pipeline at Black Mesa. They received the sum of $9,000 per year for this resource.[40]

Timber

Compared to water, the tribes have profited much more from leases on their timber, but only a smaller number of tribes have commercially attractive amounts of this resource. Fourteen reservations receive 96 percent of all timber revenues. In the early 1960s, only 2 sawmills were located on or near reservations but a decade later, nearly two dozen were in operation.[41] A number of these mills, such as the Menominee Mill in Wisconsin, received assistance from the Economic Development Administration. However, there were no mills in operation near the largest timber producing areas of the Northwest. This timber is milled outside Northwest reservations. Amid occasional allegations of mismanagement, the BIA is still responsible for overseeing timber leases on many reservations. During the decade of the 1970s timber leases steadily increased. For example, from 1972 to 1974, the value of timber produced increased from $38 million to $49 million.[42] It is yet unknown how seriously the recent sharp recession in the lumber industry has reduced tribal revenues.

Energy Minerals

Over the past ten years, no other resources have attracted as much attention as the energy-related mineral deposits belonging to Indians in Oklahoma, the mountain states, and the southwest. Rapidly escalating energy prices throughout the 1970s raised the value of these deposits to unprecedented levels. High prices, combined with the large size of these deposits, held forth the potential of unbelievable wealth beneath tribal lands. As knowledge about the size and value of these resources became available, it was followed by a flurry of activity and controversy. Emissaries from the Federal Government and from private interests actively courted the tribes known to have energy reserves. As a result, numerous leases were signed with individuals and tribal groups.

Energy resource development on Indian lands is not a new phenomenon, although it is rapidly expanding. As early as 1900, oil was discovered on the Osage reservation in western Oklahoma.[43] This discovery led to a vast number of oil leases and development sites throughout the Osage reservation (also known as Osage County). For many years, the Osage discoveries represented the only significant mineral developments on tribal land. As late as 1955, 90 percent of the $30 million in total Indian mineral revenues was received by six reservations and a few tribes in

Oklahoma. In this year, the Osage claimed 30 percent of the $30 million, another 15 percent was paid to other tribes in Oklahoma, and another 45 percent went to tribes such as the Navajo and Blackfoot in the southwest and plains states.[44] Almost 15 years later, this situation had changed very little. In 1969, nine reservations received 85 percent of the royalties from mineral development, and the Osage and Navajo accounted for about half of all royalties paid.[45]

Unlike water, there are relatively few disputes over the ownership of mineral rights. Instead, there are intense controversies arising from the terms in lease agreements and the overall handling of energy development on Indian lands. Managing energy resource development and effectively negotiating lease agreements requires highly specialized technical skills and information about geological formations and market behavior. Most tribes, and BIA officials, lack this expertise. They find themselves seriously disadvantaged in dealing with large corporations which possess an abundance of technical information. This lopsided arrangement has produced a series of lease negotiations which virtually have given away Indian resources and have drawn bitter criticism from groups inside and outside the Federal Government.

An extended litany of abuses and incompetence can be recited about the handling of energy developments on Indian lands. They range from outright fraud and theft to simple mismanagement. For example, lacking the resources to do otherwise, the BIA and most tribes rely on oil company reports of how much oil is taken from a lease. Most tribes are too understaffed to oversee pumping operations, and the BIA (as of 1983) has a staff of eight in its division of Energy and Minerals. An example of the abuses that this encourages is that an audit of a major oil company at a single field showed that the company failed to account for 1.38 million barrels of oil between 1971 and 1982. Another example is that in 1981, the Navajo were receiving 15 to 38 cents per ton for coal at the same time foreign buyers were paying American suppliers $70 per ton. This resulted from extremely liberal leases negotiated in the 1950s and 1960s that the BIA declined to renegotiate, even after its own Office of Audit and Investigation urged in 1978 that these leases be reconsidered.[46]

The critics of these leases include numerous authorities within the Federal Government. The Indian Policy Review Commission, the Federal Trade Commission, and the Senate Select Committee on Indian Affairs have been most vocal. After an extensive review of lease agreements and leasing policy in the BIA, the Indian Policy Review Commission concluded that "the leases negotiated on behalf of Indians are among the poorest agreements ever made."[47] Senate and FTC investigations also uncovered widespread incompetence and legally questionable practices. The FTC warned that "it is imperative that the Department of Interior clarify the role of the BIA in a way that leaves no doubt that the BIA's primary responsibility is to the Indians only and not to the developers."[48]

Energy development and its abuses are especially significant in crystallizing a growing recognition of the neo-colonial relationship between American Indians and mainstream American society. Taking note of problems among the Navajos, the U.S. Commission on Civil Rights[49] forthrightly labeled the Navajo reservation an American colony. In an overview of energy development, the American Indian Policy Review Commission[50] compared Indian reservations with developing nations and found numerous similarities, except that lease terms are usually less favorable for Indians.

American Indians are responding by reasserting their tribal sovereignty. Americans for Indian Opportunity, an influential Indian advocacy organization, sponsored a series of conferences in 1974 and 1975 aimed at promoting greater control over reservation resource development. These conferences emphasized the common problems which tribes shared with Third World countries, and urged tribal leaders to adopt strategies which would lead to greater control over tribal resources. The problems arising from colonial exploitation, namely inequitable bargains and dependence, were the central issues addressed at these meetings. Among the solutions proposed were methods for developing tribal expertise in energy resource management, and greater tribal involvement in development pro-

jects. These measures were offered as a way of reshaping the "lease mentality" which facilitates the exploitation of Indian resources by non-Indians.[51]

Taking lessons from these conferences, a group of tribal leaders from 22 tribes, many of whom attended these meetings, formed the Council of Energy Resource Tribes (CERT) in 1975. CERT was organized as a means for improving Indian control over reservation energy projects. Between 1975 and 1977, CERT was virtually unknown among non-Indians until June 1977. At this time, CERT opened discussions with leaders from the Organization of Petroleum Exporting Countries (OPEC). These meetings raised the possibility of having OPEC involved with tribal energy projects. Amid energy shortages allegedly caused by OPEC, the political implications of OPEC sponsored energy development within U.S. boundaries were intolerable to the Federal Government. To avert this possibility, CERT was soon receiving $2 million annually to develop tribal capacities in energy resource management.[52]

Since its creation, CERT's membership has grown to 43 tribes and it continues to develop tribal management skills and advises tribes on the leasing of their lands. CERT advised the Laguna Pueblo to decline $191,000 for a pipeline right of way; they eventually settled for $1.5 million. In another case, the ARCO Company offered the Navajo $280,000 for a pipeline easement which the BIA routinely approved. CERT urged the Navajo to renegotiate and a lease worth $70 million over 20 years was later signed. Recently [as of 1986], oil surpluses and a conservative political climate have adversely affected CERT's prodevelopment positions. The Reagan administration cut two thirds of CERT's 1984 budget and a complete termination of federal support was slated for 1985.[53]

Besides CERT, another important measure designed to capture the benefits of development relies on the exercise of tribal sovereignty. Using this authority, some tribes have enacted *ad valorem* severance taxes on resources leaving the reservation. The Jicarilla Apache were the first to use this power and were immediately confronted with legal challenges from concerned oil companies. In a key 1977 decision, the Supreme Court upheld Apache taxation powers. Since then, several tribes such as the Navajo and the Crow have established tribal tax codes for energy development.[54]

IV. CLOSING REMARKS

The structure of Indian-White relations over the past two centuries is composed of a complex web of events and processes, inextricably linked to the rise of capitalism and industrial society in the U.S. and elsewhere. The complexity of such circumstances defy simplification and easy generalization; it certainly escapes any single inquiry. A comprehensive rendering of U.S.-Indian relations was not intended in the preceding discussion. However, it should be evident from the narrative that the development of natural resources on tribal lands heralds a new era in relations between American Indian tribes and the United States.

This observation is often made but the conceptual framework for understanding this transition is poorly developed. Most observers ignore the special historical circumstances of American Indians and borrow heavily from other theoretical contexts. In response, this and the preceding article outline in historical and conceptual terms, a different way of thinking about the changing status of American Indians. This approach explicitly acknowledges historic events in the development of relations between Indian tribes and the United States by refocusing the underdevelopment perspective. Instead of dwelling on neocolonial relations like most discussions of underdevelopment, this approach attempts to understand these relations by focusing on conditions before and after development. Risking oversimplification, resource development delineates two distinct historical eras in White-Indian relations, suggesting several conclusions about the captive nation–internal colony typology, and about the specific historic events from which it arises.

The early history of Indian-White relations is a period of military actions and other measures consciously used to subordinate Indian tribes, forcing them to recognize the authority of the United States. During this period of history, American Indians very nearly vanished and most tribes escaping annihilation did so by accommodating the demands for their land. American Indians also were not without allies. The survival of American Indians through the 19th century was aided by sympathizers who believed in the integrity of native cultures and the legitimacy of tribal organization. Compromising between the advocates and opponents of Indian rights evolved a political status for American Indian tribes that recognizes them as legitimate authorities but with highly circumscribed rights of sovereignty – captive nations.

Since 1900 and especially in recent years, the bargaining table has replaced the battleground and lease agreements have replaced treaty negotiation, but the outcomes of these encounters are not very different from earlier times. Many American Indian tribes have access to large amounts of increasingly scarce resources in the form of energy minerals, farm land, timber, and water. These resources have grown increasingly scarce throughout the 20th century and as the end of this century nears, it is almost certain that these resources will become even more depleted.

Land that was once considered worthless and "fit only for Indians" is now highly valued and intensely coveted. Rising valuation of Indian lands has spawned a new dimension of Indian-White relations that is as much economic as it is political. Akin to political events of the preceding century, Indian tribes are burdened with disadvantages in developing economic relations with non-Indians. The disadvantages of Indian tribes resemble the conditions associated with internal colonialism, which, as noted earlier, leads a growing number of observers to describe Indian tribes as bona fide internal colonies.

The captive nation–internal colony distinction described in this article, and discussed at length in another essay, should not be seen as an attempt to gloss over a long and complex history of Indian-White political and economic relations. In the most fundamental sense, this typology calls attention to how the political and economic roles of American Indians have been, and remain in a state of flux since the very earliest days of American history. It illustrates how the legacies of Andrew Jackson and John Marshall have been reflected in the policy vacillations that eventually created the politically ambiguous and economically marginal status of "captive nations." It also shows how the economic exploitation associated with natural resource development now qualifies many tribes for the designation of "internal colony." Captive nationhood, by creating the poverty, dependence, and isolation of most tribes, is an indispensable element in the process by which tribes become colonial outposts for outside non-Indian interests.

In relation to development models, especially underdevelopment or dependency theory, this typology is especially useful. These models were originally intended to explain conditions in Third World nations. Their historic and geographic specificity causes them to reveal unseemly gaps when applied to American Indians. The typology in this paper is presented as a minor amendment to the standard underdevelopment prospective, making it resemble more closely the experiences and circumstances of Indian tribes.

The most apparent weakness of this typology is its simplicity in the face of the complexity of Indian-White and Indian-Indian relationships. However appealing the traditional lifestyle of American Indians, contacts with other cultures have also proved beneficial; the introduction of modern scientific medicine is a clear example. A credible complaint is that it reduces a long, complex process into two discrete categories, themselves imprecisely defined. In defense of such a scheme, the face validity and conceptual implications of this typology should recommend it for reasons other than conceptual precision. As a heuristic device, it is intended to reflect the political, economic, and social status of American Indians in U.S. society, and how this status has been changing as a consequence of natural resource development. Regarding empirical realities, two further qualification are crucial. One is that the transformation from captive nation to internal colony is anything but discrete. For some tribes, the transition is likely to be rapid and for others, the process is less abrupt or evolutionary. A second consideration is that not all tribes have made the transition from one status to another. Some tribes are far along in their development as internal colonies, some are not and are actively resisting, other tribes are seeking to reverse the process by expelling development.

These qualifications raise important questions for empirical research. The causal forces shaping the rate of development on Indian reservations is an important research issue with significant implications for theoretical and applied work. A related problem concerns the extent of uneven development across Indian reservations. Systematic documentation is unavailable from any source, public or private. Little is known about why some tribes, resources being equal, choose to exploit their assets while other tribes firmly resist. Space prevents a thorough, in-depth consideration of the evidence which would fully support the implications of this typology. At best, the supporting details are sketchy and await further examination. Answers to these questions will enlarge our knowledge about the political and economic status of American Indians in particular, and provide insights about development processes in general.

ENDNOTES

1. C. Matthew Snipp, "The Changing Political and Economic Status of American Indians: From Captive Nations to Internal Colonies," *American Journal of Economics and Sociology,* Vol. 45, No. 2 (April, 1986), pp. 145–57.

2. The following discussion relies very heavily on D'Arcy McNickle, Mary E. Young, and W. Roger Buffalohead, "Captives within a Free Society," in American Indian Policy Review Commission (AIPRC), *Final Report of the American Indian Policy Review Commission* (Washington, D.C.: U.S. Government Printing Office, 1977), pp. 51–82; Harold E. Fey and D'Arcy McNickle, *Indians and Other Americans: Two Ways of Life Meet* (New York: Harper and Brothers, 1959); Joseph G. Jorgenson, "A Century of Political Economic Effects on American Indian Society, 1880–1980," *Journal of Ethnic Studies* 6: 1–82 (1978).

3. Fey and McNickle, *op. cit.,* p. 50.

4. *Ibid.,* pp. 49–51.

5. *Ibid.,* p. 52.

6. *Ibid.,* p. 53.

7. U.S. Bureau of the Census, *Historical Statistics of the United States, Colonial Times to 1970, Bicentennial Edition, Parts 1 and 2* (Washington, D.C.: U.S. Government Printing Office, 1975): Series A 1–5, p. 8.

8. William T. Hagan, *American Indians,* revised ed. (Chicago, IL: University of Chicago Press, 1979). pp. 59–61; S. Lyman Tyler, *History of Indian Policy* (Washington, D.C.: United States Department of the Interior, Bureau of Indian Affairs, 1973), pp. 56–60.

9. 30 U.S. (5 Pet.) 1 (1831).

10. 21 U.S. (6 Pet.) 515 (1832).

11. Fey and McNickle, *op. cit.*, p. 31.

12. Jorgenson, *op. cit.*, p. 10.

13. Fey and McNickle, *op. cit.*, p. 67.

14. Tyler, *op. cit.*, pp. 95–124.

15. *Ibid.*, pp. 125–150; Jorgenson, *op. cit.*, pp. 17–22.

16. James E. Officer, "The American Indian and Federal Policy," in Jack O. Waddell and O. Michael Watson (eds.), *The American Indian in Urban Society* (Boston: Little, Brown and Company, 1971), pp. 8–65.

17. Raymond V. Butler, "The Bureau of Indian Affairs: Activities since 1945," *The Annals,* 436: 359–69 (1978), p. 52.

18. *Ibid.*, p. 58.

19. AIPRC, *op. cit.*, pp. 3–9 EFNS.

20. These data are taken from U.S. Bureau of the Census, *op. cit.*. Series J 16–19, p. 430.

21. These numbers are illustrative but they should be regarded with caution. Even in recent censuses, federal data are notoriously inaccurate for American Indians. The 1880 population figure is taken from Russell Thornton and Joan Marsh-Thornton, "Estimating Prehistoric American Indian Population Size for United States Area: Implications of the Nineteenth Century Population Decline and Nadir," *American Journal of Physical Anthropology,* 55: 47–53 (1981); Thornton and Thornton, U.S. Bureau of the Census, *op. cit.,* Series A 91–104, p. 14.

22. The 1873 Culture Act, the Desert Land Act of 1877, the Timber and Stone Act of 1878, the Homestead Act of 1862.

23. Jorgenson, *op. cit.*, p. 13.

24. In the late nineteenth century, the Bureau of Indian Affairs was transformed from the War Department to the Interior Department.

25. Edna Bonacich, "A Theory of Ethnic Antagonism: the Split Labor Market," *American Sociological Review,* 37: 547–59 (1972).

26. Jorgenson, *op. cit.*, p. 11–2.

27. William A. Brophy and Sophie D. Aberle, *The Indian: America's Unfinished Business* (Norman, OK: Univ. of Oklahoma Press, 1966), p. 74.

28. *Ibid.*, p. 79; Sar A. Levitan and William B. Johnston, *Indian Giving: Federal Programs for Native Americans* (Baltimore: Johns Hopkins Univ. Press, 1975), p. 21; Stephen W. Fuller, "Indians' Problems in Acquiring Development Capital," Four Corners Agriculture and Forestry Development Study. Special Report No. 11, 1971, p. 28.

29. Public Laws PL 86–326 and PL 88–167.

30. Levitan and Johnston, *op. cit.*, p. 21.

31. *Ibid.*

32. Brophy and Aberle, *op. cit.*, p. 80.

33. Levitan and Johnston, *op. cit.*, p. 20.

34. *Ibid.*, p. 23.

35. 207 U.S. 564 (1908).

36. Jim Richardson and John A. Farrell, "The New Indian Wars," *Denver Post,* Special Reprint. November 20–27 (1983), p. 44.

37. Richardson and Farrell, *op. cit.*, p. 45.

38. *Ibid.*, p. 45.

39. *Ibid.*

40. Joseph G. Jorgenson, Richard O. Clemmer, Ronald L. Little, Nancy J. Owens, and Lynn A. Robbins, *Native Americans and Energy Development* (Cambridge, MA: Anthropology Resource Center, 1978), p. 43.

41. Levitan and Johnston, *op. cit.*, pp. 25–26.

42. *Ibid.*, pp. 20–25.

43. H. Craig Miner, *The Corporation and the Indian: Tribal Sovereignty and Industrial Civilization in Indian Territory, 1865–1907* (Columbia, MO: Univ. of Missouri Press, 1976), p. 171.

44. Brophy and Aberle, *op. cit.*, p. 85.

45. Levitan and Johnston, *op. cit.*, p. 26.

46. Richardson and Farrell, *op. cit.*, p. 17.

47. AIPRC, *op. cit.*, p. 339.

48. Quoted in Richardson and Farrell, *op. cit.*, p. 30.

49. U.S. Commission on Civil Rights, *The Navajo Nation, an American Colony* (Washington, D.C.: U.S. Government Printing Office, 1975).

50. AIPRC, *op. cit.*, p. 344.

51. See Americans for Indian Opportunity (AIO), *Indian Tribes as Developing Nations; A Question of Power: Indian Control of Indian Resource Development* (Albuquerque, NM: Americans for Indian Opportunity, Inc., 1975).

52. Mark Kellogg, "Indian Rights: Fighting Back with White Man's Weapons," *Saturday Review,* November 25, 1978, pp. 24–27; Mary Olson, "Native American Resource Development," unpublished manuscript (1978); Richard Nafziger, "Transnational Corporations and American Indian Development," pp. 9–38 in Roxanne Dunbar, ed., *American Indian Energy Resources and Development* (Santa Fe, NM: Native American Studies, University of New Mexico, 1980).

53. Richardson and Farrell, *op. cit.*, p. 68.

54. *Ibid.*, pp. 17–18.

The Social Organization of Mexican Migration to the United States

Douglas S. Massey

During the 1970s, Mexican immigration to the United States became a mass phenomenon involving millions of people on both sides of the border. Annual legal immigration rose from just over 44,000 in 1970 to more than 100,000 in 1981, while the number of undocumented Mexicans annually apprehended increased from about 277,000 to nearly 900,000. It has been estimated that some 931,000 undocumented Mexicans were counted in the 1980 U.S. census, 81 percent of whom entered during the prior decade. Overall, the population of the United States that is of Mexican origin increased by 93 percent during the 1970s, and about one-third of this increase was attributable to immigration.

Whatever figures one considers, it is obvious that there was a sharp upswing in Mexican immigration during the 1970s, one not adequately explained by economic conditions alone. In the United States, the 1970s brought rising unemployment and falling real wages for American workers, while in Mexico an oil-driven economic boom increased wages and lowered unemployment. If anything, economic conditions predicted a dampening of migration during the late 1970s. The large upsurge in migration between Mexico and the United States reflects the inevitable culmination of a long social process, one intrinsic to the migration enterprise itself.

Massive Mexican migration today reflects the prior development of social networks that support and sustain it. These networks consist of kin and friendship relations that link Mexican sending communities to particular destinations in the United States. People from the same family or town are enmeshed in a web of reciprocal obligations. New migrants draw upon these obligations in order to enter and find work in the United States. As these networks develop and mature, they dramatically reduce the costs of migration, inducing others to enter the migrant work force. The entry of additional migrants, in turn, leads to more extensive networks, which encourages still more migration. Over time, therefore, international migration tends to become a self-perpetuating social phenomenon.

Mature migrant networks provide a social infrastructure capable of supporting mass migration. They have put a U.S. job within reach of nearly all people in western Mexico, the traditional source region for migration to the United States. Temporary migration to the United States is now an integral part of economic strategies in households throughout the region and has become a common event in the family life cycle.

This article examines the structure and development of migrant networks using ethnographic and survey data collected in four Mexican communities between November 1982 and February 1983 and in California between August and September of 1983. A random sample of 200 households was gathered in each of two rural and two urban Mexican communities located in the states of Michoacán and Jalisco. These data were supplemented by nonrandom samples of 60 households that had settled permanently in California. In both the United States and in Mexico, the surveys were administered by Mexican anthropologists, who also conducted extensive ethnographic field work.

THE SOCIAL BASES
OF NETWORK MIGRATION

Migration from Mexico to the United States is an inherently social enterprise. Migrants do not go north alone, but travel in groups comprised of relatives, neighbors, and friends. In moving to a strange and often hostile land, these people naturally draw upon the existing ties of kinship and friendship to share the problems of life abroad. Over time, these basic human relationships acquire new meanings and social functions. They are transformed into a set of social relations the meaning of which is defined within the migrant context. Shared understandings develop about what it means to be a friend, relative, or neighbor within a community of migrants, and eventually these understandings crystallize into a web of interrelationships that constitute a migrant network. Migrant networks grow out of universal human relations that are adapted to the special circumstances of international migration. The relations are not created by the migratory process, but molded to it, and over time they are strengthened by the common bond of the migrant experience itself.

Kinship is the most important base of migrant social organization, and family connections provide the most secure network connections. Male relatives, in particular, have evolved well-established expectations of mutual aid and cooperation in the United States. The strongest relationship is between migrant fathers and sons. Long after they have grown up to form their own families, fathers and sons migrate together. Out of this common experience, the paternal bond is strengthened, and a new relationship between migrant fathers and sons develops. Throughout their lives, migrant fathers and sons are more likely to offer help, information, and services to one another, both at home and abroad.

Between brothers there is also a continual exchange of favors. Facing many demands for assistance from friends and relatives while abroad, migrants favor brothers. To a brother arriving in the United States without money, job, or documents, there is a series of obligations. A place to stay, help in finding work, a loan of money, and the payment of trip expenses are common ways that fraternal ties are strengthened in the migrant context. This relationship between migrant brothers carries over to their sons, with nephews similarly being given preferred treatment over other relatives. A new migrant arriving in the United States can generally count on the help of his father's brother, and many uncles take it upon themselves to initiate their nephews into the migratory process. The strength of the brotherly tie also extends to cousins linked by common male relatives. When young men strike out together for the United States, they are often parallel cousins.

Because of its explosive growth, migration has outgrown a social organization based solely on kinship, and networks have increasingly incorporated other close social relations. The closest bonds outside of the family are those formed by people as they grow up together. These are typically friendships between people of roughly the same age who shared formative experiences as children. A lifetime of shared experiences creates a disposition to exchange favors and to provide mutual assistance, and friends who find themselves sharing another formative experience – international migration – assist one another in a variety of ways: finding an apartment in the United States, sharing information about jobs, pooling resources, borrowing or loaning money.

Although a migrant's friendship connections are initially concentrated among those of the same age, ties gradually extend to other generations as migrants of all ages are drawn together in the United States. If friends from the same town migrate repeatedly, their relations eventually overlap with circles of friends from other communities, greatly expanding the range of the community's network.

The most diffuse type of social relations in the networks is that of *paisanaje,* the sharing of a community of origin, and it has become an increasingly important base of migrant social organization. As with friends and relatives, migrant *paisanos* call upon one another for mutual assistance during their time abroad. *Paisanos* have an obligation to one another not shared with acquaintances from other communities.

Moreover, *paisanaje* reinforces the network in another way. The most important representation of *paisanaje* is the patron saint. Every Mexican town holds an annual fiesta in honor of its benefactor. This celebration represents a reaffirmation of the community and its people, and it has traditionally been an important integrative mechanism in rural Mexico. With the advent of U.S. migration, however, the symbolic value of the patron saint has been shaped to the new reality of a migrant community, and the traditional importance of the fiesta has been greatly augmented.

The saint's fiesta provides a very practical framework within which to reunite families and friends. It is now more a celebration of the return of *los ausentes,* the absent ones, than a ceremony in honor of a saint. By sponsoring the periodic reunion of *los ausentes* and nonmigrant *paisanos,* the fiesta facilitates the reintegration of the former into the community and reaffirms their continuing place in social life by providing a very public demonstration of the community's commitment to them as true *paisanos.*

In the two rural towns under study, a special day in the fiesta has been set aside to honor *los ausentes.* On this day, migrants pay the costs of music, church decorations, fireworks displays, and other diversions. Those who have been able to return are featured in the processions and liturgic acts, and in his sermon for that day, the town priest reaffirms the collective sentiment of unity, speaking of a single community and of a great family with a patron saint that looks over them. In this way, a concrete cultural manifestation of *paisanaje,* the saint's fiesta, has become a very important social institution supporting migration. Symbolically, it reaffirms the existence of an international network of *paisanos* linked together by a common heritage, and, practically, it strengthens the network by facilitating contact between active migrants and prospective migrants at home.

Other institutional mechanisms besides the saint's fiesta have evolved to enable migrants to use the social connections of the network. Although migrants belong to a variety of voluntary organizations in the United States, the most important is the soccer club. One of the two urban communities under study provides a particularly good example of how an organization apparently unrelated to the migrant process, a soccer club, has been adapted to serve the needs of a binational migrant community. Although its manifest functions are recreational, its latent functions are to strengthen and expand the social connections within the network, thereby supporting the migrant enterprise.

The vast majority of migrants from this community go to Los Angeles, a large and sprawling city, where it is not easy to maintain regular contact with friends, relatives, and *paisanos.* Migrants from the community under consideration have resolved this problem through their soccer club, to which all *paisanos* belong as a right. The club was formed to support a team of hometown players competing in a California soccer league. The team trains every Sunday in a public park and has won its league championship for five consecutive years.

The team's success on the playing field has made the club so popular that nearly all *paisanos* in the Los Angeles area are involved. Indeed, the practice field has become an obligatory place of reunion for all out-migrant *paisanos.* It is the place where dates are made, work obtained, friends located, new arrivals welcomed, and news of the town exchanged. Sunday after Sunday, townspeople meet to watch soccer and to socialize. This weekly reunion not only breaks up the routine of work, but it also provides a regular forum for communication and exchange. By sponsoring the regular interaction of townspeople, the soccer club serves as a clearinghouse for jobs, housing, and other information.

These encounters also facilitate the formation of friendly relations with people from other communities in Mexico, who also frequent the athletic fields. On some occasions, when there is a scarcity of hometown players, these people join the team and share in the party mood that prevails after each game, permitting them to take advantage of the information and offers of assistance that spring from these reunions. Their incorporation into the circle of friends, relatives, and *paisanos* from another home community further extends the range of the migrant network.

A QUALITATIVE STUDY
OF NETWORK DEVELOPMENT

One of the two rural communities under study provides a good case study of network development. The first migrants went north at the turn of the century through the efforts of U.S. labor recruiters, who put them in touch with railroad track crews in the southwestern United States. Toward the end of the 1920s, migrants began entering the steel mills around Chicago. These migrants, in turn, got jobs for their friends and relatives, and the flow of migrants shifted primarily to the upper Midwest. Recent arrivals were informed of opportunities for work and housing and were incorporated into the social life of migrants in Chicago. By 1929, a large daughter community of permanent out-migrants had emerged in that city. However, with the onset of the depression, and the subsequent repatriation and return of many families, the social network into Chicago was ruptured. Between 1930 and 1942, this network withered away and died.

With the advent of the *bracero* program in 1942, new contacts were established with agricultural work sites in California, and the flow of migrants was redirected there. These California-directed networks were different from the earlier ones going into Chicago. The *bracero* program permitted the immediate resumption of large-scale international migration because it did not require an extensive social infrastructure of contacts and previous experience. The socio-economic organization of migrants was accomplished through institutional channels sponsored by the U.S. and Mexican governments.

Within a few years, the demand for *bracero* permits greatly exceeded their supply, and undocumented migration began to grow. While U.S. employment was initially arranged through government channels, these soon became irrelevant to migrant recruitment. Government-regulated contracts were replaced by personal relationships between migrants and employers. Information flowed back into the home communities from agricultural areas in California, bypassing the official *bracero* recruitment centers.

Undocumented migration initially developed among men with prior *bracero* experience, whose knowledge, contacts, and experience enabled them to go north with some assurance of finding work. These contacts were encouraged by the growers themselves, who preferred dealing directly with undocumented workers to arranging contracts through the government. By establishing personal relationships with particular migrants, the growers assured themselves of a stable and reliable labor force, without incurring any legal obligations to the workers and above all without having to pay the transportation costs that were stipulated in the *bracero* treaty.

In these direct relations between migrants and growers, intermediaries such as foremen or labor contractors played a key role. They drew upon their kin and friendship connections with townspeople and recruited those people into U.S. agricultural work. These *contratistas,* the intermediaries, tended to settle in the United States and serve as permanent U.S. anchors for the emerging migrant networks. Many of them were former *braceros* who managed to arrange their legal papers before restrictive amendments to U.S. immigration law took effect in 1968. These settlers allowed the development of a pattern of migration typified by the predominance, in a particular place, of a core of settled migrants surrounded by a larger free-floating population of temporary *paisanos.*

Relations between the hometown and the various California communities gradually developed into a stable configuration, and by the end of the *bracero* program in 1964, several specific migrant networks were in place. The maturation of the networks after 1964 coincided with a wave of capital-intensive agricultural modernization in rural Mexico, giving rise to a massive upsurge in out-migration, most of it undocumented. Townspeople turned to international rather than internal migration because the networks put a U.S. job within easy reach. For a resident of this particular town, the networks meant that it was easier to go to California and find a job than to go to Mexico City or Guadalajara.

A QUANTITATIVE STUDY
OF NETWORK DEVELOPMENT

The development of the migrant networks is clearly indicated by quantitative survey data from the four sample communities. Table 1 ex-

TABLE 1   *Social Ties to the United States by Period of Trip and Rural/Urban Status: Migrants from Four Mexican Communities*

Social Tie	Period of Trip			
	Pre-1940	1940–64	1965–82	Pre-1940 to 1982
Rural Communities				
Personal ties to the United States				
Mean number of relatives in the United States	9.9	10.3	15.9	14.3
Mean number of *paisanos* in the United States	29.9	19.9	25.6	24.1
Percentage with migrant parent	0.0%	25.7%	52.9%	43.9%
Percentage with migrant grandparent	0.0%	4.3%	11.2%	8.9%
Organizational ties to the United States				
Percentage in a U.S. social club	0.0%	4.1%	6.0%	5.4%
Percentage in a U.S. religious club	0.0%	5.7%	5.0%	5.1%
Percentage in a U.S. sports club	0.0%	4.1%	16.1%	12.7%
Number of migrants	6	75	208	289
Urban Communities				
Personal ties to the United States				
Mean number of relatives in the United States	15.7	23.3	20.7	21.2
Mean number of *paisanos* in the United States	6.3	7.8	19.1	15.3
Percentage with migrant parent	14.3%	13.9%	27.6%	23.0%
Percentage with migrant grandparent	0.0%	2.8%	7.0%	5.4%
Organizational ties to the United States				
Percentage in a U.S. social club	0.0%	2.7%	3.8%	3.3%
Percentage in a U.S. religious club	0.0%	5.4%	5.7%	5.3%
Percentage in a U.S. sports club	0.0%	5.4%	40.6%	29.8%
Number of migrants	8	37	106	151

amines a variety of social ties to the United States reported by migrants on their most recent U.S. trip. In order to show the development of the networks over time, the data are broken down by period of trip.

As networks matured over time, migrants reported a growing number of family connections in the United States. Those migrating before 1940 generally had the fewest family connections abroad, with rural-origin migrants reporting about 10 relatives in the United States, and urban-origin migrants about 16. Prior to 1940 no one had a grandparent with prior migrant experience, and no rural dweller had a migrant parent.

Only 14 percent of the urban dwellers reported a parent with migrant experience.

During the *bracero* period from 1942 to 1964, however, the foundations for modern network migration were established and the number of family connections grew. After 1965, migrants could count on a much larger set of kinship ties to assist them in getting established and securing employment in the United States. In the most recent period, migrants of rural origin reported about 16 U.S. relatives and urban-origin migrants about 21. Similarly, those with migrant parents had risen to 53 percent in rural areas and to 28 percent in urban areas, and the percentage with migrant grandparents increased in both places as well.

Survey data also show that friendship connections increased over time. Before 1940 urban dwellers reported knowing only 6 *paisanos* on their latest trip to the United States, but after 1965 the number had increased to 19. Among rural dwellers, however, the number of U.S. *paisanos* started high at around 30 before 1940, fell to 20 during the 1940–64 period, and then rose to 26 after 1965. The high number before 1940 reflects the relatively well-developed Chicago network that flowered before the depression.

Ties to voluntary organizations based in the United States grew steadily over time, especially ties to sports clubs. Among urban-origin migrants, soccer clubs grew to become key organizational elements of the migrant network, with the share reporting membership in a sports club increasing from zero percent before 1940 to 41 percent after 1965, and among rural migrants the increase was from zero percent to 16 percent. In the urban community whose soccer club we described earlier, a majority of post-1965 migrants, 53 percent, reported membership in the sports club, compared to under 20 percent before 1965.

The maturation of the networks is also indicated by the emergence of daughter communities in the United States. Around these daughter communities, a social and economic organization grows, channeling migrants in ever increasing numbers to specific points of destination. This channeling occurs as the social networks focus increasingly on specific communities. As the daughter communities develop, the social infrastructure linking them to the parent community becomes ever more complex and reified, and the network becomes increasingly self-sustaining. More migrants move to a particular place because that is where the networks lead and because that is where social connections afford them the greatest chance for success. As more migrants arrive, the range of social connections expands, making subsequent migration to that place even more likely.

This channeling of migrants is evident in . . . the share of new migrants going to different areas of California at various points in time. One rural and one urban community were chosen to illustrate the process. In the rural town,

destinations fluctuated considerably up through the 1950s. After 1960, however, the range of U.S. destinations steadily dwindled, when Los Angeles and the middle San Joaquin Valley emerged as the two predominant poles of attraction, capturing between 50 percent and 80 percent of all migrants. Data for the urban community also show the progressive channeling of migrants into Los Angeles. While the *bracero* program recruited townspeople into agricultural areas during the 1940s, after 1950 Los Angeles became the overwhelmingly favorite destination of new U.S. migrants. By the most recent period, about 90 percent of new urban-origin migrants went to work in the Los Angeles area.

The importance of network connections to the migrant enterprise is suggested in Table 2, which shows how migrants got their U.S. jobs and to whom they turned for financial assistance while in the United States. Of the rural-origin migrants, 35 percent found a job in the United States through a friend, relative, or *paisano,* while 46 percent of urban-origin migrants did so. When rural migrants needed money while abroad, 82 percent fell back on one of these network connections, and 61 percent of the urban migrants did so.

Perhaps the best indication of the important role that networks have played in migration between Mexico and the United States is the effect they have had on the likelihood of out-migration, especially from rural areas. Figure 1 presents the lifetime probability of out-migration for males in the two rural communities under study, estimated for successive five-year periods from 1940 to 1982. These figures were derived from an age-period-cohort analysis of first migration to the United States. The lifetime probability of out-migration represents the hypothetical probability of going to the United States at least once before age 60. It was estimated for successive five-year periods by asking what would happen if men born in that interval went through life subject to the out-migration rates prevailing at the time.

The end of the *bracero* program in 1964 coincided with two events of great importance to rural areas. First, the migrant networks matured and began to acquire increasing momentum. Second, a wave of agricultural modernization mechanized farm production and supplanted tradi-

THE SOCIAL ORGANIZATION OF MEXICAN MIGRATION TO THE UNITED STATES

TABLE 2 *How Migrants Obtained Their U.S. Job and to Whom They Turned for Financial Assistance in the United States: Migrants from Four Mexican Communities (Percentage)*

Source of Aid	Rural Communities	Urban Communities
How U.S. job was obtained		
Through migrant's own search	44.9	42.2
Through friend, relative, *paisano*	34.5	45.8
Through labor contractor	18.9	10.1
Through coyote*	1.1	0.8
Other	0.6	1.1
Number of jobs	(740)	(353)
Where migrant turned for financial help on last trip		
Friend	63.1	28.9
Relative	15.4	23.7
Paisano	3.0	7.9
Employer	7.7	2.7
Bank	7.7	18.4
Other	3.1	18.4
Number needing financial help	(65)	(38)

*A coyote is a person who guides undocumented migrants across the border between Mexico and the United States.

tional crops, displacing farm workers from the traditional sources of sustenance. The result of these developments was a massive upswing in the likelihood of migration after 1965. Modernization spurred migration and the networks directed it northward. A man born in the period 1960–64 had a 56 percent chance of going to the United States at some point in his life, but in the ensuing years the probability of migration rose steadily, and by 1975–79 it reached nearly 90 percent. In other words, by the late 1970s, migration had become universal among men in the communities studied.

CONCLUSION

Prior sections have shown how migration is a social process in which basic human relationships are adapted to play new roles in the migratory enterprise. The familiar relations of kinship, friendship, and *paisanaje* are woven into a social fabric that provides migrants with a valuable adaptive resource in a strange new environment. Through networks of interpersonal relations, people and information circulate to create a social continuum linking communities in Mexico with daughter settlements in the United States. The networks are strengthened by a variety of institutional mechanisms, ranging from the fiesta of the patron saint to United States-based soccer clubs. Social networks provide aspiring migrants with food, housing, transport, work, and a social life in the United States. Their existence greatly reduces the cost of U.S. migration, permitting its regular and repeated use by Mexican families in a conscious economic strategy.

Thus, networks are key elements in understanding Mexican migration to the United States. While the displacement of farm labor by agricultural modernization may cause out-migration, networks direct it to the united States. Over time, the operation of networks tends to be self-perpetuating, so that international migration continues independently of the conditions that originally

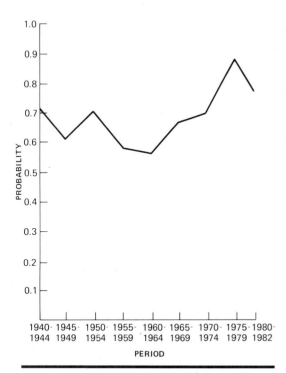

FIGURE 1 *Lifetime Probability of Becoming a Migrant by Period: Males from Two Rural Mexican Towns*

sparked it. Expansion of the networks leads to more migration, which leads to expansion of the networks. Thus, in the late 1970s, when economic conditions in Mexico dramatically improved and those in the United States deteriorated, the likelihood of U.S. migration continued to climb to the point where it became virtually universal among men.

The increasing probability of migration during the past decade occurred in spite of an increasingly restrictive U.S. immigration policy toward Mexico. American policies have not always been so ineffectual, however. In the regeneration of migrant networks after the Great Depression, the *bracero* program sponsored by the United States was pivotal. It permitted the instantaneous resumption of mass migration without developed networks. The program's duration for 22 years, between 1942 and 1964, provided the time necessary for new networks to take hold and grow, so that by the time it ended, it was largely irrelevant to the ongoing migrant process. Migration to the United States had become a self-sustaining social enterprise. Perhaps the most important lesson of this study is that migration is much easier to start than to stop.

A Common Destiny
Blacks and American Society

Gerald David Jaynes
Robin M. Williams, Jr.

Just five decades ago, most black Americans could not work, live, shop, eat, seek entertainment, or travel where they chose. Even a quarter century ago – 100 years after the Emancipation Proclamation of 1863 – most blacks were effectively denied the right to vote. A large majority of blacks lived in poverty, and very few black children had the opportunity to receive a basic education; indeed, black children were still forced to attend inferior and separate schools in jurisdictions that had not accepted the 1954 decision of the Supreme Court declaring segregated schools unconstitutional.

Today the situation is very different. In education, many blacks have received college degrees from universities that formerly excluded them. In the workplace, blacks frequently hold professional and managerial jobs in desegregated settings. In politics, most blacks now participate in elections, and blacks have been elected to all but the highest political offices. Overall, many blacks have achieved middle-class status.

Yet the great gulf that existed between black and white Americans in 1939 has only been narrowed; it has not closed. One of three blacks still live in households with incomes below the poverty line. Even more blacks live in areas where ineffective schools, high rates of dependence on public assistance, severe problems of crime and drug use, and low and declining employment prevail. Race relations, as they affect the lives of inhabitants of these areas, differ considerably from black-white relations involving middle-class blacks. Lower status blacks have less access to desegregated schools, neighborhoods, and other institutions and public facilities. Their interactions with whites frequently emphasize their subordinate status – as low-skilled employees, public agency clients, and marginally performing pupils.

The status of black Americans today can be characterized as a glass that is half full – if measured by progress since 1939 – or as a glass that is half empty – if measured by the persisting disparities between black and white Americans since the early 1970s. Any assessment of the quality of life for blacks is also complicated by the contrast between blacks who have achieved middle-class status and those who have not.

The progress occurred because sustained struggles by blacks and their allies changed American law and politics, moving all governments and most private institutions from support of principles of racial inequality to support of principles of racial equality. Gradually, and often with much resistance, the behaviors and attitudes of individual whites moved in the same direction. Over the 50-year span covered by this study, the social status of American blacks has *on average* improved dramatically, both in absolute terms and relative to whites. The growth of the economy and public policies promoting racial equality led to an erosion of segregation and discrimination, making it possible for a substantial fraction of blacks to enter the mainstream of American life.

Reprinted from *A Common Destiny*, 1989, by permission of The National Academy Press.

The reasons for the continuing distress of large numbers of black Americans are complex. Racial discrimination continues despite the victories of the civil rights movement. Yet, the problems faced today by blacks who are isolated from economic and social progress are less directly open to political amelioration than were the problems of legal segregation and the widely practiced overt discrimination of the few decades past. Slow overall growth of the economy during the 1970s and 1980s has been an important impediment to black progress; in the three previous decades economic prosperity and rapid growth had been a great help to most blacks. Educational institutions and government policies have not successfully responded to underlying changes in the society. Opportunities for upward mobility have been reduced for all lower status Americans, but especially for those who are black. If all racial discrimination were abolished today, the life prospects facing many poor blacks would still constitute major challenges for public policy.

SUMMARY OF MAJOR FINDINGS

. . . We write at a time 20 years after the Kerner Commission, following the summer riots of 1967, warned that ours was becoming a racially divided and unequal nation. We write 45 years after Gunnar Myrdal in *An American Dilemma* challenged Americans to bring their racial practices into line with their ideals. Despite clear evidence of progress against each problem, Americans face an unfinished agenda: many black Americans remain separated from the mainstream of national life under conditions of great inequality. The American dilemma has not been resolved.

The new "American dilemma" that has emerged after the civil rights era of the 1960s results from two aspirations of black Americans: equal opportunity—the removal of barriers to employment, housing, education, and political activities—and the actual attainment of equality in participation in these sectors of life.

Central to the realization of these aspirations are national policies promoting equality of opportunity for the most disadvantaged blacks (especially in areas such as employment and education) and the preservation among black people of

attitudes and behaviors toward self-help and individual sacrifice that have enabled them to benefit from such opportunities. Black-white relations are important in determining the degree to which equal opportunity exists for black Americans. Whites desire equality of treatment in social institutions and in governmental policy; however, many whites are less likely to espouse or practice equality of treatment for blacks in their personal behavior. Thus, at the core of black-white relations is a dynamic tension between many whites' expectations of American institutions and their expectations of themselves. This state of relations is a significant improvement from 45 years ago when majorities of white people supported discrimination against blacks in many areas of life. But the divergence between social principle and individual practice frequently leads to white avoidance of blacks in those institutions in which equal treatment is most needed. The result is that American institutions do not provide the full equality of opportunity that Americans desire.

Foremost among the reasons for the present state of black-white relations are two continuing consequences of the nation's long and recent history of racial inequality. One is the negative attitudes held toward blacks and the other is the actual disadvantaged conditions under which many black Americans live. These two consequences reinforce each other. Thus, a legacy of discrimination and segregation continues to affect black-white relations.

In the context of American history, this continuing legacy is not surprising. Racial and ethnic differences have had crucial effects on the course of American history. In particular, black Americans' central role in several constitutional crises—their past status as slaves and the debates over slavery during the Constitutional Convention of 1787; the fighting of the Civil War; the denial of blacks' basic citizenship until the civil rights movement of the 1950s and 1960s—has frequently focused international attention on black-white relations in the United States. In view of this history, race is likely to retain much of its saliency as a feature of American society for some time.

Indeed, as the twenty-first century nears, demographic conditions will increase Americans' awareness that theirs is a multiracial society. The Bureau of the Census projects that the black population will increase from 11.7 percent of the U.S. total in 1980 to 15 percent in 2020; blacks will be nearly 1 of 5 children of school age and 1 of 6 adults of prime working age (25–54). Rising numbers of blacks will be represented both in influential occupations and positions, and among the poor, the least educated, and the jobless. At the same time, immigration trends are also increasing the numbers and proportions of Asian-Americans and Hispanics in the U.S. population. Thus, the importance of racial and ethnic minorities in general to the nation's well-being is growing.

We can summarize our main findings on the status of blacks in America in the late 1980s succinctly:

- By almost all aggregate statistical measures – incomes and living standards; health and life expectancy; educational, occupational, and residential opportunities; political and social participation – the well-being of both blacks and whites has advanced greatly over the past five decades.
- By almost all the same indicators, blacks remain substantially behind whites.

Beyond this brief picture lies a more complex set of changes that affect the *relative* status of black Americans:

- The greatest economic gains for blacks occurred in the 1940s and 1960s. Since the early 1970s, the economic status of blacks relative to whites has, on average, stagnated or deteriorated.
- The political, educational, health, and cultural statuses of blacks showed important gains from the 1940s through the 1960s. In addition, some important indicators continued to improve after the early 1970s.
- Among blacks, the experiences of various groups have differed, and status differences among those groups have increased. Some blacks have attained high-status occupations, income, education, and political positions, but a substantial minority remain in disadvantaged circumstances.

These patterns of change have been largely determined by three factors:

- Political and social activism among black Americans and their white allies led to changes in governmental policies; particularly important were sweeping improvements in the legal status of blacks.
- Resistance to social change in race relations continues in American society.
- Broad changes in overall economic conditions, especially the post-1973 slowdown in the nation's economic growth, have significantly affected social and economic opportunities for all Americans. . . .

Blacks and Whites in a Changing Society

Two general developments in the status of black Americans stand out; each is reflective of a near-identical development in the population at large. First, for the period 1940–1973, real earnings of Americans improved steadily, but they stagnated and declined after 1973. Similarly, over these same periods, there was a clear record of improving average material status of blacks relative to whites followed by stagnation and decline. Second, during the post-1973 period, inequality increased among Americans as the lowest income and least skilled people were hurt most by changes in the overall economy. Similarly, there were increasing differences in material well-being and opportunities among blacks, and they have been extremely pronounced.

These developments may be understood as consequences of four interdependent events that have altered the status of blacks, relative black-white status, and race relations in the United States. These events were the urbanization and northern movement of the black population from 1940 to 1970; the civil rights movement that forced the nation to open its major institutions to black participation during the same three decades; the unprecedented high and sustained rate of national economic growth for roughly the same period; and the significant slowdown in the U.S. economy since the early 1970s.

The civil rights movement, blacks' more proximate location near centers of industrial activity, and high economic growth enabled those blacks best prepared to take advantage of new opportunities to respond with initiative and success. Increases in educational opportunities were seized by many blacks who were then able to translate better educations into higher status occupations than most blacks had ever enjoyed. Black incomes and earnings rose generally, with many individuals and families reaching middle-class and even upper middle income status. The new black middle class moved into better housing, frequently in the suburbs, and sometimes in desegregated neighborhoods. Despite much confrontation between whites and blacks as blacks abandoned traditional approaches to black-white relations, race relations eventually advanced closer to equal treatment.

At the same time, many blacks were not able to take advantage of the new conditions that developed: some were still located in areas relatively untouched by the changes; some lacked the family support networks to provide assistance; for some, better opportunities simply did not arise. Those who were left behind during the 1960s and 1970s faced and still face very different situations than poor blacks immediately before that period.

A major reason is the performance of the economy. Real weekly earnings (in constant 1984 dollars) of all American men, on average, fell from $488 in 1969 to $414 in 1984; real weekly earnings of women fell from $266 in 1969 to $230 in 1984. For the first time since the Great Depression of the 1930s, American men born in one year (e.g., 1960) may face lower lifetime real earnings than men born 10 years earlier. Among the myriad and complex responses to these economic conditions have been rising employment rates among women, but falling rates among men, while the unemployment rates of both men and women have been on an upward trend for three decades.

A generation ago, a low-skilled man had relatively abundant opportunity to obtain a blue-collar job with a wage adequate to support a family at a lower middle class level or better. Today the jobs available to such men – and women – are often below or just barely above the official poverty line for a family of four. For example, black males aged 25–34, with some high school but no diploma, earned on average $268 weekly in 1986; in 1969, black male dropouts of that age had averaged $334 weekly (in constant 1984 dollars). For white men of the same age and education, work conditions have been better, but changes over time cannot be said to have been good: in the years 1969 and 1986, mean weekly earnings were $447 and $381. Thus, among men who did not complete high school, blacks and whites had lower real earnings in 1986 than in 1969.

Obtaining a well-paying job increasingly requires a good education or a specific skill. Many young blacks and whites do not obtain such training, and the educational system in many locations is apparently not equipped to provide them. Recent reports on the state of American education sound great alarm about the future status of today's students. One in six youths dropped out of high school in 1985, and levels of scholastic achievement are disturbingly low by many measures. Young men with poor credentials, finding themselves facing low-wage job offers and high unemployment rates, frequently abandon the labor force intermittently or completely. Some choose criminal activity as an alternative to the labor market.

Greater numbers of people are today susceptible to poverty than in the recent past. With some year-to-year variation, the percentage of Americans living in poverty has been on an upward trend: from 11.2 percent in 1974 to 13.5 percent in 1986. In addition, the poor may be getting poorer in the 1980s: the average poor family has persistently had a yearly income further below the poverty line than any year since 1963.

More and more of the poor are working family heads, men and women who are employed or seeking employment but who cannot find a job that pays enough to prevent their families from sliding into or near poverty. For the more fortunate, reasonably secure from the fear of poverty, such middle-class advantages as a home in the suburbs and the ability to send their children to the best college for which they qualify are goals that were reached by their parents but may be unattainable for many of them.

Perhaps the most important consequences of the stagnating U.S. economy have been the effects on the status of children. Many members of the next generation of young adults live in conditions ill suited to prepare them to contribute to the nation's future. In 1987, 1 of 5 (20 percent) American children under age 18 – white, black, Hispanic, Native American, and Asian-American – were being raised in families with incomes below official poverty standards. Among minorities the conditions were worse: for example, 45 percent of black children and 39 percent of Hispanic children were living in poverty. During the 1970s, approximately 2 of every 3 black children could expect to live in poverty for at least 1 of the first 10 years of their childhood, while an astounding 1 of 3 could expect at least 7 of those 10 years to be lived in poverty.

We cannot emphasize too much the gravity of the fact that in any given year more than two-fifths of all black children live under conditions of poverty as the 1980s draw to a close. As fertility rates decrease, the total youth population of the United States will contain a larger proportion of comparatively disadvantaged youths from minority ethnic and racial groups. This change may in turn lead to major changes in labor markets, childbearing, the armed forces, and education.

Under conditions of increasing economic hardship for the least prosperous members of society, blacks, because of their special legacy of poverty and discrimination, are afflicted sooner, more deeply, and longer. But the signs of distress that are most visible in parts of the black population are becoming more discernible within the entire population. This distress should be viewed in the context of the underlying changes within American society that affect not only black-white differences, but all disadvantaged blacks and whites who face the difficult economic conditions of the late 1980s.

Determinants of Black Status

One major determinant of black status has been noted in the previous sections: the stagnation of the U.S. economy since 1973, which has particularly hurt lower class blacks. In this section we note two other determinants: organizational and individual resistance to change, intended and otherwise, that has erected and maintained barriers to black opportunities; and the policies of governments and private organizations aimed at improving blacks' position, which have resulted in large measure from black activism, initiative, and self-identity.

Barriers and disadvantages persist in blocking black advancement. Three such barriers to full opportunity for black Americans are residential segregation, continuance of diffuse and often indirect discrimination, and exclusion from social networks essential for full access to economic and educational opportunities. These barriers also existed for blacks who overcame them in earlier decades, but those successes were achieved in an economy that was growing rapidly and providing good wage opportunities even to low-skilled and less educated job seekers. In the 1960s, blacks seeking to help themselves also were benefited by a society more willing to expend energy and resources toward improving opportunities for the poor and minorities.

The past five decades have shown that purposeful actions and policies by governments and private institutions make a large difference in the opportunities and conditions of black Americans. Such purposeful actions and policies have been essential for past progress, and further progress is unlikely without them. Many blacks attained middle-class status because government and private programs enabled them to achieve better educations and jobs, through employment and education programs and government enforcement of equal employment opportunity.

Black initiative and identity have increasingly played primary roles in bringing about changes in government and private institutions and improvements in blacks' economic, social, and political status. This is of course evident in blacks' leadership of the civil rights movement and in their response to industrial opportunity during the great rural-to-urban migration of 1940–1970. But it is also evident in the strivings of individuals to finish high school or attain higher education; to enter a predominantly white factory, secretarial pool, or corporate law office; or to desegregate an entire institution, such as a professional sport, military combat corps, or legislative body.

Many blacks who have not succeeded live in environments in which social conditions and individual behavioral patterns are often detrimental to self-improvement. Such behaviors may be natural responses to group conditions and social forces perceived as beyond personal control. One-half of black families with children must manage their affairs with only one parent—almost always a mother. These families are overwhelmingly poor (59 percent were below the poverty line in 1987), have high rates of dependence on family assistance benefits, and live in areas with a high percentage of families in similar circumstances.

Why do such behaviors and conditions persist? There are no simple answers to this crucial question and no answers that can be validated as scientific findings. We can say, however, that the evidence does not support some popular hypotheses that purport to explain female-headed households, high birth rates to unmarried women, low labor force participation by males, or poor academic performance solely on the basis of government support programs or, more generally, on the existence of a "culture of poverty" among the black poor. Black-white cultural differences have narrowed since 1960, not widened.

Our analysis of the problem does identify a number of important contributory factors. Discrimination plays an important role in the lives of many blacks, and even in the absence of discrimination the opportunities of many blacks are limited. Black youths in poor environments probably anticipate little payoff from working for academic achievement and may underestimate their opportunities. Those in poorly staffed, dilapidated schools populated with underachieving students can easily fall into the trap of perceiving the pursuit of academic excellence as a poor investment. Inequalities in economic status to a large extent cause and interact with other status features to maintain overall black-white differences in status. Consequently, status gaps between blacks and whites will remain as long as blacks' economic status lags behind that of whites. For example, differences in black-white voting patterns result from persistent economic and social inequalities that impede electoral participation regardless of race; individual blacks now participate as much or more than whites of comparable socioeconomic status. Similarly, differences in socioeconomic status account for the entire black-white difference in high school dropout rates. In health, differences in black and white infant mortality are similarly linked to differences in economic status. In the criminal justice system, much of the differential sentencing of blacks and whites can be attributed to differences between sentences for defendants of higher and lower economic status.

Yet the status of blacks is determined by the presence of both racial stratification and class (position within the socioeconomic structure of society). Changes in black-white relations and social opportunities do not affect blacks of different status in similar ways. For example, because of higher geographic concentrations of poor households among blacks, segregated residential areas affect the quality of schools and medical care available to low-income blacks more than they affect the availability of these resources to higher income blacks or low-income whites. And we have already noted that changes in the national economy have had particularly negative effects on lower status Americans, white and black. But changes have been most detrimental to the fortunes of blacks, and opportunities were curtailed most for blacks of lowest status.

A RECORD OF THE STATUS OF BLACK AMERICANS

Attitudes, Participation, Identity, and Institutions

Large majorities of blacks and whites accept the principles of equal access to public institutions and equal treatment in race relations. For whites this is the result of a long upward trend from a low base in the 1940s; blacks have favored equality since survey data have been collected. Yet there remain important signs of continuing resistance to full equality of black Americans. Principles of equality are endorsed less when they would result in close, frequent, or prolonged social contact, and whites are much less prone to endorse policies meant to implement equal participation of blacks in important social institutions. In practice, many whites refuse or are reluctant to participate in social settings (e.g., neighborhoods and schools) in which significant numbers of blacks are present; see Figures 1, 2, and 3.

Whether one considers arts and entertainment, religious institutions, public schools, or a number of other major institutions, black participation has increased significantly since 1940 and since 1960. Yet increased black participation has

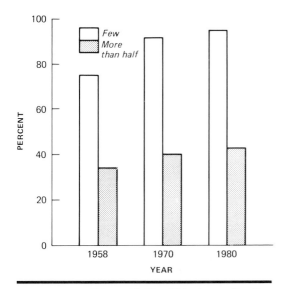

FIGURE 1 *Whites with No Objection to Sending Their Children to a School in Which a Few or More than Half of the Children are Black*

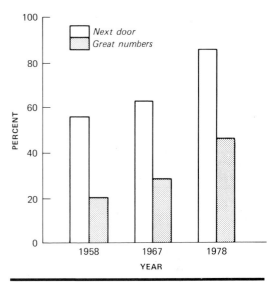

FIGURE 2 *Whites Who Would Not Move If Black People Came to Live Next Door or in Great Numbers in the Neighborhood*

not produced substantial integration. An exception is the U.S. Army, where a true modicum of integration – significant numerical participation on terms of equal treatment – has been accomplished. The other three military services, although generally ahead of the civilian sector, have not attained the level of equality found in the Army. Although large-scale desegregation of public schools occurred in the South during the late 1960s and early 1970s – and has been substantial in many small and medium-sized cities elsewhere – the pace of school desegregation has slowed, and racial separation in education is significant, especially outside the South. And residential separation of whites and blacks in large metropolitan areas remains nearly as high in the 1980s as it was in the 1960s.

These findings suggest that a considerable amount of remaining black-white inequality is due to continuing discriminatory treatment of blacks. The clearest evidence is in housing. Discrimination against blacks seeking housing has been conclusively demonstrated. In employment and public accommodations, discrimination, although greatly reduced, is still a problem.

The long history of discrimination and segregation produced among blacks a heightened

sense of group consciousness and a stronger orientation toward collective values and behavior than exists generally among Americans, and group consciousness remains strong among blacks today. Contemporary conditions in the United States reinforce a recognition of group identity and position among blacks, who continue to be conspicuously separated from the white majority. This separation is manifested in a range of specific findings: two findings of special importance are separation of blacks and whites in residential areas and public schools. The residential separation of blacks and whites is nearly twice the rate of whites and Asian-Americans, and it is often much greater than residential separation between Hispanic Americans and whites in many cities.

These past experiences and current conditions have important consequences for the status of blacks and the manner in which they attempt to improve their status. Blacks overwhelmingly believe in values such as individual responsibility and free competition, but they are more likely to disapprove of the ubiquity of individualism and market autonomy throughout American society than are whites. This disapproval has appeared primarily in black support, at levels higher than

483

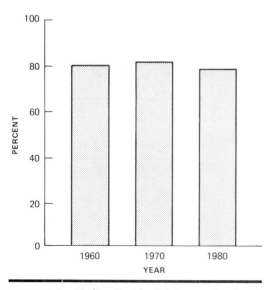

FIGURE 3 *Median Residential Segregation in 29
Metropolitan Areas with the Largest Black
Populations.*

Note: 100 = total segregation; 0 = no segregation.

whites, of such federal policies as guaranteed full employment, guaranteed income floors, and national health care.

Given blacks' history, the sources of this desire for change are not difficult to identify. Data show that blacks generally believe that basic social institutions are biased in favor of whites and against blacks. Many blacks believe that their relative position in society cannot be improved without government policies to intervene with social institutions on behalf of minorities and the disadvantaged. In contrast with whites, blacks have highly favorable views of the high activity years of government policy intervention of the 1960s.

As a consequence of their heightened group consciousness, their belief that racial discrimination remains a major deterrent to black progress, and their history of collective social expression, black Americans vote at the same or higher rates than whites of comparable socioeconomic status, support redistributive policies more often than do whites, and participate in a wider variety of political activity.

This political participation has had some im-

portant effects on American politics. After the legislative and judicial successes of the civil rights movement during the 1960s, there have been continuous struggles to enforce laws and administrative measures aimed at eliminating discrimination and improving opportunities. As a result, blacks' right of access to public facilities and accommodations is now widely accepted. Arbitrary harassment and intimidation of blacks by legal authorities, by organized antiblack organizations, and by unorganized individuals have greatly diminished, although there are regular reports of such incidents.

The changes since 1940 – and particularly since the 1960s – have had important effects on the nature of black communities. The organizations and institutions created by blacks, as well as changing concepts of black identity, were two crucial foundations on which the achievement of sweeping improvements in blacks' legal and political status were attained. Changes in black social structure have resulted from the rising incomes, occupations, and educations of many blacks. The exit of higher status blacks from inner cities has accentuated problems of increasing social stratification among blacks. The service needs of poorer blacks have placed strains on many black institutions, including schools, churches, and voluntary service organizations. These strains have resulted in a proliferation of activities devoted to the material needs of poor blacks by black organizations.

Other effects on black institutions and organizations have been produced by the civil rights movement. Greater access to majority white institutions by higher status blacks' has led to alterations in black leadership structure, problems of recruitment and retention of black talent by black organizations, and reduced participation in many spheres of black life by those blacks. As a result, the often well-knit, if poor and underserviced, black communities of the past have lost some of their cultural cohesion and distinct identity. However, most blacks retain a high degree of racial pride and a conscious need to retain aspects of black culture as a significant component of their American identity. Because of these desires and needs, black institutions continue to play important roles in the lives of most blacks.

Political Participation

Until the 1960s, black political activity was primarily directed toward the attainment of basic democratic rights. Exclusion of black Americans from voting and office holding meant that blacks had to seek political and civil rights through protest and litigation. The civil rights movement arose out of long-standing grievances and aspirations. It was based on strong networks of local organizations and given a clear focus and direction by articulate leadership. Because most blacks were unable to vote, move freely, or buy and sell property as they wished, their efforts were directed to the objective of attaining these basic rights of citizenship. During the civil rights movement, civic equality and political liberty came to be viewed by increasing percentages of Americans as basic human rights that blacks should enjoy. By the 1960s, the federal executive branch and a congressional coalition backed by a sufficient public opinion was finally able to legislate black civil equality.

Active participation by blacks in American political life has had a major impact on their role in the society. Figures 4 to 7 highlight some of the effects. The number of black elected officials has risen from a few dozen in 1940 to over 6,800 in 1988. However, blacks comprise only about 1.5

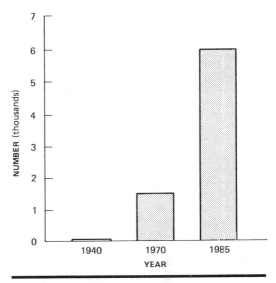

FIGURE 5 *Black Elected Officials*

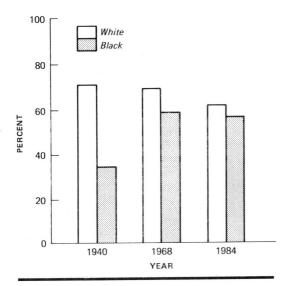

FIGURE 4 *Reported Voter Participation as a Percentage of the Voting-Age Population, by Race*

percent of all elected officials. The election of black officials does result in additional hiring and higher salaries for blacks in public-sector jobs and more senior positions for blacks in appointive public office. The black proportion of federal, state, and local public administrators rose from less than 1 percent in 1940 to 8 percent in 1980; even so, it was less than blacks' 13 percent proportion of the U.S. population. As measured by the proportion of delegates to the national party conventions, black participation in the political party organizations has increased dramatically among Democrats since 1940, while black participation in Republican party affairs, after declining during the 1960s and 1970s, has returned to be about the same level as in 1940.

Blacks' desires for political rights were not merely based on abstract principles of equality, but also on the practical fruits of political participation. Blacks sought democratic rights because they believed that direct access to political institutions through voting, lobbying, and office holding would lead to greater material equality between themselves and the rest of society. However, changes in blacks' socioeconomic status, although complex, have not attained levels commensurate to black-white equality with respect to civil rights. But black influence in the political sector has been an important factor in determin-

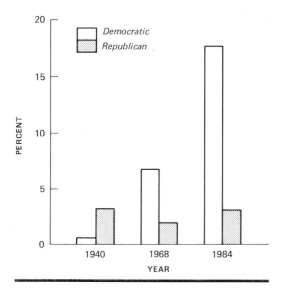

FIGURE 6 *Black National Convention Delegates, by Party*

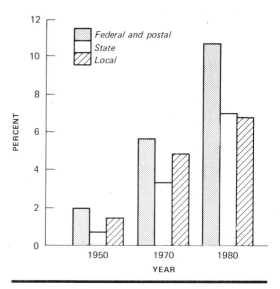

FIGURE 7 *Black Officials and Administrators, by Level of Government*

ing many of the important gains that have occurred. In particular, the extensive development of equal opportunity law has improved the status of blacks (as well as that of women and other minorities) in the areas of education, occupations, health care, criminal justice, and business enterprise. Blacks have also benefited from increased public-sector provision of job training, health care, Social Security, and other cash and in-kind benefit programs.

Although political participation has not been the only important determinant of changes in black opportunities, resulting alterations in American politics have had influence in many areas of life. A review of blacks' status shows that increased civil rights have been important in all areas of society.

Economic Status

Changes in labor market conditions and social policies of governments have had many beneficial effects on the economic status of black Americans. Yet the current economic prospects are not good for many blacks. Adverse changes in labor market opportunities and family conditions—falling real wages and employment, increases in one-parent families with one or no working adults—have made conditions especially difficult for those blacks from the most disadvantaged backgrounds. However, among blacks, changes in family structures per se have not been a major cause of continuing high poverty rates since the early 1970s.

Black-white differences are large despite significant improvements in the absolute and relative positions of blacks over the past 50 years. After initial decades of rising relative black economic status, black gains stagnated on many measures after the early 1970s. Lack of progress in important indicators of economic status during the past two decades is largely a consequence of two conflicting trends: while blacks' weekly and hourly wages have risen relative to whites, blacks' relative employment rates have deteriorated significantly. Figures 8 to 11 present some key data.

In terms of per capita incomes, family incomes, and male workers' earnings, blacks gained relative to whites fairly steadily from 1939 to 1969; measures of relative status peaked in the early to mid-1970s and since have remained stagnant or declined. Women earn much less than men, but the gap between black and white women decreased steadily throughout the period until, by 1984, black women had earnings very close to those of white women. Employment

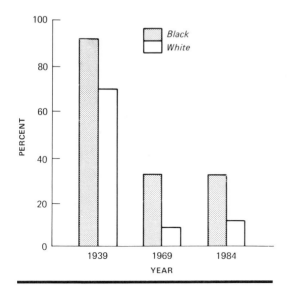

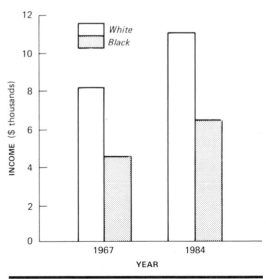

FIGURE 8 *Persons Below the Poverty Level, by Race*

FIGURE 9 *Per Capita Income, by Race*
Note: Per capita income is calculated in 1984 constant dollars.

rates of adult black men and women have been falling relative to those of white men and women throughout the period; black unemployment rates remain approximately twice those of white rates. The proportion of working black men and women in white-collar occupations and in managerial and professional positions increased throughout the period, but these gains show signs of slowing in the 1980s.

Uneven change in the average economic position of blacks has been accompanied, especially during the past 25 years, by accentuated differences in status among blacks. An important aspect of the polarization in the incomes of black families has been the growth of female-headed black families since 1960. It is among such families that the incidence of poverty is highest. It is no exaggeration to say that the two most numerically important components of the black class structure have become a lower class dominated by female-headed families and a middle class largely composed of two-parent families. The percentage of both blacks and whites living in households with incomes below the poverty line declined during the 1939–1975 period. But poverty rates have risen in the past decade, and black poverty rates have been 2 to 3 times higher than white rates at all times.

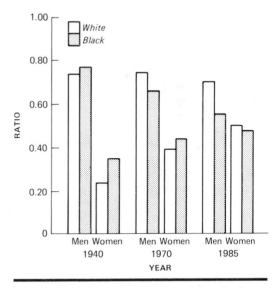

FIGURE 10 *Employment to Population Ratios, by Race*

The major developments accounting for black gains in earnings and occupation status from 1939 to 1969 were South-to-North migration and concurrent movement from agricultural to non-

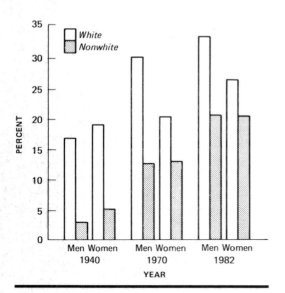

FIGURE 11 *Employed Workers Holding Professional or Managerial Jobs, by Race*

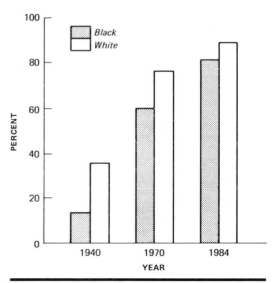

FIGURE 12 *High School Graduates Aged 25–29, by Race*

agricultural employment, job creation, and national economic growth. After 1965, major factors responsible for improvements in blacks' status have been government policies against discrimination, government incentives for the equal employment opportunity of minorities, general changes in race relations, and higher educational attainment.

Schooling

Substantial progress has been made toward the provision of educational resources to blacks. Yet black and white educational opportunities are not generally equal. Standards of academic performance for teachers and students are not equivalent in schools that serve predominantly black students and those that serve predominantly white students. Nor are equal encouragement and support provided for the educational achievement and attainment of black and white students. Figures 12, 13, and 14 highlight some of the effects of the progress that has been made and the gaps that remain.

Measures of educational outcomes – attainment and achievement – reveal substantial gaps between blacks and whites. Blacks, on average, enter the schools with substantial disadvantages in socioeconomic backgrounds and tested achieve-

ment. American schools do not compensate for these disadvantages in background: on average, students leave the schools with black-white gaps not having been appreciably diminished.

There remain persistent and large gaps in the schooling quality and achievement outcomes of education for blacks and whites. At the pinnacle of the educational process, blacks' life opportunities relative to whites' are demonstrated by the fact that the odds that a black high school graduate will enter college within a year of graduation are less than one-half the odds that a white high school graduate will do so. College enrollment rates of high school graduates, after rising sharply since the late 1960s, declined in the mid-1970s; while white enrollment rates have recovered, black rates in the 1980s remain well below those of the 1970s. The proportion of advanced degrees awarded to blacks has also decreased. While we cannot conclude with certainty that the cause has been the decline in (real) financial aid grants to students, other reasonable hypotheses can explain only a negligible component of this change.

Segregation and differential treatment of blacks continue to be widespread in the elementary and secondary schools. We find that school desegregation does not substantially affect the aca-

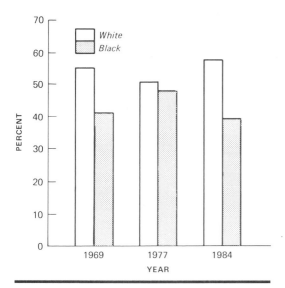

FIGURE 13 *High School Graduates Enrolled in College, by Race*

Note: Percentages are smoothed 3-year averages.

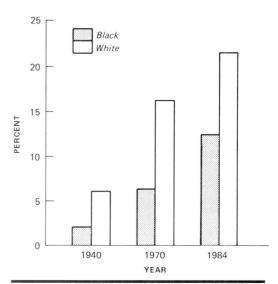

FIGURE 14 *College Graduates Aged 25–29, by Race*

demic performance of white students, but it does modestly improve black performance (in particular, reading). When several key conditions are met, intergroup attitudes and relations improve after schools are desegregated. And desegregation is most likely to reduce racial isolation as well as improve academic and social outcomes for blacks when it is part of a comprehensive and rapid desegregation plan.

Differences in the schooling experienced by black and white students contribute to black-white differences in achievement. These difference are closely tied to teacher behavior; school climate; and the content, quality, and organization of instruction. Early intervention compensatory education programs, such as Head Start, have had positive effects on blacks' educational performance. Among the most recent cohorts to complete their education – people born in the late 1950s and early 1960s – blacks have a median education close to that of whites, 12.6 years, compared with 12.9 years for whites. But a remaining substantial gap in overall educational attainment is noncompletion: high school dropout rates for blacks are double those for whites.

Changes in academic achievement test scores show that, while black students' average scores

remain well below white students' average scores, black performance has improved faster, and black-white differences have become somewhat smaller.

Health

There have been substantial improvements in life expectancy and health status for Americans since 1940. However, overall gains have not been evenly shared. Poor blacks, people on Medicaid, and uninsured groups have unmet needs despite expanded health services. Since 1982, access to health care may be worsening for these groups: 22 percent of blacks and 14 percent of whites under age 65 are not covered by private health insurance or Medicaid.

Persisting wide gaps in the mortality and morbidity of blacks compared to whites remain at all ages except among the oldest old (people 85 and older). Figures 15, 16, and 17 highlight a few aspects of the health status of black Americans. Infant mortality rates have dropped steadily since 1940, for both whites and blacks, but the odds of dying shortly after birth are consistently twice as high for blacks as for whites.

Blacks are underrepresented in the health professions (as compared to their population percentage); this is important since access to care by

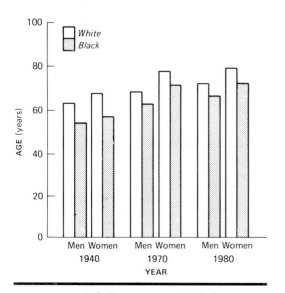

FIGURE 15 *Life Expectancy at Birth, by Race*

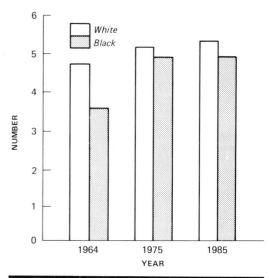

FIGURE 16 *Annual Number of Physician Visits Per Capita, by Race*

minorities and the poor increases with the availability of minority providers.

Preventive or remedial interventions could reduce black-white health gaps at each period of the life cycle. Access to early and appropriate prenatal care prevents low birthweight, infant mortality, and infant neurological damage and other morbidity and reduces maternal mortality. Prenatal care for black mothers lags behind that for whites.

Significant improvement in the health status of blacks will also depend on reducing health-damaging personal behaviors such as substance abuse, injuries (accidental and nonaccidental), homicide, and sexual activities that can cause ill-timed pregnancy or risk infection with sexually transmitted diseases. Slowing the transmission rate of the acquired immune deficiency syndrome (AIDS) in the black community is critical. This will require preventive strategies tailored to the special needs of intravenous drug users and other groups at high risk for human immunodeficiency virus (HIV) infection. Risky behavior is an increasing health problem among young blacks: for example, the homicide rate is more than 6 times higher for black men than for white men.

In adulthood, the cumulative effects of health disadvantages and delaying medical visits until

conditions are serious predispose black adults to higher incidences of chronic illness and disability. Preventive health services as well as assured continuity in management of chronic health conditions would reduce deaths and disability. Poverty and limited bed capacity in care centers, combined with discrimination, pose special problems of access to long-term health care for elderly blacks.

Crime and Criminal Justice

Among black Americans, distrust of the criminal justice system is widespread. Historically, discrimination against blacks in arrests and sentencing was ubiquitous. Prior to the 1970s, very few blacks were employed as law enforcement officials, but in the 1980s, the percentage of blacks in police forces has increased to substantial levels. Black representation among attorneys and judges has also increased, although it is not as high as that in the police.

Blacks are arrested, convicted, and imprisoned for criminal offenses at rates much higher than are whites. Currently, blacks account for nearly one-half of all prison inmates in the United States; thus, blacks' representation in prisons is about 4 times their representation in

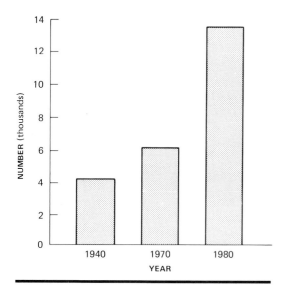

FIGURE 17 *Black Physicians*

the general population. Compared with the total population, black Americans are disproportionately victims of crime: they are twice as likely to be victims of robbery, vehicle theft, and aggravated assault, and 6 to 7 times as likely to be victims of homicide, the leading cause of death among young black males. Blacks also suffer disproportionately from injuries and economic losses due to criminal actions.

Most black offenders victimize other blacks. But offenders and victims are often in different socioeconomic strata: most offenders are poor; many victims are not. Consequently, middle-income and near-poor blacks have greater economic losses due to criminal acts than the black poor or than whites at any income level.

The role of discrimination in criminal justice has apparently varied substantially from place to place and over time. Some part of the unexplained differences in black-white arrest rates may be due to racial bias and the resulting differential treatment. Current black-white differences in sentencing appear to be due less to overt racial bias than to socioeconomic differences between blacks and whites: people of lower socioeconomic status – regardless of race – receive more severe sentences than people of higher status. An important exception may be bias in sentencing

that is related to the race of the victim: criminals whose victims are white are on average punished more severely than those whose victims are black.

As long as there are great disparities in the socioeconomic status of blacks and whites, blacks will continue to be overrepresented in the criminal justice system as victims and offenders. And because of these disparities, the precise degree to which the overrepresentation reflects racial bias cannot be determined.

Children and Families
Changes since the mid-1960s among both blacks and whites have brought higher rates of marital breakup, decreased rates of marriage, rapidly rising proportions of female-headed households, and increasing proportions of children being reared in single-parent families. The changes have been much greater among blacks than among whites. Some characteristics of families are shown in Figures 18, 19, and 20.

Birthrates for both the white and black populations have fallen since the baby boom of the 1950s, and fertility rates have declined for women of all ages. By the mid-1980s, the lifetime fertility rates were similar for black and white women. Contrary to popular myth, birthrates

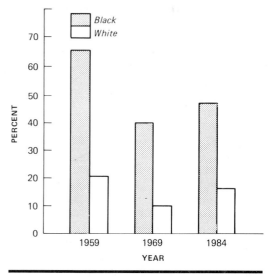

FIGURE 18 *Children in Poverty, by Race*

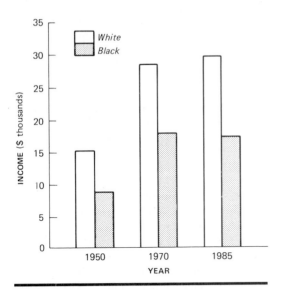

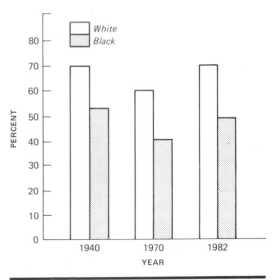

FIGURE 19 *Median Family Income, by Race*
Note: Median family income is calculated in 1985 constant dollars.

FIGURE 20 *Childless Women Aged 20–24, by Race*

among black teenagers – although still an important problem – have declined significantly during the past two decades.

In 1970, about 18 percent of black families had incomes over $35,000 (1987 constant dollars); by 1986 this proportion had grown to 22 percent. The increase in well-to-do families was matched by an increase in low-income families. During the same 1970–1980 period, the proportion of black families with incomes of less than $10,000 grew from about 26 to 30 percent. After declining during earlier decades, the percentage of black and white children in poverty began to increase in the 1970s. In 1986, 43 percent of black children and 16 percent of white children under age 18 lived in households below the poverty line.

Black and white children are increasingly different with regard to their living arrangements. As we noted above, a majority of black children under age 18 live in families that include their mothers but not their fathers; in contrast, four of every five white children live with both parents. (Although some fathers who are not counted as household members may actually aid in child rearing, there are no data to estimate the number, and it is believed to be small.) In the course of

their childhood, 86 percent of black children and 42 percent of white children are likely to spend some time in a single-parent household.

The greater inequality between family types among blacks has important consequences for the welfare of future generations. Black female-headed families were 50 percent of all black families with children in 1985, but had 25 percent of total black family income, while 70 percent of black family income was received by black husband-wife families.

The data and analyses we have examined throw doubt on the validity of the thesis that a culture of poverty is a major cause of long-term poverty. Although cultural factors are important in social behavior, arguments for the existence of unalterable behaviors among the poor are not supported by empirical research. The behaviors that are detrimental to success are often responses to existing social barriers to opportunity. The primary correlates of poverty are macroeconomic conditions of prosperity or recession and changes in family composition. However, increases in female-headed families have had only negligible effects on increasing black poverty rates since the mid-1970s. Importantly, attitudes toward work and the desire to succeed are not very different among the poor and the non-poor.

Black-white differences in family structures result from a complex set of interrelated factors. The most salient are black-white differences in income and employment, greater (relative) economic independence of black women, and a more limited pool of black men who are good marriage prospects.

THE FUTURE: ALTERNATIVES AND POLICY IMPLICATIONS

Blacks' Status in the Near Future

In assessing the status of black Americans, we have asked what roles blacks play in the nation today and what role they are likely to play in the near future. Our conclusion is largely positive, but it is mixed. The great majority of black Americans contribute to the political, economic, and social health of the nation. The typical black adult – like the typical white adult – is a full-time employee or homemaker who pays taxes, votes in public elections, and sends children to school. Blacks make important contributions to all forms of American life, from the sciences and health care, to politics and education, to arts and entertainment.

However, this role is not available to a sizable minority of black – and of a small but growing group of white – Americans. The evidence for this assessment is clear. High school dropout rates among young black adults have risen, and attaining high standards of academic competence seems unavailable to millions of poor black youths attending school systems that are not able to teach them. During the 1980s, thousands of young black men who were not enrolled in school have also not been active participants in the labor market. Many of these men are incarcerated or have dropped out of society into the escape offered by alcohol and drug addiction. And, on the basis of the fertility rates of 1986, 170 of 1,000 black females become mothers before the age of 20, often disrupting or discontinuing their secondary educations. These young mothers are likely to be poor as they establish households, and they will frequently have to receive family assistance benefits. These alarming developments are mirrored by similar, if more modest, trends among whites.

Barring unforeseen events or changes in present conditions – that is, no changes in educational policies and opportunities, no increased income and employment opportunities, and no major national programs to deal directly with the problems of economic dependency – our findings imply several negative developments for blacks in the near future, developments that in turn do not bode well for American society:

- A substantial majority of black Americans will remain contributors to the nation, but improvements in their status relative to whites are likely to slow even more as the rate of increase of the black middle class is likely to decline.
- Approximately one-third of the black population will continue to be poor, and the relative employment and earnings status of black men is likely to deteriorate further.
- Drugs and crime, teenage parenthood, poor educational opportunities, and joblessness will maintain their grip on large numbers of poor and near-poor blacks.
- High rates of residential segregation between blacks and whites will continue.
- The United States is faced with the prospect of continued great inequality between whites and blacks and a continuing division of social status within the black population.
- A growing population of poor and under-educated citizens, disproportionately black and minority, will pose challenges to the nation's abilities to solve the emerging economic and social problems of the twenty-first century.

These short-term projections emerge as important implications of our assessment of the status of black Americans and of black-white relations since 1940. They are especially crucial to the future well-being of the United States, as a common destiny continues to connect black and other Americans. Throughout the last five decades, all Americans have been affected by the same general social processes: technological change, national and international economic developments, and large population movements. Generally, when conditions have been improving for blacks, they have been improving for the entire population. Yet while the same general factors affect all Americans in similar ways, blacks—who as a group still carry many of the effects of systematic discrimination and segregation—are especially sensitive both to changes in the national economy and to changes in public policies.

Residential Segregation

Time alone does not resolve America's racial problems. When the status of blacks has improved, it has not been simply because time has passed. Two reasons for the continuing exclusion of many blacks from the economic mainstream are persisting discriminatory barriers and the residential concentration of poor blacks. It is therefore appropriate to consider the future prospects for reducing current levels of black residential separation.

Black-white residential segregation declined more in the 1970s than in previous decades. Despite these changes, however, levels of black-white segregation remain very high. Considering the 16 metropolitan areas that had the largest black populations in 1980 and using an index for which 100 means all blacks and all whites live in distinct racially homogeneous neighborhoods and zero if all people are randomly distributed, the average index value for black-white residential segregation was about 80. This reflects a drop of about 6 points, on average, from the segregation level of 1970. In contrast, one can compare the indices for Hispanic and Asian-Americans, who entered many metropolitan areas in large numbers during the 1970s. One might expect them to be highly segregated from whites, but their segregation indices average about 45 points. If the historically high 1970s pace of reduction in black-white segregation were to persist, it would take about 60 years for the black-white index to fall to the values currently observed for Hispanic and Asian-Americans.

Income and Poverty

Between 1940 and 1974, poverty as officially measured by cash income declined sharply. The percentage of blacks living in poor households fell from 92 percent in 1939 to 30 percent in 1974; among whites, the change was from 65 to 9 percent. If that trend had continued, the percentage of poor people in the year 2000 would be about 1 percent among whites and 9 percent among blacks. However, the trends toward lower poverty rates came to an end in the early 1970s; since 1974 rates have stagnated or even increased. If the post-1974 trend is extrapolated to the year 2000, the poverty rate among blacks will be about 32 percent and the rate among whites about 15 percent. These are approximately the rates of the late 1960s. Of course such predictions are tentative, since economic conditions or government policies could change.

A similar picture results from the projection of current trends in the incomes of black families vis-à-vis those of white families. When the Bureau of the Census first measured family incomes in 1947, blacks' median incomes were 51 percent of whites'. During the years of economic expansion and civil rights legislation, the status of blacks improved: by 1974, the median income of black families was 62 percent that of white families. A projection of 1947–1974 trends to the year 2000 shows black families with median income about 70 percent of whites. But in fact the median income of black families has not gone up quite as rapidly as that of whites in the past 15 years. Projection of the 1974–1986 trend implies that in the year 2000, the median income of black families would be 54 percent of that of white families—the same as that in 1960.

During the decades from the 1940s through the 1970s, the hourly wage rates and annual earnings of employed black men rose more rapidly than those of white men. Between 1960 and 1980, the relative annual earnings of black men increased from 49 percent of those of white men to 64 percent.

With respect to the relative annual earnings of men aged 25–64, the trend of improvement ended in the 1980s. Between 1960 and 1980, the black/white ratio rose from 49 to 64 percent, but it then fell back to 62 percent by 1987. This reversal arose from an increasing black-white difference in hours of employment. In 1960, black men averaged annually about 8 fewer hours of work per week than white men; this difference declined to about 5 hours per week in 1980, but it then moved up to 7 hours in 1987. If these trends continue to the year 2000, the decrease in black men's employment will offset their gains in hourly wage rates, and the average annual earnings of black men will be 58 percent those of white men, the level observed in the early 1970s.

Policy Alternatives

It was not part of the mandate of this committee to make specific recommendations for public policy. It is, however, an implication of our analyses that such rapid progress as that attained by black Americans in the 1960s will not be attainable in the immediate future without both public and private programs to increase opportunities and to reduce race-connected constraints and disadvantages. On the basis of the findings and analyses of this study, we have identified four areas of national life in which there are major options for constructive social policies to improve opportunities for disadvantaged Americans and especially to reduce impediments to black advancement:

- Provision of education, health care, and other services to enhance people's skills and productive capabilities;
- Facilitation of national economic growth and full employment;
- Reduction of discrimination and involuntary segregation; and
- Development and reform of income-maintenance and other family assistance social welfare programs to avoid long-term poverty.

Each type of policy contains many complex possibilities. Feasible alternatives necessarily must be developed through the political processes by which collective decisions are made. Here we wish only to note some salient options.

Several specific policy interventions have been effective in promoting black advancement and greater opportunities for all Americans. Most successful have been employment and training programs such as the Job Corps; early intervention and other compensatory education programs such as Head Start; government financial aid for postsecondary education; increased access to health care, particularly for pre- and postnatal clinical service for low-income women; and greater health insurance coverage for all poor and near-poor people. These specific policy interventions have been shown to work and to be beneficial to the nation. Improvements in program design are surely possible and should be given the highest priority by policy makers and practitioners.

The one issue that stands out above all others in this study is that of bringing the black population into gainful full employment. This is a major task for public policy. Economic opportunity alone will not solve all problems, of course, but it is the essential ground for other constructive developments. All the evidence reviewed in this report points to the central importance of jobs for men and women at pay levels that permit families to live above the poverty line.

Macroeconomic growth and reduced joblessness create favorable conditions, but they do not remove some crucial barriers that exist for blacks. Improvement depends also on active promotion and vigorous enforcement of antidiscrimination laws and administrative measures to reduce discrimination in employment, education, and housing. Carefully designed programs intended to increase black participation in social institutions can be useful in counteracting the persisting effects of past exclusion, discrimination, and segregation. Both the removal of barriers and compensatory programs are needed for full equality of opportunity. Persistent segregation in neighborhoods and schools, for example, are barriers to equal opportunity, and they cannot be ameliorated without large-scale efforts—national, state, and local.

Economic growth and removal of barriers create many opportunities. To take advantage of such opportunities, however, black Americans must further develop their education, skills, health, and other "human capital." The efforts of individuals and of voluntary associations and groups are likely to increase in the near term. But these efforts can be fully effective only when public programs provide access to job training and education for children and youths from low-income families. The decreases in black college enrollment in the late 1970s and 1980s that followed reductions in federal financial aid to students attest to the importance of such support.

This brings us to the fourth type of social policy on our list: policies to reduce extreme and long-term poverty. Income-maintenance and family assistance programs have developed to meet residual problems not solved by general economic growth and equal opportunity measures. For example, although better education and job training programs have a potential for helping to place workers into available jobs, they will not overcome all the barriers that keep many single mothers and men out of the labor force.

Furthermore, the provision of employment is not enough, by itself, to raise all families out of poverty. Three-fourths of recipients of family assistance and other benefits are unable to find work at wages sufficient to produce incomes above the poverty level even if they worked year-long at full-time jobs. To reduce the extreme poverty of such families—primarily mothers and children in female-headed households—thus requires supplementary programs and changes in tax policies and child support programs. The Family Support Act of 1988 was passed by Congress late in the year, and we were not able to assess its likely effects.

Programs specifically aimed at the reduction of poverty may take two contrasting approaches: a single comprehensive program such as the negative income tax or a set of programs directed to different categories of individuals and families, such as child allowances, Social Security for the aged, special aid for the ill and disabled, and so on. The latter approach characterizes the present situation in the United States. Although this diversity is often criticized, plausible arguments can be advanced that the more differentiated approach can be made both more efficient and politically feasible.

Black Perspectives

The historical record of black people in America shows a persisting tension between the goals of social separation from whites and inclusion within the broader society. This tension differs from—although it has some similarities to—the tension between cultural assimilation and pluralism among groups of different national origins. Black Americans have long debated the merits of integrated participation with whites as opposed to the development of autonomous organizations and communities.

In the past, segregation and discrimination helped to create strong currents of so-called "black nationalism," illustrated in separatist politics as well as in cultural autonomy movements. But blacks' political and economic interdependence with white Americans is very great and is growing. Our data show that black separatism is not a dominant orientation. The likelihood appears low that separatism will be important in the near future, with the exception of some use of separatist ideology in political debate. Yet there is much evidence that racial identities and interests are likely to remain significant in political affairs, and in public life generally, for the foreseeable future. We do not find convincing evidence that such identities and interests are diminishing in importance.

Full assimilation of blacks in a "color-blind" society is unlikely in any foreseeable future. Existing social and economic separation, very low rates of intermarriage, and group preferences and images ensure the continued existence of distinct racial groups. It does not mean a continuation of discrimination in public life, but it does mean that black Americans will claim acceptance and equality on their own terms. Although a "color-blind" society is not foreseen, integrated participation in public affairs is becoming more acceptable. Indeed, political and civic coalitions and joint collective activities are now common. A high degree of cooperation and coalition between blacks and whites has been and is now important on selective issues of legislative and administrative politics. Coalitions with other racial and ethnic minorities will likely grow in importance as such minorities become an increasing proportion of the total citizenry.

We cannot exclude the possibility of confrontation and violence. The urban revolts and civil disorders of the 1960s and later are still vividly present in memory; the 1980s had barely begun when blacks in Miami exploded in anger and dissatisfaction. The ingredients are there: large populations of jobless youths, an extensive sense of relative deprivation and injustice, distrust of the legal system, frequently abrasive police-community relations, highly visible inequalities, extreme concentrations of poverty, and great racial awareness. Such conditions sometimes produce apathy when disadvantaged persons feel that their situation is hopeless. But the surface calm can disappear very quickly. A specific source of possible social turbulence is widespread dissatisfaction with the operation of the criminal justice system, which is evident among black Americans. The allegations of bias are two-sided: that law enforcement officials, judicial proceedings, and the correctional system treat blacks with undue harshness, and that the system is too lenient with whites who commit criminal offenses against blacks. Given the high likelihood that young urban males, blacks and whites, will continue on occasion to find themselves in confrontational situations, and given the continuing high incidence of street crime, it is realistic to expect future episodes of racial violence, followed by concentrated pressures on legal and correctional institutions to deal with alleged racial bias.

CONCLUSION

After our intensive review, the committee has a concluding reflection on the wider implications of the findings. We believe it is consistent with the research data and the best available historical understandings of how American society functions.

Every society to survive has to adapt to its environment and maintain its resources over time. It must cope with the basic economic problem—the efficient allocation of scarce resources—as well as with its external relations to other societies. Every society must also develop practical arrangements for the internal distribution of power, economic goods, and social prestige and respect. Finally, societies over the long term must safeguard their own legitimacy and historical meaning. These latter tasks of social integration and cultural maintenance tend to be discounted and neglected in a task-oriented society that focuses attention on short-run payoffs. In the United States of the coming decades, any agenda for these basic needs will have to give high priority to dealing with the fissures that have been created by the history of relations among black and white Americans. Our review leads us to believe that now is an appropriate time for a serious national effort to grasp the means at hand to accomplish this vital assignment.

The Cost of Racial and Class Exclusion in the Inner City

Loïc J.D. Wacquant
William Julius Wilson

After a long eclipse, the ghetto has made a stunning comeback into the collective consciousness of America. Not since the riots of the hot summers of 1966–68 have the black poor received so much attention in academic, activist, and policymaking quarters alike.[1] Persistent and rising poverty, especially among children, mounting social disruptions, the continuing degradation of public housing and public schools, concern over the eroding tax base of cities plagued by large ghettos and by the dilemmas of gentrification, the disillusions of liberals over welfare have all combined to put the black inner-city poor back in the spotlight. Owing in large part to the pervasive and ascendant influence of conservative ideology in the United States, however, recent discussions of the plight of ghetto blacks have typically been cast in individualistic and moralistic terms. The poor are presented as a mere aggregation of personal cases, each with its own logic and self-contained causes. Severed from the struggles and structural changes in the society, economy, and polity that in fact determine them, inner-city dislocations are then portrayed as a self-imposed, self-sustaining phenomenon. This vision of poverty has found perhaps its most vivid expression in the lurid descriptions of ghetto residents that have flourished in the pages of popular magazines and on televised programs devoted to the emerging underclass.[2] Descriptions and explanations of the current predicament of inner-city blacks put the emphasis on individual attributes and the alleged grip of the so-called culture of poverty.

This article, in sharp contrast, draws attention to the specific features of the proximate social structure in which ghetto residents evolve and strive, against formidable odds, to survive and, whenever they can, escape its poverty and degradation. We provide this different perspective by profiling blacks who live in Chicago's inner city, contrasting the situation of those who dwell in low-poverty areas with residents of the city's ghetto neighborhoods. Beyond its sociographic focus, the central argument running through this article is that the interrelated set of phenomena captured by the term "underclass" is primarily social-structural and that the ghetto is experiencing a "crisis" not because a "welfare ethos" has mysteriously taken over its residents but because joblessness and economic exclusion, having reached dramatic proportions, have triggered a process of hyperghettoization.

Indeed, the urban black poor of today differ both from their counterparts of earlier years and from the white poor in that they are becoming increasingly concentrated in dilapidated territorial enclaves that epitomize acute social and economic marginalization. In Chicago, for instance, the proportion of all black poor residing in extreme-poverty areas—that is, census tracts with a population at least 40 percent of which

"The Cost of Racial and Class Exclusion in the Inner City," by Loïc J.D. Wacquant and William Julius Wilson, THE ANNALS of the American Academy of Political and Social Science (501), pp. 8–26, © 1989 by the American Academy of Political and Social Science. Reprinted by permission of Sage Publications, Inc.

comprises poor persons – shot up from 24 percent to 47 percent between 1970 and 1980. By this date, fully 38 percent of all poor blacks in the 10 largest American cities lived in extreme-poverty tracts, contrasted with 22 percent a decade before, and with only 6 percent of poor non-Hispanic whites.[3]

This growing social and spatial concentration of poverty creates a formidable and unprecedented set of obstacles for ghetto blacks. As we shall see, the social structure of today's inner city has been radically altered by the mass exodus of jobs and working families and by the rapid deterioration of housing, schools, businesses, recreational facilities, and other community organizations, further exacerbated by government policies of industrial and urban laissez-faire[4] that have channeled a disproportionate share of federal, state, and municipal resources to the more affluent. The economic and social buffer provided by a stable black working class and a visible, if small, black middle class that cushioned the impact of downswings in the economy and tied ghetto residents to the world of work has all but disappeared. Moreover, the social networks of parents, friends, and associates, as well as the nexus of local institutions, have seen their resources for economic stability progressively depleted. In sum, today's ghetto residents face a closed opportunity structure.

The purpose of this article is to begin to highlight this specifically sociological dimension by the changing reality of ghetto poverty by focusing on Chicago's inner city. Using data from a multistage, random sample of black residents of Chicago's poor communities,[5] we show that ghetto dwellers do face specific obstacles owing to the characteristics of the social structure they compose. We begin, by way of background, by sketching the accelerating degradation of Chicago's inner city, relating the cumulation of social dislocations visited upon its South and West sides to changes in the city's economy over the last thirty years.

DEINDUSTRIALIZATION AND HYPERGHETTOIZATION

Social conditions in the ghettos of Northern metropolises have never been enviable, but today they are scaling new heights in deprivation, oppression, and hardship. The situation of Chicago's black inner city is emblematic of the social changes that have sown despair and exclusion in these communities. As Table 1 indicates, an unprecedented tangle of social woes is now gripping the black communities of the city's South Side and West Side. In the past decade alone, these racial enclaves have experienced rapid increases in the number and percentage of poor families, extensive out-migration of working- and middle-class households, stagnation – if not real regression – of income, and record levels of unemployment. As of the last census, over two-thirds of all families living in these areas were headed by women; about half of the population had to rely on public aid, for most adults were out of a job and only a tiny fraction of them had completed college.[6]

The single largest force behind this increasing social and economic marginalization of large numbers of inner-city blacks has been a set of mutually enforcing spatial and industrial changes in the country's urban political economy[7] that have converged to undermine the material foundations of the traditional ghetto. Among these structural shifts are the decentralization of industrial plants, which commenced at the time of World War I but accelerated sharply after 1950, and the flight of manufacturing jobs abroad, to the Sunbelt states, or to the suburbs and exurbs at a time when blacks were continuing to migrate en masse to Rustbelt central cities; the general deconcentration of metropolitan economies and the turn toward service industries and occupations, promoted by the growing separation of banks and industry; and the emergence of post-Taylorist, so-called flexible forms of organizations and generalized corporate attacks on unions – expressed by, among other things, wage cutbacks and the spread of two-tier wage systems and labor contracting – which has intensified job competition and triggered an explosion of low-pay, part-time work. This means that even mild forms of racial discrimination – mild by historical standards – have a bigger impact on those at the bottom of the American class order. In the labor-surplus environment of the 1970s, the weakness of unions and the retrenchment of civil rights enforcement aggravated the structuring of un-

TABLE 1   *Selected Characteristics of Chicago's Ghetto Neighborhood, 1970–80*

Area	Families below Poverty Line (percentage)		Unemployed (percentage)		Female-Headed Families (percentage)		Median Family Income*		Residents with Four-Year College Degree (percentage)	
	1970	1980	1970	1980	1970	1980	1970	1980	1970	1980
West Side										
Near West Side	35	47	8	16	37	66	6.0	7.5	5	13†
East Garfield Park	32	40	8	21	34	61	6.4	9.7	1	2
North Lawndale	30	40	9	20	33	61	7.0	9.9	2	3
West Garfield Park	25	37	8	21	29	58	7.5	10.9	1	2
South Side										
Oakland	44	61	13	30	48	79	4.9	5.5	2	3
Grand Boulevard	37	51	10	24	40	76	5.6	6.9	2	3
Washington Park	28	43	8	21	35	70	6.5	8.1	2	3
Near South Side	37	43	7	20	41	76	5.2	7.3	5	9†

Source: Chicago Fact Book Consortium, *Local Community Fact Book: Chicago Metropolitan Area* (Chicago: Chicago Review Press, 1984).

*In thousands of dollars annually.
†Increases due to the partial gentrification of these areas.

skilled labor markets along racial lines,[8] marking large numbers of inner-city blacks with the stamp of economic redundancy.

In 1954, Chicago was still near the height of its industrial power. Over 10,000 manufacturing establishments operated within the city limits, employing a total of 616,000, including nearly half a million production workers. By 1982, the number of plants had been cut by half, providing a mere 277,000 jobs for fewer than 162,000 blue-collar employees—a loss of 63 percent, in sharp contrast with the overall growth of manufacturing employment in the country, which added almost 1 million production jobs in the quarter century starting in 1958. This crumbling of the city's industrial base was accompanied by substantial cuts in trade employment, with over 120,000 jobs lost in retail and wholesale from 1963 to 1982. The mild growth of services—which created an additional 57,000 jobs during the same period, excluding health, financial, and social services—came nowhere near to compen-

sating for this collapse of Chicago's low-skilled employment pool. Because, traditionally, blacks have relied heavily on manufacturing and blue-collar employment for economic sustenance,[9] the upshot of these structural economic changes for the inhabitants of the inner city has been a steep and accelerating rise in labor market exclusion. In the 1950s, ghetto blacks had roughly the same rate of employment as the average Chicagoan, with some 6 adults in 10 working (see Table 2). While this ratio has not changed citywide over the ensuing three decades, nowadays most residents of the Black Belt cannot find gainful employment and must resort to welfare, to participation in the second economy, or to illegal activities in order to survive. In 1980, two persons in three did not hold jobs in the ghetto neighborhoods of East Garfield Park and Washington Park, and three adults in four were not employed in Grand Boulevard and Oakland.[10]

As the metropolitan economy moved away from smokestack industries and expanded out-

TABLE 2 *The Historic Rise of Labor Market Exclusion in Chicago's Ghetto Neighborhoods, 1950–80*

	Adults Not Employed (percentage)		
	1950	1970	1980
City of Chicago	43.4	41.5	44.8
West Side			
Near West Side	49.8	51.2	64.8
East Garfield Park	38.7	51.9	67.2
North Lawndale	43.7	56.0	62.2
South Side			
Oakland	49.1	64.3	76.0
Grand Boulevard	47.5	58.2	74.4
Washington Park	45.3	52.0	67.1

Source: Computed from Chicago Fact Book Consortium, *Local Community Fact Book: Chicago Metropolitan Area;* Philip M. Hauser and Evelyn M. Kitagawa, *Local Community Fact Book for Chicago, 1950* (Chicago: University of Chicago, Chicago Community Inventory, 1953).

Note: Labor market exclusion is measured by the percentage of adults not employed, aged 16 years and older for 1970 and 1980, 14 years and older for 1950.

In the 1960s, 47th Street was still the social hub of the South Side black community. Sue's eyes light up when she describes how the street used to be filled with stores, theaters and nightclubs in which one could listen to jazz bands well into the evening. Sue remembers the street as "soulful." Today the street might be better characterized as "soulless." Some stores, currently exchanges, bars and liquor stores continue to exist on 47th. Yet, as one walks down the street, one is struck more by the death of the street than by its life. Quite literally, the destruction of human life occurs frequently on 47th. In terms of physical structures, many stores are boarded up and abandoned. A few buildings have bars across the front and are closed to the public, but they are not empty. They are used, not so secretly, by people involved in illegal activities. Other stretches of the street are simply barren, empty lots. Whatever buildings once stood on the lots are long gone. Nothing gets built on 47th. . . . Over the years one apartment building after another has been condemned by the city and torn down. Today many blocks have the bombed-out look of Berlin after World War II. There are huge, barren areas of Kenwood, covered by weeds, bricks, and broken bottles.[11]

Duncan reports how this disappearance of businesses and loss of housing have stimulated the influx of drugs and criminal activities to undermine the strong sense of solidarity that once permeated the community. With no activities or organizations left to bring them together or to present them as a collectivity, with half the population gone in 15 years, the remaining residents, some of whom now refer to North Kenwood as the "Wild West," seem to be engaged in a perpetual *bellum omnium contra omnes* for sheer survival. One informant expresses this succinctly: " 'It's gotten worse. They tore down all the buildings, deterioratin' the neighborhood. All your friends have to leave. They are just spreading out your mellahs [close friends]. It's not no neighborhood anymore.' "[12] With the ever-present threat of gentrification – much of the area is prime lakefront property that would bring in huge profits if it could be turned over to upper-class condominiums and apartment complexes to cater to the needs of the higher-income clientele of Hyde Park, which lies just to the south – the future of the community appears gloomy. One resident explains: " 'They want to put all the blacks in the projects. They want to build buildings for the rich, and not us poor people. They are trying to

side of Chicago, emptying the Black Belt of most of its manufacturing jobs and employed residents, the gap between the ghetto and the rest of the city, not to mention its suburbs, widened dramatically. By 1980, median family income on the South and West sides had dropped to around one-third and one-half of the city average, respectively, compared with two-thirds and near parity thirty years earlier. Meanwhile, some of the city's white bourgeois neighborhoods and upper-class suburbs had reached over twice the citywide figure. Thus in 1980, half of the families of Oakland had to make do with less than $5500 a year, while half of the families of Highland Park incurred incomes in excess of $43,000.

A recent ethnographic account of changes in North Kenwood, one of the poorest black sections on the city's South Side, vividly encapsulates the accelerated physical and social decay of the ghetto and is worth quoting at some length:

move us all out. In four or five years we will all be gone.' "[13]

Fundamental changes in the organization of America's advanced economy have thus unleashed irresistible centrifugal pressures that have broken down the previous structure of the ghetto and set off a process of hyperghettoization.[14] By this, we mean that the ghetto has lost much of its organizational strength – the "pulpit and the press," for instance, have virtually collapsed as collective agencies – as it has become increasingly marginal economically; its activities are no longer structured around an internal and relatively autonomous social space that duplicates the institutional structure of the larger society and provides basic minimal resources for social mobility, if only within a truncated black class structure. And the social ills that have long been associated with segregated poverty – violent crime, drugs, housing deterioration, family disruption, commercial blight, and educational failure – have reached qualitatively different proportions and have become articulated into a new configuration that endows each with a more deadly impact than before.

If the "organized," or institutional, ghetto of forty years ago described so graphically by Drake and Cayton[15] imposed an enormous cost on blacks collectively,[16] the "disorganized" ghetto, or hyperghetto, of today carries an even larger price. For, now, not only are ghetto residents, as before, dependent on the will and decisions of outside forces that rule the field of power – the mostly white dominant class, corporations, realtors, politicians, and welfare agencies – they have no control over and are forced to rely on services and institutions that are massively inferior to those of the wider society. Today's ghetto inhabitants comprise almost exclusively the most marginal and oppressed sections of the black community. Having lost the economic underpinnings and much of the fine texture of organizations and patterned activities that allowed previous generations of urban blacks to sustain family, community, and collectivity even in the face of continued economic hardship and unflinching racial subordination, the inner-city now presents a picture of radical class and racial exclusion. It is to a sociographic assessment of the latter that we now turn.

THE COST OF LIVING IN THE GHETTO

Let us contrast the social structure of ghetto neighborhoods with that of low-poverty black areas of the city of Chicago. For purposes of this comparison, we have classified as low-poverty neighborhoods all those tracts with rates of poverty – as measured by the number of persons below the official poverty line – between 20 and 30 percent as of the 1980 census. Given that the overall poverty rate among black families in the city is about one-third, these low-poverty areas can be considered as roughly representative of the average non-ghetto, non-middle-class, black neighborhood of Chicago. In point of fact, nearly all – 97 percent – of the respondents in this category reside outside traditional ghetto areas. Extreme-poverty neighborhoods comprise tracts with at least 40 percent of their residents in poverty in 1980. These tracts make up the historic heart of Chicago's black ghetto: over 82 percent of the respondents in this category inhabit the West and South sides of the city, in areas most of which have been all black for half a century and more, and an additional 13 percent live in immediately adjacent tracts. Thus when we counterpose extreme-poverty areas with low-poverty areas, we are in effect comparing ghetto neighborhoods with other black areas, most of which are moderately poor, that are not part of Chicago's traditional Black Belt. Even though this comparison involves a truncated spectrum of types of neighborhoods,[17] the contrasts it reveals between low-poverty and ghetto tracts are quite pronounced.

It should be noted that this distinction between low-poverty and ghetto neighborhoods is not merely analytical but captures differences that are clearly perceived by social agents themselves. First, the folk category of ghetto does, in Chicago, refer to the South Side and West Side, not just to any black area of the city; mundane usages of the term entail a social-historical and spatial referent rather than simply a racial dimension. Furthermore, blacks who live in extreme-poverty areas have a noticeably more negative opinion of their neighborhood. Only 16 percent rate it as a "good" to "very good" place to live in, compared to 41 percent among inhabitants of low-poverty tracts; almost 1 in 4 find their neighborhood "bad or very bad" compared to fewer than 1 in 10 among the latter. In short, the contrast between ghetto and non-ghetto poor areas is one that is socially meaningful to their residents.

The Black Class Structure in and out of the Ghetto

The first major difference between low- and extreme-poverty areas has to do with their class structure (See Figure 1). A sizeable majority of blacks in low-poverty tracts are gainfully employed: two-thirds hold a job, including 11 percent with middle-class occupations and 55 percent with working-class jobs, while one-third do not work.[18] These proportions are exactly opposite in the ghetto, where fully 61 percent of adult residents do not work, one-third have working-class jobs and a mere 6 percent enjoy middle-class status. For those who reside in the urban core, then, being without a job is by far the most likely occurrence, while being employed is the exception. Controlling for gender does not affect this contrast, though it does reveal the greater economic vulnerability of women, who are twice as likely as men to be jobless. Men in both types of neighborhoods have a more favorable class mix resulting from their better rates of employment: 78 percent in low-poverty areas and 66 percent in the ghetto. If women are much less frequently employed—42 percent in low-poverty areas and 69 percent in the ghetto do not work—they have comparable, that is, severely limited, overall access to middle-class status: in both types of neighborhood, only about 10 percent hold credentialed salaried positions or better.

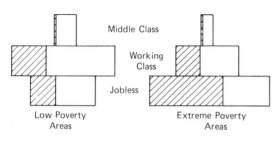

FIGURE 1 *The Black Class Structure in Chicago's Low- and Extreme-Poverty Areas*
Source: Urban Poverty and Family Structure Survey.

These data are hardly surprising. They stand as a brutal reminder that joblessness and poverty are two sides of the same coin. The poorer the neighborhood, the more prevalent joblessness and the lower the class recruitment of its residents. But these results also reveal that the degree of economic exclusion observed in ghetto neighborhoods during the period of sluggish economic growth of the late 1970s is still very much with us nearly a decade later, in the midst of the most rapid expansion in recent American economic history.

As we would expect, there is a close association between class and educational credentials. Virtually every member of the middle class has at least graduated from high school; nearly two-thirds of working-class blacks have also completed secondary education; but less than half— 44 percent—of the jobless have a high school diploma or more. Looked at from another angle, 15 percent of our educated respondents—that is, high school graduates or better—have made it into the salaried middle class, half have become white-collar or blue-collar wage earners, and 36 percent are without a job. By comparison, those without a high school education are distributed as follows: 1.6 percent in the middle class, 37.9 percent in the working class, and a substantial majority of 60.5 percent in the jobless category. In other words, a high school degree is a *conditio sine qua non* for blacks for entering the world of work, let alone that of the middle class. Not finishing secondary education is synonymous with economic redundancy.

Ghetto residents are, on the whole, less educated than the inhabitants of other black neighborhoods. This results in part from their lower class composition but also from the much more modest academic background of the jobless: fewer than 4 in 10 jobless persons on the city's South Side and West Side have graduated from high school, compared to nearly 6 in 10 in low-poverty areas. It should be pointed out that education is one of the few areas in which women do not fare worse than men: females are as likely to hold a high school diploma as males in the ghetto—50 percent—and more likely to do so in low-poverty areas—69 percent versus 62 percent.

Moreover, ghetto residents have lower class origins, if one judges from the economic assets of their family of orientation.[19] Fewer than 4 ghetto dwellers in 10 come from a family that owned its home and 6 in 10 have parents who owned nothing, that is, no home, business, or land. In low-poverty areas, 55 percent of the inhabitants are from a home-owning family while only 40 percent had no assets at all a generation ago. Women, both in and out of the ghetto, are least likely to come from a family with a home or any other asset – 46 percent and 37 percent, respectively. This difference in class origins is also captured by differential rates of welfare receipt during childhood: the proportion of respondents whose parents were on public aid at some time when they were growing up is 30 percent in low-poverty tracts and 41 percent in the ghetto. Women in extreme-poverty areas are by far the most likely to come from a family with a welfare record.

Class, Gender, and Welfare Trajectories in Low- and Extreme-Poverty Areas

If they are more likely to have been raised in a household that drew public assistance in the past, ghetto dwellers are also much more likely to have been or to be currently on welfare themselves. Differences in class, gender, and neighborhood cumulate at each juncture of the welfare trajectory to produce much higher levels of welfare attachments among the ghetto population (Table 3).

In low-poverty areas, only one resident in four are currently on aid while almost half have never personally received assistance. In the ghetto, by contrast, over half the residents are current welfare recipients, and only one in five have never been on aid. These differences are consistent with what we know from censuses and other studies: in 1980, about half of the black population of most community areas on the South Side and West Side was officially receiving public assistance, while working- and middle-class black neighborhoods of the far South Side, such as South Shore, Chatham, or Roseland, had rates of welfare receipt ranging between one-fifth and one-fourth.[20]

None of the middle-class respondents who live in low-poverty tracts were on welfare at the time they were interviewed, and only one in five had ever been on aid in their lives. Among working-class residents, a mere 7 percent were on welfare and just over one-half had never had any welfare experience. This same relationship be-

TABLE 3 *Incidence of Welfare Receipt and Food Assistance among Black Residents of Chicago's Low- and Extreme-Poverty Areas (Percentage)*

	All Respondents		Males		Females	
	Low Poverty	Extreme Poverty	Low Poverty	Extreme Poverty	Low Poverty	Extreme Poverty
On aid when child	30.5	41.4	26.3	36.4	33.5	43.8
Currently on aid	25.2	57.6	13.4	31.8	32.4	68.9
Never had own grant	45.9	22.0	68.6	44.5	31.3	11.9
Expects to remain on aid*						
Less than 1 year	52.9	29.5	75.0	56.6	46.1	25.0
More than 5 years	9.4	21.1	5.0	13.0	10.8	22.0
Receives food stamps	33.5	60.2	22.2	39.1	40.4	70.0
Receives at least one of five						
forms of food assistance†	51.1	71.1	37.8	45.0	59.6	85.2

Source: Urban Poverty and Family Structure Survey, University of Chicago, Chicago, IL.

*Asked of current public-aid recipients only.

†Including pantry or soup kitchen, government food surplus program, food stamps, Special Supplemental Food Program for Women, Infants and Children, free or reduced-cost school lunches.

tween class and welfare receipt is found among residents of extreme-poverty tracts, but with significantly higher rates of welfare receipt at all class levels: there, 12 percent of working-class residents are presently on aid and 39 percent received welfare before; even a few middle-class blacks – 9 percent – are drawing public assistance and only one-third of them have never received any aid, instead of three-quarters in low-poverty tracts. But it is among the jobless that the difference between low- and extreme-poverty areas is the largest: fully 86 percent of those in ghetto tracts are currently on welfare and only 7 percent have never had recourse to public aid, compared with 62 percent and 20 percent, respectively, among those who live outside the ghetto.

Neighborhood differences in patterns of welfare receipt are robust across genders, with women exhibiting noticeably higher rates than men in both types of areas and at all class levels. The handful of black middle-class women who reside in the ghetto are much more likely to admit to having received aid in the past than their male counterparts: one-third versus one-tenth. Among working-class respondents, levels of current welfare receipt are similar for both sexes – 5.0 percent and 8.5 percent, respectively – while levels of past receipt again display the greater economic vulnerability of women: one in two received aid before as against one male in five. This gender differential is somewhat attenuated in extreme-poverty areas by the general prevalence of welfare receipt, with two-thirds of all jobless males and 9 in 10 jobless women presently receiving public assistance.

The high incidence and persistence of joblessness and welfare in ghetto neighborhoods, reflecting the paucity of viable options for stable employment, take a heavy toll on those who are on aid by significantly depressing their expectations of finding a route to economic self-sufficiency. While a slim majority of welfare recipients living in low-poverty tracts expect to be self-supportive within a year and only a small minority anticipate receiving aid for longer than five years, in ghetto neighborhoods, by contrast, fewer than 1 in 3 public-aid recipients expect to be welfare-free within a year and fully 1 in 5 anticipate needing assistance for more than five years. This difference of expectations increases

among the jobless of both genders. For instance, unemployed women in the ghetto are twice as likely as unemployed women in low-poverty areas to think that they will remain on aid for more than five years and half as likely to anticipate getting off the rolls within a year.

Thus if the likelihood of being on welfare increases sharply as one crosses the line between the employed and the jobless, it remains that, at each level of the class structure, welfare receipt is notably more frequent in extreme-poverty neighborhoods, especially among the unemployed, and among women. This pattern is confirmed by the data on the incidence of food assistance presented in Table 3 and strongly suggests that those unable to secure jobs in low-poverty areas have access to social and economic supports to help them avoid the public-aid rolls that their ghetto counterparts lack. Chief among those are their financial and economic assets.

Differences in Economic and Financial Capital

A quick survey of the economic and financial assets of the residents of Chicago's poor black neighborhoods (Table 4) reveals the appalling degree of economic hardship, insecurity, and deprivation that they must confront day in and day out.[21] The picture in low-poverty areas is grim; that in the ghetto is one of near-total destitution.

In 1986, the median family income for blacks nationally was pegged at $18,000, compared to $31,000 for white families. Black households in Chicago's low-poverty areas have roughly equivalent incomes, with 52 percent declaring over $20,000 annually. Those living in Chicago's ghetto, by contrast, command but a fraction of this figure: half of all ghetto respondents live in households that dispose of less than $7500 annually, twice the rate among residents of low-poverty neighborhoods. Women assign their households to much lower income brackets in both areas, with fewer than 1 in 3 in low-poverty areas and 1 in 10 in extreme-poverty areas enjoying more than $25,000 annually. Even those who work report smaller incomes in the ghetto: the proportion of working-class and middle-class households falling under the $7500 mark on the South and West sides – 12.5 percent and 6.5 percent, respectively – is double that of other black

TABLE 4 *Economic and Financial Assets of Black Residents of Chicago's Low- and Extreme-Poverty Areas (Percentage)*

	All Respondents		Males		Females	
	Low Poverty	Extreme Poverty	Low Poverty	Extreme Poverty	Low Poverty	Extreme Poverty
Household income						
Less than $7,500	27.2	51.1	16.1	33.6	34.5	59.0
More than $25,000	34.1	14.3	41.4	22.7	29.8	10.5
Finances have improved	32.3	21.1	35.7	23.4	30.4	20.1
Financial assets						
Has checking account	34.8	12.2	33.3	17.6	36.4	9.9
Has savings account	35.4	17.8	40.4	26.6	33.1	14.1
Has none of six assets*	48.2	73.6	40.7	63.1	52.6	78.3
Has at least three of six assets*	23.3	8.3	26.8	13.5	21.3	5.8
Respondent owns nothing†	78.7	96.6	75.6	93.7	80.5	98.0
Material assets of household						
Owns home	44.7	11.5	49.7	19.8	41.5	7.8
Has a car	64.8	33.9	75.9	51.4	57.7	25.7

Source: Urban Poverty and Family Structure Survey.

*Including personal checking account, savings account, individual retirement account, pension plan, money in stocks and bonds, and prepaid burial.

†Home, business, or land.

neighborhoods, while fully one-half of jobless respondents in extreme-poverty tracts do not reach the $5000 line. It is not surprising that ghetto dwellers also less frequently report an improvement of the financial situation of their household, with women again in the least enviable position. This reflects sharp class differences: 42 percent of our middle-class respondents and 36 percent of working-class blacks register a financial amelioration as against 13 percent of the jobless.

Due to meager and irregular income, those financial and banking services that most members of the larger society take for granted are, to put it mildly, not of obvious access to the black poor. Barely one-third of the residents of low-poverty areas maintain a personal checking account; only one in nine manage to do so in the ghetto, where nearly three of every four persons report no financial asset whatsoever from a possible list of six and only 8 percent have at least three of those six assets. (See Table 4.) Here, again, class and neighborhood lines are sharply

drawn: in low-poverty areas, 10 percent of the jobless and 48 percent of working-class blacks have a personal checking account compared to 3 percent and 37 percent, respectively, in the ghetto; the proportion for members of the middle class is similar – 63 percent – in both areas.

The American dream of owning one's home remains well out of reach for a large majority of our black respondents, especially those in the ghetto, where barely 1 person in 10 belong to a home-owning household, compared to over 4 in 10 in low-poverty areas, a difference that is just as pronounced within each gender. The considerably more modest dream of owning an automobile is likewise one that has yet to materialize for ghetto residents, of which only one-third live in households with a car that runs. Again, this is due to a cumulation of sharp class and neighborhood differences: 79 percent of middle-class respondents and 62 percent of working-class blacks have an automobile in their household, contrasted with merely 28 percent of the jobless.

But, in ghetto tracts, only 18 percent of the jobless have domestic access to a car – 34 percent for men and 13 percent for women.

The social consequences of such a paucity of income and assets as suffered by ghetto blacks cannot be overemphasized. For just as the lack of financial resources or possession of a home represents a critical handicap when one can only find low-paying and casual employment or when one loses one's job, in that it literally forces one to go on the welfare rolls, not owning a car severely curtails one's chances of competing for available jobs that are not located nearly or that are not readily accessible by public transportation.

Social Capital and Poverty Concentration

Among the resources that individuals can draw upon to implement strategies of social mobility are those potentially provided by their lovers, kin, and friends and by the contacts they develop within the formal associations to which they belong – in sum, the resources they have access to by virtue of being socially integrated into soli-

darity groups, networks, or organizations, what Bourdieu calls "social capital."[22] Our data indicate that not only do residents of extreme-poverty areas have fewer social ties but also that they tend to have ties of lesser social worth, as measured by the social position of their partners, parents, siblings, and best friends, for instance. In short, they possess lower volumes of social capital.

Living in the ghetto means being more socially isolated: nearly half of the residents of extreme-poverty tracts have no current partner – defined here as a person they are married to, live with, or are dating steadily – and one in five admits to having no one who would qualify as a best friend, compared to 32 percent and 12 percent, respectively, in low-poverty areas. It also means that intact marriages are less frequent (Table 5). Jobless men are much less likely than working males to have current partners in both types of neighborhoods: 62 percent in low-poverty neighborhoods and 44 percent in extreme-poverty areas. Black women have a slightly better chance

TABLE 5 *Social Capital of Black Residents of Chicago's Low- and Extreme-Poverty Areas (Percentage)*

	All Respondents		Males		Females	
	Low Poverty	Extreme Poverty	Low Poverty	Extreme Poverty	Low Poverty	Extreme Poverty
Current partner						
Respondent has no current partner	32.4	42.0	23.3	39.1	38.0	43.1
Respondent married*	35.2	18.6	40.9	27.0	31.2	14.9
Partner completed high school	80.9	72.1	83.8	83.0	88.4	71.5
Partner works steadily	69.0	54.3	50.0	34.8	83.8	62.2
Partner is on public aid	20.4	34.2	38.6	45.5	16.2	28.6
Best friend						
Respondent has no best friend	12.2	19.0	14.3	21.1	10.7	18.1
Best friend completed high school	87.4	76.4	83.7	76.3	87.2	76.3
Best friend works steadily	72.3	60.4	77.2	72.8	65.6	54.8
Best friend is on public aid	14.0	28.6	3.0	13.6	20.5	35.3

Source: Urban Poverty and Family Structure Survey.

*And not separated from his or her spouse.

of having a partner if they live in a low-poverty area, and this partner is also more likely to have completed high school and to work steadily; for ghetto residence further affects the labor-market standing of the latter. The partners of women living in extreme-poverty areas are less stably employed than those of female respondents from low-poverty neighborhoods: 62 percent in extreme-poverty areas work regularly as compared to 84 percent in low-poverty areas.

Friends often play a crucial role in life in that they provide emotional and material support, help construct one's identity, and often open up opportunities that one would not have without them – particularly in the area of jobs. We have seen that ghetto residents are more likely than other black Chicagoans to have no close friend. If they have a best friend, furthermore, he or she is less likely to work, less educated, and twice as likely to be on aid. Because friendships tend to develop primarily within genders and women have much higher rates of economic exclusion, female respondents are much more likely than men to have a best friend who does not work and who receives welfare assistance. Both of these characteristics, in turn, tend to be more prevalent among ghetto females.

Such differences in social capital are also evidenced by different rates and patterns of organizational participation. While being part of a formal organization, such as a block club or a community organization, a political party, a school-related association, or a sports, fraternal, or other social group, is a rare occurrence as a rule – with the notable exception of middle-class blacks, two-thirds of whom belong to at least one such group – it is more common for ghetto residents – 64 percent, versus 50 percent in low-poverty tracts – especially females – 64 percent, versus 46 percent in low-poverty areas – to belong to no organization. As for church membership, the small minority who profess to be, in Weber's felicitous expression, "religiously unmusical" is twice as large in the ghetto as outside: 12 percent versus 5 percent. For those with a religion, ghetto residence tends to depress church attendance slightly – 29 percent of ghetto inhabitants attend service at least once a week compared to 37 percent of respondents from low-poverty tracts – even though women tend to attend more regularly than men in both types of areas. Finally, black women who inhabit the ghetto are also slightly less likely to know most of their neighbors than their counterparts from low-poverty areas. All in all, then, poverty concentration has the effect of devaluing the social capital of those who live in its midst.

CONCLUSION: THE SOCIAL STRUCTURING OF GHETTO POVERTY

The extraordinary levels of economic hardship plaguing Chicago's inner city in the 1970s have not abated, and the ghetto seems to have gone unaffected by the economic boom of the past five years. If anything, conditions have continued to worsen. This points to the asymmetric causality between the economy and ghetto poverty[23] and to the urgent need to study the social and political structures that mediate their relationship. The significant differences we have uncovered between low-poverty and extreme-poverty areas in Chicago are essentially a reflection of their different class mix and of the prevalence of economic exclusion in the ghetto.

Our conclusion, then, is that social analysts must pay more attention to the extreme levels of economic deprivation and social marginalization as uncovered in this article before they further entertain and spread so-called theories[24] about the potency of a ghetto culture of poverty that has yet to receive rigorous empirical elaboration. Those who have been pushing moral-cultural or individualistic-behavioral explanations of the social dislocations that have swept through the inner city in recent years have created a fictitious normative divide between urban blacks that, no matter its reality – which has yet to be ascertained[25] – cannot but pale when compared to the objective structural cleavage that separates ghetto residents from the larger society and to the collective material constraints that bear on them.[26] It is the cumulative structural entrapment and forcible socioeconomic marginalization resulting from the historically evolving interplay of class, racial, and gender domination, together with the changes in the organization of American capitalism and failed urban and social policies, not a "welfare ethos," that explain the plight of today's ghetto blacks. Thus, if the concept of underclass is used, it must be a structural concept: it must denote a new sociospatial patterning of class and racial domination, recognizable by the unprecedented concentration of the most socially excluded and economically marginal members of the dominated racial and economic group. It should not be used as a label to designate a new breed of individuals molded freely by a mythical and all-powerful culture of poverty.

ENDNOTES

This article is based on data gathered and analyzed as part of the University of Chicago's Urban Poverty and Family Structure Project, whose principal investigator is W.J. Wilson. We gratefully acknowledge the financial support of the Ford Foundation, the Carnegie Corporation, the U.S. Department of Health and Human Services, the Institute for Research on Poverty, the Joyce Foundation, the Lloyd A. Fry Foundation, the Rockefeller Foundation, the Spencer Foundation, the William T. Grant Foundation, and the Woods Charitable Fund.

1. For instance, Sheldon H. Danziger and Daniel H. Weinberg, eds., *Fighting Poverty: What Works and What Doesn't* (Cambridge, MA: Harvard University Press, 1986); William Kornblum, "Lumping the Poor: What *Is* the Underclass?" *Dissent*, Summer 1984, pp. 275–302; William Julius Wilson, *The Truly Disadvantaged: The Inner City, the Underclass and Public Policy* (Chicago: University of Chicago Press, 1987); Rose M. Brewer, "Black Women in Poverty: Some Comments on Female-Headed Families," *Signs: Journal of Women in Culture and Society*, 13(2):331–39 (Winter 1988); Fred R. Harris and Roger T. Wilkins, eds., *Quiet Riots: Race and Poverty in the United States* (New York: Pantheon, 1988). Martha A. Gephart and Robert W. Pearson survey recent research in their "Contemporary Research on the Urban Underclass," *Items*, 41(1–2):1–10 (June 1988).

2. William Julius Wilson, "The American Underclass: Inner-City Ghettos and the Norms of Citizenship" (Godkin Lecture, John F. Kennedy School of Government, Harvard University, Apr. 1988), offers a critical dissection of these accounts.

3. A detailed analysis of changes in population, poverty, and poverty concentration in these 10 cities is presented in Loïc J.D. Wacquant and William Julius Wilson, "Poverty, Joblessness and the Social Transformation of the Inner City," in *Reforming Welfare Policy*, ed. D. Ellwood and P. Cottingham (Cambridge, MA: Harvard University Press, forthcoming).

4. See Gregory D. Squires et al., *Chicago: Race, Class, and the Response to Urban Decline* (Philadelphia: Temple University Press, 1987).

5. The following is a summary description of the sample design and characteristics of the data for this article. The data come from a survey of 2490 inner-city residents of Chicago fielded by the National Opinion Research Center in 1986–87 for the Urban Poverty and Family Structure Project of the University of Chicago. The sample for blacks was drawn randomly from residents of the city's 377 tracts with poverty rates of at least 20.0 percent, the citywide average as of the last census. It was stratified by parental status and included 1184 respondents – 415 men and 769 women – for a completion rate of 83.0 percent for black parents and 78.0 percent for black nonparents. Of the 1166 black respondents who still lived in the city at the time they were interviewed, 405, or 34.7 percent, resided in low-poverty tracts – that is, tracts with poverty rates between 20.0 and 29.9 percent – to which were added 41 individuals, or 3.5 percent, who had moved into tracts with poverty rates below 20.0 percent; 364, or 31.2 percent, lived in high-poverty tracts – tracts with poverty rates of 30.0 to 39.9 percent – and are excluded from the analyses reported in this article; and 356, or 30.5 percent, inhabited extreme-poverty areas, including 9.6 percent in tracts with poverty rates above 50.0 percent. The latter include 63 persons, or 17.7 percent of all extreme-poverty-area residents, dwelling in tracts with poverty rates in excess of 70.0 percent – public housing projects in most cases. All the results presented in this article are based on unweighted data, although weighted data exhibit essentially the same patterns.

6. A more detailed analysis of social changes on Chicago's South Side is in William Julius Wilson et al., "The Ghetto Underclass and the Changing Structure of Urban Poverty," in *Quite Riots*, ed. Harris and Wilkins.

7. Space does not allow us to do more than allude to the transformations of the American economy as they bear on the ghetto. For provocative analyses of the systemic disorganization of advanced capitalist economies and polities and the impact, actual and potential, of postindustrial and flexible-specialization trends on cities and their labor markets, see Scott Lash and John Urry, *The End of Organized Capitalism* (Madison: University of Wisconsin Press, 1988); Claus Offe, *Disorganized Capitalism: Contemporary Transformations of Work and Politics*, ed. John Keane (Cambridge: MIT Press, 1985); Fred Block, *Revising State Theory: Essays on Politics and Postindustrialism* (Philadelphia: Temple University Press, 1987); Donald A Hicks, *Advanced Industrial Development* (Boston: Oelgeschlager, Gun and Hain, 1985); Barry Bluestone and Bennett Harrison, *The Great U-Turn* (New York: Basic Books, 1988); Michael J. Piore and Charles F. Sabel, *The Second Industrial Divide: Possibilities for Prosperity* (New York: Basic Books, 1984).

8. See, for instance, Norman Fainstein, "The Underclass/Mismatch Hypothesis as an Explanation for Black

Economic Deprivation," *Politics and Society*, 15(4):403–52 (1986–87); Wendy Wintermute, "Recession and 'Recovery': Impact on Black and White Workers in Chicago" (Chicago: Chicago Urban League, 1983); Bruce Williams, *Black Workers in an Industrial Suburb: The Struggle against Discrimination* (New Brunswick, NJ: Rutgers University Press, 1987).

9. In 1950, fully 60 percent of employed black men and 43 percent of black women in Chicago had blue-collar occupations, skilled and unskilled combined, compared to 48 percent and 28 percent of white men and women, respectively. See "Black Metropolis 1961, Appendix," in St. Clair Drake and Horace R. Cayton, *Black Metropolis: A Study of Negro Life in a Northern City*, 2 vols., rev. and enlarged ed. (originally 1945; New York: Harper & Row, 1962).

10. Rates of joblessness have risen at a much faster pace in the ghetto than for blacks as a whole. For comparative data on the long-term decline of black labor force participation, esp. among males, see Reynolds Farley and Walter R. Allen, *The Color Line and the Quality of Life in America* (New York: Russell Sage Foundation, 1987); Katherine L. Bradbury and Lynn E. Brown, "Black Men in the Labor Market," *New England Economic Review*, Mar.–Apr. 1986, pp. 32–42.

11. Arne Duncan, "The Values, Aspirations, and Opportunities of the Urban Underclass" (B.A. honors thesis, Harvard University, 1987). pp. 18ff.

12. In ibid., p. 21.

13. In ibid., p. 28.

14. See Gary Orfield, "Ghettoization and Its Alternatives," in *The New Urban Reality*, ed. P. Peterson (Washington, DC: Brookings Institution, 1985), for an account of processes of ghettoization; and Wacquant and Wilson, "Poverty, Joblessness and Social Transformation," for a preliminary discussion of some of the factors that underlie hyperghettoization.

15. Drake and Cayton, *Black Metropolis*.

16. Let us emphasize here that this contrast between the traditional ghetto and the hyperghetto of today implies no nostalgic celebration of the ghetto of yesteryear. If the latter was organizationally and socially integrated, it was not by choice but under the yoke of total black subjugation and with the threat of racial violence looming never too far in the background. See Arnold Hirsch, *Making the Second Ghetto: Race and Housing in Chicago, 1940–1960* (New York: Cambridge University Press, 1983), for an account of riots and violent white opposition to housing desegregation in Chicago in the two decades following World War II. The organized ghetto emerged out of necessity, as a limited, if creative, response to implacable white hostility; separatism was never a voluntary development, but a protection against unyielding pressures from without, as shown in Allan H. Spear, *Black Chicago: The Making*

of a Negro Ghetto, 1890–1920 (Chicago: University of Chicago Press, 1968).

17. Poverty levels were arbitrarily limited by the sampling design: areas with less than 20 percent poor persons in 1980 were excluded at the outset, and tracts with extreme levels of poverty, being generally relatively underpopulated, ended up being underrepresented by the random sampling procedure chosen.

18. Class categories have been roughly defined on the basis of the respondent's current occupation as follows: the middle class comprises managers, administrators, executives, professional specialists, and technical staff; the working class includes both blue-collar workers and noncredentialed white-collar workers; in the jobless category fall all those who did not hold a job at the time of the interview. Our dividing line between middle and working class, cutting across white-collar occupations, is consistent with recent research and theory on class—for example, Erik Olin Wright, *Classes* (New York: Verso, 1985); Nicholas Abercrombie and John Urry, *Capital, Labour and the Middle Classes* (London: George Allen & Unwin, 1983)—and on contemporary perceptions of class in the black community—see Reeve Vanneman and Lynn Cannon Weber, *The American Perception of Class* (Philadelphia: Temple University Press, 1987), chap. 10. The category of the jobless is admittedly heterogeneous, as it should be given that the identity of those without an occupational position is ambiguous and ill-defined in reality itself. It includes people actively looking for work (half the men and 1 women in 10), keeping house (13 percent of the men and 61 percent of the women), and a minority of respondents who also attend school part- or full-time (16 percent of the males, 14 percent of the females). A few respondents without jobs declared themselves physically unable to work (6 percent of the men, 3 percent of the women).

19. And from the education of their fathers: only 36 percent of ghetto residents have a father with at least a high school education, compared to 43 percent among those who live outside the ghetto. The different class backgrounds and trajectories of ghetto and non-ghetto blacks will be examined in a subsequent paper.

20. See Wacquant and Wilson, "Poverty, Joblessness and Social Transformation," fig. 2.

21. Again, we must reiterate that our comparison excludes *ex definitio* the black upper- and the middle-class neighborhoods that have mushroomed in Chicago since the opening of race relations in the 1960s. The development of this "new black middle class" is surveyed in Bart Landry, *The New Black Middle Class* (Berkeley: University of California Press, 1987).

22. Pierre Bourdieu, "The Forms of Capital," in *Handbook of Theory and Research for the Sociology of Education*, ed. J.G. Richardson (New York: Greenwood Press,

1986). The crucial role played by relatives, friends, and lovers in strategies of survival in poor black communities is documented extensively in Carol B. Stack, *All Our Kin: Strategies for Survival in a Black Community* (New York: Harper & Row, 1974). On the management of relationships and the influence of friends in the ghetto, see also Elliot Liebow, *Tally's Corner: A Study of Negro Street Corner Men* (Boston: Little, Brown, 1967); Ulf Hannerz, *Soulside: Inquiries into Ghetto Culture and Community* (New York: Columbia University Press, 1969); Elijah Anderson, *A Place on the Corner* (Chicago: University of Chicago Press, 1978); Terry Williams and William Kornblum, *Growing Up Poor* (Lexington, MA: Lexington Books, 1985).

23. By this we mean that when the economy slumps, conditions in the ghetto become a lot worse but do not automatically return to the *status quo ante* when macroeconomic conditions improve, so that cyclical economic fluctuations lead to stepwise increases in social dislocations.

24. We say "so-called" here because, more often than not, the views expressed by scholars in this regard are little more than a surface formalization of the dominant American ideology – or commonsense notion – of poverty that assigns its origins to the moral or psychological deficiencies of individual poor persons. See Robert Castel, "La 'guerre à la pauvreté' et le statut de l'indigence dans une société d'abondance," *Actes de la recherche en sciences sociales,* 19 Jan. 1978, pp. 47–60, for a pungent critical and historical analysis of conceptions of poverty in the American mind and in American welfare policy.

25. Initial examination of our Chicago data would appear to indicate that ghetto blacks on public aid hold basically the same views as regards welfare, work, and family as do other blacks, even those who belong to the middle class.

26. Let us emphasize in closing that we are not suggesting that differences between ghetto and nonghetto poor can be explained by their residence. Because the processes that allocate individuals and families to neighborhoods are highly socially selective ones, to separate neighborhood effects – the specific impact of ghetto residence – from the social forces that operate jointly with, or independently of, them cannot be done by simple controls such as we have used here for descriptive purposes. On the arduous methodological and theoretical problems posed by such socially selective effects, see Stanley Lieberson, *Making It Count: The Improvement of Social Theory and Social Research* (Berkeley: University of California Press, 1985), pp. 14–43 and passim.

Family, Race, and Poverty in the Eighties

Maxine Baca Zinn

The 1960s Civil Rights movement overturned segregation laws, opened voting booths, created new job opportunities, and brought hope to Black Americans. As long as it could be said that conditions were improving, Black family structure and life-style remained private matters. The promises of the 1960s faded, however, as the income gap between whites and Blacks widened. Since the middle 1970s, the Black underclass has expanded rather than contracted, and along with this expansion emerged a public debate about the Black family. Two distinct models of the underclass now prevail – one that is cultural and one that is structural. Both of them focus on issues of family structure and poverty.

THE CULTURAL DEFICIENCY MODEL

The 1980s ushered in a revival of old ideas about poverty, race, and family. Many theories and opinions about the urban underclass rest on the culture-of-poverty debate of the 1960s. In brief, proponents of the culture-of-poverty thesis contend that the poor have a different way of life than the rest of society and that these cultural differences explain continued poverty. Within the current national discussion are three distinct approaches that form the latest wave of deficiency theories.

The first approach – culture as villain – places the cause of the swelling underclass in a value system characterized by low aspirations, exces-sive masculinity, and the acceptance of female-headed families as a way of life.

The second approach – family as villain – assigns the cause of the growing underclass to the structure of the family. While unemployment is often addressed, this argument always returns to the causal connections between poverty and the disintegration of traditional family structure.

The third approach – welfare as villain – treats welfare and antipoverty programs as the cause of illegitimate births, female-headed families, and low motivation to work. In short, welfare transfer payments to the poor create disincentives to work and incentives to have children out of wedlock – a self-defeating trap of poverty.

Culture as Villain

Public discussions of urban poverty have made the "disintegrating" Black family the force most responsible for the growth of the underclass. This category, by definition poor, is overwhelmingly Black and disproportionately composed of female-headed households. The members are perceived as different from striving, upwardly mobile whites. The rising number of people in the underclass has provided the catalyst for reporters' and scholars' attention to this disadvantaged category. The typical interpretation given by these social commentators is that the underclass is permanent, being locked in by its own unique but maladaptive culture. This thinking, though flawed, provides the popular rationale for treating the poor as the problem.

The logic of the culture-of-poverty argument is that poor people have distinctive values, aspirations, and psychological characteristics that inhibit their achievement and produce behavioral deficiencies likely to keep them poor not only within generations but also across generations, through socialization of the young.[1] In this argument, poverty is more a function of thought processes than of physical environment.[2] As a result of this logic, current discussions of ghetto poverty, family structure, welfare, unemployment, and out-of-wedlock births connect these conditions in ways similar to the 1965 Moynihan Report.[3] Because Moynihan maintained that the pathological problem within Black ghettos was the deterioration of the Negro family, his report became the generative example of blaming the victim.[4] Furthermore, Moynihan dismissed racism as a salient force in the perpetuation of poverty by arguing that the tangle of pathology was "capable of perpetuating itself without assistance from the white world."[5]

The reaction of scholars to Moynihan's cultural-deficiency model was swift and extensive although not as well publicized as the model itself. Research in the sixties and seventies by Andrew Billingsley, Robert Hill, Herbert Gutman, Joyce Ladner, Elliot Leibow, and Carol Stack, to name a few, documented the many strengths of Black families, strengths that allowed them to survive slavery, the enclosures of the South, and the depression of the North.[6] Such work revealed that many patterns of family life were not created by a deficient culture but were instead "a rational adaptational response to conditions of deprivation."[7]

A rapidly growing literature in the eighties documents the disproportionate representation of Black female-headed families in poverty. Yet, recent studies on Black female-headed families are largely unconcerned with questions about adaptation. Rather, they study the strong association between female-headed families and poverty, the effects of family disorganization on children, the demographic and socioeconomic factors that are correlated with single-parent status, and the connection between the economic status of men and the rise in Black female-headed families.[8] While most of these studies do not advance a social-pathology explanation, they do

signal a regressive shift in analytic focus. Many well-meaning academics who intend to call attention to the dangerously high level of poverty in Black female-headed households have begun to emphasize the family structure and the Black ghetto way of life as contributors to the perpetuation of the underclass.

The popular press, on the other hand, openly and enthusiastically embraced the Moynihan thesis both in its original version and in Moynihan's restatement of the thesis in his book *Family and Nation*.[9] Here Moynihan repeats his assertion that poverty and family structure are associated, but now he contends that the association holds for Blacks and whites alike. This modification does not critique his earlier assumptions; indeed, it validates them. A profoundly disturbing example of this is revealed in the widely publicized television documentary, CBS Reports' "The Vanishing Family."[10] According to this refurbished version of the old Moynihan Report, a breakdown in family values has allowed Black men to renounce their traditional breadwinner role, leaving Black women to bear the economic responsibility for children.[11] The argument that the Black community is devastating itself fits neatly with the resurgent conservatism that is manifested among Black and white intellectuals and policymakers.

Another contemporary example of the use of the culture of poverty is Nicholas Lemann's two-part 1986 *Atlantic Monthly* article about the Black underclass in Chicago.[12] According to Lemann, family structure is the most visible manifestation of Black America's bifurcation into a middle class that has escaped the ghetto and an underclass that is irrevocably trapped in the ghetto. He explains the rapid growth of the underclass in the seventies by pointing to two mass migrations of Black Americans. The first was from the rural South to the urban North and numbered in the millions during the forties, fifties, and sixties; the second, a migration out of the ghettos by members of the Black working and middle classes, who had been freed from housing discrimination by the civil rights movement. As a result of the exodus, the indices of disorganization in the urban ghettos of the North (crime, illegitimate births) have risen, and the underclass has flourished.[13] Loose attitudes toward marriage, high illegitimacy rates, and family disintegration are said to be a heritage of the rural South. In Lemann's words, they represent the power of culture to produce poverty:

> The argument is anthropological, not economic; it emphasizes the power over people's behavior that culture, as opposed to economic incentives, can have. Ascribing a society's condition in part to the culture that prevails there seems benign when the society under discussion is England or California. But as a way of thinking about black ghettos it has become unpopular. Twenty years ago ghettos were often said to have a self-generating, destructive culture of poverty (the term has an impeccable source, the anthropologist Oscar Lewis). But then the left equated cultural discussions of the ghetto with accusing poor blacks of being in a bad situation that was of their own making. . . . The left succeeded in limiting the terms of the debate to purely economic ones, and today the right also discusses the ghetto in terms of economic "incentives to fail," provided by the welfare system. . . . In the ghettos, though, it appears that the distinctive culture is now the greatest barrier to progress by the black underclass, rather than either unemployment or welfare.[14]

Lemann's essay, his "misreading of left economic analysis, and cultural anthropology itself"[15] might be dismissed if it were atypical in the debate about the culture of poverty and the underclass. Unfortunately, it shares with other studies the problems of working "with neither the benefit of a well-articulated theory about the impact of personality and motivation on behavior nor adequate data from a representative sample of the low-income population."[16]

The idea that poverty is caused by psychological factors and that poverty is passed on from one generation to the next has been called into question by the University of Michigan's Panel Study of Income Dynamics (PSID), a large-scale data collection project conceived, in part, to test many of the assumptions about the psychological and demographic aspects of poverty. This study has gathered annual information from a representative sample of the U.S. population. Two striking discoveries contradict the stereotypes stemming from the culture-of-poverty argument. The first is the high turnover of individual families in poverty and the second is the finding that motivation cannot be linked to poverty. Each year the number of people below the poverty line remains about the same, but the poor in one year are not necessarily the poor in the following year. "Blacks from welfare dependent families were no more likely to become welfare dependent than similar Blacks from families who had never received welfare. Further, measures of parental sense of efficacy, future orientation, and achievement motivation had no effects on welfare dependency for either group."[17] This research has found no evidence that highly motivated people are more successful at escaping from poverty than those with lower scores on tests.[18] Thus, cultural deficiency is an inappropriate model for explaining the underclass.

The Family as Villain

A central notion within culture-of-poverty arguments is that family disintegration is the source and sustaining feature of poverty. Today, nearly six out of ten Black children are born out of wedlock, compared to roughly three out of ten in 1970. In the 25–34-year age bracket, today the probability of separation and divorce for Black women is twice that of white women. The result is a high probability that an individual Black woman and her children will live alone. The so-called "deviant" mother-only family, common among Blacks, is a product of "the feminization of poverty," a shorthand reference to women living alone and being disproportionately represented among the poor. The attention given to increased marital breakups, to births to unmarried women, and to the household patterns that accompany these changes would suggest that the bulk of contemporary poverty is a family-structure phenomenon. Common knowledge – whether true or not – has it that family-structure changes cause most poverty, or changes in family structure have led to current poverty rates that are much higher than they would have been if family composition had remained stable.[19]

Despite the growing concentration of poverty among Black female-headed households in the past two decades, there is reason to question the conventional thinking. Research by Mary Jo Bane finds that changes in family structure have less causal influence on poverty than is commonly thought.[20] Assumptions about the correlation and association between poverty and family breakdown avoid harder questions about the character and direction of causal relations between the two phenomena.[21] Bane's longitudinal research on household composition and poverty suggests that much poverty, especially among Blacks, is the result of already-poor, two-parent households that break up, producing poor female-headed households. This differs from the event transition to poverty that is more common for whites: "Three-quarters of whites who were poor in the first year after moving into a female-headed or single person household became poor simultaneously with the transition; in contrast, of the Blacks who were poor after the transition, about two-thirds had also been poor before. Reshuffled poverty as opposed to event-caused poverty for Blacks challenges the assumption that changes in family structure have created ghetto poverty. This underscores the importance of considering the ways in which race produces different paths to poverty."[22]

A two-parent family is no guarantee against poverty for racial minorities. Analyzing data from the PSID, Martha Hill concluded that the long-term income of Black children in two-parent families throughout the decade was even lower than the long-term income of non-Black children who spent most of the decade in mother-only families: "Thus, increasing the proportion of Black children growing up in two-parent families would not by itself eliminate very much of the racial gap in the economic well-being of children; changes in the economic circumstances of the parents are needed most to bring the economic status of Black children up to the higher status of non-Black children."[23]

Further studies are required if we are to understand the ways in which poverty, family structure, and race are related.

Welfare as Villain

An important variant of the family-structure and deficient-culture explanations, one especially popular among political conservatives, is the argument that welfare causes poverty. This explanation proposes that welfare undermines incentives to work and causes families to break up by allowing Black women to have babies and encouraging Black men to escape family responsibilities. This position has been widely publicized by Charles Murray's influential book,

Losing Ground.[24] According to Murray, liberal welfare policies squelch work incentives and thus are the major cause of the breakup of the Black family. In effect, increased AFDC benefits make it desirable to forgo marriage and live on the dole.

Research has refuted this explanation for the changes in the structure of families in the underclass. Numerous studies have shown that variations in welfare across time and in different states have not produced systematic variation in family structure.[25] Research conducted at the University of Wisconsin's Institute for Research on Poverty found that poverty increased after the late sixties due to a weakening economy through the seventies. No support was found for Murray's assertion that spending growth did more harm than good for Blacks because it increased the percentage of families headed by women. Trends in welfare spending increased between 1960 and 1972, and declined between 1970 and 1984; yet there were no reversals in family-composition trends during this period. The percentage of these households headed by women increased steadily from 10.7 percent to 20.8 percent between 1968 and 1983.[26]

Further evidence against the "welfare-dependency" motivation for the dramatic rise in the proportion of Black families headed by females is provided by William Darity and Samuel Meyers. Using statistical causality tests, they found no short-term effects of variations in welfare payments on female headship in Black families.[27]

Other research draws similar conclusions about the impact of welfare policies on family structure. Using a variety of tests, David Ellwood and Lawrence Summers dispute the adverse effects of AFDC.[28] They highlight two facts that raise questions about the role of welfare policies in producing female-headed households. First, the real value of welfare payments has declined since the early 1970s, while family dissolution has continued to rise. Family-structure changes do not mirror benefit-level changes. Second, variations in benefit levels across states do not lead to corresponding variations in divorce rates or numbers of children in single-parent families. Their comparison of groups collecting AFDC with groups that were not, found that the effects of welfare benefits on family structures were small.[29] In sum, the systematic research on welfare and family structure indicates that AFDC has far less effect on changes in family structure than has been assumed.

OPPORTUNITY STRUCTURES IN DECLINE

A very different view of the underclass has emerged alongside the popularized cultural-deficiency model. This view is rooted in a substantial body of theory and research. Focusing on the opportunity structure of society, these concrete studies reveal that culture is not responsible for the underclass.

Within the structural framework there are three distinct strands. The first deals with transformations of the economy and the labor force that affect Americans in general and Blacks and Hispanics in particular. The second is the transformation of marriage and family life among minorities. The third is the changing class composition of inner cities and their increasing isolation of residents from mainstream social institutions.

All three are informed by new research that examines the macrostructural forces that shape family trends and demographic patterns that expand the analysis to include Hispanics.

Employment

Massive economic changes since the end of World War II are causing the social marginalization of Black people throughout the United States. The shift from an economy based on the manufacture of goods to one based on information and services has redistributed work in global, national, and local economies. While these major economic shifts affect all workers, they have more serious consequences for Blacks than whites, a condition that scholars call "structural racism."[30] Major economic trends and patterns, even those that appear race neutral, have significant racial implications. Blacks and other minorities are profoundly affected by (1) the decline of industrial manufacturing sectors and the growth of service sectors of the economy; and (2) shifts in the geographical location of jobs from central cities to the suburbs and from the traditional manufacturing cities (the rustbelt) to the sunbelt and to other countries.

In their classic work *The Deindustrialization of*

America, Barry Bluestone and Bennett Harrison revealed that "minorities tend to be concentrated in industries that have borne the brunt of recent closing. This is particularly true in the automobile, steel, and rubber industries."[31] In a follow-up study, Bluestone, Harrison, and Lucy Gorham have shown that people of Color, particularly Black men, are more likely than whites to lose their jobs due to the restructuring of the U.S. economy and that young Black men are especially hard hit.[32] Further evidence of the consequences of economic transformation for minority males is provided by Richard Hill and Cynthia Negrey.[33] They studied deindustrialization in the Great Lakes region and found that the race-gender group that was hardest hit by the industrial slump was Black male production workers. Fully 50 percent of this group in five Great Lakes cities studied lost their jobs in durable-goods manufacturing between 1979 and 1984. They found that Black male production workers also suffered the greatest rate of job loss in the region and in the nation as a whole.

The decline of manufacturing jobs has altered the cities' roles as opportunity ladders for the disadvantaged. Since the start of World War II, well-paying blue-collar jobs in manufacturing have been a main avenue of job security and mobility for Blacks and Hispanics. Movement into higher-level blue-collar jobs was one of the most important components of Black occupational advancement in the 1970s. The current restructuring of industries creates the threat of downward mobility for middle-class minorities.[34]

Rather than offering opportunities to minorities, the cities have become centers of poverty. Large concentrations of Blacks and Hispanics are trapped in cities in which the urban employment base is shifting. Today inner cities are shifting away from being centers of production and distribution of physical goods toward being centers of administration, information, exchange, trade, finance, and government service. Conversely, these changes in local employment structures have been accompanied by a shift in the demographic composition of large central cities away from European white to predominantly Black and Hispanic, with rising unemployment. The transfer of jobs away from central cities to the suburbs has created a residential job opportunity mismatch that literally leaves minorities behind in the inner city. Without adequate training or credentials, they are relegated to low-paying, nonadvancing exploitative service work or they are unemployed. Thus, Blacks have become, for the most part, superfluous people in cities that once provided them with opportunities.

The composition and size of cities' overall employment bases have also changed. During the past two decades most older, larger cities have experienced substantial job growth in occupations associated with knowledge-intensive service industries. However, job growth in these high-skill, predominantly white-collar industries has not compensated for employment declines in manufacturing, wholesale trade, and other predominantly blue-collar industries that once constituted the economic backbone of Black urban employment.[35]

While cities once sustained large numbers of less skilled persons, today's service industries typically have high educational requisites for entry. Knowledge and information jobs in the central cities are virtually closed to minorities given the required technological education and skill level. Commuting between central cities and outlying areas is increasingly common; white-collar workers commute daily from their suburban residences to the central business districts while streams of inner-city residents are commuting to their blue-collar jobs in outlying nodes.[36]

An additional structural impediment innercity minorities face is their increased distance from current sources of blue-collar and other entry-level jobs. Because the industries that provide these jobs have moved to the suburbs and nonmetropolitan peripheries, racial discrimination and inadequate incomes of inner-city minorities now have the additional impact of preventing many from moving out of the inner city in order to maintain their access to traditional sources of employment. The dispersed nature of job growth makes public transportation from inner-city neighborhoods impractical, requiring virtually all city residents who work in peripheral areas to commute by personally owned automobiles. The severity of this mismatch is documented by John Kasarda: "More than one half of the minority households in Philadelphia and Boston are without a means of personal transportation. New York City's proportions are even higher with only three of ten black or Hispanic households having a vehicle available."[37]

This economic restructuring is characterized by an overall pattern of uneven development. Manufacturing industries have declined in the North and Midwest while new growth industries, such as computers and communications equipment, are locating in the southern and southwestern part of the nation. This regional shift has produced some gains for Blacks in the South, where Black poverty rates have declined. Given the large minority populations in the sunbelt, it is conceivable that industrial restructuring could offset the economic threats to racial equality. However, the sunbelt expansion has been based largely on low-wage, labor-intensive enterprises that use large numbers of underpaid minority workers, and a decline in the northern industrial sector continues to leave large numbers of Blacks and Hispanics without work.

Marriage

The connection between declining Black employment opportunities (especially male joblessness) and the explosive growth of Black families headed by single women is the basis of William J. Wilson's analysis of the underclass. Several recent studies conducted by Wilson and his colleagues at the University of Chicago have established this link.[38] Wilson and Kathryn Neckerman have documented the relationship between increased male joblessness and female-headed households. By devising an indicator called "the index of marriageable males," they reveal a long-term decline in the proportion of Black men, and particularly young Black men, who are in a position to support a family. Their indicators include mortality and incarceration rates, as well as labor-force participation rates, and they reveal that the proportion of Black men in unstable economic situations is much higher than indicated in current unemployment figures.[39]

Wilson's analysis treats marriage as an opportunity structure that no longer exists for large numbers of Black people. Consider, for example, why the majority of pregnant Black teenagers do not marry. In 1960, 42 percent of Black teenagers who had babies were unmarried; by 1970 the rate jumped to 63 percent and by 1983 it was 89 percent.[40] According to Wilson, the increase is tied directly to the changing labor-market status of young Black males. He cites the well-established relationship between joblessness and marital instability in support of his argument that "pregnant teenagers are more likely to marry if their boyfriends are working."[41] Out-of-wedlock births are sometimes encouraged by families and absorbed into the kinship system because marrying the suspected father would mean adding someone who was unemployed to the family's financial burden.[42] Adaptation to structural conditions leaves Black women disproportionately separated, divorced, and solely responsible for their children. The mother-only family structure is thus the consequence, not the cause, of poverty.

Community

These changes in employment and marriage patterns have been accompanied by changes in the social fabric of cities. "The Kerner Report Twenty Years Later," a conference of the 1988 Commission on the Cities, highlighted the growing isolation of Blacks and Hispanics.[43] Not only is inner-city poverty worse and more persistent than it was twenty years ago, but ghettos and barrios have become isolated and deteriorating societies with their own economies and with increasingly isolated social institutions, including schools, families, businesses, churches, and hospitals. According to Wilson, this profound social transformation is reflected not only in the high rates of joblessness, crime, and poverty but also in a changing socioeconomic class structure. As Black middle-class professionals left the central city, so too did working-class Blacks. Wilson uses the term "concentration effects" to capture the experiences of low-income families who now make up the majority of those who live in inner cities. The most disadvantaged families are disproportionately concentrated in the sections of the inner city that are plagued by joblessness, lawlessness, and a general milieu of desperation. Without working-class or middle-class role models these families have little in common with mainstream society.[44]

The departure of the Black working and middle classes means more than a loss of role models, however. As David Ellwood has observed, the flight of Black professionals has meant the loss of connections and networks. If successfully employed persons do not live nearby, then the informal methods of finding a job, by which one worker tells someone else of an opening and recommends her or him to the employer, are lost.[45] Concentration and isolation describe the processes that systematically entrench a lack of opportunities in inner cities. Individuals and families are thus left to acquire life's necessities though they are far removed from the channels of social opportunity.

THE CHANGING DEMOGRAPHY OF RACE AND POVERTY

Hispanic poverty, virtually ignored for nearly a quarter of a century, has recently captured the attention of the media and scholars alike. Recent demographic and economic patterns have made "the flow of Hispanics to urban America among the most significant changes occurring in the 1980s."[46]

As the Hispanic presence in the United States has increased in the last decade, Hispanic poverty rates have risen alarmingly. Between 1979 and 1985, the percentage of Latinos who were poor grew from 21.8 percent to 29.0 percent. Nationwide, the poverty rate for all Hispanics was 27.3 percent in 1986. By comparison, the white poverty rate in 1986 was 11 percent; the Black poverty rate was 31.1 percent.[47] Not only have Hispanic poverty rates risen alarmingly, but like Black poverty, Hispanic poverty has become increasingly concentrated in inner cities. Hispanics fall well behind the general population on all measures of social and economic well-being: jobs, income, educational attainment, housing, and health care. Poverty among Hispanics has become so persistent that, if current patterns continue, Hispanics will emerge in the 1990s as the nation's poorest racial-ethnic group.[48] Hispanic poverty has thus become a trend to watch in national discussions of urban poverty and the underclass.

While Hispanics are emerging as the poorest minority group, poverty rates and other socioeconomic indicators vary widely among Hispanic groups. Among Puerto Ricans, 39.9 percent of the population lived below the poverty level in 1986. For Mexicans, 28.4 percent were living in poverty in 1986. For Cubans and Central and South Americans, the poverty rate was much lower: 18.7 percent.[49] Such diversity has led scholars to question the usefulness of this racial-ethnic category that includes all people of Latin American descent.[50] Nevertheless, the labels Hispanic or Latino are useful in general terms in describing the changing racial composition of poverty populations. In spite of the great diversity among Hispanic nationalities, they face common obstacles to becoming incorporated into the economic mainstream of society.

Researchers are debating whether trends of rising Hispanic poverty are irreversible and if those trends point to a permanent underclass among Hispanics. Do macrostructural shifts in the economy and the labor force have the same effects on Blacks and Latinos? According to Joan W. Moore, national economic changes do affect Latinos, but they affect subgroups of Latinos in different ways:

> The movement of jobs and investments out of Rustbelt cities has left many Puerto Ricans living in a bleak ghetto economy. This same movement has had a different effect on Mexican Americans living in the Southwest. As in the North, many factories with job ladders have disappeared. Most of the newer Sunbelt industries offer either high paying jobs for which few Hispanics are trained or low paying ones that provide few opportunities for advancement. Those industries that depend on immigrant labor (such as clothing manufacturing in Los Angeles) often seriously exploit their workers, so the benefits to Hispanics in the Southwest of this influx of industries and investments are mixed. Another subgroup, Cubans in Miami, work and live in an enclave economy that appears to be unaffected by this shift in the national economy.[51]

Because shifts in the subregional economies seem more important to Hispanics than changes in the national economy, Moore is cautious about applying William Wilson's analysis of how the underclass is created.

Opportunity structures have not declined in a uniform manner for Latinos. Yet Hispanic poverty, welfare dependence, and unemployment rates are greatest in regions that have been transformed by macrostructural economic changes. In some cities, Puerto Rican poverty and unemployment rates are steadily converging with, and in some cases exceeding, the rates of Blacks. In 1986, 40 percent of Puerto Ricans in the United States lived below the poverty level and 70 percent of Puerto Rican children lived in poverty.[52]

Family structure is also affected by economic dislocation. Among Latinos, the incidence of female-headed households is highest for Puerto Ricans – 43.3 percent – compared to 19.2 percent for Mexicans, 17.7 for Cubans, and 25.5 percent for Central and South Americans.[53] The association between national economic shifts and high rates of social dislocation among Hispanics provides further evidence for the structural argument that economic conditions rather than culture create distinctive forms of racial poverty.

FAMILY, POVERTY, AND GENDER

The structural model described above advances our understanding of poverty and minority families beyond the limitations of the cultural model. It directs attention away from psychological and cultural issues and toward social structures that allocate economic and social rewards. It has generated a substantial body of research and findings that challenge culture-of-poverty arguments.

On matters of gender, however, the structural model would benefit from discussion, criticism, and rethinking. This is not to deny the structural model's value in linking poverty to external economic conditions but, rather, to question the model's assumptions about gender and family structure and to point to the need for gender as a specific analytic category.

Although several key aspects of the structural model distinguish it from the cultural model, both models are remarkably close in their thinking about gender. Patricia Hill Collins, in her viewpoint in this issue, exposes the gender ideologies that underlie cultural explanations of racial inferiority. Those same ideologies about women and men, about their place in the family and their relationship to the public institutions of the larger society, reappear, albeit in modified ways, in the structural model.

Collins shows how assumptions about racial deficiency rest on cultural notions about unfit men and women. In contrast, the structural approach focuses on the social circumstances produced by economic change. It therefore avoids drawing caricatures of men who spurn work and unmarried women who persist in having children. Yet both models find differences between mainstream gender roles and those of the underclass. Indeed, some of the most striking and important findings of the structural approach focus on this difference. Clearly, the reasons for the difference lie in the differing economic and social opportunities of the two groups, yet the structural model assumes that the traditional family is a key solution for eliminating racial poverty. Although the reasons given for the erosion of the traditional family are very different, both models rest on normative definitions of women's and men's roles. Two examples reveal how the structural perspective is locked into traditional concepts of the family and women's and men's places within it.

Wilson identifies male joblessness and the resulting shortage of marriageable males as the conditions responsible for the proliferation of female-headed households. His vision of a solution is a restoration of marital opportunities and the restoration of family structures in which men provide for their families by working in the labor force and women have children who can then be assured of the economic opportunities afforded by two-parent families. He offers no alternative concept of the family, no discussion of lesbian families or other arrangements that differ from the standard male-female married pair. Instead of exploring how women's opportunities and earning capacities outside of marriage are affected by macrostructural economic transformations, instead of calling "for pay equity, universal day care and other initiatives to buttress women's capacities for living independently in the world . . . Wilson goes in exactly the opposite direction."[54]

Ellwood's comprehensive analysis of American family poverty and welfare, *Poor Support: Poverty in the American Family,* contains a discussion that says a great deal about how women, men, and family roles are viewed by authoritative scholars working within the structural tradition. Looking at the work of adults in two-parent families, Ellwood finds that all families must fulfill two roles—a nurturing/child-rearing role and a provider role—and that in two-parent families

these responsibilities are divided along traditional gender lines. Therefore, Ellwood raises the question "Do we want single mothers to behave like husbands or like wives? Those who argue that single mothers ought to support their families through their own efforts are implicitly asking that they behave like husbands."[55] While Ellwood's discussion is meant to illustrate that single mothers experience difficulty in having to fulfill the dual roles of provider and nurturer, it confuses the matter by reverting to a gendered division of labor in which women nurture and men provide. By presenting family responsibilities as those of "husbands" and "wives," even well-meaning illustrations reproduce the ideology they seek to challenge.

Structural approaches have failed to articulate gender as an analytic category even though the conditions uncovered in contemporary research on the urban underclass are closely intertwined with gender. In fact, the problems of male joblessness and female-headed households form themselves around gender. Although these conditions are the result of economic transformations, they change gender relations as they change the marital, family, and labor arrangements of women and men. Furthermore, the economic disenfranchisement of large numbers of Black men, what Clyde Franklin calls "the institutional decimation of Black men,"[56] is a gender phenomenon of enormous magnitude. It affects the meanings and definitions of masculinity for Black men, and it reinforces the public patriarchy that controls Black women through their increased dependence on welfare. Such gender issues are vital. They reveal that where people of Color "end up" in the social order has as much to do with the economic restructuring of gender as with the economic restructuring of class and race.

The new structural analyses of the underclass reveal that the conditions in which Black and Hispanic women and men live are extremely vulnerable to economic change. In this way, such analyses move beyond "feminization of poverty" explanations that ignore class and race differences among women and ignore poverty among minority men.[57] Yet many structural analyses fail to consider the interplay of gender-based assumptions with structural racism. Just as the "feminization of poverty" approach has tended to neglect the way in which race produces different routes to poverty, structural discussions of the underclass pay far too little attention to how gender produces different routes to poverty for Black and Hispanic women and men. Many social forces are at work in the current erosion of family life among Black and Hispanic people. Careful attention to the interlocking systems of class, race, and gender is imperative if we are to understand and solve the problems resulting from economic transformation.

ENDNOTES

1. Mary Corcoran, Greg J. Duncan, Gerald Gurin, and Patricia Gurin, "Myth and Reality: The Causes and Persistence of Poverty," *Journal of Policy Analysis and Management* 4, no. 4 (1985): 516–36.
2. Mary Corcoran, Greg J. Duncan, and Martha S. Hill, "The Economic Fortunes of Women and Children: Lessons from the Panel Study of Income Dynamics," *Signs: Journal of Women in Culture and Society* 10, no. 2 (Winter 1984): 232–48.
3. Daniel P. Moynihan, "The Negro Family: The Case for National Action," in *The Moynihan Report and the Politics of Controversy,* ed. L. Rainwater and W.L. Yancey (Cambridge, Mass.: MIT Press, 1967), 39–132.
4. Margaret Cerullo and Marla Erlien, "Beyond the 'Normal Family': A Cultural Critique of Women's Poverty," in *For Crying Out Loud,* ed. Rochelle Lefkowitz and Ann Withorn (New York: Pilgrim Press, 1986), 246–60.
5. Moynihan, 47.
6. Leith Mullings, "Anthropological Perspectives on the Afro-American Family," *American Journal of Social Psychiatry* 6, no. 1 (Winter 1986): 11–16; see the following revisionist works on the Black family: Andrew Billingsley, *Black Families in White America* (Englewood Cliffs, N.J.: Prentice-Hall, 1968); Robert Hill, *The Strengths of Black Families* (New York: Emerson-Hall, 1972); Herbert Gutman, *The Black Family in Slavery and Freedom* (New York: Pantheon, 1976); Joyce Ladner, *Tomorrow's Tomorrow: The Black Woman* (New York: Doubleday, 1971); Elliot Leibow, *Talley's Corner: A Study of Negro Street Corner Men* (Boston: Little, Brown, 1967); Carol Stack, *All Our Kin* (New York: Harper & Row, 1974).
7. William J. Wilson and Robert Aponte, "Urban Poverty," *Annual Review of Sociology* 11 (1985): 231–58, esp. 241.
8. For a review of recent studies, see ibid.
9. Daniel Patrick Moynihan, *Family and Nation* (San Diego: Harcourt, Brace, Jovanovich, 1986).
10. "The Vanishing Family: Crisis in Black America,"
narrated by Bill Moyers, Columbia Broadcasting System (CBS) Special Report, January 1986.
11. "Hard Times for Black America," *Dollars and Sense,* no. 115 (April 1986), 5–7.
12. Nicholas Lemann, "The Origins of the Underclass: Part 1," *Atlantic Monthly* (June 1986), 31–55; Nicholas Lemann, "The Origins of the Underclass: Part 2," *Atlantic Monthly* (July 1986), 54–68.
13. Lemann, "Part 1," 35.
14. Ibid.
15. Jim Sleeper, "Overcoming 'Underclass': More Jobs Are Still the Key," *In These Times* (June 11–24, 1986), 16.
16. Corcoran et al. (n. 1 above), 517.
17. Martha S. Hill and Michael Ponza, "Poverty and Welfare Dependence across Generations," *Economic Outlook U.S.A.* (Summer 1983), 61–64, esp. 64.
18. Anne Rueter, "Myths of Poverty," *Research News* (July–September 1984), 18–19.
19. Mary Jo Bane, "Household Composition and Poverty," in *Fighting Poverty,* ed. Sheldon H. Danziger and Daniel H. Weinberg (Cambridge, Mass.: Harvard University Press, 1986), 209–31.
20. Ibid.
21. Betsy Dworkin, "40% of the Poor are Children," *New York Times Book Review* (March 2, 1986), 9.
22. Bane, 277.
23. Martha Hill, "Trends in the Economic Situation of U.S. Families and Children, 1970–1980," in *American Families and the Economy,* ed. Richard R. Nelson and Felicity Skidmore (Washington, D.C.: National Academy Press, 1983), 9–53, esp. 38.
24. Charles Murray, *Losing Ground* (New York: Basic, 1984).
25. David T. Ellwood, *Poor Support* (New York: Basic, 1988).
26. Sheldon Danziger and Peter Gottschalk, "The Poverty of *Losing Ground,"* *Challenge* 28 (May/June 1985): 32–38.
27. William A. Darity and Samuel L. Meyers, "Does Welfare Dependency Cause Female Headship? The Case of the Black Family," *Journal of Marriage and the Family* 46, no. 4 (November 1984): 765–79.
28. David T. Ellwood and Lawrence H. Summers, "Poverty in America: Is Welfare the Answer or the Problem?" in *Fighting Poverty* (n. 19 above), 78–105.
29. Ibid., 96.
30. "The Costs of Being Black," *Research News* 38, nos. 11–12 (November–December 1987): 8–10.
31. Barry Bluestone and Bennett Harrison, *The Deindustrialization of America* (New York: Basic, 1982), 54.
32. Barry Bluestone, Bennett Harrison, and Lucy Gorham, "Storm Clouds on the Horizon: Labor Market Crisis and Industrial Policy," 68, as cited in "Hard Times for Black America" (n. 11 above).
33. Richard Child Hill and Cynthia Negrey, "Dein-

dustrialization and Racial Minorities in the Great Lakes Region, U.S.A.," in *The Reshaping of America: Social Consequences of the Changing Economy,* ed. D. Stanley Eitzen and Maxine Baca Zinn (Englewood, N.J.: Prentice-Hall, 1989), 168–77.

34. Elliot Currie and Jerome H. Skolnick, *America's Problems: Social Issues and Public Policy* (Boston: Little, Brown, 1984), 82.

35. John D. Kasarda, "Caught in a Web of Change," *Society* 21 (November/December 1983): 41–47.

36. Ibid., 45–47.

37. John D. Kasarda, "Urban Change and Minority Opportunities," in *The New Urban Reality,* ed. Paul E. Peterson (Washington, D.C.: Brookings Institution, 1985), 33–68, esp. 55.

38. William J. Wilson with Kathryn Neckerman, "Poverty and Family Structure: The Widening Gap between Evidence and Public Policy Issues," in *The Truly Disadvantaged,* by William J. Wilson (Chicago: University of Chicago Press, 1978), 63–92.

39. Ibid.

40. Jerelyn Eddings, "Children Having Children," *Baltimore Sun* (March 2, 1986), 71.

41. As quoted in ibid., 71.

42. Noel A. Cazenave, "Alternate Intimacy, Marriage, and Family Lifestyles among Low-Income Black Americans," *Alternate Lifestyles* 3, no. 4 (November 1980): 425–44.

43. "The Kerner Report Updated" (Racine, Wis.: Report of the 1988 Commission on the Cities, March 1, 1988).

44. Wilson, *The Truly Disadvantaged* (n. 38 above), 62.

45. Ellwood (n. 25 above), 204.

46. Paul E. Peterson, "Introduction: Technology, Race, and Urban Policy," in *The New Urban Reality,* ed. Paul E. Peterson (Washington, D.C.: Brookings Institution, 1985), 1–35, esp. 22.

47. Jennifer Juarez Robles, "Hispanics Emerging as Nation's Poorest Minority Group," *Chicago Reporter* 17, no. 6 (June 1988): 1–3.

48. Ibid., 2–3.

49. Ibid., 3.

50. Alejandro Portes and Cynthia Truelove, "Making Sense of Diversity: Recent Research on Hispanic Minorities in the United States," *Annual Review of Sociology* 13 (1987): 359–85.

51. Joan W. Moore, "An Assessment of Hispanic Poverty: Does a Hispanic Underclass Exist?" *Tomás Rivera Center Report* 2, no. 1 (Fall 1988): 8–9.

52. Robles, 3.

53. U.S. Bureau of the Census, *Current Population Reports,* Series P-20, nos. 416, 422 (Washington, D.C.: Government Printing Office, March 1987).

54. Adolph Reed, Jr., "The Liberal Technocrat," *Nation* (February 6, 1988), 167–70.

55. Ellwood (n. 25 above), 133.

56. Clyde W. Franklin II, "Surviving the Institutional Decimation of Black Males: Causes, Consequences, and Intervention," in *The Making of Masculinities,* ed. Harry Brod (Winchester, Mass.: Allen & Unwin, 1987), 155–69, esp. 155.

57. See Maxine Baca Zinn, "Minority Families in Crisis: The Public Discussion," Working Paper no. 6 (Memphis, Tenn.: Memphis State University, Center for Research on Women, 1987), for an extended critique of the culture-of-poverty model.

The Next Waves
Migration Theory for a Changing World

Aristide R. Zolberg

Twenty-five years is a long time in the history of both international migrations and migration theory. The most striking change since the founding of *International Migration Review* is the fundamentally altered relationship between the two. When the journal started, migration theory was still very much confined to the "classic" genre initiated by Ravenstein in the 1880s (e.g. Lee, 1966), which conceptualized migration as relocation of human beings across space, within or between countries, and strove to achieve an elegant formal model that would account for such movements. Theoretical developments of the subsequent period, many of which first appeared in IMR or in works by members of the extensive international and interdisciplinary network it fostered, challenged conventional theoretical discourse in the light of ongoing processes in the world at large. Despite many differences, attributable to different intellectual traditions and disciplinary backgrounds, the most stimulating newer approaches share a number of common features: (1) they are generally historical, not in the sense of dealing mostly with a more distant past, but rather in paying appropriate attention to the changing specificities of time and space; (2) they are generally structural rather than individualistic, focusing on the social forces that constrain individual action, with special emphasis on the dynamics of capitalism and of the state; (3) they are generally globalist, in that they see national entities as social formations as interactive units within an encompassing international social field, permeable to determination by transnational and international economic and political processes; and (4) they are generally critical, sharing to some degree a commitment to social science as a process of demystification and rectification, and in particular are concerned with the consequences of international migrations for the countries of origin and destination, as well as the migrants themselves. (A particularly interesting development is the emergence of migration as an explicit concern of political and social philosophy.) The historicization of migration theory implies that theoretical concerns and emphases must be modified in the light of changing social realities. What follows therefore reviews the links between history and theory of the past quarter century, and tries to project what we might expect in the next. We can obtain an inkling of "the next waves" by asking in what ways each of the major features of recent epochal patterns is likely to change in the foreseeable future.

GLOBAL INEQUALITY

No corner of the globe is now left that has not been restructured by market forces, uprooting the last remnants of subsistence economies and propelling ever growing numbers to search for work. Despite some of the good news regarding the decline of the rate of growth of world population since 1970, the annual addition to the world total is expected to continue increasing until the end of the century (U.N., 1989:3). Although con-

Reprinted by permission of Aristide R. Zolberg and the *International Migration Review,* published by the Center for Migration Studies of N.Y., Inc.

trary to expectations, several of the largest LDCs managed to resolve their subsistence problems, and in the next quarter of a century more of them will undoubtedly rise to the status of "NICs"; however, most LDCs will remain unable to provide jobs for rising generations. Concurrently, information about variation in opportunities will continue to spread, and the relative cost of transportation will further decrease. Most people will in fact move within their own country; but for the unfortunate who find themselves born in Burundi rather than Belgium, Chihuahua rather than Chicago, it will make sense to try in every way possible to relocate abroad. The worst conditions will probably continue to prevail in sub-Saharan Africa, which has the highest rate of population growth.

One might anticipate a regionalization of migration pressures from each "south" to its particular "north," determined not only by geographical proximity but also by political and economic linkages which contributed to the formation of migratory networks (Portes and Walton, 1981). Most obviously, within the Western Hemisphere they will intensify on the one hand from Latin America and the Caribbean to the United States and Canada; and on the other from Africa (both north and south of the Sahara) to Western-Central Europe. In Asia, there will be strong pressures for relocation from the less to the more dynamic countries within each of the continent's major regions. Given the rapidly increasing differentiation of conditions among countries of the developing world more generally, south-to-south pressures will undoubtedly intensify in the coming decades.

Yet migratory pressures do not automatically result in massive migrations, because border control usually intervenes as a determinative factor. Independently of other conditions, it is state actions with respect to these borders that determine whether any international migration will take place at all: if the world consisted of Albania on the one hand and Japan on the other, there would be no *International Migration Review* at all. This helps to make sense of the statistical finding that high rates of population growth and low economic growth rates do not induce emigration (e.g. Weiner, 1987:176–177).

BORDERS AS BARRIERS TO MOVEMENT

In retrospect, it is quite strange that classical migration theory altogether ignored borders and their effects. This egregious omission goes back to the founder. Although E.G. Ravenstein (1889:241) acknowledged in his second paper that "currents of migration which would flow naturally in a certain direction traced out for them in the main by geographical features, may . . . be diverted, or stopped altogether, by legislative enactments," his sole example is the enactment in the reign of Elizabeth I of a law to restrain the growth of London. He left out of consideration measures to control immigration then recently legislated by the United States which, as revealed in the discussion that followed presentation of his paper, were widely known in Britain and legitimatized demands to enact similar laws. These culminated a decade and a half later in the passage of a highly restrictive Aliens Act which contributed to keep immigration to Britain well below the European level until after World War II (Gainer, 1972). Whatever the reasons for Ravenstein's omission, he thereby erroneously concluded that international migrations were governed by the same "laws" as migrations within countries. The result was a theoretical tradition which bore only a tenuous relationship to reality.

One important theoretical development of the past quarter of a century is recognition that it is precisely the control which states exercise over borders that defines international migration as a distinctive social process. This arises from their irreducible political element, in that the process entails not only physical relocation, but a change of jurisdiction and membership (Zolberg, 1981a).

Overall, the policies they have adopted allow for only very limited international movement (Dowty, 1987). Although some states restrict exit, generally, those containing the population most prone to relocate in keeping with the trend noted above do not. On the other hand, all the countries to which people would like to go restrict entry. This means that, in the final analysis, it is the policies of potential receivers which determine whether movement can take place, and of what kind. This has been noted as well by Bhagwati

(1984), who has concluded that the process of international migrations is therefore characterized by "disincentives" rather than "incentives," and surmised that were socialist countries to let people out, "the effective constraint on the numbers migrating would soon become the immigration legislations of the destination countries" (p. 684).

The observation is applicable to refugees as well as to economic migrations. Regardless of what violence people may be subjected to in the country of origin, this produces a flow of refugees only if people have a place to go; if not, the violence has other consequences, as dramatically demonstrated by the fate of so many Armenians and Jews in the first half of the twentieth century, Biafrans in the 1960s, or the population of West Irian under Indonesian occupation today.

It is now well understood also that in a world characterized by widely varying conditions, international borders serve to maintain global inequality. Arghiri Emmanuel (1972) has observed that they prevent labor from commanding the same price everywhere, while from a very different theoretical perspective, Carruthers and Vining (1982) have proposed a conceptualization of states as dispensers of widely varying bundles of collective goods. Hamilton and Whalley (1984) have sought to demonstrate the dramatic effects of the elimination of borders (see also Petras 1980b). On the normative side, the importance of borders as a device for maintaining inequality has been emphasized by Nett (1971).

In recent decades, the capitalist democracies have reaffirmed their long-established immigration policies which, collectively, constitute a protective wall against self-propelled migration, but with small doors that allow for specific flows. One of the doors was provided to allow for the procurement of certain types of labor; and the other to let in a small number of asylum-seekers. The future shape of international migrations depends in large part on how these doors are manipulated.

THE EXPLOITATION OF FOREIGN LABOR

One of the sharpest contrasts between the old and new literatures is the conceptual shift from a view of "ordinary" international migration as the aggregate movements of individuals in response to differential opportunities, to a view of this process as a movement of workers propelled by the dynamics of the transnational capitalist economy, which simultaneously determine both the "push" and the "pull." The shift is no mere artifact of intellectual fashion, but reflects a reinterpretation of the American experience as well as a broadening of the theoretical domain to encompass the contemporary experience of other countries.

In the United States, at the time the IMR was launched, those concerned with international migration focused their attention almost exclusively on the "main gate" – i.e., immigration from Europe – which, in consequence of the laws adopted in the 1920s, no longer figured as a significant source of labor (e.g. Jones, 1960). Although population movements originating in the Western Hemisphere (Mexico, the Caribbean, and eastern Canada) arose as substitutes, together with internal migrations (including Puerto Rico), in the 1960s the United States appeared determined to further relinquish the use of alien labor. The Kennedy-Johnson Reforms (1965, effective 1968) imposed for the first time a quantitative limit on Western Hemisphere immigration, and the extensive *bracero* program was also brought to halt (Craig, 1971; Garcia y Griego, 1983). In reality, however, massive procurement of foreign workers continued by way of undocumented border crossers, at no risk whatsoever to the employers and under conditions that facilitated more extreme exploitation.

By the early 1970s, the consequences of these arrangements were quite evident. In one of the earliest theoretical analyses in the new vein, Burawoy (1976) drew attention to similarities between labor procurement systems in California and southern Africa. The fact that the countries supplying labor were Latin American or Caribbean, a region that constitutes the periphery of the U.S. dominated sector of the world economy, also suggested a linkage between the migratory process and dependency. As demonstrated by Portes (1978), dependent development effected structural distortions that exacerbated "push" conditions and triggered the onset of migrations from the peripheral to the core country, subsequently expanding by way of the formation of networks.

Far from being unique, the bracero program as well as its informal successor had many features in common with European guestworker systems. In Europe, the early 1960s were also an important turning point in that immigration moved to the fore as a major social phenomenon and emerged for the first time as a subject of interest to social scientists. Under prevailing regulations, European countries did not receive "immigrants" in the American sense, but persons whose admission and residence were conditional on economic performance. This reflected, by and large, the implementation of a deliberate policy based on Arthur Lewis's analysis of economic growth with an unlimited supply of labor, derived from American historical experience and applied to post-war Europe by Charles Kindleberger (1967). The theory emphasized the advantages of using foreign labor in the face of slower population growth and as a "conjunctural buffer," and in the late 1960s emerged as the official doctrine of the OECD.

Because the population movements in question were so explicitly functional, they could be encompassed within an essentially economic analysis, either of an institutional sort (e.g. Tapinos, 1974), or of a more Marxist cast, with an emphasis on the dynamics of production and reproduction of labor and the necessity of a disposable "industrial reserve army" (e.g. Castles and Kosack, 1973; Castells, 1975). Approaching the phenomenon from a different theoretical tradition, Piore (1979) also demonstrated on the basis of observations of the United States and Western Europe how the use of foreign labor was functional to capitalism, permitting the structuring of a segmented labor market (see also Gordon, 1988).

In retrospect, however, as Cohen (1987:144) has suggested, "both orthodox economists and a number of Marxists became trapped into a timeless functionality and exaggerated the extent to which migrant labor was a permanent solution for European capital." Much as strategic theorists are generally one war behind, the new *problematique* emerged as the ruling paradigm at a moment when new conditions brought about a change in the calculation of costs and benefits of

the system, and ultimately a questioning of the further suitability of these arrangements. Considered in a longer and more historical vision, the period under consideration can be thought of as

> one where importing labor of a subordinate status was a preferred and helpful solution for European capital. . . . The mix between free and unfree labor is spatially redistributed in complex and continuously changing ways in response to the mix of market opportunities, comparative labor-power costs, the course of struggles between capital and labor and the historically specific flows and supplies of migrant and other forms of unfree labor. (Cohen, 1978:144)

That this abrupt about-face was triggered by the energy crisis of 1973, which signaled the onset of slower growth and was followed by a depression, suggested that the explanation for it was essentially conjunctural. However, hesitations and second thoughts concerning the balance of costs and benefits of foreign workers had in fact surfaced before the crisis. Even at their height, policies designed to import temporary alien labor were cast against a background of strictly limited immigration. The coexistence of these seemingly contradictory stances suggests they are interrelated, so that if we wish to understand the overall role of industrial capitalist countries in the determination of international migrations, it is necessary to account for the wall they have erected as well as for the small doors they have provided in it.

The benefits capitalists derive from foreign labor have been well analyzed, and need not be restated here. However, much less attention has been given to the other side of the question — given the advantages of an "unlimited supply of labor," why don't capitalists deploy their clout to import many, many more, or even to obtain completely open borders? In order to be rendered productive, labor must be combined with capital. Beyond a certain point, capital becomes very scarce and hence much more costly, wages reach some minimal floor, and demand for additional output dies out. Should the labor supply continue to increase beyond this, the social costs of income transfers to the excess portion — borne by employers and employed workers — will begin to mount.

Reubens (1983:179) has suggested that the lesson Ricardo and Malthus drew from the natural increase of the local population may be extended to international migration. Given worldwide disparities, free entry would induce unlimited flows, leading to a drastic jump toward worldwide equalization, and hence a violent tumble in employment and consumption levels among the more developed countries. The income gap for individuals living in countries at very different levels of development stems not only from wage differentials, but also from substantial differences in the bundles of collective goods provided by the respective countries (Carruthers et al., 1982). Capitalist economies with democratic regimes provide their residents many more of the universally prized conditions than do less developed countries, ranging from abundant and safe water as well as relatively disease-free environments, to educational facilities and freedom from arbitrary exactions by government officials. Beyond this, within the world economy, when rich countries experience a bad conjuncture, the situation is likely to be much worse in the peripheral countries that normally supply them with imported labor. Under those circumstances, incentives to move remain in effect or become perhaps even more acute than before.

The difficulty of reducing the costs of the welfare state in bad times has sharpened awareness of the inefficiencies involved in the labor procurement policies under consideration and prompted widespread questioning of their wisdom. It is, of course, possible to deny income transfers to unemployed alien workers; but if this were done, their efforts to survive would inevitably be translated into other social costs. In fact, foreign workers have in many cases been able to overcome restrictions on their rights, and hence managed to bargain for conditions closer to those of native labor. However, to the extent that this has been achieved, they have significantly reduced the advantage of this form of labor to capital.

In any case, although capitalists carry a great deal of weight in the determination of economic policies, in liberal democracies public policy seldom reflects the interests of capitalists alone. As pithily suggested by Przeworski and Wallerstein (1982:215), "If workers opt for capitalism under some conditions, then . . . the state institutional-

izes, coordinates and enforces compromises reached by a class coalition that encompasses both workers and capitalists." In most capitalist democracies, organized labor was able to achieve some market protection by imposing limiting conditions on labor importation. If we add to this that workers and capitalists also have interests as "native taxpayers" it is possible to make sense of immigration policies as particular outcomes of such compromises, sometimes forged vociferously within a free-for-all legislative arena, as in the United States, or far from the public eye by way of a quiet corporatist settlement, as in West Germany or Sweden.

The issue of future demand in the countries of the "core" remains moot. According to the recently elaborated theory of a "new international division of labor," industrial capital from the core is moving to the periphery, where cheaper labor is located, establishing factories to produce manufactured goods for export to the worldwide market (Frobel et al., 1980). Accordingly, it has been suggested that, beyond the current conjuncture, structural changes in the labor market of both Europe and the United States have reduced the demand for massive industrial labor of the sort hitherto filled by immigrants (Piore, 1986). As against this, however, a number of analysts have pointed out that the much-touted "New International Division of Labor" still leaves the overwhelming bulk of industrial production within the "core" (e.g. Cohen, 1987:233–251; Gordon, 1988). Furthermore, Sassen-Koob (1984) projects a continuing polarization of the employment structure of global cities, with the lower segment to be filled largely by immigrants. Yet this need not necessarily be the case, as the expanding demand for low-skilled labor in the service sector could be met in large part from internal sources, including the residue of recent waves of immigration, particularly in the face of pressures to force the "idle" to work in order to control the costs of the welfare state.

As it is, opposition to labor importation is not founded on economic grounds alone. A group of independent experts who reviewed policy trends in Europe for the OECD in 1978 concluded that:

the second primary objective of implementing restrictions . . . was a desire to minimize the growing social tensions created by the presence of a large number of foreigners. It is hard to be precise about such a nebulous topic, but history is replete with examples of the seriousness of problems resulting from cultural conflicts, competing claims for jobs, or miscommunication due to language problems. (OECD, 1979:22)

Manifestations of what these experts euphemistically term a "desire to minimize . . . social tensions" were visible in many receiving countries well before the energy crisis and subsequent downturn. For example, in Britain immigration policy rose to the fore of political controversy as early as 1958, and remained on the agenda until very restrictive measures were legislated in 1983.

Yet there were also countertrends. In 1965, the United States eliminated the blatantly discriminatory national origins quota system, and equivalent measures were enacted around the same period by the immigration countries of the "white Commonwealth." Writing shortly afterwards, Nett (1971:224) went so far as to suggest that limits on immigration founded on arguments of cultural compatibility "could no longer have the same ideological push." But while there is no gainsaying the significance of these enactments, in the light of subsequent developments, it is evident that he underestimated the persistent thrust of "cultural compatibility" concerns.

The negative reactions of natives obviously express xenophobia and racism, but explanation cannot be found at the level of individual attitudes alone. The analytic starting point is that transnational migration brings about the encounter of culturally different groups hitherto separated from each other in space. However, these are not just any groups. As is well known, in the course of establishing their hegemony Europeans and their descendants stressed their common distinctiveness from the subjected populations, founded in part on phenotypical distinctions, and assigned to these differences values that legitimized in their own eyes relationships of superiority and inferiority. *Mutatis mutandis*, a similar process of cultural coding has tended to develop with respect to labor imported from the periphery.

Once established, this configuration of beliefs serves as a foundation for calculations concerning the putative political and cultural impact of various groups on the receiving countries. In ef-

fect, the very characteristics that make these human beings suitable as labor renders them undesirable from the perspective of membership in the receiving society. Although conventional social psychological studies tend to suggest that racism and xenophobia are associated with low education and social status, it should be remembered that racist doctrines were wrought by intellectuals, and that social elites concerned to maintain the cultural status quo have often played a major role in institutionalizing discrimination and in initiating restrictive immigration policies.

If we strip away the layers of prejudice that surround discussion of the issues involved, we come to the considerations evoked by Michael Walzer in his exploration of the moral justification for maintaining national boundaries (Walzer, 1981). In the world as presently constituted, nation-states constitute the most comprehensive level at which human beings have been able to develop liberal and democratic forms of political organization. In relation to this, it is necessary to limit membership in some fashion so as to preserve a functioning political community. Massive immigration of any kind poses special problems to which it is legitimate to pay attention, but the problems are compounded if the newcomers are culturally very different people who have not been socialized into the same political traditions. It is evident that even under the best of circumstances, the arrival of a large wave of immigrants who speak a different language, practice a different religion or merely have very different habits, does challenge the cultural status quo of the receiving country and induces some collective stress. Accordingly, liberal democracies have a right to be prudent and hence to restrict their intake to a manageable level.

The ethical implications of Walzer's position are further discussed in this article's conclusion. For the time being, his observations suggest that under current conditions, considerations of membership are likely to reinforce the economically induced trend to severely restrict permanent immigration. However, there is a broadening of the notion of "membership" to encompass on the one hand citizens of larger economic entities that are in the making throughout the capitalist world (the European Community, the coming U.S.-Canadian market), and on the other hand, groups considered members of the receiving society by virtue of their ancestral origins (e.g. "patrials" in Britain, "volksdeutsche" in Germany, Jews in Israel).

This means, in effect, that despite mounting pressures in the foreseeable future, south to north migrations involving workers and refugees will remain very limited. As against this, both types will continue to take place within the south. Reports suggest that current labor migrations, from one part of the developing world to another, often entail extreme exploitation because of the paucity of institutionalized protection for the rights of workers and, more generally, the prevalence of authoritarian political regimes.

LIBERALIZATION OF EXIT
FROM THE SOCIALIST WORLD

The prohibition of exit that prevailed among socialist states during the past quarter of a century has acted as a negative determinant of the world migratory configuration. However, these restrictive emigration policies have begun to change, and it is likely that the trend will be further accentuated in the near future. To understand why this is occurring, we need to understand why the prohibitions were established in the first place.

The classic case is the Soviet Union. Before the gates were shut, about one million people left the boundaries of the old Russian empire, a flow far exceeding any triggered by violent regime changes in earlier historical experience, not only because the state affected had a much larger population than any of the others, but also because the upheaval took place within the context of the collapse and transformation of the empire of the Tsars (Marrus, 1985:53–61). However, in the mid-1920s, the Soviet Union adopted a no-exit policy which, with minor exceptions, it maintained until very recently.

Alan Dowty (1987:63–67,208) has pointed out that the roots of this stance can be traced to prerevolutionary Russia, which never evolved a tradition of freedom of movement, both internal and external, because this was incompatible with the maintenance of serfdom. Although prerevolutionary Marxists advocated lifting such restrictions, Lenin's views of the state "laid the basis for future controls" in that all citizens were to be considered as "hired employees" of the state and required to serve. The Bolshevik attitude was also shaped by civil war and foreign intervention: "It was feared that those leaving the country would swell the ranks of the White armies and other enemies abroad. From there it was a short step to equating the wish to emigrate with opposition to the socialist state" (Dowty, 1987:68).

Adopted later by many others, this outlook emerged as the common feature of a disparate array of modern authoritarian regimes, including not only those of the Marxist-Leninist persuasion, but also during much of their life Fascist Italy, Nazi Germany, Spain, and Portugal (as late as the 1960s). More generally, prohibition of emigration arises as a concomitant of state-directed economic autarchy, particularly in the case of states that seek to catch up by imposing great sacrifices on the current generation. But the prohibition also serves more purely political objectives; since exit is tantamount to "voting with one's feet," an alternative to protest, authoritarian regimes which claim to rest on democratic consent cannot afford such concrete evidence of deep alienation (Hirschman, 1981:246–265). This is reinforced by tense international conjunctures, including the Cold War and more limited regional conflicts such as the one between the United States and Cuba.

Against this background, emigration may be used exceptionally to relieve tensions or to rid the state of some unwanted ethnic or national minority; however, permission to leave may be disguised as expulsion or coupled with humiliating measures, so as to avoid appearing to grant to the minority a privilege refused to the majority of nationals. However, this is a double-edged sword; by the same token, the imposition of barriers on emigration has the effect of calling into question the legitimacy of the regime. For example, at the conclusion of his memoirs, Khrushchev characterized the policy as a "disgraceful heritage . . . which lies like a chain on the consciousness of the Soviet state" (Dowty, 1987:209).

It follows that political liberalization – *glasnost* – is likely to be accompanied by some relaxation of exit policy, and that a reduction of international tensions lowers the costs of doing so.

This assuages pressures from dissidents, and hence makes internal politics more manageable. In addition, we might anticipate additional weight in the same direction from *perestroika*. The relevant precedent here is Yugoslavia in the mid-1960s, when it shifted to a decentralized form of socialist self-management (Dowty, 1987:206). No longer able to guarantee full employment, the state encouraged its citizens to enlist as guest-workers in the Federal Republic and their hard currency remittances also facilitated Yugoslavia's reentry into the capitalist world economy.

Within the world of the Cold War, Western states regarded emigration from the Soviet Union and its satellites as "defection," a demonstration that Communist regimes lacked support. Adoption of an immigration policy welcoming defectors carried little cost, since most people could not get out. Except for Hungarians in 1956, those who did emigrate were largely Germans who were absorbed by the Federal Republic. However, little note was taken of the fact that even at the height of the Cold War Western states did not adopt the same welcoming stance with respect to Asian defectors.[1] U.S. policy regarding Cubans evolved from a "European" to an "Asian" stance — the first wave (1959–63) was welcome, the second (freedom flights, 1965–73) evoked some doubts and the third (Mariel, 1980) was initially resisted. In recent years, the Asian policy has prevailed, as indicated by efforts to discourage emigration from Poland at the time of the military coup of 1984.

We are thus faced with a paradoxical situation. Reduction in international tensions makes exit from the Socialist countries more likely, but it also lessens the propaganda value of "defection," and hence leads to the treatment of people desiring to leave as ordinary immigrants, having to face severe restrictions. In short, unless something is done, the human beings involved will be just as immobilized after the lifting of barriers to exit as before. It appears that Bhagwati's surmise is unfortunately in the course of being confirmed.

THE REFUGEE CRISIS
IN THE DEVELOPING WORLD[2]

Myron Weiner has suggested that "there may be as many refugees in the world as there are people who migrated in response to employment opportunities" (Weiner, 1987:177). In the mid-1970s, there appeared massive new flows in both Asia and Africa, attributable to complex conflicts that engulfed entire regions — the countries that composed former Indochina, the Horn of Africa and southern Africa. For the first time, large bodies of refugees also materialized in Latin America's Southern Cone. This was compounded in the early 1980s by the explosion of long-standing ethnic confrontations in Sri Lanka and Lebanon, the resumption of violence following the breakdown of earlier settlements in Sudan, Chad and Uganda, as well as the flaring up of revolutionary conflicts in hitherto quiescent regions of Central America and West Asia (Afghanistan).

One measure of the crisis is that in the late 1970s there was a step-level increase in the total number of refugees in need at a given time from a previous range of between five and ten million, to a higher one of between ten and fifteen million; at the end of 1988, the estimate was about 18.5 million (USCR, 1989). Moreover, refugees abroad constitute but one segment of the total number of persons uprooted by violence; the same upheavals also produced millions of internally displaced, with estimates of the major concentrations as follows:

- Southern Africa: 10.5 million uprooted (including 3.6 million forcibly relocated within the Republic of South Africa), of whom 1.4 are abroad.
- Afghanistan: 7–8 million uprooted, of whom 5.8 million are abroad.
- Palestinians: 2.8 million abroad (of whom 2.2 million are under UNWRA jurisdiction).
- Other Middle East: 2.8–3.2 million uprooted (including by Iran-Iraq war), of whom 1.3 million are abroad. Sub-Saharan Africa: 2.7–2.9 million uprooted, of whom 1.1 million are abroad.
- Ethiopia: 1.8–2.6 million uprooted, of whom 1.1 million are abroad.
- Central America: 1.9 million uprooted, of whom 850,000 are abroad (including 600,000 unrecognized in the United States, mostly from El Salvador).
- Former Indochina: residual 440,000 abroad within region.

The sense of crisis stemmed not only from the increase of the total number of people in the world at large who might be classified as refugees, but also from a perceptible expansion of the burdens they impose on the international community. This is attributable in part to the decision of the UNHCR in the early 1960s to assume responsibility for populations displaced by wars of national liberation under the "good offices" doctrine, a move that was itself stimulated by the accession of a steady stream of former colonies to U.N. membership. In addition, a mounting proportion of the new refugees appeared destined to linger on indefinitely, unable either to return to their country of origin or to find a permanent haven. Also, the swelling of the refugee population in the 1970s came at a period of economic retrenchment for all but oil-producers. In the face of rapidly mounting unemployment, the affluent liberal countries imposed more severe restrictions on general immigration and were more reluctant to take in refugees for permanent asylum. Largely in consequence of the preceding, a sizable proportion of the new refugees were parked in rag-tag camps in some of the world's poorest countries, themselves badly hit by the global economic downturn. With little opportunity to fend for themselves, the refugees constituted a mounting burden for the UNHCR, which itself depended on constant handouts from a limited number of governments and voluntary agencies, in some cases lacking the capacity to protect those under its jurisdiction. Violent conflicts are likely to be more destructive today than in the past because both governments and their opponents have access to firepower in all its forms. Furthermore, the impact of violence on poor and densely populated countries is particularly catastrophic because it often reduces agricultural production below the subsistence level. Given the availability of roads, bicycles and trucks, even very poor peasants are today much more able to move in the face of violence than their forebears. How many of them become refugees is largely a function of location in relation to international borders, existing migratory networks and the disposition of relevant neighbors.

As the summary overview indicates, refugees in the developing world arise mostly as a by-product of two major historical processes – the formation of new states and confrontations over the social order in both old and new states. These are analytically distinguishable, but often combined in reality to generate complex and extremely violent conflicts. Although the processes are akin to those that produced earlier crises in Europe, they are unfolding in very different settings and under extremely different historical circumstances, so that the outcome is likely to be quite different as well.

It is noteworthy that in contrast with what happened in Europe earlier in this century, relatively few people in the developing world have been uprooted by ordinary wars between sovereign states. However, this is not to say that the root causes of the crisis can therefore be characterized as "domestic" rather than "international." Indeed, a distinctive feature of the contemporary epoch is the formation of a world within which national societies persist, but are internationalized to a higher degree than ever before. Consequently the conflicts with which we are concerned arise as a product of what constitute from the perspective of a given society both internal and external forces, inextricably linked to form distinctive transnational patterns.

This is reflected most dramatically in the prominent role of external intervention in the conflicts that produced the major concentrations found today (Zolberg, Suhrke, and Aguayo, 1986). These major categories can be disaggregated and their likely incidence in the foreseeable future examined.

FORMATION OF NEW STATES IN ASIA AND AFRICA

One important source of refugees in recent decades were wars of national liberation, but all the possible cases have already surfaced and reached a definitive outcome including now Namibia. Following the assumption of power by the nationalists, the refugees rapidly returned to their homes. However, this was foreclosed in Angola by the internationalization of the conflict, which subsequently added major new flows. A similar situation later emerged in Mozambique as well. Transfers of power triggered, in turn, the massive flight or expulsion of Europeans as well as their indigenous auxiliaries and allies, who often included a stratum of mixed racial ascendancy, now living as near-exiles in the former imperial countries (e.g. Algerian Harkis in France). The major exception so far is Zimbabwe, which retained approximately half its European settler population after independence. Namibia will soon become independent under black rule, but the ongoing conflict in the Republic of South Africa itself is bound to develop further and is likely to generate larger flows of refugees to neighboring countries.

"Ethnic diversity" is generally regarded as a leading root cause of recent movements in Asia and Africa. However, it is evident that only some of the numerous differences of language, religion, and social organization encountered in the societies in question have given rise to conflicts, and that in turn only some of these conflicts produce significant flows of refugees.

Ethnicity is not merely a projection or revival of traditional attachments, but a contemporary social construct used as an organizational resource in struggles over the allocation of resources and power (Horowitz, 1985). Although the ethnic and cultural heterogeneity of the new states of Asia and Africa generally exceeds even that of the European "successor" states of the interwar period, the formation of classic "target minorities" as the result of persecution by the state on the grounds that they constitute an obstacle to the formation of a successful nation is quite rare because, in contrast with many of their European predecessors, most of the new states accepted from the outset the reality of a multinational or multiethnic political community. Somewhat paradoxically, extreme ethnic diversity normally imposes constraints on political elites, providing incentives to build multiethnic governing coalitions, even in the absence of open political competition. However, over the long run, the various components cooperate only if they reap tangible benefits from ruling together, as was generally the case during the expansive "development" epoch up to the early 1970s. Under conditions of greater scarcity brought about by the worldwide economic crisis, whose effects were multiplied for the heavy debtor nations, the incentives for cooperation were considerably weakened, precipitating a scramble for power.

One particularly explosive type of formation is "ethnic hierarchies," in which social class coincides with ethnic membership. Focusing on com-

prehensive relationships between the dominant and subjected groups, conflict takes on an explosive character akin to a social revolution. Most ethnic hierarchies encompassing whole national societies exploded early on, soon after introduction of the principle of majority rule, as in Rwanda and Burundi. In the former case a successful revolution resulted in the massacre or flight of most of the ruling group; in the latter, the revolution was unsuccessful, leading to violent retaliation by the dominant group against the majority. Many were killed or fled, but most remained behind, providing the potential for recurrent confrontations and additional refugee waves, as occurred again in mid-1988.

Minorities relying on kinship and ethnic solidarity to develop far-flung networks engaging in intercultural trade were ubiquitous among ancient societies, including Europe, and are still found throughout Asia and Africa (Curtin, 1984). These diasporas traditionally operated under the protection of a ruling stratum in exchange for a share of the profits in the form of tribute, taxation or bribery. However, from the perspective of the new ruling elites, they are seen as ruthless exploiters, who usurp positions that could be filled by genuine nationals or fail to perform any valid economic function at all. Massive departures can be triggered by outright expulsions, pogroms, or their equivalent, notably regulations that deprive the minority of the possibility of making a living. Alternatively, if they have access to some homeland or other country that will receive them as immigrants, the minority may leave in anticipation of such measures. Many of these situations have already exploded, and remaining trading minorities throughout the developing world may be considered in jeopardy.

Groups that are not hierarchically related may be regionally concentrated or spatially interspersed. The presence of regionally concentrated groups tends to exacerbate conflicts over the distribution of power and resources between center and periphery. Separatism is especially likely to arise in situations involving a small number of large groups and if reformist action is impossible by virtue of the authoritarian character of the state or because the configuration renders territorial minorities permanently impotent. Regions that became "backward" as a consequence of the uneven impact of social change during the colonial period are particularly likely to spawn secessionist movements. A major exception is Eritrea, attributable to the region's formative experience as a separate colony and later trusteeship, with the prospect of achieving independence in the foreseeable future, but whose progress along this path was abruptly arrested when turned over by the United Nations to Ethiopia.

It is remarkable that, so far, only one of the numerous separatist movements that have arisen in the new states – Bangladesh – has resulted in a permanent actual separation of the ethnic group's homeland from the established political community. In some cases, this is attributable to the movement's success in achieving some of its objectives. Where the conflict escalated to the level of armed struggle, as in Nigeria, the absence of secession is mostly attributable to the capacity of the state to defend its integrity and defeat the challengers. In this respect, international factors are clearly decisive. By virtue of the legitimacy of established states in the international political system, the governmental side possesses inherent advantages, including external support in the form of diplomatic recognition, financial and legal facilities for the acquisition of weapons, and the like. The success of separatist movements is, in turn, contingent on obtaining a level of external support that is in fact seldom available. The most likely source of support is "irredentist" neighbors. Yet the only clear cases to emerge so far are Somalia in relation to the Ogaden and Libya in relation to northern Chad. In this respect again, the multiethnic character of the new states acts as a constraint – irredentist initiatives are likely to be taken only by fairly homogeneous states, Horowitz suggests, because otherwise the interventionist policy would constitute a divisive issue.

Successful separatism triggers temporary flight from violence and subsequently an unmixing with settlement in the new homeland, but the more commonplace unsuccessful challenges tend to produce refugees of a more problematic kind. There is usually an initial trickle of activist exiles who have little difficulty finding havens but if and when the struggle moves into a military phase, actions by the antagonists foster much larger waves. The separatists encourage able men to leave in order to join the struggle, while states facing separatist guerrillas typically exercise violence against the source group as a whole, any member of which is considered an actual or potential supporter of insurgency. As the separatist group is usually located near a state's international borders, many in the target group often succeed in escaping. Entire populations may flee the fire zone and systematized repression, as in Eritrea and the Ogaden. International assistance to the antagonistic camps has the effect of enhancing their respective capacity and hence widening the firezone as well to prolong the conflict.

CONFLICTS OVER THE SOCIAL ORDER

Rooted in inequality and oppression, conflicts over the social order involve a struggle between dominant and subordinate classes, whose most dramatic manifestations are full-scale social revolutions (Skocpol, 1979). All the successful revolutions that have taken place in Asia, Africa and Latin America since the end of World War II, as well as most attempted ones, have produced major international population movements. Conversely, of the eight major refugee concentrations found today, five are attributable in whole or in part to revolutionary conflicts. Moreover, revolution breeds counterrevolution, and the fear of revolution fosters pre-emptive authoritarian regimes that may also spawn refugees.

Refugees are generated in the first instance by the generalized violence and dislocation that typically accompany the onset of the revolutionary upheaval process itself, regardless of outcome. The prospect of a successful revolution often triggers the exodus of the old ruling class and their associates, threatened with or afraid of retribution. This falls within the distinctive type Kunz has termed "anticipatory refugee movement" (Kunz, 1973:131). The elite wave is likely to be numerically small and irreversible. This is often followed by a second outflow, larger than the first, and extending downward to encompass a variety of groups and strata negatively affected by the exigencies of revolutionary reconstruction. The hardships are exacerbated by the fact that such policies are generally carried out in a hostile international economic environment. Discontent is more likely to materialize into refugee flows because states that oppose the revolution are likely to provide the necessary havens, but as noted earlier, in anticipation or in response to this, most revolutionary states have imposed severe obstacles on exit. A variation on the scenario occurs when the problems of revolutionary reconstruction are compounded by the military operations of counterrevolutionary forces. The resulting insecurity and added impositions by the revolutionary regime, especially military mobilization, cause additional people to leave. These flows may be encouraged by the counterrevolutionaries and their patrons because they provide a source of military manpower as well.

It is now generally recognized that, contrary to the hopes and fears of the 1960s, full-scale revolution in largely peasant societies are rare historical events (Goldstone, 1980; Goldstone, 1982; Skocpol, 1982). Social revolution is best understood as a phenomenon specific to "agrarian bureaucracies" such as traditional China and tsarist Russia, i.e., relatively well-integrated societies with centralized states and as a phenomenon of the transition to capitalism, rather than of industrial capitalism itself. They may also occur among "neo-patrimonial" personalistic patronage states, very vulnerable to economic downturns or military pressures, and particularly when these dictatorships are land-based, i.e., with a socioeconomic order featuring an upper class essentially dependent on direct control over land and unable to give up more of the product without reducing their own share (Paige, 1975; Eisenstadt, 1978).

Whether the revolutionary potential among the peasantry becomes politically effective depends on the possibility of an alliance with other strata with grievances of their own and a vanguard organization that can channel peasant anger (Moore, 1966:480; Jenkins, 1983:512; Scott, 1987). The geopolitical configuration can also hamper or favor the antagonists (e.g. Tilly, 1975a:503; Skocpol, 1982:302), as illustrated by variation among recent upheavals in Central America. Revolutionary conflict almost always attracts significant foreign involvement because of the linkages within the global state system between regime orientation and international strategic alignments.

Most revolution-prone agrarian-bureaucratic states either had their revolution long ago, or underwent some profound changes that took them out of the category, usually in the form of a "revolution from above." Eastern Asia, which had the most appropriate conditions for revolution outside the European orbit, indeed gave rise to a number of them, but their refugee-generating potential is now largely spent. Leaving aside the oil rich kingdoms and principalities of the Middle East, by 1960 there were only a handful of ancient agrarian states which, for one reason or another, were not subjected to full-scale colonial transformation and survived more or less intact. Subsequently, Ethiopia and Afghanistan did experience revolutions. Although both approximated Eisenstadt's hybrid agglomerate of patrimonial and feudal structures with a weak center, which tends to fall apart and smolder without explosion, in both cases timely Soviet intervention propped up the center during the critical phase. In both cases as well, the revolutionary regime's radical actions provoked peasant uprisings under the leadership of local notables. Whereas in Ethiopia they were left to their own devices, in Afghanistan massive assistance from the United States and the collaboration of Pakistan transformed rebellious peasants into the world's largest and most effective refugee-warrior community.[3]

With no Ethiopias or Afghanistans remaining for revolutions to happen, except perhaps in the Middle East, land-based dictatorships are left as the most likely candidates for major social upheavals. The combination is encountered in Pakistan, and the Latin American countries that have not had the benefit of significant land reform. These include the troubled trio in Central America, Nicaragua under the Somosas, El Salvador and Guatemala, as well as possibly Colombia and Paraguay.

Since conditions for a successful peasant revolution rarely occur in the appropriate combination, low-legitimacy regimes of this sort more commonly persist amidst considerable instability, experiencing occasional intra-elite coups and recurrent popular rebellions. They are able to carry on protracted internal wars, often with aid from the United States or some other patron within the western camp, but unable to extinguish the rebellion. It will be noted that this largely mirrors the situation of weak revolutionary regimes that survive only with support from the Soviet Union or other socialist power, and that the situation is similarly conducive to endemic violence. An important feature, inherent in the underlying socioeconomic conditions, is that the exodus is co-determined by acute economic need as well as manifest violence, thus allowing potential receivers to question whether the victims are "genuine" refugees.

Under ordinary circumstances, the "bureaucratic-authoritarian" regimes that arise among countries in the middle-range of the world income distribution, particularly the "NICs" (Linz, 1975; Collier, 1979; Feith, 1980), do not generate massive refugee flows but rather an intermittent trickle of activist exiles. However, the regimes that came to power in the Southern Cone of Latin America and Brazil in the 1970s constructed especially brutal "national security states," unleashing terror against targets that extended well beyond activists to groups and strata from which they might be expected to emerge, in a manner strikingly reminiscent of European fascism and of the Stalinist phase in the Soviet Union (Dassin, 1986; Fagen, forthcoming). More recently there has been a trend toward democratization, both in Latin America and Asia, but this is unlikely to go very far and remains subject to reversal.

Revolutions are not likely to occur in postcolonial states that are recent amalgams of disparate, small-scale societies, composed mostly of smallholders, as in most of black Africa. Intra-elite competition leads to structural instability at the center, manifested by frequent coups and counter-coups, while popular protest tends to be very localized. However, under the stress occasioned by the exhaustion of political spoils, deteriorating international conjuncture and continuing rapid population growth, relatively broadly-based authoritarian rule has tended to degenerate into more brutal "gangster government" or "kleptocracy" (e.g. Haiti under the Duvaliers). The African version is ethnic tyranny, as occurred in Uganda (Amin and Obote), Chad, the Central African Republic and Equatorial Guinea.

If the international configuration allows, oppressed urban and rural masses literally vote with their feet—i.e., resort to "exit" as an alternative to "voice" (Hirschman, 1970). This may result in massive exodus, as for example in ex-French and ex-Spanish Guinea in the 1960s—one-fourth of the population in the one case, one-third in the other. Substantial numbers fled Haiti in a similar manner to neighboring Caribbean countries or the United States, until harsh measures were taken by the receivers to stem the flow. An alternative path is internal withdrawal, where peasants concentrate on production for subsistence while withholding from the state what it claims as its due. Albeit in appearance apolitical, "exit" constitutes one of the most effective weapons the weak can wield against an exploitative state (Scott, 1985 and 1987). Because extortion is their primary source of livelihood, the rulers cannot afford to give in, much like landlords. Notwithstanding their rational preference for dodging, peasants may thus find themselves in confrontation with the state and have no choice but to use violence in self-defense.

In this manner, withdrawal from the state may trigger a violent implosion, a disaggregation of both rulers and ruled into primary solidarity groups vying with one another in a desperate search for security and subsistence. As violence becomes a major means of survival, it tends to feed on itself. This process may foster the proliferation of armed factions, leading to the emergence of a warlord system, as occurred in seventeenth-century Germany, in China at the beginning of the twentieth century, and more recently in Chad and Uganda. The violence unleashed by this process is more likely to result in massive deaths, but it may produce refugees as well if the populations in question are located near international borders.

If the superpowers reach a better *modus vivendi*, as currently appears likely, some of the conflicts that contributed to the crisis of the 1970s and early 1980s will be settled and many refugees will be going home. However, the structural conditions that exacerbate the tensions of state formation among the new states of Asia and Africa, and which fuel perennial brushfires as well as intermittent social explosions within the developing world as a whole, are unlikely to change very profoundly in the foreseeable future. We should therefore expect some of the old refugee-producing conflicts to revive, and new ones to emerge occasionally as well. Given the drastic restrictions on the admission of refugees in the more affluent countries, most of these victims are likely to remain confined, as they are today, in neighboring countries of the developing world.

CONCLUSION

The dynamics that have propelled international population movements to the forefront of humanistic and political concerns during the past quarter century are likely to be amplified in the next. Given the persistence of huge disparities of conditions among rich and poor countries, the pool of potential international migrants will continue to grow; and since the affluent countries have erected a collective protective wall, we should anticipate a rise in "north-south" tensions over the issue of migration, leading to demands for inclusion of more equitable arrangements within the "new international order." Concurrently, political liberalization in the socialist countries will present the capitalist democracies with a dilemma as well. Yet, despite its significance, international migration has attracted relatively little attention as a subject for ethical reflection (see Gibney, 1986).

In this perspective, two issues are of special importance: (1) aid to the mass of refugees who are in effect confined within the developing world itself; and (2) guidelines for admission policy in the capitalist democracies. Since the first of these properly belongs to a discussion of how best to carry out the general obligation to aid the unfortunate abroad (e.g. Shue, 1980), this conclusion shall focus on the second. Although the relevant philosophical literature originated almost exclusively in the United States, its implications are obviously relevant for the capitalist democracies as a whole.

Ethical analysis in this field is rendered extremely complex by the problem of calculating costs and benefits of emigration and immigration. The mainstream economic literature basically argues that departure raises average incomes in the countries of origin and does not lower and may even raise incomes of the poorest there, so that it can be assumed that from their perspective emigration is basically a positive good (e.g. King, 1983). As against this, the thrust of much of the critical literature has been to demonstrate that the benefits of labor migrations have been distributed unequally, to the advantage of the already more fortunate receivers. It has therefore been proposed that the senders should be compensated by the receivers (e.g. Bohning, 1982). Some have gone so far as to argue that the balance to the already unfortunate sending countries is altogether negative. If so, then the current trend among the affluent countries to further restrict immigration would in effect constitute a major contribution to global social justice!

Similar controversies occur with respect to the impact on the receivers, especially if this is disaggregated by class or strata. Nevertheless, there appears to be a growing consensus that most members of the "native" population are better off as a result, with the exception of those already in the bottom-most position. If so, any argument in favor of relatively open immigration should be coupled with proposals for compensation for the least well off.

The most intractable problem pertains to the choice of entity in relation to which the calculus of costs and benefits is to be made. Even when the same guiding principles are used (e.g. utilitarianism, or the Rawlsian "difference principle"), one reaches drastically different conclusions depending on whether one applies the principle to the national community or to the world as a whole. Adoption of a national approach provides ethical grounds for liberal states to adopt a limited immigration policy designed to preserve the established community (Walzer, 1981): in short, the gates can be shut if additional immigrants would threaten its stability. Within this, priorities are to be allocated on the basis of (1) family reunion, because we have special obligations to our own; and (2) asylum to refugees, whom Walzer identifies as people whose predicament is such that they cannot be helped within their own country. He also suggests that those who have been exploited as temporary workers must be granted the right to stay permanently.

In effect, this position legitimizes a "liberal" version of contemporary American immigration policy, as might be institutionalized in a more even-handed administration of the Refugee Act of 1980 and a generous application of the "amnesty" provisions of the Immigration Reform and Control Act of 1986. However, although it is by no means intended to justify a national origins approach, the Walzer approach lends itself to this because the community-preservation principle can easily be invoked to attribute priority to "patrials." Under conditions of scarcity, if this is done it is unlikely that there will be room for many others. This possibility was in fact reflected in legislative proposals before the 100th Congress providing "points" for knowledge of English, and to grant additional admissions to countries which have "traditionally" sent immigrants to the United States (especially Ireland, Italy and Poland).

As against this, a "cosmopolitan" approach permits no restrictions unless they can be shown to be essential to the maintenance of the total system of equal basic liberties; although a liberal state still has the right to protect itself against destruction, the burden of proof is on the receiver, and while stopping short of unlimited immigration, adoption of this principle would lead in practice to a significantly larger intake. It is possible to argue that the "cosmopolitan" approach must be chosen over the "national" because of what liberal theory has to say with respect to exit. Liberal principles prescribe the almost unqualified right of individuals to leave their country, and even to relinquish membership in their political community of origin. However, given the social organization of the globe, emigration is impossible in the absence of a place to enter. Liberal states are thus under collective obligation to provide at the least a sufficient number of entries to foreigners so as to enable them to exercise their right to exit (Zolberg, 1987).

That still leaves the question of how priorities for admission are to be ordered. Gibney (1986) has advanced two principles for judgment: (1) the "Harm Principle," whereby those who caused harm have a special duty of restitution; and (2) the "Basic Rights Principle," which obligates nations to play some part in meeting the basic rights of individuals in other societies, even if they were not the cause of their need. When applied to ongoing U.S. immigration policy, for example, these principles provide grounds for a radical reordering of priorities. In effect, U.S. policy (including both the legal and "informal" components) has been dominated by three considerations: family reunion (i.e., exercise of a "right" by members of the U.S. community to bring in close relatives); admission of people originating in Communist countries (i.e., foreign policy objectives); and labor procurement. If Gibney's principles were to be applied, however, the highest priority must be attributed instead to people who have been harmed by the United States (e.g. Chileans following the Pinochet coup), and secondly to those whose admission contributes to the meeting of a "fair share" obligation toward those in greatest need—many of whom would presumably be refugees in the Walzer sense noted above. Unless there were a general willingness to vastly expand immigration, this would leave little room for relatives and probably none at all for labor procurement.

The debate at this level has only begun, and thoughtful political theorists are continuing to explore the implications of various normative considerations (e.g. Carens, 1988). However, it is evident that scholars of international migration have a special responsibility to clarify for themselves, political theorists, as well as decision makers, the choices we face in an area which, in the next quarter of a century, will continue to rise on the world agenda of critical issues.

ENDNOTES

1. This point was brought to my attention by Astri Suhrke. In addition to the departure of KMT elites and their dependents to Taiwan, many went from China to Hong Kong in the 1950s and again 1960s.
2. This section is based on collaborative research (see Zolberg, Suhrke and Aguayo, 1989).
3. Most of Ethiopia's refugees were generated by the separatist conflicts in the Ogaden and Eritrea rather than by anti-revolutionary uprisings.

Bibliography

The articles reprinted in this volume are drawn from a wide range of sources and reflect many different reference formats. I have provided some uniformity of reference style. Where the references are numbered in the original publication I have placed them at the end of each article ("Endnotes"). Where the system of identifying references by last name of author, year of publication, and page numbers (for example, Bonacich 1972:553) has been used, I have placed all reference sources in this bibliography. An asterisk (*) next to a citation in this bibliography indicates that the selection or portions of it are reprinted in this volume.

Abbott, Edith. 1924. *Immigration: Select Documents and Case Records.* Chicago: University of Chicago Press.

Abramson, Harold J. 1973. *Ethnic Diversity in Catholic America.* New York: Wiley.

_____. 1975. "The Religioethnic Factor and the American Experience: Another Look at the Three Generation Hypothesis." *Ethnicity.* 2.

Adams, David Wallace. 1988. "Fundamental Considerations: The Deep Meaning of Native American Schooling, 1880–1900." *Harvard Educational Review.* 58.

Alba, Richard D. 1976. "Social Assimilation among American Catholic National Origin Groups." *American Sociological Review.* 41.

*_____. 1981. "The Twilight of Ethnicity among American Catholics of European Ancestry." *Annals of the American Academy of Political and Social Science.* 454.

_____. 1985. *Italian Americans: Into the Twilight of Ethnicity.* Englewood Cliffs, NJ: Prentice-Hall.

_____. 1988. "Cohorts and the Dynamics of Ethnic Change." In Matilda White Riley, Bettina Huber, and Beth Hess, eds., *Social Structures and Human Lives.* Newbury Park, CA: Sage.

Alba, Richard D., and Chamlin, Mitchell B. 1983. "A Preliminary Examination of Ethnic Identification among Whites." *American Sociological Review.* 48.

Alba, Richard D., and Moore, Gwen. 1982. "Ethnicity in the American Elite." *American Sociological Review.* 47.

Alba, Richard D., and Golden, Reid M. 1986. "Patterns of Ethnic Marriage in the United States." *Social Forces.* 65.

Alba, Richard, and Kessler, Ronald C. 1979. "Patterns of Interethnic Marriage among American Catholics." *Social Forces.* 57.

Aldrich, Howard, and Weiss, Jane. 1981. "Differentiation within the U.S. Capitalist Class." *American Sociological Review.* 46.

Allen, Robert L. 1970. *Black Awakening in Capitalist America.* Garden City, NY: Doubleday.

Allen, Walter R., and Farley, Reynolds. 1986. "The Shifting Social and Economic Tides of Black America, 1950–1980." *Annual Review of Sociology.* 12.

Allport, Gordon W. 1958. *The Nature of Prejudice.* Garden City, NY: Doubleday.

Allworth, Edward. 1977. *Nationality Group Survival in Multi-ethnic States.* New York: Praeger.

Alvarez, R. R. 1985. "A Profile of the Citizenship Process among Hispanics in the United States: An Anthropological Perspective." Special Report to the National Association of Latin Elected Officials.

Alvarez, Rodolfo. 1973. "The Psycho-Historical and Socioeconomic Development of the Chicano Community in the United States." *Social Science Quarterly.* 53.

American Council on Education. 1988. *One Third of a Nation.* Washington, DC: American Council on Education.

Amin, Samir. 1974. *Accumulation on a World Scale: A Critique of the Theory of Underdevelopment.* New York: Monthly Review Press.

Amin, Samir. 1976. *Unequal Development: An Essay on the Social Formations of Peripheral Capitalism.* New York: Monthly Review Press.

Anderson, Patrick. 1976. "On Working Closely with Jimmy Carter." *New York Times.* July 19.

Archdeacon, Thomas J. 1983. *Becoming American: An Ethnic History*. New York: The Free Press.

Armstrong, Edward G. 1975. "The System Paradigm and the Sociological Study of Racial Conflict." *Phylon*. 36.

Aronowitz, Stanley. 1973. *False Promises*. New York: McGraw-Hill.

Asian Women United of California. 1989. *Making Waves*. Boston: Beacon Press.

Auletta, Ken. 1982. *The Underclass*. New York: Random House.

Auster, Ellen, and Aldrich, Howard. 1984. "Small Business Vulnerability, Ethnic Enclaves, and Ethnic Enterprise." In Robin Ward, ed., *Ethnic Business in Britain*. Cambridge: Cambridge University Press.

Ayal, Eliezer B., and Chiswick, Barry R. 1983. "The Economics of the Diaspora Revisited." *Economic Development and Cultural Change*. 31.

Awolowo, Chief Obafemi. 1960. *Awo*. London: Cambridge University Press.

Azkin, Benjamin. 1964. *State and Nation*. London: Hutchinson University Library.

Bach, Robert L. 1985. "Socialist Construction and Cuban Emigration: Explorations into Mariel." *Cuban Studies*. 15.

Bach, Robert L.; Gordon, L. W.; Haines, D. W.; and Howell, D. R. 1984. "The Economic Adjustment of Southeast Asian Refugees in the U.S." In *U.N. Commission for Refugees, World Refugee Survey 1983*. Geneva: United Nations.

Bade, K. 1985. "German Emigration to the U.S. and Continental Immigration to Germany in the Late Nineteenth and Early Twentieth Centuries." In Dirk Hoerder, ed., *Labor Migration in the Atlantic Economies*. Westport, CT: Greenwood.

Bailey, Thomas A. 1934. *Theodore Roosevelt and the Japanese-American Crisis*. Stanford: Stanford University Press.

Bailyn, Bernard. 1955. *The New England Merchants in the Seventeenth Century*. Cambridge, MA: Harvard University Press.

Baker, Ray Stannard. 1964. *Following the Color Line: American Negro Citizenship in the Progressive Era*. New York: Harper Torchbooks.

Bancroft, Hubert Howe. 1888. *California Inter Pocula*. San Francisco: The History Company.

———. 1890. *Essays and Miscellany*. San Francisco: The History Company.

———. 1912. *Retrospection, Political and Personal*. New York: The Bancroft Company.

Banton, Michael. 1974. "1960: A Turning Point in the Study of Race Relations." *Daedalus*. 103.

Baran, Paul, and Sweezy, Paul. 1966. *Monopoly Capital*. New York: Monthly Review Press.

Baratz, Stephen S., and Baratz, Joan C. 1970. "Early Childhood Intervention: The Social Science Base of Institutional Racism." *Harvard Educational Review*. 40.

Barkan, E., and Khoklov, N. 1980. "Socioeconomic Data as Indices of Naturalization Patterns in the United States: A Theory Revisited." *Ethnicity*. 7.

Barkow, J. H. 1978. "Culture and Sociobiology." *American Anthropologist*. 80.

Baron, Harold M. 1968. "Black Powerlessness in Chicago." *Transaction*. 6.

———. 1969. "The Web of Urban Racism." In Louis Knowles and Kenneth Prewitt, eds., *Institutional Racism in America*. Englewood Cliffs, NJ: Prentice-Hall.

Barr, A. 1970. "Occupations and Geographic Mobility in San Antonio: 1870–1900." *Social Science Quarterly*. 51.

Barrera, Mario. 1980. *Labor and Class in the Southwest: A Theory of Racial Inequality*. Notre Dame, IN: Notre Dame University Press.

Barrett, J. R. 1986. "Unity and Fragmentation: Class, Race, and Ethnicity on Chicago's South Side, 1900–22." In Dirk Hoerder, ed., *Struggle a Hard Battle*.

Barth, Ernest A. T., and Noel, Donald L. 1972. "Conceptual Frameworks for the Analysis of Race Relations: An Evaluation." *Social Forces*. 50.

Barth, Frederick. 1962. *The Role of Entrepreneur in Social Change in Northern Norway*. Bergen: Norwegian Universities Press.

———, ed. 1969a. *Ethnic Groups and Boundaries*. Boston: Little, Brown and Company.

———. 1969b. "Ecological Relationships of Ethnic Groups in Swat, Pakistan." In A. Vayda, ed., *Environment and Cultural Behavior*. Austin: University of Texas Press.

Barth, Gunther. 1964. *Bitter Strength: A History of the Chinese in the United States, 1850–1870*. Cambridge, MA: Harvard University Press.

Barton, Josef. 1975. *Peasants and Strangers*. Cambridge, MA: Harvard University Press.

Bean, Frank D.; King, A. G.; and Passel, J. S. 1983. "The Number of Illegal Migrants of Mexican Origin in the United States: Sex Ratio Based Estimates for 1980." *Demography*. 20.

———. 1986. "Estimates of the Size of the Illegal Migrant Population of Mexican Origin in the United States: An Assessment, Review, and Proposal." In Harley L. Browning and Rudolfo de la Garza, eds., *Mexican Immigrants and Mexican Americans: An Evolving Relation*. Austin: Center for Mexican American Studies, University of Texas.

Bean, Frank D., and Marcum, J. P. 1978. "Differential Fertility and the Minority Group Status Hypothesis: An Assessment and Review." In Frank D. Bean and

W. P. Frisbie, eds., *The Demography of Racial and Ethnic Groups.* New York: Academic Press.

Bean, Frank D.; Swicegood, C. G.; and King, A. G. 1985. "Role Incompatibility and the Relationship between Fertility and Labor Supply among Hispanic Women." In George J. Borjas and Marta Tienda, eds., *Hispanics in the U.S. Economy.* Orlando, FL: Academic Press.

Bean, Frank D., and Tienda, Marta. 1987. *The Hispanic Population of the United States.* New York: Russell Sage Foundation.

Bechofer, Frank; Elliott, Brian; Rushforth, Monica; and Bland, Richard. 1974. "Small Shopkeepers: Matters of Money and Meanings." *Sociological Review* 22.

Bell, Daniel. 1975. "Ethnicity and Social Change." In Nathan Glazer and Daniel P. Moynihan, eds., *Ethnicity: Theory and Experience.* Cambridge, MA: Harvard University Press.

Bell, Daniel. 1976. *The Cultural Contradictions of Capitalism.* New York: Basic Books.

Bell, David A. 1985. "The Triumph of Asian-Americans." *The New Republic.* July 15 and 22.

Bellah, Robert. 1957. *Tokugawa Religion.* New York: Free Press.

Bellah, Robert N.; Madsen, Richard; Sullivan, William M.; Swidler, Ann; and Tipton, Stephen M. 1985. *Habits of the Heart: Individualism and Commitment in American Life.* New York: Harper & Row.

Belshaw, Cyril. 1955. "The Cultural Milieu of the Entrepreneur." *Explorations in Entrepreneurial History.* 7.

Benedict, Barton. 1968. "Family Firms and Economic Development." *Southwest Journal of Anthropology.* 24.

Berelson, Bernard, and Salter, Patricia J. 1946. "Majority and Minority Americans: An Analysis of Magazine Fiction." *Public Opinion Quarterly.* 10.

Berk, Richard A. 1983. "An Introduction to Sample Selection Bias in Sociological Data." *American Sociological Review.* 48.

Bernard, W. S. 1936. "Cultural Determinants of Naturalization." *American Sociological Review.* 1.

Berreman, Gerald D. 1969. "Caste in India and the United States." In J. Roach, L. Gross, and O. Gursslin, eds., *Social Stratification in the United States.* Englewood Cliffs, NJ: Prentice-Hall.

*_____. 1972. "Race, Caste, and Other Invidious Distinctions in Social Stratification." *Race.* 12.

Berrol, S. 1976. "Education and Economic Mobility: The Jewish Experience in New York City, 1880–1920." *American Jewish Historical Quarterly.* 65.

Bettelheim, Charles. 1970. "Economic Inequalities between Nations and International Solidarity." *Monthly Review.* 22.

Beveridge, Andrew A., and Oberschall, Anthony R. 1979. *African Businessmen and Development in Zambia.* Princeton, NJ: Princeton University Press.

Bhagwati, J. N. 1984. "Incentives and Disincentives: International Migration." *Weltwirtschafliches Archiv.* 120.

Bierstedt, Robert. 1948. "The Sociology of Majorities." *American Sociological Review.* 13.

Blackstone, Kevin B. 1981. "Arab Entrepreneurs Take Over Inner City Grocery Stores." *Chicago Reporter* 10.

Blalock, H. M., Jr. 1967. *Toward a Theory of Minority-Group Relations.* New York: Wiley.

Blassingame, John W. 1972. *The Slave Community: Plantation Life in the Antebellum South.* New York: Oxford University Press.

Blau, F. 1980. "Immigration and Labor Earnings in Early Twentieth Century America." In J. Simon and J. DaVanzo, eds., *Research in Population Economics.* Greenwich, CT: JAI.

Blau, Peter M., and Duncan, Otis Dudley. 1967. *The American Occupational Structure.* New York: Free Press.

Blauner, Robert. 1969. "Internal Colonialism and Ghetto Revolt." *Social Problems.* 16.

_____. 1972. *Racial Oppression in America.* New York: Harper and Row.

_____. n.d. "Marxist Theory, Nationality, and Colonialism." Unpublished manuscript.

Blumer, Herbert. 1958. "Race Prejudice as a Sense of Group Position." *Pacific Sociological Review.* 1.

_____. 1965. "Industrialization and Race Relations." In G. Hunter, ed., *Industrialization and Race Relations: A Symposium.* Institute of Race Relations. New York: Oxford University Press.

Bodnar, John. 1985. *The Transplanted.* Bloomington, IN: Indiana University Press.

Bodnar, John; Simon, R.; and Wever, M. 1982. *Lives of Their Own.* Urbana, IL: University of Illinois Press.

Bogardus, Emory S. 1930. "Race-Relations Cycle." *American Journal of Sociology.* 35.

_____. 1943. "Culture Conflicts in Relocation Center." *Sociology and Social Research.* 27.

Bogen, Elizabeth. 1987. *Immigration in New York.* New York: Praeger.

Bohning, W. R. 1972. *The Migration of Workers in the United Kingdom and the European Community.* London: Oxford University Press.

Boissevain, Jeremy. 1984. "Small Entrepreneurs in Contemporary Europe." In Robin Ward, ed., *Ethnic Business in Britain.* Cambridge: Cambridge University Press.

Bonacich, Edna. 1972. "A Theory of Ethnic Antagonism: The Split Labor Market." *American Sociological Review.* 37.

_____. 1973. "A Theory of Middleman Minorities." *American Sociological Review.* 38.

_____. 1975a. "Abolition, the Extent of Slavery and the

Position of Free Blacks: A Study of Split Labor Markets in the United States, 1830–1863." *American Journal of Sociology.* 81.

———. 1975b. "Small Business and Japanese American Ethnic Solidarity." *Amerasia Journal.* 3.

———. 1976. "Advanced Capitalism and Black/White Relations in the United States: A Split Labor Market Interpretation." *American Sociological Review.* 41.

———. 1978a. "Korean Immigrant Small Business in Los Angeles." In Roy S. Bryce-Laporte, ed., *Sourcebook on the New Immigration.* New Brunswick, NJ: Transaction Books.

———. 1978b. "U. S. Capitalism and Korean Immigrant Small Business." Mimeographed. Riverside, CA: University of California.

———. 1979. "The Past, Present, and Future of Split Labor Market Theory." In Cora B. Marrett and C. Leggon, eds., *Research in Race and Ethnic Relations,* 1. Greenwich, CT: JAI.

*———. 1980a. "Class Approaches to Ethnicity and Race." *Insurgent Sociologist.* 10.

———. 1980b. "The Development of U.S. Capitalism and Its Influence on Asian Immigration." Unpublished manuscript.

———. 1984a. "Some Basic Facts: Patterns of Asian Immigration and Exclusion." In Lucie Cheng and Edna Bonacich, eds., *Labor Migration under Capitalism.* Berkeley: University of California Press.

———. 1984b. "Asian Labor in the Development of California and Hawaii." In Lucie Cheng and Edna Bonacich, eds., *Labor Migration under Capitalism.* Berkeley: University of California Press.

Bonacich, Edna, and Hirata, Lucie Cheng. 1979. "International Labor Migration: A Theoretical Orientation." Unpublished manuscript.

Bonacich, Edna, and Jung, Tae Hwan. 1982. "A Portrait of Korean Small Business in Los Angeles: 1977." In Eeui-Young Yu, Earl H. Phillips, and Eun Sik Yang, eds., *Koreans in Los Angeles.* Los Angeles: Koryo Research Institute and Center for Korean-American and Korean Studies, California State University.

Bonacich, Edna and Light, Ivan H. 1988. *Immigrant Entrepreneurs: Koreans in Los Angeles, 1965–1982.* Berkeley and Los Angeles: University of California Press.

Bonacich, Edna, and Modell, John. 1980. *The Economic Basis of Ethnic Solidarity: Small Business in the Japanese-American Community.* Berkeley: University of California Press.

Bonilla, F. A., and Campos, R. 1981. "A Wealth of Poor: Puerto Ricans in the New Economic Order." *Daedalus.* 110.

———. 1982. Imperialist Initiatives and the Puerto Rican Workers: From Foraker to Reagan. *Contemporary Marxism.* 5.

Bonnett, Aubrey W. 1980. "An Examination of Rotating Credit Associations among Black West Indian Immigrants in Brooklyn." In Roy S. Bryce-Laporte, ed., *Sourcebook on the New Immigration.* New Brunswick, NJ: Transaction Books.

Borhek, J.T. 1970. "Ethnic Group Cohesion." *American Journal of Sociology.* 76.

Borjas, George J., and Tienda, Marta, eds. 1985. *Hispanics in the U.S. Economy.* Orlando, FL: Academic Press.

Borrie, W. D. 1954. *Italians and Germans in Australia.* Melbourne: Chesire.

Bose, Christine E. 1984. "The Employment of Black and Ethnic Women in 1900." Paper presented at the Annual Meetings of the American Sociological Association, San Antonio.

Boswell, Thomas D. 1984. "Cuban-Americans." In J. O. McKee, ed., *Ethnicity in Contemporary America.* Dubuque, IA: Kendall-Hunt.

Boswell, Thomas D., and Curtis, J. R. 1984. *The Cuban-American Experience.* Totowa, NJ: Rowman & Allanheld.

Bosworth, Allen R. 1967. *America's Concentration Camps.* New York: W. W. Norton.

Botifoll, L. J. 1984. "How Miami's New Image Was Created." *Occasional Paper #1985-1.* Miami: Institute of Interamerican Studies, University of Miami.

Bottomore, Thomas B. 1966. *Classes in Modern Society.* New York: Pantheon.

Bouvier, Leon F., and Agresta, Anthony J. 1987. "The Future Asian Population of the United States." In James T. Fawcett and Benjamin V. Carino, eds., *Pacific Bridges: The New Immigration from Asia and the Pacific Islands.* Staten Island: Center for Migration Studies.

Bouvier, Leon F., and Gardner, Robert W. 1986. "Immigration to the U.S.: The Unfinished Story." *Population Bulletin.* 41:4.

Brenner, Reuven, and Kiefer, Nicholas. 1981. "The Economics of the Disapora: Discrimination and Occupational Structure." *Economic Development and Culture Change.* 29.

Briggs, Dennis I. 1954. "Social Adaptation among Japanese American Youth: A Comparative Study." *Sociology & Research.* 38.

Briggs, J. 1978. *An Italian Passage.* New Haven, CT: Yale University Press.

Briggs, Vernon M. 1990. "Immigration Policy Sends Blacks Back to South." *New York Times.* February 1.

Brody, David. 1971. "The Expansion of the American Labor Movement: Institutional Sources of Stimulus and Restraint." In David Brody, ed., *The American Labor Movement.* New York: Harper & Row.

Brooke, James. 1988. "In Africa, Tribal Hatreds Defy the Borders of State." *New York Times.* August 28.

Browning, Harley L., and Rodríguez, N. 1985. "The Migration of Mexican Indocumentados as a Settlement Process: Implications for Work." In George J. Borjas & Marta Tienda, eds., *Hispanics in the U.S. Economy.* Orlando, FL: Academic Press.

Brumberg, S. 1986. *Going to America, Going to School.* New York: Praeger.

Bryce-Laporte, Roy Simon. 1969. "The American Slave Plantation and Our Heritage of Communal Deprivation." *American Behavioral Scientist.* 4.

Bukowczyk, J. 1984. "The Transformation of Working Class Ethnicity: Corporate Control, Americanization, and the Polish Immigrant Middle Class in Bayonne, N.J., 1915–1925." *Labor History.* 25.

Buraway, Michael. 1976. "The Functions and Reproduction of Migrant Labor: Comparative Material from Southern Africa and the United States." *American Journal of Sociology,* 81.

Burchell, R. A. 1980. *The San Francisco Irish, 1848–1880.* Berkeley, CA: University of California Press.

Bureau of Indian Affairs. 1983. Indian Tribal Entities Recognized and Eligible to Receive Services from the United States Bureau of Indian Affairs. *Federal Register.* December 10.

Burgess, M. Elaine. 1978. "The Resurgence of Ethnicity: Myth or Reality?" *Ethnic and Racial Studies.* 1:3.

Burgess, Thomas. 1913. *Greeks in America: An Account of Their Coming, Progress, Customs, Living and Aspirations with an Historical Introduction on the Stories of Some Famous American Greeks.* Boston: German, Fr. & Co.

Burma, John H. 1951. "Background on the Current Situation of Filipino-Americans." *Social Forces.* 30.

Cahan, Abraham. 1917/1966. *The Rise of David Levinsky.* New York: Harper Torchbooks.

California Assembly Office of Research. 1986. *California 2000: A People in Transition.* Sacramento Assembly Office of Research.

Callao, Maximo Jose. 1973. "Culture Shock – West, East and West Again." *Personnel & Guidance Journal.* 51.

Camarillo, Albert. 1979. *Chicanos in a Changing Society.* Cambridge, MA: Harvard University Press.

Capek, Thomas. 1920. *The Czechs (Bohemians) in America: A Study of Their National, Cultural, Political, Social, Economic and Religious Life.* Boston: Houghton, Mifflin Company.

Cardona, Ramiro C., and Cruz, Carmen I. 1980. *El Exodo de Colomianos.* Bogotá: Ediciones Tercer Mundo.

Carens, J. H. 1988. "Immigration and the Welfare State." In A. Gutmann, ed., *Democracy and the Welfare State.* Princeton, NJ: Princeton University Press.

Carmichael, Stokely, and Hamilton, Charles V. 1967. *Black Power: The Politics of Liberation in America.* New York: Vintage Books.

Carpenter, Niles. 1927. *Immigrants and Their Children.* Washington, DC: Government Printing Office, Census Monograph VII.

Carruthers, N., and Vining, A. R. 1982. "International Migration: An Application of the Urban Location Choice Model." *World Politics.* 35.

Castells, Manuel. 1975. "Immigrant Workers and Class Struggles in Advanced Capitalism: The Western European Experience." *Politics and Society.* 5.

Castles, S., and Kosack, G. 1973. *Immigrant Workers and Class Structure in Western Europe.* London: Oxford University Press.

Caudill, William. 1952. "Japanese-American Personality and Acculturation." *Genetic Psychology Monographs.* 45:1.

Caudill, William, and DeVos, George. 1956. "Achievement, Culture, and Personality: The Case of the Japanese Americans." *American Anthropologist.* 58.

Centro de Estudios Puertorriquenos. 1979. *Labor Migration under Capitalism.* New York: Monthly Review.

Chai, Alice Yun. 1987. "Adaptive Strategies of Recent Korean Immigrant Women in Hawaii." In Janet Sharistanian, ed., *Beyond the Public/Domestic Dichotomy: Contemporary Perspectives on Women's Lives.* Westport, CT: Greenwood Press.

Chan, Janet B. L., and Cheung, Yuet-Wah. 1982. "Ethnic Resources and Business Enterprise: A Study of Chinese Business in Toronto." Paper presented at the Annual Meeting of the American Sociological Association, San Francisco.

Chan, Sucheng. 1986. *This Bitter Sweet Soil: The Chinese in California Agriculture, 1860–1910.* Berkeley: University of California Press.

Chang, Francis Y. 1934. "An Accommodation Program for Secondary-Generation Chinese." *Sociology and Social Research.* 18.

Charsley, S. R. 1974. "The Formation of Ethnic Groups." In Abner Cohen, ed., *Urban Ethnicity.* London: Tavistock.

Chen, Anita Beltran. 1977. "Selectivity in Philippine Migration." In Gordon P. Means, ed., *Development and Underdevelopment in Southeast Asia.* Canadian Society for Asian Studies.

Cheng, Ch'eng-K'un. 1953. "A Study of Chinese Assimilation in Hawaii." *Social Forces.* 32:2.

Cheng, Lucie, and Bonacich, Edna. 1984. *Labor Migration under Capitalism: Asian Workers in the United States before World War II.* Berkeley: University of California Press.

Child, Irwin L. 1943. *Italian or American? Second Generation in Conflict.* New Haven, CT: Yale University Press.

"The Children of Immigrants in Schools." 1911. *Reports*

of the Immigration Commission, vol. 1. Washington, DC: U.S. Government Printing Office.

Chinoy, Ely. 1952. "The Tradition of Opportunity and the Aspirations of Automobile Workers." *American Journal of Sociology.* 57.

Chiswick, Barry. 1979. "The Economic Progress of Immigrants: Some Apparently Universal Patterns." In William Fellner, ed., *Contemporary Economic Problems.* Washington, DC: American Enterprise Institute.

_____. 1982. "Immigrants in the U.S. Labor Market." *The Annals of the American Academy of Political and Social Sciences.* March.

_____. 1983a. "An Analysis of the Earnings and Employment of Asian-American Men." *Journal of Labor Economics.* 1.

_____. 1983b. "The Earnings and Human Capital of American Jews." *Journal of Human Resources.* 18.

_____. 1985. "The Labor Market Status of American Jews: Patterns and Determinants." In W. Van Horne, ed., *Ethnicity and the Work Force.* Madison, WI: University of Wisconsin System.

_____. 1986a. *Differences in Education and Economics among Racial and Ethnic Groups: Testing Alternative Hypotheses.* Center for the Study of Economics and the State, University of Chicago.

_____. 1986b. "Labor Supply and Investment in Child Quality: A Study of Jewish Women." *Review of Economic Statistics.* 68.

Chock, Phyllis P. 1981. "The Greek-American Small Businessman: A Cultural Analysis." *Journal of Anthropological Research.* 37.

Chun, Ki-Taek. 1980. "The Myth of Asian American Success and Its Educational Ramifications." *IRCD Bulletin.* XV:1&2.

Cinel, D. 1982. *From Italy to San Francisco.* Stanford, CA: Stanford University Press.

Cingolani, Cindy. 1973. "Avoiding Management Pitfalls." *Bank of America Small Business Reporter.* 11.

Cizmik, I. 1983. "Yugoslav Immigrants in the U.S. Labor Movement, 1880–1920." In Dirk Hoerder, ed., *American Labor and Immigration History, 1877–1920s.* Urbana, IL: University of Illinois Press.

Clark, Juan M. 1977. "The Cuban Exodus: Why?" Mimeographed. Miami: Cuban Exile Union.

Clark, Kenneth B. 1965. *Dark Ghetto.* New York: Harper and Row.

Clark, William A. V. 1986. "Residential Segregation in American Cities: A Review and Interpretation." *Population Research and Policy Review.* 5.

Clay, P. L. 1979. "The Process of Black Suburbanization." *Urban Affairs Quarterly.* 14.

Clemens, Samuel L. 1972. *Roughing It: The Works of Mark Twain.* Vol. 2. Berkeley: University of California Press.

Cobas, Jose. 1984. "Participation in the Ethnic Economy, Ethnic Solidarity and Ambivalence Toward the Host Society: The Case of Cuban Emigres in Puerto Rico." Paper presented at the American Sociological Association Meeting, San Antonio.

Cohen, Abner, 1969. *Custom and Politics in Urban Africa: A Study of Hausa Migrants in Yoruba Towns.* Berkeley: University of California Press.

_____, ed. 1974. *Urban Ethnicity.* London: Tavistock.

Cohen, M. 1988. *From Workshop to Office.* Urbana, IL: University of Illinois Press.

Cohen, Robin. 1986. *Endgame in South Africa?* Paris: Unesco Press.

_____. 1987. *The New Helots: Migrants in the International Division of Labor.* Aldershot: Avebury/Gower.

Cohen, Steven M. 1988. *American Assimilation or Jewish Revival?* Bloomington: Indiana University Press.

Cole, Stewart G., and Cole, Mildred Wiese. 1954. *Minorities and the American Promise.* New York: Harper.

Coleman, James. 1958. *Nigeria: Background to Nationalism.* Berkeley: University of California Press.

_____. 1966. *Equality of Educational Opportunity.* Washington, DC: U.S. Government Printing Office.

Collier, D., ed. 1979. *The New Authoritarianism in Latin America.* Princeton, NJ: Princeton University Press.

Commager, Henry Steele. 1962. "The Study of Immigration." In Henry Steele Commager, ed. *Immigration and American History.* Minneapolis: University of Minnesota Press.

Conk, M. 1978. *The U.S. Census and Labor Force Change.* Ann Arbor, MI: UMI Research Press.

_____. 1981. "Immigrant Workers in the City, 1870–1930: Agents of Growth or Threats to Democracy?" *Social Science Quarterly.* 62.

Connor, John W. 1975. "Changing Trends in Japanese American Academic Achievement." *The Journal of Ethnic Studies.* 2.

Connor, Walker. 1977. "Ethnonationalism in the First World." In Milton Esman, ed., *Ethnic Pluralism and Conflict in the Western World.* Ithaca, NY: Cornell University Press.

Conroy, Hilary, and Miyakawa, T. Scott, eds. 1972. *East across the Pacific.* Santa Barbara: Clio Press.

Conzen, Kathleen N. 1976. *Immigrant Milwaukee.* Cambridge, MA: Harvard University Press.

Coolidge, Mary R. 1909. *Chinese Immigration.* New York: Henry Holt and Company.

Cordova, Fred. 1973. "The Filipino-American, There's Always an Identity Crisis." In Stanley Sue and Nathaniel N. Wagner, eds., *Asian-American Psychological Perspectives.* Palo Alto: Science & Behavior Books.

Corey, Lewish. 1966. "The Middle Class." In Reinhard Bendix and Seymour Lipset, eds., *Class, Status, and Power,* 2d ed. Glencoe, IL: Free Press.

Cornelius, Wayne A. 1977. *Illegal Immigration to the*

United States: Recent Research Findings, Policy Implications, and Research Priorities. Working Paper. Center for International Studies, MIT.

———. 1981. "The Future of Mexican Immigrants in California: A New Perspective for Public Policy." *Working Papers on Public Policy # 6.* Center for U.S.-Mexico Studies, University of California-San Diego.

Corrigan, Samuel W. 1970. "The Plains Indian Powwow: Cultural Integration in Manitoba and Saskatchewan." *Anthropologica.* 12.

Cox, Oliver Cromwell. 1948. *Caste, Class and Race: A Study in Social Dynamics.* New York: Doubleday.

Craig, R. B. 1971. *The Bracero Program: Interest Groups and Foreign Policy.* Austin, TX: University of Texas Press.

Crawford, James. 1979. *The Creation of States in International Law.* Oxford: Clarendon Press.

Crèvecoeur, Hector St. John de. 1782/1957. *Letters from an American Farmer.* New York: E. P. Dutton.

Cross, Ira B. 1935. *A History of the Labor Movement in California.* Berkeley: University of California Press.

Cummings, Scott A., ed. 1980. *Self-Help in Urban America.* Port Washington, NY: Kennikat.

Curtin, Philip D. 1984. *Cross-Cultural Trade in World History.* Cambridge: Cambridge University Press.

Daedalus. 1961. "Ethnic Groups in American Life."

———. 1965. "The Negro American."

———. 1981. "American Indians, Blacks, Chicanos, and Puerto Ricans."

Dahrendorf, Ralf. 1959. *Class and Class Conflict in Industrial Society.* Stanford, CA: Stanford University Press.

Daniels, Roger. 1962/1966/1977. *The Politics of Prejudice: The Anti-Japanese Movement in California and the Struggle for Japanese Exclusion.* Berkeley: University of California Press.

———. 1971. *Concentration Camps USA: Japanese Americans and World War II.* New York: Holt, Rinehart and Winston.

———. 1975. *The Decision to Relocate the Japanese Americans.* Philadelphia: J. B. Lippincott Co.

———. 1977. "The Japanese-American Experience: 1890–1940." In Leonard Dinnerstein and F. C. Jaher, eds., *Uncertain Americans.* New York: Oxford University Press.

———. 1988. *Asian America: Chinese and Japanese in the United States since 1850.* Seattle: University of Washington Press.

Daniels, Roger, and Kitano, Harry H. L. 1970. *American Racism.* Englewood Cliffs, NJ: Prentice-Hall.

Dann, Uriel. 1969. *Iraq under Qassem.* New York: Praeger.

Das Gupta, Jyotirindra. 1970. *Language, Conflict and National Development.* Berkeley: University of California Press.

———. 1975. "Ethnicity, Language Demands, and National Development in India." In Nathan Glazer and Daniel Patrick Moynihan, eds., *Ethnicity: Theory and Experience.* Cambridge, MA: Harvard University Press.

Dassin, J. 1986. "The Culture of Fear." *Items.* 40.

Davis, A.; Gardner, B.; and Gardner, M. 1941. *Deep South: A Social Anthropological Study of Caste and Class.* Chicago: University of Chicago Press.

Davis, Cary; Haub, Carl; and Willette, Joanne. 1983. "U.S. Hispanics: Changing the Face of America." *Population Bulletin.* 38.

Davis, David Brian. 1966. *The Problem of Slavery in Western Culture.* Ithaca, NY: Cornell University Press.

———. 1975. *The Problem of Slavery in the Age of Revolution.* Ithaca, NY: Cornell University Press.

Dawson, A. 1983. "The Parameters of Craft Consciousness: The Social Outlook of the Skilled Worker 1890–1929." In Dirk Hoerder, ed., *American Labor and Immigration History, 1877–1920s.* Urbana, IL: University of Illinois Press.

de la Garza, R., and Flores, A. 1986. "The Impact of Mexican Immigrants on the Political Behavior of Chicanos." In H. L. Browning and R. de la Garza, eds., *Mexican Immigrants and Mexican Americans: An Evolving Relation.* Austin: Center for Mexican American Studies, University of Texas.

Decker, P. 1978. *Fortunes and Failures: White Collar Mobility in Nineteenth Century San Francisco.* Cambridge, MA: Harvard University Press.

Dedman, Bill. 1989. "Blacks Turned Down for Home Loans from S & Ls Twice as Often as Whites." *Atlanta Constitution.* January 22.

DeFleur, Melvin L., and Cho, Chang-Soo. 1957. "Assimilation of Japanese-Born Women in an American City." *Social Problems.* 4.

Degler, Carl N. 1971. *Neither Black Nor White.* New York: Macmillan.

Department of Commerce. 1974. "Federal and State Indian Reservations and Indian Trust Areas." Washington, DC: Government Printing Office.

Desai, Rashmi. 1963. *Indian Immigrants in Britain.* London: Oxford University Press.

Despres, Leo. 1967. *Cultural Pluralism and Nationalist Politics in British Guiana.* Chicago: Rand-McNally.

———. 1975. "Toward a Theory of Ethnic Phenomena." In Leo Despres, ed., *Ethnicity and Resource Competition.* The Hague: Mouton.

Deutsch, Karl. 1966. "Nation-Building and National Development." In Karl Deutsch and W. Foltz, eds., *Nation-Building.* New York: Atherton.

DeVos, George. 1955. "A Quantitative Rorschach Assessment of Maladjustment and Rigidity in Acculturating Japanese Americans." *Genetic Psychology Monographs.* 52.

DeVos, George, and Wagatsuma, Hiroshi. 1966. *Ja-*

pan's *Invisible Race: Caste in Culture and Personality*. Berkeley: University of California Press.

DeWind, J.; Seidl, T.; and Shenk, J. 1977. "Contract Labor in U.S. Agriculture." *NACLA Report on Americas*. 11.

DeWolfe, Evelyn, 1982. "Fund Pools Blocked by Postal Law." *Los Angeles Times*. February 21, VII

Díaz-Briquets, Sergio. 1985. "Cuban-Owned Businesses in the United States: A Research Note." *Cuban Studies*. 14.

Díaz-Briquets, Sergio, and Pérez, Lisandro. 1981. "Cuba: The Demography of Revolution." *Population Bulletin*. 36.

DiLeonardo, M. 1984. *The Varieties of the Ethnic Experience*. Ithaca, NY: Cornell University Press.

Dimaggio, Paul. 1982. "Cultural Capital and School Success: The Impact of Status Culture Participation on the Grades of U.S. High School Students." *American Sociological Review*. 47.

Dinnerstein, Leonard. 1977. "The East European Jewish Migration." In L. Dinnerstein and F. C. Jaher, eds., *Uncertain Americans*. New York: Oxford University Press.

———. 1982. "Education and the Advancement of American Jews." In B. Weiss, ed., *American Education and the European Immigrant*. Urbana, IL: University of Illinois Press.

Dinnerstein, Leonard, and Jaher, Frederick Cople. 1977. *Uncertain Americans*. New York: Oxford University Press.

Dinnerstein, Leonard, and Reimers, David M. 1975/1983/1987. *Ethnic Americans: A History of Immigration and Assimilation*. New York: Harper and Row.

Dollard, John. 1937. *Caste and Class in a Southern Town*. New Haven, CT: Yale University Press.

Dorris, Michael A. 1981. "The Grass Still Grows, The Rivers Still Flow: Contemporary Native Americans." *Daedalus*. 110.

Dowty, A. 1987. *Closed Borders: The Contemporary Assault on Freedom of Movement*. New Haven, CT: Yale University Press.

Doyle, D. 1983. "Unestablished Irishmen: Immigrants and Industrial America 1870–1910." In Dirk Hoerder ed., *American Labor and Immigration History*. Urbana, IL: University of Illinois Press.

Drake, St. Clair, and Cayton, Horace. 1945. *Black Metropolis: A Study of Negro Life in a Northern City*. New York: Harcourt, Brace.

Dresang, Dennis. 1974. "Ethnic Politics, Representative Bureaucracy, and Development Administration: The Zambian Case." *American Political Science Review*. 69.

DuBois, W. E. B. 1961. *The Souls of Black Folk*. Greenwich, CT: Fawcett.

———. 1899/1967. *The Philadelphia Negro: A Social Study*. New York: Schocken.

Duncan, Beverly. 1967. "Education and Social Background." *American Journal of Sociology*. 72.

Duncan, Beverly, and Duncan, Otis D. 1968. "Minorities and the Process of Stratification." *American Sociological Review*. 33.

Duncan, Otis D., and Duncan, Beverly. 1955. "Residential Distribution and Occupational Stratification." *American Journal of Sociology*. 60.

Duncan, Otis Dudley; Featherman, David L.; and Duncan, Beverly. 1972. *Socioeconomic Background and Achievement*. New York: Seminar Press.

Dushkin, Lelah. 1972. "Scheduled Caste Politics." In J. Michael Mahan, ed., *The Untouchables in Contemporary India*. Tucson: The University of Arizona Press.

Eckland, Bruce K. 1968. "Retrieving Mobile Cases in Longitudinal Surveys." *Public Opinion Quarterly*. 32.

Eckstein, Susan. 1977. *The Poverty of Revolution: The State and the Urban Poor in Mexico*. Princeton, NJ: Princeton University Press.

Economic Commission for Latin America. 1974. "Economic Survey of Latin America, Part 3." United Nations Document E/CN.12/974/Add. 3.

The Economist. May 13, 1985.

Edwards, Richard C. 1975. "The Social Relations of Production in the Firm and Labor Market Structure." In Richard C. Edwards, Michael Reich, and David M. Gordon, eds., *Labor Market Segmentation*. Lexington, MA: D. C. Heath.

Edwards, Richard C.; Reich, Michael; and Gordon, David M., eds. 1975. *Labor Market Segmentation*. Lexington, MA: D. C. Heath.

Eisenstadt, S. N. 1970. "The Process of Absorbing New Immigrants in Israel." In S. N. Eisenstadt, ed., *Integration and Development in Israel*. Jerusalem: Israel University Press.

———. 1978. *Revolution and the Transformation of Societies: A Comparative Study of Civilizations*. New York: Free Press.

Eitzen, D. Stanley, and Yetman, Norman R. 1977. "Immune from Racism?" *Civil Rights Digest*. 9.

Elkins, Stanley M. 1959. *Slavery: A Problem in American Institutional and Intellectual Life*. Chicago: University of Chicago Press.

Emmanuel, Arghiri. 1972. *Unequal Exchange: A Study of the Imperialism of Free Trade*. New York: Monthly Review Press.

Engelhardt, Tom. 1971. "Ambush at Kamikaze Pass." *Bulletin of Concerned Asian Scholars*. 3.

Enloe, Cynthia. 1973. *Ethnic Development and Political Conflict*. Boston: Little, Brown.

———. 1981. "The Growth of the State and Ethnic Mobilization: The American Experience." *Ethnic and Racial Studies*. 4.

Epstein, A. L. 1967. "Urbanization and Social Change in Africa. *Current Anthropology.* October.

Erdrich, Louise, and Dorris, Michael. 1988. "Who Owns the Land?" *New York Times Magazine.* September 4.

Erickson, Charlotte. 1957. *American Industry and the European Immigrant, 1860–1885.* New York: Russell & Russell.

*Estrada, Leobardo F.; García, F. Chris; Macías, Reynaldo Flores; and Maldonado, Lionel. 1981. *Daedalus.* 110:2.

Ewen, E. 1985. *Immigrant Women in the Land of Dollars.* New York: Monthly Review Press.

Fagen, P. (forthcoming) "Repression and State Security." In J. Carradi, ed., *Fear and Society.* New York: Monthly Review Press.

Fagen, Richard; Brody, Richard A.; and O'Leary, Thomas J. 1968. *Cubans in Exile: Disaffection and the Revolution.* Stanford, CA: Stanford University Press.

Fain, T. Scott. 1980. "Self-Employed Americans: Their Number Has Increased." *Monthly Labor Review.* 103.

Fairbank, John King. 1969. "Assignment for the '70's." *American Historical Review.* 74.

———. 1972. "America and China: The Mid-Nineteenth Century." In Ernest R. May and James C. Thomson, Jr., eds., *American-East Asian Relations: A Survey,* Cambridge, MA: Harvard University Press.

Faires, N. 1983. "Occupational Patterns of German-Americans in Nineteenth Century Cities." In H. Keil and J. Jentz, eds., *German Workers in Industrial Chicago, 1850–1910.* De Kalb, IL: Northern Illinois University Press.

Falcón, A. 1983. "Puerto Rican Politics in Urban America: An Introduction to the Literature." *La Red.* July.

Fallows, James. 1983. "Immigration." *The Atlantic.* 252:5.

Fanon, Frantz. 1968. *The Wretched of the Earth.* New York: Grove.

Farley, Reynolds. 1970. "The Changing Distribution of Negroes within Metropolitan Areas: The Emergence of Black Suburbs." *American Journal of Sociology.* 75.

———. 1977a. "Trends in Racial Inequalities: Have the Gains of the 1960s Disappeared in the 1970s?" *American Sociological Review.* 42.

———. 1977b. "Residential Segregation in Urbanized Areas of the United States in 1970: An Analysis of Social Class and Racial Differences." *Demography.* 14.

———. 1978. "School Integration in the United States." In Frank D. Bean and W. Parker Frisbie, eds., *The Demography of Racial and Ethnic Groups.* New York: Academic Press.

———. 1984. *Blacks and Whites: Narrowing the Gap?* Cambridge, MA: Harvard University Press.

Farley, Reynolds, and Allen, William. 1987. *The Color Line and the Quality of Life: The Problem of the Twentieth Century.* New York: Russell Sage Foundation.

Farley, Reynolds, and Bianchi, Suzanne. 1985. "Social Class Polarization: Is It Occurring among Blacks?" *Research in Race and Ethnic Relations.* 4.

Farley, Reynolds; Bianchi, Suzanne; and Colasanto, Diane. 1979. "Barriers to the Racial Integration of Neighborhoods: The Detroit Case." *Annals of the American Academy of Political and Social Science.* 441.

Farley, Reynolds; Schuman, Howard; Bianchi, Suzanne; Colasanto, Diane; and Hatchett, S. 1978. "Chocolate City, Vanilla Suburbs: Will the Trend toward Racially Separate Communities Continue?" *Social Science Research.* 7.

Faust, Albert. 1909. *The German Element in the United States with Special Reference to its Political, Moral, Social and Educational Influence.* Boston: Houghton Mifflin.

Feagin, Joe R., and Feagin, Clairece Booher. 1978. *Discrimination American Style.* Englewood Cliffs, NJ: Prentice-Hall.

Featherman, David. 1971. "The Socioeconomic Achievements of White Religio-ethnic Subgroups: Social and Psychological Explanations." *American Sociological Review.* 36.

Featherman, David, and Hauser, Robert. 1976. "Changes in the Socioeconomic Stratification of the Races, 1962–1973." *American Journal of Sociology.* 82.

———. 1978. *Opportunity and Change.* New York: Academic Press.

Feith, H. 1980. "Repressive-Developmentalist Regimes in Asia: Old Strengths, New Vulnerabilities." *Prisma.* 19.

Fernández, C. 1984. "The Causes of Naturalization and Nonnaturalization for Mexican Immigrants: An Empirical Study Based on Case Studies." Report Project Participar.

Firebaugh, Glenn, and Davis, Kenneth E. 1988. "Trends in Antiblack Prejudice 1972–1984: Region and Cohort Effects." *American Journal of Sociology.* 94.

Firey, Walter. 1974. *Land Use in Central Boston.* Cambridge, MA: Harvard University Press.

Fishman, Joshua; Nahirny, Vladimir C.; Hofman, John E.; and Hayden, Robert G. 1966. *Language Loyalty in the United States.* The Hague: Mouton.

Fisk University. 1946. *Orientals and Their Cultural Adjustment.* Nashville: Fisk University Press. Social Science Source Documents No. 4.

Fitzpatrick, Joseph P. 1971. *Puerto Rican Americans: The Meaning of Migration to the Mainland.* Englewood Cliffs, NJ: Prentice-Hall.

Fitzpatrick, Joseph P., and Gurak, D. 1979. *Hispanic Intermarriage in New York City.* New York: Fordham University Hispanic Research Center.

Flaming, Karl H., et al. 1972. "Black Powerlessness in

Policy-Making Positions." *The Sociological Quarterly.* 13.

Fogel, Robert William, and Engerman, Stanley L. 1974. *Time on the Cross: The Economics of American Negro Slavery.* Boston: Little, Brown.

Foner, Laura, and Genovese, Eugene, eds. 1969. *Slavery in the New World.* Englewood Cliffs, NJ: Prentice-Hall.

Fong, Stanley L. M. 1965. "Assimilation of Chinese in America: Changes in Orientation and Social Perspective." *American Journal of Sociology.* 71:3.

Francis, E. K. 1976. *Interethnic Relations: An Essay in Sociological Theory.* New York: Elsevier.

Frank, Andre Gunder. 1967. *Capitalism and Underdevelopment in Latin America.* New York: Monthly Review Press.

_____. 1969. *Latin America: Underdevelopment or Revolution?* New York: Monthly Review Press.

Frazier, E. Franklin. 1947. "Sociological Theory and Race Relations." *American Sociological Review.* 12.

_____. 1949. *The Negro in the United States.* New York: MacMillan.

Freeman, James A. 1989. *Hearts of Sorrow: Vietnamese-American Lives.* Stanford: Stanford University Press.

Freeman, Richard B. 1976. *Black Elite: The New Market for Highly Educated Black Americans.* New York: McGraw-Hill.

Freedman, Maurice. 1959. "The Handling of Money: A Note on the Background to the Economic Sophistication of the Overseas Chinese." *Man.* 59.

Frey, William H. 1985. "Mover Destination Selectivity and the Changing Suburbanization of Metropolitan Whites and Blacks." *Demography.* 22.

Friedman, Samuel. 1969. "How is Racism Maintained?" *Et al.* 2 (Fall).

Friedman, Thomas L. 1985. "Kahane Appeal to Oust Arabs Gains in Israel." *New York Times.* August 5.

Frobel, F.; Heinrichs, J.; and Kreye, O. 1980. *The New International Division of Labor.* Cambridge: Cambridge University Press.

Fuchs, Estelle, and Havighurst, Robert J. 1973. *To Live on This Earth: American Indian Education.* Garden City, NY: Doubleday.

Fuguitt, Glenn V. 1985. "The Nonmetropolitan Turnaround: A Review." *Annual Review of Sociology.* 11.

Gabaccia, D. 1984. *From Sicily to Elizabeth Street.* Albany, NY: SUNY Press.

Gainer, Bernard. 1972. *The Alien Invasion: The Origin of the Aliens Act of 1905.* London: Heinemann Educational Books.

Galarza, Ernesto. 1964. *Merchants of Labor: The Mexican Bracero Story.* Santa Barbara: McNally & Loflin.

_____. 1970. *Spiders in the House and Workers in the Field.* Notre Dame, IN: Notre Dame University Press.

_____. 1977. *Farm Workers and Agri-Business in California, 1947–1960.* Notre Dame, IN: University of Notre Dame Press.

Gans, Herbert. 1962. *The Urban Villagers.* New York: Free Press.

_____. 1968. "Social Protest of the 1960's Takes the Form of the Equality Revolution." *New York Times Magazine.* November 3.

*_____. 1979. "Symbolic Ethnicity: The Future of Ethnic Groups and Culture in America." *Ethnic and Racial Studies.* 2.

García, J. A. 1981. "Political Integration of Mexican Immigrants: Explorations into the Naturalization Process." *International Migration Review.* 15.

Gardner, Robert W.; Robey, Bryant; and Smith, Peter C. 1985. "Asian Americans: Growth, Change, and Diversity." *Population Bulletin.* 4.

Geertz, Clifford. 1963. "The Integrative Revolution: Primordial Sentiments and Civil Politics in New States." In Geertz, ed., *Old Societies and New States.* New York: Free Press.

Gelfand, Mitchell Brian. 1981. "Chuzpah in El Dorado: Social Mobility of Jews in Los Angeles, 1900–1920." Ph.D. Dissertation, Carnegie-Mellon University, Pittsburgh, PA.

Genovese, Eugene D. 1974. *Roll, Jordon, Roll: The World the Slaves Made.* New York: Pantheon Books.

Gerry, Chris, and Birkbeck, Chris. 1981. "The Petty Commodity Producer in Third World Cities: Petit-Bourgeois or Disguised Proletarian?" in Frank Bechofer and Brian Elliott, eds., *The Petite Bourgeoisie.* New York: St. Martin's Press.

Geschwender, James A. 1978. *Racial Stratification in America.* Dubuque, IA: William C. Brown.

Geschwender, James A., and Carroll-Seguin, Rita. 1990. "Exploding the Myth of African-American Progress." *Signs.* 15:2.

Gibney, Mark. 1986. *Strangers or Friends: Principles for a New Alien Admission Policy.* Westport, CT: Greenwood Press.

Giddens, Anthony. 1973. *The Class Structure of the Advanced Societies.* New York: Harper and Row.

Girdner, Audrey, and Loftis, Anne. 1969. *The Great Betrayal: The Evacuation of the Japanese-Americans during World War II.* New York: Macmillan.

Gittler, Joseph B. 1956. *Understanding Minority Groups.* New York: Wiley.

Glaessel-Brown, W. 1985. *Colombian Immigrants in the Industries of the Northeast.* Ph.D. thesis. Boston: Department of Political Science, Massachusetts Institute of Technology.

Glasgow, Douglas G. 1980. *The Black Underclass: Poverty, Unemployment and Entrapment of Ghetto Youth.* San Francisco: Jossey-Bass.

Glazer, Nathan. 1954. "Ethnic Groups in America." In

M. Berger, T. Abel, and C. Page, eds., *Freedom and Control in Modern Society*. New York: Van Nostrand.

_____. 1955. "Social Characteristics of American Jews, 1654–1954." *American Jewish Yearbook*. 56. Philadelphia: The American Jewish Committee and the Jewish Publication Society of America.

_____. 1975. *Affirmative Discrimination*. New York: Basic Books.

_____. 1981. "Pluralism and the New Immigrants." *Society* 19.

_____. 1987. "New Perspectives on American Jewish Sociology." In David Singer, ed., *American Jewish Yearbook, 1987*. 87. Philadelphia: The American Jewish Committee.

Glazer, Nathan, and Moynihan, Daniel Patrick. 1963 /1970. *Beyond the Melting Pot*. Cambridge, MA: Massachusetts Institute of Technology Press and the Harvard University Press.

_____. 1975. *Ethnicity: Theory and Experience*. Cambridge, MA: Harvard University Press.

Glenn, C. 1977. *Immigrant Destinations*. Philadelphia: Temple University Press.

Glenn, E. 1984. "The Dialectics of Wage Work: Japanese Women and Domestic Service, 1905–1940." In Lucie Cheng and Edna Bonacich, *Labor Migration under Capitalism*. Berkeley: University of California Press.

Glick, Clarence. 1938. "Transition from Familism to Nationalism among Chinese in Hawaii." *American Journal of Sociology*. 43:5.

Glyn, Andrew, and Sutcliffe, Bob. 1971. "The Critical Condition of British Capital." *New Left Review*. 66.

_____. 1972. *British Capitalism, Workers and the Profit Squeeze*. Hammondsworth: Penguin.

Goering, John M. 1971. "The Emergence of Ethnic Interests: A Case of Serendipity." *Social Forces*. 49.

Goffman, Erving. 1961. *Asylums*. New York: Doubleday.

Golab, Caroline. 1973. "The Immigrant and the City: Poles, Italians, and Jews in Philadelphia, 1870–1920." In Allen F. Davis and Mark H. Haller, eds., *The Peoples of Philadelphia*. Philadelphia: Temple University Press.

_____. 1977. *Immigrant Destinations*. Philadelphia: Temple University Press.

Golant, Stephen M., and Jacobsen, Christian W. 1978. "Factors Underlying the Decentralized Residential Locations of Chicago's Ethnic Population." *Ethnicity*. 5.

Goldberg, Milton M. 1941. "A Qualification of the Marginal Man Theory." *American Sociological Review*. 6.

Goldin, Claudia. 1981. "Family Strategies and the Family Economy in the Late Nineteenth Century: The Role of Secondary Workers." In Theodore Hershberg, ed., *Philadelphia: Work, Space, Family, and Group Experience in the Nineteenth Century*. New York: Oxford University Press.

Goldschneider, Calvin. 1986. *Jewish Continuity and Change*. Bloomington, IN: Indiana University Press.

Goldschneider, Calvin, and Kobrin, Frances, 1980. "Ethnic Continuity and the Process of Self-Employment." *Ethnicity*. 7.

Goldstein, Ira, and White, Clark. 1985. "Residential Segregation and Color Stratification among Hispanics in Philadelphia: Comment on Massey and Mullan." *American Journal of Sociology*. 89.

Goldstone, Jack A. 1980. "Theories of Revolution: The Third Generation." *World Politics*.

_____. 1982. "The Comparative and Historical Study of Revolutions." *Annual Review of Sociology*. 8.

Golovensky, David L. 1952. "The Marginal Man Concept." *Social Forces*. 30.

Gonzalo, D. F. 1929. "Social Adjustments of Filipinos in America." *Sociology and Social Research*. 14:2.

Gordon, David M. 1971. *Class Productivity and the Ghetto*. Ph.D. dissertation, Cambridge, MA: Harvard University.

_____. 1972. *Theories of Poverty and Underemployment*. Lexington, MA: D. C. Heath.

_____. 1988. "The Global Economy: New Edifice or Crumbling Foundations?" *New Left Review*. 168.

Gordon, David; Edwards, Richard; and Reich, Michael. 1982. *Segmented Work, Divided Workers*. New York: Cambridge University Press.

*Gordon, Milton M. 1961. "Assimilation in America: Theory and Reality." *Daedalus*. 90:2.

*_____. 1964. *Assimilation in American Life*. New York: Oxford University Press.

_____. 1978. *Human Nature, Class, and Ethnicity*. New York: Oxford University Press.

Gorelick, Sherry 1981. *City College and the Jewish Poor*. New Brunswick, NJ: Rutgers University Press.

Granovetter, Mark. 1974. *Getting a Job: A Study of Contacts and Careers*. Cambridge, MA: Harvard University Press.

Granovetter, Mark, and Tilly, Charles. 1988. "Inequality and Labor Process." In Neil Smelser, ed., *Handbook of Sociology*. Newbury Park, CA: Sage.

Grasmuck, S. 1984. "Immigration, Ethnic Stratification, and Native Working-Class Discipline: Comparisons of Documented and Undocumented Dominicans." *International Migration Review*. 18.

Grebler, Leo. 1966. "The Naturalization of the Mexican Immigrant in the U.S." *International Migration Review*. 1.

Grebler, Leo; Moore, Joan W.; and Guzman, Ralph. 1970. *The Mexican-American People, The Nation's Second Largest Minority*. New York: Free Press.

Greeley, Andrew M. 1971/1975. *Why Can't They Be Like Us?* New York: E. P. Dutton.

_____. 1974. *Ethnicity in the United States: A Preliminary Reconnaissance.* New York: Wiley.

*_____. 1976a. "The Ethnic Miracle." *The Public Interest.* 45.

_____. 1976b. *Ethnicity, Denomination, and Inequality.* Beverly Hills, CA: Sage.

_____. 1977. *The American Catholic: A Social Portrait.* New York: Basic Books.

_____. 1978. "Group Formation and the Cultural Division of Labor." *American Journal of Sociology.* 84.

_____. 1982. "Immigration and Religioethnic Groups: A Sociological Reappraisal." In Barry Chiswick, ed., *The Gateway: U.S. Immigration Issues and Policies.* Washington: American Enterprise Institute.

Greeley, Andrew M., and Sheatsley, Paul B. 1974. "Attitudes towards Racial Integration." In Lee Rainwater, ed., *Social Problems and Public Policy: Inequality and Justice.* Chicago: Aldine.

Green, Arnold W. 1947. "A Re-examination of the Marginal Man Concept." *Social Forces.* 26.

Green, J. 1980. *The World of the Worker.* New York: Hill & Wang.

Greene, J. E. 1974. *Race vs. Politics in Guyana.* Jamaica: Institute of Social and Economic Research, University of West Indies.

Greer, Colin, ed., 1974. *The Divided Society.* New York: Basic Books.

Grier, Eunice, and Grier, Scott. 1965. "Equality and Beyond: Housing Segregation in the Great Society." *Daedalus.* 95.

Griffen, Sally, and Griffen, Clyde. 1977. "Family and Business in a Small City: Poughkeepsie, N.Y., 1850–1880." In Tamara Hareven, ed., *Family and Kin in Urban Communities, 1700–1930.* New York: New Viewpoints.

Griffen, Clyde, and Griffen, Sally. 1978. *Natives and Newcomers.* Cambridge, MA: Harvard University Press.

Grimshaw, Allen D. 1959. "Lawlessness and Violence in America and Their Special Manifestations in Changing Negro-White Relationships." *Journal of Negro History.* 44.

Grodzins, Morton. 1956/1966. *Americans Betrayed: Politics and the Japanese Evacuation.* Chicago: University of Chicago Press.

Guest, Avery. 1978. "The Changing Racial Composition of Suburbs: 1950–1970." *Urban Affairs Quarterly.* 19.

Gutman, Herbert G. 1976. *The Black Family in Slavery and Freedom, 1750–1925.* New York: Pantheon Books.

Haaland, G. 1969. Economic Determinants in Ethnic Processes. In F. Barth, ed., *Ethnic Groups and Boundaries.* Boston: Little, Brown and Company.

Haberman, Clyde. 1989. "Flow of Turks Leaving Bulgaria Swells to Hundreds of Thousands." *New York Times.* August 15.

Hagen, Everett E. 1962. *On the Theory of Social Change: How Economic Growth Begins.* Homewood, IL: Dorsey.

_____. 1968. *The Economics of Development.* Homewood, IL: Richard D. Irwin.

Hall, Peter Dobkin. 1977. "Family Structure and Economic Organization: Massachusetts Merchants, 1700–1850." In Tamara Hareven, ed., *Family and Kin in Urban Communities 1700–1930.* New York: New Viewpoints.

Hamilton, Gary. 1978. "Pariah Capitalism: A Paradox of Power and Dependence." *Ethnic Groups.* 2.

Handlin, Oscar. 1941/1959. *Boston's Immigrants: A Study of Acculturation.* Cambridge, MA: Harvard University Press.

_____. 1951. *The Uprooted: The Epic Story of the Great Migration That Made the American People.* New York: Grossett and Dunlap.

_____. 1956. *The Newcomers: Negroes and Puerto Ricans in a Changing Metropolis.* Cambridge, MA: Harvard University Press.

_____. 1957. *Race and Nationality in American Life.* Garden City, NY: Doubleday.

_____. 1961. "Historical Perspectives on the American Ethnic Group." *Daedalus.* 90.

Hannan, Michael T. 1979. "The Dynamics of Ethnic Boundaries in Modern States." In John Meyer and Michael T. Hannan, eds., *National Development and the World System.* Chicago: University of Chicago Press.

Hansen, Marcus Lee. 1938. *The Problem of the Third Generation Immigrant.* Rock Island, IL: Augustana Historical Society.

_____. 1940a. *The Atlantic Migration, 1607–1860.* Cambridge, MA: Harvard University Press.

_____. 1940b. *The Immigrant in American History.* Cambridge: Harvard University Press.

Harbison, Frederick. 1956. "Entrepreneurial Organization as a Factor in Economic Development." *Quarterly Journal of Economics.* 70.

Hareven, Tamara. 1982. *Family Time and Industrial Time.* New York: Cambridge University Press.

Harris, Donald J. 1972. "The Black Ghetto as a Colony: A Theoretical Critique and Alternative Formulation." *Review of Black Political Economy.* 2.

Harris, Marvin. 1964. *Patterns of Race in the Americas.* New York: Walker.

Hartwig, M. C. 1972. "Aborigines and Racism: An Historical Perspective." In F. S. Stevens, ed., *Racism: The Australian Experience.* vol. 2. New York: Taplinger.

Harwood, Edwin. 1986. "American Public Opinion and

U.S. Immigration Policy." *Annals of the American Academy of Political and Social Science.* 487.

Harzig, C. 1983. "Chicago's German North Side, 1880–1990: The Structure of a Gilded Age Neighborhood." In Keil & Jentz, eds., *German Workers in Industrial Chicago, 1850–1910.* De Kalb: Northern Illinois University Press.

Hauser, R. 1982. Occupational Status in the Nineteenth and Twentieth Centuries. *Historical Methods.* 15.

Hauser, Robert M., and Featherman, David L. 1976. "Equality of Schooling: Trends and Prospects." *Sociology of Education.* 49.

Hechter, Michael. 1975. *Internal Colonialism.* Berkeley: University of California Press.

Heisler, Martin. 1977. Managing Ethnic Conflict in Belgium. *Annals.* 433.

Hendricks, G. L. 1974. *The Dominican Diaspora: From the Dominican Republic to New York City.* New York: Teacher's College Press, Columbia University.

Henrietta, J. 1977. "The Study of Social Mobility: Ideological Assumptions and Conceptual Bias." *Labor History.* 18.

Henry, Frances. 1976. *Ethnicity in the Americas.* Chicago: Aldine.

Henry, Jeannette. 1965. "White People's Time, Colored People's Time." *Transaction.* (March-April).

_____. 1967. "Our Inaccurate Textbooks." *The Indian Historian.* 1.

Herberg, Will. 1955/1960. *Protestant-Catholic-Jew.* New York: Doubleday.

Herman, Edward S. and Chomsky, Noam. 1988. *Manufacturing Consent: The Political Economy of the Mass Media.* New York: Pantheon Books.

Herman, Harry Vjekoslav. 1979. "Dishwashers and Proprietors: Macedonians in Toronto's Restaurant Trade." in Sandra Wallman, ed., *Ethnicity at Work.* London: Macmillan.

*Hershberg, Theodore; Burstein, Alan N.; Ericksen, Eugene P.; Greenberg, Stephanie; and Yancey, William L. 1979. "A Tale of Three Cities: Blacks, Immigrants and Opportunity in Philadelphia: 1850–1880, 1930 and 1970." *The Annals of the American Academy of Political and Social Science.* 441.

Hershberg, Theodore, and Dockhorn, R., 1976. "Occupational Classification." *Historical Methods Newsletter.* 9.

Hertzberg, Hazel W. 1977. *The Search for An American Indian Identity: Modern Pan-Indian Movements.* Syracuse: Syracuse University Press.

Hess, Gary R. 1974. "The Forgotten Asian Americans: The East Indian Community in the United States." *Pacific Historical Review.* 43.

Higgs, Robert. 1977. *Competition and Coercion.* Cambridge: Cambridge University Press.

Higham, John. 1963/1965. *Strangers in the Land.* New Brunswick, NJ: Rutgers University Press.

_____. 1973. *History.* New York: Harper & Row.

_____. 1975. *Send These To Me.* New York: Atheneum.

Hill, Robert B. 1981. "The Economic Status of Black Americans." In *The State of Black America.* New York: National Urban League.

Himes, Joseph. 1966. "The Functions of Racial Conflict." *Social Forces.* 46.

Hirschman, A. O. 1970. *Exit, Voice, and Loyalty: Responses to Decline in Firms, Organizations, and States.* Cambridge: Harvard University Press.

_____. 1981. "Exit, Voice, and the State." *Essays in Trespassing: Economics to Politics and Beyond.* Cambridge: Cambridge University Press.

Hirschman, Charles. 1983. "America's Melting Pot Reconsidered." *Annual Review of Sociology.* 9.

Hirschman, Charles, and Falcón, L. M. 1985. "The Educational Attainment of Religio-ethnic Groups in the United States." *Research in Sociology of Education and Socialization.* 5.

Hirschman, Charles, and Kraly, E. P. 1986a. "Immigrants, Minorities, and Earnings in 1950." Paper presented at the American Sociological Association Meetings, New York.

_____. 1986b. "Racial and Ethnic Inequality and Labor Markets in the U.S., 1940 and 1950." Paper presented at the Meetings of the Population Studies Association of America, San Francisco.

Hirschman, Charles, and Wong, Morrison G. 1981. "Trends in Socioeconomic Achievement among Immigrant and Native-Born Asian-Americans, 1960–1976." *Sociological Quarterly.* 22:495–513.

_____. 1984. "Socioeconomic Gains of Asian-Americans, Blacks, and Hispanics: 1960–1976." *American Journal of Sociology.* 90.

*_____. 1986. "The Extraordinary Educational Attainment of Asian-Americans: A Search for Historical Evidence and Explanations." *Social Forces.* 65:1.

Hispanic Review of Business. 1985. *Annual Survey of Hispanic Business, 1984.* June-July.

Hobsbawm, Eric. 1977. "Some Reflections on 'The Break-up of Britain.' " *New Left Review.* 105.

Hodson, R., and Kaufman, R. 1982. "Economic Dualism: A Critical Review." *American Sociological Review* 47.

Hoerder, Dirk., ed. 1983. *American Labor and Immigration History, 1877–1920s.* Urbana, IL: University of Illinois Press.

_____. 1986. *Struggle a Hard Battle.* De Kalb, IL: Northern Illinois University Press.

Hoetink, Harry. 1967. *Caribbean Race Relations.* London: Oxford University Press.

Hopkins, R. 1968. "Occupational and Geographic Mobility in Atlanta, 1870–96." *Journal of Southern History.* 34.

Horowitz, Donald. 1971. "Three Dimensions of Ethnic Politics." *World Politics.* XXIII.

———. 1975. "Ethnic Identity." In Nathan Glazer and Daniel Patrick Moynihan, eds., *Ethnicity: Theory and Experience.* Cambridge, MA: Harvard University Press.

———. 1977. "Cultural Movements and Ethnic Change." *Annals.* 433.

*———. 1985. *Ethnic Groups in Conflict.* Berkeley: University of California Press.

Horton, John. 1966. "Order and Conflict Theories of Social Problems as Competing Ideologies." *American Journal of Sociology.* 71.

Horvat, Branko. 1982. *The Political Economy of Socialism.* Armonk, N.Y.: M. E. Sharpe.

Hosokawa, Bill. 1969. *Nisei: The Quiet Americans.* New York: William Morrow.

Hough, Joseph C., Jr. 1968. *Black Power and White Protestants: A Christian Response to the New Negro Pluralism.* New York: Oxford University Press.

Howe, Irving, 1976. *World of Our Fathers.* New York: Harcourt, Brace, Jovanovich.

———. 1977. "The Limits of Ethnicity." *The New Republic.* June 25.

Howe, Irving, and Libo, Kenneth. 1979. *How We Lived: A Documentary History of Immigrant Jews in America.* New York: Richard March.

Hraba, Joseph. 1979. *American Ethnicity.* Itasca, IL: F. E. Peacock.

Hsu, Francis L. K. 1971. *The Challenge of the American Dream: The Chinese in the United States.* Belmont, CA: Wadsworth.

Hughes, Everett C. 1963. "Race Relations and the Sociological Imagination." *American Sociological Review.* 28.

*Hune, Shirley. 1977. "Pacific Migration to the United States: Trends and Themes in Historical and Sociological Literature." *RIIES Bibliographic Studies.* 2. Washington, DC: Smithsonian Institution.

———. 1989. "Opening the American Mind and Body: The Role of Asian American Studies." *Change.* November/December.

Hune, Shirley; Kim, Hyung-Chan; Fujuta, Stephen S.; and Ling, Amy. 1990. *Asian Americans: Comparative and Global Perspectives.* Pullman: Washington State University Press.

Hurh, Won Moo, and Kim, Kwang Chung. 1983. "Korean Americans and the 'Success' Image: A Critique." *Amerasia Journal.* 10.

Hurh, Won Moo, and Kim, Kwang Chung. 1989. "The 'Success' Image of Asian Americans: Its Validity and Its Practical and Theoretical Implications." *Ethnic and Racial Studies.* 12.

Hutchinson, Edward P. 1956. *Immigrants and Their Children, 1850–1950.* New York: Wiley.

Ianni, F. 1972. *A Family Business.* New York: Russell Sage Foundation.

Ichihashi, Yamato. 1932. *Japanese in the United States.* Stanford, CA: Stanford University Press.

Ichioka, Yuji. 1988. *The Issei: The World of the First Generation Japanese Immigrants, 1885–1924.* New York: The Free Press.

Issacs, Harold R. 1963. *The New World of Negro Americans.* New York: Viking.

———. 1975. "Basic Group Identity: The Idols of the Tribe." In Nathan Glazer and Daniel Patrick Moynihan, eds., *Ethnicity: Theory and Experience.* Cambridge, MA: Harvard University Press.

Jackson, Peter. 1981. "Paradoxes of Puerto Rican Segregation in New York." In Ceri Peach, Vaughn Robinson, and Susan Smith, eds., *Ethnic Segregation in Cities.* London: Croom-Helm.

Jackson, R. M. 1984. *The Formation of Craft Labor Markets.* New York: Academic Press.

James, David R. 1989. "City Limits on Racial Equality: The Effects of City-Suburban Boundaries on Public-School Desegregation, 1968–1976." *American Sociological Review.* 54.

James, David R., and Taeuber, Karl E. 1985. "Measures of Segregation." In Nancy Tuma, ed., *Sociological Methodology 1985.* San Francisco: Jossey-Bass.

Jarvenpa, Robert. 1985. "The Political Economy and Political Ethnicity of American Indian Adaptations and Identities." *Ethnic and Racial Studies.* 8.

Jarvenpa, Robert, and Zenner, Walter P. 1979. "Scot Trader/Indian Worker Relations and Ethnic Segregation: A Subarctic Example." *Ethnos.* 44.

Jasso, Guillermo, and Rosenzweig, M. R. 1985. "What's in a Name? Country-of-Origin Influences on the Earnings of Immigrants in the United States." Bulletin # 85–4. Economic Development Center, University of Minnesota.

*Jaynes, Gerald David, and Williams, Robin M., Jr., ed. 1989. *A Common Destiny: Blacks and American Society.* Washington, DC: National Academy Press.

Jencks, Christopher. 1972. *Inequality: A Reassessment of the Effects of Family and Schooling in America.* New York: Harper and Row.

———. 1983. "Discrimination and Thomas Sowell." *New York Review of Books.* 30.

Jenkins, J. C. 1983. "Why Do Peasants Rebel? Structural and Historical Theories of Modern Peasant Rebellions." *American Journal of Sociology.* 88.

Jenkins, Richard. 1984. "Ethnicity and the Rise of Capitalism." In Robin Ward, ed., *Ethnic Business in Britain*. Cambridge: Cambridge University Press.

Jenkins, J. Craig, and Perrow, Charles. 1977. "Insurgency of the Powerless: Farm Worker Movements (1946–1972)." *American Sociological Review*. 48.

Jennings, J. 1977. *Puerto Rican Politics in New York City*. Washington, DC: University Press of America.

Jensen, Arthur R. 1969. "How Much Can We Boost I.Q. and Scholastic Achievement?" *Harvard Educational Review*. Reprint Series No. 2.

Jensen, Joan M. 1988. *Passage from India: Asian Indian Immigrants in North America*. New Haven: Yale University Press.

Jiobu, Robert M. 1976–77. "Earnings Differentials between Whites and Ethnic Minorities: The Cases of Asian-Americans, Blacks, and Chicanos." *Sociology and Social Research*. 61.

Johnson, Charles S. 1934. *Shadow of the Plantation*. Chicago: University of Chicago Press.

Jones, Faustine C. 1981. "External Crosscurrents and Internal Diversity: An Assessment of Black Progress, 1960–1980." *Daedalus*. 110:2.

Jones, LeRoy, and Sakong, I. 1980. *Government, Business and Entrepreneurship in Economic Development: The Korean Case*. Cambridge, MA: Harvard University Council on East Asian Studies.

Jones, Maldwyn Allen. 1960. *American Immigration*. Chicago: University of Chicago Press.

———. 1976. *Destination America*. New York: Holt, Rinehart, and Winston.

Jorge, Antonio, and Moncarz, Raul. 1981. "International Factor Movement and Complementarity: Growth and Entrepreneurship under Conditions of Cultural Variation." *R.E.M.P. Bulletin, Supplement*. 14.

———. 1982. "The Future of the Hispanic Market: The Cuban Entrepreneur and the Economic Development of the Miami SMSA." Discussion Paper 6, International Banking Center, Florida International University.

Jorgensen, Joseph G. 1971. "Indians and the Metropolis." In J. O. Waddell and O. M. Watson, eds., *The American Indian in Urban Society*. Boston: Little, Brown.

———. 1978. "A Century of Political Economic Effects on American Indian Society, 1880–1980." *The Journal of Ethnic Studies*. 6.

Journal of Social Issues. 1973.

Kain, John F. 1968. "Housing Segregation, Negro Employment, and Metropolitan Decentralization." *Quarterly Journal of Economics*. 82.

———. 1974. "Housing Segregation, Black Employment, and Metropolitan Decentralization: A Retrospective View." In George M. von Furstenberg, ed.,

Patterns of Racial Discrimination. Lexington, MA: Lexington Books.

Kain, John F., and Quigley, J. M. 1975. *Housing Markets and Racial Discrimination: A Microeconomic Analysis*. New York: National Bureau of Economic Research.

Kallen, Horace. 1915. "Democracy *versus* the Melting Pot." *The Nation*. February 18–25.

———. 1924. *Culture and Democracy in the United States*. NY: Boni and Liveright.

Kallenberg, Arne L., and Sorenson, Aage B. 1979. "The Sociology of Labor Markets." *Annual Review of Sociology*. 5.

Kane, Jean Ellen. 1980. "Flemish and Walloon Nationalism: Devolution of a Previously Unitary State." In U. Ra'anan, ed., *Ethnic Resurgence in Modern Democratic States*. New York: Pergamon.

Karsh, Norman C. 1977. *What Is a Small Business?* Washington, DC: Small Business Administration.

Kasfir, Nelson. 1979. Explaining Ethnic Political Participation. *World Politics*.

Keely, Charles B. 1979. *U.S. Immigration: A Policy Analysis*. New York: The Population Council.

———. 1981. *Global Refugee Policy: The Case for a Development-Oriented Strategy*. New York: The Population Council.

Keil, Charles. 1966. *Urban Blues*. Chicago: University of Chicago Press.

Keil, H. 1983. "Chicago's German Working Class in 1900." In H. Keil and J. Jentz, eds., *German Workers in Industrial Chicago, 1850–1910*. De Kalb: Northern Illinois University Press.

Keil, H., and Jentz, J., eds. 1983. *German Workers in Industrial Chicago, 1850–1910*. De Kalb: Northern Illinois University Press.

Kennedy, Rose J. 1943. "Premarital Propinquity and Ethnic Endogamy." *American Journal of Sociology*. 48.

Kennedy, Ruby Jo Reeves. 1944. "Single or Triple Melting Pot? Intermarriage Trends in New Haven, 1870–1940." *American Journal of Sociology*. 49.

———. 1952. "Single or Triple Melting Pot? Intermarriage in New Haven, 1870–1950." *American Journal of Sociology*. 58.

Kessler-Harris, Alice, and Yans-McLaughlin, Virginia. 1978. "European Immigrant Groups." In Thomas Sowell, ed., *Essays and Data on American Ethnic Groups*. Washington, DC: Urban Institute.

Kessner, Thomas. 1977. *The Golden Door*. New York: Oxford University Press.

Kiernan, Ben. 1988. "Orphans of Genocide: The Cham Muslims of Kampuchea under Pol Pot." *Bulletin of Concerned Asian Scholars*. 20:4.

Kiljunen, Kimmo. 1985. "Power Politics and the Tragedy of Kampuchea during the Seventies." *Bulletin of Concerned Asian Scholars*. 17:2.

Killian, Lewis M. 1968. *The Impossible Revolution.* New York: Random House.

———. 1970. *White Southerners.* New York: Random House.

Kilson, Martin. 1975. *New States in the Modern World.* Cambridge, MA: Harvard University Press.

Kim, Hyung-Chan. 1977. "Ethnic Enterprises among Korean Immigrants in America." In Hyung-Chan Kim, ed., *The Korean Diaspora.* Santa Barbara, CA: ABC:CLIO.

———. 1989. *Asian-American Studies: An Annotated Bibliography and Research Guide.* Westport, CT: Greenwood Press.

Kim, Illsoo. 1981. *New Urban Immigrants: The Korean Community in New York.* Princeton, NJ: Princeton University Press.

———. 1988. "A New Theoretical Perspective on Asian Enterprises." *Amerasia Journal.* 14.

Kim, Warren Y. 1971. *Korean in America.* Seoul: Po Chin Chai Printing Company.

Kindleberger, C. P. 1967. *Europe's Postwar Growth: The Role of Labor Supply.* Cambridge, MA: Harvard University Press.

King, Martin Luther, Jr. 1964. *Why We Can't Wait.* New York: Harper and Row.

———. 1967. *Where Do We Go From Here? Chaos or Community.* New York: Harper and Row.

King, S. W. 1962. *Chinese in American Life.*

King, T. 1983. "Immigration from Developing Countries: Some Philosophical Issues." *Ethics.* 93.

Kinton, Jack. 1977. *American Ethnic Revival.* Aurora, IL: Social Service and Sociological Resources.

Kirk, G., and Kirk, C. 1978. "Immigrant Economic Opportunity and Type of Settlement in Nineteenth Century America." *Journal of Economic History.* 38.

Kirk-Green, A. H. M. 1971. *Crisis and Conflict in Nigeria,* Vols. I and II. London: Oxford University Press.

Kitano, Harry H. L. 1969/1976. *Japanese Americans: The Evolution of a Subculture.* Englewood Cliffs, NJ: Prentice-Hall.

———. 1974. "Japanese Americans: The Development of a Middleman Minority." *Pacific Historical Review.* 43.

Kitano, Harry, and Stanley, Sue. 1973. "The Model Minorities." *The Journal of Social Issues.* 29.

Klineberg, Otto. 1963. "Children's Readers: Life Is Fun in a Smiling, Fair-Skinned World." *Saturday Review.* February.

Kluegel, James R., and Smith, Eliot R. 1982. "Whites' Beliefs about Black Opportunity." *American Sociological Review.* 47.

Kobrin, Frances E., and Goldschneider, Calvin. 1978. *The Ethnic Factor in Family Structure and Mobility.* Cambridge, MA: Ballinger.

Korman, Gerd. 1967. *Industrialization, Immigrants, and Americanization: The View from Milwaukee, 1866–1921.* Madison, WI: State Historical Society.

Kunz, E. F. 1973. "The Refugee in Flight: Kinetic Models and Forms of Displacement." *International Migration Review.* 7.

Kuo, Wen H. 1981. "Colonized Status of Asian Americans." *Ethnic Groups.* 3.

Kuper, Leo, and Smith, M. G. 1969. *Pluralism in Africa.* Berkeley: University of California Press.

Lake, Robert W. 1981. *The New Suburbanites: Race and Housing in the Suburbs.* New Brunswick, NJ: Rutgers University Center for Urban Policy Research.

Landis, Joseph B. 1974. "Racial Polarization and Political Conflict in Guyana." In W. Bell and Walter R. Freeman, eds., *Ethnicity and Nation-Building: Comparative, International and Historical Perspectives.* Beverly Hills, CA: Sage.

Langberg, Mark. 1986. *Residential Segregation of Asians in the United States.* Ph.D. dissertation. Ann Arbor: University of Michigan.

Langberg, Mark, and Farley, Reynolds. 1985. "Residential Segregation of Asian Americans in 1980." *Sociology and Social Research.* 69.

Larrick, Nancy. 1965. "The All-White World of Children's Books." *Saturday Review.* September 11.

Lasker, Bruno. 1931. *Philipino Immigration to the United States and Hawaii.* Chicago: University of Chicago Press.

Lauwagie, B. 1979. "Ethnic Boundaries in Modern States." *American Journal of Sociology.* 85.

Layng, Anthony. 1985. "The Caribs of Dominica: Prospects for Structural Assimilation of a Territorial Minority." *Ethnic Groups.* 6.

Lazerwitz, B., and Rowitz, L. 1964. "The Three-Generation Hypothesis." *American Journal of Sociology.* 69.

Lee, Barrett A.; Spain, Daphne; and Umberson, Debra J. 1985. "Neighborhood Revitalization and Racial Change: The Case of Washington, D.C." *Demography* 22.

Lee, Everett S. 1966. "A Theory of Migration." *Demography.* 3.

Lee, Robert. 1952. "Acculturation of Chinese Americans." *Sociology and Social Research.* 36.

Lee, Rose Hum. 1960. *The Chinese in the United States of America.* Hong Kong: Hong Kong University Press.

Leff, Nathaniel. 1978. "Industrial Organization and Entrepreneurship in the Developing Countries: The Economic Groups." *Economic Development and Cultural Change.* 26.

Leggett, John C. 1968. *Class, Race, and Labor: Working Class Consciousness in Detroit.* New York: Oxford University Press.

Legum, Colin. 1967. "Color and Power in the South African Situation." *Daedalus.* 96:2.

Lemarchand, Rene. 1975. "Ethnic Genocide." *Society.* 12.

Lenin. V. I. 1939. *Imperialism: The Highest State of Capitalism.* New York: International Publishers.

——. 1968. *National Liberation, Socialism, and Imperialism: Selected Writings.* New York: International Publishers.

Lenski, Gerhard. 1961. *The Religious Factor.* Garden City, NY: Doubleday.

Leon, Abram. 1970. *The Jewish Question: A Marxist Interpretation.* New York: Pathfinder.

Levine, Barry. 1986. "In the Heat of Two Revolutions: The Forging of German-American Radicalism." In Dirk Hoerder, ed., *American Labor and Immigration History, 1877–1920s.* Urbana, IL: University of Illinois Press.

Levine, Barry, ed., 1976. *The Caribbean Exodus.* New York: Praeger.

——. 1987. "The Puerto Rican Exodus: Development of the Puerto Rican Circuit." In Barry Levine, ed., *The Caribbean Exodus.* New York: Praeger.

Levine, Gene N. 1989. "Review of *American Assimilation or Jewish Revival* by Steven M. Cohen." *Contemporary Sociology.* 18:5.

Levine, Gene N., and Montero, Darrel M. 1973. "Socioeconomic Mobility Among Three Generations of Japanese Americans." *Journal of Social Issues.* 29.

Levine, Lawrence W. 1977. *Black Culture and Black Consciousness.* New York: Oxford University Press.

Lewis, Oscar. 1966. *La Vida: A Puerto Rican Family in the Culture of Poverty.* New York: Random House.

Li, Peter S. 1977. "Ethnic Businesses among Chinese in the United States." *Journal of Ethnic Studies.* 4:3.

Liddle, R. William. 1970. *Ethnicity, Party, and National Integration.* New Haven, CT: Yale University Press.

Lieberson, Stanley. 1961. "A Societal Theory of Race and Ethnic Relations." *American Sociological Review.* 26.

——. 1963. *Ethnic Patterns in American Cities.* New York: Free Press.

——. 1973. "Generational Differences among Blacks in the North." *American Journal of Sociology.* 79.

——. 1975. "Rank Sum Comparisons between Groups." In David R. Heise, ed., *Sociological Methodology 1976.* San Francisco: Jossey-Bass.

——. 1980. *A Piece of the Pie: Blacks and White Immigrants since 1900.* Berkeley: University of California Press.

——. 1981. "An Asymmetrical Approach to Segregation." In Ceri Peach, Vaughn Robinson, and Susan Smith, eds., *Ethnic Segregation in Cities.* London: Croom-Helm.

*——. 1985. "A New Ethnic Group in the United States." In Norman R. Yetman, ed., *Majority and Minority: The Dynamics of Race and Ethnicity in American Life,* 4th ed. Boston: Allyn and Bacon.

Lieberson, Stanley, and Carter, Donna K. 1982a. "A Model for Inferring the Voluntary and Involuntary Causes of Residential Segregation." *Demography.* 19.

——. 1982b. "Temporal Changes and Urban Differences in Residential Segregation: A Reconsideration." *American Journal of Sociology.* 88.

Lieberson, Stanley; Dalto, Guy; and Johnston, Mary Ellen. 1975. "The Course of Mother-Tongue Diversity in Nations." *American Journal of Sociology.* 81.

Liebow, Elliot. 1967. *Tally's Corner.* Boston: Little, Brown.

Light, Ivan. 1972. *Ethnic Enterprise in America: Business and Welfare among Chinese, Japanese, and Blacks.* Berkeley: University of California Press.

——. 1977a. "The Ethnic Vice District, 1880–1944." *American Sociological Review.* 44.

——. 1977b. "Numbers Gambling: A Financial Institution." *American Sociological Review.* 43.

——. 1979. "Disadvantaged Minorities in Self-Employment." *International Journal of Comparative Sociology.* 20.

——. 1980. "Asian Enterprise in America." In Scott A. Cummings, ed., *Self-Help in Urban America.* Port Washington, NY: Kennikat.

*——. 1984. "Immigrant and Ethnic Enterprise in North America." *Ethnic and Racial Studies.* 7:2.

Light, Ivan, and Bonacich, Edna. 1988. *Immigrant Entrepreneurs: Koreans in Los Angeles, 1965–1982.* Berkeley: University of California Press.

Light, Ivan H., and Wong, Charles. 1975. "Protest or Work: Dilemmas of the Tourist Industry in American Chinatown." *American Journal of Sociology.* 80.

Lijphart, Arendt. 1977. *Democracy in Plural Societies.* New Haven, CT: Yale University Press.

Lincoln, C. Eric. 1961. *The Black Muslims in America.* Boston: Beacon.

Linz, J. 1975. "Totalitarian and Authoritarian Regimes." In Fred I. Greenstein and Nelson W. Polsby, eds., *Handbook of Political Science.* Reading, MA: Addison Wesley.

Lipset, Seymour Martin, and Bendix, Reinhard, eds. 1953/1966. "Social Mobility and Occupational Career Pattern." In *Class, Status, and Power.* Glencoe, IL: Free Press.

——. 1959. *Social Mobility in Industrial Society.* Berkeley and Los Angeles: University of California Press.

Lipset, Seymour M., and Rokkan, Stein. 1967. *Party Systems and Voter Alignments.* New York: Free Press.

Litwak, Leon. 1961. *North of Slavery: The Negro in the Free States, 1790–1860.* Chicago: University of Chicago Press.

Llanes, J. 1982. *Cuban-Americans, Masters of Survival.* Cambridge, MA: Abt.

Lodge, Henry Cabot. 1896. Speech in the United States Senate, *Congressional Record* 54th Congress, Second Session. March 16.

Loewen, James W. 1971. *The Mississippi Chinese: Between Black and White.* Cambridge, MA: Harvard University Press.

Logan, John R., and Schneider, Mark. 1984. "Racial Segregation and Racial Change in American Suburbs." *American Journal of Sociology.* 89.

Logan, John R., and Stearns, Linda B. 1981. "Suburban Racial Segregation as a Non-ecological Process." *Social Forces.* 60.

Lohman, J. D., and Reitzes, D. C. 1952. "Note on Race Relations in Mass Society." *American Journal of Sociology.* 58.

Long, Larry H. 1974. "Poverty Status and Receipt of Welfare among Migrants and Non-migrants in Large Cities." *American Sociological Review.* 39.

Lopez, Manuel Mariano. 1981. "Patterns of Interethnic Residential Segregation in the Urban Southwest." *Social Science Quarterly.* 62.

Lopreato, Joseph. 1970. *Italian Americans.* New York: Random House.

Louis, Kit K. 1932. "Program for Second-Generation Chinese." *Sociology and Social Research.* 16.

Lovell-Troy, Lawrence A. 1980. "Clan Structure and Economic Activity: The Case of Greeks in Small Business Enterprise." In Scott Cummings, ed., *Self-Help in Urban America.* Port Washington, NY: Kennikat Press.

_____. 1981. "Ethnic Occupational Structures: Greeks in the Pizza Business." *Ethnicity.* 8.

Lukes, Timothy J., and Okihiro, Gary Y. 1985. *Japanese Legacy: Farming and Community Life in California's Santa Clara Valley.* Cuperton, CA: California History Center.

*Lurie, Nancy Oestreich. 1965/1968. "The American Indian: Historical Background." In Stuart Levine and Nancy Lurie, eds., *The American Indian Today.* Deland FL: Everett/Edwards.

Lyman, Stanford M. 1968. "Contrasts in the Community Organization of Chinese and Japanese in North America." *Canadian Review of Sociology and Anthropology.* 5:2.

_____. 1968. "The Race Relations Cycle of Robert E. Park." *Pacific Sociological Review.* 11.

_____. 1973. *The Black American in Sociological Thought.* New York: Capricorn Books.

_____. 1974. *Chinese Americans.* New York: Random House.

Lynd, Robert S., & Lynd, Helen M. 1937. *Middletown in Transition.* New York: Harcourt Brace.

McCaffrey, L. 1985. "Ghetto to Suburbs: Irish Occupational and Social Mobility." In W. Van Horne, ed., *Ethnicity and the Work Force.* Madison, WI: University Wisconsin System.

McCarthy, John, and Zald, Mayer. 1973. *The Trend of Social Movements in America: Professionalization and Resource Mobilization.* Morristown, NJ: General Learning Press.

_____. 1977. "Resource Mobilization and Social Movements: A Partial Theory." *American Journal of Sociology.* 82.

McGouldrick, P., and Tannen, M. 1977. "Did American Manufacturers Discriminate against Immigrants before 1914?" *Journal Economic History.* 37.

McKenzie, R. D. 1928. *Oriental Exclusion.* University of Chicago Press.

McLemore, S. Dale. 1973. "The Origins of Mexican American Subordination in Texas." *Social Science Quarterly.* 53.

_____. 1983. *Racial and Ethnic Relations in America,* 2nd ed. Boston: Allyn and Bacon.

McMillan, Penelope. 1982. "Vietnamese Influx: It's Chinatown with Subtitles." *Los Angeles Times.* February 14.

McWilliams, Carey. 1944. *Prejudice: Japanese-Americans.* Boston: Little, Brown.

Magner, Denis K. 1989. "Blacks and Whites on Campuses: Behind Ugly Racist Incidents, Student Isolation and Insensitivity." *The Chronicle of Higher Education.* April 26.

Malcolm X. 1967. *Malcolm X on Afro-American History.* New York: Merit Publishers.

Mandel, Ernest. 1972. "Nationalism and the Class Struggle." *International Socialist Review.* 33.

Manley, Robert H. 1979. *Guyana Emergent.* Boston: Hall.

Marable, Manning. 1983. *How Capitalism Underdeveloped Black America: Problems in Race, Political Economy and Society.* Boston: South End.

Marrus, M. 1985. *The Unwanted: European Refugees in the Twentieth Century.* New York: Oxford University Press.

Marson, Wilfred G., and Van Valey, Thomas L. 1979. "The Role of Residential Segregation in the Assimilation Process." *The Annals of the American Academy of Political and Social Science.* 441.

Maruyama, Magoroh. 1973. "The Development of Ethnic Identifications among Third-Generation Japanese Americans." In Sallie TeSelle, ed., *The Discovery of Ethnicity.* New York: Harper Colophon Books.

Massarik, Fred. n.d. "Intermarriage: Factors for Planning." National Jewish Population Study. New York: Council of Jewish Federation and Welfare Funds.

Massey, Douglas S. 1979a. "Effects of Socio-economic Factors on the Residential Segregation of Blacks and Spanish Americans in the U.S. Urbanized Areas." *American Sociological Review.* 44.

_____. 1979b. "Residential Segregation of Spanish

Americans in United States Urbanized Areas." *Demography*. 16.

_____. 1981a. "Dimensions of the New Immigration to the United States and the Prospects for Assimilation." *Annual Review of Sociology*.

_____. 1981b. "Hispanic Residential Segregation: A Comparison of Mexicans, Cubans, and Puerto Ricans." *Sociology and Social Research*. 65.

_____. 1981c. "Social Class and Ethnic Segregation: A Reconsideration of Methods and Conclusions." *American Sociological Review*. 46.

_____. 1985. "Ethnic Residential Segregation: A Theoretical Synthesis and Empirical Review." *Sociology and Social Research*. 60.

_____. 1986a. "The Settlement Process among Mexican Immigrants to the United States." *American Sociological Review*. 51.

*_____. 1986b. "The Social Organization of Mexican Migration to the United States." *The Annals of the American Academy of Political and Social Science*. 487.

_____. 1987. "Understanding Mexican Migration to the United States." *American Journal of Sociology*. 92.

_____. 1990. "American Apartheid: Segregation and the Making of the Underclass." *American Journal of Sociology*. 96.

Massey, Douglas S.; Alarcon, Rafael; Durand, Jorge; and Gonzalez, Humberto. 1987. *Return to Aztlan: The Social Process of International Migration from Western Mexico*. Berkeley: University of California Press.

Massey, Douglas S., and Bitterman, Brooks. 1985. "Explaining the Paradox of Puerto Rican Segregation." *Social Forces*. 64.

Massey, Douglas S., and Blakeslee, Laura. 1983. "An Ecological Perspective on Assimilation and Stratification." Paper presented at the Annual Meetings of the American Sociological Association.

Massey, Douglas S.; Condran, Gretchen A.; and Denton, Nancy A. 1987. "The Effect of Residential Segregation on Black Social and Economic Well-Being." *Social Forces*. 66:1.

Massey, Douglas S., and Denton, Nancy A. 1985. "Spatial Assimilation as a Socioeconomic Outcome." *American Sociological Review*. 50.

_____. 1987a. "The Dimensions of Residential Segregation." Unpublished manuscript. Population Studies Center, University of Pennsylvania.

*_____. 1987b. "Trends in the Residential Segregation of Blacks, Hispanics, and Asians: 1970–1980." *American Sociological Review*. 52.

Massey, Douglas S., and Mullan, Brendan P. 1984. "Processes of Hispanic and Black Spatial Assimilation." *American Journal of Sociology*. 89:4.

_____. 1985. "Reply to Goldstein and White: *American Journal of Sociology*. 89.

Mathews, Fred H. 1964. "White Community and Yellow Peril." *Mississippi Valley Historical Review*. 50.

Mathews, Linda. 1987. "When Being Best Isn't Good Enough." *Los Angeles Times Magazine*. July 19.

Mayer, Egon. 1983. "Children of Intermarriage." New York: American Jewish Committee.

Mayhew, Leon. 1968. "Ascription in Modern Societies." *Sociological Inquiry*. 38.

Mazrui, Ali A. 1979. "Soldiers as Traditionalizers: Military Rule and the Re-Africanization of Africa." *World Politics*. January.

Means, Gordon P. 1976. *Malaysian Politics*. London: Hodder and Stoughton.

Mehrlaender, Ursula. 1980. "The 'Human Resource' Problem in Europe: Migrant Labor in the Federal Republic of Germany." In Uri Ra'anan, ed., *Ethnic Resurgence in Modern Democratic States*. New York: Pergamon.

Melendy, H. Brett. 1972. *The Oriental Americans*. New York: Hippocrene Books.

Melson, Robert, and Wolpe, Howard, eds. 1971. *Nigeria: Modernization and the Politics of Communalism* East Lansing, MI: Michigan State University Press.

Merton, Robert K. 1949. "Discrimination and the American Creed." In Robert MacIver, ed., *Discrimination and the National Welfare*. New York: Institute for Religious and Social Studies and Harper and Row.

Metzger, L. Paul. 1971. "American Sociology and Black Assimilation: Conflicting Perspectives." *American Journal of Sociology*. 76.

Meyer, Kurt, 1947. "Small Business as a Social Institution." *Social Research*. 14.

_____. 1953. "Business Enterprise: Traditional Symbol of Opportunity." *British Journal of Sociology*. 4.

Meyer, John W.; Boli-Bennett, John; and Chase-Dunn, Christopher. 1975. "Convergence and Divergence in Development." *Annual Review of Sociology*. 1.

Miller, Daniel R., and Swanson, Guy E. 1958. *The Changing American Parent*. New York: John Wiley.

Mills, C. Wright. 1951. *White Collar*. New York: Oxford University Press.

_____. 1956. *Power Elite*. New York: Oxford University Press.

_____. 1966. "The Middle Classes in Middle-Sized Cities." In Seymour Martin Lipset and Reinhard Bendix, eds., *Class, Status, and Power* 2nd ed. New York: Free Press.

Mills, C. Wright; Senior, Clarence; and Goldsen, Rose. 1950. *Puerto Rican Journey*. New York: Harper & Row.

Mindel, Charles H., and Habenstein, Robert W. 1976. *Ethnic Families in America: Patterns and Variations*. New York: Elsevier.

Mirandé, Alfredo. 1985. *The Chicano Experience, an Al-*

ternative Perspective. Notre Dame, IN: Notre Dame University Press.

Miyamoto, Samuel F. 1972. "An Immigrant Community in America." In Hilary Conroy and T. Scott Miyakawa, eds., *East across the Pacific.* Santa Barbara: CLIO Press.

Model, Suzanne. 1988a. "Italian and Jewish Intergenerational Mobility in 1910 New York." *Social Science History 11.* 12.

———. 1988b. "Mode of Job Entry and the Ethnic Composition of Firms: Early Twentieth Century Migrants to New York City." *Sociological Forum.*

*———. 1988. "The Economic Progress of European and East Asian Americans." *Annual Review of Sociology.* 14.

Modell, John, 1969. "Class or Ethnic Solidarity: The Japanese American Company Union." *Pacific Historical Review.* 38.

———. 1977. *The Economics and Politics of Racial Accommodation: The Japanese of Los Angeles, 1900–1942.* Urbana, IL: University of Illinois Press.

Montero, Darrel, 1981. "The Japanese Americans: Changing Patterns of Assimilation over Three Generations." *American Sociological Review.* 46.

Montero, Darrel, and Tsukashima, Ronald. 1977. "Assimilation and Educational Achievement: The Case of the Second-Generation Japanese American." *Sociological Quarterly.* 18.

Montgomery, D. 1986. "Nationalism, American Patriotism, and Class Consciousness among Immigrant Workers in the U.S. in the Epoch of World War I." In Dirk Hoerder, ed., *American Labor and Immigration History.* Urbana, IL: University of Illinois Press.

Moore, Barrington. 1966. *Social Origins of Dictatorship and Democracy: Lord and Peasant in the Making of the Modern World.* Boston: Beacon.

Moore, D. D. 1981. *At Home in America: Second Generation New York Jews.* New York: Columbia University Press.

Moore, Joan W. 1970. "Colonialism: The Case of the Mexican Americans." *Social Problems.* 17.

———. 1981. "Minorities in the American Class System." *Daedalus.* 110.

Moore, Joan, and Pachón, Henry. 1985. *Hispanics in the United States.* Englewood Cliffs, NJ: Prentice-Hall.

Morawska, Ewa. 1985. *For Bread with Butter.* New York: Cambridge University Press.

———. 1988a. "Labor Migrations in the World Systems." *Comparative Studies in Society and History.*

———. 1988b. "The Sociology and Historiography of Immigration." In *Myth, Reality and History: Interdisciplinary Perspectives on Immigration.* New York: Oxford University Press.

Morley, Charles. 1955. Translation of Henry Sienkie-

wicz's Report, "The Chinese in California." *California Historical Society Quarterly.* 34.

Morris, Aldon. 1984. *The Origins of the Civil Rights Movement.* New York: Free Press.

Moynihan, Daniel Patrick. 1966. "Employment, Income and the Ordeal of the Negro Family." In Talcott Parsons and Kenneth B. Clark, eds., *The Negro American.* Boston: Houghton Mifflin.

Muller, Thomas, and Espenshade, Thomas J. 1985. *The Fourth Wave: California's Newest Immigrants.* Washington, DC: The Urban Institute.

Murguía, E. 1975. *Assimilation, Colonialism, and the Mexican American People.* Austin: Center for Mexican-American Studies, University of Texas.

Murray, Charles. 1984. *Losing Ground: American Social Policy, 1950–1980.* New York: Basic.

Musolf, Lloyd D., and Springer, J. Frederick. 1979. *Malaysia's Parliamentary System: Representative Politics and Policy-Making in a Divided Society.* Boulder, CO: Westview Press.

Myrdal, Gunnar. 1944/1962. *An American Dilemma: The Negro Problem and Modern Democracy.* New York: Harper and Row.

Nafziger, W., and Richter, W. 1976. "Biafra and Bangladesh: The Political Economy of Secessionist Conflict." *Journal of Peace Research.* XIII.

Nagel, Joane. 1982. "Political Mobilization of Native Americans." *Social Science Journal.* 19.

*Nagel, Joane. 1986. "The Political Construction of Ethnicity." In Susan Olzak and Joane Nagel, eds., *Competitive Ethnic Relations.* Orlando, FL: Academic Press.

Nagel, Joane, and Olzak, Susan. 1982. "Ethnic Mobilization in New States and Old States: An Extension of the Competition Model." *Social Problems.* 30:2.

Nagel, Joane; Ward, Carol; and Knapp, Timothy. 1986. "The Politics of American Indian Economic Development: The Reservation/Urban Nexus." In Matthew Snipp, ed., *American Indian Economic Development: Policy Impacts and Unresolved Problems.* Albuquerque: University of New Mexico Press.

Nairn, Tom. 1975. "The Modern Janus." *New Left Review.*

Nash, Manning. 1962. "Race and the Ideology of Race." *Current Anthropology.* 3:3.

National Advisory Commission on Civil Disorders. 1968. *Report.* Washington, DC: Government Printing Office.

National Advisory Council on Indian Education. 1974. *First Annual Report.* Washington, DC: U.S. Government Printing Office.

National Research Council. 1985. *Immigration Statistics: A Story of Neglect. Report of the Panel on Immigration Statistics.* Washington, DC: National Academy of Sciences.

Navarro, Jovina. 1974. "The Plight of the Newly-Arrived Immigrants." In Jovina Navarro, ed., *Diwang Pilipino*. Davis, CA: University of California.

Nayar, Baldev Raj. 1966. *Politics in the Punjab*. New Haven, CT: Yale University Press.

Nazario, S. 1983. "After a Long Holdout, Cubans in Miami Take a Role in Politics." *Wall Street Journal*. June 7.

Neary, Ian J. 1986. "Socialist and Communist Party Attitudes toward Discrimination against Japan's *Burakumin*." *Political Studies*. 34.

Nee, Victor G., and Nee, Brett DeBary. 1972. *Longtime Californ': A Documentary Study of an American Chinatown*. Boston: Houghton Mifflin.

Nee, Victor, and Sanders, Jimy. 1985. "The Road to Parity: Determinants of the Socioeconomic Attainments of Asian Americans." *Ethnic and Racial Studies*. 8.

Nee, Victor, and Wong, Herbert Y. 1985. "Asian American Socioeconomic Achievement: The Strength of the Family Bond." *Sociological Perspectives*. 28.

Neidert, Lisa, and Farley, Reynolds. 1985. "Assimilation in the United States: An Analysis of Ethnic and Generation Differences in Status and Achievement." *American Sociological Review*. 50.

Neilsen, François. 1980. "The Flemish Movement in Belgium after World War II." *American Sociological Review*. 45.

Nelli, Humbert S. 1970. *The Italians in Chicago: 1880–1930*. New York: Oxford University Press.

_____. 1985. "The Economic Activities of Italian Americans." In W. Van Horne, ed., *Ethnicity and the Work Force*. Madison, WI: University Wisconsin System.

Nelson, Candace, and Tienda, Marta. 1985. "The Structuring of Hispanic Ethnicity: Historical and Contemporary Perspectives." *Ethnic and Racial Studies*. 8.

Nett, R. 1971. "The Civil Right We Are Not Ready For: The Right of Free Movement of People on the Face of the Earth." *Ethics*. 8.

Nettl, J. P. 1967. *Political Mobilization*. London: Faber and Faber.

Newcomer, Mabel. 1961. "The Little Businessman: A Study of Business Proprietors in Poughkeepsie, N.Y." *Business History Review* 35.

Newman, William M. 1973. *American Pluralism: A Study of Minority Groups and Social Theory*. New York: Harper and Row.

New York Times. 1990. "Mid and Low-Income Minorities on Decline on College Rolls." January 15.

Niebuhr, H. Richard. 1929. *The Social Sources of Denominationalism*. New York: Henry Holt.

*Noel, Donald L. 1968. "A Theory of the Origin of Ethnic Stratification." *Social Problems*. 16.

_____. 1972. *The Origins of American Slavery and Racism*. Columbus, OH: Charles E. Merrill.

Nomura, Gail M.; Endo, Russel; Sumida, Stephen H.; and Leong, Russell C., eds. 1989. *Frontiers of Asian American Studies*. Pullman: Washington State University Press.

North, David. 1974. *Immigrants and the American Labor Market*. Manpower Research Monograph No. 31. Department of Labor.

_____. 1985. "The Long Gray Welcome: A Study of the American Naturalization Program." Monograph of the National Association of Latin Elected Officials (Mimeo).

Norton, Robert. 1977. *Race and Politics in Fiji*. New York: St. Martin's Press.

Novak, Michael. 1971. *The Rise of the Unmeltable Ethnics*. New York: Macmillan.

_____. 1974. "The New Ethnicity." *The Center Magazine*. vii:4.

_____. 1975. "Black and White in Catholic Eyes." *New York Times Magazine*. November 16.

_____. 1978. *Novak Report on the New Ethnicity*. Washington, DC.

Oates, Stephen B. 1982. *Let the Trumpet Sound: The Life of Martin Luther King, Jr*. New York: Mentor Books.

Oberschall, Anthony. 1973. *Social Conflict and Social Movements*. Englewood Cliffs, NJ: Prentice-Hall.

O'Brien, William V. 1968. "International Crimes." In D. L. Sills, ed., *International Encyclopedia of the Social Sciences*. New York: Macmillan.

O'Connor, James. 1973. *The Fiscal Crisis of the State*. New York: St. Martin's Press.

Oestreicher, R. 1983. "Industrialization, Class, and Competing Cultural Systems: Detroit Workers, 1875–1900." In Keil & Jentz, ed. *German Workers in Industrial Chicago, 1850–1910*. De Kalb: Northern Illinois University Press.

Ogbu, John U. 1978. *Minority Education and Caste: The American System in Cross-Cultural Perspective*. New York: Academic Press.

Okihiro, Gary Y.; Hune, Shirley; Hansen, Arthur A.; and Liu, John M., eds. 1988. *Reflections on Shattered Windows*. Pullman: Washington State University Press.

Oliver, Melvin L., and Shapiro, Thomas M. 1989a. "Wealth of a Nation: A Reassessment of Asset Inequality in America." *American Journal of Economics and Sociology*. 48.

_____. 1989b. "Race and Wealth." *Review of Black Political Economy*. 17:4.

Olsen, Randall J. 1980. "A Least Squares Correction for Selectivity Bias." *Econometrica*. 48.

Olzak, Susan. 1982. "Ethnic Mobilization in Quebec." *Ethnic and Racial Studies*. July.

_____. 1987. "Ethnic Conflict and Protest in Urban America." *Social Science Research*. 16.

Olzak, Susan, and Nagel, Joane, eds. 1986. *Competitive Ethnic Relations.* Orlando, FL: Academic Press.

Oppenheimer, Martin. 1974. "The Sub-Proletariat: Dark Skins and Dirty Work." *Insurgent Sociologist.* 4.

Opperman, Hubert. 1966. "Australia's Immigration Policy." Paper delivered to the Youth and Student Seminar, Canberra, Australia, May 28.

Orfield, Gary, and Monfort, Franklin. 1988. "Racial Change and Desegregation in Large School Districts: Trends through the 1986–1987 School Year." Report of the Council of Urban Boards of Education and the National School Desegregation Project of the University of Chicago.

Orfield, Gary; Monfort, Franklin; and Aaron, Melissa. 1989. "Status of School Desegregation, 1968–1986." Report of the Council of Urban Boards of Education and the National School Desegregation Research Project of the University of Chicago.

Organization for Economic Co-operation and Development. 1979. *Migrations, Growth, and Development.* Paris: OECD.

Orsi, R. A. 1985. *The Madonna of 115th Street.* New Haven, CT: Yale University Press.

Paden, John. 1973. *Religion and Political Culture in Kano.* Berkeley: University of California Press.

Padilla, E. 1958. *Up from Puerto Rico.* New York: Columbia University Press.

Padilla, Feliz. 1986. "Latino Ethnicity in the City of Chicago." In Susan Olzak and Joane Nagel, eds., *Competitive Ethnic Relations.* Orlando, FL: Academic Press.

Paige, J. 1975. *Agrarian Revolution.* New York: Free Press.

Parenti, Michael. 1967. "Ethnic Politics and the Persistence of Ethnic Identification." *American Political Science Review.* 61.

Park, Robert E. 1928. "Human Migration and the Marginal Man." *American Journal of Sociology.* 33.

———. 1939. "The Nature of Race Relations." In E. T. Thompson, ed., *Race Relations and the Race Problem.* Durham, NC: Duke University Press.

———. 1950. *Race and Culture.* Glencoe, IL: Free Press.

Parker, S. 1976. "The Precultural Basis of the Incest Taboo." *American Anthropologist.* 73:2.

Parot, J. J. 1981. *Polish Catholics in Chicago, 1850–1920.* De Kalb: Northern Illinois University Press.

Parsons, Talcott. 1954. *Essays in Sociological Theory.* Glencoe, IL: Free Press.

———. 1957. "The Distribution of Power in American Society." *World Politics.* 10.

———. 1966. "Full Citizenship for the Negro American?" In Talcott Parsons and Kenneth B. Clark, eds., *The Negro American.* Boston: Houghton Mifflin.

Parsons, Talcott, and Shils, Edward A. 1954. *Toward a General Theory of Action.* Cambridge, MA: Harvard University Press.

Passel, Jeffrey S. 1985. "Undocumented Immigrants: How Many?" Presented at Annual Meeting of the American Statistical Association, Las Vegas.

Passel, Jeffrey S., and Woodrow, Karen A. 1984. "Geographic Distribution of Undocumented Immigrants: Estimates of Undocumented Aliens Counted in the 1980 Census by State." *International Migration Review.* 18.

Patterson, Orlando. 1977. *Ethnic Chauvinism: The Reactionary Impulse.* New York: Stein and Day.

Peach, Ceri. 1981. "Ethnic Segregation and Ethnic Intermarriage: A Reexamination of Kennedy's Triple Melting Pot in New Haven, 1900–1950." In Ceri Peach, ed., *Ethnic Segregation in Cities.* London: Croom-Helm.

Pear, Robert. 1984. "Cuban Aliens, but Not Haitians Will Be Offered Residency Status." *New York Times.* February 12.

Pearce, Diana M. 1979. "Gatekeepers and Homeseekers: Institutional Factors in Racial Steering." *Social Problems.* 26.

Pedraza-Bailey, Silvia. 1981. "Cubans and Mexicans in the United States: The Functions of Political and Economic Migration." *Cuban Studies.* 11.

———. 1985a. *Political and Economic Migrants in America: Cubans and Mexicans.* Austin: University of Texas Press.

———. 1985b. "Cuba's Exiles: Portrait of a Refugee Migration." *International Migration Review.* 19.

Penn, Steve. 1989. "Racial Incidents Reported on Rise in KC Area." *Kansas City Times.* March 6.

Pérez, Lisandro. 1986. "Immigrant Economic Adjustment and Family Organization: The Cuban Success Story Reexamined." *International Migration Review.* 20.

———. 1986. "Cubans in the United States." *The Annals of the American Academy of Political and Social Sciences.* 487.

Perlez, Jane. 1988. "Burundi's Army May Have Inflamed a Deadly Tribal Revenge Born in Fear." *New York Times.* August 29.

Pernia, Ernesto M. 1976. "The Question of the Brain Drain from the Philippines." *International Migration Review.* 10.

Pessar, P. R. 1982. "The Role of Households in International Migration and the Case of U.S.-Bound Migration from the Dominican Republic." *International Migration Review.* 16.

Petersen, M. F., and Maidique, M. A. 1986. *Success Patterns of the Leading Cuban-American Entrepre-*

neurs. Innovation and Entrepreneurship Institute, University of Miami. (Mimeo).

Petersen, William. 1966. "Success Story, Japanese-American Style." *New York Times Magazine.* January 9.

———. 1969. "The Classification of Subnations in Hawaii: An Essay in the Sociology of Knowledge." *American Sociological Review.* 34.

———. 1971. *Japanese Americans: Oppression and Success.* New York: Random House.

———. 1978. "Chinese Americans and Japanese Americans." In Thomas Sowell, ed., *Essays and Data on American Ethnic Groups.* Washington, DC: Urban Institute.

Petras, Elizabeth M. 1980a. "Toward a Theory of International Migration: The New Division of Labor." In R. S. Bryce-Laporte, ed., *Sourcebook on the New Immigration.* New Brunswick, NJ: Transaction Books.

———. 1980b. "The Role of National Boundaries in a Cross-National Labour Market," *International Journal of Urban and Regional Research.* 4.

Petra, James F. 1975. "Sociology of Development or Sociology of Exploitation?" Paper presented at the Meeting of the American Sociological Association.

Pettigrew, Thomas F. 1969. "Racially Separate or Together?" *Journal of Social Issues.* 25.

———. 1973. "Attitudes on Race and Housing: A Social Psychological View." In Amos H. Hawley and Vincent P. Rock, eds., *Segregation in Residential Areas.* Washington, DC: National Academy of Sciences.

———. 1979. "Racial Change and Social Policy." *The Annals of the American Academy of Political and Social Science.* 441.

Piore, Michael J. 1975. "Notes for a Theory of Labor Market Stratification." In Richard Edwards, Michael Reich, and David Gordon, eds., *Labor Market Segmentation.* Lexington, MA: D. C. Heath.

———. 1979. *Birds of Passage: Migrant Labor and Industrial Societies.* Cambridge: Cambridge University Press.

———. 1986. "The Shifting Grounds for Immigration." *Annals of the American Academy of Political and Social Science.* 485.

Pitt-Rivers, Julian. 1967. "Race, Color, and Class in Central America and the Andes." *Daedalus.* 92:2.

Piven, Frances F., and Cloward, Richard A. 1971. *Regulating the Poor.* New York: Pantheon.

Polenberg, Richard. 1980. *One Nation Divisible: Class, Race and Ethnicity in the United States since 1938.* New York: Viking.

Ponting, J. Rick, and Gibbons, Roger. 1980. *Out of Irrelevance.* Toronto: Butterworths.

Portes, Alejandro. 1976. "Determinants of the Brain Drain." *International Migration Review.* 10.

———. 1978. "Migration and Underdevelopment." *Politics and Society.* 8:1.

———. 1979. "Illegal Immigration and the International System, Lessons from Recent Legal Mexican Immigrants to the United States." *Social Problems.* 26.

———. 1981. "Modes of Structural Incorporation and Present Theories of Labor Immigration." In Mary M. Kritz and Charles B. Keely, eds., *Global Trends in Migration: Theory and Research on International Population Movements.* New York: Center for Migration Studies.

———. 1984. "The Rise of Ethnicity: Determinants of Ethnic Perceptions among Cuban Exiles in the United States." *American Sociological Review* 49.

Portes, Alejandro, and Bach, Robert L. 1980. "Immigrant Earnings: Cuban and Mexican Immigrants in the United States." *International Migration Review.* 14.

———. 1985. *Latin Journey, Cuban and Mexican Immigrants in the United States.* Berkeley: University of California Press.

Portes, Alejandro; Clark, Juan M.; and Bach, Robert L. 1977. "The New Wave: A Statistical Profile of Recent Cuban Exiles in the United States." *Cuban Studies.* 7.

Portes, Alejandro; Clark, Juan M.; and Lopez, Manuel M. 1981–82. "Six Years Later: The Process of Incorporation of Cuban Exiles in the United States: 1973–1979." *Cuban Studies.* 11–12.

Portes, Alejandro, and Curtis, J. 1986. "Changing Flags: Naturalization and Its Determinants among Mexican Immigrants." Unpublished Research Report. Program in Comparative International Development, Johns Hopkins University.

Portes, Alejandro, and Ferguson, D. Frances. 1977. "Comparative Ideologies of Poverty and Equity: Latin America and the United States." In Irving Louis Horowitz, ed., *Equity, Income, and Policy: Comparative Studies in Three Worlds of Development.* New York: Praeger.

Portes, Alejandro, and Jensen, Leif. 1989. "The Enclave and the Entrants: Effects of Ethnic Market Size and Isolated Labor Pool." *American Sociological Review.* 54.

*Portes, Alejandro, and Manning, Robert D. 1986. "The Immigrant Enclave: Theory and Empirical Examples." In Susan Olzak and Joane Nagel, eds., *Competitive Ethnic Relations.* New York: Academic Press.

Portes, Alejandro, and Mozo, Rafael. 1985. "The Political Adaptation Process of Cubans and Other Ethnic Minorities in the United States." *International Migration Review.* 19.

Portes, Alejandro, and Rumbaut, Ruben G. 1990. *Immigrant America: A Portrait.* Berkeley and Los Angeles: University of California Press.

Portes, Alejandro, and Stepick, Alex. 1985. "Unwelcome Immigrants: The Labor Market Experiences of 1980 (Mariel) Cuban and Haitian Refugees in South Florida." *American Sociological Review.* 50.

*Portes, Alejandro, and Truelove, Cynthia. 1987. "Making Sense of Diversity: Recent Research on Hispanic Minorities in the United States." *Annual Review of Sociology.* 13.

Portes, Alejandro, and Walton, John. 1981. *Labor, Class, and the International System.* Orlando, FL: Academic Press.

Portes, Alejandro, and Wilson, Kenneth L. 1976. "Black-White Differences in Educational Attainment." *American Sociological Review.* 41.

Prosen, Rose Mary. 1976. "Looking Back." In Michael Novak, ed., *Growing Up Slavic in America.* Bayville, NY: EMPAC.

Prosterman, R. L. 1976. "A Simplified Index of Rural Instability." *Comparative Politics.* 16.

Przeworski, A., and Wallerstein, M. 1982. "The Structure of Class Conflict in Democratic Capitalist Societies." *American Political Science Review.* 76:2.

Quality Education for Minorities Project. 1990. *Education That Works: An Action Plan for the Education of Minorities.* Cambridge, MA: Massachusetts Institute of Technology.

Ragin, C. 1979. "Ethnic Political Mobilization: The Welsh Case." *American Sociological Review.* 44.

Rainwater, Lee, and Yancey, William L. 1967. *The Moynihan Report and the Politics of Controversy.* Cambridge, MA: M.I.T. Press.

Ramirez, Anthony. 1980. "Cubans and Blacks in Miami." *Wall Street Journal,* May 29.

Ravenstein, E. G. 1889. "The Laws of Migration." *Journal of the Royal Statistical Society.* 52.

Rawick, George P. 1972. *From Sundown to Sunup: The Making of the Black Community.* Westport, CT: Greenwood Press.

Ray, Robert N. 1975. "A Report on Self-Employed Americans in 1973." *Monthly Labor Review.* 98.

Reich, Michael. 1971. "The Economics of Racism." In D. M. Gordon, ed., *Problems in Political Economy.* Lexington, MA: D. C. Heath.

———. 1981. *Racial Inequality.* Princeton, NJ: Princeton University Press.

Reichert, J. S. 1981. "The Migrant Syndrome: Seasonal U.S. Wage Labor and Rural Development in Central Mexico." *Human Organization.* 40.

Reichert, J. S. and Massey, D. S. 1979. "Patterns of U.S. Migration from a Mexican Sending Community: A Comparison of Legal and Illegal Migrants." *International Migration Review.* 13.

———. 1980. "History and Trends in U.S. Bound Migration from a Mexican Town." *International Migration Review.* 14.

Reimers, C. W. 1985. "A Comparative Analysis of the Wages of Hispanics, Blacks, and Non-Hispanic Whites." In George J. Borjas & Marta Tienda, eds., *Hispanics in the U.S. Economy.* Orlando, FL: Academic Press.

Reitz, Jeffrey G. 1980. *The Survival of Ethnic Groups.* Toronto: McGraw-Hill.

———. 1982. "Ethnic Group Control of Jobs." Paper presented at the Annual Meeting of the American Sociological Association, San Francisco, September 6.

Reports of the Immigration Commission, 41 vols. 1911/1970. Washington, DC: U.S. Government Printing Office. Reprinted by Arno Press, New York.

Reports of the Industrial Commission on Immigration, vol. 15. 1901. Washington, DC: U.S. Government Printing Office.

Research News. 1987. "The Costs of Being Black." 38.

Reubens, E. P. 1983. "International Migration Models and Policies." *American Economic Review.* 73.

Rex, John. 1970. *Race Relations in Sociological Theory.* New York: Schocken.

Riesman, David. 1950. *The Lonely Crowd: A Study of the Changing American Character.* New Haven, CT: Yale University Press.

Rinder, Irwin D. 1958–59. "Strangers in the Land: Social Relations in the Status Gap." *Social Problems.* 6.

Rischin, Moses. 1962. *The Promised City: New York Jews, 1870–1914.* Cambridge, MA: Harvard University Press.

Rist, Ray C. 1980. "Guestworkers and Post-World War II European Migrations." *Studies in Comparative International Development.* 14.

Robinson, Patricia. 1985. "Language Retention among Canadian Indians: A Simultaneous Equations Model with Dichotomous Endogenous Variable." *American Sociological Review.* 50.

Rodriguez, Richard. 1981. *Hunger of Memory.* New York: Godine.

Rogg, Eleanor. 1971. "The Influence of a Strong Refugee Community on the Economic Adjustment of Its Members." *International Migration Review.* 5.

Rogg, Eleanor, and Cooney, R. 1980. *Adaptation and Adjustment of Cubans: West New York.* New York: Fordham University Hispanic Research Center.

Rojo, Trinidad A. 1937. "Social Maladjustment among Pilipinos in the United States." *Sociology and Social Research.* 21.

Roof, Wade Clark. 1979a. "Race and Residence: The Shifting Basis of American Race Relations." *The Annals of the American Academy of Political and Social Science.* 441.

———. 1979b. "Socioeconomic Differentials among White Socioreligious Groups in the U.S." *Social Forces.* 58.

_____. 1981. "Unresolved Issues in the Study of Religion and the National Elite: Response to Greeley." *Social Forces.* 59.

Roof, Wade C.; Van Valey, Thomas L.; and Spain, Daphne. 1976. "Residential Segregation in Southern Cities: 1970." *Social Forces.* 55.

Roos, P., and Hennessy, J. 1987. "Assimilation or Exclusion? Japanese and Mexican Americans in California." *Sociological Forum* 2.

Rose, Harold. 1976. *Black Suburbanization.* Cambridge, MA: Harvard University Press.

Rose, Jerry D. 1976. *Peoples: The Ethnic Dimension in Human Relations.* Chicago: Rand McNally.

Rosen, Bernard C. 1959. "Race, Ethnicity, and the Achievement Syndrome." *American Sociological Review.* 24.

Rosenblum, Gerald. 1973. *Immigrant Workers: Their Impact on American Labor Radicalism.* New York: Basic Books.

Rosenthal, Erich. 1975. "The Equivalence of United States Census Data for Persons of Russian Stock or Descent with American Jews: An Evaluation." *Demography.* 12.

Rothschild, Joseph. 1981. *Ethnopolitics.* New York: Columbia University Press.

Roucek, Joseph S. 1969. "The Image of the Slav in U.S. History and in Immigration Policy." *American Journal of Economics and Sociology.* 28.

Roy, Prodipto. 1972. "The Measurement of Assimilation: The Spokane Indians." In Howard M. Bahr, Bruce A. Chadwick, and Robert C. Day, eds., *Native Americans Today: Sociological Perspectives.* New York: Harper and Row.

Roybal, E. R. 1984. "Welcome Statement." In *Proceedings of the First National Conference on Citizenship and the Hispanic Community.* Washington, DC: National Association of Latin Elected Officials.

Rubinow, Israel. 1907. "The Economic Condition of Jews in Russia." *Bulletin of the Bureau of Labor.* 72. Washington, DC: U.S. Government Printing Office.

Rudolph, Lloyd, and Rudolph, Susanne. 1967. *The Modernity of Tradition: Political Development in India.* Chicago: University of Chicago Press.

Ruhlen, Merritt. 1987. "The First Americans: Voices From the Past." *Natural History.* 96.

Russell, Raymond. 1982. "Ethnic and Occupational Cultures in the New Taxi Cooperatives of Los Angeles." Paper presented at the Annual Meeting of the American Sociological Association, San Francisco, September 6.

Ryan, William. 1971. *Blaming the Victim.* New York: Pantheon Books.

Ryder, Norman B. 1955. "The Interpretation of Origin Statistics." *Canadian Journal of Economics and Political Science.* 21.

Samora, Julian. 1971. *Los Mojados: The Wetback Story.* Notre Dame, IN: University of Notre Dame Press.

Sánchez-Korrol, V. 1983. *From Colonia to Community.* Westport, CT: Greenwood.

Sandberg, Neil C. 1974. *Ethnic Identity and Assimilation: The Polish American Community.* New York: Praeger.

Sanders, Jimy M. and Nee, Victor. 1987. "Limits of Ethnic Solidarity in the Ethnic Enclave." *American Sociological Review.* 52:6.

Sandmeyer, Elmer C. 1939. *The Anti-Chinese Movement in California.* Urbana: University of Illinois Press.

Saniel, Joseph, ed. 1967. *The Filipino Exclusion Movement, 1929–1935.* Quecon City: Institute of Asian Studies.

Sanjian, Avedis K. 1965. *The Armenian Communities in Syria under Ottoman Dominion.* Cambridge, MA: Harvard University Press.

Santibanez, Enrique. 1930. *Ensayo Acerca de la Immigracion Mexicana a Estados Unidos.* San Antonio, TX: The Clegg Co.

Sassen-Koob, Saskia. 1979. "Formal and Informal Associations: Dominicans and Colombians in New York." *International Migration Review.* 13.

_____. 1980. "Immigrant and Minority Workers in the Organization of the Labor Process." *Journal of Ethnic Studies.* 1.

_____. 1981. "Exporting Capital and Importing Labor: The Role of Caribbean Migration to New York City." New York: Center for Latin American and Caribbean Studies, Occasional Papers No. 28, New York University.

_____. 1984. "Notes on the Incorporation of Third World Women into Wage Labor through Immigration and Off-Shore Production." *International Migration Review.* 18.

Saul, John S. 1979. "The Dialectic of Class and Tribe." *Race and Class.* 20.

Saveth, Edward N. 1948. *American Historians and European Immigrants.* New York: Columbia University Press.

Saxon, Alexander. 1971. *The Indispensable Enemy: Labor and the Anti-Chinese Movement in California.* Berkeley: University of California Press.

Schermerhorn, Richard A. 1970. *Comparative Ethnic Relations: A Framework for Theory and Research.* New York: Random House.

_____. 1974. "Ethnicity in the Perspective of Sociology of Knowledge." *Ethnicity.* 1.

_____. 1978. *Ethnic Plurality in India.* Tucson: University of Arizona Press.

Schlesinger, Arthur M. 1921. "The Significance of Immigration in American History." *American Journal of Sociology.* 27.

Schmid, Calvin F., and Nobbe, Charles E. 1965. "Socioeconomic Differentials among Non-white Races." *American Sociological Review.* 30.

Schmitt, Robert C. 1968. *Demographic Statistics of Hawaii: 1778–1965.* Honolulu: University of Hawaii Press.

Schneider, Mark, and Logan, John R. 1982. "Suburban Racial Segregation and Black Access to Local Public Resources." *Social Science Quarterly.* 63.

Schooler, Carmi. 1976. "Serfdom's Legacy: An Ethnic Continuum." *American Journal of Sociology.* 81.

Schuman, Howard. 1969. "Sociological Racism." *Transaction.* 7.

Schuman, Howard; Steeh, Charlotte; and Bobo, Lawrence. 1985. *Racial Attitudes in America: Trends and Interpretations.* Cambridge, MA: Harvard University Press.

Schumpeter, Joseph. 1934. *The Theory of Economic Development,* trans. Redvers Opie. Cambridge, MA: Harvard University Press.

Schwartz, Audrey James. 1970. *Traditional Values and Contemporary Achievement of Japanese American Pupils.* California Center for the Study of Evaluation.

———. 1971. "The Culturally Advantaged: A Study of Japanese-American Pupils." *Sociology and Social Research.* 55.

Scott, J. C. 1985. *Weapons of the Weak: Everyday Forms of Peasant Resistance.* New Haven, CT: Yale University Press.

———. 1987. "Resistance without Protest and without Organization." *Comparative Studies in Society and History.* 29.

Seller, Maxine. 1977. *To Seek America: A History of Ethnic Life in the United States.* Englewood, NJ: Jerome S. Ozer.

Sengstock, Mary Catherine. 1967. "Maintenance of Social Interaction Patterns in an Ethnic Group." Ph.D. dissertation, Washington University.

Sewell, William H., and Hauser, Robert M. 1975. *Education, Occupation, and Earnings: Achievement in the Early Career.* New York: Academic Press.

Sharma, Miriam. 1984. "The Philippines: A Case of Migration to Hawaii, 1906 to 1946." In Lucie Cheng and Edna Bonacich, eds., *Labor Immigration under Capitalism: Asian Workers in the United States before World War II.* Berkeley: University of California Press.

Sharpless, J., and Rury, J. 1980. "The Political Economy of Women's Work, 1900–1920." *Social Science History.* 4.

Sheatsley, Paul B. 1966. "White Attitudes toward the Negro." In Talcott Parsons and Kenneth B. Clark, eds., *The Negro American.* Boston: Houghton Mifflin.

Shue, H. 1980. *Basic Rights: Subsistence, Affluence and U.S. Foreign Policy.* Princeton: Princeton University Press.

Sidell, Scott. 1981. "The United States and Genocide in East Timor." *Journal of Contemporary Asia.* 11:1.

Simkus, Albert A. 1978. "Residential Segregation by Occupation and Race in Ten Urbanized Areas, 1950–1970." *American Sociological Review.* 43.

Simon, Julian L. 1989. *The Economic Consequences of Immigration.* Cambridge, MA: Basil Blackwell.

Simpson, George E., and Yinger, J. Milton. 1954/1972/1985. *Racial and Cultural Minorities: An Analysis of Prejudice and Discrimination,* 4th ed. New York: Harper and Row.

Singer, Lester. 1962. "Ethnogenesis and Negro Americans Today." *Social Research.* 29.

Sitkoff, Harvard. 1981. *The Struggle for Black Equality: 1945–1980.* New York: Hill and Wang.

Siu, Paul. 1962. "The Sojourner." *American Journal of Sociology.* 8.

Sklair, Leslie. 1989. *Assembling for Development: The Maquila Industry in Mexico and the United States.* Boston: Unwin Hyman.

Sklar, Richard. 1963. *Nigerian Political Parties.* Princeton, NJ: Princeton University Press.

Sklar, Richard, and Whitaker, C. S., Jr. 1964. "Nigeria." In James S. Coleman and Carl G. Rosberg, eds., *Political Parties and National Integration in Tropical Africa.* Berkeley: University of California Press.

Skocpol, Theda. 1979. *States and Social Revolutions: A Comparative Analysis of France, Russia, and China.* Cambridge: Cambridge University Press.

———. 1982. "What Makes Peasants Revolutionary?" *Comparative Politics.*

Skolnick, Jerome. 1969. *The Politics of Protest: A Staff Report to the National Commission on the Causes and Prevention of Violence.* Washington, DC: U.S. Government Printing Office.

Slavin, S. L., and Pradt, M. A. 1982. *The Einstein Syndrome.* Lanham, MD: University Press of America.

Smiley, Donald V. 1977. "French-English Relations in Canada and Consociational Democracy." In Milton J. Esman, ed., *Ethnic Conflict in the Western World.* Ithaca, NY: Cornell University Press.

Smith, J. 1985. *Family Connections.* Albany, NY: SUNY Press.

Smith, Michael G. 1965. *The Plural Society in the British West Indies.* Berkeley: University of California Press.

Smith, R. T. 1970–1971. "Race and Political Conflict in Guyana." *Race.* 12.

Smith, William C. 1925. "The Second Generation Oriental American." *Journal of Applied Sociology.* 10.

———. 1936. *American in Process.* Ann Arbor: Edwards Brothers.

Smitherman-Donaldson, Geneva, and Van Dijk, Teun A. 1988. *Discourse and Discrimination.* Detroit: Wayne State University Press.

*Snipp, C. Matthew. 1986. "American Indians and Natural Resource Development." *American Journal of Economics and Sociology.* 45.

Solomon, Barbara. 1956/1965. *Ancestors and Immigrants.* New York: Wiley.

Sombart, Werner. 1914/1951. *The Jews and Modern Capitalism.* Glencoe, IL: The Free Press.

Sommers, Vita S. 1960. "Identity Conflict and Acculturation Problems in Oriental-Americans." *American Journal of Orthopsychiatry.* 30.

Sorensen, Annemette; Taeuber, Karl E.; and Hollingsworth, L. J., Jr. 1975. "Indexes of Residential Segregation for 109 Cities in the United States: 1940–1970." *Sociological Focus.* 8.

Southern Poverty Law Center. 1987. " 'Move-In' Violence: White Resistance to Neighborhood Integration in the 1980s." Montgomery, AL: Southern Poverty Law Center.

Sowell, Thomas. 1978. *Essays and Data on American Ethnic Groups.* Washington, DC: Urban Institute.

_____. 1980. *Ethnic America: A History.* New York: Basic Books.

_____. 1981. *Markets and Minorities.* New York: Basic Books.

Spain, Daphne, and Long, Larry H. 1981. *Black Movers to the Suburbs: Are They Moving to Predominantly White Suburbs?* Washington, DC: U.S. Bureau of the Census, Special Demographic Analysis.

Spear, H. 1961. "Marcus Lee Hansen and the Historiography of Immigration." *Wisconsin Magazine of History.* Summer.

_____. 1969. *A Short History of the Indians of the United States.* New York: Van Nostrand Reinhold.

Special Task Force to the Secretary of Health, Education, and Welfare. 1973. *Work in America.* Cambridge, MA: MIT Press.

Stampp, Kenneth M. 1956. *The Peculiar Institution: Slavery in the Ante-Bellum South.* New York: Random House.

Stampp, Kenneth M., et al. 1968. "The Negro in American History Textbooks." *Negro History Bulletin.* 31.

Stearns, Linda B., and Logan, John R. 1986. "Measuring Trends in Segregation: Three Dimensions, Three Measures." *Urban Affairs Quarterly.* 22.

Steinberg, Stephen. 1974. *The Academic Melting Pot: Catholics and Jews in American Higher Education.* New York: McGraw-Hill.

*_____. 1981/1989. *The Ethnic Myth: Race, Ethnicity, and Class in America.* New York: Atheneum.

_____. 1989. *The Ethnic Myth: Race, Ethnicity and Class in America.* Boston: Beacon Press.

Stephenson, George M. 1926. *A History of American Immigration, 1820–1924.* Boston: Ginn.

Stevens, Rosemary; Goodman, Louis W.; and Mick, Stephen S. 1978. *The Alien Doctors: Foreign Medical Graduates in American Hospitals.* New York: Wiley.

Stewart, Omer C. 1972. "The Native American Church and the Law." In Deward E. Walker, ed., *The Emergent Native Americans.* Boston: Little, Brown.

Stinchcombe, Arthur. 1975. "Social Structure and Politics." In Fred I. Greenstein and Nelson W. Polsby, eds., *Handbook of Political Science.* Reading, MA: Addison Wesley.

Stocking, George W. 1968. *Race, Culture, and Evolution: Essays in the History of Anthropology.* New York: Free Press.

Stolarik, Mark. 1985. *Growing Up on the South Side.* Lewisburg, PA: Bucknell University Press.

Stolzenberg, R. M. 1982. "Occupational Differences between Hispanics and Non-Hispanics." Report of the National Commission Employment Policy. Santa Monica, CA: Rand.

Stonequist, E. V. 1935. "The Problem of the Marginal Man." *American Journal of Sociology.* 41.

_____. 1937. *The Marginal Man.* New York: Charles Scribner's Sons.

Straszheim, M. 1980. "Discrimination and the Spatial Characteristics of the Urban Labor Market." *Journal of Urban Economics.* 7.

Strodtbeck, Fred L. 1958. "Family Interaction, Values and Achievement." In Marshall Sklare, ed., *The Jews: Social Patterns in An American Group.* New York: Free Press.

Strong, Edward K. 1934/1970. *The Second Generation Japanese Problem.* New York: Arno Press.

Stryker, Robin. 1984. "Religio-Ethnic Effects on Attainment in the Early Career." *American Sociological Review.* 46.

Sue, Derald Wing. 1973. "Ethnic Identity: The Impact of Two Cultures on the Psychological Development of Asians in America." In Stanley Sue and Nathaniel N. Wagner, eds., *Asian-Americans: Psychological Perspectives.* Ben Lomond, CA: Science and Behavior Books.

Sue, Stanley, and Sue, Derald W. 1971. "Chinese-American Personality and Mental Health." *Amerasia Journal.* 1:2.

Suhrbur, T. 1983. "Ethnicity in the Formation of the Chicago Carpenters' Union: 1855–1890." In H. Keil and J. Jentz, eds., *German Workers in Industrial Chicago, 1850–1910.* De Kalb, Northern Illinois University.

Sung, Betty Lee. 1967. *Mountain of Gold: The Story of the Chinese in America.* New York: Macmillan.

Suttles, Gerald D. 1968. *The Social Order of the Slum.* Chicago: University of Chicago Press.

Suzuki, Bob H. 1977. "Education and the Socialization of Asian Americans: A Revisionist Analysis of the 'Model Minority' Thesis." *Amerasia Journal.* 4:2.

Sway, Marlene. 1983. "Gypsies as a Middleman Minority." Ph.D. dissertation, University of California, Los Angeles.

Swinton, David H. 1990. "The Economic Status of Black Americans during the 1980s: A Decade of Limited Progress." *The State of Black America.* New York: National Urban League.

Szymanski, Albert. 1976. "Racial Discrimination and White Gain." *American Sociological Review.* 41.

Tabb, William. 1970. *The Political Economy of the Black Ghetto.* New York: Norton.

Taeuber, Karl. 1983. "Racial Residential Segregation, 28 Cities, 1970–1980." *CDE Working Paper 83–12,* University of Wisconsin, Madison.

———. 1990. "Race and Residence, 1619 to 2019." In Winston A. Van Horne and T. V. Tonnesen, eds., *Race: Twentieth Century Dilemmas—Twentieth-First Century Prognoses.* Milwaukee: University of Wisconsin Institute on Race and Ethnicity.

Taeuber, Karl E., and Taeuber, Alma F. 1965. *Negroes in Cities.* Chicago: Aldine.

Takaki, Ronald. 1989. *Strangers from a Different Shore: A History of Asian Americans.* Boston: Little, Brown.

Tapinos, G. 1974. *L'economie des Migrations Internationales.* Paris: Armand Colin.

Task Force on the Administration of Military Justice in the Armed Forces. 1972. *Report.* Washington, DC: U.S. Government Printing Office.

Taylor, D. Garth; Sheatsley, Paul B.; and Greeley, Andrew M. 1978. "Attitudes toward Racial Integration." *Scientific American.* 238.

Taylor, Philip. 1971. *The Distant Magnet: European Emigration to the U.S.A.* New York: Harper and Row.

Teague, Bob. 1968. "Charlie Doesn't Even Know His Daily Racism Is a Sick Joke." *New York Times Magazine.* September 15.

tenBroek, Jacobus, *et al.* 1954. *Prejudice, War and the Constitution.* Berkeley, University of California Press.

Tenenbaum, S. 1986. "Immigrants and Capital: Jewish Loan Societies in the U.S., 1890–1945." *American Jewish History.* 76.

Tentler, L. 1979. *Wage Earning Women: Industrial Work and Family Life in the U.S., 1900–1930.* New York: Oxford University Press.

Thernstrom, Stephan. 1973. *The Other Bostonians: Poverty and Progress in the American Metropolis, 1880–1970.* Cambridge, MA: Harvard University Press.

———, ed. 1980. *Harvard Encyclopedia of American Ethnic Groups.* Cambridge, MA: Harvard University Press.

Thomas, Dorothy Swaine, and Nishimoto, Richard S. 1969. *The Spoilage: Japanese American Evacuation and Resettlement.* Berkeley: University of California Press.

Thomas, Robert K. 1968. "Pan-Indianism." In Stuart Levine and Nancy O. Lurie, eds., *The American Indian Today.* Deland, FL: Everett/Edwards.

Thomas, John F., and Huyck, Earl E. 1967. "Resettlement of Cuban Refugees in the United States." Paper presented at the Meetings of the American Sociological Association. San Francisco.

Thompson, Richard H. 1979. "Ethnicity vs. Class: Analysis of Conflict in a North American Chinese Community." *Ethnicity* 6.

Thornton, Russell. 1987. *American Indian Holocaust and Survival.* Norman, OK: University of Oklahoma Press.

Tienda, Marta, and Jensen, Leif. 1985. "Immigration and Public Assistance Participation: Dispelling the Myth of Dependency." Discussion Paper #777–85. Institute for Research into Poverty, University of Wisconsin-Madison (Mimeo).

Tienda, Marta, and Lee, D. T. 1986. "Migration, Market Insertion, and Earnings Determination of Mexicans, Puerto Ricans, and Cubans." Presented at the Annual Meeting of the American Sociological Association, New York.

Tilly, Charles. 1975a. "Revolutions and Collective Violence." In Fred I. Greenstein and Nelson W. Polsby, eds., *Handbook of Political Science.* Reading, MA: Addison-Wesley.

———, ed. 1975b. *The Formation of National States in Europe.* Princeton, NJ: Princeton University Press.

———, ed. 1978. *From Mobilization to Revolution.* Reading, MA: Addison-Wesley.

Tilly, Louise. 1974. "Comments on the Yans-McLaughlin and Davidoff Papers." *Journal of Social History.* 7.

Time. 1975. "America's Rising Black Middle Class." June 17.

———. 1978. "Hispanic Americans Soon the Biggest Minority." *Special Report.* October 16.

———. 1987. "Racism on the Rise." February 2.

Tinker, John N. 1973. "Intermarriage and Ethnic Boundaries: The Japanese American Case." *Journal of Social Issues.* 29:2.

Toll, William. 1982. *The Making of an Ethnic Middle Class: Portland Jewry over Four Generations.* Albany, NY: SUNY Press.

Tow, J. S. 1923. *The Real Chinese in America.* New York: The Academy Press.

Treiman, David. 1977. *Occupational Status in Comparative Perspective.* New York: Academic.

Trillin, Calvin. 1986. "Black or White." *The New Yorker.* 62.

Tucker, M. Belinda and Mitchell-Kernan, Claudia. 1990. "New Trends in Black American Interracial Marriage: The Social Structural Context." *Journal of Marriage and the Family.* 52.

Tumin, Melvin M. 1969. *Comparative Perspectives on Race Relations.* Boston: Little, Brown.

Turner, Frederick Jackson. 1894/1966. "The Significance of the Frontier in American history." In Ray Allen Billington, ed., *The Frontier Thesis: Valid Interpretation of American History?* New York: Holt, Rinehart, and Winston.

Turner, Jonathan H., and Bonacich, Edna. 1980. "Toward a Composite Theory of Middleman Minorities." *Ethnicity* 7.

Turner, Jonathan H.; Singleton, Royce, Jr., and Musick, David. 1984. *Oppression: A Social-History of Black Relations in America.* Chicago: Nelson-Hall.

Tuttle, William M., Jr. 1972. *Race Riot: Chicago in the Red Summer of 1919.* New York: Atheneum.

Uhlenberg, Peter. 1972. "Demographic Correlates of Group Achievement: Contrasting Patterns of Mexican-Americans and Japanese-Americans." *Demography.* 9.

United Nations. 1974. "Report on the World Social Situation – Social Trends in the Developing Countries, Latin America and the Caribbean." U.N. Document E/CN.5/512/Add. 1.

United Nations Department of International Economic and Social Affairs. 1989. *World Population Trends and Policies: 1988 Monitoring Report.* ST/ESA/SER. A/103. New York: United Nations.

United States Committee for Refugees. 1989. *World Refugee Survey: 1988 in Review.* Washington, DC: American Council on Nationalities Service.

U.S. Bureau of the Census. 1904. *Special Reports: Occupations at the Twelfth Census.* Washington, DC: U.S. Government Printing Office.

_____. 1922. *Fourteenth Census of the United States Taken in the Year 1920. Volume II. Population, 1920. General Report and Analytical Tables.* Washington, DC: U.S. Government Printing Office.

_____. 1923. *Fourteenth Census of the United States Taken in the Year 1920. Volume IV. Population, 1920. Occupations. Washington, DC: U.S. Government Printing Office.*

_____. 1933a. *Fifteenth Census of the United States: 1930. Population. Volume II. General Report. Statistics by Subjects.* Washington, DC: U.S. Government Printing Office.

_____. 1933b. *Fifteenth Census of the United States: 1930. Population. Volume V. General Report on Occupations.* Washington, DC: U.S. Government Printing Office.

_____. 1943a. *Sixteenth Census of the United States: 1940. Population. Second Series. Characteristics of the Population. U.S. Summary.* Washington, DC: U.S. Government Printing Office.

_____. 1943b. *Sixteenth Census of the United States: 1940. Population. Comparative Occupation Statistics for the United States, 1870 to 1940.* Washington, DC: U.S. Government Printing Office.

_____. 1943c. *Sixteenth Census of the United States: 1940. Population. The Labor Force: Occupational Characteristics.* Washington, DC: U.S. Government Printing Office.

_____. 1943d. *Sixteenth Census of the United States: 1940. Population. Characteristics of the Nonwhite Population by Race.* Washington, DC: U.S. Government Printing Office.

_____. 1953. *U.S. Census of the Population: 1950. Special Reports, Nonwhite Population by Race.* Washington, DC: U.S. Government Printing Office.

_____. 1963a. *U.S. Census of the Population: 1960. Characteristics of the Population. Part 1. U.S. Summary.* Washington, DC: U.S. Government Printing Office.

_____. 1963b. *U.S. Census of the Population: 1960. Subject Reports. Nonwhite Population by Race. Final Report IC(2)-1C.* Washington, DC: U.S. Government Printing Office.

_____. 1963c. *U.S. Census of the Population: 1960. Subject Reports. Nonwhite Population by Race.* Washington, DC: U.S. Government Printing Office.

_____. 1969. *Statistical Abstract of the United States,* 90th ed. Washington, DC: U.S. Government Printing Office.

_____. 1970a. *1970 Census Users Guide, Part I.* Washington, DC: U.S. Government Printing Office.

_____. 1970b. *Census of Population and Housing 1970, Fourth Count Summary Tape File A.* [MRDF] NPDC ed. Washington, DC: U.S. Bureau of the Census [producer]. Ithaca, NY: National Planning Data Corporation (NPDC) [distributor].

_____. 1971. *One in a 100: A Public Sample of Basic Records from the 1960 Census: Description and Technical Documentation.* Washington, DC: U.S. Government Printing Office.

_____. 1973a. *U.S. Census of the Population: 1970. Characteristics of the Population.* Vol. 1, Part I. U.S. Summary Section 2. Washington, DC: U.S. Government Printing Office.

_____. 1973b. *U.S. Census of the Population: 1970. Subject Reports PC(2)-1G: Japanese, Chinese, Filipinos.* Washington, DC: U.S. Government Printing Office.

_____. 1975. *Historical Statistics of the United States.* Washington, DC: U.S. Government Printing Office.

_____. 1979. *The Social and Economic Status of the Black Population in the United States: An Historical View, 1790–1978.* Series P-23 (80). Washington, DC: U.S. Government Printing Office.

_____. 1980. *Census of Population and Housing 1980, Summary Tape File 4A.* [MRDF] NPDC ed. Washington, DC: U.S. Bureau of the Census [producer].

567

Ithaca, NY: National Planning Data Corporation (NPDC) [distributor].

_____. 1981. *U.S. Census of the Population: 1980. Supplementary Report PC80-S1-3: Race of the Population by States.* Washington, DC: U.S. Government Printing Office.

_____. 1982a. *1980 Census of Housing and Population Users' Guide, Part A. Text.* Washington, DC: U.S. Government Printing Office.

_____. 1982b. *Current Population Reports.* Series P-23. No. 116. Washington, DC: U.S. Government Printing Office.

_____. 1982c. *Statistical Abstract of the United States: 1982–83.* Washington, DC: U.S. Government Printing Office.

_____. 1983a. *1980 Census of the Population. Volume I. Characteristics of the Population. General Social and Economic Characteristics. U.S. Summary.* Washington, DC: U.S. Government Printing Office.

_____. 1983b. *U.S. Census of the Population: 1980. Characteristics of the Population. General Social and Economic Characteristics. Hawaii.* PC80-1-C13. Washington, DC: U.S. Government Printing Office.

U.S. Bureau of the Census. 1983c. *Condition of Hispanics in America Today.* Special Release. Sept. 13. Washington, DC: U.S. Government Printing Office.

_____. 1984. *1980 Census of the Population. Volume I. Characteristics of the Population. Chapter D. Detailed Population Characteristics. Part 1. U.S. Summary.* PC80-1-D1-A. Washington, DC: U.S. Government Printing Office.

_____. 1985. *1980 Census of Population.* Vol. 2. "Subject Reports: Marital Characteristics." Washington, DC: U.S. Government Printing Office.

_____. 1986. "Money Income of Households, Families and Persons in the United States: 1985." *Current Population Reports.* Series P-60, No. 156. Washington, DC: U.S. Government Printing Office.

_____. 1988a. "Educational Attainment in the United States: March 1987 and 1986." *Current Population Reports.* Series P-20. No. 428. Washington, DC: U.S. Government Printing Office.

_____. 1989a. "The Hispanic Population of the U.S., March 1988." *Current Population Reports.* Series P-20; No. 438. Washington, DC: U.S. Government Printing Office.

_____. 1989b. "Money Income and Poverty Status in the United States: 1988." *Current Population Reports.* Series P-60. No. 166. Washington, DC: U.S. Government Printing Office.

_____. 1990a. "United States Population Estimates by Age, Sex, Race, and Hispanic Origin: 1980 to 1988." *Current Population Reports.* Series P-25, No. 1045. Washington, DC: U.S. Government Printing Office.

_____. 1990b. "The Hispanic Population of the United States: March 1989." *Current Population Reports.* Series P-20, No. 444. Washington, DC: U.S. Government Printing Office.

_____. 1990c. "U. S. Population Estimates by Age, Sex, Race, and Hispanic Origin, 1989." *Current Population Reports.* Series P-25, No. 1057. Washington, DC: U.S. Government Printing Office.

_____. 1990d. "Money Income and Poverty Status in the United States: 1989." *Current Population Reports.* Series P-60, No. 168. Washington, DC: U.S. Government Printing Office.

U.S. Commission on Civil Rights. 1961. *Report: Justice* 5. Washington, DC: U.S. Government Printing Office.

_____. 1978. *Social Indicators of Equality for Minorities and Women.* Washington, DC: U.S. Government Printing Office.

_____. 1983a. *Ancestry of the Population by State: 1980. Supplementary Report.* Washington, DC: U.S. Government Printing Office.

_____. 1983b. *General Population Characteristics, United States Summary.* Washington, DC: U.S. Government Printing Office.

_____. 1983c. *General Social and Economic Characteristics. United States Summary.* Washington, DC: U.S. Government Printing Office.

_____. 1983d. *Conditions of Hispanics in America Today.* Special Release. September 13, Washington, DC: U.S. Government Printing Office.

_____. 1988. *The Economic Status of Americans of Asian Descent.* Washington, DC: U.S. Government Printing Office.

U.S. Department of Health and Human Services. 1985. *Black and Minority Health.* Washington, DC: U.S. Government Printing Office.

U.S. Department of Labor. 1979. *Seven Years Later: The Experiences of the 1970 Cohort of Immigrants in the United States.* Washington, DC: Department of Labor.

U.S. Immigration Commission. 1911. *Abstracts of Reports of the Immigration Commission.* Vol. 2. Washington, DC: U.S. Government Printing Office.

U.S. Immigration and Naturalization Service. 1984. *Annual Report.* Washington, DC: U.S. Government Printing Office.

U.S. Immigration and Naturalization Service. 1989. *Statistical Yearbook of the Immigration and Naturalization Service 1988.* Washington, DC: U.S. Government Printing Office.

U.S. Indian Claims Commission. 1980. *Final Report.* House Report No. 96-383. Washington, DC: Government Printing Office.

U.S. News and World Report. 1985. "When Blocks Battle to Stay Lily-White." December 9.

U.S. Small Business Administration, Office of Advocacy. 1980. *The Small Business Data Base*. Washington, DC: Small Business Administration.

U.S. Statistical Abstract. 1981. Washington, DC: U.S. Government Printing Office.

Useem, Michael. 1980. "Corporations and the Corporate Elite." *Annual Review of Sociology* 6.

Uys, Pieter-Dirk. 1988. "Chameleons Thrive under Apartheid." *New York Times*. September 23.

Valdivieso, Rafael, and Davis, Cary. 1988. *Population Trends and Public Policy*. Washington, DC: Population Reference Bureau.

Valentine, Bettylou. 1978. *Hustling and Other Hard Work*. New York: Macmillan.

van den Berghe, Pierre L. 1966. "Paternalistic versus Competitive Race Relations: An Ideal-Type Approach." In Bernard E. Segal, ed., *Racial and Ethnic Relations*. New York: Crowell.

_____. 1967/1978a. *Race and Racism: A Comparative Perspective*. New York: Wiley.

_____. 1970. *Race and Ethnicity*. New York: Basic Books.

_____. 1971. "Ethnicity: The African Experience." *International Social Science Journal*. 23.

_____. 1978a. *Man in Society*. New York: Elsevier.

_____. 1978b. "Race and Ethnicity: A Sociobiological Perspective." *Ethnic and Racial Studies*. 1.

_____. 1981. *The Ethnic Phenomenon*. New York: Elsevier.

Van Horne, W., ed. 1985. *Ethnicity and the Work Force*. Madison, WI: University of Wisconsin System.

Van Valey, Thomas L.; Roof, Wade C.; and Wilcox, J. E. 1977. "Trends in Residential Segregation 1960–1970." *American Journal of Sociology*. 82.

Vecoli, Rudolph J. 1964. "Contadini in Chicago: A Critique of the Uprooted." *Journal of American History*. 51.

_____. 1970. "Ethnicity: A Neglected Dimension of American History." In Herbert J. Bass, ed., *The State of American History*. Chicago: Quadrangle Books.

_____. 1977. "The Italian Americans." In Leonard Dinnerstein and Frederick C. Jaher, eds., *Uncertain Americans*. New York: Oxford University Press.

Veltman, Calvin. 1981. "Language Planning in the United States: The Politics of Ignorance." Paper presented at the annual meeting of the American Sociological Association. Toronto.

Venable, Abraham S. 1972. *Building Black Business: An Analysis and a Plan*. New York: Earl G. Graves.

Vernon, Philip E. 1982. *The Abilities and Achievement of Orientals in North America*. New York: Academic Press.

Vidich, Arthur, and Bensman, Joseph. 1960. *Small Town in Mass Society*. Garden City, N.Y.: Doubleday Anchor Books.

Vinyard, J. 1976. *The Irish on the Urban Frontier*. New York: Arno.

*Wacquant, Loïc J. D., and Wilson, William Julius. 1989. "The Cost of Racial and Class Exclusion in the Inner City." *The Annals of the American Academy of Political and Social Science*. 501.

Wagatsuma, Hiroshi. 1976. "Political Problems of a Minority Group in Japan: Recent Conflicts in Buraku Liberation Movements." In Willem A. Veenhoven and Winifred Crum Ewing, eds., *Case Studies on Human Rights and Fundamental Freedoms*. Vol. III. The Hague: Martinus Nijhoff.

Wagley, Charles, and Harris, Marvin. 1958. *Minorities in the New World*. New York: Columbia University Press.

Waldinger, Roger. 1982. "Immigrant Enterprise and Labor Market Structure." Paper Presented at the Annual Meeting of the American Sociological Association, San Francisco.

_____. 1985. "Immigration and Industrial Change in the New York City Apparel Industry." In George J. Borjas and Marta Tienda, eds., *Hispanics in the U.S. Economy*. Orlando, FL: Academic Press.

_____. 1986. *Through the Eye of the Needle*. New York: New York University Press.

*_____. 1986/87. "Changing Ladders and Musical Chairs: Ethnicity and Opportunity in Post-Industrial New York." *Politics and Society*. 15.

Walker, Charles and Guest, Robert. 1952. *The Man on the Assembly Line*. Cambridge, MA: Harvard University Press.

Wallerstein, Immanuel. 1960. "Ethnicity and National Integration." *Cahiers d'Etudes Africaines*. 3.

_____. 1976. *The Modern World-System*. New York: Academic Press.

Wallman, Sandra, ed. 1979. *Ethnicity at Work*. London: Macmillan.

Walsh, E. J. 1980. "Resource Mobilization Theory and the Dynamics of Local Anti-Nuclear Coalition Formation in the Wake of the Three-Mile Island Accident." Paper presented at the annual meeting of the American Sociological Association, New York.

Walton, John. 1975. "Internal Colonialism: Problems of Definition and Measurement." In W. A. Cornelius and F. Trueblood, eds., *Latin American Urban Research*. Vol. 5. Beverly Hills, CA: Sage.

Walzer, M. 1981. "The Distribution of Membership," In Peter G. Brown and H. Shue, eds., *Boundaries: National Autonomy and Its Limits*. Totowa, NJ: Rowan and Littlefield.

Warner, W. Lloyd, and Srole, Leo. 1945. *The Social Systems of American Ethnic Groups*. New Haven, CT: Yale University Press.

569

Warren, Ronald. 1979. "Status Report on Naturalization Rates." Working Paper #CO 1326. 6C U.S. Bureau of the Census. Washington, DC: U.S. Government Printing Office.

Washburn, Wilcomb. 1964. *The Indian and the White Man.* New York: Anchor Books.

_____. 1975. *The Indian in America.* New York: Harper and Row.

Wax, Murray L. 1971. *Indian Americans: Unity and Diversity.* Englewood Cliffs, NJ: Prentice-Hall.

Weber, Max. 1958a. *The Protestant Ethic and the Spirit of Capitalism.* New York: Scribner.

_____. 1958b. "The Protestant Sects and the Spirit of Capitalism." In Hans H. Gerth and C. W. Mills, eds., *From Max Weber.* New York: Oxford University Press.

Weinberg, Meyer. 1983. *The Search for Quality Integration Education: Policy and Research on Minority Studies in School and College.* Westport, CT: Greenwood Press.

Weiner, W. 1987. "International Emigration and the Third World." In W. Alonso, ed., *Population in an Interacting World.* Cambridge, MA: Harvard University Press.

White, Michael J. 1986. "Segregation and Diversity Measures in Population Distribution." *Population Index.* 52.

Wilcox, Preston, 1970. "Social Policy and White Racism." *Social Policy.* 1.

Wilensky, Harold L., and Lawrence, Anne T. 1979. "Job Assignment in Modern Societies: A Reexamination of the Ascription-Achievement Hypothesis." In Amos H. Hawley, ed., *Societal Growth.* New York: Free Press.

Wilhelm, Sidney M. 1970. "Who Needs the Negro?" *Transaction.* 1.

_____. 1971. *Who Needs the Negro?* New York: Doubleday.

Williams, Eric. 1944. *Capitalism and Slavery.* Chapel Hill, NC: University of North Carolina Press.

Williams, Robin M. 1964. *Strangers Next Door: Ethnic Relations in American Communities.* Englewood Cliffs, NJ: Prentice-Hall.

Willie, Charles V. 1979. *Caste and Class Controversy.* Bayside, NY: General Hall.

Wilson, A. Jeyaratnam. 1975. *Electoral Politics in an Emergent State.* Cambridge: Cambridge University Press.

Wilson, Kenneth L., and Martin, W. Allen. 1982. "Ethnic Enclaves: A Comparison of the Cuban and Black Economies in Miami." *American Journal of Sociology.* 88.

Wilson, Kenneth L., and Portes, Alejandro. 1980. "Immigrant Enclaves: An Analysis of the Labor Market Experience of Cubans in Miami." *American Journal of Sociology.* 86.

Wilson, William Julius. 1973. *Power, Racism, and Privilege: Race Relations in Theoretical and Sociohistorical Perspectives.* New York: Macmillan.

*_____. 1978a. *The Declining Significance of Race: Blacks and Changing American Institutions.* Chicago: University of Chicago Press.

_____. 1978b. "The Declining Significance of Race; Revisited but not Revised." *Society.* 15:5.

_____. 1981a. "The Black Community in the 1980s: Questions of Race, Class, and Public Policy." *Annals of the American Academy of Political and Social Science.* 454.

_____. 1981b. "Shifts in the Analysis of Race and Ethnic Relations." In J. F. Short, Jr., ed., *The State of Sociology: Problems and Prospects.* Beverly Hills, CA: Sage.

_____. 1987. *The Truly Disadvantaged: Essays on Inner City Woes and Public Policy.* Chicago: University of Chicago Press.

Wilson, William Julius, and Aponte, Robert. 1985. "Urban Poverty." *Annual Review of Sociology.* 11.

Wirth, Louis. 1928/1956. *The Ghetto.* Chicago: University of Chicago Press.

Wittke, Carl. 1940. *We Who Built America.* Englewood Cliffs, NJ: Prentice-Hall.

_____. 1952. *Refugees of Revolution: The German Forty-Eighters in America.* Philadelphia: University of Pennsylvania Press.

Wolpe. Harold. 1970. "Industrialism and Race in South Africa." In Sami Zubaida, ed., *Race and Racialism.* London: Tavistock.

_____. 1974. *Urban Politics in Nigeria.* Los Angeles: University of California Press.

Wong, Charles Choy, 1977. "Black and Chinese Grocery Stores in Los Angeles' Black Ghetto." *Urban Life* 5.

Wong, Morrison G. 1977. "The Japanese in Riverside, 1890 to 1945: A Special Case in Race Relations." Ph.D. dissertation, University of California, Riverside.

_____. 1980a. "Changes in Socioeconimc Status of the Chinese Male Population in the United States from 1960 to 1970." *International Migration Review.* 14:4.

_____. 1980b. "Model Students?: Teachers' Perceptions and Expectations of Their Asian and White Students." *Sociology of Education.* 53.

_____. 1981. "Chinese Sweatshops in the United States: A Look at the Garment Industry." In Ida H. Simpson and Richard L. Simpson, eds., *Research in the Sociology of Work,* Vol. 2. Greenwich, CT: JAI Press.

_____. 1982. "The Cost of Being Chinese, Japanese, and Filipino in the United States: 1960, 1970, and 1976." *Pacific Sociological Review.* 25.

———. 1986. "Post-1965 Asian Immigrants: Where Do They Come From, Where Are They Now, and Where Are They Going?" *Annals of the American Academy of Political and Social Science.* 487.

Wong, Morrison G. 1989. "A Look at Intermarriage among the Chinese in the United States in 1980." *Sociological Perspectives.* 32.

Wong, Morrison G., and Hirschman, Charles. 1983. "The New Asian Immigrants." In William C. McCready, ed., *Culture, Ethnicity and Identity: Current Issues in Research.* New York: Academic Press.

Wood, C. H. 1984. "Caribbean Cane Cutters in Florida: A Study of the Relative Cost of Foreign and Domestic Labor." Presented at the Annual Meeting of the American Sociological Association, San Antonio.

Woodrum, Eric. 1981. "An Assessment of Japanese American Assimilation, Pluralism and Subordination." *American Journal of Sociology.* 87.

———. 1985. "Religion and Economics among Japanese Americans: A Weberian Study." *Social Forces.* 64.

Woodrum, Eric; Rhodes, Colbert; and Feagin, Joe R. 1980. "Japanese American Economic Behavior: Its Types, Determinants and Consequences." *Social Forces* 58.

Woodward, C. Vann. 1957. *The Strange Career of Jim Crow.* New York: Oxford University Press.

World Bank. 1987. *World Development Report 1987.* New York: Oxford University Press.

Wright, Eric O.; Costello, Cynthia; Hachen, David; and Sprague, Joey. 1982. "The American Class Structure." *American Sociological Review* 47.

Xenos, Peter S.; Gardner, Robert W.; Barringer, Herbert R.; and Levin, Michael J. 1987. "Asian Americans: Growth and Change in the 1970s." In James T. Fawcett and Benjamin V. Carino, eds., *Pacific Bridges: The New Immigration from Asia and the Pacific Islands.* Staten Island, NY: Center for Migration Studies.

Yancey, William L.; Ericksen, Eugene P.; and Juliani, Richard N. 1976. "Emergent Ethnicity: A Review and Reformulation." *American Sociological Review.* 41.

Yancey, William L.; Ericksen, Eugene P.; and Leon, George H. 1985. "The Structure of Pluralism: 'We're All Italian around Here, Aren't We Mrs. O'Brien?' " *Ethnic and Racial Studies.* 8.

Yans-McLaughlin, Virginia. 1971. "Patterns of Work and Family Organization among Buffalo's Italians." *Journal of Interdisciplinary History.* 2.

———. 1977. *Family and Community: Italian Immigrants in Buffalo, 1880–1930.* Ithaca, NY: Cornell University Press.

Yetman, Norman R. 1970. *Life under the "Peculiar Institution."* New York: Holt, Rinehart and Winston.

———. 1975. "The Irish Experience in America." In Hal Orel, ed., *Irish History and Culture.* Lawrence, KS: University Press of Kansas.

———. 1984. "Ethnic Pluralism in the 1970s." *American Studies in Scandinavia.* 16:2.

Yetman, Norman R., and Eitzen, E. Stanley. 1977, 1982. "Racial Dynamics in American Sport: Continuity and Change." In Norman R. Yetman, ed., *Majority and Minority: The Dynamics of Race and Ethnicity in American Life.* Boston: Allyn and Bacon.

Yinger, J. Milton. 1968. "Prejudice: Social Discrimination." In D. L. Sills, ed., *International Encyclopedia of the Social Sciences.* New York: Macmillan.

Young, Crawford. 1965. *Politics in the Congo.* Princeton: Princeton University Press.

———. 1976. *The Politics of Cultural Pluralism.* Madison, WI: University of Wisconsin Press.

Young, Frank W. 1971. "A Macrosociological Interpretation of Entrepreneurship." In Peter Kilby, ed., *Entrepreneurship and Economic Development.* New York: Free Press.

Yu, Eui-Young. 1982. "Occupation and Work Patterns of Korean Immigrants." In Eui-Young Yu, Earl H. Phillips, and Eun-Sik Yang, eds., *Koreans in Los Angeles.* Los Angeles: Koryo Research Institute and Center for Korean-American and Korean Studies, California State University.

Zenner, Walter P. 1980. "Middleman Minority Theories: A Critical Review." In Roy S. Bryce-Laporte, ed., *Sourcebook on the New Immigration.* New Brunswick, NJ: Transaction Books.

———. 1982. "Arabic-Speaking Immigrants in North America as Middlemen Minorities." *Ethnic and Racial Studies* 5.

*Zinn, Maxine Baca. 1989. "Family, Race, and Poverty in the Eighties." *Signs.* 14.

Zolberg, Aristide R. 1968. "The Structure of Political Conflict in New States of Tropical Africa." *American Political Science Review.* 62.

———. 1981a. "International Migrations in Political Perspective." In Mary Kritz, Charles Keely, and Silvio Tomasi, eds., *Global Trends in Migration.* Staten Island, NY: Center for Migration Studies.

———. 1981b. "The Origins of the Modern World-System: A Missing Link." *World Politics.* 33.

———. 1983. "Contemporary Transnational Migration in Historical Perspective: Patterns and Dilemmas." In Mary M. Kritz, ed., *U.S. Immigration and Refugee Policy.* Lexington, MA: D. C. Heath.

———. 1987. "Keeping Them Out: Ethnical Dilemmas of Immigration Policy." In R. J. Meyers, ed., *International Ethics in the Nuclear Age.* Lanham, MD: University Press of America.

*_____. 1989a. "The Next Waves: Migration Theory for a Changing World." *International Migration Review.* 23.

_____. 1989b. "The Politics of Immigration Reform." *Revue Française D'Etudes Americaines.* 41.

Zolberg, Aristide R.; Suhrke, A.; and Aguayo, S. 1986. "International Factors in the Formation of Ref-ugee Movements." *International Migration Review.* 20.

_____. 1989. *Escape from Violence: Conflict and the Refugee Crisis in the Developing World.* New York: Oxford University Press.

Zunz, Oliver. 1982. *The Changing Face of Inequality.* Chicago: University of Chicago Press.

List of Contributors

Richard D. Alba is Professor of Sociology and Public Policy at the State University of New York at Albany.

Gerald D. Berreman is Professor of Anthropology at the University of California, Berkeley.

Edna Bonacich is Professor of Sociology at the University of California, Riverside.

Alan N. Burstein is Vice President of Singer/Wenger Trading Company, Chicago, Illinois.

Nancy A. Denton is Research Associate at the University of Chicago.

Eugene P. Ericksen is Professor of Sociology at Temple University.

Leobardo F. Estrada is Associate Professor of Architecture and Urban Planning at the University of California, Los Angeles.

Herbert J. Gans is Professor of Sociology at Columbia University.

F. Chris García is Vice President for Academic Affairs and Professor of Political Science at the University of New Mexico.

Milton M. Gordon is Emeritus Professor of Sociology at the University of Massachusetts.

Andrew M. Greeley is Professor of Sociology at the University of Arizona and is affiliated with the National Opinion Research Center.

Theodore Hershberg is Professor of Public Policy and History at the University of Pennsylvania.

Charles Hirschman is Professor of Sociology at the University of Washington.

Donald L. Horowitz is Charles S. Murphy Professor of Law and Professor of Political Science at Duke University.

Shirley Hune is Professor in the Department of Educational Foundations and Counseling Programs at Hunter College of the City University of New York.

Gerald David Jaynes is Professor in the Department of Economics and in the Program of African and African-American Studies at Yale University.

Stanley Lieberson is Professor of Sociology at Harvard University.

Ivan Light is Professor of Sociology at the University of California, Los Angeles.

Nancy Oestreich Lurie is Curator of Anthropology at the Milwaukee Public Museum and Adjunct Professor of Anthropology at The University of Wisconsin, Milwaukee.

Reynaldo Flores Macías is Associate Professor of Education at the University of Southern California.

Lionel Maldonado is Professor of Ethnic Studies at California State University, San Marcos.

Robert D. Manning is Assistant Professor of Sociology at The American University.

Douglas S. Massey is Professor of Sociology at the University of Chicago.

Suzanne Model is Assistant Professor of Sociology at the University of Massachusetts, Amherst.

Joane Nagel is Associate Professor of Sociology at the University of Kansas.

Donald L. Noel is Professor of Sociology at the University of Wisconsin, Milwaukee.

Alejandro Portes is John Dewey Professor of Sociology and International Relations at Johns Hopkins University.

C. Matthew Snipp is Associate Professor of Rural Sociology and Sociology at the University of Wisconsin, Madison.

Stephen Steinberg is Professor of Sociology and Urban Studies at Queens College and the Graduate School of the City University of New York.

Cynthia G. Truelove is Assistant Professor of Rural Sociology at the University of Wisconsin, Madison.

Loïc J. D. Wacquant is Lavoisier Fellow in the Department of Sociology, The University of Chicago and Ecole des Hautes Etudes en Sciences Sociales, Paris.

Roger Waldinger is Associate Professor of Sociology at the City College and the Graduate School of the City University of New York.

Robin M. Williams, Jr. is Henry Scarborough Professor of Social Science, Emeritus, at Cornell University.

William Julius Wilson is Lucy Flower University Professor of Sociology and Public Policy at the University of Chicago.

Morrison G. Wong is Associate Professor of Sociology at Texas Christian University.

William L. Yancey is Professor of Sociology at Temple University.

Norman R. Yetman is Professor of Sociology and American Studies at the University of Kansas.

Maxine Baca Zinn is Professor of Sociology at the University of Michigan, Flint.

Aristide R. Zolberg is University-in-Exile Professor in the Department of Political Science at the New School for Social Research.